An Introduction to the Flight Dynamics of Rigid Aeroplanes

An Introduction to the Flight Dynamics of Rigid Aeroplanes

G.J. Hancock

Ellis Horwood
New York London Toronto Sydney Tokyo Singapore

First published 1995 by
Ellis Horwood Limited
Campus 400, Maylands Avenue
Hemel Hempstead
Hertfordshire, HP2 7EZ
A division of
Simon & Schuster International Group

Printed and bound in Great Britain by
Hartnolls, Bodmin

Library of Congress Cataloging-in-Publication Data

Available from the publisher

British Library Cataloguing in Publication Data

A catalogue record for this book is available
from the British Library

ISBN 0-13-319450-7

1 2 3 4 5 99 98 97 96 95

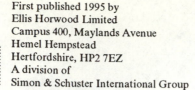

Dedicated to H. H. B. M. Thomas, known as Beaument to his countless colleagues, for his inspiration, friendship and encouragement over many years.

Table of contents

APPENDICES

Preface

To its devotees, which includes the author as one of its keenest addicts, aerospace flight dynamics is a fascinating, stimulating and challenging technology, embracing the disciplines of mathematics, mechanics, aerodynamics, structural dynamics, mechanical and electronic systems, instrumentation, computer hardware and software, simulation, pilot handling qualities, ergonomics, safety and reliability, atmospheric environment, wind tunnel testing, flight testing, overall design and operational monitoring. As a major pace setter, flight dynamics plays a dominant role in the continuing expansion of the frontiers of aerospace endeavour.

After a career in academe, during which considerable time has been spent pondering on, and lecturing on, flight dynamics, the author, now retired with time on his hands but with enthusiasm undiminished, feels that perhaps his lecture material, suitably amplified, may be of interest to a wider audience.

Many books, or parts of books, have been written on the topic of flight dynamics over the past eighty years; refs. P.1–P.22 list those known to the author. The book by Etkin (ref. P.15) deserves special mention; it has passed the test of time to become accepted as an authoritative text around the world, east and west, for the instruction of undergraduates and graduates. The author also has a high regard for the books by Kolk (ref. P.7) for its enduring topicality and readability, Dickinson (ref. P.13) for its pragmatic approach based on personal experience of flying aeroplanes and Roskam (ref. P.17) for its emphasis on control hardware. The most individualistic book, and also the most mathematical, is the book by Hacker (ref. P.14) with its insight, not found elsewhere, its introduction to the Russian literature, and for an elegance of style which foreign nationals often manage to achieve but which many native English-speaking authors, including this one, fail to emulate.

With so many books on flight dynamics overloading the bookshelf it is necessary to justify a further publication.

(i) With due respect to all of the above authors there is a feeling, at least in the UK, that a definitive and readable text, suitable for students, has yet to appear.

(ii) Most books in the list of references were written some years ago; in a new book, topics of contemporary importance can be introduced—for example, flight dynamics at high angles of incidence.

(iii) A common approach in the literature is to concentrate on the concepts of flight dynamics of aeroplanes at low speeds and then to introduce the effects of Mach number as a subsequent modification. In this book a different approach is adopted, namely to develop the principles of flight dynamics of aeroplanes in high speed flight, *ab initio*, from subsonic through to supersonic speeds; the low speed characteristics then appear as a limiting case as Mach number becomes small. A more unified approach gives a fresh perspective to many fundamental concepts, particularly to the topic of static stability.

(iv) This book provides the author with an opportunity to present his thoughts on the role of unsteady aerodynamics in flight dynamics, and to clarify what is meant by 'aerodynamic derivatives'.

According to the title this book is confined to the flight dynamics of rigid aeroplanes (the word 'aeroplane' is preferred to the word 'aircraft' because 'aircraft' encompasses a wider class of aerospace vehicles: aeroplanes, helicopters and missiles). The reason is that it is intended that there should be a follow-up book on the flight dynamics of flexible aeroplanes. Although not immediately apparent, the representation of rigid aeroplane dynamics in this book is compatible with a unified representation of the flight dynamics of both flexible and rigid aeroplanes.

This book is written as a student text at the level of a final year undergraduate course or a first year graduate course. It is also aimed at the lecturers of those courses, because often, at least in the UK, these lecturers are not experts in flight dynamics but are experts in related fields, either aerodynamics or control systems. It is hoped also that the book will interest and stimulate more experienced flight dynamicists.

There is always a problem in broaching the subject of flight dynamics; namely, knowing where to start, how to develop the principles of the basic disciplines (theory of differential equations, applied aerodynamics, dynamics and automatic systems), how to integrate them into a unified course and how far to go. The aim here is to make the book self-contained (although some prior elementary knowledge of aerodynamics is expected) and to develop a base of knowledge which allows the reader to appraise contemporary literature. This book covers the role, application and importance of automatic flight control systems but their detailed design based on the Laplace transform and conventional transfer functions is not included; for this topic the reader is referred to an excellent brief account by Roskam (ref. P.17), or to the fuller accounts by McRuer *et al.* (ref. P.20), or by McClean (ref. P.21), or by Stevens & Lewis (ref. P.22).

Concepts of the flight dynamics of rigid aeroplanes are to be derived in general terms and then, to reinforce appreciation and understanding, it is left to the reader to apply these concepts to three basic aeroplane configurations which represent different types of aeroplane:

(i) a low speed, propeller driven, light aeroplane,
(ii) a high subsonic transport aeroplane, with twin turbo-fan engines underslung beneath the wings,
(iii) a combat aeroplane with supersonic capability, with interior turbo-fan engines.

Of the basic disciplines, dynamics is the one which students newly attending engineering classes at university level find the most difficult to comprehend. There are a number of reasons. One reason is that intuition is either at variance with the mathematics and reality, or of little help, for example in the directions of inertial forces, in rolling problems, in accepting Coriolis forces, and in understanding gyroscopic moments. Another reason is that to solve most problems it is necessary to return to first principles, rote learning has no place in dynamics. A third reason is the way the topic is taught. In the author's experience a full treatment of fundamental dynamics using the elegance and conciseness of vector algebra presented at too early a stage, and then applied to solve simplistic motions, erodes interest and enthusiasm and creates the illusion that dynamics has a mystique which only a select élite can unravel. Confidence, expertise, reliance on mathematical formulations and mathematical manipulations, understanding and familiarity can best be built up by proceeding through elementary considerations as a preparation for more advanced treatments. Thus, in this book vector algebra is introduced at a later, rather than an early, stage.

There is a dilemma on how to integrate the dynamic and aerodynamic components in formulating the basic equations of flight dynamics. One can start with dynamics, break off in mid-flight to introduce the topic of aerodynamic loads, and return to the dynamics; but students complain about the lack of continuity. Alternatively, one can describe first the nature of aerodynamic loads, and then the subsequent treatment of the dynamics is a straight run; but students grumble initially, studying aerodynamics when their timetable says flight dynamics. It is a no-win situation. For better or worse the second approach is adopted here.

To the consternation of many students mathematics plays a central role in the description of flight dynamics, but there really is no alternative. Mathematical formulae express concise relationships between variables and parameters; the interpretation of formulae in physical terms provides qualitative understanding while the substitution of numerical values provides quantitative insight. Qualitative understanding and quantitative insight are prerequisites for reducing complex flight behaviour, by valid approximations, to more simplified and useful forms. The feel for number, the order of numerical magnitude of all variables and parameters, is the key to comprehension. These themes represent the pedagogical philosophy throughout this book. Although there are many formulae, and some formulae are undoubtedly formidable, the actual level of the mathematics is not too advanced and is within the scope of a second year engineering undergraduate student in the UK. In this book

'$=$' denotes 'equal to',
'$\simeq$' denotes 'approximately equal to', which means within $\pm 20\%$,
'$= O[\ ]$' denotes 'of the order of', which means within -50% to $+100\%$.

Nomenclature is the nightmare of flight dynamics; not only is the stream of notation endless but notation varies from country to country. In the UK a major effort was expended by Hopkins [ref. P. 23] to standardize notation in the field of flight dynamics, but the end result was so exhaustive in its attention to rigour, consistency and detail that the extensive range of recommendations tended to be indigestible. The recommendations were ignored primarily because they were alien to the more acceptable USA notation.

The notation used in this book is not totally standard, it has evolved over the years to be self-evident in the teaching of flight dynamics to undergraduate students; in the main the notation is consistent with that used in the USA.

Because there is such an extensive list of notation it is often difficult for the student to remember which terms are positive and which are negative. To help in this regard coefficients or derivatives which are positive are distinguished from coefficients or derivatives which are negative. For example, if C_{ab} denotes a coefficient,

if	$C_{ab} > 0$	then it appears as	C_{ab},	which is positive,
if	$C_{ab} < 0$	then it appears as	$(-C_{ab})$,	which is also positive,

and in an equation,

$+ C_{ab}$	is written as	$+ C_{ab}$	when	$C_{ab} > 0$,
	is written as	$- (-C_{ab})$	when	$C_{ab} < 0$,

while

$- C_{ab}$	is written as	$- C_{ab}$	when	$C_{ab} > 0$
	is written as	$+ (-C_{ab})$	when	$C_{ab} < 0$.

In this way the signs of the various terms in an expression are clearly identified.

The number of different axis systems adds to the confusion. Although the different axis systems are described, the fuselage body axis system is used throughout this book, preserving consistency of approach over the entire angle of incidence range.

SI units are used because they are used exclusively in all engineering courses in the UK. For those readers not totally conversant with SI units, Imperial units are also included where appropriate. However, most of the parameters to be quantified are non-dimensional, in which case the question of units will not arise.

Examples are interposed in the text to help the reader reflect on the subject matter. Some of the examples are trivial, some are substantial, and some require an ability to read between the lines of the text. The main purpose is to stimulate the reader to formulate his or her own independent lines of enquiry.

ACKNOWLEDGEMENTS

The author expresses his sincere thanks and gratitude to colleagues who have made available their time, expertise and advice: to John Gibson (B.Ae. Warton) for so many informative and enjoyable sessions; to Ranjan Vepa (Queen Mary and Westfield College) for the computations; to Glynn Jones, Charles O'Leary, Denis Mabey (Defence Research Agency), Mike Graham (Imperial College), Dave Butter, Barry Haines (Aircraft Research Establishment) for their willing support; and last, but by no means least, to Len Bernstein, Dave Clark, Harry Horton, Dave Petty, Dave Sharpe, Dave Sweeting and Alec Young (Aero. Dept. at Queen Mary and Westfield College) for their tolerance and good humour in innumerable discussions over the years when their valued opinions helped the author evolve his understanding.

Part I

Introduction

Flight mechanics is the branch of aerospace engineering concerned with the motion of aerospace vehicles; it comprises the three complementary and interrelated technologies of performance, guidance and navigation, and flight dynamics.

Performance deals with trajectories and their optimization: take-off, climb, cruise, range, endurance, manoeuvres, descent and landing. The main parameters which influence performance are the forces of all-up weight, engine thrust, overall lift and overall drag.

Guidance and navigation are concerned with establishing and maintaining a designated flight path, using on-board instrumentation together with reference to ground based, or satellite, signals.

The task of flight dynamics is to ensure that the full complement of performance, guidance and navigational missions and tasks can be performed successfully and safely in virtually all atmospheric conditions by a pilot, either human or automatic, through appropriate changes to the engine(s) throttle and to deflections of control surfaces. The main parameters which influence flight dynamics are the inertial and aerodynamic moments acting on an aerospace vehicle, the control surfaces' aerodynamic effectiveness, and the vehicle response to commands from the human pilot and the automatic control system.

An aeroplane operates within its flight envelope which defines the Mach number range and altitude range. Typical flight envelopes are shown in Fig. I.1 for a transport aeroplane and a combat aeroplane. For the transport aeroplane the altitude ceiling and maximum speed are determined by the maximum thrust available from the engine, while the minimum speeds are determined from the stall characteristics, which include any buffeting limit. For the combat aeroplane the altitude ceiling and the maximum speeds at higher altitudes are similarly determined by the maximum engine thrust, although at higher supersonic Mach numbers, above 2.5, aerodynamic heating is the limiting factor; the maximum speeds at lower altitudes may be determined by limits on structural deformations due to excessive dynamic pressure; again minimum speeds are determined by the stall/buffeting characteristics.

An aeroplane also operates within the manoeuvre envelope which defines the operational maximum and minimum normal accelerations (i.e. the accelerations in the

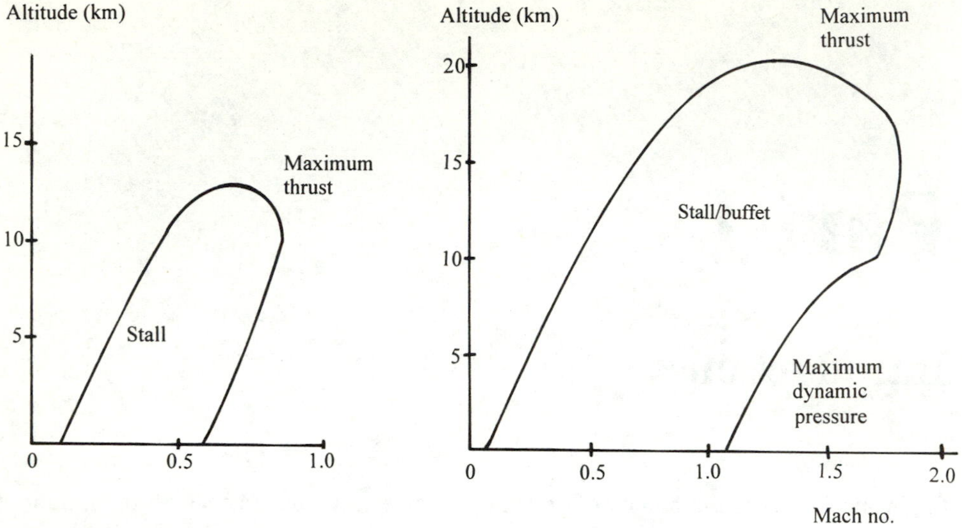

Fig. I.1. Typical flight envelopes.

direction normal to the wing plan form). The structural strength of an aeroplane is designed to withstand the range of normal accelerations within these limits.

Structural loads on an aeroplane are proportional to the load factor (= 1 + (normal acceleration/g)); a load factor equal to 1 represents steady level flight; a load factor greater than 1 occurs during a pull-out from a dive into a climb; a load factor less than 1, including –1, occurs during a push-over from a climb into a dive; a load factor of –1 also represents steady level inverted flight. The range for the load factor is usually –1.5 to +2.5 for a transport aeroplane and –4.0 to +9.0 for a combat aeroplane. Conventional manoeuvre envelopes are shown in Fig. I.2 which plot the limits of load factor against equivalent air speed; at low speeds the maximum and minimum accelerations are determined by the maximum and minimum aerodynamic lifts which can be generated. For a

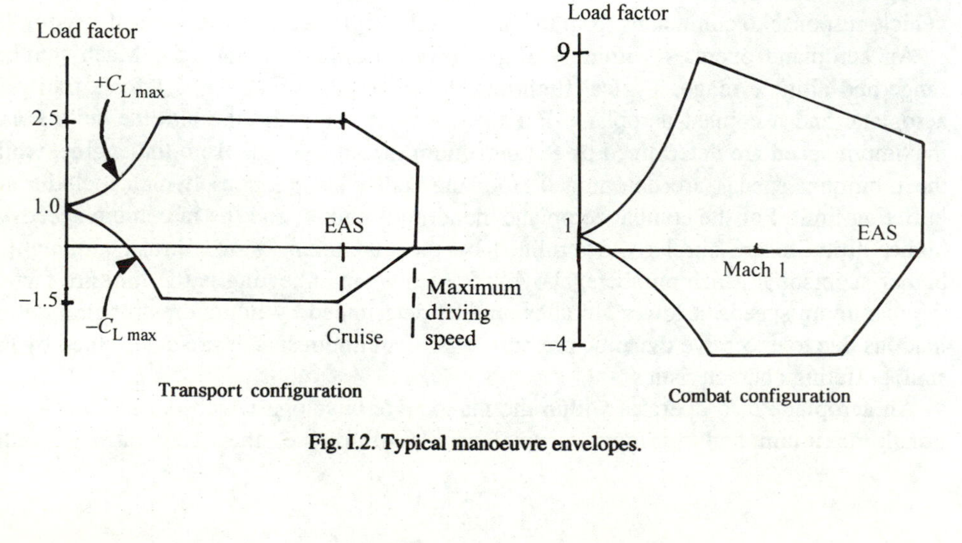

Fig. I.2. Typical manoeuvre envelopes.

transport aeroplane the maximum load factor of 2.5 is regarded as the limit for providing manoeuvring capability in emergencies such as aborted landings and evasion from collisions whereas the minimum load factor of –1.5 is an empirical value which gives a reasonable factor in inverted flight with a 'negative' strength of 60% of the 'positive' strength. These limits have stood the test of time, demonstrating adequate safety margins. In combat the human pilot, wearing appropriate anti-*g* clothing, can safely tolerate +7*g* for 5–10 seconds, but the ability to track an adversary begins to deteriorate in the range 4–5*g*; the structural limit of 9*g* for a combat aeroplane is the limit of human consciousness, only to be experienced in extreme emergencies.

Aeroplane flight dynamics involve

— static equilibrium
— stability
— trim
— manoeuvrability
— controllability
— flying qualities
— ride qualities
— agility (for combat aeroplanes).

It is thought that a preliminary introduction to these terms, and their interdependence, would be useful.

An aeroplane is said to be in a state of **static equilibrium** when the total aerodynamic, propulsive and gravity loads acting on the aeroplane in a steady flight condition (i.e. steady level flight, steady climb, steady descent), with the throttle and control surfaces fixed at appropriate settings, satisfy the equations of static equilibrium (i.e. zero resultant force and zero resultant moment acting on the aeroplane).

To define **stability**, consider an aeroplane, initially in a state of static equilibrium, which is subjected to a pulse disturbance, from either an atmospheric gust or an elevator input (i.e. a rapid flick of the elevator angle, up and back again). The aeroplane responds in a time varying motion. If this aeroplane response dies away with time and the aeroplane returns to its initial condition of static equilibrium without the intervention of the human pilot, the aeroplane is said to be (asymptotically) stable. If, on the other hand, the aeroplane response builds up with time without the intervention of human pilot, the aeroplane does not return to its initial condition of static equilibrium and is then said to be (asymptotically) unstable.

There are other types of stability apart from asymptotic stability (see Etkin, ref. P.15, and Hacker, ref. P.14). An aeroplane may be stable to a small pulse disturbance but unstable to a large pulse disturbance (e.g. the phenomenon of deep stall). An aeroplane may be unstable to a pulse disturbance, but the resulting flight condition does not build up indefinitely and becomes oscillatory with a finite amplitude, a so-called limit cycle oscillation (e.g. the phenomenon of wing rock). When gust disturbances are continuous, stability may need to be defined in terms of the level of continuous aeroplane response. Unless specified otherwise, stability in this book implies asymptotic stability.

Stability, as defined above, requires that the human pilot does not intervene during the aeroplane response, but the control surfaces do not necessarily remain fixed. If, on a light aeroplane, the pilot is flying 'hands-off', the control surfaces will float during the response; on commercial and combat aeroplanes any stability augmentation system or active control system moves the control surfaces during the aeroplane response as dictated by the on-board computer/control system.

Inherent stability of an aeroplane is its stability when the actual control surfaces (elevators, ailerons and rudder) are kept fixed during the aeroplane response, following the pulse disturbance. Most contemporary combat aeroplanes are inherently unstable but are stabilized by an active control system.

An aspect of stability can be extracted and labelled 'overall static stability'. As a formal definition, we can state that with a single degree of freedom, mass–spring–damper, system the condition of static stability is that the spring stiffness be positive; with a multi-degree of freedom system, consisting of many mass–spring–damper subsystems all coupled together, the condition of overall static stability is that the product of all the spring stiffnesses be positive. Overall static stability occurs when all the spring stiffnesses are positive, but also occurs when an even number of the spring stiffnesses are negative and the system is unstable, so a knowledge of overall static stability can be misleading. In the context of aeroplane dynamics, overall static stability is not, in itself, a parameter of importance.

It is often said that stability can be separated into two complementary aspects, namely (overall) static stability and dynamic stability, implying that static stability plus dynamic stability guarantee overall stability. This concept is not worth pursuing. Stability, by its definition, is determined by the time varying response to a pulse disturbance, so stability and 'dynamic stability' are synonymous. Also, ('dynamic') stability means that static stability is automatically satisfied.

An aeroplane is said to be **'trimmed'** when it maintains a condition of nominal steady flight with the pilot flying 'hands-off' the stick. In order to trim an aeroplane a static equilibrium condition must exist, and that condition of static equilibrium must be stable. A real atmosphere is never still, as gust disturbances of varying intensity are always present. The flight condition is therefore steady on the average, but interrupted by responses to atmospheric disturbances—hence the phrase 'nominal steady flight'. Horizontal cruise, climb and descent are the usual trimmed flight conditions.

In some textbooks trimmed flight is treated under the heading of static stability. Apart from static equilibrium and static stability having the word 'static' in common, they are totally distinct concepts. Misunderstanding has been perpetuated from the early days of flight, stemming primarily from unmanned gliders where, as explained later, balancing and stability are closely interlinked.

An aeroplane is said to be **manoeuvrable** when it can perform a range of standard manoeuvres (pull-ups, rolls and turns) throughout the flight envelope at sufficiently high rates to meet specifications. For a transport aeroplane maximum manoeuvrability is determined by emergency conditions, e.g. aborting a landing or avoiding a collision. For a combat aeroplane, for survival, manoeuvres need to be executed more quickly than those of an adversary.

Controllability of an aeroplane refers to the ability of the human pilot to initiate a manoeuvre, to change from one manoeuvre to another, and to maintain a manoeuvre in the presence of atmospheric disturbances (e.g. descending down a designated approach path in gust conditions). Controllability depends on two factors: first, the stick (and/or pedal) displacement and force needed to achieve and maintain a desired manoeuvre and, second, how fast the aeroplane responds to changes in stick (and/or pedal), displacement and force.

Stability, manoeuvrability and controllability are closely linked, but the relationships between them are complex. It has been said that 'the more stable an aeroplane the more difficult it is to manoeuvre, so, reducing the level of stability, even down to the level of instability, improves the manoeuvrability', which is another legacy from the early days of flight. As explained later, there is some validity in this statement, although it depends on what is meant by manoeuvrability. In general, as the level of stability is reduced, manoeuvrability may be enhanced but controllability becomes more difficult.

Flying qualities are assessed by the subjective opinion of pilots on the ease and precision by which flight missions can be completed; flying qualities are an amalgam of ability to trim, stability, manoeuvrability, controllability, external vision, comprehensibility of displays, physical workload (pulling and pushing the controls) and mental concentration in taking decisions and coordinating all piloting tasks.

Ride quality refers to the number and severity of bumps and jolts experienced by the pilot and passengers during flight in turbulence. It is unfortunate, especially for combat aeroplanes, that design features which improve ride quality (i.e. reduce the level of bumps) tend to reduce the ability to manoeuvre.

Agility refers to how quickly a fighter aeroplane can react to the ever changing demands in a combat scenario. To optimize agility it is necessary to minimize stability response times, to maximize manoeuvring capability, to maximize the acceleration/deceleration performance, and to define the time varying piloting strategies which combine all of the above factors to ensure combat superiority. Carefree agility implies that whatever the pilot input, the flight control system prevents the pilot from damaging the aeroplane either through structural failure at excessive normal accelerations or from going beyond the limits of the flight envelope or from losing control.

In describing stability and control the terms 'static, dynamic, steady, unsteady, and quasi-steady' appear often; their meanings are listed below.

(i) Static and dynamic refer to motions; static implies a motion with constant (i.e. time independent) forward speed, constant angles of incidence, sideslip, pitch, bank, yaw and constant control surface angles; dynamic implies a motion in which at least one of the above variables varies with time.

(ii) Steady and unsteady refer to aerodynamic loads: steady implies that the aerodynamic loads are independent of time, neglecting the very high frequency unsteadiness associated with the turbulence inside attached boundary layers; unsteady implies that the aerodynamic loads vary with time.

(iii) A static condition does not necessarily lead to steady loads. On a stationary model in a wind tunnel, the loads are steady when the flow is attached; but at a high angle of incidence, when there is flow separation and flow breakdown, the aerodynamic loads are unsteady, although the unsteady aerodynamic loads can be time-averaged to give mean, steady, loads.

(iv) A dynamic motion does not necessarily lead to unsteady loads. A dynamic motion with a constant rate of change of pitch or roll—all other variables remaining constant—gives steady loads.

(v) A general dynamic motion results in unsteady loads, and unsteady loads result in a dynamic motion.

(vi) A dynamic motion which is 'slowly varying' leads to quasi-steady loads; what is meant by 'a slowly varying motion' and quasi-steady loads is a question of considerable importance in the flight dynamics of aeroplanes, and the answer depends on an elementary knowledge of unsteady aerodynamics, to be presented later.

Part II

Elementary mathematical theory of stability and response

II.1 INTRODUCTION

Understanding what is meant by stability of a system, how that stability is assessed, the relationship between stability and the response to a wide range of standard inputs, coupled with familiarity and expertise in the mathematical techniques of calculating stability and response, are essential prerequisites to the study of aeroplane flight dynamics.

Quantitative considerations of stability and response involve the analysis of differential equations. In this part the characteristics are described of a range of standard differential equations of linear systems, which are typical of the equations which represent the motion of an aeroplane at low angles of incidence and sideslip. For a more comprehensive account and for supplementary reading, see Pontryagin (ref. II.1).

In the parlance of stability theory, stability analysis and synthesis is carried in three 'planes': the 'time plane', the 'frequency plane' and the '*s* plane' using the Laplace transform. Only the time 'plane' approach is used in this book, mainly because the time 'plane' approach is sufficient for all the applications; the frequency response is introduced as one particular time dependent response. The '*s* plane' analysis is not mentioned. For the wider scenario of all three approaches, which is required for an analysis of automatic systems, see refs. P.20–P.22.

II.2 SINGLE DEGREE OF FREEDOM, FIRST ORDER, SYSTEM

Consider the differential equation

$$(\mathrm{D} + A_0)\, y(t) = B_0 x(t), \tag{II.1}$$

where D is the differential operator $\mathrm{d}/\mathrm{d}t$, A_0 and B_0 are real constants, $y(t)$ is the output or response and $x(t)$ is the input.

Eqn. (II.1) represents the behaviour of a system which is:

- — first order, because the highest order time derivative is the first order derivative, $\mathrm{d}y(t)/\mathrm{d}t$;
- — single degree of freedom, because there is only one output, or response, variable, $y(t)$;
- — linear, because there are no product terms involving $y(t)$ or its derivatives;
- — with constant coefficients, since A_0 and B_0 are independent of time.

It is assumed that the system is quiescent for $t < 0$, and that the input and response start at time $t = 0$, so

$$y(t) = 0, \qquad x(t) = 0 \quad \text{for} \quad t < 0. \tag{II.2}$$

The response $y(t)$ can be expressed in the form

$$\begin{aligned} y(t) &= \text{transient response} + \text{`steady state' response} \\ &= y_{tr}(t) + \big(y(t)\big)_{ss}. \end{aligned} \tag{II.3}$$

The transient response is a non-zero solution of the homogeneous equation

$$(\mathrm{D} + A_0)y_{tr}(t) = 0, \qquad t > 0. \tag{II.4}$$

For the relatively simple inputs used in this book the 'steady state' response can be determined by inspection. The phrase 'steady state', which is standard terminology, is rather unfortunate because, in general, $(y(t))_{ss}$ varies with time.

The system is stable when the response, $y(t)$, tends to the steady state response, $(y(t))_{ss}$, as time t increases. The system is unstable when the response does not tend to the steady state response as time increases.

It follows that the system stability is determined by the transient response, $y_{tr}(t)$. From eqn. (II.3)

if $\quad y_{tr}(t) \to 0 \quad$ as $t \to \infty$, $\quad$ the system is stable;

if $\quad y_{tr}(t) \to \infty \quad$ as $t \to \infty$, $\quad$ the system is unstable.

II.2.1 Stability

To solve for the transient response, eqn. (II.4), try a solution

$$y_{tr}(t) = a\exp(\lambda t) \tag{II.5}$$

where a and λ are arbitrary constants. Substitution of eqn. (II.5) into eqn. (II.4) gives

$$a[\lambda + A_0]\exp(\lambda t) = 0. \tag{II.6}$$

Since a must be non-zero for a solution to exist, eqn. (II.6) is satisfied when

$$\lambda + A_0 = 0 \tag{II.7}$$

which gives

$$\lambda = -A_0. \tag{II.8}$$

Combining eqns. (II.5) and (II.8)

$$y_{tr}(t) = a\exp(-A_0 t). \tag{II.9}$$

The equation for λ (eqn. (II.7)) is known as the characteristic equation. The value of λ which satisfies the characteristic equation (II.8) is known as the stability root or eigenvalue.

From eqn. (II.9)

(i) when A_0 is positive $y_{tr}(t)$ decreases to zero exponentially with time, as shown in Fig. II.1; this form of time decay is known as a pure subsidence; the system is stable;

(ii) when A_0 is negative $y_{tr}(t)$ grows exponentially with time, as shown in Fig. II.1; this form of growth is known as a pure divergence; the system is unstable;

(iii) when A_0 is zero $y_{tr}(t)$ is a constant, i.e. it neither grows nor decays, and the system is said to have neutral stability.

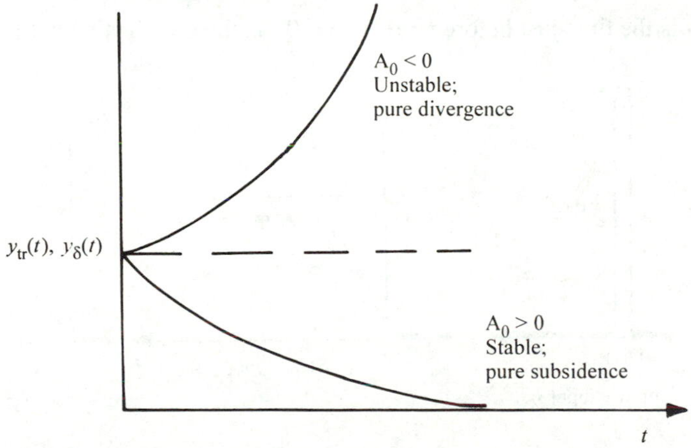

Fig. II.1. Transient (or impulse) response of a first order system.

To assess stability it is not necessary to know the value of the arbitrary constant a in eqn. (II.9). To calculate the response $y(t)$ $(= y_{tr}(t) + (y(t))_{ss})$ the value of a in eqn. (II.9) is given by the initial boundary value of $y(t)$ at time t equal to zero.

For a stable system with a pure subsidence (i.e. $A_0 > 0$) a relative measure of the level of stability is given by the time taken for the response to decay to half amplitude, $t_{1/2}$, which is given by

$$\exp(-A_0 t_{1/2}) = \tfrac{1}{2} \quad \text{or} \quad t_{1/2} = (\ln 2)/A_0 \simeq 0.7/A_0 = 0.7t_c \tag{II.10}$$

where t_c, which denotes the first order system time constant, is defined as

$$t_c = 1/A_0 \,. \tag{II.11}$$

As t_c decreases, the time to half amplitude decreases, and the system is said to become more stable.

For an unstable system with a pure divergence (i.e. $A_0 < 0$) the level of instability is given by the time taken for the response to build up to double amplitude, t_2, which is given by

$$\exp(-A_0 t_2) = 2 \quad \text{or} \quad t_2 = (\ln 2)/(-A_0) \simeq 0.7/(-A_0). \tag{II.12}$$

As $(-A_0)$ increases, the time to double amplitude decreases, and the system is said to become less stable or more unstable.

II.2.2 Impulse response

A unit impulse applied at time $t = 0$, as sketched in Fig. II.2, is represented by the impulse function

$$x(t) = \delta(t) \tag{II.13}$$

where $\delta(t) = 0$ when $t < 0$ and when $t > 0$, and

$$\int_{0-}^{0+} \delta(t)\, dt = 1.0 \tag{II.14}$$

where $t = 0-$ is the time just before $t = 0$ and $t = 0+$ is the time just after $t = 0$.

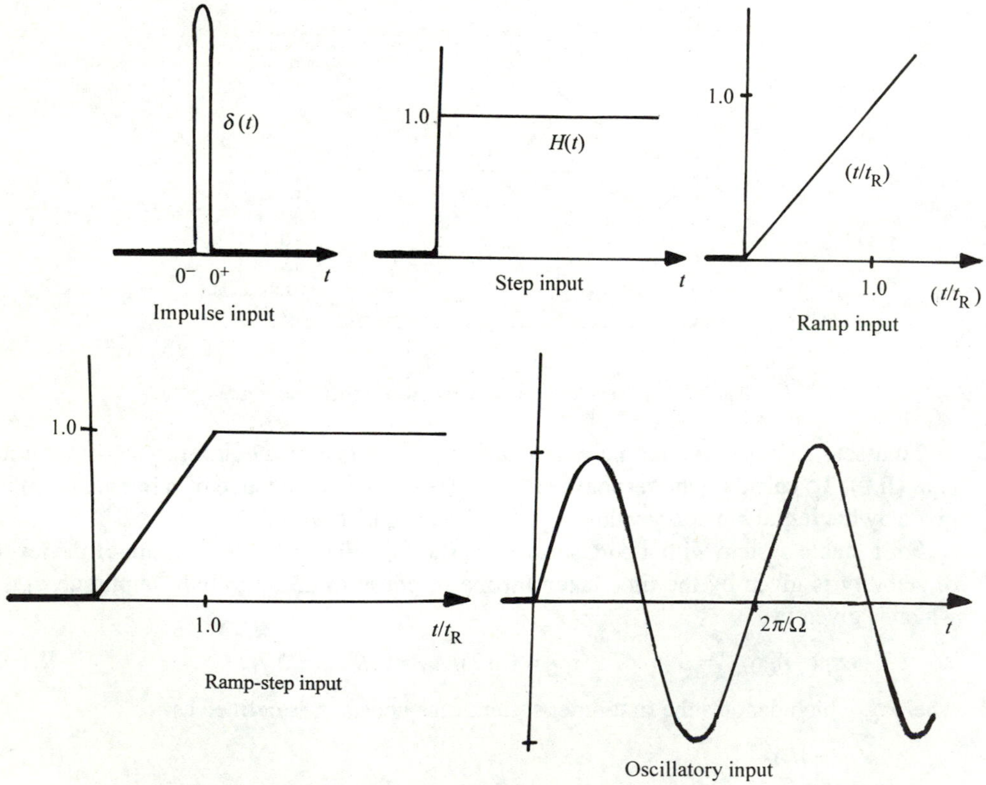

Fig. II.2. Standard inputs.

The response of a system to the impulse input $(x(t) = \delta(t))$ is known as the impulse response and is denoted by $y_\delta(t)$.

The impulse response of the system represented by eqn. (II.1) is the solution of the differential equation

$$(\mathrm{D}+A_0)y_\delta(t) = B_0\,\delta(t). \tag{II.15}$$

Thus $y_\delta(t)$ is the solution of the differential equation

$$(\mathrm{D}+A_0)y_\delta(t) = 0 \quad \text{for } t>0 \tag{II.16}$$

which satisfies an initial boundary value at time $t = 0+$.

This initial boundary value is calculated by integrating eqn. (II.15) with respect to time from $t = 0-$ to $t = 0+$, namely,

$$\int_{0-}^{0+}\left[(\mathrm{D}+A_0)y_\delta(t)\right]\mathrm{d}t = B_0\int_{0-}^{0+}\delta(t)\,\mathrm{d}t,$$

which gives

$$y_\delta(t=0+) - y_\delta(t=0-) + A_0\int_{0-}^{0+} y_\delta(t)\,\mathrm{d}t = B_0. \tag{II.17}$$

Now $y_\delta(t = 0-)$ is zero because the system is quiescent for $t < 0$, and the integral involving $y_\delta(t)$ is zero because $y_\delta(t)$, although discontinuous, is finite across $t = 0$, so

$$y_\delta(t=0+) = B_0. \tag{II.18}$$

Because eqns. (II.4) and (II.16) are the same, it follows that

$$y_\delta(t) = y_{\mathrm{tr}}(t) = B_0\exp(-A_0 t) \tag{II.19}$$

where the arbitrary constant a is determined from the initial boundary value, eqn. (II.18).

The impulse responses are the same as those shown in Fig. II.1.

Stability is deduced mathematically from the transient response, whereas in practice stability can be measured from the response to an impulse input, or as close to an impulse as physically possible. Eqn. (II.19) shows the equivalence between the transient and impulse responses for a first order system.

II.2.3 Step response

A unit step input, as sketched in Fig. II.2, is defined by

$$x(t) = H(t) \tag{II.20}$$

where

$$H(t) = 0 \quad \text{for } t<0, \qquad H(t) = 1 \quad \text{for } t>0.$$

The response of a system to a step input is the step response $y_\mathrm{H}(t)$. The step response of the system represented by eqn. (II.1) is the solution of the differential equation

$$(\mathrm{D}+A_0)\,y_\mathrm{H}(t) = B_0\,H(t). \tag{II.21}$$

Thus $y_\mathrm{H}(t)$ is the solution of the differential equation

$$(\mathrm{D}+A_0)\,y_\mathrm{H}(t) = B_0, \quad t>0 \tag{II.22}$$

which satisfies the initial boundary value

$$y_H(t = 0+) = 0. \qquad \text{(II.23)}$$

This initial boundary value is obtained by following the same procedure as that indicated in eqns (II.17) and (II.18).

The steady state step response is a constant, so from eqn. (II.22)

$$\left(y_H(t)\right)_{ss} = \text{constant} = B_0/A_0. \qquad \text{(II.24)}$$

The step response, namely the steady state step response, eqn. (II.24), plus the transient response, eqn. (II.9), is

$$y_H(t) = \left(B_0/A_0\right) + a\exp(-A_0 t) = \left(B_0/A_0\right)\left(1 - \exp(-A_0 t)\right), \qquad \text{(II.25)}$$

which satisfies the initial boundary condition, eqn. (II.23).

Note, because

$$H(t) = \int_{-\infty}^{t} \delta(\tau)\, d\tau$$

then

$$y_H(t) = \int_{-\infty}^{t} y_\delta(\tau)\, d\tau. \qquad \text{(II.26)}$$

The step response for a stable first order system is shown in Fig. II.3(i). The values of the step response at t equal to $t_{1/2}$ and t_c are indicated.

As an indicator of how close the response is to its steady state value, t_c is a poor guide; for example, when t is equal to t_c the step response is approximately 65% of its final steady state value. A more informative rise time would be the time for the step response to reach 95% of its steady state value, $t_{0.95}$, say, which is the time for the transient effectively to disappear, and then $\exp(-A_0\, t_{0.95}) = 0.05$, that is,

$$t_{0.95} = 3.0/A_0 = 3.0t_c. \qquad \text{(II.27)}$$

II.2.4 Ramp response

A unit ramp input, as sketched in Fig. II.2, is represented by

$$x(t) = \left(t/t_R\right)H(t) \qquad \text{(II.28)}$$

where $1/t_R$ is the ramp rate. If t_R is small the ramp rate is fast; if t_R is large the ramp rate is slow.

The ramp response, denoted by $y_R(t/t_R)$, for the system represented by eqn. (II.1), is the solution of the differential equation

$$(D + A_0)y_R(t) = B_0\left(t/t_R\right) \quad \text{for } t > 0 \qquad \text{(II.29)}$$

which satisfies the initial boundary value

$$y_R(t = 0+) = 0. \qquad \text{(II.30)}$$

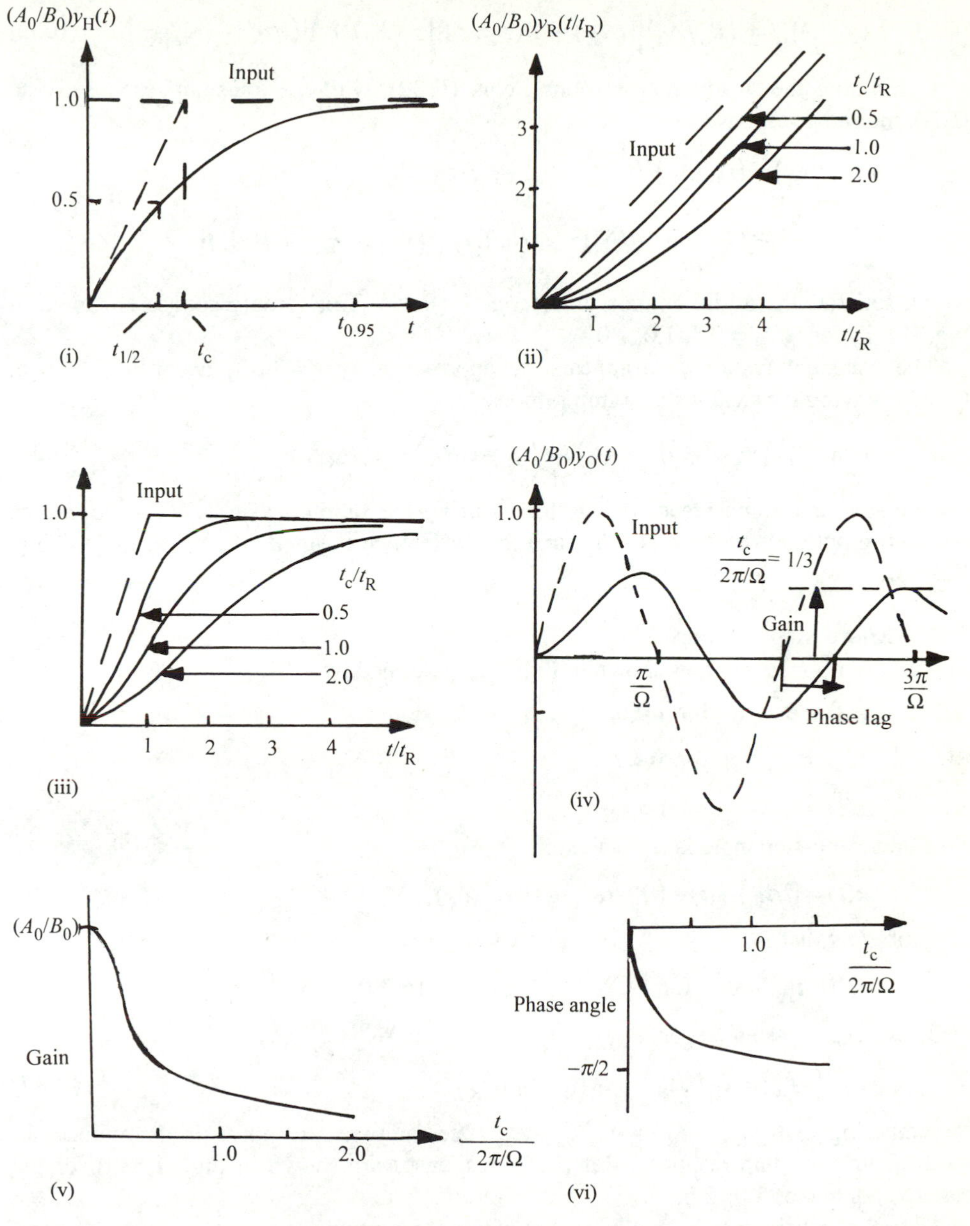

Fig. II.3. Responses of stable first order system.

The steady state ramp response is of the form

$$\left(y_R(t)\right)_{ss} = \text{const}\left(t/t_R\right) + \text{const}. \tag{II.31}$$

On substitution of eqn. (II.31) into eqn. (II.29) it follows that

$$(y_R(t))_{ss} = (B_0/A_0)[(t/t_R) - (1/(A_0 t_R))] = (B_0/A_0)[(t/t_R) - (t_c/t_R)]. \qquad \text{(II.32)}$$

Combining the steady state response, eqn. (II.32), with the transient response, eqn. (II.9), the ramp response is

$$\begin{aligned} y_R(t/t_R) &= (B_0/A_0)((t - t_c)/t_R) + a\exp(-A_0 t) \\ &= (B_0/A_0)\left[(t/t_R) - (t_c/t_R)\left(1 - \exp[-(t/t_R)(t_R/t_c)]\right)\right] \end{aligned} \qquad \text{(II.33)}$$

which satisfies the initial boundary value, eqn. (II.30). This ramp response is shown in Fig. II.3(ii) for $t_c/t_R = 0.5, 1.0, 2.0$.

The transient response disappears by approximately $t = 3.0t_c$, according to eqn. (II.27), leaving the steady state ramp response

$$(A_0/B_0)\,(y_R(t/t_R))_{ss} = (t - t_c)/t_R = (t/t_R) - (t_c/t_R). \qquad \text{(II.34)}$$

The steady state ramp response lags the input by the time constant, t_c. The difference between input and response is t_c/t_R, and this difference is small when $t_c \ll t_R$ (see Fig. II.3(ii)).

II.2.5 Ramp-step response

The unit ramp-step input, as shown in Fig. II.2, is defined by

$$\begin{aligned} x(t) &= 0 && \text{for } t < 0, \\ x(t) &= t/t_R && \text{for } 0 < t < t_R, \\ x(t) &= 1 && \text{for } t > t_R. \end{aligned} \qquad \text{(II.35)}$$

This unit ramp-step input is equivalent to

$$x(t) = (t/t_R)H(t) - ((t - t_R)/t_R)H(t - t_R) \qquad \text{(II.36)}$$

remembering that

$$H(t - t_R) = 0 \quad \text{for } t < t_R, \qquad H(t - t_R) = 1.0 \quad \text{for } t > t_R.$$

Thus the ramp-step response $y_{RH}(t/t_R)$ is

$$y_{RH}(t/t_R) = y_R(t/t_R) - y_R((t - t_R)/t_R), \qquad \text{(II.37)}$$

remembering that $y_R(t - t_R) = 0$ for $t < t_R$. The ramp-step response is determined directly from the ramp response. Ramp-step responses are shown in Fig. II.3(iii) for the cases $t_c/t_R = 0.5,\ 1.0,\ 2.0$.

Note that when t_c/t_R is small—that is, when the system time constant is small compared with ramp rise time—the response follows the input closely; in this case the response is regarded as quasi-steady.

II.2.6 Oscillatory response

A unit oscillatory input starting at t equal to zero is

$$x(t) = (\sin \Omega t)H(t). \qquad \text{(II.38)}$$

The oscillatory response, denoted by $y_O(t)$, for the system represented by eqn. (II.1) is the solution of the differential equation

$$(D + A_0)y_O(t) = B_0 \sin \Omega t \quad \text{for } t > 0 \tag{II.39}$$

which satisfies the initial boundary value

$$y_O(0+) = 0. \tag{II.40}$$

It is assumed that the steady state oscillatory response, known as the steady state frequency response, is of the form

$$\left(y_O(t)\right)_{ss} = a \sin \Omega t + b \cos \Omega t. \tag{II.41}$$

Substitution of eqn. (II.41) into eqn. (II.39) gives

$$\begin{aligned} a(A_0/B_0) &= 1\Big/\left[1 + (\Omega/A_0)^2\right], \\ b(A_0/B_0) &= (-\Omega/A_0)\Big/\left[1 + (\Omega/A_0)^2\right]. \end{aligned} \tag{II.42}$$

Hence

$$\begin{aligned} (A_0/B_0)\left(y_O(t)\right)_{ss} &= \left[\sin \Omega t - (\Omega/A_0)\cos \Omega t\right]\Big/\left[1 + (\Omega/A_0)^2\right] \\ &= \sin(\Omega t + \varphi)\Big/\left[1 + (\Omega/A_0)^2\right]^{1/2} \end{aligned} \tag{II.43}$$

where $\varphi = \tan^{-1}(-\Omega/A_0) = -\tan^{-1}(\Omega/A_0)$.

The oscillatory response, namely the steady state frequency response, eqn. (II.43), plus the transient response, eqn. (II.9), which satisfies the initial boundary value, eqn. (II.40), is

$$(A_0/B_0)y_O(t) = \left[\sin(\Omega t + \varphi) - (\sin \varphi)(\exp(-A_0 t))\right]\Big/\left[1 + (\Omega/A_0)^2\right]^{1/2}. \tag{II.44}$$

A parameter of importance is

$$\Omega/A_0 = 2\pi\left(t_c/(2\pi/\Omega)\right) \tag{II.45}$$

where $2\pi/\Omega$ is the period of the input.

The oscillatory response when $t_c/(2\pi/\Omega)$ is equal to 1/3 is sketched in Fig. II.3(iv); $t_c/(2\pi/\Omega)$ equal to 1/3 is equivalent to $t_{0.95}/(2\pi/\Omega)$ equal to 1, which implies that the transient response dies away within one period of the input.

Some nomenclature:

steady state frequency response amplitude ratio, or modulus, or gain

$$= \frac{\text{amplitude of steady state frequency response}}{\text{amplitude of input}}$$

$$= (B_0/A_0)\Big/\left[1+(\Omega/A_0)^2\right]^{1/2}$$

$$= (B_0/A_0)\Big/\left[1+\left(2\pi t_c/(2\pi/\Omega)\right)^2\right]^{1/2} \qquad \text{(II.46a)}$$

steady state frequency response phase angle

$$= \text{phase angle of steady state frequency response relative to input}$$

$$= \varphi = -\tan^{-1}(\Omega/A_0) \qquad \text{(II.46b)}$$

$$= -\tan^{-1}\left(2\pi t_c/(2\pi/\Omega)\right)$$

from eqn. (II.43); $\varphi > 0$ is a phase advance, $\varphi < 0$ is a phase lag.

Variations of the gain and phase angle with $t_c/(2\pi/\Omega)$ are shown in Fig. II.3(v). The gain decreases with $t_c/(2\pi/\Omega)$, becoming less than 0.1 for $t_c/(2\pi/\Omega)$ greater than 1.6. The phase angle is negative for all values of $t_c/(2\pi/\Omega)$.

The amplitude of the steady state frequency response is small for high frequency inputs relative to the system time constant, so this first order system filters out high frequencies, that is, it acts as a low frequency band-pass filter.

The steady state frequency response gain and phase angle are more easily obtained by assuming a complex input, namely

$$x(t) = \exp(\mathrm{i}\Omega t) \qquad \text{(II.47)}$$

where $\mathrm{i} = \sqrt{-1}$.

The complex steady state response is simply obtained by replacing the operator D by $\mathrm{i}\Omega$ in the system equation (eqn. (II.1)),

$$(\mathrm{i}\Omega + A_0)\left(y_O(t)\right)_{ss} = B_0 \exp(\mathrm{i}\Omega t). \qquad \text{(II.48)}$$

Thus,

$$(A_0/B_0)\left(y_O(t)\right)_{ss} = \frac{\exp(\mathrm{i}\Omega t)}{1+(\mathrm{i}\Omega/A_0)} = \frac{\exp(\mathrm{i}\Omega t)}{\left[1+(\Omega/A_0)^2\right]^{1/2}\exp(\mathrm{i}\varphi_1)}$$

$$= \frac{\exp(\mathrm{i}(\Omega t + \varphi))}{\left[1+(\Omega/A_0)^2\right]^{1/2}} \qquad \text{(II.49)}$$

where $\varphi_1 = \tan^{-1}(\Omega/A_0)$, $\varphi = -\varphi_1$.

Eqn. (II.49) gives the same gain and phase angle as eqns. (II.46).

Because

$$\sin \Omega t = \text{imaginary part of } \exp(-\mathrm{i}\Omega t) \tag{II.50}$$

the steady state frequency response to input $\sin \Omega t$ is the imaginary part of eqn. (II.49), which is consistent with eqn. (II.43).

II.2.7 Convolution integral

By definition of the impulse function for a function of time $f(t)$,

$$\int_{-\infty}^{+\infty} f(\tau)\delta(\tau - t)\, \mathrm{d}\tau = \int_{\tau=t-}^{\tau=t+} f(\tau)\delta(\tau - t)\, \mathrm{d}\tau = f(t). \tag{II.51}$$

Hence

$$x(t) = \int_{\tau=0}^{\tau=t+} x(\tau)\delta(\tau - t)\, \mathrm{d}\tau, \qquad t > 0. \tag{II.52}$$

Now $[x(\tau)\delta(\tau - t)]$ denotes an impulse at time τ of magnitude $x(\tau)$; thus, according to eqn. (II.52), an input $x(t)$ at time t can be regarded as a sequence, or superposition, of impulses of magnitude $[x(\tau)\delta(\tau - t)]$ at all earlier times $\tau < t$.

The response at time t of a system to the impulse $[x(\tau)\delta(\tau - t)]$ at an earlier time τ is the impulse response $[x(\tau)y_\delta(t - \tau)]$. Hence, summing all these impulse responses, for $0 < \tau < t$,

$$y(t) = \int_0^{t+} x(\tau)\, y_\delta(t - \tau)\, \mathrm{d}\tau \tag{II.53}$$

where $y(t)$ is the response to an arbitrary time input $x(t)$; the initial boundary value at $y(0+)$ is automatically incorporated.

Eqn. (II.53) allows responses to arbitrary time varying inputs to be built up from a knowledge of the impulse response.

It is sometimes more convenient to obtain these responses from the step response, rather than the impulse response; this can be done by noting that

$$\left.\begin{aligned} &\delta(t) = \mathrm{d}H(t)/\mathrm{d}t, \qquad y_\delta(t) = \mathrm{d}y_{\mathrm{H}}(t)/\mathrm{d}t, \\ &y_\delta(t - \tau) = -\mathrm{d}\big(y_{\mathrm{H}}(t - \tau)\big)/\mathrm{d}\tau. \end{aligned}\right\} \tag{II.54}$$

On substitution of eqns. (II.54) into eqn. (II.53), integrating by parts, and assuming $x(0)$ is zero,

$$y(t) = \int_0^{t+} \big(\mathrm{d}x(\tau)/\mathrm{d}\tau\big)\, y_{\mathrm{H}}(t - \tau)\, \mathrm{d}\tau. \tag{II.55}$$

It will be seen that the principle of convolution plays a most important role in aerodynamic theory as well as in dynamics.

EXAMPLES II.1

1. Relate the dimensions of $x(t)$, $y(t)$, A_0 and B_0 in eqn. (II.1).
2. Does the stability of a system depend on the input?

3. Determine the step response and the steady state frequency response when $A_0 = 0$; is this system physically acceptable?
4. Prove eqn. (II.23). What is the value of $\mathrm{D}y_H(0+)$?
5. Show that the response of the system represented by eqn. (II.1) to the trapezoidal input defined by

$$\begin{aligned} x(t) &= 0, & t &< 0 \\ &= t/t_R, & 0 &< t/t_R < 1 \\ &= 2 - (t/t_R), & 1 &< t/t_R < 2 \\ &= 0, & t/t_R &> 2 \end{aligned}$$

is given by

$$y(t) = y_{RS}(t/t_R) - y_{RS}((t/t_R) - 1).$$

By reference to Fig. II.3(iii) sketch the trapezoidal response when $t_c/t_R = 0.5, 1.0, 2.0$.
6. Prove eqn. (II.48).
7. Sketch the oscillatory response $(A_0/B_0)y_O(t)$ from eqn. (II.44) when $t_c/(2\pi/\Omega) = 2/3$.
8. Sketch the response to the input, when $t_c/(2\pi/\Omega) = \frac{1}{3}$,

$$\begin{aligned} x(t) &= 0, & t &< 0 \\ &= \sin \Omega t, & 0 &< t < \pi/\Omega \\ &= 0, & t &> \pi/\Omega. \end{aligned}$$

9. Determine the step response, the ramp-step response, and the oscillatory response for the first order system from the impulse response, using the convolution integral.
10. For the system

$$(\mathrm{D} + A_0)\,y(t) = B_1\,\mathrm{D}x(t)$$

determine (i) the step response when $x(t) = H(t)$ and (ii) the steady state frequency response gain and phase.

II.3 SINGLE DEGREE OF FREEDOM, SECOND ORDER, SYSTEM

Consider the differential equation

$$(\mathrm{D}^2 + A_1\,\mathrm{D} + A_0)\,y(t) = B_0 x(t) \tag{II.56}$$

where $\mathrm{D}^2 = \mathrm{d}^2/\mathrm{d}t^2$, $\mathrm{D} = \mathrm{d}/\mathrm{d}t$ and A_1, A_0, B_0 are constants.

Eqn. (II.56) represents the behaviour of a system which is

— single degree of freedom, since there is only one output, or response variable, $y(t)$,
— second order, since the highest time differential is $\mathrm{d}^2/\mathrm{d}t^2$,
— linear, since there are no products of $y(t)$ with its derivatives,
— with constant coefficients, A_0, A_1 and B_0.

The system is quiescent (i.e. $y(t) = 0$) for $t < 0$, and the input $x(t)$ starts at $t = 0$.

Again the response $y(t)$ can be expressed as a steady state response $(y(t))_{ss}$ plus a transient response $y_{tr}(t)$. Stability is determined by the transient response; for a stable system, the transient response decays to zero as $t \to \infty$, leaving the steady state response.

II.3.1 Stability

The transient response $y_{tr}(t)$ of the system represented by eqn. (II.56) is a non-zero solution of the differential equation

$$(\mathrm{D}^2 + A_1 \mathrm{D} + A_0) y_{tr}(t) = 0, \qquad t > 0. \tag{II.57}$$

To solve eqn. (II.57) try a solution

$$y_{tr}(t) = a \exp(\lambda t) \tag{II.58}$$

where a and λ are arbitrary constants. Substitution of eqn. (II.58) into eqn. (II.57) leads to the characteristic equation,

$$\lambda^2 + A_1 \lambda + A_0 = 0. \tag{II.59}$$

Eqn. (II.59) has two stability roots, namely,

$$\begin{aligned} \lambda = \lambda_1 &= \left[-A_1 + \left(A_1^2 - 4A_0\right)^{1/2}\right] \Big/ 2, \\ \lambda = \lambda_2 &= \left[-A_1 - \left(A_1^2 - 4A_0\right)^{1/2}\right] \Big/ 2. \end{aligned} \tag{II.60}$$

From eqns. (II.58) and (II.60) the transient response $y_{tr}(t)$ is of the form

$$y_{tr}(t) = a_1 \exp(\lambda_1 t) + a_2 \exp(\lambda_2 t) \tag{II.61}$$

where a_1 and a_2 are arbitrary constants.

For stability, both $\exp(\lambda_1 t)$ and $\exp(\lambda_2 t)$ must tend to zero with time. If either $\exp(\lambda_1 t)$ or $\exp(\lambda_2 t)$ grows with time, then the system is unstable.

The relationships between λ_1, λ_2 and A_1, A_0 are now examined.

If $A_1^2 > 4A_0$, $A_0 > 0$ and $A_1 > 0$, then both λ_1 and λ_2 are real and negative, both $\exp(\lambda_1 t)$ and $\exp(\lambda_2 t)$ are pure subsidences, and the system is stable.

If $A_1^2 > 4A_0$, $A_0 > 0$ and $A_1 < 0$, then both λ_1 and λ_2 are real and positive, both $\exp(\lambda_1 t)$ and $\exp(\lambda_2 t)$ are pure divergences, and the system is unstable.

If $A_1^2 > 4A_0$ and $A_0 < 0$, then, irrespective of the sign of A_1, λ_1 is real and positive, λ_2 is real and negative, $\exp(\lambda_1 t)$ is a pure divergence and $\exp(\lambda_2 t)$ is a pure subsidence, and the system is unstable.

If $A_1^2 < 4A_0$, which implies that $A_0 > 0$, then λ_1 and λ_2 are a complex conjugate pair, defined by

$$\lambda_1 = \mu + \mathrm{i}\omega, \qquad \lambda_2 = \mu - \mathrm{i}\omega, \tag{II.62}$$

where $\mathrm{i} = \sqrt{-1}$, $\mu = -A_1/2$ and $\omega = +(A_0 - (A_1/2)^2)^{1/2}$. In this case the transient response, eqn. (II.61), is

$$y_{tr}(t) = a_1 \exp((\mu + i\omega)t) + a_2 \exp((\mu - i\omega)t) \tag{II.63}$$

where a_1 and a_2 are now complex arbitrary constants.

Remembering that $\exp(i\omega t) = \cos\omega t + i\sin\omega t$, eqn. (II.63) becomes

$$\begin{aligned} y_{tr}(t) &= a_1 \exp(\mu t)\exp(i\omega t) + a_2 \exp(\mu t)\exp(-i\omega t) \\ &= \exp(\mu t)(a_1 + a_2)\cos\omega t + i(a_1 - a_2)\sin\omega t \\ &= \exp(\mu t)(b_1 \cos\omega t + b_2 \sin\omega t) \end{aligned} \quad \text{(II.64}$$

where b_1 and b_2 are real arbitrary constants because the transient response must be real (i.e. a_1 and a_2 must be complex conjugates).

The transient response in eqn. (II.64) is oscillatory with frequency ω rad/s, where

(i) if $\mu > 0$ (i.e. $A_1 < 0$) then the amplitude of the oscillation grows with time, a divergent oscillation, which implies instability,
(ii) if $\mu < 0$ (i.e. $A_1 > 0$) the amplitude of the oscillation decreases with time, tending to zero, a damped oscillation, which implies stability,
(iii) if $\mu = 0$ (i.e. $A_1 = 0$) the amplitude of the oscillation remains constant.

These oscillatory responses are shown in Fig. II.4.

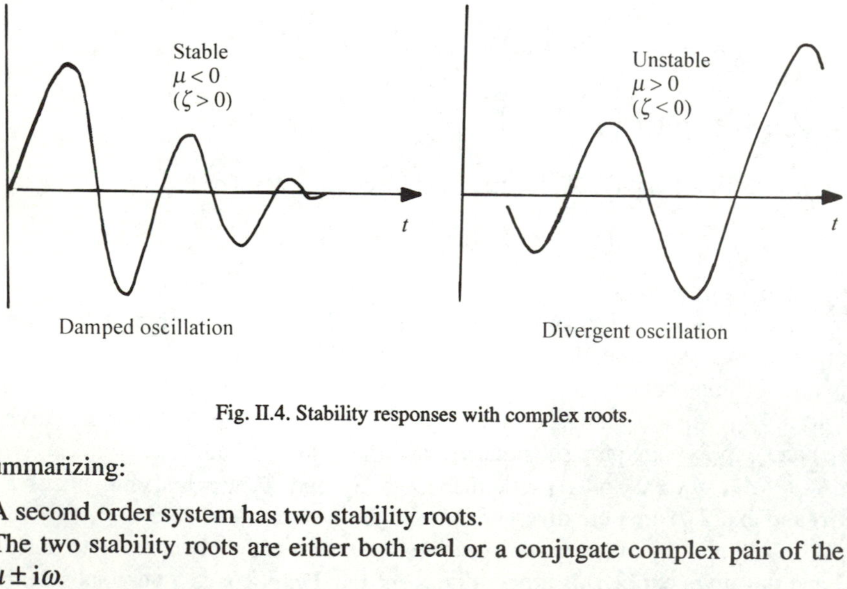

Fig. II.4. Stability responses with complex roots.

Summarizing:

1. A second order system has two stability roots.
2. The two stability roots are either both real or a conjugate complex pair of the form $\mu \pm i\omega$.
3. The system is stable when the real parts of both stability roots are negative.
4. From consideration of all possible values of A_1 and A_0, the second order system, represented by eqn. (II.56), is stable when

$$A_1 > 0 \quad \text{and} \quad A_0 > 0. \tag{II.65}$$

5. Corresponding to each stability root (λ_1, λ_2) there is a stability response ($\exp(\lambda_1 t)$, $\exp(\lambda_2 t)$).

There are different interpretations in the literature of the concept of neutral stability. In the control systems fraternity neutral stability usually refers to an oscillation with zero damping (i.e. $A_0 > 0$, $A_1 = 0$, $\mu = 0$). But traditionally in the flight dynamics fraternity neutral stability refers to zero stiffness (i.e. $A_0 = 0$) which implies one zero stability root.

The system equation, eqn. (II.56), can be interpreted physically as a mass–spring–viscous damper system with stiffness A_0 and damping A_1; stability is obtained with positive stiffness and damping. These parameters are often written in the alternative form

$$A_0 = \omega_0^2 \tag{II.66a}$$

where ω_0 is the system undamped frequency,

$$A_1 = 2\zeta\omega_0 \tag{II.66b}$$

where ζ is the system damping ratio, often quoted as a percentage of critical damping ($\zeta = 1.0$). The stability roots are then

$$\begin{aligned} \zeta < 1, \qquad & \mu = -\zeta\omega_0, \qquad \omega = \omega_0(1-\zeta^2)^{1/2} \\ \zeta > 1, \qquad & \lambda_1 = \omega_0\left[-\zeta + (\zeta^2-1)^{1/2}\right], \\ & \lambda_2 = \omega_0\left[-\zeta - (\zeta^2-1)^{1/2}\right]. \end{aligned} \tag{II.67}$$

The second order system is stable when $\zeta > 0$, $\omega_0 > 0$.

II.3.2 Impulse response

The impulse response $y_\delta(t)$, due to the impulse input $x(t) = \delta(t)$, is the transient response $y_{tr}(t)$ (eqns. (II.61) and (II.64)), which satisfies the initial boundary values

$$y_\delta(0+) = 0, \qquad \mathrm{D}y_\delta(0+) = B_0. \tag{II.68}$$

These initial conditions are obtained by a first integration of eqn. (II.56) across ($0- < t < 0+$), with $x(t) = \delta(t)$, which gives

$$\mathrm{D}y_\delta(0+) + A_1 y_\delta(0+) = B_0$$

followed by a second integration of eqn. (II.56) across ($0- < t < 0+$), which gives

$$y_\delta(0+) = 0.$$

Hence

$$\begin{aligned} y_\delta(t) &= B_0\left[\exp(\lambda_1 t) - \exp(\lambda_2 t)\right]/(\lambda_1 - \lambda_2) \quad \text{for real roots} \\ &= B_0\left[\exp(\mu t)\sin\omega t\right]/\omega \quad \text{for complex roots} \\ &= B_0 t\exp(\mu t) \quad \text{for two equal roots.} \end{aligned} \tag{II.69}$$

These formulae are interrelated; the response with complex roots is obtained from the response with real roots, substituting $\lambda_1 = \mu + \mathrm{i}\omega$, $\lambda_2 = \mu - \mathrm{i}\omega$; and the roots become equal as $\zeta \to 1$, then from eqns. (II.67), $\omega \to 0$.

II.3.3 Step response

The step response $y_H(t)$ of the second order system denoted by eqn. (II.56) to a step input ($x(t) = H(t)$) satisfies the initial boundary values

$$y_H(0+) = 0, \qquad Dy_H(0+) = 0. \tag{II.70}$$

The steady state step response is a constant, so from eqn. (II.56),

$$\left(y_H(t)\right)_{ss} = \text{const} = B_0/A_0. \tag{II.71}$$

Adding the transient response, eqns. (II.61) and (II.64), to the steady state step response, eqn. (II.71), the step response which satisfies the initial boundary values of eqns. (II.70) is

$$\begin{aligned}(A_0/B_0)y_H(t) &= 1-\left[(\lambda_1\exp(\lambda_2 t)-\lambda_2\exp(\lambda_1 t))/(\lambda_1-\lambda_2)\right]\\ &= 1-\left[\exp(\mu t)\left(\cos\omega t-(\mu/\omega)\sin\omega t\right)\right]\\ &= 1-\left[\exp(-\zeta\omega_0 t)\left[-\cos\left((1-\zeta^2)^{1/2}\omega_0 t\right)\right.\right.\\ &\qquad\left.\left.-\left(\zeta/(1-\zeta^2)^{1/2}\right)\sin\left((1-\zeta^2)^{1/2}\omega_0 t\right)\right]\right].\end{aligned} \tag{II.72}$$

The step response is sketched in Fig. II.5(i) against $\omega_0 t (= A_0^{1/2} t)$ for a stable system with $\zeta\,(= A_1/2A_0^{1/2})$ equal to 0.3, 0.7, 1.2. Note the large overshoot at low values of ζ.

When the stability roots comprise a pair of complex conjugate roots the time to 95% of the steady state value is given by

$$\begin{aligned}t_{0.95} &= (\ln 20)/(-\mu) = 3.0/(A_1/2)\\ &= 3.0/\zeta\omega_0 = \left[3/(2\pi\zeta)\right]\left(2\pi/\omega_0\right).\end{aligned} \tag{II.73}$$

When $\zeta = 0.5$, the transient dies out in approximately one period of the undamped frequency. As $\zeta \to 1$ the transient dies out in approximately half of one period of the undamped frequency.

When there are two real stability roots the time to 95% of the steady state value is determined by the smallest (in numerical magnitude) stability root. Taking $(-\lambda_1) < (-\lambda_2)$, then the time to 95% of the steady state value is approximately

$$t_{0.95} \simeq (\ln 20)/(-\lambda_1) = 3\Big/\left[\omega_0\left(\zeta-(\zeta^2-1)^{1/2}\right)\right]. \tag{II.74}$$

When $\zeta = 1.25$, the transient dies out in approximately one period of the undamped frequency. As ζ increases, the decay of the transient takes longer.

II.3.4 Ramp response

The ramp response $y_R(t)$ of the second order system denoted by eqn. (II.56) to a ramp input ($x(t) = (t/t_R)\,H(t)$) satisfies the initial boundary values

$$y_R(0+) = 0, \qquad Dy_R(0+) = 0. \tag{II.75}$$

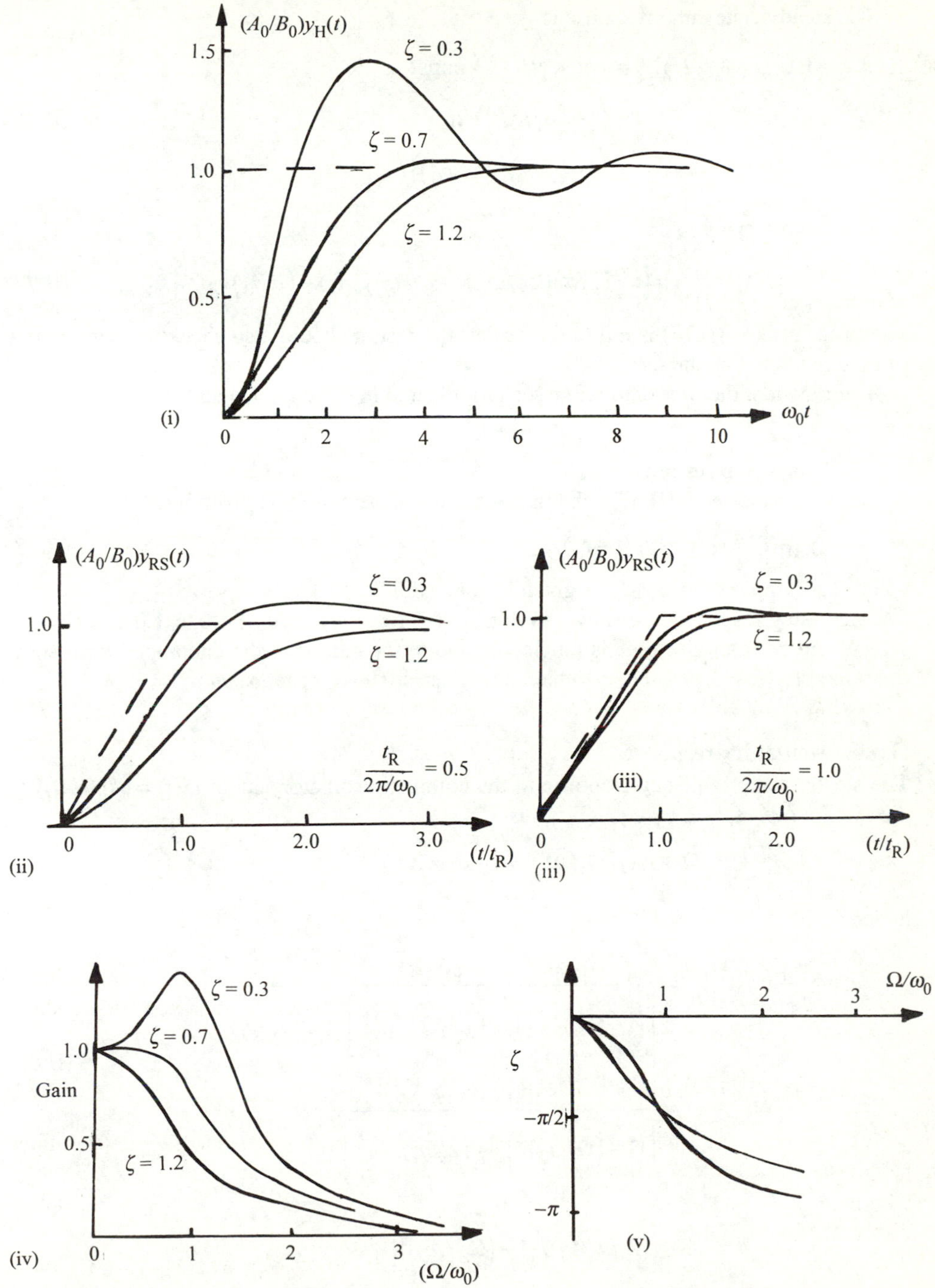

Fig. II.5. Responses of stable second order system.

The steady state ramp response is

$$\begin{aligned}(A_0/B_0)(y_R(t))_{ss} &= \text{const}\,(t/t_R) + \text{const}\\ &= \big(t-(A_1/A_0)\big)/t_R\\ &= \big(t-(\zeta/\pi)(2\pi/\omega_0)\big)/t_R\,.\end{aligned} \tag{II.76}$$

The ramp response is

$$(A_0/B_0)y_R(t) = \big[t-(\zeta/\pi)(2\pi/\omega_0)\;(A_0/B_0)y_H(t)-(1/B_0)y_\delta(t)\big]/t_R\,. \tag{II.77}$$

The proof of eqn. (II.77) is left to the reader; the reader should also check the consistency of dimensions of all the terms.

The transient dies out in the time scales indicated in eqns. (II.73) and (II.74).

II.3.5 Ramp-step response

By definition (see eqn. (II.37)), the ramp-step response $y_{RH}(t)$ is given by

$$y_{RH}(t) = y_R(t) - y_R(t-t_R) \tag{II.78}$$

where the ramp response $y_R(t)$ is given by eqn. (II.77).

Ramp-step responses are shown in Fig. II.5(ii) for $t_R/(2\pi/\omega_0) = 0.5$, 1.0 and $\zeta = 0.3$, 1.2. When the ramp rise time is long compared to the period of the undamped frequency, the ramp-step response is close to the input, a quasi-steady response.

II.3.6 Oscillatory response

The steady state frequency response to the complex oscillatory input ($x(t) = \exp(i\Omega t)$) of the system represented by eqn. (II.56) is

$$(-\Omega^2 + A_1\,i\Omega + A_0)\big(y_O(t)\big)_{ss} = B_0\exp(i\Omega t) \tag{II.79}$$

hence

$$\begin{aligned}\frac{A_0}{B_0}\big(y_O(t)\big)_{ss} &= \frac{\exp(i\Omega t)}{\Big[\big(1-(\Omega^2/A_0)\big)^2+(A_1\Omega/A_0)^2\Big]^{1/2}\exp(i\varphi_1)}\\ &= \frac{\exp(i(\Omega t+\varphi))}{\Big[\big(1-(\Omega/\omega_0)^2\big)^2+(2\zeta\Omega/\omega_0)^2\Big]^{1/2}}\end{aligned} \tag{II.80}$$

where

$$\begin{aligned}\varphi_1 = -\varphi &= \tan^{-1}\Big[(A_1\Omega/A_0)\big/\big(1-(\Omega^2/A_0)\big)\Big]\\ &= \tan^{-1}\Big[(2\zeta\Omega/\omega_0)\big/\big(1-(\Omega/\omega_0)^2\big)\Big].\end{aligned}$$

The gain and phase angle of the steady state frequency response, plotted against (Ω/ω_0) for $\zeta = 0.3$, 0.7, 1.2, are shown in Fig. II.5(iii). Note the large gain at low damping ratios when $(\Omega/\omega_0) \simeq 1.0$, the phenomenon of resonance; such resonance peaks disappear for $\zeta > 0.7$. Note that the phase angle, φ, is equal to $-\pi/2$ when $\Omega/\omega_0 = 1.0$, irrespective of the value of ζ.

The oscillatory response $y_O(t)$ to the input $(\sin \Omega t)\, H(t)$, satisfying the initial boundary values

$$y_O(0+) = 0, \qquad \mathrm{D}y_O(0+) = 0$$

is

$$\left[\frac{A_0}{B_0}\right] y_O(t) = \frac{\sin(\Omega t + \varphi) - (\exp(-\mu t)) \times [\sin\varphi \cos\omega t + (\Omega\cos\varphi + \mu\sin\varphi)\sin\omega t/\omega]}{\left[\left(1-(\Omega/\omega_0)^2\right)^2 + (2\zeta\,\Omega/\omega_0)^2\right]^{1/2}}. \tag{II.81}$$

II.3.7 Generalized input

Consider the system described by eqn. (II.56) but with a more general input of the form

$$(\mathrm{D}^2 + A_1\,\mathrm{D} + A_0) y(t) = (B_1\,\mathrm{D} + B_0) x(t). \tag{II.82}$$

The stability roots and response are not affected by the form of the input, so the stability characteristics are the same as those described in section II.3.1.

The step response of eqn. (II.82) is the solution of

$$(\mathrm{D}^2 + A_1\,\mathrm{D} + A_0) y_H(t) = B_1\delta(t) + B_0 H(t), \qquad t > 0 \tag{II.83}$$

so the step response of eqn. (II.82) can be obtained by adding the impulse response of section II.3.2, changing B_0 to B_1, to the step response of section II.3.3.

For the steady state frequency response

steady state frequency response gain

$$= \left[\frac{(B_1\Omega)^2 + B_0^2}{(A_0 - \Omega^2)^2 + (A_1\Omega)^2}\right]^{1/2} \tag{II.84a}$$

steady state frequency response phase angle

$$= \varphi = \tan^{-1}\left[\frac{B_1\Omega}{B_0}\right] - \tan^{-1}\left[\frac{A_1\Omega}{A_0 - \Omega^2}\right] \tag{II.84b}$$

EXAMPLES II.2

1. Determine the stability roots and describe the stability response for the following systems.

$$(D^2 + 6D + 8)y(t) = x(t)$$
$$(D^2 + 6D + 5)y(t) = x(t)$$
$$(D^2 - 6D + 8)y(t) = x(t)$$
$$(D^2 + 6D - 8)y(t) = x(t).$$

2. Sketch the step response of each of the systems in Example 1.
3. Sketch the steady state frequency response gain and phase angle against frequency for each of the systems in Example 1.
4. Derive the step response to the system

$$(D^2 + 6D + 9)y(t) = x(t).$$

5. Sketch, by reference to Fig. II.5(i), the response of a second order system against $\omega_0 t$, when $\zeta = 0.3$, for the square input defined by

$$x(t) = 0,\ t < 0; \quad x(t) = 1.0,\ 0 < \omega_0 t < 1.0; \quad x(t) = 0,\ \omega_0 t > 1.0.$$

6. Two statements in the text are deduced from eqns. (II.73) and (II.74):

— when $\zeta = 0.5$ the transient decays in approximately one period of the system undamped frequency,
— when $\zeta = 1.25$ the transient decays in approximately one period of the system undamped frequency.

Explain how these two statements are reconcilable.

7. Check that the steady state frequency response $(y_O(t))_{ss}$ given by eqn. (II.80) satisfies the system differential equation (II.56).
8. Sketch the oscillatory response $y_O(t)$, eqn. (II.81), taking $(\Omega/\omega_0) = 1.0$ and $\zeta = 0.3$.
9. For the system

$$(D^2 + 0.6D + 1.0)\,y(t) = (D + 1)\,x(t)$$

(i) sketch the step response,
(ii) sketch the steady state frequency response gain and phase angle against frequency.

10. Derive the ramp response, eqn. (II.77), from the step response, eqn. (II.72), using the convolution integral.

II.4 SINGLE DEGREE OF FREEDOM, HIGH ORDER, SYSTEM

Consider the differential equation

$$(D^n + A_{n-1} D^{n-1} + \ldots + A_1 D + A_0)y(t) = B_0 x(t) \qquad \text{(II.85)}$$

where D^j = differential operator = d^j/dt^j, $j = 1, \ldots, n$, and the coefficients $A_0, A_1, \ldots, A_{n-1}, B_0$ are all real constants. The system represented by eqn. (II.85) is a single degree of freedom, nth order, linear system.

The stability characteristic equation of the system represented by eqn. (II.85), by analogy with earlier arguments (see eqns. (II.56), (II.57), and (II.59)) can be written immediately, equating the differential operator to zero, replacing D^j by λ^j, hence

$$\lambda^n + A_{n-1}\lambda^{n-1} + \ldots + A_1\lambda + A_0 = 0. \tag{II.86}$$

The n stability roots of this polynomial characteristic equation, say m pairs of complex conjugate roots and $(n-2m)$ real roots, can be denoted as

$$\begin{aligned} \lambda &= \mu_j + \mathrm{i}\omega_j, \quad && j = 1,\ldots, m \\ &= \mu_j - \mathrm{i}\omega_j, && \\ &= \lambda_j, && j = 2m+1,\ldots, n. \end{aligned} \tag{II.87}$$

Standard software programs are available to calculate roots of polynomials (e.g. refs. II.2, II.3).

The transient response is then of the form

$$y_{\mathrm{tr}}(t) = \sum_{j=1}^{m} \exp(\mu_j t)(a_j \cos\omega_j t + b_j \sin\omega_j t) + \sum_{j=2m+1}^{n} c_j \exp(\lambda_j t) \tag{II.88}$$

where a_j, b_j are c_j are arbitrary real constants.

The system is stable if, and only if,

$$\mu_j < 0 \quad (j = 1,\ldots, m) \quad \text{and} \quad \lambda_j < 0 \quad (j = 2m+1,\ldots, n) \tag{II.89}$$

that is, if, and only if, the real part of each and every stability root is negative.

In sections II.2 and II.3 it is shown that the stability of a first order system and of a second order system can be assessed by the sign of the system's coefficients. These criteria for stability are

$$\begin{aligned} &\text{first order system,} && A_0 > 0. \\ &\text{second order system,} && A_1 > 0, \quad A_0 > 0. \end{aligned} \tag{II.90}$$

Similar criteria for stability exist for higher order systems:

$$\begin{aligned} &\text{third order system,} && A_1 > 0, \quad A_0 > 0, \quad A_2A_1 > A_0, \\ &\text{fourth order system,} && A_2 > 0, \quad A_1 > 0, \quad A_0 > 0, \\ & && A_1(A_3A_2 - A_1) - A_3^2A_0 > 0 \end{aligned} \tag{II.91}$$

The criteria for higher order systems are given in Etkin (ref. P.15).

These criteria were first derived by Routh in his classic 'Essay on the stability of a given state of motion' which won the Adams Prize Essay Contest in 1877 when the subject was 'The Criterion of Dynamical Stability' set by Clerk Maxwell and other examiners.

Knowing whether or not a system is stable or unstable by application of the Routh criteria may be useful at a preliminary stage. However, it is usually necessary to quantify that stability, or instability, and then the actual values of the stability roots are required.

Estimations of response characteristics of this type of higher order system are left as examples.

EXAMPLES II.3

1. Prove eqn. (II.86).
2. For a third order system, state the types of instability when

   (i) $A_2 > 0, \quad A_1 > 0, \quad A_0 < 0$
   (ii) $A_2 > 0, \quad A_1 < 0, \quad A_0 > 0$
   (iii) $A_2 < 0, \quad A_1 > 0, \quad A_0 > 0$
   (iv) $A_2 > 0, \quad A_1 > 0, \quad A_0 > 0, \quad A_2 A_1 < A_0.$

   Hint: regard the cubic characteristic equation as

   $$(\lambda + \lambda_1)(\lambda^2 + 2\zeta\omega_0\lambda + \omega_0^2) = 0.$$

3. Consider the system

   $$(\mathrm{D}^3 + 5\mathrm{D}^2 + 11\mathrm{D} + 7)y(t) = 7x(t).$$

   (i) Assess the system stability from the Routh criteria.
   (ii) Show that the stability roots are $\lambda = -1, -2 \pm \mathrm{i}\sqrt{3}$.
   (iii) Show that the initial boundary values for a step response ($x(t) = H(t)$) are

   $$\mathrm{D}^2 y_{\mathrm{H}}(0+) = \mathrm{D}y_{\mathrm{H}}(0+) = y_{\mathrm{H}}(0+) = 0.$$

   Derive an expression for, and sketch, the step response; determine $t_{0.95}$; which root essentially determines $t_{0.95}$?
   (iv) Derive expressions for, and sketch, the variation of the steady state frequency response gain and phase angle with input frequency.
4. Consider the system

   $$(\mathrm{D}^3 + 5\mathrm{D}^2 + 11\mathrm{D} + 7)y(t) = (2\mathrm{D}^2 + \mathrm{D} + 7)\, x(t).$$

   (i) Describe the system stability (note Example 3).
   (ii) Show that the initial boundary values for a step input ($x(t) = H(t)$) are

   $$\mathrm{D}^2 y_{\mathrm{H}}(0+) = -9, \quad \mathrm{D}y_{\mathrm{H}}(0+) = 2, \quad y_{\mathrm{H}}(0+) = 0.$$

   Derive an expression for, and sketch, the step response.
   (iii) Derive expressions for, and sketch, the variation of the steady state frequency response gain and phase angle with input frequency.

II.5 TWO DEGREE OF FREEDOM, SECOND ORDER, SYSTEM

To illustrate the analysis of a two degree of freedom system two simple examples are worked through.

II.5.1 First example

Consider the system

$$\begin{aligned}(\mathrm{D}+3)\,y_1(t)+\quad 2\,y_2(t)&=x_1(t)\\ y_1(t)+(\mathrm{D}+2)y_2(t)&=x_2(t).\end{aligned} \tag{II.92}$$

where $y_1(t)=y_2(t)=x_1(t)=x_2(t)=0$ when $t<0$.

Eqns. (II.92) represent a system with two degrees of freedom; there are two independent response variables, $y_1(t)$ and $y_2(t)$. It is a second order system since, as shown later, the characteristic equation is a quadratic polynomial with two stability roots. Two independent input variables $x_1(t)$ and $x_2(t)$ are assumed.

The transient response is a non-zero solution of the homogeneous equations

$$\begin{aligned}(\mathrm{D}+3)\big(y_1(t)\big)_{\mathrm{tr}}+\quad 2\,\big(y_2(t)\big)_{\mathrm{tr}}&=0,\qquad t>0\\ \big(y_1(t)\big)_{\mathrm{tr}}+(\mathrm{D}+2)\big(y_2(t)\big)_{\mathrm{tr}}&=0.\end{aligned} \tag{II.93}$$

To obtain the solution of eqns. (II.93) try

$$\big(y_1(t)\big)_{\mathrm{tr}}=a\exp(\lambda t),\qquad \big(y_2(t)\big)_{\mathrm{tr}}=b\exp(\lambda t) \tag{II.94}$$

where a, b are arbitrary constants.

On substitution of eqns. (II.94), eqns. (II.93) become

$$\begin{aligned}(\lambda+3)\,a+\quad 2\,b&=0\\ a+(\lambda+2)\,b&=0.\end{aligned} \tag{II.95}$$

Eqns. (II.95) are satisfied when either $a=b=0$, which implies a zero transient response, or one equation is a simple multiple of the other equation, and then the determinant of the coefficients is zero, so

$$\begin{vmatrix}\lambda+3 & 2\\ 1 & \lambda+2\end{vmatrix}=0 \tag{II.96}$$

which gives the characteristic equation

$$\lambda^2+5\lambda+4=0. \tag{II.97}$$

There are two real roots of the characteristic equation (II.97):

$$\lambda=\lambda_1=-4,\qquad \lambda=\lambda_2=-1. \tag{II.98}$$

Thus the system is stable with a transient response, substituting eqn. (II.98) into eqn. (II.94), of the form

$$\begin{aligned}\big(y_1(t)\big)_{\mathrm{tr}}&=a_1\exp(-4t)+a_2\exp(-t)\\ \big(y_2(t)\big)_{\mathrm{tr}}&=b_1\exp(-4t)+b_2\exp(-t)\end{aligned} \tag{II.99}$$

where a_1, a_2, b_1 and b_2 are arbitrary real constants.

Now a_1 and b_1 are related. Substitution of the response

$$\lambda_1 = -4, \quad (y_1(t))_{tr} = a_1 \exp(-4t), \quad (y_2(t))_{tr} = b_1 \exp(-4t)$$

into eqns. (II.95) gives,

$$\left.\begin{aligned} -a_1 + 2b_1 &= 0 \\ a_1 - 2b_1 &= 0 \end{aligned}\right\} \quad b_1 = a_1/2. \tag{II.100}$$

Because the determinant of the coefficients has been set to zero in eqn. (II.96) the two equations in (II.100) are effectively the same.

Stability mode 1 is described by

— the stability root, or modal root, or eigenvalue, $\lambda = -4$;
— the modal response, $\exp(-4t)$ (a pure subsidence, time to half amplitude $\simeq (0.7/4)$ s);
— the modal shape, or eigenvector, $(a : b) = (1 : 0.5)$.

Similarly a_2 and b_2 are related. Substitution of the response

$$\lambda_2 = -1, \quad (y_1(t))_{tr} = a_2 \exp(-t), \quad (y_2(t))_{tr} = b_2 \exp(-t)$$

into eqns. (II.95) gives,

$$\left.\begin{aligned} 2a_2 + 2b_2 &= 0 \\ a_2 + \ b_2 &= 0 \end{aligned}\right\} b_2 = -a_2. \tag{II.101}$$

Again because the determinant of the coefficients has been set to zero in eqn. (II.96) the two equations in (II.101) are effectively the same.

Stability mode 2 is described by:

— the stability root, or modal root, or eigenvalue, $\lambda = -1$;
— the modal response $\exp(-t)$ (a pure subsidence, time to half amplitude $\simeq$ 0.7 s);
— the modal shape, or eigenvector, $(a : b) = (1 : -1)$.

The transient response, from eqns. (II.99)–(II.101),

$$\begin{aligned} (y_1(t))_{tr} &= \quad a_1 \exp(-4t) + a_2 \exp(-t) \\ (y_2(t))_{tr} &= 0.5a_1 \exp(-4t) - a_2 \exp(-t), \end{aligned} \tag{II.102}$$

involves only two arbitrary real constants, a_1 and a_2, which is consistent with the fact that a second order system requires two initial boundary values.

To study the responses, the response variables $y_1(t)$ and $y_2(t)$ can be decoupled by regarding eqns. (II.92) as two simultaneous equations and solving for $y_1(t)$ and $y_2(t)$. It follows that

$$\begin{aligned} (\mathrm{D}^2 + 5\mathrm{D} + 4)y_1(t) &= (\mathrm{D}+2)x_1(t) \qquad - 2\,x_2(t) \\ (\mathrm{D}^2 + 5\mathrm{D} + 4)y_2(t) &= \quad - \quad x_1(t) + (\mathrm{D}+3)x_2(t). \end{aligned} \tag{II.103}$$

Responses can then be obtained using the methods described in section II.3.

Note that the characteristic equations for both $y_1(t)$ and $y_2(t)$ in eqns. (II.103) are the same as the characteristic equation for the overall system, given by eqn. (II.97).

Consider the responses to the particular input

$$x_1(t) = 2H(t), \qquad x_2(t) = 0. \tag{II.104}$$

And then from eqns. (II.103)

$$\begin{aligned} &Dy_1(0+) = 2.0, \qquad y_1(0+) = 0, \qquad (y_1(t))_{ss} = 1.0 \\ &Dy_2(0+) = 0, \qquad y_2(0+) = 0, \qquad (y_2(t))_{ss} = -0.5, \end{aligned} \tag{II.105}$$

and

$$\begin{aligned} y_1(t) &= 1.0 - \left[\tfrac{1}{3}(\exp(-4t)) + \tfrac{2}{3}(\exp(-t))\right] \\ y_2(t) &= -0.5 - \left[\tfrac{1}{6}(\exp(-4t)) - \tfrac{2}{3}(\exp(-t))\right]. \end{aligned} \tag{II.106}$$

Note that these responses, eqns. (II.106), incorporate the modal shape of the transient response, eqn. (II.102).

Responses in each of the separate stability modes can be generated by appropriate inputs. For example:

(i) the response

$$y_1(t) = \exp(-4t), \qquad y_2(t) = 0.5\exp(-4t), \tag{II.107}$$

which is the modal response of stability root 1 (see eqn. (II.102)), can be generated by the input

$$x_1(t) = \delta(t), \qquad x_2(t) = 0.5\delta(t), \tag{II.108}$$

by reference to eqns. (II.92) or to eqns. (II.103);

(ii) the response

$$y_1(t) = \exp(-t), \qquad y_2(t) = -\exp(-t), \tag{II.109}$$

which is the modal response of stability root 2 (see eqn. (II.102)), can be generated by the input

$$x_1(t) = \delta(t), \qquad x_2(t) = -\delta(t). \tag{II.110}$$

II.5.2 Second example

Consider the system given by

$$\begin{aligned} (D+4)y_1(t) - \quad 2\,y_2(t) &= x_1(t) \\ 9\,y_1(t) + (D-2)y_2(t) &= x_2(t) \end{aligned} \tag{II.111}$$

where $y_1(t) = y_2(t) = x_1(t) = x_2(t) = 0$ when $t < 0$.

The transient response is given by a solution to the equations

$$\begin{aligned}(\mathrm{D}+4)\,(y_1(t))_{\mathrm{tr}} - 2\,(y_2(t))_{\mathrm{tr}} &= 0, \quad t>0\\ 9\,(y_1(t))_{\mathrm{tr}} + (\mathrm{D}-2)(y_2(t))_{\mathrm{tr}} &= 0.\end{aligned} \tag{II.112}$$

To obtain the solution of eqns. (II.112) try

$$(y_1(t)_{\mathrm{tr}}) = a\exp(\lambda t), \qquad (y_2(t))_{\mathrm{tr}} = b\exp(\lambda t), \tag{II.113}$$

where a, b are arbitrary constants.

On substitution of eqns. (II.113), eqns. (II.112) become

$$\begin{aligned}(\lambda+4)a - \quad 2\,b &= 0\\ 9\,a+(\lambda-2)b &= 0.\end{aligned} \tag{II.114}$$

Eqns. (II.114) are satisfied when either $a = b = 0$, which implies a zero transient response, or the determinant of the coefficients is zero, namely

$$\begin{vmatrix}\lambda+4 & -2\\ 9 & \lambda-2\end{vmatrix} = 0$$

which gives the characteristic equation

$$\lambda^2+2\lambda+10=0. \tag{II.115}$$

The two stability roots of eqn. (II.115) are

$$\lambda=\lambda_1=-1+\mathrm{i}3, \qquad \lambda=\lambda_2=-1-\mathrm{i}3. \tag{II.116}$$

The system is stable since the real parts of both λ_1 and λ_2 are negative.

For this second order response, from eqn. (II.115),

$$\begin{aligned}\omega_0 &= \text{undamped frequency} = (10)^{1/2}\ \text{rad/s} = 3.16\ \text{rad/s}\\ \omega &= \text{stability frequency} = 3\,\text{rad/s}\\ \zeta &= \text{damping ratio} = 0.32.\end{aligned} \tag{II.117}$$

From eqns. (II.113) and (II.116) the transient response is of the form

$$\begin{aligned}(y_1(t))_{\mathrm{tr}} &= a_1\exp[(-1+\mathrm{i}3)t]+a_2\exp[(-1-\mathrm{i}3)t]\\ (y_2(t))_{\mathrm{tr}} &= b_1\exp[(-1+\mathrm{i}3)t]+b_2\exp[(-1-\mathrm{i}3)t]\end{aligned} \tag{II.118}$$

where a_1, a_2, b_1 and b_2 are complex arbitrary constants.

To obtain the modal shape corresponding to λ_1, namely the ratio b_1/a_1, substitute $\lambda=\lambda_1=-1+\mathrm{i}3$ into eqns. (II.114), and both equations give

$$b_1 = 1.5(1+\mathrm{i})a_1 = 1.5\left(\sqrt{2}\exp(\mathrm{i}\pi/4)\right)a_1. \tag{II.119}$$

Hence the stability mode corresponding to stability root λ_1, with modal shape (b_1/a_1), eqn. (II.119), is

$$\begin{aligned} (y_1(t))_{tr} &= \quad a_1 \exp[(-1+i3)t] \\ (y_2(t))_{tr} &= 2.12a_1 \exp[(-1+i3)t + i\pi/4] \end{aligned} \qquad (II.120)$$

To obtain the modal shape corresponding to λ_2, namely the ratio b_2/a_2, substitute $\lambda = \lambda_2 = -1 - i3$ into eqns. (II.113), both equations give

$$b_2 = 1.5(1-i)a_2 = 1.5\left(\sqrt{2}\exp(-i\pi/4)\right). \qquad (II.121)$$

Hence the stability mode corresponding to stability root λ_2, with modal shape (b_2/a_2), eqn. (II.121), is

$$\begin{aligned} (y_1(t))_{tr} &= \quad a_2 \exp[(-1-i3)t] \\ (y_2(t))_{tr} &= 2.12a_2 \exp[(-1-i3)t - i\pi/4]. \end{aligned} \qquad (II.122)$$

The total transient response is the sum of the two stability responses, so from eqns. (II.121) and (II.122),

$$\begin{aligned} (y_1(t))_{tr} &= a_1 \exp[(-1+i3)t] + a_2 \exp[(-1-i3)t] \\ &= [\exp(-t)][c_1 \cos 3t + c_2 \sin 3t] \\ (y_2(t))_{tr} &= 2.12[a_1 \exp[(-1+i3)]t + i\pi/4] \\ &\qquad + a_2 \exp[(-1-i3)t - i\pi/4)] \\ &= 2.12[\exp(-t)][c_1 \cos(3t+\pi/4) + c_2 \sin(3t+\pi/4)] \end{aligned} \qquad (II.123)$$

where c_1 and c_2 are arbitrary real constants, see eqn. (II.64).

A pair of stability roots which are complex conjugates (i.e. of the form $\mu \pm i\omega$) combine to form one stability mode. In this example the stability mode is described by

— the stability roots, or modal roots, or eigenvalues, $-1 \pm i3$,
— the modal response, a damped oscillation with damping $\exp(-t)$ and frequency 3 rad/s,
— the modal shape, or eigenvector, $(a : b) = (1 : 2.12 \exp(i\pi/4))$.

The modal shape incorporates an amplitude ratio and phase difference.

The responses to particular inputs for the system represented by eqns. (II.111) can be obtained by decoupling the degrees of freedom as explained in section II.5.1, eqns. (II.103).

EXAMPLES II.4

1. Determine inputs $x_1(t)$ and $x_2(t)$ in eqns. (II.103) which make the response $y_2(t)$ equal to zero.
2. Determine the responses $y_1(t)$, $y_2(t)$ for the system in eqns. (II.111) to the input

$$x_1(t) = H(t), \qquad x_2(t) = 0.$$

3. For the system in eqns. (II.111) compare the steady state frequency responses of $y_1(t)$ and $y_2(t)$, taking

$$x_1(t) = x_2(t) = \exp(\mathrm{i}\Omega t).$$

4. Derive the stability mode for the system:

$$\begin{aligned} (\mathrm{D}^2 + 2\mathrm{D} + 2)y_1(t) + (\mathrm{D}+1)y_2(t) &= x_1(t) \\ y_1(t) + \quad 2\, y_2(t) &= x_2(t). \end{aligned}$$

Determine the responses to inputs $x_1(t) = H(t)$, $x_2(t) = 0$.

II.6 THREE DEGREE OF FREEDOM, THIRD ORDER, SYSTEM

The analysis of a more advanced system is again demonstrated by an example. Consider the system

$$\begin{aligned} (\mathrm{D}+1)y_1(t) - \quad y_2(t) - \quad 2\, y_3(t) &= x_1(t) \\ 2\, y_1(t) + (\mathrm{D}+2)y_2(t) + \quad 4\, y_3(t) &= x_2(t) \\ y_1(t) \quad + (\mathrm{D}+2)y_3(t) &= x_3(t) \end{aligned} \tag{II.124}$$

This system has three degrees of freedom, because there are three response variables; it is a third order system because, as shown later, the characteristic equation is a cubic polynomial, with three stability roots.

The transient response is a non-zero solution of the equations,

$$\begin{aligned} (\mathrm{D}+1)\big(y_1(t)\big)_{\mathrm{tr}} - \quad \big(y_2(t)\big)_{\mathrm{tr}} - \quad 2\,\big(y_3(t)\big)_{\mathrm{tr}} &= 0 \\ 2\,\big(y_1(t)\big)_{\mathrm{tr}} + (\mathrm{D}+2)\big(y_2(t)\big)_{\mathrm{tr}} + \quad 4\,\big(y_3(t)\big)_{\mathrm{tr}} &= 0 \\ \big(y_1(t)\big)_{\mathrm{tr}} \quad + (\mathrm{D}+2)\big(y_3(t)\big)_{\mathrm{tr}} &= 0. \end{aligned} \tag{II.125}$$

As before, assume that the transient response is of the form

$$\big(y_1(t)\big)_{\mathrm{tr}} = a\exp(\lambda t), \quad \big(y_2(t)\big)_{\mathrm{tr}} = b\exp(\lambda t), \quad \big(y_3(t)\big)_{\mathrm{tr}} = c\exp(\lambda t). \tag{II.126}$$

On substitution of eqns. (II.126), eqns. (II.125) become

$$\begin{aligned} (\lambda+1)a - \quad b - \quad 2\, c &= 0 \\ 2\, a + (\lambda+2)b + \quad 4\, c &= 0 \\ a \quad + (\lambda+2)c &= 0. \end{aligned} \tag{II.127}$$

The solution of eqns. (II.126) is either $a = b = c = 0$, which implies zero response, or one equation is a linear combination of the other two, in which case the determinant of the coefficients is zero; that is,

$$\begin{vmatrix} (\lambda+1) & -1 & -2 \\ 2 & (\lambda+2) & 4 \\ 1 & 0 & (\lambda+2) \end{vmatrix} = 0. \tag{II.128}$$

The characteristic equation is

$$\lambda^3 + 5\lambda^2 + 12\lambda + 8 = 0. \tag{II.129}$$

By reference to the Routh criteria, eqn. (II.91), the system is stable.
Eqn. (II.129) can be factorized

$$(\lambda+1)(\lambda^2 + 4\lambda + 8) = 0. \tag{II.130}$$

The stability roots are

$$\lambda = \lambda_1 = -1, \qquad \lambda = \lambda_2 = -2 + \mathrm{i}2, \qquad \lambda = \lambda_3 = -2 - \mathrm{i}2. \tag{II.131}$$

The real parts of all the stability roots are negative, confirming that the system is stable.
There are two stability modes with modal responses

— a pure subsidence, $\exp(-t)$,
— a damped oscillation, damping $\exp(-2t)$ and frequency 2 rad/s. (II.132)

The modal shape corresponding to pure subsidence is obtained by substituting $\lambda = -1$ into eqns. (II.127), and then determining two of the coefficients in terms of the third coefficient; this modal shape satisfies all three equations; in this case

$$b = 2a, \qquad c = -a \tag{II.133}$$

The contribution of this mode to the transient response is

$$\begin{aligned} (y_1(t))_{\mathrm{tr}} &= a_1 \exp(-t), \\ (y_2(t))_{\mathrm{tr}} &= 2a_1 \exp(-t), \\ (y_3(t))_{\mathrm{tr}} &= -a_1 \exp(-t) \end{aligned} \tag{II.134}$$

where a_1 is an arbitrary real constant.

The modal shape corresponding to the damped oscillation is obtained by substituting $\lambda = (-2 + \mathrm{i}2)$ into eqns. (II.127), and determining two of the coefficients in terms of the third coefficient; this modal shape satisfies all three equations; in this case

$$\begin{aligned} b &= a(-1+\mathrm{i}) = a\sqrt{2}\exp(\mathrm{i}3\pi/4), \\ c &= a(\mathrm{i}0.5) = a.0.5\exp(\mathrm{i}\pi/2). \end{aligned} \tag{II.135}$$

The contribution of this mode to the transient response is

$$\begin{aligned}
(y_1(t))_{\text{tr}} &= [\exp(-2t)][a_2 \cos 2t + a_3 \sin 2t] \\
(y_2(t))_{\text{tr}} &= \sqrt{2}[\exp(-2t)][a_2 \cos(2t+3\pi/4) + a_3 \sin(2t+3\pi/4)] \\
(y_3(t))_{\text{tr}} &= 0.5[\exp(-2t)][a_2 \cos(2t+\pi/2) + a_3 \sin(2t+\pi/2)]
\end{aligned} \tag{II.136}$$

where a_2 and a_3 are arbitrary real constants.

To study the responses of the above system the degrees of freedom can be decoupled by regarding eqns. (II.124) as three simultaneous equations and solving for $y_1(t)$, $y_2(t)$ and $y_3(t)$. For example,

$$\begin{aligned}
(\mathrm{D}^3 + 5\mathrm{D}^2 + 12\mathrm{D} + 8)y_1(t) = (\mathrm{D}+2)^2 x_1(t) \\
+ (\mathrm{D}+2)x_2(t) + 2\mathrm{D}x_3(t).
\end{aligned} \tag{II.137}$$

Eqn. (II.137) can then be treated by the methods described in sect. II.4.

EXAMPLES II.5

1. For the system represented by eqns. (II.124) with inputs

$$x_1(t) = k_1\delta(t), \qquad x_2(t) = k_2\delta(t), \qquad x_3(t) = k_3\delta(t)$$

   (i) determine k_1, k_2 and k_3 such that the response gives stability mode 1 (eqns. (II.134)) only;
   (ii) determine k_1, k_2 and k_3 such that the response gives stability mode 2 (eqns. (II.136)) only.

2. Determine the decoupled equations for $y_2(t)$ and $y_3(t)$, corresponding to eqn. (II.137).
3. For the system represented by eqns. (II.124) with inputs

$$x_1(t) = 0, \qquad x_2(t) = 0, \qquad x_3(t) = H(t)$$

   (i) determine the steady state response from eqns. (II.124);
   (ii) check the steady state response from eqn. (II.137) and Example 2;
   (iii) determine the response $y_1(t)$;
   (iv) write down, without derivation, the responses $y_2(t)$ and $y_3(t)$.

4. Derive the stability modes of the system represented by

$$\begin{aligned}
y_1(t) - y_2(t) - 2\,y_3(t) &= x_1(t) \\
2y_1(t) + (\mathrm{D}+2)y_2(t) + 4\,y_3(t) &= x_2(t) \\
y_1(t) + (\mathrm{D}+2)y_3(t) &= x_3(t).
\end{aligned}$$

   Determine the responses to the input

$$x_1(t) = H(t), \qquad x_2(t) = 0, \qquad x_3(t) = 0.$$

II.7 GENERAL THEORY OF LINEAR SYSTEMS

For completeness a summary is given of the general theory of linear systems.

All linear systems with constant coefficients can be expressed as a set of coupled first order systems which can be written in matrix notation:

$$[\mathbf{A}_1]_{n\times n}[\mathbf{D}\mathbf{y}(t)]_{n\times 1}+[\mathbf{A}_0]_{n\times n}[\mathbf{y}(t)]_{n\times 1}=[\mathbf{B}_0]_{n\times m}[\mathbf{x}(t)]_{m\times 1} \tag{II.138}$$

where $[\mathbf{A}_1]_{n\times n}$ and $[\mathbf{A}_0]_{n\times n}$ are square matrices of n rows $\times$ n columns; $[\mathbf{B}_0]_{n\times m}$ is a matrix of n rows $\times$ m columns; $[\mathbf{y}(t)]_{n\times 1}$ is a column vector, listing the n response variables $y_1(t), y_2(t),\ldots, y_n(t)$; and $[\mathbf{x}(t)]_{m\times 1}$ is a column vector, listing the m independent input variables $x_1(t), x_2(t),\ldots, x_m(t)$.

Eqn. (II.138) can be rearranged into the form

$$[\mathbf{D}\mathbf{y}(t)]_{n\times 1}+[\mathbf{A}]_{n\times n}[\mathbf{y}(t)]_{n\times 1}=[\mathbf{B}]_{n\times m}[\mathbf{x}(t)]_{m\times 1} \tag{II.139}$$

where

$$[\mathbf{A}]=[\mathbf{A}_1]^{-1}[\mathbf{A}_0], \qquad [\mathbf{B}]=[\mathbf{A}_1]^{-1}[\mathbf{B}_0].$$

The characteristic equation is given by the determinant

$$\left|\lambda[\mathbf{I}]_{n\times n}+[\mathbf{A}]_{n\times n}\right|=0 \tag{II.140}$$

where $[\mathbf{I}]$ is the unit diagonal square ($n\times n$) matrix (i.e. all diagonal terms are unity, all other terms are zero). The solution of eqn. (II.140) gives the stability roots, or eigenvalues, λ_j ($j = 1,\ldots, n$).

The modal shape, or eigenvector, $[\mathbf{y}_j]$ corresponding to stability root λ_j, is obtained from

$$\left[\lambda_j[\mathbf{I}]+[\mathbf{A}]\right]_{n\times n}[\mathbf{y}_j]_{n\times 1}=0. \tag{II.141}$$

Standard subroutines are available to invert matrices, and to determine eigenvalues and eigenvectors, e.g. the NAG library in the UK (ref. II.2); the algorithms are based on linear algebra, see for example Wilkinson & Reinsch (ref. II.4).

Responses can be computed directly without recourse to eigenvalues or eigenvectors. The solution of eqn. (II.139), omitting the brackets and subscripts, is formally

$$\mathbf{y}(t)=\exp\left(-\mathbf{A}(t-t_0)\right)\mathbf{y}(t_0)+\int_{t_0}^{t}\exp(-\mathbf{A}(t-\tau))\mathbf{B}\mathbf{x}(\tau)\,\mathrm{d}\tau \tag{II.142}$$

for $t > t_0$, where

$$\exp(-\mathbf{A}t)=\mathbf{I}-\mathbf{A}t+\mathbf{A}^2t^2/2-\ldots \tag{II.143}$$

Hence

$$\begin{aligned}\mathbf{y}(t_n+\Delta t)&=\exp(-\mathbf{A}\,\Delta t)\mathbf{y}(t_n)+\int_{t_n}^{t_n+\Delta t}\exp\left(-\mathbf{A}(t_n+\Delta t-\tau)\right)\mathbf{B}\mathbf{x}(\tau)\,\mathrm{d}\tau\\&=\exp(-\mathbf{A}\,\Delta t)\mathbf{y}(t_n)+\int_{0}^{\Delta t}\exp\left(-\mathbf{A}(\tau')\right)\mathbf{B}\mathbf{x}(t_n+\Delta t-\tau')\,\mathrm{d}\tau'.\end{aligned} \tag{II.144}$$

When Δt is small a reasonable approximation for $x(t_n + \Delta t - \tau')$ is

$$\mathbf{x}(t_n + \Delta t - \tau') = \mathbf{x}(t_{n+1})(1 - \tau'/\Delta t) + \mathbf{x}(t_n)\tau'/\Delta t. \qquad \text{(II.145)}$$

On substitution of eqns. (II.143) and (II.145) eqn. (II.144) becomes, for small Δt,

$$\begin{aligned}\mathbf{y}(t_n + \Delta t) = {} & \left(\mathbf{I} - \mathbf{A}\,\Delta t + \mathbf{A}^2\,\Delta t^2/2\ \ldots\right)\mathbf{y}(t_n) \\ & + \left(\mathbf{I}\,\Delta t/2 - \mathbf{A}\,\Delta t^2/3 + \mathbf{A}^2\,\Delta t^3/8\ \ldots\right)\mathbf{B}\mathbf{x}(t_n) \\ & + \left(\mathbf{I}\,\Delta t/2 - \mathbf{A}\,\Delta t^2/6 + \mathbf{A}^2\,\Delta t^3/24\ \ldots\right)\mathbf{B}\mathbf{x}(t_{n+1}).\end{aligned} \qquad \text{(II.146)}$$

The increment Δt must be chosen to be sufficiently small for the expansions to converge.

The accuracy could be improved by expressing $\mathbf{x}(t_n + \Delta t - \tau')$ between t_n and $t_n + \Delta t$ as an interpolation between $\mathbf{x}(t_{n-1})$, $\mathbf{x}(t_n)$, $\mathbf{x}(t_{n+1})$ and $\mathbf{x}(t_{n+2})$.

EXAMPLES II.6

1. For the system in sect. II.5.1, eqns. (II.92), what are $[\mathbf{A}_1]$, $[\mathbf{A}_0]$ and $[\mathbf{B}_0]$?
2. Reduce the following system to first order form:

$$\begin{aligned}(D^2 + 2D + 3)y_1(t) + {} & (2D + 1)y_2(t) = x_1(t) \\ y_1(t) + {} & (D^2 + D + 1)y_2(t) = x_2(t)\end{aligned}$$

and determine $[\mathbf{A}_1]_{4\times4}$, $[\mathbf{A}_0]_{4\times4}$, $[\mathbf{B}_0]_{4\times2}$.
Hint: introduce variables $y_3(t) = Dy_1(t)$, $y_4(t) = Dy_2(t)$, then

$$[\mathbf{y}(t)]_{4\times1} = \begin{bmatrix} y_1(t) \\ y_2(t) \\ y_3(t) \\ y_4(t) \end{bmatrix}.$$

Part III

Longitudinal motions at low angles of incidence

III.1 LONGITUDINAL MOTIONS

An aeroplane of conventional configuration comprises (main) wing, fuselage, aft tailplane and fin, and control surfaces (elevator, rudder and ailerons), sometimes known as motivators.

The notation which describes the symmetric geometry of a conventional aeroplane, relevant to longitudinal motions, is shown and defined in Fig. III.1; the remaining notation required for lateral motions is defined later. Note:

(i) The suffix 'w' refers to wing, the suffix 't' refers to tailplane.
(ii) There is a conceptual extension of the wing through the fuselage, which is included in the gross wing area S_w; the wing root chord is measured on the extended wing along the fuselage centre line.
(iii) The geometric mean wing chord, denoted by c_w, is equal to $S_w/2s_w$, where $2s_w$ is the total span from wing tip to wing tip.
(iv) The gross tailplane area S_t includes the elevator surface area.
(v) A fuselage longitudinal axis is defined along the length of the fuselage, passing through the overall aeroplane centre of mass (in a uniform gravitational field, which can be assumed to apply to aeroplanes, but not to spacecraft, the all-up weight acts through the centre of mass, and the centre of gravity and the centre of mass then coincide).
(vi) The setting angle of the wing, i_w, and the setting angle of the tailplane, i_t, are measured positive nose-up (i.e. trailing edge down) relative to the fuselage longitudinal axis.
(vii) The elevator angle η, positive nose-up (i.e. trailing edge down), is measured normal to the elevator hinge line, and relative to the tailplane surface.

The wing can be either a low wing or a high wing relative to the fuselage longitudinal axis. The wing setting angle, i_w, is fixed for all types of aeroplanes, apart from tilt-wing aeroplanes.

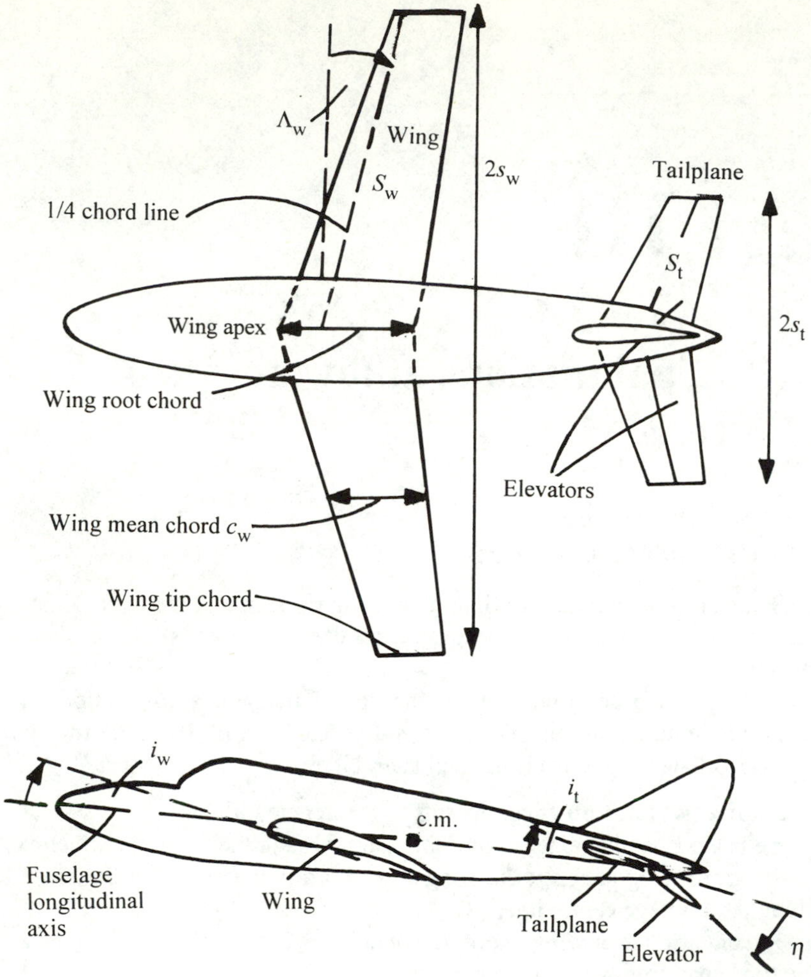

Wing gross area S_w, span $2s_w$, mean chord $c_w = S_w/2s_w$
taper ratio λ_w = (wing tip chord/wing root chord)
aspect ratio $AR_w = 2s_w/c_w = (2s_w)^2/S_w$
wing sweep angle (of 1/4 chord line) = Λ_w
wing setting angle i_w

Tailplane gross area, including elevator S_t, span $2s_t$
mean chord c_t, taper ratio λ_t, aspect ratio AR_t
tailplane setting angle i_t
elevator angle η

Fig. III.1. Notation of configuration geometry.

The tailplane can also be either low or high, with the extreme high location on top of the fin. The tailplane setting angle, i_t, is fixed on all light aeroplanes and on some transport aeroplanes (e.g. Fokker 50, B.Ae 146). But on most contemporary transport aeroplanes the tailplane angle is adjustable in flight.

All light and transport aeroplanes have elevators for longitudinal control. Combat aeroplanes invariably have all-moving tailplanes. In this case the tailplane setting angle defines a datum. In the following text the word 'elevator' covers both conventional elevators and all-moving tailplanes.

Longitudinal motions of a conventional aeroplane comprise horizontal and vertical translation of the aeroplane centre of mass in the plane of symmetry of the aeroplane, together with rotation about the pitch axis (i.e. an axis normal to the aeroplane plane of symmetry) through the centre of mass.

By reference to Fig. III.2(i) the longitudinal motion of an aeroplane is defined by

(i) the absolute velocity, $U(t)$, of the centre of mass, where t is time (an absolute velocity is a velocity relative to inertial axes, which are hypothesized to be axes fixed in space; for the purposes of aeroplane flight dynamics inertial axes can be identified with axes fixed in the earth's surface);

(ii) the flight path angle, $\gamma(t)$, which is the angle between the flight path, namely the direction of the absolute velocity $U(t)$, and the horizontal; $\gamma(t)$ is positive for climb and negative for descent;

(iii) the pitch angle, $\theta(t)$, which is the angle between the fuselage longitudinal axis and the horizontal, taken to be positive in the nose-up direction.

When the atmosphere is stationary the angle of incidence of the aeroplane (or the angle of attack of the aeroplane, the author regards these two expressions as synonymous), $\alpha(t)$, is defined as the angle of the fuselage longitudinal axis from the flight path, again positive nose-up. By reference to Fig. III.2(i),

$$\alpha(t) = \theta(t) - \gamma(t). \qquad \text{(III.1.1)}$$

For an alternative definition of the angle of incidence, take axes ox and oz fixed in the aeroplane, with origin at the centre of mass, along and normal to the fuselage longitudinal axis respectively. The absolute velocity $U(t)$ can be resolved into the components $U_x(t)$ in the ox direction and $U_z(t)$ in the oz direction, where, by reference to Figs. III.2(i, ii),

$$U_x(t) = U(t)\cos\alpha(t), \qquad U_z(t) = U(t)\sin\alpha(t). \qquad \text{(III.1.2)}$$

Hence the angle of incidence is related to the components of the aeroplane velocity along and normal to the aeroplane fuselage by the relationship,

$$\tan\alpha(t) = U_z(t)/U_x(t); \qquad \text{(III.1.3)}$$

this relationship is the one usually used in aeroplane flight dynamics. When $\alpha(t)$ is small,

$$\tan\alpha(t) \simeq \alpha(t). \qquad \text{(III.1.4)}$$

An atmosphere in motion due to winds or gusts affects the angle of incidence. As shown in Fig. III.2(iii), $U_g(t)$ is the absolute velocity of the atmosphere in the vicinity of

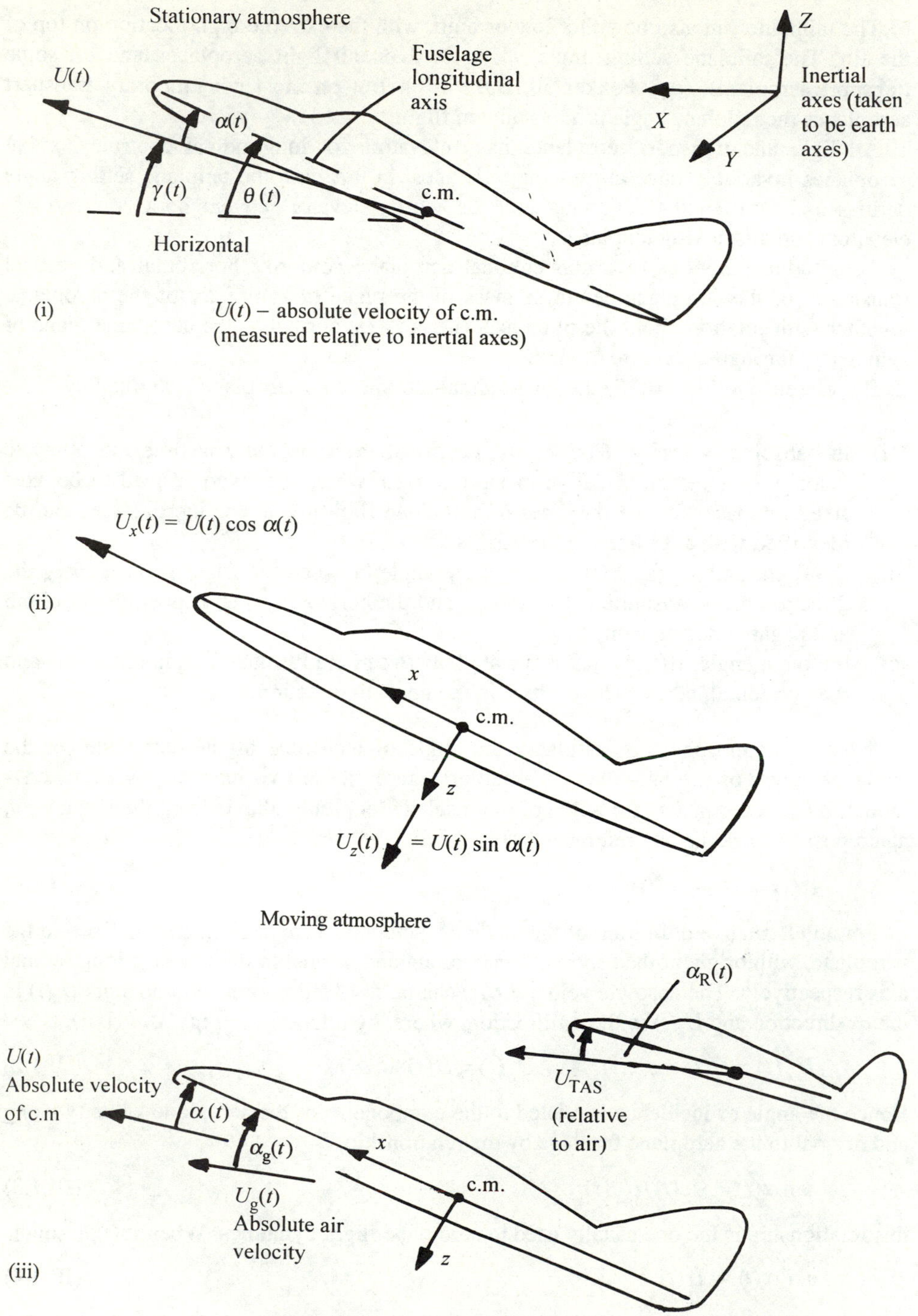

Fig. III.2. Longitudinal motions.

the aeroplane, $\alpha_g(t)$ is the angle from the direction of $U_g(t)$ to the fuselage longitudinal axis, again positive nose-up, and $\alpha(t)$ is the angle of incidence of the aeroplane in stationary air, as defined in eqn. (III.1.1). The velocity of the aeroplane centre of mass relative to the moving atmosphere is known as the true air speed, and denoted by $U_{TAS}(t)$. The components of the true air speed in the *ox* and *oz* directions are

$$\begin{aligned}(U_{TAS})_x(t) &= U(t)\cos\alpha(t) - U_g(t)\cos\alpha_g(t)\\ (U_{TAS})_z(t) &= U(t)\sin\alpha(t) - U_g(t)\sin\alpha_g(t).\end{aligned} \qquad \text{(III.1.5)}$$

Hence

$$\begin{aligned}U^2_{TAS}(t) = &\left[U(t)\cos\alpha(t) - U_g(t)\cos\alpha_g(t)\right]^2\\ &+\left[U(t)\sin\alpha(t) - U_g(t)\sin\alpha_g(t)\right]^2\end{aligned} \qquad \text{(III.1.6)}$$

and the resultant angle of incidence $\alpha_R(t)$ is

$$\tan\alpha_R(t) = \frac{U(t)\sin\alpha(t) - U_g(t)\sin\alpha_g(t)}{U(t)\cos\alpha(t) - U_g(t)\cos\alpha_g(t)}. \qquad \text{(III.1.7)}$$

In a stationary atmosphere the true air speed $U_{TAS}(t)$ is identical to the absolute velocity $U(t)$, and $\alpha_R(t)$ is identical to $\alpha(t)$. Unless stated to the contrary, the atmosphere is taken to be stationary.

EXAMPLES III.1

1. What is $\alpha_R(t)$ when the direction of $U_g(t)$ is in the same direction as $U(t)$?
2. What is $\alpha_R(t)$ when the direction of $U_g(t)$ is 90° to the direction of $U(t)$, assuming both $\alpha(t)$ and $(U_g(t)/U(t))$ small?
3. What does eqn. (III.1.7) become when the direction of $U_g(t)$ is in the opposite direction to that shown in Fig. III.2(iii)?

Performance calculations are usually carried out using the variables $U(t)$ and $\gamma(t)$, which determine the aeroplane flight path, whereas stability, control and response calculations are usually carried out using the variables $U(t)$, $\alpha(t)$ and $\theta(t)$, which are more relevant in manoeuvring flight.

It is important to realize that the angle of incidence, $\alpha(t)$, and the pitch angle, $\theta(t)$, are independent variables. A motion with $\alpha(t)$ constant but $\theta(t)$ increasing with time is a typical pull-up manoeuvre, as shown in Fig. III.3(i). A motion with $\theta(t)$ constant but $\alpha(t)$ increasing with time is a descending flight path at a constant attitude, as shown in Fig. III.3(ii).

Longitudinal motions are initiated primarily through changes in elevator angle and in thrust.

In conventional aeroplanes the human pilot changes the elevator angle by displacement of a central (hand) stick; an aft displacement of the stick (i.e. 'pulling the stick back') rotates the elevator nose-down (i.e. elevator trailing edge up), a forward displacement of the stick rotates the elevator nose-up (i.e. elevator trailing edge down). The

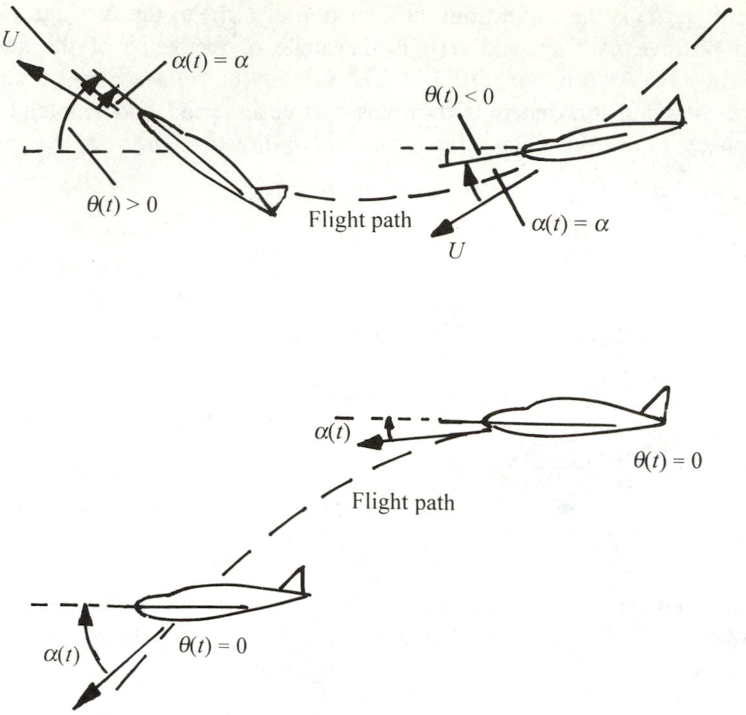

Fig. III.3. Independence of angles of pitch and incidence.

human pilot moves the throttle to control the fuel flow rate to the engines; for propeller driven aeroplanes, including turbo-prop propulsion, the throttle varies power, while for turbo-jets and turbo-fan propulsion the throttle varies thrust. In addition, the human pilot has a secondary control, a trim control, which can reduce the stick force to zero in steady flight. The human pilot also has the responsibility of deploying, and retracting, the high lift system and the undercarriage.

The connection between the pilot's stick and the elevator depends on the type of aeroplane.

In a light, low speed, aeroplane, there is a direct mechanical linkage system, usually a cable, between stick and elevator, as shown in Fig. III.4(i), known as a manual control. With this arrangement there is a simple gearing ratio between stick displacement and elevator angle deflection and between stick force and the elevator hinge moment due to the aerodynamic loading on the elevator surface.

As aeroplane size increases, the elevator hinge moments due to the aerodynamic loadings on the elevator surface increase. Also in transonic flight the elevator hinge moments can be erratic with small changes in Mach number. And at supersonic speeds the elevator hinge moments become excessively large. The stick forces to react these hinge moments in a manual system are beyond the capability of a human pilot, and so it is necessary to introduce a hydraulic power unit to rotate the elevator.

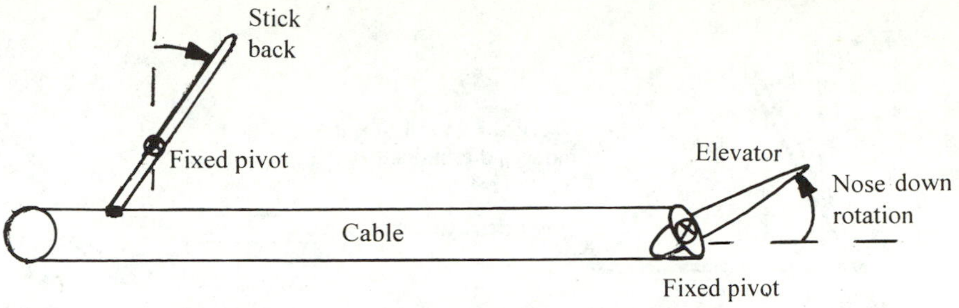

Fig. III.4(i). Direct linkage in light aeroplane.

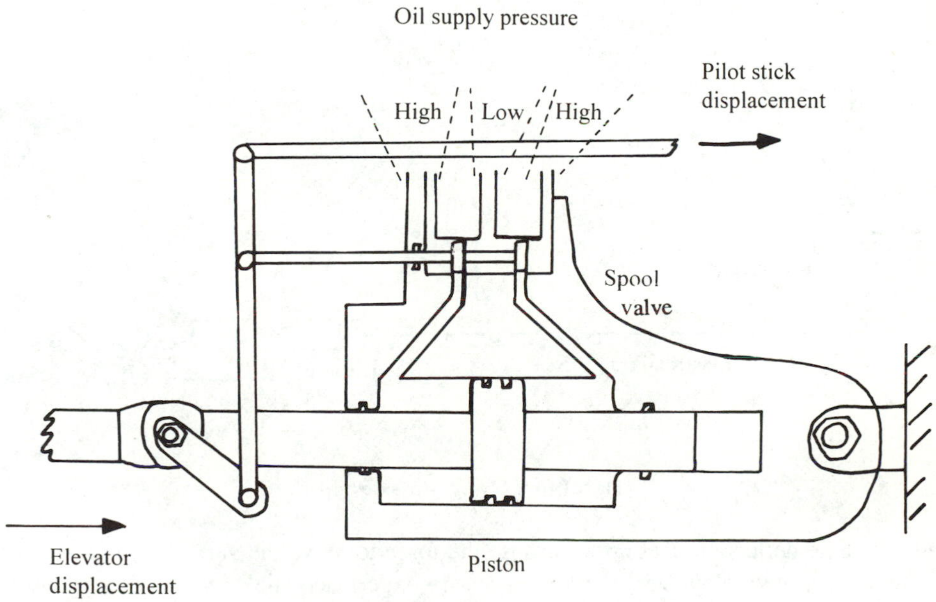

Fig. III.4(ii). Moving piston hydraulic servo unit.

The features of a hydraulic unit are sketched in Fig. III.4(ii). The hydraulic jack, which is connected to the elevator, is powered by the differential pressure of oil across a piston in the main cylinder, the flow of oil into the main cylinder is controlled by a spool valve. When the valve is displaced oil flows through the opened apertures moving the jack in the direction to close the apertures, thus in this design the displacement of the jack follows the displacement of the spool. Typically the high pressure of the oil is of the order of 200 atmospheres, the jack normally rotates the elevator up to a rate in the order of 200°/s; for some active control applications rotations up to 400°/s are possible. Accounts of hydraulic systems are given by Green (ref. III.1) and Neese (ref. III.2).

The stick may be connected mechanically to the valve in the hydraulic unit, as shown in Fig. III.4(iii). Again there is a simple gearing ratio between stick displacement and

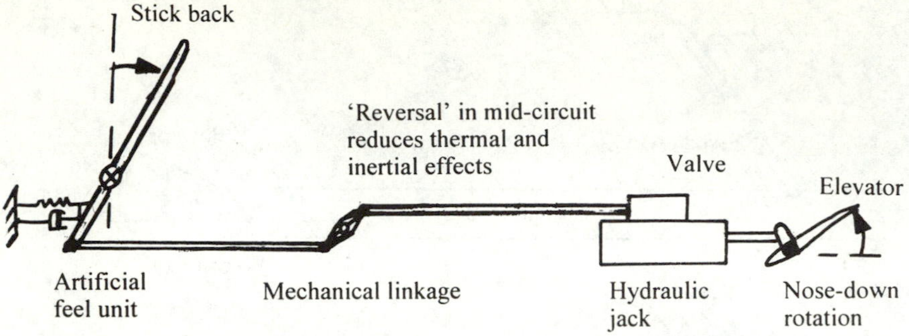

Fig. III.4(iii). Mechanical system with powered control.

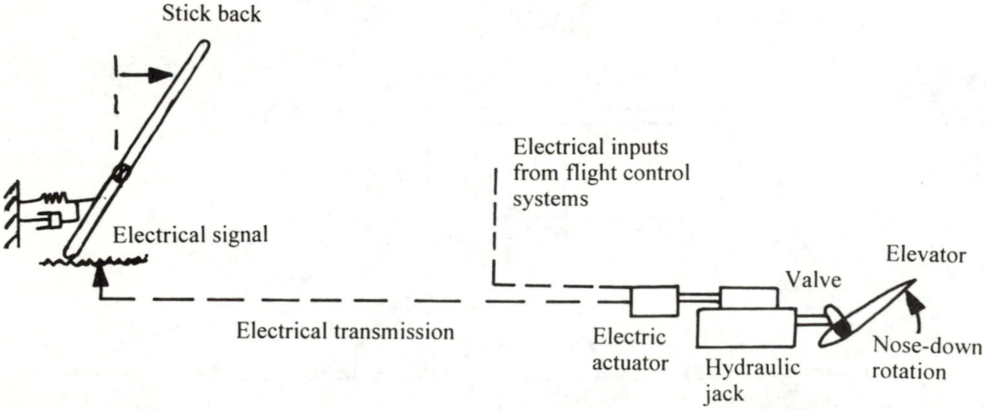

Fig. III.4(iv). Fly-by-wire system.

elevator angle deflection. But now, because the force to move the valve is low, the force on the stick is low. However, a pilot expects to experience stick forces comparable to those required to operate manual control systems, hence an artificial 'feel system' to the stick is introduced. A contemporary artificial feel system usually comprises a spring–damper arrangement which is connected to the stick where the spring stiffness is variable depending on the flight condition.

Alternatively, the connection between the stick and the valve in the hydraulic unit may be electrical, as shown in Fig. III.4(iv). An electrical signal proportional to stick displacement, generated by a potentiometer, is transmitted via an electrical connection to an electric actuator which drives the spool valve in the hydraulic servo-unit. Such a system is known as 'fly-by-wire'.

A fly-by-wire system is compatible with automatic flight control systems where sensors which respond to aeroplane motions produce electrical signals which are also relayed as inputs into the electric actuator to move the elevator. In the past, fly-by-wire systems had a mechanical reversion back-up system in case of electrical signal failure (e.g. Concorde) but with experience of the increasing reliability of electrical/electronic systems, mechanical reversion is being dispensed with, saving weight, complexity and design time.

In modern fly-by-wire systems the pilot's input does not go directly to the elevator but, instead, it is one input into the central flight control computer. The stick would be reduced in size and replaced by a smaller hand controller, situated to the side of the pilot, in which the electrical signal from the side controller would be proportional to the applied force; there is virtually no displacement of the side controller. An applied longitudinal force to the side controller would now be a command signal either for a normal acceleration at high speed or a pitch rate at low speed; the central computer would evaluate and implement the appropriate changes in the elevator angle, in other all-moving surfaces, such as wing trailing edge flaps and wing leading edge slats, and in the throttle; a so-called 'manoeuvre demand system'.

Over the past decade there have been several detailed studies on the possible benefits of the all-electrical aeroplane, replacing hydraulic units by electrical actuators—see, for example, refs. II.3–II.5. The hardware technology is reaching the stage of feasibility. Benefits are claimed to accrue from integrating all of the power requirements of the aeroplane; although electrical actuators tend to be heavier than their hydraulic counterparts there is a net saving of weight when all of the hydraulic fluid, pumps and piping are replaced by electrical connections.

A measure of understanding of aeroplane flight dynamics is the ability to explain how a pilot with two controls, stick and throttle, can manoeuvre and control an aeroplane in longitudinal motions involving three degrees of freedom. It is hoped that the reader will soon be able to provide this explanation.

EXAMPLES III.2

1. What is the largest aeroplane currently flying to have a manual control elevator system? (Browse through Janes *All the Worlds Aircraft*.)
2. What is the fastest aeroplane currently flying to have a manual control elevator system?
3. What factors decide the size of a hydraulic jack?
4. In Fig. III.4(iii) a reverse switch is included to compensate for inertial and thermal effects. How does it work?

III.2 BASIC CONFIGURATIONS

As stated in the Introduction, flight dynamic concepts are to be applied to three different types of aeroplane, namely:

(i) a low speed, light aeroplane, powered by a single propeller at the front of the fuselage,
(ii) a transport aeroplane powered by two high by-pass, turbo-fan engines underslung beneath the wing, designed to cruise at altitude at a high subsonic Mach number,
(iii) a combat aeroplane powered by a low by-pass turbo-fan engine, installed inside the fuselage, and capable of supersonic speeds, of the order of Mach 1.8, at altitude.

The configuration and operation details of these three basic aeroplanes are shown in Figs. III.5.

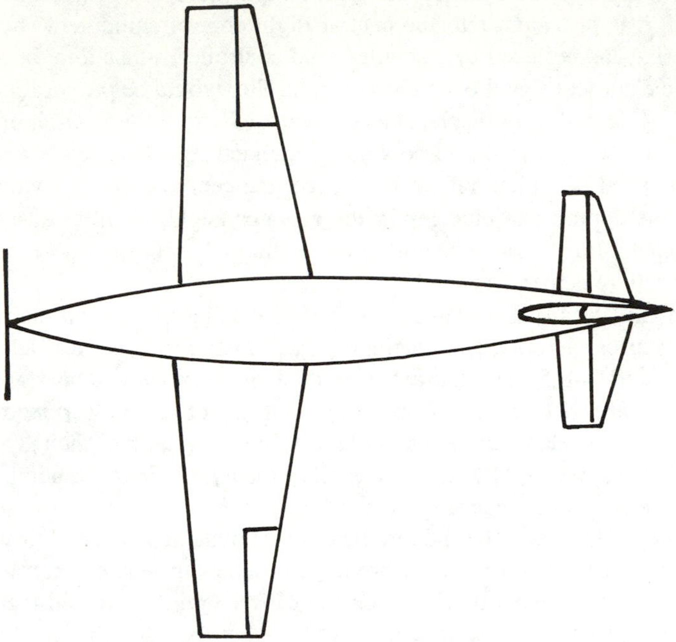

Wing: $c_w = 1.75$ m (5.74 ft), $2s_w = 11.5$ m (37.7 ft), $S_w = 20.125$ m^2 (216.6 ft^2), $AR_w = 6.6$, $s_a/s_w = 0.25$, $\Lambda_w = 0°$, $\lambda_w = 0.5$, $i_w = 1°$, $i_d = 3$

Tailplane: $c_t = 1.05$ m (3.44 ft), $2s_t = 4.0$ m (31.1 ft), $S_t = 4.2$ m^2 (45.26 ft^2) $AR_f = 3.8$, $c_e/c_t = 0.35$, $\Lambda_t = 0°$, $\lambda_t = 0.5$, $i_t = -15°$

Fin: $c_f = 1.0$ m (3.28 ft), $s_f = 2.0$ m (6.56 ft), $S_f = 2.0$ m^2 (21.5 ft^2) $AR_f = 2.0$ (21.5 ft), $c_{rudder}/c_f = 0.4$, $\Lambda_f = 15°$, $\lambda_f = 0.5$

Fuselage: distance of tailplane apex aft of wing apex = 3.5 c_w
distance of fin apex aft of wing apex = 3.2 c_w
distance of wing apex aft of fuselage nose = 1.5 c_w
(these distances are measured along the fuselage centre line)
max. radius of fuselage nose = 0.35 c_w located 0.7 c_w aft of fuselage nose

Propulsion: fuselage propeller
$l_{Th} = 0$, $c_{prop} = 0.75\ c_w$ (81.5 kg/n^2, 16.7 lb$_f$)/ft^2)

Inertias: wing loading = 0.8 kN/m^2
$i_{xx} = 0.040$, $i_{yy} = 0.65$, $i_{zz} = 0.09$, $i_{xz} = 0$

Performance: cruise at 2.75 km altitude at 80 m/s (≈156 knots)
Approach at $C_{L\ max} = 1.2$.

Fig. III.5(i). Basic configuration: Light aeroplane.

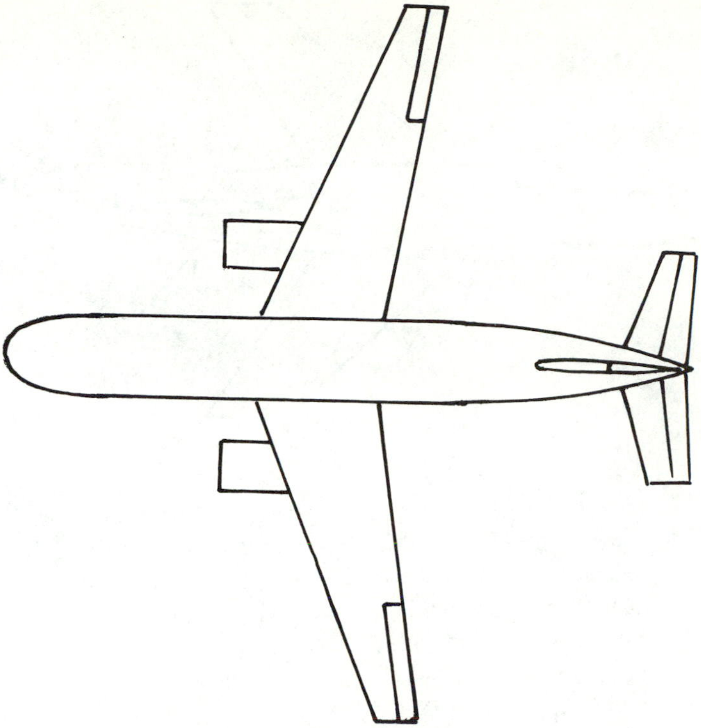

Low wing: $c_w = 5.5$ m (18.04 ft), $2s_w = 41.3$ m (135.5 ft), $S_w = 227$ m^2 (2445.0 ft^2), $AR_w = 7.5$, $s_a/s_w = 0.2$, $\Lambda_w = 25°$, $\lambda_w = 0.5$, $i_w = 1°$, $i_d = 1.5°$

Adjustable tailplane: $c_t = 3.6$ m (11.8 ft), $2s_t = 12.0$ m (39.4 ft), $S_t = 43.5$ m^2 (465 ft^2) $AR_t = 3.33$, $c_e/c_t = 0.35$, $\Lambda_t = 25°$, $\lambda_t = 0.5$

Fin: $c_f = 5.0$ m (16.4 ft), $s_f = 8.5$ m (27.9 ft), $S_f = 42.5$ m^2 (457.5 ft^2) $AR_f = 1.7$, $c_{rudder}/c_f = 0.40$, $\Lambda_f = 25°$, $\lambda_f = 0.5$

Fuselage: distance of tailplane apex aft of wing apex = 4.25 c_w
distance of fin apex aft of wing apex = 3.5 c_w
distance of wing apex aft of fuselage nose = 2.5 c_w
(these distances are measured along the fuselage centre line)
max. radius of fuselage nose = 0.35 c_w located 0.85 c_w aft of fuselage nose se

Propulsion: 2 turbofans, underslung beneath the wing,
$l_{Th} = 0.2$ Lift, $c_{rad} = 0.1f\, c_w$ ' (560 kg/m^2, 115 lb$_f$/ft^2)

Inertias: wing loading = 5.5 kN/m^2
$i_{xx} = 0.09$, $i_{yy} = 2.2$, $i_{zz} = 0.23$, $i_{xz} = 0$

Performance: Cruise at 11 km altitude at Mach 0.85
flaps up $C_{L\,max} = 1.25$, flaps down $C_{L\,max} = 2.0$

Fig. III.5(ii). Basic configuration: Transport aeroplane.

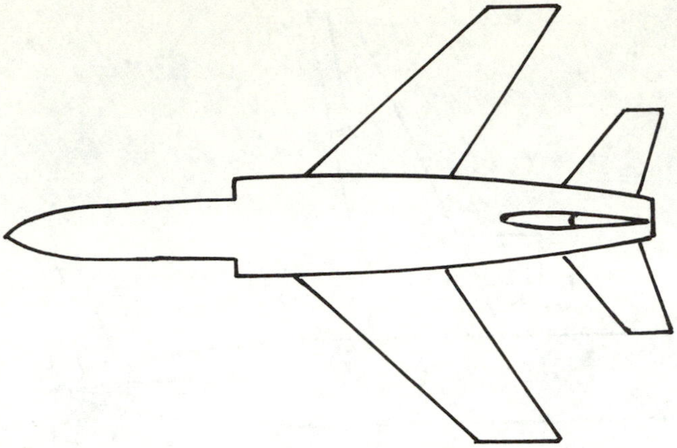

Wing: $c_w = 3.5$ m (11.98 ft), $2s_w = 12$ m (39.37 ft), $S_w = 42.0\ \text{m}^2$ (1452 ft^2), $AR_w = 3.43$, $\Lambda_w = 45°$, $\lambda_w = 0.5$, $i_w = 1°$, $i_d = 0$

All-moving tailplane (symmetric and differential):
$c_t = 2.0$ m (16.56 ft), $2s_t = 6.5$ m (21.32 ft), $S_t = 13.0\ \text{m}^2$ (140 ft^2)
$AR_f = 3.25$, $\Lambda_f = 45°$, $\lambda_f = 0.5$

Fin: $c_f = 2.8$ m (9.19 ft), $s_f = 4.5$ m (14.76 ft), $S_f = 12.6\ \text{m}^2$ (135.6 ft^2)
$AR_f = 1.61$, $\Lambda_f = 45°$, $\lambda_f = 0.5$

Fuselage: distance of tailplane apex aft of wing apex = 2.35 c_w
distance of fin apex aft of wing apex = 2.0 c_w
distance of 1/4 root chord aft of fuselage nose = 2.0 c_w
(these distances are measured along the fuselage centre line)
max. radius of fuselage nose = 0.22 c_w located 0.75 c_w aft of fuselage nose

Propulsion: internal turbo-fan. $l_{Th} = 0$

Inertias: wing $l_{Th} = 0$, neglect ?? loading = 3.5 kN/m^2 (356.7 kg/m^2, 16f/ft^2)
$i_{xx} = 0.05$, $i_{yy} = 0.85$, $i_{zz} = 0.33$, $i_{xz} = 0$

Performance: maximum Mach number at 11 km altitude = 1.8
maximum Mach number at sea level = 0.9
on the approach $C_{L\ max} = 1.4$

Fig. III.5(iii). Basic configuration: Combat aeroplane.

Aerodynamic loads depend on the ambient atmospheric conditions: density, ρ_{at}, pressure p_{at}, and temperature T_{at}, the suffix 'at' denoting atmosphere. Standard values at sea level are

$$\begin{aligned} \rho_{at} &= 1.225\ \text{kg/m}^3\ (= 0.00238\ \text{slug/ft}^3) \\ p_{at} &= 101.32\ \text{kN/m}^2\ (= 2116.2\ \text{lb}_f/\text{ft}^2) \\ T_{at} &= 288.2\,\text{K} \qquad (= 15°\text{C}). \end{aligned} \tag{III.2.1}$$

Density, pressure and temperature all decrease with increase in altitude in the troposphere which extends in the western hemisphere to approximately 11 km altitude ($\simeq$ 36 000 ft). The temperature then remains constant in the stratosphere but the density and pressure continue to fall.

An abbreviated table of the standard atmosphere, sufficient for the applications in this book, is given in Table III.1; extensive tables can be found in ref. III.6.

Table III.1. Standard atmosphere

Altitude h		Pressure ratio $p_{at}/(p_{at})_{sl}$ $\bar{\omega}$	Density ratio $\rho_{at}/(\rho_{at})_{sl}$ $\bar{\sigma}$	Temperature ratio $T_{at}/(T_{at})_{sl}$ $\bar{\theta}$
0.0 km	↑	1.0	1.0	1.0
2.75 km (9000 ft)		0.715	0.762	0.938
5.5 km (18 000 ft)		0.500	0.570	0.876
8.25 km (27 000 ft)		0.340	0.418	0.815
	Troposphere			
11.0 km (36 000 ft)		0.224	0.298	0.752
	Stratosphere			
13.75 km (45 000 ft)	↓	0.146	0.235	0.752

The speed of sound is given by the formula (see McCormick, ref. III.7)

$$a_{at} = (\gamma p_{at}/\rho_{at})^{1/2} \tag{III.2.2}$$

where γ= ratio of specific heats of air = 1.4. From the equation of state (see ref. III.7), (p_{at}/ρ_{at}) is proportional to T_{at}, so the speed of sound varies as $(T_{at})^{1/2}$, hence the speed of sound decreases with altitude in the troposphere and then remains constant in the stratosphere.

At sea level

$$a_{at} = 340 \text{ m/s}. \tag{III.2.3}$$

The speed of sound decreases with altitude as $\bar{\theta}^{1/2}$, where $\bar{\theta}$ is given in Table III.1.

III.3 SYMMETRIC AERODYNAMICS

Because aerodynamic loads play such a crucial role in aeroplane flight dynamics, an extensive account is presented in this section of the steady and unsteady aerodynamic loadings experienced by an aeroplane in longitudinal static and dynamic motions at subsonic, transonic and low supersonic speeds, at low angles of incidence. By definition, longitudinal motions are restricted to the plane of symmetry of the aeroplane, so the aerodynamic loadings described in this section are symmetric with respect to that plane of symmetry.

Although this section is intended to be self-contained some prior elementary knowledge of aerodynamics is desirable (e.g. definitions of camber, thickness distributions, pressure coefficients, lift, drag and moment coefficients; concepts of centre of pressure, aerodynamic centre, circulation, vorticity, shock waves, supersonic zones of influence). The books on traditional aerodynamics by McCormick (ref. III.7) and by Schlichting & Truckenbrodt (ref. III.8), together with the text by Moran (ref. III.9), which includes an introduction to computational aerodynamics, are particularly commended.

The topics to be described in this section cover:

(i) steady loads on an isolated wing due to static conditions,
(ii) steady loads due on an isolated wing due to a constant rate of pitch,
(iii) unsteady loads on an isolated wing due to time varying angle of incidence, pitch angle and forward speed,
(iv) interference effects between the main wing and fuselage,
(v) aerodynamic loads on the tailplane where the downwash effects behind the main wing play an important role; an account is given of these downwash effects in unsteady conditions,
(vi) elevator hinge moments,
(vii) interference effects of the propulsion unit on the aerodynamic loads,
(viii) interference effects of weapons and stores.

Finally the total symmetric loads on a complete aeroplane undergoing longitudinal dynamic motions are assembled, bringing together all the above data.

The flight dynamics of take-off and landing in the proximity of the ground are not covered in this book because this rather difficult topic deserves a fuller account than is possible in an introductory text.

For purposes of stability and control analysis the aerodynamic loads are conventionally represented and formulated in terms of so-called 'aerodynamic derivatives'; particular emphasis is given to the definitions and validity of these 'aerodynamic derivatives'.

In this section all the aerodynamic derivatives arising from typical aeroplane motions are described irrespective of their subsequent individual contributions in determining flight dynamic characteristics.

III.3.1 Steady aerodynamics of a wing under static conditions

III.3.1.1 Introduction

Consider an isolated wing of sweep angle Λ_w, taper ratio λ_w, aspect ratio AR_w and wing area S_w, moving with a constant speed U into a stationary atmosphere of density ρ_{at}, pressure p_{at} and temperature T_{at}, at a constant angle of incidence, α, as shown in Fig. III.6. Note that the angle of incidence, α, of an isolated wing is defined by the angle of the wing root section relative to the direction of motion.

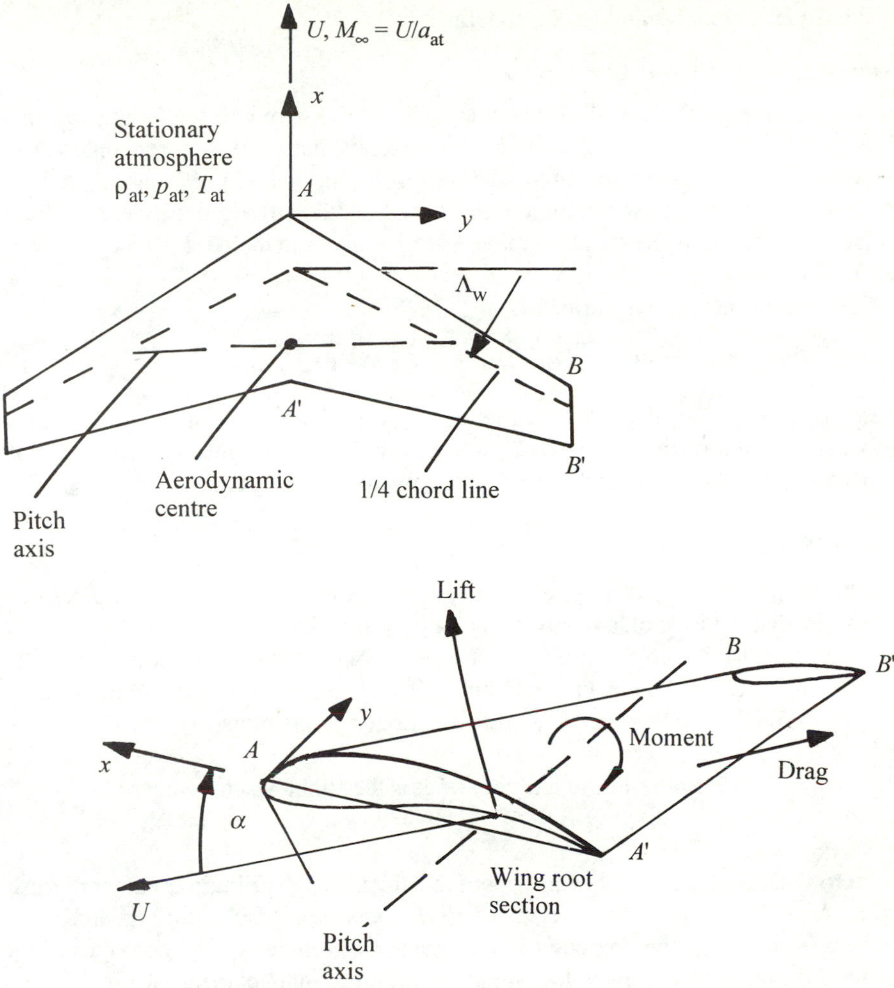

Fig. III.6. Static isolated wing.

In the past a swept wing would have been cambered to improve the (lift/drag) ratio at cruise, and twisted nose-down along its span, so-called 'wash-out', to ensure an inboard flow separation and acceptable stall characteristics. Contemporary wings designed for high speed flight will have optimized supercritical aerofoil sections along the span effectively incorporating camber and wash-out.

The flight Mach number, M_∞, is defined by

$$M_\infty = U/a_{at} \qquad (III.3.1)$$

where a_{at} is the speed of sound in the stationary atmosphere in the vicinity of the aeroplane. The subscript ∞ is convention in aerodynamics; it distinguishes the flight Mach number from the Mach number in the flow around the wing; the suffix ∞ also helps to distinguish Mach number, M_∞, from the pitching moment M.

The flight Reynolds number, *Re*, is defined by

$$Re = \rho_{at} U c_w / \mu_{at} = U c_w / \nu_{at} \qquad \text{(III.3.2)}$$

where μ_{at} is the coefficient of viscosity (= 1.789 10^{-5} kg/m s at sea level); μ_{at} varies as $(T_{at})^{3/4}$, and so decreases with altitude in the troposphere and then remains constant in the stratosphere; ν_{at} is the dynamic viscosity ($= \mu_{at}/\rho_{at} = 1.461\ 10^{-5}\ \text{m}^2/\text{s}$). All viscous effects (viscous drag, flow separation and flow breakdown) are dependent on Reynolds number. An account of Reynolds number effects is given in the book edited by Lachmann (ref. III.10).

The dynamic pressure is defined as

$$\text{dynamic pressure} = \tfrac{1}{2}\rho_{at} U_{TAS}^2 = \tfrac{1}{2}(\rho_{at})_{sl} U_{EAS}^2 \qquad \text{(III.3.3)}$$

where $(\rho_{at})_{sl}$ is the air density at sea level, U_{TAS} is the true air speed and U_{EAS} is the equivalent air speed. In still air U_{TAS} is equal to *U*, the absolute velocity. Operational speeds are invariably expressed in terms of equivalent air speeds.

EXAMPLES III.3

1. Check the value of the speed of sound given in eqn. (III.2.3) from eqn. (III.2.2).
2. Check that the Reynolds number is non-dimensional.
3. Calculate the Reynolds number of a Boeing 747 (mean wing chord = c_w = 8.5 m) cruising at Mach 0.80 at 11 km altitude. Calculate the Reynolds number of a 1/10th scale model of a Boeing 747, in a pressurized wind tunnel ($\rho = 4(\rho_{at})_{sl}$) at Mach 0.80.
4. If $U_{EAS} = 240$ m/s at 11 km altitude, what is the flight Mach number?

The aerodynamic loads on a wing depend on thickness distribution, camber, wash-out, angle of incidence, plan form, size, dynamic pressure, Mach number and Reynolds number. In this book the emphasis is on typical magnitudes of the aerodynamic loads, and to this order of accuracy the variation of aerodynamic loads at small angles of incidence with Reynolds number is ignored. For more accurate quantitative estimates of the aerodynamic loads, especially drag, the effects of Reynolds number must be included.

At low angles of incidence at subsonic ($M_\infty < 1$) and supersonic ($M_\infty > 1$) speeds the total aerodynamic lift on a wing can be taken as the sum of two separate lifts:

(i) the lift due to angle of incidence alone, assuming zero camber and zero wash-out,
(ii) the lift due to camber plus wash-out, assuming zero angle of incidence and zero wash-out.

At transonic speeds ($M_\infty \simeq 1$) this simple superposition of two separate lift contributions does not hold because of non-linear interference effects between the two contributions.

The centre of pressure of the wing lift distribution is defined as the point on the wing root chord through which the resultant wing lift acts.

The aerodynamic centre is the centre of pressure of the lift due to angle of incidence alone, assuming zero camber and zero wash-out. For all practical purposes, at a given subsonic or supersonic Mach number the position of the aerodynamic centre does not change over a range of low angles of incidence.

It follows that the pitching moment on a wing with camber and wash-out about a pitch axis through the aerodynamic centre is independent of angle of incidence at low angles of incidence (the subsequent loose phraseology 'pitching moment about the aerodynamic centre' means the pitching moment about a pitch axis through the aerodynamic centre).

For a planar symmetric wing (i.e. a wing with zero camber and zero wash-out), the aerodynamic centre and the centre of pressure coincide.

The overall forces on the wing are expressed in the form

$$\begin{aligned}\text{wing lift} &= L_\mathrm{w} = \tfrac{1}{2}\rho_\mathrm{at}U^2 S_\mathrm{w}(C_\mathrm{L})_\mathrm{w}\\ \text{wing drag} &= D_\mathrm{w} = \tfrac{1}{2}\rho_\mathrm{at}U^2 S_\mathrm{w}(C_\mathrm{D})_\mathrm{w}\end{aligned} \qquad \text{(III.3.4)}$$

where $(C_\mathrm{L})_\mathrm{w}$ and $(C_\mathrm{D})_\mathrm{w}$ are the non-dimensional wing lift coefficient and non-dimensional wing drag coefficient respectively.

By definition the lift acts normal to, and the drag acts parallel to, the direction of motion (i.e. the direction of U), as shown in Fig. III.6.

When the wing lift and drag are taken to act through the wing aerodynamic centre, the pitching moment about the aerodynamic centre can be expressed in the form

$$\text{wing pitching moment} = \mathcal{M}_\mathrm{w} = \tfrac{1}{2}\rho_\mathrm{at}U^2 S_\mathrm{w} c_\mathrm{w}(m_0)_\mathrm{w} \qquad \text{(III.3.5)}$$

where $(m_0)_\mathrm{w}$, the non-dimensional pitching moment coefficient of the wing loading about the wing aerodynamic centre, is independent of angle of incidence, α; $(m_0)_\mathrm{w}$ depends only on the wing camber and wash-out. If the wing camber and wash-out are both zero, then $(m_0)_\mathrm{w}$ is zero.

Some further terminology is now introduced:

(i) Wing surface loading distribution $\Delta p(x, y)$, where

$$\Delta p(x, y) = p(x, y)_\text{lower surface} - p(x, y)_\text{upper surface}; \qquad \text{(III.3.6)}$$

$p(x, y)$ is the static pressure normal to the wing surface, the coordinates (x, y) are shown in Fig. III.6.

(ii) Non-dimensional wing surface loading distribution $\Delta c_p(x, y)$, where

$$\Delta c_p(x,y) = \Delta p(x,y)\big/\left(\tfrac{1}{2}\rho_\mathrm{at}U^2\right). \qquad \text{(III.3.7)}$$

(iii) Wing spanwise lift distribution $L(y)$, where

$$L(y) = \int_{\text{section}(y)} \Delta p(x,y)\,\mathrm{d}x. \qquad \text{(III.3.8)}$$

(iv) Non-dimensional spanwise lift distribution $C_\mathrm{L}(y)$, where

$$C_\mathrm{L}(y) = L(y)\big/\left(\tfrac{1}{2}\rho_\mathrm{at}U^2 c(y)\right), \qquad \text{(III.3.9)}$$

where $c(y)$ is the sectional chord length, thus

$$C_\mathrm{L}(y)c(y) = L(y)\big/\left(\tfrac{1}{2}\rho_\mathrm{at}U^2\right) = \int_{\text{section}(y)} \Delta c_p(x,y)\,\mathrm{d}x.$$

(v)

$$\text{Wing lift} = L_{\mathrm{w}} = \int_{-s_{\mathrm{w}}}^{+s_{\mathrm{w}}} L(y)\,\mathrm{d}y = \iint_{\text{wing area}} \Delta p(x, y)\,\mathrm{d}x\,\mathrm{d}y$$

$$(C_{\mathrm{L}})_{\mathrm{w}} = \left[\int_{+s_{\mathrm{w}}}^{-s_{\mathrm{w}}} C_{\mathrm{L}}(y) c(y)\,\mathrm{d}y\right] \Big/ S_{\mathrm{w}}$$

$$= \left[\iint_{\text{wing area}} \Delta c_p(x, y)\,\mathrm{d}x\,\mathrm{d}y\right] \Big/ S_{\mathrm{w}}. \qquad \text{(III.3.10)}$$

Conceptually the lift on a wing can be regarded as arising from a rotation of the air around the wing, as shown in Fig. III.7 (see ref. III.7). This rotation, which varies along the wing span, is known as the circulation, and is denoted by $\Gamma(y)$. The lift distribution $L(y)$ is related to the circulation distribution by the relationship

$$L(y) = \rho_{\mathrm{at}} U \Gamma(y) \qquad \text{(III.3.11)}$$

see ref. III.7. Trailing vorticity proportional to $\mathrm{d}\Gamma(y)/\mathrm{d}y$ is shed into the wake behind the wing, as shown in Fig. III.7; this trailing vorticity rolls up to form the wing tip trailing vortices; the circulation around each trailing vortex in practice is approximately $\Gamma(y = 0.7 s_{\mathrm{w}})$.

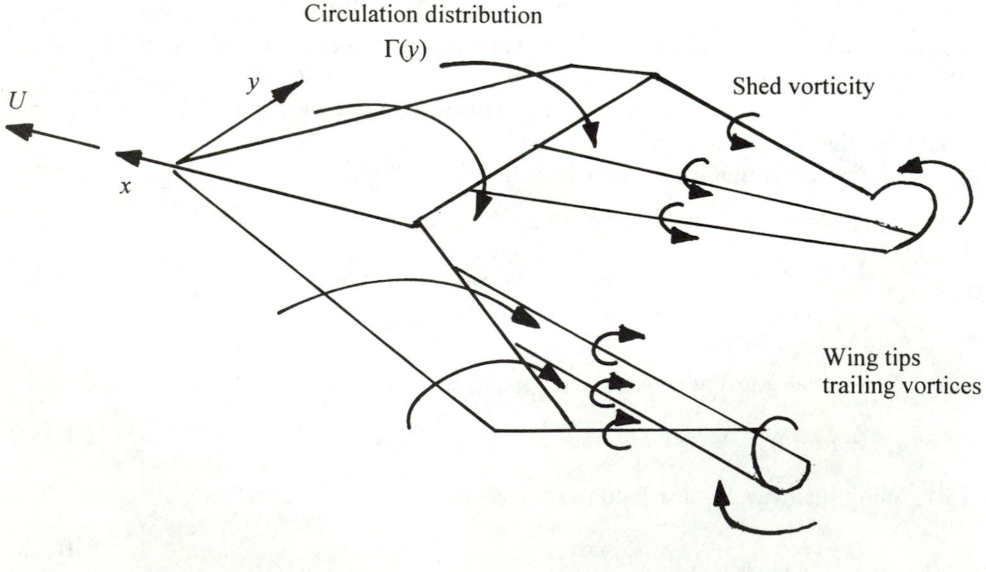

Fig. III.7. Wing circulation and formation of wing tip trailing vortices.

III.3.1.2 Wing loading distributions

Typical wing loading distributions due to angle of incidence alone, assuming zero camber and wash-out, are shown in Figs. III.8 and III.9.

For a non-swept wing at low Mach numbers, as shown in Fig. III.8(i), the chordwise load distributions are similar at different spanwise stations, the magnitude decreasing

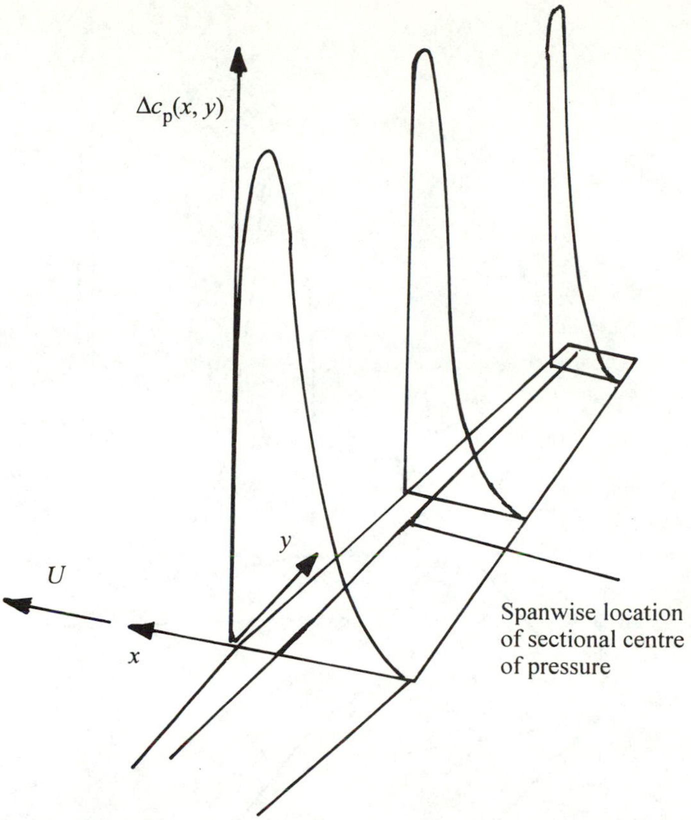

Fig. III.8(i). Loading distribution on non-swept wing due to angle of incidence alone at low Mach numbers.

towards the wing tips. The sectional centre of pressure (i.e. the centre of pressure of $\Delta c_p(x, y)$ across a chord at a spanwise station y) is close to the 1/4 chord line.

For a wing with a sweep angle of the order of 40° at low Mach numbers (see Fig. III.8(ii), taken from Kuchemann, ref. III.11), the chordwise loading distributions become higher towards the wing tip regions and more concentrated towards the leading edge. The sectional centre of pressure tends to be about 0.35 = (root chord) aft of the wing apex on the root chord, about $0.25c_w$ aft of the leading edge in the mid-span regions and about 0.10 = (tip chord) aft of the leading edge in the wing tip regions.

The integration of the chordwise load distributions in Figs. III.8(i, ii) gives the spanwise lift distribution $C_L(y)c(y)$; typical variations are shown in Fig. III.8(iii), taken from ref. III.8. The spanwise lift distribution tends to increase towards the wing tip for higher aspect ratio wings as sweep angle increases; however, this effect reduces as aspect ratio decreases. The area under the $C_L(y)c(y) \sim (y/s_w)$ curve over a wing semi-span is equal to $(C_L)_w c_w$; in Fig. III.8(iii) $(C_L)_w$ decreases with increase in wing sweep.

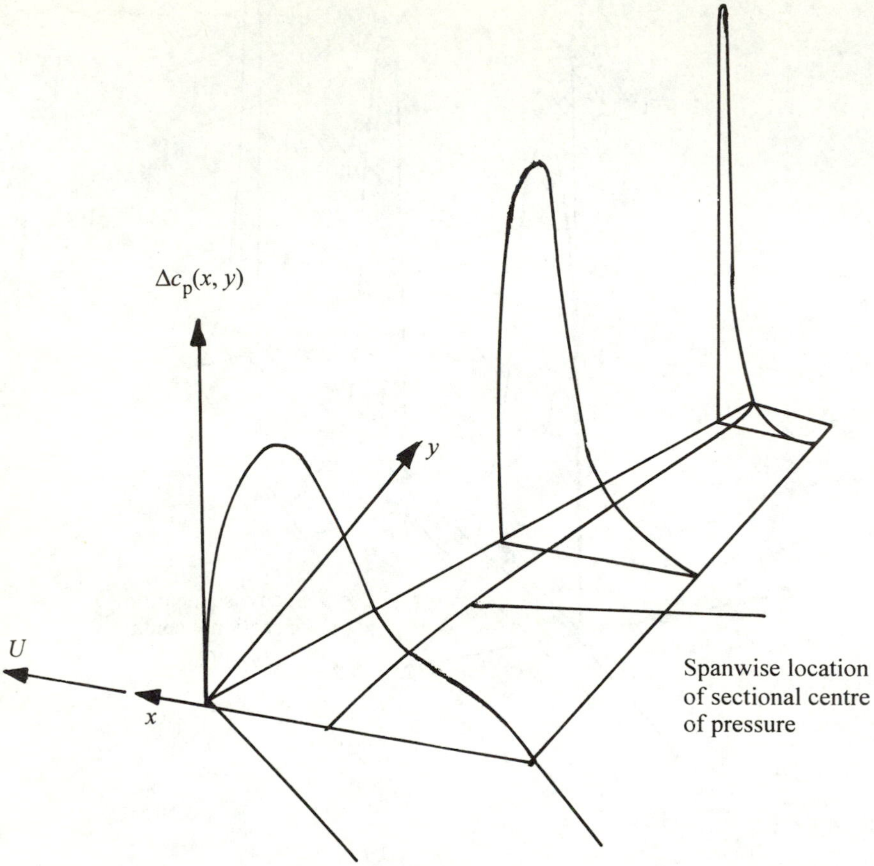

Fig. III.8(ii). Loading distribution on swept wing due to angle of incidence alone at low Mach numbers.

At subsonic speeds, as a first approximation, the non-dimensional lifting distribution $\Delta c_p(x, y)$, and the spanwise lift distribution $C_L(y)c(y)$, as shown in Figs. III.8(i, ii, iii), increase uniformly with increase in Mach number; the positions of the sectional centres of pressure are then unaffected by (subsonic) Mach number.

The loadings at transonic speeds are much more complicated (see Nixon, ref. III.12). For a transport aeroplane, wing design, using supercritical aerofoils, aims to extend the high subsonic characteristics into the transonic range before encountering unacceptable drag and buffet limits. For a well designed supersonic combat aeroplane the transonic aerodynamic forces can be faired in between the high subsonic and low supersonic values.

At supersonic speeds, loadings are determined by zones of influence. A disturbance moving at a supersonic speed only affects the region within its downstream Mach cone, where the Mach angle μ is equal to $\sin^{-1}(1/M_\infty)$, as shown in Fig. III.9(i). For a fuller discussion see ref. III.7.

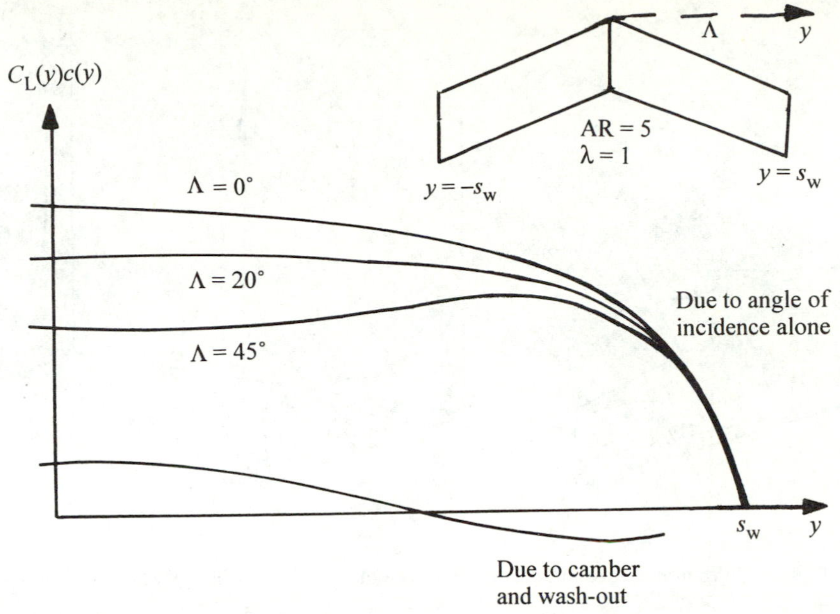

Fig. III.8(iii). Typical spanwise lift distributions at low Mach numbers.

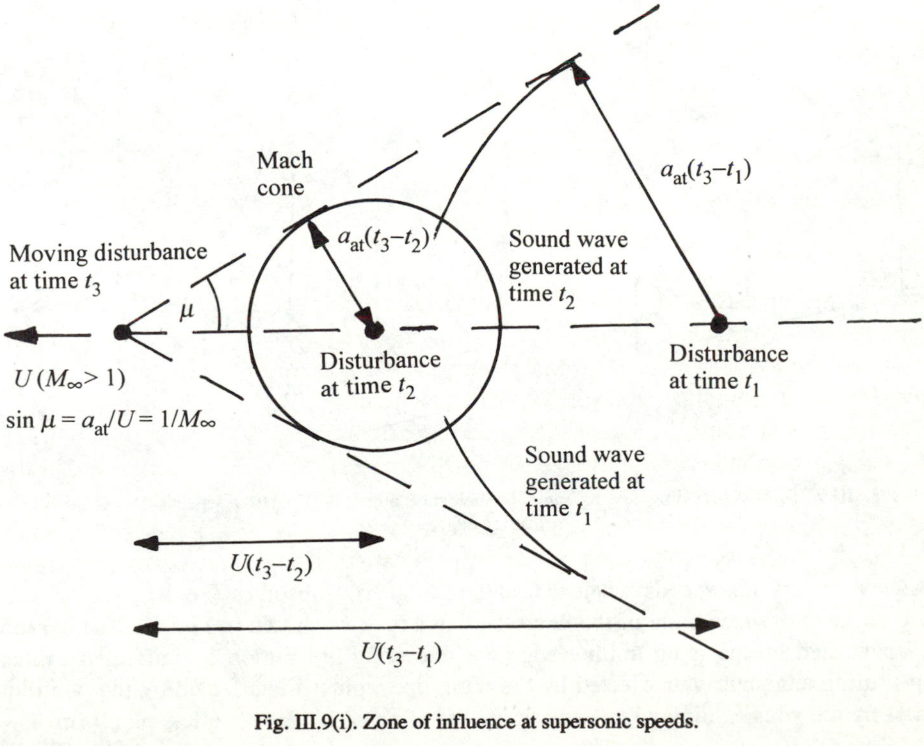

Fig. III.9(i). Zone of influence at supersonic speeds.

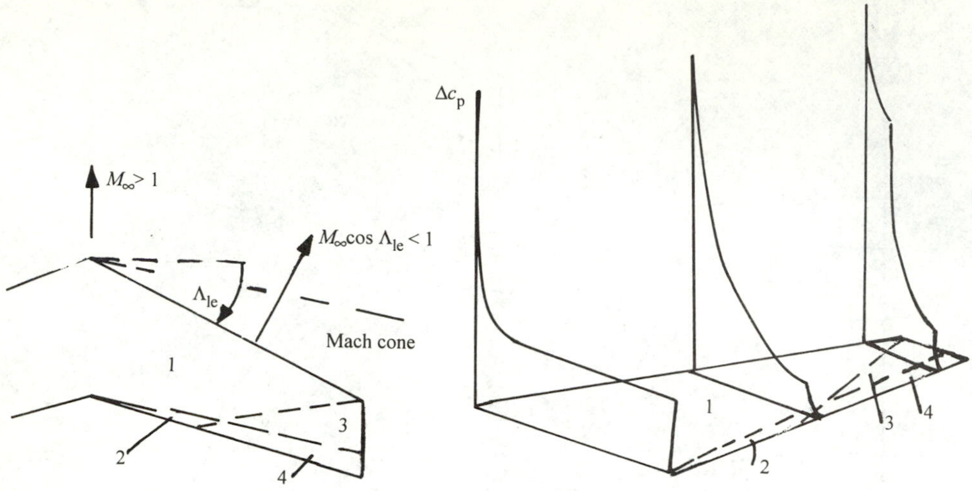

Fig. III.9(ii). Wing loading due to angle of incidence alone at supersonic speeds (subsonic leading edge).

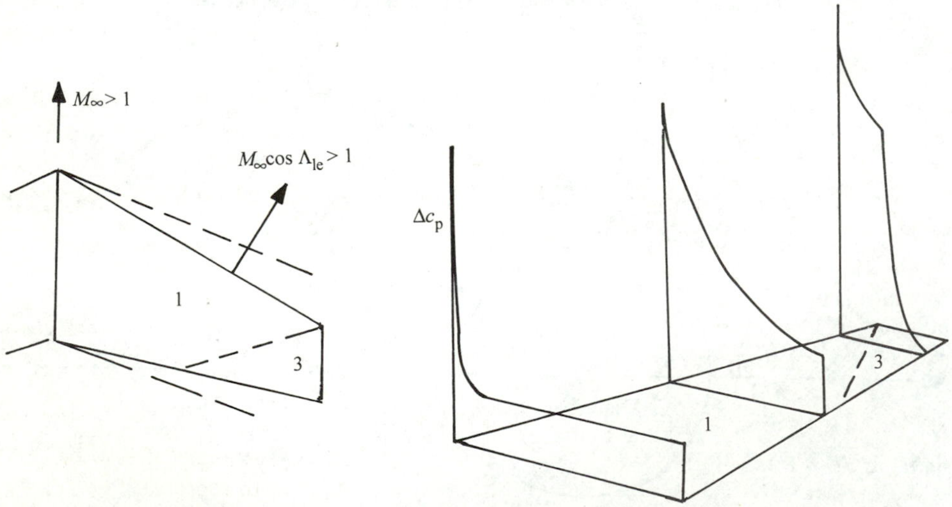

Fig. III.9(iii). Wing loading due to angle of incidence alone at supersonic speeds (subsonic leading edge).

At low supersonic speeds when the leading edge is 'subsonic' (i.e. $M_\infty \cos \Lambda_{le} < 1$, where Λ_{le} is the sweep angle of the wing leading edge), as shown in Fig. III.9(ii), region 1 is unaffected by the wing trailing edge and the wing tip, region 2 is affected by the wing trailing edge but is unaffected by the wing tip, region 3 is affected by the wing tip but not by the wing trailing edge, and region 4 is affected by the complete planform. The

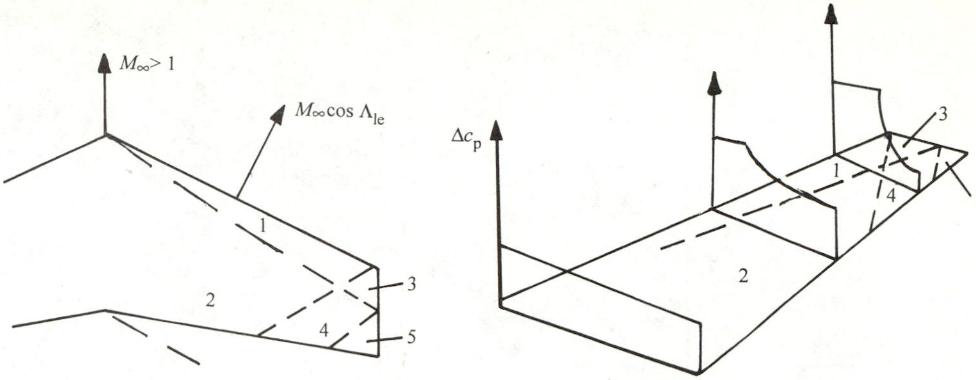

Fig. III.9(iv). Wing loading due to angle of incidence alone at supersonic speeds (supersonic leading edge).

loading in region 1 is conical (i.e. Δc_p is constant along rays, or lines, through the wing apex, with Δc_p theoretically infinite along the wing leading edge), the loadings in regions 2 and 3 are much smaller than in region 1, while the loading in region 4 is extremely small.

At a slightly higher supersonic speed, but with the leading edge still subsonic, only regions 1 and 3 exist, as shown in Fig. III.9(iii); note that there is a finite loading at the trailing edge in region 1.

With further increase in Mach number the leading edge becomes supersonic (i.e. $M_\infty \cos \Lambda_{le} > 1$). As shown in Fig. III.9(iv), region 1 is unaffected by the rest of the wing, region 2 is unaffected by the wing tip, region 3 is affected by the wing tip, while regions 4 and 5 are reflected zones. Note that the high leading edge suctions have disappeared with a constant loading over region 1.

III.3.1.3 Wing lift

At low angles of incidence the wing lift coefficient $(C_L)_w$ can be regarded as a linear function of angle of incidence, as shown in Fig. III.10, hence

$$(C_L)_w = (a_\alpha)_w(\alpha - \alpha_{0w}), \quad \alpha < \alpha_b \tag{III.3.12}$$

where $(a_\alpha)_w$ is the wing lift curve slope = $d(C_L)_w/d\alpha$, α_{0w} is the angle of zero lift, and α_b is the break angle of incidence where the linearity of $(C_L)_w$ with α breaks down due to flow separation.

The angle of zero lift, α_{0w}, is usually negative, as shown in Fig. III.10; its value depends on the amount of camber and wash-out. If camber and wash-out are both zero, then α_{0w} is zero.

An approximate formula for the wing lift curve slope at subsonic speeds is (from ref. III.8),

$$(a_\alpha)_w = 2\pi \frac{AR_w}{[(AR_w^2+4)^{1/2}+2]} \frac{(AR_w \cos \Lambda_w)+1}{[AR_w(1-M_\infty^2 \cos^2 \Lambda_w)^{1/2}+1]} \text{ per radian} \tag{III.3.13}$$

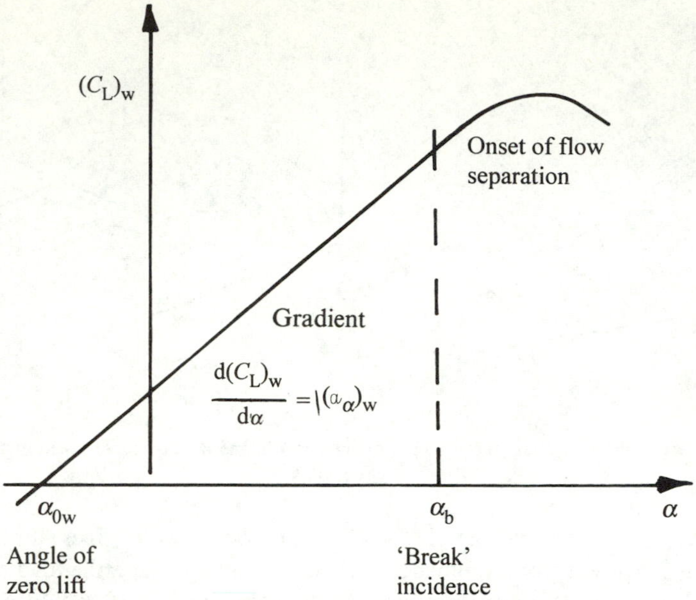

Fig. III.10. Wing lift coefficient variation with angle of incidence.

Values of $(a_\alpha)_w$ are usually quoted per radian, whereas angles are usually quoted in degrees, so it is necessary to remember to convert when estimating $(C_L)_w$.

Eqn. (III.3.13) is an amalgam of standard formulae:

$$
\begin{aligned}
(a_\alpha)_w &= 2\pi \quad \text{when } \Lambda_w = 0,\ M_\infty = 0,\ AR_w = \infty;\\
&= 2\pi\cos\Lambda_w \quad \text{when } M_\infty = 0,\ AR_w = \infty;\\
&= 2\pi\cos\Lambda_w/[1 - M_\infty^2\cos^2\Lambda_w]^{1/2} \quad \text{when } M_\infty > 0,\ AR_w = \infty;\\
&= 2\pi/[1 + 2/AR_w] \quad \text{when } M_\infty = 0,\ \Lambda_w = 0,\ AR_w > 4;\\
&= \pi AR_w/2 \quad \text{as } AR_w \to 0.
\end{aligned}
$$

An approximate formula for the lift curve slope for a wing with a subsonic leading edge at supersonic speeds, based on the formula for a delta wing (see ref. III.7), is

$$(a_\alpha)_w = \frac{\pi AR_w/2}{\left[1 + (M_\infty^2 - 1)^{1/2}/\pi\right]\left[\ 1 + 0.2\lambda_w\ \right]}. \qquad \text{(III.3.14)}$$

An approximate formula for the lift curve slope for a wing with a supersonic leading edge, based on the formula for a delta wing (from ref. III.8), is

$$(a_\alpha)_w = \frac{4}{(M_\infty^2 - 1)^{1/2}}. \qquad \text{(III.3.15)}$$

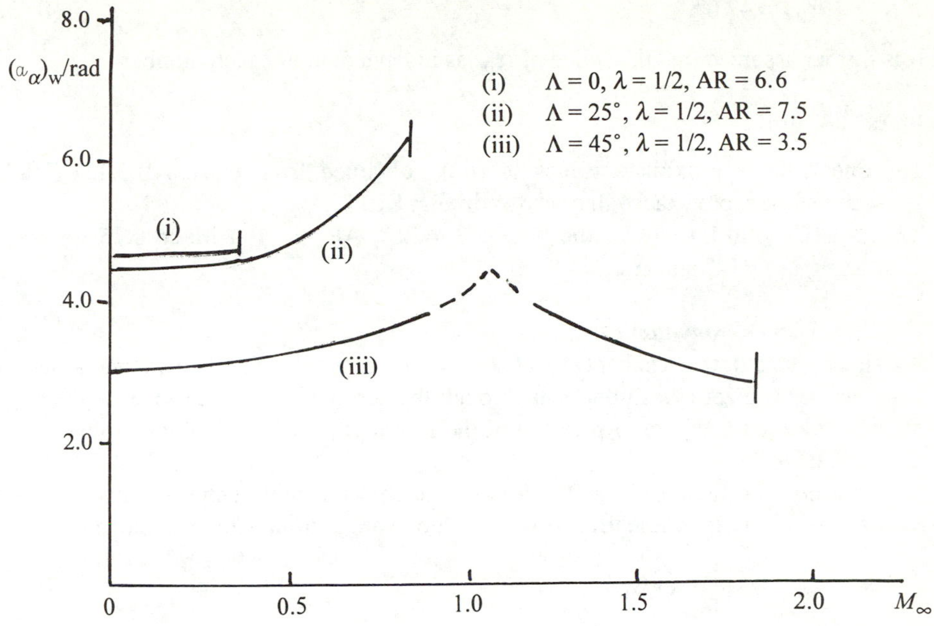

Fig. III.11. Lift curve slope of wings of basic configurations.

More accurate data for the wing lift curve slope, $(a_\alpha)_w$, for the wings of the three basic configurations (Figs. III.5) are shown in Fig. III.11, based on the ESDU Data Sheets (ref. III.13).

Note the following in Fig. III.11:

(i) $(a_\alpha)_w$ decreases with increase in wing sweep;
(ii) there is little variation of $(a_\alpha)_w$ with Mach number at low Mach numbers, say for $M_\infty < 0.4$;
(iii) $(a_\alpha)_w$ increases with Mach number at subsonic speeds;
(iv) $(a_\alpha)_w$ reaches a maximum at a low supersonic Mach number before decreasing at higher supersonic speeds.

The fairing of $(a_\alpha)_w$ for the combat configuration through the transonic speed range is reasonable for contemporary highly swept wings with thin sections. In the early days of transonic flight with wings of low sweep angle and relatively thick sections, the variations of wing lift with Mach number at transonic speeds were highly non-linear, sometimes with lift curve slopes which were effectively negative.

The linear variation of $(C_L)_w \sim \alpha$ occurs over the range $\alpha < \alpha_b$. In qualitative terms, at subsonic speeds α_b is of the order of 12°, at transonic speeds α_b is much smaller, of the order of 3°, and at supersonic speeds α_b is of the order of 15°.

To complete the static lift data for the wings of the basic configurations (Figs. III.5), all these wings are assumed to have the same angle of zero lift, namely

$$\alpha_{0w} = -2.0°. \tag{III.3.16}$$

It is further assumed that this value of α_{0w} is independent of Mach number.

EXAMPLES III.4

1. Check the approximate values of $(a_\alpha)_w$ obtained from eqns. (III.3.13)–(III.3.15) against the more exact values shown in Fig. III.11.
2. Plot $(C_L)_w$ against α for the wing ($\Lambda_w = 25°$, $AR_w = 7$) at Mach 0.75 for $\alpha < \alpha_b$, taking $\alpha_b = 14°$ and $\alpha_{0w} = -1°$.

III.3.1.4 Wing aerodynamic centre

As already stated, the resultant lift of the loading due to angle of incidence alone, with zero camber and zero wash-out, acts through the aerodynamic centre. Hence the aerodynamic centre is the centre of pressure of the resultant lift of the loadings shown in Figs. III.8 and III.9.

For a crude estimate of the location of the aerodynamic centre at subsonic speeds, assume an elliptic spanwise lift distribution due to angle of incidence alone, namely

$$L(y) = L_0\left[1-(y/s_w)^2\right]^{1/2}, \tag{III.3.17}$$

where L_0 is a constant. Furthermore, assume that $L(y)$ acts through the local $\frac{1}{4}$ chord point at spanwise position y. Then, by reference to Fig. III.12, the distance of the aerodynamic centre aft of the wing apex, $h_w\,c_r$, where c_r is the wing root chord, is given by

$$h_w\,c_r = \frac{\text{nose-down moment about pitch axis through wing apex of lift due to angle of incidence}}{\text{total lift due to angle of incidence}}$$

$$= \left[\int_{-s_w}^{+s_w}[(c_r)_w/4) + y\tan\Lambda_w]L(y)\,dy\right]\Big/\left[\int_{-s_w}^{+s_w}L_\alpha(y)\,dy\right]$$

$$= \left[\tfrac{1}{4} + (2/3\pi)AR_w\tan\Lambda_w c_w/c_r\right]c_r. \tag{III.3.18}$$

According to eqn. (III.3.18),

$$h_w = 0.25 \quad \text{when } \Lambda_w = 0,$$

$$= 0.70 \quad \text{when } \Lambda_w = 35°,\ AR_w = 4.0,\ \lambda_w = 0.5.$$

More exact estimates of the locations of the aerodynamic centres of the wings of the basic configurations (Figs. III.5) and their variation with increase in Mach number, based on the ESDU Data Sheets (ref. III.13), are shown in Fig. III.13. Note:

(i) h_w is the non-dimensional distance with respect to the wing root chord, not the wing mean chord;

(ii) the aerodynamic centre for the non-swept wing is located close to the $\frac{1}{4}$ chord point;

(iii) wing sweep moves the aerodynamic centre aft;

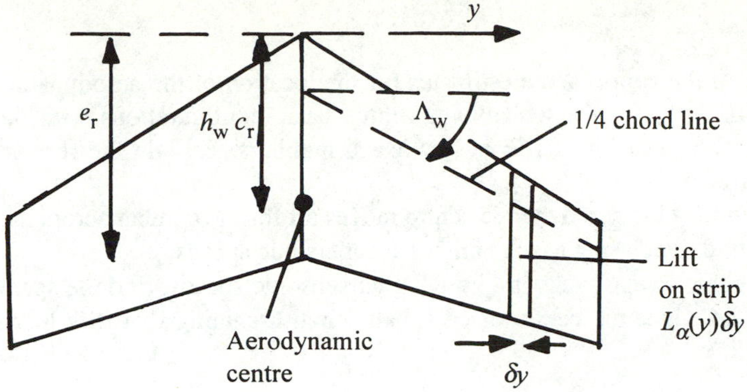

Fig. III.12. Calculation of aerodynamic centre.

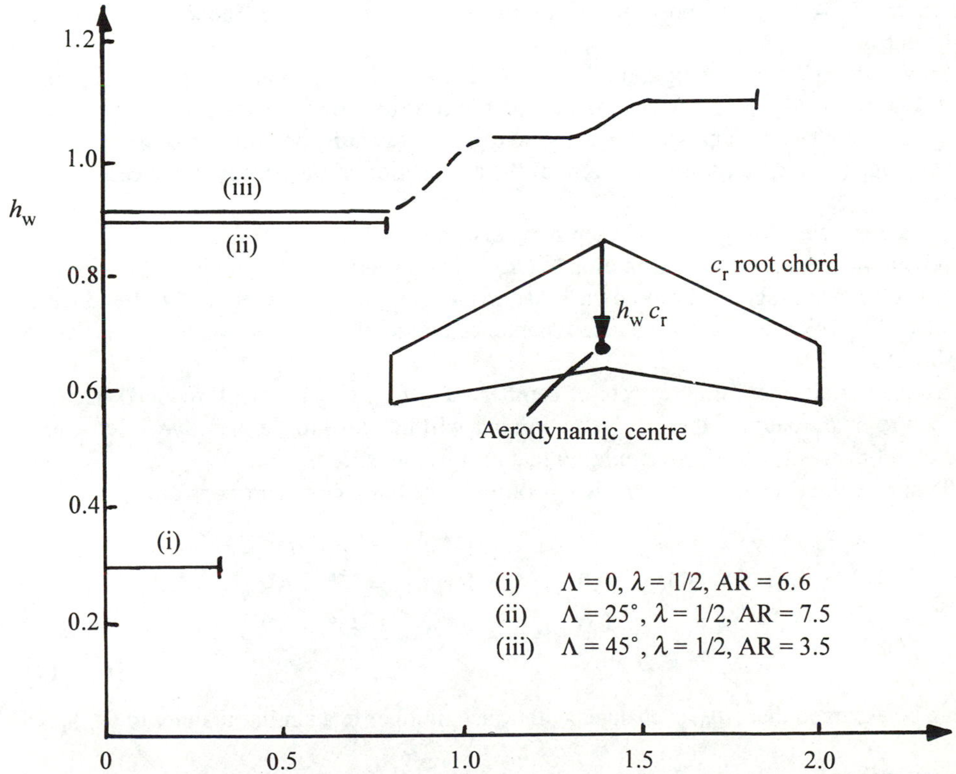

Fig. III.13. Location of aerodynamic centre of wing of basic configurations.

(iv) the location of the aerodynamic centre can be assumed independent of Mach number at subsonic speeds;

(v) the aft displacement of the aerodynamic centre with increasing Mach number at transonic and at supersonic speeds to behind the trailing edge of the wing root section.

EXAMPLES III.5

1. Compare the approximate estimates for the location of the aerodynamic centre from eqn. (III.3.18) for the wings of the three basic configurations with the more exact values shown in Fig. III.13 at low Mach numbers. Explain the reason for the poor comparison.
2. Explain why the aerodynamic centre moves aft for the combat aeroplane wing in Fig. III.13 with increasing Mach number at supersonic speeds.
3. For the two swept wings in Fig. III.13 at subsonic speeds, find the spanwise position of the aerodynamic centre of each half wing, assuming that it is located on the $\frac{1}{4}$ chord line.

III.3.1.5 Wing pitching moment at zero lift

On a non-swept wing, at low Mach numbers, positive camber gives a resultant lift which acts near the 40% chord position, aft of the aerodynamic centre, inducing a negative contribution to $(m_0)_w$.

Similarly on a swept wing a uniform camber along the full span will give a negative contribution to $(m_0)_w$. If, however, the camber is confined to the inboard stations near the wing root on a swept wing with virtually no cambers towards the wing tips, the contribution to $(m_0)_w$ could be positive because of the aft location of the aerodynamic centre on a swept wing.

On a non-swept wing, at low Mach numbers, the lift due to wash-out acts close to the aerodynamic centre so the contribution to $(m_0)_w$ from wash-out is virtually zero.

On a swept wing the nose-down twist from wing root to wing tip will induce a negative lift which acts aft of the aerodynamic centre, so the contribution to $(m_0)_w$ due to wash-out is positive.

At supersonic speeds the effects of camber on $(m_0)_w$ will be much reduced because the centre of pressure of the lift due to camber will be close to the aerodynamic centre. The effect of wash-out will be similar to that at subsonic speeds.

Typical values for $(m_0)_w$ for the wings of the three basic configurations are

$$\begin{aligned} (m_0)_w &= -0.02 && \text{for } \Lambda_w = 0, && AR_w = 6.6, \ \lambda_w = 0.5 \\ &= +0.04 \text{ at } M_\infty = 0.0 && \text{for } \Lambda_w = 25°, && AR_w = 7.5, \ \lambda_w = 0.5 \\ &= +0.02 \text{ at } M_\infty = 0.0,\ 1.2 && \text{for } \Lambda_w = 45°, && AR_w = 3.5, \ \lambda_w = 0.5. \end{aligned} \tag{III.3.19}$$

It can be assumed that $(m_0)_w$ changes with Mach number in a similar manner to $(a_\alpha)_w$.

EXAMPLES III.6

1. Why, for a non-swept wing, at low Mach numbers, does the lift due to wash-out act close to the aerodynamic centre?
2. Why, for a swept wing, at low Mach numbers, does the lift due to wash-out act behind the aerodynamic centre?
3. On a non-swept wing if $(C_L)_w = 0.1$ when $\alpha = 0$, and the centre of pressure of the wing lift is $0.4c_r$ from the wing apex, what is $(m_0)_w$?

4. Show that a crude estimate for the contribution of wash-out to $(m_0)_w$ at low Mach numbers is

$$\left[-(a_\alpha)_w\left(\theta_{tip}/2\right)\, 0.075\ AR_w \tan\Lambda_w\right],$$

taking

θ_{tip} = nose-up twist angle at wing tip relative to wing root

$(a_\alpha)_w\left(\theta_{tip}/2\right)$ = approximate wing lift coefficient due to wash-out, assuming mean angle of incidence of wing is $\theta_{tip}/2$,

overall centre of pressure of half wing lift due to wash-out

$= \frac{1}{4}$ chord at the spanwise station 0.65 s_w

location of aerodynamic centre

$= \frac{1}{4}$ chord at the spanwise station 0.5 s_w.

Estimate the contribution of wash-out to $(m_0)_w$, when

(i) $\theta_{tip} = -3°$, $AR_w = 7.5$, $\Lambda_w = 25°$.
(ii) $\theta_{tip} = -3°$, $AR_w = 3.5$, $\Lambda_w = 45°$.

III.3.1.6 Wing drag

The wing drag coefficient can be expressed in the form

$$(C_D)_w = (C_{D0})_w + (C_{DL})_w \qquad \text{(III.3.20)}$$

where $(C_{D0})_w$ is the wing drag coefficient at zero lift and $(C_{DL})_w$ is the wing lift-dependent drag coefficient.

Typical variations of $(C_{D0})_w$ with Mach number for wings with different angles of sweep are shown in Fig. III.14. At low subsonic speeds $(C_{D0})_w$, which is due primarily to the viscous stresses on the wing surface, is virtually independent of Mach number and of wing sweep; note that the value of $(C_{D0})_w$ at low Mach numbers is approximately 0.010. At a particular subsonic Mach number, $(M_\infty = M_D)$, $(C_{D0})_w$ begins to rise rapidly due to the formation of shock waves over the wing upper and lower surfaces in the wing tip regions, together with a bow shock, as shown in Fig. III.15 (taken from Rogers & Hall, ref. III.14); the force required to push these shock waves through the air is reacted by an additional normal pressure drag force on the wing, known as the wave drag. M_D is known as the drag rise Mach number. Note that M_D increases with sweep angle.

The shock waves on the wing grow in strength and move aft towards the trailing edge as the Mach number increases above M_D. When these shock waves reach the trailing edge they stay there and incline backwards to the stream direction, and $(C_{D0})_w$ then decreases with increase in Mach number.

Speed ranges may be now defined as follows:

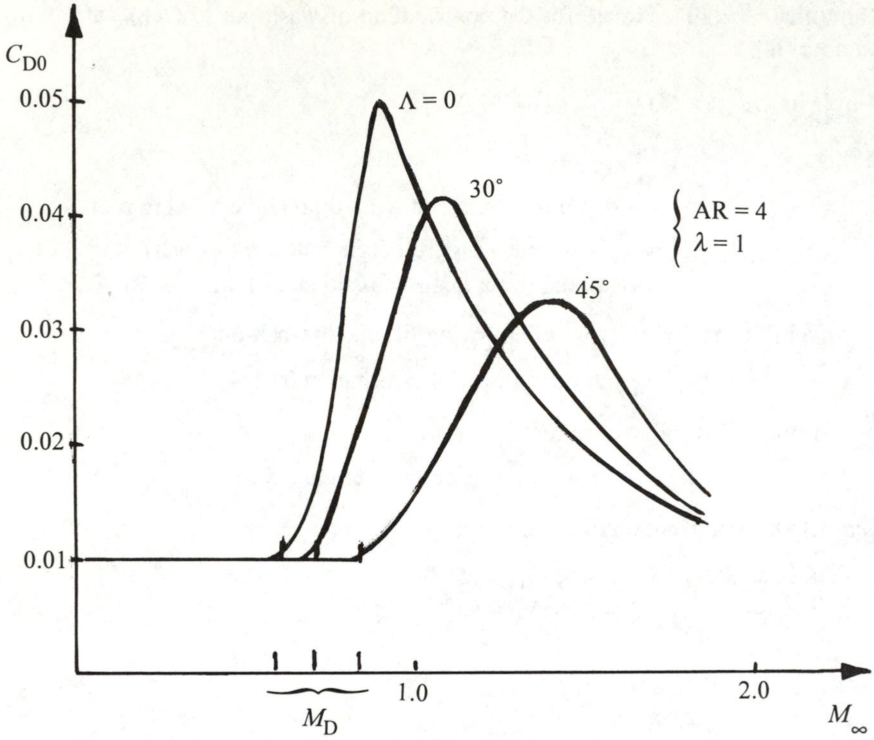

Fig. III.14. Variation of $(C_{D0})_w$ with wing sweep and Mach number.

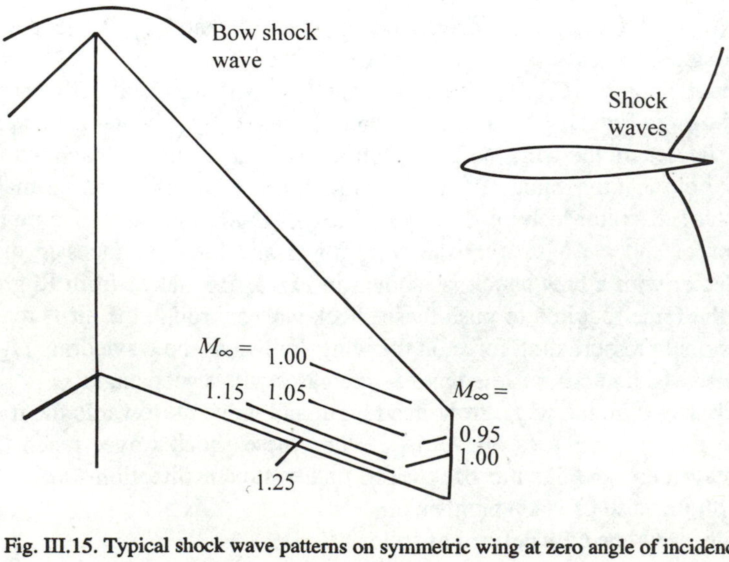

Fig. III.15. Typical shock wave patterns on symmetric wing at zero angle of incidence.

— subsonic speed range, $M_\infty < M_D$,
— supersonic speed range, when C_{D0} decreases with M_∞ at $M_\infty > 1$,
— transonic speed range, the intermediate Mach numbers through Mach 1.0.

With these definitions, subsonic, transonic and supersonic are different for different wings.

At supersonic speeds, although $(C_{D0})_w$ decreases with increase in Mach number (see Fig. III.14), the drag force at zero lift increases with increase in Mach number. The reason is that

$$\begin{aligned}\text{wing drag at zero lift} &= \tfrac{1}{2}\rho_{at}U^2 S_w (C_{D0})_w \\ &= \tfrac{1}{2}\gamma\, p_{at} M_\infty^2 S_w (C_{D0})_w\end{aligned} \qquad \text{(III.3.21)}$$

after substituting for the speed of sound, eqn. (III.2.2), and $\left(M_\infty^2 (C_{D0})_w\right)$ increases with increase in M_∞.

The drag rise Mach number M_D is a most important design parameter. M_D is increased by wing sweep (see Fig. III.14), together with efficient wing section design, using supercritical sections. Wing sweep delays the appearance of shock waves and increases M_D because, in broad terms, the flow characteristics are determined by the component of the flight Mach number normal to the wing leading edge.

For transport aeroplanes the higher M_D the higher the cruise Mach number.

For combat aeroplanes the aim is not only to increase M_D but also to minimize the large increase in wave drag at transonic and supersonic speeds. Wing sweep increases M_D and reduces the maximum value of $(C_{D0})_w$ at transonic speeds, but at supersonic speeds $(C_{D0})_w$ increases with wing sweep (see Fig. III.14), and so a compromise wing sweep angle has to be sought.

From the point of view of reducing wave drag, sweep forward is as effective as sweep back, but swept forward wings tend to suffer from excessive structural deformations unless constructed of composite materials.

The lift-dependent drag coefficient $(C_{DL})_w$ is proportional to $(C_L)_w^2$. At subsonic speeds the lift-dependent drag, which arises from the work done by the wing in forming the wing tip vortices (see Fig. III.7) is often referred to as the induced drag or vortex drag. At low angles of incidence, at subsonic speeds,

$$(C_{DL})_w \simeq (C_L)_w^2/(\pi AR_w). \qquad \text{(III.3.22)}$$

Included in eqn. (III.3.22) is a thrust on the wing leading edge which arises from the high suction pressures acting around the wing leading edge.

At transonic and supersonic speeds an increase in the angle of incidence increases the net strength of the shock waves, increasing the wave drag and so adding a wave drag contribution to the vortex drag, thus increasing the total wing lift-dependent drag.

At supersonic speeds when the wing leading edge becomes supersonic (i.e. when $M_\infty \cos \Lambda_{le} > 1.0$), the leading edge thrust is completely lost, and then

$$(C_L)_w = (C_N)_w \cos\alpha, \qquad (C_{DL})_w = (C_N)_w \sin\alpha, \qquad \text{(III.3.23)}$$

where $(C_N)_w$ is the force coefficient normal to the wing surface. At low angles of incidence,

$$(C_{DL})_w \simeq (C_L)_w \alpha \simeq (C_L)_w^2/(a_\alpha)_w, \tag{III.3.24}$$

ignoring α_{0w}.

The supersonic value of $(C_{DL})_w$ in eqn. (III.3.24) is approximately three times the subsonic value of $(C_{DL})_w$ in eqn. (III.3.22); this increase takes place over the Mach number range ($M_D < M_\infty < \sec \Lambda_{le}$).

EXAMPLES III.7

1. Plot drag against Mach number for the combat basic configuration in steady level flight (i.e. lift = weight) at 11 km altitude.
2. Plot the wing (lift/drag) ratio (= $(C_L/C_D)_w$) against α for $0 < \alpha < 10°$, at low Mach number, for the three basic configurations.
3. What is the effect of Mach number on the maximum wing (lift/drag) ratio at (i) subsonic speeds and (ii) supersonic speeds?

III.3.1.7 Effect of high lift system

Incorporated within a wing will be a high lift system, comprising trailing edge flaps and leading edge slats (see ref. III.7). When the high lift system is deployed for take-off or landing, the wing lift is considerably increased due to two effects: a large increase in wing camber, significantly decreasing the angle of zero lift, and an increase in wing area (see Fig. III.16). The wing lift can be written in the form

$$(C_L + \Delta C_L)_w = (a_\alpha)_w(\alpha - \alpha_{0w} - \Delta\alpha_{0w})\left(1 + \Delta S_w/S_w\right) \tag{III.3.25}$$

where Δ refers to the change due to the high lift system. The angle of incidence, α, is the initial angle of incidence of the wing before the high lift system is deployed.

According to eqn. (III.3.25), the lift curve slope, $d(C_L + \Delta C_L)_w/d\alpha$, is increase by a factor $\left(1 + \Delta S_w/S_w\right)$. This lift curve slope decreases at higher flap angles when the flow separates over the flap.

On substitution of typical numbers

$$(C_L)_w = (a_\alpha)_w(\alpha - \alpha_{0w}) = 1.0, \qquad (a_\alpha)_w = 4.75$$

$$(C_L + \Delta C_L)_w = 2.5, \qquad \left(1 + \Delta S_w/S_w\right) = 1.15,$$

then, from eqn. (III.3.25),

$$\Delta\alpha_{0w} = -14°. \tag{III.3.26}$$

A high lift system, slats and flaps, extends over about 70% of the inner exposed span (i.e. exterior to the fuselage) of a transport aeroplane and sometimes extends across 100% of the exposed span of a combat aeroplane. The increase in lift acts behind the aerodynamic centre, giving a nose-down moment about the aerodynamic centre; typically if $(\Delta C_L)_w$ ($\simeq$ 1.5) acts $0.1c_w$ aft of the aerodynamic centre, then

$$(\Delta m_0)_w \simeq -0.15. \tag{III.3.27}$$

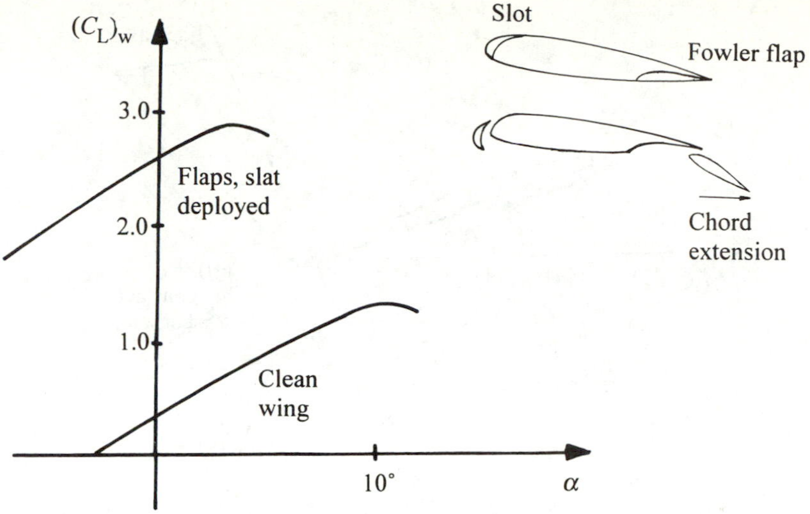

Fig. III.16. Lift effectiveness of high lift system.

At take-off a high C_L is required to minimize speed together with a low C_D to minimize drag; in this case a low flap angle, with an increase in wing area, is used. To land at low speeds again a high C_L is required, but now for flight dynamics reasons, as explained later, a high C_D is also necessary; in this case large flap angles are used with flow separations over the flaps to provide the additional drag.

III.3.2 Steady aerodynamics of a wing due to constant rate of pitch

Consider a wing in a dynamic motion consisting of constant forward speed U, constant angle of incidence α, and constant rate of pitch q (i.e. $\theta = qt$, where t is time) about a specified pitch axis, as shown in Fig. III.17(i). Such a motion occurs in a pull-up manoeuvre, as shown in Fig. III.3.

To explain how a steady aerodynamic loading is generated by a constant rate of pitch, consider a planar wing (i.e. zero geometric camber and zero geometric twist) at a zero angle of incidence. As shown in Fig. III.17(ii), a point on the wing section, distance x from the axis of pitch, has a velocity normal to the chord surface equal to qx; this velocity is upwards for points ahead of the pitch axis ($x > 0$) and downward for points behind the pitch axis ($x < 0$). From the definition of angle of incidence, eqn. (III.1.4) a local angle of incidence is therefore induced at point x equal to $-qx/U$, which is negative for x positive, and positive for x negative, producing an effective positive camber, as shown in Fig. III.17(iii). Since this effective camber is independent of time, the aerodynamic loading is steady. A lift force is generated together with a pitching moment; both are directly proportional to q. There is also a contribution to the lift-dependent drag.

The wing lift force, taken to act through the steady state aerodynamic centre of the wing, and the wing pitching moment about the steady state aerodynamic centre of the wing, can be expressed in the form

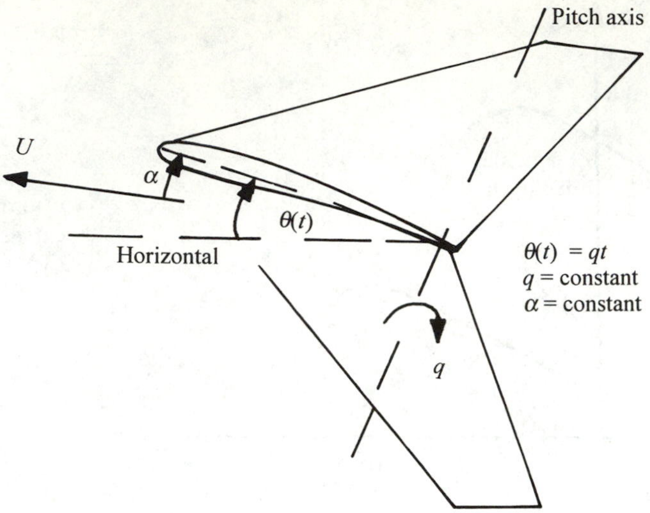

Fig. III.17(i). Notation for constant rate of pitch.

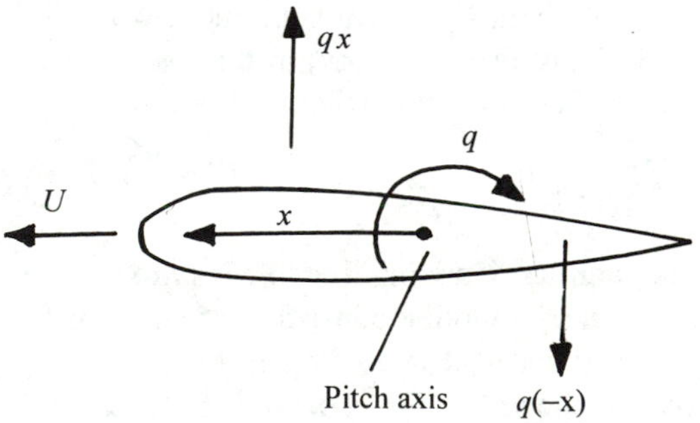

Fig. III.17(ii). Wing section in rate of pitch.

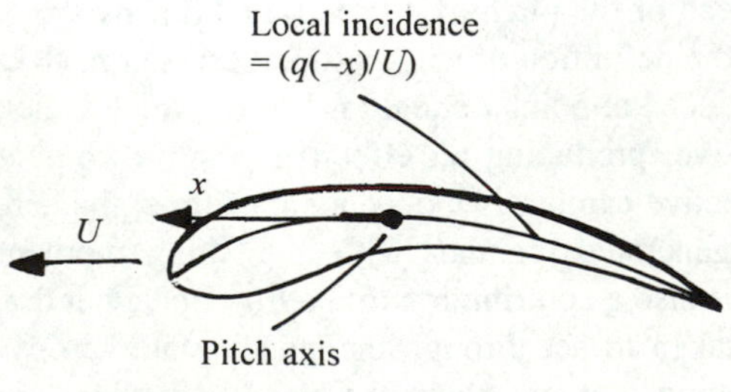

Fig. III.17(iii). Effective camber due to rate of pitch.

$$\begin{aligned}\text{wing lift due to } q &= \tfrac{1}{2}\rho_{at}U^2 S_w\left[(a_q)_w\left(qc_w/U\right)\right]\\ (\text{wing moment due to } q)_{ac} &= \tfrac{1}{2}\rho_{at}U^2 S_w c_w\left[(m_q)_w\left(qc_w/U\right)\right].\end{aligned} \tag{III.3.28}$$

The terms in the square brackets are non-dimensional, qc_w/U is the non-dimensional rate of pitch, and $(a_q)_w$ and $(m_q)_w$ are the non-dimensional pitch rate coefficients which depend on the wing plan form geometry, location of the pitch axis and Mach number.

The induced camber due to rate of pitch for a swept wing, shown in Fig. III.18, introduces three effects:

(i) a curved camber profile which is independent of sweep or position of the pitch axis,
(ii) a spanwise twist which increases the sectional angle of incidence from wing root to tip; this effect depends on wing sweep but not on the position of the pitch axis,
(iii) an overall angle of incidence which depends on the position of the pitch axis.

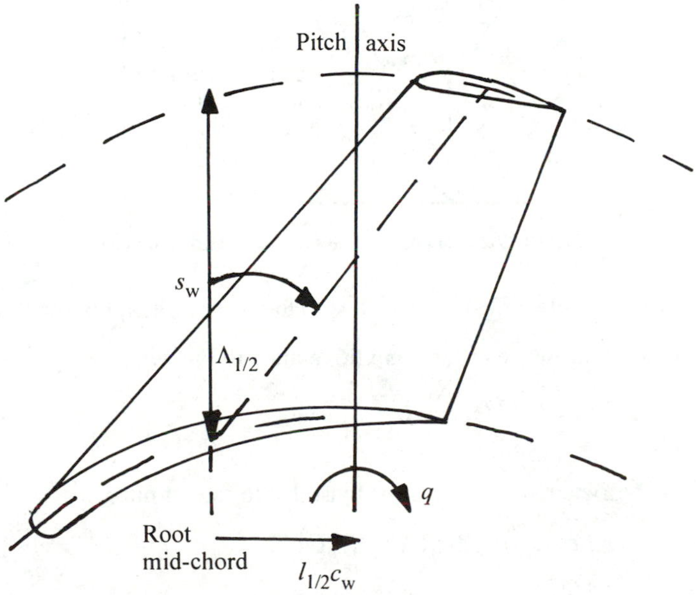

Fig. III.18. Wing in constant rate of pitch.

Approximate values of $(a_q)_w$ and $(m_q)_w$ can be estimated at subsonic speeds.

For the lift due to the effective camber due to the rate of pitch, the local incidence is $q(-x)/U$, in Fig. III.17(iii), so the camber shape, which is the integral of the local incidence, is $qx^2/2U$. By definition

camber = (maximum displacement of camber shape from chord line)/chord

hence,

$$\text{average camber over the span} \simeq \left(q\left(c_w/2\right)^2/2U\right)\Big/c_w = qc_w/8U.$$

Typically a 10% camber gives a lift coefficient of $0.2(a_\alpha)_w$, so

lift coefficient due to effective camber induced by rate of pitch

$$\simeq 0.2(a_\alpha)_w\left[\left(qc_w/8U\right)/0.1\right] \simeq 0.25(a_\alpha)_w\, qc_w/U. \qquad \text{(III.3.29)}$$

The lift on a half wing due to effective camber can be assumed to act through the mid-chord point at 0.5 semi-span (see Fig. III.19).

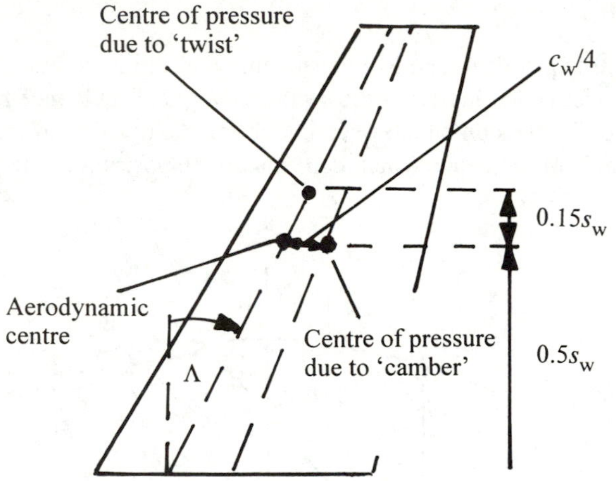

Fig. III.19. Locations of centres of pressures due to rate of pitch.

For the lift due to the effective twist due to the rate of pitch, by reference to Fig. III.18,

angle of incidence of the wing tip relative to the wing root

$$= \left(qs_w \tan\,(\Lambda_{1/2})_w\right)/U. \qquad \text{(III.3.30)}$$

Then crudely

lift coefficient due to effective twist due to rate of pitch

$$\simeq (a_\alpha)_w\left(qs_w \tan(\Lambda_{1/2})_w/U\right)/2.5 \qquad \text{(III.3.31)}$$

taking a mean wing incidence equal to

$$\left[\left(qs_w \tan\,(\Lambda_{1/2})_w/U\right)/2.5\right].$$

The lift on a half wing due to effective twist can be assumed to act through the $\frac{1}{4}$ chord point at 0.65 semi-span (see Fig. III.19).

For the lift due to the effective incidence due to the rate of pitch, by reference to Fig. III.18

$$\text{effective angle of incidence} = -ql_{1/2}c_w/U \qquad \text{(III.3.32)}$$

where $l_{1/2}c_w$ is the distance of the wing root mid-chord ahead of the pitch axis. Hence lift coefficient due to effective angle of incidence

$$= (a_\alpha)_w\left(-q l_{1/2} c_w / U\right). \tag{III.3.33}$$

The lift on a half wing due to effective angle of incidence acts at the wing aerodynamic centre which can be taken to be the $\frac{1}{4}$ chord point at 0.5 semi-span (see Fig. III.19).

Combining eqns. (III.3.29), (III.3.31) and (III.3.33), and by reference to eqns. (III.3.28), at low Mach numbers

$$(a_q)_w \simeq (a_\alpha)_w\left[0.25 + \left(AR_w \tan(\Lambda_{1/2})_w / 5\right) - l_{1/2}\right]. \tag{III.3.34}$$

For a non-swept wing the second term in eqn. (III.3.34) is negligible, while $l_{1/2}$ will be small, either positive or negative, for usual positions of the pitch axis close to the mid-chord. For wings with sweep angles greater than 25° the term $\left(AR_w \tan(\Lambda_{1/2})_w / 5\right)$ is approximately 0.7, independent of the sweep angle on the argument that as sweep angle increases the aspect ratio decreases, while $l_{1/2}$ is approximately 0.8 with a typical pitch axis $0.3c_w$ aft of the aerodynamic centre, so these terms tend to cancel, leaving

$$(a_q)_w \simeq 0.15(a_\alpha)_w. \tag{III.3.35}$$

For the pitching moment, by reference to Fig. III.19, from eqns. (III.3.28), (III.3.29) and (III.3.31),

$$(m_q)_w \simeq (a_\alpha)_w\left[-(0.25/4) - \left(AR_w \tan(\Lambda_{1/2})_w / 5\right)\left(0.075 AR_w \tan(\Lambda_{1/4})_w\right)\right]. \tag{III.3.36}$$

Note that $(m_q)_w$ is negative, and is independent of the location of the pitch axis. At subsonic speeds,

$$\left.\begin{array}{ll} \text{for a non-swept wing,} & (m_q)_w \simeq -0.06(a_\alpha)_w \\ \text{for a swept wing, } \Lambda_w > 25°, & (m_q)_w \simeq -0.25(a_\alpha)_w. \end{array}\right\} \tag{III.3.37}$$

It is not so straightforward to formulate similar simple order of magnitude formulae for supersonic speeds; in general $(a_q)_w$ peaks at transonic speeds and then decreases with increase of Mach number, going negative at high supersonic speeds; $(m_q)_w$ reduces in magnitude at supersonic speed.

Data for $(a_q)_w$ and $(m_q)_w$ for the wings of the three basic configurations (Figs. III.5), with the pitch axis located at $0.3c_w$ aft of the subsonic aerodynamic centre, are shown in Fig. III.20; the subsonic results are from ref. III.15, the supersonic results from ref. III.16.

EXAMPLES III.8

1. Compare the approximate values for $(a_q)_w$ and $(m_q)_w$ from eqns. (III.3.34) and (III.3.36) with the more accurate values given in Fig. III.20.

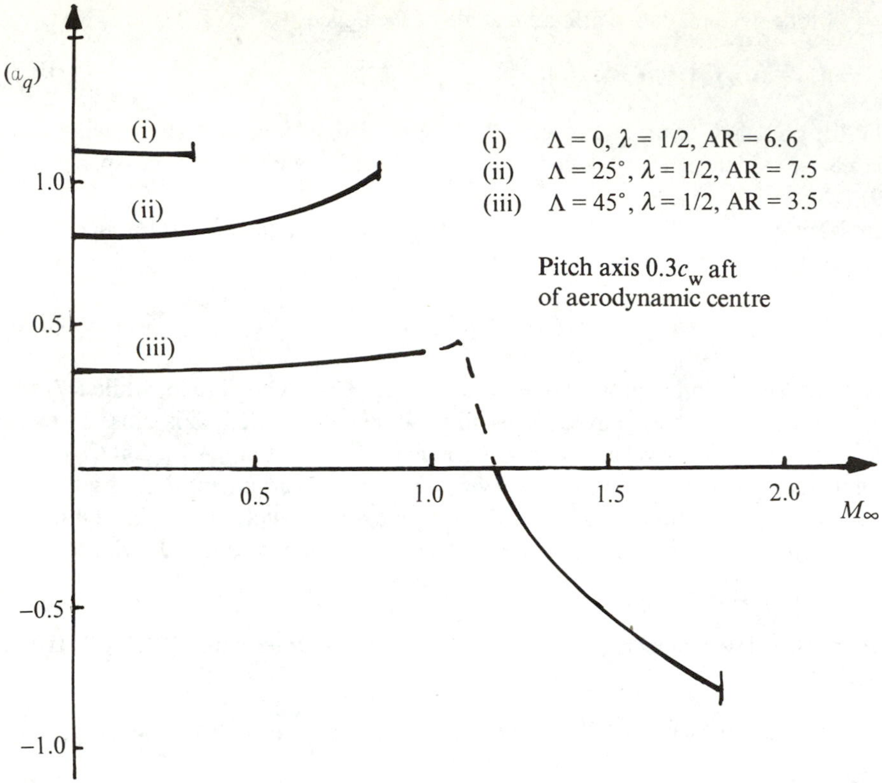

Fig. III.20(i). Coefficient a_q for wings of basic configurations.

2. Sketch $(a_q)_w \sim M_\infty$, and $(m_q)_w \sim M_\infty$ for the wing of the basic combat aeroplane configuration when the pitch axis is located $0.2c_w$ aft of the subsonic aerodynamic centre.

III.3.3 Unsteady aerodynamics of a wing in dynamic motions

In this section the unsteady loads on an isolated wing, moving in a time varying manner typical of aeroplane longitudinal dynamic motions, are described. The concepts originate from the classic work of Tobak (ref. III.17).

Unsteady aerodynamics need a time base for reference. The standard unit of aerodynamic time, $\hat{t}$, is taken as the time for a wing, moving with a constant velocity U, to travel the distance of one mean wing chord length, c_w, hence

$$\hat{t} = c_w/U. \qquad \text{(III.3.38)}$$

This unit of aerodynamic time is extremely small, for example, when

$$c_w = 3 \text{ m and } U = 85 \text{ m/s} \quad (\text{i.e. } M_\infty = 0.25),$$

$$\hat{t} = 0.035 \text{ s} \qquad \text{(III.3.39a)}$$

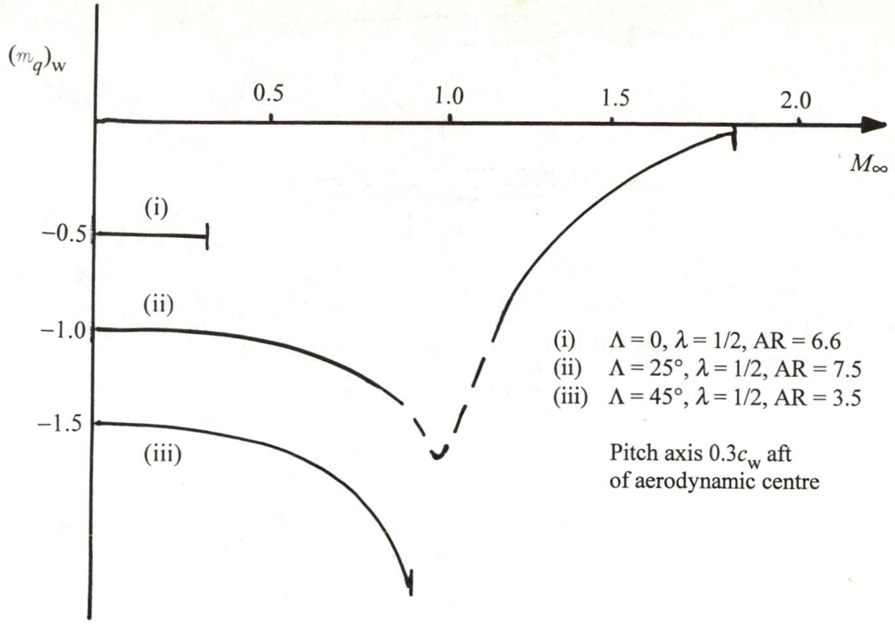

Fig. III.20(ii). Coefficient m_q for wings of basic configurations.

and when

$$c_W = 3 \text{ m and } U = 340 \text{ m/s} \quad (\text{i.e. } M_\infty = 1.0),$$

$$\hat{t} = 0.0088 \text{ s} \tag{III.3.39b}$$

Non-dimensional time $\hat{t}$ is defined as

$$\bar{t} = t/\hat{t}. \tag{III.3.40}$$

Thus, for example, $\bar{t} = 4$ represents the time taken for the wing to travel forward a distance of 4 mean wing chord lengths.

III.3.3.1 Time varying angle of incidence

The first dynamic motion to be considered is a planar wing (i.e. no camber or twist) moving at a constant speed, U, at low Mach number, with zero angles of incidence and pitch ($\alpha = 0$, $\theta = 0$), when at a datum time, taken to be $\bar{t} = 0$, the angle of incidence suddenly changes to α_s and then stays constant at α_s for $\bar{t} > 0$, the speed and pitch angle remaining unchanged at U and zero respectively. This step change in angle of incidence is shown in Fig. III.21.

The main features of the flow development with increasing time, sketched in Fig. III.22, are as follows.

1. Immediately following the sudden change in incidence a starting vortex forms rapidly along the wing span in the neighbourhood of the trailing edge; the circulation around this starting vortex is equal and opposite to the circulation around the wing, because,

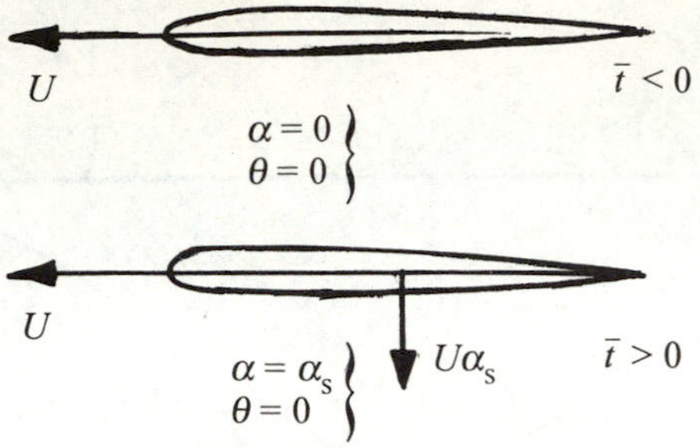

Fig. III.21. Sudden change in angle of incidence.

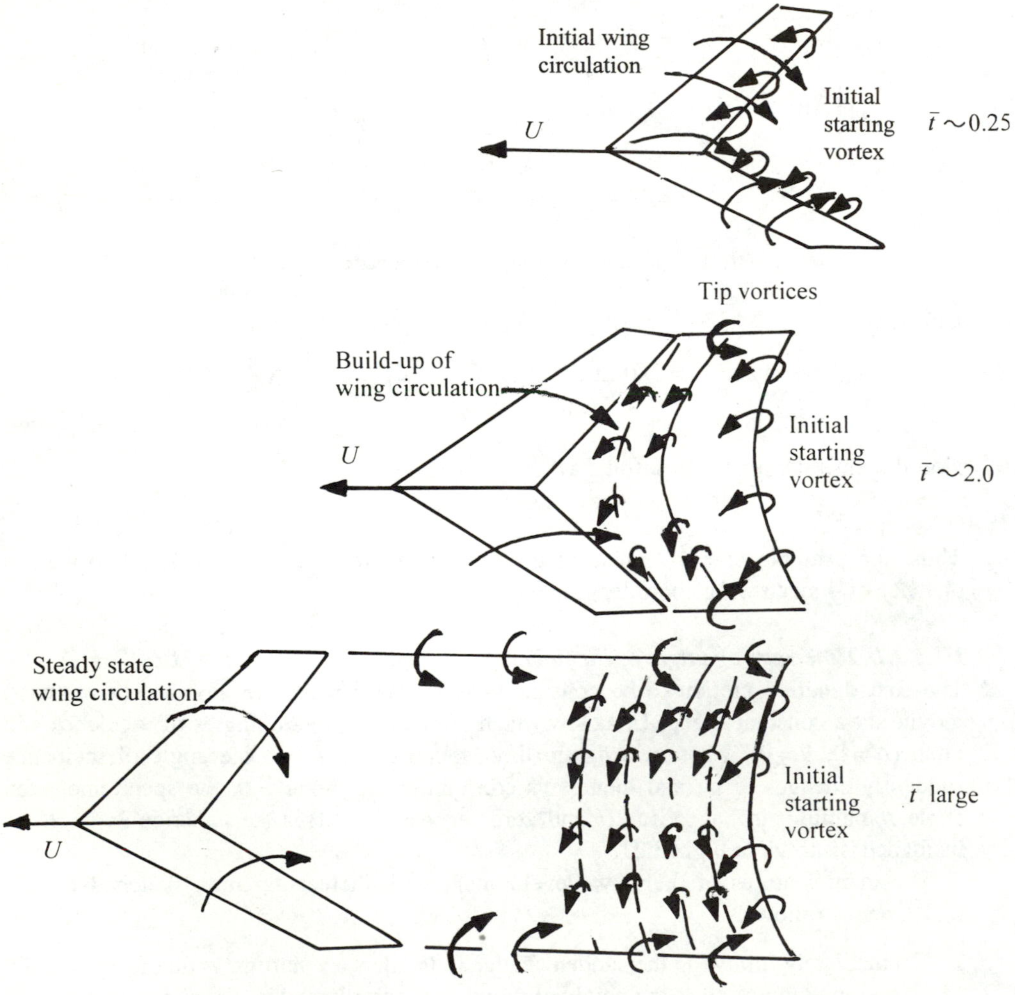

Fig. III.22. Flow development following sudden change in angle of incidence.

according to the Helmholtz theorem (see ref. III.7), no net spanwise circulation can be created by an unsteady motion.

2. About $\bar{t} = 0.25$ the starting vortex leaves the wing trailing edge, remaining stationary in space while the wing moves forward with velocity U; the distance between the wing and the starting vortex increases with time as $Ut\,(= c_{\mathrm{w}}\bar{t}\,)$. To complete the vortex pattern, wing tip vortices connect the circulation around the wing to the starting vortex.
3. For $\bar{t} > 0.25$ the circulation around the wing continues to build up but at a much slower rate and so a continuous sequence of weaker vortices are shed from the wing trailing edge, and then left behind in the wing wake. All are connected to the wing via additional wing tip vortices.
4. As $\bar{t}$ becomes large the strength of the circulation around the wing, the strength of the wing tip vortices in the vicinity of the wing and the wing lift all approach their respective steady state values associated with a steady angle of incidence, α_{s}; little further wake vorticity is shed and all the vorticity shed earlier, including the starting vortex, is then far downstream behind the wing.

The essential character of unsteady aerodynamics at low speeds is the formation of a wake, and the effect of that developing wake on the flow around the wing, resulting in time varying circulation, lift, drag and moment.

An approximation at low speeds for the build-up of the circulation $\Gamma(t)$ around a wing, where $\Gamma(t)$ is the average circulation along the wing span, following a sudden change in angle of incidence, α_{s}, at time equal zero, as derived in Appendix 1, is

$$\begin{aligned}\bar{\Gamma}(\bar{t}) &= \Gamma(t)/(c_{\mathrm{w}}U)\\ &\simeq \bar{\Gamma}_{\mathrm{s}}\left(1-1\big/\left[2.5+\left(10\bar{t}^{2}/\mathrm{AR}_{\mathrm{w}}\cos\Lambda_{\mathrm{w}}\right)\right]\right)H(\bar{t})\end{aligned} \tag{III.3.41}$$

where $\bar{\Gamma}(\bar{t})$ is the non-dimensional circulation, $\bar{\Gamma}_{\mathrm{s}}$ is the asymptotic value of $\bar{\Gamma}(\bar{t})$ as $\bar{t} \to \infty$, and $H(\bar{t})$ is the unit step function (see Part II).

In unsteady aerodynamics at low speeds the time varying lift coefficient $(C_{\mathrm{L}}(\bar{t}))_{\mathrm{w}}$ is related to the time varying circulation $\bar{\Gamma}(\bar{t})$ by the approximate relationship

$$(C_{\mathrm{L}}(\bar{t}))_{\mathrm{w}} \simeq 2\left(\bar{\Gamma}(\bar{t}) + 0.7\ \mathrm{d}\bar{\Gamma}(\bar{t})/\mathrm{d}\bar{t}\right) \tag{III.3.42}$$

as outlined in Appendix 1.

On substituting eqn. (III.3.41), eqn. (III.3.42) gives the build-up of the wing lift coefficient, $(C_{\mathrm{L}}(\bar{t}))_{\mathrm{w}}$, for $\bar{t} > 0$, following a sudden change in angle of incidence, namely

$$\begin{aligned}(C_{\mathrm{L}}(\bar{t}))_{\mathrm{w}} \simeq (a_{\alpha})_{\mathrm{w}}\alpha_{\mathrm{s}}\Big[1-\left(1\big/\left[2.5+\left(10\bar{t}^{2}/\mathrm{AR}_{\mathrm{w}}\cos\Lambda_{\mathrm{w}}\right)\right]\right)+0.7(0.6)\,\delta(\bar{t})\\ +\left(14\bar{t}/\mathrm{AR}_{\mathrm{w}}\cos\Lambda_{\mathrm{w}}\right)\big/\left[2.5+\left(10\bar{t}^{2}/\mathrm{AR}_{\mathrm{w}}\cos\Lambda_{\mathrm{w}}\right)\right]^{2}\Big],\end{aligned} \tag{III.3.43}$$

where $\delta(\bar{t})$ $\left(= dH(\bar{t})/D\bar{t}\right)$ is the standard impulse function, and $\left((a_\alpha)_w \alpha_s\right)$ is the asymptotic value of $\left(C_L(\bar{t})\right)_w$ as $\bar{t} \to \infty$.

Typical step incidence responses of $\left(C_L(\bar{t})\right)_w$ at low speeds are shown in Fig. III.23.

Four important points arise from eqn. (III.3.43) and Fig. III.23:

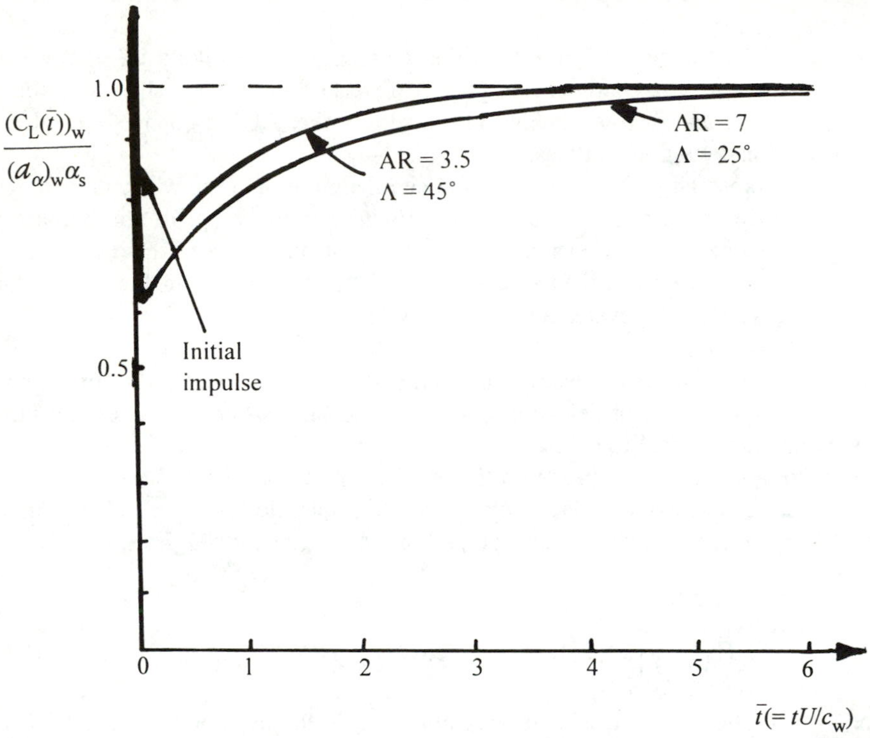

Fig. III.23. Lift response to step change in angle of incidence at low speeds.

(i) at time $\bar{t} = 0$ there is a pulse of positive lift as the wing instantaneously moves with an infinite (downward) acceleration;

(ii) after the initial pulse the lift jumps to about 60% of its final steady state value;

(iii) as $\bar{t}$ becomes large, the asymptotic steady state $\left((C_W)_w = (a_\alpha)_w \alpha_s\right)$ is approached as $1/\bar{t}^2$;

(iv) the wing lift reaches 99% of its final steady state value in time $\bar{t}_{0.99}$ when

$$2.5 + 10\bar{t}_{0.99}^2/(AR_w \cos \Lambda_w) \simeq 100,$$

that is, when

$$\begin{aligned} \bar{t}_{0.99} &\simeq (10AR_w \cos \Lambda_w)^{1/2} \\ &= 8 \quad \text{when } AR_w = 7, \quad \Lambda_w = 25° \\ &= 5 \quad \text{when } AR_w = 3.7, \quad \Lambda_w = 45°. \end{aligned} \tag{III.3.44}$$

In real time, at low speeds, from eqns. (III.3.38) and (III.3.44), the lift on a wing of aspect ratio 7 reaches 99% of its final steady state value in less than 0.3 s; this time decreases with decrease in aspect ratio.

When a sudden change of angle of incidence occurs at higher subsonic speeds the wake forms in exactly the same way as that described above at low speeds. Communication in compressible flows is by the generation and propagation of sound waves. The unsteady wake generates a sequence of sound waves in the stationary atmosphere, so the faster the wing travels the longer it takes for sound waves from the wake to reach the neighbourhood of the wing, delaying the build-up of the circulation around the wing. Hence the non-dimensional time taken for the lift to reach its steady state value increases with increase in Mach number at subsonic speeds.

Fig. III.24(i) shows the lift response to a sudden change in angle of incidence on a wing of AR = 7, sweep angle 30°, at Mach numbers 0.4 and 0.8, estimated from linearized unsteady wing theory and presented in ref. III.18. The times to reach 99% of the final steady state value are approximately

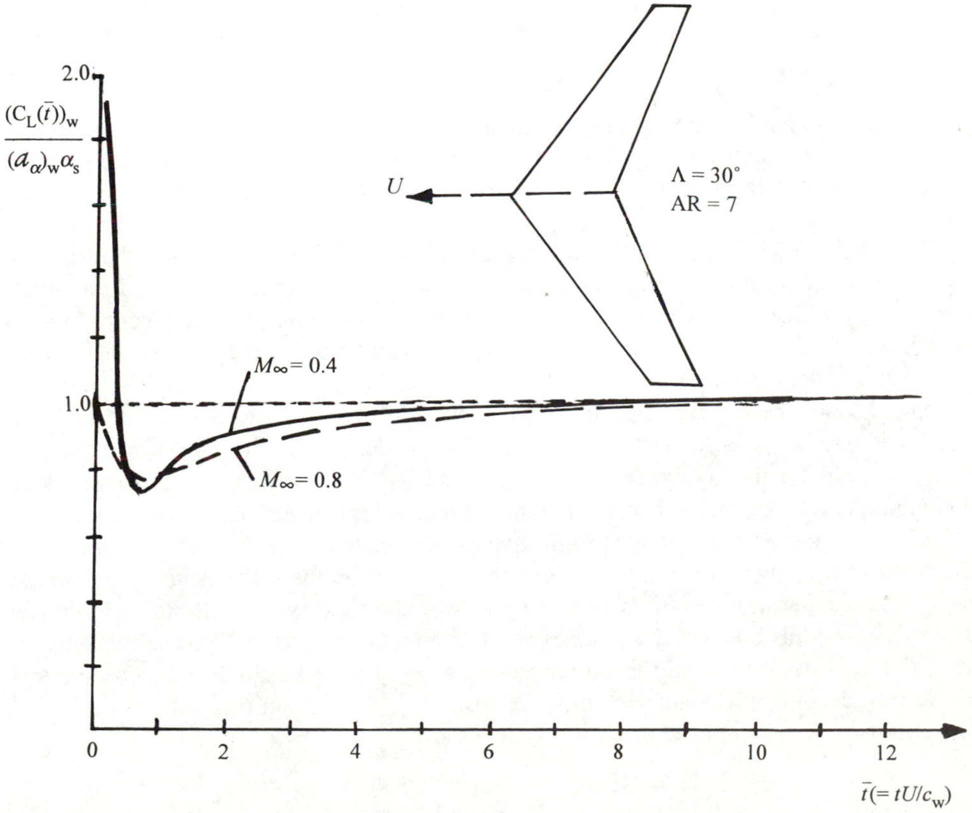

Fig. III.24(i). Lift response to step change in angle of incidence at subsonic speeds.

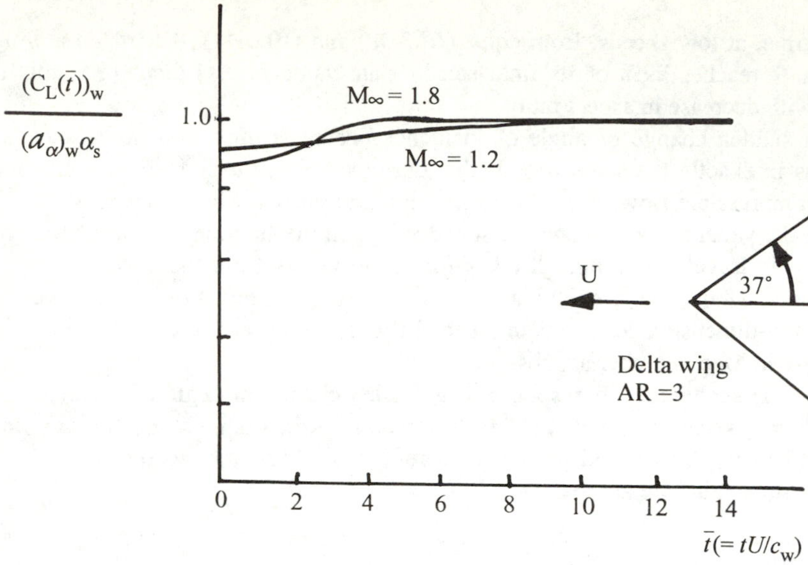

Fig. III.24(ii). Lift response to step change in angle of incidence at supersonic speeds.

$$M_\infty = 0.4, \quad \bar{t}_{0.99} \simeq 10; \qquad M_\infty = 0.8, \quad \bar{t}_{0.99} \simeq 20. \qquad \text{(III.3.45)}$$

Note that the corresponding non-dimensional build-up time from the approximate analysis at low Mach number given in eqn. (III.3.44) for the wing with $AR_w = 7$ and sweep angle 25° is close to the non-dimensional build-up time at $M_\infty = 0.4$ in eqn. (III.3.45).

Comparing Figs. III.23 and III.24(i), the initial pulse at $\bar{t} = 0$ at low speeds becomes 'spread out' as Mach number increases: at Mach 0.8 the initial pulse is hardly discernible. The reason is that those acoustic waves generated by the wing at time $\bar{t}$ equal to zero which move forward ahead of the wing remain more and more in the vicinity of the wing as Mach number increases.

At subsonic speeds, although the non-dimensional time $\bar{t}_{0.99}$ to reach a steady state increases with M_∞, the unit of aerodynamic time $\hat{t}$ decreases with M_∞, hence the real time to build up to the steady state, $t_{0.99}$ $(= \hat{t}\,\bar{t}_{0.99})$ is relatively insensitive to M_∞, remaining less than 0.3 s, a short time in the context of typical aeroplane manoeuvres.

When the wing travels at supersonic speeds what happens in the wake cannot affect flow conditions around the wing because sound waves from the wake cannot overtake the wing. There is, however, a finite time delay to form the shock wave patterns and to reach a steady state; this time delay decreases as Mach number increases. Typical build-ups of the lift forces at a supersonic speed for a delta wing of aspect ratio 3 with subsonic and supersonic leading edges are shown in Fig. III.24(ii), taken from refs. III.17 and III.18; the non-dimensional times to reach steady states are

$$M_\infty = 1.2, \quad \bar{t}_{0.99} \simeq 12; \qquad M_\infty = 1.8, \quad \bar{t}_{0.99} \simeq 4. \qquad \text{(III.3.46)}$$

From a knowledge of the lift step response to a sudden change in angle of incidence it is possible to estimate the lift response to the more realistic situation of an arbitrary time variation of the angle of incidence by the principle of convolution, which was introduced in Part II.

For a dynamic motion with a time varying angle of incidence defined by

$$\begin{aligned} U &= \text{constant}, \qquad \theta = 0, \qquad \alpha(\bar{t}) = 0 \qquad \bar{t} < 0 \\ & \qquad\qquad\qquad\qquad\quad \alpha(\bar{t}) = \alpha(\bar{t}), \qquad \bar{t} > 0 \end{aligned} \tag{III.3.47}$$

the corresponding time varying wing lift coefficient is denoted as $\left(C_L\left(\alpha(\bar{t}) \mid \bar{t}\right)\right)_W$; this notation indicates the wing lift coefficient response at time $\bar{t}$ due to an angle of incidence $\alpha(\bar{t})$.

When $\alpha(\bar{t})$ is a unit step change in angle of incidence, that is, when

$$\begin{aligned} \alpha(\bar{t}) = H(\bar{t}) &= 0, \quad \bar{t} < 0 \\ &= 1, \quad \bar{t} > 0 \end{aligned}$$

the wing lift coefficient response can be expressed in the form

$$\left(C_L\left(H(\bar{t}) \mid \bar{t}\right)\right)_W = (a_\alpha)_W f_H(\bar{t}) \tag{III.3.48}$$

where $(a_a)_W$ is the steady state lift curve slope and $f_H(\bar{t})$ is the step response function as shown in Figs. (III.23, III.24(i) and (ii)). At low speeds the delta function pulse at $= 0$ is included in the definition of $f_H(\bar{t})$.

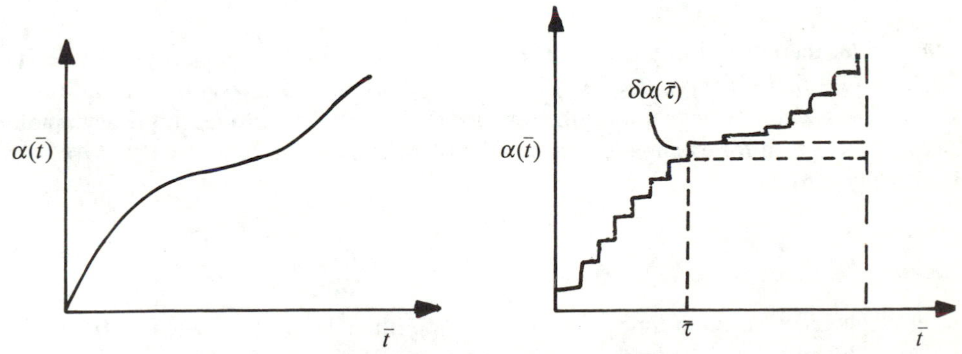

Fig. III.25. Principle of convolution.

A general time variation of the angle of incidence, for starting from zero incidence (i.e. for is shown in Fig. III.25(i). Then:

(i) suppose that the continuous $\alpha(\bar{t})$ is approximated by a sequence of small discrete steps, as shown in Fig. III.25(ii);

(ii) let the amplitude of the small step at time $\bar{\tau}$ be $\delta\alpha(\bar{\tau})$;

(iii) the lift coefficient at time $\bar{t}$ due to $\delta\alpha(\bar{\tau})$ at time $\bar{\tau}$, is given by eqn. (III.3.51), namely

$$\left(\delta C_L\left(\delta\alpha(\bar{\tau}) H(\bar{t} - \bar{\tau}) \mid \bar{t}\right)\right)_W = (a_\alpha)_W \delta\alpha(\bar{\tau}) \;\; f_H(\bar{t} - \bar{\tau}); \tag{III.3.49}$$

(iv) the total lift coefficient at time $\bar{t}$ is then the sum of all the incremental lift coefficients, each given by eqn. (III.3.49), due to all the steps $\delta\alpha(\tau)$ from $\bar{\tau}=0$, when the motion started, up to $\bar{\tau}=\bar{t}$. Hence

$$\begin{aligned}\left(C_L\left(\alpha(\bar{t})\mid\bar{t}\right)\right)_w &= \sum_{\bar{\tau}=0}^{\bar{\tau}=\bar{t}} (a_\alpha)_w \delta\alpha(\bar{\tau})\ f_H(\bar{t}-\bar{\tau}) \\ &= (a_\alpha)_w \int_0^{\bar{t}} f_H(\bar{t}-\bar{\tau}) \frac{d\alpha}{d\bar{\tau}}(\bar{\tau})\ d\bar{\tau}.\end{aligned} \tag{III.3.50}$$

Eqn. (III.3.50) can be rearranged as follows:

$$\begin{aligned}\left(C_L\left(\alpha(\bar{t})\mid\bar{t}\right)\right)_w &= (a_\alpha)_w\left[\int_0^{\bar{t}} \frac{d\alpha}{d\bar{\tau}}(\bar{\tau})\ d\bar{\tau} - \int_0^{\bar{t}} \left(1-f_H(\bar{t}-\bar{\tau})\right)\frac{d\alpha}{d\bar{\tau}}(\bar{\tau})\ d\bar{\tau}\right] \\ &= (a_\alpha)_w\left[\alpha(\bar{t}) - \int_0^{\bar{t}}\left(1-f_H(\bar{t}-\bar{\tau})\right)\left(\frac{d\alpha}{d\bar{t}}(\bar{t}) - \frac{d\alpha}{d\bar{t}}(\bar{t}) + \frac{d\alpha}{d\bar{\tau}}(\bar{\tau})\right) d\bar{\tau}\right] \\ &= (a_\alpha)_w\left[\alpha(\bar{t}) - \frac{d\alpha}{d\bar{t}}(\bar{t})\int_0^{\bar{t}}\left(1-f_H(\bar{t}-\bar{\tau})\right) d\bar{\tau}\right. \\ &\qquad \left. + \frac{d\alpha}{d\bar{t}}(\bar{t})\int_0^{\bar{t}}\left(1-f_H(\bar{t}-\bar{\tau})\right)\left\{1-\left(\frac{d\alpha}{d\bar{\tau}}(\bar{\tau})\Big/\frac{d\alpha}{d\bar{t}}(\bar{t})\right)\right\} d\bar{\tau}\right].\end{aligned} \tag{III.3.51}$$

Consider the integral in the second term in the square bracket in eqn. (III.3.51). The function $\left(1-f_H(\bar{t}-\bar{\tau})\right)$ for $0<\bar{\tau}<\bar{t}$, by reference to Fig. III.24, is shown in Fig. III.26. When $\bar{\tau}<\bar{t}-\bar{t}_{0.99}$, where $\bar{t}_{0.99}$ is the time for the step response to reach the asymptotic steady state, given for example by eqns. (III.3.44)–(III.3.46) the function $\left(1-f_H(\bar{t}-\bar{\tau})\right)$ is virtually zero, so

$$\int_0^{\bar{t}}\left(1-f_H(\bar{t}-\bar{\tau})\right) d\bar{\tau} \simeq \int_{\bar{t}-\bar{t}_{0.99}}^{\bar{t}}\left(1-f_H(\bar{t}-\bar{\tau})\right) d\bar{\tau} = k_H \tag{III.3.52}$$

where k_H is independent of time, as long as $\bar{t}>\bar{t}_{0.99}$ (in real time $\bar{t}>\bar{t}_{0.99}$, $\bar{t}\simeq 0.3$ s).

The value of k_H is given by the area under the curve in Fig. III.26. By inspection of the step responses shown in Figs. III.24 for those wings

$$\begin{aligned} &\text{when } M_\infty = 0.4, && k_H \simeq 0.5 \\ &\qquad\ \ M_\infty = 0.8, && k_H \simeq 1.0 \\ &\qquad\ \ M_\infty = 1.2, && k_H \simeq 0.35 \\ &\qquad\ \ M_\infty = 1.8, && k_H \simeq 0.3. \end{aligned} \tag{III.3.53}$$

The value of k_H is not estimated from Fig. III.23 at low speeds, as $M_\infty \to 0$, because the area under the impulse at time $t=0$ is not obvious; the area under the impulse is related to the so-called 'apparent mass' force (see refs. III.19 and III.20), a phenomenon which only exists in incompressible fluid dynamics.

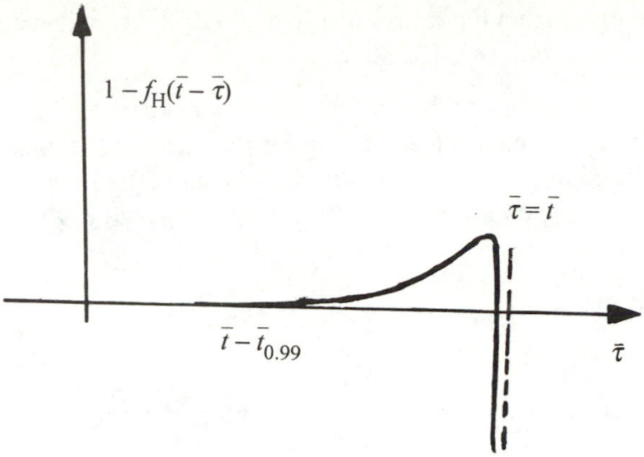

Fig. III.26. Form of integrating function.

According to eqn. (III.3.51), the wing lift coefficient response to a time varying angle of incidence $\alpha(t)$ can be expressed in the form

$$\left(C_L\left(\alpha(t)\,|t\right)\right)_w = (a_\alpha)_w \alpha(t) - \left[(a_\alpha)k_H + (\text{residual term }(t))\right]\left[\dot{\alpha}(t)c_w/U\right] \tag{III.3.54}$$

where $(a_\alpha)_w$ is the steady state lift curve slope, k_H is defined and quantified in eqns. (III.3.52), (III.3.53) and where the dot denotes differentiation with respect to time, so

$$\dot{\alpha}(t) = d\alpha(t)/dt = \left(U/c_w\right)\, d\alpha(\bar{t})/d\bar{t}. \tag{III.3.55}$$

The main point of interest in eqn. (III.3.54) is whether or not (residual term (t)) is small compared with $(a_\alpha)_w k_H$ in typical aeroplane motions. Unfortunately the answer is far from conclusive. For example, the ratio $\left[(\text{residual term }(t))/(a_\alpha)_w k_H\right]$ is

(i) zero when is constant, see eqn. (III.3.51);
(ii) of the order of 10% for low frequency undamped motions (frequency $\simeq$ 0.5 Hz), and for exponential divergent motions (time to double amplitude $\simeq$ 0.5 s);
(iii) small in the early stages of an exponential decaying motion (time to half amplitude $\simeq$ 0.5 s), but increases with time, becoming of the order of 1.0 by the time the motion has totally subsided.

EXAMPLES III.9

1. Prove statements (ii) and (iii) above. (Substitute the motion into eqn. (III.3.54) and integrate the third term; for (ii) take the range of integration $(\bar{t} - 10) < \bar{\tau} < \bar{t}$, while for (iii) take the range of integration $0 < \bar{\tau} < \bar{t}$, and understand why; assume the approximate form

$$f_H(\bar{t}) = (\text{impulse at } \bar{t} = 0) + \left[1 - 1/(3 + \bar{t}^2)\right]$$

and $k_H = 0.4$.)

2. Find the value of k_H from the expression in eqn. (III.3.43), when $AR_w = 7$, $\Lambda_w = 30°$; compare the answer with eqn. (III.3.53).

Ordinary differential equations with constant coefficients can be readily solved, as demonstrated in Part II. So a standard methodology is available if the equations of motion of an aeroplane can be represented by ordinary differential equations with constant coefficients. But such a representation requires that the time varying wing lift coefficient be expressed in the form

$$\left(C_L\left(\alpha(t)\,|\,t\right)\right)_w = (a_\alpha)_w\alpha(t) + (\alpha_{\dot{\alpha}})_w\left(\dot{\alpha}(t)c_w/U\right) \tag{III.3.56}$$

where $(\alpha_{\dot{\alpha}})_w$ is a constant independent of time.

Eqn. (III.3.56) can be obtained from eqn. (III.3.54) if (residual term (t)) can be neglected, and then

$$(a_{\dot{\alpha}})_w \simeq -(a_\alpha)_w k_H. \tag{III.3.57}$$

From the comments above, for damped motions typical of aeroplane motions, this assumption is reasonable at the beginning of the motion, becomes less valid as the motion continues, and breaks down by the time the motion has subsided by which time any error is inconsequential. In aeroplane dynamics at low angles of incidence $\dot{\alpha}(t)$ terms play a minor role so a ball-park estimate for $(a_{\dot{\alpha}})$ is usually adequate.

Eqns. (III.3.56) and (III.3.57) may be used but it should be remembered that the value of $(a_{\dot{\alpha}})_w$ denotes an order of magnitude, not an exact value. It is not possible to be more precise because a more accurate representation of $(a_{\dot{\alpha}})_w$ varies with time and is different for different types of motion; for this reason it is difficult to measure $(a_{\dot{\alpha}})_w$ experimentally.

In the literature $(a_\alpha)_w$ and $(a_{\dot{\alpha}})_w$ are referred to as 'quasi-steady aerodynamic derivatives'.

The phrase 'quasi-steady' is acceptable; it implies that $(a_\alpha)_w$ and $(a_{\dot{\alpha}})_w$ apply to slowly varying motions, which are typical of rigid aeroplane flight dynamics.

But the word 'derivative' is unfortunate, mainly for its connotation. The word 'derivative' implies that $(a_\alpha)_w$ is the derivative of $(C_L)_w$ with respect to α, which it is (in static conditions), and that $(a_{\dot{\alpha}})_w$ is the derivative of $(C_L)_w$ with respect to $\dot{\alpha}$, which it is not. Such 'derivatives' could only have any meaning if α and $\dot{\alpha}$ were independent variables, which they are not. Furthermore, the word 'derivatives' implies that the relationship

$$\left(C_L\left(\alpha(t)\,|\,t\right)\right)_w = (a_\alpha)_w\alpha(t) + (a_{\dot{\alpha}})_w\left(\dot{\alpha}(t)c_w/U\right)$$

is obtained from the first two terms of an infinite Taylor series expansion, a common misconception; no next term,

$$(a_{\ddot{\alpha}})_w\ddot{\alpha}(t)c_w^2/U^2,$$

or subsequent terms, exist. In fact it would be more apt to describe $(a_{\dot{\alpha}})_w$ as an 'integral' since its value depends on k_H, which is given by the integral of the step function response. Having made this protestation, since convention is now so firmly enshrined in the flight dynamics literature, the word 'derivative' is used throughout this book.

Another observation follows from the preceding paragraph. Some individuals who argue (erroneously) that the relationship

$$\left(C_L\left(\alpha(t)\,|t\right)\right)_W = (a_\alpha)_W\alpha(t) + (a_{\dot\alpha})_W\left(\dot\alpha(t)c_W/U\right) \qquad \text{(III.3.58)}$$

derives from a Taylor series expansion interpret the term $[(a_\alpha)_W\alpha(t)]$ as an 'instantaneous' lift and the term $(a_{\dot\alpha})_W\left(\dot\alpha(t)c_W/U\right)$ as the one which incorporates the history effects of unsteady aerodynamics. But the term $(a_\alpha)_W\alpha(t)$ is not an 'instantaneous' lift, it is a steady state lift after the transient has decayed, implying a past history. The rationale of eqn. (III.3.56) is that for slowly varying motions the wing lift effectively progresses through a sequence of steady states because the transient effects decay rapidly in comparison with the time scale of the slowly varying wing motions; roughly 90% of the unsteady history effects are incorporated in the steady state term $(a_\alpha)_W\alpha(t)$, the remaining 10% in the $(a_{\dot\alpha})_W\dot\alpha(t)c_W/U$ term.

The computationally minded reader might ask: 'Why approximate the exact unsteady lift relationship, eqn. (III.3.50), by eqn. (III.3.56) in order to force the equations of motion into the mould of ordinary differential equations when direct digital computation of the equations of motion, incorporating eqn. (III.3.50), is nowadays relatively trivial?' The answer is that the derivative formulation, which has been around for 90 years, is the bedrock of contemporary language and understanding of aeroplane flight dynamics and design applications. More exact computations at low angles of incidence could serve as validation exercises, aiming to explain any differences between flight tests and predictions based on the derivative formulation.

The effect of aspect ratio on $(a_{\dot\alpha})_W$ deserves comment. According to eqn. (III.3.44), following a step change in angle of incidence, the time delay to attain a steady state increases with aspect ratio as $AR_W^{1/2}$. Thus k_H, and hence $(a_{\dot\alpha})_W$, tend to infinity as aspect ratio tends to infinity, as a finite wing becomes a two dimensional aerofoil. This result is compatible with two dimensional unsteady aerofoil theory. It is therefore inadvisable to apply two dimensional aerofoil unsteady aerodynamics in a strip theory manner to calculate the unsteady aerodynamics of finite aspect ratio wings at the low frequencies of overall aeroplane motions.

Although the quasi-steady derivative $(a_{\dot\alpha})_W$, as defined by eqn. (III.3.57), has been expressed in the form of an integral of the step function response, quantitative values are not obtained in this manner. One technique is to calculate both $(a_\alpha)_W$ and $(a_{\dot\alpha})_W$ directly from linearized steady wing theory (see Garner & Milne, ref. III.21). Another technique is to obtain $(a_{\dot\alpha})_W$ as a limiting value of oscillatory derivatives, as explained below.

When $\alpha(t)$ is oscillatory with amplitude α_0 and frequency Ω (rad/s) then

$$\alpha(t) = \alpha_0\exp(\mathrm{i}\Omega t) = \alpha_0\exp(\mathrm{i}\Omega\hat t\,\bar t) = \alpha_0\exp(\mathrm{i}\nu\bar t) \qquad \text{(III.3.59)}$$

where the non-dimensional frequency parameter $= \nu = \Omega\hat t = \Omega c_W/U$ (or the non-dimensional reduced frequency parameter $= k = \nu/2$). The resulting oscillatory wing lift coefficient can be expressed in the form

$$\left(C_L\left(\alpha_0\exp(\mathrm{i}\Omega t)\,|t\right)\right)_W = \left[\left(\tilde a_\alpha(\nu, M_\infty)\right)_W + \mathrm{i}\nu\left(\tilde a_{\dot\alpha}(\nu, M_\infty)\right)_W\right]\alpha_0\exp(\mathrm{i}\Omega t) \qquad \text{(III.3.60)}$$

where $\left(\tilde{a}_{\alpha}(\nu, M_{\infty})\right)_{\mathrm{w}}$ and $\left(\tilde{a}_{\dot{\alpha}}(\nu, M_{\infty})\right)_{\mathrm{w}}$ are so-called oscillatory aerodynamic derivatives, denoting the in-phase and out-of-phase components of the wing oscillatory lift coefficient due to oscillatory angle of incidence. The variations of $(\tilde{a}_{\alpha})_{\mathrm{w}}$ and $(\tilde{a}_{\dot{\alpha}})_{\mathrm{w}}$ with ν over the range of ν typical of aeroplane motions for a 30° swept wing and aspect ratio 7 at M_{∞} equal to 0.4 (from ref. III.14) are shown in Fig. III.27. Note that $(\tilde{a}_{\alpha})_{\mathrm{w}}$ is constant while $(\tilde{a}_{\dot{\alpha}})_{\mathrm{w}}$ varies with ν over the range of frequencies typical of aeroplane motions.

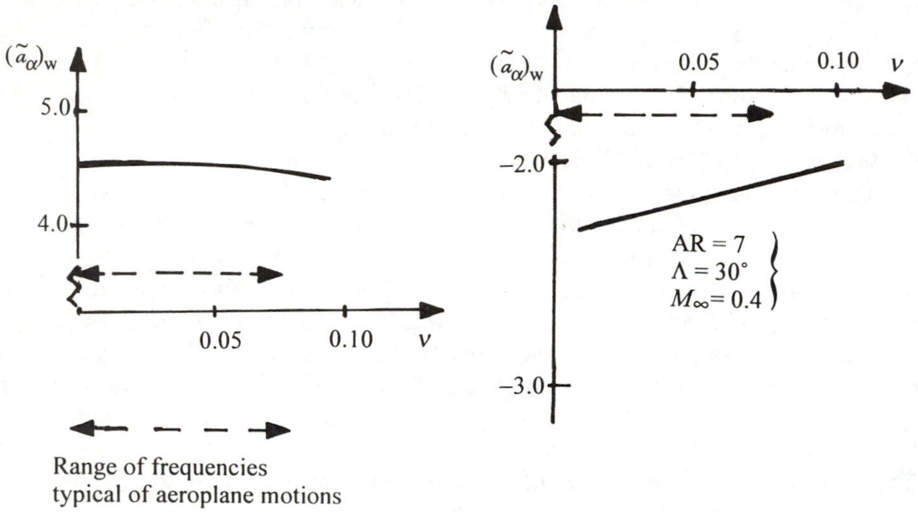

Fig. III.27. Oscillatory derivatives at low frequencies.

Quasi-steady derivatives and oscillatory derivatives are related, namely

$$\left(a_{\alpha}(M_{\infty})\right)_{\mathrm{w}} = \left(\tilde{a}_{\alpha}(0, M_{\infty})\right)_{\mathrm{w}}$$

and

$$\left(a_{\dot{\alpha}}(M_{\infty})\right)_{\mathrm{w}} = \left(\tilde{a}_{\dot{\alpha}}(0, M_{\infty})\right)_{\mathrm{w}}. \qquad \text{(III.3.61)}$$

The theoretical variation of $(a_{\dot{\alpha}})_{\mathrm{w}}$ with subsonic Mach number for the wings of the basic configurations are given in Fig. III.28(i); these graphs have been obtained by Vepa (ref. III.15).

Oscillatory derivatives have been extensively investigated and tabulated for applications to structural vibrations in flight and their stability (e.g. flutter). Unfortunately these oscillatory derivatives are presented in terms of standard aeroelasticity notation which differs from the notation of aeroplane flight dynamics. It is therefore necessary to convert from one notation to the other; this conversion is given in Appendix 2.

For the pitching moment derivatives, at low speeds the lift due to $\dot{\alpha}(t)$ (> 0) has, by reference to Fig. III.23, two contributions: an upward lift associated with the initial pulse which acts close to the centre of (plan form) area, and a downward lift, relative to the

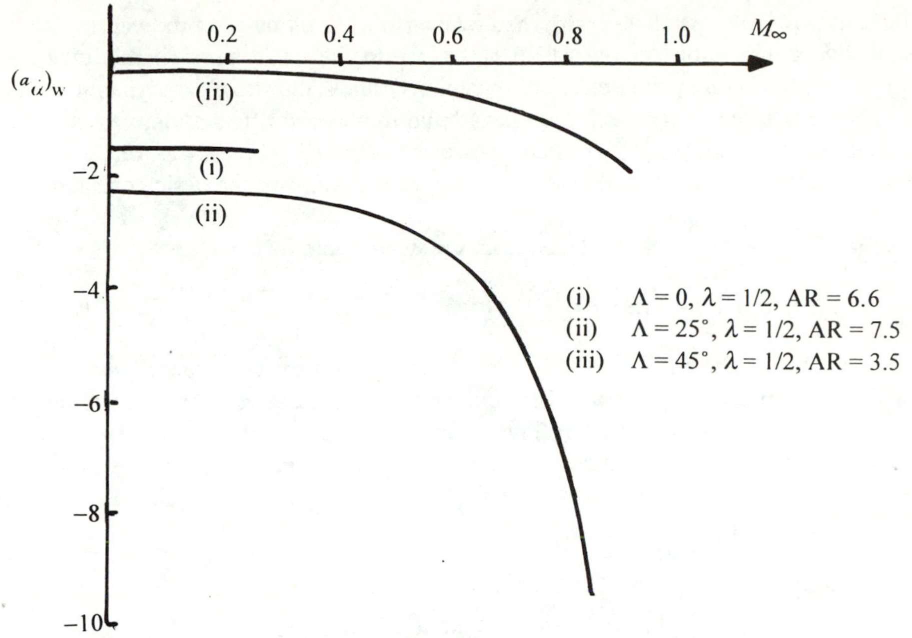

Fig. III.28(i). Coefficient for wings of basic configurations.

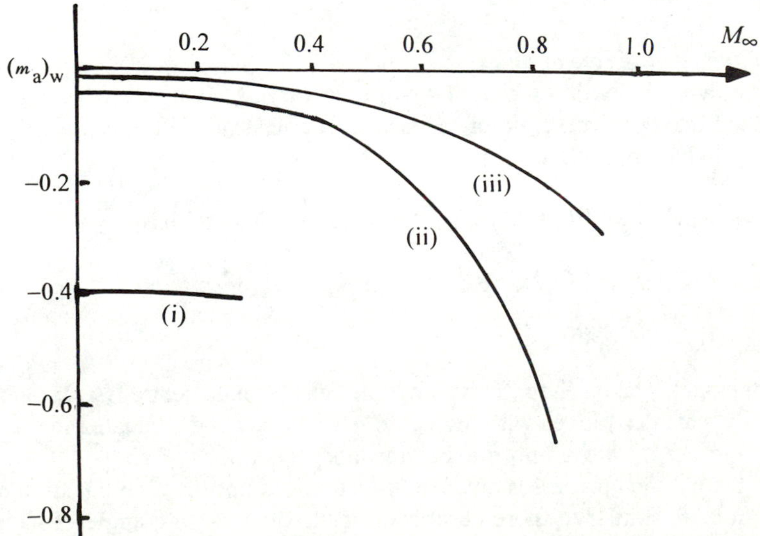

Fig. III.28(ii). Coefficient for wings of basic configurations.

final steady state lift, associated with the downwash induced by the time varying wake. For non-swept wings the downward lift acts close to the static aerodynamic centre so $(m_{\dot{\alpha}})_{\mathrm{w}}$, the pitching moment derivative due to $\dot{\alpha}(t)$ about the static aerodynamic centre, is negative. For swept wings both the upward and downward lifts act close to the static aerodynamic centre so $(m_{\dot{\alpha}})_{\mathrm{w}}$ is small; however $(-m_{\dot{\alpha}})_{\mathrm{w}}$ increases as Mach number increases at subsonic speeds. Values for $(m_{\dot{\alpha}})_{\mathrm{w}}$ for the wings of the basic configurations are shown in Fig. III.28(ii).

The lift-dependent drag can be taken from the steady state formula,

$$\left(C_{\mathrm{D}}\left(\alpha(t)\,|\,t\right)\right)_{\mathrm{w}} \simeq \left(C_{\mathrm{L}}\left(\alpha(t)\,|\,t\right)\right)_{\mathrm{w}}^{2} \Big/ (\pi \mathrm{AR}_{\mathrm{w}}). \qquad \text{(III.3.62)}$$

It should be emphasized that the above discussion on unsteady aerodynamics, the physical explanations and the order of magnitude of the parameters apply only to motions at low angles of incidence where the flow around the wing remains attached at all times. When flow separation and breakdown occurs in unsteady conditions the physical processes, the time delays, and the values of the parameters are dramatically different, as described later in Part V.

EXAMPLES III.10

1. Check the value of k_{H} in eqn. (III.3.53) with the value of k_{H} from eqns. (III.3.61) and Fig. III.27.
2. Does Fig. III.27 confirm statement (ii) prior to Examples III.9?
3. Why in Fig. III.28(i) is the value of $(a_{\dot{\alpha}})_{\mathrm{w}}$ at low Mach numbers less for the combat wing than for the transport wing?
4. Extend the variation of $(a_{\dot{\alpha}})_{\mathrm{w}}$ for the combat configuration in Fig. III.28 to supersonic speeds; use eqn. (III.3.53).

III.3.3.2 Time varying rate of pitch

Consider the dynamic motion which involves time varying pitch rate, $q(t)$, with constant forward speed and constant angle of incidence. The unsteady lift and pitching moment coefficients can be expressed as

$$\begin{aligned}
\left(C_{\mathrm{L}}\left(\theta(t)\,|\,t\right)\right)_{\mathrm{w}} &= (a_q)_{\mathrm{w}}\left(q(t)c_{\mathrm{w}}/U\right) + (a_{\dot{q}})_{\mathrm{w}}\left(\dot{q}(t)c_{\mathrm{w}}^{2}/U^{2}\right),\\
\left(C_{m}\left(\theta(t)\,|\,t\right)\right)_{\mathrm{w}} &= (m_q)_{\mathrm{w}}\left(q(t)c_{\mathrm{w}}/U\right) + (m_{\dot{q}})_{\mathrm{w}}\left(\dot{q}(t)c_{\mathrm{w}}^{2}/U^{2}\right),\\
q(t) &= \dot{\theta}(t)
\end{aligned} \qquad \text{(III.3.63)}$$

where the moment is taken about the steady state aerodynamic centre, $(a_q)_{\mathrm{w}}$ and $(m_q)_{\mathrm{w}}$ are the steady state derivatives with respect to q, described and evaluated in sect. III.3.2, and $(a_{\dot{q}})_{\mathrm{w}}$ and $(m_{\dot{q}})_{\mathrm{w}}$ are assumed to be time independent.

Because the physical processes of wake formation and upstream propagation of acoustic information are similar to those described for the time varying angle of incidence, it would be expected that

$$(a_{\dot{q}})_{\mathrm{w}}/(a_q)_{\mathrm{w}} \simeq (a_{\dot{\alpha}})_{\mathrm{w}}/(a_{\alpha})_{\mathrm{w}}\,. \qquad \text{(III.3.64)}$$

Furthermore, the loading distribution due to $\dot{q}(t)$ should be similar to the loading distribution due to $\dot{\alpha}(t)$, and then it would be expected

$$(m_{\dot{q}})_w/(a_q)_w \simeq (m_{\dot{\alpha}})_w/(a_\alpha)_w\,. \qquad \text{(III.3.65)}$$

These orders of magnitude relationships for $(a_{\dot{q}})_w$ and $(m_{\dot{q}})_w$ are of sufficient accuracy for aeroplane flight dynamics.

III.3.3.3 Time varying forward speed

In the presentation so far the dynamic motions have involved a wing moving in a stationary atmosphere, rather than a wing in an oncoming stream, which is the more usual textbook situation. One reason is that the motion of a wing into still air is literally what happens, and so has physical realism. A second reason is that the concept of relative air motion needs care in application.

Consider two cases with the same relative air motion, as shown in Fig. III.29:

(i) a wing, with constant angles of incidence and pitch, moving forward with a horizontal velocity $U(t)$ into a still atmosphere;
(ii) a wing, with the same constant angles of incidence and pitch, held stationary in an air stream which is moving with a horizontal velocity $U(t)$.

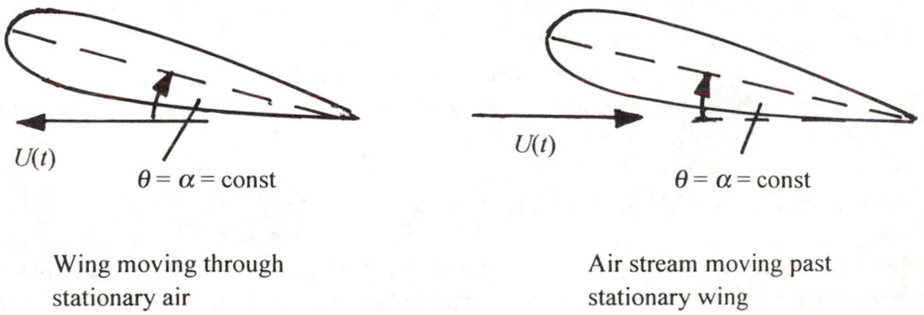

Fig. III.29. Relative motion.

All aerodynamic loads on the wings in these two cases are equal when $U(t)$ is constant, independent of time, but the aerodynamic loads on the wings in these two cases are not equal when $U(t)$ varies with time.

In case (ii), when $U(t)$ increases with time, there is an atmospheric pressure gradient from upstream of the wing to downstream of the wing to accelerate the air stream velocity $U(t)$. This pressure gradient in the air stream direction acts on the wing surface and generates an additional normal pressure drag force compared with the drag force acting on the wing in case (i) (see ref. III.20). So the drag forces are different in the two cases.

However, at low speeds the unsteady lift force and pitching moment are throught to be the same in the two cases (on physical grounds this statement appears plausible but, as far as the author is aware, this statement has not been proved). But at higher subsonic speeds even the unsteady lift force and pitching moment are different in the two cases because the speed of sound in the still atmosphere, in case (i), remains constant, whereas the speed of sound in the moving stream, in case (ii), varies in space and time because the 'atmospheric' pressure, density and temperature associated with the moving stream vary in space and time; the time of propagation of disturbances from the wake to the wing will be different in the two cases.

When forward speed varies with time the concept that aerodynamic loads depend on the relative motion between the air and the wing is not strictly valid.

To understand the effect of a time varying forward speed, suppose that a wing suddenly moves forward from zero velocity to velocity U at a datum time $t = 0$, keeping the angles of incidence, α, and pitch, θ, constant. The physical development of the unsteady wake, the effect of that wake on the flow around the wing and the build-up of circulation around the wing are exactly the same as those for the step change in incidence. The time lag to reach the new steady state associated with a step change in forward speed is the same as the time lag to reach the new steady state following a step change in incidence. Hence the time varying wing lift for $t > 0$ can be written in the form

$$\text{wing lift} = \tfrac{1}{2}\rho_{\text{at}}U^2 S_{\text{w}} f_{\text{H}}(t)(a_\alpha)_{\text{w}}\alpha \tag{III.3.66}$$

where $f_{\text{H}}(t)$ is a lift coefficient response function due to step change in angle of incidence (shown, for example, in Fig. III.24), with the unit of aerodynamic time equal to c_{w}/U.

For a general time varying forward speed $U(t)$ the principle of convolution cannot be applied using eqn. (III.3.66), firstly because the U^2 term makes the problem non-linear, and secondly because the unit of aerodynamic time changes with $U(t)$.

By analogy with the lift response to a time varying angle of incidence, the lift response to a time varying forward speed $U(t)$ might be written in the form

$$\text{wing lift} = \tfrac{1}{2}\rho_{\text{at}}U^2(t)S_{\text{w}}(a_\alpha)_{\text{w}}\alpha\left[1+(a_{\dot{U}})_{\text{w}}\left(\dot{U}(t)c_{\text{w}}/U^2(t)\right)\right] \tag{III.3.67}$$

where $\dot{U}(t)c_{\text{w}}/U^2(t)$ is the non-dimensional longitudinal acceleration. But this non-dimensional longitudinal acceleration is extremely small even for a combat aeroplane with a $1g$ longitudinal acceleration, and so the effect of longitudinal acceleration is usually ignored.

III.3.3.4 General dynamic motion

All of the above unsteady aspects can be brought together to give the aerodynamic loads on a wing moving in a general time varying manner, defined by

$$U(t)\ \left(=\left(M_\infty(t)a_{\text{at}}\right), q(t), \alpha(t)\right),$$

typical of aeroplane longitudinal motions.

At low angles of incidence the lift and moment responses due to $q(t)$ and $\alpha(t)$ can be regarded as independent (i.e. there are no non-linear aerodynamic interference effects in combined motions), with the effect of $U(t)$ confined to the dynamic pressure, apart from defining the time varying Mach number $M_\infty(t)$.

The lift and drag forces, and the pitching moment about the steady state wing aerodynamic centre, acting on a wing in a general time varying motion can be expressed in the form

$$\begin{aligned}\text{wing lift} &= \tfrac{1}{2}\rho_{\text{at}}U^2(t)S_{\text{w}}\left[C_{\text{L}}\left(M_\infty(t),\ \alpha(t),\ q(t)\,|\,t\right)\right]_{\text{w}}\\ &= \tfrac{1}{2}\rho_{\text{at}}U^2(t)S_{\text{w}}\Big[(a_\alpha)_{\text{w}}\left(\alpha(t)-\alpha_{0\text{w}}\right)+(a_{\dot\alpha})_{\text{w}}\left(\dot\alpha(t)c_{\text{w}}/U(t)\right)\\ &\quad + (a_q)_{\text{w}}\left(q(t)c_{\text{w}}/U(t)\right)+(a_{\dot q})_{\text{w}}\left(\dot q(t)c_{\text{w}}^2/U^2(t)\right)\Big],\end{aligned} \tag{III.3.68}$$

$$\text{wing drag} = \tfrac{1}{2}\rho_{\text{at}}U^2(t)S_{\text{w}}\left[C_{\text{D0}}+\left(C_{\text{L}}\left(M_\infty(t),\ \alpha(t),\ q(t)\,|\,t\right)\right)^2\Big/\pi\text{AR}_{\text{w}}\right], \tag{III.3.69}$$

wing pitching moment about the wing steady state aerodynamic centre

$$\begin{aligned}&= \tfrac{1}{2}\rho_{\text{at}}U^2(t)S_{\text{w}}c_{\text{w}}\left[C_{\text{m}}\left(M_\infty(t),\ \alpha(t),\ q(t)\,|\,t\right)\right]_{\text{w}}\\ &= \tfrac{1}{2}\rho_{\text{at}}U^2(t)S_{\text{w}}\Big[(m_0)_{\text{w}}+(m_{\dot\alpha})_{\text{w}}\left(\dot\alpha(t)c_{\text{w}}/U(t)\right)\\ &\quad + (m_q)_{\text{w}}\left(q(t)c_{\text{w}}/U(t)\right)+(m_{\dot q})_{\text{w}}\left(\dot q(t)c_{\text{w}}^2/U^2(t)\right)\Big]\end{aligned} \tag{III.3.70}$$

where all derivatives depend on $M_\infty(t)$.

III.3.4 Aerodynamics of wing–fuselage combination

In this section an outline is given of the aerodynamic loads on a configuration comprising a wing on a fuselage, but with no tailplane, in symmetric flight at low angles of incidence. This section applies to all aeroplanes except light aeroplanes with a propeller in front of the fuselage.

First consider a symmetric fuselage, rounded at the front and pointed at the rear, moving forward with constant velocity U, at a small constant angle of incidence, α, as shown in Fig. III.30. The flow fields relative to the fuselage at subsonic speeds are shown in Fig. III.31; the flow field in the plane of symmetry resembles that past an aerofoil, leading to high suction pressures around the upper surface of the nose; the flow field out of the plane of symmetry curves up and around the sides of the fuselage, forming thick boundary layers over the upper surface of the aft fuselage in which the viscous flows are complex and highly three dimensional.

These flow field effects lead to a lengthwise lift distribution along the fuselage, as shown in Fig. III.32. Effectively the lift is concentrated in the nose region. On the aft fuselage the lift is usually small.

On the basis of slender body theory (see ref. III.8):

$$\text{fuselage nose lift} = \tfrac{1}{2}\rho_{\text{at}}U^2 r_{\text{max}}^2\, 2\pi\alpha \tag{III.3.71}$$

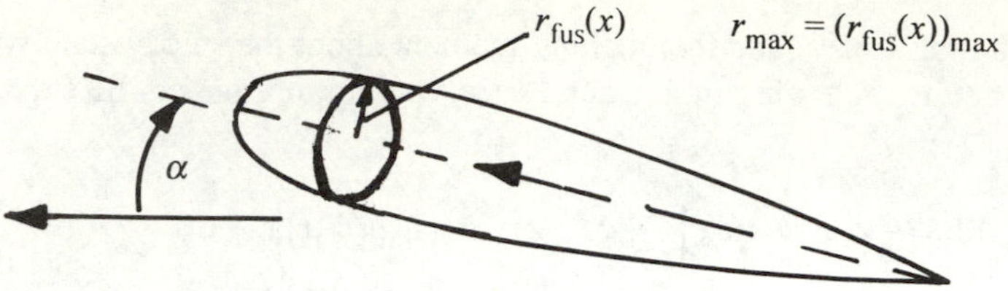

Symmetric fuselage

Fig. III.30. Notation for fuselage.

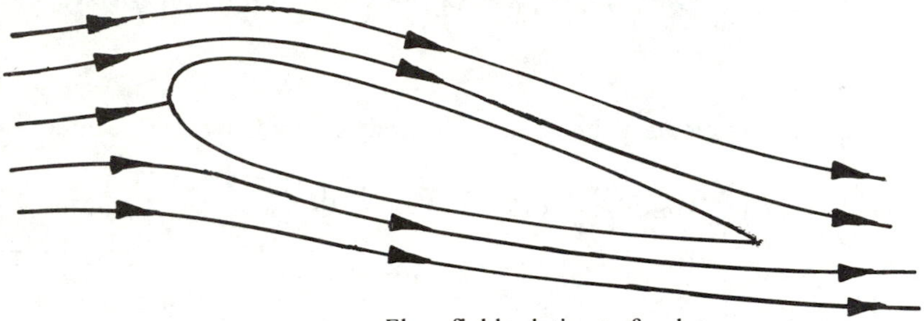

Flow field relative to fuselage in plane of symmetry

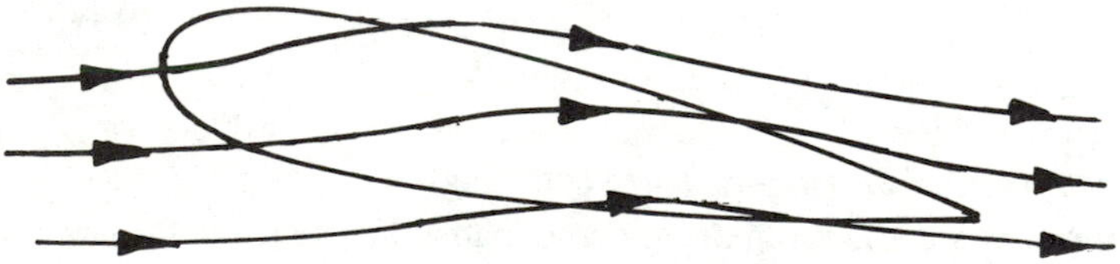

Flow field relative to fuselage out of plane of symmetry

Fig. III.31. Flow field about fuselage.

where r_{max} is the maximum radius of the fuselage (see Fig. III.30). According to slender body theory this fuselage nose lift is independent of Mach number.

By reference to eqns. (III.3.13) and (III.3.71), with typical values for a transport aeroplane $\left(r_{max}/s_w = 1/7,\ AR_w = 7,\ \Lambda_w = 30°\right)$

$$\frac{\text{fuselage nose lift}}{\text{wing lift due to incidence}} \simeq 0.05. \tag{III.3.72}$$

The centre of pressure of the fuselage nose lift depends on the shape of the fuselage nose; for a rounded nose this centre of pressure lies on the fuselage axis about [1/3

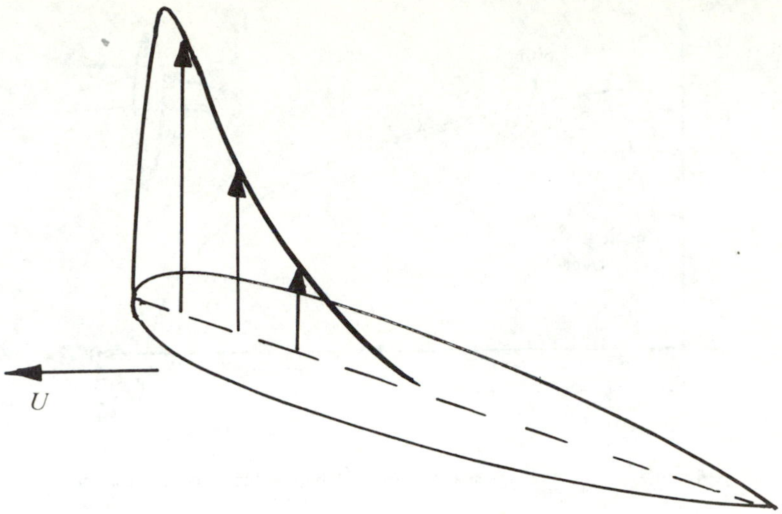

Fig. III.32. Lift distribution along fuselage.

(distance from the nose to the position of r_{max})] aft of the nose; for a pointed nose this factor would be closer to 2/3.

Next consider a symmetric fuselage with a symmetric planar wing attached at the mid-fuselage position, with zero setting angle, as shown in Fig. III.33. At a low angle of incidence, at subsonic Mach numbers, there are two primary flow interference effects on the wing lift, as shown in Fig. III.34:

(i) the up-wash in the neighbourhood of the sides of the fuselage, shown in Fig. III.31, increases slightly the distribution of local angle of incidence along the wing span in the region of the wing–fuselage junction, increasing the wing lift in these regions;
(ii) compared to the wing alone there is a loss of lift across the fuselage; this loss of lift is approximately 8% of the total lift on the wing alone.

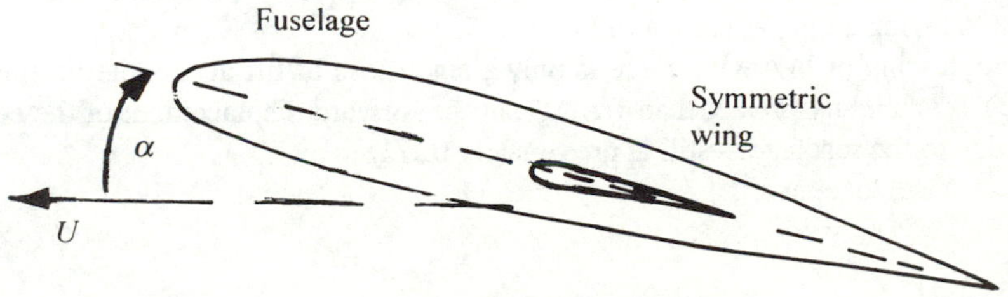

Fig. III.33. Wing–fuselage combination.

The 8% loss of wing lift across the fuselage is offset by the small increase in lift on the inboard part of the wing plus the 5% lift on the fuselage nose (eqn. (III.3.72)). It is

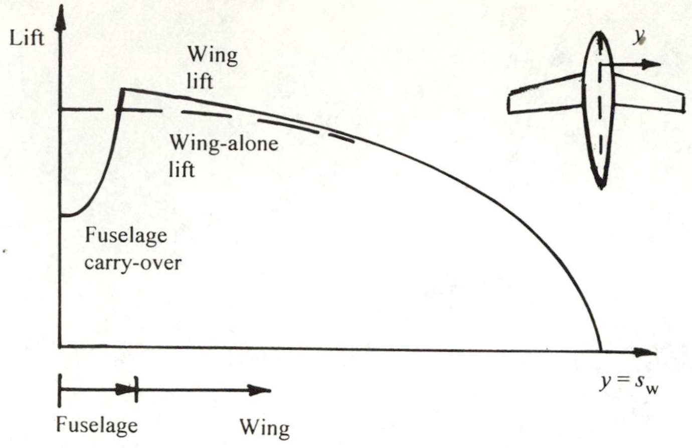

Fig. III.34. Wing–fuselage spanwise lift distribution due to incidence alone.

therefore a reasonable approximation to take the lift on the mid-wing–fuselage combination equal to the lift on the wing alone throughout the Mach number range. Hence

$$(a_\alpha)_{\mathrm{wf}} \simeq (a_\alpha)_{\mathrm{w}} \tag{III.3.73}$$

where the suffix 'wf' denotes wing–fuselage combination, without tailplane, and suffix 'w' denotes wing alone.

For a swept wing the location of the centre of pressure of the total lift on the above wing–fuselage combination (Fig. III.33) depends on two opposing trends:

1. Because of the loss in wing lift across the fuselage, the centre of pressure of the lift on the wing and its carry-over lift on the fuselage will lie slightly aft of the centre of pressure of the lift on the wing alone.
2. The lift on the fuselage nose will move the centre of pressure of the lift on the wing–fuselage combination forward relative to the centre of pressure of the lift on the wing alone.

The combined effect of 1 and 2 is that the centre of pressure of the lift on a swept mid-wing–fuselage combination lies approximately $0.1c_{\mathrm{w}}$ ahead of the centre of pressure of the lift on the wing alone, as shown in Fig. III.35.

For a high wing or low wing there is only a small loss of lift across the fuselage, and then $(a_\alpha)_{\mathrm{wf}}$ is slightly greater than $(a_\alpha)_{\mathrm{w}}$ but the forward displacement of the centre of pressure due to the fuselage is still approximately $0.1c_{\mathrm{w}}$.

EXAMPLES III.11

1. Check the statement concerning the relative positions of the centres of pressure of the lifts on the swept mid-wing–fuselage combination and the swept wing alone.
2. Repeat 1 for a non-swept wing–fuselage combination.
3. What might eqn. (III.3.72) become for a combat aeroplane?

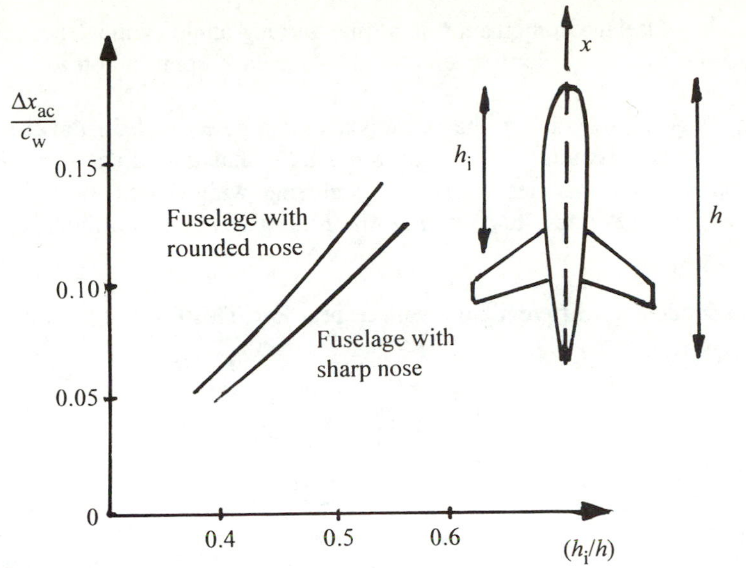

Fig. III.35. Forward displacement of wing–fuselage aerodynamic centre relative to wing-alone aerodynamic centre.

4. Explain the reason for the difference in the two curves shown in Fig. III.35; is the quantitative difference what you might expect?

The discussion so far is concerned with the lift, and its centre of pressure, on a symmetric mid-wing–fuselage combination due to angle of incidence. This centre of pressure is therefore the aerodynamic centre of a more general mid-wing–fuselage combination.

If the loss of lift due to wing setting angle, wing camber and wash-out across the fuselage is neglected, then

$$(m_0)_{wf} \simeq (m_0)_w - 0.1(a_\alpha)_w(i_w - \alpha_{0w}) \qquad \text{(III.3.74)}$$

where $(m_0)_w$ is the moment coefficient of the wing alone about the aerodynamic centre of the wing alone, and $(m_0)_{wf}$ is the moment coefficient of the wing–fuselage combination about the aerodynamic centre of the wing–fuselage combination.

For a wing–fuselage combination in a rate of pitch, q (= $d\theta/dt$), because of the effective camber of the fuselage, the lift on the fuselage nose due to q is small and can be neglected. Fuselage interference effects on the q derivatives can also be neglected as a first approximation. Hence,

$$(a_q)_{wf} \simeq (a_q)_w, \quad (m_q)_{wf} \simeq (m_q)_w - 0.1(a_q)_w \qquad \text{(III.3.75)}$$

where $(m_q)_{wf}$ is the moment coefficient due to q on the wing–fuselage combination about the wing–fuselage aerodynamic centre and $(m_q)_w$ is the moment coefficient due to q on the wing alone about the wing alone aerodynamic centre.

For a wing–fuselage combination in a time varying angle of incidence an acceptable approximation for the $\dot{\alpha}$ derivative is to add a fuselage contribution to the wing alone value.

The fuselage contribution to the $\dot{\alpha}$ derivative can be estimated from cross flow considerations. It is a standard result (see ref. III.20) that the 'drag' force F on a two dimensional circular cylinder of radius r_c, moving with velocity $w(t)$ in an inviscid incompressible fluid of density ρ (see Fig. III.36), is given by the formula

$$F = \rho\pi r_c^2 \dot{w}(t) \qquad \text{(III.3.76)}$$

where the dot denotes differentiation with respect to t. This force is known as the apparent mass.

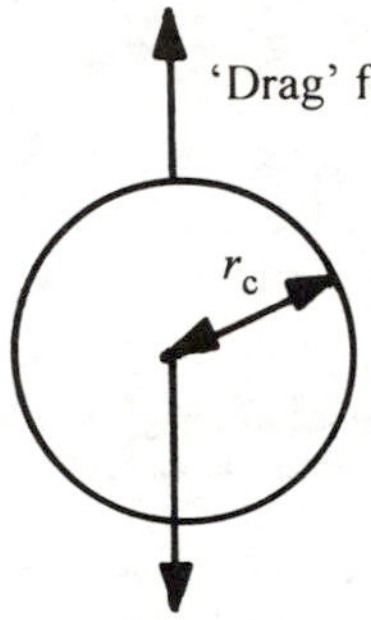

Fig. III.36. Inviscid drag force on circular cylinder.

Thus, at low Mach numbers, the lift on a fuselage arising from the transverse velocity $w(t)\ (= U\alpha(t))$ is approximately

$$\text{fuselage lift} = \pi\rho_{at}\left(U\dot{\alpha}(t)\right)\int_{\text{fuselage nose}}^{\text{fuselage tail}} r_{fus}^2(x)\,dx \qquad \text{(III.3.77)}$$

where $r_{fus}(x)$ is the variation of the fuselage radius along the fuselage length, see Fig. III.30. Hence the fuselage lift rate derivative due to $\dot{\alpha}(t)c_w/U$ is given by

$$\begin{aligned}(a_{\dot{\alpha}})_{fus} &= \text{fuselage lift}\Big/\left\{\left(\tfrac{1}{2}\rho_{at}U^2S_w\right)\left(\dot{\alpha}(t)c_w/U\right)\right\} \\ &\simeq 5/AR_w\end{aligned} \qquad \text{(III.3.78)}$$

taking typical values (mean $r_{fus}(x)/c_w \simeq \frac{1}{3}$, fuselage length $\simeq 8c_w$). This fuselage lift due to $\dot{\alpha}(t)c_w/U$ can be assumed to act at the centre of area of the fuselage plan form.

According to slender body theory the loads on a fuselage can be assumed to be independent of Mach number, hence as a first approximation eqn. (III.3.78) can be applied throughout the Mach number range.

For the wing–fuselage combination,

$$(a_{\dot{\alpha}})_{wf} \simeq (a_{\dot{\alpha}})_w + (a_{\dot{\alpha}})_{fus}. \qquad \text{(III.3.79)}$$

Now $(a_{\dot{\alpha}})_w$ is of the order of –2.5 and $(a_{\dot{\alpha}})_{fus}$ is approximately equal to $5/AR_w$ so the contribution of the fuselage to $(a_{\dot{\alpha}})_{wf}$ can be significant, especially for configurations with low aspect ratio wings.

Also, for the wing–fuselage combination

$$(m_{\dot{\alpha}})_{wf} \simeq (m_{\dot{\alpha}})_w - 0.1(a_{\dot{\alpha}})_w + (5/AR)l_{fus} \qquad \text{(III.3.80)}$$

where $(m_{\dot{\alpha}})_{wf}$ is the moment coefficient of the wing–fuselage combination due to $\dot{\alpha}(t)$ about the wing–fuselage aerodynamic centre; $(m_{\dot{\alpha}})_w$ is the moment coefficient of the wing alone due to $\dot{\alpha}(t)$ about the wing alone aerodynamic centre; and $l_{fus}c_w$ is the distance of centre of the area of fuselage plan form ahead of the aerodynamic centre of the wing–fuselage combination.

Although l_{fus} is usually small, of the order of 0.2, the fuselage contribution to $(m_{\dot{\alpha}})_{wf}$ can be comparable to the wing contribution.

There is a fuselage contribution to the $\dot{q}$ derivatives. Following the arguments in eqns. (III.3.76)–(III.3.78), taking $w(t)$ equal to $(-x\dot{q}(t))$, where x is measured forward from the pitch axis, then approximately,

$$(a_{\dot{q}})_{fus} \simeq 0, \qquad (m_{\dot{q}})_{fus} = O[-30/AR_w] \qquad \text{(III.3.81)}$$

assuming that the pitch axis and aerodynamic centres are all in the vicinity of the mid-fuselage. Hence

$$(a_{\dot{q}})_{wf} \simeq (a_{\dot{q}})_w, \qquad (m_{\dot{q}})_{wf} \simeq (m_{\dot{q}})_w + (m_{\dot{q}})_{fus}. \qquad \text{(III.3.82)}$$

EXAMPLES III.12

1. How do $(a_{\dot{\alpha}})_{wf}$ and $(m_{\dot{\alpha}})_{wf}$ vary with Mach number?
2. Estimate typical values of $(m_0)_{wf}$ and $(m_0)_w$.
3. Estimate typical values of $(m_q)_{wf}$ and $(m_q)_w$.
4. Check eqns. (III.3.81).

Wing–fuselage interference plays a crucial role in the drag rise Mach number and the subsequent increase in wave drag at higher Mach numbers. The drag rise Mach number is now much more dependent on the formation of shock waves about the fuselage, rather than about the wing. As shown in Fig. III.37, the strength of these fuselage shock waves, which form in the region of the wing–fuselage junction, can be reduced by appropriate shaping of the fuselage by expanding the flow where the compressive shock waves appear and so reducing their intensity.

In all of the above discussion an idealized fuselage shape has been assumed, namely a body of revolution. In practice the fuselage shape is not a body of revolution; for transport aeroplanes the difference is small but for combat aeroplanes the fuselage shape can be significantly different from a body of revolution. As a first approximation the above orders of magnitude are applicable. Extraneous shapings such as the canopy of the cockpit can induce local suction pressures, leading to a small local lift force.

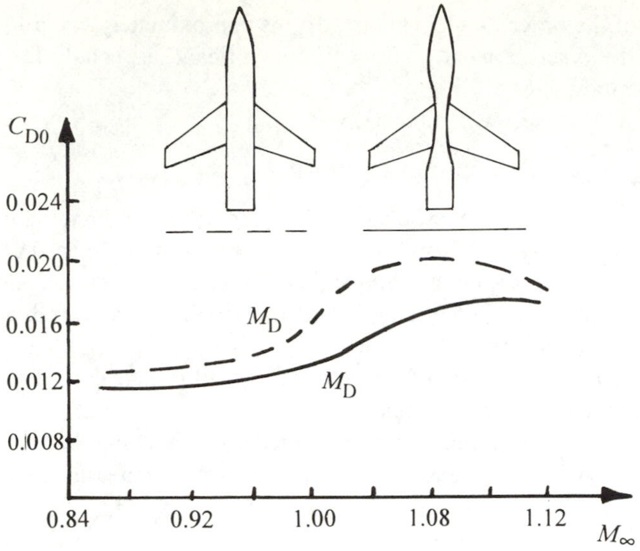

Fig. III.37. Effect of fuselage 'waisting' on drag.

III.3.5 Static aerodynamics of tailplane

When an aeroplane is moving with a constant forward speed U, at a constant angle of incidence and zero rate of pitch, the steady lift on the tailplane can be expressed as

$$\text{tailplane lift} = \tfrac{1}{2}\rho_{at}U^2 S_t (C_L)_t \tag{III.3.83}$$

where S_t is the tailplane area, $(C_L)_t$ is the tailplane lift coefficient $\left(= (a_\alpha)_t\alpha_t + a_\eta\eta\right)$, α_t is the static net angle of incidence of tailplane, η is the static elevator angle, $(a_\alpha)_t\left(= \partial(C_L)_t/\partial\alpha_t\right)$ is the rate of change of $(C_L)_t$ with α_t, keeping η constant, and $a_\eta\left(= \partial(C_L)_t/\partial\eta\right)$ is the rate of change of $(C_L)_t$ with η, keeping α_t constant.

The suffix 't' denotes 'tailplane', hopefully not to be confused with the variable, time, t. The linear form of eqn. (III.3.83) is valid for small angles of tailplane incidence, α_t, and elevator angle, η, when the effects of flow separation and breakdown are absent or small.

Typical chordwise load distributions on a tailplane and elevator are shown in Fig. III.38. In Fig. III.38(i) the load distribution at subsonic speeds due to tailplane incidence with zero elevator angle is compared with the lift distribution due to elevator angle with zero angle of incidence. Note that when the elevator is deflected, approximately 25% of the lift acts on the elevator, and the other 75% acts on the tailplane surface ahead of the elevator. At transonic speeds there are shock waves on the upper and lower surfaces of the tailplane or elevator, as indicated in Fig. III.38(ii), leading to large variations in elevator hinge moment with small changes in Mach number. At supersonic speeds the lift on the tailplane ahead of an elevator is zero, as shown in Fig. III.38(iii).

Because of the erratic hinge moment characteristics at transonic speeds and the loss of elevator efficiency at supersonic speeds, combat aeroplanes have all-moving tailplanes.

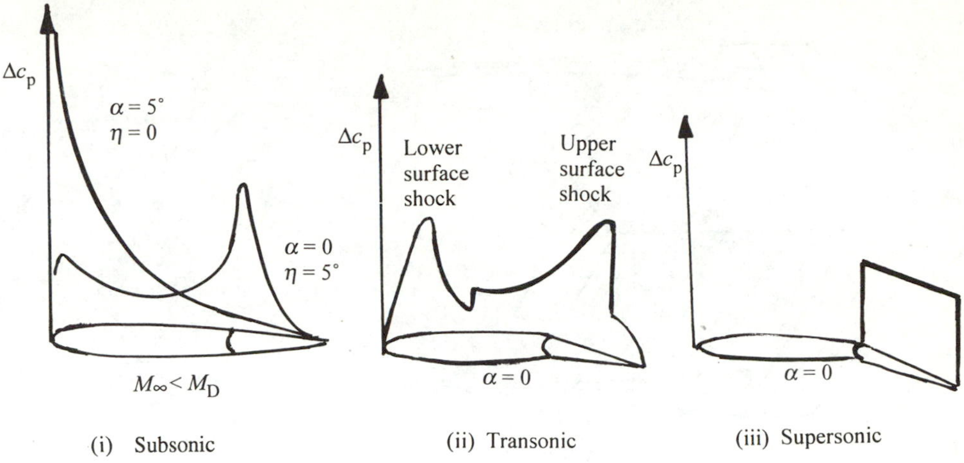

Fig. III.38. Chordwise loading due to elevator.

The value of $(a_\alpha)_t$ can be taken as the lift curve slope of the isolated wing, applied to the tailplane, eqns. (III.3.13)–(III.3.15), or ref. III.13. When the main wing and tailplane have identical aspect ratio, taper ratio and sweep angle then

$$(a_\alpha)_t = (a_\alpha)_w. \qquad \text{(III.3.84)}$$

Usually the tailplane has a lower aspect ratio than the wing, with

$$(a_\alpha)_t \simeq 0.9(a_\alpha)_w. \qquad \text{(III.3.85)}$$

The value of a_η depends on the size of the elevator, its plan form and sectional profile. At subsonic speeds, from the areas under the curves in Fig. III.38(i),

$$a_\eta \simeq 0.6(a_\alpha)_t. \qquad \text{(III.3.86)}$$

For an all-moving tailplane, at all speeds,

$$a_\eta = (a_\alpha)_t. \qquad \text{(III.3.87)}$$

Under static conditions the tailplane angle of incidence α_t is

$$\alpha_t = \alpha + i_t - \varepsilon, \qquad \text{(III.3.88)}$$

where α is the angle of incidence of the aeroplane (see Fig. III.2(i)), i_t is the tailplane setting angle (see Fig. III.1) and ε is the steady downwash angle in the wake of the main wing.

The flow field behind the main wing is dominated by the wing tip vortices, as shown in Fig. III.39. These counter-rotating vortices induce downwash field in the air in the vicinity of the tailplane. The average downwash velocity across the tailplane is denoted by w_t. The magnitude of w_t is proportional to the strength of each of the main wing tip vortices, which, in turn, is proportional to the lift on the main wing. This downwash induces a downward angle of incidence ε $(= w_t/U)$ on the tailplane.

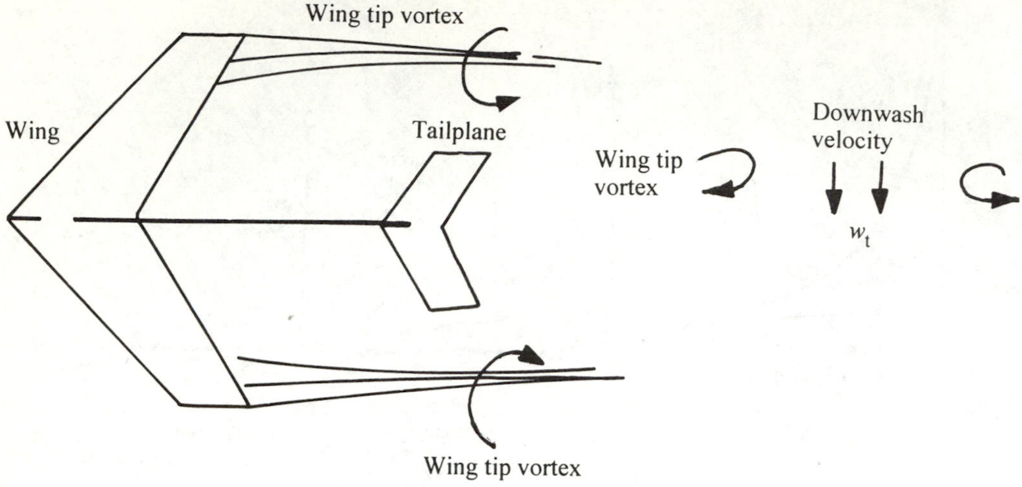

Fig. III.39. Downwash at subsonic speeds.

On the basis of dimensional analysis, the downwash angle, ε, is a function of the non-dimensional wing lift coefficient, $(C_L)_w$, and Mach number M_∞. At low angles of incidence ε can be taken to be directly proportional to $(C_L)_w$, hence

$$\varepsilon = \text{constant}\,(C_L)_w = \text{constant}\,(a_\alpha)_w(\alpha + i_w - \alpha_{0w}). \tag{III.3.89}$$

The constant of proportionality in eqn. (III.3.89) depends on the main wing sweep angle, aspect ratio, position of the tailplane relative to the main wing (i.e. a low tailplane or high tailplane) and Mach number, M_∞.

(i) At subsonic speeds, $M_\infty < M_D$, the variation of the constant of proportionality with Mach number can be neglected if it is assumed that the pattern of wake vorticity does not change significantly with Mach number, an acceptable assumption.
(ii) At supersonic speeds only that part of the wing tip vortices within the Mach cone of influence affects the downwash at the tailplane (see Fig. III.40), thus the constant of proportionality is much smaller than at subsonic speeds and, furthermore, it decreases with increase in (supersonic) Mach number.

In stability and control analysis it is convenient to express the steady state downwash characteristics in terms of $\partial\varepsilon/\partial\alpha$, so

$$\varepsilon = (\partial\varepsilon/\partial\alpha)\,(\alpha + i_w - \alpha_{0w}). \tag{III.3.90(i)}$$

At subsonic speeds, $M_\infty < M_D$, from eqn. (III.3.89),

$$\partial\varepsilon/\partial\alpha = \partial\varepsilon/\partial\alpha(M_\infty = 0)\left[a_\alpha(M_\infty)/a_\alpha(M_\infty = 0)\right]_w. \tag{III.3.90(ii)}$$

Data for $\partial\varepsilon/\partial\alpha$ are given in ref. III.22.

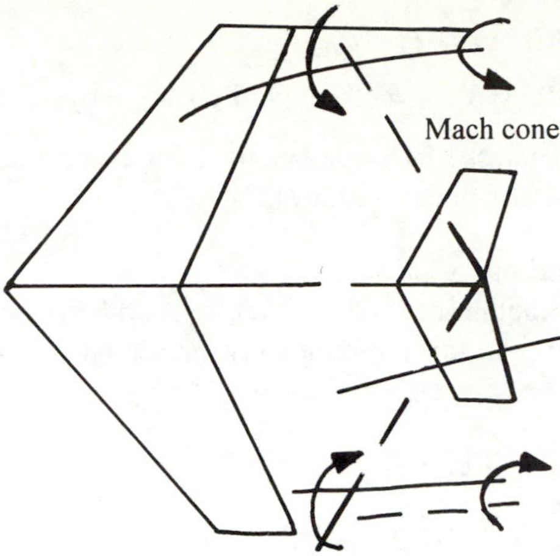

Fig. III.40. Downwash at supersonic speeds.

For the basic configurations, the following values may be taken:

$$\begin{aligned}
&\text{light aeroplane} && \partial\varepsilon/\partial\alpha = 0.45\\
&\text{transport aeroplane} && \partial\varepsilon/\partial\alpha\,(M_\infty = 0) = 0.45\\
&\text{combat aeroplane} && \partial\varepsilon/\partial\alpha\,(M_\infty = 0) = 0.55,\\
& && \partial\varepsilon/\partial\alpha\,(M_\infty = 1.2) = 0.2,\\
& && \partial\varepsilon/\partial\alpha\,(M_\infty > 1.5) = 0.0
\end{aligned} \tag{III.3.91}$$

Note from eqns. (III.3.90(ii)) and (III.3.91) the relatively large value $\partial\varepsilon/\partial\alpha$ at subsonic speeds.

The tailplane lift is taken to act through the tailplane aerodynamic centre (see Sect. III.3). The effect of the tailplane pitching moment about the tailplane aerodynamic centre is usually neglected.

The tailplane zero lift drag is incorporated in the overall aeroplane zero lift drag, whereas the tailplane lift-dependent drag is incorporated in the trim drag.

Tailplanes can be low, situated below the plane of the main wing as on the Lightning, or mid, slightly above the plane of the wing, as on Airbus, or high, on top of the fin as on the VC 10. The advantage of the high tailplane is that at low angles of incidence the downwash effect is considerably reduced, the disadvantage is that as the angle of incidence increases the tailplane comes closer to the wing tip vortices so the downwash angle increases and the tailplane loses its efficiency. The opposite trends occur with a low tailplane. If the tailplane becomes immersed in the wake of the main wing there is a loss in dynamic pressure at the tailplane, reducing the effective magnitude of $(\frac{1}{2}\rho_{at}U^2)$, decreasing the tailplane efficiency.

EXAMPLES III.13

1. Estimate η, taking $M_\infty = 0.7$,

$(C_L)_w = 0.6,\ \Lambda_w = 30°,\ AR_w = 7,\ i_w - \alpha_{0w} = 2°,$

$(C_L)_t = 0.2,\ \Lambda_t = 30°,\ AR_t = 6,\ i_t = -2°.\ \partial\varepsilon/\partial\alpha(M_\infty = 0) = 0.45.$

2. Sketch the variation of $\partial\varepsilon/\partial\alpha$ against Mach number for the transport and combat basic configurations, taking the values in eqn. (III.3.91).

III.3.6 Unsteady aerodynamics of tailplane

Consider an aeroplane in a dynamic motion defined by $U(t)$, $\alpha(t)$ and $\theta(t)$ with a time varying elevator angle $\eta(t)$. Following the same arguments as presented in Sect. III.3.3, the unsteady lift on the tailplane may be expressed in the form

$$\text{tailplane lift} = \tfrac{1}{2}\rho_{at}U^2(t)S_t\Big[(a_\alpha)_t(\alpha(t))_t + (a_{\dot\alpha})_t(\dot\alpha(t))_t\, c_t/U(t) + a_\eta\eta(t) + a_{\dot\eta}\dot\eta(t)c_t/U(t)\Big] \tag{III.3.92}$$

where

(i) the dot denotes differentiation with respect to time,
(ii) $(a_\alpha)_t$ is the steady state lift curve slope of the tailplane with respect to static α,
(iii) $(\alpha(t))_t$ is the time varying tailplane angle of incidence,
(iv) the rate derivative $(a_{\dot\alpha})_t$ can be taken independent of time for typical aeroplane responses and manoeuvres, with the proviso that $(a_{\dot\alpha})_t$ is an order of magnitude rather than an exact value; a reasonable approximation is

$$(a_{\dot\alpha})_t = (a_{\dot\alpha})_w\big((a_\alpha)_t/(a_\alpha)_w\big), \tag{III.3.93}$$

(v) a_η is the steady state lift curve slope due to elevator angle,
(vi) $a_{\dot\eta}$ is the rate derivative of the time varying elevator angle.

The derivative $a_{\dot\eta}$ may pose problems. Elevator motions associated with human pilot input, stability augmentation systems, and relaxed stability systems will be similar in frequency and damping to those of the aeroplane response and so $a_{\dot\eta}$ can be taken to be independent of time. But elevator motions on a rigid aeroplane will also include the much higher frequencies associated with the actuators' response. At these higher frequencies $a_{\dot\eta}$ cannot be assumed independent of time (or frequency); consideration of these high frequency time varying effects is beyond the scope of this book. For the present purposes it is assumed, following eqns. (III.3.86) and (III.3.87), that

$$\begin{aligned} a_{\dot\eta} &= 0.6\,(a_{\dot\alpha})_t \quad \text{for an elevator,}\\ &= (a_{\dot\alpha})_t \quad \text{for an all-moving tailplane.} \end{aligned} \tag{III.3.94}$$

The tailplane angle of incidence is given by

$$(\alpha(t))_t = \alpha(t) + i_t + l_t\big(q(t)c_w/U(t)\big) - \varepsilon(t). \tag{III.3.95}$$

There is now an additional term due to the rate of pitch. Denoting the distance of the aerodynamic centre of the tailplane aft of the aeroplane centre of mass as $l_t c_w$ (see Fig. III.41), the tailplane moves downward, relative to the centre of the mass, with velocity

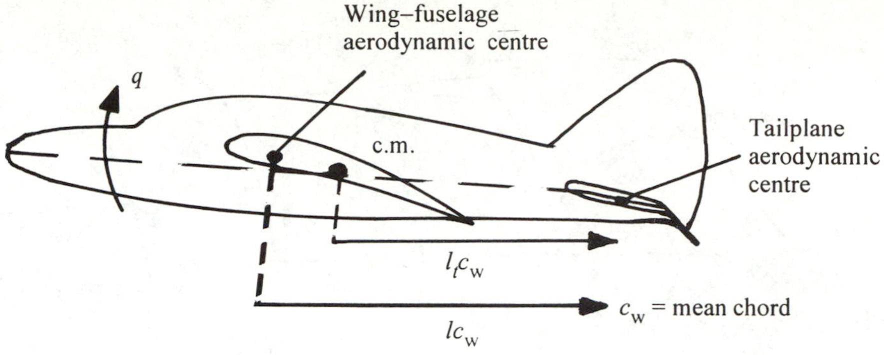

Fig. III.41. Notation for tailplane.

$(q(t)l_t c_w)$, due to the rate of pitch q, inducing a positive angle of incidence of the tailplane equal to $(q(t)l_t c_w/U(t))$.

It is convention to express the time varying downwash angle $\varepsilon(t)$ in the form

$$\varepsilon(t) = (\partial\varepsilon/\partial\alpha)\alpha\left(t - lc_w/U(t)\right) \tag{III.3.96}$$

where lc_w is the distance from the aerodynamic centre of the main wing to the aerodynamic centre of the tailplane (see Fig. III.41) on the argument that the downwash at the tailplane at time t is determined by the angle of incidence of the main wing at the earlier time $\left(t - lc_w/U(t)\right)$, where $lc_w/U(t)$ is the time taken for the relative airstream to travel from the main wing to the tailplane. It is implicitly assumed in eqn. (III.3.96), and reasonably so, that any time variation in $U(t)$ in the period of time $lc_w/U(t)$ can be neglected.

Eqn. (III.3.96) can be criticized on two counts:

1. The downwash depends on the time varying circulation about the main wing rather than on the time varying angle of incidence.
2. The physical basis for the time lag, $lc_w/U(t)$, is obscure.

As described in Sect. III.3.3, when the circulation $\Gamma(t)$ about the main wing changes with time then 'starting vortices', of strength proportional to $d\Gamma(t)/dt$, are shed continuously from the wing trailing edge and left behind the main wing as the main wing moves forward with velocity $U(t)$. These shed 'starting vortices' are 'connected' to the main wing by the wing tip vortices (see Fig. III.42). The strength of the shed 'starting vortices' at a distance X downstream of the wing will be equal to the strength of the shed 'starting vortices' formed at the wing trailing edge at the earlier time $t - X/U$; the strength of the wing tip vortices varies with X and is given by the integral of the shed vortices with respect to X.

Suppose, for simplicity, that the mean, spanwise, circulation $\Gamma(t)$ around the wing increases linearly with time (i.e. $\Gamma(t) = \Gamma_0 t$, where Γ_0 is a constant). Then, the strength of the distribution of the shed 'starting vortices' is constant, equal to Γ_0, and the strength of the wing tip vortices decreases linearly downstream.

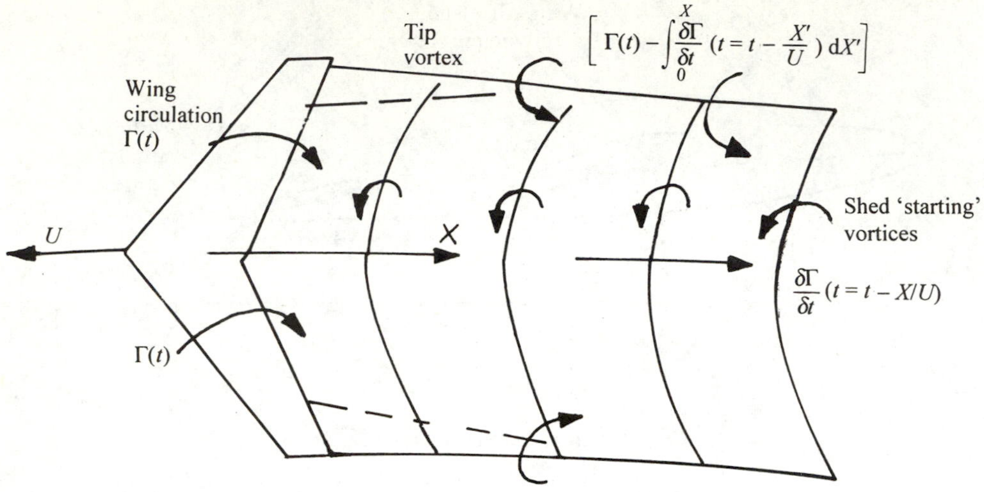

Fig. III.42. Unsteady wake aft of wing.

Consider the downwash at a tailplane, located a distance lc_w downstream of the main wing, for the two extreme cases of very large and very small aspect ratio.

1. When the aspect ratio of the main wing is very large, as shown in Fig. III.43, the downwash at the tailplane is dominated by the shed 'starting vortices'. The downwash at the tailplane at time t is the (positive) downwash due to $\Gamma(t)$ around the wing plus the (positive) downwash due to the shed 'starting vortices' downstream of $2\,lc_w$, since, by symmetry about the tailplane location, the downwash due to the uniform shed 'starting vortices' from the main wing to a distance $2\,lc_w$ is zero. Thus the downwash formula is of the form

$$\varepsilon(t) \propto \Gamma_0(t + t_1) \qquad \text{(III.3.97)}$$

where $t_1 > 0$. In this case there is not a time lag as expected from eqn. (III.3.96) but a time advance.
2. When the aspect ratio is very small, as shown in Fig. III.43, the downwash at the tailplane is dominated by the strength of the wing tip vortices at the tailplane location; in this case

$$\varepsilon(t) \propto \Gamma_0\left(t - lc_w/U\right). \qquad \text{(III.3.98)}$$

There is a superficial resemblance between eqns. (III.3.96) and (III.3.98) but it must be remembered that $\Gamma(t)$ lags behind $\alpha(t)$.

Eqn. (III.3.98) can be modified to include the effect of aspect ratio, namely

$$\varepsilon(t) \propto \Gamma_0\left(t - k_\varepsilon\, lc_w/U\right) \qquad \text{(III.3.99)}$$

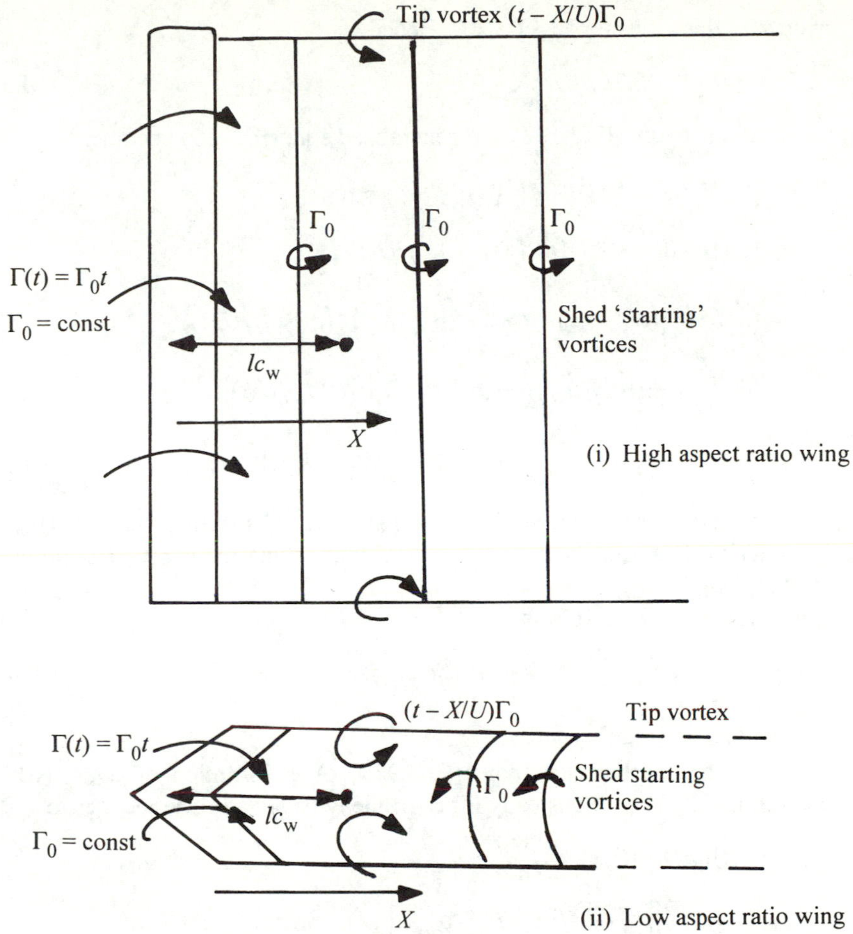

Fig. III.43. Unsteady downwash at tailplane.

where k_ε depends on aspect ratio and Mach number. It is argued in Appendix 3 that an approximation for k_ε is

$$k_\varepsilon = 1 - \left[\mathrm{AR}_\mathrm{w}^2\left(1 - M_\infty^2\right)/150\right], \qquad \mathrm{AR}_\mathrm{w} < 10. \tag{III.3.100}$$

Although the above analysis of the unsteady downwash characteristics has been derived for the particular time variation of constant $\dot{\Gamma}(t)$ it is assumed that eqn. (III.3.99) can be applied to the more general time variations, $\Gamma(t)$, typical of aeroplane motions.

According to eqn. (III.3.38), as derived in Appendix 1,

$$\begin{aligned}\left(C_\mathrm{L}(t)\right)_\mathrm{w} &\propto \Gamma(t) + 0.7\left(\mathrm{d}\Gamma(t)/\mathrm{d}t\right)c_\mathrm{w}/U,\\ &\propto \Gamma\left(t + 0.7c_\mathrm{w}/U\right)\end{aligned} \tag{III.3.101}$$

by an inverse Taylor series for small c_w/U. Hence

$$\Gamma(t) \propto \left[C_L\left(t - 0.7c_w/U\right)\right]_w. \tag{III.3.102}$$

On substitution of eqn. (III.3.102), the generalized eqn. (III.3.99) becomes

$$\begin{aligned}
\varepsilon(t) &\propto \left[C_L\left(t-(0.7+k_\varepsilon l)c_w/U(t)\right)\right]_w \\
&\propto \left[C_L\left(t-(0.7+k_\varepsilon l)\left(\mathrm{d}C_L(t)/\mathrm{d}t\right)c_w/U(t)\right)\right]_w \\
&= (\partial\varepsilon/\partial\alpha)\left[\left(\alpha(t)+i_w-\alpha_{0w}\right)+\left(a_q/a_\alpha\right)_w\left(q(t)c_w/U(t)\right)\right. \\
&\qquad +\left[\left(a_{\dot\alpha}/a_\alpha\right)_w-(0.7+k_\varepsilon l)\right]\left(\dot\alpha(t)c_w/U(t)\right) \\
&\qquad \left.+\left[\left(a_{\dot q}/a_\alpha\right)_w-\left(a_q/a_\alpha\right)_w(0.7+k_\varepsilon l)\right]\left(\dot q(t)c_w^2/U^2(t)\right)\right]
\end{aligned} \tag{III.3.103}$$

taking the first two terms in the Taylor expansion, substituting for $[C_L(t)]_w$, eqn. (III.3.68), ignoring the terms due to $\ddot\alpha$, $\ddot q$ and $\dot U$, and taking the constant of proportionality to be $(\partial\varepsilon/\partial\alpha)/(a_\alpha)_w$.

It follows from eqn. (III.3.103) that

$$\dot\varepsilon(t) = (\partial\varepsilon/\partial\alpha)\left[\dot\alpha(t)+\left(a_q/a_\alpha\right)_w\left(\dot q(t)c_w/U\right)\right] \tag{III.3.104}$$

again ignoring the $\ddot\alpha$, $\ddot q$ and $\dot U$ terms.

Returning to the tailplane lift (eqn. (III.3.92)), on substitution of eqns. (III.3.95), (III.3.103) and (III.3.104), the unsteady lift coefficient of the tailplane reduces to

$$\begin{aligned}
&\left[C_L\left(\alpha(t),q(t),\eta(t),\varepsilon(t)\,|\,t\right)\right]_t \\
&\simeq (a_\alpha)_t\left[\left[i_t-(\partial\varepsilon/\partial\alpha)(i_w-\alpha_{0w})\right]+(1-\partial\varepsilon/\partial\alpha)\alpha(t)\right. \\
&\qquad \left.+\,l_t\left(q(t)c_w/U(t)\right)+(\partial\varepsilon/\partial\alpha)(0.7+k_\varepsilon l)\left(\dot\alpha(t)c_w/U(t)\right)\right] \\
&\quad +(a_{\dot\alpha})_t l_t\left(c_t/c_w\right)\left(\dot q(t)c_w^2/U^2(t)\right) \\
&\quad +a_\eta\eta(t)+a_{\dot\eta}\left(\dot\eta(t)c_w/U(t)\right),
\end{aligned} \tag{III.3.105}$$

assuming that

(i) $\left(c_t/c_w\right)\left(a_{\dot\alpha}/a_\alpha\right)_t(1-\partial\varepsilon/\partial\alpha)-\left(a_{\dot\alpha}/a_\alpha\right)_w\partial\varepsilon/\partial\alpha \simeq 0$

(ii) $l_t-(\partial\varepsilon/\partial\alpha)\left(a_q/a_\alpha\right)_w \simeq l_t$

(iii) $l_t-(\partial\varepsilon/\partial\alpha)\left[\left(a_q/a_\alpha\right)_w\left(1-\left(c_w/c_t\right)\left(a_\alpha/a_{\dot\alpha}\right)_t(0.7+k_\varepsilon l)\right)\right]$
$\quad -\left(c_w/c_t\right)\left(a_\alpha/a_{\dot\alpha}\right)_t\left(a_{\dot q}/a_\alpha\right)_w = \mathrm{O}[l_t]$.

At the end of this extended analysis eqn. (III.3. 105) differs from the standard formula for the tailplane lift coefficient in the literature in the following respects:

(i) for the $\dot{\alpha}$ term $[(\partial\varepsilon/\partial\alpha)(0.7+k_\varepsilon l)]$ replaces $[(\partial\varepsilon/\partial\alpha)l]$, thus when $l = 3.0$ the conventional value is 10% too high for a wing with a higher aspect ratio but is 20% too low for a wing with a lower aspect ratio;

(ii) there is now a $\dot{q}$ derivative.

EXAMPLES III.14

1. How does Mach number affect (i) above for a wing of $AR_w = 7$ at subsonic speeds?
2. In the text it states: 'the strength of the wing tip vortices varies with X and is given by the integral of the shed vortices with respect to X'. Prove this statement.
3. What is the basis of the assumption that eqn. (III.3.99) can be applied to more general time variations, typical of aeroplane motions?
4. Sketch the time variation of $\varepsilon(t)$ due to a step change in wing incidence α. What is the relevance of this behaviour to the above text?

III.3.7 Elevator hinge moment

The aerodynamic moment on the elevator about the elevator hinge line is an important design parameter. On a light, low speed, aeroplane the range of elevator hinge moments required throughout the flight envelope has to be reacted manually by the human pilot and must remain within comfortable bounds of human capability at all times. On a larger, high speed, aeroplane the range of elevator hinge moments required throughout the flight envelope, and their time varying behaviour, determines the size, power and response characteristics of the elevator actuator.

At the trailing edge of the elevator there is sometimes a small chord, small span, control surface, known as the tab, as shown in Fig. III.44. The role of the tab angle is explained later.

The loads on the elevator arise from the tailplane incidence, the elevator angle, and the tab angle. The elevator hinge moment may be expressed in the form

$$\text{elevator hinge moment} = \tfrac{1}{2}\rho_{at}U(t)^2 S_e c_e\left(b_\alpha(\alpha(t))_t + b_\eta\eta(t) + b_\delta\delta\right), \quad \text{(III.3.106)}$$

taken to be positive in the nose-up direction, where S_e is the elevator surface area; c_e is the mean elevator chord; $(\alpha(t))_t$ is the time varying tailplane angle of incidence, namely,

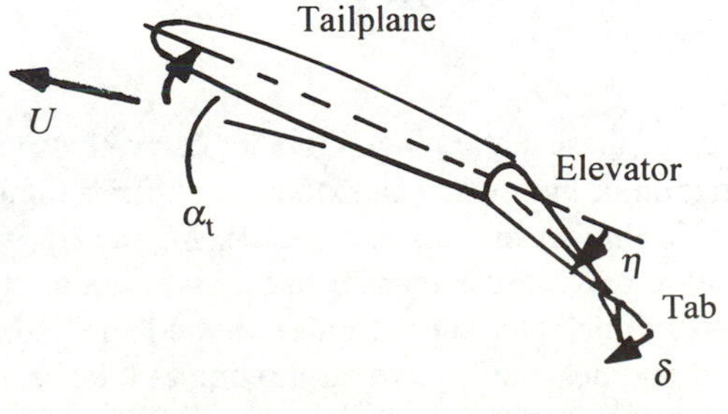

Fig. III.44. Tailplane–elevator–tab.

$$(\alpha(t))_t = \alpha(t) + i_t + l_t(q(t)c_w/U) - \varepsilon(t)$$

from eqn. (III.3.95) and $\varepsilon(t)$ is given by eqn. (III.3.103); $\eta(t)$ is the time varying elevator angle; δ is the static tab angle (the tab angle does not vary with time); and b_α, b_η and b_δ are the steady state hinge moment derivatives.

The effects of the rate derivatives $b_{\dot{\alpha}}$ and $b_{\dot{\eta}}$ are ignored; their contributions to the elevator hinge moment are thought to be small.

The range of validity of eqn. (III.3.106), which implies linearity of the elevator hinge moment with respect to α_t, η and δ, needs to be checked experimentally for each tailplane–elevator–tab configuration because it is difficult to predict the onset of flow separation on such configurations.

An order of magnitude of the value of b_η can be estimated. By inspection of Fig. III.38(i), at low Mach numbers,

$$\begin{aligned} \text{lift on elevator} &\simeq \left(\tfrac{1}{3}\right)(\text{total lift on (tailplane + elevator) due to } \eta) \\ &\simeq \left(\tfrac{1}{3}\right)\tfrac{1}{2}\rho_{at}U^2 S_t a_\eta \eta. \end{aligned} \qquad \text{(III.3.107)}$$

Taking the centre of pressure of the load on the elevator due to the elevator deflection at $0.25c_e$ aft of the elevator leading edge, for a forward hinge line at $0.05c_e$,

$$\text{elevator hinge moment} \simeq -\,(\text{lift on elevator})\ (0.2c_e). \qquad \text{(III.3.108)}$$

Hence, taking $S_e/S_t = 0.35$, $a_\eta = 2.5$,

$$b_\eta \simeq -0.067(S_t/S_e)\,a_\eta \simeq -0.45. \qquad \text{(III.3.109)}$$

To estimate an order of magnitude of the value of b_α, according to Fig. III.38(ii), the lift on the elevator due to angle of incidence, α_t, is less than the lift on the elevator due to elevator angle, η, when α_t is equal to η, by a factor of approximately 0.25, but the centre of pressure of the lift on the elevator due to α_t lies about $0.35c_e$ aft of the elevator leading edge, so

$$b_\alpha \simeq 0.4\,b_\eta \simeq -0.18. \qquad \text{(III.3.110)}$$

Empirical values have to be taken for the tab derivative, b_δ, because the flow about the tab is dominated by viscous effects; typically,

$$b_\delta \simeq -0.15. \qquad \text{(III.3.111)}$$

More accurate values of these static hinge moment derivatives are given in ref. III.23, derived from a combination of theory and an extensive experimental database.

With increasing Mach number at subsonic speeds, $M_\infty < M_D$, it can be assumed that b_α, b_η and b_δ increase in a similar manner to the increase in a_α with M_∞. There is no need to discuss elevator characteristics at transonic and supersonic speeds; aeroplanes which fly in these speed regimes would have all-moving tailplanes.

There are two main strategies to reduce the magnitude of the elevator hinge moment in steady and manoeuvring flight:

(i) aerodynamic balancing,
(ii) use of a tab.

Two types of aerodynamic balance are possible, external or internal.

To achieve an external aerodynamic balance the hinge axis can be moved aft from the front of the elevator, as shown in Fig. III.45(i), but the nose of the elevator has to be shaped so that when the elevator is rotated the nose does not protrude unduly above the tailplane surface. Although the magnitude of the hinge moment is reduced by this arrangement there is a loss in the lifting effectiveness of the elevator.

An alternative form of external aerodynamic balance is the horn elevator, as shown in Fig. III.45(ii).

An internal balance is shown in Fig. III.45(iii). The suction pressures around the upper surface of the elevator nose act on the upper surface of the internal balance arm while the higher static pressures around the lower surface of the elevator nose act on the lower surface of the internal balance arm, giving a balancing hinge moment.

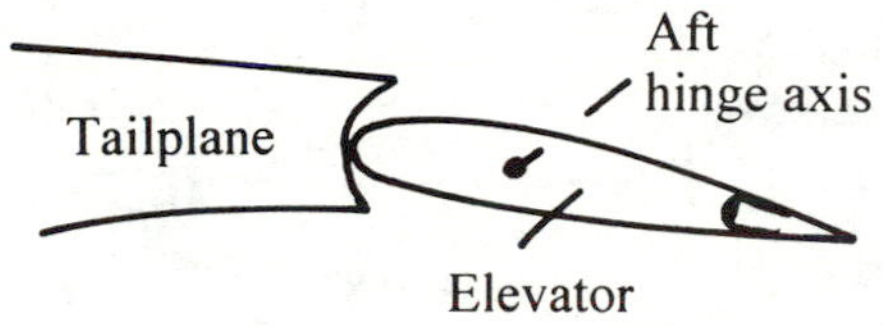

Fig. III.45(i). External aerodynamic balance (aft hinge axis)

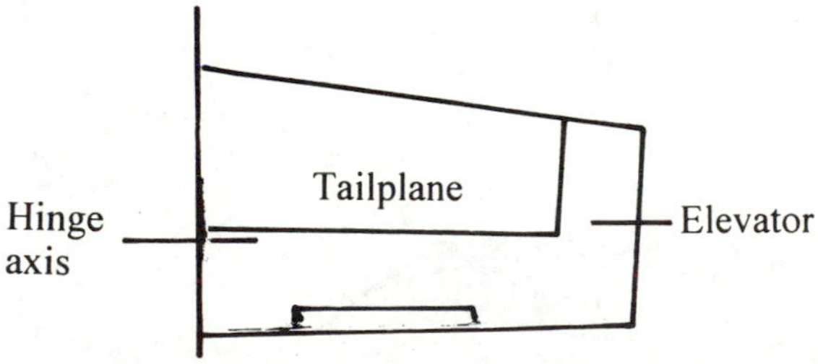

Fig. III.45(ii). External aerodynamic balance (horn balance).

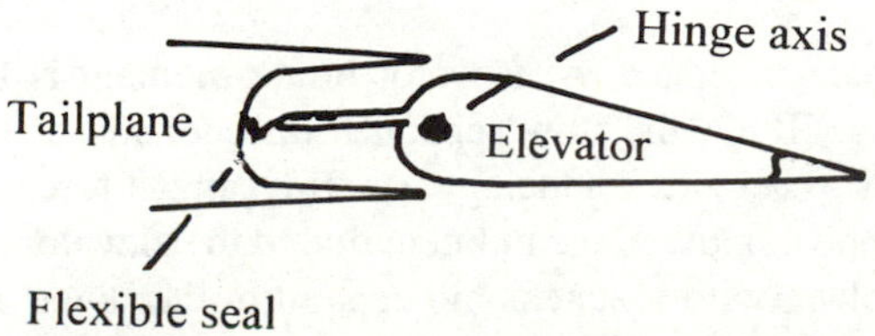

Fig. III.45(iii). Internal aerodynamic balance.

A tab can be used to reduce the elevator hinge moment by rotating the tab in the opposite direction to that of the elevator. Deflection of the tab has only a minor effect on the overall tailplane lift but a major effect on the elevator hinge moment.

In steady trimmed flight, for a specified tailplane angle of incidence and elevator angle, the elevator hinge moment can be reduced to zero by setting the tab at an appropriate angle; this arrangement is known as a trim tab. With a manual system the pilot has, in addition to the stick which moves the elevator, a separate control, either a button on the stick or a small wheel, to vary the tab angle independently of the elevator. With a powered control system there is usually no trim tab.

It is also necessary with manual control systems to minimize the elevator hinge moments in manoeuvring flight. There have been many ingenious tab designs to meet this objective (see Figs. III.46). Basically it is necessary to gear the tab deflection to the elevator deflection: a fixed gearing ratio is incorporated in the geared tab arrangement; a variable gearing ratio is incorporated into spring tab arrangement; a servo tab is a limiting case of a spring tab with zero spring stiffness in which the elevator is free floating and the stick is connected directly to the tab so the pilot only has to offset the tab hinge moment.

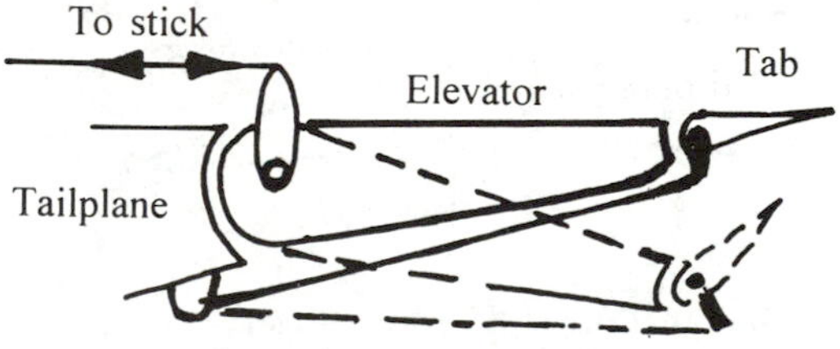

Fig. III.46(i). Geared tab.

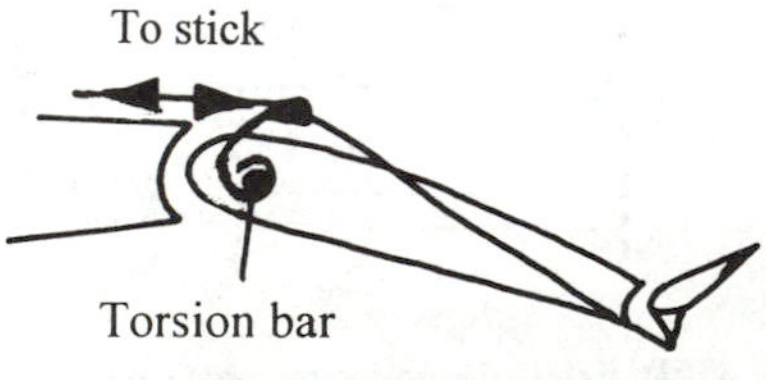

Fig. III.46(ii). Spring tab.

Yet another approach to reduce the elevator hinge moment is by a bevelled trailing edge. As shown in Fig. III.47, the flow separates on one side of the bevelled edge but remains attached on the other side, inducing a small localized force which gives a significant hinge moment, opposing the hinge moment due to the elevator angle.

On a combat aeroplane with a supersonic capability the hinge axis of an all-moving tailplane would be located approximately half way between the subsonic and supersonic aerodynamic centres.

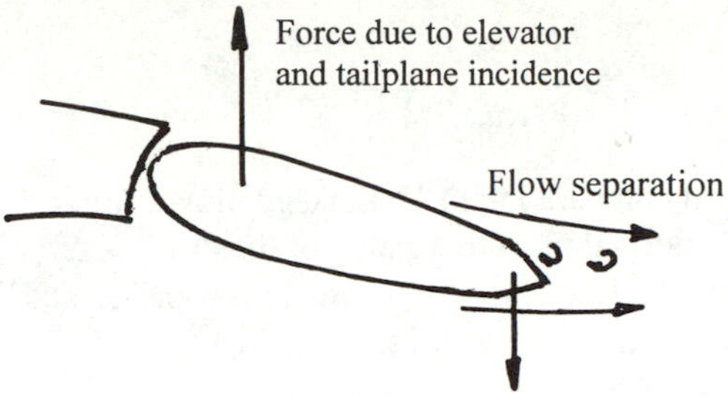

Fig. III.47. Bevelled trailing edge.

EXAMPLES III.15

1. The steady tailplane lift at 5.5 km altitude at Mach 0.6 is 2.5 kN. For an elevator–tab arrangement with a forward hinge axis determine the tab angle to reduce the elevator hinge moment to zero, given

$$AR_t = 4, \quad \Lambda_t = 15°, \quad S_t = 4 \text{ m}^2, \quad \alpha_t = 1°.$$

2. In regard to the aft hinge axis for an external balance the above text says: 'the nose of the elevator has to be shaped so that when the elevator is rotated the nose does not protrude unduly above the tailplane surface'. What happens if the nose does protrude unduly above the tailplane surface?
3. What are the relative merits of external balancing, internal balancing and the use of tabs to reduce elevator hinge moments?
4. What are the relative merits of servo, geared and spring tabs?
5. What kinds of tab system are currently fashionable?

III.3.8 Interference effects of propulsion unit

In this section the interference effects of the propulsion unit on the longitudinal aerodynamic forces and moments on an aeroplane are summarized.

III.3.8.1 Propeller

Consider first a light aeroplane with a propeller situated at the front of the fuselage. According to the principle of conservation of linear momentum, as expressed in actuator disc theory (see ref. III.7) the thrust on the propeller is given by,

$$\begin{aligned} \text{Thrust} = \text{Th} &= \tfrac{1}{2}\rho_{at}U^2 S_w C_{Th} = m_{Th}u_p, \\ m_{Th} &= \rho_{at}(\pi r_p^2)\left(U + u_p/2\right) \end{aligned} \qquad \text{(III.3.112)}$$

where, by reference to Fig. III.48, C_{Th} is the thrust coefficient, r_p is the propeller disc radius, U is the air velocity ahead of the propeller relative to the propeller, $(U + u_p)$ is the air velocity in the slipstream downstream of the propeller, relative to the propeller, and m_{Th} is the mass flow rate of air through the propeller disc, taking the velocity through the propeller disc as the mean of the upstream and downstream velocities.

Thus

$$C_{Th} \simeq (\pi/2)(r_p/s_w)^2 AR_w(u_p/U). \tag{III.3.113}$$

assuming that u_p is small compared with U. In steady level flight C_{Th} is equal to C_D, and $0.02 < C_D < 0.12$ over a normal operating range of linear $C_L \sim \alpha$.

There are a number of effects arising from the propeller and its slipstream on the aerodynamic lift and moment characteristics.

(i) When the aeroplane is at an angle of incidence, α, a normal force, N_{prop}, acts on the propeller, as indicated in Fig. III.48. From ref. III.7,

$$N_{prop} = O\left[\tfrac{1}{2}\rho_{at}U^2 S_w C_{Th}\alpha\right]. \tag{III.3.114}$$

The normal force N_{prop} is small, and negligible, compared with the main wing lift but its contribution to the pitching moment about the centre of mass may not be negligible at low speeds, high C_L.

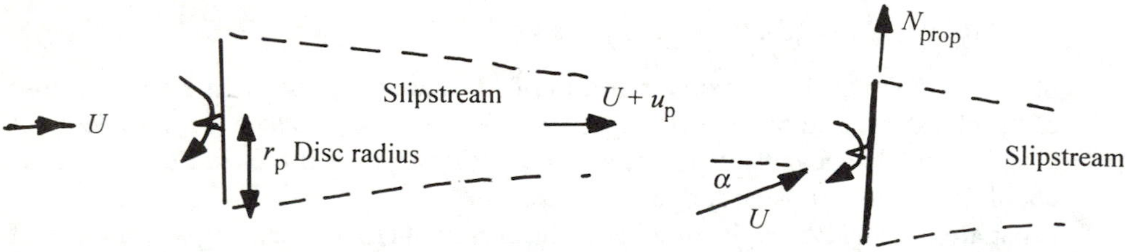

Fig. III.48. Propeller characteristics.

(ii) Because the slipstream remains more-or-less parallel to the fuselage with change of angle of incidence, there is virtually no nose lift on the fuselage nose similar to that described in sect. III.3.4.

(iii) The increase in relative velocity in the slipstream behind the propeller disc increases the lift on that part of the span of the wing immersed in the slipstream; hence the effective change in the wing lift curve slope can be approximated by

$$(a_\alpha)_{w+p} = (a_\alpha)_w\left[\left(1-(r_p/s_w)\right)+\left(1+(u_p/U)\right)^2(r_p/s_w)\right] \tag{III.3.115}$$

where the suffix 'w + p' refers to the wing plus slipstream.

For non-swept wings, which are the norm on propeller driven aeroplanes, the slipstream will not affect the wing aerodynamic centre. For non-swept wings similar formulae to eqn. (III.3.115) apply to $(m_0)_{w+p}$, $(a_q)_{w+p}$ and $(m_q)_{w+p}$.

(iv) With a single propeller there is a swirl in the slipstream which induces a higher lift on one wing, a lower lift on the other, and an overall small rolling moment.

(v) Assuming that the tailplane is totally immersed in the slipstream, the derivatives $(a_\alpha)_t$, a_η, b_α, b_η and b_δ are all increased by the factor $\left(1+(u_p/U)\right)^2$.

(vi) The author is not aware of any reference in the literature on the effect of slipstream on the wing contribution to the $\dot{\alpha}$ derivative.

(vii) There are two opposing effects of the propeller slipstream on the downwash angle at the tailplane, as shown in Fig. III.49:

(a) Because of the slipstream velocity there is a higher lift on the main wing inside the propeller slipstream than on the main wing outside the slipstream, thus a pair of trailing vortices are formed on the slipstream boundary which induce an additional downwash at the tailplane.

(b) The induced downwash velocity at the tailplane due to the trailing vortices from the wing tips of the main wing is unaffected by the propeller slipstream, but the downwash angle is reduced because of the higher streamwise velocity inside the slipstream.

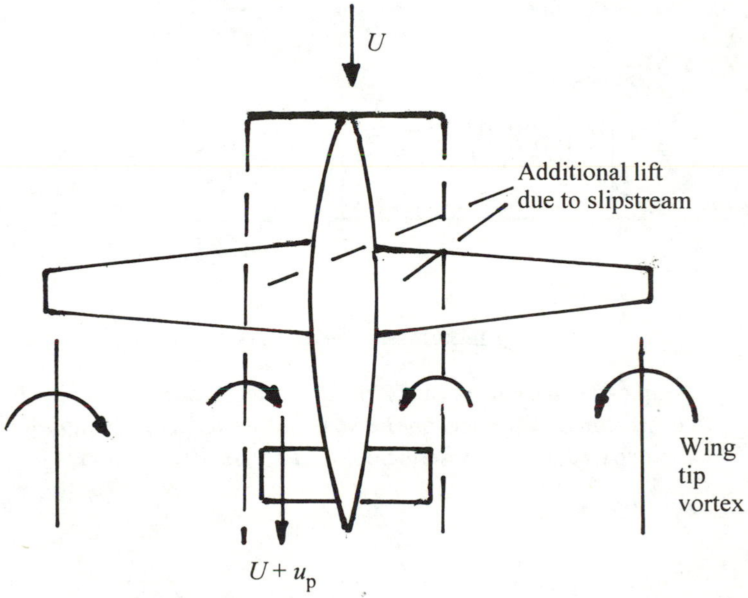

Fig. III.49. Slipstream effects.

Effect (a) tends to be larger than effect (b) so the downwash angle at the tailplane is slightly increased by the propeller slipstream.

(viii) Because of the high slipstream velocity the lag in the downwash at the tailplane is slightly reduced.

EXAMPLES III.16

1. Does the concept of aerodynamic centre still hold when N_p is taken into account? If not, how should its contribution to the pitching moment be included?
2. Calculate the increase in $(a_\alpha)_w$ and $(a_\alpha)_t$ due to slipstream effects when $C_{Th} = 0.05$, $\left(r_p/s_w\right) = \frac{1}{3}$ and $AR_w = 7$.
3. What is the effect of a slipstream on drag?
4. What is the effect of a slipstream on the tab angle to trim?

5. Derive approximate magnitudes for the two downwash effects given in (vii) (a) and (b) above.
6. Is the change in downwash lag due to the slipstream significant?

III.3.8.2 Turbo-fan

Consider an isolated nacelle, enclosing a turbo-fan engine, as shown in Fig. III.50. The net thrust is given by

$$\mathrm{Th} = \dot{m}_{\mathrm{Th}}(u_{\mathrm{j}} - U), \qquad \text{(III.3.116)}$$

where $\dot{m}_{\mathrm{Th}}$ is the mass flow rate of air through the engine, U is the speed of air ahead of the engine relative to the engine, and u_{j} is the mean exhaust velocity downstream of the engine relative to the engine.

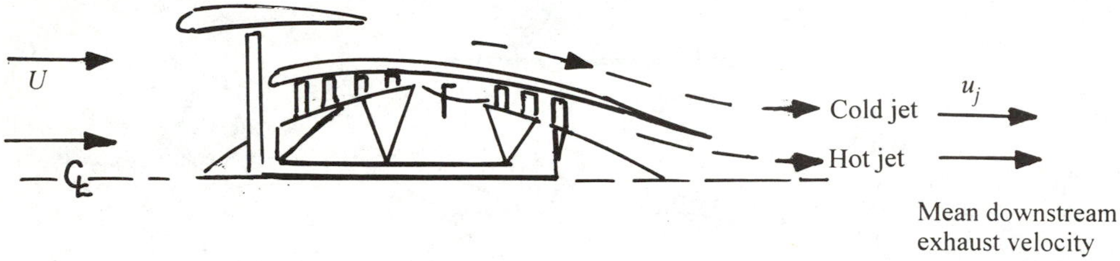

Fig. III.50. Notation for turbo-fan engine.

When the turbo-fan nacelle is at an angle of incidence, α, to the forward speed direction, a normal force, N_{nac}, acts on the nose of the intake of the nacelle, as shown in Fig. III.51, where, based on the conservation of transverse momentum,

$$N_{\mathrm{nac}} = \dot{m}_{\mathrm{Th}} U \alpha. \qquad \text{(III.3.117)}$$

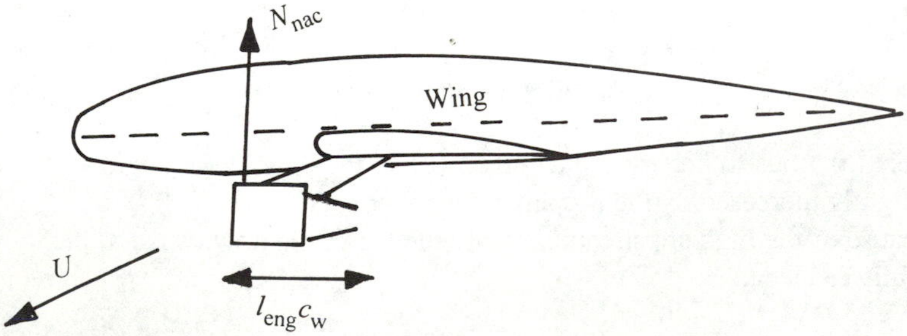

Fig. III.51. Nacelle load.

Physically N_{nac} arises from the difference in the normal pressure distributions around the upper and lower surfaces of the intake in the region of the nacelle nose. The force N_{nac} acts normal to its nacelle because the suction force around the lip of the intake is regarded as part of the thrust.

To a first order

$$\dot{m}_{Th} = O[\rho_{at}\pi r_{nac}^2 U] \tag{III.3.118}$$

where r_{nac} is the inlet radius of the nacelle.

Then, from eqns. (III.3.117) and (III.3.118), for small angles of incidence, for each engine,

$$\begin{aligned}(a_\alpha)_{nac} &= N_{nac}\Big/\left(\tfrac{1}{2}\rho_{at}U^2 S_w \alpha\right) \\ &= O\left[(\pi/2)(r_{nac}/s_w)^2 \, AR_w\right].\end{aligned} \tag{III.3.119}$$

Typically,

$$r_{nac}/s_w \simeq \tfrac{1}{18}, \; AR_w \simeq 7, \tag{III.3.120}$$

so, with two engines,

$$(a_\alpha)_{nac} = O\left[0.015(a_\alpha)_{wf}\right]. \tag{III.3.121}$$

Although $(a_\alpha)_{nac}$ can be neglected compared with $(a_\alpha)_{wf}$, the pitching moment due to N_{nac} is not necessarily negligible, as shown later.

When the aeroplane is pitching at rate $q\,(= d\theta/dt)$, the normal force acting on the nacelle is given by eqn. (III.3.117), replacing α by $(ql_{eng}c_w/U)$, where $(l_{eng}c_w)$ is the overall length of the engine nacelle (see Fig. III.50).

With the above numbers

$$(a_q)_{nac} = O\left[0.015 l_{eng}(a_\alpha)_{wf}\right] \tag{III.3.122}$$

for two engines.

When α varies with time the quasi-steady rate derivative due to $\dot{\alpha}$ is negligible because the engine in its nacelle is effectively a very low aspect ratio configuration with virtually no aerodynamic lag effects. A preliminary investigation on the effects of pitching oscillations on the loads on an engine/nacelle is described by Sheu & Hancock (ref. III.24).

The above orders of magnitude for the derivatives associated with an engine/nacelle can be applied to combat aeroplanes.

Another engine characteristic which can play a role in the aerodynamic loads is jet entrainment, whereby air in the vicinity of the jet is entrained, or 'sucked', into the main jet stream, as the jet diameter expands downstream of the jet exhaust, sketched in Fig. III.52.

On a transport aeroplane, where the engine nacelles are underslung beneath the main wing, connected by a pylon (see Fig. III.51), there are two interference effects at low angles of incidence:

(i) the (pylon + nacelle) without thrust induces a suction pressure field on the wing lower surface which tends to decrease slightly the wing lift;

(ii) with thrust, entrainment increases the velocities marginally on the lower surface of the wing, again reducing slightly the wing lift.

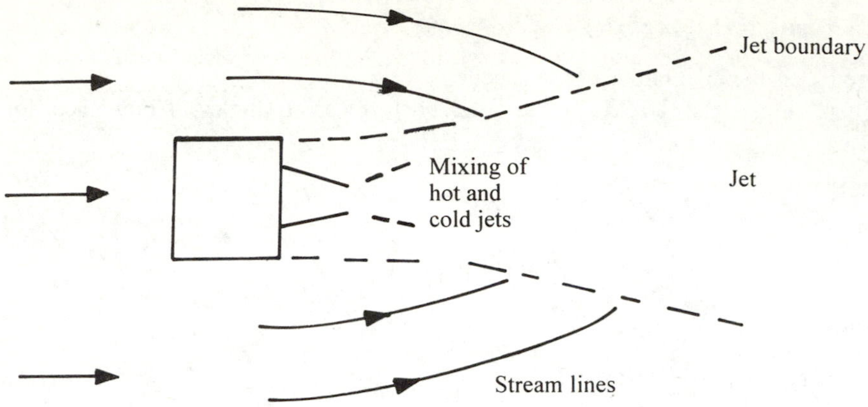

Fig. III.52. Jet entrainment.

The combined effect is small in respect of both lift and moment. The main entrainment effect associated with underslung engines arises with flaps down where the trailing edge of the flaps comes close to the jet boundary.

On a combat aeroplane, where the engine(s), enclosed within the fuselage, exhausts from a jet pipe from the back end of the fuselage, entrainment can affect the tailplane characteristics. Usually these effects are negligible at low angles of incidence, but on configurations like the Jaguar, where the tailplane is situated over the jet exhaust, entrainment effects are important (when reheat is switched on in the Jaguar the tailplane requires retrimming by approximately 1°).

EXAMPLES III.17

1. Estimate typical values of (u_j/U) for a turbo-fan engine:

   at take-off when $(\mathrm{Th}/L)\simeq\frac{1}{4}$,

   at cruise when $(\mathrm{Th}/L)\simeq\frac{1}{12}$,

   on approach when $(\mathrm{Th}/L)\simeq\frac{1}{20}$.

2. Is eqn. (III.3.118) reasonable at cruise? at low speeds? If not, what are the consequences for N_{nac}?
3. Could jet entrainment affect the downwash at the tailplane?
4. An annular wing of length c_a and radius s_a at incidence has a lift given by

   $$\text{lift}\simeq\tfrac{1}{2}\rho_{at}U^2(2s_ac_a).1.0\alpha$$

   which acts a distance 0.06 aft of the leading edge; α is in radians.

   Scaled annular wings plus pylons are sometimes used on wind tunnel models to represent the effects of the turbo-fan engines plus pylons.

   Comment on the realism of this technique.

III.3.9 Interference effects of weapons or stores

Weapons and/or stores are carried externally on combat aeroplanes, beneath the fuselage, below wings and at wing tips, as shown in Fig. III.53. The main aerodynamic effect is a large increase in drag, sometimes doubling C_{D0}, affecting performance. But there are effects on aerodynamic lift and pitching moment which influence the longitudinal flight dynamic characteristics.

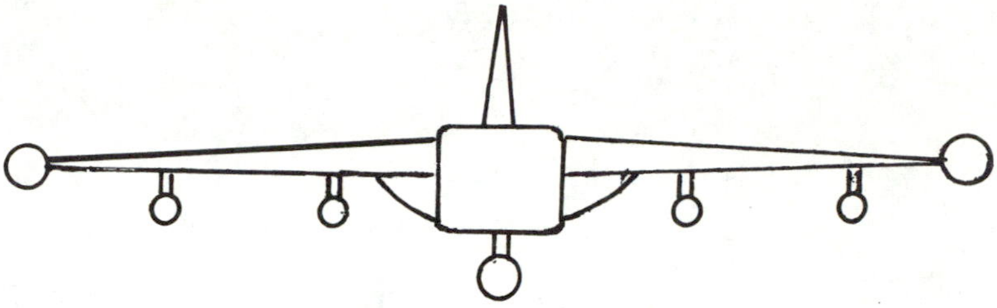

Fig. III.53. External weapons/stores.

Weapons attached to the undersurface of the fuselage do not introduce any significant changes in the fuselage lift or moment.

When a weapon is attached to the lower surface of a wing in-board of the wing tip, as shown in Fig. III.54(i), the weapon tends to 'straighten out' the flow, reducing the lift on the wing in the vicinity of the weapon. A typical lift curve is sketched in Fig. III.54(ii).

If it is assumed that this loss of lift acts through the $\frac{1}{4}$ chord point of the wing chord above the weapon, then the spanwise location of the weapon can alter the pitching moment characteristics at zero lift (i.e. $(m_0)_{wf}$), as shown in Fig. III.54(iii).

Underwing weapons also introduce two other effects:

(i) The value of the break incidence α_b is reduced because flow separation and breakdown occur at a lower angle of incidence.

(ii) Part of a low tailplane can be immersed in the thick wake of lower dynamic pressure behind the weapon(s), reducing the tailplane efficiency.

A weapon, or store, located at a wing tip (Fig. III.55) has a different effect. The weapon acts as a partial wing tip fence increasing the lift on the wing in the region of the wing tip. Thus there is a positive contribution to $(a_\alpha)_{wf}$ and, for a swept wing, an aft movement of the aerodynamic centre.

For further information see refs III.25–III.27.

EXAMPLES III.18

1. Estimate the change in $(m_0)_{wf}$ for weapons situated

   (a) at 35% semi-span,
   (b) at 70% semi-span,

   on a combat wing ($AR_w = 3.5$, $\Lambda_w = 45°$, $\lambda_w = \frac{1}{2}$), assuming that the change in lift coefficient due to the weapons is $\Delta C_L = -0.1$.

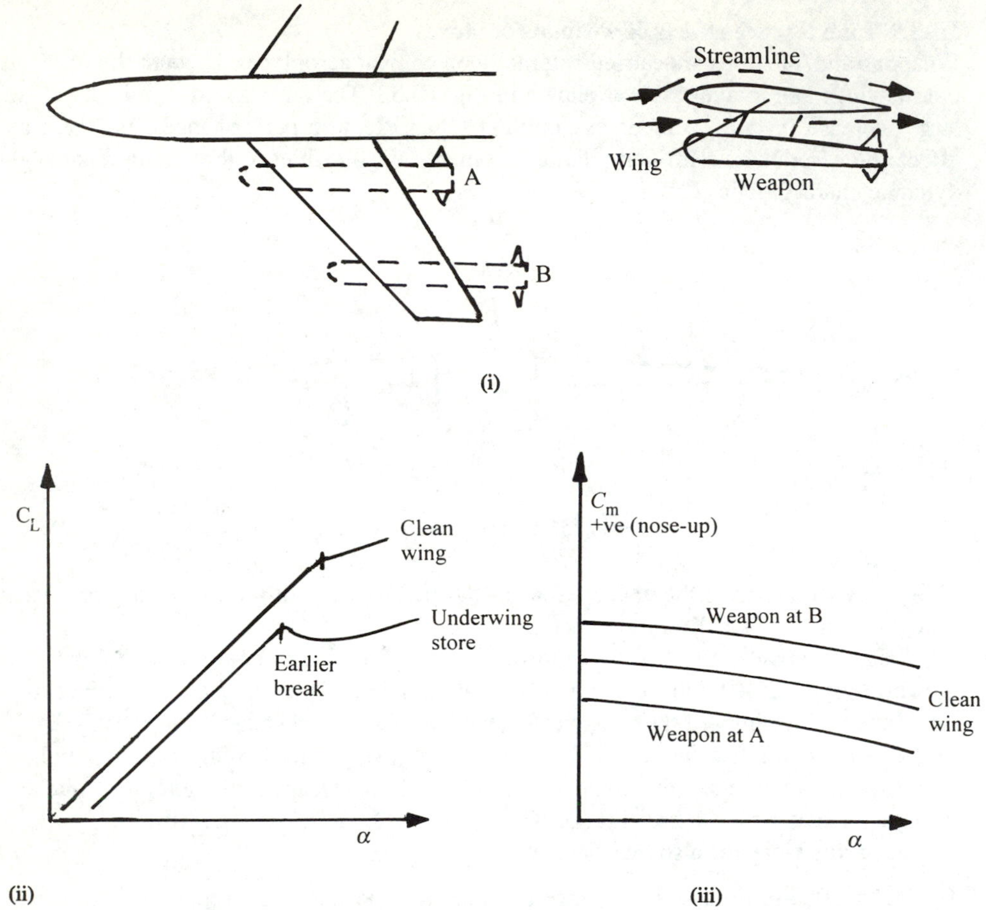

Fig. III.54. Effects of underwing weapons.

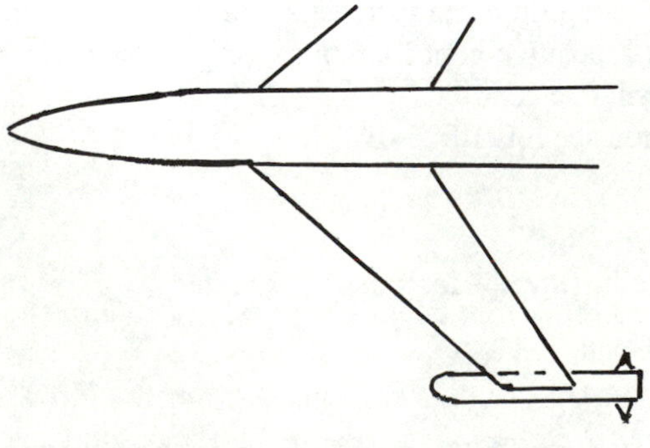

Fig. III.55. Weapons/stores at wing tip.

2. Estimate the changes in aerodynamic centre and $(m_0)_{wf}$ for weapons situated at the wing tips on a combat wing which increase $(a_\alpha)_{wf}$ by 5%.

III.3.10 Overall aeroplane aerodynamic longitudinal loads

The overall aerodynamic loads on an aeroplane undergoing a motion defined by $U(t)$, $\alpha(t)$ and $\theta(t)$ are now assembled from the separate loads described in the previous sections. This exercise is a piece of bookkeeping; it is rather tedious, but unavoidable. There is an element of arbitrariness in the formulation of the assembly procedure concerning which reference aerodynamic centre to take (e.g. aerodynamic centre of wing alone or aerodynamic centre of wing–fuselage combination or the aerodynamic centre of the wing–fuselage–nacelle/engine combination) but as long as the bookkeeping is done properly there should be no ambiguity in the final equations.

At this stage

(i) for the light aeroplane, all effects of the propeller slipstream on lift and pitching moment are omitted,
(ii) for the combat aeroplane, the effects of weapons and stores are omitted.

The aerodynamic lifts, moments and where they act are shown in Fig. III.56.

(i) L_{wf} is the lift on the wing–fuselage combination, no tailplane, no propeller, no engines or nacelles or pylons, and no weapons or stores.
(ii) L_{wf} is taken to act through the (static) aerodynamic centre of the wing–fuselage combination, which is located a distance $l_{wf}c_w$ ahead of the overall aeroplane centre of mass.
(iii) The pitching moment $\mathcal{M}_{wf}$ on the wing–fuselage combination, which acts about a pitch axis through the aerodynamic centre of the wing–fuselage combination, is, by definition, independent of the static angle of incidence, α.
(iv) On a light aeroplane the normal force on the propeller, N_{prop}, acts at the propeller disc which is located a distance $l_{prop}c_w$ ahead of the overall aeroplane centre of mass.

   On a transport or combat aeroplane N_{nac} is the normal force acting on the engines' nacelles. The small mutual interference on lift between nacelle–pylon–wing is neglected here. The normal force N_{nac} acts through its centre of pressure which is located a distance $l_{nac}c_w$ ahead of the overall aeroplane centre of mass.
(v) The lift L_t is the lift on the tailplane, which is located a distance $l_t c_w$ aft of the overall aeroplane centre of mass.
(vi) The pitching moment acting on the tailplane about the tailplane aerodynamic centre, M_t, is usually small and is ignored.

In the above listing of lifts and where they act, the moment arms, $l_{wf}c_w$, $l_{prop}c_w$, $l_{nac}c_w$ and $l_t c_w$ are all measured from the datum of the overall aeroplane centre of mass. It should be noted that the centre of mass is not a fixed position; it can vary from flight to flight, depending how the payload is distributed through the airframe, and it can vary during flight as fuel is burnt and as weapons are launched. On Concorde, fuel is transferred during flight from one part of the aeroplane to another in order to locate the centre

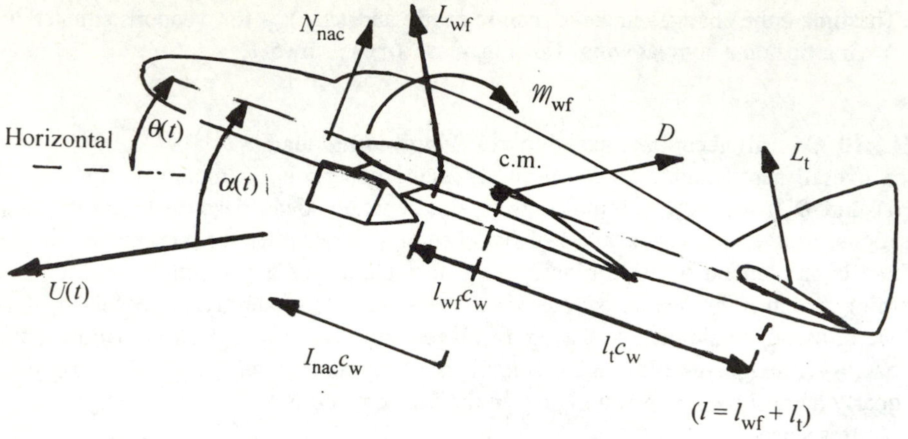

Fig. III.56(i). Aerodynamic loads on transport aeroplane.

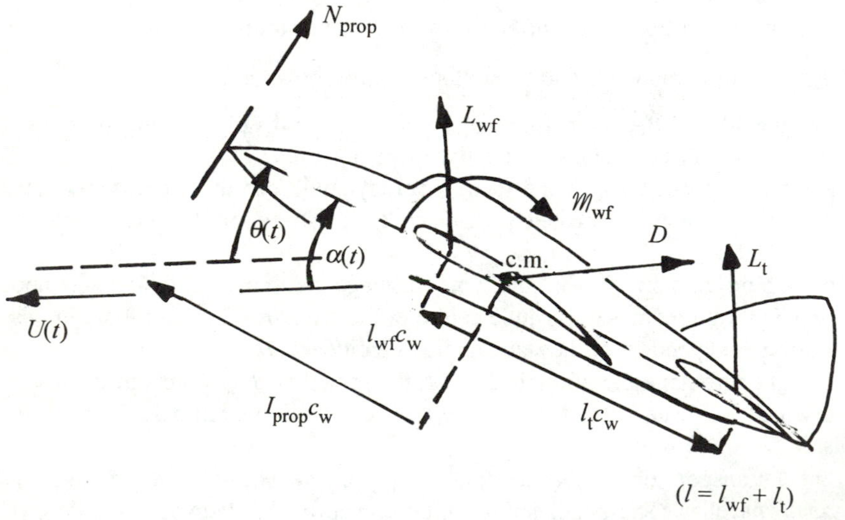

Fig. III.56(ii). Aerodynamic loads on light aeroplane.

of mass at an appropriate place for the flight Mach number. Although $l_{wf}c_w$ and $l_t c_w$ depend on the position of the centre of mass, lc_w (= $(l_{wf}c_w + l_t c_w)$, the distance from the aerodynamic centre of the wing–fuselage combination to the position of the aerodynamic centre of the tailplane (see Fig. III.56)) is independent of the position of the centre of mass, but varies slightly between subsonic and supersonic speeds.

Typically

$$l \simeq 4.0, \quad l_{prop} \simeq 2.0, \quad l_{nac} = 2.0, \tag{III.3.123}$$

at subsonic speeds $l_{wf} \simeq 0.20$; at supersonic speeds (with the same centre of mass) $l_{wf} \simeq 0.0$.

The wing–fuselage lift can be expressed in the form

$$L_{\mathrm{wf}} = \tfrac{1}{2}\rho_{\mathrm{at}}U^2(t)S_{\mathrm{w}}\Big[(a_\alpha)_{\mathrm{wf}}\big(\alpha(t)+i_{\mathrm{w}}-\alpha_{0\mathrm{w}}\big)+(a_{\dot\alpha})_{\mathrm{wf}}\big(\dot\alpha(t)c_{\mathrm{w}}/U(t)\big)$$
$$+\,(a_q)_{\mathrm{wf}}\big(q(t)c_{\mathrm{w}}/U(t)\big)+(a_{\dot q})_{\mathrm{wf}}\big(\dot q(t)c_{\mathrm{w}}^2/U^2(t)\big)\Big] \qquad \text{(III.3.124)}$$

where all derivatives vary with Mach number $M_\infty(t)$. At low Mach numbers

$$(a_\alpha)_{\mathrm{wf}} = \mathrm{O}[4.5], \quad (a_{\dot\alpha})_{\mathrm{wf}} = \mathrm{O}[-1.5],$$
$$(a_q)_{\mathrm{wf}} = \mathrm{O}[0.6], \quad (a_{\dot q})_{\mathrm{wf}} = \mathrm{O}[-0.30]. \qquad \text{(III.3.125)}$$

The wing–fuselage moment can be expressed in the form

$$\mathcal{M}_{\mathrm{wf}} = \tfrac{1}{2}\rho_{\mathrm{at}}U^2(t)S_{\mathrm{w}}c_{\mathrm{w}}\Big[(m_0)_{\mathrm{wf}}+(m_{\dot\alpha})_{\mathrm{wf}}\big(\dot\alpha(t)c_{\mathrm{w}}/U(t)\big)$$
$$+(m_q)_{\mathrm{wf}}\big(q(t)c_{\mathrm{w}}/U(t)\big)+(m_{\dot q})_{\mathrm{wf}}\big(\dot q(t)c_{\mathrm{w}}^2/U^2(t)\big)\Big]. \qquad \text{(III.3.126)}$$

At low Mach numbers

$$(m_0)_{\mathrm{wf}} = \mathrm{O}[0.01], \quad (m_{\dot\alpha})_{\mathrm{wf}} = \mathrm{O}[0.3],$$
$$(m_q)_{\mathrm{wf}} = \mathrm{O}[-1.0], \quad (m_{\dot q})_{\mathrm{wf}} = \mathrm{O}[-5.0]. \qquad \text{(III.3.127)}$$

The normal force from the propulsion unit can be expressed in the form

$$N_{\mathrm{prop}} = \mathrm{O}\big[\tfrac{1}{2}\rho_{\mathrm{at}}U^2(t)S_{\mathrm{w}}C_{\mathrm{Th}}\alpha\big]. \qquad \text{(III.3.128)}$$

$$N_{\mathrm{nac}} = \tfrac{1}{2}\rho_{\mathrm{at}}U^2(t)S_{\mathrm{w}}\big[(a_\alpha)_{\mathrm{nac}}\alpha(t)+(a_q)_{\mathrm{nac}}\,q(t)c_{\mathrm{w}}/U(t)\big]. \qquad \text{(III.3.129)}$$

At low Mach numbers, per engine,

$$(a_\alpha)_{\mathrm{nac}} \simeq (a_q)_{\mathrm{nac}} = \mathrm{O}[0.035]. \qquad \text{(III.3.130)}$$

The tailplane lift can be expressed in the form

$$L_{\mathrm{t}} = \tfrac{1}{2}\rho_{\mathrm{at}}U^2(t)S_{\mathrm{t}}\Big[(a_\alpha)_{\mathrm{t}}\big[i_{\mathrm{t}}-(\partial\varepsilon/\partial\alpha)(i_{\mathrm{w}}-\alpha_{0\mathrm{w}})+(1-\partial\varepsilon/\partial\alpha)\alpha(t)$$
$$+(\partial\varepsilon/\partial\alpha)(0.7+k_\varepsilon l)\big(\dot\alpha(t)c_{\mathrm{w}}/U(t)\big)$$
$$+l_{\mathrm{t}}\big(q(t)c_{\mathrm{w}}/U(t)\big)\big]$$
$$+(a_{\dot\alpha})_{\mathrm{t}}l_{\mathrm{t}}\big(\dot q(t)c_{\mathrm{w}}^2/U^2(t)\big)$$
$$+a_\eta\eta(t)+a_{\dot\eta}\big(\dot\eta(t)c_{\mathrm{w}}/U(t)\big)\Big] \qquad \text{(III.3.131)}$$

At low Mach numbers

$$(a_\alpha)_t = O[4.0], \quad (a_{\dot\alpha})_t = O[-2.0], \quad \partial\varepsilon/\partial\alpha \simeq 0.5, \quad k_\varepsilon \simeq 0.75$$
$$a_\eta = O[2.4], \quad a_{\dot\eta} = O[-1.2]. \qquad \text{(III.3.132)}$$

Summing the above lifts, assuming all angles small, the overall aerodynamic lift, L, for a transport or combat aeroplane is given by

$$\begin{aligned} L &= L_{wf} + N_{nac} + L_t \\ &= \tfrac{1}{2}\rho_{at}U^2(t)S_w\left[C_L\left(M_\infty(t), \alpha(t), q(t)\,|t\right)\right] \\ &= \tfrac{1}{2}\rho_{at}U^2(t)S_w\Big[C_{L0} + C_{L\alpha}\alpha(t) + C_{L\dot\alpha}\left(\dot\alpha(t)(c_w/2)/U(t)\right) \\ &\qquad + C_{Lq}\left(q(t)(c_w/2)/U(t)\right) + C_{L\dot q}\left(\dot q(t)(c_w/2)^2/U^2(t)\right) \\ &\qquad + C_{L\eta}\eta(t) + C_{L\dot\eta}\left(\dot\eta(t)(c_w/2)/U(t)\right)\Big] \end{aligned}$$

(III.3.133)

where

$$\begin{aligned} C_{L0} &= (a_\alpha)_{wf}(i_w - \alpha_{0w}) + (S_t/S_w)(a_\alpha)_t\left[i_t - (\partial\varepsilon/\partial\alpha)(i_w - \alpha_{0w})\right] && = O[0.2] \\ C_{L\alpha} &= (a_\alpha)_{wf} + (a_\alpha)_{nac} + (S_t/S_w)(a_\alpha)_t(1 - \partial\varepsilon/\partial\alpha) && = O[5.0] \\ C_{L\dot\alpha} &= 2\left[(a_{\dot\alpha})_{wf} + (S_t/S_w)(a_\alpha)_t(\partial\varepsilon/\partial\alpha)(0.7 + k_\varepsilon l)\right] && = O[-0.6] \\ C_{Lq} &= 2\left[(a_q)_{wf} + (a_q)_{nac} + (S_t/S_w)(a_\alpha)_t l_t\right] && = O[6.0] \\ C_{L\dot q} &= 4\left[(a_{\dot q})_{wf} + (S_t/S_w)(a_{\dot\alpha})_t l_t\right] && = O[-6.0] \\ C_{L\eta} &= (S_t/S_w)a_\eta && = O[0.5] \\ C_{L\dot\eta} &= 2(S_t/S_w)a_{\dot\eta}. && = O[-0.5]. \end{aligned}$$

The orders of magnitude quoted are for low Mach numbers.

For a light aeroplane, replace $(a_\alpha)_{nac}$ by C_{Th}.

The form of eqn. (III.3.133), with its definition of overall derivatives, is consistent with USA notation; the reason for the unit of length being taken as $c_w/2$ goes back to the earliest days of elementary aerofoil theory based on conformal mapping techniques.

Some observations on the above overall aeroplane lift derivatives are:

C_{L0} is composed of two terms; the first is positive, because $(i_w - \alpha_{0w})$ is positive, the second is negative because i_t is negative;

$C_{L\alpha}$ the overall aeroplane lift derivative due to angle of incidence, is dominated by the main wing contribution; the tailplane contributes about 10%, the nacelle contribution is negligible;

$C_{L\dot\alpha}$ is the overall lift derivative due to rate of change of angle of incidence; the wing–fuselage contribution is negative while the tailplane contribution is positive; the net value is small;

C_{Lq} is the overall aeroplane lift derivative due to rate of pitch; the main contribution arises from the tailplane; plus an additional contribution from the wing–fuselage of approximately 20%;

$C_{L\dot{q}}$ is the overall aeroplane lift due to pitch acceleration; the main contribution arises from the tailplane;

$C_{L\eta}$ is the overall lift derivative due to elevator deflection;

$C_{L\dot{\eta}}$ is the overall lift derivative due to the rate of elevator deflection.

The overall drag force, D, is assumed to act through the centre of mass where

$$D = \tfrac{1}{2}\rho_{at}U^2(t)S_w C_D, \qquad C_D = C_{D0} + C_{DL}. \tag{III.3.134}$$

Below the drag rise Mach number,

$$C_{D0} \simeq 0.02, \qquad C_{DL} \simeq C_L^2/(\pi AR_w).$$

Above the drag rise Mach number, through the transonic range, C_{D0} increases by a factor of approximately 2.5 before decreasing with increase in Mach number; and C_{DL} increases to $(C_L\alpha)$ when the wing leading edge goes sonic.

The overall aerodynamic pitching moment, $\mathcal{M}$, about the centre of mass is denoted by

$$\begin{aligned}\mathcal{M} &= \tfrac{1}{2}\rho_{at}U^2(t)S_w c_w\Big[C_m\big(M_\infty(t),\alpha(t),q(t)\,|\,t\big)\Big]\\ &= \tfrac{1}{2}\rho_{at}U^2(t)S_w c_w\Big[C_{m0} + C_{m\alpha}\alpha(t) + C_{m\dot{\alpha}}\big(\dot{\alpha}(t)(c_w/2)/U(t)\big)\\ &\qquad + C_{mq}\big(q(t)(c_w/2)/U(t)\big) + C_{m\dot{q}}\big(\dot{q}(t)(c_w/2)^2/U^2(t)\big)\\ &\qquad + C_{m\eta}\eta(t) + C_{m\dot{\eta}}\big(\dot{\eta}(t)c_w/U(t)\big)\Big]\end{aligned} \tag{III.3.135}$$

where

$$\begin{aligned}
C_{m0} &= (m_0)_{wf} + l_{wf}(a_\alpha)_{wf}(i_w - \alpha_{0w})\\
&\qquad - l_t(S_t/S_w)(a_\alpha)_t\big[i_t - (\partial\varepsilon/\partial\alpha)(i_w - \alpha_{0w})\big] && = O[0.2]\\
C_{m\alpha} &= l_{wf}(a_\alpha)_{wf} + l_{nac}(a_\alpha)_{nac} - l_t(S_t/S_w)(a_\alpha)_t(1 - \partial\varepsilon/\partial\alpha)\\
&= l_{wf}C_{L\alpha} + l_{nac}(a_\alpha)_{nac} - l(S_t/S_w)(a_\alpha)_t(1 - \partial\varepsilon/\partial\alpha)\\
C_{m\dot{\alpha}} &= 2\big[(m_{\dot{\alpha}})_{wf} + l_{wf}(a_{\dot{\alpha}})_{wf} - l_t(S_t/S_w)(a_\alpha)_t(\partial\varepsilon/\partial\alpha)(0.7 + k_\varepsilon l)\big] && = O[-7.0]\\
C_{mq} &= 2\big[(m_q)_{wf} + l_{wf}(a_q)_{wf} + l_{nac}(a_q)_{nac} - l_t\big[(S_t/S_w)(a_\alpha)_t l_t\big]\big] && = O[-16.0]\\
C_{m\dot{q}} &= 4\big[(m_{\dot{q}})_{wf} + l_{wf}(a_{\dot{q}})_{wf} - l_t\big[(S_t/S_w)(a_{\dot{\alpha}})_t l_t\big]\big] && = O[-6.0]\\
C_{m\eta} &= -(S_t/S_w)l_t a_\eta && = O[-1.5]\\
C_{m\dot{\eta}} &= 2(S_t/S_w)l_t a_{\dot{\eta}} && = O[1.5]
\end{aligned}$$

The order of magnitude of $C_{m\alpha}$ is discussed later in section III.3.12.

The orders of magnitude are for low Mach numbers.

For a light aeroplane replace $(a_\alpha)_{\text{nac}}$ and l_{nac} by C_{Th} and l_{prop} respectively.

Some observations on the above overall aeroplane moment derivatives are:

C_{m0} for a swept wing all of the contributions are positive, for a non-swept wing all of the contributions except $(m_0)_{\text{wf}}$ are positive;

$C_{m\alpha}$ the overall pitching moment derivative due to angle of incidence is primarily a small difference between a positive wing contribution and a negative tailplane contribution;

$C_{m\dot{\alpha}}$ the overall pitching moment derivative due to the rate of change of angle of incidence arises primarily from the downwash lag at the tailplane; the wing–fuselage contribution is negligible;

C_{mq} the overall pitching moment derivative due to rate of pitch is dominated by the negative tailplane contribution; the $(a_q)_{\text{wf}}$ and $(a_q)_{\text{nac}}$ terms are negligible; for a swept wing the negative $(m_q)_{\text{wf}}$ term contributes approximately 10%, for a non-swept wing the $(m_q)_{\text{wf}}$ term is negligible;

$C_{m\dot{q}}$ the overall pitching moment due to pitch acceleration is the difference between two approximately equal contributions from the fuselage and tailplane;

$C_{m\eta}$ is the overall pitching moment derivative due to elevator angle,

$C_{m\dot{\eta}}$ is the overall pitching moment derivative due to rate of change of elevator angle.

In practice the estimation and validation of derivatives is an intensive, thorough and expensive activity in manpower and facilities, involving

(i) preliminary estimates from empirical data as presented in the ESDU Data Sheets and the USAAF Dat(a) Com(pendium); all aerospace companies have their own in-house files of empirical data,

(ii) computational aerodynamics,

(iii) comprehensive wind tunnel tests,

(iv) comprehensive flight tests on the prototype aeroplanes.

EXAMPLES III.19

1. On the basis of the data given in this book plot the following derivatives against Mach number for the three basic configurations, taking $l_{\text{wf}} = 0.12$ at subsonic speeds:

$$C_{L0},\ C_{L\alpha},\ C_{Lq},\ C_{L\dot{\alpha}},\ C_{L\eta},\ C_{m0},\ C_{m\alpha},\ C_{m\dot{\alpha}},\ C_{mq},\ C_{m\dot{q}},\ C_{m\dot{\eta}}.$$

III.3.11 Overall aeroplane aerodynamic loads in perturbed motions

Consider an aeroplane in trimmed steady level flight with

$$U(t) = U_{\text{trim}}, \quad \alpha(t) = \theta(t) = \alpha_{\text{trim}}, \quad \eta(t) = \eta_{\text{trim}}. \qquad \text{(III.3.136)}$$

And then

$$L_{\text{trim}} = \tfrac{1}{2}\rho_{\text{at}}U_{\text{trim}}^2 S_{\text{w}}(C_{\text{L}})_{\text{trim}}, \qquad (C_{\text{L}})_{\text{trim}} = C_{\text{L0}} + C_{\text{L}\alpha}\alpha_{\text{trim}} + C_{\text{L}\eta}\eta_{\text{trim}}$$
$$D_{\text{trim}} = \tfrac{1}{2}\rho_{\text{at}}U_{\text{trim}}^2 S_{\text{w}}(C_{\text{D}})_{\text{trim}}, \qquad (C_{\text{D}})_{\text{trim}} \simeq C_{\text{D0}} + (C_{\text{L}})_{\text{trim}}^2/(\pi \text{AR}_{\text{w}})$$
$$M_{\text{trim}} = \tfrac{1}{2}\rho_{\text{at}}U_{\text{trim}}^2 S_{\text{w}}c_{\text{w}}(C_m)_{\text{trim}}, \qquad (C_m)_{\text{trim}} = C_{m0} + C_{m\alpha}\alpha_{\text{trim}} + C_{m\eta}\eta_{\text{trim}}$$
(III.3.137)

The derivatives C_{L0}, $C_{\text{L}\alpha}$, $C_{\text{L}\eta}$, C_{D0}, C_{m0}, $C_{m\alpha}$ and $C_{m\eta}$, and the trim angles α_{trim} and η_{trim} all depend on the (trim) Mach number M_∞ $(= U_{\text{trim}}/a_{\text{at}})$.

Consider this trimmed state to be perturbed in a time varying motion defined by

$$U(t) = U_{\text{trim}} + \Delta U(t), \qquad \alpha(t) = \alpha_{\text{trim}} + \Delta\alpha(t),$$
$$\theta(t) = \alpha_{\text{trim}} + \Delta\theta(t), \qquad q(t) = \Delta\dot{\theta}(t), \qquad \eta(t) = \eta_{\text{trim}} + \Delta\eta(t)$$
(III.3.138)

assuming that $(\Delta U(t)/U_{\text{trim}})$, $\Delta\alpha(t)$, $\Delta\theta(t)$ and $\Delta\eta(t)$ are all small.

Then

$$\begin{aligned}
L(t) &= \tfrac{1}{2}\rho_{\text{at}}U^2(t)S_{\text{w}}\big[C_{\text{L}}\big(M_\infty(t),\ \alpha(t),\ \theta(t)|\ t\big)\big] \\
&= \tfrac{1}{2}\rho_{\text{at}}\big[U_{\text{trim}} + \Delta U(t)\big]^2 S_{\text{w}} \\
&\quad \times\big[(C_{\text{L}})_{\text{trim}} + \big(\partial(C_{\text{L}})_{\text{trim}}/\partial M_\infty\big)\Delta M_\infty(t) \\
&\qquad + C_{\text{L}\alpha}\Delta\alpha(t) + C_{\text{L}\dot{\alpha}}\big(\Delta\dot{\alpha}(t)(c_{\text{w}}/2)/U_{\text{trim}}\big) \\
&\qquad + C_{\text{L}q}\big(q(t)(c_{\text{w}}/2)/U_{\text{trim}}\big) + C_{\text{L}\dot{q}}\big(\dot{q}(t)(c_{\text{w}}/2)^2/U_{\text{trim}}^2\big) \\
&\qquad + C_{\text{L}\eta}\Delta\eta(t) + C_{\text{L}\dot{\eta}}\big(\Delta\dot{\eta}(t)(c_{\text{w}}/2)/U(t)\big)\big] \\
&= \tfrac{1}{2}\rho_{\text{at}}U_{\text{trim}}^2 S_{\text{w}} \\
&\quad \times\big[(C_{\text{L}})_{\text{trim}} + C_{\text{L}U}\big(\Delta U(t)/U_{\text{trim}}\big) \\
&\qquad + C_{\text{L}\alpha}\Delta\alpha(t) + C_{\text{L}\dot{\alpha}}\big(\Delta\dot{\alpha}(t)(c_{\text{w}}/2)/U_{\text{trim}}\big) \\
&\qquad + C_{\text{L}q}\big(q(t)(c_{\text{w}}/2)/U_{\text{trim}}\big) + C_{\text{L}\dot{q}}\big(\dot{q}(t)(c_{\text{w}}/2)^2/U_{\text{trim}}^2\big) \\
&\qquad + C_{\text{L}\eta}\Delta\eta(t) + C_{\text{L}\eta}\big(\Delta\dot{\eta}(t)(c_{\text{w}}/2)/U_{\text{trim}}\big)\big]
\end{aligned}$$
(III.3.139)

neglecting all products of small terms, where

$$C_{\text{L}U} = \big[2(C_{\text{L}})_{\text{trim}} + M_\infty\big(\partial(C_{\text{L}})_{\text{trim}}/\partial M_\infty\big)\big]$$

Similarly,

$$D(t) = \tfrac{1}{2}\rho_{\text{at}}U_{\text{trim}}^2 S_{\text{w}}\big[(C_{\text{D}})_{\text{trim}} + C_{\text{D}U}\big(\Delta U(t)/U_{\text{trim}}\big) + C_{\text{D}\alpha}\Delta\alpha(t)\big] \qquad \text{(III.3.140)}$$

where

$$C_{DU} = 2(C_D)_{trim} + M_\infty\big(\partial(C_D)_{trim}/\partial M_\infty\big),$$

$$C_{D\alpha} = \partial C_{DL}/\partial\alpha \simeq 2(C_L)_{trim}\, C_{L\alpha}/(\pi AR_w) \text{ at subsonic speeds},$$

ignoring the effects of $\Delta\dot{\alpha}(t)$, $q(t)$, and $\Delta\eta(t)$ on drag.

And

$$\begin{aligned}\mathcal{M}(t) = \tfrac{1}{2}\rho_{at}U_{trim}^2 S_w\\ \times\Big[(C_m)_{trim} + C_{mU}\big(\Delta U(t)/U_{trim}\big)\\ + C_{m\alpha}\Delta\alpha(t) + C_{m\dot{\alpha}}\big(\Delta\dot{\alpha}(t)(c_w/2)/U_{trim}\big)\\ + C_{mq}\big(q(t)(c_w/2)/U_{trim}\big) + C_{m\dot{q}}\big(\dot{q}(t)(c_w/2)^2/U_{trim}^2\big)\\ + C_{m\eta}\Delta\eta(t) + C_{m\dot{\eta}}\big(\Delta\dot{\eta}(t)(c_w/2)/U_{trim}\big)\Big]\end{aligned} \quad \text{(III.3.141)}$$

where

$$C_{mU} = 2(C_m)_{trim} + M_\infty\big(\partial(C_m)_{trim}/\partial M_\infty\big).$$

III.3.12 Incidence stiffness

An incidence stiffness, K_α, is introduced, defined by the relationship

$$\begin{aligned}K_\alpha &= (-C_{m\alpha})/C_{L\alpha}\\ &= -l_{wf} - \big[l_{nac}(a_\alpha)_{nac}/C_{L\alpha}\big]\\ &\quad + \big[l(S_t/S_w)(1-\partial\varepsilon/\partial\alpha)\big]\big[(a_\alpha)_t/C_{L\alpha}\big]\end{aligned} \quad \text{(III.3.142)}$$

from the formula for $C_{m\alpha}$ in eqn. (III.3.135).

As demonstrated later, the condition $K_\alpha > 0$ plays a fundamental role in ensuring satisfactory stability and control characteristics.

In the literature on flight dynamics one of the most popular parameters is the static margin, but there are different interpretations of its definition and usage at higher Mach numbers. Hence an alternative parameter, the incidence stiffness, is introduced; this incidence stiffness as defined in eqn. (III.3.142), which is identical to the conventional static margin at low Mach numbers, is unambiguous throughout the Mach number range. Etkin (ref. P.15), refers to K_α as the 'pitch stiffness'; the phrase 'incidence stiffness' is thought to be more appropriate because incidence, not pitch, is the variable involved.

For the incidence stiffness, eqn. (III.3.142), at low Mach numbers,

(i) the positive tailplane contribution

$$\big[l(S_t/S_w)(1-\partial\varepsilon/\partial\alpha)\big]\big[(a_\alpha)_t/C_{L\alpha}\big] = O[0.30], \quad \text{(III.3.143)}$$

is independent of the position of the centre of mass,

(ii) the negative engines/nacelle contribution for two engines

$$-l_{\mathrm{nac}}\,(a_\alpha)_{\mathrm{nac}}/C_{\mathrm{L}\alpha} = \mathrm{O}[-0.025] \qquad \text{(III.3.144)}$$

is relatively insensitive to small changes in the position of the centre of mass,

(iii) the negative wing–fuselage contribution

$$(-l_{\mathrm{wf}}) = \mathrm{O}[-0.2] \qquad \text{(III.3.145)}$$

is extremely sensitive to small changes in the position of the centre of mass.

As the centre of mass is moved aft l_{wf} increases so K_α decreases. On the basis of the above numbers, eqns. (III.3.143) and (III.3.144),

$$\begin{aligned} &\text{when } l_{\mathrm{wf}} = 0.1, && K_\alpha = +0.175 \\ &\text{when } l_{\mathrm{wf}} = 0.275, && K_\alpha = \ \ 0.0 \\ &\text{when } l_{\mathrm{wf}} = 0.4, && K_\alpha = -0.125. \end{aligned} \qquad \text{(III.3.146)}$$

Hence $K_\alpha > 0$ when $l_{\mathrm{wf}} < 0.275$, which determines an aft limit on the centre of mass location for positive incidence stiffness at low Mach numbers.

By its definition K_α is zero when the centre of mass coincides with the overall aeroplane aerodynamic centre. And so K_α can be re-expressed by the alternative formula

$$K_\alpha = -l_{\mathrm{wf}} + h_{\mathrm{ac}} \qquad \text{(III.3.147)}$$

where $h_{\mathrm{ac}}c_{\mathrm{w}}$ is the distance of the overall aeroplane aerodynamic centre aft of the wing fuselage aerodynamic centre.

The variation of incidence stiffness with Mach number can be deduced.

(i) At low Mach numbers typically $l_{\mathrm{wf}} = 0.10$, $(lS_{\mathrm{t}}/S_{\mathrm{w}}) = 0.7$, $l_{\mathrm{nac}} = 2.0$, $(a_\alpha)_{\mathrm{nac}}/C_{\mathrm{L}\alpha} = 0.015$, $(a_\alpha)_{\mathrm{t}}/C_{\mathrm{L}\alpha} = 0.8$, and $\partial\varepsilon/\partial\alpha = 0.45$, then

$$K_\alpha = 0.18. \qquad \text{(III.3.148)}$$

(ii) With increase in Mach number at subsonic speeds the positions of the aerodynamic centres and the ratios $(a_\alpha)_{\mathrm{nac}}/C_{\mathrm{L}\alpha}$ and $(a_\alpha)_{\mathrm{t}}/C_{\mathrm{L}\alpha}$ can be assumed to remain constant, but the downwash $\partial\varepsilon/\partial\alpha$ increases. At a high subsonic Mach number if $\partial\varepsilon/\partial\alpha$ has increased by a factor 1.2 then

$$K_\alpha = 0.13; \qquad \text{(III.3.149)}$$

a substantial reduction compared to the low speed value.

(iii) At supersonic speeds there is a substantial aft displacement of the wing–fuselage aerodynamic centre and a significant reduction in the downwash; typically, keeping the position of the centre of mass unchanged $(l_{\mathrm{wf}} = -0.15$, $(lS_{\mathrm{t}}/S_{\mathrm{w}}) = 0.65$, $\partial\varepsilon/\partial\alpha = 0.15)$, with the other parameters $(((a_\alpha)_{\mathrm{nac}}/C_{\mathrm{L}\alpha})$, $((a_\alpha)_{\mathrm{t}}/C_{\mathrm{L}\alpha}))$ retaining their subsonic values, then

$$K_\alpha = 0.56; \qquad \text{(III.3.150)}$$

a four-fold increase relative to its high subsonic value.

The parameter (lS_t/S_w) is conventionally known as the 'tail volume', denoted by $\overline{V}$. The value of the tail volume is roughly the same for different aeroplanes even though there are large differences in l and (S_t/S_w), for example,

$$\begin{aligned} &\text{for a light aeroplane,} && l \simeq 3, \quad S_t/S_w \simeq 1/5 \\ &\text{for a transport aeroplane,} && l \simeq 5, \quad S_t/S_w \simeq 1/5 \\ &\text{for a combat aeroplane,} && l \simeq 2, \quad S_t/S_w \simeq 1/3. \end{aligned} \tag{III.3.151}$$

EXAMPLES III.20

1. On the basis of the values given in eqns. (III.3.148)–(III.3.150) sketch the variation of the location of the overall aeroplane aerodynamic centre with Mach number.
2. What flight condition determines the aft centre of mass location?
3. For a light aeroplane, what are the effects of the propeller slipstream on the incidence stiffness K_α?
4. For a combat aeroplane, what are the effects of underwing weapons on the incidence stiffness K_α?

III.4 INTRODUCTION TO PLANAR DYNAMICS

A cursory introduction to planar dynamics is presented here, sufficient to provide a background to the subsequent applications. For a wider reading the excellent text by Meriam & Kraige (ref. III.28) is highly commended.

III.4.1 Planar motion of a particle

Newton's first and second laws of motion describe the motion of a particle of mass *m*, expressed by the formula,

$$\text{applied force} = m\ (\text{absolute acceleration}) \tag{III.4.1}$$

where the absolute acceleration is in the same direction as the applied force.

Absolute acceleration refers to the acceleration relative to hypothetical axes 'fixed in space'. For the purposes of aeroplane stability and control axes 'fixed in space' can be taken to be axes fixed in the earth's surface, say in the vertical and horizontal directions, because aeroplane manoeuvres take place over a relatively short distance compared to the radius of the earth. For navigation around the earth, axes 'fixed in space' would need to be taken at the earth's centre. For interplanetary flight axes 'fixed in space' would need to be taken at the centre of the solar system.

Newton's third law of motion states that 'action and reaction are equal and opposite'. This third law is far from trivial, it is the basis of the free-body diagram in which action and reaction forces are clearly identified; the application of the free-body diagram plays a pivotal role in the derivation of solutions in virtually all problems in statics and dynamics (see Fig. III.61).

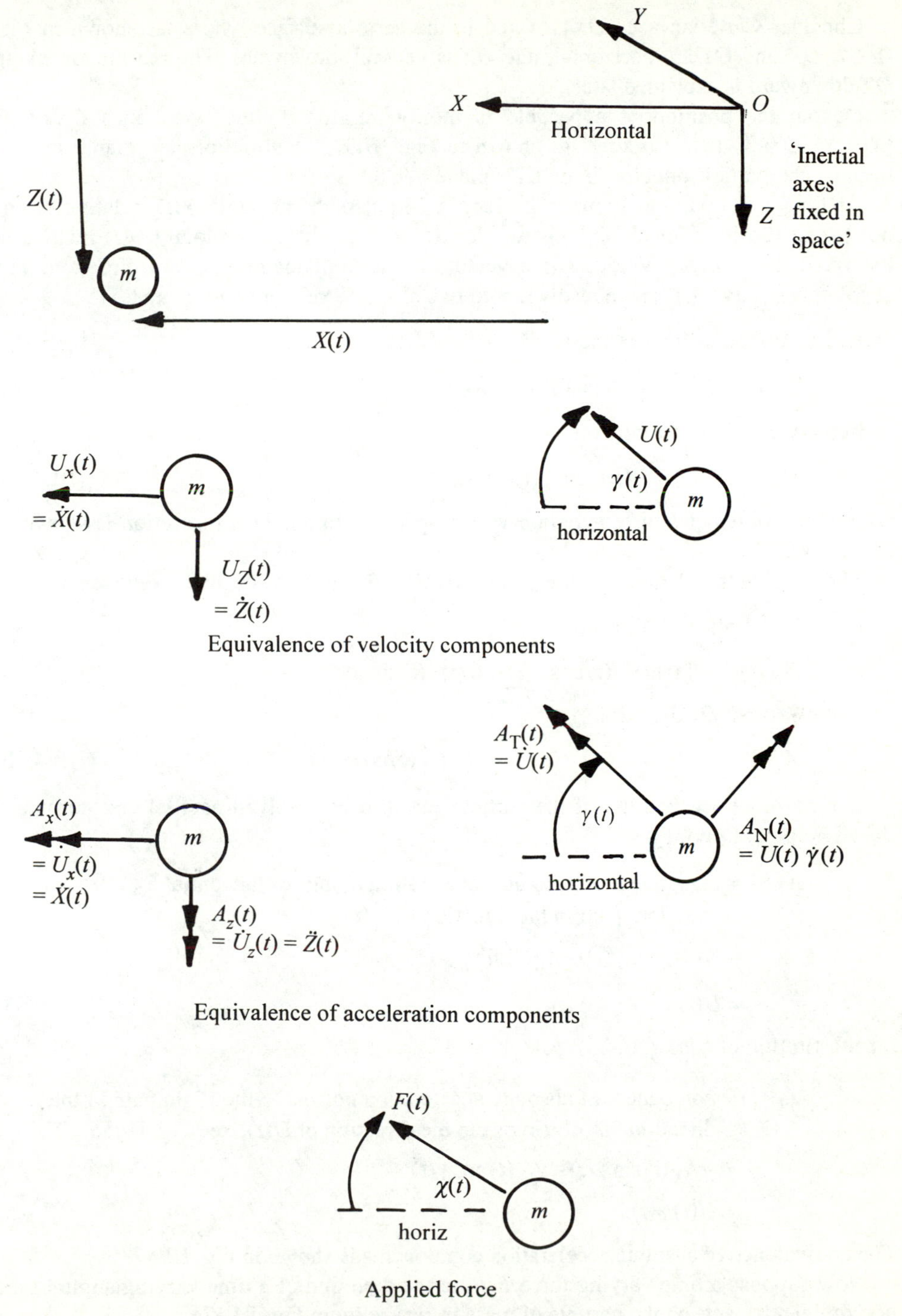

Fig. III.57. Notation for planar motion of a particle.

Consider Cartesian axes *OXYZ* fixed in the earth's surface where, as shown in Fig. III.57, *OX* and *OY* are horizontal, and *OZ* is vertical, downward. The reason for taking *OZ* downward is explained later.

Denote the position of a particle in motion relative to the fixed axes *OXYZ* as $(X(t), O, Z(t))$, where t is time, as shown in Fig. III.57. This motion is a planar motion because the particle remains in the *OXZ* plane.

At time t the particle is moving along a 'flight path' at angle $\gamma(t)$, relative to the horizontal (positive for climb, negative for descent) at absolute velocity $U(t)$ relative to the fixed axes *OXYZ*. Velocity is a vector; it has both magnitude and direction. The absolute velocity $U(t)$ can be resolved into two absolute velocity components:

in the horizontal *OX* direction,

$$U_X(t) = \dot{X}(t) = U(t)\cos\gamma(t) = \dot{X}(t) \qquad \text{(III.4.2a)}$$

in the vertical *OZ* direction,

$$U_Z(t) = \dot{Z}(t) = -U(t)\sin\gamma(t) = \dot{Z}(t) \qquad \text{(III.4.2b)}$$

where the dot denotes differentiation with respect to time t. This resolution is shown in Fig. III.57.

The absolute acceleration of the particle, which also is a vector, has components:

in the horizontal *OX* direction,

$$A_X(t) = \dot{U}_X(t) = \dot{U}(t)\cos\gamma(t) - U(t)\dot{\gamma}(t)\sin\gamma(t) \qquad \text{(III.4.3a)}$$

in the vertical *OZ* direction,

$$A_Z(t) = \dot{U}_Z(t) = -\dot{U}(t)\sin\gamma(t) - U(t)\dot{\gamma}(t)\cos\gamma(t). \qquad \text{(III.4.3b)}$$

The absolute acceleration of the particle can also be resolved parallel and normal to the flight path. Denoting

$$\begin{aligned} A_T(t) &= \text{component of absolute acceleration along, or tangential to,} \\ &\quad\ \text{the flight path in the direction of } U(t) \\ &= A_X(t)\cos\gamma(t) - A_Z(t)\sin\gamma(t) \\ &= \dot{U}(t) \qquad \text{(III.4.4)} \end{aligned}$$

on substitution of eqns. (III.4.3). And

$$\begin{aligned} A_N(t) &= \text{component of absolute acceleration normal to the flight path in the} \\ &\quad\ \text{direction } 90^\circ \text{ clockwise to the direction of } U(t)\text{, see Fig. III.56} \\ &= -A_X(t)\sin\gamma(t) - A_Z(t)\cos\gamma(t) \\ &= U(t)\dot{\gamma}(t). \qquad \text{(III.4.5)} \end{aligned}$$

The equivalence of absolute acceleration components is shown in Fig. III.57.

Now suppose a time varying force $F(t)$, in the direction of a time varying angle to the horizontal $\chi(t)$, acts on the particle of mass m, as shown in Fig. III.57.

The component equations of motion are either

$$mA_X(t) = F(t)\cos\chi(t), \qquad mA_Z(t) = -F(t)\sin\chi(t) \tag{III.4.6}$$

or

$$mA_T(t) = F(t)\cos\big(\chi(t) - \gamma(t)\big), \qquad mA_N(t) = F(t)\sin\big(\chi(t) - \gamma(t)\big). \tag{III.4.7}$$

The problem is: given $F(t)$ and its direction $\chi(t)$, determine the motion of the particle, $X(t)$ and $Z(t)$. Which pair of equations of motion to take depends on the type of force; if the force direction is defined relative to the *OXYZ* axis system then eqns. (III.4.6) are the most appropriate, whereas if the force direction is defined relative to the 'flight path' then eqns. (III.4.7) are the most convenient.

It should be emphasized that a gravitational body force is an applied force to be incorporated in the force term $F(t)$.

EXAMPLES III.21

1. Sketch the motion of a particle of mass m (i.e. determine $X(t)$, $Z(t)$, assuming $X(0) = Z(0) = 0$, $\dot{X}(0) = \dot{Z}(0) = 1$) when

   (i) $F(t) = F$, $\chi(t) = \pi/4$;
   (ii) $F(t) = F$, $\chi(t) = t$;
   (iii) $F(t) = F$, $\chi(t) = \gamma(t)$;
   (iv) $F(t) = F$, $\chi(t) = \gamma(t) + \pi/2$.

2. What is the answer to (iv) if the initial conditions are changed to

$$X(0) = Z(0) = 0, \qquad \dot{X}(0) = \dot{Z}(0) = 0\,?$$

3. Repeat Example 1 above when a gravitational field acts in the positive *OZ* direction.

III.4.2 Planar motion of a rigid body

Consider a solid body in planar motion as shown in Fig. III.58.

(i) The time varying coordinates of the centre of mass of the body are denoted $(X_{cm}(t), O, Z_{cm}(t))$ relative to axes *OXYZ* fixed in space; the motion is planar when the motion of the centre of mass remains in the *OXZ* plane.

(ii) An axis system *oxyz* is taken fixed in the body. This axis system moves and rotates with the body as that body moves through the air; the origin is located at the centre of mass, the axis *ox* points forward (for an aeroplane the *ox* axis is identified with the fuselage longitudinal axis) and the *oz* axis, perpendicular to the *ox* axis, points downward. The *oz* axis is taken downward because when the body is an aeroplane a positive component of velocity in the *oz* direction induces a positive angle of incidence; the *OZ* axis is taken downward for compatibility.

(iii) The pitch angle $\theta(t)$ is the angle from the horizontal (i.e. in the direction *OX*) to the *ox* axis, positive nose-up.

(iv) The position of the body and its orientation in space at each instant of time are defined by $X_{cm}(t)$, $Z_{cm}(t)$ and $\theta(t)$.

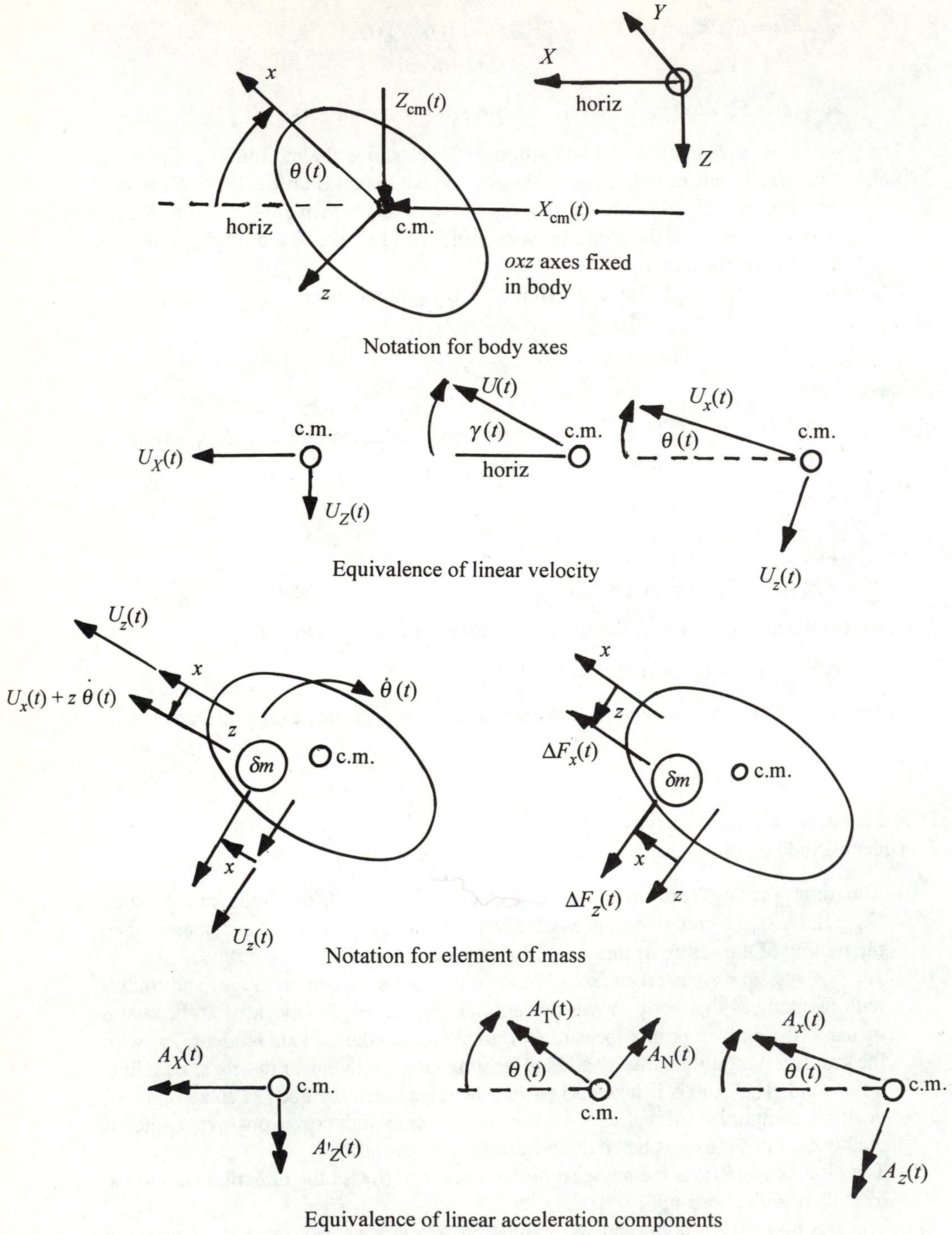

Fig. III. 58. Notation for planar motion of rigid body.

The absolute velocity of the centre of mass is $U(t)$ in the direction of the flight path, $\gamma(t)$, measured from the horizontal, positive nose-up. The components of the absolute velocity in the OX and OZ directions are

$$U_X(t) = \dot{X}_{cm}(t) = U(t)\cos\gamma(t),$$
$$U_Z(t) = \dot{Z}_{cm}(t) = -U(t)\sin\gamma(t). \quad \text{(III.4.8)}$$

The components of the absolute velocity in the (instantaneous) ox and oz directions are

$$U_x(t) = U(t)\cos\big(\theta(t)-\gamma(t)\big) = U_X(t)\cos\theta(t) - U_Z(t)\sin\theta(t)$$
$$U_z(t) = U(t)\sin\big(\theta(t)-\gamma(t)\big) = U_X(t)\sin\theta(t) + U_Z(t)\cos\theta(t) \quad \text{(III.4.9)}$$

The equivalence of these velocity components is shown in Fig. III.57.

To derive the equations of motion of a body consider a small element of mass δm located at position $P(x, y, z)$ relative to the $oxyz$ axis system; the coordinates (x, y, z) are independent of time. By definition of the centre of mass

$$\sum \delta m\, x = \sum \delta m\, y = \sum \delta m\, z = 0, \quad \text{(III.4.10)}$$

where the summation is over the totality of elements which make up the body.

The absolute velocity components of the element resolved in the ox and oz directions are denoted by $U_{Px}(t)$ and $U_{Pz}(t)$, where, by reference to Fig. III.58,

$$U_{Px}(t) = U_x(t) + z\dot{\theta}(t)$$
$$U_{Pz}(t) = U_z(t) - x\dot{\theta}(t) \quad \text{(III.4.11)}$$

where $U_x(t)$ and $U_z(t)$ are the absolute velocity components of the centre of mass resolved in the ox and oz directions given in eqns. (III.4.9).

The absolute velocity components of the element resolved in the OX and OZ directions, denoted by $U_{PX}(t)$ and $U_{PZ}(t)$, are

$$U_{PX}(t) = U_{Px}(t)\cos\theta(t) + U_{Pz}(t)\sin\theta(t),$$
$$U_{PZ}(t) = -U_{Px}(t)\sin\theta(t) + U_{Pz}(t)\cos\theta(t). \quad \text{(III.4.12)}$$

The absolute acceleration components of the element resolved in the OX and OZ directions, denoted by $A_{PX}(t)$ and $A_{PZ}(t)$, are

$$\begin{aligned}
A_{PX}(t) &= \dot{U}_{PX}(t) \\
&= \dot{U}_{Px}(t)\cos\theta(t) + \dot{U}_{Pz}(t)\sin\theta(t) \\
&\quad + \big[-U_{Px}(t)\sin\theta(t) + U_{Pz}(t)\cos\theta(t)\big]\dot{\theta}(t) \\
A_{PZ}(t) &= \dot{U}_{PZ}(t) \\
&= -\dot{U}_{Px}(t)\sin\theta(t) + \dot{U}_{Pz}(t)\cos\theta(t) \\
&\quad + \big[-U_{Px}(t)\cos\theta(t) - U_{Pz}(t)\sin\theta(t)\big]\dot{\theta}(t).
\end{aligned} \quad \text{(III.4.13)}$$

The absolute acceleration components of the element resolved in the *ox* and *oz* directions, denoted by $A_{Px}(t)$ and $A_{Pz}(t)$, are

$$\begin{aligned} A_{Px}(t) &= A_{PX}(t)\cos\theta(t) - A_{PZ}(t)\sin\theta(t) \\ &= \dot{U}_{Px}(t) + U_{Pz}\dot{\theta}(t) \\ &= \dot{U}_x(t) + z\ddot{\theta}(t) + \left[U_z(t) - x\dot{\theta}(t)\right]\dot{\theta}(t) \\ A_{Pz}(t) &= A_{PX}(t)\sin\theta(t) + A_{PZ}(t)\cos\theta(t) \\ &= \dot{U}_{Pz}(t) - U_{Px}\dot{\theta}(t) \\ &= \dot{U}_z(t) - x\ddot{\theta}(t) - \left[U_x(t) + z\dot{\theta}(t)\right]\dot{\theta}(t) \end{aligned} \tag{III.4.14}$$

on substitution of eqns. (III.4.11) and (III.4.13).

Suppose that the force components acting on the element of mass δm in the directions *ox* and *oz* are $\delta F_x(t)$ and $\delta F_z(t)$ respectively (see Fig. III.57).

The equations of motion of the element are

$$\begin{aligned} \delta F_x(t) &= \delta m\, A_{Px}(t) \\ \delta F_z(t) &= \delta m\, A_{Pz}(t). \end{aligned} \tag{III.4.15}$$

Summing over all elements,

$$\begin{aligned} \sum \delta F_x(t) &= \sum \delta m\left[\dot{U}_x(t) + z\ddot{\theta}(t) + \left[U_z(t) - x\dot{\theta}(t)\right]\dot{\theta}(t)\right] \\ \sum \delta F_z(t) &= \sum \delta m\left[\dot{U}_z(t) - x\ddot{\theta}(t) - \left[U_x(t) + z\dot{\theta}(t)\right]\dot{\theta}(t)\right] \end{aligned} \tag{III.4.16}$$

on substitution of eqns. (III.4.14); thus

$$\begin{aligned} F_x(t) &= m\left(\dot{U}_x(t) + U_z(t)\dot{\theta}(t)\right) \\ F_z(t) &= m\left(\dot{U}_z(t) - U_x(t)\dot{\theta}(t)\right) \end{aligned} \tag{III.4.17}$$

where $F_x(t)$ and $F_z(t)$ are the external force components applied to the body in the *ox* and *oz* directions on the assumption that all of the internal forces between elements cancel out in the summation process, and m is the total mass of the body $(= \sum \delta m)$—remembering that the centre of mass is located at the origin of the axes, eqn. (III.4.10).

Multiplying the first equation in eqns. (III.4.15) by z and the second equation by x, subtracting the two equations, and then summing over all elements,

$$\begin{aligned} \sum\left(z\,\delta F_x(t) - x\,\delta F_z(t)\right) &= \sum \delta m\left(zA_{Px}(t) - xA_{Pz}(t)\right) \\ &= \sum \delta m\Big[z\left[\dot{U}_x(t) + z\ddot{\theta}(t) + \left(U_z(t) - x\dot{\theta}(t)\right)\dot{\theta}(t)\right] \\ &\qquad - x\left[\dot{U}_z(t) - x\ddot{\theta}(t) - \left(U_x(t) + z\dot{\theta}(t)\right)\dot{\theta}(t)\right]\Big], \end{aligned}$$

which reduces to

$$M = I_{yy}\ddot{\theta}(t) \tag{III.4.18}$$

where M is the total pitching moment applied by the external forces and external moments about a pitch axis through the centre of mass (see Fig. III.57) and I_{yy} $(= \sum \delta m\,(x^2 + z^2))$ is the moment of inertia about the pitch axis through the centre of mass.

Eqns. (III.4.17) and (III.4.18) are the equations of motion relative to axes *oxyz* fixed in the body.

The translational equations of motion can be re-expressed relative to other axes:

1. Relative to axes *OXYZ* fixed in space

$$F_X(t) = m\dot{U}_X(t), \qquad F_Z(t) = m\dot{U}_Z(t) \tag{III.4.19}$$

   where $F_X(t)$ and $F_Z(t)$ are the components of the resultant external force in the *OX*, horizontal, and *OZ*, vertical, directions.
2. Relative to axes along and normal to the flight path

$$F_T(t) = m\dot{U}(t), \qquad F_N(t) = mU(t)\dot{\gamma}(t) \tag{III.4.20}$$

   where $F_T(t)$ and $F_N(t)$ are the components of the resultant external force along and normal to the flight path (note eqns. (III.4.4) and (III.4.5)).

However, the rotational equation is invariably expressed in terms of the body axes *oxz* (eqn. (III.4.18)).

Eqns. (III.4.17) are the most convenient for stability and control calculations. Eqns. (III.4.19) are the most convenient for navigation calculations. Eqns. (III.4.20) are used for complex manoeuvring flight.

Before beginning any calculation in dynamics it is necessary to determine the position of the centre of mass and the value of the moment of inertia—a formidable task as the mass distribution on an aeroplane is highly complex. In the design process there is continual modification in the mass distribution as the aerodynamics, engine, structures, and systems groups update their designs; every element of mass must be included, even the coats of paint on the aeroplane surface.

As an extremely simple example consider the body shown in Fig. III.59, comprising four masses δm, $2\delta m$, $3\delta m$ and $4\delta m$ at the corners of a square framework of length l and of negligible mass. Introduce a datum axis system $o_d x_d z_d$ taken parallel to the sides of the square. Let the coordinates of the centre of mass relative to the datum axis system be $(\bar{x}_d, \bar{z}_d)$. Then by definition

$$\begin{aligned} \bar{x}_d\left(\sum \delta m\right) &= \left(\sum x_d\,\delta m\right) = \delta m l + (2\delta m)l, \quad \text{so } \bar{x}_d = 0.3l, \\ \bar{z}_d\left(\sum \delta m\right) &= \left(\sum z_d\,\delta m\right) = \delta m l + (4\delta m)l, \quad \text{so } \bar{z}_d = 0.5l. \end{aligned} \tag{III.4.21}$$

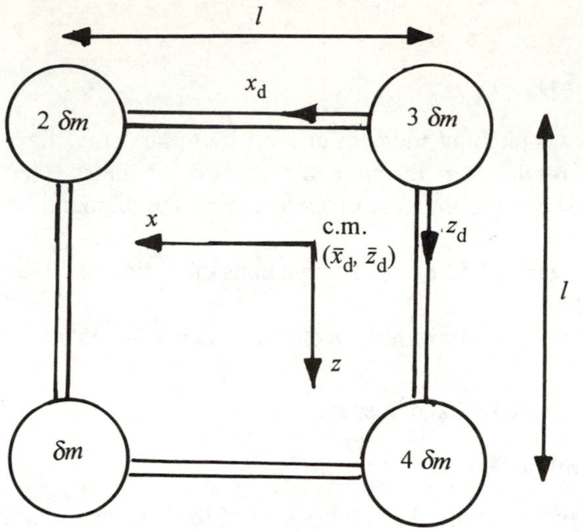

Fig. III.59. Simple body.

The moment of inertia about the centre of mass is

$$I_{yy} = \sum \delta m(x^2 + z^2) = \delta m(0.74 + 2(0.74) + 3(0.34) + 4(0.34))l^2$$
$$= 4.6\delta ml^2 = m(0.68l)^2 \qquad \text{(III.4.22)}$$

where m (= $10\delta m$) is the total mass.

The moment of inertia is often expressed in the form

$$I_{yy} = mr_g^2 \qquad \text{(III.4.23)}$$

where r_g is the radius of gyration. In the above example

$$r_g = 0.68l.$$

The calculation of the centre of mass and the moment of inertia of a complete aeroplane essentially follows the above procedure, except that the number of elements can be of the order of 50 000.

In the calculation of the moment of inertia the parallel axis theorem is extremely useful. This theorem states that

$$I_{yy} = (I_{yy})_1 - m(x_1^2 + z_1^2) \qquad \text{(III.4.24)}$$

where

I_{yy} = the moment of inertia about a pitch axis through the centre of mass as defined in eqn. (III.4.18), and

$(I_{yy})_1$ = the moment of inertia about a pitch axis through the point (x_1, z_1)

$$= \sum \delta m\left[(x - x_1)^2 + (z - z_1)^2\right]$$

III.4.3 Statics

Statics is the special case of dynamics when all accelerations are zero, thus the motion is proceeding with constant linear and angular velocities; the body is then said to be in a state of static equilibrium.

The equations of static equilibrium, from eqns. (III.4.17)–(III.4.18), are

$$F_x = F_z = M = 0. \tag{III.4.25}$$

There is one important difference between statics and dynamics. In dynamics the moment, M, in eqn. (III.4.18), must be taken about the pitch axis through the centre of mass and not about a pitch axis through any other point, whereas in statics the moment, $M = 0$, can be taken about a pitch axis through any arbitrary point.

III.4.4 D'Alembert's principle

The D'Alembert principle reduces a dynamic problem of a body in motion to an equivalent problem of static equilibrium by introducing a force on each element of body mass proportional to the mass of that element multiplied by its acceleration and acting in the opposite direction to the acceleration. The application of the D'Alembert principle to a body in motion is illustrated in Fig. III.60 where the overall equations of 'static equilibrium' are the same as the dynamic equations (eqns. (III.4.17)–(III.4.18)).

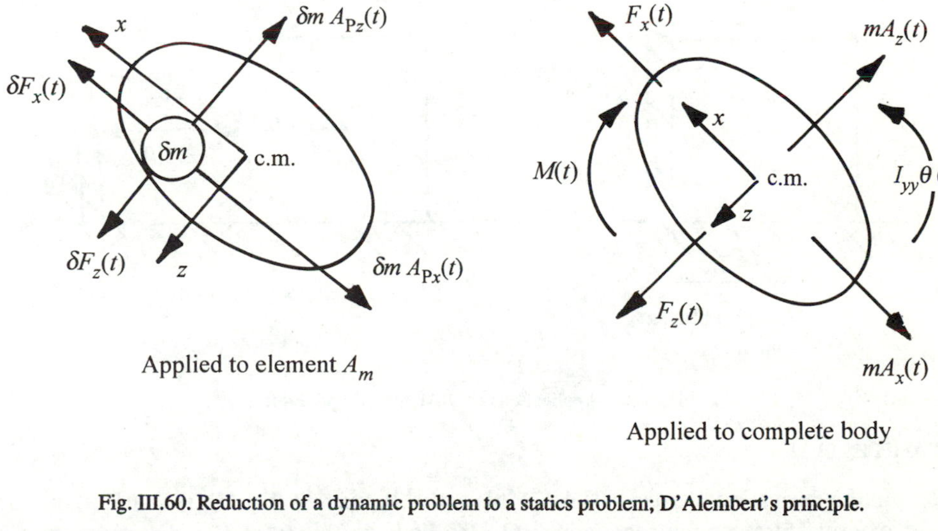

Fig. III.60. Reduction of a dynamic problem to a statics problem; D'Alembert's principle.

The D'Alembert principle is often dismissed as an irrelevancy by those applied mathematicians who regard themselves as dynamicists, and this opinion is justified in their fields of interest and application. And for the analysis of the motion of a rigid body the difference between treating the problem as one in dynamics or as one in statics, via D'Alembert, is minor. However, to understand and to analyse the flexible internal loading body in motion, D'Alembert's principle is invaluable; two simple examples are shown in Fig. III.61.

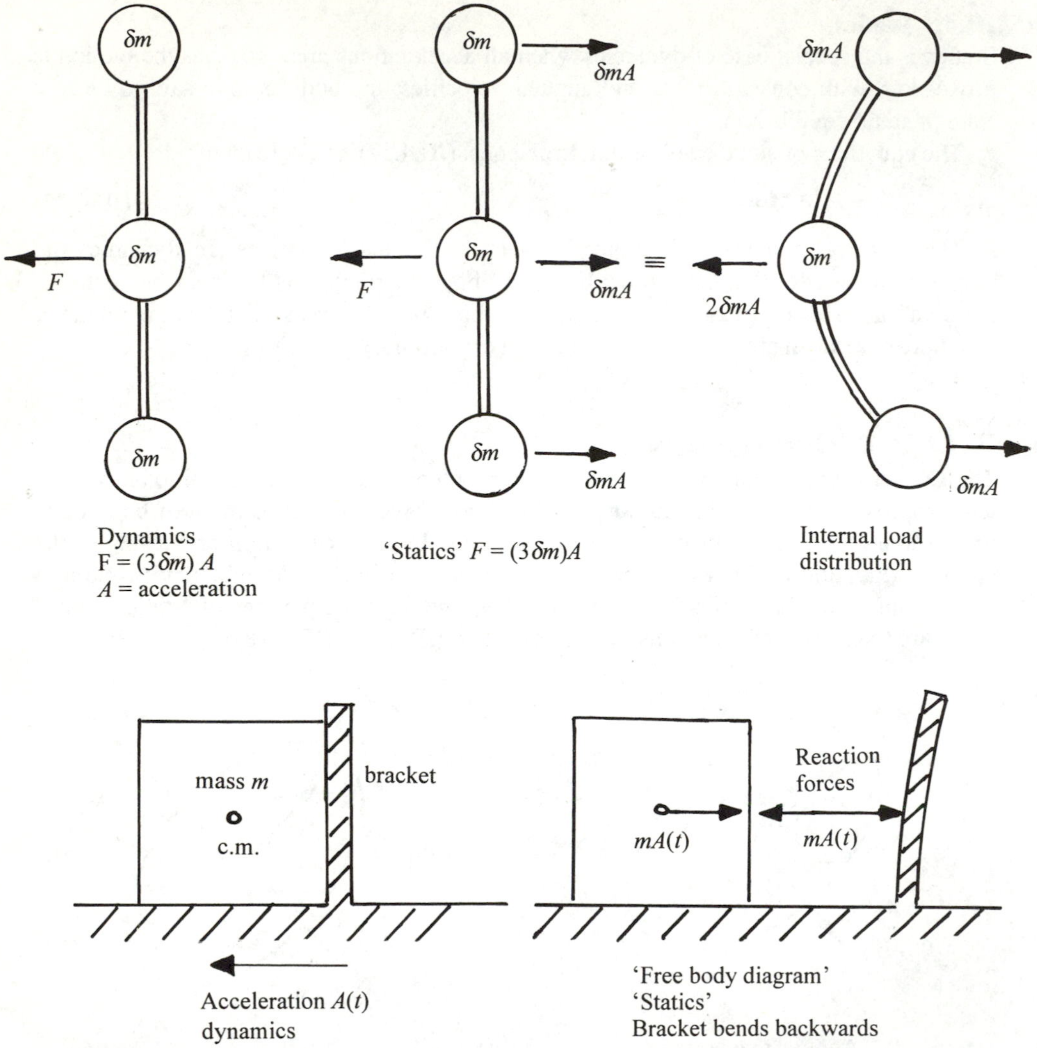

Fig. III.61. Applications of D'Alembert's principle.

EXAMPLES III.22

1. In the derivation of eqns. (III.4.17) it is stated in the text that '$F_x(t)$ and $F_z(t)$ are the external force components applied to the body in the *ox* and *oz* directions on the assumption that all of the internal forces between elements cancel out in the summation process'. Prove this statement.
2. Prove the definition of the centre of mass used in eqns. (III.4.21).
3. It is said in the text following eqn. (III.4.25) that: 'In dynamics the moment, *M*, in eqn. (III.4.18), must be taken about the pitch axis through the centre of mass and not about a pitch axis through any other point, whereas in statics the moment, $M = 0$, can be taken about a pitch axis through any arbitrary point.' Explain why.

4. The body shown in Fig. III.59, and described in the text, is stationary and then at time $t = 0$ an impulse force $F\delta(t)$ is applied as shown in Fig. III.62. Describe the subsequent motion.

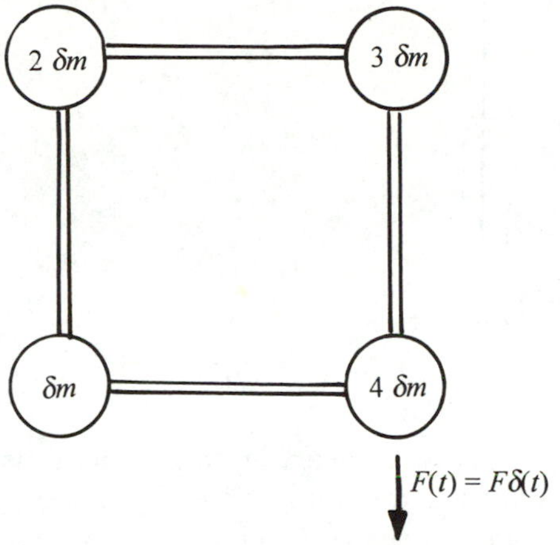

Fig. III.62. Example III.22.4.

5. The mass distribution of an aeroplane is assumed to be a set of lumped masses all in one plane, as shown in Fig. III.63. Determine
   (i) the position of the centre of mass,
   (ii) the moment of inertia.

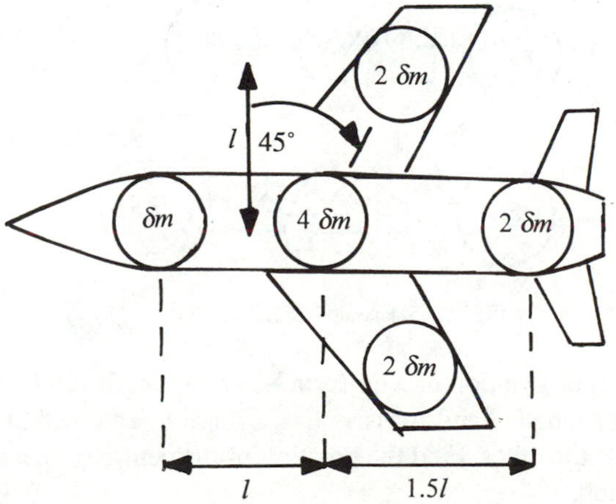

Fig. III.63. Example III.22.5.

6. Prove the parallel axis theorem, eqn. (III.4.24); apply the parallel axis theorem to derive eqn. (III.4.22).
7. The space vehicle shown in Fig. III.64 has four reaction jets at the four corners of the vehicle; each of the four jets is a bang-bang system (i.e. either on or off) and

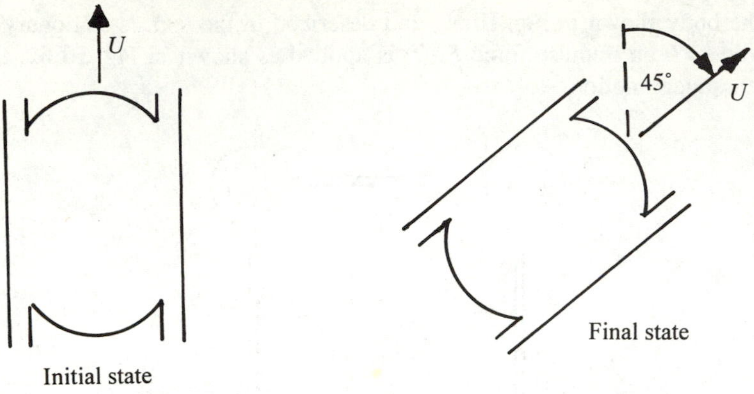

Fig. III.64. Example III.22.7.

each of the four jets can be activated separately and collectively in any combination. Initially the vehicle is travelling at constant speed U. It is desired to change flight direction by 45°, as shown in Fig. III.64, and to proceed with the same constant speed. Describe the sequence of jet activations to achieve this manoeuvre (neglect gravity).

8. A spring-damper system connects two equal masses as shown in Fig. III.65. Each mass is δm, the spring stiffness is k and the spring length is l. A constant force F is applied to one of the masses. By application of D'Alembert's principle, and the free-body diagram, estimate the extension of the spring.

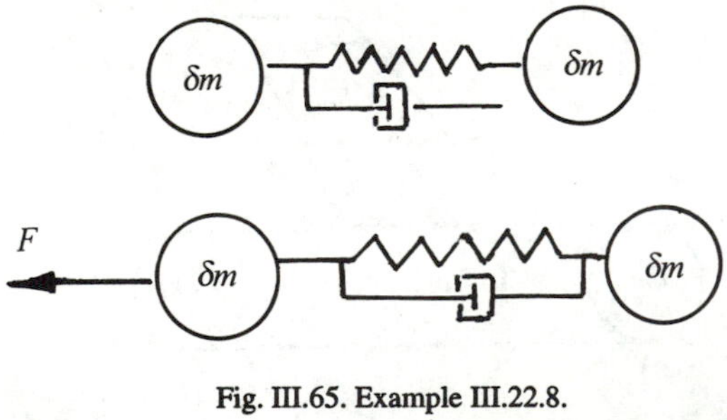

Fig. III.65. Example III.22.8.

9. Show that the radius of gyration of a uniform beam of length l is $l/\sqrt{12}$.
10. A uniform beam of length l and mass m has a mass m attached at one end and a mass $2m$ attached at the other. Find the position of the centre of mass and determine the radius of gyration.

III.5 TRIMMED FLIGHT

For trimmed flight the overall steady loads on an aeroplane must be in static equilibrium, and that condition of static equilibrium must be stable. Trimmed flight usually refers to steady level flight, steady climb and steady descent, and possibly to a steady horizontal turn.

The (human) pilot must be able to trim the aeroplane, that is,

(i) adjust the throttle and stick displacements to obtain a required steady flight condition,
(ii) once the appropriate throttle and stick displacement are set, reduce the stick force to zero and then fly 'hands-off' (this procedure is different from switching on the auto-pilot and flying 'hands-off').

In addition, the forces on the stick to change trim speed should be neither too small nor too large.

In this section static equilibrium is considered; stability is presumed and dealt with later.

III.5.1 Steady level flight

Steady level flight is concerned with an aeroplane, of given all-up weight and location of centre of mass, flying at a constant forward speed (i.e. constant Mach number) at a constant altitude with appropriate constant settings of the pilot primary controls of throttle and stick displacement.

The loads on an aeroplane in steady horizontal flight, at an angle of incidence α_{trim} (= θ_{trim}, the pitch angle), and forward speed U_{trim}, shown in Fig. III.66, can be represented by

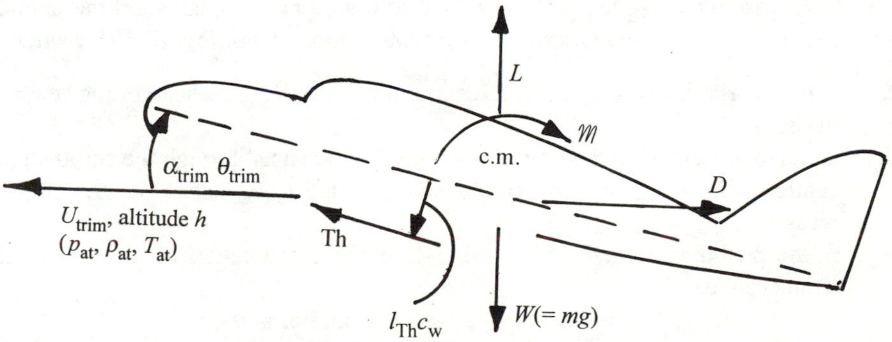

Fig. III.66. Overall forces and moments on an aeroplane in steady level flight.

— total aerodynamic lift L acting vertically upward through the centre of mass,
— total aerodynamic drag D acting horizontally backward through the centre of mass,
— total aerodynamic pitching moment $\mathcal{M}$ (positive nose-up) acting about a pitch axis through the centre of mass,
— all-up weight W (= mg, where m is the all-up mass) acting vertically downward through the centre of mass,
— net thrust Th, which is assumed to act parallel to the fuselage longitudinal axis,

— a pitching moment (positive nose-up) due to the Thrust–Drag couple, denoted by (Th $l_{\mathrm{Th}}\, c_{\mathrm{w}}$).

On virtually all light aeroplanes l_{Th} is small and negligible. On transport aeroplanes with engines underslung beneath the wings l_{Th} is positive, of the order of 0.2. On combat aeroplanes l_{Th} is small and negligible, apart from when laden with underwing weapons, then l_{Th} becomes negative due to lowering of the overall centre of mass.

By reference to Fig. III.66 the equations of static equilibrium are

$$\begin{aligned} \mathrm{Th}\cos\alpha_{\mathrm{trim}} &= D, \\ L + \mathrm{Th}\sin\alpha_{\mathrm{trim}} &= W, \\ \mathcal{M} + \mathrm{Th}\, l_{\mathrm{Th}} c_{\mathrm{w}} &= 0. \end{aligned} \tag{III.5.1}$$

When l_{Th} is zero the aerodynamic pitching moment, $\mathcal{M}$, is zero for static equilibrium and then the forces L, D, W and Th all act through the centre of mass. This simple concept of static equilibrium, which would appear to be self evident and irrefutable, is not universally accepted. In the light aeroplane fraternity, as demonstrated for example in the Shell Film 'How an aeroplane flies', and in elementary instruction courses for pilots, it is stated that the lift L must act aft of the centre of mass 'so that if the thrust fails the aeroplane will pitch nose down'; an erroneous concept for a debatable practical flight requirement. At the appropriate stage in this book the reader should explain what happens to a trimmed light aeroplane when the thrust fails.

Conditions which influence the sign of the tailplane lift in trimmed flight as described next.

Taking the case when l_{Th} is zero the vertical forces on an aeroplane and the pitching moment about the wing–fuselage aerodynamic centre are shown in Fig. III.67(i), where

- L_{nac} is the nacelle lift which acts at its centre of pressure $l_{\mathrm{nac}} c_{\mathrm{w}}$ ahead of the centre of mass,
- L_{wf} is the lift on the wing–fuselage combination which acts through the aerodynamic centre of the wing–fuselage combination located $l_{\mathrm{wf}} c_{\mathrm{w}}$ ahead of the centre of mass,
- $\mathcal{M}_{\mathrm{wf}}$ is the pitching moment of the wing–fuselage combination about the aerodynamic centre,
- L_{t} is the tailplane lift which acts $l_{\mathrm{t}} c_{\mathrm{w}}$ aft of the centre of mass.

The small component of the thrust Th in the vertical direction is neglected. Relating Figs. III.66 and III.67(i), assuming all angles small,

$$\begin{aligned} L &= L_{\mathrm{nac}} + L_{\mathrm{wf}} + L_{\mathrm{t}} \\ \mathcal{M} &= \mathcal{M}_{\mathrm{wf}} + L_{\mathrm{nac}} l_{\mathrm{nac}} c_{\mathrm{w}} + L_{\mathrm{wf}} l_{\mathrm{wf}} c_{\mathrm{w}} - L_{\mathrm{t}} l_{\mathrm{t}} c_{\mathrm{w}}. \end{aligned} \tag{III.5.2}$$

An alternative representation of these loads is shown in Fig. III.67(ii) where the resultant lift force ($L_{\mathrm{nac}} + L_{\mathrm{wf}}$) acts through its centre of pressure located $l_{\mathrm{cp}} c_{\mathrm{w}}$ ahead of the centre of mass, so

$$(L_{\mathrm{nac}} + L_{\mathrm{wf}})\, l_{\mathrm{cp}} c_{\mathrm{w}} = \mathcal{M}_{\mathrm{wf}} + L_{\mathrm{nac}} l_{\mathrm{nac}} c_{\mathrm{w}} + L_{\mathrm{wf}} l_{\mathrm{wf}} c_{\mathrm{w}}. \tag{III.5.3}$$

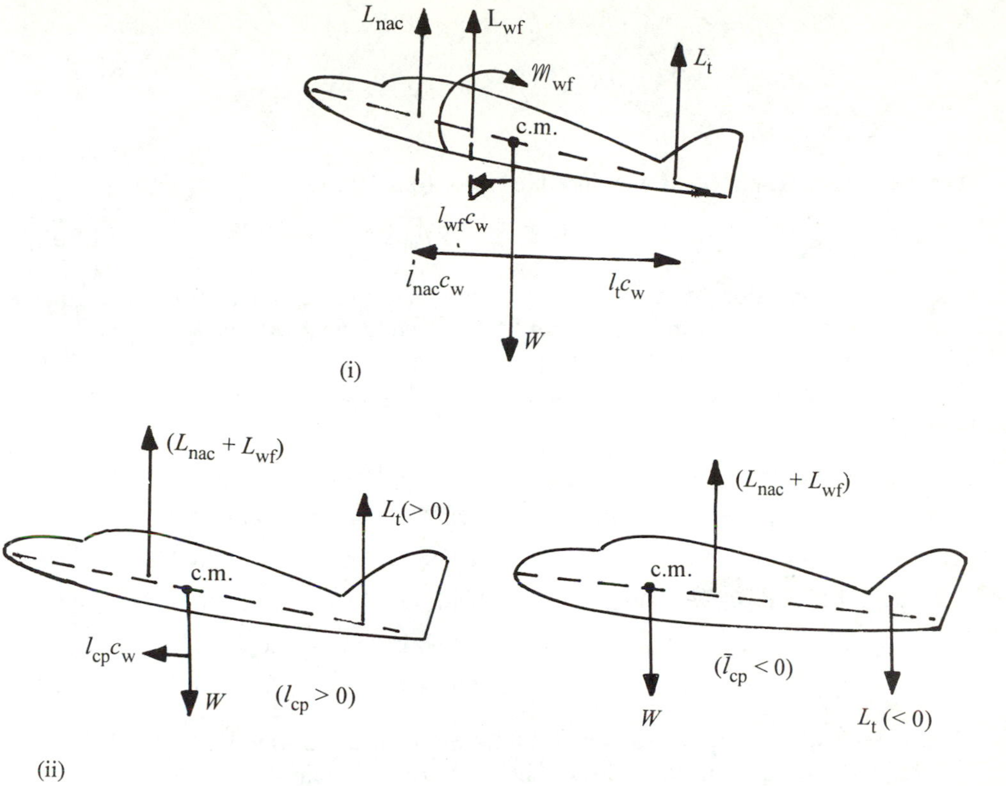

Fig. III.67. Alternative arrangements of aeroplane loads in steady level flight.

By reference to Fig. III.67(ii), when the centre of pressure of $(L_{nac} + L_{wf})$ is forward of the centre of mass, that is, when $l_{cp} > 0$, L_t is positive (i.e. upward) for static equilibrium. When the centre of pressure of $(L_{nac} + L_{wf})$ is aft of the centre of mass, that is, when $l_{cp} < 0$, L_t is negative (i.e. downward) for static equilibrium. The centre of pressure location varies with the flight condition so it is not immediately obvious whether in any specific flight condition L_t is positive or negative. At low speeds l_{cp} is usually positive (i.e. L_t positive); l_{cp} decreases with increase in speed, sometimes going negative at higher speeds (i.e. L_t negative). At supersonic speeds l_{cp} is invariably negative (i.e. L_t negative). On transport aeroplanes a design aim is to make L_t small at the cruise condition to minimize trim drag.

Another common misunderstanding is that the tailplane lift must be negative for all trimmed flight conditions. Although this concept is incorrect, and in fact potentially dangerous, as explained later when stability is described, it is possible to discern its origins.

Returning to the equations of static equilibrium, eqns. (III.5.1), dividing the two force equations by $(\frac{1}{2}\rho_{at}U_{trim}^2S_w)$ and the pitching moment equation by $(\frac{1}{2}\rho_{at}U_{trim}^2S_wc_w)$, replacing cos α_{trim} by 1 and sin α_{trim} by α_{trim} for small α_{trim}, the non-dimensional forms of eqns. (III.5.1) are

$$C_{\text{Th}} = C_{\text{D}},$$
$$C_{\text{L}} + C_{\text{Th}}\alpha_{\text{trim}} = W\Big/\left(\tfrac{1}{2}\rho_{\text{at}}U_{\text{trim}}^2 S_{\text{w}}\right) = C_{\text{W}} \qquad \text{(III.5.4)}$$
$$C_{\text{m}} + C_{\text{Th}}l_{\text{Th}} = 0.$$

The weight coefficient C_{W} is introduced in eqns. (III.5.4) where

$$C_{\text{W}} = (W/S_{\text{w}})\Big/\left(\tfrac{1}{2}\rho_{\text{at}}U_{\text{trim}}^2\right) = (W/S_{\text{w}})\Big/\left(\tfrac{1}{2}\gamma\, p_{\text{at}}M_\infty^2\right) \qquad \text{(III.5.5)}$$

C_{W} is the non-dimensional independent variable which represents the variation of the trim dynamic pressure or of trim speed or of trim Mach number ($M_\infty = U_{\text{trim}}/a_{\text{at}}$). Note that C_{W} decreases as speed, or Mach number, increases.

The ratio (W/S_{w}) is known as the wing loading. Typical values of maximum wing loadings are:

Galaxy, Boeing 747, A310-300	$O[6.5\ \text{kN/m}^2 \simeq 130\ \text{lb}_\text{f}/\text{ft}^2]$
Boeing 767, A320, B.Ae 146, Concorde	$O[5.5\ \text{kN/m}^2 \simeq 110\ \text{lb}_\text{f}/\text{ft}^2]$
Jet Stream, Short 330	$O[2.5\ \text{kN/m}^2 \simeq 50\ \text{lb}_\text{f}/\text{ft}^2]$
Cessna Skyhawk, Piper Warrion II	$O[0.7\ \text{kN/m}^2 \simeq 14\ \text{lb}_\text{f}/\text{ft}^2]$
Jaguar, Harrier	$O[6.0\ \text{kN/m}^2 \simeq 120\ \text{lb}_\text{f}/\text{ft}^2]$
EFA	$O[3.5\ \text{kN/m}^2 \simeq 70\ \text{lb}_\text{f}/\text{ft}^2]$

To convert kN/m^2 to $\text{lb}_\text{f}/\text{ft}^2$ multiply by 20.89. Sometimes the wing loading is defined as (m/S_{w}) and expressed in the units kg/m^2 ($1\ \text{kN/m}^2$ is equivalent to $101.9\ \text{kg/m}^2$; $1\ \text{lb}_\text{f}/\text{ft}^2$ is equivalent to $1\ \text{lb}_\text{m}/\text{ft}^2$).

The equations of static equilibrium, eqns. (III.5.4), can be expanded into the form

$$C_{\text{Th}} = C_{\text{D}}$$
$$C_{\text{L}0} + (C_{\text{L}\alpha} + C_{\text{D}})\alpha_{\text{trim}} + C_{\text{L}\eta}\,\eta_{\text{trim}} = C_{\text{W}} \qquad \text{(III.5.6)}$$
$$(C_{m0} + C_{\text{D}}l_{\text{Th}}) + C_{m\alpha}\alpha_{\text{trim}} + C_{m\eta}\eta_{\text{trim}} = 0,$$

expressing C_{L} and C_m in terms of their derivatives, see eqns. (III.3.133) and (III.3.135); in steady level flight there are no $\dot{\alpha}(t)$ or $q(t)$ or $\dot{q}(t)$ or $\dot{\eta}(t)$ terms.

Solving eqns. (III.5.6) for α_{trim},

$$\alpha_{\text{trim}} \simeq -\frac{1}{C_{\text{L}\alpha}}\left[C_{\text{L}0} + \frac{C_{m0} + l_{\text{Th}}C_{\text{D}}(C_{\text{W}})}{l_{\text{t}}}\right] + \left[\frac{C_{\text{W}}}{C_{\text{L}\alpha}}\right] \qquad \text{(III.5.7)}$$

where, from eqns. (III.3.133) and (III.3.135), $C_{\text{L}\eta}/(-C_{m\eta}) = l_{\text{t}}$, assuming $1 + (C_{\text{D}}/C_{\text{L}\alpha}) - (K_\alpha/l_{\text{t}}) \simeq 1$, $C_{\text{D}}(C_{\text{L}}) \simeq C_{\text{D}}(C_{\text{w}})$, remembering that K_α = incidence stiffness = $(-C_{m\alpha})/C_{\text{L}\alpha}$.

As explained in the Preface, to aid comprehension of equations all negative derivatives such as $C_{m\eta}$ and $C_{m\alpha}$ are expressed in the form $(-C_{m\eta})$ and $(-C_{m\alpha})$ and then the signs of various terms can be more easily identified.

At low speeds, when the effects of Mach number on the aerodynamic derivatives can be neglected, and when l_{Th} is zero, from eqn. (III.5.7), α_{trim} is a linear function of C_W, with positive gradient, $(1/C_{L\alpha})$, as shown in Fig. III.68. In steady level flight the lift, which is proportional to $(\frac{1}{2}\rho_{at}U^2_{trim}\alpha_{trim})$, is equal to the weight so α_{trim} increases as $(\frac{1}{2}\rho_{at}U^2_{trim})$ decreases, that is, as C_W increases. When l_{Th} is positive the gradient reduces slightly as C_W increases.

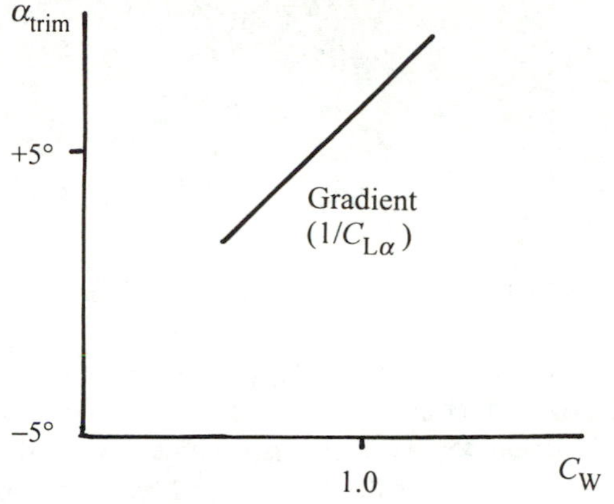

Fig. III.68. α_{trim} ~ C_W at low Mach numbers.

Over the range $0.7 < C_W < 1.2$, with $C_{L\alpha}$ of the order of 4.5, the range of α_{trim} is approximately 6°.

Solving eqns. (III.5.6) for η_{trim}

$$\eta_{trim} \simeq \left[\frac{C_{m0} + K_\alpha C_{L0} + l_{Th}C_D(C_W)}{(-C_{m\eta})}\right] - \left[\frac{K_\alpha}{(-C_{m\eta})}\right]C_W \tag{III.5.8}$$

assuming $1+(C_D/C_{L\alpha}) \simeq 1$ and $1+K_\alpha/l_t \simeq 1$.

The variation of η_{trim} ~ C_W at low Mach numbers, taking l_{Th} to be zero, is shown in Fig. III.69.

Positive trim control, based on traditional piloting techniques, requires that 'pulling the stick back' and closing the throttle decreases the trim speed. 'Pulling the stick back' decreases the elevator angle while decreasing the trim speed increases C_W, so the gradient of η_{trim} ~ C_W must be negative for positive trim control. Closing the throttle decreases the thrust, or power, to offset the decrease in drag with decrease in speed.

For positive trim control at low Mach numbers when l_{Th} is zero, from eqn. (III.5.8),

$$d\eta_{trim}/dC_W = -K_\alpha/(-C_{m\eta}) < 0. \tag{III.5.9}$$

Since $(-C_{m\eta})$ is positive, K_α must be positive.

Typically, at low Mach numbers,

$$K_\alpha = 0.2, \quad (-C_{m\eta}) = 1.5, \tag{III.5.10}$$

then over the range $0.7 < C_W < 1.2$ the range of η_{trim} is approximately 4°.

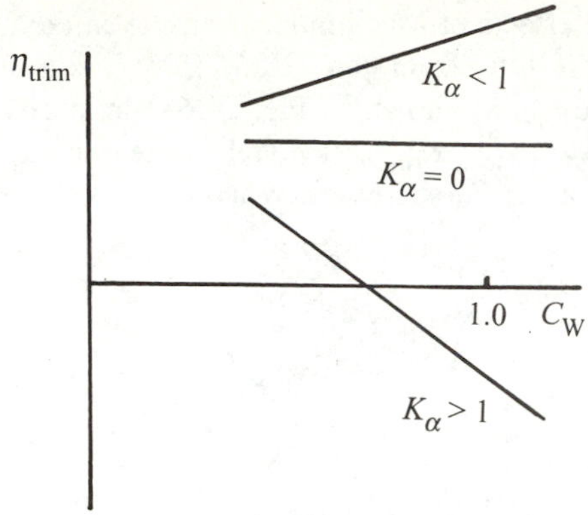

Fig. III.69. $\eta_{trim} \sim C_W$ at low Mach numbers.

The magnitude of the negative gradient of $\eta_{trim} \sim C_W$ must not be too small, otherwise a specified change in C_W would require too small a change in elevator angle, and consequently too fine an adjustment to the stick displacement which the pilot would find disconcerting; the pilot would say that the trim control was too sensitive. Neither must the magnitude of the negative gradient of $\eta_{trim} \sim C_W$ be too large, otherwise a required change in C_W would involve a large change in elevator angle, and consequently a large stick displacement; the pilot would regard excessive stick displacements, especially if compounded with large stick forces, as a contributory factor to a higher pilot work load. Another consequence of a large gradient is that the range of elevator angle to trim over a range of C_W is increased, possibly taking the elevator angle beyond the limits of attached flow, hence losing elevator effectiveness.

The pilot controls the elevator angle, η_{trim}; the pilot has no direct control over the angle of incidence, α_{trim}. Effectively the pilot uses the elevator to rotate the aeroplane to the appropriate angle of incidence at which the lift equals weight. At the same time the pilot adjusts the throttle to obtain the appropriate thrust to counteract the drag. Note that the relationship between η_{trim} and α_{trim}, given by the moment equation in eqns. (III.5.6), is independent of C_W, that is, independent of the trim speed when l_{Th} is zero.

The value of η_{trim} can be altered without affecting the gradient of $\eta_{trim} \sim C_W$ by a change in the tailplane setting angle i_t. A negative change in tailplane setting angle implies an increase in the elevator angle to trim if the same tailplane trim lift is to be maintained. A change in tailplane setting angle of –1° leads to an incremental change in η_{trim} of approximately +1.5°, as shown in Fig. III.70.

For the effect of underslung engines on η_{trim} at low Mach numbers, from eqn. (III.5.8),

$$\begin{aligned}(\mathrm{d}\eta_{trim}/\mathrm{d}C_W) &= \left[-K_\alpha + (l_{Th}\,\mathrm{d}C_D(C_W)/\mathrm{d}C_W)\right]/(-C_{m\eta}) \\ &\simeq \left[-K_\alpha + (l_{Th}\,2C_W)/(\pi \mathrm{AR_w})\right]/(-C_{m\eta}).\end{aligned} \tag{III.5.11}$$

The magnitude of the negative gradient of $\eta_{trim} \sim C_W$ decreases as speed decreases, typically by the order of 10% at low speeds (see Fig. III.71).

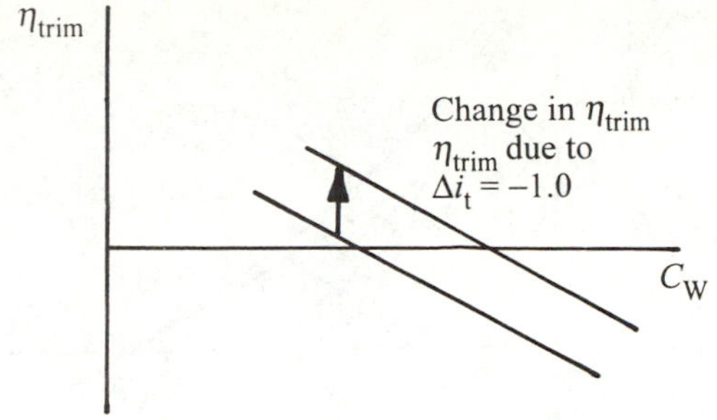

Fig. III.70. Effect of tailplane setting angle.

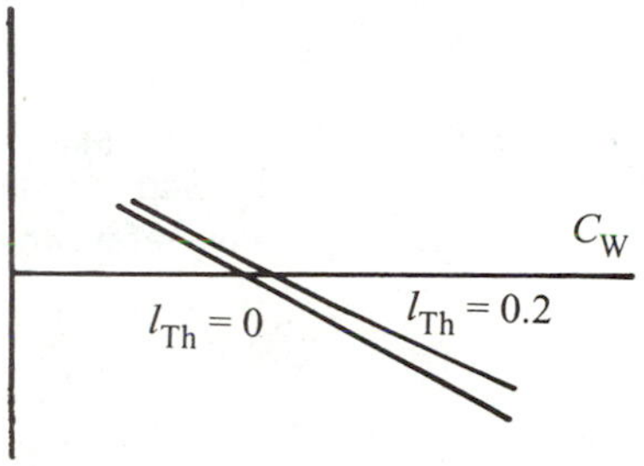

Fig. III.71. Effect of underslung engines.

At low Mach numbers the plot of $\eta_{trim} \sim C_W$ is the same at all altitudes, thus η_{trim} varies with equivalent air speed only. This result does not hold at higher Mach numbers.

From eqn. (III.5.5),

$$M_\infty = \left[(W/S_w)/\left(\tfrac{1}{2}\gamma\, p_{at} C_W\right)\right]^{1/2}. \qquad \text{(III.5.12)}$$

Taking $W/S_w = 4.5\,\text{kN/m}^2$,

at sea level,

when $C_W = 1.0$, $M_\infty = 0.25$; when $C_W = 0.4$, $M_\infty = 0.40$,

at 11 km,

when $C_W = 1.0$, $M_\infty = 0.53$; when $C_W = 0.4$, $M_\infty = 0.84$.

With increasing Mach number at subsonic speeds, in eqn. (III.5.8), K_α decreases with increase in Mach number (see eqns. (III.3.148) and (III.3.149)) while C_{m0}, C_{L0} and $(-C_{m\eta})$ all tend to increase with Mach number; the net effect is that the negative gradient of $\eta_{trim} \sim C_W$ steepens with increase in Mach number. Typical variations of $\eta_{trim} \sim C_W$ at two altitudes are shown in Fig. III.72, taking l_{Th} equal to zero.

It is of interest to note that the effects of underslung engines tend to counter the effects of Mach number to give a more linear curve for $\eta_{trim} \sim C_W$ at subsonic speeds.

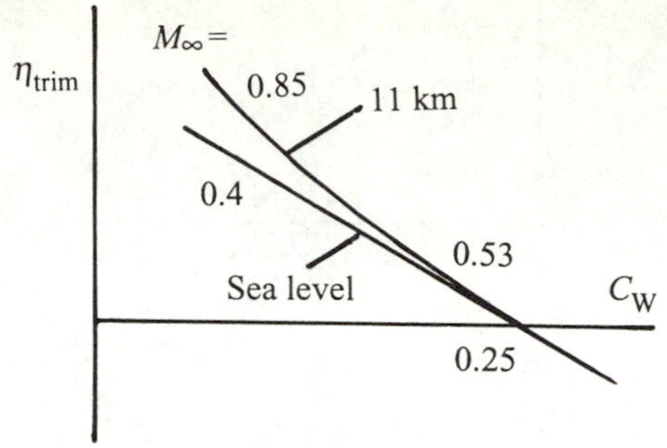

Fig. III.72. $\eta_{trim} \sim C_W$ for transport aeroplane.

At supersonic speeds there are dramatic effects on η_{trim} due to the large increase in K_α (see eqn. (III.3.149)), and decrease in $(-C_{m\eta})$. Typical variations of $\eta_{trim} \sim C_W$ are shown in Fig. III.73 for a combat aeroplane; η_{trim} now refers to the angle of an all-moving tailplane.

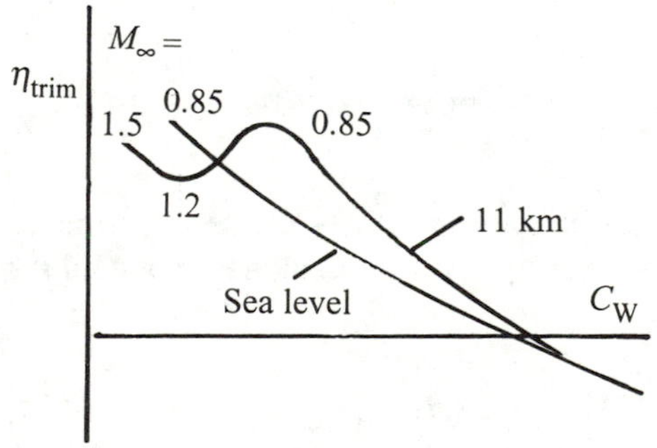

Fig. III.73. $\eta_{trim} \sim C_W$ for combat aeroplane.

For transport aeroplanes with adjustable tailplanes the trim elevator is reduced to zero by changing the tailplane setting angle, keeping the tailplane lift constant. Hence

$$(\Delta i_t)_{trim} = \left(a_\eta / (a_\alpha)_t\right) \eta_{trim} \tag{III.5.13}$$

measured relative to a datum tailplane setting angle.

When full flaps are deployed at low speeds typical incremental changes are, from eqns. (III.3.26) and (III.3.27)

$$\begin{aligned} (\Delta m_0)_w &= \Delta C_{m0} = -0.125, \\ (\Delta C_L)_w &= \Delta C_{L0} = 1.25, \\ \Delta \alpha_0 &= -14°. \end{aligned} \tag{III.5.14}$$

Hence from eqn. (III.5.8),

$$\text{when } K_\alpha = 0.1, \quad \Delta\eta_{\text{trim}} \simeq 0°;$$
$$\text{when } K_\alpha = 0.2, \quad \Delta\eta_{\text{trim}} \simeq 4°. \qquad \text{(III.5.15)}$$

Elevator angles to trim, flaps up and flaps down, are sketched in Fig. III.74.

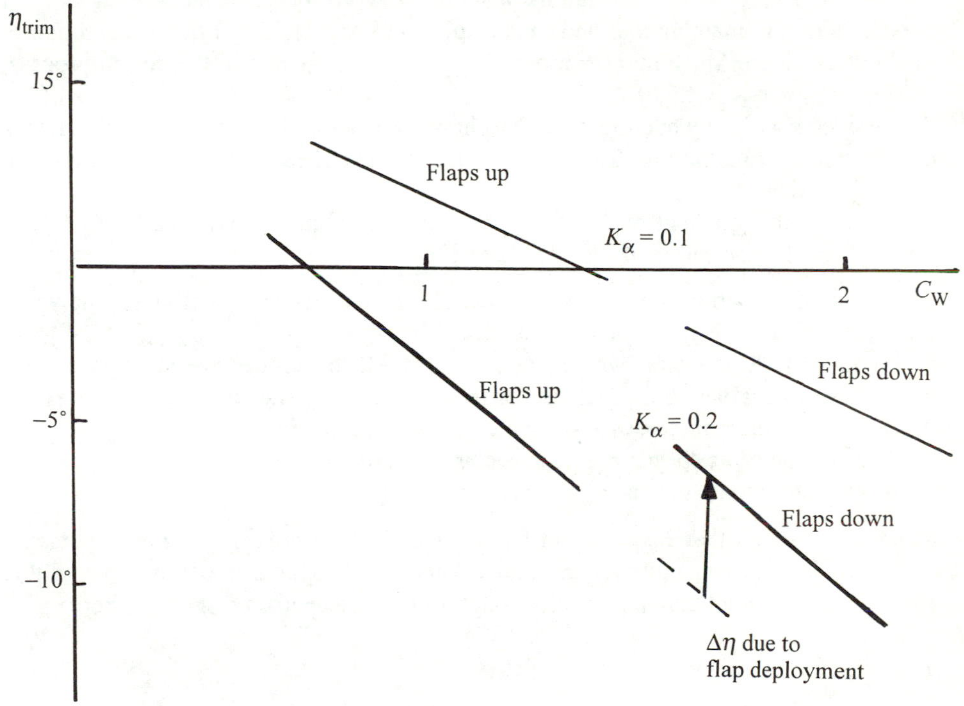

Fig. III.74. Effect of flaps on elevator to trim.

To explain these trends, if flaps were deployed at constant C_W, to maintain constant wing lift, with the numbers of eqn. (III.5.14), the angle of incidence must be reduced by 14°. Because the wing lift is unchanged there is no change in downwash at the tailplane. Two effects contribute to $\Delta\eta_{\text{trim}}$ which tend to cancel:

(i) the nose-down pitching moment due to the flaps must be countered by a negative change in elevator angle,

(ii) the decrease in aeroplane angle of incidence gives a nose-up pitching moment proportional to $(C_{m\alpha}\Delta\alpha)$ $(= C_{L\alpha}K_\alpha(-\Delta\alpha))$ which must be countered by a positive change in elevator angle.

Thus for higher values of K_α (i.e. forward locations of the centre of mass) a positive change in $\Delta\eta_{\text{trim}}$ is required.

III.5.2 Elevator trim margin

A measure of the trim control is the amount of elevator displacement required to change C_W. The parameter E_{tri}, called the elevator trim margin, is introduced where

$$E_{trim} = -(d\eta_{trim}/dC_W). \tag{III.5.16}$$

As already explained, E_{trim} must be positive for positive trim control; furthermore, E_{trim} must be neither too small nor too large for satisfactory trim control.

The notation E_{trim} is not conventional notation. The advantage of introducing E_{trim} is that its definition is unambiguous and can be applied to both rigid and flexible aeroplanes throughout the entire Mach number range. E_{trim} can be calculated in the design process, and measured directly in flight.

The reader may be wondering why the phrase 'elevator trim margin' is used rather than the simpler 'trim margin'. The reason is that for flexible aeroplanes an 'aileron trim margin' also exists.

E_{trim} is the local gradient of the $\eta_{trim} \sim C_W$ curve. The qualitative behaviour of E_{trim} can be deduced by inspection of Figs. III.72 and III.73:

(i) At low Mach numbers, where the effects of Mach number are negligible, and when l_{Th} is zero, E_{trim} is a constant independent of C_W.
(ii) At low Mach numbers, where the effects of Mach number are negligible, with underslung engines, E_{trim} decreases with increase in C_W (i.e. as speed decreases).
(iii) As Mach number increases at subsonic speeds, E_{trim} increases.
(iv) At low supersonic speeds E_{trim} can become negative.
(v) At high supersonic speeds E_{trim} is positive.

It has been stated that E_{trim} should be positive for trim control. At low supersonic speeds E_{trim} is negative; however, as shown later the aeroplane is controllable in this speed range so the pilot can accelerate through to higher supersonic speeds where again E_{trim} is positive.

Although mathematically

$$E_{trim} = -(d\eta_{trim}/dC_W) = -\left[\partial/\partial C_W - (M_\infty/2C_W)\partial/\partial M_\infty\right]\eta_{trim}, \tag{III.5.17}$$

the derivation of an expression for E_{trim} is most easily obtained directly from the equations of static equilibrium. As derived in Appendix 4,

$$2C_W(-C_{m\eta})E_{trim} \simeq K_\alpha C_{LU} + C_{mU} + l_{Th}\left[C_{DU} - 2\left(C_W(dC_D/dC_L)_{trim}\right)\right] \tag{III.5.18}$$

where C_{LU}, C_{mU} and C_{DU} are the perturbation speed derivatives introduced in section III.3.11. And then

$$\begin{aligned}2C_W(-C_{m\eta})E_{trim} \simeq{}& K_\alpha\left[2C_W + M_\infty(\partial C_L/\partial M_\infty)_{trim}\right] + M_\infty(\partial C_m/\partial M_\infty)_{trim} \\ &- l_{Th}\left[2C_W(dC_D/dC_L)_{trim} - M_\infty(\partial C_D/\partial M_\infty)_{trim}\right]\end{aligned} \tag{III.5.19}$$

on cancelling the moment trim condition ($[C_m + l_{Th}C_D]_{trim} = 0$).

Expressions for $(\partial C_L/\partial M_\infty)_{trim}$, $(\partial C_m/\partial M_\infty)_{trim}$ and $(\partial C_D/\partial M_\infty)_{trim}$ are derived in Appendix 4. In general,

— $(\partial C_L/\partial M_\infty)_{trim}$ and $(\partial C_m/\partial M_\infty)_{trim}$ are positive at subsonic speeds, below the drag rise Mach number,
— $(\partial C_L/\partial M_\infty)_{trim}$ and $(\partial C_m/\partial M_\infty)_{trim}$ are large and negative at low supersonic speeds,
— $(\partial C_L/\partial M_\infty)_{trim}$ and $(\partial C_m/\partial M_\infty)_{trim}$ are smaller and negative at higher supersonic speeds.

At low Mach numbers, from eqn. (III.5.19),

$$E_{trim} = \left[K_\alpha - l_{Th}(dC_D/dC_L)_{trim}\right]/(-C_{m\eta})$$
$$= \left[K_\alpha - l_{Th}(2C_W/\pi\, AR_w)\right]/(-C_{m\eta}). \qquad (III.5.20)$$

This formula is consistent with eqn. (III.5.11). When l_{Th} is zero E_{trim} is a constant, independent of C_W. For underslung engines l_{Th} is positive and then E_{trim} decreases with increase in C_W.

At subsonic Mach numbers both $(\partial C_L/\partial M_\infty)_{trim}$ and $(\partial C_m/\partial M_\infty)_{trim}$ are positive, while K_α decreases and $(-C_{m\eta})$ increases with increase in Mach number. Hence from eqn. (III.5.19), E_{trim} can increase with increase in Mach number.

At low supersonic speeds, although in eqn. (III.5.19) K_α is large and positive, $[1+(M_\infty(\partial C_L/\partial M_\infty)_{trim}/2C_W)]$ can be negative, and then E_{trim} becomes negative.

At higher supersonic speeds the magnitude of $(\partial C_L/\partial M_\infty)_{trim}$ reduces, although still negative, while $(\partial C_m/\partial M_\infty)_{trim}$ becomes small, so E_{trim} becomes positive.

III.5.3 Trim point

The trim point is defined as the location of the centre of mass at which the elevator trim margin is zero ($E_{trim} = 0$).

Denoting the position of the trim point aft of the wing–fuselage aerodynamic centre as $h_{trim}c_w$, it follows from eqn. (III.5.19) that

$$E_{trim} = [h_{trim} - l_{wf}]\left[1+\left(M_\infty(\partial C_L/\partial M_\infty)_{trim}/2C_W\right)\right]/(-C_{m\eta}). \qquad (III.5.21)$$

At subsonic speeds, because $[1+(M_\infty(\partial C_L/\partial M_\infty)_{trim}/2C_W)]$ is positive, E_{trim} is positive when the centre of mass lies forward of the trim point (i.e. $h_{trim} > l_{wf}$).

The concept of a trim point loses all sense of reality at supersonic speeds because with increasing Mach number from Mach 1, $[2C_W + M_\infty(\partial C_m/\partial M_\infty)_{trim}]$ goes zero, then negative, zero again, and finally positive, but E_{trim} remains finite, so h_{trim} can go infinite. At low supersonic speeds, when $[2C_W + M_\infty(\partial C_m/\partial M_\infty)_{trim}]$ is negative, E_{trim} is positive only if the centre of mass lies *aft* of the trim point.

III.5.4 Manual control system

With a manual control system the stick displacement is directly proportional to the elevator deflection and the stick force is directly proportional to the elevator hinge moment; a separate control is available to the pilot to vary the tab angle.

For a fixed tailplane with elevator and trim tab

$$\text{elevator trim hinge moment}$$
$$= \tfrac{1}{2}\rho_{at}U_{trim}^2 S_e c_e \big[b_\alpha[\alpha_{trim} + i_t - (\partial\varepsilon/\partial\alpha)(\alpha_{trim} + i_w - \alpha_{0w})]$$
$$+ b_\eta \eta_{trim} + b\delta\big] \qquad \text{(III.5.22)}$$

$$= (W/S_w)S_e c_e \Big[\big[(\text{term independent of } C_W)/C_W\big]$$
$$+ (-b_\eta)\Big[\big(K_\alpha/(-C_{m\eta})\big) - \big((b_\alpha/b_\eta)\big(1 - \partial\varepsilon/\partial\alpha\big)/C_{L\alpha}\big)\Big]$$
$$+ \big((b_\delta\delta)/C_W\big)\Big] \qquad \text{(III.5.23)}$$

where δ is the tab angle, on substitution for α_{trim} from eqn. (III.5.7) and η_{trim} from eqn. (III.5.8).

The pilot trims the aeroplane by changing the tab angle until the elevator hinge moment, and the stick force, are zero. The trim tab angle δ_{trim} for zero elevator trim hinge moment is, from eqn. (III.5.22),

$$\delta_{trim} = \big[b_\alpha[\alpha_{trim} + i_t - (\partial\varepsilon/\partial\alpha)(\alpha_{trim} + i_w - \alpha_0)] + b_\eta\eta_{trim}\big]/(-b_\delta) \qquad \text{(III.5.24)}$$

assuming that the tab angle contribution to the elevator lift can be neglected. In the design process it is necessary to ensure that δ_{trim} remains within reasonable limits throughout the flight envelope.

When changing from one trim speed to another the pilot will move the stick and alter the throttle; when the new trim speed is established the pilot will retrim, namely, relax the stick force. From a pilot's point of view the relevant trim control parameters are the stick displacement per unit change in trim speed and stick force per unit change in trim speed.

Now the elevator displacement per unit change in trim speed is

$$\Delta\eta_{trim}/\Delta U_{trim} = (-2C_W/U_{trim})(d\eta_{trim}/dC_W)$$
$$= \big[E_{trim}2(W/S_w)\big]/\big(\tfrac{1}{2}\rho_{at}U_{trim}^3\big), \qquad \text{(III.5.25)}$$

so $(\Delta\eta_{trim}/\Delta U_{trim})$ increases with E_{trim}, wing loading and altitude but decreases dramatically with increase in U_{trim}.

The stick displacement per unit change in trim speed is

$$\text{stick displacement}/\Delta U_{trim} = G_d\,(+\Delta\eta_{trim})/\Delta U_{trim}, \qquad \text{(III.5.26)}$$

where G_d is the displacement gearing between the stick displacement and elevator angle and $(\Delta\eta_{trim}/\Delta U_{trim})$ is given by eqn. (III.5.25). A forward stick displacement, defined as positive, gives a positive change in elevator angle, which explains the $(+\Delta\eta_{\text{trim}})$ term. A forward stick displacement must increase trim speed, so E_{trim} must be positive, as already described.

The elevator hinge moment per unit change in trim speed is

$$\begin{aligned}
&\Delta(\text{elevator hinge moment})/\Delta U_{\text{trim}} \\
&\quad = -(2C_W/U_{\text{trim}})[\Delta(\text{elevator hinge moment})/\Delta C_W] \\
&\quad = -[2(W/S_w)S_e c_e/U_{\text{trim}}] \\
&\qquad \times(-b_\eta)\left[(K_\alpha/(-C_{m\eta})) - [((-b_\alpha)/(-b_\eta))(1-\partial\varepsilon/\partial\alpha)/C_{L\alpha}]\right] \qquad \text{(III.5.27)}
\end{aligned}$$

at low Mach numbers. Eqn. (III.5.27) is obtained from eqn. (III.5.23), remembering that initially the elevator trim hinge moment is zero, and that the tab angle is fixed during the trim speed increase.

Note that the [Δ(elevator hinge moment)/ΔU_{trim}] is independent of altitude, proportional to (Wc_e) and decreases with increase of trim speed as $(1/U_{\text{trim}})$.

The stick force per unit change in trim speed is

$$\text{stick force}/\Delta U_{\text{trim}} = G_f[-\Delta(\text{elevator hinge moment})/\Delta U_{\text{trim}}] \qquad \text{(III.5.28)}$$

where G_f is the force gearing between stick force and elevator hinge moment. A forward stick force must push the stick forward rotating the elevator down, so a forward stick force counteracts a negative (nose-down) elevator hinge moment which explains the (−Δ(elevator trim hinge moment)) term.

A forward stick force must increase the trim speed, so

$$(-b_\eta)[(K_\alpha/(-C_{m\eta})) - ((-b_\alpha)/(-b_\eta))(1-\partial\varepsilon/\partial\alpha)/C_{L\alpha}] > 0 \qquad \text{(III.5.29)}$$

Thus $(-b_\eta)$ must be positive. And then the condition

$$K_\alpha/(-C_{m\eta}) > ((-b_\alpha)/(-b_\eta))(1-\partial\varepsilon/\partial\alpha)/C_{L\alpha} \qquad \text{(III.5.30)}$$

must also be satisfied. Typically

$$(-b_\alpha)/(-b_\eta) \simeq 0.5, \quad (1-\partial\varepsilon/\partial\alpha) \simeq 0.5, \quad C_{L\alpha} \simeq 5.0, \quad -C_{m\eta} \simeq 1.5$$

so eqn. (III.5.30) is satisfied when $K_\alpha > 0.075$.

Eqn. (III.5.29) suggests that any balancing must be done with care to ensure that $(-b_\eta)$ is positive, which implies that the hinge line is not too far aft, and that $(-b_\alpha)/(-b_\eta)$ does not become too large.

III.5.5 Powered controls

When powered controls were first introduced they operated a conventional elevator on a fixed tailplane, but there was no tab; the hydraulic actuator held the elevator at the required trim angle, reacting the elevator trim hinge moment given by eqn. (III.5.23). The pilot reduced the stick force to zero via an artificial feel system, leaving the trim elevator angle unaffected. Artificial feel systems are described in more detail later.

With this system the stick displacement per unit change in trim speed is given by eqns. (III.5.25) and (III.5.26). The stick force per unit change in trim speed is now provided by an artificial feel system with its magnitude following the trends of eqn. (III.5.28), thus providing continuity of 'feel' for the pilot between a manual control system and a powered control system.

III.5.5.1 Adjustable tailplane

As seen in Fig. III.74, the trim angle of a conventional elevator can become large with a forward centre of mass and flaps down; this angle can become sufficiently large that the tailplane loses its lifting efficiency through flow separation. An adjustable tailplane can provide the required tailplane lift but at a lower angle.

An advantage of the adjustable tailplane is that when the pilot trims at a fixed trim speed the elevator trim angle is reduced to zero; the tailplane incidence is adjusted to retain the same tailplane trim lift, consequently the stick returns to its zero position.

Two power systems are necessary, one to move the tailplane, the other to move the elevator. Once trimmed the tailplane is at its setting angle with zero elevator angle. Hence if the tailplane hinge line passes close to the centre of pressure of the tailplane loading and if the elevator hinge line passes close to the elevator loading, both tailplane and elevator trim hinge moments will be small. Since these centres of pressure vary little with Mach number at subsonic speeds the trim hinge moments remain small throughout the subsonic speed range.

With an adjustable tailplane a change in trim speed is obtained by a change in elevator angle so the elevator angle and elevator hinge moment per unit change in trim speed are given by eqns. (III.5.25) and (III.5.27). The stick displacement per unit change in trim speed is given by eqn. (III.5.26) while the stick force per unit change in trim speed is provided by an artificial feel system.

III.5.5.2 All-moving tailplane

With an all-moving tailplane on a combat aeroplane the hydraulic jack holds the tailplane at its trim angle, reacting the tailplane trim hinge moment. Now

$$\begin{aligned}&\text{tailplane trim hinge moment}\\&\quad= \mathcal{b}_\alpha\left[(W/S_\mathrm{w})S_\mathrm{t}c_\mathrm{t}/C_\mathrm{W}\right]\\&\qquad\times\left[\alpha_\mathrm{trim}+i_\mathrm{t}-(\partial\varepsilon/\partial\alpha)(\alpha_\mathrm{trim}+i_\mathrm{w}-\alpha_{0\mathrm{w}})+\eta_\mathrm{trim}\right].\end{aligned} \tag{III.5.31}$$

This tailplane trim hinge moment can be minimized by locating the hinge axis such that $\mathcal{b}_\alpha$ is small. Unfortunately the centre of pressure of the tailplane loading moves aft as the combat aeroplane goes supersonic. A compromise is to place the hinge axis half way between the subsonic and supersonic centres of pressure.

Again the stick displacement per unit change in trim speed is given by eqns. (III.5.25) and (III.5.26) while the stick force per unit change in trim speed is provided by an artificial feel system.

EXAMPLES III.23

1. From the data in Figs. III.5(i)–(iii) and Example III.19, No. 1:
   (i) Plot $\eta_{\text{trim}} \sim C_W$ for the light aeroplane basic configuration.
   (ii) Plot $\eta_{\text{trim}} \sim C_W$ for the transport aeroplane basic configuration at sea level and at 11 km altitude.
   (iii) Plot $\eta_{\text{trim}} \sim C_W$ for the combat aeroplane basic configuration at sea level and 11 km altitude.
   (iv) Plot $\eta_{\text{trim}} \sim M_\infty$ for the combat aeroplane basic configuration at sea level and 11 km altitude.
2. In the text (p. 145) it says that l_{cp} decreases as speed increases. Explain why.
3. Why does the wing loading tend to increase with aeroplane size?
4. Are C_L and C_W interchangeable? Can C_L be a function of C_W? Can C_W be a function of C_L?
5. Check that eqn. (III.5.19) gives the quantitative behaviour of E_{trim}.
6. What is the effect of propeller slipstream on E_{trim}?
7. What are the effects of underwing weapons on E_{trim}?
8. Under what conditions do the trim point and the overall aerodynamic centre coincide?
9. For the light aeroplane basic configuration plot $\delta_{\text{trim}} \sim C_W$.
10. Plot the variation of the position of the trim point with Mach number at sea level and 11 km altitude for the combat aeroplane basic configuration measured from the wing apex.
11. Estimate the order of magnitude of the maximum trim hinge moment on the basic combat aeroplane configuration (check flaps up and down).

III.5.6 Steady climb or descent

Consider an aeroplane in either a steady climb (i.e. constant positive flight path angle γ_{trim}) or a steady descent (i.e. constant negative flight path angle γ_{trim}), as shown in Fig. III.75. The forward speed U_{trim}, angle of incidence α_{trim}, pitch angle θ_{trim} (= $\alpha_{\text{trim}} + \gamma_{\text{trim}}$), elevator angle η_{trim}, lift L, drag D, thrust Th, and the aerodynamic moment $\mathcal{M}$, are all assumed constant during the climb or descent.

The aeroplane is in a state of static equilibrium, so the resultant force components parallel and normal to the flight path are zero, and the overall moment is zero. Hence

$$\begin{aligned} \text{Th}\cos\alpha_{\text{trim}} &= D + W\sin\gamma_{\text{trim}}, \\ L + \text{Th}\sin\alpha_{\text{trim}} &= W\cos\gamma_{\text{trim}}, \\ \mathcal{M} + \text{Th}\ l_{\text{Th}}c_{\text{w}} &= 0. \end{aligned} \tag{III.5.32}$$

By reference to eqns. (III.5.4), (III.5.6)–(III.5.8), the trim angle of incidence from eqns. (III.5.32) is

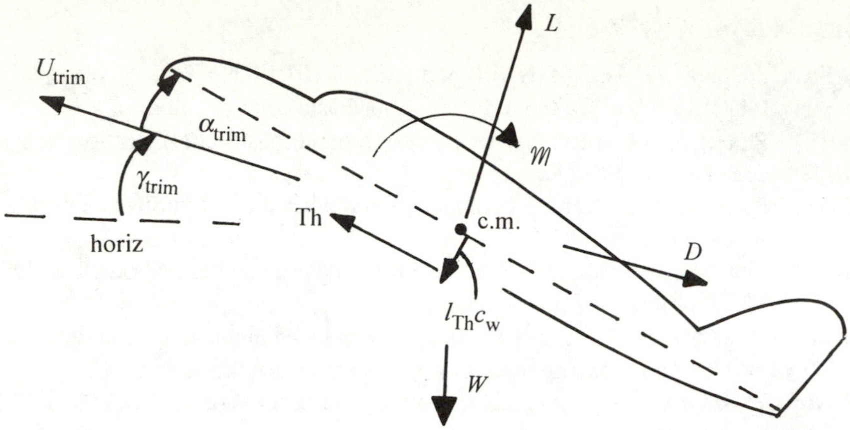

Fig. III.75. Aeroplane in steady climb.

$$\alpha_{\text{trim}} \simeq -\frac{1}{C_{L\alpha}}\left[C_{L0} + \frac{C_{m0} + l_{\text{Th}}\left(C_D(C_W) + C_W \sin\gamma_{\text{trim}}\right)}{l_t}\right] + \left[\frac{C_W \cos\gamma_{\text{trim}}}{C_{L\alpha}}\right] \qquad \text{(III.5.33)}$$

assuming

$$1 + \left((C_D + C_W \sin\gamma_{\text{trim}})/C_{L\alpha}\right) - \left(K_\alpha / l_t\right) \simeq 1.$$

And

$$\eta_{\text{trim}} \simeq \left[\frac{C_{m0} + K_\alpha C_{L0} + l_{\text{Th}}\left(C_D(C_W) + C_W \sin\gamma_{\text{trim}}\right)}{(-C_{m\eta})}\right] - \left[\frac{K_\alpha \cos\gamma_{\text{trim}}}{-C_{m\eta}}\right] C_W. \qquad \text{(III.5.34)}$$

For light aeroplanes and transport aeroplanes the flight path angle γ_{trim} is usually less than 10°, so cos γ_{trim} is approximately 1.0.

When l_{Th} is zero and γ_{trim} is small the relationship between η_{trim} and C_W is independent of γ_{trim}. This result leads to the important observation that in this case η_{trim} is the trim speed control while the throttle is the trim angle of climb, or descent, control.

When l_{Th} is non-zero and γ_{trim} is small,

$$\eta_{\text{trim}} = (\eta_{\text{trim}})_{\gamma=0} + \left[l_{\text{Th}}\, C_W/(-C_{m\eta})\right]\gamma_{\text{trim}}. \qquad \text{(III.5.35)}$$

Now η_{trim} depends on both C_W and γ_{trim}, so η_{trim} is not strictly the trim speed control but is regarded as such.

The elevator trim margin, eqn. (III.5.17), is, from eqn. (III.5.34), when γ_{trim} is small

$$E_{\text{trim}} = (E_{\text{trim}})_{\gamma=0} - \left[l_{\text{Th}}\, \gamma_{\text{trim}}/(-C_{m\eta})\right]$$
$$\times\left[1 + \left((M_\infty/2)\left(\partial(-C_{m\eta})/\partial M_\infty\right)/(-C_{m\eta})\right)\right]. \qquad \text{(III.5.36)}$$

When l_{Th} is zero E_{trim} is unaffected by angle of climb, or descent, but when l_{Th} is positive E_{trim} is reduced in a climb and increased in a descent.

Climb of light aeroplanes is usually carried out with a fixed, open, throttle at a constant equivalent air speed with a constant elevator, η_{trim}. Because engine power decreases with altitude the rate of climb decreases with altitude, so the climb is not strictly steady, but the rates of change are sufficiently small that it is reasonable to assume quasi-steady conditions. Descent will also be at a constant equivalent air speed with the appropriate constant elevator trim setting and a fixed, reduced, throttle.

A transport aeroplane could climb at the constant equivalent airspeed which produces the maximum rate of climb; this maximum rate of climb decreases with altitude because thrust decreases with altitude, but again quasi-steady conditions may be assumed. A constant C_W implies that $(p_{\text{at}}M_\infty^2)$ remains constant with change of altitude; typically in a climb from sea level to 11 km altitude at constant C_W, if the starting Mach number is 0.35 the finishing Mach number is 0.74, thus a small change in η_{trim} during the climb is required to take account of the change in Mach number to maintain C_W constant. An alternative climb strategy could minimize fuel consumption. Sometimes the climb at low altitudes must not exceed specified noise levels over built-up areas. Descent is a low speed flight condition flown at a constant equivalent airspeed with constant trim elevator angle along a prescribed descending flight path.

A combat aeroplane is capable of high angles of climb, up to 90° when the available thrust is greater than the all-up weight, but such manoeuvres are rarely steady. It is of interest to note that as γ approaches 90°, taking l_{Th} equal to zero, both α_{trim} and η_{trim} become independent of C_W, so E_{trim} in these circumstances is zero. The climb strategy depends on the mission: for patrol the climb strategy may aim for minimum fuel consumption and maximum endurance whereas for interception the climb strategy would aim to minimize time to climb to altitude, based on dynamic energy height techniques.

EXAMPLES III.24

1. If a light aeroplane climbs at constant C_W, why does the angle of climb change?
2. What are typical magnitudes of the effect of underslung engines on the value of E_{trim} in a climb or descent, including the effect of Mach number?
3. If a transport aeroplane climbs at constant C_W from sea level to 11 km altitude, what is the approximate change in η_{trim}?
4. On a light aeroplane does steady climb, or descent, affect (i) the elevator trim hinge moment, (ii) the stick force/ΔU_{trim}?

III.6 PULL-OUT MANOEUVRE

The pull-out is the manoeuvre by which a pilot pulls-up from a dive and enters a climb, or alternatively pushes-over from a climb and enters a dive. The pull-out manoeuvre includes entering a climb, or dive, from steady level flight.

Consider an aeroplane initially trimmed in steady level flight at forward speed U_{trim}, with trim angle of incidence α_{trim}, a trim angle of pitch θ_{trim} ($= \alpha_{trim}$), and a trim elevator angle η_{trim}, as shown in Fig. III.76.

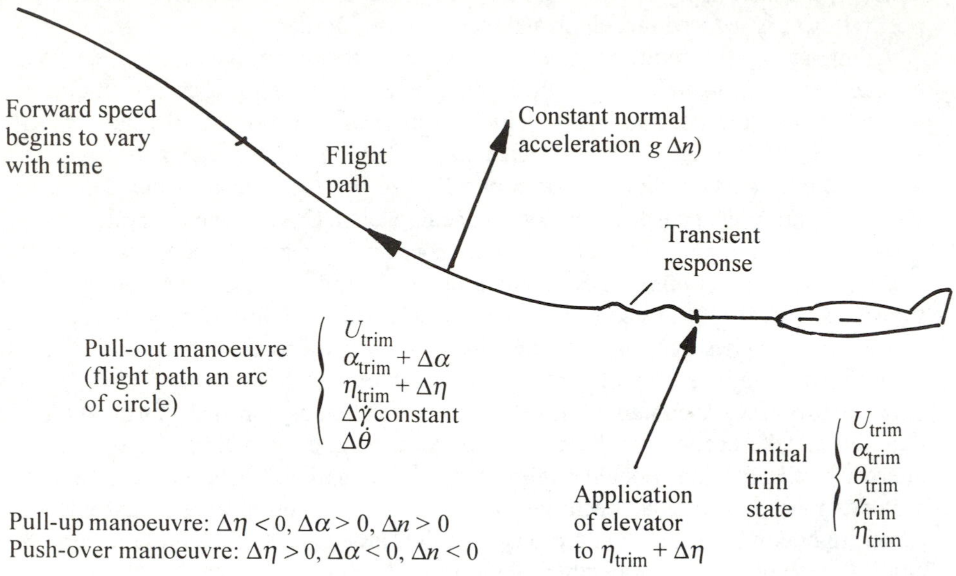

Fig. III.76. Pull-out manoeuvre.

At a particular instant of time the pilot displaces the stick and holds it in its displaced position, leaving the throttle unaltered. The elevator angle is changed quickly to $(\eta_{trim} + \Delta\eta)$, where $\Delta\eta$ is an incremental elevator angle. The aeroplane responds in a time varying manner denoted by speed $(U_{trim} + \Delta U(t))$, angle of incidence $(\alpha_{trim} + \Delta\alpha(t))$, flight path angle $\Delta\gamma(t)$, and angle of pitch $(\theta_{trim} + \Delta\theta(t))$, where

$$\Delta\theta(t) = \Delta\alpha(t) + \Delta\gamma(t). \tag{III.6.1}$$

Hence the rate of pitch $q(t)$ is

$$q(t) = \dot{\theta}(t) = \Delta\dot{\alpha}(t) + \Delta\dot{\gamma}(t). \tag{III.6.2}$$

Immediately following the application of the incremental elevator angle (see Fig. III.76) the aeroplane responds in a damped oscillatory motion which, for a stable aeroplane, decays in the order of 2–5 s, depending on the size of the aeroplane. The aeroplane then enters a dynamic motion which is virtually steady; the aeroplane follows closely a circular flight path. After about 10–20 s this 'steady state' dynamic motion degenerates into a slowly varying unsteady dynamic motion. The pull-out manoeuvre refers to that intermediate 'steady state' motion along the circular flight path, after the initial transient oscillatory motion has decayed but before the slow unsteady dynamic motion has had time to build up.

As shown later, it is an acceptable assumption to neglect changes in forward speed during the initial transient response and the 'steady state' pull-out, so $\Delta U(t)$ can be taken to be zero during this period.

In the 'steady state' pull-out $\Delta\alpha(t)$, $\Delta\dot{\gamma}(t)$ and $q(t)$ can be assumed to be independent of time. The assumptions of constant $U(t)$ and constant $\Delta\dot{\gamma}(t)$ are compatible with flight along an arc of a circle.

From the elementary dynamics of a particle in motion at constant speed U_{trim} along a circular path, a constant normal acceleration, denoted by $g\,\Delta n$, acts towards the centre of the circular flight path, where

$$g\,\Delta n = U_{\text{trim}}\dot{\gamma}(t). \qquad \text{(III.6.3)}$$

And then from eqn. (III.6.2), because $\Delta\dot{\alpha}(t)$ is assumed zero,

$$q(t) = g\,\Delta n / U_{\text{trim}}. \qquad \text{(III.6.4)}$$

From a control point of view the aim is to establish the relationship between the normal acceleration ($g\,\Delta n$) and the incremental elevator angle $\Delta\eta$. An upward change in elevator angle (i.e. a negative $\Delta\eta$) obtained by pulling the stick back, gives an incremental download on the tailplane, inducing a positive nose-up rate of pitch to the aeroplane, increasing the angle of incidence, which leads to a positive normal acceleration, as shown in Fig. III.76; a pull-up. A downward change in elevator angle obtained by pushing the stick forward gives the opposite effect; a push-over.

The forces and pitching moment on the aeroplane during the 'steady state' pull-out are shown in Fig. III.77.

(i) The forces L_{trim}, D_{trim}, Th_{trim} and the aerodynamic pitching moment $\mathcal{M}_{\text{trim}}$, associated with trim variables U_{trim}, α_{trim}, and η_{trim}, refer to conditions in the initial trim state, taken to be steady level flight, before the application of $\Delta\eta$.

(ii) The 'steady' aerodynamic forces $(L_{\text{trim}} + \Delta L)$ and $(D_{\text{trim}} + \Delta D)$, and the steady aerodynamic pitching moment $(\mathcal{M}_{\text{trim}} + \Delta\mathcal{M})$, associated with constant U_{trim}, $(\alpha_{\text{trim}} + \Delta\alpha)$, $(\eta_{\text{trim}} + \Delta\eta)$, and q, refer to conditions in the pull-out manoeuvre.

(iii) The thrust Th remains equal to its initial trim value when the throttle is not changed; this condition holds both for the turbo-fan engine when the throttle controls thrust directly, and for the turbo-prop and piston engines when the throttle controls the power directly (with forward speed constant).

(iv) Reducing the dynamic problem to an equivalent statics problem by the application of D'Alembert's principle, an inertial reaction force $(m(g\,\Delta n))$ acts in the opposite direction to Δn. There is no inertial reaction pitching moment because the pitching acceleration $(= \dot{q})$ is zero.

The equations of static equilibrium in the initial steady state are

$$\begin{aligned} \text{Th}_{\text{trim}}\cos\alpha_{\text{trim}} &= D_{\text{trim}} \\ \text{Th}_{\text{trim}}\sin\alpha_{\text{trim}} + L_{\text{trim}} &= W \\ \text{Th}_{\text{trim}} l_{\text{Th}} c_{\text{w}} + \mathcal{M}_{\text{trim}} &= 0. \end{aligned} \qquad \text{(III.6.5)}$$

The equations of static equilibrium in the pull-out manoeuvre are

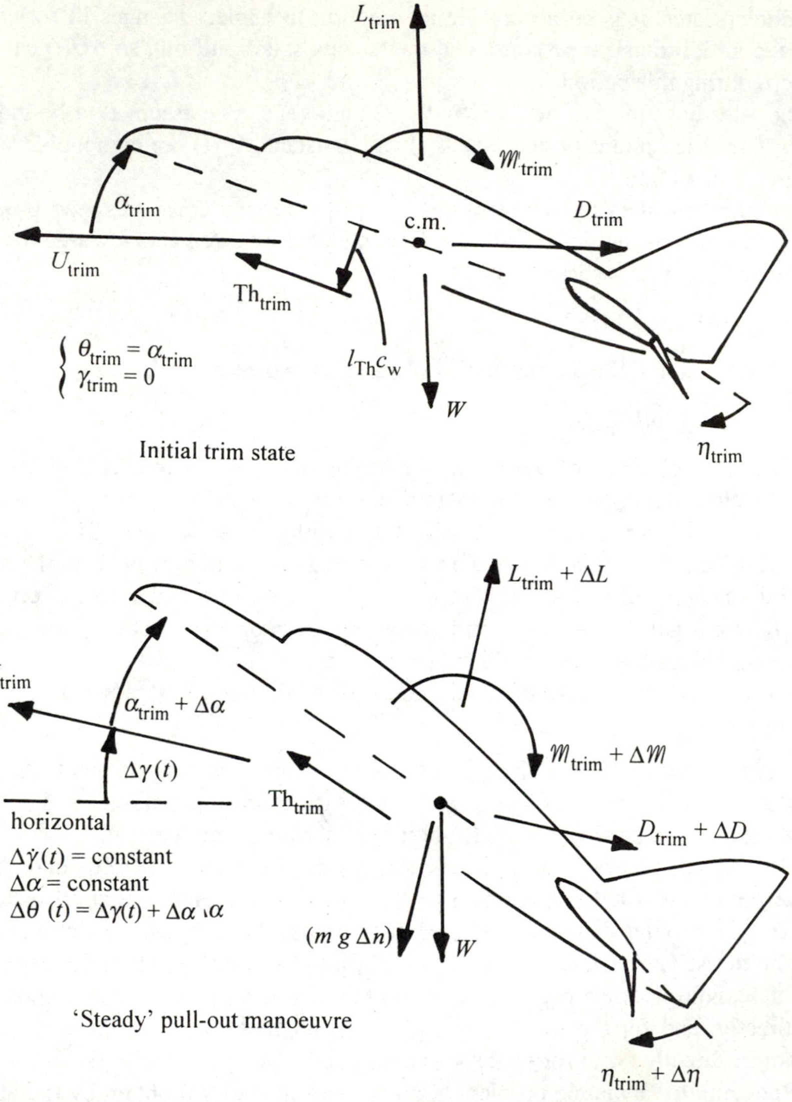

Fig. III.77. Loads in pull-out manoeuvre.

$$
\begin{aligned}
\text{Th}_{\text{trim}} \cos(\alpha_{\text{trim}} + \Delta\alpha) &= D_{\text{trim}} + \Delta D + W \sin \Delta\gamma(t) \\
\text{Th}_{\text{trim}} \sin(\alpha_{\text{trim}} + \Delta\alpha) + L_{\text{trim}} + \Delta L &= W \cos \Delta\gamma(t) + m(g\,\Delta n) \\
\text{Th}_{\text{trim}} l_{\text{Th}} c_{\text{w}} + \mathcal{M}_{\text{trim}} + \Delta\mathcal{M} &= 0.
\end{aligned}
\tag{III.6.6}
$$

Subtracting the equations in (III.6.5) from their counterparts in (III.6.6), assuming that all angles are small, and dividing by $(\frac{1}{2}\rho_{\text{at}} U_{\text{trim}}^2 S_{\text{w}})$,

$$0 = \Delta C_D + C_W\,\Delta\gamma(t)$$

$$\begin{aligned}(C_D)_{trim}\Delta\alpha + \Delta C_L &= \left[(C_D)_{trim} + C_{L\alpha}\right]\Delta\alpha + C_{L\eta}\Delta\eta \\ &\quad + C_{Lq}\left(g\,\Delta n/U_{trim}\right)\left((c_w/2)/U_{trim}\right) \\ &= C_W\Delta n\end{aligned} \tag{III.6.7}$$

$$C_{m\alpha}\Delta\alpha + C_{m\eta}\Delta\eta + C_{mq}\left(g\,\Delta n/U_{trim}\right)\left((c_w/2)/U_{trim}\right) = 0$$

substituting ΔC_L and ΔC_m in terms of their derivatives, noting that there are no $\dot{\alpha}$ nor $\dot{q}$ nor $\dot{\eta}$ terms because $\Delta\alpha$, q and $\Delta\eta$ are taken to be constant, and substituting for q from eqn. (III.6.3).

The second and third equations, the lift and moment equations, in eqns. (III.6.7) can be solved for $\Delta\alpha$ and $\Delta\eta$ in terms of ($g\,\Delta n$). But then the first equation is not satisfied; however, this equation may be ignored because the out-of-balance force in the flight direction is sufficiently small not to significantly affect the forward velocity during the pull-out manoeuvre. As time progresses it is the cumulative effect of this deceleration which decreases the forward velocity and effectively ends the 'steady state' pull-out.

Solving eqns. (III.6.7), remembering that $C_{m\eta} = -l_t\,C_{L\eta}$ and $K_\alpha = (-C_{m\alpha})/C_{L\alpha}$

$$\Delta\alpha = \frac{C_W\,\Delta n\left[1 - \left[C_{Lq} - (-C_{mq})/l_t\right]/2\overline{m}\right]}{C_{L\alpha}\left(1 - K_\alpha/l_t\right) + (C_D)_{trim}} \simeq \frac{C_W\Delta n}{C_{L\alpha}} \tag{III.6.8}$$

where

$$\begin{aligned}\overline{m} &= \text{non-dimensional mass parameter} \\ &= m/\left(\tfrac{1}{2}\rho_{at}S_w c_w\right) = (W/S_w)/\left(\tfrac{1}{2}g\rho_{at}c_w\right).\end{aligned} \tag{III.6.9}$$

At sea level $\overline{m} = O[150]$ for aeroplanes; note that $\overline{m}$ increases with altitude.

Eqn. (III.6.8) indicates the incremental change in angle of incidence, $\Delta\alpha$, which induces the incremental lift, which leads to the normal acceleration ($g\,\Delta n$). It is implicit in the above analysis that ($\alpha_{trim} + \Delta\alpha$) does not exceed α_b, the break incidence at which aerodynamic linearity ceases due to flow breakdown. Manoeuvrability at high angles of incidence above α_b is described later, in Part V.

On substitution of the approximation for $\Delta\alpha$ from eqn. (III.6.8) into the moment equation of eqns. (III.6.7),

$$\Delta\eta \simeq -C_W\Delta n\left[\frac{K_\alpha + \left((-C_{mq})/2\overline{m}\right)}{(-C_{m\eta})}\right]. \tag{III.6.10}$$

The ratio ($\Delta\eta/\Delta n$), known as the (elevator angle/g), depends on C_W, the incidence stiffness K_α, the smaller term $\left((-C_{mq})/2\overline{m}\right)$, and the pitch control 'power' ($-C_{m\eta}$).

III.6.1 Elevator manoeuvre margin

An elevator manoeuvre margin E_m is now introduced, defined by

$$E_m = -\Delta\eta/(C_W \Delta n). \qquad (III.6.11)$$

For positive manoeuvre control, stick back produces a pull-up, or stick forward produces a push-over, hence

$$\Delta n > 0 \text{ with } \Delta\eta < 0 \quad \text{or} \quad \Delta n < 0 \text{ with } \Delta\eta > 0,$$

which is obtained when

$$E_m > 0. \qquad (III.6.12)$$

For acceptable pitch control

(i) $(\Delta\eta/\Delta n)$ must not be too small, otherwise a unit change in $\Delta\eta$ could lead to a large normal acceleration which could overstress the aeroplane structure and lead to structural failure, or alternatively lead to pilot blackout.

(ii) $(\Delta\eta/\Delta n)$ must not be too large, otherwise the stick displacement needed to produce a required normal acceleration would become excessive, exacerbating the pilot work load.

From eqns. (III.6.10) and (III.6.11)

$$E_m \simeq \left[K_\alpha + \left((-C_{mq})/2\overline{m}\right)\right] / (-C_{m\eta}). \qquad (III.6.13)$$

In the literature the conventional manoeuvre margin H_m is defined as

$$H_m = \left[K_\alpha + \left((-C_{mq})/2\overline{m}\right)\right] = E_m(-C_{m\eta}). \qquad (III.6.14)$$

According to eqn. (III.6.14), E_m and H_m are the same parameter but of differing magnitudes; $(-C_{m\eta})$ is of the order of 1.5. But H_m is essentially a rigid aeroplane parameter, there are difficulties in defining a conventional manoeuvre margin for flexible aeroplanes, especially when tailplane and elevator flexibilities are included. On the other hand, the definition of the elevator manoeuvre margin E_m applies equally well to both rigid and flexible aeroplanes, and can be estimated in the design process and measured directly in flight.

An important result is that, because $\left((-C_{mq})/2\overline{m}\right)$ is positive, positive incidence stiffness, K_α, ensures positive conventional manoeuvre margin, H_m, and hence positive elevator manoeuvre margin, E_m, whatever the Mach number.

For typical values:

at low Mach numbers,

$$K_\alpha \simeq 0.15, \quad (-C_{mq}) \simeq 15.0, \quad (-C_{m\eta}) \simeq 1.5, \quad \overline{m} \text{ (sea level)} \simeq 150,$$

so

$$H_m \simeq 0.20, \qquad E_m \simeq 0.13; \qquad (III.6.15)$$

at high subsonic speeds at altitude,

$$K_\alpha \simeq 0.10, \quad (-C_{mq}) \simeq 18.0, \quad (-C_{m\eta}) \simeq 1.8, \quad \overline{m}(11 \text{ km}) \simeq 670,$$

so

$$H_m \simeq 0.11, \quad E_m \simeq 0.063; \tag{III.6.16}$$

at supersonic speeds at altitude,

$$K_\alpha \simeq 0.5, \quad (-C_{mq}) \simeq 15.0, \quad (-C_{m\eta}) \simeq 1.6, \quad \overline{m}(11 \text{ km}) \simeq 670,$$

so

$$H_m \simeq 0.51, \quad E_m \simeq 0.32. \tag{III.6.17}$$

From a control point of view (i.e. elevator angle/$g = C_W E_m$) the large increase in H_m, and E_m, from high subsonic to low supersonic speeds is partially compensated by the decrease in C_W.

Two control margins have been defined: the elevator trim margin E_{trim} in eqn. (III.5.16) and the elevator manoeuvre margin E_m in eqn. (III.6.11). It is of interest to compare their behaviour with increasing Mach number.

(i)   At low Mach numbers, when l_{Th} is zero, E_{trim} and E_m are simply related and are roughly equal.

(ii) At subsonic speeds with increase in Mach number, E_{trim} increases while E_m decreases.

(iii) At low supersonic speeds, E_{trim} can be negative while E_m can be large and positive.

(iv) At higher supersonic speeds, E_{trim} and E_m are both positive.

It should be noted that E_{trim} depends on l_{Th}, whereas E_m is independent of l_{Th}.

III.6.2 Manoeuvre point

The manoeuvre point is the location of the centre of mass at which E_m (and H_m) is zero.

Denoting the distance of the manoeuvre point aft of the wing–fuselage aerodynamic centre as $h_m c_w$, then from eqns. (III.6.14) and (III.3.146)

$$h_m = h_{ac} + \left((-C_{mq})/2\overline{m} \right) \tag{III.6.18}$$

where $h_{ac} c_w$ is the distance of the overall aerodynamic centre aft of the wing–fuselage aerodynamic centre. Hence

$$H_m = E_m(-C_{m\eta}) = (h_m - l_{wf}). \tag{III.6.19}$$

For positive E_m and positive H_m the centre of mass must be located ahead of the manoeuvre point.

The manoeuvre point lies aft of the overall aerodynamic centre, irrespective of Mach number, the difference decreasing with altitude. The manoeuvre point and the overall aerodynamic centre tend to move together with change in Mach number.

At subsonic speeds the wing–fuselage aerodynamic centre is insensitive to Mach number so the manoeuvre point moves forward relative to the airframe with increasing Mach number. At supersonic speeds the manoeuvre point relative to the airframe moves back dramatically because the wing–fuselage aerodynamic centre moves aft and h_m also increases.

III.6.3 Manoeuvre control loads

The incremental elevator hinge moment per unit normal acceleration, or (elevator manoeuvre hinge moment/g), is, by reference to Fig. III.78,

$$\begin{aligned}
&(\text{elevator manoeuvre hinge moment}/g)\\
&= \Delta(\text{elevator hinge moment})/\Delta n\\
&= \tfrac{1}{2}\rho_{\text{at}}U^2 S_e c_e\left[b_\alpha \Delta\alpha(1-\partial\varepsilon/\partial\alpha)+b_\eta\Delta\eta\right]+\left[(m_e g\,\Delta n)\,h_e c_e\right]/\Delta n\\
&= Wc_e(S_e/S_W)\left[(-b_\eta)E_m-((-b_\alpha)(1-\partial\varepsilon/\partial\alpha)/C_{L\alpha})+((m_e/S_e)/(m/S_W))\,h_e\right]
\end{aligned}$$

(III.6.20)

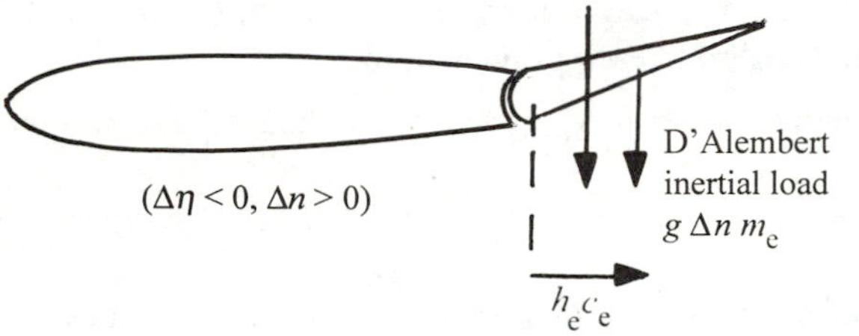

Fig. III.78. Manoeuvre elevator loads.

where m_e is the elevator mass and $h_e c_e$ is the distance of the elevator centre of mass aft of the elevator hinge line, substituting for $\Delta\alpha$ and $\Delta\eta$ from eqns. (III.6.8) and (III.6.11). Eqn. (III.6.20) assumes no manoeuvre (i.e. geared, or servo, or spring) tab arrangement.

A most important observation arises from eqn. (III.6.20), the (elevator manoeuvre hinge moment/g) is independent of C_W. The effect of speed is confined to the effects of Mach number on $(-b_\eta)$, E_m, $(-b_\alpha)$, $\partial\varepsilon/\partial\alpha$ and $C_{L\alpha}$. The variation of the (elevator manoeuvre hinge moment/g) with Mach number closely parallels the variation of E_m with Mach number. At subsonic speeds the (elevator manoeuvre hinge moment/g) decreases significantly with increase in Mach number and decreases marginally with increase in altitude. At supersonic speeds there is a large increase in the (elevator manoeuvre hinge moment/g) not only because E_m increases but also because, for an all-moving tailplane, c_e and S_e become c_t and S_t respectively; combat manoeuvrability is limited in the range of Δn at supersonic speeds compared with the range of Δn at subsonic speeds, see the manoeuvre envelope, Fig. I.2.

It is also noted from eqn. (III.6.20) that for aeroplanes of similar geometries the (elevator manoeuvre hinge moment/g) is proportional to (Wc_e). Hence the need to resort to power controls on subsonic aeroplanes depends on aeroplane size rather than on forward speed. Power controls are necessary at transonic speeds because the elevator hinge moments can vary rapidly and erratically with small changes of speed and elevator angles. Power controls are necessary at supersonic speeds because of the large elevator manoeuvre hinge moments.

For all aeroplanes a backward stick displacement moves the elevator up (i.e. $\Delta\eta < 0$), giving a positive normal acceleration ($\Delta n > 0$) and *vice versa* with a forward stick displacement. To move the stick backward a backward force must be applied and to move the stick forward a forward force must be applied. These stick forces must be neither too small (i.e. too sensitive) nor too large (i.e. too heavy). From a pilot's point of view the (stick force/g) is a more important parameter than (stick displacement/g).

III.6.3.1 Manual controls

For aeroplanes with manual controls a backward stick force for positive g reacts a positive, nose-up, elevator manoeuvre hinge moment, so the (stick force/g) is given by

$$(\text{stick force}/g) = G_f\,(\text{elevator manoeuvre hinge moment}/g) \qquad \text{(III.6.21)}$$

where G_f is the force gearing between the stick and the elevator.

A positive (stick force/g) requires

$$\left[(-b_\eta)E_m + \left[(m_e/S_e)/(m/S_w)h_e\right]\right] > (-b_\alpha)(1-\partial\varepsilon/\partial\alpha)/C_{L\alpha}. \qquad \text{(III.6.22)}$$

When the elevator is mass balanced (i.e. $h_e = 0$) ($-b_\eta$) must be positive and then eqn. (III.6.22) imposes a condition on E_m, which automatically satisfies the condition $E_m > 0$.

Two manoeuvre points can be defined:

(i) stick displacement manoeuvre point, namely the manoeuvre point defined in sect. III.6.3, when the location of the centre of mass satisfies the condition E_m equal to zero;

(ii) stick force manoeuvre point, when the location of the centre of mass satisfies the condition

$$E_m - \left[\left((-b_\alpha)(1-\partial\varepsilon/\partial\alpha)/C_{L\alpha}\right) - \left((m_e/S_e)/(m/S_w)h_e\right)\right]/(-b_\eta) = 0. \qquad \text{(III.6.23)}$$

The stick force manoeuvre point, which lies in front of the stick displacement manoeuvre point, defines a design criterion for the most aft location of the centre of mass for aeroplanes with manual controls.

There are a range of design options to ensure that the range of (stick force/g) lies within specified limits: aerodynamic balance (see Fig. III.45) reduces both ($-b_\eta$) and ($-b_\alpha$); geared tabs or spring tabs (see Fig. III.46) reduce ($-b_\eta$) but not ($-b_\alpha$); bob weights attached to the elevator ahead of the elevator hinge line, or in the control run, can make h_e negative. The design of a manual system of elevator, trim tab, manoeuvre tab and mechanical linkages is far from straightforward and is time consuming; the design process is more an art than a precise scientific methodology, relying on past experience and folklore. The introduction of powered controls simplifies these design difficulties but at the expense of increased weight.

III.6.3.2 Powered controls

For aeroplanes with powered controls there is no requirement that the elevator manoeuvre hinge moment remains positive; the hydraulic jack moves the elevator in the desired direction irrespective of the sign of the elevator hinge moment. A knowledge of the maximum elevator hinge manoeuvre moment is necessary to size the actuators.

Although there is still a direct gearing between the stick displacement and elevator angle the force on the stick, which is directly proportional to the force on the valve in the hydraulic unit, is extremely small. The (stick force/g) felt by the pilot is now provided by an artificial feel system.

In a 'Q-feel' system the stick is connected to a spring of variable stiffness, as shown in Fig. III.79(i), where the spring stiffness is proportional to the dynamic pressure ($\frac{1}{2}\rho_{at}U^2$). The spring is a hydraulic device in which the stiffness depends on hydraulic pressure and the hydraulic pressure is controlled by the dynamic pressure as measured by the pitot-static tube in the air data system. Hence

$$\begin{aligned}(\text{stick force}/g) &\propto (\text{dynamic pressure})\ (\text{stick displacement}/g)\\ &\propto (\text{dynamic pressure})\ (\Delta\eta/g)\\ &\propto E_m. \qquad \text{(III.6.24)}\end{aligned}$$

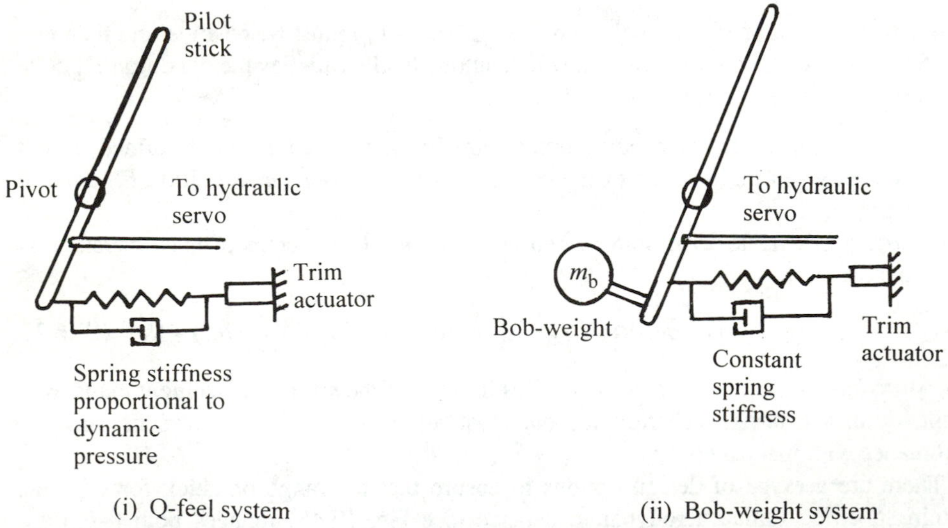

Fig. III.79. Artificial feel systems.

Although there is no attempt to reproduce a stick force proportional to the actual hinge moment, compare eqns. (III.6.20) and (III.6.24), the (stick force/g) from the artificial feel system is independent of C_W, but depends on Mach number and altitude through E_m, conforming broadly to manual control system experience.

A trim actuator is included to reduce the stick force to zero in trimmed flight.

At supersonic speeds the dynamic pressure can become large so the dependency of the spring stiffness on dynamic pressure is switched out and the spring stiffness then remains constant.

An alternative artificial feel system to the Q-feel system is by simply attaching a bob-weight to the stick, as shown in Fig. III.79(ii). In this case the stick force is directly proportional to the normal acceleration, irrespective of the stick displacement, under all conditions of flight. Traditionally bob-weights have been troublesome because of their inertial effects in time varying manoeuvres.

On a combat aeroplane with an all-moving tailplane $(-b_\eta)$ and $(-b_\alpha)$ are equal, so for a mass-balanced tailplane the (elevator manoeuvre hinge moment/g) is directly proportional to $(-b_\alpha)$. As explained in sect. III.5.2.2, the hinge axis is usually located about half way between the subsonic and supersonic centres of pressure.

III.6.4 Range of elevator angle

The range of required elevator angle must encompass the full range of elevator trim angles, together with additional elevator angles to cover the full range of design manoeuvres, throughout the entire flight envelope, for a designated range of locations of the centre of mass, flaps up and flaps down.

The range of required elevator angle can be obtained by superimposing $\Delta\eta\ (= -C_W E_m\, \Delta n)$, for the maximum and minimum values of Δn, on $\eta_{trim} \sim C_W$, for the most forward and most aft locations of the centre of mass, flaps up and flaps down, as shown in Fig. III.80.

There is an additional 'flight condition' which affects the range of elevator angle, namely the ground run at take-off.

During the ground run the stick is held forward to generate an up-load (positive lift) on the tailplane to ensure that the nose wheel remains attached to the ground to maintain adequate steering capability.

At the end of the ground run the stick is pulled hard back to generate a download on the tailplane to rotate the aeroplane for lift-off. The maximum tailplane download for rotation is dictated by the most forward location of the centre of mass relative to the main wheels. Usually,

- —the maximum positive elevator angle is determined by providing the required manoeuvre capability at maximum speed, flaps up, with the most aft location of the centre of mass;
- —the minimum negative elevator angle is determined by providing the required tailplane download at rotation with the most forward location of the centre of mass, with flaps down.

The range should not extend beyond the bounds of losing tailplane lift through flow separation. In general, to arrange for the elevator angle to extend from positive to negative values the tailplane setting angle will be negative.

Typical ranges for the elevator are $+10° \rightarrow -20°$.

III.6.5 Extended pull-ups

The above analysis is based on the assumption that the flight path angle remains small. For a combat aeroplane, or aerobatic light aeroplane, a pull-up manoeuvre may continue

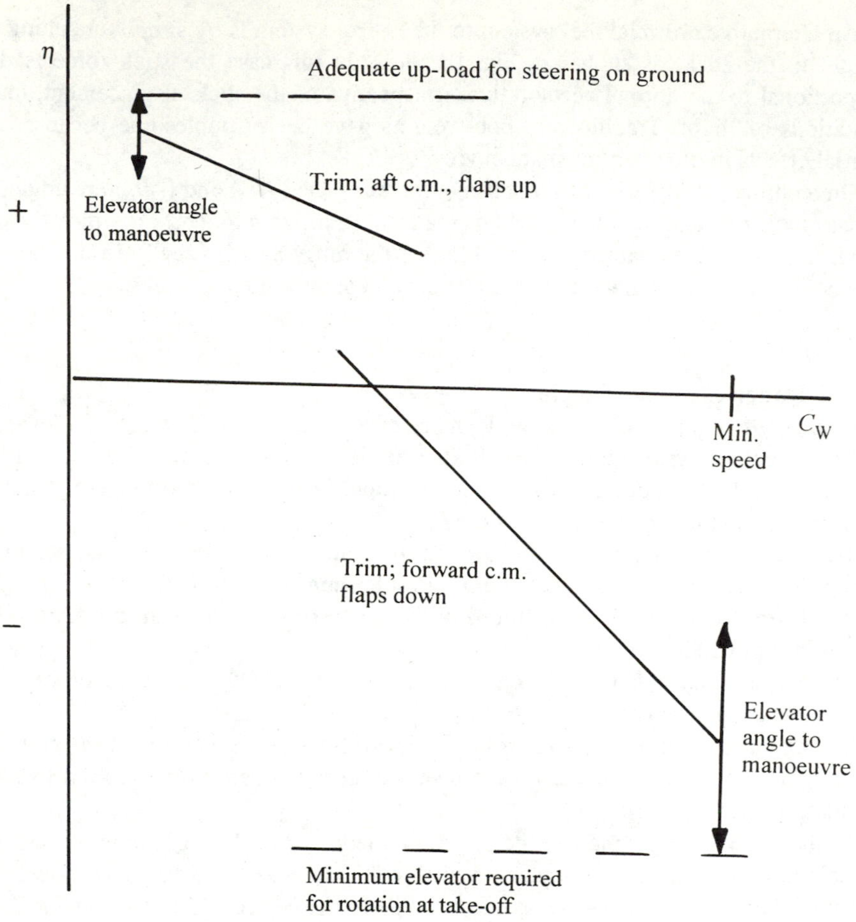

Fig. III.80. Range of elevator angle.

up to a well inclined flight path angle especially if the pilot also opens the throttle. There are two options.

(i) The pilot can maintain a constant normal acceleration Δn with the flight path continuing along an arc of a circle; in this case the component of all-up weight normal to the flight path decreases as $W \cos \gamma$ so the lift must be decreased accordingly to maintain a constant normal acceleration, thus the stick must be gradually eased forward to rotate the aeroplane nose-down as the flight path angle builds up.

(ii) The pilot can fly 'by the seat of his pants' and maintain the sensation of being pushed down in his seat by a constant force. From D'Alembert's principle the force on the pilot into his seat is $[m_P (\Delta n + \cos \gamma)g]$, where m_P is the mass of the pilot. To keep this force constant as γ increases, Δn must increase, so the lift must increase, so the stick must be gradually eased back to rotate the nose up as the flight path angle builds up.

EXAMPLES III.25

1. Determine typical values of $\Delta\eta/\Delta n$ in degrees$/\Delta n$ for the three basic configurations.
2. Plot the variations of the overall aerodynamic centre and manoeuvre points with Mach number measured from the wing apex for the three basic configurations.
3. Describe in qualitative terms the effect of propeller slipstream on E_m.
4. Describe in qualitative terms the effect of underwing weapons on E_m.
5. Does the deployment of the high lift system affect E_{trim} or E_m; if so, how?
6. Estimate the maximum value of (elevator manoeuvre hinge moment$/g$) for the combat aeroplane basic configuration.
7. Determine the range of elevator angle required for trim and manoeuvrability for the three basic configurations throughout their flight envelope .

III.7 LONGITUDINAL STATIC WEATHERCOCK STABILITY

Longitudinal static weathercock stability is a simplified and qualitative concept which plays a central role in longitudinal flight dynamics. Contrary to what is said in much of the literature, longitudinal static weathercock stability is not overall static stability, see sect. III.16.

Consider an aeroplane in steady level flight in a state of static equilibrium at speed U_{trim}, angle of incidence α_{trim}, angle of pitch θ_{trim} (= α_{trim}) and elevator angle η_{trim}.

Suppose that this aeroplane is given a static longitudinal weathercock disturbance, namely a static pitch angle disturbance, $\Delta\theta$, without changing the forward speed or its direction, as shown in Fig. III.81, so the static angle of incidence ($\alpha_{trim} + \Delta\alpha$) and the static angle of pitch ($\theta_{trim} + \Delta\theta$) remain the same (i.e. $\alpha_{trim} = \theta_{trim}$, $\Delta\alpha = \Delta\theta$).

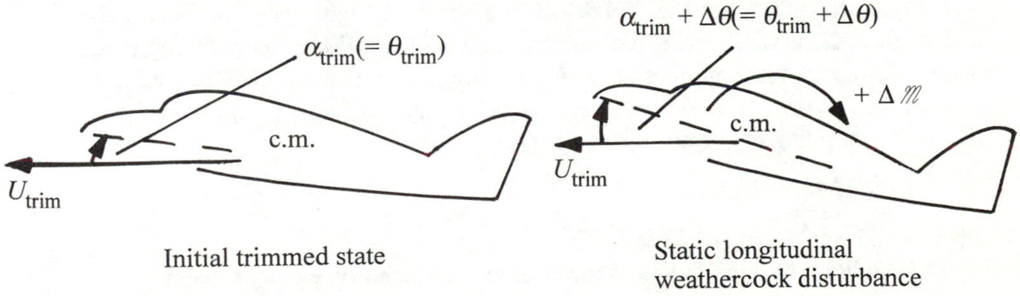

Fig. III.81. Static longitudinal weathercock stability.

If the static aerodynamic moment on the aeroplane tends to return the aeroplane to its initial trimmed condition the aeroplane is said to have positive longitudinal static weathercock stability. Hence

(i) if $\Delta\theta\,(= \Delta\alpha) > 0$, a nose-down static incremental aerodynamic moment, $\Delta\mathcal{M} < 0$, should act to reduce the angle of pitch and incidence, tending to return the aeroplane to its original trim state;

(ii) if $\Delta\theta\,(=\Delta\alpha) < 0$, a nose-up static incremental aerodynamic moment, $\Delta\mathcal{M} > 0$, should act to increase the angle of pitch and incidence, tending to return the aeroplane to its original trim state.

The static incremental aerodynamic moment $\Delta\mathcal{M}$ depends on angle of incidence but not on the angle of pitch. Hence the condition

$$\Delta\mathcal{M}/\Delta\alpha < 0 \qquad \text{(III.7.1)}$$

satisfies both (i) and (ii).

For aeroplanes with powered controls with the pilot flying hands-off in trimmed flight, the elevator is locked in its trim position by the hydraulic actuator. Therefore, during any disturbance, the elevator angle remains fixed in its initial trim position. So then

$$\Delta\mathcal{M} = \tfrac{1}{2}\rho_{\text{at}} U_{\text{trim}}^2 S_{\text{w}} C_{m\alpha}\,\Delta\alpha. \qquad \text{(III.7.2)}$$

By reference to eqns. (III.7.1) and (III.7.2), the condition for longitudinal static weathercock stability, elevator fixed, becomes

$$C_{m\alpha} < 0; \qquad \text{(III.7.3)}$$

or alternatively

$$\text{incidence stiffness} = K_\alpha = (-C_{m\alpha})/C_{\text{L}\alpha} > 0. \qquad \text{(III.7.4)}$$

Positive incidence stiffness ensures longitudinal static weathercock stability, elevator fixed; this statement applies at all Mach numbers, subsonic through to supersonic.

For an aeroplane with manual controls the longitudinal static weathercock stability, elevator fixed, as expressed by eqns. (III.7.3) and (III.7.4) would apply if the pilot held the stick in its trimmed position throughout a disturbance. But if, for an aeroplane with manual controls, the pilot flies hands-off in a trimmed flight condition, and if the pilot does not touch the stick during a disturbance, the elevator floats freely during that disturbance. Zero stick force implies zero elevator hinge moment, so when the angle of incidence becomes $(\alpha_{\text{trim}} + \Delta\alpha)$ the elevator angle changes to $(\eta_{\text{trim}} + \Delta\eta)$, where, from eqn. (III.5.22), assuming only static disturbances,

$$\mathcal{b}_\alpha\,\Delta\alpha(1 - \partial\varepsilon/\partial\alpha) + \mathcal{b}_\eta\,\Delta\eta = 0 \qquad \text{(III.7.5)}$$

since the tab angle remains fixed.

The condition for longitudinal static weathercock stability, elevator free, is

$$\Delta\mathcal{M}/\Delta\alpha = \tfrac{1}{2}\rho_{\text{at}} U_{\text{trim}}^2 S_{\text{w}}\,(C_{m\alpha}\,\Delta\alpha + C_{m\eta}\Delta\eta)/\Delta\alpha < 0 \qquad \text{(III.7.6)}$$

that is, from eqn. (III.7.5), when,

$$C_{m\alpha} - C_{m\eta}\left(\mathcal{b}_\alpha/\mathcal{b}_\eta\right)(1 - \partial\varepsilon/\partial\alpha) < 0;$$

or alternatively, when

$$K_\alpha - \left((-C_{m\eta})/C_{\text{L}\alpha}\right)\left((-\mathcal{b}_\alpha)/(-\mathcal{b}_\eta)\right)(1 - \partial\varepsilon/\partial\alpha) > 0. \qquad \text{(III.7.7)}$$

Typical low speed values are

$$K_\alpha \simeq 0.15, \quad \big((-C_{m\eta})/C_{L\alpha}\big)\big((-b_\alpha)/(-b_\eta)\big)(1-\partial\varepsilon/\partial\alpha) \simeq 0.05. \qquad \text{(III.7.8)}$$

Eqn. (III.7.6) also applies to high subsonic transport and combat aeroplanes when stability augmentation systems or active control systems are operative, then $\Delta\eta/\Delta\alpha$ depends on the feed-back control law, as described later.

The arguments above describe the longitudinal static weathercock stability of an aeroplane given a steady disturbance from an initial condition of steady level flight. The same arguments apply when the initial aeroplane state is any condition of static equilibrium: steady climb, steady descent and the pull-out manoeuvre.

Positive, elevator fixed, longitudinal static weathercock stability (i.e. $K_\alpha > 0$) is an important design criterion because it ensures

(i) positive elevator manoeuvre margin (i.e. $E_m > 0$) at all Mach numbers;
(ii) positive elevator trim margin (i.e. $E_{trim} > 0$) at low Mach numbers when l_{Th} is zero.

Positive, elevator free, longitudinal static weathercock stability, eqn. (III.7.7), is an important design criterion for aeroplanes with manual controls because it ensures

(i) positive (stick force/g) for a mass balanced elevator in the pull-out manoeuvre, eqns. (III.6.20) and (III.6.21);
(ii) positive (stick force/ΔU_{trim}) in trimmed flight, eqn. (III.5.30) at low Mach numbers, when l_{Th} is zero.

The above two paragraphs demonstrate that positive stability and positive control are closely interlinked.

From the definition of incidence stiffness, namely,

$$K_\alpha = -l_{wf} + l(S_t/S_w)\,\big((a_\alpha)_t/C_{L\alpha}\big)\,(1-\partial\varepsilon/\partial\alpha)$$

it should be noted that longitudinal static weathercock stability does not depend on main wing camber or wash-out, or on main wing or tailplane setting angles.

In the light aeroplane fraternity it is often said that the setting angle of the main wing relative to the tailplane, the so-called longitudinal dihedral, plays a role in longitudinal static weathercock stability, elevator fixed. This long-standing piece of folklore stems from the early days of model glider flight where static equilibrium and stability were interrelated.

Consider, as shown in Fig. III.82(i), a glider model where a symmetric wing and symmetric tailplane are aligned. For this model the total lift at any angle of incidence acts through the overall model aerodynamic centre, so to balance this model in steady flight the centre of mass must be located at the overall aerodynamic centre, but then the longitudinal static weathercock stability would be zero. For satisfactory flight characteristics it is necessary to ensure both static equilibrium and positive longitudinal static weathercock stability, that is, the centre of mass must coincide with the overall centre of pressure of the total lift, and the centre of mass must be located ahead of the overall aerodynamic centre. If the tailplane angle is reduced relative to the main wing angle, as shown in Fig. III.82(ii), the overall centre of pressure of the total lift moves forward

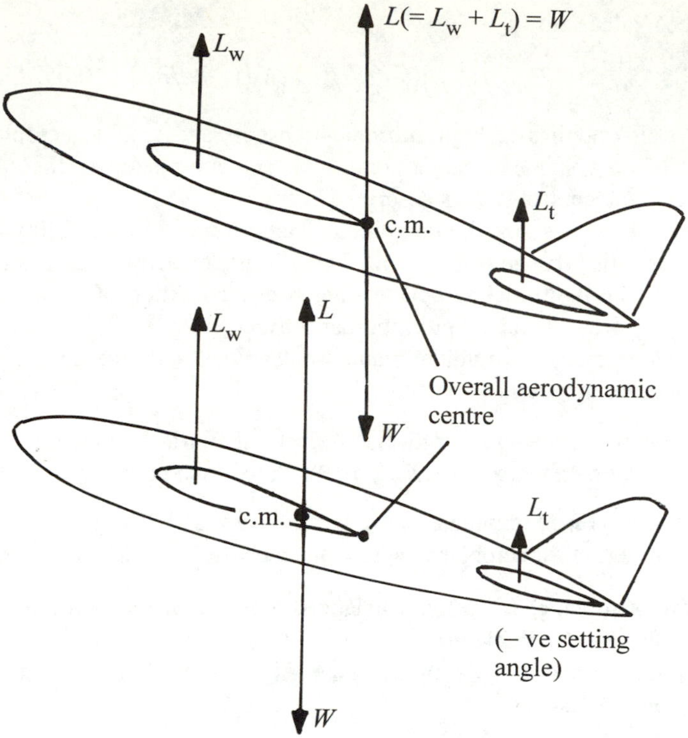

Fig. III.82. Trim and stability of a glider model.

relative to the overall aerodynamic centre, so if the centre of mass is moved forward to coincide with the overall centre of pressure, the glider model is both balanced and stable. Thus longitudinal dihedral, which does not affect the position of the overall aerodynamic centre, is necessary to push the overall centre of pressure of the total lift forward of the overall aerodynamic centre to ensure stable, steady, flight. For this configuration a download on the tailplane occurs with a large longitudinal dihedral; a download on the tailplane would guarantee stable flight but the incidence stiffness, and manoeuvre margin, would become high, leading to pitching oscillations in turbulence.

III.8 LONGITUDINAL SMALL PERTURBATIONS ABOUT A STEADY STATE

In this section the basic equations are derived for an aeroplane perturbed from an initial steady state (level flight, climbing flight, descending flight) when a pilot moves the stick to change the elevator angle and/or changes the throttle.

Consider an aeroplane trimmed in steady flight, as shown in Fig. III.83(i), at forward speed U_{trim}, angle of incidence α_{trim}, pitch angle θ_{trim}, flight path angle γ_{trim} (= $(\theta_{trim} - \alpha_{trim})$) and elevator angle η_{trim}. The aerodynamic trim lift, L_{trim}, and trim drag, D_{trim}, act through the centre of mass, and the aerodynamic pitching moment is

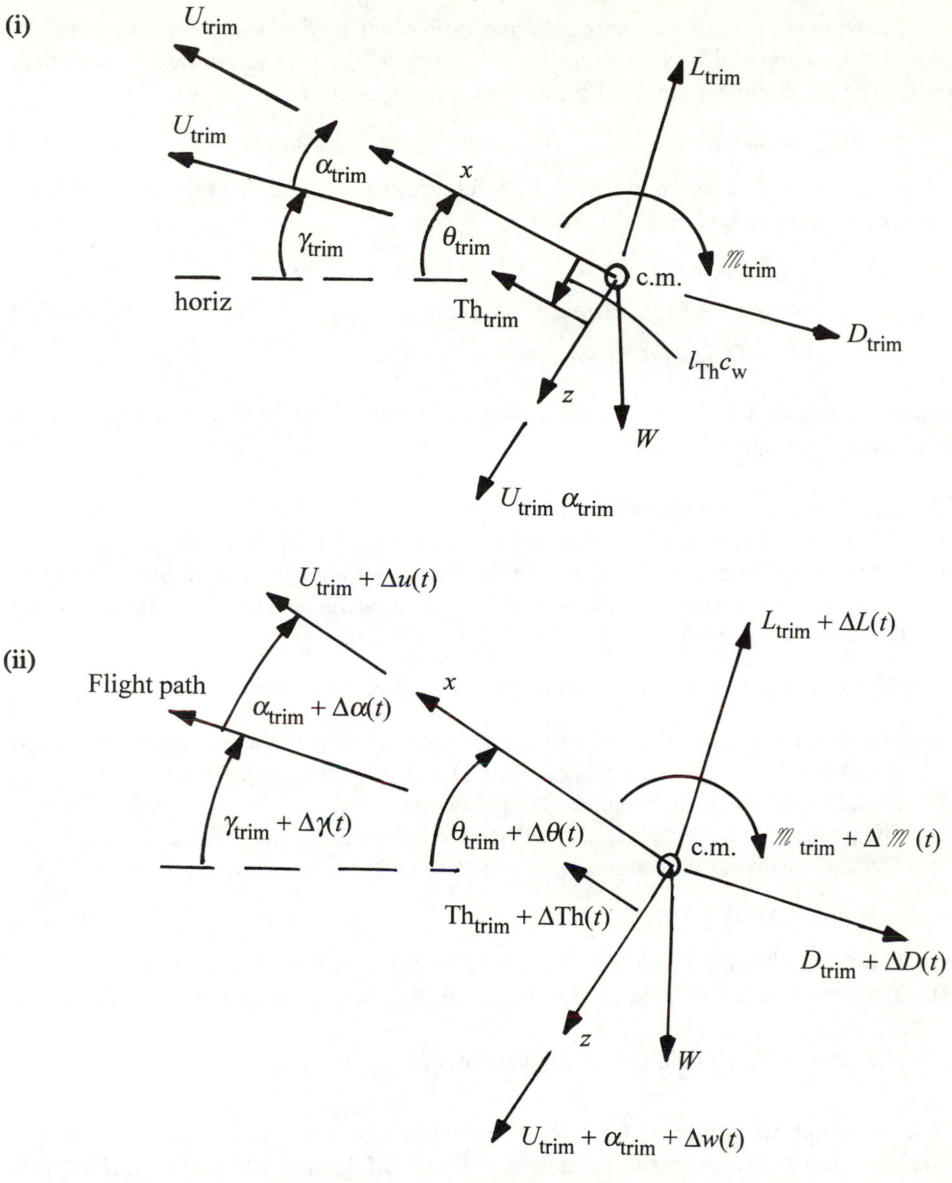

Fig. III.83. Loads on perturbed motions. (i) Initial trimmed state. (ii) Perturbed state.

$\mathcal{M}_{trim}$. The thrust Th_{trim} acts parallel to the fuselage longitudinal axis at a distance $l_{Th}c_w$ below it.

Fuselage body axes *oxyz* are taken fixed in the aeroplane with the origin at the centre of mass. The *ox* axis, which coincides with the fuselage longitudinal axis, points forward. The *oz* axis, perpendicular to the *ox* axis, points downward. The *oy* axis points to starboard; by definition the *oy* axis remains horizontal during any longitudinal motion.

In the trimmed state the components of absolute velocity of the aeroplane centre of mass in the *ox*, *oy* and *oz* directions are ($U_{trim}\cos\alpha_{trim}$, 0, $U_{trim}\sin\alpha_{trim}$). Assuming trim α to be small, the longitudinal components are denoted by

$$U_{trim}\cos\alpha_{trim} \simeq U_{trim}, \qquad U_{trim}\sin\alpha_{trim} \simeq U_{trim}\alpha_{trim}. \tag{III.8.1}$$

The equations of static equilibrium, by reference to Fig. III.83(i), resolving the force components in the *ox* and *oz* directions, are:

$$\begin{aligned} \mathrm{Th}_{trim} + L_{trim}\sin\alpha_{trim} &= D_{trim}\cos\alpha_{trim} + W\sin\theta_{trim}, \\ L_{trim}\cos\alpha_{trim} + D_{trim}\sin\alpha_{trim} &= W\cos\theta_{trim}, \\ \mathrm{Th}_{trim} l_{Th} c_w + \mathcal{M}_{trim} &= 0. \end{aligned} \tag{III.8.2}$$

Suppose that the pilot changes the elevator angle and throttle in a time varying manner starting at a datum time, $t = 0$. Then:

(i) the elevator angle becomes $\eta_{trim} + \Delta\eta(t)$;
(ii) with a turbo-fan engine a change in throttle changes the thrust to $(\mathrm{Th}_{trim} + \Delta\mathrm{Th}(t))$;
(iii) with a propeller propulsion unit, whether driven by a turbo-prop engine or reciprocating engine, a change in throttle changes the power, leading to a change in the thrust of the form $[\mathrm{Th}_{trim}(1 + \Delta u(t)/U_{trim}) + \Delta\mathrm{Th}(t)]$.

The dynamic response of the aeroplane is shown in Fig. III.83(ii).

(i) The absolute velocity components at any instant of time in the instantaneous *ox* and *oz* directions are denoted as $(U_{trim} + \Delta u(t))$ and $(U_{trim}\alpha_{trim} + \Delta w(t))$.
(ii) The angle of incidence becomes $(\alpha_{trim} + \Delta\alpha(t))$.
(iii) The pitch angle becomes $(\theta_{trim} + \Delta\theta(t))$; the rate of pitch $q(t)$ is equal to $\Delta\dot{\theta}(t)$.
(iv) The flight path angle becomes $(\gamma_{trim} + \Delta\gamma(t))$, so

$$\Delta\gamma(t) = \Delta\theta(t) - \Delta\alpha(t). \tag{III.8.3}$$

(v) The aerodynamic lift becomes $(L_{trim} + \Delta L(t))$ acting normal to the flight path.
(vi) The aerodynamic drag becomes $(D_{trim} + \Delta D(t))$ acting aft in the direction of the flight path.
(vii) The aerodynamic pitching moment becomes $(\mathcal{M}_{trim} + \Delta\mathcal{M}(t))$.

For an aeroplane with turbo-fan engines the equations of longitudinal motion relative to the body axis system *oxyz* are, by reference to sect. III.4, eqns. (III.4.17) and (III.4.18):

$$\begin{aligned} m\left[\Delta\dot{u}(t) + \left(U_{trim}\alpha_{trim} + \Delta w(t)\right)\Delta\dot{\theta}(t)\right] &= F_x(t) \\ m\left[\Delta\dot{w}(t) - \left(U_{trim} + \Delta u(t)\right)\Delta\dot{\theta}(t)\right] &= F_z(t) \\ I_{yy}\Delta\ddot{\theta}(t) &= M(t) \end{aligned} \tag{III.8.4}$$

where

m = the total aeroplane mass

$$F_x(t) = \text{resultant force in the direction } ox$$
$$= \left(\text{Th}_{\text{trim}} + \Delta\text{Th}(t)\right) + \left(L_{\text{trim}} + \Delta L(t)\right)\sin\left(\alpha_{\text{trim}} + \Delta\alpha(t)\right)$$
$$- \left(D_{\text{trim}} + \Delta D(t)\right)\cos\left(\alpha_{\text{trim}} + \Delta\alpha(t)\right) - W\sin\left(\theta_{\text{trim}} + \Delta\theta(t)\right)$$
$$F_z(t) = \text{resultant force in the direction } oz$$
$$= W\cos\left(\theta_{\text{trim}} + \Delta\theta(t)\right) - \left(L_{\text{trim}} + \Delta L(t)\right)\cos\left(\alpha_{\text{trim}} + \Delta\alpha(t)\right)$$
$$- \left(D_{\text{trim}} + \Delta D(t)\right)\sin\left(\alpha_{\text{trim}} + \Delta\alpha(t)\right)$$
$$M(t) = \mathcal{M}_{\text{trim}} + \Delta\mathcal{M}(t) + \left(\text{Th}_{\text{trim}} + \Delta\text{Th}(t)\right)l_{\text{Th}}c_{\text{w}}.$$

It is assumed that the terms $(\Delta u(t)/U_{\text{trim}})$, $(\Delta w(t)/U_{\text{trim}})$, $\Delta\alpha(t)$, $\Delta\gamma(t)$, $\Delta\theta(t)$, $(\Delta L(t)/L_{\text{trim}})$, and $(\Delta D(t)/D_{\text{trim}})$ are small; so-called small perturbations. And then products of all small perturbations (e.g. $(\Delta L(t)/L_{\text{trim}})\Delta\alpha(t)$, $\Delta w(t)\Delta\theta(t)$), the second order terms, can be neglected.

Furthermore, when α_{trim} is small

$$\begin{aligned} \sin\left(\alpha_{\text{trim}} + \Delta\alpha(t)\right) &\simeq \alpha_{\text{trim}} + \Delta\alpha(t) \\ \cos\left(\alpha_{\text{trim}} + \Delta\alpha(t)\right) &\simeq 1 \end{aligned} \tag{III.8.5}$$

assuming $(\alpha_{\text{trim}}\,\Delta\alpha\,(t))$ to be a second order term and negligible.

Neglecting all second order perturbation quantities and cancelling out the trim conditions, eqns. (III.8.2), the equations of motion (eqns. (III.8.4)) become

$$\begin{aligned} m\left(\Delta\dot{u}(t) + U_{\text{trim}}\alpha_{\text{trim}}\Delta\dot{\theta}(t)\right) &= \Delta\text{Th}(t) + L_{\text{trim}}\left[\Delta\alpha(t) + \left(\Delta L(t)/L_{\text{trim}}\right)\alpha_{\text{trim}}\right] \\ &\quad - \Delta D(t) - W\cos\theta_{\text{trim}}\,\Delta\theta(t) \\ m\left(\Delta\dot{w}(t) - U_{\text{trim}}\Delta\dot{\theta}(t)\right) &= -W\sin\theta_{\text{trim}}\,\Delta\theta(t) - \Delta L(t) \\ &\quad - D_{\text{trim}}\left[\Delta\alpha(t) + \left(\Delta D(t)/D_{\text{trim}}\right)\alpha_{\text{trim}}\right] \\ I_{yy}\Delta\ddot{\theta}(t) &= \Delta\mathcal{M}(t) + \Delta\text{Th}(t)\,l_{\text{Th}}c_{\text{w}} \end{aligned} \tag{III.8.6}$$

Assuming α_{trim} to be small, the terms

$$\alpha_{\text{trim}}\Delta\theta(t), \quad \left(\Delta L_{\text{trim}}/L_{\text{trim}}\right)\alpha_{\text{trim}}, \quad \left(\Delta D_{\text{trim}}/D_{\text{trim}}\right)\alpha_{\text{trim}} \tag{III.8.7}$$

are of second order and can be neglected.

By definition, see eqn. (II.1.3),

$$\begin{aligned} \alpha_{\text{trim}} + \Delta\alpha(t) &= \left(U_{\text{trim}}\alpha_{\text{trim}} + \Delta w(t)\right)/\left(U_{\text{trim}} + \Delta u(t)\right) \\ &= \left(\alpha_{\text{trim}} + (\Delta w(t)/U)\right)\left(1 - (\Delta u(t)/U_{\text{trim}})\ldots\right) \end{aligned}$$

so

$$\Delta\alpha(t) = \Delta w(t)/U_{\text{trim}}, \tag{III.8.8}$$

when all second order terms are neglected.

Next the perturbation aerodynamic forces and moment $\Delta L(t)$, $\Delta D(t)$ and $\Delta M(t)$ are expanded out in terms of their aerodynamic derivatives, see sect. III.3.11.

$$\Delta D(t) = \tfrac{1}{2}\rho_{\mathrm{at}} U_{\mathrm{trim}}^2 S_{\mathrm{w}} \left[C_{\mathrm{D}U}\left(\Delta u(t)/U_{\mathrm{trim}}\right) + C_{\mathrm{D}\alpha}\Delta\alpha(t) \right]$$

$$\begin{aligned} \Delta L(t) = {} & \tfrac{1}{2}\rho_{\mathrm{at}} U_{\mathrm{trim}}^2 S_{\mathrm{w}} \\ & \times \Big[C_{\mathrm{L}U}\left(\Delta u(t)/U_{\mathrm{trim}}\right) + C_{\mathrm{L}\alpha}\Delta\alpha(t) + C_{\mathrm{L}\dot{\alpha}}\left(\Delta\dot{\alpha}(t)\left(c_{\mathrm{w}}/2\right)/U_{\mathrm{trim}}\right) \\ & + C_{\mathrm{L}q}\left(q(t)\left(c_{\mathrm{w}}/2\right)/U_{\mathrm{trim}}\right) + C_{\mathrm{L}\dot{q}}\left(\dot{q}(t)\left(\left(c_{\mathrm{w}}/2\right)/U_{\mathrm{trim}}\right)^2\right) \\ & + C_{\mathrm{L}\eta}\Delta\eta(t) + C_{\mathrm{L}\dot{\eta}}\left(\Delta\dot{\eta}(t)\left(c_{\mathrm{w}}/2\right)/U_{\mathrm{trim}}\right)\Big]. \end{aligned} \qquad \text{(III.8.9)}$$

$$\begin{aligned} \Delta \mathcal{M}(t) = {} & \tfrac{1}{2}\rho_{\mathrm{at}} U_{\mathrm{trim}}^2 S_{\mathrm{w}} c_{\mathrm{w}} \\ & \times \Big[C_{mU}\left(\Delta u(t)/U_{\mathrm{trim}}\right) + C_{m\alpha}\Delta\alpha(t) + C_{m\dot{\alpha}}\left(\Delta\dot{\alpha}(t)\left(c_{\mathrm{w}}/2\right)/U_{\mathrm{trim}}\right) \\ & + C_{mq}\left(q(t)\left(c_{\mathrm{w}}/2\right)/U_{\mathrm{trim}}\right) + C_{m\dot{q}}\left(\dot{q}(t)\left(\left(c_{\mathrm{w}}/2\right)/U_{\mathrm{trim}}\right)^2\right) \\ & + C_{m\eta}\Delta\eta(t) + C_{m\dot{\eta}}\left(\Delta\dot{\eta}(t)\left(c_{\mathrm{w}}/2\right)/U_{\mathrm{trim}}\right)\Big]. \end{aligned}$$

Combining eqns. (III.8.6)–(III.8.9)

$$\begin{aligned} & \left[U_{\mathrm{trim}}\, C_{\mathrm{W}}/g\right]\left[\Delta\dot{u}(t)/U_{\mathrm{trim}}\right] \\ & \quad = -C_{\mathrm{D}U}\left(\Delta u(t)/U_{\mathrm{trim}}\right) + \left((C_{\mathrm{L}})_{\mathrm{trim}} - C_{\mathrm{D}\alpha}\right)\Delta\alpha(t) \\ & \quad - C_{\mathrm{W}}\cos\theta_{\mathrm{trim}}\Delta\theta(t) + C_{\mathrm{W}}\left(\Delta \mathrm{Th}(t)/W\right) \\ & \left[U_{\mathrm{trim}}\, C_{\mathrm{W}}/g\right]\left[\Delta\dot{\alpha}(t) - q(t)\right] \\ & \quad = -C_{\mathrm{L}U}\left(\Delta u(t)/U_{\mathrm{trim}}\right) - \left(C_{\mathrm{L}\alpha} + (C_{\mathrm{D}})_{\mathrm{trim}}\right)\Delta\alpha(t) \\ & \quad - C_{\mathrm{L}\dot{\alpha}}\,\Delta\dot{\alpha}(t)\left(c_{\mathrm{w}}/2\right)/U_{\mathrm{trim}} - C_{\mathrm{L}q}q(t)\left(c_{\mathrm{w}}/2\right)/U_{\mathrm{trim}} \\ & \quad - C_{\mathrm{L}\dot{q}}\,\dot{q}(t)\left(\left(c_{\mathrm{w}}/2\right)/U_{\mathrm{trim}}\right)^2 - C_{\mathrm{L}\eta}\Delta\eta(t) \\ & \quad - C_{\mathrm{L}\dot{\eta}}\,\Delta\dot{\eta}(t)\left(c_{\mathrm{w}}/2\right)/U_{\mathrm{trim}} - C_{\mathrm{W}}\sin\theta_{\mathrm{trim}}\Delta\theta(t) \\ & \left[c_{\mathrm{w}}\, C_{\mathrm{W}}/g\right]\left[i_{yy}\dot{q}(t)\right] \\ & \quad = C_{mU}\left(\Delta u(t)/U_{\mathrm{trim}}\right) + C_{m\alpha}\,\Delta\alpha(t) + C_{m\dot{\alpha}}\,\Delta\dot{\alpha}(t)\left(c_{\mathrm{w}}/2\right)/U_{\mathrm{trim}} \\ & \quad + C_{mq}q(t)\left(c_{\mathrm{w}}/2\right)\big/U_{\mathrm{trim}} + C_{m\dot{q}}\,\dot{q}(t)\left(\left(c_{\mathrm{w}}/2\right)/U_{\mathrm{trim}}\right)^2 \\ & \quad + C_{m\eta}\,\Delta\eta(t) + C_{m\dot{\eta}}\,\Delta\dot{\eta}(t)\left(c_{\mathrm{w}}/2\right)/U_{\mathrm{trim}} + C_{\mathrm{W}}\left(\Delta \mathrm{Th}(t)/W\right) l_{\mathrm{Th}} \\ & q(t) = \Delta\dot{\theta}(t) \end{aligned} \qquad \text{(III.8.10)}$$

writing

$$i_{yy} = \text{non-dimensional pitching moment of inertia} = I_{yy}/(mc_{\mathrm{w}}^2).$$

For a typical aeroplane configuration the radius of gyration about the pitch axis is of the order of c_{w}, so i_{yy} is of the order of 1.0. More precisely

$$\begin{aligned} &\text{for light aeroplanes,} && i_{yy} = \mathrm{O}[0.75], \\ &\text{for combat aeroplanes,} && i_{yy} = \mathrm{O}[0.50], \\ &\text{for transport aeroplanes,} && i_{yy} = \mathrm{O}[2.0]. \end{aligned} \tag{III.8.11}$$

A number of further approximations can be introduced into eqns. (III.8.10):

$$\begin{aligned} (C_{\mathrm{L}})_{\mathrm{trim}} &\simeq C_{\mathrm{W}} \cos\theta_{\mathrm{trim}} \\ C_{\mathrm{L}\alpha} + (C_{\mathrm{D}})_{\mathrm{trim}} &\simeq C_{\mathrm{L}\alpha} \\ \left(1 - \left(gc_{\mathrm{w}}/(C_{\mathrm{W}}U_{\mathrm{trim}}^2)\right)C_{\mathrm{L}q}/2\right) = \left(1 - \left(C_{\mathrm{L}q}/2\overline{m}\right)\right) &\simeq 1 \\ \left(1 + \left(gc_{\mathrm{w}}/(C_{\mathrm{W}}U_{\mathrm{trim}}^2)\right)C_{\mathrm{L}\dot{\alpha}}/2\right) = \left(1 - \left(C_{\mathrm{L}\dot{\alpha}}/2\overline{m}\right)\right) &\simeq 1 \\ \left(i_{yy} - \left(gc_{\mathrm{w}}/(C_{\mathrm{W}}U_{\mathrm{trim}}^2)\right)C_{m\dot{q}}/4\right) = \left(i_{yy} - \left(C_{m\dot{q}}/4\overline{m}\right)\right) &\simeq i_{yy}. \end{aligned} \tag{III.8.12}$$

It is only at this stage that the aerodynamic terms involving $C_{\mathrm{L}\dot{\alpha}}$, $C_{\mathrm{L}q}$ and $C_{m\dot{q}}$ can be neglected because these aerodynamic terms are small in comparison with their inertial acceleration counterparts. Strictly, the term involving $C_{\mathrm{L}\dot{q}}$ still has to be retained because it cannot be compared with any inertial term, but the magnitude of the term involving $C_{\mathrm{L}\dot{q}}$ is small and, in the context of the later stability analysis, its effect is then negligible and so it is omitted for convenience at this stage.

Incorporating the approximations (eqns. (III.8.12)), the equations of motion (eqns. (III.8.10)) become finally

$$\begin{aligned} &\Delta\dot{u}(t)/U_{\mathrm{trim}} + \left(g/(U_{\mathrm{trim}}C_{\mathrm{W}})\right)\left[C_{\mathrm{D}U}\left(\Delta u(t)/U_{\mathrm{trim}}\right) + (C_{\mathrm{D}\alpha} - C_{\mathrm{W}}\cos\theta_{\mathrm{trim}})\Delta\alpha(t)\right. \\ &\qquad\qquad \left. + C_{\mathrm{W}}\cos\theta_{\mathrm{trim}}\,\Delta\theta(t)\right] \\ &\quad \simeq \left(g/U_{\mathrm{trim}}\right)\left(\Delta\mathrm{Th}(t)/W\right) \\ &\left(g/(U_{\mathrm{trim}}C_{\mathrm{W}})\right)C_{\mathrm{L}U}\left(\Delta u(t)/U_{\mathrm{trim}}\right) + \Delta\dot{\alpha}(t) + \left(g/(U_{\mathrm{trim}}C_{\mathrm{W}})\right)C_{\mathrm{L}\alpha}\,\Delta\alpha(t) \\ &\quad - q(t) + \left(g/U_{\mathrm{trim}}\right)\sin\theta_{\mathrm{trim}}\Delta\theta(t) \\ &\quad \simeq -\left(g/(U_{\mathrm{trim}}C_{\mathrm{W}})\right)\left[C_{L\eta}\Delta\eta(t) + C_{L\dot{\eta}}\Delta\dot{\eta}(t)\left(c_{\mathrm{w}}/2\right)/U_{\mathrm{trim}}\right] \\ &-C_{mU}\left(\Delta u(t)/U_{\mathrm{trim}}\right) - C_{m\dot{\alpha}}\Delta\dot{\alpha}(t)\left(c_{\mathrm{w}}/2\right)/U_{\mathrm{trim}} - C_{m\alpha}\Delta\alpha(t) \\ &\qquad + \left(c_{\mathrm{w}}C_{\mathrm{W}}i_{yy}/g\right)\dot{q}(t) - C_{mq}q(t)\left(c_{\mathrm{w}}/2\right)/U_{\mathrm{trim}} \\ &\quad \simeq C_{m\eta}\Delta\eta(t) + C_{m\dot{\eta}}\Delta\dot{\eta}(t)\left(c_{\mathrm{w}}/2\right)/U_{\mathrm{trim}} + C_{\mathrm{W}}\left(\Delta\mathrm{Th}(t)/W\right)l_{\mathrm{Th}} \\ &q(t) = \Delta\dot{\theta}(t). \end{aligned} \tag{III.8.13}$$

In the literature there are slight differences in these equations due to the treatment of the second order terms.

Solutions of eqns. (III.8.13) are developed and described in the following sections.

EXAMPLES III.26

1. Derive the equations of longitudinal motion taking axes along and normal to the flight path for the translational equations but axes fixed in the aeroplane for the rotational equation. Show that by appropriate approximations these equations reduce to eqns. (III.8.13).
2. Derive the equations of longitudinal motion for an aeroplane with a propeller propulsion unit.

III.9 SHORT PERIOD STABILITY MODE

An aeroplane disturbed from trimmed flight usually incorporates two longitudinal stability modes, known as the short period mode and phugoid mode. In this section the short period mode is described.

The short period mode usually extends over the first few seconds of an aeroplane response. The accelerations and decelerations along the flight path are sufficiently slow that during these few seconds the forward speed does not have time to change significantly and so the forward speed can be assumed to remain constant, equal to U_{trim}, so $(\Delta u(t)/U)$ can be neglected. And then the equation of motion in the direction of the flight path can be ignored.

The two remaining equations of motion, from eqns. (III.8.13), taking the initial steady state as level flight, hence neglecting the term $\sin\theta_{\text{trim}}\Delta\theta(t)$, are

$$\left[\mathrm{D}+(g/(U_{\text{trim}}C_{\mathrm{W}}))C_{\mathrm{L}\alpha}\right]\Delta\alpha(t)-q(t)$$
$$=-\left(g/(U_{\text{trim}}C_{\mathrm{W}})\left[\left(C_{\mathrm{L}\dot{\eta}}\,(c_{\mathrm{w}}/2)/U_{\text{trim}}\right)\mathrm{D}+C_{\mathrm{L}\eta}\right]\Delta\eta(t)\right), \qquad \text{(III.9.1)}$$

$$\left[(-C_{m\dot{\alpha}})\left((c_{\mathrm{w}}/2)/U_{\text{trim}}\right)\mathrm{D}+(-C_{m\alpha})\right]\Delta\alpha(t)$$
$$+\left[\left(c_{\mathrm{w}}C_{\mathrm{W}}i_{yy}/g\right)\mathrm{D}+(-C_{mq})\left((c_{\mathrm{w}}/2)/U_{\text{trim}}\right)\right]q(t)$$
$$=\left[\left(C_{m\dot{\eta}}\,(c_{\mathrm{w}}/2)/U_{\text{trim}}\right)\mathrm{D}+C_{m\eta}\right]\Delta\eta(t)+C_{\mathrm{W}}\left(\Delta\mathrm{Th}(t)/W\right)l_{\mathrm{Th}} \qquad \text{(III.9.2)}$$

where D is the differential operator $\mathrm{d}/\mathrm{d}t$.

Eqns. (III.9.1) and (III.9.2) denote a system, coupling the two degrees of freedom $\Delta\alpha(t)$ and $q(t)$. The stability of this system, see Part II, is given by the transient response, which is a non-zero solution when the input terms on the right hand sides are put equal to zero. The stability characteristic equation, obtained by replacing D by λ and then equating the determinant of the coefficients of $\Delta\alpha(t)$ and $q(t)$ to zero, is

$$\lambda^2 + \frac{g}{U_{\text{trim}} C_W} \left[C_{L\alpha} + \frac{(-C_{m\dot{\alpha}}) + (-C_{mq})}{2i_{yy}} \right] \lambda + \frac{g\, C_{L\alpha} H_m}{c_w C_W i_{yy}} = 0, \qquad \text{(III.9.3)}$$

substituting, from eqn. (III.6.14),

$$(-C_{m\alpha}) + (-C_{mq}) C_{L\alpha}/2\overline{m} = C_{L\alpha} H_m$$

where H_m is the conventional manoeuvre margin.

Eqn. (III.9.3), one of the important formulae in aeroplane flight dynamics, describes the short period modal response. The main features are described.

Eqn. (III.9.3) denotes a second order system; the damping is always positive because $C_{L\alpha}$, $(-C_{m\dot{\alpha}})$ and $(-C_{mq})$ are all positive; the stiffness is positive as long as the conventional manoeuvre margin, H_m, is positive; and then the short period mode is stable.

The undamped frequency $(\omega_0)_{sp}$ is

$$\begin{aligned}(\omega_0)_{sp} &= \left[(g C_{L\alpha} H_m)/(c_w C_W i_{yy}) \right]^{1/2} \\ &= \left[(C_{L\alpha} H_m)/(\overline{m} i_{yy}) \right]^{1/2} \left[U_{\text{trim}}/c_w \right].\end{aligned} \qquad \text{(III.9.4)}$$

The undamped frequency $(\omega_0)_{sp}$

— is proportional to $H_m^{1/2}$,
— increases with forward speed, becoming relatively high at supersonic speeds,
— decreases with altitude,
— decreases with increase in aeroplane size.

With typical values, for a transport aeroplane, of $C_{L\alpha} = 5.0/\text{rad}$, $H_m = 0.2$, $c_w = 6$ m, $i_{yy} = 1.5$:

$$(\omega_0)_{sp} = \left[1.1/C_W \right]^{1/2} \text{ rad/s.} \qquad \text{(III.9.5)}$$

At $C_W = 2.0$ on an approach with flaps down

$$(\omega_0)_{sp} = 0.74 \text{ rad/s (period} = 8.4 \text{ s);}$$

at $C_W = 0.5$ in subsonic cruise

$$(\omega_0)_{sp} = 1.48 \text{ rad/s (period} = 4.2 \text{ s).}$$

With typical values, for a combat aeroplane, of $C_{L\alpha} = 4.0/\text{rad}$, $H_m = 0.2$, $c_w = 3$ m, $i_{yy} = 0.75$:

$$(\omega_0)_{sp} = \left[3.5/C_W \right]^{1/2} \text{ rad/s.} \qquad \text{(III.9.6)}$$

At $C_W = 1.5$ on an approach

$$(\omega_0)_{sp} = 1.5 \text{ rad/s (period} = 4.1 \text{ s);}$$

at $C_W = 0.5$ at subsonic cruise

$$(\omega_0)_{sp} = 2.6 \text{ rad/s (period} = 2.4 \text{ s);}$$

at $C_W = 0.1$ at supersonic speeds with increased H_m,

$$(\omega_0)_{sp} \simeq 8.7 \text{ rad/s (period} = 0.7 \text{ s).}$$

The short period damping coefficient is

$$\left[\frac{g}{U_{trim} C_W}\right]\left[C_{L\alpha} + \frac{(-C_{m\dot{\alpha}}) + (-C_{mq})}{2i_{yy}}\right]$$
$$= \left[\frac{U_{trim}}{c_W \overline{m}}\right] C_{L\alpha}\left[1 + \frac{(-C_{m\dot{\alpha}}) + (-C_{mq})}{2C_{L\alpha} i_{yy}}\right]. \qquad \text{(III.9.7)}$$

The short period damping coefficient

— increases with forward speed,
— decreases with altitude,
— decreases with increase in aeroplane size.

The time to half amplitude is $t_{1/2} \simeq 0.7$ (2/damping coefficient).
Broadly,

$$\begin{array}{ll} \text{on the approach,} & t_{1/2} = O[0.8 \text{ s}] \\ \text{at } C_W = 0.5 \text{ at low altitude,} & t_{1/2} = O[0.4 \text{ s}] \\ \text{at } C_W = 0.5 \text{ at 11 km altitude,} & t_{1/2} = O[0.8 \text{ s}] \\ \text{at } C_W = 0.1 \text{ at 11 km altitude,} & t_{1/2} = O[0.35 \text{ s}]. \end{array} \qquad \text{(III.9.8)}$$

The time for the stability oscillatory response to decay is approximately 4 × (time to half amplitude). Thus at subsonic speeds the short period response decays within one undamped period. At supersonic speeds the short period response decays within two undamped periods.

The damping ratio, ζ_{sp}, where $2(\zeta\omega_0)_{sp}$ = damping coefficient, is

$$\zeta_{sp} = \frac{1}{2}\left[\frac{i_{yy} C_{L\alpha}}{H_m \overline{m}}\right]^{1/2}\left[1 + \frac{(-C_{m\dot{\alpha}}) + (-C_{mq})}{C_{L\alpha}\ 2i_{yy}}\right]. \qquad \text{(III.9.9)}$$

The damping ratio ζ_{sp}

— is proportional to $(1/H_m)^{1/2}$
— increases with Mach number at subsonic speeds
— is considerably reduced at supersonic speeds
— decreases with altitude
— tends to be greater for transport aeroplanes than for combat aeroplanes.

Typically, at sea level,

$$\zeta_{sp} = O[0.7]. \qquad \text{(III.9.10)}$$

When $\zeta_{sp} < 1$, the normal condition, the short period mode is a damped oscillation with frequency

$$\omega_{sp} = (\omega_0)_{sp}(1-\zeta_{sp}^2)^{1/2}. \qquad \text{(III.9.11)}$$

From eqn. (III.9.10), at sea level, $\omega_{sp} \simeq 0.7(\omega_0)_{sp}$.

If $\zeta_{sp} > 1.0$ the damped oscillation degenerates into two subsidences, assuming that $(\omega_0)_{sp}$ is positive. The short period mode is not necessarily oscillatory, despite the fact that the phrase 'short period' implies an oscillatory response.

Variation in the location of the centre of mass affects H_m. As the centre of mass is moved aft, H_m reduces; $(\omega_0)_{sp}$ then decreases and ζ_{sp} increases, leaving the damping coefficient $(= 2(\omega_0\zeta)_{sp})$ unaffected. As H_m decreases to zero the validity of the short period mode as formulated in this section breaks down for the following reason: as H_m decreases, the short period mode degenerates into two subsidences, and as H_m tends to zero one of these subsidences decays so slowly that it is affected by the change in forward speed, which violates the initial assumptions.

The modal shape for the short period mode, namely the amplitude and phase relationship between $\Delta\theta(t)$ and $\Delta\alpha(t)$, or alternatively, between $\Delta\gamma(t)$ and $\Delta\alpha(t)$, can be obtained from eqns. (III.9.1) and (III.9.2), where, with zero input,

$$q(t) - \Delta\dot{\alpha}(t) = \Delta\dot{\gamma}(t) = \left[g/(U_{trim}C_W)\right]C_{L\alpha}\,\Delta\alpha(t). \qquad \text{(III.9.12)}$$

Writing

$$\Delta\alpha(t) = \Delta\alpha_0 \exp\left[\left[(\omega_0)_{sp}\left(-\zeta_{sp} + i(1-\zeta_{sp}^2)^{1/2}\right)\right]t\right]_{sp}$$

$$\Delta\gamma(t) = \Delta\gamma_0 \exp\left[\left[(\omega_0)_{sp}\left(-\zeta_{sp} + i(1-\zeta_{sp}^2)^{1/2}\right)\right]t + i\varphi\right]_{sp},$$

then, from eqn. (III.9.12),

$$\text{amplitude ratio} = \Delta\gamma_0/\Delta\alpha_0 = \left[g/(U_{trim}C_W)\right]C_{L\alpha}/(\omega_0)_{sp}$$
$$= \left[(i_{yy}C_{L\alpha})/(\overline{m}H_m)\right]^{1/2}$$

$$\text{phase angle} = \varphi = -\tan^{-1}\left[(1-\zeta_{sp}^2)^{1/2}/(-\zeta_{sp})\right].$$

With typical values, $\Delta\gamma_0/\Delta\alpha_0 = O[0.4]$, $\varphi = O[-135°]$,

And then $\Delta\theta_0/\Delta\alpha_0 = O[0.8]$, $\varphi = O[-20°]$. (III.9.13)

Thus $\Delta\theta(t)$ and $\Delta\alpha(t)$ have approximately the same amplitude and are approximately in phase, implying a damped oscillatory weathercock type of motion with the centre of mass continuing approximately in a horizontal direction.

Following on from the last observation, if it is assumed that there is no change in the flight path angle during the short period motion with the forward velocity remaining horizontal, together with the relationship that the pitch angle remains equal to the angle of incidence $(\Delta\theta(t) = \Delta\alpha(t))$, a dynamic weathercock motion, then only the pitching moment equation, eqn. (III.9.2) need be considered. The characteristic equation now becomes

$$\lambda^2 + \frac{g}{U_{\text{trim}} C_{\text{W}}} \left[\frac{(-C_{m\dot{\alpha}}) + (-C_{mq})}{2i_{yy}} \right] \lambda + \frac{g C_{\text{L}\alpha} K_\alpha}{c_{\text{w}} C_{\text{W}} i_{yy}} = 0. \qquad \text{(III.9.14)}$$

There are two important differences between the approximate equation for the short period characteristic equation, eqn. (III.9.14), and the exact characteristic equation, eqn. (III.9.3):

(i) the damping in eqn. (III.9.14) is approximately 35% less than the damping in eqn. (III.9.3), because the term $C_{\text{L}\alpha}$ is missing;
(ii) the incidence stiffness, K_α, in eqn. (III.9.14) replaces H_{m} in the stiffness term in eqn. (III.9.3); it is not a serious quantitative difference unless K_α is very small.

If an aeroplane model in a wind tunnel is pivoted at its centre of mass and balanced by the tailplane or elevator for static equilibrium, then its stability response to a pitch disturbance is given by eqn. (III.9.14).

It is now possible to interpret longitudinal static weathercock stability. As explained in sect. III.7, longitudinal static weathercock stability, elevator fixed, is satisfied when the incidence stiffness K_α is positive. But positive K_α ensures positive stiffness of the approximation to the short period motion, eqn. (III.9.14). Thus longitudinal static weathercock stability, elevator fixed, is an approximation for the condition of positive stiffness of the short period motion, that is, the condition $K_\alpha > 0$ is an approximation for the condition $H_{\text{m}} > 0$. As already pointed out, since $H_{\text{m}} > K_\alpha$, positive K_α guarantees positive H_{m} at all Mach numbers.

The above short period mode can be initiated by an impulsive elevator input, associated with an impulsive stick input, namely a quick pull-back on the stick followed by an immediate return of the stick to its original stick position and then holding the stick in that position. The resulting aeroplane response is the elevator-fixed short period mode; the stick, and elevator angle, are kept constant during the time of this response.

Whether an aeroplane has manual or power controls, whenever a pilot manoeuvres the aeroplane by moving the stick the initial transient response, superimposed on the 'steady state' response, will be the elevator-fixed short period mode.

But with a manual control system another short period mode can be initiated by an impulsive elevator input, associated with an impulsive stick input, namely a quick pull-back on the stick followed by an immediate return of the stick to its original position, and then releasing the stick so that the elevator floats freely. This response is the elevator-free short period modal response.

To study elevator-free stability, assume that when the elevator floats freely the static elevator hinge moment is zero, and then

$$b_\eta \, \Delta\eta(t) + b_\alpha \{(1 - \partial\varepsilon/\partial\alpha)\Delta\alpha(t) + q(t) l_t c_{\text{w}}/U\} = 0, \qquad \text{(III.9.15)}$$

ignoring any geared or spring tab arrangements. On substitution of $\Delta\eta(t)$ from eqn. (III.9.15) into eqns. (III.9.1) and (III.9.2), transferring the terms depending on $\Delta\alpha(t)$ and $q(t)$ from the right hand sides to the left hand sides of the equations, then

(i) the damping of the elevator-free short period response is of the order of 10% less than the damping of the elevator-fixed short period mode;

(ii) the formula for the stiffness of the elevator-free short period response is the same as that for the elevator-fixed short period mode in eqn. (III.9.3), except that H_{m} is replaced by

$$\left[H_{\mathrm{m}}-\left((-\mathcal{b}_{\alpha})/(-\mathcal{b}_{\eta})\right)(1-\partial\varepsilon/\partial\alpha)/C_{\mathrm{L}\alpha}\right]; \qquad \text{(III.9.16)}$$

the undamped frequency of the elevator-free short period response is of the order of 70% of the undamped frequency of the elevator-fixed short period response.

For a more accurate estimate of the elevator-free stability it is necessary to include the dynamic motion of the (free) elevator. There are now three coupled equations, involving the three degrees of freedom $\Delta\alpha(t)$, $q(t)$ and $\Delta\eta(t)$. The characteristic equation becomes a quartic polynomial in λ which can be factorized into two quadratic polynomials; one quadratic polynomial represents the elevator-free short period response, the second quadratic polynomial represents an oscillatory response in a mode which is primarily of elevator rotation. It is necessary to ensure that both the short period mode and the elevator response mode are stable.

EXAMPLES III.27

1. Can an impulsive change in thrust, $\Delta\mathrm{Th}(t)$, initiate a short period mode response?
2. Do the same short period equations, eqns. (III.9.1) and (III.9.2), apply to both propeller propulsion and turbo-fan propulsion?
3. What is the approximate value of H_{m} when the short period damped oscillation degenerates into two subsidences?
4. Describe the short period modal response in physical terms (i.e. interpret eqn. (III.9.13)).
5. From the data in Figs. III.5(i)–(iii) and Examples III.19, No. 1:

   (i) Sketch the variation of the short period undamped frequency and damping ratio, elevator fixed and elevator free, against C_{W} for the basic propeller configuration. What effect does propeller slipstream have on these short period characteristics?

   (ii) Sketch the variation of the short period mode undamped frequency and damping ratio for the basic transport configuration, against Mach number at sea level and 11 km altitude.

   (iii) Sketch the variation of the short period mode undamped frequency and damping ratio for the basic combat configuration, against Mach number at sea level and 11 km altitude. What is the effect of underwing weapons on these short period characteristics?

III.10 PHUGOID STABILITY MODE

The second longitudinal stability mode, known as the phugoid mode, has a much lower frequency than the short period mode, with changes primarily in forward speed, altitude and attitude but with little change in angle of incidence.

As a first approximation it is assumed that during the phugoid modal response the perturbation angle of incidence $\Delta\alpha(t)$ is taken to be zero and the pitching moment equation is ignored. The two remaining equations of translational motion of small perturbations from an initial trimmed state of steady level flight, so $\sin\theta_{\rm trim}\Delta\theta \simeq \sin\gamma_{\rm trim}\Delta\theta \simeq 0$, for an aeroplane with turbo-fan engines are, from eqns. (III.8.1),

$$\begin{aligned}&\left[\mathrm{D}+(g/(C_{\rm W}U_{\rm trim}))C_{\rm D\mathit{U}}\right](\Delta u(t)/U_{\rm trim})+(g/U_{\rm trim})\Delta\theta(t)\\&\quad\simeq (g/U_{\rm trim})(\Delta\mathrm{Th}(t)/W)\\&-(g/(C_{\rm W}U_{\rm trim}))C_{\rm L\mathit{U}}(\Delta u(t)/U_{\rm trim})+\mathrm{D}\,\Delta\theta(t)\\&\quad=(g/(U_{\rm trim}C_{\rm W}))\left[\left(C_{\rm L\dot{\eta}}(c_{\rm w}/2)/U_{\rm trim}\right)\mathrm{D}+C_{\rm L\eta}\right]\Delta\eta(t).\end{aligned} \qquad \text{(III.10.1)}$$

Eqns. (III.10.1) denote a system coupling the two degrees of freedom $(\Delta u(t)/U_{\rm trim})$ and $\Delta\theta\,(t)$; the stability characteristic equation is

$$\lambda^2+(g/(U_{\rm trim}C_{\rm W}))C_{\rm D\mathit{U}}\lambda+(g/U_{\rm trim})^2(C_{\rm L\mathit{U}}/C_{\rm W})=0 \qquad \text{(III.10.2)}$$

where

$$C_{\rm D\mathit{U}}=\left[2C_{\rm D}+M_\infty\,\partial C_{\rm D}/\partial M_\infty\right]_{\rm trim},$$

$$C_{\rm L\mathit{U}}=\left[2C_{\rm L}+M_\infty\,\partial C_{\rm L}/\partial M_\infty\right]_{\rm trim}$$

are described in Appendix 4.

Eqn. (III.10.2) describes a second order system which gives an approximation to the phugoid modal response.

(i) At low Mach numbers where the effects of Mach number can be neglected, $C_{\rm D\mathit{U}}=(2C_{\rm D})_{\rm trim}$, $(C_{\rm L\mathit{U}}/C_{\rm W})=2$, and the phugoid stability response is then stable as a damped oscillation with

$$\text{undamped frequency}=(\omega_0)_{\rm ph}=(g/U_{\rm trim})\sqrt{2} \qquad \text{(III.10.3)}$$

$$\text{damping ratio}=\zeta_{\rm ph}=((C_{\rm D})_{\rm trim}/C_{\rm W})/\sqrt{2}$$

Irrespective of the size of the aeroplane, when $U_{\rm trim}=100$ m/s,

$$(\omega_0)_{\rm ph}=0.17\,\text{rad/s}, \qquad \zeta_{\rm ph}=O[0.05],$$

so time of one period $\simeq$ 37 s. The damping ratio, 5% of critical damping, implies that the time to half amplitude is approximately twice the time of one period, an extremely low rate of convergence.

(ii) Both $C_{\rm L\mathit{U}}$ and $C_{\rm D\mathit{U}}$ are positive at subsonic speeds so the phugoid mode is stable; $(\omega_0)_{\rm ph}$ decreases with increase in Mach number mainly due to the $U_{\rm trim}$ term.

(iii) Both C_{LU} and C_{DU} can go negative at low supersonic speeds, and then the phugoid mode is unstable as a relatively slow divergence.

It is of interest to note that if the small phugoid damping is neglected (i.e. C_{DU} is put equal to zero) the first of eqns. (III.10.1) becomes

$$\mathrm{D}\Delta u(t) + g\,\Delta\theta(t) = 0 \tag{III.10.4}$$

which can be re-expressed in the form

$$\mathrm{D}\left[\left(U(t)^2/2\right) + gh(t)\right] = 0 \tag{III.10.5}$$

noting that $\mathrm{D}h(t) = U(t)\theta(t)$.

Eqn. (III.10.5) states the conservation of mechanical energy, namely that the sum of the kinetic energy and potential energy is constant. Thus the phugoid motion is, crudely, a flight path oscillation in altitude about the initial trimmed altitude where the speed falls as altitude is gained and increases as altitude is lost.

A more accurate, albeit more complicated, expression for the phugoid motion can be derived. The change in angle of incidence $\Delta\alpha(t)$ is now included but $\Delta\dot{\alpha}(t)$ and $\dot{q}(t)$ may be neglected because the rate of change in the phugoid response is extremely low. With this assumption the characteristic equation of eqns. (III.8.13) becomes

$$\lambda^2 + \frac{g}{U_{\text{trim}} C_{\text{W}}}\left[C_{DU} + \frac{\left((C_{\text{W}} - C_{\text{D}\alpha})/C_{\text{L}\alpha}\right)\left(C_{mU} - C_{\text{L}U}\left(-C_{mq}/2\overline{m}\right)\right)}{K_\alpha + \left(-C_{mq}/2\overline{m}\right)}\right]\lambda$$

$$+\, g^2\left[\frac{K_\alpha C_{\text{L}U} + C_{mU}}{U_{\text{trim}}^2 C_{\text{W}} H_{\text{m}}}\right] = 0 \tag{III.10.6}$$

where

$$C_{mU} = \left[2C_m + M_\infty\,\partial C_m/\partial M_\infty\right]_{\text{trim}},$$

$$(C_m)_{\text{trim}} = -l_{\text{th}}(C_{\text{Th}})_{\text{trim}}.$$

As shown later, although derived from an approximate analysis, eqn. (III.10.6) gives the 'exact' phugoid stiffness. Eqn. (III.10.6) gives a ball-park prediction of the trends of the damping but the value of the damping, compared to the 'exact' value, is poor.

By reference to eqn. (III.5.18) the phugoid stiffness reduces to the relationship,

$$(\omega_0)_{\text{ph}}^2 = 2\left[\frac{g}{U_{\text{trim}}}\right]^2\left[\frac{E_{\text{trim}} - \left(l_{\text{Th}}/(-C_{m\eta})\right)\left[\left(C_{\text{D}U}/2C_{\text{L}}\right) - \left(\mathrm{d}C_{\text{D}}/\mathrm{d}C_{\text{L}}\right)\right]_{\text{trim}}}{E_{\text{m}}}\right] \tag{III.10.7}$$

which involves the elevator trim margin, E_{trim}, eqn. (III.5.17) and the elevator manoeuvre margin, E_{m}, eqns. (III.6.13) and (III.6.14).

When l_{Th} is zero

$$(\omega_0)_{\text{ph}} = [g/U_{\text{trim}}][2E_{\text{trim}}/E_{\text{m}}]^{1/2}. \tag{III.10.8}$$

(i) At low speeds

$$E_{\text{trim}}/E_{\text{m}} = K_\alpha/H_{\text{m}}. \tag{III.10.9}$$

With a forward location of the centre of mass this ratio is close to unity, which is the basis of the approximate phugoid stiffness at low speeds given by eqn. (III.10.3).

(ii) With increase in Mach number at subsonic speeds E_{trim} increases while E_{m} decreases.

(iii) At supersonic speeds E_{trim} decreases, usually going negative at low supersonic speeds, while E_{m} increases substantially; the phugoid mode is then unstable in the form of a slow divergence.

Positive l_{Th} reduces the phugoid mode stiffness.

The above analysis applies to an aeroplane with turbo-fan engines where a change in forward speed does not change the thrust when the throttle is kept constant. For propeller driven aeroplanes a change in forward speed causes a change in thrust when the throttle is kept constant, because constant throttle maintains constant power (= Th U); in this case the undamped frequency of the phugoid mode is given by the same equation, eqn. (III.10.9), when l_{Th} is zero, but the damping is increased.

The phugoid mode described above is essentially the stick-fixed phugoid mode. There is also a stick-free phugoid mode where the stick-free incidence stiffness, defined in eqn. (III.7.7), replaces K_α in eqn. (III.10.6).

The above analysis has been based on the assumption that the initial trimmed state was steady level flight. Extending the analysis, the phugoid undamped frequency and damping are increased when the initial trimmed state is a shallow descent, with the opposite effect in a shallow ascent.

During a phugoid motion the change in altitude can be sufficiently large that the variation in atmospheric density can affect the phugoid modal response. As shown in ref. P.15, the effect of the atmospheric density variation is to increase slightly the phugoid frequency and to decrease the damping; these trends are amplified at higher speeds.

The phugoid mode with its long period and extremely low damping, possibly negative, is ever present, but does not usually pose problems for a pilot as long as there is adequate short period stability. The pilot who is flying hands-off in trimmed flight in cruise keeps an eye on the altimeter; if significant altitude changes appear through a phugoid response the pilot can quickly and easily return the aeroplane to its trimmed state through a short period response by use of the elevator. Problems with a phugoid can arise if pilot attention is occupied with emergencies, for example, if the pilot is sorting out options in case of system or engine malfunction or in case of navigational problems.

EXAMPLES III.28

1. By reference to eqns. (III.10.1) show that the phugoid undamped frequency is the same for both turbo-fan and turbo-prop propulsion when l_{Th} is zero, but that the damping is higher for the turbo-prop case.
2. Show that the effect of positive l_{Th} at low Mach numbers decreases $(\omega_0)_{\text{ph}}$ at speeds above the minimum drag speed but increases ω_0 at speeds below the minimum drag speed.
3. Derive the modal shape $((\Delta u(t)/U_{\text{trim}}) : \Delta\theta(t))$ for the phugoid mode from eqns. (III.10.1), then derive the corresponding modal shape $((\Delta u(t)/U) : \Delta h(t))$; interpret this result.
4. The text states: 'the phugoid undamped frequency and damping are increased when the initial trimmed state is a shallow descent, with the opposite effect in a shallow ascent'. Prove this statement by extending eqns. (III.10.1).

III.11 SMALL PERTURBATION LONGITUDINAL STABILITY

In this section the exact longitudinal stability modes for small perturbations about a trimmed state are derived. The conditions for the existence of the short period and phugoid stability modes are obtained.

The basic equations of motion of small perturbations have been derived in sect. III.8.

In sects. III.9 and III.10 the short period and phugoid modal equations are solved in dimensional form and their characteristics expressed in real time. For many applications, particularly in simulators or when the effects of automatic systems and their hardware are to be incorporated, the equations of motion need to be solved in their dimensional form; such solutions are readily obtained on the digital computer. But traditionally non-dimensional analysis has been a central discipline in providing an understanding of an engineering problem, identifying the groups of non-dimensional parameters and their interrelationships. Conforming to this tradition the basic equations of aeroplane motion have usually been derived in non-dimensional form, providing a concise methodology in the era before the advent of the digital computer. In this section a non-dimensional approach is described to complement the dimensional approaches in sects. III.8–III.10. Unfortunately there are many versions of the non-dimensional equations, and the UK versions in particular are over-complicated and confusing; the approach presented here is thought to be compatible with the current literature.

First, a non-dimensional unit of time is required. In sect. II.3.3 the unit of aerodynamic time $\hat{t}$ $(= c_{\text{w}}/U_{\text{trim}})$ is introduced. This unit of aerodynamic time is extremely small (= O[0.03 s]) compared with the typical period of the short period mode (= O[3.0 s]), so a larger reference unit of non-dimensional time is sought. A unit of dynamic time $\hat{t}_{\text{d}}$ is defined where

$$\hat{t}_{\text{d}} = \overline{m}\hat{t} = \overline{m}\, c_{\text{w}}/U_{\text{trim}}, \tag{III.11.1}$$

and $\overline{m}$ is the mass parameter $\left(=m/(\tfrac{1}{2}\rho_{\text{at}}S_{\text{w}}c_{\text{w}}) = \text{O}[150]\right)$ at sea level), so $\hat{t}_{\text{d}} = \text{O}[4.5\text{ s}]$. Another advantage of using $\hat{t}_{\text{d}}$ is that at altitude the increase in $\overline{m}$ is counteracted by the higher speed U_{trim}.

Non-dimensional time relative to the unit of dynamic time is defined as

$$\bar{t}_{\mathrm{d}} = t/\hat{t}_{\mathrm{d}}\,. \tag{III.11.2}$$

Thus

$$\mathrm{d}/\mathrm{d}t = \left(1/\hat{t}_{\mathrm{d}}\right)\mathrm{d}/\mathrm{d}\bar{t}_{\mathrm{d}} = \left(U_{\mathrm{trim}}/\bar{m}c_{\mathrm{w}}\right)\mathrm{d}/\mathrm{d}\bar{t}_{\mathrm{d}} = g/(U_{\mathrm{trim}}C_{\mathrm{W}})\,\mathrm{d}/\mathrm{d}\bar{t}_{\mathrm{d}}. \tag{III.11.3}$$

Writing $\Delta\bar{u}(\bar{t}_{\mathrm{d}}) = \Delta u(t)/U_{\mathrm{trim}}$, the equations of motion, eqns. (III.8.13) are, assuming initial steady level flight,

$$\begin{aligned}
&[\bar{\mathrm{D}} + C_{\mathrm{D}U}]\Delta\bar{u}(\bar{t}_{\mathrm{d}}) - (C_{\mathrm{W}} - C_{\mathrm{D}\alpha})\Delta\alpha(\bar{t}_{\mathrm{d}}) + C_{\mathrm{W}}\,\Delta\theta(\bar{t}_{\mathrm{d}}) \\
&\qquad = C_{\mathrm{W}}\;\Delta\mathrm{Th}(\bar{t}_{\mathrm{d}})/W \\
&C_{\mathrm{L}U}\,\Delta\bar{u}(\bar{t}_{\mathrm{d}}) + [\bar{\mathrm{D}} + C_{\mathrm{L}\alpha}]\Delta\alpha(\bar{t}_{\mathrm{d}}) - \bar{\mathrm{D}}\,\Delta\theta(\bar{t}_{\mathrm{d}}) \\
&\qquad = -\left[C_{\mathrm{L}\eta} + \left(C_{\mathrm{L}\dot{\eta}}/2\bar{m}\right)\mathrm{D}\right]\Delta\eta(\bar{t}_{\mathrm{d}}), \\
&-C_{mU}\,\Delta\bar{u}(\bar{t}_{\mathrm{d}}) + \left[\left(-C_{m\dot{\alpha}}/2\bar{m}\right)\bar{\mathrm{D}} - C_{m\alpha}\right]\Delta\alpha(\bar{t}_{\mathrm{d}}) \\
&\qquad + \left[\left(i_{yy}/\bar{m}\right)\bar{\mathrm{D}}^2 - \left(C_{mq}/2\bar{m}\right)\bar{\mathrm{D}}\right]\Delta\theta(\bar{t}_{\mathrm{d}}) \\
&\qquad = \left(C_{\mathrm{W}}\,\Delta\mathrm{Th}(\bar{t}_{\mathrm{d}})/W\right)l_{\mathrm{Th}} + \left[C_{m\eta} + \left(C_{m\dot{\eta}}/2\bar{m}\right)\bar{\mathrm{D}}\right]\Delta\eta(\bar{t}_{\mathrm{d}})
\end{aligned} \tag{III.11.4}$$

where $\bar{\mathrm{D}} = \mathrm{d}/\mathrm{d}\bar{t}_{\mathrm{d}}$.

As explained in Part II the stability of a system is determined from a transient response which is obtained by putting inputs equal to zero, and then solving the resulting homogeneous equations.

For eqns. (III.11.4), putting the right hand sides equal to zero, substitution of a solution of the form

$$\Delta\bar{u}(\bar{t}_{\mathrm{d}}) = a\exp(\bar{\lambda}\bar{t}_{\mathrm{d}}), \quad \Delta\alpha(\bar{t}_{\mathrm{d}}) = b\exp(\bar{\lambda}\bar{t}_{\mathrm{d}}), \quad \Delta\theta(\bar{t}_{\mathrm{d}}) = c\exp(\bar{\lambda}\bar{t}_{\mathrm{d}}) \tag{III.11.5}$$

leads to

$$\begin{aligned}
(\bar{\lambda} + C_{\mathrm{D}U})\;a - \quad & (C_{\mathrm{W}} - C_{\mathrm{D}\alpha})\;b + \quad & C_{\mathrm{W}}\,c = 0 \\
C_{\mathrm{L}U}\;a + \quad & (\bar{\lambda} + C_{\mathrm{L}\alpha})\;b - \quad & \lambda\,c = 0 \\
-\,\bar{m}C_{mU}\;a + \quad & \left[\left(-C_{m\dot{\alpha}}/2\right)\bar{\lambda} + \bar{m}(-C_{m\alpha})\right]b + \quad & \left[i_{yy}\bar{\lambda}^2 + \left(-C_{mq}/2\right)\bar{\lambda}\right]c = 0
\end{aligned} \tag{III.11.6}$$

For a non-zero solution the determinant of the coefficients in eqns. (III.11.6) must be zero, that is

$$\begin{vmatrix}
\bar{\lambda} + C_{\mathrm{D}U} & -(C_{\mathrm{W}} - C_{\mathrm{D}\alpha}) & +C_{\mathrm{W}} \\
C_{\mathrm{L}U} & \bar{\lambda} + C_{\mathrm{L}\alpha} & -\bar{\lambda} \\
-\bar{m}C_{mU} & \left(-C_{m\dot{\alpha}}/2\right)\lambda + \bar{m}(-C_{m\alpha}) & i_{yy}\bar{\lambda}^2 + \left(-C_{mq}/2\right)\bar{\lambda}
\end{vmatrix} = 0. \tag{III.11.7}$$

Expanding out this determinant, the characteristic equation is

$$i_{yy}\bar{\lambda}^4 + A_3\bar{\lambda}^3 + A_2\bar{\lambda}^2 + A_1\bar{\lambda} + A_0 = 0 \qquad \text{(III.11.8)}$$

where

$$A_3 = C_{DU}i_{yy} + C_{L\alpha}i_{yy} + \left(-C_{m\dot{\alpha}}/2\right) + \left(-C_{mq}/2\right),$$

$$A_2 = C_{L\alpha}\left(-C_{mq}/2\right) + \bar{m}(-C_{m\alpha})$$
$$+ C_{DU}\left[C_{L\alpha}i_{yy} + \left(-C_{m\dot{\alpha}}/2\right) + \left(-C_{mq}/2\right)\right] + i_{yy}(C_W - C_{D\alpha})C_{LU},$$

$$A_1 = C_{DU}\left[(C_{L\alpha})\left(-C_{mq}/2\right) + \bar{m}(-C_{m\alpha})\right]$$
$$+ (C_W - C_{D\alpha})\left[C_{LU}\left(-C_{mq}/2\right) - \bar{m}C_{mU}\right] + C_W\left[C_{LU}\left(-C_{m\dot{\alpha}}/2\right) + \bar{m}C_{mU}\right],$$

$$A_0 = \bar{m}C_W\left[C_{LU}(-C_{m\alpha}) + C_{mU}C_{L\alpha}\right].$$

Eqn. (III.11.8) is known as the longitudinal stability quartic. There are four stability roots. Usually there are two pairs of complex conjugate roots; one pair represents the short period modal response, the other pair the phugoid modal response. Substitution of the stability roots into eqn. (III.11.6) gives the modal shapes.

To illustrate these features an example is presented for low speed flight where Mach number effects can be neglected. Taking the typical values

$$\begin{gathered} i_{yy} = 1.5, \quad \bar{m} = 150, \quad l_{Th} = 0, \quad \gamma_{trim} = 0 \\ C_W = 0.8, \quad C_{L\alpha} = 5.0, \quad (-C_{m\alpha}) = 1.0 \text{ (i.e. } K_\alpha = 0.2) \\ (-C_{m\dot{\alpha}}) = 10.0, \quad (-C_{mq}) = 20.0, \quad C_D = 0.02 + 0.05C_L^2 = 0.052 \\ C_{DU} = 0.104, \quad C_{LU} = 1.6, \quad C_{mU} = 0.0, \quad C_{D\alpha} = 0.4 \end{gathered} \qquad \text{(III.11.9)}$$

the characteristic equation, eqn. (III.11.8), becomes

$$1.5\bar{\lambda}^4 + 22.66\bar{\lambda}^3 + 203.3\bar{\lambda}^2 + 33.6\bar{\lambda} + 192 = 0. \qquad \text{(III.11.10)}$$

Eqn. (III.11.10) can be factorized by a simple algorithm, see Appendix 5, giving

$$(1.5\bar{\lambda}^2 + 22.57\bar{\lambda} + 200.5)(\bar{\lambda}^2 + 0.0598\bar{\lambda} + 0.9578) = 0. \qquad \text{(III.11.11)}$$

There are two pairs of complex conjugate roots: from the first bracket in eqn. (III.11.11)

$$\bar{\lambda}_{1,2} = -7.52 \pm i8.78 \qquad \text{(III.11.12)}$$

with modal shape

$$\begin{aligned} (a:b:c)_{1,2} &= (\quad \Delta\bar{u} \quad : \quad \Delta\alpha \quad : \quad \Delta\theta) \\ &= (0.035\exp(i18°) \; : \; 1.27\exp(i25°) \; : \; 1.0); \end{aligned} \qquad \text{(III.11.13)}$$

from the second bracket in eqn. (III.11.11)

$$\bar{\lambda}_{3,4} = -0.03 \pm i0.98 \qquad \text{(III.11.14)}$$

with modal shape

$$(a:b:c)_{3,4} = (\quad \Delta\bar{u} \quad : \quad \Delta\alpha \quad : \quad \Delta\theta)$$
$$= (0.82\exp(\mathrm{i}90°) \quad : \quad 0.06\exp(-\mathrm{i}82°) \quad : \quad 1.0). \tag{III.11.15}$$

Stability roots $\bar{\lambda}_{1,2}$ and their associated modal shapes, eqns. (III.11.12)–(III.11.13), denote a well damped oscillatory mode, namely the short period stability mode. According to the modal shape (eqn. (III.11.13)), the change in forward speed is negligible compared to the changes in $\Delta\alpha$ and $\Delta\theta$; this result is the basis of the approximation to the short period stability motion described in section III.9. That approximation—which neglects $\Delta\bar{u}$ in the lift and moment equations and ignores the drag equation—when applied to eqn. (III.11.4), leads to the non-dimensional short period equations,

$$[\bar{\mathrm{D}} + C_{\mathrm{L}\alpha}]\Delta\alpha(\bar{t}_{\mathrm{d}}) - \bar{q}(\bar{t}_{\mathrm{d}})$$
$$= -\left[\left(C_{\mathrm{L}\dot{\eta}}/2\bar{m}\right)\bar{\mathrm{D}} + C_{\mathrm{L}\eta}\right]\Delta\eta(\bar{t}_{\mathrm{d}}),$$
$$\left[\left(-C_{m\dot{\alpha}}/2\right)\bar{\mathrm{D}} - \bar{m}C_{m\alpha}\right]\Delta\alpha(\bar{t}_{\mathrm{d}}) + \left[i_{yy}\bar{\mathrm{D}} - \left(C_{mq}/2\right)\right]\bar{q}(\bar{t}_{\mathrm{d}}) \tag{III.11.16}$$
$$= \left(C_{\mathrm{W}}\,\Delta\mathrm{Th}(t_{\mathrm{d}})/W\right)l_{\mathrm{Th}} + \left[\left(C_{m\dot{\eta}}/2\right)\bar{\mathrm{D}} + \bar{m}C_{m\eta}\right]\Delta\eta(\bar{t}_{\mathrm{d}}).$$

The short period characteristic equation from eqns. (III.11.16) is, in non-dimensional form,

$$i_{yy}\bar{\lambda}^2 + \left[i_{yy}C_{\mathrm{L}\alpha} + \left(-C_{m\dot{\alpha}}/2\right) + \left(-C_{mq}/2\right)\right]\bar{\lambda} + \bar{m}\left[(-C_{m\alpha}) + C_{\mathrm{L}\alpha}(-C_{mq})/2\bar{m}\right] = 0. \tag{III.11.17}$$

On substitution of the typical values of eqns. (III.11.9), eqn. (III.11.17) becomes

$$1.5\bar{\lambda}^2 + 22.5\bar{\lambda} + 200 = 0$$

which gives stability roots

$$\lambda_{1,2} = -7.5 \pm \mathrm{i}8.78 \tag{III.11.18}$$

and modal shape

$$(a:b:c)_{1,2} = (\Delta\bar{u} \quad : \quad \Delta\alpha \quad : \quad \Delta\theta)$$
$$= (0.0 \quad : \quad 1.27\exp(\mathrm{i}25°) \quad : \quad 1.0) \tag{III.11.19}$$

which are virtually the same as the exact values in eqns. (III.11.12) and (III.11.13).

Stability roots $\lambda_{3,4}$ and their associated modal shape, eqns. (III.11.14) and (III.11.15), denote a lightly damped, low frequency, oscillatory mode, namely the phugoid stability mode. According to the modal shape, eqn. (III.11.15), the change in angle of incidence is small compared with the changes in $\Delta\bar{u}$ and $\Delta\theta$; this result is the basis of the second approximation to the phugoid stability motion mentioned in sect. III.10. That approximation, which assumes $\Delta\alpha$ to be small and the rates of change sufficiently low that

$\overline{D}\Delta\alpha$ and $\overline{D}^2\Delta\theta$ can be neglected, leads to the approximate non-dimensional phugoid equations

$$[\overline{D}+C_{DU}]\Delta\bar{u}(\bar{t}_d)-(C_W-C_{D\alpha})\Delta\alpha(\bar{t}_d)+C_W\Delta\theta(\bar{t}_d) = C_W\Delta Th(\bar{t}_d)/W$$

$$C_{LU}\Delta\bar{u}(\bar{t}_d)+C_{L\alpha}\Delta\alpha(\bar{t}_d)-\overline{D}\,\Delta\theta(\bar{t}_d) = -\left[\left(C_{L\dot{\eta}}/2\bar{m}\right)D+C_{L\eta}\right]\Delta\eta(\bar{t}_d) \tag{III.11.20}$$

$$-C_{mU}\,\Delta\bar{u}(\bar{t}_d)-C_{m\alpha}\,\Delta\alpha(\bar{t}_d)-\left(C_{mq}/2\bar{m}\right)\overline{D}\,\Delta\theta(\bar{t}_d) = \left(C_W\,\Delta Th(\bar{t}_d)/W\right)l_{Th}+\left[\left(C_{m\dot{\eta}}/2\bar{m}\right)D+C_{m\eta}\right]\Delta\eta(\bar{t}_d).$$

The approximate phugoid characteristic equation from eqns. (III.11.20) is

$$\left[(-C_{m\alpha})+C_{L\alpha}(-C_{mq})/2\bar{m}\right]\lambda^2+A_1'\lambda+A_0'=0 \tag{III.11.21}$$

where

$$A_1' = C_{DU}\left[\left(C_{L\alpha}(-C_{mq})/2\bar{m}\right)+(-C_{m\alpha})\right] +(C_W-C_{D\alpha})\left[\left(C_{LU}(-C_{mq})/2\bar{m}\right)-C_{mU}\right]$$

$$A_0' = C_W\left[C_{Lu}(-C_{m\alpha})+C_{mU}C_{L\alpha}\right].$$

On substitution of the typical values of eqns. (III.11.9), eqn. (III.11.21) becomes

$$1.33\lambda^2+0.182\bar{\lambda}+1.28=1.33(\bar{\lambda}^2+0.137\bar{\lambda}+0.960)=0$$

which gives stability roots

$$\lambda_{3,4}=-0.069\pm i0.98 \tag{III.11.22}$$

with modal shape

$$(a:b:c)_{3,4} = (\Delta\bar{u} : \Delta\alpha : \Delta\theta) = (0.83\exp(i92°) : 0.064\exp(-i86°) : 1.0) \tag{III.11.23}$$

By comparison of eqns. (III.11.22) and (III.11.23) with eqns. (III.11.14) and (III.11.15) this approximation for the phugoid mode gives an exact value for the non-dimensional frequency but a poor estimate for the non-dimensional damping, although qualitatively the magnitudes of both the exact and approximate dampings are extremely small. The modal shape is well predicted.

Next the important effect of changing the location of the centre of mass on the stability modes is outlined.

A typical variation of the dampings of the stability roots of an aeroplane (with $l_{Th} = 0$) in low speed flight as the centre of mass is moved aft is shown in Fig. III.84. The dampings are shown in terms of real time to either half or double amplitude, while the periods of the stability responses are quoted in seconds. The location of the centre of mass is denoted by l_{wf}, the non-dimensional distance of the centre of mass aft of the aerodynamic centre of the wing–fuselage combination.

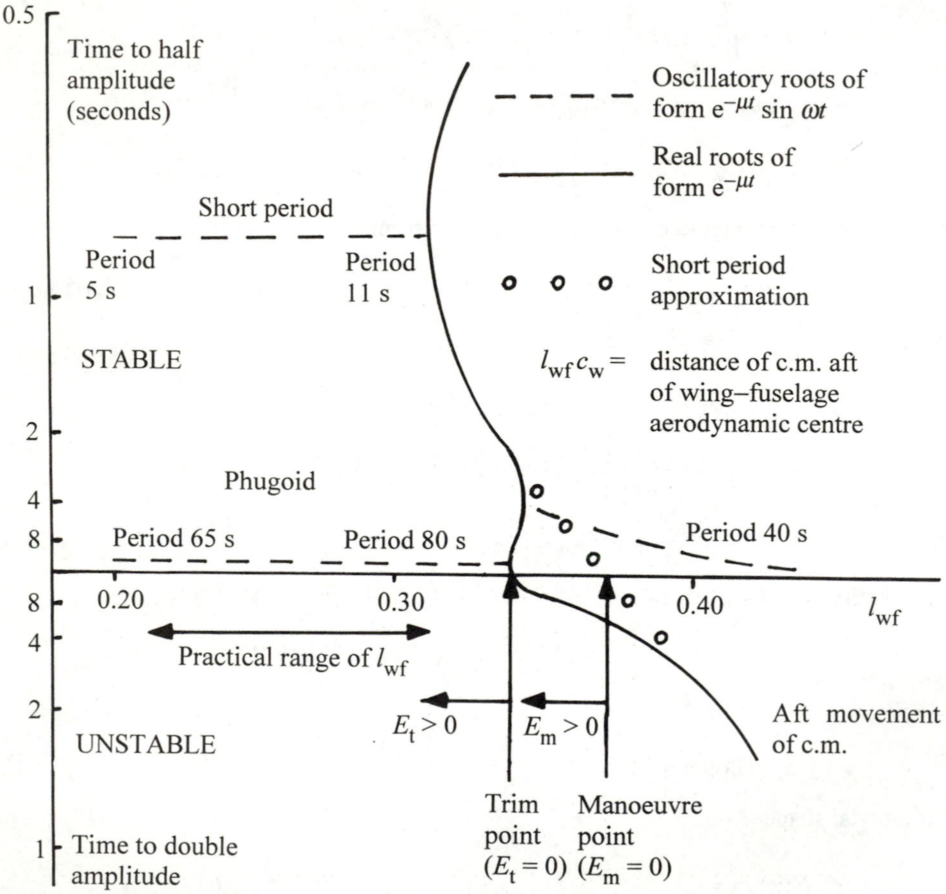

Fig. III.84. Dampings of longitudinal stability roots at low speeds.

(i) With a forward centre of mass location, $l_{wf} = 0.20$, the oscillatory, damped short period and oscillatory, damped phugoid stability modes are clearly identified.

(ii) As the centre of mass moves aft (i.e. as l_{wf} increases from 0.20 to 0.30) the damping of the short period motion is unaltered, while the damping of the phugoid motion actually increases but this increase is not discernible on the scale shown. The frequency of the short period mode decreases (i.e. period increases), because

E_m decreases. The frequency of the phugoid mode also decreases (i.e. period increases), because (E_{trim}/E_m) decreases.

(iii) When the centre of mass reaches the location $l_{wf} = 0.32$ the short period mode ceases to be a damped oscillation and degenerates into two real subsidences, one slow and one rapid.

(iv) With a small further aft movement of the centre of mass the slow short period subsidence becomes slower, while the rapid subsidence becomes even more rapid.

(v) At $l_{wf} = 0.335$, the phugoid oscillation degenerates into two subsidences. The short period and phugoid modes are said to have become coupled, generating four new modes which are all pure subsidences, where the rates of subsidence of two of the modes are extremely slow (i.e. long times to double amplitude). Coupling of two modes always occurs when the response times of the two modes become approximately the same.

(vi) At $l_{wf} = 0.34$, the low speed trim point when l_{Th} is zero, one of the stability roots becomes zero with an infinite time to half, or double, amplitude.

(vii) For $l_{wf} > 0.34$ the aeroplane is unstable; one stability root is real and positive indicating a pure divergence, the time to double amplitude decreases as l_{wf} increases.

(viii) At $l_{wf} = 0.35$, a slowly damped oscillation mode (the phugoid mode) reappears, but the aeroplane is unstable.

(ix) A pilot would be able to control an unstable aeroplane with a time to double amplitude greater than 5 s, so the maximum value of l_{wf} would be approximately 0.38.

The range of l_{wf} covered in items (i) to (ix) above is of the order of 0.20 (i.e. 20% of the mean wing chord). The practical range of the location of the centre of mass is usually about 10% of the mean wing chord; in the example shown in Fig. III.84 typically $0.2 < l_{wf} < 0.3$.

Fig. III.84 also includes the stability roots of the approximation of the short period mode, see sect. III.9. The zero stability root of the short period approximation occurs when the centre of mass is located at the manoeuvre point. The short period approximation breaks down for centre of mass locations

$$0.34 < l_{wf} < 0.40; \qquad \text{(III.11.24)}$$

this range is where coupling of the short period and phugoid modes occur. The instability when $l_{wf} > 0.40$ is effectively a divergence of the short period mode.

At low Mach numbers, when l_{Th} is zero, since $E_m > E_{trim}$, the manoeuvre point lies aft of the trim point, as indicated in Fig. III.84.

With increasing Mach number at subsonic speeds, E_{trim} tends to increase whereas E_m tends to decrease. At high subsonic speeds it is possible for the manoeuvre point to lie in front of the trim point. Fig. III.85 shows typical trends of the stability roots at a high subsonic speed as the location of the centre of mass is moved aft. The overall trends are similar to the low Mach number case (Fig. III.84) apart from some differences (of considerable academic interest, as explained later in the section on static stability, but of little practical importance) when the centre of mass lies close to the trim or manoeuvre points.

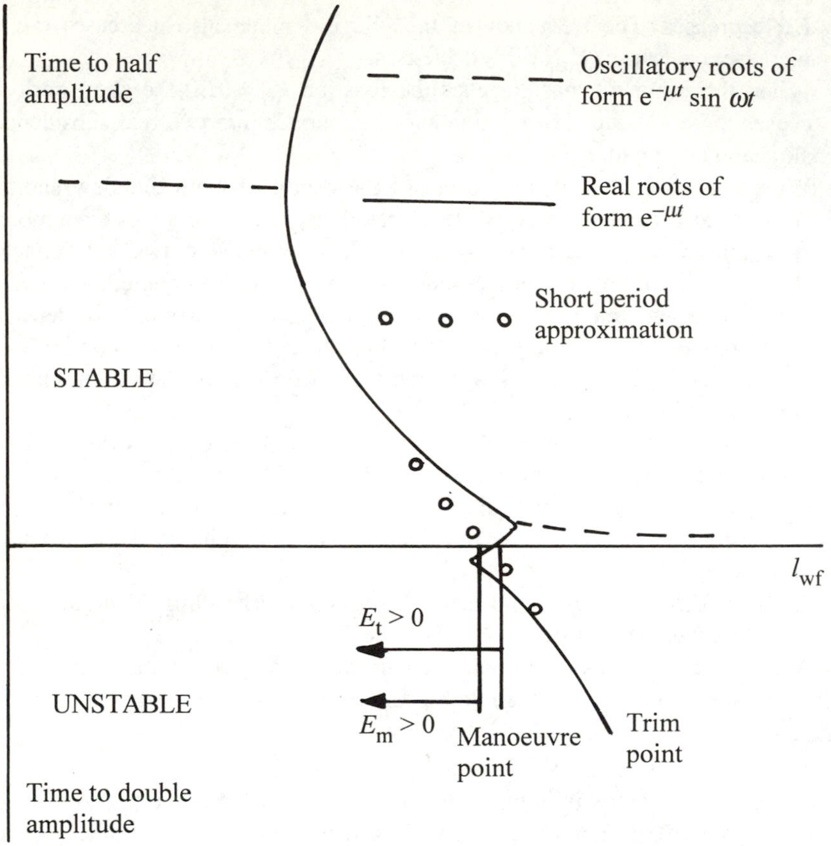

Fig. III.85. Dampings of longitudinal stability roots at high subsonic speed.

In this example the aeroplane first becomes unstable as the centre of mass moves aft as a slowly divergent phugoid oscillation; the critical instability is, as always, the pure divergence associated with an unstable short period mode.

At low supersonic speeds typical values for a combat aeroplane at high altitude are:

$$\begin{aligned} &i_{yy} = 0.7, \quad \overline{m} = 600, \quad l_{\text{Th}} = 0, \\ &C_{\text{W}} = 0.2, \quad C_{\text{L}\alpha} = 3.5, \quad (-C_{m\alpha}) = 2.1 \text{ (i.e. } K_\alpha = 0.6) \\ &(-C_{m\dot{\alpha}}) = 2.0, \quad (-C_{mq}) = 12.0, \quad C_{\text{D}} = 0.1, \\ &C_{\text{D}U} = 0.2, \quad C_{\text{L}U} = 0.0, \quad C_{mU} = -0.05, \quad C_{\text{D}\alpha} = 0.3. \end{aligned} \tag{III.11.25}$$

In this case the four non-dimensional stability roots are:

$$\begin{aligned} &\lambda = +0.07, \quad -0.25 \text{ (phugoid)} \\ &\lambda = -6.75 \pm \text{i}41.0 \quad \text{(short period).} \end{aligned} \tag{III.11.26}$$

The phugoid has degenerated into two real roots (both small), one positive, one negative, leading to a weak divergence. The short period response is a damped oscillatory motion of high relative frequency, due to the high value of the manoeuvre margin, and relatively low damping ratio.

It is concluded that the elevator manoeuvre margin E_m (= $H_m/(-C_{m\eta})$) is the crucial parameter for longitudinal stability at all Mach numbers. For positive values of E_m, say $E_m > 0.05$, the aeroplane is stable with separate short period and phugoid modes. This type of criterion would serve as a preliminary design stability criterion. However, the practical limits on the manoeuvre margin and on the damping ratio are determined by the control and handling characteristics, as explained later.

The stability characteristics of an aeroplane trimmed in a shallow descent or climb differ only slightly from those described above for an aeroplane in trimmed steady level flight.

EXAMPLES III.29

1. Does l_{Th} affect the longitudinal stability characteristics?
2. Eqn. (III.11.24) gives the range of l_{wf} when the approximation for the short period mode breaks down. What is the corresponding range of H_m and E_m?
3. Convert the non-dimensional undamped frequencies and damping ratios in eqns. (III.11.3), (III.11.12) and (III.11.14) into real time; compare with the values in sects. III.9 and III.10.
4. Solve for the stability roots and modal shapes for the basic light aeroplane configuration.
5. Describe the stability characteristics of an aeroplane which is performing a 'steady' pull-out manoeuvre.

III.12 LONGITUDINAL RESPONSE TO CONTROLS

In this section the longitudinal response to elevator and throttle inputs are described, assuming small perturbations from the initial trim state.

It is now possible to give a qualitative explanation of what happens to a stable aeroplane in trimmed flight when the elevator angle is moved slightly from its trim position and held there, without changing the throttle. First the aeroplane responds with a short period stability motion which decays in the order of a few seconds, leaving the aeroplane in a motion with a virtually constant normal acceleration in which the forward velocity has hardly changed from its initial trim value and where the angle of incidence and rate of pitch have settled down to steady values. This quasi-steady pull-out manoeuvre slowly changes as a phugoid stability motion develops. If the pilot continues to hold the elevator angle for about 5 minutes until the phugoid response finally decays, the aeroplane will settle down into a new steady state, either in steady climb or descent, depending on the sign of the change in elevator angle, with a speed different from the initial trimmed state.

Alternatively when the throttle is opened, increasing the thrust, leaving the elevator angle unchanged at its trimmed setting, there is virtually no short period response, but a phugoid stability motion is initiated. After about 5 minutes the phugoid motion decays and the aeroplane then climbs steadily at the initial trim speed. The angle of climb depends on the increase in thrust. This procedure for implementing a climb is not practical as it takes too long; practical procedures are explained later in sect. III.14.

In this section the responses to elevator angle and throttle are derived; there is no attempt to explain how a pilot uses these responses; this aspect is dealt with in section III.14.

III.12.1 Response to elevator

A stick displacement changes the elevator angle and initiates:

(i) a normal acceleration response
(ii) a rate of pitch response
(iii) a pitch attitude response
(iv) a flight path angle response.

These responses can be determined from the short period approximation because they occur sufficiently quickly before the phugoid mode has time to build up.

The short period response equations are derived in Appendix 6.

III.12.1.1 Normal acceleration response

The equation for the normal acceleration response to an elevator input is, from Appendix 6,

$$\left[\mathrm{D}^2 + 2\zeta_{\mathrm{sp}}(\omega_0)_{\mathrm{sp}}\mathrm{D} + (\omega_0)^2_{\mathrm{sp}}\right]\Delta n(t)$$
$$\simeq \left[-\left(C_{\mathrm{L}\eta}/C_{\mathrm{W}}\right)\mathrm{D}^2 + (\omega_0)^2_{\mathrm{sp}}/(E_{\mathrm{m}}C_{\mathrm{W}})\right](-\Delta\eta(t)) \qquad \text{(III.12.1)}$$

where D is the differential operator d/dt;

$$(\omega_0)^2_{\mathrm{sp}} = \left[g/(c_{\mathrm{w}}C_{\mathrm{W}}i_{yy})\right]C_{\mathrm{L}\alpha}H_{\mathrm{m}} = \left[g/(c_{\mathrm{w}}C_{\mathrm{W}}i_{yy})\right]C_{\mathrm{L}\alpha}(-C_{m\eta})E_{\mathrm{m}},$$

$$2\zeta_{\mathrm{sp}}(\omega_0)_{\mathrm{sp}} = \left(g/U_{\mathrm{trim}}C_{\mathrm{W}}\right)\left[C_{\mathrm{L}\alpha} + \left[\left(\left(-C_{m\dot{\alpha}}/2\right) + \left(-C_{mq}/2\right)\right)/i_{yy}\right]\right].$$

Consider the aeroplane normal acceleration response to the step input

$$\Delta\eta(t) = \Delta\eta_{\mathrm{s}}H(t), \qquad \text{(III.12.2)}$$

where $\Delta\eta_{\mathrm{s}}$ is the amplitude of the step input. It is not unreasonable to assume this idealized step input as a first approximation because the time taken in practice to pull back the stick rapidly, and then hold it, is small compared to the time of the short period response.

The initial mathematical values of the normal acceleration are, from eqn. (III.12.1),

$$\mathrm{D}\,\Delta n(0+) + 2\zeta_{\mathrm{sp}}(\omega_0)_{\mathrm{sp}}\,\Delta n(0+) = 0, \qquad \Delta n(0+) = \left(C_{\mathrm{L}\eta}/C_{\mathrm{W}}\right)\Delta\eta_{\mathrm{s}} \qquad \text{(III.12.3)}$$

(these values are obtained by integration(s) of eqn. (III.12.1) across $-0 < t < +0$—see Part II, eqns. (II.17) and (II.68)). Note that when $\Delta\eta_{\mathrm{s}}$ is negative the initial normal acceleration $\Delta n(0+)$ is (theoretically) negative due to the fact that at time $t = 0+$ the only incremental load on the aeroplane is the download on the tailplane. There is a delay in the build-up of a positive normal acceleration while the aeroplane rotates to increase the aeroplane incidence. The magnitude of the negative normal acceleration at small time will be much reduced in practice because of aerodynamic lag effects, but the prediction of the time lag for the aeroplane to rotate and build up positive lift should be realistic.

In eqn. (III.12.1), as $t \to \infty$ the steady state normal acceleration response

$$\Delta n_{ss} = (-\Delta\eta_s)/(C_W E_m) \quad \left(= (-\Delta\eta_s)(-C_{m\eta})/(C_W H_m)\right) \qquad \text{(III.12.4)}$$

which is consistent with the definition of E_m.

The normal acceleration step response from eqns. (III.12.1) and (III.12.3), when the damping is subcritical (i.e. when $\zeta_{sp} < 1.0$), is

$$\begin{aligned}\left(E_m C_W/(-\Delta\eta_s)\right)\Delta n(t) \\ &= 1.0 - \left[1.0 + (E_m C_{L\eta})\right]\exp\left(-\zeta_{sp}(\omega_0)_{sp} t\right)\cos\omega t \\ &\quad - \left[1.0 - (E_m C_{L\eta})\right]\left(\zeta_{sp}/\left(1-\zeta_{sp}^2\right)\right)^{1/2}\exp\left(-\zeta_{sp}(\omega_0)_{sp} t\right)\sin\omega t\end{aligned} \qquad \text{(III.12.5)}$$

where

$$\omega = (\omega_0)_{sp}(1-\zeta_{sp}^2)^{1/2}.$$

When the damping is supercritical (i.e. when $\zeta_{sp} > 1.0$)

$$\begin{aligned}\left(E_m C_W/(-\Delta\eta_s)\right)\Delta n(t) \\ &= 1.0 - \left[1.0 + (E_m C_{L\eta})\right]\left[\lambda_2\exp(\lambda_1 t) - \lambda_1\exp(\lambda_2 t)/(\lambda_2 - \lambda_1)\right] \\ &\quad - (E_m C_{L\eta})\left[(\lambda_1+\lambda_2)/(\lambda_1-\lambda_2)\right]\left[\exp(\lambda_1 t) - \exp(\lambda_2 t)\right]\end{aligned} \qquad \text{(III.12.6)}$$

where

$$\lambda_1 = (\omega_0)_{sp}\left(-\zeta_{sp} + (\zeta_{sp}^2 - 1)^{1/2}\right), \qquad \lambda_2 = (\omega_0)_{sp}\left(-\zeta_{sp} - (\zeta_{sp}^2 - 1)^{1/2}\right).$$

Fig. III.86(i) shows the response for $(E_m C_W/(-\Delta\eta_s))\,\Delta n(t)$ plotted against $(\zeta_{sp}(\omega_0)_{sp} t)$ for an aeroplane with $W/S_w = 4.0\ \text{kN/m}^2$, $C_W = 0.85$, at sea level, taking $\zeta_{sp}(\omega_0)_{sp} = \text{constant} = 1.0/\text{s}$, with

$$\left((\omega_0)_{sp},\ \zeta_{sp}\right) = (2.5,\ 0.4),\ (1.67,\ 0.6),\ (1.25,\ 0.8),\ (0.625,\ 1.6).$$

This variation of $(\omega_0)_{sp}$ and ζ_{sp} is obtained by varying the elevator manoeuvre margin E_m in the ratio (4.0 : 1.78 : 1.0 : 0.25), by changing the location of the centre of mass. It is important to appreciate that a change in elevator manoeuvre margin, E_m, affects both the undamped frequency, $(\omega_0)_{sp}$, and the damping ratio, ζ_{sp}, but not the damping coefficient.

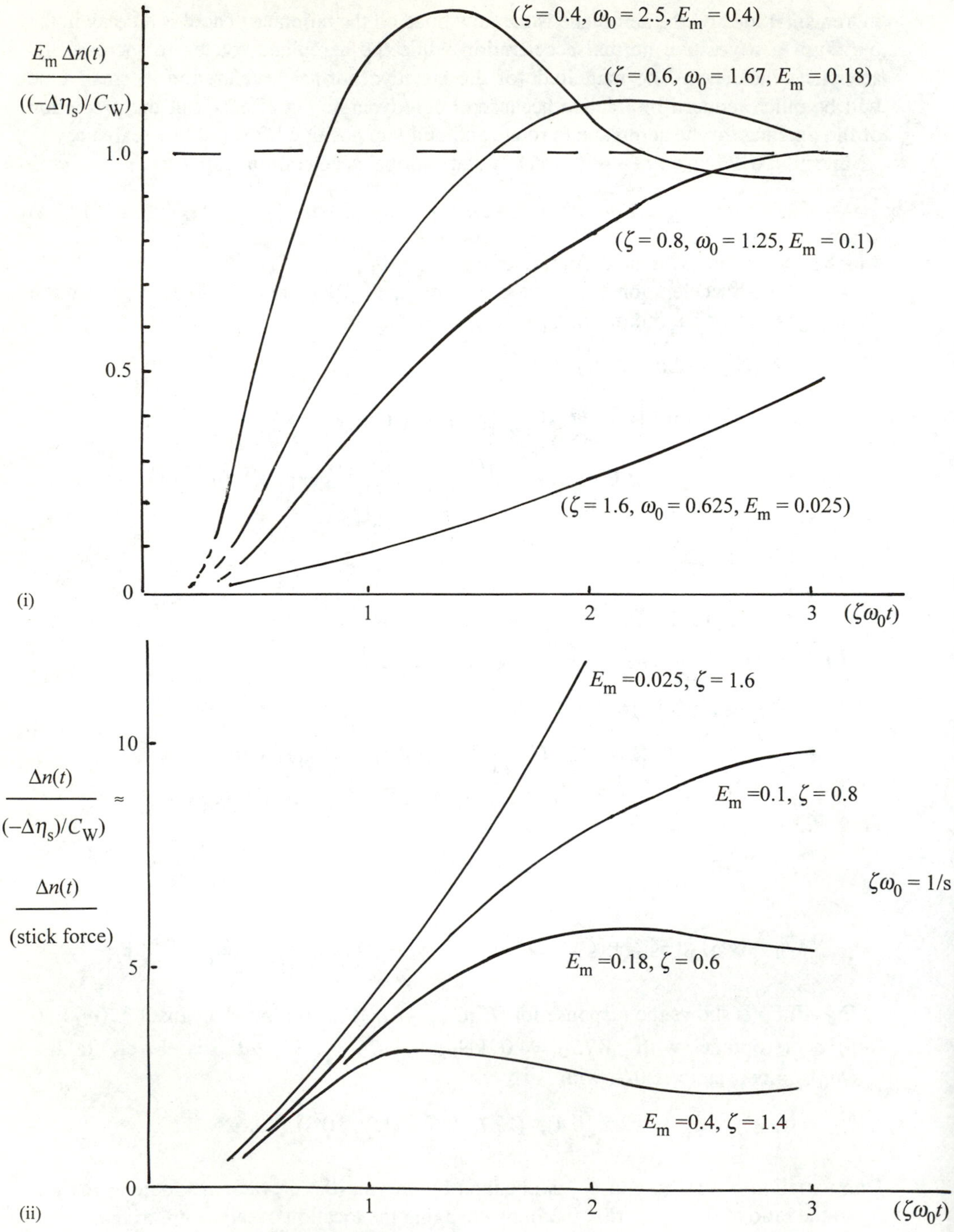

Fig. III.86. (i) Normal acceleration responses to step elevator angle. (ii) Normal acceleration responses to step elevator input.

Note that $(\Delta\eta_s/C_W)$ is proportional to the stick force for both manual controls and powered controls with an artificial Q-feel system.

In Fig. III.86(i) the normal acceleration responses at small time are dotted in to represent the practical situation; the time lag before the positive normal acceleration starts is approximately 0.25 s.

In Fig. III.86(i)

(i) the response with the lowest damping ratio, ζ_{sp} (= 0.4), that is with the highest E_m, first reaches the steady state value in under 1.0 s, but then overshoots by approximately 30% before settling down to its asymptotic steady state in about 3 s;

(ii) when the damping ratio ζ_{sp} is 0.6 the response first reaches the steady state value in approximately 1.5 s and then overshoots by approximately 10%, again settling down to its asymptotic state in about 3 s;

(iii) virtually no overshoot occurs with ζ_{sp} greater than 0.8;

(iv) for subcritical damping, $\zeta_{sp} < 1$, the time to reach the asymptotic state is independent of $(\omega_0)_{sp}$ (and E_m), about 3 s;

(v) for supercritical damping, $\zeta > 1$, the time to reach the asymptotic state increases as $(\omega_0)_{sp}$ (and E_m) decreases.

From the point of view of how quickly a step response reaches its asymptotic steady state, low values of E_m imply a 'sluggish' response while higher values of E_m imply a fast rise time.

Fig. III.86(i) is redrawn in Fig. III.86(ii) where the response per unit stick force is plotted against time for different E_m. In Fig. III.86(ii) the fastest response, for $t > 0.5$ s, occurs with the smallest E_m; there is the danger, however, that large values of Δn may build up, leading either to excessive inertial loads, which may cause structural damage, or to pilot blackout.

From the point of view of how quickly a step response per unit force builds up, higher values of E_m imply a 'sluggish' response while lower values of E_m imply a faster response, the opposite conclusion from that deduced from Fig. III.86(i). When describing response characteristics as fast or sluggish it is imperative that the context is clearly understood.

III.12.1.2 Pitch rate response

The pitch rate response equation, from Appendix 6, is

$$\left[D^2 + 2\zeta_{sp}(\omega_0)_{sp}D + (\omega_0)_{sp}^2\right]q(t)$$
$$\simeq \left((\omega_0)_{sp}^2/E_m\right)\left[\left(1/C_{L\alpha}\right)D + \left(g/(U_{trim}C_W)\right)\right]\left(-\Delta\eta(t)\right). \qquad \text{(III.12.7)}$$

Consider the pitch rate response to the step input

$$\Delta\eta(t) = \Delta\eta_s H(t).$$

The initial values of the pitch acceleration and pitch rate at time $t = 0+$, from eqn. (III.12.7), are

$$q(0+) = 0$$

$$\begin{aligned} Dq(0+) &= \left[(\omega_0)^2_{sp}/(E_m C_{L\alpha})\right](-\Delta\eta_s) \\ &= \left[g/(c_w C_W i_{yy})\right](-C_{m\eta})(-\Delta\eta_s) \\ &= \left[\tfrac{1}{2}\rho_{at} U^2_{trim} S_w c_w (-C_{m\eta})(-\Delta\eta_s)\right]/I_{yy}. \end{aligned} \tag{III.12.8}$$

The right hand side of eqn. (III.12.8) denotes the 'instantaneous' aerodynamic pitching moment at time $t = 0+$ divided by the pitch moment of inertia, hence eqn. (III.12.8) expresses the initial pitch acceleration, neglecting aerodynamic lag effects.

From eqn. (III.12.7), as $t \to \infty$ the steady state pitch rate response is

$$q_{ss} = \left[(g/U_{trim})/(C_W E_m)\right](-\Delta\eta_s) = (g/U_{trim})\Delta n_{ss}. \tag{III.12.9}$$

The pitch rate step response from eqn. (III.12.7), when the damping is subcritical (i.e. $\zeta_{sp} < 1$), is

$$\begin{aligned} &(E_m C_W/(-\Delta\eta_s))(U_{trim} q(t)/g) \\ &\quad = 1.0 - \exp\left(-(\zeta\omega_0)_{sp} t\right)\left[\cos\omega t + K_1\left(\zeta/(1-\zeta^2)^{1/2}\right)_{sp} \sin\omega t\right] \end{aligned} \tag{III.12.10}$$

where

$$\omega = (\omega_0)_{sp}(1-\zeta^2_{sp})^{1/2}$$

$$K_1 = 1 - (E_m C_W/(-\Delta\eta_s))(U_{trim}/g)\left(Dq(0+)/(\zeta\omega_0)_{sp}\right).$$

The pitch rate step response when the damping is supercritical (i.e. $\zeta_{sp} > 1$) is

$$\begin{aligned} &(E_m C_W/(-\Delta\eta_s))(U_{trim} q(t)/g) \\ &\quad = 1 - \left[\lambda_2 \exp(\lambda_1 t) - \lambda_1 \exp(\lambda_2 t)\right]/(\lambda_2 - \lambda_1) \\ &\quad\quad + (1 - K_1)\left[\exp(\lambda_1 t) - \exp(\lambda_2 t)\right]/(\lambda_1 - \lambda_2) \end{aligned} \tag{III.12.11}$$

where

$$\lambda_1 = (\omega_0)_{sp}\left(-\zeta_{sp} + (\zeta^2_{sp} - 1)^{1/2}\right), \qquad \lambda_2 = (\omega_0)_{sp}\left(-\zeta_{sp} - (\zeta^2_{sp} - 1)^{1/2}\right).$$

Fig. III.87(i) shows the pitch rate responses for the same range of parameters as in Fig. III.86(i). In Fig. III.87(i):

(i) for the case ($\zeta_{sp} = 0.4$, $(\omega_0)_{sp} = 2.5/\text{s}$, $E_m = 0.4$) the overshoot is extreme with a maximum pitch rate approximately four times q_{ss}; the initial positive pitch acceleration is followed by a large pitch deceleration;

(ii) the level of overshoot decreases as ζ_{sp} is increased;

(iii) the levels of overshoot in pitch rate are substantially greater than the corresponding levels of overshoot in normal acceleration (compare Figs. III.86(i) and III.87(i));

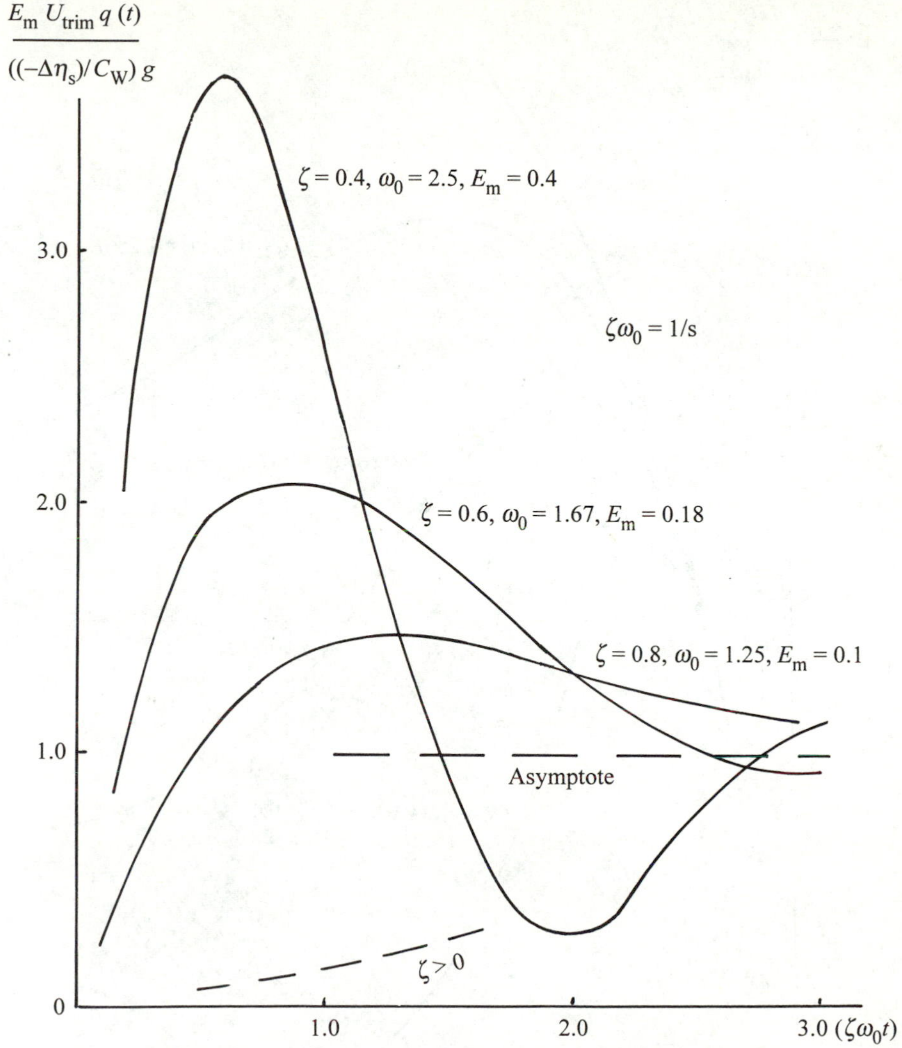

Fig. III.87(i). Pitch rate responses to step elevator input.

(iv) for subcritical damping all asymptotic steady states of normal acceleration, pitch rate and angle of incidence, are reached in approximately 3 s, leading into the steady state pull-out manoeuvre;

(v) for supercritical damping the build-up time to all asymptotic states increases with increase in ζ_{sp}.

Fig. III.87(ii) , based on the same information as Fig. III.87(i), shows the pitch rate per unit stick force:

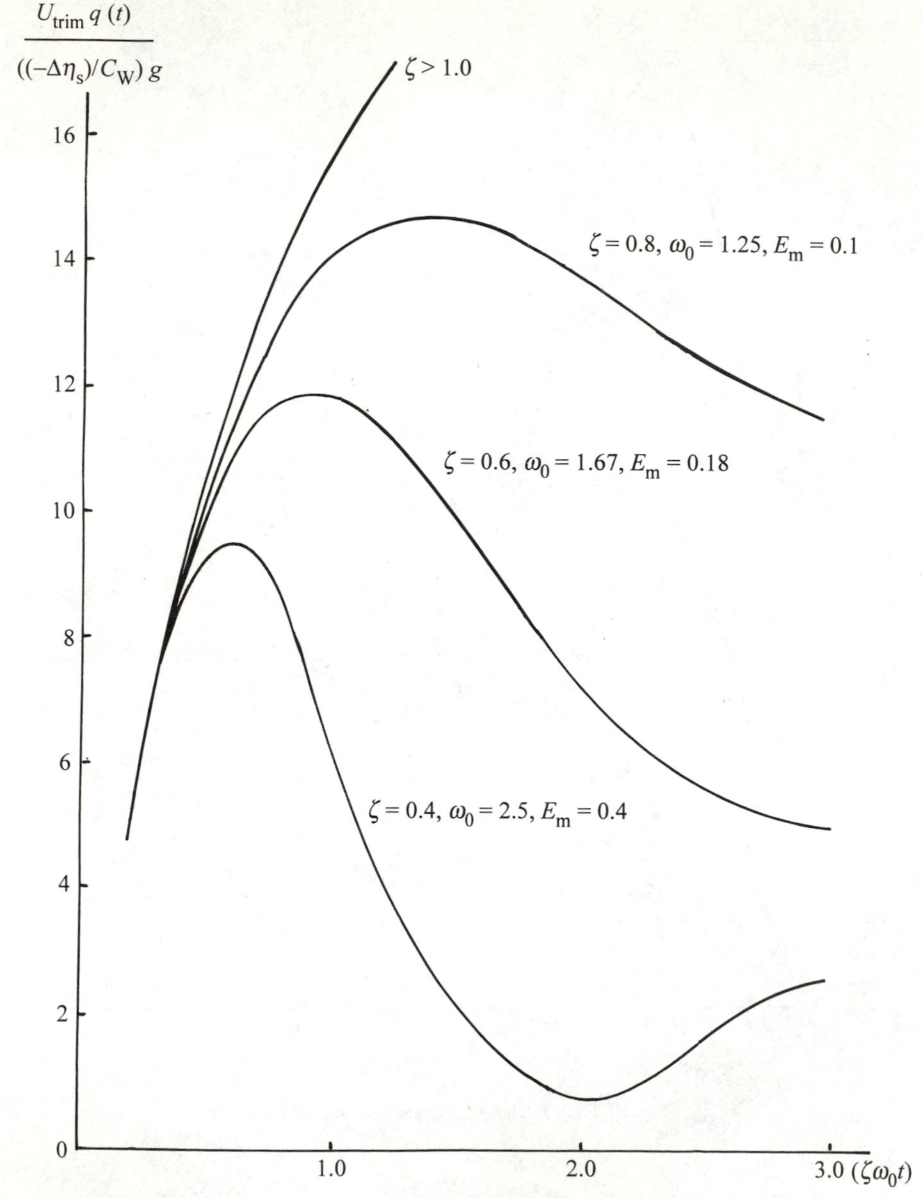

Fig. III.87(ii). Pitch rate responses to step elevator input.

(i) all cases have the same initial pitch acceleration, which is independent of ζ_{sp} and $(\omega_0)_{sp}$ from eqn. (III.12.8);

(ii) again the pitch rate response increases as the damping ratio increases, that is, as E_m decreases.

III.12.1.3 Pitch attitude angle response

Pitch attitude responses, obtained by integration of the pitch rate responses in Fig. III.87(i), are shown in Fig. III.88.

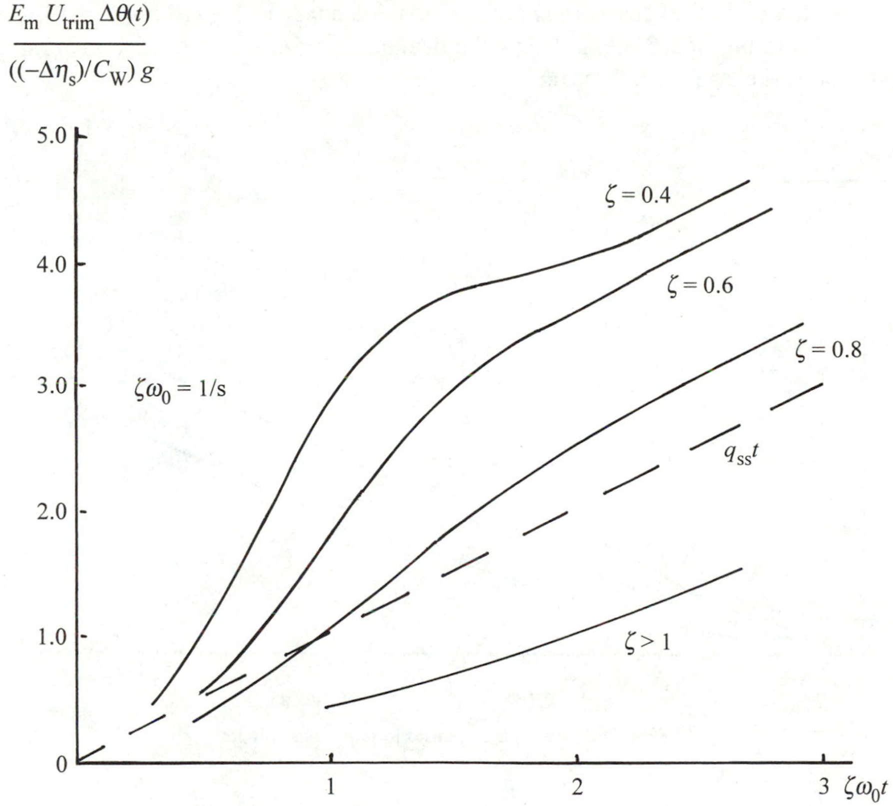

Fig. III.88. Pitch attitude responses to step elevator input.

The main point of interest is the pitch attitude response relative to a datum response, $q_{ss}t$, which assumes a steady state pitch rate response q_{ss} from zero time. By inspection of the 'areas under the curves' of the pitch rate responses in Fig. III.87(i), the pitch attitude responses for $\zeta_{sp} = 0.4$, 0.6 are significantly higher than the datum response, the pitch attitude for $\zeta_{sp} = 0.8$ is slightly higher than the datum response, and the pitch attitude response is below the datum for $\zeta_{sp} > 1$.

All curves ultimately have the same gradient because $(\Delta\dot{\theta}(t))_{ss}$ is equal to q_{ss}.

III.12.1.4 Flight path angle response

Because

$$U_{trim}\Delta\dot{\gamma}(t) = g\,\Delta n(t) \tag{III.12.12}$$

flight path angle responses are obtained by the integration of the normal acceleration responses.

Flight path angle responses are sketched in Fig. III.89. Again the main point of interest is the flight path angle response relative to the datum response $q_{ss}t$. By inspection of the 'areas under the curves' of the normal acceleration responses in Fig. III.86(i), the flight path responses in Fig. III.89 are all below the datum response, the difference increasing as ζ_{sp} increases (i.e. as E_m decreases).

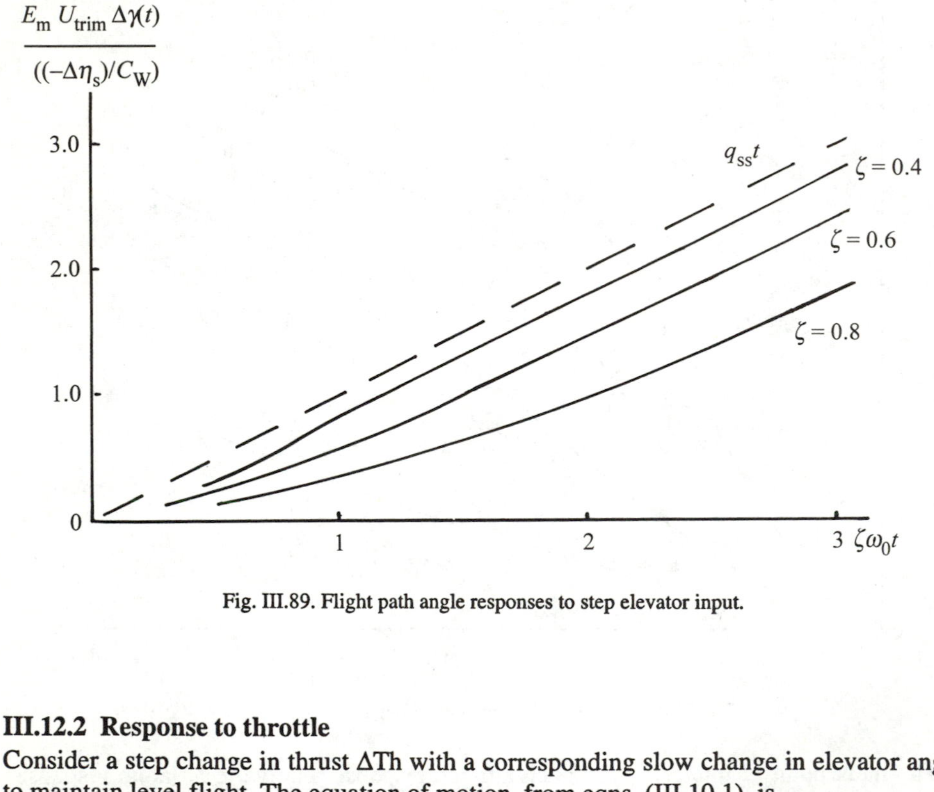

Fig. III.89. Flight path angle responses to step elevator input.

III.12.2 Response to throttle

Consider a step change in thrust ΔTh with a corresponding slow change in elevator angle to maintain level flight. The equation of motion, from eqns. (III.10.1), is

$$\left[D + \left(g/(C_W U_{trim})\right) C_{DU}\right]\left(\Delta u(t)/U_{trim}\right)$$
$$= \left(g/U_{trim}\right)\left((C_D)_{trim}/C_W\right)\left(\Delta Th/Th_{trim}\right) H(t). \qquad \text{(III.12.13)}$$

The speed builds up from U_{trim} to a steady state value

$$\left(\Delta u/U_{trim}\right)_{ss} = \tfrac{1}{2}\left(\Delta Th/Th_{trim}\right) \qquad \text{(III.12.14)}$$

because $C_{DU} = 2C_D$, neglecting Mach number effects. The time constant of this first order response is

$$t_c = \left(C_W/(2(C_D)_{trim})\right)\left(U_{trim}/g\right) = O\left[(7.5U_{trim}/g)\ \mathrm{s}\right] = O[1.0\ \mathrm{min}]. \qquad \text{(III.12.15)}$$

If a step change in thrust ΔTh is applied keeping elevator fixed then the phugoid response equations, assuming no change in angle of incidence, from eqns. (III.10.1) are, at low Mach number,

$$\left(\mathrm{D}^2 + 2(g/U_{\text{trim}})(C_\mathrm{D}/C_\mathrm{L})_{\text{trim}}\mathrm{D} + 2(g/U_{\text{trim}})^2\right)(\Delta u(t)/U_{\text{trim}})$$
$$= (g/U_{\text{trim}})((C_\mathrm{D})_{\text{trim}}/C_\mathrm{W})(\Delta\text{Th}/\text{Th}_{\text{trim}})\delta(t)$$
$$\left(\mathrm{D}^2 + 2(g/U_{\text{trim}})(C_\mathrm{D}/C_\mathrm{L})_{\text{trim}}\mathrm{D} + 2(g/U_{\text{trim}})^2\right)\Delta\theta(t) \qquad \text{(III.12.16)}$$
$$= 2(g/U_{\text{trim}})^2((C_\mathrm{D})_{\text{trim}}/C_\mathrm{W})(\Delta\text{Th}/\text{Th}_{\text{trim}})H(t).$$

The initial conditions are

$$\Delta\dot{u}(0+)/U_{\text{trim}} = (g/U_{\text{trim}})((C_\mathrm{D})_{\text{trim}}/C_\mathrm{W})(\Delta\text{Th}/\text{Th}_{\text{trim}}),$$
$$\Delta u(0+)/U_{\text{trim}} = 0, \qquad \Delta\dot{\theta}(0+) = \Delta\theta(0+) = 0. \qquad \text{(III.12.17)}$$

The steady state conditions after the decay of the phugoid mode, after approximately 5 minutes, are

$$(\Delta u/U_{\text{trim}})_{ss} = 0, \qquad \Delta\theta_{ss} \simeq \Delta\gamma_{ss} = ((C_\mathrm{D})_{\text{trim}}/C_\mathrm{W})(\Delta\text{Th}/\text{Th}_{\text{trim}}). \qquad \text{(III.12.18)}$$

There is no ultimate change in forward speed; the aeroplane then climbs at a steady angle, as expected from the opening remarks to this section.

For a propeller propulsion unit a change in throttle gives a change in power, ΔP, where

$$\Delta P = U_{\text{trim}}\Delta\text{Th} + \text{Th}_{\text{trim}}\Delta u \qquad \text{(III.12.19a)}$$

or

$$(\Delta P/P_{\text{trim}}) = (\Delta\text{Th}/\text{Th}_{\text{trim}}) + (\Delta u/U_{\text{trim}}). \qquad \text{(III.12.19b)}$$

Hence, for a step change in power, with a change in elevator to maintain level flight, from eqn. (III.12.14),

$$(\Delta u/U_{\text{trim}})_{ss} = \tfrac{2}{3}(\Delta P/P_{\text{trim}}). \qquad \text{(III.12.20)}$$

For a step change in power, with zero change in elevator, the steady states are given by eqns. (III.12.18), replacing $(\Delta\text{Th}/\text{Th}_{\text{trim}})$ by $(\Delta P/P_{\text{trim}})$. However, the damping is increased by 50% so the time to reach the steady states is reduced by 1/3.

EXAMPLES III.30

1. Derive the short period response equation for the flight path angle due to a step elevator deflection.
2. When $\zeta_{sp} = 0.8$, $C_\mathrm{W} = 1.0$, from Fig. III.86(i), what change in elevator angle gives a steady state normal acceleration of $1g$?
3. Give a physical explanation for the high overshoot in the pitch rate response when $\zeta_{sp} = 0.4$ shown in Fig. III.87(i).

4. Sketch the normal acceleration response, the pitch rate response, the pitch attitude response and the flight path angle response to the pulse input

$$\Delta\eta(t) = 0, \quad t < 0; \qquad \Delta\eta(t) = -\Delta\eta_s, \quad 0 < t < 2\text{ s}; \qquad \Delta\eta(t) = 0, \quad t > 2\text{ s}$$

when $\zeta_{sp} = 0.6$.

5. Check the statement in the text: 'For a step change in power, with zero change in elevator, the steady states are given by eqns. (III.12.18), replacing $(\Delta Th/Th_{trim})$ by $(\Delta P/P_{trim})$. However, the damping is increased by 50% so the time to reach the steady states is reduced by 1/3.'

III.13 LONGITUDINAL RESPONSE TO ATMOSPHERIC GUSTS

III.13.1 Introduction

A number of important effects arise during aeroplane flight in turbulence.

(i) Airframe and equipment experience accelerations and (gust) loads; the aeroplane structure is designed to withstand, with an adequate safety margin, the most extreme gust loading condition expected during the lifetime of that aeroplane. The cumulative effect of gust loads also contributes to the structural fatigue life.
(ii) Acceleration responses subject crew and passengers to bumps and jolts, affecting the ability of the crew to carry out their flying duties and causing discomfort to passengers. These bumps and jolts vary in intensity and type from the extremely rare large single jolt, caused by entering a so-called air pocket in which all unrestrained bodies can hit the cabin roof, to the more common continuous bumpiness, which is mostly light, occasionally moderate, and infrequently severe.
(iii) Atmospheric turbulence disturbs an aeroplane from its flight path. It is the job of the pilot, human or auto, to ensure that a designated flight path is maintained as closely as possible, for example on a low speed approach or on a high speed ground attack or during terrain following.
(iv) Atmospheric turbulence increases the human pilot workload.
(v) Unless an aeroplane is controllable by a pilot, human and/or auto, in virtually all wind and gust conditions, the aeroplane will be rejected as unairworthy by statutory authorities (e.g. CAA, MoD, FAA, USAAF).

The main sources of atmospheric turbulence have been identified.

(i) Clouds, at all altitudes, are continually in turmoil from internal thermal currents and mixing processes.
(ii) Extreme turbulence, superimposed on large up-and-down draughts, is found in thunderstorm clouds. At the base of a thunderstorm, close to the ground, the up-and-down draughts can induce changes in direction in horizontal winds, a phenomenon known as wind shear.
(iii) Clear air turbulence, which by definition is not visible (as distinct from clouds, which are), can be generated as winds flow past high mountain peaks, and then convected with the winds over long distances.

(iv) Clear air turbulence can develop in inversions due to instabilities between stratified air layers, so-called Kelvin–Helmholtz instabilities.
(v) Clear air turbulence is present at the edges of high altitude jet streams which, in the northern hemisphere, are part of the high altitude westerlies patterns of winds.
(vi) Below an altitude of 500 m, turbulence is associated with the ground boundary layer, and then the character of the turbulence depends on the local terrain.

For descriptions of these meteorological phenomena, see refs. III.29 and III.30.

The essential feature of atmospheric turbulence is that it is a random phenomenon, it defies exact representation, and can only be described in terms of its statistical parameters. Consequently, all aeroplane responses to turbulence are random. The problem is to relate the statistical properties of the aeroplane responses to the statistical properties of atmospheric turbulence.

The effects of atmospheric turbulence on structural strength or fatigue are not covered in this book.

From the point of view of flight dynamics, turbulence affects:

(i) ride quality, usually defined in statistical terms as the number of bumps, or peak accelerations, exceeding a specified g level per unit time (a typical criterion is the number of bumps exceeding $\frac{1}{2}g$ per minute—about 5 would indicate moderate turbulence, more than 20 would indicate severe turbulence);
(ii) the effectiveness of the pilot/aeroplane combination to complete specific flying tasks such as landing, tracking during combat, terrain following or lining up an aeroplane for a ground attack;
(iii) the workload of the human pilot when attempting flying tasks, such as those listed in (ii);
(iv) the effectiveness of a combat aeroplane as a weapon aiming platform, either in combat or in ground attack;
(v) in severe turbulence, the ability of a pilot to see the instruments.

Passenger and crew comfort also depend on the physiology of the human body; extended periods of time at very low frequencies can induce nausea (air sickness), frequencies of the order of 5 Hz induce resonance of the intestines, frequencies of the order of 20 Hz induce resonance of the eyeballs.

Structural flexibility is a major factor in determining the frequencies and amplitudes of responses, especially at frequencies higher than 2 Hz on transport aeroplanes and 8 Hz on combat aeroplanes; structural flexibility is not considered in this book, which is confined to rigid aeroplanes.

To build up an understanding of aeroplane response to atmospheric turbulence it is helpful, first, to consider aeroplane response to different types of discrete gust profiles before attempting consideration of aeroplane responses to sequences of random gusts.

III.13.2 Response to discrete gusts

III.13.2.1 Normal acceleration response to discrete vertical gusts

A basic reference gust profile is an idealized sharp edged up-gust of uniform velocity w_{gs}, as shown in Fig. III.90. An aeroplane trimmed in steady level flight, travelling at forward speed U_{trim}, encounters this sharp edged gust at a datum time, $t = 0$.

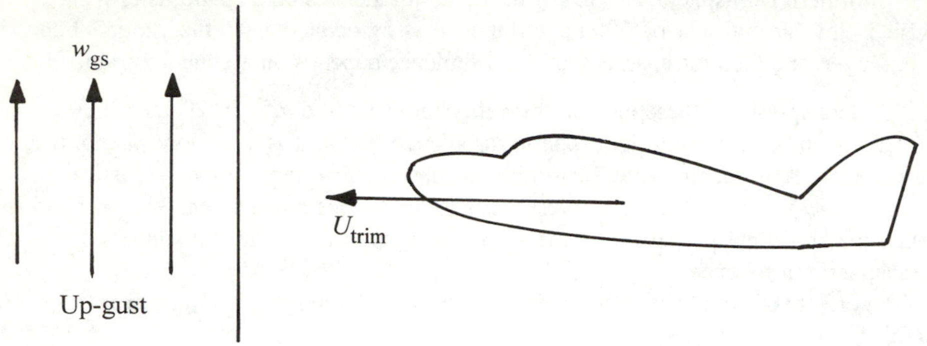

Fig. III.90. Entry into sharp edged vertical gust.

As a crude approximation:

(i) the time for the aeroplane to pass through the gust front is neglected; it is assumed that the aeroplane is instantaneously engulfed in the gust as it flies into the gust; the constant up-gust velocity introduces a sudden incremental angle of incidence, $\Delta\alpha_{gs}$, equal to (w_{gs}/U_{trim});
(ii) unsteady lag effects in the build-up of the aerodynamic lift due to the gust are neglected.

On the basis of these assumptions, as the aeroplane enters the gust, there is a sudden increase in lift, with the incremental lift, ΔL_g, given by

$$\Delta L_g = \tfrac{1}{2}\rho_{at}U_{trim}^2 S_w C_{L\alpha}\left(w_{gs}/U_{trim}\right) \tag{III.13.1}$$

together with a sudden pitching moment, $\Delta\mathcal{M}_g$, given by

$$\Delta\mathcal{M}_g = \tfrac{1}{2}\rho_{at}U_{trim}^2 S_w c_w C_{m\alpha}\left(w_{gs}/U_{trim}\right). \tag{III.13.2}$$

Thus

instantaneous normal acceleration of centre of mass on entering the gust

$$\begin{aligned} &= g\,\Delta n(0+) = \left[\tfrac{1}{2}\rho_{at}U_{trim}^2 S_w C_{L\alpha}\left(w_{gs}/U_{trim}\right)\right]/m \\ &= g\tfrac{1}{2}\rho_{at}U_{trim}C_{L\alpha}\,w_{gs}/\left(W/S_w\right), \end{aligned} \tag{III.13.3}$$

instantaneous pitching acceleration on entering the gust

$$= \dot{q}(0+)$$

$$= \left[\tfrac{1}{2}\rho_{at}U_{trim}^2 S_w c_w C_{m\alpha}\left(w_{gs}/U_{trim}\right)\right]/I_{yy} \qquad \text{(III.13.4)}$$

$$= -\left[g\tfrac{1}{2}\rho_{at}U_{trim}(-C_{m\alpha})w_{gs}\right]/\left[(W/S_w)c_w i_{yy}\right].$$

For a point distance x ahead of the centre of mass,

instantaneous normal acceleration on entering the gust

$$= g\,\Delta n(0+) + x\dot{q}(0+)$$

$$= \left[g\tfrac{1}{2}\rho_{at}U_{trim}C_{L\alpha}\,w_{gs}/(W/S_w)\right]\left[1 - K_\alpha(x/c_w)/i_{yy}\right] \qquad \text{(III.13.5)}$$

$$= \left[g(C_{L\alpha}/C_W)(w_{gs}/U_{trim})\right]\left[1 - K_\alpha(x/c_w)/i_{yy}\right]$$

where K_α $(= -C_{m\alpha}/C_{L\alpha})$ is the incidence stiffness.

The increase in lift as the aeroplane enters the gust moves the aeroplane upwards, inducing a negative angle of incidence, which decreases the lift which, in turn, decreases the upward acceleration. The maximum, or peak, acceleration occurs at entry into a sharp edged gust before the response has time to develop; it is the peak acceleration encountered on entering the gust which is felt as a bump by passengers and crew.

Eqns. (III.13.3) and (III.13.5) are instructive:

(i) for a given gust intensity w_{gs}, at a given forward speed U_{trim}, the peak normal acceleration decreases with altitude;
(ii) the peak normal acceleration can be reduced by reducing forward speed, U_{trim}, a standard operational procedure;
(iii) the peak normal acceleration is less for aeroplanes with low $C_{L\alpha}$, that is, for highly swept wings (e.g. Concorde); one of the advantages of variable sweep on combat aeroplanes is the reduction of the gust response with high wing sweep in ground attack missions at high subsonic speeds;
(iv) the peak normal acceleration is reduced as wing loading (W/S_w) increases;
(v) passengers who sit at the rear of the fuselage (i.e. $x/c_w < 0$) suffer higher accelerations than the crew on a transport aeroplane who sit forward of the centre of mass (i.e. $x/c_w > 0$); it is not unusual for the crew to be unaware of the rough ride of the passengers in the aft cabin; it is no coincidence that the first class cabin is forward.

The peak normal acceleration quoted in eqn. (III.13.3) is regarded as a reference value. The peak normal acceleration arising from the response to a general discrete gust is usually quoted in terms of a gust alleviation factor K_g where

$$K_g = \left[\frac{\text{peak normal acceleration in response to a discrete gust}}{\text{reference value given by eqn. (III.13.3)}}\right]. \qquad \text{(III.13.6)}$$

The gust alleviation factor, K_g, depends on the type of discrete gust, on the aerodynamic lag in the build-up of the gust lift on entering the gust, and on the initial aeroplane response.

The time lags associated with the build-up of the aerodynamic loads are similar to those described in sect. III.3.3 for the build-up of lift due to a sudden change of incidence, apart from a difference in the very early stages. In the case of the sudden change of incidence there is an initial impulse and then the lift jumps immediately to approximately 60% of its final steady state and reaches that steady state in the time the aeroplane travels the order of 10 mean chord lengths, or less for lower aspect ratios. However, when a wing enters a sharp edged gust there is no initial impulse, the lift builds up rapidly from zero as the gust front travels across the wing chord to approximately half the final steady state value by the time the gust front reaches the wing trailing edge; the final steady state is again reached in the time the aeroplane travels the order of 10 mean chord lengths. The build-up of lift due to a sudden change of incidence is known as the Wagner effect; the build-up of lift due to entry into a sharp edged gust is known as the Kussner effect.

When the Kussner lag is taken into account, together with the response of the aeroplane, the peak acceleration following entry into a sharp edged gust occurs about $5\hat{t}$, where $\hat{t}$ is the time for the aeroplane to travel one mean wing chord, with a gust alleviation factor approximately equal to 0.92.

A general upward vertical gust profile in space along the flight path can be denoted as $w_g(X)$, as shown in Fig. III.91. Relative to an aeroplane moving with forward speed U_{trim}, then the upward vertical gust velocity becomes a function of time, $w_g(U_{trim}t)$, inducing an incremental angle of incidence $\Delta\alpha_g(t)$ $(= w_g(U_{trim}t)/U_{trim})$.

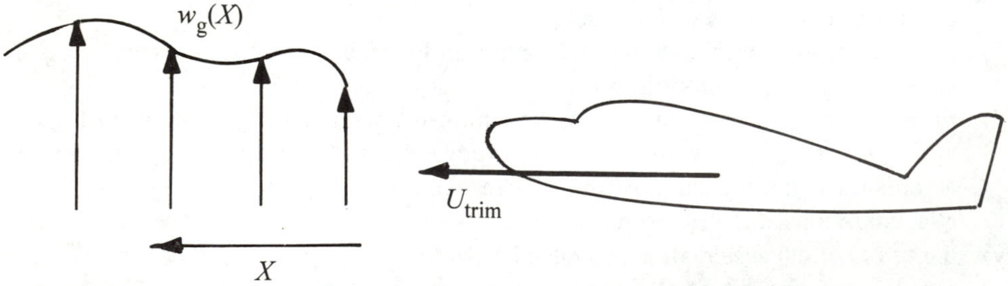

Fig. III.91. Entry into general vertical gust.

The lift and pitching moment due to $\Delta\alpha_g(t)$ can be expressed in the approximate form

$$\Delta L_g(t) \simeq \tfrac{1}{2}\rho_{at}U_{trim}^2 S_w\left[C_{L\alpha}\,\Delta\alpha_g(t) + (C_{L\dot{\alpha}} + C_{L\dot{\alpha}g})\Delta\dot{\alpha}_g(t)(c_w/2)/U_{trim}\right]$$

$$\Delta\mathcal{M}_g(t) \simeq \tfrac{1}{2}\rho_{at}U_{trim}^2 S_w c_w\left[C_{m\alpha}\,\Delta\alpha_g(t) + (C_{m\dot{\alpha}} + C_{m\dot{\alpha}g})\Delta\dot{\alpha}_g(t)(c_w/2)/U_{trim}\right] \quad \text{(III.13.7)}$$

$C_{L\alpha}$, $C_{m\alpha}$, $C_{L\dot{\alpha}}$ and $C_{m\dot{\alpha}}$ are the conventional derivatives, which now represent the quasi-steady gust lift, including the time lag in the downwash at the tailplane due to the gust lift on the main wing. New rate derivatives $C_{L\dot{\alpha}g}$ and $C_{m\dot{\alpha}g}$ are added to account for the time delay as a gust front travels from the main wing to the tailplane; writing

$$\text{gust incidence at tailplane } = \Delta\alpha_g(t - lc_w/U)$$
$$\simeq \Delta\alpha_g(t) - (lc_w/U)\Delta\dot{\alpha}_g(t) \qquad \text{(III.13.8)}$$

hence

$$C_{L\dot{\alpha}g} \simeq -2l(a_\alpha)_t(S_t/S_w), \quad C_{m\dot{\alpha}g} \simeq +2ll_t(a_\alpha)_t(S_t/S_w). \qquad \text{(III.13.9)}$$

Eqns. (III.13.7) are strictly only valid when $\Delta\alpha_g(t)$ is slowly varying with respect to aerodynamic time; typically, gust rise times greater than 0.3 s can be regarded as slowly varying. For faster rise times the full Kussner effects need to be included.

The aeroplane response to a time varying vertical gust is given by the short period response when it assumed that the forward speed does not change.

The normal acceleration response $g\,\Delta n(t)$ to a time varying vertical gust, as derived in Appendix 7, is given by

$$\left[D^2 + 2\zeta_{sp}(\omega_0)_{sp}D + (\omega_0)^2_{sp}\right]\Delta n(t)$$
$$= (C_{L\alpha}/C_W)\left[D^2 + 2\zeta_{ng}(\omega_0)_{sp}D\right]\Delta\alpha_g(t) \qquad \text{(III.13.10)}$$

where

$$2\zeta_{sp}(\omega_0)_{sp} = (g/U_{trim}\,C_W)\left[C_{L\alpha} + \left(\left((-C_{m\dot{\alpha}}) + (-C_{mq})\right)/2i_{yy}\right)\right],$$
$$\omega_0^2 = gC_{L\alpha}\left(K_\alpha + \left(-C_{mq}/2\overline{m}\right)\right)/(c_w C_W i_{yy}),$$
$$\frac{\zeta_{ng}}{\zeta_{sp}} = \frac{(-C_{mq}) + C_{m\dot{\alpha}g}}{2C_{L\alpha}i_{yy} + (-C_{m\dot{\alpha}}) + (-C_{mq})} = O[1.0].$$

On the argument that the peak normal acceleration of the centre of mass occurs before the pitch rate has time to build up, the pitch degree of freedom is sometimes neglected, calculating the normal acceleration assuming a vertical heave motion only. The validity of this approximation is left to the reader to analyse as one of the later examples.

Consider the ramp-step vertical gust as shown in Fig. III.92, defined in space by

$$\begin{aligned} w_g(X) &= 0, & X &< 0 \\ &= w_{gs}\,X/H_g, & 0 &< X < H_g \\ &= w_{gs}, & X &> H_g \end{aligned}$$

where H_g is the ramp length. For an aeroplane flying at speed U_{trim}, $X = U_{trim}t$, and the incremental gust incidence input then becomes

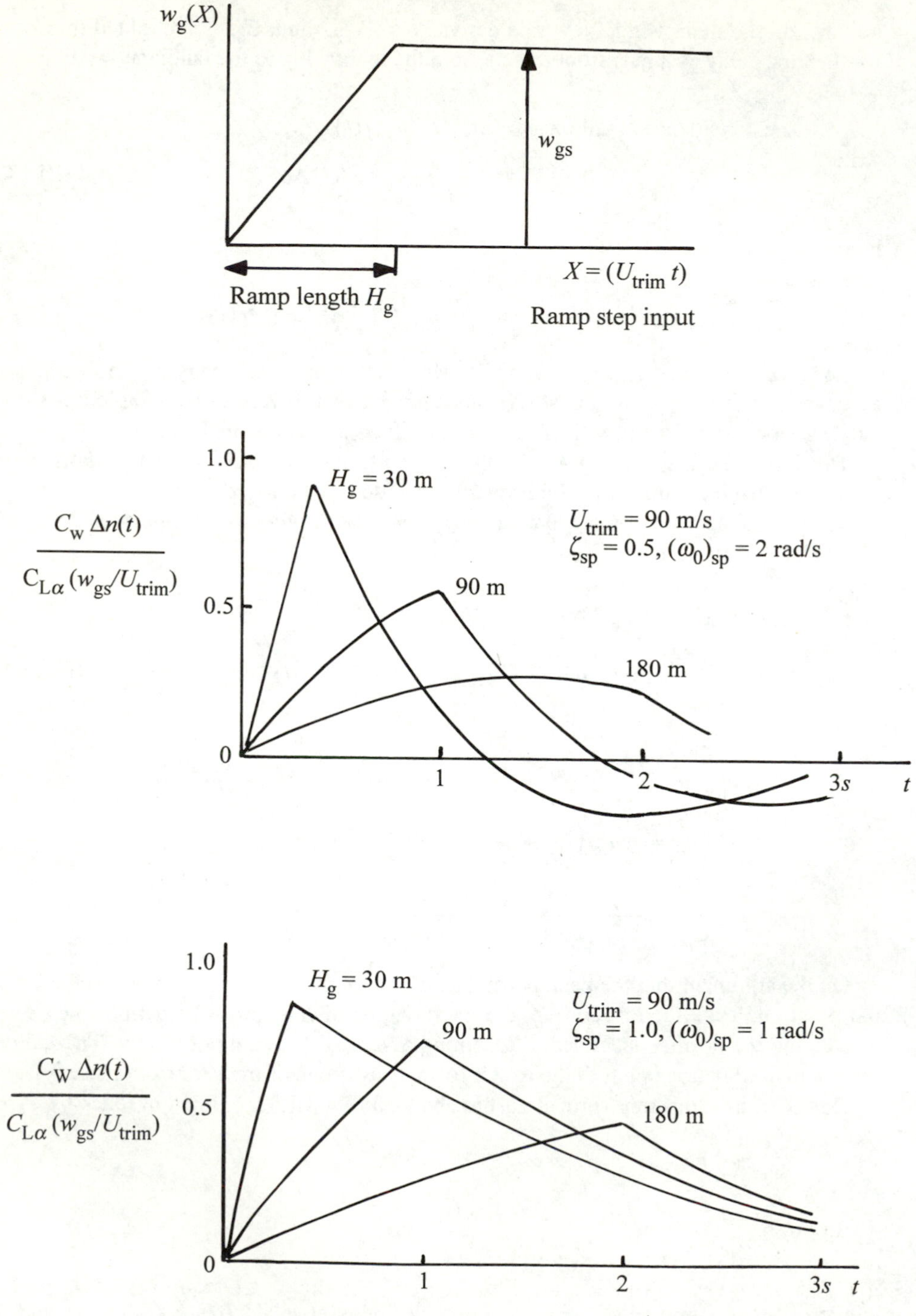

Fig. III.92. Normal acceleration response to discrete ramp-step vertical gust.

$$\begin{aligned}
\Delta\alpha_{g}(t) &= 0, && t<0 \\
\Delta\alpha_{g}(t) &= \Delta\alpha_{gs}\left(U_{trim}/H_{g}\right)t, && 0<t<H_{g}/U_{trim} \\
\Delta\alpha_{g}(t) &= \Delta\alpha_{gs}, && t>H_{g}/U_{trim}
\end{aligned} \quad \text{(III.13.11)}$$

where

$$\Delta\alpha_{gs} = w_{gs}/U_{trim}.$$

With the input defined by eqns. (III.13.11) the initial (theoretical) boundary values for the normal acceleration $g\,\Delta n(t)$ from eqn. (III.13.10) are

$$\Delta n(0+) = 0, \qquad \mathrm{D}\Delta n(0+) = \left(C_{L\alpha}/C_{W}\right)\Delta\alpha_{gs}\left(U_{trim}/H_{g}\right). \quad \text{(III.13.12)}$$

The ramp-step acceleration response $\Delta n_{RS}(t)$ is

$$\begin{aligned}
\Delta n_{RS}(t) &= \Delta n_{R}(t), && 0<t<H_{g}/U_{trim} \\
&= \Delta n_{R}(t) - \Delta n_{R}\left(t - H_{g}/U_{trim}\right), && t>H_{g}/U_{trim}
\end{aligned} \quad \text{(III.13.13)}$$

where $\Delta n_{R}(t)$, the corresponding ramp response of eqn. (III.13.10), is given by

$$\frac{\Delta n_{R}(t)}{\left(C_{L\alpha}/C_{W}\right)\Delta\alpha_{gs}} = \frac{U_{trim}}{H_{g}}\,\frac{2\zeta_{ng}}{(\omega_{0})_{sp}} \times\left[1-\exp\left(-(\zeta\omega_{0})_{sp}t\right)\frac{\cos\omega t-(1-2\zeta_{sp}\zeta_{ng})\sin\omega t}{2\zeta_{ng}(1-\zeta_{sp}^{2})^{1/2}}\right] \quad \text{(III.13.14)}$$

where

$$\omega = (\omega_{0})_{sp}(1-\zeta_{sp}^{2})^{1/2}.$$

The ramp-step acceleration responses

$$\left[\Delta n_{RS}(t)/\left[\left(C_{L\alpha}/C_{W}\right)\left(w_{gs}/U_{trim}\right)\right]\right]$$

are sketched in Fig. III.92, taking $\zeta_{ng}/\zeta = 0.75$.

For the two cases,

$$\zeta = 0.5, \quad \omega_{0} = 2 \text{ rad/s} \quad \text{and} \quad \zeta = 1.0, \quad \omega_{0} = 1 \text{ rad/s},$$

for ramp lengths,

$$H_{g}/U_{trim} = 0.33, \quad 1.0, \quad 2.0 \text{ s}.$$

In Figs. III.92, note:

(i) in general the peak acceleration occurs at the end of the ramp input, but for low damping ($\zeta = 0.5$) and a long ramp length ($H_{g}/U_{trim} = 2.0$ s) the peak acceleration occurs before the end of the ramp input;

(ii) the peak accelerations give the gust alleviation factors

$\zeta_{sp} = 0.5, \ (\omega_0)_{sp} = 2$ rad/s,	$\zeta_{sp} = 1.0,$	$(\omega_0)_{sp} = 1$ rad/s,
$H_g/U_{trim} = 0.33$ s	$K_g = 0.90$	$K_g = 0.92$
$= 1.0$ s	$= 0.53$	$= 0.76$
$= 2.0$ s	$= 0.265$	$= 0.58.$

The peak accelerations are higher for the higher damping ratio, as might be expected, because the more 'rigid' a system the higher the acceleration to a rapid input.

The most rapid rise time in the above examples is 0.33 s, which is marginally 'slowly varying', so eqns. (III.13.7) are valid for all of the above ramp-step applications. For ramp-step gusts with rise times (H_g/U_{trim}) less than 0.3 s the gust aerodynamics need to be modified to incorporate more exact unsteady aerodynamics; with these more rapid ramp rates and using more exact unsteady aerodynamics the peak acceleration occurs after the ramp input has reached its maximum value.

The next gust profile is trapezoidal, which is generated by a positive ramp-step imput followed by a negative ramp-step input of the same magnitude, as shown in Fig. III.93. Therefore,

the trapezoidal gust normal acceleration response

$$\begin{aligned} &= \Delta n_{RS}(t) && 0 < t < H_g/U_{trim}, \\ &= \Delta n_{RS}(t) - \Delta n_{RS}\left(t - H_g/U_{trim}\right), && t > H_g/U_{trim}. \end{aligned} \tag{III.13.15}$$

The normal acceleration responses to these trapezoidal gusts, deduced directly from Fig. III.92, are shown in Fig. III.93. Note:

(i) for the aeroplane configuration with the higher damping ratio ($\zeta_{sp} = 1.0$) the response is broadly trapezoidal with a positive response peak corresponding with the peak of the trapezoidal gust input; the gust alleviation factor for the trapezoidal gust input is the same as the gust alleviation factor for the ramp-step gust input with the same value of H_g/U_{trim};

(ii) for the aeroplane configuration with the lower damping ($\zeta_{sp} = 0.5$) there are two distinct response peaks, one positive and one negative; in certain circumstances the magnitude of the negative peak can be greater than the magnitude of the positive peak (see the case when $H_g/U_{trim} = 1$ s); when this phenomenon occurs the gust is said to be 'tuned' to the short period modal frequency.

Normal acceleration responses to a sequence of trapezoidal gusts can be built up from Fig. III.93.

III.13.2.2 Flight path response to discrete vertical gusts

The change in the flight path angle, $\Delta\gamma(t)$, is related to the normal acceleration, $g\,\Delta n(t)$, by the relationship

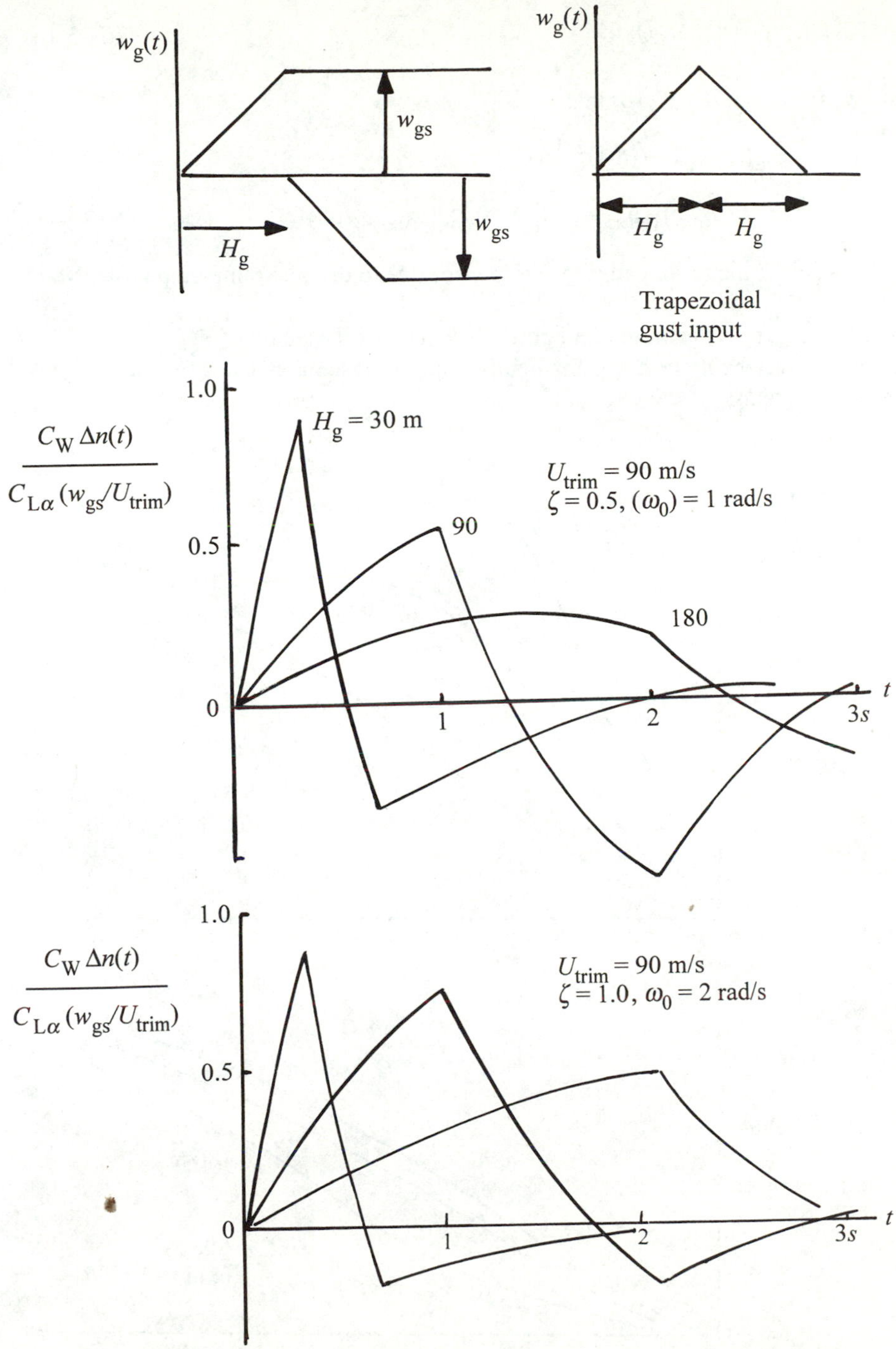

Fig. III.93. Normal acceleration response to discrete trapezoidal vertical gust.

$$U_{\text{trim}}\Delta\gamma(t) = \int g\,\Delta n(t)\,\mathrm{d}t. \tag{III.13.16}$$

It follows from eqn. (III.13.10) that

$$\left[\mathrm{D}^2 + 2\zeta_{sp}(\omega_0)_{sp}\mathrm{D} + (\omega_0)^2_{sp}\right]\Delta\gamma(t)$$
$$= (g/U_{\text{trim}})(C_{L\alpha}/C_W)\left[\mathrm{D} + 2\zeta_{ng}(\omega_0)_{sp}\right]\Delta\alpha_g(t). \tag{III.13.17}$$

Fig. III.94 shows the flight path angle responses due to discrete ramp-step gusts. Note:

(i) $\Delta\gamma(t)$ is larger for the more rapid gust inputs, i.e. for the smaller (H_g/U_{trim});
(ii) there are overshoots in $\Delta\gamma(t)$ for lightly damped systems but not for more highly damped systems;

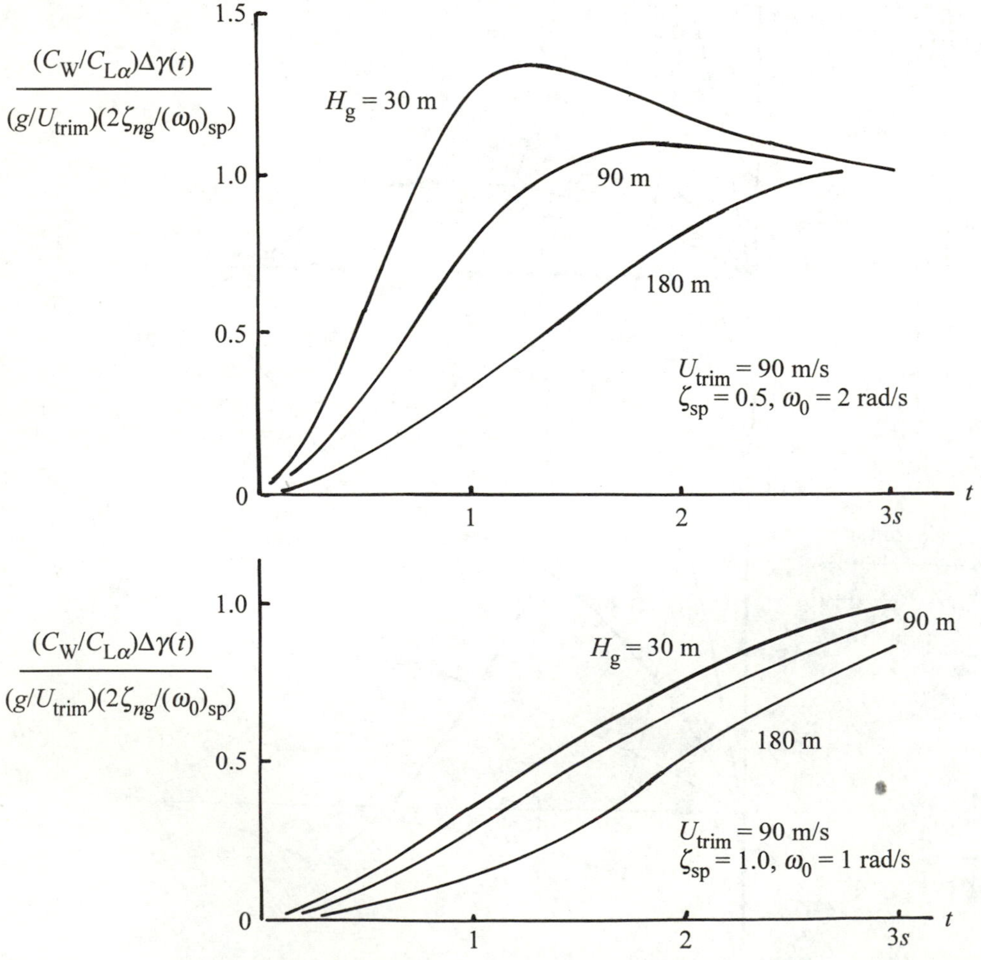

Fig. III.94. Flight path angle response to discrete ramp-step vertical gust.

(iii) The steady state response, $\Delta\gamma(t)_{ss}$, is greater for the higher value of damping ζ_{sp}, or lower value of $(\omega_0)_{sp}$, assuming a constant ratio (ζ_{ng}/ζ_{sp}).

III.13.2.3 Pitch attitude response to discrete vertical gusts

The equation for the short period pitch attitude response $\Delta\theta(t)$ to a gust input, $\Delta\alpha_g(t)$, from Appendix 7, is

$$\left[D^2 + 2\zeta_{sp}(\omega_0)_{sp}D + (\omega_0)^2_{sp}\right]\Delta\theta(t)$$
$$= \left[2\zeta_{\theta g}(\omega_0)_{sp}D - \bar{K}_{\alpha g}(\omega_0)^2_{sp}\right]\Delta\alpha_g(t) \qquad \text{(III.13.18)}$$

where

$$\bar{K}_{\alpha g} = \left(K_\alpha - C_{m\dot{\alpha}g}/2\bar{m}\right)\Big/\left(K_\alpha + (-C_{mq})/2\bar{m}\right)$$

$$\zeta_{\theta g}/\zeta_{sp} = O[0.2], \qquad C_{m\dot{\alpha}g}/(-C_{mq}) = O[1.0], \qquad (-C_{mq})/2\bar{m} = O[0.05].$$

Crudely

$$\bar{K}_{\alpha g} = 0.5 \text{ corresponds to } (\omega_0)_{sp} = 2 \text{ rad/s}$$

$$\bar{K}_{\alpha g} = 0.0 \text{ corresponds to } (\omega_0)_{sp} = 1 \text{ rad/s;}$$

As a first approximation the effect of the term involving $\zeta_{\theta g}$ can be neglected. Typical pitch attitude responses $[\Delta\theta(t)/\Delta\alpha_{gs}]$ to ramp-step gust inputs are sketched in Fig. III.95. Note:

(i) the pitch attitude response is negative;
(ii) the steady state pitch attitude $\Delta\theta_{ss}/\Delta\alpha_{gs}$ is equal to $\bar{K}_{\alpha g}$;
(iii) when $\bar{K}_{\alpha g} = 0.5$, which corresponds to the lightly damped short period mode with $(\omega_0)_{sp} = 2.0$ rad/s and $\zeta_{sp} = 0.5$, there are overshoots in the responses; although not shown, as $\bar{K}_{\alpha g}$ decreases (i.e. $(\omega_0)_{sp}$ decreases and ζ_{sp} increases) the overshoots disappear.

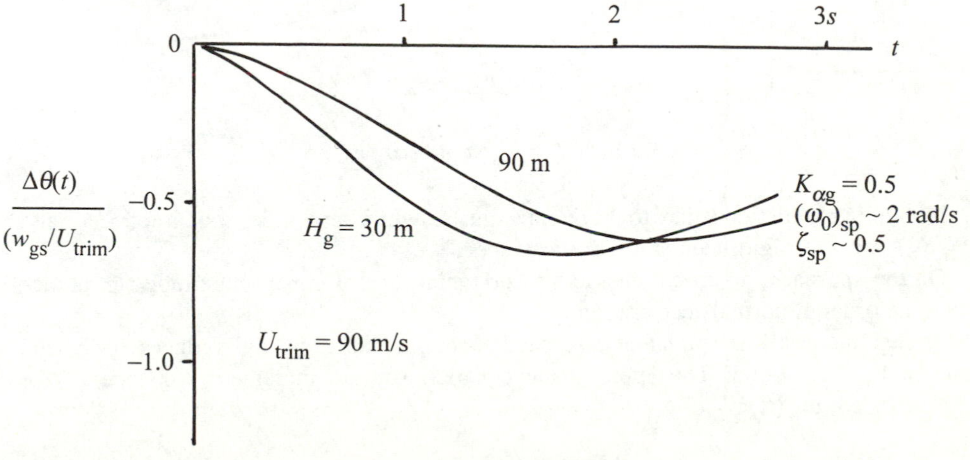

Fig. III.95. Pitch attitude response to discrete ramp-step vertical gust.

Comparing Figs. III.94 and III.95, on entering an up-gust, as might be anticipated, for usual values of K_α (or manoeuvre margin, H_m), the flight path angle response increases due to upward normal acceleration, while the pitch angle response decreases due to the negative $C_{m\alpha}$. In general, as the manoeuvre margin decreases, the magnitude of the flight path angle response increases while the magnitude of the pitch attitude response decreases.

In the literature the pitch attitude response equation (eqn. (III.13.18)) is often approximated further to the form

$$\left[\mathrm{D}^2 + 2\zeta_{sp}(\omega_0)_{sp}\,\mathrm{D} + (\omega_0)^2_{sp}\right]\Delta\theta(t) \simeq -(\omega_0)^2_{sp}\,\Delta\alpha_g(t). \qquad \text{(III.13.19)}$$

This approximation is valid for high values of K_α, or at high altitude.

III.13.2.4 Response to a discrete horizontal gust

Consider a step discrete headwind gust with uniform velocity u_{gs}, as shown in Fig. III.96. On entering the gust there is a step increase in the equivalent air speed which gives an incremental lift, ΔL_g, of

$$\Delta L_g = \tfrac{1}{2}\rho_{at}U^2_{trim}S_w 2(C_L)_{trim}\left(u_{gs}/U_{trim}\right) \qquad \text{(III.13.20)}$$

from eqn. (III.3.141), neglecting aerodynamic lag and Mach number effects. The corresponding normal acceleration is then

$$g\,\Delta n = \Delta L_g/m = g2u_{gs}/U_{trim}. \qquad \text{(III.13.21)}$$

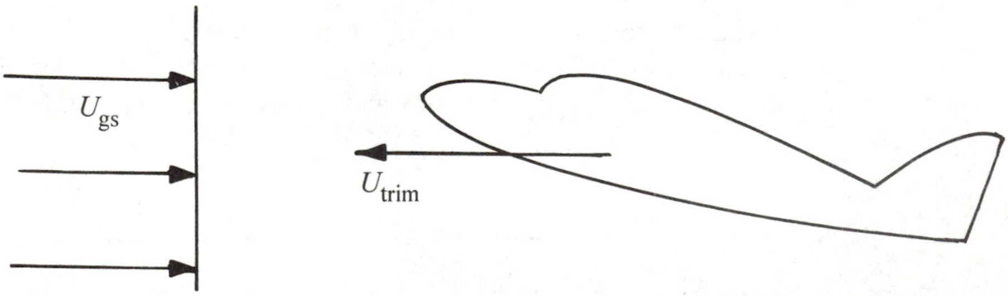

Fig. III.96. Entry into horizontal gust.

Normal accelerations due to horizontal gusts, which are independent of $C_{L\alpha}$ and (W/S_w), are only significant at low forward speeds.

On the approach, a vertical gust and a horizontal gust of equal magnitude can induce the same order of normal acceleration.

A step increase in equivalent air speed increases the drag and reduces the speed relative to the ground. The approximate equation for the incremental change in the ground speed, $\Delta u_g(t)$, is

$$m\,\Delta\dot{u}_g(t) = -\tfrac{1}{2}\rho_{at}U^2_{trim}S_w\,2C_D\left[\left(\Delta u_g(t) + u_{gs}\right)/U_{trim}\right] \qquad \text{(III.13.22)}$$

keeping the thrust constant. Thus $\Delta u_g(t)$ decreases with time to $(-u_{gs})$, with a delay time constant equal to $[(U_{trim}/2g)\,(C_L/C_D)_{trim}]$ s, which, on the approach, is of the order of 1 minute.

EXAMPLES III.31

1. What is the normal acceleration for an aeroplane

$$W/S_w = 4.0 \;\; \text{kN/m}^2, \quad C_{L\alpha} = 5.0, \quad U_{trim} = 150 \;\; \text{m/s}$$

on entering a sharp edge gust at sea level of magnitude $w_{gs} = 10$ m/s?
2. From eqn. (III.13.5) plot a typical variation of the normal acceleration along the length of a fuselage.
3. If the Kussner function is approximated by

build-up of lift due to unit step gust

$$= \tfrac{1}{2}\rho_{at} U_{trim}^2 S_w C_{L\alpha}\left(1 - 1/(1+\bar{t}^2)\right); \quad \bar{t} = t/\hat{t},$$

show that the equation for the vertical response of an aeroplane entering a sharp edged gust, neglecting the pitch response, is

$$\Delta\ddot{h}(t) = \left(gC_{L\alpha}/C_W\right)\left[-\left(\Delta\dot{h}(t)/U_{trim}\right) + \left(1 - 1/(1+\bar{t}^2)\right)\Delta\alpha_{gs}\right].$$

Determine and plot the acceleration $\Delta\ddot{h}(t)$ for small time $(0 < \bar{t} < 10)$. Find the time for the maximum acceleration and the value of the gust alleviation factor.
4. In eqns. (III.13.7) for the gust aerodynamics, is it correct to include the conventional derivatives $C_{L\dot{\alpha}}$ and $C_{m\dot{\alpha}}$? If not, is it a reasonable approximation?
5. Check the ramp response given by eqn. (III.13.14).
6. Show that the equation for the vertical response, neglecting the pitch response, is

$$\left[U_{trim}(c_w/g)D + C_{L\alpha}\right]D\left(\Delta h(t)/U_{trim}\right)$$
$$\simeq \left[(C_{L\dot{\alpha}} + C_{L\dot{\alpha}g})\left((c_w/2)/U_{trim}\right)D + C_{L\alpha}\right]\Delta\alpha_g(t).$$

Derive the normal acceleration ramp-step responses, neglecting the pitch response, for the cases shown in Fig. III.92, and compare the results. Any comments?
7. Sketch the normal acceleration responses to
   (i) a positive trapezoidal gust input followed immediately by a second positive trapezoidal gust input, as shown in Fig. III.97(i),
   (ii) a positive trapezoidal gust input followed immediately by a negative trapezoidal input as shown in Fig. III.97(ii)

   from Fig. III.93 for $H_g/U_{trim} = 0.33$, 1.0 s. Comment on the results.
8. Check the statement in the text: 'In general, as the manoeuvre margin decreases, the magnitude of the flight path angle response increases while the magnitude of the pitch attitude response decreases.'
9. Sketch the flight path angle response to a trapezoidal gust.
10. Sketch the pitch attitude response to a trapezoidal gust.

11. Check the statement: 'On the approach, a vertical gust and a horizontal gust of equal magnitude can induce the same order of normal acceleration.'

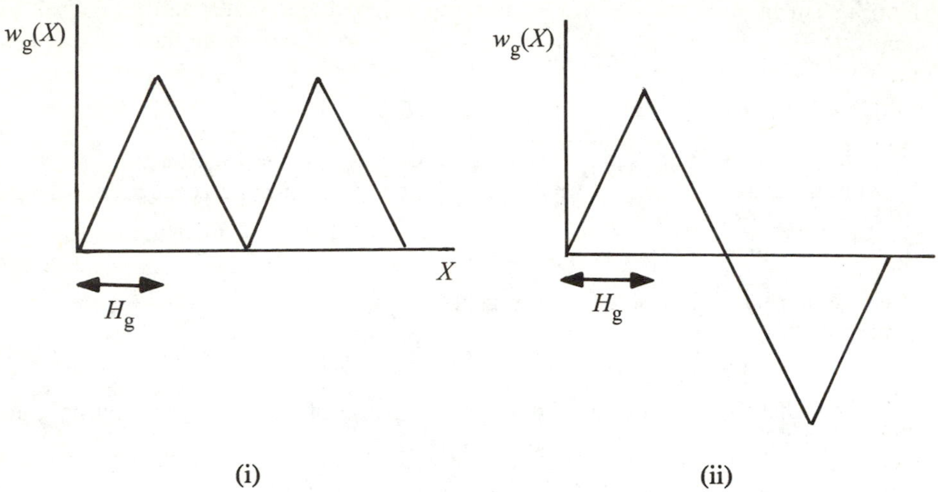

Fig. III.97. Combination of trapezoidal gusts.

III.13.3 Philosophy of turbulence modelling

The estimation of aeroplane accelerations and disturbances in turbulence involves a mathematical model of atmospheric turbulence applied to the aeroplane response equations. This procedure implies that the nature of the turbulence, the magnitudes of all the turbulence parameters, and the formulation of a turbulence input in mathematical terms is known. Unfortunately, although the physics of the atmosphere is broadly understood by meteorologists, the quantitative modelling of atmospheric turbulence for flight dynamics applications is relatively elementary and the database limited, mainly because it is not possible to measure the full range of turbulence characteristics at all altitudes, in all weather conditions, all around the world. There is a large body of turbulence data at low altitudes from anemometer measurements at the tops of tall masts and some similar data at altitude from measurements on balloons. There have been a number of research investigations using aeroplanes specially instrumented to record simultaneously both the turbulence input, using probes in front of the aeroplane, and the three linear and three angular acceleration aeroplane responses to that turbulence (an inevitable consequence of Murphy's law is that an aeroplane designated to investigate extreme turbulence has difficulty in finding it). What are available in abundance are normal acceleration responses of commercial aeroplanes in turbulence in operational flying (covering over five million flying miles in the 1950s alone) from flight recorders which measure the vertical acceleration responses at the centre of mass by either the Vgh recorder (normal acceleration is measured by a linear accelerometer, the forward speed by the air data system, and the altitude by the altimeter), or by a counting accelerometer (which counts the number of g accelerations above a range of levels). Commercial aeroplanes still carry flight recorders which monitor continuously the normal accelerations and store those records of the more violent encounters for subsequent analysis.

The approach to predict characteristics of flight in turbulence is to formulate a mathematical model of a 'turbulence input' involving a number of empirical constants. Normal acceleration responses are calculated for past aeroplanes and the values of the empirical constants determined by fitting the predicted responses to the measurements of the normal acceleration responses on those past aeroplanes. It may be necessary to formulate a number of different turbulent models for different types of turbulence (e.g. continuous turbulence and patches of extreme turbulence) and to modify the values of the empirical constants for different applications (e.g. design gust loads, fatigue loads, ride quality). Once the models are established the aeroplane designer is then able to estimate the structural strength and fatigue life, the ride quality and response characteristics of future aeroplanes. This approach does not aim to reproduce the aerodynamics of real atmospheric turbulence, instead it aims to bridge, in a consistent manner, past experience to future design.

The above approach is satisfactory if the response characteristics of a future aeroplane are similar to the response characteristics of past aeroplanes. But application of this approach to radically new types of aeroplane configurations needs to be treated with caution. It is true to say that the better a gust model represents real turbulence the more reliable its predictions of aeroplane responses. But improved realism is nearly always accompanied by increased mathematical and computational complexity without necessarily improving the design effectiveness, so simplified models may still be preferred. Controversy still simmers over the relative merits of different models.

Estimation of aeroplane response to turbulence is highly mathematical because of the need to represent turbulence as a random process, compounded with the difficulty of estimating aeroplane response to random inputs. The following discourse is oversimplified and far from rigorous, nevertheless it is hoped that the flavour of the methodologies can be appreciated.

III.13.4 Discrete 'derived gust' model

The earliest 'turbulence' model was the discrete 'derived gust' model, aimed at quantifying the magnitudes of the rare high intensity discrete gusts which are responsible for the largest structural loading cases, see Zbrozek (ref. III.31) and Donely (ref. III.32).

It was assumed that each peak acceleration response was due to a single discrete ramp-step gust (ramp gust length $H_g = 12.5c_w$ in the USA; $H_g = 30.5$ m (100 ft) in the UK). From the magnitude of each measured acceleration peak, positive and negative, and using the appropriate gust alleviation factor, a value of the corresponding gust velocity amplitude w_{gs} which produces each peak can be deduced. By analysis of extensive flight records the average frequency of occurrences of derived ramp-step gusts of varying magnitudes of w_{gs} were established. Typical results, indicating measured level of occurrence of 'derived' gust amplitudes are shown in Fig. III.98; large amplitude gusts occur at higher altitudes up to the troposphere, but then diminish in the stratosphere; there are more small amplitude gusts at lower altitudes than at higher altitudes.

The basic premise of the 'derived gust' model is that each acceleration peak is associated with one ramp-step gust of fixed ramp length, implicitly assuming that the response

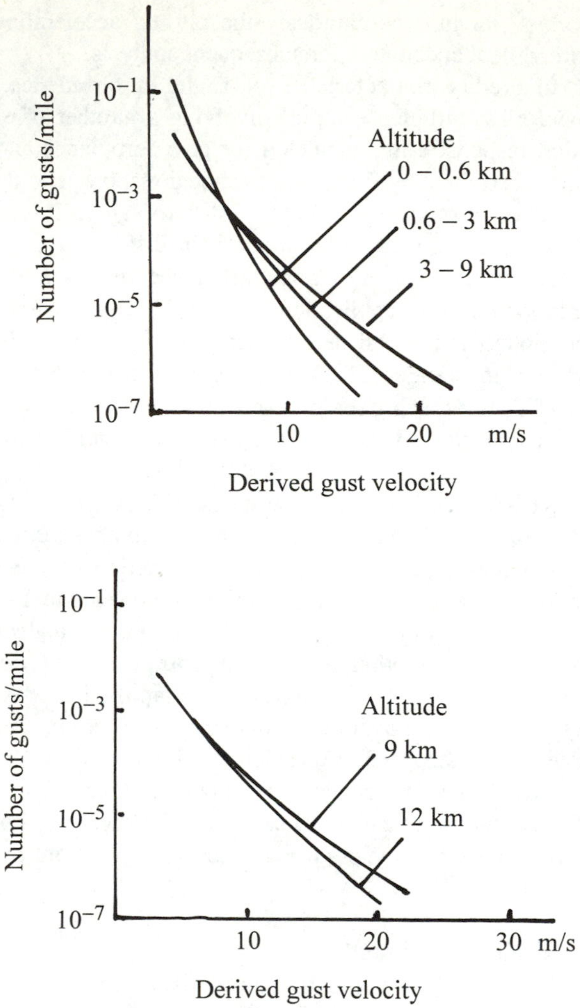

Fig. III.98. Derived gust probabilities.

to one ramp-step gust dies away before the next ramp-gust is encountered. There are two main criticisms of the 'derived' gust model.

(i) The effects of closely coupled ramp-step gusts are ignored. For example, when a positive ramp-step gust is followed closely by an equal and negative ramp-step gust, forming a trapezoidal gust, then by reference to Fig. III.93 for ramp rises of the order of H_g/U_{trim} equal to 0.33 s, the magnitude of the negative peak associated with the negative ramp-step gust is much reduced. On the other hand, for longer ramp trapezoidal gusts, for the 'tuned' gust case, as shown in Fig. III.93, the magnitude of the first positive peak can be less than the magnitude of the second, negative, peak.

(ii) The effect of variation of the gust ramp length, H_g, is ignored. There is no distinction between an acceleration peak associated with a gust of small H_g of lower gust velocity and the acceleration peak associated with a gust of longer H_g and higher gust velocity.

To remedy these defects it is necessary to consider more complicated models which take into account gusts of all wavelengths, including closely coupled gusts, and the random nature of turbulence.

EXAMPLES III.32

1. An aeroplane with characteristics $W/S_w = 4.0\,\text{kN/m}^2$, $C_{L\alpha} = 5.0$, $c_w = 4$ m, when flying at 150 m/s at low altitude, experiences a peak normal acceleration of $0.75g$. Estimate the derived discrete gust velocity from both the UK and USA criteria.
2. Can you give a possible explanation for the different reference ramp lengths in the UK and USA derived discrete gust formulations?
3. How does the concept of a 'derived' gust cope with the double trapezoidal inputs, obtained in Example III.31, No. 7?

III.13.5 Introduction to random variable theory

As all air travellers are acutely aware, turbulence is irregular and patchy; periods of turbulence are interspersed with periods of no turbulence; and even in patches of turbulence there are sometimes periods of intense turbulence interspersed with periods of low turbulence.

The time variation of a random vertical gust velocity cannot be expressed by a deterministic formula. A gust velocity can only be quantified in terms of a number of statistical parameters, the main ones being: the mean, the intensity, the auto-correlation function, the power spectral density, the probability density distribution and the number of exceedances over a prescribed threshold. These parameters are defined in this section.

Let $w_g(X, t)$ denote the random vertical air velocity in a patch of turbulence which varies in space ($X_0 < X < X_N$) and time (t). A typical patch length (i.e. $X_N - X_0$) is of the order of 8 km. It is assumed that the statistical properties of $w_g(X, t)$ with respect to X are the same at each instant of time and then it is only necessary to consider $w_g(X, t)$ at one instant of time (say, $t = t_1$), denoting it as $w_g(X)$; this property is known as 'stationarity'.

An aeroplane flies through $w_g(X, t)$. It is assumed that $w_g(X, t)$ in a patch of turbulence does not change significantly during the time it takes for an aeroplane to pass through that patch (the visible change in shape of a cloud is a relatively slow process). Thus, it is assumed that an aeroplane flies through $w_g(X, t)$ 'frozen' at a time t ($= t_1$), so the turbulence can be denoted as a function of X only, namely $w_g(X)$.

Mean

The mean, $\overline{w}_g$, is defined by

$$\overline{w}_g = \frac{1}{X_N - X_0} \int_{X_0}^{X_N} w_g(X)\,\mathrm{d}X. \qquad \text{(III.13.23)}$$

A mean velocity over a patch of turbulence plays an important role in the overall displacement of an aeroplane from a designated flight path.

Intensity
The gust intensity, σ_w^2, is defined by

$$\sigma_w^2 = \frac{1}{X_N - X_0} \int_{X_0}^{X_N} \left[w_g(X) - \overline{w}_g \right]^2 \, dX. \tag{III.13.24}$$

The gust intensity, σ_w^2, is proportional to the average energy per unit distance and has dimensions $(m/s)^2$.

Power spectral density
As a preliminary to the definition of the power spectral density, suppose that the gust variable $w_g(X)$, with zero mean, can be regarded as the superposition of a large number of harmonic components, namely

$$w_g(X) = \sum_{j=1}^{J} a_j \cos(\Omega_j X + \varphi_j), \qquad \Omega_j = 2\pi / X_j = 2\pi j / (X_N - X_0) \tag{III.13.25}$$

where $[a_j \cos(\Omega_j X + \varphi_j)]$ denotes a single simple harmonic gust of spatial wavelength X_j with amplitude a_j, and phase angle φ_j.

Eqns. (III.13.25) can be inverted for a long patch length, namely,

$$a_j \cos \varphi_j = \frac{2}{X_N - X_0} \int_{X_0}^{X_N} w_g(X) \cos \Omega_j X \, dX, \tag{III.13.26}$$

$$a_j \sin \varphi_j = -\frac{2}{X_N - X_0} \int_{X_0}^{X_N} w_g(X) \sin \Omega_j X \, dX \tag{III.13.27}$$

because

$$\begin{aligned} \int_{X_0}^{X_N} \cos \Omega_m X \cos \Omega_n X \, dX &= \int_{X_0}^{X_N} \sin \Omega_m X \sin \Omega_n X \, dX \\ &= 0 \qquad \text{when } m \neq n \\ &= (X_N - X_0)/2 \qquad \text{when } m = n \end{aligned} \tag{III.13.28}$$

$$\int_{X_0}^{X_N} \cos \Omega_m X \sin \Omega_n X \, dX = 0 \quad \text{for all } m, n.$$

From eqns. (III.13.26) and (III.13.27)

$$\begin{aligned} a_j^2 &= \left(\frac{2}{X_N - X_0} \right)^2 \left[\left[\int_{X_0}^{X_N} w_g(X) \cos \Omega_j X \, dX \right]^2 + \left[\int_{X_0}^{X_N} w_g(X) \sin \Omega_j X \, dX \right]^2 \right] \\ &= \frac{4}{(X_N - X_0)^2} \left[\int_{X_0}^{X_N} w_g(X) \exp(i \Omega_j X) \, dX \right] \left[\int_{X_0}^{X_N} w_g(X) \exp(-i \Omega_j X) \, dX \right] \end{aligned} \tag{III.13.29}$$

where

$$\exp(\mathrm{i}\,\Omega_j X) = \cos\,\Omega_j X + \mathrm{i}\,\sin\,\Omega_j X,$$
$$\exp(-\mathrm{i}\,\Omega_j X) = \cos\Omega_j X - \mathrm{i}\,\sin\,\Omega_j X.$$

The intensity, or energy, of a single harmonic gust, $a_j\cos(\Omega_j X + \varphi_j)$, is, from eqn. (III.13.24),

$$(\sigma_\mathrm{w})_j^2 = \frac{1}{X_N - X_0}\int_{X_0}^{X_N}\left[a_j\cos\,\Omega_j X + \varphi_j\right]^2\,\mathrm{d}X = a_j^2/2. \tag{III.13.30}$$

The total intensity of $w_\mathrm{g}(X)$ is

$$\sigma_\mathrm{w}^2 = \frac{1}{X_N - X_0}\int_{X_0}^{X_N}\left[w_\mathrm{g}(X)\right]^2\,\mathrm{d}X = \sum_{j=1}^{J}\left(a_j^2/2\right) \tag{III.13.31}$$

on substitution of eqn. (III.13.25), and using eqns. (III.13.28).

The total intensity is the sum of the intensities of each of the harmonic components of the random signal, and is independent of the phase angles.

As J tends to infinity the summation in eqn. (III.13.31) becomes an integral, namely

$$\sigma_\mathrm{w}^2 = \int_{j=1}^{\infty}\left((a_j)^2/2\right)\,\mathrm{d}j \tag{III.13.32}$$

which is usually written in the form

$$\sigma_\mathrm{w}^2 = \int_{[2\pi/(X_N - X_0)]}^{\infty}\Phi_\mathrm{w}(\Omega_j)\,\mathrm{d}\Omega_j \tag{III.13.33}$$

where

$$\Phi_\mathrm{w}(\Omega_j)\,\mathrm{d}\Omega_j = \text{the energy contained in the frequency band } \Omega_j \to (\Omega_j + \mathrm{d}\Omega_j). \tag{III.13.34}$$

$\Phi_\mathrm{w}(\Omega_j)$ is known as the vertical gust power spectral density.

The power spectral density $\Phi_\mathrm{w}(\Omega_j)$ can be expressed in terms of $w_\mathrm{g}(X)$:

from eqns. (III.13.32), (III.13.33), $\quad\left((a_j)^2/2\right)\mathrm{d}j = \Phi_\mathrm{w}(\Omega_j)\,\mathrm{d}\Omega_j;$

from eqn. (III.13.25), $\quad\mathrm{d}\Omega_j = \left[2\pi/(X_N - X_0)\right]\mathrm{d}j;$

then, from eqn. (III.13.29),

$$\Phi_\mathrm{w}(\Omega_j) = \frac{1}{\pi(X_N - X_0)}\left[\int_{X_0}^{X_N} w_\mathrm{g}(X)\exp(\mathrm{i}\,\Omega_j X)\,\mathrm{d}X\right] \times \left[\int_{X_0}^{X_N} w_\mathrm{g}(X)\exp(-\mathrm{i}\,\Omega_j X)\,\mathrm{d}X\right]. \tag{III.13.35}$$

Auto-correlation function

An alternative, more practical, technique for obtaining the power spectral density from $w_g(X)$ is via the auto-correlation function $R_w(\chi)$, defined as

$$\sigma_w^2 R_w(\chi) = \frac{1}{X_N - X_0} \int_{-\infty}^{+\infty} w_g(X)\, w_g(X+\chi)\, dX \qquad (III.13.36)$$

taking $w_g(X) = 0$ for $X > X_N$ and for $X < X_0$.

Thus

$$R_w(0) = 1.0. \qquad (III.13.37)$$

In a random process, as $|\chi|$ increases $R(\chi)$ tends to zero. The two signals $w_g(X)$ and $w_g(X+\chi)$ are said to be uncorrelated when $R_w(\chi)$ is zero.

The scale length L is defined as

$$L = \int_{-\infty}^{+\infty} R_w(\chi)\, d\chi = 2\int_0^{+\infty} R_w(\chi)\, d\chi \qquad (III.13.38)$$

assuming that $R_w(\chi) = R_w(-\chi)$. The scale length L gives the order of distance over which $w_g(X)$ is correlated.

It has been stated previously that the definitions for the mean intensity and power spectral density can only be applied if the patch length should be 'sufficiently long'; this condition is satisfied when

$$(X_N - X_0) \gg L. \qquad (III.13.39)$$

For the relationship between the auto-correlation function and the power spectral density, from eqn. (III.13.36)

$$\begin{aligned}\sigma_w^2 &\int_{-\infty}^{+\infty} R_w(\chi) \exp(i\Omega_j \chi)\, d\chi \\ &= \frac{1}{X_N - X_0}\left[\int_{-\infty}^{+\infty} w_g(X+\chi)\exp\left(i\Omega_j(X+\chi)\right) d\chi\right]\left[\int_{-\infty}^{+\infty} w_g(X)\exp(-i\Omega_j X)\, dX\right] \\ &= \pi\Phi(\Omega_j)\end{aligned} \qquad (III.13.40)$$

from eqn. (III.13.35). Thus,

$$\Phi_w(\Omega_j) = \left(2\sigma_w^2/\pi\right) \int_0^{\infty} R_w(\chi) \cos \Omega_j \chi\, d\chi. \qquad (III.13.41)$$

Now $R_w(\chi)$ tends to zero for large χ, say for $\chi > L$. While for $\chi < L$, $\cos \Omega_j \chi \simeq 1$ for the range of long wavelengths $\Omega_j L\,(= 2\pi L/X_j) \ll 1$. Thus from eqns. (III.13.38) and (III.13.41) for wavelengths substantially greater than the scale length, the power spectral density is constant namely

$$\Phi_w(\Omega_j) = \sigma_w^2\, L/\pi. \qquad (III.13.42)$$

The power spectral density decreases with Ω_j for wavelengths less than the scale length.

The concept of correlation needs care in interpretation. The existence of a single wave by definition implies correlation over the entire wavelength, even when that wavelength is far greater than the scale length L. But when waves of different wavelength are superimposed the correlation over a length χ, as defined in eqn. (III.13.36), depends on the amplitudes of the waves. When waves of the same amplitude but different wavelength are superimposed, the correlation $R(\chi)$ is zero, down to small χ (i.e. small L); this statement can be proved from the above equations. White noise has a constant power spectral density (i.e. all waves have equal amplitude) with a zero scale length. In general, waves with wavelengths greater than the scale length L have the same amplitude (e.g. eqn. (III.13.42)) and do not contribute to the value of L.

First order probability density distribution

The first order probability density distribution $p(w_g, X)$ is defined as

$$p(w_g, X)\,\Delta w_g = \text{probability that } w_g(X) \text{ lies between } w_g \text{ and } (w_g + \Delta w_g). \tag{III.13.43}$$

For a stationary process, $p(w_g, X)$ is the same for all X, and then, by reference to Fig. III.99, $p(w_g)\,\Delta w_g$ is obtained, in principle, from

$$p(w_g)\,\Delta w_g = \left[\frac{\text{area of } w_g(X) \text{ between } w_g \text{ and } (w_g + \Delta w_g) \text{ over } X_0 < X < X_N}{\text{area of } \left|w_g(X)\right| \text{ over } X_0 < X < X_N}\right]. \tag{III.13.44}$$

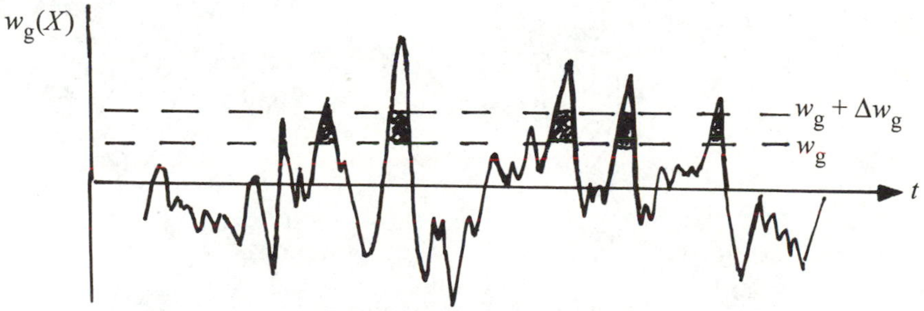

Fig. III.99. Derivation of $p(w_g)$.

It follows from eqn. (III.13.44) that

$$\int_{-\infty}^{+\infty} p(w_g)\,\mathrm{d}w_g = 1.0. \tag{III.13.45}$$

The shape of $p(w_g)$ is completely defined by the set of moments

$$m_n = \int_{-\infty}^{+\infty} w_g^n\, p(w_g)\,\mathrm{d}w_g, \qquad m = 0, 1, \dots, \infty. \tag{III.13.46}$$

In particular,

$$m_0 = 1.0, \quad m_1 = \overline{w}_g, \quad m_2 = \sigma_w^2. \tag{III.13.47}$$

It is important to appreciate that, in general, the power spectral density and first order probability density distribution are independent parameters. To illustrate this statement consider the combination of two sinusoidal gusts

$$w_g(t) = \sin \Omega X + \sin(2\Omega X + \varphi) \tag{III.13.48}$$

where φ is a phase angle; $w_g(t)$ is sketched in Fig. III.100 for two phase angles ($\varphi = 0, 45°$). Although both of these gusts have the same mean and intensity, they have different probability densities. When φ is zero the probability density is symmetric for positive and negative values of w_g, whereas when φ is equal to 45° the probability density is asymmetric; the curve when φ is equal to zero has a greater probability density for larger positive w_g than the curve when φ is equal to 45°, with the opposite trend at larger negative values of w_g.

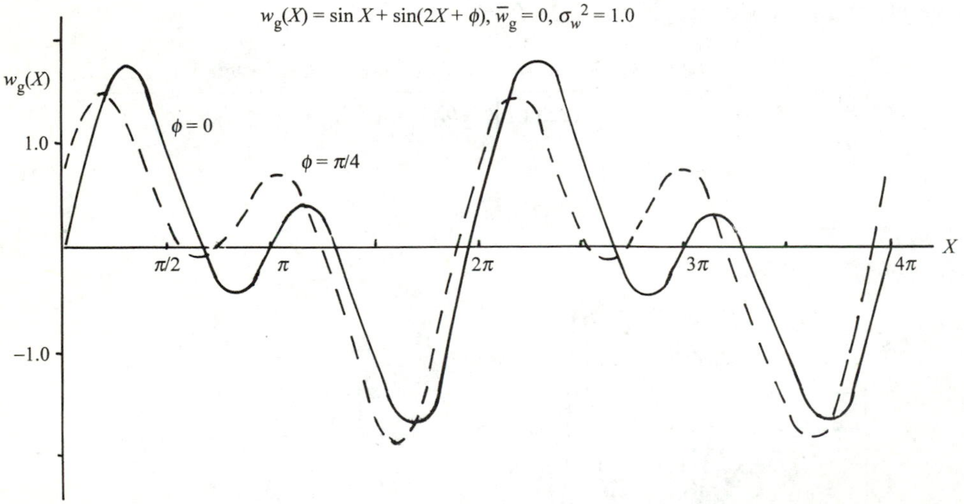

Fig. III.100. Effect of phase angle.

According to eqn. (III.13.31) the intensity, σ_w^2, depends on the amplitudes of the gust harmonic components only; the intensity is independent of the phase angles. The probability first order density distribution, however, as illustrated in the above example, depends on both the amplitudes and the phase angles of the harmonic components.

In a Gaussian process, with zero mean (i.e. $\overline{w} = 0$), the first order probability density distribution is the normal probability density distribution

$$p(w_g) = \left(1/(2\pi\sigma_w^2)^{1/2}\right)\exp\left(-w_g^2/2\sigma_w^2\right). \tag{III.13.49}$$

This probability density distribution covers symmetrically both positive and negative values of w_g. And then the moments

$$m_{2k+1} = 0, \qquad m_{2k} = (2k-1)\sigma_w^{2k}. \tag{III.13.50}$$

In a Gaussian process the first order probability density distribution is a function of the gust intensity (i.e. σ_w^2) only, which implies that the phase angles of the harmonic components are uncorrelated.

To complete the statistical description of a random process it is necessary to define a sequence of higher order probability density distributions; a second order probability density distribution relates the probability of occurrences at X_1 to the probability of occurrences at X_2; a third order probability density distribution relates the probability of occurrences at X_1, the probability of occurrences at X_2 to the probability of occurrences at X_3; and so on. These higher order distributions are not described further because they are not used in this elementary introduction.

For further information on random variable theory, see refs. III.33 and III.34.

EXAMPLES III.33

1. Determine the mean and intensity when

$$w_g(X) = \sum_{j=1}^{J} a_j \cos^2(\Omega_j X + \varphi_j). \tag{III.13.51}$$

2. Does the auto-correlation function depend on phase angle?
3. Plot out the normal probability density distribution, eqn. (III.13.49).
4. Sketch the first order probability density distributions for the two phase angles from the curves shown in Fig. III.100.
5. If, in eqn. (III.13.25),

$$a_j = a = \text{constant for } j = 1, \ldots, 5 \tag{III.13.52}$$

$$a_j = a(5/j)^3 \quad \text{for } j = 6, \ldots, 10, \tag{III.13.53}$$

taking $X_N - X_0 = 6$ km, $J = 10$, then
(i) sketch the power spectral density, $\Phi(\Omega_j)$,
(ii) derive, and sketch, the auto-correlation function $R(\chi)$,
(iii) estimate the scale length L.

III.13.6 Atmospheric turbulence

The formula used in practice for the power spectral density of vertical gusts is based on a formula derived by von Karman, with empirical factors by Houbolt (ref. III.35), namely

$$\Phi_w(\Omega_j) = \frac{\sigma_w^2 L}{\pi} \frac{1 + (8/3)(1.339 L\Omega_j)^2}{[1 + (1.339 L\Omega_j)^2]^{11/6}}. \tag{III.13.54}$$

The scale length L, as defined in eqn. (III.13.38), is taken to be equal to altitude at low altitudes and constant at higher altitudes; a consensus of opinion, after a long debate over many years, is that

$L = 750$ m (2500 ft) above an altitude of 750 m. (III.13.55)

As an aeroplane flies through turbulence, then

$$X = U_{\text{trim}}t,$$

so the spatial wavelength X_j corresponds to a temporal wavelength (X_j/U_{trim}) and the spatial scale length L corresponds to a temporal scale length $T\,(= L/U_{\text{trim}})$. Thus to convert from space to time, because

$$\begin{aligned}\sigma_{\text{w}}^2 &= \int_0^\infty \Phi_{\text{w}}(\Omega_j)\,\mathrm{d}\Omega_j \text{ in the space domain with } \Omega_j = 2\pi/X_j \\ &= \int_0^\infty \Phi_{\text{w}}(\Omega_j)\,\mathrm{d}\Omega_j \text{ in the time domain with } \Omega_j = 2\pi/\left(X_j/U_{\text{trim}}\right)\end{aligned} \tag{III.13.56}$$

the power spectral density in the time domain is given by eqn. (III.13.54) with

$$\Omega_j = 2\pi/\left(X_j/U_{\text{trim}}\right) \tag{III.13.57}$$

and L is replaced by $T\,(= L/U_{\text{trim}})$.

A sketch of $\Phi_{\text{w}}(\Omega) \propto \Omega$, omitting the subscript j, in the time plane, on a log–log scale, is shown in Fig. III.101 for different altitudes and forward speeds. The effect of altitude can be minimal because at low altitudes the decrease in L is usually compensated by a decrease in forward speed, leaving T more-or-less constant. The ranges of the short period modal frequency (from 0.5 to 6 rad/s) and phugoid modal frequency (less than 0.2 rad/s) are indicated.

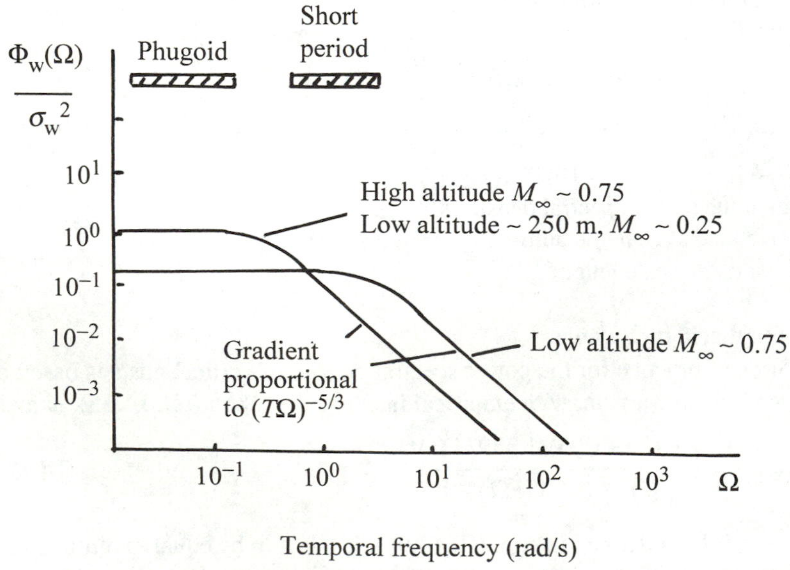

Fig. III.101. Power spectra for vertical gusts.

In Fig. III.101 the power spectral density is uniform at lower frequencies, consistent with eqn. (III.13.42), and decreases as $(T\Omega)^{-5/3}$ at higher frequencies. The frequency range where the power spectral density decreases as $(T\Omega)^{-5/3}$ is known as the inertial subrange. Note that the short period mode response tends to lie in the inertial subrange apart for high speed ground attack at low altitude.

Measurements of atmospheric turbulence on specially instrumented aeroplanes confirm the power spectral characteristics of the inertial subrange, as shown in Fig. III.102.

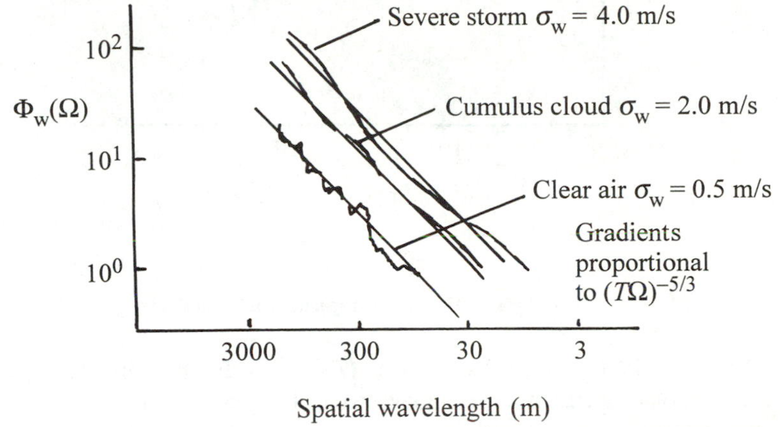

Fig. III.102. Measured spectra.

Experimental verification of the power spectral density in the band of longer wavelengths around the knee of the power spectral curve, where, according to eqn. (III.13.54), $L\Omega$ is of the order of unity, is sparse. Measurements at extremely low altitudes made at the tops of towers suggest that, in the low frequency band, there is an intermediate range where the power spectrum is proportional to $(L\Omega)^{-1}$, as shown in Fig. III.103, based on Jones (ref. III.36); note that the spatial wavelength of 200 m, the knee of the inertial subrange, is compatible with L equal to the tower height multiplied by 2π. There are considerable difficulties in making measurements at altitude where the relevant spatial wavelengths at altitude are greater than 4.5 km $(=2\pi/\Omega = 2\pi L)$, because many long patches of turbulence need to be tested before the statistical behaviour emerges. The USA launched a programme of such measurements in the mid-1970s, see Murrow *et al.* (ref. III.37); the results are not incompatible with the trends in Fig. III.103.

The form of the power spectral density at very long wavelengths has not been verified. It has been conjectured that the spectrum does not level off at long wavelengths, as predicted by the von Karman spectrum and shown in Fig. III.101, but continues to increase. However, such long wavelengths play little part in aeroplane flight dynamics.

An approximation for $\Phi_w(\Omega)$ in eqn. (III.13.54), due to Dryden, is

$$\Phi_w(\Omega) = \frac{\sigma_w^2 L}{\pi} \frac{1 + 3(L\Omega)^2}{[1 + (L\Omega)^2]^2}. \qquad \text{(III.13.58)}$$

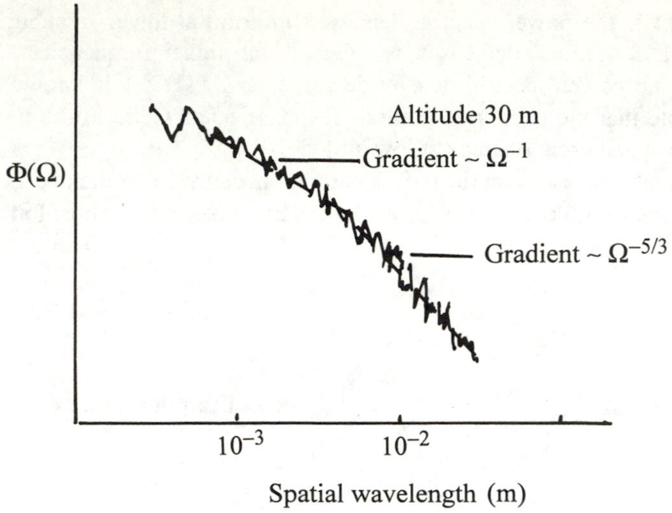

Fig. III.103. Measured spectrum at low altitude.

This Dryden formula, which decreases as $(T\Omega)^{-2}$ in the inertial subrange, is more convenient for some practical applications; it can be generated easily by analogue means from white noise and a linear filter.

Because aeroplane response is determined primarily by the inertial subrange, the probability densities of interest are the probability densities of the gust input in the inertial subrange. Thus, if the low frequency content of $w_g(X)$ is filtered out, leaving a higher frequency signal $w_g'(X)$, the first order probability density distribution $p(w_g')$ can be defined and obtained from eqn. (III.13.44). For a Gaussian process both $p(w_g)$ and $p(w_g')$ are normal probability density distributions.

From measurements it is observed that the first order probability density distribution of $w_g'(X)$ in a patch of turbulence is not a normal distribution; there are more larger peaks and more smaller peaks but fewer middle size peaks compared with the normal distribution, as indicated in Fig. III.104. This behaviour is reflected in the moment m_4, see eqn. (III.13.47):

for a Gaussian process, $\left(m_4/\sigma_w^4\right) = 3$

from measurements, $\left(m_4/\sigma_w^4\right)$ ranges from 2.5 to 5.0.

Measurements indicate that the variation of $p(w_g')$ for larger values of $\left|w_g'\right|$, with zero mean, tends to be exponential, that is,

$$p(w_g') \propto \exp\left(-\text{const}\left|w_g'\right|\right). \qquad \text{(III.13.59)}$$

There is a further non-Gaussian characteristic of turbulence, namely the clustering together of the larger gusts, as sketched in Fig. III.105, giving the effect of intermittency.

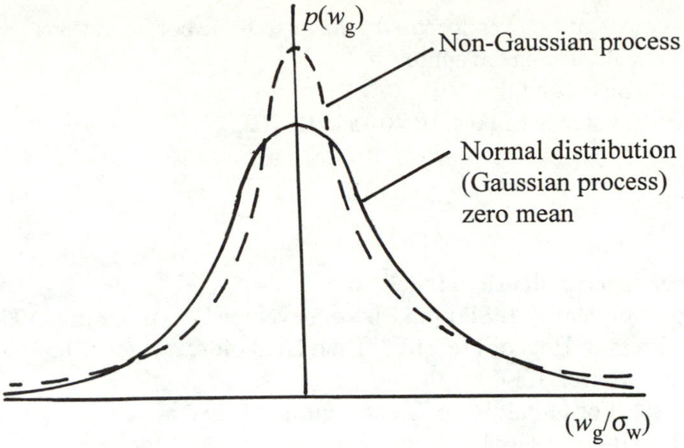

Fig. III.104. Probability density distribution.

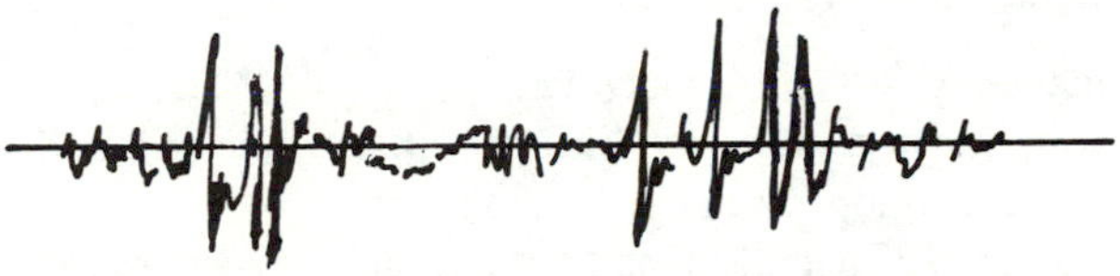

Fig. III.105. Clustering of large gusts.

The above description of vertical gusts can be carried over to horizontal gusts. Horizontal gusts have a different power spectral density given by

von Karman, $$\Phi_u(\Omega) = \frac{\sigma_u^2 2T}{\pi} \frac{1}{\left[1+(1.339T\Omega)^2\right]^{5/6}} \qquad \text{(III.13.60)}$$

Dryden $$\Phi_u(\Omega) = \frac{\sigma_u^2 2T}{\pi} \frac{1}{1+(T\Omega)^2} \qquad \text{(III.13.61)}$$

where $T\,(= L/U_{\text{trim}})$ is the same in both horizontal and vertical spectra.

EXAMPLES III.34

1. Plot the von Karman and Dryden power spectral densities and note the differences.
2. Taking the probability density distribution

$$p(w_g) = \mathscr{K}_1 \exp\left(-\mathscr{K}_2 \left| w_g \right|\right)$$

(i) is it reasonable to take $\mathscr{K}_2 = 1/\sigma_w$?
(ii) calculate $\mathscr{K}_1$.

3. Plot the vertical gust power spectra for the three basic configurations
   (i) at 250 m altitude on the approach
   (ii) at their cruise condition.
4. Check the consistency of Figs. III.101 and III.102.

III.13.7 Power spectral density model

The power spectral density (PSD) model was developed from the mid-1950s at NASA, Langley—see Press & Houbolt (ref. III.38) and Houbolt *et al.* (ref. III.39)—based on the classic work of Rice (ref. III.40).

Consider a patch of turbulence of vertical gusts; assume a Gaussian process, an intensity σ_{w}^2, and a power spectral density, either the von Karman, eqn. (III.13.54), or the Dryden, eqn. (III.13.58).

The statistical characteristics of the random response of a variable (e.g. normal acceleration, pitch attitude) can be estimated

(i) assuming that the gust input is Gaussian,
(ii) when the response equations are linear (both the phugoid and short period mode equations so far developed satisfy this condition),
(iii) when the patch is sufficiently long for the transient response initiated at entry into the patch to have decayed relatively quickly so as not to affect the statistical characteristics of the response.

On the basis that the gust input, $w_{\mathrm{g}}(t)$, is a Gaussian process, the aeroplane response is also a Gaussian process.

For the normal acceleration response, $g\,\Delta n(t)$, the power spectral density of the short period normal acceleration response, $\Phi_{\Delta n}(\Omega)$, is related to the power spectral density of the gust input, $\Phi_{\mathrm{w}}(\Omega)$, by the relationship

$$\Phi_{\Delta n}(\Omega) = \Phi_{\mathrm{w}}(\Omega)\left|G_{\Delta n}(\mathrm{i}\Omega)\right|^2, \qquad \text{(III.13.62)}$$

where $G_{\Delta n}(\mathrm{i}\Omega)$ is the steady state short period harmonic response of the normal acceleration to a harmonic gust input.

By reference to Appendix 7

$$\Phi_{\Delta n}(\Omega) = \frac{\Phi_{\mathrm{w}}(\Omega)}{U_{\mathrm{trim}}^2}\left[\frac{C_{\mathrm{L}\alpha}}{C_{\mathrm{W}}}\right]^2\left[\frac{(\Omega^2)^2 + \left(2\zeta_{ng}(\omega_0)_{\mathrm{sp}}\Omega\right)^2}{\left(\Omega^2 - (\omega_0)_{\mathrm{sp}}^2\right)^2 + \left(2\zeta_{\mathrm{sp}}(\omega_0)_{\mathrm{sp}}\Omega\right)^2}\right]. \qquad \text{(III.13.63)}$$

The intensity of the normal acceleration response is

$$\sigma_{\Delta n}^2 = \int_0^\infty \Phi_{\Delta n}(\Omega)\,\mathrm{d}\Omega = A_{n\mathrm{w}}^2\sigma_{\mathrm{w}}^2. \qquad \text{(III.13.64)}$$

By definition $\sigma_{\Delta n}$ is dimensionless, so $A_{n\mathrm{w}}$ has the dimension (1/velocity).

With the Dryden vertical gust spectrum, eqn. (III.13.59)

$$A_{nw}^2 = \frac{T}{\pi U_{\text{trim}}^2}\left[\frac{C_{L\alpha}}{C_W}\right]^2 \int_0^\infty \frac{1+3(T\Omega)^2}{\left[1+(T\Omega)^2\right]^2}\left[\frac{(\Omega^2)^2+\left(2\zeta_{ng}(\omega_0)_{sp}\Omega\right)^2}{\left(\Omega^2-(\omega_0)_{sp}^2\right)^2+\left(2\zeta_{sp}(\omega_0)_{sp}\Omega\right)^2}\right] d\Omega. \tag{III.13.65}$$

Taking

$$\zeta_{sp} = 0.5, \quad \zeta_{ng} = 0.5, \quad T(\omega_0)_{sp} = O[6.0],$$

sketching the integrand in eqn. (III.13.65) with respect to $(\Omega/(\omega_0)_{sp})$, and estimating the area under the curve, then

$$A_{nw}^2 = \left(T/(\pi U_{\text{trim}}^2)\right)\left(C_{L\alpha}/C_W\right)^2\left(3/\left(T(\omega_0)_{sp}\right)^2\right) \quad O[3.0(\omega_0)_{sp}]$$

so

$$A_{nw} = \left(C_{L\alpha}/(U_{\text{trim}}C_W)\right)\left(1/\left(T(\omega_0)_{sp}\right)^{1/2}\right) \quad O[1.7]. \tag{III.13.66}$$

The concept of the threshold exceedance rate above a prescribed level $N(\Delta n)$ is now introduced. Denoting $N(\Delta n)$ as the average number of peaks of acceleration response per unit time greater than $(g\,\Delta n)$, for a Gaussian process,

$$\begin{aligned} N(\Delta n) &= N_0 \exp\left(-(\Delta n)^2/2\sigma_{\Delta n}^2\right) \\ &= N_0 \exp\left(-(\Delta n)^2/2A_{nw}^2\sigma_w^2\right) \end{aligned} \tag{III.13.67}$$

where

$$\begin{aligned} N_0 &= \text{number of upward zero crossings per unit time} \\ &= (1/2\pi)\left[\left[\int_0^\infty \Omega^2\Phi_{\Delta n}(\Omega)\, d\Omega\right]\Big/\left[\int_0^\infty \Phi_{\Delta n}(\Omega)\, d\Omega\right]\right]^{1/2}. \end{aligned} \tag{III.13.68}$$

Unfortunately, on substitution of either the von Karman spectral density, eqn. (III.13.54), or the Dryden spectral density, eqn. (III.13.58), into eqn. (III.13.68), N_0 is mathematically infinite. And so to make N_0 finite a high frequency cut-off must be imposed. It is implicit in the assumptions so far that the gust profile is two dimensional, varying along the length of the fuselage but not across the wing span. At high spatial frequencies where the harmonic wavelength is less than the wing span, the gust amplitude may well vary over the wing span. When more accurate representations of the atmospheric gusts are made in terms of wavelengths both along and spanwise to the flight path, a finite value of N_0 is obtained (see Kaynes, ref. III.41).

To obtain an order of magnitude for N_0 from eqn. (III.13.68), let the cut-off frequency be $[2\pi/(c_w/U_{\text{trim}})]$ rad/s, where c_w is the wing mean chord; then, following a similar crude estimation to that leading to eqn. (III.13.66),

$$N_0 = (1/2\pi)\left[(\omega_0)_{sp}2\pi U_{\text{trim}}/c_w\right]^{1/2} \quad O\left[\left(\frac{1}{3.0}\right)^{1/2}\right] \text{ per second} \tag{III.13.69}$$

An example:

$$C_{L\alpha} = 4.5, \quad W/S_w = 4.0\,\text{kN/m}^2, \quad (\omega_0)_{sp} = 2\,\text{rad/s}, \quad C_W = 4.0\,\text{m}$$

$$U_{trim} = 150\,\text{m/s at 300 m altitude (i.e. } T = 2\text{ s)}$$

moderate turbulence $\sigma_w = 2\,\text{m/s}$,

from eqn. (III.13.66), $A_{nw} = 0.087\,\text{s/m}$

from eqn. (III.13.49), $N_0 = 130/\text{min}$

number of $\frac{1}{2}g$ bumps $\simeq$ 2/minute. (III.13.70)

For constant U_{trim} and $(\omega_0)_{sp}$, from eqn. (III.13.66), A_{nw} decreases as

— altitude increases,
— $C_{L\alpha}$ decreases, with increasing wing sweep and low aspect ratio,
— wing loading, (W/S_w), increases,

while, from eqn. (III.13.69), N_0 remains constant. When A_{nw} decreases and N_0 remains constant the frequency of high level bumps is reduced, see Fig. III.106.

At constant altitude for a given configuration both A_{nw} and N_0 decrease with decrease in U_{trim}, reducing the number of both low and high level bumps, see Fig. III.106.

At a constant altitude and constant speed, a reduction in the manoeuvre margin reduces $(\omega_0)_{sp}$, which reduces N_0 and increases A_{nw}, thus decreasing the number of small bumps but increasing the number of large bumps, see Fig. III.106.

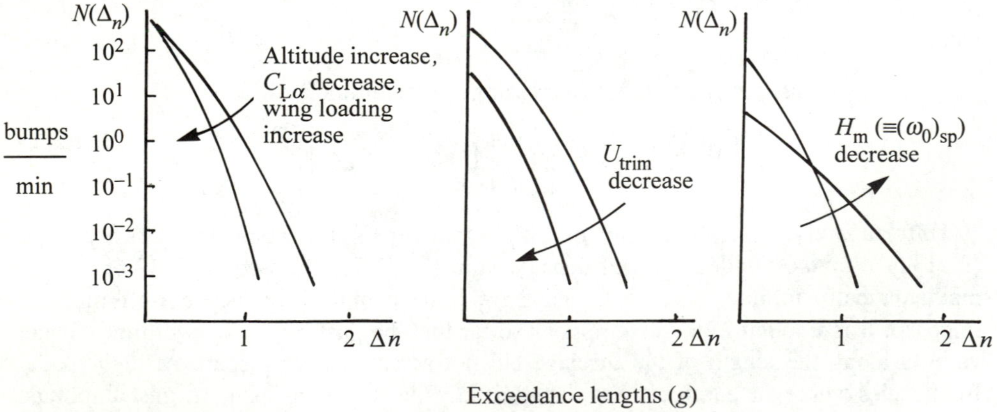

Fig. III.106. Ride quality.

Because of the assumption that the turbulence is expressed in terms of a Gaussian process, eqn. (III.13.67) underestimates the occurrence of large bumps in a patch of turbulence, a serious criticism. As already stated, in practice, in each patch of turbulence, measurements of $N(\Delta n)$ behave as $\exp(-\text{const}\,|\Delta n|)$ rather than $\exp(-\text{const}\,(\Delta n)^2)$, as predicted by eqn. (III.13.67).

Although the PSD model does not predict the levels of acceleration in each separate patch of turbulence, the model has been adapted to estimate the averages of the cumulative levels of acceleration from travelling through patches of turbulence of different intensities in an overall flight mission. If it is assumed that the gust intensity, σ_w^2, varies between patches of turbulence according to a probability distribution of the form

$$p(\sigma_w^2) = \sqrt{(2/\pi)}\ (P/B)\exp\left(-\sigma_w^2/2B^2\right) \tag{III.13.71}$$

where P and B are variable constants depending on type of turbulence and altitude (P denotes a (non-dimensional) probability and B an intensity, with dimensions of velocity) then, combining eqns. (III.13.67) and (III.13.71), integration over all possible values of σ_w^2 gives the total number of exceedances, that is,

$$\begin{aligned} N(\Delta n) &= \int_0^\infty p(\sigma_w^2) N_0 \exp\left(-(\Delta n)^2/2\sigma_w^2 A_{nw}^2\right) d\sigma_w \\ &= N_0 P \exp\left(-|\Delta n|/BA_{nw}\right). \end{aligned} \tag{III.13.72}$$

This final equation now gives an exponential form which tallies with flight experience.

Variations of (P, B) with altitude for non-storm turbulence and storm turbulence are shown in Fig. III.107. $N(\Delta n)$ for a given flight mission is obtained from Fig. III.107, summing the contributions to $N(\Delta n)$ at different altitudes weighted according to the time spent at those altitudes in storm and non-storm turbulence.

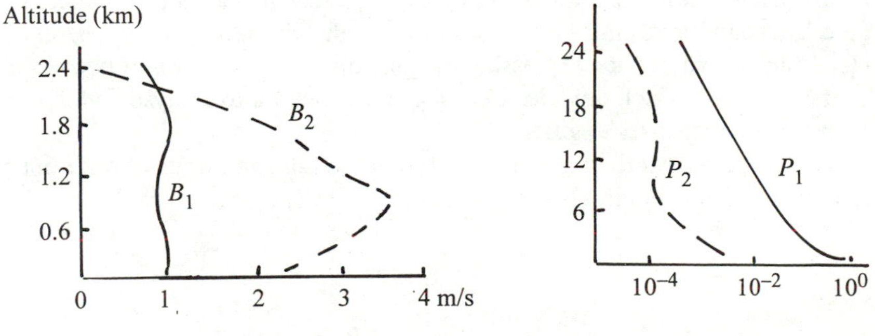

Fig. III.107. PSD parameters.

All of the above analysis is concerned with the determination of the normal acceleration responses to vertical gusts using the PSD method. It is left to the reader in the following examples to analyse the pitch attitude response and the flight path angle response to vertical gusts.

The PSD method can be applied to determine the power spectral densities of the normal acceleration, flight path angle and pitch attitude responses to horizontal gusts, combining the appropriate steady state frequency response to sinusoidal horizontal gusts, with $\Phi_u(\Omega)$ from eqns. (III.13.60) and (III.13.61).

There are a number of reservations concerning the PSD method.

(i) The assumption of a Gaussian probability distribution in each patch of turbulence with a given intensity predicts responses which do not match measurements. Noback (ref. III.42) has attempted to establish a more realistic mathematical formulation; the main difficulty is that there is no established technique for estimating responses of systems to non-Gaussian inputs.
(ii) There is a continuing debate whether or not the very large but exceedingly rare gusts which impose the extreme peak accelerations and structural loads are covered by the mission analysis PSD statistics. It is common practice to treat the rare large gust encounters separately, using a derived gust approach.
(iii) The method is restricted to linear systems, which covers the conventional short period and phugoid responses as derived so far. The method cannot be applied if the responses extend to higher angles of incidence when non-linear aerodynamic effects appear. Neither can the method be applied to active control systems, including gust alleviation systems, when non-linear effects due to saturation occur—for example, when the control system demands elevator angles beyond the stops or demands rates of change higher than the actuators can supply.
(iv) When pilots fly simulators with PSD gust inputs the consensus of pilot opinion is that the input is not realistic; the bumps are too regular compared with the clustering of large bumps as experienced in flight.

Nevertheless the PSD method has virtues.

(i) The method is straightforward to apply; only A_{nw} and $N(0)$ need be calculated.
(ii) There is a sound mathematical basis which, as already intimated, can be extended to two dimensional inputs, expressing the gust input as a function of two variables, e.g. $w_g(X, Y)$, and which provides a consistent framework to analyse both longitudinal and lateral responses to gusts.
(iii) The method is used extensively for comparing the relative merits of different aeroplanes and different control laws of automatic flight systems.

EXAMPLES III.35

1. Estimate the number of $\frac{1}{2}g$ bumps/min for the three basic configurations on the approach in severe turbulence (take $L = 200$ m, $\sigma_w = 4.0$ m/s). Comment on the results.
2. Estimate the number of $\frac{1}{2}g$ bumps/min for the basic transport configuration at its cruise condition in moderate turbulence ($\sigma_w = 2$ m/s).
3. Estimate the number of $\frac{1}{2}g$ bumps/min for the basic combat configuration in its ground attack role at Mach 0.7 at 200 m altitude in moderate turbulence ($\sigma_w = 2$ m/s).
4. Show that the power spectral density $\Phi_{\Delta\theta}(\Omega)$ of the pitch attitude response, using the Dryden power spectral density for vertical gusts, is

$$\Phi_{\Delta\theta}(\Omega) = \frac{\sigma_w^2}{U_{\text{trim}}^2}\frac{1+3(\Omega T)^2}{[1+(\Omega T)^2]^2}\left[\frac{\left(2\zeta_{\theta g}(\omega_0)_{sp}\Omega\right)^2 - \overline{K}_{\alpha g}^2(\omega_0)_{sp}^4}{\left((\omega_0)_{sp}^2-\Omega^2\right)^2+\left(2\zeta_{sp}(\omega_0)_{sp}\Omega\right)^2}\right].$$

Analyse the pitch attitude response to vertical gusts, for the case $\overline{K}_{\alpha g} = 0.5$.

5. Analyse the flight path angle response to vertical gusts.
6. Analyse the normal acceleration response due to horizontal gusts.

III.13.8 Statistical discrete gust model

The statistical discrete gust (SDG) method was formulated in the late 1960s by Jones in the UK; recent developments of the method and its applications are surveyed in ref. III.43.

The SDG method is aimed at the representation of gusts in the inertial subrange where the von Karman spectrum decreases as $(L\Omega)^{-5/3}$. A key feature of the inertial subrange is the property of self-similarity, where gusts of smaller wavelength are scaled down versions of gusts of larger wavelength and occur with equal probability.

In the SDG method the vertical gust input is represented by a sequence of discrete vertical gusts. Each discrete gust is of the form of a ramp-step gust profile, or a smoother (1 – cosine) profile, with ramp length H_g and maximum gust velocity w_g, as shown in Fig. III.108.

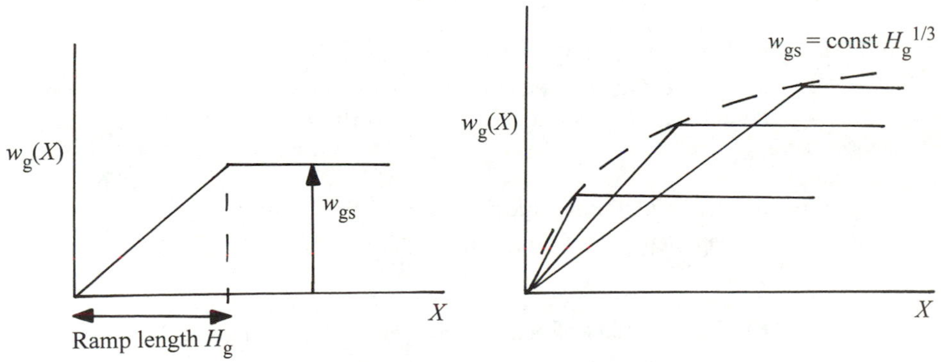

Fig. III.108 Family of ramp-step gusts.

Each discrete gust belongs to a family of gusts defined by

$$\frac{w_{gs}}{H_g^{1/3}} = \frac{u_k}{(H_{ref})^{1/3}} \tag{III.13.73}$$

where u_k is a constant, of dimension m/s, and H_{ref} is a reference ramp length, taken to be 1 m. A family of gusts with u_k constant is shown in Fig. III.108. Different families have different values of u_k.

Jones has shown that the $H_g^{1/3}$ variation is compatible with the von Karman $\Omega^{-5/3}$ spectrum.

The fundamental assumption, arising from the concept of self-similarity, is that all the discrete gusts in one family have equal probability of occurrence. It is then necessary to formulate the probability of occurrence of each family of gusts in a patch of turbulence, typically of the order of 8 km.

Let

$$N_1(H_g, U_k)\Delta H_g = \text{number of occurrences per unit distance of discrete gusts with ramp lengths between } H_g \text{ and } H_g + \Delta H_g \text{ in the families } u_k > U_k. \tag{III.13.74}$$

To conform to the exponential trends of measured data it is assumed that

$$N_1(H_g, U_k) = \left(a/H_g^2\right)\exp(-U_k/b), \tag{III.13.75}$$

where a is a non-dimensional number which determines whether the fluctuations are densely packed (i.e. continuous turbulence) or are relatively sparse (i.e. intermittent turbulence); from measurements a varies between 0.8 for continuous turbulence to 0.1 for intermittent turbulence.

The factor H_g^2 ensures the correct dimensions since $N(H_g, U_k)$ has dimension $(1/(\text{distance})^2)$, and b is proportional to gust intensity, with dimensions of velocity; from measurements, $b \simeq 0.1\sigma_w$.

Denoting

$$\gamma(H_g) = \text{peak acceleration by an aeroplane travelling at } U_{trim} \text{ through a discrete ramp-step gust of ramp length } H_g \text{ from family } u_k = 1.0\,\text{m/s} \tag{III.13.76}$$

For a linear system,

$$u_k\gamma(H_g) = \text{peak acceleration experienced through discrete ramp-step gust of ramp length } H_g \text{ from family } u_k. \tag{III.13.77}$$

Let

$$N_2(H_g, \Delta n)\Delta H_g = \text{number of occurrences per unit distance of peak accelerations greater than } (g\,\Delta n) \text{ due to discrete ramp-step gusts with ramp lengths between } H_g \text{ and } H_g + \Delta H_g \tag{III.13.78}$$

$$= \text{number of occurrences per unit distance that } u_k > \left[\left(g\,\Delta n/\gamma(H_g)\right)\text{m/s}\right] \text{ due to discrete ramp-step gusts with ramp lengths between } H_g \text{ and } H_g + \Delta H_g \tag{III.13.79}$$

from eqn. (III.13.77), on the basis of the important assumption that one acceleration peak corresponds to one discrete ramp-step gust.

Comparing eqns. (III.13.74) and (III.13.79),

$$\begin{aligned} N_2(H_g, \Delta n) &= N_1\left(H_g, \left[\left(g\,\Delta n/\gamma(H_g)\right)\text{m/s}\right]\right) \\ &= \left(a/H_g^2\right)\exp\left(-\left[\left(g\,\Delta n/\gamma(H_g)\right)\text{m/s}\right]/b\right) \end{aligned} \qquad \text{(III.13.80)}$$

from eqn. (III.13.75).

Then

$$\begin{aligned} N(\Delta n) &= \text{number of acceleration peaks per unit distance} \\ &\quad\ \text{greater than } (g\,\Delta n) \\ &= \int_0^L N_2(H_g, \Delta n)\,\mathrm{d}H_g \qquad \text{(III.13.81)} \\ &= \int_0^L \left(a/H_g^2\right)\exp\left[-\left((g\,\Delta n)/\gamma(H_g)\right)/b\right]\,\mathrm{d}H_g \end{aligned}$$

from eqns. (III.13.79) and (III.13.80), where $0 < H_g < L$ covers the inertial subrange, assuming that discrete gusts with $H_g > L$ do not contribute to $N(\Delta n)$.

Jones shows that an acceptable approximation of eqn. (III.13.81) for larger values of Δn is

$$N(\Delta n) \simeq (\alpha/\lambda H_{max})\exp\left[-\left[\left((g\,\Delta n)/\gamma_{max}\right)\text{m/s}\right]/\beta\right] \qquad \text{(III.13.82)}$$

where $\alpha = 0.89a$, $\beta = b/1.12$, γ_{max} is the maximum value of $\gamma(H_g)$, H_{max} is the value of H_g when $\gamma(H_g)$ is equal to γ_{max}, and λ is the parameter which depends on the curvature of $\gamma(H_g)$ at $H_g = H_{max}$ (a value 0.2 is usually taken).

Eqn. (III.13.82) is mathematically valid only for larger values of Δn; however, eqn. (III.13.82) agrees with experimental data over the practical range of values of interest of Δn and so is used as a general formula.

An example:

$$U_{trim} = 150\,\text{m/s}, \quad C_{L\alpha} = 4.5, \quad W/S_w = 4\,\text{kN/m}^2$$

at sea level with $\sigma_w = 2\,\text{m/s}$ in continuous turbulence.

Derivations of γ_{max} and H_{max} are shown in Fig. III.109.

$$\begin{aligned} H_{max} &\simeq 100\ \text{m}, \\ \gamma_{max} &\simeq 0.80g\left(\left[150^{1/3}\ \text{m/s}\right]/U_{trim}\right)\left(C_{L\alpha}/C_W\right) \\ &= 0.80g.150^{1/3}.\tfrac{1}{2}\rho_{at}U_{trim}\,C_{L\alpha}/\left(W/S_w\right) = 0.44\ \text{g} \\ N(\Delta n) &= (0.7/0.2/100.0)\exp(-\Delta n/0.44/0.18)/\text{m} \\ &= 315\exp(-12.6\Delta n)/\text{minute}; \end{aligned} \qquad \text{(III.13.83)}$$

number of bumps exceeding $\tfrac{1}{2}g = 0.6/\text{minute}$. (III.13.84)

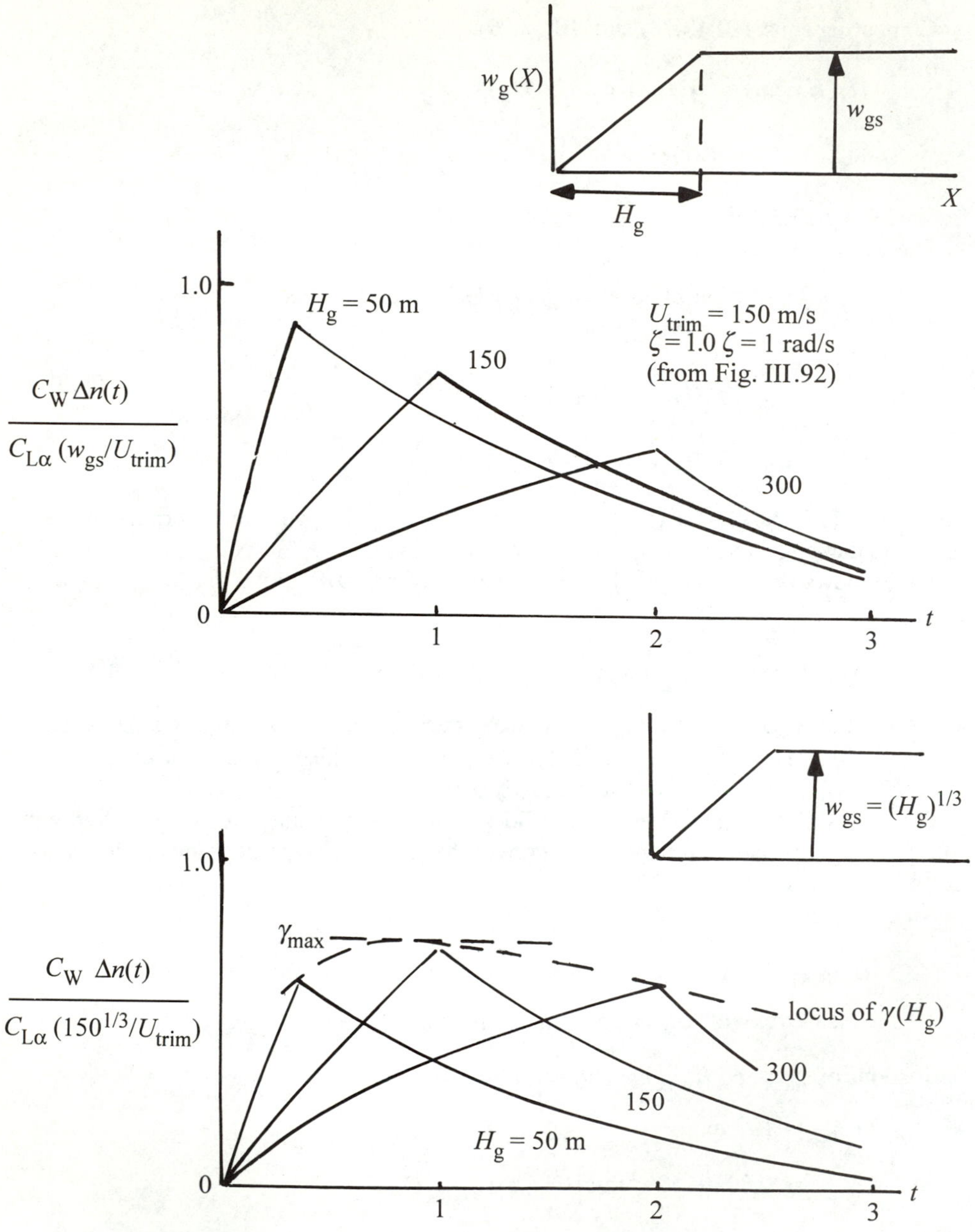

Fig. III.109. Estimation of γ_{max}.

In general the PSD method (eqn. (III.13.70)) and the SDG method (eqn. (III.13.84)) give the same ball-park numbers for $\frac{1}{2}g$ bumps/min in moderate turbulence.

So far it has been assumed that the discrete gusts are well separated so that each peak response can be identified with one discrete gust. But gusts can be closely coupled, so the range of gust profiles is extended.

A combination of a positive ramp-step gust followed by a negative ramp-step gust forms a trapezoidal gust. Single ramp-step gusts are known as Pattern 1 type gusts; trapezoidal gusts are known as Pattern 2 type gusts.

A family of gusts denoted by u_k includes Pattern 1 and Pattern 2 type gusts. Pattern 1 and Pattern 2 type gusts of one family have equal probability; from the analysis of turbulence records there is a relative amplitude factor between Pattern 1 and Pattern 2 type gusts denoted by

$$\begin{aligned} p_1 &= 1.0 = \text{datum amplitude of Pattern 1 type gusts of family } u_k \\ p_2 &= 0.85 = \text{relative amplitude of Pattern 2 type gusts of family } u_k. \end{aligned} \qquad \text{(III.13.85)}$$

Jones has shown that when the two patterns of gusts are taken into account, then

$$N(\Delta n) = (\alpha/\lambda H_{\max})\exp\left(-\left[(g\,\Delta n/\gamma_{\max})\,\text{m/s}\right]/\beta\right) \qquad \text{(III.13.86)}$$

where

$$\begin{aligned} \gamma_{\max} &= \text{maximum of } (p_1\gamma_{1\max}, p_2\gamma_{2\max}) \\ \gamma_1(H_g) &= \text{peak acceleration for Pattern 1 gust with ramp length } H_g \\ &\quad\ \text{when } u_k = 1\,\text{m/s} \\ \gamma_{1\max} &= \text{maximum value of } \left|\gamma_1(H_g)\right| \\ \gamma_2(H_g) &= \text{peak acceleration for Pattern 2 gust with ramp length } H_g \\ &\quad\ \text{when } u_k = 1\,\text{m/s} \\ \gamma_{2\max} &= \text{maximum value of } \left|\gamma_2(H_g)\right|, \\ H_{\max} &= \text{value of } H_g \text{ corresponding to } \gamma_{\max}. \end{aligned}$$

For the example shown in Fig. III.110, deduced from Figs. III.92 and III.93, $\gamma_{2\max} > \gamma_{1\max}$ but $p_2\gamma_{2\max} < p_1\gamma_{1\max}$ so $\gamma_{\max} = \gamma_{1\max}$ with $H_{\max}$ approximately 100 m. In practice, for lightly damped short period responses, $\gamma_{\max}$ is often given by $p_2\gamma_{2\max}$.

In the full version of the SDG method further patterns of gusts are included; Pattern 4 gusts comprise two positive trapezoidal gusts while Pattern 8 gusts comprise four positive trapezoidal gusts. The method then involves a search for $\gamma_{\max}$ from the weighted maximum accelerations from all the patterns of gusts.

The trends in the variations of the normal acceleration responses with configuration and operational parameters described for the PSD method, as sketched in Fig. III.106, are reproduced by the SDG method.

According to Jones, the analysis of flight test results indicates that the rare gusts of extremely large amplitude satisfy different similarity relationships, in particular, that a family of equi-probable large gusts satisfy the condition that $(w_g/(H_g)^{1/6})$ is constant.

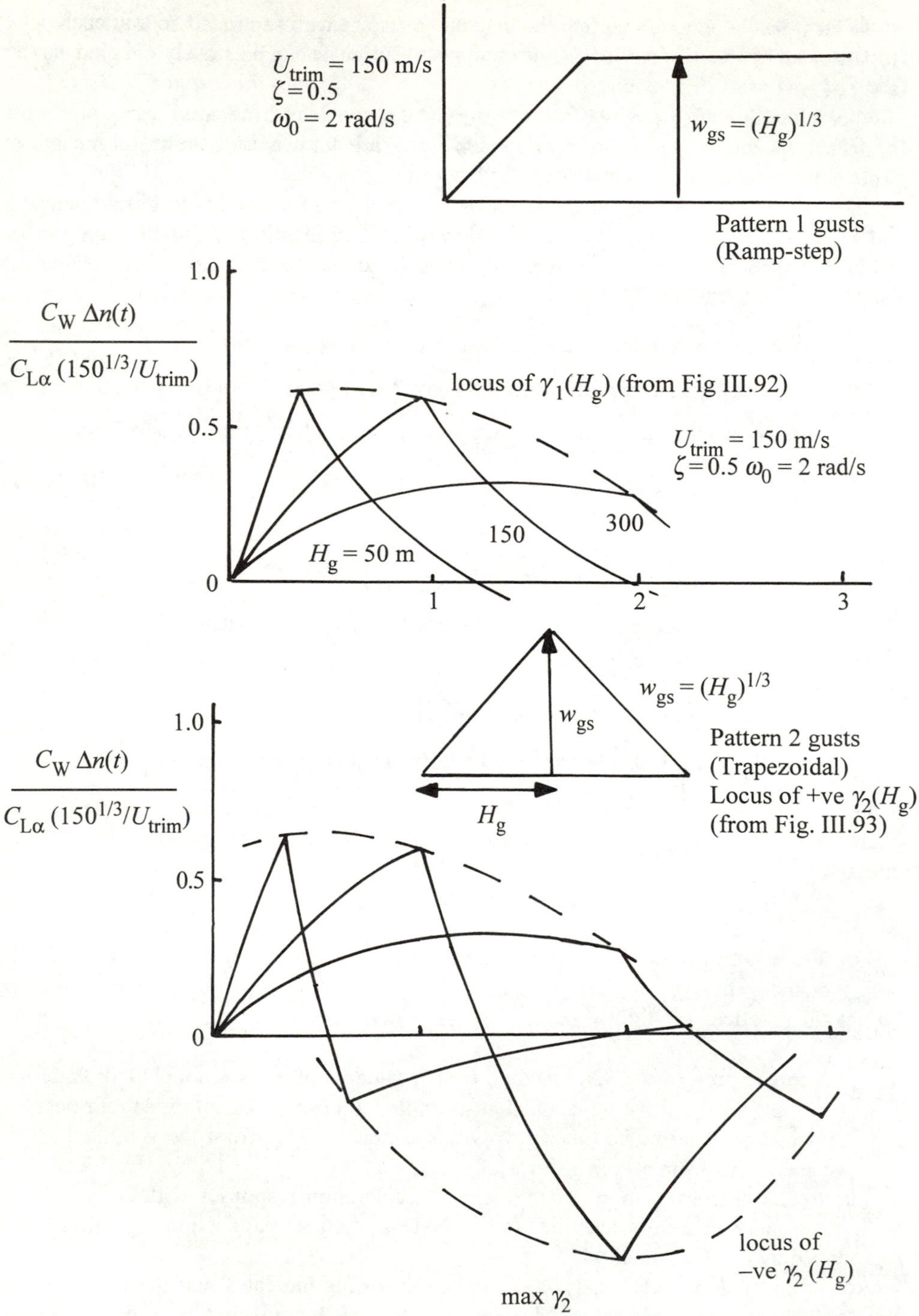

Fig. III.110. Estimation of γ_{max}.

It was pointed out in sect. III.13.6 that at the low frequencies in the region of the knee of the power spectral density the power spectral density varied as $(L\Omega)^{-1}$. In this region the families of equi-probable ramp-step gusts satisfy the condition that (w_g/H_g) is constant; furthermore, in this frequency range the gusts are more Gaussian.

By incorporating all of these features into his later applications, Jones claims to have formulated a unified model covering all types of turbulence.

The SDG method, at least at present, does not have the universality of the PSD method for expressing gust inputs, including multi-dimensional inputs, and for the estimation of all responses (normal acceleration, pitch attitude, flight path deviation) across the full frequency range within a coherent mathematical framework. However, it is claimed that the main advantages of the SDG approach are its sounder physical background, its application to individual patches of turbulence with their non-Gaussian behaviour, its incorporation of the large discrete gusts and its ability to cope with non-linear response behaviour, including non-linear active control systems.

According to recent work on the PSD and SDG methods (e.g. Perry *et al.*, ref. III.44), there can be areas of overlap between the two methods with a relationship between A_{nw} and γ_{max}.

EXAMPLES III.36

1. Is it reasonable to assume that discrete gusts with $H_g > L$ do not contribute to $N(\Delta n)$?
2. Plot $N(\Delta n)$ for the example in eqn. (III.13.83) for $\sigma_w = 3.0$ m/s.
3. Derive and plot $N(\Delta n)$ for the example in eqn. (III.13.83) but with $U_{trim} = 60$ m/s in severe turbulence ($\sigma_w = 4$ m/s).

III.13.9 Wind shear and microbursts

When a wind is blowing and gusting close to the ground the mean horizontal wind speed increases with altitude due to the boundary layer effect. A crude approximation for the mean wind velocity, u_g, is

$$u_g/(u_g)_{ref} = (h/h_{ref})^a \qquad \text{(III.13.87)}$$

where $(u_g)_{ref}$ is the mean horizontal wind speed at the reference height, h_{ref}, taken as 7.5 m, and a varies between 0.1 over a smooth terrain to approximately 0.4 over an urban terrain. There can be a problem in formulating the wind shear profile in the neighbourhood of an airport where a relatively smooth terrain is surrounded by built-up areas. In general, $(u_g)_{ref}$ is proportional to the horizontal gust intensity, σ_u.

On the approach, as an aeroplane descends into a headwind shear, the equivalent air speed decreases and lift is lost unless corrective action is taken by the pilot, in addition the phygoid frequency and damping are reduced (see Etkin, ref. P.15). The opposite trends occur when descending into tailwind shear.

Extreme wind shear conditions can arise in the proximity of thunderstorms. The main features of a mature thunderstorm, as sketched in Fig. III.111, are

(i) a central, cold, downdraught;
(ii) the conversion of this downdraught into horizontal wind shear close to the ground;

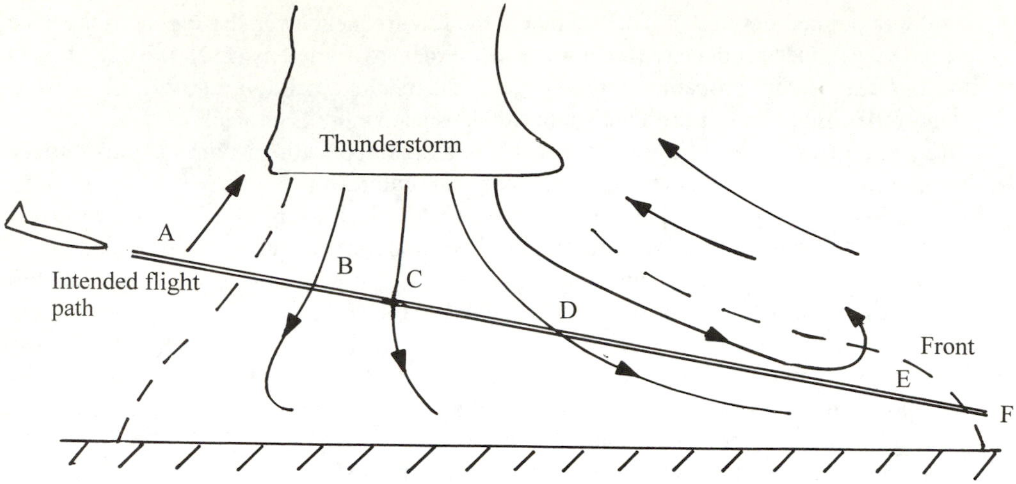

Fig III.111. Flight through a microburst.

(iii) the induction of warm updraughts on the periphery of the thunderstorm;
(iv) a front as the thunderstorm moves along.

As indicated in Fig. III.111 there are severe problems in maintaining control in a descent through a 'microburst'; an upwash gust field is suddenly replaced by a downwash gust field from *A* to *B*, the downwash field is converted to a large tailwind between *C* and *D*, and the tailwind is lost between *E* and *F*; unfortunately the pilot does not know in advance where *A*, *B*, *C*, *D*, *E* and *F* are along the flight path.

For further information on flight through microbursts, see refs. III.45–III.49.

III.13.10 Turbulence input to simulators

Flight simulators are widely used for research, design and pilot training. The more advanced simulators have five degrees of freedom (heave, sideslip, pitch, roll and yaw), moved by hydraulic actuators, a digital visual display and a complete cockpit with all controls and instruments. The associated computer carries a mathematical model of the aeroplane dynamics and all the systems; the pilot's control inputs are fed to the computer which calculates in real time the predicted aeroplane response, which is transmitted to the hydraulic servos to move the cockpit accordingly and change the visual display. A separate input feeds in any particular pattern of turbulence.

For realism the time varying signal input representing turbulence must incorporate the main features of actual turbulence: the correct power spectral density, the non-Gaussian probability distribution and the clustering of large gusts.

When white noise, from a random number generator, is passed through an appropriate linear filter, a 'continuous' time varying signal is produced which is Gaussian with a Dryden power spectral density. Such an input, as shown in Fig. III.112(i), together with the square of the signal to highlight those gusts with higher energy levels, would be regarded as unacceptable because the signal is 'too regular'.

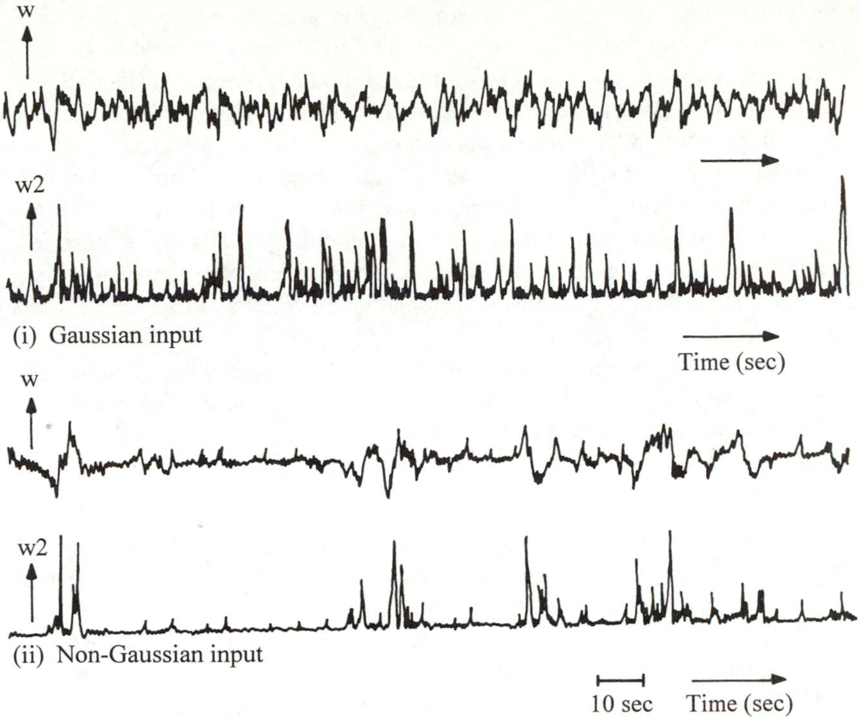

Fig. III.112. Simulated gust inputs.

A non-Gaussian input signal with a required power spectral density, and with features of clustering, can be generated by first multiplying two signals and then adding a third, where each of these signals is generated from a white noise source and passed through a linear filter, as described by Gerlach *et al.* (ref. III.50), following the initial ideas of Reeves (ref. III.51). A typical input signal, which now more closely resembles real turbulence, is shown in Fig. III.112(ii).

In the UK (Tomlinson, ref. III.52), turbulence inputs are obtained in accordance with the SDG model. An input signal is generated from a random sequence of discrete ramp gusts with an appropriate balance of large and small peaks to satisfy the non-Gaussian probability criterion, and with suitable phasing to obtain the effects of clustering.

For further reading on topics related to turbulence, see refs. III.53–III.56.

III.14 LONGITUDINAL FLYING QUALITIES

III.14.1 Introduction

In operational flying it is mandatory that the pilot–aeroplane combination shall be able to complete safely all specified performance tasks in virtually all weather conditions: take-off, climb, cruise, descend, land, abort, avoid collisions, together with, for a combat aeroplane, loiter, supersonic dash, intercept, tracking a moving target, weapon firing, ground attack and terrain following. The completion of all tasks relevant to an aeroplane must be well within the capabilities of an average pilot after appropriate training.

The topic of Flying Qualities is concerned with providing the aeroplane designer with an understanding of how pilots fly aeroplanes and how to design aeroplanes which pilots regard as satisfactory. This topic is far from straightforward. The human pilot is not an automaton; the human pilot is highly adaptive in overcoming challenges, making it difficult to anticipate or predict pilots' behaviour and opinion, especially when those opinions differ widely. Yet the human pilot is the only constant factor throughout the history of powered flight while the technologies of aeronautics have evolved beyond all recognition.

In this section the flying qualities of conventional aeroplanes without advanced automatic control systems are described. The aim is to introduce some elementary concepts underlying this topic and to help the reader to come to grips with a bewildering range of literature built up over many years of flying experience.

The basic terminology may be defined.

(i) Flying qualities of a particular aeroplane are assessed by the subjective opinions of pilots on the ease and precision with which those pilots complete the range of performance tasks.
(ii) Handling qualities refer to those features of the aeroplane flight characteristics which govern the flying qualities.
(iii) Handling qualities criteria are concerned with the identification and quantification of specific parameters and variables which describe the handling qualities.
(iv) Flying qualities requirements are statutory regulations laid down by the certifying authorities in terms of qualitative specifications deemed to provide acceptable levels of flying qualities; in the UK military requirements of these qualitative specifications are satisfied by 'means of compliance', which define the ranges of values of the basic flight dynamic variables.

The terminology in the literature is not so clear cut; often flying qualities and handling qualities are regarded as synonymous, combining definitions (i) and (ii).

Handling qualities criteria provide the rationale for the requirements. Both criteria and requirements have evolved over many years, primarily by establishing and analysing the correlations between the flying qualities of operational aeroplanes, prototype aeroplanes, research (variable stability) aeroplanes and 'paper aeroplanes' in ground based simulators, with quantitative values of basic flight response parameters. A thorough presentation of military requirements by the United States Air Force (USAF) was published in 1969, with updates in 1980 and 1987 (see refs. III.57). Similar requirements have been formulated in the UK by the Ministry of Defence (MoD). Civil requirements have been formulated in the USA by the Federal Aviation Authority (FAA), in the UK by the Civil Aviation Authority (CAA) and also by the Joint Airworthiness Authority (JAA), which is a collective of seventeen European countries, including the UK.

It is recognized that flying qualities depend on the type of aeroplane, on the type of flight task or flight phase, on the possible failure states, and on the atmospheric environment.

It is customary to classify aeroplanes as follows:

Class I—light aeroplanes
Class II—medium size transport, low to medium manoeuvrability (e.g. B.Ae 146, Boeing 757).
Class III—large size transport, low to medium manoeuvrability (e.g. Boeing 747, B52).
Class IV—high-manoeuvrability combat aeroplanes.

It is then customary to distinguish between three different types of flight tasks or flight phases.

Category A—flight phases requiring rapid manoeuvrability for precision tracking or precise flight path control (e.g. air-to-air combat, ground attack, weapon launch, terrain following, in-flight refuelling (receiver), close formation flying).
Category B—flight phases requiring gradual manoeuvres without precision tracking although accurate flight path control may be required (e.g. climb, cruise, loiter, descent, in-flight refuelling (tanker)).
Category C—flight phases associated with take-off and landing involving gradual manoeuvres with accurate flight path control (e.g. take-off, approach, landing, abort).

From a pilot's point of view, flying qualities are reflected in the pilot workload required to complete the above categories of flight phases. Pilot workload is a combination of

- —pilot compensation to overcome deficiencies in the basic aeroplane response characteristics (the mechanism of pilot compensation is explained later);
- —physical exertion, pushing and pulling the controls;
- —atmospheric environment; wind variations and intensity of turbulence;
- —taking decisions on the timing of appropriate control inputs, on navigation, routes and flight paths, on timing of weapons' launching;
- —psychological stress and mental concentration, monitoring and relating visual cues from all instruments and external observation, with, in combat, a heightened awareness of danger;
- —layout of the cockpit, external visibility, ease of comprehension of information displayed by a welter of instruments;
- —physiological reactions to angular and linear disturbances;
- —communication with aircrew and A(ir) T(raffic) C(control);
- —a pilot's familiarity with, and confidence in, the aeroplane, including an awareness of all potential hazards.

Flying qualities are graded qualitatively.

Level 1—task achieved with acceptable workload.
Level 2—task effectiveness degraded, or significant increase in workload, or both.
Level 3—task cannot be completed although aeroplane controllable; workload at the limit of pilot's ability.
Below Level 3— aeroplane uncontrollable.

Aeroplanes of all classes must be capable of satisfying level 1 flying qualities for all categories of flight phases within the operational flight envelope. Relaxation to level 2 or level 3 flying qualities is allowed within the operational flight envelope for specific malfunctions of low probability (e.g. augmentation system failure) or in extreme turbulence. Combat aeroplanes are allowed to operate beyond the operational flight envelope within the service envelope, where level 2 flying qualities must be satisfied, or within a permissible flight envelope where level 3 flying qualities must be satisfied (see Fig. III.113). It is mandatory that at all times a pilot must be able to retain controllability, even with severe malfunctions, and be able to land the aeroplane.

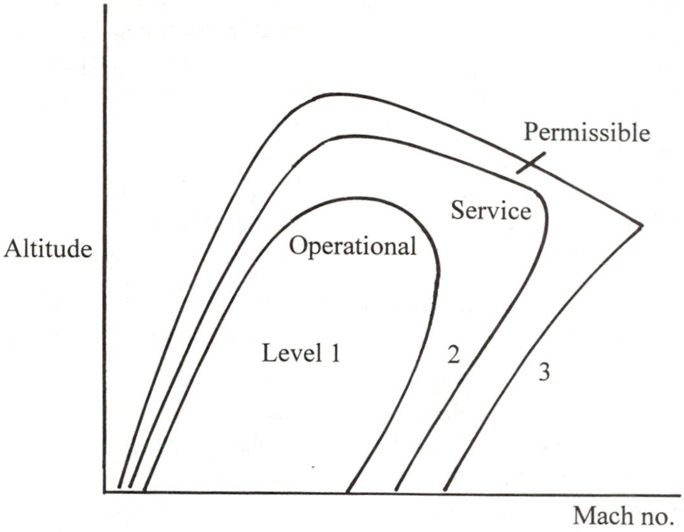

Fig. III.113. Flight envelopes for military aeroplanes.

Pilots are asked to grade their assessments of the flying qualities of an aeroplane using the Cooper–Harper rating scale, as set out in Table III.2. The Cooper–Harper rating system identifies ten sublevels within the four basic levels of flying qualities.

Handling qualities depend on the combination of longitudinal and lateral flight dynamic characteristics, but at this stage only those handling qualities relevant to longitudinal motions are described.

III.14.2 Piloting techniques

Before describing handling quality criteria and flying qualities requirements some comments on how pilots fly aeroplanes are offered by an author who is not a pilot himself but who has sought advice.

Exactly how pilots fly aeroplanes, what they look for, how they formulate their views, and the variations in technique between pilots cannot be precisely quantified, sometimes introducing a communication gap between pilot and designer. Apparently before the Second World War it was the custom in Japan that the chief designer piloted his

Table III.2. Cooper–Harper rating

Aeroplane characteristics	Demands on pilot in meeting given task	Level of flying qualities	Pilot rating
Excellent	Pilot compensation not a factor for required task	1	1
Good, negligible deficiencies	Pilot compensation not a factor for required task	1	2
Fair, mildly unpleasant deficiencies	Minimal pilot compensation needed to complete task	1	3
Minor but annoying deficiencies	Moderate pilot compensation needed to complete task	2	4
Moderate objectionable deficiencies	Considerable pilot compensation needed to complete task	2	5
Very objectionable but tolerable deficiencies	Extensive pilot compensation needed to complete task	2	6
Major deficiencies	Task not attainable with maximum tolerable pilot compensation; aeroplane controllable	3	7
Major deficiencies	Considerable pilot compensation needed for control	3	8
Major deficiencies	Intense pilot compensation needed to retain control	3	9
Major deficiencies	Control lost	below 3	10

prototype aeroplane on its maiden flight; this custom was presumably highly effective because virtually all of the Japanese chief designers of that era are noted for their longevity.

A pilot explores the capabilities of an aeroplane, often in unsuspected directions. Navy Phantoms were found to be suffering excessive fin fatigue compared to Air Force Phantoms; after some time it was observed that navy pilots could more comfortably clear the sea mist from their windscreens by a flick of the rudder pedal than by switching the windscreen wipers on and off. And pilots sometimes have different priorities to designers; on the Spitfire a lead bob-weight, painted black, was installed to maintain stability and structural limits; pilots were known to replace this bob-weight by a balsa wood replica, painting it black, in order to retain the option of exceeding those limits when in danger of being shot down.

Apparently 65% of aviation disasters are attributed to pilot error. It is therefore of considerable importance to understand the reasons why such accidents occur, and to seek design improvements to reduce them. This area of expertise is known as 'human factors' (see Wiener & Nagel, ref. III.58).

The pilot flies by visual reference to external sources and/or to instruments, and by sensing motions.

External visual sources are the horizon, ground terrain, and landing aids.

Basic instruments which are relevant to flight dynamics are laid out in a traditional 'T' panel, as shown in Fig. III.114:

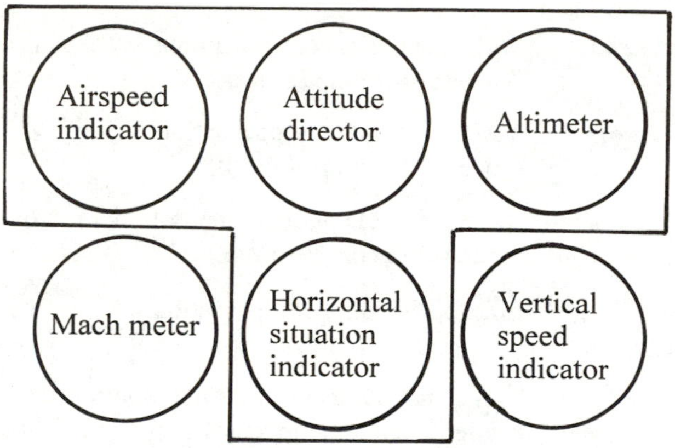

Fig. III.114. Basic instrument panel.

Air speed indicator—indicates 'indicated air speed' in knots (1 knot $\simeq$ 0.5 m/s); for now 'indicated air speed' can be taken equal to 'equivalent air speed': a fuller explanation of these speeds is given later.
Attitude director—indicates both pitch attitude and bank angle.
Altimeter—indicates the altitude (in ft).
Vertical speed indicator—indicates the rate of climb (in ft/min).
Horizontal situation indicator—gives the compass heading.
Mach meter—indicates the Mach number.

Other instruments relate to navigation, radio communication, radar, fuel and power plant, and the hydraulic, electrical and air conditioning systems.

A pilot senses dynamic motions physiologically. Semicircular channels in the inner ear contain fluid; hairlike cells monitor any fluid movement caused by dynamic motions; accelerations are detected extremely quickly. Linear accelerations are also sensed by the entire body, essentially by the 'heaviness' in the seat. But the interpretation of these senses by the brain can be ambiguous, for example, between the effect of gravity in a change of static pitch attitude and a longitudinal acceleration.

Physiological senses are coordinated in the brain with visual inputs; physiological senses need to 'match' a visual reference for the brain to interpret correctly the motion that is happening. If there is no visual reference—for example, in a cloud—a pilot can become totally disorientated, not knowing which way the aeroplane is turning, or even whether the aeroplane is upside down. In instrument flying, pilots must learn to rely on their instruments and to distrust their senses.

For longitudinal motions the pilot has two inputs, fore-and-aft stick displacement, and throttle, to control the three degrees of freedom, forward speed, flight path angle and pitch attitude angle.

To increase speed at constant altitude, keeping an eye on the horizon but cross checking with vertical speed indicator, the pilot will gradually push the stick forward, putting the elevator down, rotating the aeroplane nose-down, decreasing the angle of incidence, while at the same time gradually opening the throttle to increase thrust. By correct matching of the forward stick displacement and the throttle opening, which is learned as part of the pilot training, the aeroplane accelerates forward at constant altitude, maintaining lift equal to weight, through, effectively, a continuous sequence of trimmed states.

To climb, the pilot would pull the stick back to initiate a short period motion for a pull-out manoeuvre, to rotate the aeroplane and to incline its flight path; at the same time the pilot would open the throttle. As the aeroplane enters the steady pull-out manoeuvre the stick is pushed back to an appropriate setting for the speed in climb; if the speed in climb is to be the same as in the initial trimmed state then the stick is returned to its initial trimmed setting. The pilot checks his rate of climb on the vertical speed indicator and forward speed on the airspeed indicator.

To descend the pilot reverses the above procedure.

For trimmed flight (steady level flight, steady climb and steady descent at low angles) the elevator is the trim speed control and the throttle is the trimmed flight path control. In manoeuvring flight the roles are reversed: the elevator is the manoeuvre flight path control and the throttle is the manoeuvre speed control.

Changes in flight path angle and pitch attitude result from pulling 'g'; the pilot moves the stick back, holds the stick fixed, and then sits tight while the aeroplane normal acceleration, pitch rate, pitch attitude and flight path angle build up. Pilots look for a fairly rapid response to a steady state without excessive overshoots.

If the aeroplane response is sluggish a pilot can improve the rate of response. As shown in Fig. III.115, to obtain a required normal acceleration corresponding to a steady state elevator displacement $(-\Delta\eta_s)$, if a pilot pulls the stick back for a $2(-\Delta\eta_s)$ elevator displacement, holds it there for a time t equal to t_1, and then pushes the stick forward a distance for an elevator displacement $\Delta\eta_s$, and holds it there, the response is significantly faster, but with an overshoot, than if the pilot had initially pulled the stick back for an elevator displacement $(-\Delta\eta_s)$ and held it there. Such a technique is known as pilot compensation. For optimum response the pilot could first overcompensate and then undercompensate, to reduce the overshoot, before returning the stick at its final position.

Stick force, whether manual or artificial, increases with stick deflection so the amount of physical effort to implement compensation can be considerable, contributing to the workload.

Once the idea of pilot compensation is appreciated, then the concept of controllability can be discussed (controllability here refers to human pilot controllability of an aeroplane, which differs from the concept of controllability in the theory of feedback systems).

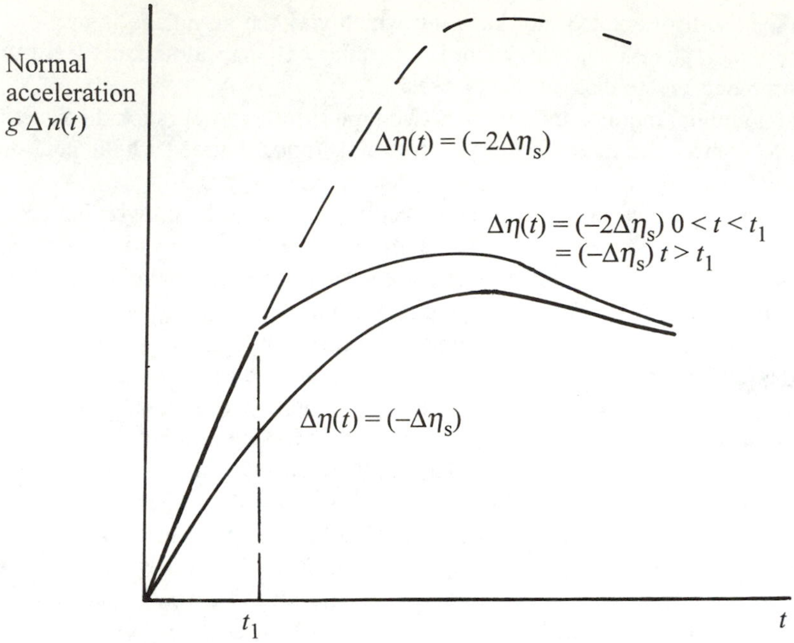

Fig. III.115. Pilot compensation.

The most rapid initial normal acceleration response per unit step per unit stick force, is given by a low value of the manoeuvre margin (see Fig. III.116, which reproduces Fig. III.86(ii)).

With a small manoeuvre margin, to prevent a high normal acceleration from building up, the pilot would need to react and compensate fairly quickly, in the order of 1 s in the specific case of Fig. III.116. When the manoeuvre margin is small, either positive or negative, the short period mode may not exist, the steady state pull-out normal acceleration, if it exists, would be unacceptably high and it would be difficult, if not impossible, to trim the aeroplane. But such an aeroplane could be controllable in the sense that in light turbulence the pilot would be able, by untiring application of compensation and by constant vigilance, to keep the levels of acceleration below the safety limits, and so maintain an approximate desired flight path.

The previous paragraph is the basis of the folklore that an aeroplane with marginal or even negative stability (i.e. small positive or negative manoeuvre margin) has optimum manoeuvrability. At the present time the lack of a steady state normal acceleration and inability to trim would render an aeroplane unairworthy. Current philosophy is to aim for a rapid response to a steady state pull-out with a high value of control power (i.e. $(-C_{m\eta})$) to obtain a satisfactory normal acceleration.

To vary the manoeuvring flight path angle and pitch attitude the pilot pulls the stick back and holds it while the pull-up manoeuvre develops; both the flight path angle and the pitch attitude angle increase, with the flight path angle lagging behind the pitch

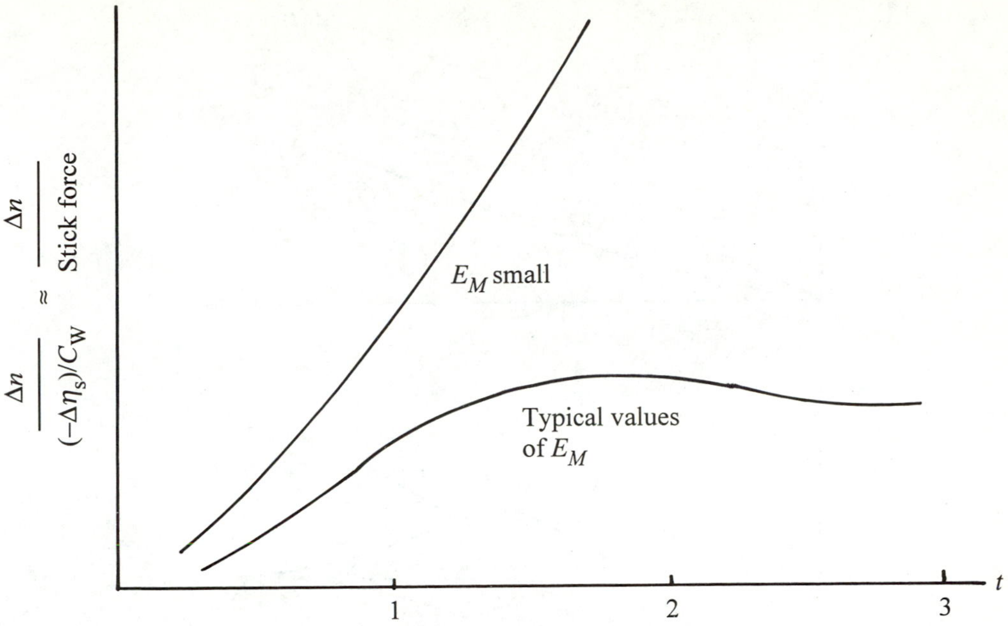

Fig. III.116. Normal acceleration response.

attitude angle, as shown in Fig. III.117(i) (taken from Figs. III.88 and III.89). After a short delay the stick is pushed back to its initial position; the resulting push-over manoeuvre decays to equal steady state changes in flight path angle and pitch attitude angle, as shown in Fig. III.117(ii). To maintain these steady state flight path and attitude angles the throttle must be opened.

In Fig. III.117(ii) the pitch attitude response shows the feature known as drop-back; the flight path angle response shows the feature of overshoot.

As shown in Fig. III.117(ii), the flight path angle 'follows' the pitch attitude angle. In general the pilot flies by reacting to pitch attitude in the knowledge that, in a transient motion, the flight path changes lag behind the pitch attitude changes, and that in the steady state manoeuvre the pitch attitude change is equal to the flight path angle change.

Particular piloting tasks are:

(i) the approach
(ii) tracking
(iii) weapon aiming
(iv) high speed ground attack
(v) terrain following

remembering that atmospheric turbulence is invariably present.

The approach involves two tasks: first, the approach must be set up initially with the appropriate speed and descent flight path; second, precise flight path and speed control during the descent. Precise flight path and speed control also implies precise angle of incidence control to avoid stall because the aeroplane will be flying close to its stall

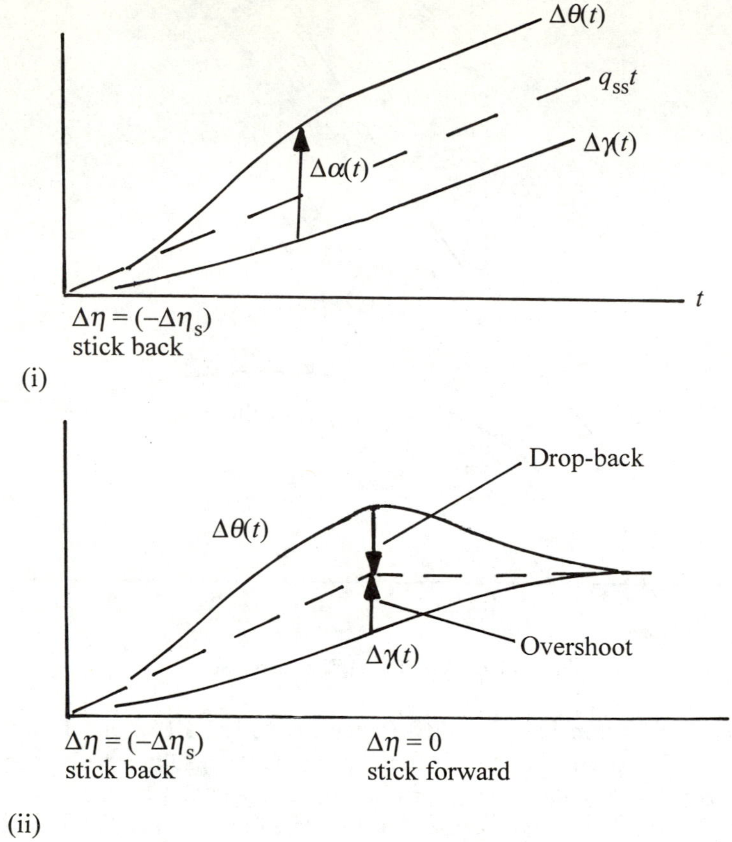

Fig. III.117. Pitch attitude and flight path angle response.

boundary. Traditionally the angle of incidence has not been monitored directly but has been monitored indirectly through the difference between pitch attitude and flight path angles; however, contemporary aeroplanes have an indicator for the angle of incidence.

For light aeroplanes pilots are taught that on the approach the stick, or elevator, is the speed control, and throttle is the flight path control. The reasoning is that a light aeroplane with its low approach speed can be adequately controlled through the phugoid mode; this technique, with its relatively slow response time, involves small stick displacements and so reduces the probability of inducing an inadvertent stall, reinforcing safety. As explained later, this technique prevents speed instability below the minimum drag speed. Nevertheless the pilot will learn to use small stick movements to induce transient flight path corrections through the short period mode.

For heavier aeroplanes the short period mode, which is relatively slow on the approach, is used extensively for short term response; pilots use the stick to control the flight path control and the throttle to control speed. But any build-up of a phugoid mode or any misalignment of the approach path must be countered by the 'light aeroplane' technique.

Atmospheric turbulence is the primary source of disturbance to the flight path and speed on the approach. Pilots do not react to every short term gust response but take gradual remedial action as flight path and speed errors build up in the longer term. Because the flight path and pitch attitude gust responses are in opposite directions, the pilot usually reacts first to pitch attitude and then corrects for the flight path.

Basic tracking is concerned with keeping an enemy aeroplane within external visual range on a constant line of sight. The primary control is the stick; throttle is brought in to maintain range.

The aiming of guns and the launch of missiles requires a tight control on pitch attitude, high speed ground attack is essentially a weapon aiming exercise, followed by a fast get-away. The delivery of bombs, which depends critically on the initial trajectory of the bomb centre of mass, requires a tight control of the flight path.

Terrain following requires an anticipation of a complicated flight path and a tight control of that flight path.

III.14.3 Stability under constraint

To maintain a designated flight path a pilot attempts to minimize deviations from that flight path, but in the process the pilot changes the stability characteristics of the aeroplane. This type of stability was called 'stability under constraint' in the classic paper by Neumark (ref. III.59).

Consider the case where a pilot is to maintain a straight and level flight path. The non-dimensional equations of perturbed motion relative to trimmed level flight in terms of $\Delta\bar{u}(\bar{t}_{\mathrm{d}})$, $\Delta\alpha(\bar{t}_{\mathrm{d}})$, and $\Delta\gamma(\bar{t}_{\mathrm{d}})$ $(=\Delta\theta(\bar{t}_{\mathrm{d}})-\Delta\alpha(\bar{t}_{\mathrm{d}}))$, from eqns. (III.11.4), with inputs $\Delta\eta(\bar{t}_{\mathrm{d}})$ and $\Delta\mathrm{Th}(\bar{t}_{\mathrm{d}})$, and gust disturbances, are

$$[\bar{\mathrm{D}}+C_{\mathrm{D}U}]\Delta\bar{u}(\bar{t}_{\mathrm{d}})+C_{\mathrm{D}\alpha}\,\Delta\alpha(\bar{t}_{\mathrm{d}})+C_{\mathrm{W}}\,\Delta\gamma(\bar{t}_{\mathrm{d}})$$
$$=C_{\mathrm{W}}\,\Delta\mathrm{Th}(\bar{t}_{\mathrm{d}})/W-\text{drag forces due to gust disturbances,}$$
$$C_{\mathrm{L}U}\,\Delta\bar{u}(\bar{t}_{\mathrm{d}})+C_{\mathrm{L}\alpha}\,\Delta\alpha(\bar{t}_{\mathrm{d}})-\bar{\mathrm{D}}\Delta\gamma(\bar{t}_{\mathrm{d}})$$
$$=-\left[\left(C_{\mathrm{L}\dot{\eta}}/\bar{m}\right)\bar{D}+C_{\mathrm{L}\eta}\right]\Delta\eta(\bar{t}_{\mathrm{d}})-\text{lift forces due to gust disturbances,}$$
$$-\bar{m}C_{mU}\,\Delta\bar{u}(\bar{t}_{\mathrm{d}})-\left[i_{yy}\bar{\mathrm{D}}^2+\left((-C_{mq})+(-C_{m\dot{\alpha}})\right)\bar{\mathrm{D}}+\bar{m}(-C_{m\alpha})\right]\Delta\alpha(\bar{t}_{\mathrm{d}})$$
$$+\left[i_{yy}\bar{\mathrm{D}}+(-C_{mq})\right]\bar{\mathrm{D}}\Delta\gamma(\bar{t}_{\mathrm{d}})$$
$$=\bar{m}\left(C_{\mathrm{W}}\,\Delta\mathrm{Th}(\bar{t}_{\mathrm{d}})/W\right)l_{\mathrm{Th}}+[C_{m\dot{\eta}}\bar{\mathrm{D}}+\bar{m}C_{m\eta}]\Delta\eta(\bar{t}_{\mathrm{d}})\Big]$$
$$+\text{pitching moments due to gust disturbances.}\tag{III.14.1}$$

Suppose that the piloting strategy is to move the stick forward if $\Delta\gamma(t)$ increases (i.e. stick forward increases the elevator angle, rotates the aeroplane nose-down, decreases the lift, and reduces the perturbation $\Delta\gamma(t)$) and to move the stick back if $\Delta\gamma(t)$ decreases, keeping the throttle unchanged. Mathematically, neglecting any lags,

$$\Delta\eta(\bar{t}_{\mathrm{d}})=\mathcal{K}\,\Delta\gamma(\bar{t}_{\mathrm{d}}),\qquad \Delta\mathrm{Th}(\bar{t}_{\mathrm{d}})=0.\tag{III.14.2}$$

On substitution of $\Delta\eta(\bar{t}_d)$ from eqns. (III.14.2) into the pitching moment equation in eqns. (III.14.1), if the coefficient $(\overline{m}C_{m\eta}\mathcal{K})$ is numerically large compared to all of the other coefficients, then $\Delta\gamma(\bar{t}_d)$ will be small, which is what is required. It is not unreasonable to expect that the coefficient $(\overline{m}C_{m\eta}\mathcal{K})$ can be made large, because $\overline{m}$ is large, $C_{m\eta}$ is of order unity and $\mathcal{K}$ can be made arbitrarily large.

Then, as a first approximation, $\Delta\gamma(\bar{t}_d)$ can be taken to be zero.

With $\Delta\gamma(\bar{t}_d)$ zero, and with $\Delta\mathrm{Th}(\bar{t}_d)$ zero, the drag and lift equations in eqns. (III.14.1) become

$$[\bar{\mathrm{D}} + C_{\mathrm{D}U}]\Delta\bar{u}(\bar{t}_d) + C_{\mathrm{D}\alpha}\,\Delta\alpha(\bar{t}_d) = -\text{drag forces due to gust disturbances,}$$
$$C_{\mathrm{L}U}\,\Delta\bar{u}(\bar{t}_d) + C_{\mathrm{L}\alpha}\,\Delta\alpha(\bar{t}_d) = -\text{lift forces due to gust disturbances.} \qquad \text{(III.14.3)}$$

The stability of these coupled drag and lift equations is determined by the characteristic equation

$$(\bar{\lambda} + C_{\mathrm{D}U})C_{\mathrm{L}\alpha} - C_{\mathrm{L}U}C_{\mathrm{D}\alpha} = 0 \qquad \text{(III.14.4)}$$

which becomes, at low speeds and neglecting Mach number effects,

$$\bar{\lambda} + 2\left(C_{\mathrm{D}0} - C_{\mathrm{W}}^2/\pi\mathrm{AR}_{\mathrm{w}}\right) = 0, \qquad \text{(III.14.5)}$$

taking

$$C_{\mathrm{D}U} = (2C_{\mathrm{D}})_{\mathrm{trim}} = 2\left(C_{\mathrm{D}0} + C_{\mathrm{L}}^2/\pi\mathrm{AR}_{\mathrm{w}}\right)_{\mathrm{trim}}$$
$$C_{\mathrm{L}U} = 2C_{\mathrm{w}}, \qquad C_{\mathrm{D}\alpha} = \left(2C_{\mathrm{W}}C_{\mathrm{L}\alpha}/\pi\mathrm{AR}_{\mathrm{w}}\right), \qquad (C_{\mathrm{L}})_{\mathrm{trim}} = C_{\mathrm{W}}.$$

The system represented by eqn. (III.14.5) is stable when

$$C_{\mathrm{W}}^2/\pi\mathrm{AR}_{\mathrm{w}} < C_{\mathrm{D}0} \qquad \text{(III.14.6)}$$

that is, at trim speeds above the minimum drag speed; the system is unstable at trim speeds below the minimum drag speed. This stability mode, a degenerate form of the phugoid mode, is known as the speed stability mode.

Speed stability above the minimum drag speed is a slow subsidence with time to half amplitude

$$t_{1/2} = 0.7\left(\overline{m}c_{\mathrm{w}}/U_{\mathrm{trim}}\right)\Big/\left(C_{\mathrm{D}0} - C_{\mathrm{W}}^2/\pi\mathrm{AR}_{\mathrm{w}}\right) = \mathrm{O}[150\ \mathrm{s}]. \qquad \text{(III.14.7)}$$

At speeds below the minimum drag speed, time to double amplitude can be of the order of 50 s.

For trim speeds below the minimum drag speed a perturbation decrease in speed would continue to decrease (i.e. $\Delta u < 0$) and $\Delta\alpha$ would be positive (since in the lift equation both $C_{\mathrm{L}U}$ and $C_{\mathrm{L}\alpha}$ are positive), building up to an aeroplane stall, while maintaining a virtually fixed flight path.

There is also a modified short period mode. As described later in the section on autopilots (III.15.4), the damping and frequency of the short period mode are decreased.

It should be emphasized that speed instability below the minimum drag speed only occurs when the pilot attempts to control flight path by using just the stick. If the pilot also changes the throttle to minimize speed changes the speed instability disappears.

It is now seen that the light aeroplane approach technique of using the stick for speed control and the thrust for flight path control also circumvents the possibility of speed instability.

Normally, on the approach, high flap angles and sometimes spoilers are deployed to induce flow separation and to generate high zero lift drag. This high drag is beneficial because

(i) it is necessary to maintain the thrust above a threshold level so that the engines can respond quickly to an emergency,
(ii) the phugoid damping is increased,
(iii) the minimum drag speed is reduced usually to a value below the approach speed, so the possibility of speed instability is diminished.

The one situation in which landings are made below the minimum drag speed are for carrier landings, and then the light aeroplane approach strategy is followed.

As a digression, the history of speed stability is of interest. As early as 1910 Painleve (ref. III.60) stated that an aeroplane was speed unstable below the minimum drag speed. The conventional argument is as follows.

The drag variation with $(\frac{1}{2}\rho_{at}U^2)$, or $((W/S_w)/C_W)$, at constant lift (= weight) is the familiar curve shown in Fig. III.118. Also shown is a thrust variation with $(\frac{1}{2}\rho_{at}U^2)$ at a particular altitude with constant throttle setting. There are two points, A and B, where the thrust is equal to the drag. These two points represent possible states of static equilibrium.

Suppose an aeroplane, flying at state A, at speed U_A, is disturbed such that the forward speed is changed. If the speed is increased relative to U_A then the drag becomes greater

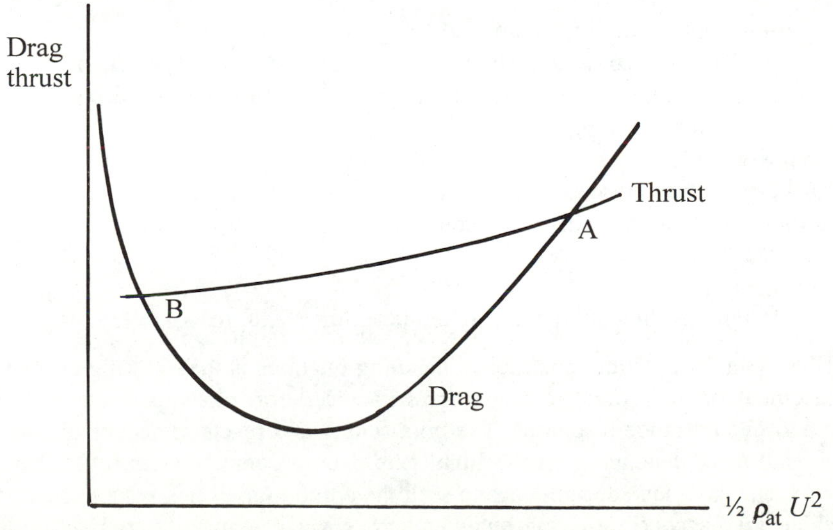

Fig. III.118. Speed stability.

than the thrust and the aeroplane slows down to its initial speed U_A. If the speed is decreased relative to U_A then the thrust is greater than the drag and the aeroplane accelerates back to its initial speed U_A. Thus state A is speed stable.

Suppose an aeroplane, flying at state B, at speed U_B, is disturbed such that the forward speed is changed. If the speed is increased relative to U_B the thrust becomes greater than the drag and the aeroplane accelerates away from U_B. If the speed is decreased relative to U_B the drag is greater than the thrust and the aeroplane decelerates away from U_B. Thus state B is speed unstable.

Thus, apparently, an aeroplane is speed unstable when it flies 'on the back side of the drag curve', that is, below the minimum drag speed.

Painleve's criterion was accepted by its plausibility and publicized by von Mises in his book in 1915 (ref. III.61).

Following the publication of the foundations of aeroplane stability by Bryan in 1911 (ref. P.1), the ramifications were explored and it was noted, for example by Fuchs & Hopf in 1922 (ref. III.62), that speed instability did not appear in the longitudinal stability equations (speed instability does not arise in the short period mode or in the phugoid stability mode as described in this book in sects. III.9 and III.10). Consequently Painleve's criterion was rejected. In 1953 Neumark published the explanation summarized above.

The fallacy in the conventional argument is to treat the aeroplane disturbance as a one degree of freedom system involving only change in forward speed, ignoring changes in angles of incidence and pitch.

III.14.4 Longitudinal handling qualities criteria

Handling qualities refer to those aeroplane flight characteristics that influence the flying qualities. Longitudinal handling qualities depend on:

(i) short period manoeuvrability in terms of
  (a) normal acceleration and pitch rate response to step stick displacement,
  (b) flight path angle and pitch attitude angle response to step stick displacement,
  (c) stick displacement/g,
  (d) stick force/g;
(ii) aeroplane response to turbulence;
(iii) the ability to trim, with positive trim control;
(iv) phugoid damping;
(v) thrust response;
(vi) cockpit design, instrument layout, ergonomic features, external visibility.

The difficulty in formulating longitudinal handling qualities is that the single input of stick displacement, or stick force, generates normal acceleration, pitch acceleration, flight path angle and pitch attitude responses. The pilot senses and reacts to accelerations and visual cues, and then, depending on the flight task, has to control either flight path or pitch attitude. The aeroplane designer has to seek the compromise stick response characteristics which give acceptable flying qualities across a wide range of stick-dependent tasks.

In this introductory text it is only possible to outline some simple ideas of handling qualities.

For longitudinal manoeuvrability (i.e. pulling '*g*'), a pilot looks for a sufficiently fast rise time of the short period response to a 'steady' state pull-out normal acceleration and rate of pitch following a step change in stick displacement, or stick force, which eliminates the need for pilot compensation. But at the same time any overshoots should be acceptable.

What constitutes a rapid manoeuvre rise time depends on the type of aeroplane and its task. Combat calls for rapid manoeuvre rise times of less than 1 s, whereas for the same aeroplane on the approach manoeuvre rise times of 2 to 3 s would be acceptable. On larger transport aeroplanes pilots accept slower manoeuvre rise times.

First the effects of the short period undamped frequency, $(\omega_0)_{sp}$, and damping ratio, ζ_{sp}, on the manoeuvre rise times are described.

Fig. III.119(i) shows the normal acceleration and pitch rate responses to a step stick input, taken from Figs. III.86 and III.87 for an example with $\zeta_{sp} = 0.6$, $(\omega_0)_{sp} = 1.65$ rad/s. The rise time for the normal acceleration to reach 90% of the steady state normal acceleration is 1.4 s, with approximately a 20% subsequent overshoot. There is, however, a 100% overshoot in the pitch rate response.

Fig. III.119(ii) sketches the normal acceleration and pitch rate responses for a step stick input, with an increased damping ratio, $\zeta_{sp} = 0.9$, keeping the same undamped frequency, $(\omega_0)_{sp} = 1.65$ rad/s. The normal acceleration reaches 90% of the steady state normal acceleration in approximately 1.7 s, somewhat longer than in Fig. III.119(i). The pitch rate overshoot is approximately 30%.

Fig. III.119(iii) sketches the normal acceleration and pitch rate responses for a step stick input, with increased undamped frequency, $(\omega_0)_{sp} = 2.5$ rad/s, reverting to the initial damping ratio, $\zeta_{sp} = 0.6$. The normal acceleration first reaches 90% of the steady state normal acceleration in approximately 1.0 s, faster than in Fig. III.119(i), but with the same overshoot, approximately 20%. The pitch rate overshoot is now approximately 250%.

It may be concluded from Fig. III.119 that, for this case:

1. An acceptable criterion for a rise time of 1.5 s, with acceptable overshoots, might be $\zeta_{sp} \simeq 0.7$, $(\omega_0)_{sp} = 1.7$ s.
2. Decreasing the undamped frequency makes the manoeuvre more sluggish, unless compensated by a decrease in the damping ratio, but then the levels of overshoots increase.
3. Increasing the damping ratio makes the manoeuvre more sluggish unless compensated by an increase in the undamped frequency.
4. Increasing the short period undamped frequency, keeping the same damping ratio, reduces the manoeuvre response time but at the cost of introducing large, and possibly unacceptable, pitch rate overshoots.

At subsonic speeds

—$(\omega_0)_{sp}$ is proportional to $(H_m/C_W)^{1/2}$; $(\omega_0)_{sp}$ increases with forward speed although the increase is tempered by the decrease of H_m with Mach number; $(\omega_0)_{sp}$ can be

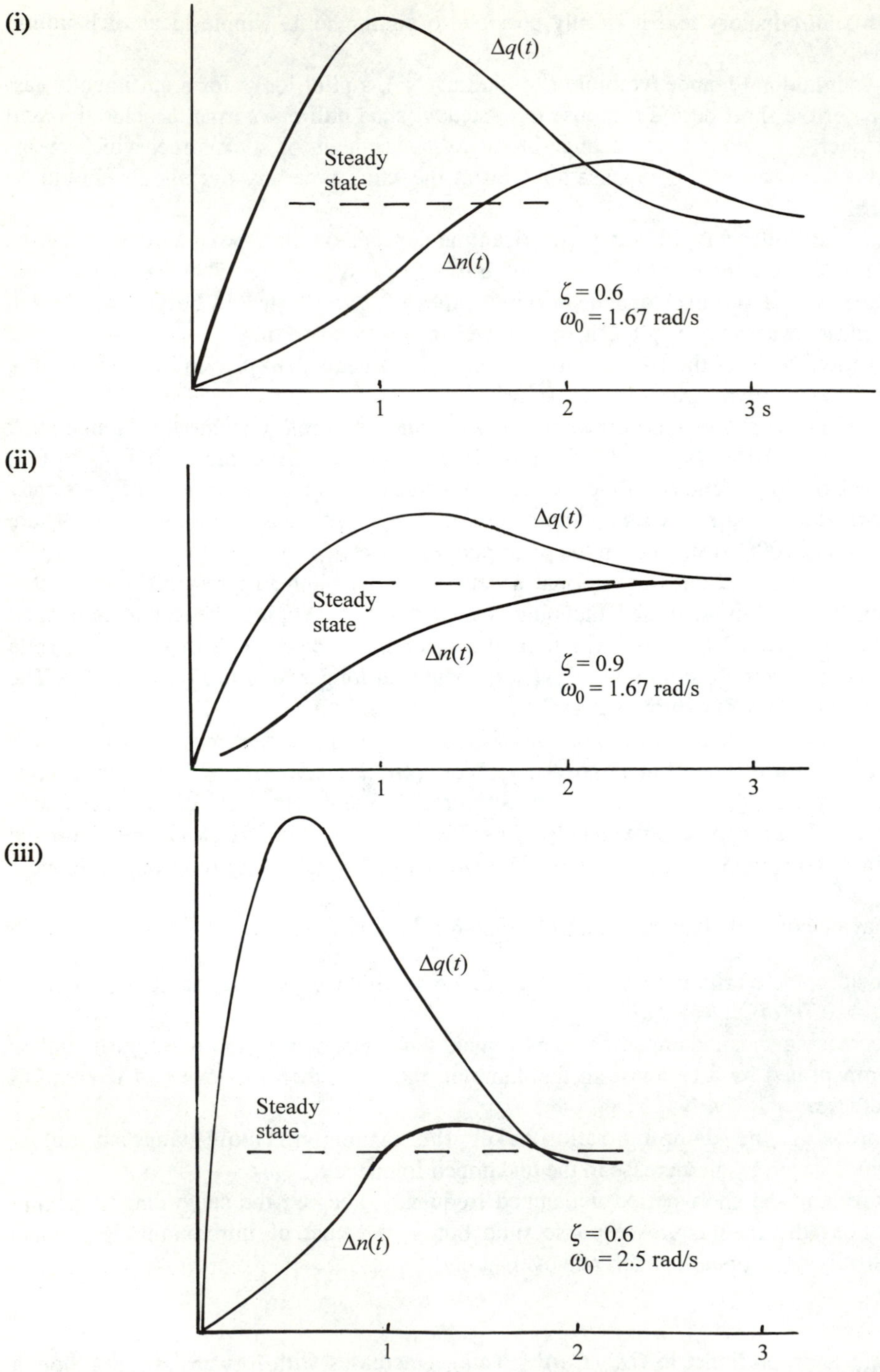

Fig. III.119. Comparison of pitch rate and normal acceleration responses.

doubled through the subsonic Mach number range, effectively halving the manoeuvre response time;
— ζ_{sp} increases with Mach number.

At low supersonic speeds the requirements for fast manoeuvring are relaxed; the main tasks are concerned with controllability, maintaining flight paths.

From pilots' ratings, typical flying qualities have been identified:

$\zeta_{sp} = 0.8,\ (\omega_0)_{sp} > 6\,\text{rad/s}$	too rapid a response to steady pull-out, aeroplane over-sensitive, danger of pilot induced oscillations (PIO), large manoeuvre stick displacement and forces;
$(\omega_0)_{sp} < 1\,\text{rad/s}$	excessive compensation required, difficult to trim;
$(\omega_0)_{sp} = O[2.0]\ \text{rad/s},\ \zeta_{sp} < 0.25$	excessive overshoots, difficult to manoeuvre;
$\zeta_{sp} > 1.5$	response too sluggish.

When the stick is pulled back quickly, and held, there is a high initial pitch acceleration; this pitch acceleration decreases with time as the normal acceleration builds up. The pilot senses the initial pitch acceleration first before sensing the subsequent build-up of the normal acceleration. It is argued that pilots anticipate the level of the subsequent steady state normal acceleration from the initial pitch acceleration.

From eqns. (III.12.8) and (III.12.4), the ratio of $\mathrm{D}q(0+)$, the initial pitch acceleration, to $(\Delta n)_{ss}$, the steady state normal acceleration factor after the decay of the short period response, is known as the control anticipation parameter (CAP), where

$$\begin{aligned} \text{CAP} &= \mathrm{D}q(0+)/(\Delta n)_{ss} \\ &= (\omega_0^2)_{sp}\, C_W/C_{L\alpha} = (gH_m)/(c_w i_{yy})\ \text{rad/s}^2 . \end{aligned} \qquad \text{(III.14.8)}$$

Pilot ratings indicate that the CAP should be greater than a minimum value of the order of 0.25 rad/s^2 (= $15°/\text{s}^2$). This minimum value for the CAP corresponds approximately to

$$(\omega_0)_{sp} = 1.5\ \text{rad/s} \quad \text{with } C_W = 0.5 \text{ and } C_{L\alpha} = 4.5. \qquad \text{(III.14.9)}$$

As a parameter the CAP is equivalent to the conventional manoeuvre margin H_m. The minimum CAP effectively dictates the minimum value of H_m. Because H_m decreases with Mach number at subsonic speeds the limiting condition on the aft location of the centre of mass is determined at high subsonic speeds.

A pilot tends to fly on stick force rather than stick displacement. The same stick force induces virtually the same initial pitch acceleration, $\mathrm{D}q(+0)$ at all subsonic flight conditions, but the steady state normal acceleration, Δn_{ss}, is inversely proportional to H_m at all flight conditions.

We shall now discuss flight path and pitch attitude control.

Two time delays related to the steady state short period response of the pitch attitude and flight path angle to a step elevator input can be identified, as shown in Fig. III.120:

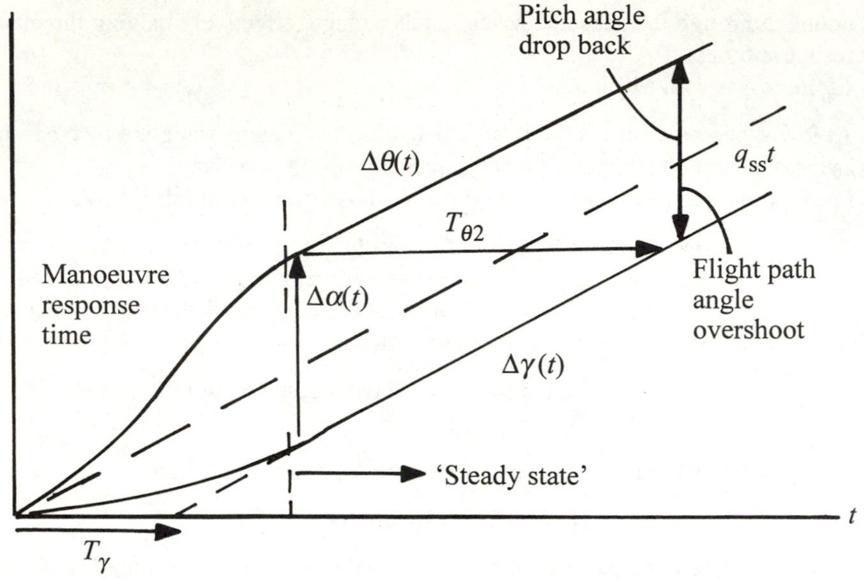

Fig. III.120. Time lags due to step elevator input.

(i) the time lag, T_γ, of the steady state flight path response relative to the datum response $q_{ss}t$, where q_{ss} is the steady state pitch rate;

(ii) the time lag, $T_{\theta 2}$, of the steady state flight path response relative to the steady state pitch attitude response.

By definition

$$U_{trim}\Delta\gamma(t) = \int (g\,\Delta n(t))\,dt. \tag{III.14.10}$$

On substitution of $\Delta n(t)$ from eqn. (III.12.5) it follows that

$$\begin{aligned} T_\gamma &= 2\zeta_{sp}/(\omega_0)_{sp} \\ &= 2\zeta_{sp}(c_w/U_{trim})\left[\overline{m}i_{yy}/(C_{L\alpha}H_m)\right]^{1/2} \end{aligned} \tag{III.14.11}$$

and, by reference to Fig. III.120,

$$\begin{aligned} T_{\theta 2} = (\Delta\alpha)_{ss}/q_{ss} &\simeq (U_{trim}/g)(C_W/C_{L\alpha}) \\ &= (c_w/U_{trim})(\overline{m}/C_{L\alpha}) \end{aligned} \tag{III.14.12}$$

because $(\Delta\alpha)_{ss} \simeq (\Delta n_{ss}C_W/C_{L\alpha})$ and $q_{ss} = (g\,\Delta n_{ss}/U_{trim})$.

Typically

$$T_\gamma = \text{O}[0.6\text{ s}], \qquad T_{\theta 2} = \text{O}[1.0\text{ s}]. \tag{III.14.13}$$

To control either flight path angle or pitch attitude angle the pilot pulls the stick back, or pushes the stick forward, equivalent to an elevator deflection $\Delta\eta_s$, followed, after a time delay, by a stick reversal, as shown in Fig. III.117. The parameters which influence the control effectiveness are

$$\text{flight path angle overshoot} \simeq q_{ss}T_\gamma, \qquad \text{(III.14.14)}$$

$$\text{pitch attitude angle drop-back} \simeq q_{ss}(T_{\theta 2} - T_\gamma). \qquad \text{(III.14.15)}$$

There is a conflict: the close control of the flight path angle requires a small T_γ (i.e. small ζ_{sp} and high H_m) whereas the close control of the pitch attitude requires a larger T_γ.

The maximum value of the conventional manoeuvre margin is usually related to the maximum value of $(\omega_0)_{sp}$ to ensure that the pitch attitude response is not too abrupt.

As already explained the ranges of acceptable conventional manoeuvre margins H_m and short period characteristics (ζ_{sp}, $(\omega_0)_{sp}$) have been obtained by correlating aeroplane characteristics with pilots' ratings; however, these broad correlations do not necessarily reflect the differences associated with particular flight tasks.

Turbulence imposes accelerations and changes pitch attitude and flight path angles.

Accelerations, or bumps, determine the ride quality. The pilot cannot influence the ride quality and so ride quality is not usually regarded as part of handling qualities, although bumpiness can degrade the flying qualities. As explained in sect. III.13, to reduce the number of severe bumps $C_{L\alpha}$ should be small, (W/S_w) should be large, ζ_{sp} should not be small, and $(\omega_0)_{sp}$ should not be small.

Pitch attitude and flight path angle response to turbulence should not be excessive. From sect. III.13, eqns. (III.13.17) and (III.13.18), the steady state responses to a step gust are

$$\begin{aligned}\Delta\gamma_{ss} &= \left(U_{trim}/c_w\right)\left(C_{L\alpha}/\overline{m}\right)\left(2\zeta_{ng}/(\omega_0)_{sp}\right)\Delta\alpha_g,\\ \Delta\theta_{ss} &= -\overline{K}_{\alpha g}\,\Delta\alpha_g.\end{aligned} \qquad \text{(III.14.16)}$$

Again a conflict: a large value of $(\omega_0)_{sp}$ (i.e. H_m) minimizes the gust flight path response $\Delta\gamma_{ss}$, whereas a small value of $(\omega_0)_{sp}$ minimizes the gust pitch attitude response $\Delta\theta_{ss}$.

Turning next to the important parameters of (stick displacement$/g$) and (stick force$/g$), particularly (stick force$/g$), these parameters should not be too small otherwise the controls would be oversensitive, nor too large otherwise the controls would be too heavy. Crudely, the maximum manoeuvring stick force will be the same for all types of aeroplane, within the range 70–250 N (= 18–56 lb_f); the stick force$/g$ will be smaller on a combat aeroplane, with its maximum load factor of 9, than on a transport aeroplane, with its maximum load factor of 2.5. The stick requires a small breakout force to move it. The corresponding maximum (conventional) stick displacement lies within the range, typically, 3–10 cm (1.5–4 in).

All aeroplanes must be trimmable with positive trim control (i.e. $\Delta\eta_{trim}/\Delta U_{trim} < 0$ with reasonable stick force$/\Delta U_{trim}$). The exception is the combat aeroplane at low supersonic speeds where the trim control parameters can go negative; there is no attempt to trim the combat aeroplane in this Mach number range but rather to accelerate through it to higher supersonic speeds where positive trim control returns. At low supersonic speeds the aeroplane must be controllable, which is practicable because control through the highly stable short period mode can contain the unstable phugoid mode.

For aeroplanes with positive trim and manoeuvre control the condition of positive phugoid stiffness will be automatically satisfied. Effectively the phugoid mode is an irrelevancy in any controlled flight because the phugoid would be incidentally suppressed. Pilots prefer aeroplanes to have positive phugoid damping in case of emergencies or distractions when their attention is taken away from their control tasks.

III.14.5 Longitudinal flying qualities requirements

The optimum handling qualities for one task may not coincide with the optimum handling qualities of another (e.g. combat and the approach). The flying qualities requirements aim to express the compromise(s) which ensure acceptable flying qualities across all phases of flight. The designer regards the requirements as minimum requirements which have to be satisfied; however, the designer may aim to optimize the flying qualities by designing to more demanding criteria developed by his organization over many years.

Both civil and military requirements are comprehensive, covering the limits of the flight envelope, probability of failures of systems, as well as the desirable piloting characteristics, all expressed in qualitative terms. In the military requirements quantitative limits on the main parameters are specified which are deemed to satisfy the requirements for all types of aeroplanes, including transport aeroplanes.

Some of the main longitudinal military requirements are briefly summarized.

(i) There shall be positive trim control. This condition is relaxed for combat aeroplanes at low supersonic speeds, where the maximum unstable gradients of the stick displacement and stick force with increase in Mach number are specified.

(ii) The phugoid oscillation shall not cause piloting difficulties; bounds on the phugoid damping ratio are specified.

Flying qualities:	*Level 1*	*Level 2*	*Level 3*
	$(\zeta)_{ph} > 0.04$	$(\zeta)_{ph} > 0.0$	Time to double amplitude > 55 s.

(iii) The bounds for the short period undamped frequency $(\omega_0)_{sp}$, are expressed in terms of $C_{L\alpha}/C_W$ ($\equiv n_{z\alpha}$) for constant CAP, or conventional manoeuvre margin, H_m, as shown in Fig. III.121. Because the CAP is equal to $((\omega_0)^2_{sp}C_{L\alpha}/C_W)$ the plot of $(\omega_0)_{sp}$ against $(C_W/C_{L\alpha})$ on a log–log scale is a straight line with gradient 0.5. Fig. III.121 indicates the flying quality levels 1, 2 and 3, for the three flight phases (categories A, B and C) and the four classes of aeroplane (I–IV).

(iv) The bounds on the short period damping are given in Table III.3.

(v) The stick force/g shall be within specified limits, essentially those given in the text.

There is a consensus of opinion that the upper boundaries for $(\omega_0)_{sp}$ in Fig. III.121 are too high, and that while the lower boundaries are satisfactory for pitch attitude control these lower boundaries may be unsatisfactory for flight path control.

For further reading on the topic of handling qualities, see refs. III.63–III.67.

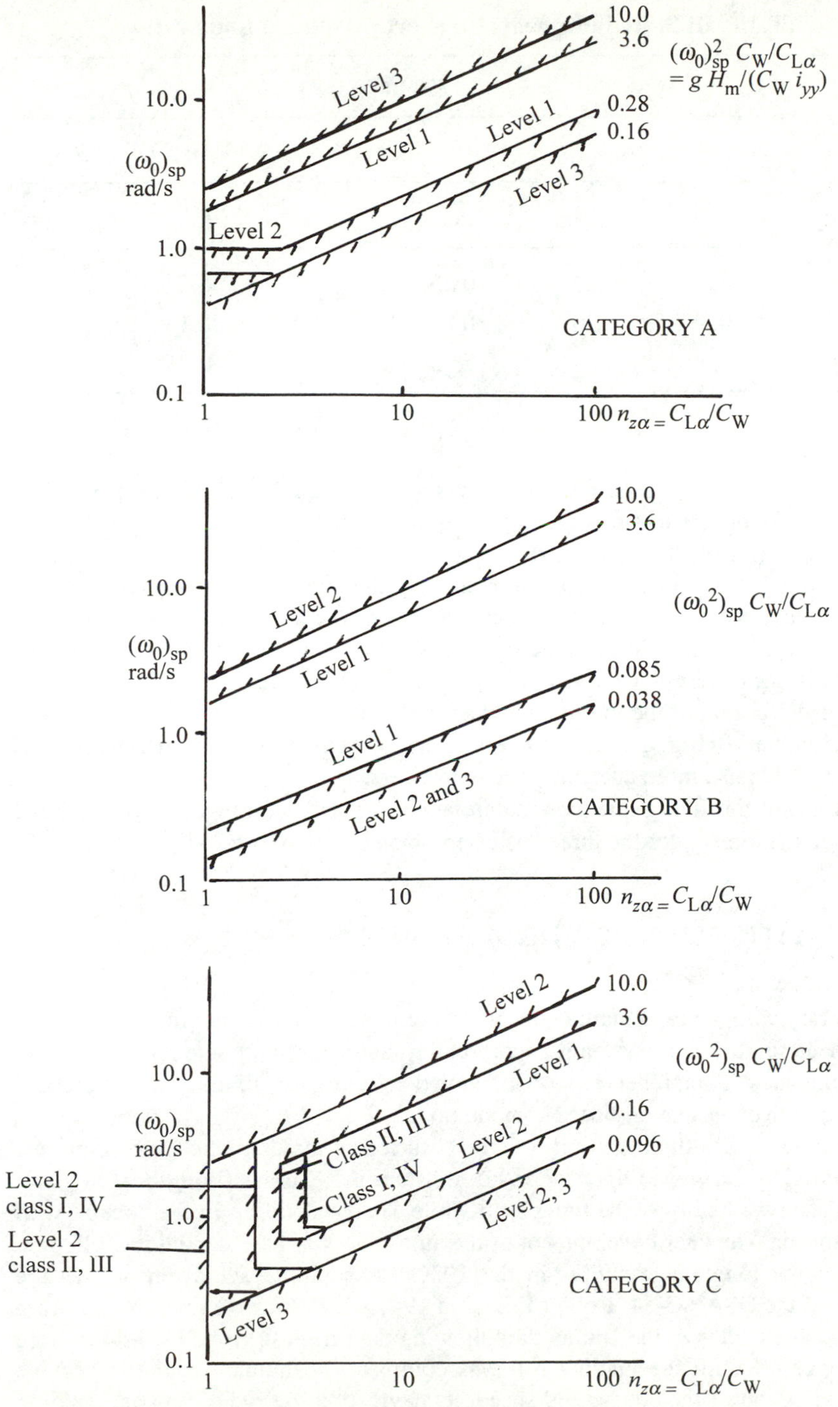

Fig. III.121. Flying quality requirements.

Table III.3. Requirements for short period damping ratio

	Flight phase					
	Level 1		Level 2		Level 3	
Category	min.	max.	min.	max.	min.	max.
A	0.35	1.3	0.25	2.0	0.1	
B	0.3	2.0	0.2	2.0	0.1	
C	0.5		0.35	2.0	0.25	

EXAMPLES III.37

1. Explain physically why speed instability does not occur on the 'back side of the drag curve' when flight path controls are not being implemented.
2. Confirm eqns. (III.14.11)–(III.14.13).
3. What are the differences in the requirements for the short period frequency for the different categories of flight phases? Comment on these differences.
4. What are the differences in the requirements for the short period frequency for the different classes of aeroplanes? Why are there these differences?
5. Relate the discussion of the longitudinal handling qualities criteria in sect. III.14.4 to the longitudinal flying qualities requirements presented in sect. III.14.5. (This exercise should raise more questions than it answers.)
6. On the basis of the flying qualities requirements, what is the range of conventional manoeuvre margin H_m for the three basic aeroplane configurations?

III.15 AUTOMATIC FLIGHT CONTROL SYSTEMS

III.15.1 Introduction

All contemporary aeroplanes contain elements of automatic control, ranging from simple auto-pilots to more advanced systems, incorporating auto-pilot and augmented stability systems, to the most comprehensive of integrated systems, combining auto-pilot and active controls with extensive on-board computation.

The birth of automatic flight control was the occasion of the dramatic flight along the Seine, near Paris, by Lawrence Sperry and his assistant in a Curtiss flying boat in 1914, when the assistant walked over the wing span while Sperry stood up in the cockpit with his hands in the air. The later development of the auto-pilot was an essential ingredient in the success of the long range flights in the 1930s. A supreme achievement was the historic flight of the USAF C-54 'Robert E.Lee' in 1947 which took off one evening from Newfoundland and landed in the UK on the following day; from the time the brakes were released for take-off until the landing roll was complete, no human hand touched the controls; the selection of the course and speed, its navigation via radio, flap and landing gear retraction and deployment, and final application of wheel brakes were accomplished automatically from a program of punched cards. As the technologies of aerodynamics, materials and power plants expanded from the 1950s, bringing rapid advances in performance, it became necessary to design an individual automatic control system for each aeroplane to optimize its flight dynamics and flying qualities throughout its flight envelope.

A primitive longitudinal automatic flight control system, involving the elevator, as shown in Fig. III.122, comprises:

(i) a sensor which responds to an aeroplane motion and generates an electrical signal proportional to that motion;
(ii) the conversion of the sensor electrical signal by an electric/electronic circuit to another electrical signal, known as the feedback control demand signal; the control law relates the sensor signal to the feedback control demand signal;
(iii) the transmission of the electrical feedback control signal to an electric motor which converts the electrical feedback control demand signal into a mechanical feedback control demand displacement;
(iv) a mechanical linkage to sum, or subtract, the mechanical displacements from the pilot's stick and the electric motor;
(v) the mechanical operation of the hydraulic actuator to give an elevator angle rotation which combines the pilot demand and the feedback control demand.

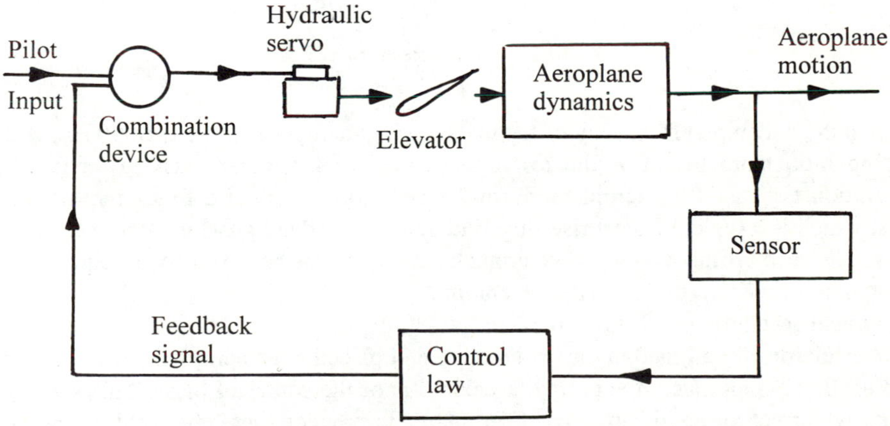

Fig. III.122. Principle of feedback system.

In a fly-by-wire system the electrical signal from the pilot's stick would be combined with the electrical feedback control demand signal prior to the electric motor which would then activate the hydraulic servo.

Open loop characteristics refer to the stability and response characteristics of the aeroplane when there is no feedback signal.

Closed loop characteristics refer to the stability and response characteristics of the aeroplane with the feedback in operation.

In this book the aim is to introduce some elementary concepts which underlie automatic flight control systems, but without recourse to standard feedback theory, and to ease the reader into the discipline of the analysis and design of automatic flight control systems as presented in refs. P.20–P.22.

III.15.2 Sensors

III.15.2.1 Linear accelerometer

Linear acceleration can be measured by an accelerometer, which is essentially a mass–spring–damper arrangement enclosed in a case, as sketched in Fig. III.123. When an absolute linear acceleration acts, aligned with the axis of the case, the reactive inertia force on the mass depresses, or extends, the spring and so the mass moves relative to the casing; this displacement can be measured electrically.

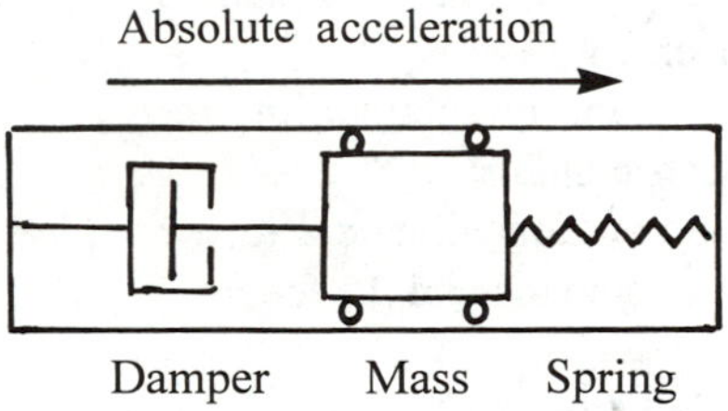

Fig. III.123. Linear accelerometer.

When the undamped frequency of the mass–spring–damper is more than 50 Hz, with a damping ratio more than 0.7, the response of the accelerometer mass to an imposed acceleration typical of an aeroplane normal acceleration (with rise times more than of 0.15 s, which is a typical fastest rise time due to a sharp edged gust) is effectively quasi-steady. Hence the time varying accelerometer reading can be taken to be equal to the instantaneous time varying normal acceleration.

A typical accelerometer mass is 0.14 kg (= 0.30 lb_m).

An accelerometer aligned in the *oz* direction and placed at an aeroplane centre of mass (see Fig. III.124) measures the normal acceleration of the centre of mass. This statement is literally correct for an idealized rigid aeroplane. In practice there are problems because an aeroplane structure is flexible; an accelerometer attached to the structure in the vicinity of the centre of mass picks up not only the normal acceleration of the centre of mass but also higher frequency accelerations associated with the vibrations of the flexible modes of the fuselage. It is necessary to filter out electrically these high frequency components from the sensor signal.

Two accelerometers can be used (Fig. III.124) both placed on the fuselage longitudinal axis, one forward, one aft, and both aligned in the *oz* direction. In principle half of the sum of the two accelerometers measures the normal acceleration of the centre of mass, whereas the difference of the two accelerometers, divided by the distance apart, measures the pitch acceleration but the effects of structural flexibility, especially fuselage bending, are now substantial.

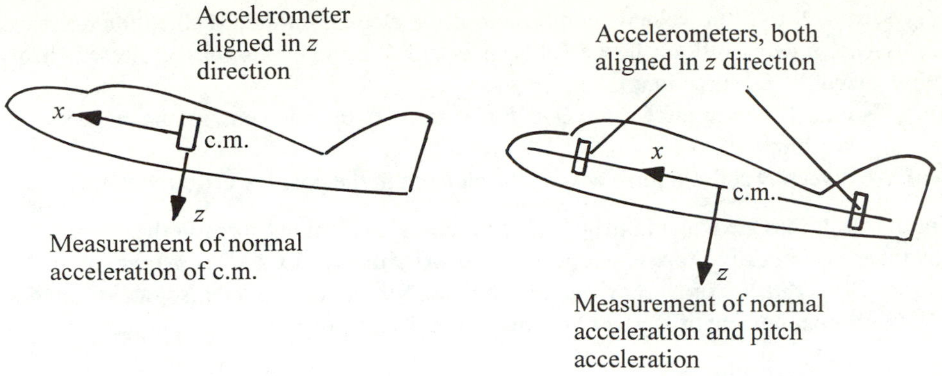

Fig. III.124. Application of linear accelerometer.

III.15.2.2 Gyroscope

The basic principle of the gyroscope is illustrated in Fig. III.125:

(i) consider a disc which is rotating rapidly at ω_1 rad/s about axis O1 normal to the disc;

(ii) suppose that this O1 axis rotates at rate ω_2 about axis O2;

(iii) consider an element of mass δm on the disc edge as it moves from A to B to C to D;

(iv) in the motion from A to B the element has an increasing velocity component (i.e. an acceleration) in the O1 direction due to the angular velocity ω_2; hence in the motion from A to B there must be a force acting on the element in the positive O1 direction;

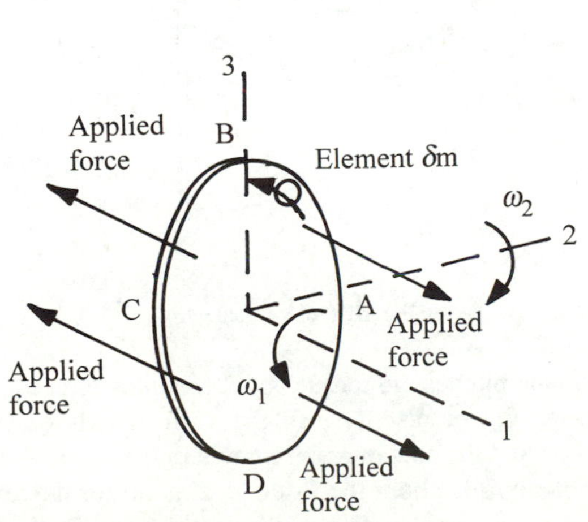

Fig. III.125. Forces on a gyroscope.

(v) from B to C the velocity component of the element in the O1 direction decreases (i.e. a deceleration); hence between B and C a force acts on the element in the negative O1 direction;

(vi) similarly, between C and D a force acts on the element in the negative O1 direction;

(vii) between D and A a force acts on the element in the positive O1 direction.

These four forces are equal in magnitude so there is no resultant force in the O1 direction but there is a negative torque about the third axis, the O3 axis. The magnitude of this torque (T_3) is directly proportional to the angular rotation, ω_2, to the disc rate of rotation, ω_1, and to the moment of inertia of the disc about its axis of rotation (I); in fact

$$T_3 = -I\omega_1\omega_2. \tag{III.15.1}$$

When a torque about the O3 axis is applied to a rotor spinning about the O1 axis, the axis of the rotor rotates, or precesses, about the O2 axis.

A vertical gyro is sketched in Fig. III.126. The rotating disc, spinning about a vertical axis, is held in a two gimbal arrangement with free pivots A, A_1, B, B_1, C and C_1 and fixed to the airframe along the fuselage longitudinal axis.

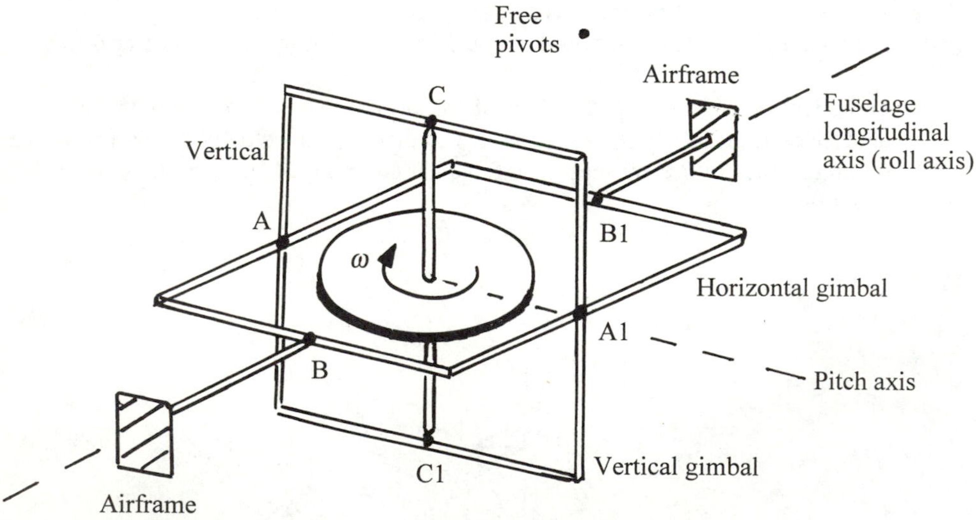

Fig. III.126. Vertical gyro.

(i) When the aeroplane pitches, no torque about the pitch axis can be transmitted to the rotor disc through the pivots A, A_1 so the vertical axis of spin does not precess about the roll axis and the axis of spin remains in the vertical direction.

(ii) When the aeroplane rolls about the fuselage axis no torque about the fuselage axis can be transmitted to the rotor disc through the pivots B, B_1 so the vertical axis of spin does not precess about the pitch axis, so again the axis of spin remains vertical.

(iii) When the aeroplane yaws about a vertical axis a torque about the vertical axis moves the horizontal gimbal, but no torque can be transmitted to the rotor through the pivots C, C_1.

As the aeroplane rotates about all three axes the spin axis remains in the vertical direction. The angle between the horizontal gimbal and the airframe is the bank angle, while the angle between the vertical gimbal and the airframe is the pitch angle; these angles can be measured.

With the above arrangement the rotor is maintained at constant speed, of the order of 600 Hz by an electric motor. Drift occurs due to friction in the pivots. There is automatic monitoring and correction to keep the axis of spin vertical, using mercury switches.

A vertical gyro will supply the pitch attitude and bank angle data for the attitude director on the instrument panel. A typical self-contained unit complete with instrument dial has approximate dimensions $7.5 \times 7.5 \times 20$ cm, with mass approximately 1.5 kg.

A directional gyro is a similar two gimbal arrangement with the spin axis aligned along the fuselage axis; changes in heading angle are measured and transmitted to the horizontal situation indicator on the instrument panel.

Another type of gyro is the rate gyro which has only one gimbal. As sketched in Fig. III.127 the rotor spins about the vertical (oz) axis in a vertical gimbal which is restrained by a linear spring plus damper from rotating about the fuselage axis. When the aeroplane pitches with pitch rate q about the oy axis, the (gyroscopic) torque about the ox axis is reacted by the restraining spring. By ensuring that the response time of the effective gyro mass–spring–damper system is extremely small, the instantaneous extension of the spring can be taken to be proportional to $q(t)$. A voltage proportional to the spring displacement can be generated by a potentiometer.

Separate rate gyros are needed to measure pitch rate, roll rate and yaw rate; these are usually packaged in one unit.

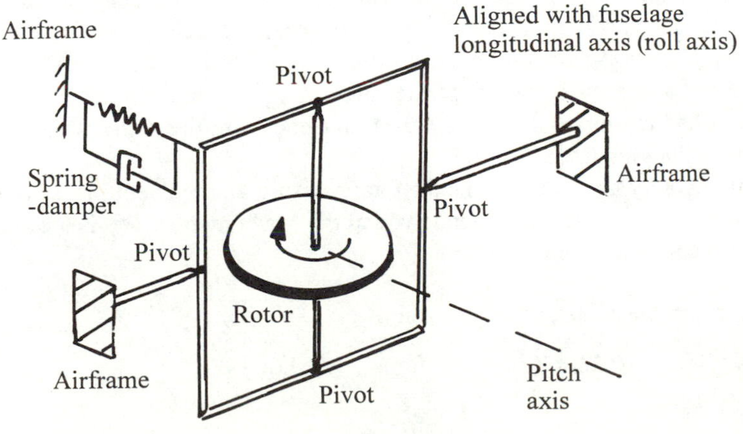

Fig. III.127. Rate gyro.

III.15.2.3 Air speed

For relative aeroplane air speed (i.e. aeroplane speed relative to the ambient air) and relative Mach number, the primary sensor is the pitot static tube as shown in Fig. III.128, which measures total pressure p_0, and static (ambient) pressure, p_{at}.

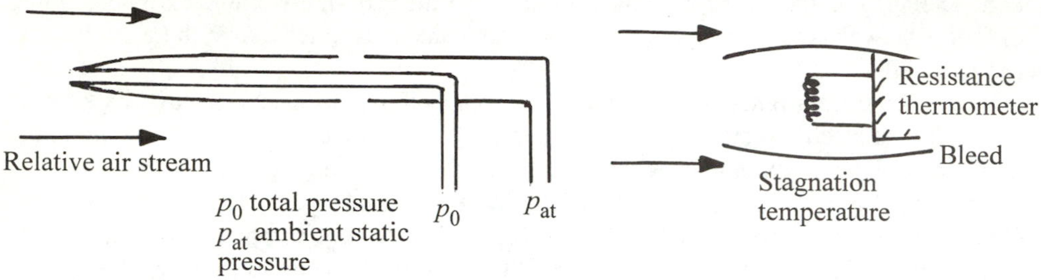

Fig. III.128. Pitot-static tube, thermometer probe.

The measurement of p_{at} in a barometer relative to sea level static pressure is the basis for a conventional altimeter.

At low Mach numbers

$$p_0 - p_{at} = \tfrac{1}{2}\rho_{at}U_{TAS}^2 = \tfrac{1}{2}(\rho_{at})_{sl}U_{EAS}^2, \qquad \text{(III.15.2)}$$

where U_{TAS} is the true (relative) air speed and U_{EAS} is the equivalent (relative) air speed. U_{TAS} is equal to the absolute velocity in the absence of winds.

Traditionally the pressures p_0 and p_{at} have been fed to either side of a diaphragm in a barometer type device, the pressure difference $(p_0 - p_{at})$ is measured, calibrated at sea level, and displayed to the pilot on the speed indicator as the indicated air speed, denoted by U_{IAS}. At low Mach numbers at all altitudes the indicated air speed, U_{IAS}, is equal to the equivalent air speed, U_{EAS}, apart from instrument errors. As Mach numbers increase the indicated air speed and equivalent airspeed diverge; at Mach 0.7 at sea level U_{IAS} is approximately 17 m/s ($\simeq$ 8.5 knots) greater than U_{EAS}; at Mach 2 at altitude U_{IAS} is approximately 160 m/s ($\simeq$ 80 knots) greater than U_{EAS}. In the early days of high speed flight the pilot had to work out his equivalent airspeed from the indicated air speed and altitude using calibration tables.

With contemporary air data systems the total pressure and ambient pressure acting on the pilot-static tube are measured separately, and the Mach number M_∞ is then calculated by an on-board computer from

$$\begin{aligned} p_0/p_{at} &= [1+0.2M_\infty^2]^{3.5} && \text{for } M_\infty < 1.0 \\ &= [1+0.2M_2^2]^{3.5} && \text{for } M_\infty > 1.0\ (M_2 < 1) \end{aligned} \qquad \text{(III.15.3)}$$

where

$$M_\infty^2 = \left[1+\left[36/(7M_2^2-1)\right]\right]/7.$$

The subsonic formula is the standard isentropic relationship between stagnation pressure and static pressure. The supersonic formula takes into account the change in Mach number across the bow shock wave in front of the pitot tube.

The stagnation temperature T_0 is measured by a resistance thermometer enclosed in an open-sided tube pointing into the relative flow field, as shown in Fig. III.128. The ambient temperature is then determined from

$$T_0/T_{at} = [1 + 0.2M_\infty^2]. \tag{III.15.4}$$

Finally

$$U_{TAS} = \text{const}\, M_\infty T_{at}^{1/2}$$
$$U_{EAS} = U_{TAS}\left[(p_{at}/T_{at})/(p_{at}/T_{at})_{sl}\right]^{1/2}. \tag{III.15.5}$$

With such an air data system the altitude, Mach number and equivalent air speed are displayed to the pilot and fed as inputs into the automatic flight control system.

III.15.2.4 Airspeed direction detector (ADD)

Angle of incidence is usually measured by two spring loaded vanes, one on each side of the front fuselage in the region of the fuselage nose. A combination of the lifts on the two vanes is calibrated to give the angle of incidence; two vanes are needed to eliminate the interference effect of sideslip. Vanes may have rather poor response characteristics, are prone to icing problems, and susceptible to handling damage and to bird strikes.

Angle of incidence can also be measured by a yawmeter, as shown in Fig. III.129. The differential pressure difference $(p_A - p_B)$ across the 'inclined' tubes is proportional to the angle of incidence and depends on the total pressure p_0; the angle of incidence is computed from $(p_A - p_B)$ and p_0. In fact the pitot tube probe will carry two further inclined tubes, p_C and p_D, as shown in Fig. III.129, which give the angle of sideslip. In general both angle of incidence and angle of sideslip are determined from $(p_A - p_B)$, $(p_C - p_D)$ and p_0; the calibration needs to be done with care. There are small time lags between the change in pressures at the probe nose and the measurement transducer, which need to be included in the analysis of any feedback signal.

Alternatively fixed vanes incorporating yawmeters have been proposed.

As explained later, the angle of incidence is not normally used as a primary feedback variable in automatic flight control systems.

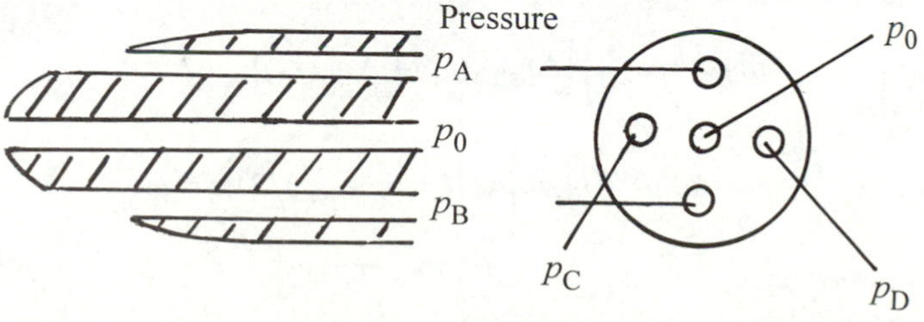

Fig. III.129. Yawmeter.

More detailed coverage of aeroplane instrumentation is given by Kranenborg (ref. III.68), Andresen (ref. III.69), and Demiel (ref. III.70).

III.15.3 Longitudinal stability augmentation

The short period stability and response characteristics have been related to the stiffness, or undamped frequency, and the damping, or damping ratio, of the short period mode. These parameters vary over the flight envelope with altitude and forward speed and so affect the handling qualities and gust responses. On a conventional aeroplane the short period undamped frequency can be kept within bounds by a restriction on the range of location of the centre of mass. However, at low speed, or at high altitude, the short period damping can become small; to restore acceptable handling characteristics the damping can be increased by a stability augmentation system.

In this case the sensor is a pitch rate gyro, which generates a signal proportional to $q(t)$; the control law converts the sensor signal to a feedback elevator demand signal $\Delta\eta_{stab}(t)$ which depends on $q(t)$; see Fig. III.130.

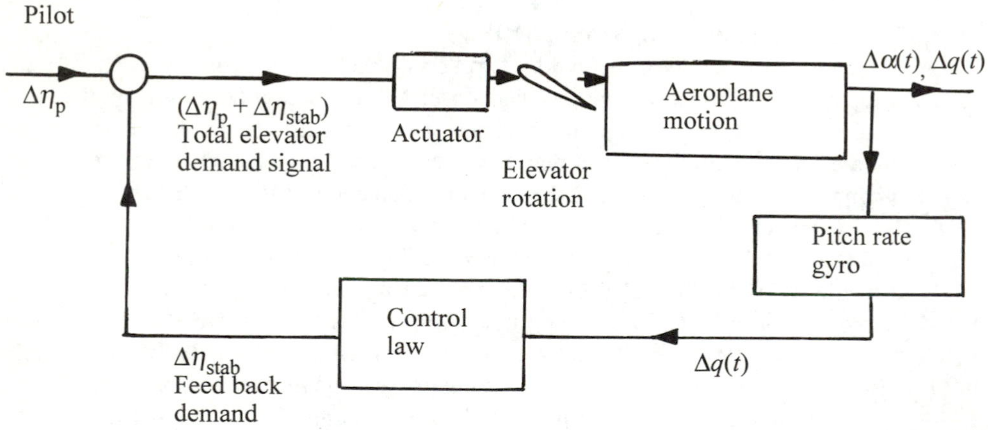

Fig. III.130. Stability augmentation system.

The equation for the short period response in non-dimensional form, from eqn. (III.11.16), is

$$[\bar{D} + C_{L\alpha}]\Delta\alpha(\bar{t}_d) - \bar{q}(\bar{t}_d) \simeq -\left[\left(C_{L\dot{\eta}}/2\bar{m}\right)\bar{D} + C_{L\eta}\right]\left[\Delta\eta_{stab}(\bar{t}_d) + \Delta\eta_p(\bar{t}_d)\right],$$

$$\left[\left((-C_{m\dot{\alpha}})/2\right)\bar{D} - \bar{m}C_{m\alpha}\right]\Delta\alpha(t_d) + \left[i_{yy}\bar{D} + \left((-C_{mq})/2\right)\right]\bar{q}(\bar{t}_d) \simeq \left[\left(C_{m\dot{\eta}}/2\right)\bar{D} + \bar{m}C_{m\eta}\right]\left[\Delta\eta_{stab}(\bar{t}_d) + \Delta\eta_p(\bar{t}_d)\right] \quad \text{(III.15.6)}$$

where

$$\Delta\eta_{stab}(\bar{t}_d) = \text{elevator demand from feedback signal}$$
$$\Delta\eta_p(\bar{t}_d) = \text{elevator demand from pilot stick.}$$

Consider first an idealized control law

$$\Delta\eta_{stab}(t) = \mathcal{K}\, q(t) = \overline{\mathcal{K}}\, \bar{q}(\bar{t}_d)/\bar{m} \tag{III.15.7}$$

since $\bar{t}_d = t(U_{trim}/c_w\bar{m})$, $q(t) = d\theta(t)/dt$, $\bar{q}(\bar{t}_d) = d\theta(\bar{t}_d)/d\bar{t}_d$, $\mathcal{K}$ is the gain and $\overline{\mathcal{K}} = \mathcal{K}\, U_{trim}/c_w$.

On substitution of eqn. (III.15.7), eqns. (III.15.6) become

$$[\bar{D} + C_{L\alpha}]\Delta\alpha(\bar{t}_d) - \bar{q}(\bar{t}_d) = -\left[\left(C_{L\dot{\eta}}/2\bar{m}\right)\bar{D} + C_{L\eta}\right]\Delta\eta_p(\bar{t}_d),$$

$$\left[\left((-C_{m\dot{\alpha}})/2\right)\bar{D} - \bar{m}C_{m\alpha}\right]\Delta\alpha(t_d) + \left[i_{yy}\bar{D} + \left((-C_{mq})/2\right) + \overline{\mathcal{K}}(-C_{m\eta})\right]\bar{q}(\bar{t}_d)$$
$$= \left[\left(C_{m\dot{\eta}}/2\right)D + \bar{m}C_{m\eta}\right]\Delta\eta_p(t_d) \tag{III.15.8}$$

neglecting $(\overline{\mathcal{K}}C_{L\dot{\eta}}/2\bar{m}^2)$, and taking $\overline{\mathcal{K}}C_{L\eta}/\bar{m} \ll 1$ and $\overline{\mathcal{K}}C_{m\dot{\eta}}/2\bar{m} \ll i_{yy}$.

The effect of the stability augmentation system is to increase the effective value of the pitch damping derivative,

$$\left((-C_{mq})/2\right) \to \left[\left((-C_{mq})/2\right) + \overline{\mathcal{K}}(-C_{m\eta})\right]. \tag{III.15.9}$$

Typically,

$$(-C_{m\eta}) = O[0.2]\left((-C_{mq})/2\right),$$

then taking,

$$\overline{\mathcal{K}} = 5.0 \tag{III.15.10}$$

the effective value of $(-C_{mq})$ is doubled, which increases the short period damping by approximately 40% and the short period stiffness, at sea level, by approximately 20% (i.e. an increase in undamped frequency of 10%).

To check whether the value of $\overline{\mathcal{K}}$ given by eqn. (III.15.10) is practicable, if

$$\Delta\theta(t) = \Delta\theta_0 \sin 2t \tag{III.15.11}$$

then, from eqn. (III.15.7)

$$\Delta\eta_{stab}(t) = \left(\overline{\mathcal{K}}c_w/U_{trim}\right)2\,\Delta\theta_0\cos 2t \simeq 0.3\,\Delta\theta_0\cos 2t. \tag{III.15.12}$$

The amplitude of the elevator angle due to the augmentation system is approximately one third of the amplitude of the pitch response, which is acceptable.

In practice, there is a lag between the sensor first measuring a pitch rate response and the elevator rotation, primarily associated with the lag in the hydraulic jack. Combining a simple first order lag, representing the hydraulic actuator lag, with the feedback gain, the relationship between $\Delta\eta_{stab}(t)$ and $q(t)$ is

$$(D + A_{act})\,\Delta\eta_{stab}(t) = A_{act}\mathcal{K}\, q(t). \tag{III.15.13}$$

A time constant (= $1/A_{\text{act}}$) equal to 0.1 s is typical.

In non-dimensional terms, eqn. (III.15.13) is

$$(\overline{\mathrm{D}} + \overline{A}_{\text{act}})\, \Delta\eta_{\text{stab}}(\bar{t}_{\text{d}}) = (\overline{A}_{\text{act}}\, \overline{\mathcal{K}}/\overline{m})\bar{q}(\bar{t}_{\text{d}}) \tag{III.15.14}$$

where $\overline{A}_{\text{act}} = A_{\text{act}}\overline{m}\, c_{\text{w}}/U_{\text{trim}} = \text{O}[50]$.

Eqns. (III.15.8) and (III.15.14) couple the short period response with the actuator response, namely

$$\begin{aligned}
&[\overline{\mathrm{D}} + C_{\mathrm{L}\alpha}]\, \Delta\alpha(\bar{t}_{\text{d}}) - \bar{q}(\bar{t}_{\text{d}}) + \left[\left(C_{\mathrm{L}\dot{\eta}}/2\overline{m}\right)\overline{\mathrm{D}} + C_{\mathrm{L}\eta}\right] \Delta\eta_{\text{stab}}(\bar{t}_{\text{d}}) \\
&\qquad = -\left[\left(C_{\mathrm{L}\dot{\eta}}/2\overline{m}\right)\overline{\mathrm{D}} + C_{\mathrm{L}\eta}\right] \Delta\eta_{\text{p}}(\bar{t}_{\text{d}}), \\
&\left[\left((-C_{m\dot{\alpha}})/2\right)\overline{\mathrm{D}} - \overline{m}C_{m\alpha}\right] \Delta\alpha(\bar{t}_{\text{d}}) + \left[i_{yy}\overline{\mathrm{D}} + \left((-C_{mq})/2\right)\right]\bar{q}(\bar{t}_{\text{d}}) \\
&\qquad -\left[\left(C_{m\dot{\eta}}/2\right)\overline{\mathrm{D}} + \overline{m}C_{m\eta}\right] \Delta\eta_{\text{stab}}(\bar{t}_{\text{d}}) \\
&\qquad = \left[\left(C_{m\dot{\eta}}/2\right)\overline{\mathrm{D}} + \overline{m}C_{m\eta}\right] \Delta\eta_{\text{p}}(\bar{t}_{\text{d}}), \\
&\qquad -\left(\overline{A}_{\text{act}}\overline{\mathcal{K}}/\overline{m}\right)\bar{q}(\bar{t}_{\text{d}}) + [\overline{\mathrm{D}} + \overline{A}_{\text{act}}]\, \Delta\eta_{\text{stab}}(\bar{t}_{\text{d}}) = 0.
\end{aligned} \tag{III.15.15}$$

The stability characteristic equation of eqns. (III.15.15) is

$$\begin{aligned}
&[\bar{\lambda} + \overline{A}_{\text{act}}]\Big[i_{yy}\bar{\lambda}^2 + \left(i_{yy}C_{\mathrm{L}\alpha} + (-C_{m\dot{\alpha}})/2 + (-C_{mq})/2\right)\bar{\lambda} \\
&\qquad + \left(\overline{m}(-C_{m\alpha}) + C_{\mathrm{L}\alpha}\left((-C_{mq})/2\right)\right)\Big] \\
&\qquad + \left[(-C_{m\eta})\,\lambda + (-C_{m\eta})C_{\mathrm{L}\alpha}\right]\overline{A}_{\text{act}}\overline{\mathcal{K}} = 0.
\end{aligned} \tag{III.15.16}$$

neglecting small terms.

The characteristic equation, eqn. (III.15.16), can be analysed by substituting typical numbers:

$$i_{yy} = 1.5, \quad \overline{m} = 150, \quad C_{\mathrm{L}\alpha} = 5.0, \quad (-C_{m\alpha}) = 1.0,$$
$$(-C_{m\dot{\alpha}}) = 12.0, \quad (-C_{mq}) = 20.0, \quad (-C_{m\eta}) = 2.5,$$

actuator rise time of 0.1 s, $\overline{A}_{\text{act}} = 50$.

The characteristic equation, eqn. (III.15.16), becomes on factorization for various values of the gain $\overline{\mathcal{K}}$:

$$\begin{aligned}
\overline{\mathcal{K}} &= 0, \quad (\bar{\lambda} + 50)\ (1.5\bar{\lambda}^2 + 23.5\bar{\lambda} + 200) = 0 \\
\overline{\mathcal{K}} &= 2, \quad (\bar{\lambda} + 45)\ (1.5\bar{\lambda}^2 + 31.0\bar{\lambda} + 221) = 0 \\
\overline{\mathcal{K}} &= 4, \quad (\bar{\lambda} + 38)\ (1.5\bar{\lambda}^2 + 41.5\bar{\lambda} + 329) = 0 \\
\overline{\mathcal{K}} &= 6, \quad (\bar{\lambda} + 9.5)(1.5\bar{\lambda}^2 + 83.0\bar{\lambda} + 1447) = 0.
\end{aligned} \tag{III.15.17}$$

When $\overline{\mathcal{K}}$ is zero there is no feedback signal and the actuator mode and short period mode are uncoupled; the quadratic bracket denotes the unaugmented (open loop) short period mode, the linear bracket denotes the pure actuator mode.

As the gain $\overline{\mathcal{K}}$ is increased the actuator mode time constant decreases while the short period damping and stiffness increase; effectively there is a transfer of damping from the actuator mode to the short period mode; the energy for increasing the damping of the aeroplane comes from the energy in the actuator system. When $\overline{\mathcal{K}}$ is equal to 4 both the (closed loop) short period damping and stiffness are increased by approximately 80% relative to their open loop values.

When the gain $\overline{\mathcal{K}}$ is increased beyond a critical value the system behaviour degenerates, becoming unacceptable, as seen when $\overline{\mathcal{K}}$ is equal to 6. As $\overline{\mathcal{K}}$ increases the response time of the actuator mode decreases while the response time of the short period mode increases; when these two response times come close together there is a strong coupling in which both the actuator mode and the short period mode lose their identities.

The critical value of $\overline{\mathcal{K}}$ decreases with increase in the actuator lag. In the above example an actuator with a time of constant of 0.2 s would be completely unacceptable; only a small gain would be feasible with limited increase in the short period damping.

Fast acting actuators are essential otherwise a significant increase in short period damping cannot be achieved.

In contemporary systems the gain $\overline{\mathcal{K}}$ will be scheduled in that its value will be changed, by computer, depending on altitude, equivalent air speed and Mach number.

A stability augmentation system is usually a low authority system which implies only one channel of information (i.e. one sensor, one feedback control signal, one actuator; no duplication of hydraulic power) and the amplitude of $\Delta\eta_{stab}$ would be limited to within approximately ±3°. If the augmentation system fails the consequences would not be catastrophic; the aeroplane would revert to its unaugmented, open loop, state which should be safe to fly.

A stability augmentation system can modify the flying qualities.

(i) The closed loop stability of the aeroplane, assuming no change in forward speed, comprises two modes: a faster actuator mode and a slower closed loop, short period mode.

(ii) The actuator mode affects the initial stages of the transient response, possibly reducing the initial pitch acceleration and increasing the lag in the build-up of the normal acceleration, thus modifying the pilot's sensing cues for anticipating the subsequent response.

(iii) The above stability augmentation system increases not only the short period damping but also the short period stiffness. And so the steady state response is altered; effectively the stick displacement/g and hence the stick force/g are reduced. If this steady state change is unacceptable a 'wash-out' term can be included in the feedback loop to gradually reduce the feedback signal to zero within a time comparable with the open loop undamped period of the short period mode. With wash-out, the steady state response $(= \Delta n_{ss}/(-\Delta\eta_p))$ is the same for both open loop and closed loop systems. Wash-out also helps prevent saturation which occurs when the elevator demand $(\eta_{\text{trim}} + \Delta\eta_{\text{p}} + \Delta\eta_{\text{stab}})$ exceeds the available elevator angle and the elevator comes up against the stops.

(iv) With wash-out the stability augmentation system only affects the transient response, not the steady state response. However, the wash-out introduces yet another degree of freedom which, for example, changes the cubic characteristic equation, eqns. (III.15.16) and (III.15.17), into a higher order characteristic equation. The full implications of the additional modal response on the flying qualities have to be analysed.

(v) The ride quality needs to be checked; changes in the transient response can affect the peak accelerations to sharp edged gusts and the character of the tuned gusts.

EXAMPLES III.38

1. Check that the approximations following eqns. (III.15.8) and (III.15.16) are reasonable.
2. If the damping and the stiffness are both increased by 60% what is the percentage increase in the damping ratio?
3. The text following eqn. (III.15.9) states: 'the effective value of $((-C_{mq})/2)$ is doubled, which increases the short period damping by approximately 40% and the short period stiffness, at sea level, by approximately 20%'. Prove this statement. How is this statement modified at 11 km altitude?
4. Determine the critical value of $\overline{\mathcal{K}}$ with the above typical values for an actuator time constant of 0.2 s. (Solve the cubic by finding the real root by trial and error.)
5. What is the effect of the stability augmentation system, eqn. (III.15.7), on the parameter A_{nw} in the PSD method for
   (i) pitch attitude gust response
   (ii) flight path angle gust response?

III.15.4 Auto-pilot systems

Auto-pilot systems, interfacing with navigation systems, were introduced initially to reduce pilot fatigue during long flights. Contemporary auto-pilots not only fulfil this role but also interface with on-board computers to minimize fuel consumption during climb and cruise for a commercial aeroplane, or to minimize time to climb for a combat aeroplane, or to land in conditions of poor visibility.

By definition an auto-pilot can be switched in, or out, by the human pilot. It is mandatory that the human pilot be able to fly the aeroplane safely with the auto-pilot switched out, albeit sometimes less effectively.

The auto-pilot is an outer feedback loop, around an inner loop comprising a stability augmentation system, as sketched in Fig. III.131. However, for the present illustrative purposes the inner loop is not included.

The case of an auto-pilot to hold a steady flight path in the presence of vertical gusts is considered.

Perturbations from a designated level flight path can be measured in a number of ways:

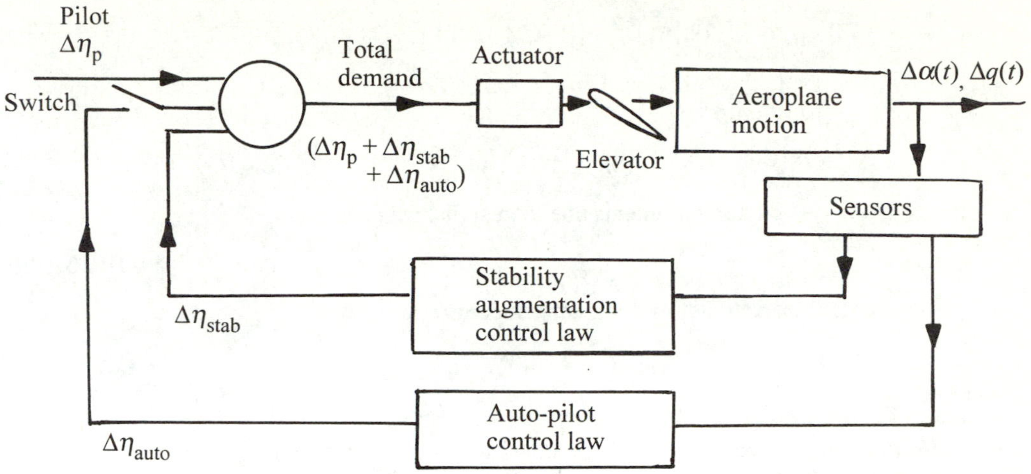

Fig. III.131. Auto-pilot loop.

(i) Height variations can be taken from the barometric pressure. A constant barometric pressure does not necessarily mean constant height, but from an air traffic point of view all aeroplanes in the same vicinity will experience the same error so any height difference between traffic lanes will be maintained.

(ii) Height variations can be extracted directly from the navigation system.

(iii) The perturbation flight path angle $\Delta\gamma(t)$ can be obtained from a dedicated sensor system comprising two linear accelerometers located at the centre of mass, one aligned in the oz direction, measuring $A_z(t)$, the other aligned in the ox direction, measuring $A_x(t)$. Then,

$$U(t) = \int A_x(t)\,dt, \qquad \Delta\gamma(t) = \int \big(A_z(t)/U(t)\big)\,dt. \qquad \text{(III.15.18)}$$

Integrations can be carried out electronically virtually instantaneously.

The non-dimensional equations of perturbed motion relative to trimmed level flight in terms of $\Delta\bar{u}(\bar{t}_d)$, $\Delta\theta(\bar{t}_d)$ and $\Delta\gamma(\bar{t}_d)$, from eqns. (III.11.4), with inputs $\Delta\eta_{auto}(\bar{t}_d)$ the auto-pilot demand, $\Delta\text{Th}(\bar{t}_d)$ and gust disturbances, are:

$$[\bar{\text{D}} + C_{DU}]\Delta\bar{u}(\bar{t}_d) + C_{D\alpha}\,\Delta\theta(\bar{t}_d) + (C_W - C_{D\alpha})\Delta\gamma(\bar{t}_d)$$
$$= C_W\,\Delta\text{Th}(\bar{t}_d)/W - \text{drag forces due to gust disturbances,}$$

$$C_{LU}\,\Delta\bar{u}(\bar{t}_d) + C_{L\alpha}\,\Delta\theta(\bar{t}_d) - (\bar{\text{D}} + C_{L\alpha})\Delta\gamma(\bar{t}_d)$$
$$= -\Big[\big(C_{L\dot{\eta}}/2\bar{m}\big)\bar{\text{D}} + C_{L\eta}\Big]\Delta\eta_{auto}(\bar{t}_d)$$
$$- \text{lift forces due to gust disturbances}$$

$$- \overline{m} C_{mU} \, \Delta\bar{u}(\bar{t}_d) + \left[i_{yy}\overline{\mathrm{D}}^2 + \left(((-C_{mq})/2) + ((-C_{m\dot{\alpha}})/2) \right)\overline{\mathrm{D}} + \overline{m}(-C_{m\alpha}) \right] \Delta\theta(\bar{t}_d)$$
$$- \left[((-C_{m\dot{\alpha}})/2)\overline{\mathrm{D}} + \overline{m}(-C_{m\alpha}) \right] \Delta\gamma(\bar{t}_d)$$
$$= \overline{m}(C_W \, \Delta\mathrm{Th}(\bar{t}_d)/W) l_{\mathrm{Th}} + \left[(C_{m\dot{\eta}}/2)\overline{\mathrm{D}} + \overline{m} C_{m\eta} \right] \Delta\eta_{\mathrm{auto}}(\bar{t}_d)$$

+ pitching moments due to gust disturbances.

(III.15.19)

Consider an idealized auto-pilot feedback control law

$$\Delta\mathrm{Th}(t) = 0, \qquad \Delta\eta_{\mathrm{auto}}(t) = +\mathcal{K}_\gamma \, \Delta\gamma(t), \tag{III.15.20}$$

where $\mathcal{K}_\gamma$ is the gain.

The plus sign in eqn. (III.15.20) is consistent with a positive upward change in the flight path angle requiring a nose-down pitching moment to reduce the angle of incidence, to decrease lift, and to return the aeroplane to its initial height.

It would be expected that, for practical elevator deflections,

$$\mathcal{K}_\gamma < 1. \tag{III.15.21}$$

On substitution of the feedback given by eqn. (III.15.20) into eqn. (III.15.19), the flight path response is given by

$$\Big[\overline{\mathrm{D}} \Big[i_{yy}\overline{\mathrm{D}}^2 + \left[i_{yy} C_{\mathrm{L}\alpha} + ((-C_{m\dot{\alpha}})/2) + ((-C_{mq})/2) \right] \overline{\mathrm{D}}$$
$$+ \left[\overline{m}(-C_{m\alpha}) + C_{\mathrm{L}\alpha}(-C_{mq})/2 \right] \Big]$$
$$+ \; \mathcal{K}_\gamma \overline{m} C_{\mathrm{L}\alpha}(-C_{m\eta}) \Big] \Delta\gamma(\bar{t}_d)$$
$$= \text{gust input,} \tag{III.15.22}$$

which is obtained from the lift and pitching moment equations, neglecting any changes in forward speed (i.e. neglecting Δu) and omitting small terms. With typical numbers eqn. (III.15.22) is

$$\left[\overline{\mathrm{D}}[1.5\,\overline{\mathrm{D}}^2 + 23.5\,\overline{\mathrm{D}} + 200] + \mathcal{K}_\gamma 1500 \right] \Delta\gamma(\bar{t}_d) = \text{gust input.} \tag{III.15.23}$$

By reference to eqn. (III.13.17) when $\mathcal{K}_\gamma$ is zero,

the steady state response $(\Delta\gamma)_{ss}$ to a ramp-step vertical gust of magnitude $\Delta\alpha_{gs}$ is proportional to $\Delta\alpha_{gs}$.

But when $\mathcal{K}_\gamma$ is non-zero it is inferred from eqns. (III.13.10) and (III.13.16) and eqns. (III.15.22) and (III.15.23) that the steady state response $(\Delta\gamma)_{ss}$ to a ramp-step vertical gust of magnitude $\Delta\alpha_{gs}$ is proportional to $\mathrm{D}\,\Delta\alpha_{gs}/(1500\,\mathcal{K}_\gamma)$, which is zero. Thus with perturbation flight path angle feedback the steady state flight path response is zero for all non-zero $\mathcal{K}_\gamma$, which is a design objective; an increase in $\mathcal{K}_\gamma$ would be expected to decrease the transient response to ramp gusts, improving the auto-pilot efficiency.

There is, however, a problem with the stability responses of eqn. (III.15.23). Solving for the characteristic roots:

$$
\begin{aligned}
\text{when} \quad \mathcal{K}_\gamma &= 0, & \lambda(1.5\lambda^2 + 23.5\lambda + 200) &= 0 \\
\mathcal{K}_\gamma &= 0.6, & (\lambda + 8.5)(1.5\lambda^2 + 10.75\lambda + 106) &= 0 \\
\mathcal{K}_\gamma &= 1.2, & (\lambda + 12.5)(1.5\lambda^2 + 4.75\lambda + 144) &= 0.
\end{aligned}
\tag{III.15.24}
$$

As the auto-pilot gain $\mathcal{K}_\gamma$ is increased to reduce the magnitude of $\Delta\gamma(t)$ the damping of the short period mode decreases, going unstable at higher values of $\mathcal{K}_\gamma$. This damping can be restored by including a term proportional to $\Delta\dot{\theta}(t)$ in the control law.

There is a long period stability mode, namely the speed stability mode, as described in sect. III.14.3, which involves slow perturbations in speed and pitch angle about a virtually steady flight path. To increase the damping of this mode some thrust feedback is necessary.

Other longitudinal auto-pilot modes include:

- —pitch attitude hold;
- —long range cruise which interfaces with the navigation system, minimizes fuel consumption and avoids weather hazards;
- —climb which may minimize fuel consumption, or minimize noise levels at low altitudes, or minimize time to climb;
- —descent;
- —terrain following.

Automatic landing systems use not only on-board systems but also ground based systems (e.g. marker beacons to indicate distance down the glide path to nominal touchdown, ILS beam).

Automatic landing systems are certified into a number of categories which are defined in terms of the ceiling for vertical visibility (DH is the vertical decision height) and the runway visual range (RVR) as specified by the control tower at the time of landing.

Category I DH = 60 m, RVR = 800 m,

Category II DH = 30 m, RVR = 400 m.

For both Categories I and II the aeroplane is steered automatically towards the centre line of the runway; at the decision height the pilot takes over for a manual landing, the landing is either executed or aborted with a go-around to another attempt at landing or diversion to another airport.

Category IIIa—allows for automatic approach and flare to touch down, the pilot takes over control at touchdown, RVR should be 200 m.

Category IIIb—allows for automatic flare, touchdown and roll-out with the pilot taking over control some distance down the runway, RVR should be 80 m.

Category IIIc—allows for automatic flare, touchdown and automatic taxi-ing.

For Categories IIIa and IIIb there must be a residual of vertical visibility, which varies from airline to airline and from airport to airport, before the automatic landing is allowed to proceed. At the time of writing, no airport is cleared for Category IIIc landings.

EXAMPLES III.39

1. Describe in qualitative terms the effect of a hydraulic actuator lag on the performance of the auto-pilot mode to hold the flight path.
2. Show that the damping of the short period mode with flight path angle feedback can be restored by including a term proportional to $\Delta\dot{\theta}(t)$ in the control law.
3. Would $\Delta\theta(t)$ feedback be effective in increasing the damping of the speed stability mode?
4. Investigate the auto-pilot mode to hold pitch attitude.

III.15.5 Active control technology

III.15.5.1 Introduction

Active control technology covers a range of automatic feedback control systems, all coordinated by a central computer system, the so-called Integrated Flight Management System. These systems operate continuously at all times when the aeroplane is airborne and cannot be switched out by the human pilot. Stick inputs from the human pilot are transmitted to the central computer by a fly-by-wire arrangement, and the central computer transmits the appropriate signals to the aerodynamic controls and engine. The auto-pilot modes listed in sect. III.15.4 can be switched in or out by the human pilot and are not usually regarded as part of an active control system, although auto-pilot modes such as terrain following and weapon aiming utilize the available active control technology.

The range of active control systems are listed below.

Flight dynamics	relaxed stability
	manoeuvre demand
	improved ride quality
	improved flying qualities
	carefree manoeuvring
Structures	gust load alleviation
	manoeuvre load alleviation
	flutter suppression
Engines	engine thrust control
	engine parameters management
	inlet and nozzle optimization.

Active control technology incorporates

sensor technology
actuator technology
computer technology

data links
interface with guidance systems
integration of all flight systems
integrity, including redundancy and reliability.

In this section only those aspects of active controls relevant to longitudinal motions of rigid aeroplanes at low angles of incidence are introduced.

III.15.5.2 Relaxed stability

The manoeuvre margin decreases as the aeroplane centre of mass is moved aft. There are a number of potential performance benefits with an aft centre of mass and negative manoeuvre margin.

(i) The role of the aft tailplane on a conventional aeroplane is to provide short period mode stability and to provide pitch control power. Strictly, the tailplane is not necessary for stability because longitudinal stability can be obtained without a tailplane as long as the aeroplane centre of mass lies ahead of the aeroplane manoeuvre point. But when a tailplane is incorporated it is sensible to use it to optimize both stability and manoeuvrability. However, the lifting effectiveness of a conventional tailplane is not fully utilized; tailplane lifts are relatively small. In an equilibrium state (trim or pull-out manoeuvre), as the centre of mass is moved aft more of the total lift is carried by the tailplane and less by the main wing; an aft movement of the centre of mass by $(0.1 l_t c_w)$ would transfer 10% of the total lift from the main wing to the tailplane. The main wing can then be reduced in size, reducing its viscous drag and saving weight.

(ii) There can be a reduction of overall induced drag by transferring lift from the wing to the tailplane. Now

$$\text{induced drag on an isolated wing} \simeq \tfrac{1}{2}\rho_{at} U^2 S_w\, C_L^2/(\pi \mathrm{AR})$$
$$= L^2\Big/\left[\pi (2s_w)^2\left(\tfrac{1}{2}\rho U^2\right)\right].$$

Thus the total induced drag on a main wing plus tailplane

$$\left[\sim \left[L_w^2/(2s_w)^2\right] + \left[L_t^2/(2s_t)^2\right]\right]\left[1\Big/\left(\pi \tfrac{1}{2}\rho U^2\right)\right] + L_t\varepsilon \qquad \text{(III.15.25)}$$

where L_w and L_t are the lifts on the main wing and tailplane, s_w and s_t are the semi-spans of the main wing and tailplane, and ε is the downwash at the tailplane due to the main wing tip vortices:

$$\varepsilon = (\partial\varepsilon/\partial\alpha)(C_L)_w/(C_{L\alpha})_w. \qquad \text{(III.15.26)}$$

So eqn. (III.15.25) becomes

$$\text{total induced drag} \sim \left[L_w^2 + (L_t s_w/s_t)^2 + \left(L_t L_w \pi (\mathrm{AR}/C_{L\alpha})_w (\partial\varepsilon/\partial\alpha)\right)\right].$$

(III.15.27)

Taking, for a combat aeroplane, $s_w/s_t = 2$, $(AR/C_{L\alpha})_w = 1$, $\partial\varepsilon/\partial\alpha = 0.5$, then,

$L_w/W = 1.1$	$L_t/W = -0.1$	$[\ \ ]/W^2 = 1.08$
$= 1.0$	$= 0.0$	$= 1.00$
$= 0.9$	$= +0.10$	$= 0.985$
$= 0.8$	$= +0.20$	$= 1.04.$

where the square brackets refer to eqn. (III.15.27). The total induced drag is a minimum when the tailplane takes 10% of the total lift.

(iii) The tailplane area may also be reduced, decreasing the viscous drag on the tailplane.

(iv) The tailplane plus elevator, or all-moving tailplane, must still be capable of rotating the aeroplane at take-off, maintaining trim with flaps down and providing adequate control power for manoeuvrability.

The cumulative effects of all of the points described above on the redesign of a combat aeroplane by moving the centre of mass aft a distance of $0.25c_w$, retaining a permissible range of the centre of mass of $0.08c_w$, is shown in Fig. III.132, taken from Burns (ref. III.71). Effectively the same mission effectiveness is achieved by an aeroplane which is 9% lighter in weight.

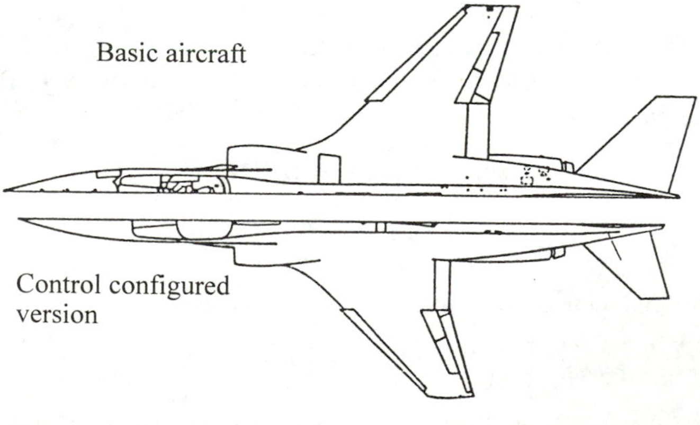

Fig. III.132. Optimized configuration.

It is claimed (ref. III.70) that an aft centre of mass location on a transport aeroplane can reduce the drag by the order of 3%, a worthwhile benefit in terms of fuel consumption.

Relaxed stability is where an inherently unstable aeroplane (i.e. a basic aeroplane with a negative manoeuvre margin) is stabilized by an automatic feedback system.

The approximate non-dimensional equations for the short period response are, from eqns. (III.15.6),

$$[\bar{D} + C_{L\alpha}]\Delta\alpha(\bar{t}_d) - \bar{q}(\bar{t}_d)$$
$$= \left[\left((-C_{L\dot{\eta}})/2\bar{m}\right)\bar{D} - C_{L\eta}\right]\left[\Delta\eta_p(\bar{t}_d) + \Delta\eta_{stab}(\bar{t}_d)\right]$$
$$\left[\left((-C_{m\dot{\alpha}})/2\right)\bar{D} - \bar{m}C_{m\alpha}\right]\Delta\alpha(\bar{t}_d) + \left[i_{yy}\bar{D} + \left((-C_{mq})/2\right)\right]\bar{q}(\bar{t}_d) \tag{III.15.28}$$
$$= \left[\left(C_{m\dot{\eta}}/2\right)\bar{D} - \bar{m}(-C_{m\eta})\right]\left[\Delta\eta_p(\bar{t}_d) + \Delta\eta_{stab}(\bar{t}_d)\right]$$

where

$\Delta\eta_p(\bar{t}_d)$ = elevator angle due to pilot input

$\Delta\eta_{stab}(\bar{t}_d)$ = elevator angle due to feedback

The characteristic equation of the basic aeroplane with $\Delta\eta_{stab}(\bar{t}_d)$ equal to zero (i.e. the open loop short period characteristic equation), from eqns. (III.15.28) is

$$i_{yy}\bar{\lambda}^2 + \left[i_{yy}C_{L\alpha} + \left((-C_{m\dot{\alpha}})/2\right) + \left((-C_{mq})/2\right)\right]\bar{\lambda}$$
$$+ \bar{m}\left[(-C_{m\alpha}) + C_{L\alpha}\left((-C_{mq})/2\right)/\bar{m}\right]$$
$$= 0. \tag{III.15.29}$$

For a basic aeroplane with aft centre of mass, the conventional manoeuvre margin

$$H_m = \left((-C_{m\alpha})/C_{L\alpha}\right) + \left((-C_{mq})/2\bar{m}\right)$$

can be of the order of –0.2, so the open loop short period mode is unstable as a pure divergence.

There are a number of options for the stabilizing feedback system.

Consider first a feedback signal proportional to the angle of incidence, taking the ideal control law,

$$\Delta\eta_{stab}(t) = \mathcal{K}_\alpha\,\Delta\alpha(t) \tag{III.15.30}$$

where $\mathcal{K}_\alpha$ is the feedback gain. A gain factor, $\mathcal{K}_\alpha$, about 1.0 would lead to acceptable changes in elevator angle.

With this feedback the characteristic equation of the closed loop short period mode is

$$i_{yy}\bar{\lambda}^2 + \left[i_{yy}(C_{L\alpha} + \mathcal{K}_\alpha C_{L\eta}) + \left((-C_{m\dot{\alpha}})/2\right) - \mathcal{K}_\alpha\left(C_{m\dot{\eta}}/2\right) + \left((-C_{mq})/2\right)\right]\bar{\lambda}$$
$$+ \bar{m}\left[(-C_{m\alpha}) + (C_{L\alpha} + \mathcal{K}_\alpha C_{L\eta})\left((-C_{mq})/2\bar{m}\right) + \mathcal{K}_\alpha(-C_{m\eta})\right] = 0 \tag{III.15.31}$$

assuming $\mathcal{K}_\alpha(-C_{L\dot{\eta}})/\bar{m} \ll 1$.

For a combat aeroplane with an all-moving tailplane

$$C_{L\eta}/C_{L\alpha} = O[0.3],$$
$$(-C_{m\eta})/C_{L\alpha} = O[0.5], \quad (-C_{mq})/2\bar{m} = O[0.05]. \tag{III.15.32}$$

Hence a gain factor, $\mathcal{K}_\alpha$, equal to 1.0 would compensate for the open loop negative H_m ($\simeq -0.2$), leading to an equivalent positive closed loop conventional manoeuvre margin approximately equal to +0.3. In addition there could be a small increase in the damping. The close loop short period mode is now stable.

An alternative automatic stability system can be based on a feedback signal proportional to the perturbation pitch angle $\Delta\theta(t)$, obtained by integrating the signal from a rate gyro. Consider the ideal feedback control law,

$$\Delta\eta_{\text{stab}}(t) = \mathcal{K}_\theta \, \Delta\theta(t). \qquad \text{(III.15.33)}$$

Again a value of $\mathcal{K}_\theta$ about 1 would lead to practical elevator angles.

Substitution of eqn. (III.15.33) into eqn. (III.15.28) leads to a cubic characteristic equation. With typical values, the open loop characteristic equation, with a negative open loop manoeuvre margin, is

$$[\bar{\lambda}^2 + 20\bar{\lambda} - 120] = 0. \qquad \text{(III.15.34)}$$

The corresponding closed loop characteristic equation, with the feedback eqn. (III.15.33) could then be

$$\bar{\lambda}[\bar{\lambda}^2 + 20\bar{\lambda} - 120] + \mathcal{K}_\theta[3\bar{\lambda}^2 + 300\bar{\lambda} + 1200] = 0. \qquad \text{(III.15.35)}$$

Eqn. (III.15.35) can be factorized:

$$\begin{aligned} \text{when} \quad \mathcal{K}_\theta &= 1.0, \quad (\bar{\lambda} + 16.5)(\bar{\lambda}^2 + 6.5\bar{\lambda} + 72.7) = 0 \\ \mathcal{K}_\theta &= 1.5, \quad (\bar{\lambda} + 8.1)(\bar{\lambda}^2 + 13.4\bar{\lambda} + 222) = 0 \\ \mathcal{K}_\theta &= 2.0, \quad (\bar{\lambda} + 6.9)(\bar{\lambda}^2 + 19.1\bar{\lambda} + 348) = 0. \end{aligned} \qquad \text{(III.15.36)}$$

The closed loop system is stable, comprising two modes: a pure subsidence and a damped oscillation.

The combination of the pure subsidence and the damped oscillation in eqns. (III.15.36) must decay at least as fast as the conventional short period mode:

(i) when $\mathcal{K}_\theta = 1.0$, the decay of the pure subsidence is satisfactory but neither the damping nor stiffness of the damped oscillation is high enough;
(ii) when $\mathcal{K}_\theta = 2.0$, the decay of the pure subsidence is too slow, the oscillation damping is acceptable, the oscillation frequency is possibly too high;
(iii) when $\mathcal{K}_\theta = 1.5$, the response is marginally acceptable, although higher dampings would be preferred.

Acceptable levels of both damping and undamped frequency for the damped oscillatory mode, together with a rapid decay rate for the pure subsidence, can be obtained with a feedback control law of the form

$$\Delta\eta_{\text{stab}}(t) = \mathcal{K}_q \, \Delta\dot{\theta}(t) + \mathcal{K}_\theta \, \Delta\theta(t) = \overline{\mathcal{K}}_{\bar{q}}\bar{q}(\bar{t}_{\text{d}}) + \mathcal{K}_\theta \Delta\theta(\bar{t}_{\text{d}}). \qquad \text{(III.15.37)}$$

The factors $\mathcal{K}_q$ and $\mathcal{K}_\theta$ will be scheduled for optimization throughout the flight envelope by computer from the air data system.

The inherently unstable aeroplane can be stabilized, in principle, by either incidence feedback or pitch feedback. So, what are their relative merits?

One important difference between the two options is that, from the pilot's point of view, the flying qualities are totally different.

(i) With $\Delta\alpha$ feedback the aeroplane response to pilot elevator input, $\Delta\eta_{\mathrm{p}}(t)$, behaves as a conventional aeroplane: a step change in pilot elevator angle gives, after the decay of the short period response, a steady rate of pitch, q_{ss}.

(ii) But with $\Delta\theta$ feedback a step change in pilot elevator angle, gives, after the decay of the closed loop short period response, a steady pitch angle $\Delta\theta_{\mathrm{ss}}$.

(The reader is asked to prove this statement in the examples.) On the grounds of preserving continuity with past aeroplanes that stick displacement and/or force leads to normal acceleration, or pitch rate, the incidence feedback would be preferred.

The second consideration concerns safety. The survival of the aeroplane depends on the integrity of the automatic stability system; if the system fails, the aeroplane is lost. Thus the automatic stability system is, at least, triplicated, and each system is completely independent. The installation of three independent pitot probes to measure angle of incidence is far more inconvenient than installing three pitch rate gyros. Four incidence vanes around the fuselage nose at 45°, 135°, 225° and 315° could provide the degree of triplication. But pitch rate gyros are regarded as more reliable than vanes. Incidence vanes are not usually used as primary sensors but are used as secondary sensors when safety is not at a premium.

Thirdly, the automatic stability feedback system is not designed in isolation from the other active control applications. As explained in the next section, a common pitch attitude feedback system can be used to stabilize the aeroplane and as a manoeuvre demand system.

EXAMPLES III.40

1. Does the elevator 'work harder' with the incidence feedback or the pitch feedback?
2. If $\overline{\mathcal{K}}_{\bar{q}} = 0.05$ in eqn. (III.5.37), taking the values in eqn. (III.15.35), what is the value of $\mathcal{K}_\theta$ which gives satisfactory stability characteristics?
3. For pitch attitude feedback, what is $(\Delta\theta)_{\mathrm{ss}}/(\Delta\eta_{\mathrm{p}})$?

III.15.5.3 Manoeuvre demand system

To illustrate the elements of a manoeuvre demand system, consider a system which implements the manoeuvre demand using the elevator only. Suppose that a certain stick force applied by the pilot commands a pitch rate q_{com}. The appropriate feedback control law for the elevator could be of the form

$$\Delta\eta_{\mathrm{man}}(t) = \mathcal{K}_\theta \int \left(q(t) - q_{\mathrm{com}}\right) \mathrm{d}t \qquad \text{(III.15.37)}$$

where $\Delta\eta_{\mathrm{man}}(t)$ is the manoeuvre demand elevator angle, $\mathcal{K}_\theta$ is the feedback gain, and $q(t)$ is the aeroplane pitch rate, measured by the pitch rate gyro.

On substitution of eqn. (III.15.37) into eqns. (III.11.16), the short period pitch rate response is of the form

$$\left[i_{yy}\bar{\mathrm{D}}^3 + (\ )\bar{\mathrm{D}}^2 + (\ )\bar{\mathrm{D}} + \mathcal{K}_\theta \bar{m}\left[C_{\mathrm{L}\alpha}(-C_{m\eta}) - C_{\mathrm{L}\eta}(-C_{m\alpha})\right]\right] \bar{q}(\bar{t}_\mathrm{d})$$
$$= \left[(\ )\bar{\mathrm{D}}^2 + (\ )\bar{\mathrm{D}} + \mathcal{K}_\theta \bar{m}\left[C_{\mathrm{L}\alpha}(-C_{m\eta}) - C_{\mathrm{L}\eta}(-C_{m\alpha})\right]\right] \bar{q}_{\mathrm{com}}. \qquad \text{(III.15.38)}$$

Thus the steady state response, after the transient has decayed, is

$$(q(t))_{\mathrm{ss}} = q_{\mathrm{com}}$$

as required.

The feedback in eqn. (III.15.37) is essentially the pitch attitude feedback for stabilizing an inherently unstable basic aeroplane, as described in sect. III.15.5.2. Thus the relaxed stability system and the pitch rate manoeuvre demand system can be integrated. To improve the stability characteristics, without affecting the steady state response, the feedback term, $\mathcal{K}_q(q_{\mathrm{com}} - q(t))$ can be added to eqn. (III.15.37).

A pitch rate manoeuvre demand system is effectively a pitch attitude control system because a positive stick force followed by a negative stick force leads to a steady state change in pitch attitude angle; the aeroplane then remains effectively trimmed at that pitch attitude.

Other types of manoeuvre demand systems have been investigated, for example, a normal acceleration demand system or a mixed system demanding a pitch rate at lower speeds and a normal acceleration at higher speeds. Pitch rate demand seems to be the current norm.

Such manoeuvre demand systems are known as 'superaugmentation'.

The handling qualities for aeroplanes with superaugmentation can be substantially different from traditional aeroplanes. With a pitch rate demand system the aeroplane is stiff in pitch attitude, with smaller pitch rate overshoot in transient responses. The flight path response, which can be sluggish, can be improved by so-called 'command path filtering'. The provision of satisfactory flying qualities for these types of aeroplane has been a topic of intense investigation (see Gibson, ref. III.66, III.67 and McRuer *et al.*, III.74).

III.15.5.4 Manoeuvre enhancement

On a transport aeroplane the time to build up a normal acceleration can be of the order of 4 s, or longer, at low speed, which is a somewhat long time, especially when manoeuvring during an approach for landing. To recap what happens in a positive pull-out manoeuvre: the elevator angle is decreased; there is a download on the tailplane, which initially actually gives the aeroplane a small negative (downward) acceleration; the tail load imposes a pitching moment which has to overcome the pitch inertia to pitch the aeroplane nose-up, increasing the angle of incidence, hence increasing the wing lift. This sequence is time consuming. Time would be saved if wing lift could be generated more quickly—for example, by using fast acting flaps on the main wings, so-called direct lift controls. If main wing flaps could be deflected over a small angular range, in the order of 1 s, the build-up of wing lift would be quasi-steady so the peak acceleration would occur in the order of 1 s, a significant improvement on the 4 s mentioned earlier. It would appear that it is not thought worth while to incorporate such direct lift controls on current transport aeroplanes, although a direct lift system using spoilers was installed on the Tristar.

The design aim for combat aeroplanes is rapid manoeuvrability combined with optimum flying qualities and good ride quality. With a conventional aeroplane the design options are severely limited because manoeuvrability and handling qualities all involve the single aerodynamic control, the all-moving tailplane. The task of enhancing manoeuvre performance, especially turning performance as explained later, together with the need to widen the range of parameters, has led to the incorporation of direct lift controls such as variable wing camber with leading edge droop and trailing edge flaps (see Fig. III.133).

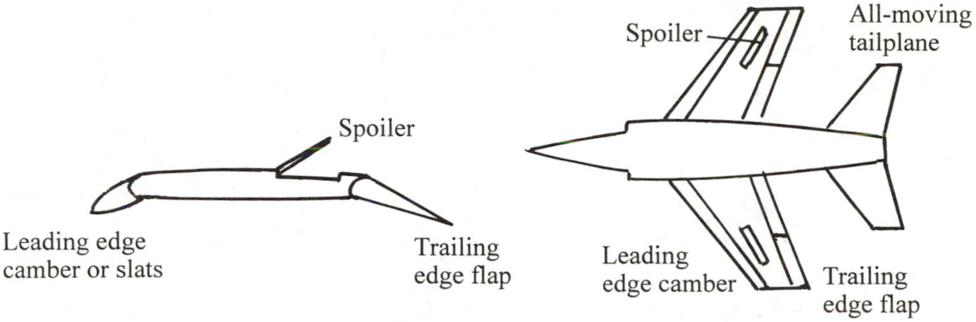

Fig. III.133. Manoeuvre surfaces.

On a combat aeroplane there could be three independent aerodynamic control surfaces (leading edge droop, trailing edge flaps and (all-moving) tailplane). Now the pilot's stick force generates an electrical signal which is a command input into the central flight control computer; the central flight control computer evaluates which aerodynamic surfaces should be activated, depending on flight Mach number and altitude, and possibly on the mission, to obtain the demanded manoeuvre. Appropriate feedback control laws would activate these surfaces to optimize the flying qualities and ride quality.

An aeroplane with a pitch rate demand system can have worse ride quality characteristics than a conventional aeroplane (see Jones and Fry, ref. III.75). The stiffness in pitch attitude with a pitch rate demand system prevents the pitch relief which is present on conventional aeroplanes, consequently the acceleration peaks are greater. Any automatic system which aims to improve ride quality must be fast acting and therefore requires a form of direct lift control, either a trailing edge flap or spoiler.

In contemporary aeroplanes a smaller side hand controller has replaced the traditional central stick and pedals. This side hand controller, as sketched in Fig. III.134, is usually stiff with little displacement and responds to primarily applied force. However, the stick is not simply for commanding aeroplane responses; it also includes switches to select missiles, guns, and bombs, for air-to-air or air-to-surface delivery, and a weapons release trigger.

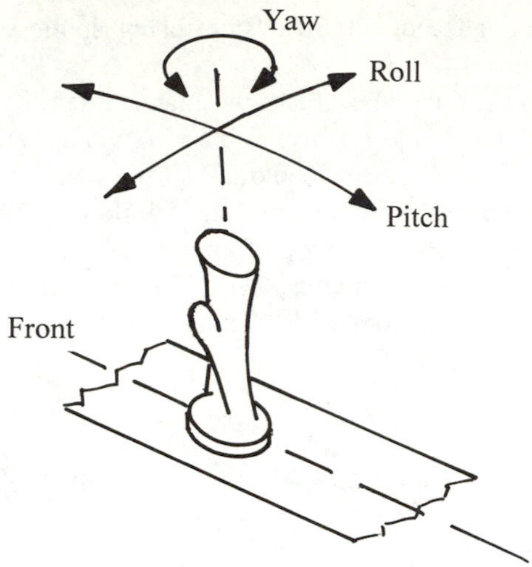

Fig. III.134. Side controller.

III.15.5.5 Safety

Safety is the overriding consideration of active control technology involving a relaxed stability system. If the feedback system were to fail the stability of the aeroplane would revert to that of the basic aeroplane which would be highly unstable, the aeroplane would become uncontrollable, and the consequences lethal.

The main design effort, testing and development is aimed at a high integrity, full authority, system. The airworthiness requirements specify the probability of failure to be 1 in 10^7 hours of operation (i.e. the order of one failure in 400 aeroplanes in 30 years of peace-time operation). To achieve this level of safety, as already mentioned, each critical feedback loop (sensor, computer, hydraulics) is, at least, triplicated with independent softwares; an on-board computer monitors all signals and cross checks all channels, taking decisions when differences appear.

In a full authority system the full range of control angle is available for the control demand from the flight control system. The system is said to be saturated when a control comes up against the stops or when a hydraulic actuator cannot move fast enough to meet a demand, say, in a gust alleviation system. The effects of saturation have to be completely analysed.

Proving the integrity of the software is a formidable task, especially with the quadruplication of many subsystems. It is said that it takes more man-hours to write the software and debug it than to design, validate and test the structure.

With all of the electrical hardware, corruption of electrical information by electromagnetic induction is a hazard, which must be designed out. The effect of a lightning strike is also potentially dangerous when composite materials are used in the external structure; composite materials offer no protection against external electrical charge unlike the all-metal skin structure.

EXAMPLES III.41

1. Which contemporary combat aeroplanes are inherently unstable?
2. Which contemporary combat aeroplanes have some form of direct lift control?
3. Which contemporary aeroplanes have side controllers?

III.16 STATIC STABILITY

The description of longitudinal motions at small angles of incidence is now complete, and all without introducing, or mentioning, the phrase or concept of 'static stability'. However, because static stability appears to be such a dominant theme in the literature of aeroplane flight dynamics, some comments on static stability are included here, covering its definition, its physical interpretation and its practical significance.

Overall static stability can be defined mathematically. The stability characteristic equation for a linear system with constant coefficients is

$$C(\lambda) = \lambda^n + A_{n-1}\lambda^{n-1} + A_{n-2}\lambda^{n-2} + \ldots + A_1\lambda + A_0 = 0. \tag{III.16.1}$$

The overall static stability of the system is governed by the sign of A_0:

$$\begin{aligned} A_0 > 0 &\quad \text{defines overall static stability,} \\ A_0 < 0 &\quad \text{defines overall static instability.} \end{aligned} \tag{III.16.2}$$

Overall static instability ($A_0 < 0$) implies that there is at least one mode which is unstable in the form of a pure divergence. The reasoning is as follows. For the stability characteristic equation, eqn. (III.16.1), when λ is very large and positive the value of $C(\lambda)$ is positive; when λ is zero then $C(\lambda)$ has the same sign as A_0. So when A_0 is negative there must be at least one real positive value of λ where $C(\lambda)$ is zero; the system is then unstable with at least one mode of instability which is a pure divergence.

When A_0 is zero there is at least one stability root which is zero ($\lambda = 0$). The stability modal displacement, relating ($\Delta u : \Delta\alpha : \Delta\theta$), corresponding to this zero stability root, neither grows nor decays with time. In the context of aeroplane flight dynamics this situation is known traditionally as neutral equilibrium (in other contexts neutral equilibrium also refers to an oscillatory stability motion with zero damping).

The characteristic polynomial, eqn. (III.16.1), can be factorized into the form

$$\begin{aligned} &(\lambda + \lambda_1) \ldots (\lambda + \lambda_m)(\lambda^2 + 2\zeta_{m+1}\omega_{m+1}\lambda + \omega_{m+1}^2) \\ &\qquad \ldots (\lambda^2 + 2\zeta_p\omega_p\lambda + \omega_p^2) = 0 \end{aligned} \tag{III.16.3}$$

where $m + 2p = n$

$\lambda_j (j = 1, \ldots, m)$ represent the real stability roots

$(\zeta_j, \omega_j^2)\ (j = m+1, \ldots, p)$ represent the oscillatory roots.

This system is completely stable when

$$\begin{aligned} &\text{all } \lambda_j > 0 && \text{for } j = 1,\ldots,n \\ &\text{all } \zeta_j > 0 && \text{for } j = m+1,\ldots,p \\ &\text{all } \omega_j^2 > 0 && \text{for } j = m+1,\ldots,p. \end{aligned} \tag{III.16.4}$$

Each stability mode has its own condition of modal static stability: from the definition, eqns. (III.16.2),

$$\begin{aligned} &\text{mode } j \ (1,\ldots,m) \text{ is statically stable when } \lambda_j > 0 \\ &\text{mode } j \ (m+1,\ldots,p) \text{ is statically stable when } \omega_j^2 > 0. \end{aligned} \tag{III.16.5}$$

By comparison of eqns. (III.16.1) and (III.16.3)

$$A_0 = \lambda_1, \lambda_2, \ldots, \lambda_m \cdot \omega_{m+1}^2, \omega_{m+2}^2, \ldots, \omega_p^2. \tag{III.16.6}$$

Hence, the important result,

overall static stability = product of all the modal static stabilities. (III.16.7)

When all the modes are statically stable the system has overall static stability.

But the converse is not true. Overall static stability ($A_0 > 0$) does not imply that all modes are statically stable; two negative modal static instabilities when multiplied together give a positive overall static stability. Hence it is possible for instabilities in the form of pure divergences to exist even when there is overall static instability. This possibility is not a remote academic abstraction, it can arise in longitudinal stability, as explained later.

It is easy to illustrate the static stability of a one degree of freedom system: the ball rolling on a curved surface is the all-time favourite. But such an oversimplified example provides little physical understanding of overall static stability for a system which comprises three or more degrees of freedom. It is probably a fruitless exercise to attempt a physical explanation of overall static stability.

In general, the stability of a system is understood, analysed theoretically, and measured experimentally in terms of the individual stability modes, their rise times, their damping ratios, their frequencies, and their modal shapes. Overall static stability then offers no further insight into the stability of the system.

Turning to the longitudinal stability of a rigid aeroplane trimmed in level flight, the condition for the overall static stability according to eqn. (III.11.8) is

$$A_0 = (\overline{m}/i_{yy})\, C_{\mathrm{W}} C_{\mathrm{L}\alpha} [C_{\mathrm{L}U} K_\alpha + C_{mU}] > 0. \tag{III.16.8}$$

At low speeds, when Mach number effects are negligible and l_{Th} is zero, $C_{\mathrm{L}U}$ is equal to $2C_{\mathrm{W}}$, C_{mU} is zero, so the condition of overall static stability reduces to

$$K_\alpha > 0 \tag{III.16.9}$$

namely positive incidence stiffness. And zero K_α gives neutral equilibrium.

At subsonic speeds below the drag rise Mach number, C_{LU} and C_{mU} are both positive; although a positive incidence stiffness ($K_\alpha > 0$) guarantees overall static stability, neutral equilibrium is not given by $K_\alpha = 0$.

At low supersonic speeds when both C_{LU} and C_{mU} can be negative, a positive incidence stiffness ($K_\alpha > 0$) then gives an overall static instability.

Overall static stability is related to changes in trim.

Consider a step change in perturbation elevator angle $\Delta \eta_s H(t)$, with zero change in throttle (assumed to be equivalent to zero change in thrust), relative to an initial trim state of steady level flight. After the decay of both the short period motion and the phugoid motion the perturbation forward velocity attains a steady state $\Delta \bar{u}_{ss} (= (\Delta U)_{ss}/U_{trim})$, together with steady state perturbations in angle of incidence, $\Delta \alpha_{ss}$, and pitch angle, $\Delta \theta_{ss}$. The relationships between $\Delta \bar{u}_{ss}$, $\Delta \alpha_{ss}$, $\Delta \theta_{ss}$ and $\Delta \eta_s$ are obtained from the perturbation equations of motion, putting all time differentials equal to zero. By reference to eqns. (III.11.4)

$$C_{DU}\, \Delta \bar{u}_{ss} - (C_W - C_{D\alpha})\Delta \alpha_{ss} + C_W\, \Delta \theta_{ss} = 0$$

$$C_{LU}\, \Delta \bar{u}_{ss} + \qquad C_{L\alpha}\, \Delta \alpha_{ss} \qquad\qquad = -C_{L\eta}\, \Delta \eta_s \qquad\qquad \text{(III.16.10)}$$

$$-C_{mU}\, \Delta \bar{u}_{ss} - \qquad C_{m\alpha}\, \Delta \alpha_{ss} \qquad\qquad = C_{m\eta}\, \Delta \eta_s.$$

From the ratio of determinants

$$\frac{\Delta \bar{u}_{ss}}{\Delta \eta_s} = \frac{C_W[-C_{L\eta}(-C_{m\alpha}) + (-C_{m\eta})C_{L\alpha}]}{C_W[C_{LU}(-C_{m\alpha}) + C_{mU}C_{L\alpha}]} \qquad\qquad \text{(III.16.11)}$$

Since $C_W = (W/S_w)/(\tfrac{1}{2}\rho_{at}U_{trim}^2)$, then $\Delta C_W = -2C_W\, \Delta u_{ss}$, and eqn. (III.16.11) becomes, by reference to eqn. (III.16.8),

$$\left[-\frac{\Delta \eta_s}{\Delta C_W}\right]_{\text{thrust constant}} = \frac{C_W[C_{LU}(-C_{m\alpha}) + C_{mU}C_{L\alpha}]}{2C_W^2[-C_{L\eta}(-C_{m\alpha}) + (-C_{m\eta})C_{L\alpha}]}$$

$$= \frac{(i_{yy}/\overline{m})A_0}{2C_W^2[-C_{L\eta}(-C_{m\alpha}) + (-C_{m\eta})C_{L\alpha}]}. \qquad\qquad \text{(III.16.12)}$$

Note that thrust is not changed, but there is a change in the flight path angle.

From sect. III.5 the definition of the elevator trim margin E_{trim} is

$$E_{trim} = [(-\Delta \eta_s)/\Delta C_W]_{\text{thrust variable}} \qquad\qquad \text{(III.16.13)}$$

evaluated in steady level flight, involving a change in thrust with change in trim speed to maintain level flight.

And the formula for the elevator trim margin E_{trim}, eqn. (III.5.18), is

$$E_{trim} \simeq \frac{C_{LU}K_\alpha + C_{mU} + l_{Th}[C_{DU} - 2(C_W(dC_D/dC_L)_{trim})]}{2C_W(-C_{m\eta})}. \qquad\qquad \text{(III.16.14)}$$

When l_{Th} is zero,

$$E_{trim} = [(-\Delta\eta_s)/\Delta C_W]_{thrust\ variable} = [(-\Delta\eta_s)/\Delta C_W]_{thrust\ constant}. \quad (III.16.15)$$

$$= \left[i_{yy}/\left(2C_W^2 C_{L\alpha}(-C_{m\eta})\overline{m}\right]A_0. \quad (III.16.16)$$

Eqn. (III.16.15) is exact; it has been assumed in the derivation of E_{trim} in eqn. (III.16.14) that

$$(-C_{L\eta})(-C_{m\alpha}) + (-C_{m\eta})\ (C_{L\alpha} + (C_D)_{trim}) \simeq (-C_{m\eta})C_{L\alpha}.$$

And in both eqns. (III.16.12) and (III.16.14) it has been assumed that $(C_D)_{trim} \ll C_{L\alpha}$.

For zero l_{Th}, positive overall static stability and positive elevator trim margin are synonymous throughout the Mach number range.

When l_{Th} is positive, at subsonic speeds,

$$C_{DU} - 2\left(C_W\left(dC_D/dC_L\right)_{trim}\right) > 0$$

so

$$E_{trim} > A_0. \quad (III.16.17)$$

Overall static stability guarantees positive trim control at higher subsonic speeds, but not *vice versa*.

For conventional aeroplanes a neutral point can be defined:

> the neutral point is the location of the centre of mass when the overall static stability is zero (i.e. $A_0 = 0$). (III.16.18)

Remembering that

> the trim point is the location of the centre of mass when $E_{trim} = 0$, the neutral point coincides with the trim point when l_{Th} is zero, but when l_{Th} is positive the neutral point lies forward of the trim point.

At subsonic speeds for overall static stability the centre of mass must lie ahead of the neutral point. At supersonic speeds the neutral point, like the trim point, loses any sense of meaning, since it can disappear to infinity.

When l_{Th} is zero,

for overall static stability, from eqn. (III.16.16), $E_{trim} > 0$

for short period static stability, from sect. III.9, $E_m > 0$

for phugoid static stability, from sect. III.10, $E_{trim}/E_m > 0$.

(III.16.19)

These three conditions are consistent with eqn. (III.16.7), namely that the overall static stability is the product of the modal static stabilities.

It is of interest to note in Fig. III.84 that at a high subsonic Mach number there is a small range of the location of the centre of mass where E_{trim} is small and positive but E_m

is small and negative, and in this range there are two small real unstable roots. Here is an example where two first order modes are both statically unstable but the overall static stability is positive.

Longitudinal stability and manoeuvrability is effectively determined by the elevator manoeuvre margin E_m. Overall static stability, *per se*, is not an important parameter from the points of view of stability or manoeuvrability. However, from a pilot handling point of view an aeroplane must be trimmable, so E_{trim} must be positive, which ensures a positive overall static stability.

The phrase 'static stability' appears often in the literature, but its usage is ambiguous. Sometimes it denotes 'overall static stability' as defined in this section. More frequently it denotes positive K_α, which can imply overall static stability at low Mach numbers, but positive K_α should be associated with positive short period static stability.

As pointed out in section III.9 the weathercock motion is an approximation of the short period mode. It is therefore a mistake to interpret longitudinal static weathercock stability as a physical explanation of overall static stability.

The phrase 'c.g. margin' also appears in the literature. Sometimes it denotes the overall static stability margin, namely the non-dimensional distance of the centre of mass forward of the neutral point. At other times it means simply K_α, which is the non-dimensional distance of the centre of mass ahead of the overall aerodynamic centre. The phrase 'c.g. margin' is unnecessary; all the relevant information is contained in K_α, E_m and E_{trim}.

In the literature overall static stability is sometimes determined from (dC_m/dC_L) evaluated under the constraint of lift equal weight. The argument leading to this formulation is somewhat obscure but the correct expression is obtained. The algebra is tedious; little additional insight is provided.

EXAMPLES III.42

1. Four reference points have been identified:
   — the overall aerodynamic centre
   — the trim point
   — the manoeuvre point
   — the neutral point.
   Describe the relationships between them as Mach number increases.
2. What happens to the relationship between A_0 and E_{trim} at supersonic speeds?
3. Do you think E_{trim} and E_m are stability or manoeuvrability margins?

Part IV

Small perturbation lateral motions at low angles of incidence

IV.1 LATERAL MOTIONS

Small perturbation lateral motions involve time variations in small angles of roll, sideslip and yaw about a steady state with constant angles of incidence, pitch and elevator, and constant throttle.

First, the notation defining a conventional aeroplane configuration is listed; by reference to Fig. IV.1:

— starboard wing, to the pilot's right; the port wing, to the pilot's left;
— main wing dihedral setting angle, i_d;
— fin area, including rudder and extension through the aft fuselage, S_f (= $c_f s_f$);
— fin span, s_f;
— fin mean chord, c_f;
— fin aspect ratio AR_f (= s_f/c_f);
— fin sweep (of 1/4 chord line), Λ_f;
— fin moment arm, the distance of the fin aerodynamic centre aft of the aeroplane centre of mass, $l_f c_w$;
— fuselage nose moment arm, the distance of the aeroplane centre of mass aft of the centre of pressure of the forces on the fuselage nose, $l_n c_w$.

Conventionally there are a pair of differential ailerons for roll control, as shown in Fig. IV.1. When the starboard aileron is rotated downward through the angle ξ_{std} and the port aileron is rotated upward through the angle ξ_{pt}, the aileron angle, ξ, is taken to be positive, and defined as $(\xi_{std} + \xi_{pt})/2$. Unless stated otherwise, ξ_{std} is taken to be equal to ξ_{pt} (i.e. $\xi = \xi_{std} = \xi_{pt}$); in practice, as explained later, there are reasons for having different ξ_{std} and ξ_{pt} although ξ is still defined as $(\xi_{std} + \xi_{pt})/2$.

On transport aeroplanes there can be two sets of ailerons, as shown in Fig. IV.2: an outer set for use at low speeds and an inboard set for use at higher speeds.

On combat aeroplanes the all-moving tailplane can be moved differentially as a roll control.

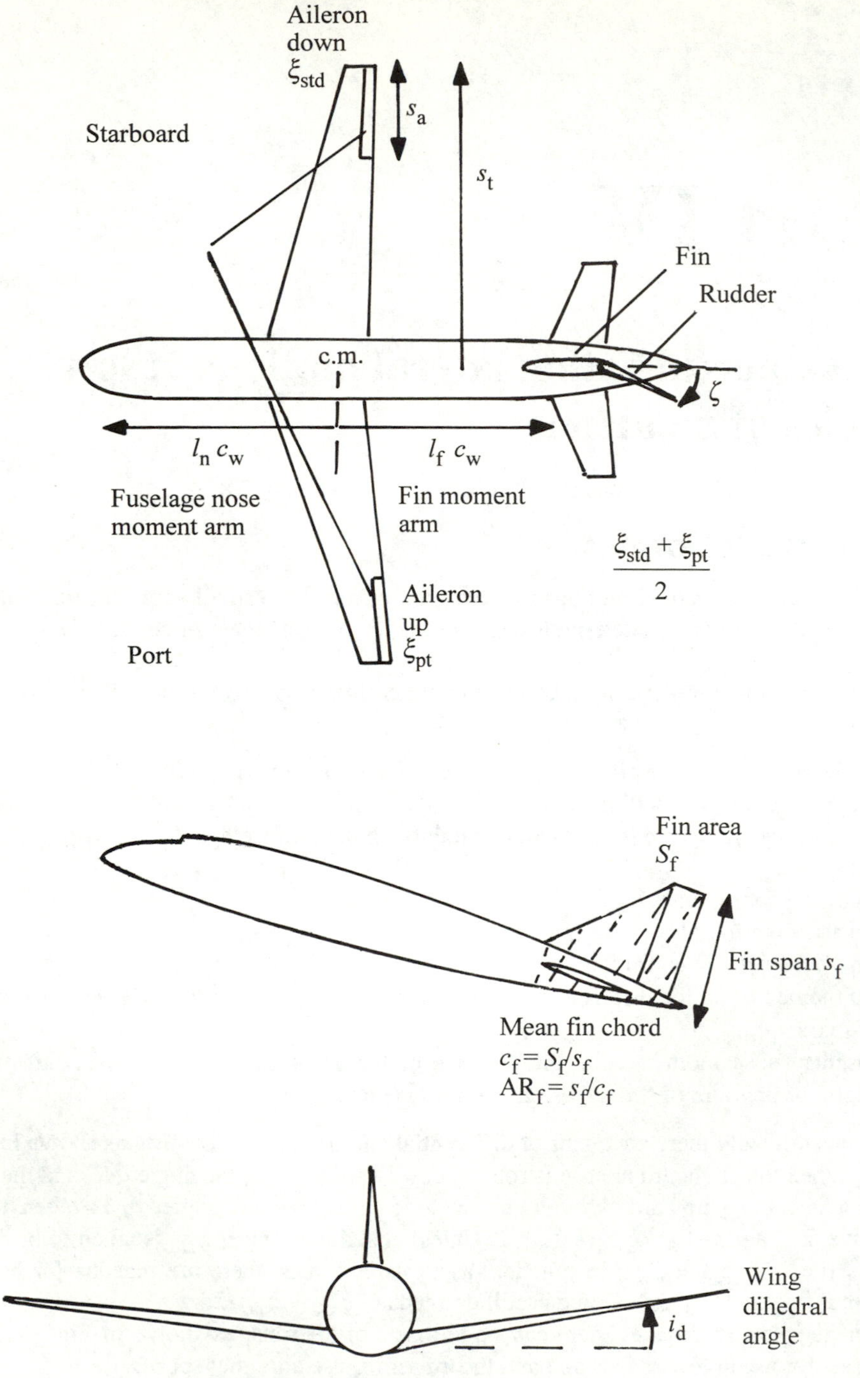

Fig. IV.1. Assymetric notation.

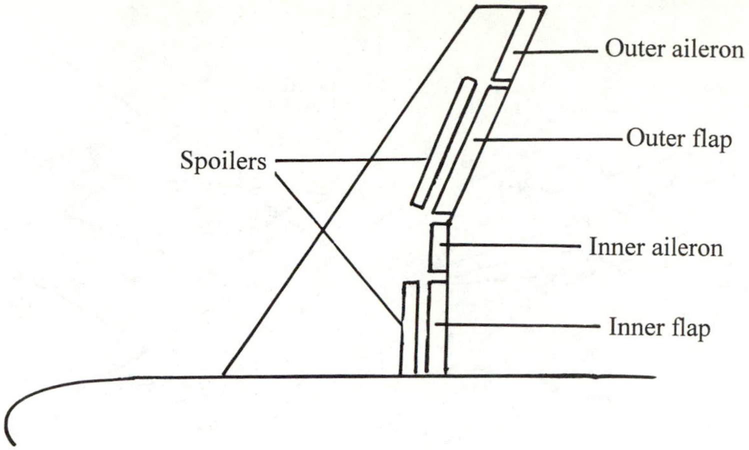

Fig. IV.2. Aileron/flap/spoiler arrangement for transport aeroplane.

Spoilers, as shown in Fig. IV.2, when deployed symmetrically act as lift dumpers (usually in conjunction with trailing edge flaps, on the approach), but when deployed singly act as aids to roll control.

Positive rudder angle, ζ, is defined in Fig. IV.1. The convention for the sign of control angles is that a positive control angle induces a negative moment; a positive elevator angle induces a nose-down, negative, pitching moment; a positive aileron angle induces a roll to port, a negative rolling moment; and a positive rudder angle induces a yaw to port, a negative yawing moment.

For the pilot's control a stick displacement, and force, to starboard (or stick wheel, right hand down) moves the ailerons in a negative sense, rolling the aeroplane, starboard wing down. A right pedal deflection, and force, moves the rudder in a negative sense, yawing the aeroplane nose to starboard.

For light aeroplanes the lateral controls are manual; transport and combat aeroplanes usually have powered lateral controls.

The fuselage body axis system, *oxyz*, defined and used for the longitudinal motions in Part III, is shown in Fig. IV.3;

— the origin is located at the centre of mass,
— the *oxz* plane is the aeroplane plane of symmetry,
— the *ox* axis, the roll axis, points forward along the fuselage axis,
— the *oz* axis, the yaw axis, points downward,
— the *oy* axis, the pitch axis, points to starboard.

The resultant absolute velocity of the centre of mass, $U(t)$, can be resolved into components $[U_x(t), U_y(t), U_z(t)]$ in the *ox*, *oy*, *oz* directions respectively.

The rotation of the aeroplane can be expressed by the components of rates of rotation $[p(t), q(t), r(t)]$, namely the roll rate, pitch rate and yaw rate, about the *ox*, *oy* and *oz* axes respectively.

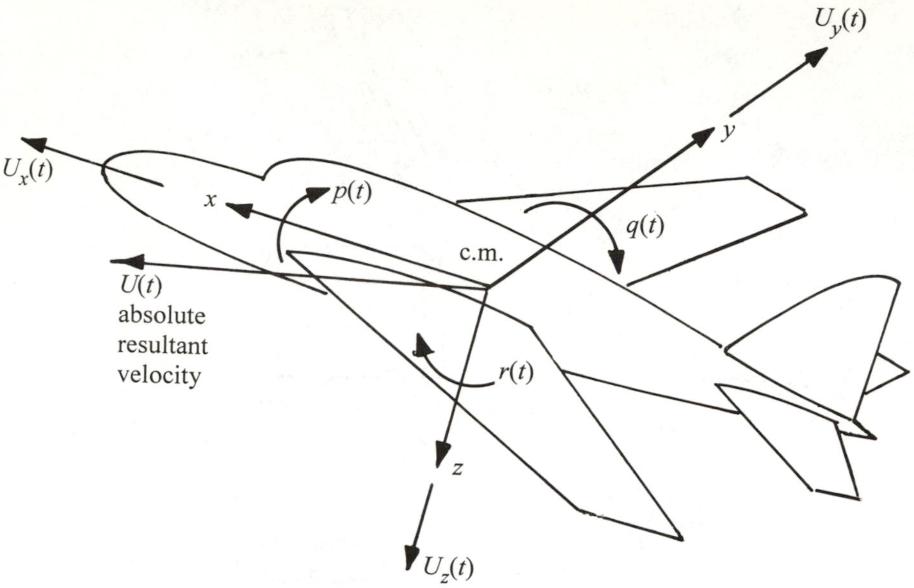

Fig. IV.3. Fuselage body axis system.

A complete set of angles $\alpha(t)$, $\beta(t)$, $\varphi(t)$, $\theta(t)$ and $\psi(t)$ can be defined, as shown in Fig. IV.4:

— in a stationary atmosphere the angle of incidence $\alpha(t)$ is the angle in the oxz plane defined by

$$\tan \alpha(t) = U_z(t)/U_x(t); \tag{IV.1.1}$$

— in a stationary atmosphere the sideslip angle $\beta(t)$ is the angle between the resultant velocity and the component of the resultant velocity in the oxz plane, hence

$$\sin \beta(t) = U_y(t)/U(t); \tag{IV.1.2}$$

— the bank angle $\varphi(t)$ is the angle of the oy axis from the horizontal, measured in the oyz plane;

— the pitch angle $\theta(t)$ is the angle of the ox axis from the horizontal, measured in the vertical plane;

— the yaw angle, $\psi(t)$, is the angle between the horizontal heading of the ox axis (i.e. the ox_H axis, as shown in Fig. IV.4) to a horizontal datum.

Atmospheric turbulence affects the definitions of $\alpha(t)$ and $\beta(t)$ since these angles depend on relative airspeed, but not $\varphi(t)$, $\theta(t)$ or $\psi(t)$.

When an aeroplane is perturbed from trimmed level flight, then

$$\begin{aligned} &U_x(t) = U_{\text{trim}} + \Delta u(t), \quad U_y(t) = \Delta v(t), \quad U_z = U_{\text{trim}}\alpha_{\text{trim}} + \Delta w(t),\\ &\alpha(t) = \alpha_{\text{trim}} + \Delta\alpha(t), \quad \theta(t) = \theta_{\text{trim}} + \Delta\theta(t),\\ &\beta(t) = \Delta\beta(t), \quad \varphi(t) = \Delta\varphi(t), \quad \psi(t) = \Delta\psi(t). \end{aligned} \tag{IV.1.3}$$

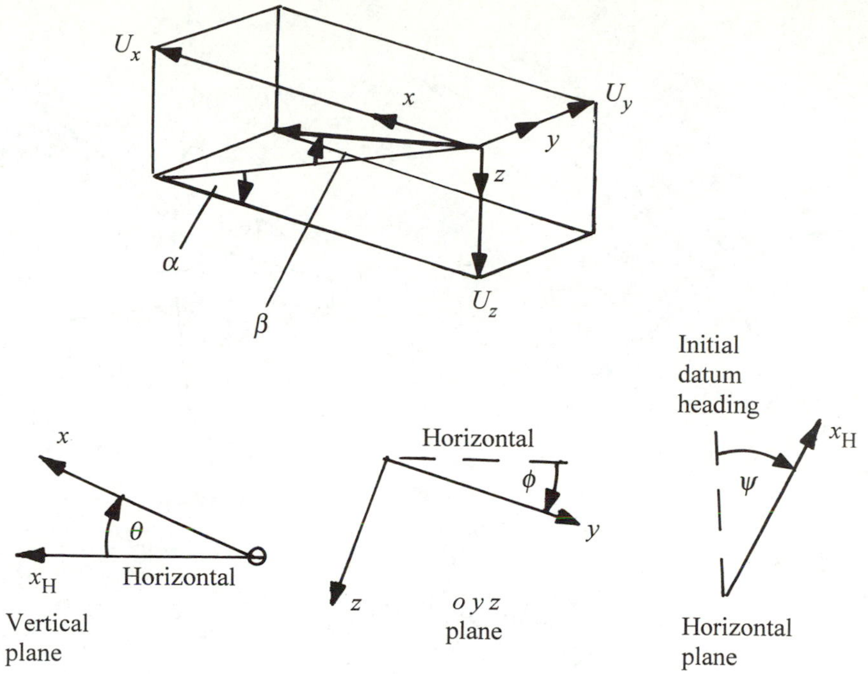

Fig. IV.4. Definition of angles.

Assuming that α_{trim}, $(\Delta u(t)/U_{\text{trim}})$, $(\Delta v(t)/U_{\text{trim}})$, $(\Delta w(t)/U_{\text{trim}})$, $\Delta\alpha(t)$, $\Delta\beta(t)$, $\Delta\varphi(t)$, $\Delta\theta(t)$ and $\Delta\psi(t)$ are all small, then

$$\Delta\alpha(t) \simeq \Delta w(t)/U_{\text{trim}}, \qquad \Delta\beta(t) \simeq \Delta v(t)/U_{\text{trim}} \tag{IV.1.4}$$

$$p(t) \simeq \Delta\dot{\varphi}(t), \qquad q(t) \simeq \Delta\dot{\theta}(t), \qquad r(t) \simeq \Delta\dot{\psi}(t). \tag{IV.1.5}$$

Eqns. (IV.1.5) can be accepted at this stage on an intuitive level; the proof is given later in Part V.

In longitudinal motions it is important to appreciate that $\alpha(t)$ and $\theta(t)$ are independent variables; in lateral motions it is equally important to appreciate that $\beta(t)$ and $\psi(t)$ are independent variables. Fig. IV.5 shows two curved flight paths, one with $\beta(t)$ zero but varying $\psi(t)$, the other with $\psi(t)$ zero and $\beta(t)$ zero. Fig. IV.5 also shows the case where the aeroplane centre of mass moves in a straight line; there is now a relationship between the perturbation sideslip and yaw angles, namely

$$\beta(t) = -\psi(t). \tag{IV.1.6}$$

Traditionally aeroplane flight dynamics have been developed in terms of the trim body axis system, $ox_1y_1z_1$ (alternatively known as the wind body axis system in the UK, or the stability body axis system in the USA), which can be defined relative to the fuselage body axis system, as shown in Fig IV.6. Axes ox_1 and oz_1 are in the plane of symmetry;

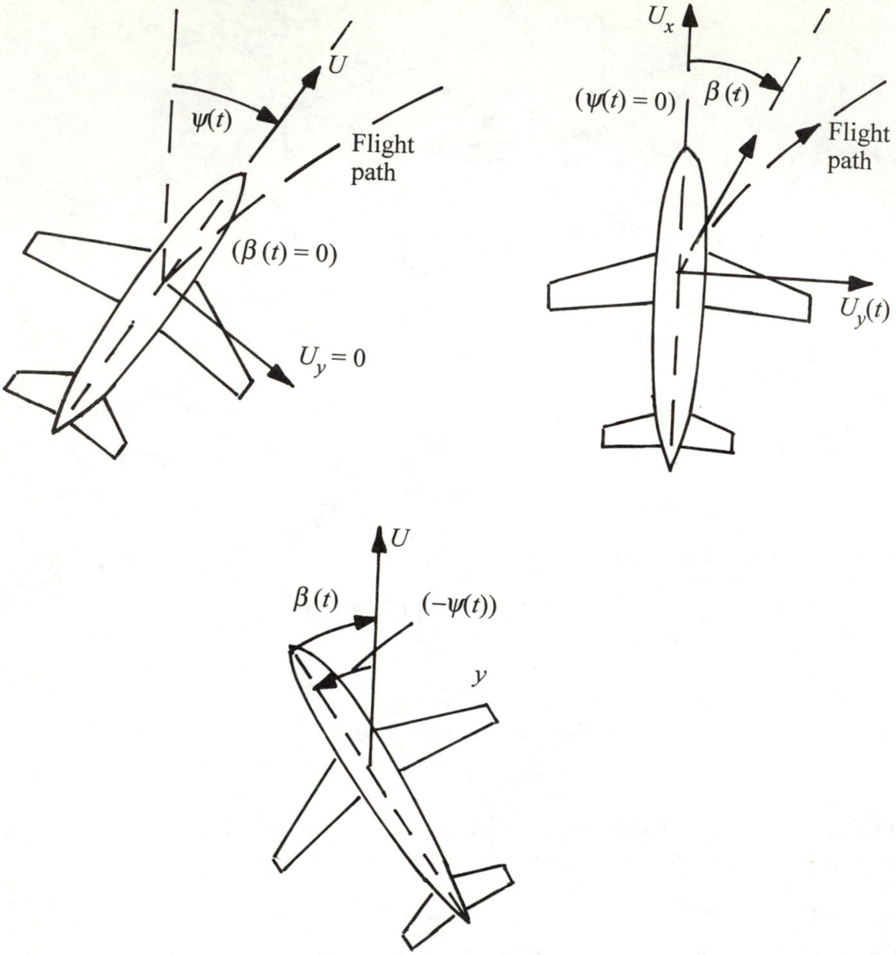

Fig. IV.5. Independence of sideslip and yaw.

the oy_1 axis coincides with the oy axis. The angle from ox_1 to ox, in the plane of symmetry, is α_{trim} where α_{trim} is the aeroplane angle of incidence in an initial trim state; the ox_1 axis is aligned with the trim velocity U_{trim} in the initial trim state, and then the axis system is 'frozen' in the airframe during any subsequent dynamic motion. The angle α_{trim} can be regarded as the fuselage setting angle relative to the ox_1 axis.

The resultant absolute velocity of the centre of mass, $U(t)$, can be resolved into components $[U_{x_1}(t), U_y(t), U_{z_1}(t)]$ in the ox_1, oy, oz_1 directions respectively. And then

$$U_{x_1}(t) = U_x(t)\cos\alpha_{trim} + U_z(t)\sin\alpha_{trim}$$
$$U_{z_1}(t) = -U_x(t)\sin\alpha_{trim} + U_z(t)\cos\alpha_{trim}$$

or

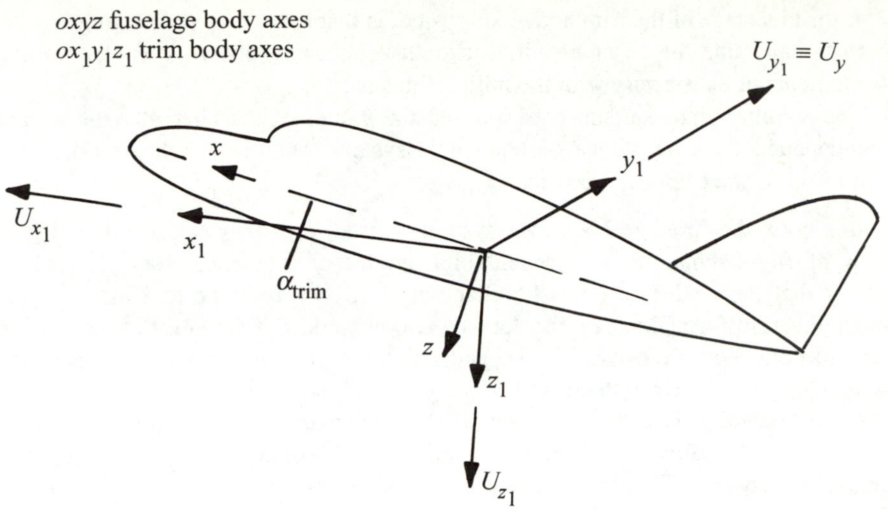

Fig. IV.6. Transformation of axes.

$$
\begin{aligned}
U_x(t) &= U_{x_1}(t)\cos\alpha_{\text{trim}} - U_{z_1}(t)\sin\alpha_{\text{trim}} \\
U_z(t) &= U_{x_1}(t)\sin\alpha_{\text{trim}} + U_{z_1}(t)\cos\alpha_{\text{trim}}
\end{aligned}
\tag{IV.1.7}
$$

The rotation of the aeroplane can be expressed by the components of rates of rotation $[p_1(t), q(t), r_1(t)]$, about the ox_1, oy and oz_1 axes, respectively. The relationships between $(p(t), r(t))$ and $(p_1(t), r_1(t))$ are identical to those between $(U_x(t), U_z(t))$ and $(U_{x_1}(t), U_{z_1}(t))$ as presented in eqns. (IV.1.7).

The set of perturbation angles $\Delta\alpha_1(t)$, $\Delta\beta_1(t)$, $\Delta\varphi_1(t)$, $\Delta\theta_1(t)$ and $\Delta\psi_1(t)$ relative to the trim body axis system follow the same definitions as their counterparts above in the fuselage body axis system.

A number of observations concerning these two body axis systems are listed:

(i) Although the values of the longitudinal aerodynamic derivatives are virtually the same in both sets of body axis systems when α_{trim} is small, some of the important lateral aerodynamic derivatives are sensitive to the choice of axis system.

(ii) The lateral aerodynamics of wings are most easily estimated using trim body axes.

(iii) The lateral aerodynamics of fuselage and fin are most easily estimated using fuselage body axes.

(iv) Because flight dynamics has evolved over many years using trim body axes, so nearly all the past literature and aerodynamic data in that literature is relative to trim body axes, for example in the ESDU and DAT COM publications.

(v) The flight dynamics of combat aeroplanes at high angles of incidence involves continuous manoeuvring with large dynamic excursions so trim body axes are inappropriate because there is no datum state.

(vi) A disadvantage of the trim body axis system is that the axis system changes relative to the airframe for different initial trim states; thus, as shown later, the values of moments of inertia vary with the initial trim state.

(vii) The stability characteristic equation and the values of the characteristic roots are independent of the choice of body axis system, but the stability modal shapes depend on the choice of body axis system.

In this book the fuselage body axis system is used, primarily because it unifies the analysis of flight dynamics at low and high angles of incidence. Nevertheless, it is important that the reader becomes familiar with both the fuselage and trim body axis systems; the transformations of the lateral aerodynamic derivatives between the two systems of body axes are derived in Appendix 8, the transformations of the equations of motion are described later in the main text.

There is a third axis system, namely flight path axes ($ox_f y_f z_f$) where the ox_f axis always points in the direction of the flight path; there is some arbitrariness in the choice of the oy_f and oz_f axes. Flight path axes are not body axes; they are not fixed in the body as that body moves. When flight path axes are used for the translational degrees of freedom fuselage body axes are retained for the rotational degrees of freedom. Flight path axes are useful in formulating the dynamics in complex dynamic motions; also pilots tend to fly relative to flight path axes.

EXAMPLES IV.1

1. How are spoilers used as roll controls?
2. When α_{trim} is small, relate $(\Delta\alpha, \Delta\beta, \Delta\varphi, \Delta\theta, \Delta\psi)$ to $(\Delta\alpha_1, \Delta\beta_1, \Delta\varphi_1, \Delta\theta_1, \Delta\psi_1)$.
3. If an aeroplane in an initial trimmed state at α_{trim} rolls through an angle of 90° about its direction of flight:
   (a) What are the angles of incidence and sideslip relative to the trim body axis system?
   (b) What are the angles of incidence and sideslip relative to the fuselage body axis system?
4. If an aeroplane in an initial trimmed state at α_{trim} rolls through an angle of 90° about the fuselage roll axis ox:
   (a) What are the angles of incidence and sideslip relative to the trim body axis system?
   (b) What are the angles of incidence and sideslip relative to the fuselage body axis system?
5. Describe the motions

$$\beta(t) = 0, \quad r(t) > 0, \quad p(t) > 0,$$
$$\psi(t) = 0, \quad \beta(t) > 0, \quad p(t) > 0.$$

6. An aeroplane is in a spin, rotating about a vertical axis at an angular rate r_{spin}; the centre of mass is a constant distance d from the vertical axis of spin and the vertical velocity of the centre of mass is V; the inclination of the fuselage ox axis to the vertical is steady at 30°, and the oy axis remains horizontal. Estimate α, β, p, q, r.

IV.2 LATERAL AERODYNAMICS

Lateral, or asymmetric, aerodynamics are concerned with the determination of the aerodynamic loadings which arise from the lateral motions of sideslip, roll and yaw. In this section lateral aerodynamics are described when the angles of incidence, sideslip, bank and yaw are small, with the flows around the aeroplane remaining attached.

Lateral aerodynamics have not received the same level of intensive research as longitudinal aerodynamics primarily because longitudinal aerodynamics determine the overall performance efficiency of the aeroplane, as well as the longitudinal flight dynamic characteristics. Lateral aerodynamics are more complicated than longitudinal aerodynamics and tend therefore to be more empirical.

The aim here is to present a qualitative framework, to identify the aerodynamic phenomena which affect lateral aerodynamics and to derive order-of-magnitude values of the lateral derivatives. But even this limited objective is fraught with difficulty, firstly because of the large number of aerodynamic effects, some of which cannot be quantified, and secondly because of the vigilance required to ensure that the aerodynamic moments consistently refer to the chosen axis system.

For more accurate empirical values of the lateral derivatives the reader is referred to the ESDU Data Sheets (ref. IV.1) or to the DAT COM (ref. IV.2).

IV.2.1 Aerodynamics of the fin

Consider a fuselage, without a main wing, but with a conventional tailplane and fin.

Suppose that this configuration is moving forward at zero angle of incidence at speed U_{trim} and sideways with a constant positive sideslip velocity (βU_{trim}). The fin 'angle of incidence' is β, so a transverse 'lift' force acts on the fin, as shown in Fig. IV.7, denoted by

$$\text{fin transverse force} = \tfrac{1}{2}\rho_{at}U_{trim}^2 S_f (a_\beta)_f \beta \qquad \text{(IV.2.1)}$$

where $(a_\beta)_f$ is the 'lift curve slope' of the fin.

According to ref. III.8, the lift curve slope of a fin is approximately equal to the lift curve slope of a wing. There is a loss of fin 'lift' around the fuselage which is compensated by an increase in fin 'lift' due to the presence of the tailplane, which acts as a reflecting plate.

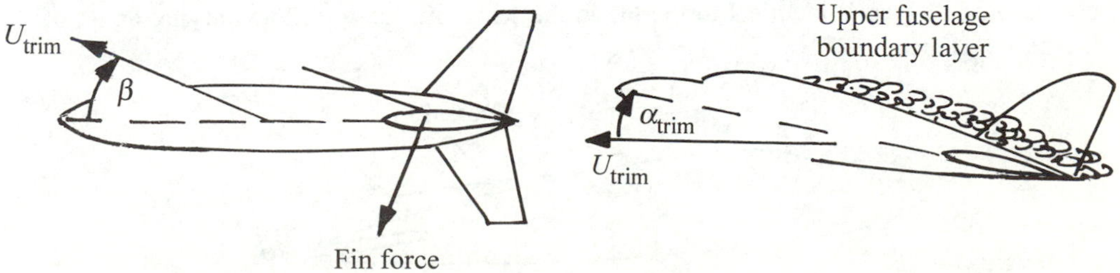

Fig. IV.7. Fin loads.

Thus an approximate value for $(a_\beta)_f$ can be taken from the formulae for $(a_\alpha)_w$, eqns. (III.3.13)–(III.3.15), namely

at subsonic speeds, $M_\infty < 0.85$,

$$(a_\beta)_f \simeq 2\pi \frac{AR_f}{(AR_f^2+4)^{1/2}+2} \frac{(AR_f \cos\Lambda_f)+1}{AR_f(1-M_\infty^2 \cos^2\Lambda_f)^{1/2}+1} \text{ per rad.,} \qquad \text{(IV.2.2a)}$$

at supersonic speeds, with subsonic leading edge,

$$(a_\beta)_f \simeq \pi \frac{AR_f/2}{\left[1+\left((M_\infty^2-1)^{1/2}/\pi\right)\right]\left[1+0.2\lambda_f\right]}, \qquad \text{(IV.2.2b)}$$

at supersonic speeds, with supersonic leading edge,

$$(a_\beta)_f \simeq \frac{4}{(M_\infty^2-1)^{1/2}}. \qquad \text{(IV.2.2c)}$$

When the initial trim state is at an angle of incidence, α_{trim}, as shown in Fig. IV.7, the fin sweep angle is effectively increased by α_{trim}. At low Mach number, because

$$\cos(\Lambda_f+\alpha_{trim}) \simeq \cos\Lambda_f - \alpha_{trim}\sin\Lambda_f,$$

$$\text{fin 'lift curve slope'} \simeq (a_\beta)_{fin}\left[1-\frac{(AR_f \sin\Lambda_f)\alpha_{trim}}{AR_f\cos\Lambda_f+1}\right] \qquad \text{(IV.2.3)}$$

taking $(a_\beta)_f$ as the fin 'lift curve slope' when α_{trim} is zero. Usually this effect of α_{trim} on the fin 'lift curve slope' is negligible, except possibly for highly swept fins at higher angles of α_{trim} (for example, there is an approximate 10% reduction in the fin 'lift curve slope', taking $AR_f = 2$, $\Lambda_f = 45°$, $\alpha_{trim} = 10°$).

Another effect associated with α_{trim} which decreases $(a_\beta)_f$ is the thickening of the boundary layer on the upper surface of the aft fuselage as α_{trim} increases, reducing the effective dynamic pressure in the flow about the fin root.

A traditional fin arrangement is the dorsal fin as shown in Fig. IV.8 where flow separation is induced in sideslip to increase the fin efficiency. The dorsal fin is a strake in modern parlance, thought of and used well before contemporary wing-strakes became fashionable.

When the sideslip angle varies with time, $\beta(t)$, there is an aerodynamic lag in the fin normal force which is identical to the lag in the wing lift due to a time varying angle of incidence. Hence

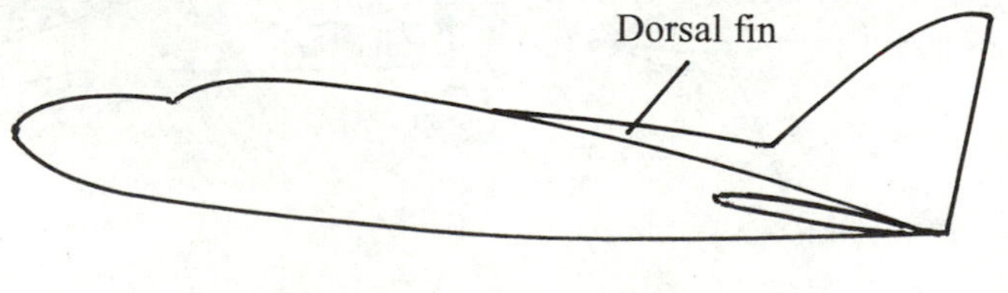

Fig. IV.8. Dorsal fin.

$$\text{fin normal force} = \tfrac{1}{2}\rho_{at}U_{trim}^2 S_f\left[(a_\beta)_f\beta(t) + (a_{\dot{\beta}})_f\left(c_f\dot{\beta}(t)/U_{trim}\right)\right] \quad \text{(IV.2.4)}$$

where $(a_{\dot{\beta}})_f$ can be obtained from sect. III.3.3, regarding the fin as an isolated wing. Because of the low aspect ratio of the fin, at low Mach numbers,

$$(a_{\dot{\beta}}/a_\beta)_f = O[-0.10]. \quad \text{(IV.2.5)}$$

EXAMPLES IV.2

1. Plot $(a_\beta)_f$ against Mach number for
   (i) the light aeroplane basic configuration,
   (ii) the transport aeroplane basic configuration, $0 < M_\infty < 0.85$,
   (iii) the combat aeroplane basic configuration, $0 < M_\infty < 1.8$.
   The lateral data for the basic configurations are given in sect. III.3.2.
2. Check the approximation for eqn. (IV.2.3). Modify this formula to account for subsonic Mach numbers; estimate typical orders of magnitude.
3. Estimate the loss in $(a_\beta)_f$ due to fuselage boundary layer at 12° angle of incidence (see Fig. IV.7), assuming typical values of fuselage/fin geometry.
4. How might eqn. (IV.2.5) vary with Mach number?

IV.2.2 Aerodynamics due to rate of roll

IV.2.2.1 Wing

Consider an isolated finite wing with camber and wash-out, and dihedral angle i_d, moving in symmetric flight at a steady trim speed U_{trim}, as shown in Fig. IV.9. By definition α_{trim} is the angle between the (fuselage) ox axis and the direction of U_{trim}; the wing is set at angle i_w relative to the ox axis.

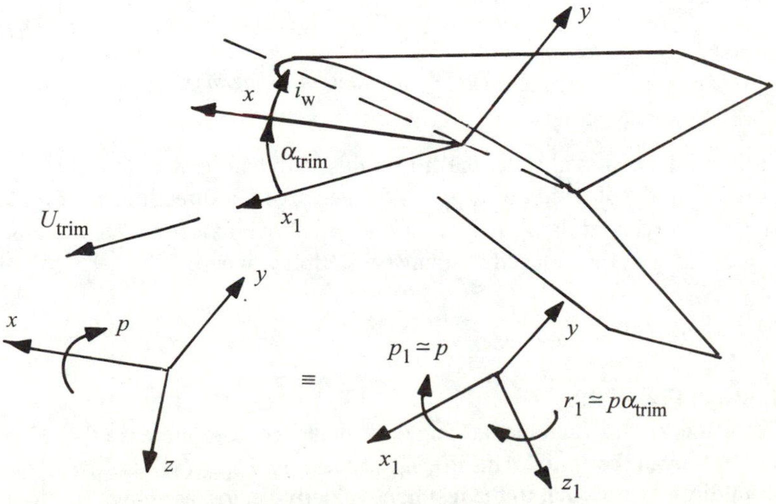

Fig. IV.9. Axes for rolling wing.

Suppose that the wing rolls about the ox axis with a constant rate of roll p. The problem is to determine the rolling moment about the ox axis, the yawing moment about the oz axis, and the side force in the y direction. To undertake this task it is necessary to refer to the trim body axis system ox_1yz_1, introduced in section IV.1, and shown again in Fig IV.9.

The rate of roll p about the ox axis can be resolved into a rate of roll p_1 ($= p \cos \alpha_{trim} \simeq p$ when α_{trim} is small) about the ox_1 axis and a rate of yaw r_1 ($= -p \sin \alpha \simeq -p\, \alpha_{trim}$) about the oz_1 axis.

Consider a geometrical strip at spanwise station y of width δy, as shown in Fig. IV.10.

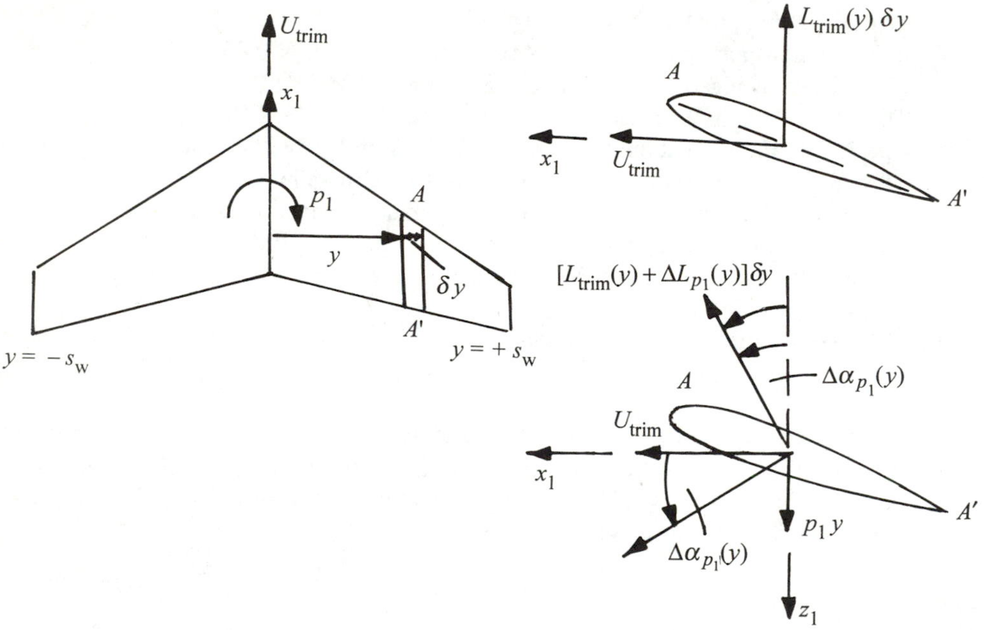

Fig. IV.10. Loading on rolling wing.

In the initial trimmed state, the lift on this strip can be denoted as ($L_{trim}(y)\, \delta y$) which acts normal to the direction of U_{trim}, in the negative oz_1 direction, see Fig. IV.10.

When the wing rolls with rate of roll p_1 about axis ox_1, an incremental angle of incidence $\Delta\alpha_{p_1}(y)$ is induced at spanwise station y, where

$$\Delta\alpha_{p_1}(y) = p_1\, y / U_{trim} \tag{IV.2.6}$$

as shown in Fig. IV.10.

The effect of this incremental angle of incidence is to increase the lift on the strip δy at station y from the initial trim lift, $L_{trim}(y)\, \delta y$, to $[L_{trim}(y) + \Delta L_{p_1}(y)]\delta y$, and to rotate this total lift to act normal to the resultant velocity vector, as shown in Fig. IV.10.

The total lift on the strip, $L(y)\, \delta y$, is

$$L(y)\,\delta y = \left[L_{\text{trim}}(y) + \Delta L_{p_1}(y)\right]\,\delta y \cos\left(\Delta\alpha_{p_1}(y)\right) \simeq \left[L_{\text{trim}}(y) + \Delta L_{p_1}(y)\right]\,\delta y, \tag{IV.2.7}$$

when $\Delta\alpha_{p_1}(y)$ is small.

The incremental lift $\Delta L_{p_1}(y)\,\delta y$ due to $\Delta\alpha_{p_1}(y)$ is given crudely by

$$\Delta L_{p_1}(y)\,\delta y \simeq \tfrac{1}{2}\rho_{\text{at}}U_{\text{trim}}^2 c(y)\,\delta y\, a_\alpha(y)\Delta\alpha_{p_1}(y) \simeq \tfrac{1}{2}\rho_{\text{at}}U_{\text{trim}}^2 c(y)\,\delta y\, a_\alpha(y)\,(p_1 y/U_{\text{trim}}) \tag{IV.2.8}$$

on substitution of eqn. (IV.2.6), where $a_\alpha(y)$ is the sectional lift curve slope at spanwise station y, corresponding to this antisymmetric loading; ($\Delta L_{p_1}(y)$ is positive on the starboard wing when y is positive, and negative on the port wing when y is negative).

The spanwise distribution $L_{\text{trim}}(y)$ is symmetric with respect to y from one wing tip ($y = -s_{\text{w}}$) to the other wing tip ($y = +s_{\text{w}}$), while the spanwise distribution $\Delta L_{p_1}(y)$, from eqn. (IV.2.8), is antisymmetric with respect to y. Hence

resultant lift in the negative oz_1 direction

$$= \int_{-s_{\text{w}}}^{+s_{\text{w}}} L(y)\,\mathrm{d}y = \int_{-s_{\text{w}}}^{+s_{\text{w}}} L_{\text{trim}}(y)\,\mathrm{d}y = \text{ initial trim lift.} \tag{IV.2.9}$$

And

rolling moment about ox_1 axis, due to rate of roll p_1 about the ox_1 axis

$$= (\mathscr{L}_{1p_1})_{\text{w}} \simeq -\int_{-s_{\text{w}}}^{+s_{\text{w}}} L(y)y\,\mathrm{d}y = -\int_{-s_{\text{w}}}^{+s_{\text{w}}} \Delta L_{p_1}(y)y\,\mathrm{d}y$$

$$\simeq -\tfrac{1}{2}\rho_{\text{at}}U_{\text{trim}}^2 S_{\text{w}} 2s_{\text{w}}(p_1 s_{\text{w}}/U_{\text{trim}})\,(1/4)\int_{y/s_{\text{w}}=-1}^{y/s_{\text{w}}=+1} a_\alpha(y)(c(y)/c_{\text{w}})\,(y/s_{\text{w}})^2\,\mathrm{d}(y/s_{\text{w}}) \tag{IV.2.10}$$

where c_{w} is the mean wing chord and S_{w} is the wing area ($= 2s_{\text{w}}c_{\text{w}}$). The negative sign arises because the moment $(\mathscr{L}_{1p_1})_{\text{w}}$ acts in the negative sense about the ox_1 axis. The form of eqn. (IV.2.10) is consistent with USA notation.

For an approximation for $(\mathscr{L}_{1p_1})_{\text{w}}$, it is necessary to formulate an order of magnitude value for $a_\alpha(y)$. If the loading on each half wing is assumed to be independent then the aspect ratio is effectively halved, then $a_\alpha(y)$ would be approximately ($0.8\ (a_\alpha)_{\text{w}}$), but there is an additional mutual interference between the two half wings which reduces the lift curve slope further. Hence

$$a_\alpha(y) = O[0.65(a_\alpha)_{\text{w}}]. \tag{IV.2.11}$$

And then, on substitution of eqn. (IV.2.11) into eqn. (IV.2.10),

$$(\mathscr{L}_{1p_1})_{\text{w}} = \tfrac{1}{2}\rho_{\text{at}}U_{\text{trim}}^2 S_{\text{w}} 2s_{\text{w}}(p_1 s_{\text{w}}/U_{\text{trim}}) \quad O[-0.09(a_\alpha)_{\text{w}}] \tag{IV.2.12}$$

for a wing with a taper ratio of $\tfrac{1}{2}$.

A rolling wing generates a side force from

(i) the suction edge forces on the wing leading edge and wing tips,
(ii) the rotation of the lift vector by the dihedral setting angle.

High suctions are created in the neighbourhood of a wing tip, leading to a wing tip suction force, due to the flow around that wing tip, similar to the leading thrust on a wing leading edge, see Fig. IV.11. If Γ is the strength of a wing tip trailing vortex then the outward suction force on that wing tip is proportional to Γ^2, say equal to (const Γ^2), on the argument that pressures are proportional to $(\text{velocity})^2$ and Γ is proportional to velocity. By reference to Fig. IV.11:

(i) in the initial trim state when each tip vortex has strength Γ_{trim}, but of opposite sign, the two wing tip side forces, both equal to const Γ_{trim}^2, cancel;
(ii) if the wing rolls at zero incidence generating tip vortices of strength Γ_p, both of the same sign, the two wing tip side forces are equal to const Γ_p^2, and again cancel;
(iii) when a wing at incidence rolls, the starboard wing tip vortex has strength $(\Gamma_{\text{trim}} + \Gamma_p)$, while the port wing tip vortex has strength $(\Gamma_{\text{trim}} - \Gamma_p)$; there is a net side force to starboard from the two wing tips equal to (const $4\Gamma_{\text{trim}}\Gamma_p$).

The leading edge suctions are also affected by roll rate. The increase in lift on the starboard wing and decrease in lift on the port wing implies an increase in the leading edge suction forces on the starboard wing and a decrease on the port wing, leading to a contribution to the net side force when the wing is swept, as sketched in Fig. IV.11.

An empirical formula from ESDU (ref. IV.1) for the net side force due to wingtip and leading edge suction forces in the direction of oy is

$$\left((Y_{p_1})_{\text{w}}\right)_{\text{I}} = \tfrac{1}{2}\rho_{\text{at}}U_{\text{trim}}^2 S_{\text{w}}(p_1 s_{\text{w}}/U_{\text{trim}}) \\ \mathrm{O}\left[((C_{\text{L}})_{\text{w}})_{\text{trim}}\left[(1/\text{AR}_{\text{w}}) + 0.8\tan\Lambda_{\text{w}}\right]\right]; \qquad \text{(IV.2.13)}$$

the two terms represent the wing tip and leading edge contributions respectively.

Any theoretical estimate for the wing side force is based on the assumption that the edge suction forces exist, which is only true when there are no flow separations around the leading edge or wing tips. But localized flow separations occur, especially in the wing tip regions of swept wings, at relatively small angles of incidence, of the order of 5°, reducing the suction forces. This effect can only be quantified by experimental measurement; but even here there is a problem because the onset and extent of flow separations depend critically on Reynolds number, so wind tunnel measurements at Reynolds numbers well below full scale Reynolds numbers may not reproduce full scale behaviour.

The second contribution to the side force is created by the wing dihedral angle, as sketched in Fig. IV.12. The increase in lift on the starboard wing and the decrease in the lift on the port wing due to rate of roll leads to a negative side force equal to

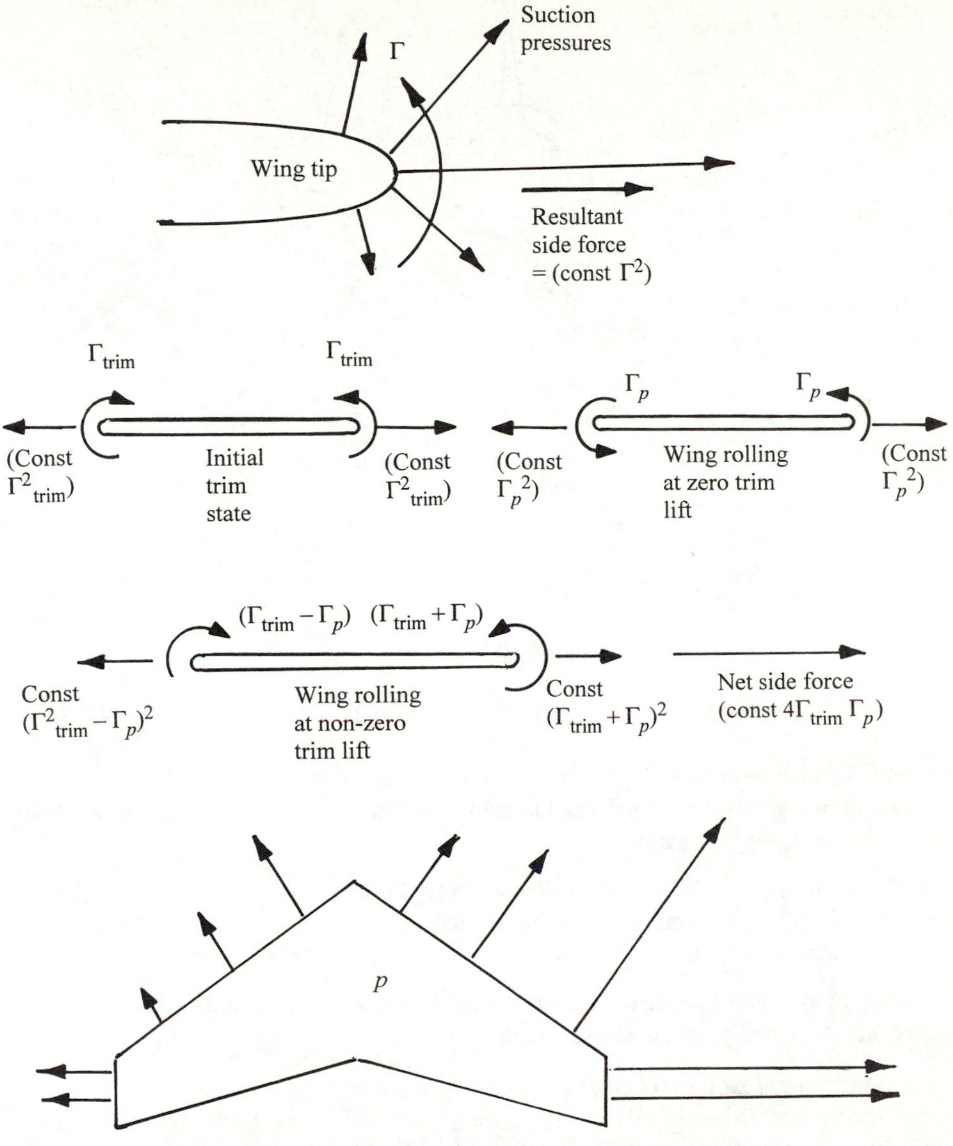

Fig. IV.11. Wing side force in roll due to edge forces.

$$\left((Y_{p_1})_{\mathrm{w}}\right)_{\mathrm{II}} = -\left(\int_0^{s_{\mathrm{w}}} \Delta L_{1p_1}(y)\,\mathrm{d}y\right) 2i_{\mathrm{d}}$$

$$= \tfrac{1}{2}\rho_{\mathrm{at}} U_{\mathrm{trim}}^2 S_{\mathrm{w}} \left(p_1 s_{\mathrm{w}}/U_{\mathrm{trim}}\right) \qquad \mathrm{O}\left[-0.3(a_\alpha)_{\mathrm{w}} i_{\mathrm{d}}\right]; \qquad \text{(IV.2.14)}$$

from eqns. (IV.2.8) and (IV.2.11).

The total wing side force, from eqns. (IV.2.13) and (IV.2.14), is

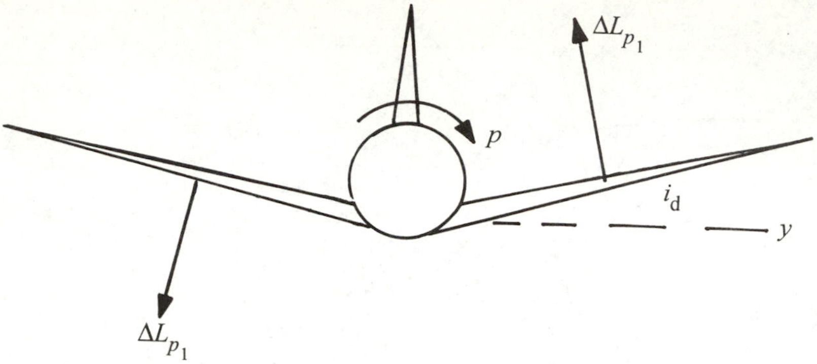

Fig. IV.12. Wing side force in roll due to dihedral.

$$(Y_{p_1})_w = \left((Y_{p_1})_w\right)_I + \left((Y_{p_1})_w\right)_{II}$$
$$= \tfrac{1}{2}\rho_{at} U_{trim}^2 S_w \left(p_1 s_w / U_{trim}\right)$$
$$\mathrm{O}\left[\left((C_L)_w\right)_{trim}\left[(1/AR_w) + 0.8 \tan \Lambda_w\right] - 0.30(a_\alpha)_w i_d\right]. \tag{IV.2.15}$$

The net wing side force will be positive when the full suction force acts.

A rolling wing generates a yawing moment about the oz_1 axis. There are three contributions to this yawing moment:

(i) the rotation of the lift vector, as shown in Fig. IV.10,
(ii) an antisymmetric vortex drag on the two half wings,
(iii) the side force $(Y_{p_1})_w$.

The rotation of the lift vector, shown in Fig. IV.10, induces a component of force in the ox_1 direction, acting on the strip at station y, equal to

$$[L_{trim}(y) + \Delta L_{p_1}(y)]\ (p_1 y / U_{trim})\delta y.$$

As already stated, $L_{trim}(y)$ is symmetric with respect to y while $\Delta L_{p_1}(y)$ is antisymmetric with respect to y, so

(i) there is a net forward thrust given by

$$\text{forward thrust} \simeq \int_{-s_w}^{+s_w} \Delta L_{p_1}(y)\left(p_1 y / U_{trim}\right) dy; \tag{IV.2.16}$$

this forward thrust, which is proportional to $(p_1 s_w / U_{trim})^2$, is second order and negligible;

(ii) there is a yawing moment about the oz_1 axis, due to rate of roll p_1 about the ox_1 axis,

$$\left((\mathcal{N}_{1p_1})_{\rm w}\right)_{\rm I} \simeq -\int_{-s_{\rm w}}^{+s_{\rm w}} \Delta L_{\rm trim}(y)\left(p_1 y/U_{\rm trim}\right) y\,{\rm d}y$$
$$\simeq -\tfrac{1}{2}\rho_{\rm at}U_{\rm trim}^2 S_{\rm w} 2s_{\rm w}\left(p_1 s_{\rm w}/U_{\rm trim}\right)$$
$$\times\left(\tfrac{1}{4}\right)\int_{y/s_{\rm w}=-1}^{y/s_{\rm w}=+1}\left(C_{\rm L}(y)\right)_{\rm trim}\left(c(y)/s_{\rm w}\right)\left(y/s_{\rm w}\right)^2 {\rm d}\left(y/s_{\rm w}\right)$$
$$\simeq \tfrac{1}{2}\rho_{\rm at}U_{\rm trim}^2 S_{\rm w} 2s_{\rm w}\left(p_1 s_{\rm w}/U_{\rm trim}\right) \quad {\rm O}\left[-0.12\left((C_{\rm L})_{\rm w}\right)_{\rm trim}\right].$$

(IV.2.17)

For the contribution of the vortex drags to the yawing moment:

(i) the trim vortex system, $\Gamma_{\rm trim}$ in Fig. IV.11, induces a symmetric spanwise incidence distribution $(\alpha_i(y))_{\rm trim}$ across the wing span, which rotates the trim lift vector, $(L(y)_{\rm trim}\,\delta y)$, aft; the integration of $[L(y)_{\rm trim}(\alpha_i(y)_{\rm trim}\,\delta y]$ across the wing span gives the trim induced drag;

(ii) the vortex system due to rate of roll, Γ_p in Fig. IV.11, induces an antisymmetric spanwise incidence distribution $\Delta\alpha_{ip}(y)$ across the wing span; $\Delta\alpha(y)$ is positive when $\Delta L_{p_1}(y)$ is positive and negative when $\Delta L_{p_1}(y)$ is negative.

Thus, there is a net yawing moment about the oz_1 axis

$$\left((\mathcal{N}_{1p_1})_{\rm w}\right)_{\rm II} = +\int_{-s_{\rm w}}^{+s_{\rm w}}\left[L_{\rm trim}(y)+\Delta L_{p_1}(y)\right]\left[\left(\alpha_i(y)\right)_{\rm trim}+\Delta\alpha_{ip_1}(y)\right] y\,{\rm d}y$$
$$= +\int_{-s_{\rm w}}^{+s_{\rm w}}\left[L_{\rm trim}(y)\Delta\alpha_{ip_1}(y)+\Delta L_{p_1}(y)\left(\alpha_i(y)\right)_{\rm trim}\right] y\,{\rm d}y. \qquad \text{(IV.2.18)}$$

Now $(\alpha_i(y))_{\rm trim}$ is approximately uniform and equal to $[((C_{\rm L})_{\rm w})_{\rm trim}/(\pi\,{\rm AR_w})]$ (see ref. III.8), so, taking the two terms in eqn. (IV.2.18) to be the same order of magnitude, from the second term, by reference to eqns. (IV.2.10) and (IV.2.12),

$$\left((\mathcal{N}_{1p_1})_{\rm w}\right)_{\rm II} \simeq \tfrac{1}{2}\rho_{\rm at}U_{\rm trim}^2 S_{\rm w} 2s_{\rm w}\left(p_1 s_{\rm w}/U_{\rm trim}\right)$$
$$\left(2\,{\rm O}\left[(0.09)\;(a_\alpha)_{\rm w}\left((C_{\rm L})_{\rm w}\right)_{\rm trim}/(\pi\,{\rm AR_w})\right]\right) \qquad \text{(IV.2.19)}$$

The third contribution to the wing yawing moment arises from the side forces, see Figs. IV.11 and IV.12. Unfortunately it is not easy to estimate where the resultant side force acts. But on the argument that its line of action passes reasonably close to the centre of mass, the yawing moment contribution from the wing side force is ignored here.

The total yawing moment on the wing about the axis oz_1 due to a rate of roll p_1 about the ox_1 axis is

$$(\mathcal{N}_{1p_1})_{\rm w} = \left((\mathcal{N}_{1p_1})_{\rm w}\right)_{\rm I} + \left((\mathcal{N}_{1p_1})_{\rm w}\right)_{\rm II}$$
$$\simeq \tfrac{1}{2}\rho_{\rm at}U_{\rm trim}^2 S_{\rm w} 2s_{\rm w}\left(p_1 s_{\rm w}/U_{\rm trim}\right) \qquad \text{(IV.2.20)}$$
$${\rm O}\left[\left(0.18(a_\alpha)_{\rm w}/(\pi\,{\rm AR_w})\right)-0.12\right]\left((C_{\rm L})_{\rm w}\right)_{\rm trim}.$$

The rolling and yawing moments due to rate of yaw r_1 ($\simeq -p\alpha_{\text{trim}}$) about the oz_1 axis can be neglected compared with the corresponding moments due to the rate of roll p_1 ($\simeq p$) about the ox_1 axis; this statement is verified later.

The wing side force $(Y_p)_{\text{w}}$, the wing rolling moment $(\mathscr{L}_p)_{\text{w}}$ and the wing yawing moment $(\mathscr{N}_p)_{\text{w}}$ about the fuselage body axes ox and oz respectively due to the rate of roll p about the ox axis for small α_{trim}, remembering that $p_1 \simeq p$, from eqns. (IV.2.15), (IV.2.12) and (IV.2.20), are

$$\begin{aligned}(Y_p)_{\text{w}} &= (Y_{p_1})_{\text{w}}\\ &= \tfrac{1}{2}\rho_{\text{at}}U_{\text{trim}}^2 S_{\text{w}}(ps_{\text{w}}/U_{\text{trim}})\\ &\quad \text{O}\Big[\big((C_{\text{L}})_{\text{w}}\big)_{\text{trim}}\big[(1/\text{AR}_{\text{w}})+0.8\tan\Lambda_{\text{w}}\big]-0.30(a_\alpha)_{\text{w}}i_{\text{d}}\Big],\end{aligned} \tag{IV.2.21}$$

$$\begin{aligned}(\mathscr{L}_p)_{\text{w}} &= (\mathscr{L}_{1p_1})_{\text{w}} - (\mathscr{N}_{1p_1})_{\text{w}}\alpha_{\text{trim}}\\ &\simeq (\mathscr{L}_{1p_1})_{\text{w}}\\ &\simeq \tfrac{1}{2}\rho_{\text{at}}U_{\text{trim}}^2 S_{\text{w}}2s_{\text{w}}(ps_{\text{w}}/U_{\text{trim}}) \quad \text{O}\big[-0.09\,(a_\alpha)_{\text{w}}\big],\end{aligned} \tag{IV.2.22}$$

$$\begin{aligned}(\mathscr{N}_p)_{\text{w}} &= (\mathscr{L}_{1p_1})_{\text{w}}\alpha_{\text{trim}} + (\mathscr{N}_{1p_1})_{\text{w}}\\ &= \tfrac{1}{2}\rho_{\text{at}}U_{\text{trim}}^2 S_{\text{w}}2s_{\text{w}}(ps_{\text{w}}/U_{\text{trim}})\\ &\quad \text{O}\Big[\big[(0.18(a_\alpha)_{\text{w}}/(\pi\,\text{AR}_{\text{w}}))-0.12\big]\big((C_{\text{L}})_{\text{w}}\big)_{\text{trim}}\\ &\qquad - 0.09(a_\alpha)_{\text{w}}\,\alpha_{\text{trim}}\Big].\end{aligned} \tag{IV.2.23}$$

With flaps up: $\quad (a_\alpha)_{\text{w}}\alpha_{\text{trim}} \simeq \big((C_{\text{L}})_{\text{w}}\big)_{\text{trim}} - (a_\alpha)_{\text{w}}(i_{\text{w}} - \alpha_{0\text{w}}),$

but with flaps down: $\quad (a_\alpha)_{\text{w}}\alpha_{\text{trim}} \simeq 0.$ (IV.2.24)

IV.2.2.2 Tailplane

The rolling moment on the tailplane due to rate of roll is given by similar expressions to that for the main wing, hence

$$(\mathscr{L}_p)_{\text{t}}/(\mathscr{L}_p)_{\text{w}} \simeq (S_{\text{t}}/S_{\text{w}})\,(s_{\text{t}}/s_{\text{w}})^2. \tag{IV.2.25}$$

For transport and light aeroplanes $(\mathscr{L}_p)_{\text{t}}$ can be neglected in comparison with $(\mathscr{L}_p)_{\text{w}}$. For a combat aeroplane with a large all-moving tailplane $(\mathscr{L}_p)_{\text{t}}$, although smaller than $(\mathscr{L}_p)_{\text{w}}$, is not necessarily negligible.

For all aeroplanes the tailplane contributions $(\mathscr{N}_p)_{\text{t}}$ and $(Y_p)_{\text{t}}$ are negligible because in the trimmed state the tailplane is less heavily loaded than the wing; this assumption may not be valid for an aeroplane with relaxed stability with a more heavily loaded tailplane.

IV.2.2.3 Fin

In roll there are two contributions to a side force on the fin:

(i) a side force arising from the 'incidence' of the fin as the aeroplane rolls;
(ii) a side force induced on the fin by the sidewash in the wake from the main wing.

As shown in Fig. IV.13, when the aeroplane rolls with a rate of roll p about the ox axis there is an increase in angle of 'incidence' along the span of the fin equal to $(p(-z)/(U_{\text{trim}}\cos\alpha_w))$. Taking the average 'incidence' to be $(p(s_f/2)/U_{\text{trim}})$ the side force on the fin in the oy direction is

$$\begin{aligned}(Y_p)_f &\simeq -\tfrac{1}{2}\rho_{at}U_{\text{trim}}^2 S_f(a_\beta)_f\big(p(s_f/2)/U_{\text{trim}}\big)\\ &= \tfrac{1}{2}\rho_{at}U_{\text{trim}}^2 S_w\big(ps_w/U_{\text{trim}}\big)\big[-0.5(S_f/S_w)(s_f/s_w)(a_\beta)_f\big]\end{aligned} \quad \text{(IV.2.26)}$$

where $(a_\beta)_f$ is given by eqns. (IV.2.2).

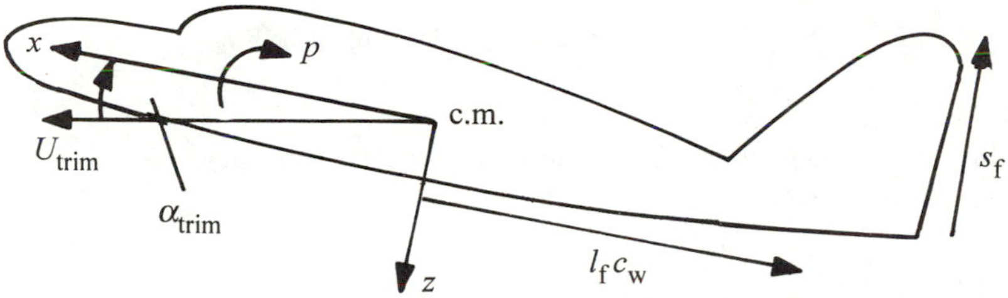

Fig. IV.13. Fin in roll.

The trailing vorticity in the wake behind the main wing for a rolling aeroplane comprises the trailing vorticity generated by the wing lift distribution due to rate of roll (i.e. $\Delta L_{p_1}(y)$) superimposed on the trailing vorticity generated by the trim wing lift distribution (i.e. $L_{\text{trim}}(y)$); see Fig. IV.14. Only the trailing vorticity associated with $\Delta L_{p_1}(y)$ induces a sidewash in the vicinity of the fin. This trailing vorticity can be regarded as a distribution of inboard continuous vorticity across the span together with two tip vortices; the net strength of trailing vorticity (i.e. inboard continuous vorticity plus tip vortices) must be zero. The inboard continuous vorticity induces a positive sidewash at the fin whereas the tip vortices induce a negative sidewash; the net sidewash is positive, but small. The side force on the fin due to the sidewash from the trailing vorticity is ignored.

The side force on the fin, $(Y_p)_f$, exerts

(i) a rolling moment about the ox axis

$$(\mathcal{L}_p)_f \simeq (Y_p)_f(0.6s_f) = (Y_p)_f 2s_w\big(0.3(s_f/s_w)\big), \quad \text{(IV.2.27)}$$

assuming that the centre of pressure of $(Y_p)_f$ acts at 60% of the fin span;

(ii) a yawing moment about the oz axis

$$(\mathcal{N}_p)_f \simeq -(Y_p)_f l_f c_w = -(Y_p)_f 2s_w\big(l_f/(\text{AR})_w\big), \quad \text{(IV.2.28)}$$

where $(l_f c_w)$ is the moment arm of the fin.

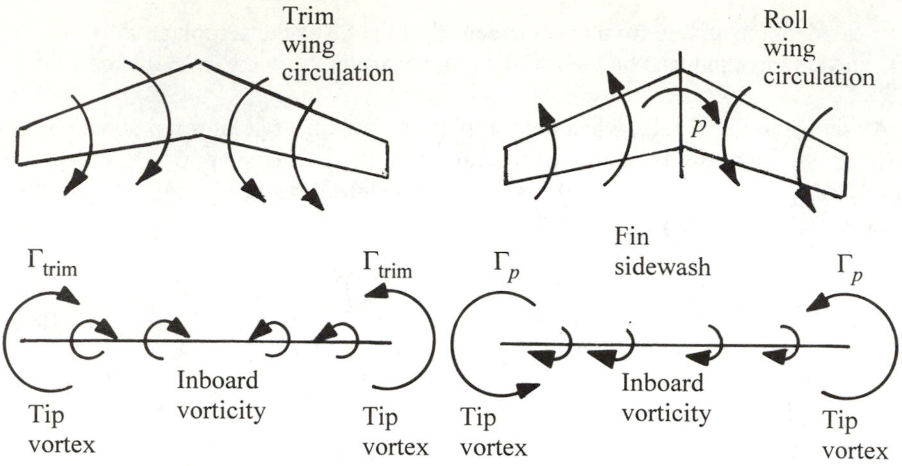

Fig. IV.14. Pattern of trailing vorticity aft of rolling wing.

IV.2.2.4 Fuselage

The loading on the fuselage, including any wing–fuselage interference effects, due to a rate of roll can be neglected.

IV.2.2.5 Propulsion unit

For a light aeroplane with a propeller at the front of a fuselage the rotating slipstream will induce a transverse load on that part of the fin immersed in the slipstream. In steady level flight the transverse fin load will be trimmed out by the rudder. When rolling the perturbation side force on the fin will be increased slightly relative to eqn. (IV.2.26) because of the increase in dynamic pressure in the slipstream.

For engines on the wing, whether propeller or turbo-fan, the increase in the angle of incidence on the starboard wing, and the decrease in angle of incidence on the port wing, results in a small rolling moment from the propeller disc or the turbo-fan nacelle, which adds to the wing rolling moment due to rate of roll.

IV.2.2.6 Effects of underwing weapons or stores

As explained in sect. III.3.9, the effect of underwing weapons is to change the angle of zero lift with little effect on the lift curve slope. Therefore the effects of underwing weapons on the roll rate derivatives are small.

Wing tip weapons or stores tend to increase loading in the wing tip regions so in this case the wing rolling moment due to rate of roll will be increased.

IV.2.2.7 Unsteady aerodynamic effects

The above analysis has been based on the premise that the rate of roll is constant. When the roll rate is varying with time, $p(t)$, there are aerodynamic lag effects.

Returning to the wing alone, consider a step change in roll rate (i.e. $p(t) = p_s H(t)$). The build-up time to the steady state rolling moment will be faster than the build-up time of the steady state wing lift following a step change in angle of incidence, as described in sect. III.3.3, because the shed vorticity into the wake following a step change in roll rate will be one sign for y positive and the opposite sign for y negative, whereas the shed vorticity into the wake following a step change in incidence is the same for y positive and y negative (see Fig. IV.15).

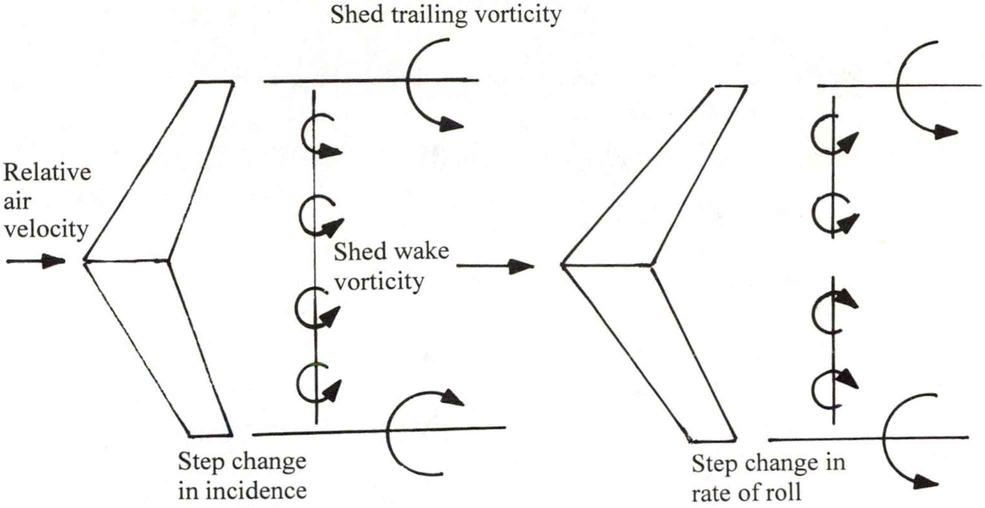

Fig. IV.15. Patterns in wake vorticity for step changes in angle of incidence and rate of roll.

Assuming that the lag effect for a rate of roll is a half of the lag effect for a change in angle of incidence, the wing rolling moment due to a time varying rate of roll, $p(t)$, can be expressed as, extending eqn. (IV.2.22),

$$(\mathcal{L}_p)_w = \tfrac{1}{2}\rho_{at}U_{trim}^2 S_w 2s_w$$

$$O[-0.09]\Big[(a_\alpha)_w\ \big(p(t)s_w/U_{trim}\big) \qquad \text{(IV.2.29)}$$

$$+\ 0.5(a_{\dot\alpha})_w\big(c_w/s_w\big)\Big(\dot p(t)\big(s_w/U_{trim}\big)^2\Big)\Big]$$

remembering that lag effects are measured in terms of the unit of time (c_w/U_{trim}).

The lag effects for the yawing moment on the main wing are more complicated because lags in vortex drags are involved. But $(\mathcal{N}_p)_w$ is relatively small so it is not unreasonable to ignore its lag effects. Hence for a time varying roll rate, $(\mathcal{N}_p)_w$ is given by eqn. (IV.3.23) replacing p by $p(t)$.

As will be seen later, the fin contributions in roll are also relatively small so again their lag effects can be ignored.

IV.2.2.8 Complete aeroplane

For the complete aeroplane, introducing the lateral derivatives,

$$
\begin{aligned}
Y_p(t) &= \text{total side force in } oy \text{ direction due to rate of roll } p(t) \\
&\quad\ \text{about } ox \text{ axis} \\
&= (Y_p)_w + (Y_p)_f, \quad \text{see eqns. (IV.2.21) and (IV.2.26)} \\
&= \tfrac{1}{2}\rho_{at}U_{trim}^2 S_w\left[C_{Yp}\left(p(t)s_w/U_{trim}\right)\right];
\end{aligned}
\tag{IV.2.30}
$$

$$
\begin{aligned}
\mathscr{L}_p(t) &= \text{total rolling moment about } ox \text{ axis due to rate of roll } p(t) \\
&\quad\ \text{about } ox \text{ axis} \\
&= (\mathscr{L}_p)_w + (\mathscr{L}_p)_f, \quad \text{see eqns. (IV.2.22) and (IV.2.27)} \\
&= \tfrac{1}{2}\rho_{at}U_{trim}^2 S_w 2s_w\Big[C_{lp}\left(p(t)s_w/U_{trim}\right) \\
&\qquad + C_{l\dot{p}}\left(\dot{p}(t)\left(s_w/U_{trim}\right)^2\right)\Big]
\end{aligned}
\tag{IV.2.31}
$$

$$
\begin{aligned}
\mathscr{N}_p(t) &= \text{total yawing moment about } ox \text{ axis due to rate of roll } p(t) \\
&\quad\ \text{about } ox \text{ axis} \\
&= (\mathscr{N}_p)_w + (\mathscr{N}_p)_f, \quad \text{see eqns. (IV.2.23) and (IV.2.28)} \\
&= \tfrac{1}{2}\rho_{at}U_{trim}^2 S_w 2s_w\left[C_{np}\left(p(t)s_w/U_{trim}\right)\right],
\end{aligned}
\tag{IV.2.32}
$$

where, taking $((C_L)_w)_{trim} \simeq (C_L)_{trim} = C_w$,

$$
\begin{aligned}
C_{Yp} &= O\Big[C_w\left[(1/AR_w) + 0.8\tan\Lambda_w\right] - 0.30(a_\alpha)_w i_d \\
&\qquad - 0.5\left(S_f/S_w\right)\left(s_f/s_w\right)(a_\beta)_f\Big] \\
C_{lp} &= O\left[-0.09(a_\alpha)_w - 0.15(a_\beta)_f\left(S_f/S_w\right)\left(s_f/s_w\right)^2\right] \\
C_{l\dot{p}} &= O\left[0.09(-a_{\dot{\alpha}})_w/AR_w\right] \\
C_{np} &= O\Big[\left[\left(0.18(a_\alpha)_w/(\pi AR_w)\right) - 0.12\right]C_w \\
&\qquad - 0.09(a_\alpha)_w\alpha_{trim} \\
&\qquad + 0.5(a_\beta)_f\left(S_f/S_w\right)\left(s_f/s_w\right)\left(l_f/AR_w\right)\Big].
\end{aligned}
\tag{IV.2.33}
$$

Taking typical values

$$
\begin{aligned}
&AR_w = 6, \quad \Lambda_w = 30°, \quad i_d = 2°, \quad (a_\alpha)_w = 4.5, \quad (a_{\dot{\alpha}})_w = -2.25, \\
&\left(S_f/S_w\right) = 0.2, \quad s_f/s_w = 0.4, \quad (a_\beta)_f = 2.5, \quad l_f = 3.0, \quad (i_w - \alpha_{0w}) = 3°
\end{aligned}
$$

then

$$C_{Yp} = O[-0.15 + 0.63C_w]$$

$$C_{lp} = O[-0.40]$$

$$C_{l\dot{p}} = O[+0.03] \qquad \text{(IV.2.34)}$$

$$C_{np} = O[0.05 - 0.17C_w] \quad \text{flaps up}$$

$$= O[0.05 - 0.08C_w] \quad \text{flaps down.}$$

The formula and value for C_{lp} are reasonable. Flow separations near the wing tip at higher angles α_{trim} can affect the values of C_{Yp} and C_{np}. The derivative C_{np} is notoriously difficult to predict, even to obtain the correct sign, because it is the difference between two quantities of the same magnitude; however, the trend from positive to negative with increasing C_w is valid.

EXAMPLES IV.3

1. Check the derivation of eqn. (IV.2.14).
2. Comment on the statement in the text: 'its line of action [of the resultant (wing) side force] passes reasonably close to the centre of mass'.
3. Is it a paradox that a rolling wing at zero angle of incidence, which generates tip vortices, has a thrust (see eqn. (IV.2.16))?
4. Explain the reasoning behind eqn. (IV.2.25).
5. In which roll rate derivatives are the fin contributions significant?
6. Estimate the rolling moment from turbo-fan engines on the wing.
7. Calculate, on the basis of eqns. (IV.2.33) the values of C_{Yp}, C_{lp}, C_{np} for the light aeroplane basic configuration. Is the effect of the propeller slipstream on these derivatives significant?
8. Plot, on the basis of eqns. (IV.2.33), the variation of C_{Yp}, C_{lp}, C_{np} against Mach number for the combat aeroplane basic configuration:

   at sea level $0.15 < M_\infty < 0.5$

   at 11 km altitude $0.5 < M_\infty < 0.85$.
9. Plot, on the basis of eqns. (IV.2.33), the variation of C_{Yp}, C_{lp}, C_{np} against Mach number for the transport aeroplane basic configuration:

   at sea level $0.15 < M_\infty < 0.7$

   at 11 km altitude $0.5 < M_\infty < 1.8$.

IV.2.3 Aerodynamics due to rate of yaw

IV.2.3.1 Wing

A rate of yaw r about the oz axis can be resolved into a rate of yaw r_1 ($= r\cos\alpha_{trim} \simeq r$) about the oz_1 axis and a rate of roll p_1 ($= r\sin\alpha_{trim} \simeq r\alpha_{trim}$) about the ox_1 axis, as shown in Fig. IV.16.

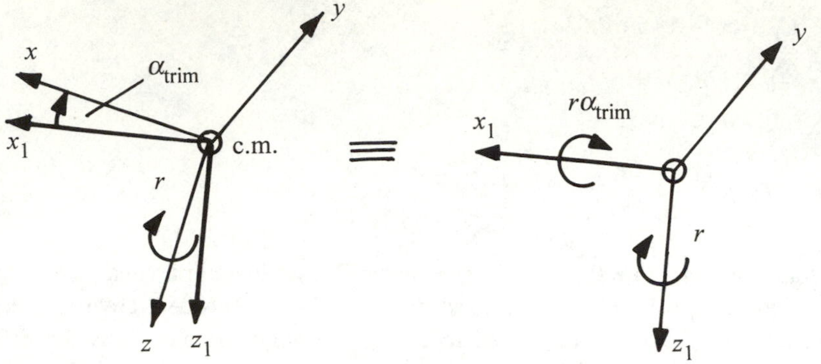

Fig. IV.16. Resolution of rate of yaw.

Consider the main wing yawing with constant rate of yaw r_1 about the oz_1 axis. As shown in Fig. IV.17, the effect of the rate of yaw is to decrease the forward relative air speed on the starboard wing and to increase the forward relative air speed on the port wing. The lift (in the $-oz_1$ direction) and the drag (in the negative ox_1 direction) on the strip at spanwise station y of width δy is approximately

$$\begin{aligned} L(y)\,\delta y &\simeq \tfrac{1}{2}\rho_{\text{at}}(U_{\text{trim}} - r_1 y)^2 (c(y)\,\delta y)(C_{\text{L}}(y))_{\text{trim}} \\ &\simeq \tfrac{1}{2}\rho_{\text{at}} U_{\text{trim}}^2 (1 - 2(r_1 y / U_{\text{trim}}))\,(c(y)\,\delta y)\,(C_{\text{L}}(y))_{\text{trim}}; \end{aligned} \quad \text{(IV.2.35)}$$

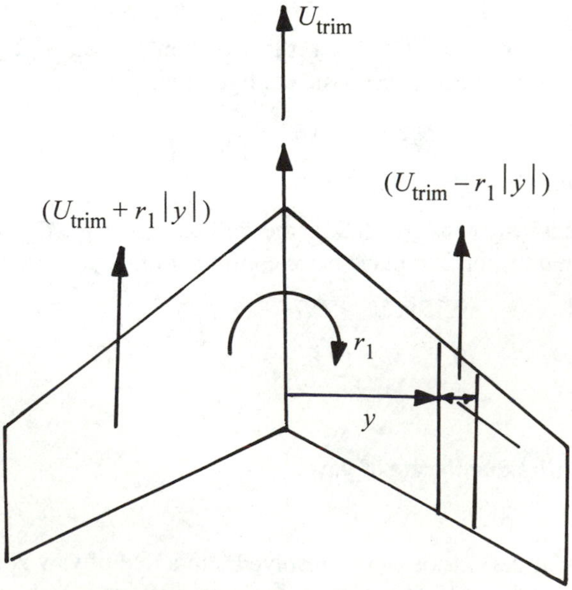

Fig. IV.17. Wing in rate of yaw.

$$D(y)\,\delta y \simeq \tfrac{1}{2}\rho_{\rm at}U_{\rm trim}^2\left(1-2\left(r_1 y/U_{\rm trim}\right)\right)\left(c(y)\,\delta y\right)\left(C_{\rm D}(y)\right)_{\rm trim}; \qquad \text{(IV.2.36)}$$

neglecting $(r_1 y/U_{\rm trim})^2$ as a second order term.

The lift distribution, eqn. (IV.2.35), induces a rolling moment on the main wing about the ox_1 axis, due to rate of yaw r_1 about the oz_1 axis, denoted by

$$\begin{aligned}(\mathscr{L}_{1r_1})_{\rm w} &= +\int_{-s_{\rm w}}^{+s_{\rm w}}\tfrac{1}{2}\rho_{\rm at}U_{\rm trim}^2\,2\left(r_1 y/U_{\rm trim}\right)\left(C_{\rm L}(y)\right)_{\rm trim}c(y)y\,{\rm d}y\\ &= \tfrac{1}{2}\rho_{\rm at}U_{\rm trim}^2 S_{\rm w}2s_{\rm w}\left(r_1 s_{\rm w}/U_{\rm trim}\right)(1/2)\\ &\qquad \int_{-1}^{+1}\left(C_{\rm L}(y)\right)_{\rm trim}\left(c(y)/c_{\rm w}\right)\left(y/s_{\rm w}\right)^2{\rm d}\left(y/s_{\rm w}\right)\\ &= \tfrac{1}{2}\rho_{\rm at}U_{\rm trim}^2 S_{\rm w}2s_{\rm w}\left(r_1 s_{\rm w}/U_{\rm trim}\right)\quad {\rm O}\left[+0.25\left((C_{\rm L})_{\rm w}\right)_{\rm trim}\right].\end{aligned} \qquad \text{(IV.2.37)}$$

The drag distribution, eqn. (IV.2.36), induces a yawing moment on the main wing about the oz_1 axis, denoted by

$$\begin{aligned}(\mathscr{N}_{1r_1})_{\rm w} &= \tfrac{1}{2}\rho_{\rm at}U_{\rm trim}^2 S_{\rm w}2s_{\rm w}\left(r_1 s_{\rm w}/U_{\rm trim}\right)\\ &\qquad {\rm O}\left[-\,0.25\left((C_{\rm D})_{\rm w}\right)_{\rm trim}\right].\end{aligned} \qquad \text{(IV.2.38)}$$

Thus,

$$\begin{aligned}(\mathscr{L}_r)_{\rm w} &= \text{rolling moment about } ox \text{ axis due to rate of yaw } r\\ &\quad\ \text{about the } oz \text{ axis}\\ &= \left[(\mathscr{L}_{1r_1})_{\rm w}+(\mathscr{L}_{1p_1})_{\rm w}\right]-\left[(\mathscr{N}_{1r_1})_{\rm w}+(\mathscr{N}_{1p_1})_{\rm w}\alpha_{\rm trim}\right]\alpha_{\rm trim}\\ &= \tfrac{1}{2}\rho_{\rm at}U_{\rm trim}^2 S_{\rm w}\,2s_{\rm w}\left(rs_{\rm w}/U_{\rm trim}\right)\\ &\qquad {\rm O}\left[+\,0.25\left((C_{\rm L})_{\rm w}\right)_{\rm trim}-0.09(a_\alpha)_{\rm w}\alpha_{\rm trim}\right],\end{aligned} \qquad \text{(IV.2.39)}$$

taking $r_1 = r$, $p_1 = r\alpha_{\rm trim}$, from eqns. (IV.2.37), (IV.2.12), (IV.2.38) and (IV.2.20), retaining terms of the same order of magnitude.

Similarly

$$\begin{aligned}(\mathscr{N}_r)_{\rm w} &= \text{yawing moment about } oz \text{ axis due to rate of yaw } r\\ &\quad\ \text{about the } oz \text{ axis}\\ &= \left[(\mathscr{L}_{1r_1})_{\rm w}+(\mathscr{L}_{1p_1})_{\rm w}\alpha_{\rm trim}\right]\alpha_{\rm trim}+\left[(\mathscr{N}_{1r_1})_{\rm w}+(\mathscr{N}_{1p_1})_{\rm w}\alpha_{\rm trim}\right]\\ &= \tfrac{1}{2}\rho_{\rm at}U_{\rm trim}^2 S_{\rm w}\,2s_{\rm w}\left(rs_{\rm w}/U_{\rm trim}\right)\\ &\qquad {\rm O}\Big[-\,0.25(C_{\rm D})_{\rm trim}+\left(0.18\left((a_\alpha)_{\rm w}/\pi{\rm AR}_{\rm w}\right)+0.13\right)\left((C_{\rm L})_{\rm w}\right)_{\rm trim}\alpha_{\rm trim}\\ &\qquad\quad -0.09(a_\alpha)_{\rm w}\alpha_{\rm trim}^2\Big].\end{aligned} \qquad \text{(IV.2.40)}$$

A side force on the wing arises from two contributions:

(i) a negative side force from the suction forces on the wing leading edge and wing tips,
(ii) a positive side force arising from the dihedral angle.

Both of these contributions are small, and of opposite sign, so the total side force is ignored.

IV.2.3.2 Fin

The rate of yaw r about the oz axis induces an angle of 'incidence' on the fin equal to $(rl_f c_w/U_{trim} \cos \alpha_w))$, as shown in Fig. IV.18, which leads to a side force $(Y_r)_f$ in the oy direction given by

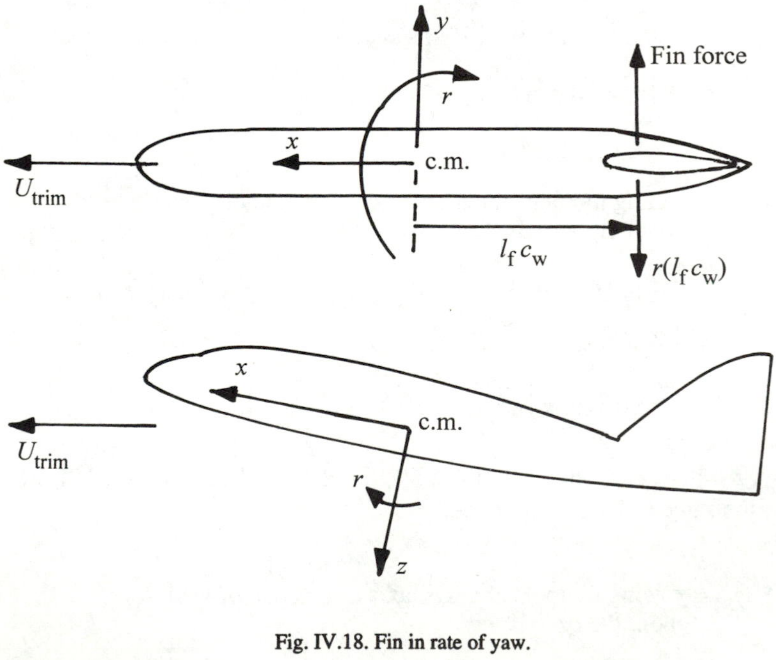

Fig. IV.18. Fin in rate of yaw.

$$(Y_r)_f = +\tfrac{1}{2}\rho_{at}U^2_{trim}S_f(a_\beta)_f(rl_f c_w/U_{trim})$$
$$= +\tfrac{1}{2}\rho_{at}U^2_{trim}S_w(rs_w/U_{trim})\left[(S_f/S_w)\,(2/(AR)_w)l_f(a_\beta)_f\right] \qquad (IV.2.41)$$

The wing tip vortices arising from the trim loading and the rolling moment due to rate of yaw, in their curved paths, induce a sidewash on the fin; the side force arising from this sidewash is small compared with the direct fin force given by eqn. (IV.2.41).

The fin side force gives a rolling moment about the *ox* axis

$$(\mathscr{L}_r)_f \simeq +(Y_r)_f \, s_f/2, \tag{IV.2.42}$$

assuming that the centre of pressure of the fin side force acts at the half span, and a yawing moment about the *oz* axis

$$(\mathscr{N}_r)_f \simeq -(Y_r)_f l_f c_w. \tag{IV.2.43}$$

IV.2.3.3 Fuselage

The fuselage contribution to the side force and yawing moment due to rate of yaw arises mainly from the side force on the fuselage nose, similar to the nose lift due to angle of incidence described in sect. III.3.4. From eqn. (III.3.71) the side force on the fuselage nose is

$$\begin{aligned}(Y_r)_{fus} &\simeq -\tfrac{1}{2}\rho_{at}U_{trim}^2\Big((r_{max})^2 2\pi\big(rl_n c_w/U_{trim}\big)\Big)\\ &\simeq -\tfrac{1}{2}\rho_{at}U_{trim}^2 S_w\big(rs_w/U_{trim}\big)\Big[\pi l_n\big(r_{max}/c_w\big)^2\big(2/\mathrm{AR}_w\big)^2\Big]\end{aligned} \tag{IV.2.44}$$

where r_{max} is the maximum fuselage radius in the neighbourhood of the fuselage nose and $l_n c_w$ is the distance of the fuselage nose side force ahead of the aeroplane centre of mass (see Fig. IV.1).

The yawing moment due to the side force on the fuselage nose is

$$(\mathscr{N}_r)_{fus} = (Y_r)_{fus} l_n c_w. \tag{IV.2.45}$$

IV.2.3.4 Propulsion unit

The contributions from the propulsion unit arising from a rate of yaw can usually be neglected.

IV.2.3.5 Effects of underwing weapons and stores

The main effect of underwing weapons is the large increase in drag, leading to a substantial increase in the C_D term in eqn. (IV.2.40)

IV.2.3.6 Unsteady aerodynamic effects

When the rate of yaw is a function of time, *r*(*t*), the lag effects on the wing rolling and yawing moments can be neglected.

The side force on the fin, $(Y_r)_f$, incorporating the lag effect, from eqn. (IV.2.4), is

$$\begin{aligned}(Y_r)_f &= +\tfrac{1}{2}\rho_{at}U_{trim}^2 S_w\big[(S_f/S_w)(2/(\mathrm{AR})_w)l_f\big]\\ &\times\Big[(a_\beta)_f\big(r(t)s_w/U_{trim}\big)+(a_{\dot\beta})_f\big(c_f/s_w\big)\Big(\dot r(t)\big(s_w/U_{trim}\big)^2\Big)\Big].\end{aligned} \tag{IV.2.46}$$

The lag effects for the loads on the fuselage nose are insignificant.

An unsteady contribution to the yawing moment arises from the fuselage 'apparent mass' due to $\dot r(t)$ similar to pitching moment due to $\dot q(t)$; so from eqns. (III.3.81)

$$(\mathcal{N}_{\dot{r}})_{\text{fus}} = \tfrac{1}{2}\rho_{\text{at}}U_{\text{trim}}^2 S_{\text{w}} c_{\text{w}} \quad \text{O}\left[-(30/\text{AR}_{\text{w}})\left(\dot{r}(t)(c_{\text{w}}/U_{\text{trim}})^2\right)\right]$$
$$= \tfrac{1}{2}\rho_{\text{at}}U_{\text{trim}}^2 S_{\text{w}}\, 2s_{\text{w}} \quad \text{O}\left[-(120/\text{AR}_{\text{w}}^4)\left(\dot{r}(t)(s_{\text{w}}/U_{\text{trim}})^2\right)\right]. \qquad \text{(IV.2.47)}$$

IV.2.3.7 Complete aeroplane

For the overall aeroplane

$$\mathcal{L}_r = \text{total rolling moment due to rate of yaw } r(t) \text{ about the } oz \text{ axis}$$
$$= (\mathcal{L}_r)_{\text{w}} + (\mathcal{L}_r)_{\text{f}} \text{ (see eqns. (IV.2.39) and (IV.2.42))} \qquad \text{(IV.2.48)}$$
$$= \tfrac{1}{2}\rho_{\text{at}}U_{\text{trim}}^2 S_{\text{w}}\, 2s_{\text{w}}\left[C_{lr}\left(r(t)\, s_{\text{w}}/U_{\text{trim}}\right) + C_{l\dot{r}}\left(\dot{r}(t)(s_{\text{w}}/U_{\text{trim}})^2\right)\right]$$

$$\mathcal{N}_r = \text{total yawing moment due to rate of yaw } r(t) \text{ about the } oz \text{ axis}$$
$$= (\mathcal{N}_r)_{\text{w}}(\mathcal{N}_r)_{\text{f}} + (\mathcal{N}_r)_{\text{fus}} + (\mathcal{N}_{\dot{r}})_{\text{fus}} \text{ (see eqns. (IV.2.40),}$$
$$\text{(IV.2.43), (IV.2.45)–(IV.2.47))} \qquad \text{(IV.2.49)}$$
$$= \tfrac{1}{2}\rho_{\text{at}}U_{\text{trim}}^2 S_{\text{w}}\, 2s_{\text{w}}\left[C_{nr}\left(r(t)\, s_{\text{w}}/U_{\text{trim}}\right) + C_{n\dot{r}}\left(\dot{r}(t)(s_{\text{w}}/U_{\text{trim}})^2\right)\right]$$

$$Y_r = \text{overall side force due to rate of yaw } r(t) \text{ about the } oz \text{ axis}$$
$$= (Y_r)_{\text{f}} + (Y_r)_{\text{fus}} \quad \text{(see eqns. (IV.2.44) and (IV.2.46))} \qquad \text{(IV.2.50)}$$
$$= \tfrac{1}{2}\rho_{\text{at}}U_{\text{trim}}^2 S_{\text{w}}\left[C_{Yr}\left(r(t) s_{\text{w}}/U_{\text{trim}}\right) + C_{Y\dot{r}}\left(\dot{r}(t)(s_{\text{w}}/U_{\text{trim}})^2\right)\right]$$

where, taking $((C_{\text{L}})_{\text{trim}}) = C_{\text{w}}$

$$C_{lr} = \text{O}\big[+0.25C_{\text{w}} - 0.09(a_\alpha)_{\text{w}}\alpha_{\text{trim}}$$
$$+ 0.5(S_{\text{f}}/S_{\text{w}})(s_{\text{f}}/s_{\text{w}})(l_{\text{f}}/\text{AR}_{\text{w}})(a_\beta)_{\text{f}}\big]$$

$$C_{l\dot{r}} = \text{O}\left[(S_{\text{f}}/S_{\text{w}})(c_{\text{f}}/c_{\text{w}})(l_{\text{f}}/\text{AR}_{\text{w}}^2)(a_{\dot{\beta}})_{\text{f}}\right]$$

$$C_{nr} = \text{O}\big[-0.25(C_{\text{D}})_{\text{trim}} + \left(0.18((a_\alpha)_{\text{w}}/\pi\text{AR}_{\text{w}}) + 0.13\right)C_{\text{w}}\alpha_{\text{trim}}$$
$$- 0.09(a_\alpha)_{\text{w}}\alpha_{\text{trim}}^2 - 2(S_{\text{f}}/S_{\text{w}})(l_{\text{f}}/\text{AR}_{\text{w}})^2(a_\beta)_{\text{f}}$$
$$- 4\pi d_{\text{n}}^2 (r_{\max}/c_{\text{w}})^2/\text{AR}_{\text{w}}^3\big]$$

$$C_{n\dot{r}} = \text{O}\left[-4(S_{\text{f}}/S_{\text{w}})(c_{\text{f}}/c_{\text{w}})(l_{\text{f}}^2/\text{AR}_{\text{w}}^3)(a_{\dot{\beta}})_{\text{f}} - 120/\text{AR}_{\text{w}}^4\right]$$

$$C_{Yr} = O\left[+ 2(S_f/S_w)\ (l_f/AR_w)\ (a_\beta)_f - \pi l_n (r_{max}/c_w)^2 (2/AR_w)^2\right]$$

$$C_{Y\dot{r}} = O\left[+ 4(S_f/S_w)(c_f/c_w)(l_f/AR_w^2)\ (a_{\dot{\beta}})_f\right]. \qquad \text{(IV.2.51)}$$

With the typical values

$$AR_w = 6, \quad \Lambda_w = 30°, \quad i_d = 2°, \quad (a_\alpha)_w = 4.5, \quad (a_{\dot{\alpha}})_w = -2.25,$$

$$(S_f/S_w) = 0.2, \quad s_f/s_w = 0.4, \quad (a_\beta)_f = 2.5, \quad (a_{\dot{\beta}})_f = -1.25,$$

$$l_f = 3.0, \quad l_n = 3.0, \quad r_{max}/c_w = 0.3,$$

then, with flaps up,

$$C_{lr} = O[+ 0.16C_w + 0.07]$$
$$C_{l\dot{r}} \simeq O[- 0.02]$$
$$C_{nr} = O[- 0.3 - 0.25(C_D)_{trim}]$$
$$C_{n\dot{r}} \simeq O[- 0.05] \qquad \text{(IV.2.52)}$$
$$C_{Yr} = O[+ 0.4]$$
$$C_{Y\dot{r}} = O[- 0.08]$$

Note:

(i) the C_{lr} derivative arises from the wing and the fin; the wing contribution grows with C_w, becoming significant at low speeds;

(ii) the contributions from the fin and fuselage nose to the derivative C_{nr} are additive; the fin contribution is dominant; the fuselage nose contribution is approximately 20% of the fin contribution;

(iii) the contributions from the fin and fuselage nose to the derivative C_{Yr} are of opposite sign; again the fuselage nose contribution is approximately 20% of the fin contribution.

EXAMPLES IV.4

1. Explain the statement in the text: 'The wing tip vortices arising from the trim loading and the rolling moment due to rate of yaw, in their curved paths, induce a sidewash on the fin.'
2. Check the statement made in the text in sect. IV.2.2.1: 'The rolling and yawing moments due to rate of yaw r_1 ($\simeq -p\ \alpha_{trim}$) about the oz_1 axis can be neglected compared with the corresponding moments due to the rate of roll p_1 ($\simeq p$) about the ox_1 axis.'
3. How might the values in eqns. (IV.2.51) be changed with flaps down?

4. Calculate, on the basis of eqns. (IV.2.51) the values of C_{Yr}, C_{lr}, C_{nr} for the light aeroplane basic configuration. Discuss the effect of the propeller slipstream on these derivatives.
5. Plot, on the basis of eqns. (IV.2.51), the variation of C_{Yr}, C_{lr}, C_{nr} against Mach number for the transport aeroplane basic configuration:

   at sea level $0.15 < M_\infty < 0.5$

   at 11 km altitude $0.5 < M_\infty < 0.85$.

6. Plot, on the basis of eqns. (IV.2.51), the variation of C_{Yr}, C_{lr}, C_{nr} against Mach number for the combat aeroplane basic configuration:

   at sea level $0.15 < M_\infty < 0.7$

   at 11 km altitude $0.5 < M_\infty < 1.8$.

   What is the effect of underwing weapons on these derivatives if $(\Delta C_D)_{weapons} = 0.02$?

IV.2.4 Aerodynamics due to sideslip

IV.2.4.1 Wing

Consider first a non-swept wing with dihedral setting angle i_d, as shown in Fig. IV.19. When this wing is sideslipping at steady sideslip angle β, there is an increase in the angle of incidence of the section AA' in the direction of the resultant velocity of the starboard wing by $(+\beta i_d)$, assuming β to be small. Similarly there is a decrease in angle of incidence of the port wing by $(-\beta i_d)$.

Thus

$$\text{change in lift on starboard wing} \simeq \tfrac{1}{2}\rho_{at}U_{trim}^2(S_w/2)\left(0.65(a_\alpha)_w\right)(+\beta i_d)$$

$$\text{change in lift on port wing} \simeq \tfrac{1}{2}\rho_{at}U_{trim}^2(S_w/2)\left(0.65(a_\alpha)_w\right)(-\beta i_d)$$

where the factor 0.65 is explained in eqn. (IV.2.11). Hence the rolling moment about the stability axis ox_1 is

$$\left((\mathscr{L}_{1\beta})_w\right)_I \simeq 2\left[-\tfrac{1}{2}\rho_{at}U_{trim}^2(S_w/2)\left(0.65(a_\alpha)_w\right)\beta i_d(s_w/2)\right] \qquad \text{(IV.2.53)}$$

taking the centre of lift of each half-wing at the mid semi-span.

Although derived for a non-swept wing, eqns. (IV.2.51) are applicable to a swept wing.

Next consider a swept wing with sweep angle Λ_w with zero dihedral angle at angle of incidence α_w, sideslipping at steady sideslip angle β, as shown in Fig. IV.20.

In symmetric flight, when β is zero, the lift on each half-wing of a wing of reasonable aspect ratio (say $AR_w > 4$) is approximately proportional to $(\tfrac{1}{2}\rho_{at}(U_{trim}\cos\Lambda_w)^2)$, the dynamic pressure based on the velocity normal to the wing sweep.

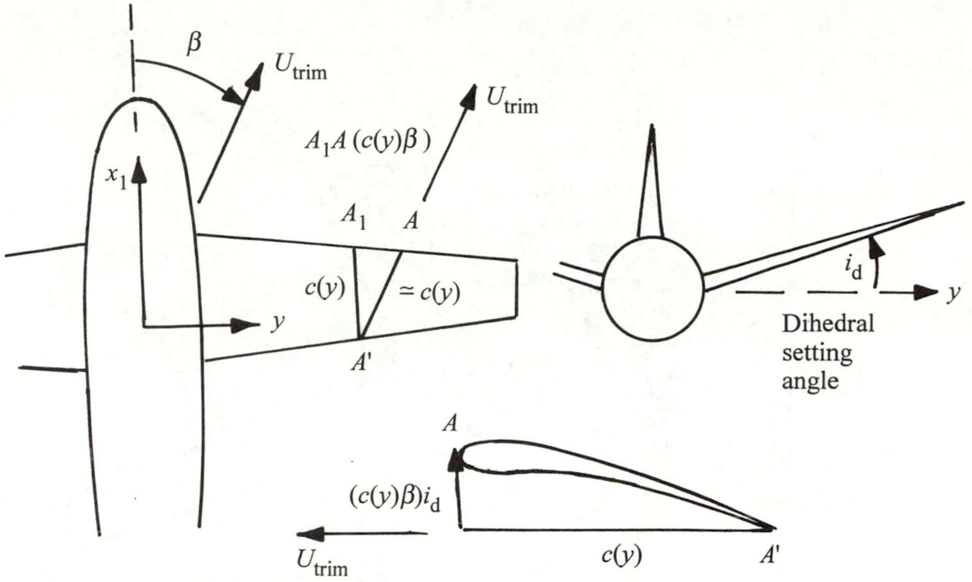

Fig. IV.19. Effect of wing dihedral in sideslip.

In sideslip:

velocity normal to the leading edge of the starboard wing

$$= U_{trim}(\cos\Lambda_w + \beta\sin\Lambda_w), \tag{IV.2.54}$$

for small β. Hence

dynamic pressure based on velocity normal to the leading edge of starboard wing

$$= \tfrac{1}{2}\rho_{at}(U_{trim}\cos\Lambda_w)^2(1 + 2\beta\tan\Lambda_w) \tag{IV.2.55(i)}$$

neglecting β^2. Similarly,

dynamic pressure based on velocity normal to the leading edge of port wing

$$= \tfrac{1}{2}\rho_{at}(U_{trim}\cos\Lambda_w)^2(1 - 2\beta\tan\Lambda_w). \tag{IV.2.55(ii)}$$

Therefore the starboard wing lift increases by a factor ($2\beta\tan\Lambda_w$) while the port wing lift decreases by a factor ($2\beta\tan\Lambda_w$), giving a rolling moment about the ox_1 axis

$$\left((\mathscr{L}_{\beta 1})_w\right)_{II} \simeq 2\left[-\tfrac{1}{2}\rho_{at}U_{trim}^2(S_w/2)\left(0.7((C_L)_w)_{trim}\right)2\beta\tan\Lambda_w(s_w/2)\right]. \tag{IV.2.56}$$

The somewhat arbitrary factor 0.7 is introduced to denote the loss in incremental lift due to sideslip across the fuselage and the fact that the above argument applies to about the

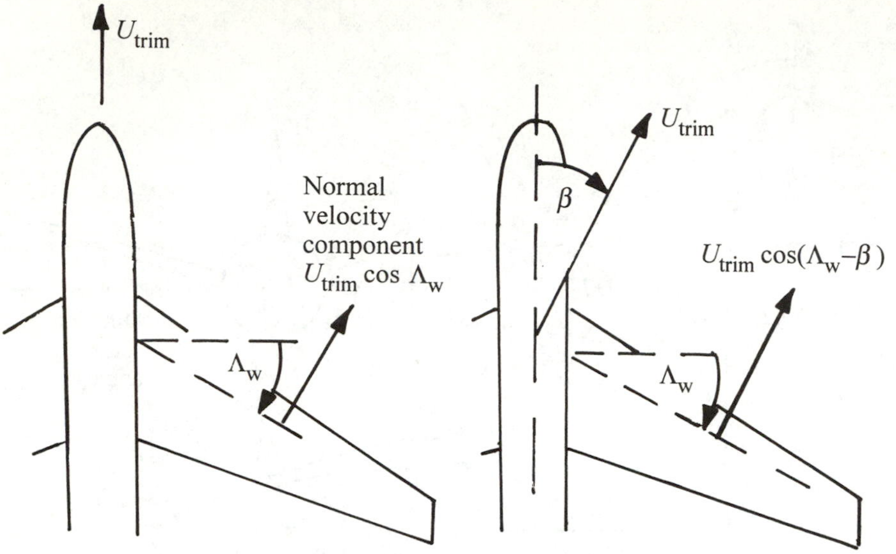

Fig. IV.20. Effect of wing sweep in sideslip.

70% of the wing span away from the wing root and wing tip, and assuming that the centre of pressure of the incremental lift on each half-wing acts at the mid semi-span, $(s_w/2)$.

The rolling moment on a swept wing with dihedral about the axis ox_1 due to sideslip is the sum of eqns. (IV.2.52) and (IV.2.56), namely

$$(\mathscr{L}_{\beta 1})_w \simeq -\tfrac{1}{2}\rho_{at} U_{trim}^2 S_w \, 2s_w \Big[0.16(a_\alpha)_w i_d + 0.35\big((C_L)_w\big)_{trim} \tan \Lambda_w\Big]\beta. \tag{IV.2.57}$$

There is a small yawing moment $(\mathscr{N}_{\beta 1})_w$ on the wing about the oz_1 axis arising from a vortex drag contribution, similar to that for the rolling wing, see eqn. (IV.2.18).

Hence the rolling and yawing moments about the fuselage body axes ox and oz are, for small α_{trim},

$$(\mathscr{L}_\beta)_w = (\mathscr{L}_{\beta 1})_w + (\mathscr{N}_{\beta 1})_w \alpha_{trim} \simeq (\mathscr{L}_{\beta 1})_w, \tag{IV.2.58}$$

$$(\mathscr{N}_\beta)_w = (\mathscr{L}_{\beta 1})_w \alpha_{trim} + (\mathscr{N}_{\beta 1})_w \simeq 0.0. \tag{IV.2.59}$$

The neglect of $(\mathscr{N}_\beta)_w$ is reasonable in comparison to the larger contributions to the yawing moment from the fin and fuselage.

A side force arises on a wing in sideslip from

(i) the antisymmetric lifts on each half-wing, inclined by the dihedral angle, which give a negative side force;
(ii) the suction forces on the leading edge and wing tips from the changes in loading on each half-wing, which give a positive side force.

The net side force on the wing is ignored here; this assumption needs to be checked in a more thorough analysis, especially at high C_L with flaps down.

IV.2.4.2 Fin

In sideslip the side force on the fin, neglecting all interference effects, is, from eqn. (IV.2.2)

$$(Y_\beta)_f = -\tfrac{1}{2}\rho_{at}U_{trim}^2 S_f(a_\beta)_f\beta. \qquad \text{(IV.2.60)}$$

In sideslip, there is a complicated pattern of sidewash in the neighbourhood of the fin:

(i) sideslip skews the trim wake from the main wing, as sketched in Fig. IV.21(i), inducing a sidewash at the fin semi-span in the negative y direction;
(ii) the antisymmetric loading on the main wing due to dihedral and wing sweep, introduces additional trailing vortices, as shown in Fig. IV.21(ii), which induces a sidewash at the fin semi-span in the positive y direction, in the opposite sense to (i).

Usually (ii) dominates over (i), increasing marginally the effective value of β. The sidewash effect is ignored here; again this assumption needs to be checked in a more thorough analysis, especially at high C_L with flaps down.

The difference between the wake patterns in Figs. IV.14 and IV.21 deserves comment. When a wing rolls, the incremental spanwise loading increases from zero at the wing root to a maximum in the region of the wing tips, and then the inboard trailing vorticity across the semi-span due to the incremental loading is virtually uniform. But for a wing in sideslip the incremental spanwise loading on each half-wing is more uniform with a virtual discontinuity in incremental loading across the wing root, thus the inboard trailing vorticity due to the incremental loading tends to become a concentrated vortex around the fuselage.

The side force on the fin gives a yawing moment about the fuselage oz axis,

$$(\mathcal{N}_\beta)_f \simeq -(Y_\beta)_f l_f c_w, \qquad \text{(IV.2.61)}$$

and a rolling moment about the fuselage ox axis

$$(\mathcal{L}_\beta)_f \simeq (Y_\beta)_f(s_f/2). \qquad \text{(IV.2.62)}$$

IV.2.4.3 Fuselage

The side force on the fuselage nose in sideslip, from eqn. (III.3.71), is

$$(Y_\beta)_{fus} = -\tfrac{1}{2}\rho_{at}U_{trim}^2 S_w\left[\pi(r_{max}/c_w)^2(2/AR_w)\right]\beta, \qquad \text{(IV.2.63)}$$

which leads to a yawing moment about the oz axis

$$(\mathcal{N}_\beta)_{fus} \simeq (Y_\beta)_{fus} l_n c_w. \qquad \text{(IV.2.64)}$$

Wing–fuselage interference affects the wing loadings due to sideslip for the two extremes of a high wing or a low wing, as sketched in Fig. IV.22.

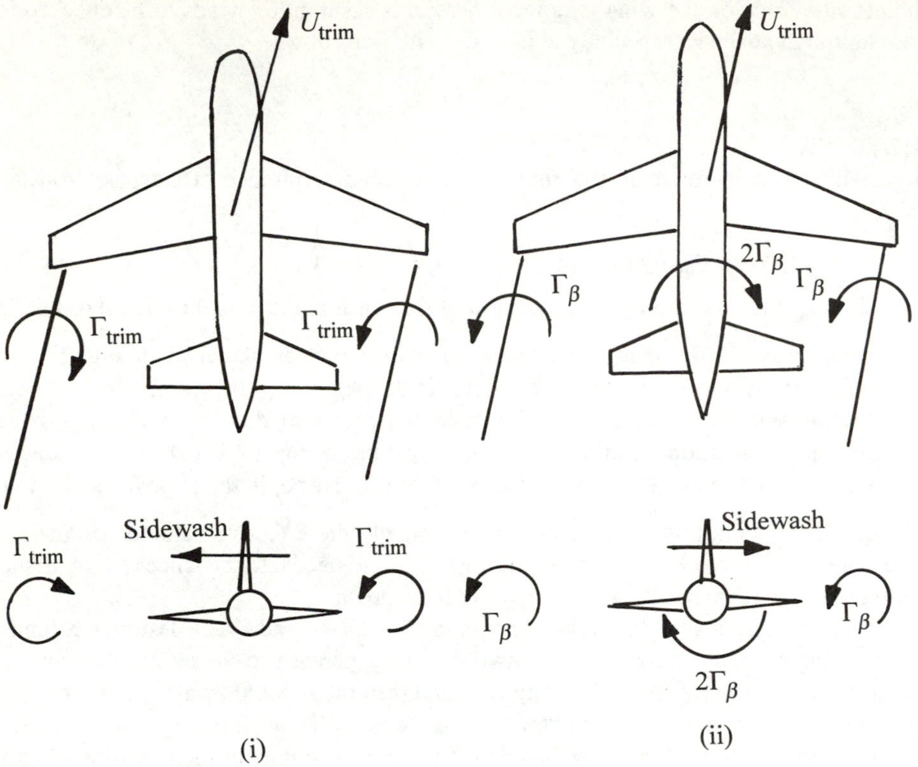

Fig. IV.21. Sidewash field in neighbourhood of fin in sideslip.

(i) On a high wing the cross flow about a fuselage due to the sideslip velocity induces a positive increment of incidence on the starboard wing and a negative increment of incidence on the port wing, increasing the lift on the starboard wing and decreasing the lift on the port wing, resulting in an incremental, negative, rolling moment; an equivalent positive dihedral effect. This rolling moment will not be large since the changes in lift act primarily in the region of the wing root.

(ii) The change in lift on the high wing across the fuselage introduces further trailing vortices which affect the sidewash patterns in the neighbourhood of the fin.

The opposite effects occur with a low wing, see Fig. IV.22.

As a first approximation these wing–fuselage contributions are ignored.

IV.2.4.4 Propulsion unit

The contributions from the propulsion unit(s) in sideslip are identical in form to the contributions of the propulsion units in the longitudinal case due to angle of incidence, as described in sect. III.3.8.

A side force due to sideslip acts on a propeller disc at the front of the fuselage, where, from eqn. (III.3.114),

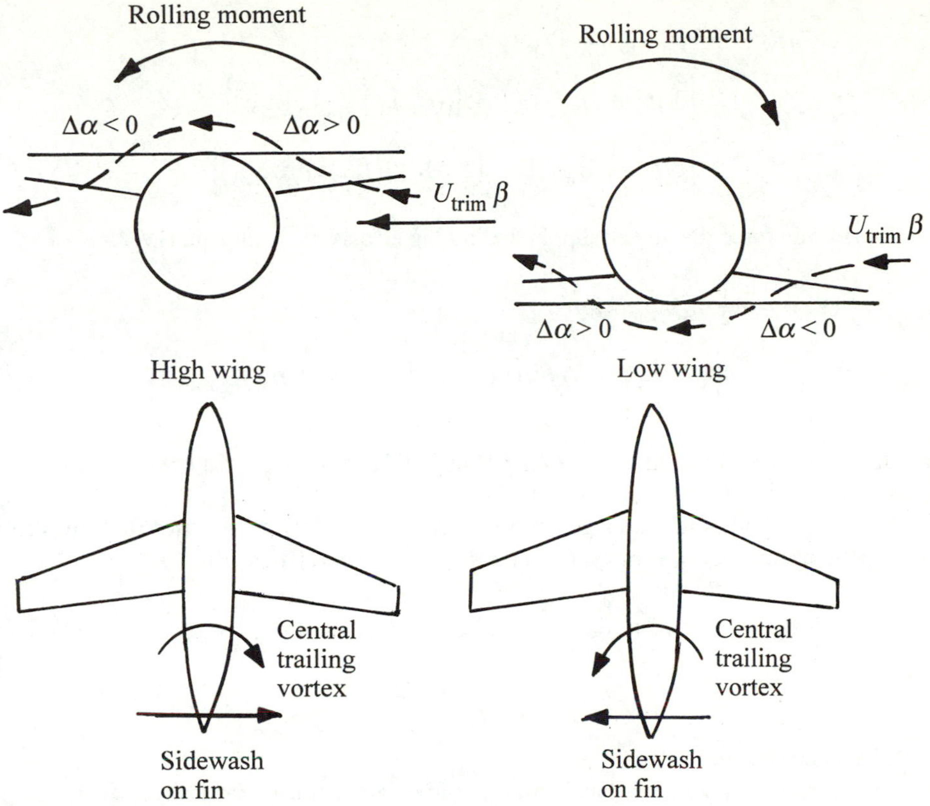

Fig. IV.22. Effect of high and low wings.

$$(Y_\beta)_{\rm prop} = -\tfrac{1}{2}\rho_{\rm at}U_{\rm trim}^2 S_{\rm w}\big(\mathrm{O}[C_{\rm Th}]\big)\beta, \tag{IV.2.65}$$

which yields a yawing moment about the oz axis

$$(\mathcal{N}_\beta)_{\rm prop} = (Y_\beta)_{\rm prop}\, l_{\rm prop} c_{\rm w}. \tag{IV.2.66}$$

A side force due to sideslip acts on each turbo-fan nacelle where, from eqn. (III.3.120),

$$(Y_\beta)_{\rm nac} = -\tfrac{1}{2}\rho_{\rm at}U_{\rm trim}^2 S_{\rm w}\Big(\mathrm{O}\big[(\pi/2)(r_{\rm nac}/s_{\rm w})^2 \mathrm{AR}_{\rm w}\big]\Big)\beta \tag{IV.2.67}$$

which yields a yawing moment about the oz axis

$$(\mathcal{N}_\beta)_{\rm nac} = (Y_\beta)_{\rm nac}\, l_{\rm nac} c_{\rm w}. \tag{IV.2.68}$$

IV.2.4.5 Unsteady aerodynamic effects

There are lag effects on the wing loadings when the sideslip varies with time, $\beta(t)$. Using the same arguments as those applied to $(\mathcal{L}_p)_{\rm w}$ (eqn. (IV.2.29)), then eqn. (IV.2.57) for $(\mathcal{L}_\beta)_{\rm w}$ can be expressed as

$$(\mathscr{L}_\beta)_\mathrm{w} \simeq -\tfrac{1}{2}\rho_\mathrm{at}U_\mathrm{trim}^2 S_\mathrm{w}\, 2s_\mathrm{w}$$
$$\times \left[0.16\big((a_\alpha)_\mathrm{w} i_\mathrm{d}\big) + 0.35\Big(\big((C_\mathrm{L})_\mathrm{w}\big)_\mathrm{trim} \tan\Lambda_\mathrm{w}\Big)\right]$$
$$\times \left[\beta(t) + \tfrac{1}{2}\left(a_{\dot\alpha}/a_\alpha\right)_\mathrm{w}(2/\mathrm{AR}_\mathrm{w})\left(\dot\beta(t)s_\mathrm{w}/U_\mathrm{trim}\right)\right]. \quad \text{(IV.2.69)}$$

The fin side force due to sideslip, including lag effects, is, from eqn. (IV.2.4)

$$(Y_\beta)_\mathrm{f} = -\tfrac{1}{2}\rho_\mathrm{at}U_\mathrm{trim}^2 S_\mathrm{w}$$
$$O\left[(S_\mathrm{f}/S_\mathrm{w})\left[(a_\beta)_\mathrm{f}\beta(t) + (a_{\dot\beta})_\mathrm{f}(c_\mathrm{f}/s_\mathrm{w})\left(\dot\beta(t)s_\mathrm{w}/U_\mathrm{trim}\right)\right]\right] \quad \text{(IV.2.70)}$$

which can be substituted in eqns. (IV.2.61) and (IV.2.62) for the fin contributions to the yawing moment and the rolling moment.

The contribution of the fuselage contribution to the $\dot\beta$ derivative arises from the cross-flow apparent mass term, namely, from eqns. (III.3.77) and (III.3.78)

$$(Y_{\dot\beta})_\mathrm{fus} = -\tfrac{1}{2}\rho_\mathrm{at}U_\mathrm{trim}^2 S_\mathrm{w}\Big(O\big[(5/\mathrm{AR}_\mathrm{w})(c_\mathrm{w}/s_\mathrm{w})\big]\Big)\left(\dot\beta(t)s_\mathrm{w}/U_\mathrm{trim}\right). \quad \text{(IV.2.71)}$$

IV.2.4.6 Complete aeroplane

Finally, for the complete aeroplane with n_nac turbo-fan engines, in sideslip,

$$Y_\beta(t) = \text{overall side force due to sideslip}$$
$$= (Y_\beta)_\mathrm{f} + (Y_\beta)_\mathrm{fus} + (Y_{\dot\beta})_\mathrm{fus} + (Y_\beta)_\mathrm{nac},$$
see eqns. (IV.2.70), (IV.2.63), (IV.2.71), (IV.2.67), (IV.2.72)
$$= \tfrac{1}{2}\rho_\mathrm{at}U_\mathrm{trim}^2 S_\mathrm{w}\left[C_{Y\beta}\beta(t) + C_{Y\dot\beta}\left(\dot\beta(t)s_\mathrm{w}/U_\mathrm{trim}\right)\right]$$

$$\mathscr{L}_\beta(t) = \text{overall rolling moment due to sideslip}$$
$$= (\mathscr{L}_\beta)_\mathrm{w} + (\mathscr{L}_\beta)_\mathrm{f}, \text{ see eqns. (IV.2.58), (IV.2.62),} \quad \text{(IV.2.73)}$$
$$= \tfrac{1}{2}\rho_\mathrm{at}U_\mathrm{trim}^2 S_\mathrm{w}\, 2s_\mathrm{w}\left[C_{l\beta}\beta(t) + C_{l\dot\beta}\left(\dot\beta(t)s_\mathrm{w}/U_\mathrm{trim}\right)\right]$$

$$\mathscr{N}_\beta(t) = \text{overall yawing moment due to sideslip}$$
$$= (\mathscr{N}_\beta)_\mathrm{w} + (\mathscr{N}_\beta)_\mathrm{f} + (\mathscr{N}_\beta)_\mathrm{fus} + (\mathscr{N}_\beta)_\mathrm{nac},$$
see eqns. (IV.2.59), (IV.2.61), (IV.2.64), (IV.2.68), (IV.2.74)
$$= \tfrac{1}{2}\rho_\mathrm{at}U_\mathrm{trim}^2 S_\mathrm{w}\, 2s_\mathrm{w}\left[C_{n\beta}\beta(t) + C_{n\dot\beta}\left(\dot\beta(t)s_\mathrm{w}/U_\mathrm{trim}\right)\right]$$

where

$$C_{Y\beta} = \mathrm{O}\Big[-(S_\mathrm{f}/S_\mathrm{w})(a_\beta)_\mathrm{f} - \pi(r_\mathrm{max}/c_\mathrm{w})^2(2/\mathrm{AR}_\mathrm{w})$$
$$-n_\mathrm{nac}(\pi/2)\ (r_\mathrm{nac}/s_\mathrm{w})^2\,\mathrm{AR}_\mathrm{w}\Big]$$

$$C_{Y\dot\beta} = \mathrm{O}\Big[-(S_\mathrm{f}/S_\mathrm{w})(a_{\dot\beta})_\mathrm{f}(c_\mathrm{f}/c_\mathrm{w})(2/\mathrm{AR}_\mathrm{w}) - 10/\mathrm{AR}_\mathrm{w}^2\Big]$$

$$C_{l\beta} = \mathrm{O}\ \Big[-0.16((a_\alpha)_\mathrm{w} i_\mathrm{d}) - 0.35 C_\mathrm{w}\tan\Lambda_\mathrm{w}$$
$$-(1/4)(s_\mathrm{f}/s_\mathrm{w})\ (S_\mathrm{f}/S_\mathrm{w})(a_\beta)_\mathrm{f}\Big]$$

$$C_{l\dot\beta} = \mathrm{O}\ \Big[-\big[0.16((a_\alpha)_\mathrm{w} i_\mathrm{d}) + 0.35\tan\Lambda_\mathrm{w}\big]$$
$$\Big[(a_{\dot\alpha}/a_\alpha)_\mathrm{w}/\mathrm{AR}_\mathrm{w}\Big] - (S_\mathrm{f}/S_\mathrm{w})^2(a_{\dot\beta})_\mathrm{f}/\mathrm{AR}_\mathrm{w}\Big] \qquad \text{(IV.2.75)}$$

$$C_{n\beta} = \mathrm{O}\Big[\Big[(S_\mathrm{f}/S_\mathrm{w}) l_\mathrm{f}\,(a_\beta)_\mathrm{f}/\mathrm{AR}_\mathrm{w}\Big] - \Big[2\pi l_\mathrm{n}(r_\mathrm{max}/c_\mathrm{w})^2/\mathrm{AR}_\mathrm{w}^2\Big]$$
$$-\ n_\mathrm{nac}(\pi/2) l_\mathrm{nac}(r_\mathrm{nac}/s_\mathrm{w})^2\Big]$$

$$C_{n\dot\beta} = \mathrm{O}\Big[\Big[(S_\mathrm{f}/S_\mathrm{w}) l_\mathrm{f}\,(a_{\dot\beta})_\mathrm{f}/\mathrm{AR}_\mathrm{w}\Big]\Big[(c_\mathrm{f}/c_\mathrm{w})\ (2/\mathrm{AR}_\mathrm{w})\Big]\Big]$$

For a propeller driven aeroplane the propeller characteristics, eqns. (IV.2.65) and (IV.2.66) replace the turbo-fan nacelle characteristics, eqns. (IV.2.67) and (IV.2.68).

With the typical values

$$\mathrm{AR}_\mathrm{w} = 6, \quad i_\mathrm{d} = 2°, \quad n_\mathrm{nac} = 2,$$
$$(S_\mathrm{f}/S_\mathrm{w}) = 0.2, \quad s_\mathrm{f}/s_\mathrm{w} = 0.4, \quad c_\mathrm{f}/c_\mathrm{w} = 1.0,$$
$$(a_\alpha)_\mathrm{w} = 4.5, \quad (a_{\dot\alpha})_\mathrm{w} = -2.25, \quad (a_\beta)_\mathrm{f} = 2.5, \quad (a_{\dot\beta})_\mathrm{f} = -1.25,$$
$$l_\mathrm{f} = 3.0, \quad l_\mathrm{n} = 3.0, \quad l_\mathrm{nac} = 2.0, \quad r_\mathrm{max}/c_\mathrm{w} = 0.3, \quad r_\mathrm{nac}/s_\mathrm{w} = 0.06,$$

with flaps up,

$$C_{Y\beta} = \mathrm{O}[-0.65]$$
$$C_{Y\dot\beta} = \mathrm{O}[-0.20]$$
$$C_{l\beta} = \mathrm{O}[-0.075 - 0.35 C_\mathrm{w}\tan\Lambda_\mathrm{w}]$$
$$C_{l\dot\beta} = \mathrm{O}[+0.01 + 0.03\,C_\mathrm{w}\tan\Lambda_\mathrm{w}] \qquad \text{(IV.2.76)}$$
$$C_{n\beta} = \mathrm{O}[+0.20]$$
$$C_{n\dot\beta} = \mathrm{O}[-0.04].$$

Note:

(i) the fin contribution dominates the values of $C_{Y\beta}$ and $C_{n\beta}$;
(ii) the wing contribution dominates the value of $C_{l\beta}$;
(iii) for $C_{Y\beta}$ the contributions from the fin, fuselage nose, and propulsion unit $C_{Y\beta}$ are cumulative;
(iv) for $C_{n\beta}$ the contributions from the fuselage nose and the propulsion unit oppose the contribution from the fin.

EXAMPLES IV.5

1. Are the values in eqn. (IV.2.76) affected by flaps down?
2. Calculate, on the basis of eqns. (IV.2.75), the values of $C_{Y\beta}$, $C_{l\beta}$, $C_{n\beta}$ for the light aeroplane basic configuration. Is the effect of the propeller slipstream on these derivatives significant?
3. Plot, on the basis of eqns. (IV.2.75), the variation of $C_{Y\beta}$, $C_{l\beta}$, $C_{n\beta}$ against Mach number for the transport aeroplane basic configuration:

   at sea level $0.15 < M_\infty < 0.5$

   at 11 km altitude $0.5 < M_\infty < 0.85$.

4. Plot, on the basis of eqns. (IV.2.75), the variation of $C_{Y\beta}$, $C_{l\beta}$, $C_{n\beta}$ against Mach number for the combat aeroplane basic configuration:

   at sea level $0.15 < M_\infty < 0.7$

   at 11 km altitude $0.5 < M_\infty < 1.8$.

IV.2.5 Aerodynamics of the rudder

The side force on the fin due to a rudder deflection $\zeta(t)$, see Fig. IV.1, is

$$(Y_\zeta)_\mathrm{f} = \tfrac{1}{2}\rho_\mathrm{at} U_\mathrm{trim}^2 S_\mathrm{f}\left(a_\zeta \zeta(t) + a_{\dot\zeta}\left(\dot\zeta(t) c_\mathrm{f}/U_\mathrm{trim}\right)\right) \qquad \text{(IV.2.77)}$$

where

at subsonic speeds $a_\zeta \simeq 0.65(a_\beta)_\mathrm{f}$,

at supersonic speeds $a_\zeta \simeq \left(c_\mathrm{rudder}/c_\mathrm{f}\right)(a_\beta)_\mathrm{f}$,

and

$$a_{\dot\zeta} \simeq a_\zeta\left(a_{\dot\beta}/a_\beta\right)_\mathrm{f}.$$

And then,

$$\text{rolling moment about } ox \text{ axis} \simeq (Y_\zeta)_\mathrm{f}\left(s_\mathrm{f}/2\right), \qquad \text{(IV.2.78)}$$

$$\text{yawing moment about } oz \text{ axis} \simeq -(Y_\zeta)_\mathrm{f} l_\mathrm{f} c_\mathrm{w}. \qquad \text{(IV.2.79)}$$

In terms of derivatives,

$$Y_\zeta(t) = \text{side force due to rudder deflection}$$

$$= \tfrac{1}{2}\rho_{at}U_{trim}^2 S_w\left[C_{Y\zeta}\zeta(t) + C_{Y\dot{\zeta}}\left(\dot{\zeta}(t)s_w/U_{trim}\right)\right], \tag{IV.2.80}$$

$$\mathscr{L}_\zeta(t) = \text{rolling moment due to rudder deflection}$$

$$= \tfrac{1}{2}\rho_{at}U_{trim}^2 S_w\, 2s_w\left[C_{l\zeta}\zeta(t) + C_{l\dot{\zeta}}\left(\dot{\zeta}(t)s_w/U_{trim}\right)\right], \tag{IV.2.81}$$

$$\mathscr{N}_\zeta(t) = \text{yawing moment due to rudder deflection}$$

$$= \tfrac{1}{2}\rho_{at}U_{trim}^2 S_w\, 2s_w\left[C_{n\zeta}\zeta(t) + C_{n\dot{\zeta}}\left(\dot{\zeta}(t)s_w/U_{trim}\right)\right], \tag{IV.2.82}$$

where

$$\begin{aligned}
C_{Y\zeta} &= (S_f/S_w)a_\zeta \\
C_{Y\dot{\zeta}} &= (S_f/S_w)\,(c_f/c_w)\,(2/AR_w)\,a_{\dot{\zeta}} \\
C_{l\zeta} &= (S_f/S_w)a_\zeta\,(1/4)(s_f/s_w) \\
C_{l\dot{\zeta}} &= (S_f/S_w)a_{\dot{\zeta}}\,(1/4)(s_f/s_w)(c_f/c_w)(2/AR_w) \\
C_{n\zeta} &= -(S_f/S_w)a_\zeta\,(l_f/AR_w) \\
C_{n\dot{\zeta}} &= -(S_f/S_w)a_{\dot{\zeta}}\,(l_f/AR_w)(c_f/c_w)(2/AR_w).
\end{aligned} \tag{IV.2.83}$$

With typical values

$$AR_w = 6, \quad (S_f/S_w) = 0.2, \quad s_f/s_w = 0.4, \quad c_f/c_w = 1.0, \quad l_f = 3.0,$$
$$a_\zeta = 1.5, \quad a_{\dot{\zeta}} = -0.7,$$

then

$$\begin{aligned}
C_{Y\zeta} &= O[0.30], & C_{Y\dot{\zeta}} &= O[-0.04] \\
C_{l\zeta} &= O[0.03], & C_{l\dot{\zeta}} &\simeq 0.0 \\
C_{n\zeta} &= O[-0.15], & C_{n\dot{\zeta}} &= O[0.02].
\end{aligned} \tag{IV.2.84}$$

EXAMPLES IV.6

1. Calculate on the basis of eqn. (IV.2.83), the values of $C_{Y\zeta}$, $C_{l\zeta}$, $C_{n\zeta}$, for the light aeroplane basic configuration. Is the effect of the propeller slipstream on these derivatives significant?

2. Plot, on the basis of eqns. (IV.2.83), the variation of $C_{Y\zeta}$, $C_{l\zeta}$, $C_{n\zeta}$ against Mach number for the transport aeroplane basic configuration.
3. Plot, on the basis of eqns. (IV.2.83), the variation of $C_{Y\zeta}$, $C_{l\zeta}$, $C_{n\zeta}$ against Mach number for the combat aeroplane basic configuration.

IV.2.6 Aerodynamics of roll control

IV.2.6.1 Aileron

When the starboard aileron is deflected (downward) through angle $\xi(t)$, and the port aileron is deflected (upward) through angle $\xi(t)$, which defines a positive aileron angle $\xi(t)$, the change in lift on the starboard wing can be denoted as

$$\Delta L_\xi = \tfrac{1}{2}\rho_{\text{at}}U_{\text{trim}}^2(S_{\text{w}}/2)\left[a_\xi\xi(t) + a_{\dot{\xi}}\left(\dot{\xi}(t)c_{\text{w}}/U_{\text{trim}}\right)\right]. \quad \text{(IV.2.85)}$$

The lift on the port wing is minus the lift on the starboard wing.

For an order-of-magnitude value of a_ξ,

$$a_\xi = \mathrm{O}\left[(0.75)(0.6)(s_{\text{a}}/s_{\text{w}})(a_\alpha)_{\text{w}}\right] = \mathrm{O}[0.6]. \quad \text{(IV.2.86)}$$

The factor 0.75 represents the loss of lift towards the wing root, the factor 0.6 is associated with the fact that the aileron is a part-chord control surface (see eqn. (III.3.86)), and s_{a} is the span of the aileron.

And for $a_{\dot{\xi}}$, when the rate of application of aileron angle is not too rapid, say a ramp-step change in 0.2 s,

$$a_{\dot{\xi}} = \mathrm{O}\left[a_\xi\; 0.5(a_{\dot{\alpha}}/a_\alpha)_{\text{w}}\right]. \quad \text{(IV.2.87)}$$

The factor of $\frac{1}{2}$ is included because the lag in the build-up of an antisymmetric loading will be less than the lag in the build-up of a symmetric loading.

The differential lifts on the starboard and port wings generate a rolling moment about the body axis ox_1, given approximately by

$$(\mathscr{L}_{l\xi})_{\text{w}} = \text{wing rolling moment due to aileron deflection}$$

$$\simeq -\Delta L_\xi\, 2(0.6 s_{\text{w}}) \quad \text{(IV.2.88)}$$

where $\mathscr{L}_{l\xi}$ is given by eqn. (IV.2.85), assuming that the centre of lift on the starboard wing due to aileron deflection acts at 0.6 semi-span.

A wing side force is generated by the deflection of the ailerons similar to the side force generated by a rate of roll as described in sect. IV.2.2. From eqn. (IV.2.13)

$$(Y_\xi)_{\text{w}} = \text{side force on wing due to aileron deflection}$$

$$\simeq \tfrac{1}{2}\rho_{\text{at}}U_{\text{trim}}^2 S_{\text{w}}\mathrm{O}\left[((C_{\text{L}})_{\text{w}})_{\text{trim}}\left((1/\text{AR}_{\text{w}}) + 0.8\tan\Lambda_{\text{w}}\right)\right]\xi(t) \quad \text{(IV.2.89)}$$

equating ξ to $(ps_{\text{w}}/U_{\text{trim}})$ on the argument that the effective angle of incidence of the section at mid-aileron is (0.65ξ) when the aileron is deflected and the effective angle of the same section for a rolling wing is of the order of $(p(0.65s_{\text{w}})/U_{\text{trim}})$.

And a yawing moment arises on the wing from

(i) the differential vortex drags on the starboard and port wings from the coupling between the trim and aileron lift distributions and their induced downwash distributions, as explained in sect. IV.2.2 in the derivation of the yawing moment due to rate of roll,
(ii) the wing side force.

The yawing moment about the body axis oz_1 due to aileron deflection from the vortex drags, by analogy with the arguments leading to eqn. (IV.2.19), is

$$(\mathcal{N}_{1\xi})_{\mathrm{w}} = -2(\mathcal{L}_{1\xi})_{\mathrm{w}}\left[((C_{\mathrm{L}})_{\mathrm{w}})_{\mathrm{trim}}/(\pi\,\mathrm{AR}_{\mathrm{w}})\right]. \qquad \text{(IV.2.90)}$$

The contribution to the yawing moment from the side force is ignored because its line of action is difficult to predict.

There are changes in the wake behind the wing when the ailerons are deflected which affects the sidewash flow in the neighbourhood of the fin. These effects are ignored.

Finally, in terms of derivatives,

$$\begin{aligned}\mathcal{L}_{\xi}(t) &= \text{rolling moment, about the fuselage body } ox \text{ axis, due to ailerons}\\ &= (\mathcal{L}_{1\xi})_{\mathrm{w}} - (\mathcal{N}_{1\xi})_{\mathrm{w}}\alpha_{\mathrm{trim}}, \quad \text{see eqns. (IV.2.88) and (IV.2.90)}\\ &= \tfrac{1}{2}\rho_{\mathrm{at}}U_{\mathrm{trim}}^2 S_{\mathrm{w}}\,2s_{\mathrm{w}}\left[C_{l\xi}\xi(t) + C_{l\dot{\xi}}\left(\dot{\xi}(t)s_{\mathrm{w}}/U_{\mathrm{trim}}\right)\right]\end{aligned} \qquad \text{(IV.2.91)}$$

$$\begin{aligned}\mathcal{N}_{\xi}(t) &= \text{yawing moment, about the } oz \text{ axis, due to ailerons}\\ &= (\mathcal{N}_{1\xi})_{\mathrm{w}} + (\mathcal{L}_{1\xi})_{\mathrm{w}}\alpha_{\mathrm{trim}}, \quad \text{see eqns. (IV.2.88) and (IV.2.90)}\\ &= \tfrac{1}{2}\rho_{\mathrm{at}}U_{\mathrm{trim}}^2 S_{\mathrm{w}}\,2s_{\mathrm{w}}\left[C_{n\xi}\xi(t) + C_{n\dot{\xi}}\left(\dot{\xi}(t)s_{\mathrm{w}}/U_{\mathrm{trim}}\right)\right]\end{aligned} \qquad \text{(IV.2.92)}$$

$$\begin{aligned}Y_{\xi}(t) &= \text{side force due to ailerons}\\ &= (Y_{\xi})_{\mathrm{w}}, \quad \text{see eqn. (IV.2.89)}\\ &= \tfrac{1}{2}\rho_{\mathrm{at}}U_{\mathrm{trim}}^2 S_{\mathrm{w}}\,2s_{\mathrm{w}}\left[C_{Y\xi}\xi(t) + C_{Y\dot{\xi}}\left(\dot{\xi}(t)s_{\mathrm{w}}/U_{\mathrm{trim}}\right)\right].\end{aligned} \qquad \text{(IV.2.93)}$$

where

$$\begin{aligned}C_{l\xi} &\simeq -0.3a_{\xi}\\ C_{l\dot{\xi}} &\simeq -0.3a_{\dot{\xi}}\,2/\mathrm{AR}_{\mathrm{w}}\\ C_{n\xi} &\simeq -0.3a_{\xi}\left(\alpha_{\mathrm{trim}} - 2C_{\mathrm{w}}/(\pi\,\mathrm{AR}_{\mathrm{w}})\right)\\ C_{n\dot{\xi}} &\simeq 0.0.\\ C_{Y\xi} &\simeq C_{\mathrm{w}}\left((1/\mathrm{AR}_{\mathrm{w}}) + 0.8\tan\Lambda_{\mathrm{w}}\right)\\ C_{Y\dot{\xi}} &\simeq 0.0.\end{aligned} \qquad \text{(IV.2.94)}$$

With typical values

$$\mathrm{AR_w} = 6, \quad a_\xi = 0.6, \quad a_{\dot{\xi}} = -0.15,$$

then, with flaps up

$$\begin{aligned} C_{l\xi} &= \mathrm{O}[-0.2] & C_{l\dot{\xi}} &= \mathrm{O}[+0.02] \\ C_{n\xi} &= \mathrm{O}[0.01 - 0.02C_\mathrm{w}] & C_{n\dot{\xi}} &\simeq 0.0 \\ C_{Y\xi} &= \mathrm{O}[C_\mathrm{w}(0.02 + 0.10\tan\Lambda_\mathrm{w})] & C_{Y\dot{\xi}} &\simeq 0.0. \end{aligned} \tag{IV.2.95}$$

The wing yawing moment due to aileron about the body axis oz_1 deserves comment. This yawing moment, given by $(\mathcal{N}_{1\xi})_\mathrm{w}$ in eqn. (IV.2.90), has the opposite sign to the rolling moment $((\mathcal{L}_{1\xi})_\mathrm{w})_1$. Thus, a positive rolling moment, due to a (negative) aileron deflection, which rolls the aeroplane, starboard wing down, and turns the aeroplane to starboard, is accompanied by a negative yawing moment, which rotates the nose of the aeroplane out of the turn, inducing a positive sideslip, which then induces a negative rolling moment, opposing the positive rolling moment resulting from the initial aileron input. This effect, known as adverse yaw due to aileron, is unwelcome by pilots.

The phenomenon of adverse yaw has been described above in terms of trim body axes which in effect, at small angles of incidence, is the motion relative to the flight path. An explanation of adverse yaw in terms of fuselage body axes is more obscure because, as seen from eqns. (IV.2.95), the yawing and rolling moments can have the same sign.

There have been various aerodynamic attempts to reduce adverse yaw due to aileron.

(i) The starboard and port aileron deflections may not be of the same magnitude. As an extreme, suppose that to induce a positive rate of roll, the starboard aileron is deflected upward through angle 2ξ while the port aileron is not altered (the magnitude of the aileron angle, by definition, is still ξ); there is a positive rolling moment accompanied by a loss in lift. This partial loss of lift, which reduces the adverse yawing moment, is of limited duration while the ailerons are deployed, introducing only a minor effect on the longitudinal motion of the aeroplane.

(ii) The spoiler as a roll control, see Fig. IV.1, extends the philosophy of (i). To obtain a positive rolling moment the spoiler on the upper surface of the starboard wing is raised, leaving the spoiler on the port wing *in situ*; lift is lost on the starboard wing but not on the port wing, as in (i) above. But there is an additional advantage of the spoiler; the flow separation aft of the spoiler increases the normal pressure drag on the starboard wing, and this increased normal pressure drag counteracts the adverse yaw, converting the adverse yaw into a proverse yaw.

  (a) Spoiler effectiveness depends critically on its chordwise location; spoilers which are too far forward are said, by pilots, to be sluggish.

  (b) A spoiler is not as effective as an aileron as a roll control. Spoilers tend to be used to augment roll effectiveness rather than as primary roll control surfaces.

  (c) A disadvantage of spoilers is that the rate of loss of lift with spoiler angle can be highly non-linear.

(d) Spoilers are popular on combat aeroplanes for then the full wing span is available for trailing edge flaps.

(iii) An ingenious aileron geometry, the Frise aileron, patented in 1924, as sketched in Fig. IV.23, is designed so that when the aileron is deflected downward there is no flow separation over the aileron surface but when the aileron is deflected upward the nose of the aileron protrudes below the surface of the wing, provoking flow separation and increasing the drag. This increase of drag acts to reduce the adverse yaw due to aileron. In addition, the aft hinge line creates an external aerodynamic balance to reduce the hinge moment.

(iv) A mechanical coupling of rudder and aileron, whereby a negative aileron is accompanied by a negative rudder angle, can also reduce the adverse yaw.

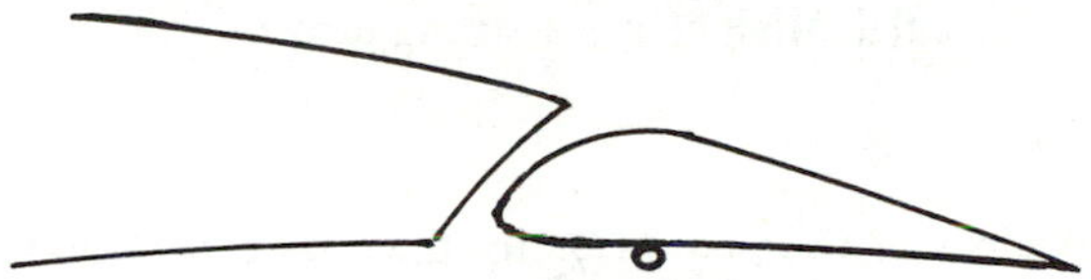

Fig. IV.23. Frise aileron.

IV.2.6.2 Differential tailplane

With a differential all-moving tailplane a nose-up starboard tailplane of angle ξ and a nose-down port tailplane of angle ξ gives a negative rolling moment on the tailplane about the ox_1 axis:

$$\begin{aligned}(\mathscr{L}_{1\xi})_t &\simeq -2\left[\tfrac{1}{2}\rho_{at}U^2_{trim}(S_t/2)(0.65(a_\alpha)_t)\xi(s_t/2)\right] \\ &= -\tfrac{1}{2}\rho_{at}U^2_{trim}S_w\,2s_w\left[0.16(a_\alpha)_t(S_t/S_w)(s_t/s_w)\right]\xi.\end{aligned} \quad \text{(IV.2.96)}$$

The factor 0.65 is explained in eqn. (IV.2.11); and it is assumed that the incremental lift on each tailplane acts at $s_t/2$.

The side force on the tailplane due to edge suction forces will be negligible because the trim tailplane lift is small.

The trailing vorticity from the differential tailplane induces a positive sidewash on the fin, generating a positive fin side force

$$(Y_\xi)_f \simeq \tfrac{1}{2}\rho_{at}U^2_{trim}S_w\left[0.05(a_\alpha)_t(a_\beta)_f(S_f/S_w)(c_t/s_f)\right]\xi. \quad \text{(IV.2.97)}$$

The proof is outlined in Appendix 9.

This fin side force generates a yawing moment and rolling moment about the oz and ox axes, namely

$$(\mathscr{N}_\xi)_f = -(Y_\xi)_f l_f c_w \quad \text{(IV.2.98)}$$

$$(\mathscr{L}_\xi)_f \simeq (Y_\xi)_f\, s_f/2. \quad \text{(IV.2.99)}$$

Hence

$$C_{Y\xi} = \mathrm{O}\left[0.05(a_\alpha)_\mathrm{t}(a_\beta)_\mathrm{f}\left(S_\mathrm{f}/S_\mathrm{w}\right)\left(c_\mathrm{t}/s_\mathrm{f}\right)\right]$$

$$C_{l\xi} = \mathrm{O}\left[-0.16(a_\alpha)_\mathrm{t}\left(S_\mathrm{t}/S_\mathrm{w}\right)\left(s_\mathrm{t}/s_\mathrm{w}\right) + 0.25C_{Y\xi}\left(s_\mathrm{f}/s_\mathrm{w}\right)\right] \qquad \text{(IV.2.100)}$$

$$C_{n\xi} = \mathrm{O}\left[-C_{Y\xi}\left(l_\mathrm{f}/\mathrm{AR}_\mathrm{w}\right) - 0.16(a_\alpha)_\mathrm{t}\left(S_\mathrm{t}/S_\mathrm{w}\right)\left(s_\mathrm{t}/s_\mathrm{w}\right)\alpha_\mathrm{trim}\right].$$

The rate derivatives can be derived using the same unsteady approximations which have been used previously.

With typical values for a combat aeroplane,

$$C_{Y\xi} = \mathrm{O}[0.06], \quad C_{l\xi} = \mathrm{O}[-0.10], \quad C_{n\xi} = \mathrm{O}[-0.03 - 0.025C_\mathrm{w}]. \qquad \text{(IV.2.101)}$$

A feature of a differential tailplane is the strong proverse yaw.

EXAMPLES IV.7

1. Calculate the values of $C_{Y\xi}$, $C_{l\xi}$, $C_{n\xi}$ for the light aeroplane basic configuration. Is the effect of the propeller slipstream on these derivatives significant?
2. Plot the variation of $C_{Y\xi}$, $C_{l\xi}$, $C_{n\xi}$ against Mach number for the transport aeroplane basic configuration:

   at sea level $0.15 < M_\infty < 0.5$

   at 11 km altitude $0.5 < M_\infty < 0.85$.
3. Plot the variation of $C_{Y\xi}$, $C_{l\xi}$, $C_{n\xi}$ against Mach number for the combat aeroplane basic configuration:

   at sea level $0.15 < M_\infty < 0.7$

   at 11 km altitude $0.5 < M_\infty < 1.8$.

IV.3 STEADY LATERAL MOTIONS

IV.3.1 Steady level symmetric flight

To maintain steady straight level flight in normal operating conditions with zero sideslip and zero bank angle, all control angles must be set at appropriate trim values. The elevator angle to trim is described in sect. III.5. But there is also an aileron angle to trim, and a rudder angle to trim.

Any asymmetry in the geometry of the wing profiles will cause asymmetry in wing loading, resulting in a small rolling moment, which needs to be counteracted by a rolling moment from the aileron angle to trim. Similarly, any asymmetry in the wing mass distribution, caused for example by asymmetric fuel usage or missile deployment, also needs to be counteracted by an aileron angle to trim. With a single rotary engine–propeller propulsion unit the inertial torque needs to be counteracted by an aileron angle to trim.

A rudder angle to trim might be necessary on a multi-engined aeroplane to offset slight differences in turbo-fan thrusts, or on a combat aeroplane to counter the drag associated with asymmetric missiles, or to offset the swirl in the slipstream behind a propeller.

For rigid aeroplanes the topic of aileron and rudder angles to trim is relatively trivial. But for flexible aeroplanes the topic of aileron and rudder angles to trim is of major importance; aeroelastic aileron reversal, rudder reversal and elevator reversal are all related to trimmed flight, determining maximum trim speeds.

IV.3.2 Steady level asymmetric flight

It is possible in principle to fly an aeroplane in steady straight level flight at a steady sideslip and with a steady bank angle.

Consider, as shown in Fig. IV.24, an aeroplane in steady level flight, with the aeroplane centre of mass moving at U_{trim}, at a small steady (positive) sideslip angle β and at a small steady (positive) bank angle φ.

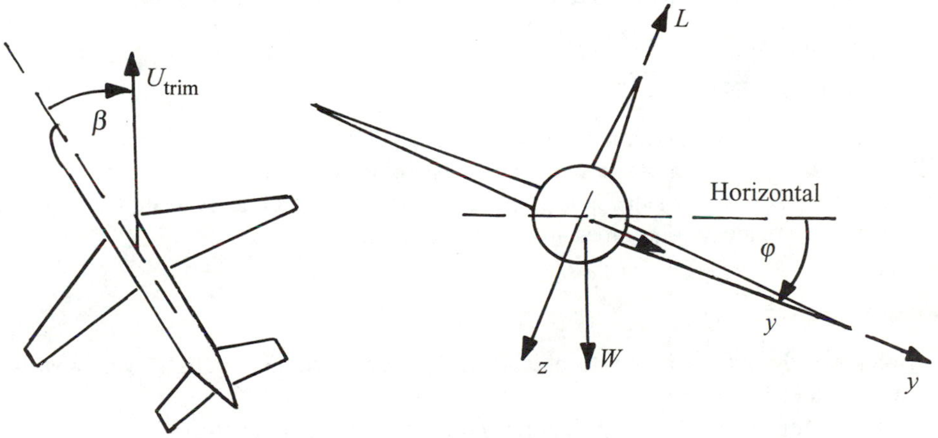

Fig. IV.24. Steady asymmetric flight.

The equations of static equilibrium are, for small α and φ,

$$
\begin{aligned}
\text{Th} &= D \\
L + \text{Th}\alpha &\simeq W \\
Y + W\varphi &= 0 \\
\mathscr{L} = \mathscr{M} &= \mathscr{N} = 0 \\
p = q &= r = 0.
\end{aligned}
\tag{IV.3.1}
$$

Assuming that the longitudinal equations are satisfied at their trim values, the lateral equations in eqns. (IV.3.1) become, in terms of the lateral derivatives,

$$C_{Y\beta}\beta + C_{Y\xi}\xi + C_{Y\zeta}\zeta = -C_W\varphi$$
$$C_{l\beta}\beta + C_{l\xi}\xi + C_{l\zeta}\zeta = 0 \qquad \text{(IV.3.2)}$$
$$C_{n\beta}\beta + C_{n\xi}\xi + C_{n\zeta}\zeta = 0.$$

As a first approximation, neglecting the small derivatives $C_{l\zeta}$ and $C_{n\xi}$, then

$$\xi/\beta \simeq -\left[(-C_{l\beta})/(-C_{l\xi})\right]$$
$$\zeta/\beta \simeq C_{n\beta}/(-C_{n\zeta}) \qquad \text{(IV.3.3)}$$
$$C_W\varphi/\beta \simeq (-C_{Y\beta}) - C_{Y\xi}(\xi/\beta) - C_{Y\zeta}(\zeta/\beta),$$

retaining the convention that the negative derivatives are expressed in a negative bracket so that the signs of the terms are more clearly apparent (e.g. $(-C_{l\beta})$ and $C_{n\beta}$ are both positive).

Typically, from eqns. (IV.2.34), (IV.2.52), (IV.2.76), (IV.2.84), (IV.2.95) (the reader should copy out the typical values of the lateral derivatives for ready reference)

$$(\xi/\beta) = O[-1.0], \quad (\zeta/\beta) = O[+1.3], \quad (C_W\varphi/\beta) = O[+0.3]. \qquad \text{(IV.3.4)}$$

From eqns. (IV.3.4):

(i) φ and β are the same sign, as drawn in Fig. IV.24;
(ii) ξ and ζ are of the opposite sign, known as crossed controls;
(iii) the maximum steady sideslip angle, and maximum bank angle, is when the required aileron or rudder angle comes up against its stops.

EXAMPLES IV.8

1. What are the pilot's inputs to obtain steady level asymmetric flight with positive sideslip and bank angles?
2. For an aeroplane with $\Lambda_w = 30°$, plot (ξ/β), (ζ/β) and (φ/β) against C_W.
3. What are the maximum steady sideslip and bank angles when the maximum aileron and transfer angles are 10°?
4. How is the above analysis changed if trim body axes are used?
5. What would the values become in eqn. (IV.3.4) for a combat aeroplane with all-moving tailplane?

IV.3.3 Sustained turn

In a sustained turn an aeroplane maintains constant altitude, at a steady forward speed, U, with a steady bank angle (i.e. zero roll rate), zero sideslip, and steady turn rate, the so-called sustained turn rate (STR).

The terminology 'sustained turn rate' is introduced to distinguish it from the 'attained turn rate' which is a transient turn rate at high angles of incidence, as described later in Part V.

By reference to Fig. IV.25, the equations of motion are, invoking D'Alembert's principle,

$$\begin{aligned} \text{Th} &\simeq D \\ L\cos\varphi &\simeq W + Y\sin\varphi \\ L\sin\varphi &= (W/g)(\text{STR})U - Y\cos\varphi \\ \mathscr{L} &= \mathscr{M} = \mathscr{N} = 0. \end{aligned} \tag{IV.3.5}$$

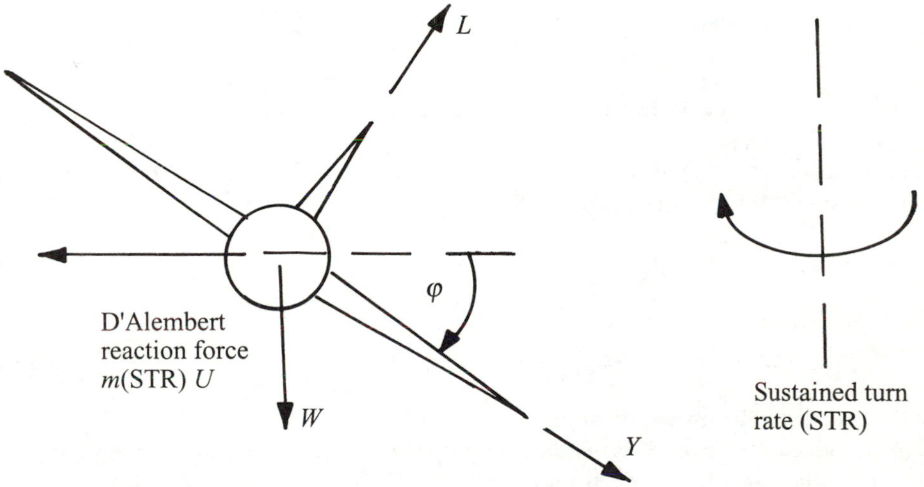

Fig. IV.25. Steady turning flight.

The fuselage body ox axis is inclined upward from the horizontal in the oxz plane at the angle of incidence α. Resolving the STR about the three fuselage body axes, by reference to Fig. IV.26,

$$p = -\text{STR}\ \sin\alpha, \quad q = \text{STR}\cos\alpha\sin\varphi, \quad r = \text{STR}\cos\alpha\cos\varphi. \tag{IV.3.6}$$

At low angles of incidence and low bank angles the rotation is primarily rate of yaw, but at low angles of incidence and high bank angles the rotation is primarily rate of pitch.

Now

$$Y = \tfrac{1}{2}\rho_{\text{at}}U^2 S_{\text{w}}\left(C_{Y\xi}\,\Delta\xi + C_{Y\zeta}\,\Delta\zeta + C_{Yp}\left(ps_{\text{w}}/U\right) + C_{Yr}\left(rs_{\text{w}}/U\right)\right)$$

where $\Delta\xi$ and $\Delta\rho$ are the incremental control angles, hence

$$Y = \text{O}\left[(W/C_{\text{W}})(\text{STR}\ s_{\text{w}}/U)\right]. \tag{IV.3.7}$$

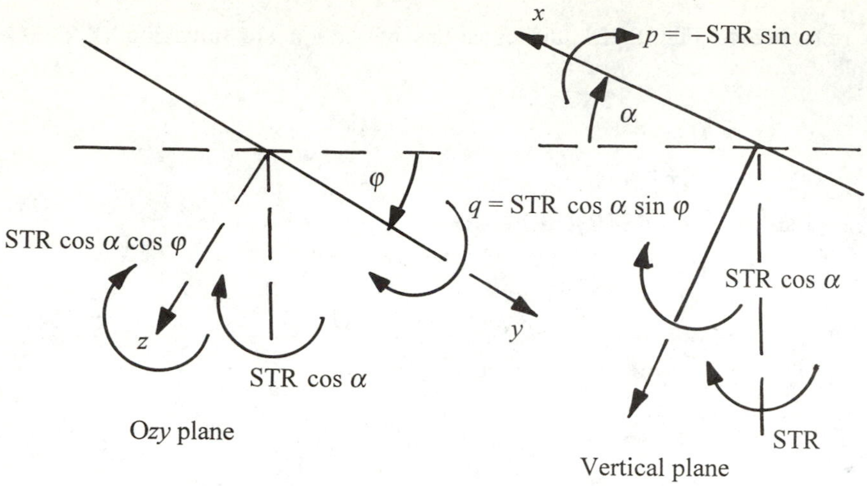

Fig. IV.26. Resolution of angular velocities in steady turn.

It then follows that with typical values of STR (< 0.3 rad/s) the effect of Y in eqns (IV.3.5) is small. When Y in eqns. (IV.3.5) is neglected

$$\mathrm{STR} \simeq (g/U)\tan\varphi \tag{IV.3.8}$$

and

$$C_\mathrm{L} = C_\mathrm{W}\sec\varphi, \qquad \alpha + i_\mathrm{w} - \alpha_{0\mathrm{w}} = C_\mathrm{W}\sec\varphi/C_{\mathrm{L}\alpha}\,; \tag{IV.3.9}$$

α will be small and below the break α_b.

The sustained turn rate (STR) is directly proportional to tan φ, and inversely proportional to U; when $U = 100$ m/s, $\varphi = 45°$, then

$$\mathrm{STR} \simeq 0.1 \ \text{rad/s} \simeq 6°/\text{s}, \qquad C_\mathrm{L} = 1.4C_\mathrm{W}. \tag{IV.3.10}$$

If an aeroplane is flying initially in trimmed steady linear flight at a forward speed U_trim, at a trim angle of incidence α_trim, with trim elevator angle η_trim, all controls, including the throttle, must be changed to fly in a sustained turn at the same altitude at the same forward speed. The changes in the controls are given by

$$\begin{aligned}
\Delta C_\mathrm{Th} &= \Delta C_\mathrm{D} \simeq \left(2C_\mathrm{W}/(\pi\,\mathrm{AR_w})\right)\Delta C_\mathrm{L}\\
C_{l\xi}\,\Delta\xi + C_{lp}(ps_\mathrm{w}/U_\mathrm{trim}) + C_{lr}(rs_\mathrm{w}/U_\mathrm{trim}) &\simeq 0\\
C_{m\eta}\,\Delta\eta + C_{m\alpha}\,\Delta\alpha + C_{mq}(qc_\mathrm{w}/2U_\mathrm{trim}) &= 0\\
C_{n\zeta}\,\Delta\zeta + C_{np}(ps_\mathrm{w}/U_\mathrm{trim}) + C_{nr}(rs_\mathrm{w}/U_\mathrm{trim}) &\simeq 0
\end{aligned} \tag{IV.3.11}$$

neglecting C_{pp} and $C_{n\xi}$, where p, q and r are given by eqns. (IV.3.6), and

$$\Delta\alpha \simeq \Delta C_\mathrm{L}/C_{\mathrm{L}\alpha} = C_\mathrm{W}(\sec\varphi - 1)/C_{\mathrm{L}\alpha}. \tag{IV.3.12}$$

From the substitution of eqns. (IV.3.6), (IV.3.8) and (IV.3.9) into eqn. (IV.3.11), the incremental control angles are

$$\Delta\eta = -\frac{\left[K_\alpha C_W(\sec\varphi - 1)\right] + \left[\left((-C_{mq})C_w/2\bar{m}\right)\tan\varphi\sin\varphi\right]}{(-C_{m\eta})}$$

$$\Delta\xi \simeq \frac{\left[C_{lr}\cos\varphi + (-C_{lp})\alpha\right]\left[(\tan\varphi)\ C_W AR_w/4\bar{m}\right]}{(-C_{l\xi})} \qquad \text{(IV.3.13)}$$

$$\Delta\zeta \simeq -\frac{\left[(-C_{nr})\cos\varphi - (-C_{np})\alpha\right]\left[(\tan\varphi)\, C_W \mathrm{AR}_w/4\bar{m}\right]}{(-C_{n\zeta})}.$$

When $C_W = 0.7$, $\varphi = 45°$, typically

$$\Delta\eta = \mathrm{O}[-2.5°], \qquad \Delta\xi = \mathrm{O}[0.6°], \qquad \Delta\zeta = \mathrm{O}[-0.6°]. \qquad \text{(IV.3.14)}$$

Note the relatively small lateral control angles; again the lateral controls are crossed.

For a combat aeroplane it is necessary to maximize the sustained turn rate. By definition

$$\text{(structural) load factor} = L/W = (L/D)\,(\mathrm{Th}/W). \qquad \text{(IV.3.15)}$$

The structure is designed to a maximum load factor of 9.

Hence, from eqns. (IV.3.5), neglecting the side force Y,

$$\begin{aligned} \mathrm{STR} &= (g/U)\left[(\text{load factor})^2 - 1\right]^{1/2} \\ &\simeq (g/U)(\text{load factor}) \text{ for load factor} > 3. \end{aligned} \qquad \text{(IV.3.16)}$$

But

$$U = \left[(\text{load factor})\ (W/S_w)/\left(\tfrac{1}{2}\rho_{at}C_L\right)\right]^{1/2}$$

so

$$\mathrm{STR} = g\left[\left(\tfrac{1}{2}\rho_{at}C_L(\text{load factor})\right)/(W/S_w)\right]^{1/2}. \qquad \text{(IV.3.17)}$$

To optimize the STR:

(i) a typical plot of $L/D\ (= C_L/C_D) \sim C_L$ is shown in Fig. IV.27;
(ii) suppose that $(\mathrm{Th}/W)_{max} = 1.0$ and $(\text{load factor})_{max} = 9$;
(iii) thus from eqn. (IV.3.15), $(\text{load factor})_{max}$ can only be obtained with Th/W less than, or equal to, 1.0, with L/D greater than, or equal to, 9, so from Fig. IV.27 C_L lies within the range

$$0.9 > C_L > 0.2; \qquad \text{(IV.3.18)}$$

(iv) over the range of C_L in eqn. (IV.3.18) the maximum STR, from eqn. (IV.3.17), is obtained with

$C_L = 0.9$, load factor = 9 (IV.3.19)

(it can be checked that with $C_L > 0.9$, $Th/W = 1.0$ and load factor < 9, the STR is less than the maximum given by condition (IV.3.19));

(v) taking the wing loading equal to 3.5 kN/m^2, then at 3 km (5000 ft) altitude,

maximum STR $\simeq$ 20°/s. (IV.3.20)

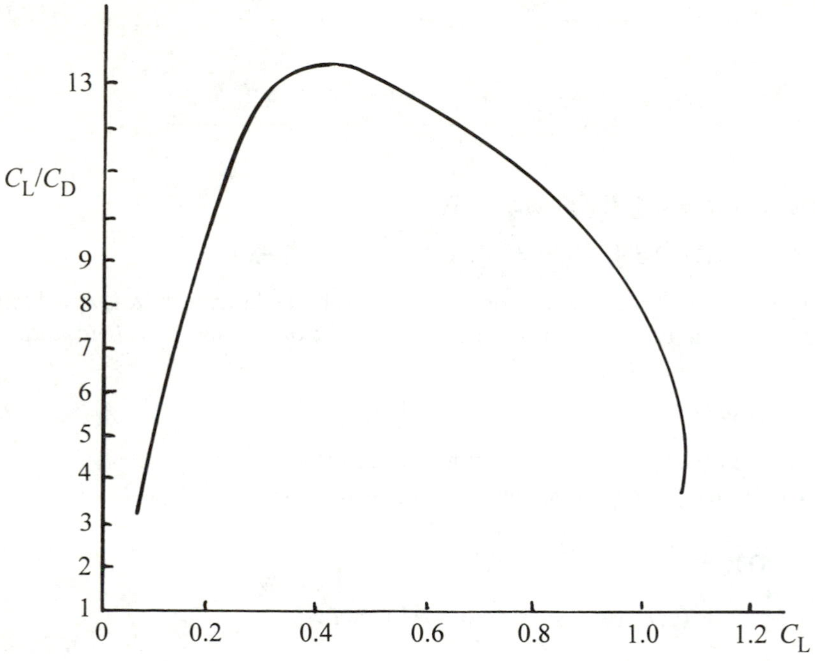

Fig. IV.27. Example: Variation of $C_L/C_D \sim C_L$.

Some observations.

(i) According to eqn. (IV.3.17) the STR can be improved by decreasing the wing loading. Thus, turn efficiency requires low wing loading. But, as already explained in sect. III.13, ride quality requires high wing loading. The search at the design stage for the compromise value of the wing loading for an optimum overall performance is far from straightforward.

(ii) Also, according to eqn. (IV.3.17), the STR is increased at lower altitudes, so combat takes place at lower rather than higher altitudes.

(iii) In practice $(Th/W)_{max}$ increases with Mach number, so the maximum STR will increase with Mach number, but (L/D) decreases significantly above the drag rise Mach number so combat takes place at high subsonic speeds.

(iv) From eqns. (IV.3.5) and (IV.3.15) the angle of bank depends only on the load factor, irrespective of Mach number or altitude; at a load factor equal to 9 the bank angle is 84°.

EXAMPLES IV.9

1. Check the statement following eqn. (IV.3.7) that Y is negligible at all operating speeds and altitudes.
2. Check that the same incremental control angles are obtained for a sustained turn when trim body axes are used.
3. What are the pilot's actions to implement the incremental angle changes in eqns. (IV.3.14)?
4. Plot $\Delta\eta$, $\Delta\xi$ and $\Delta\zeta$ against φ ($0 < \varphi < 84°$) at sea level take $C_W = 0.7$, $i_w - \alpha_{0W} = 3°$.
5. Determine $\Delta\eta$, $\Delta\xi$, $\Delta\zeta$ typical values for a differential tailplane.
6. Determine the maximum STR in the example in the text if $(\text{Th}/W)_{max} = 0.8$.

IV.3.4 Steady flight with engine out

It is a requirement that an aeroplane should be flyable when one engine fails in a two engine configuration, or two engines fail in a four engine configuration. From a control point of view it is necessary to ensure sufficient rudder power to offset the change in yawing moment on the aeroplane when an engine fails.

Suppose on a two engine configuration, as shown in Fig. IV.28, the starboard engine fails. Then for lateral static equilibrium in straight flight,

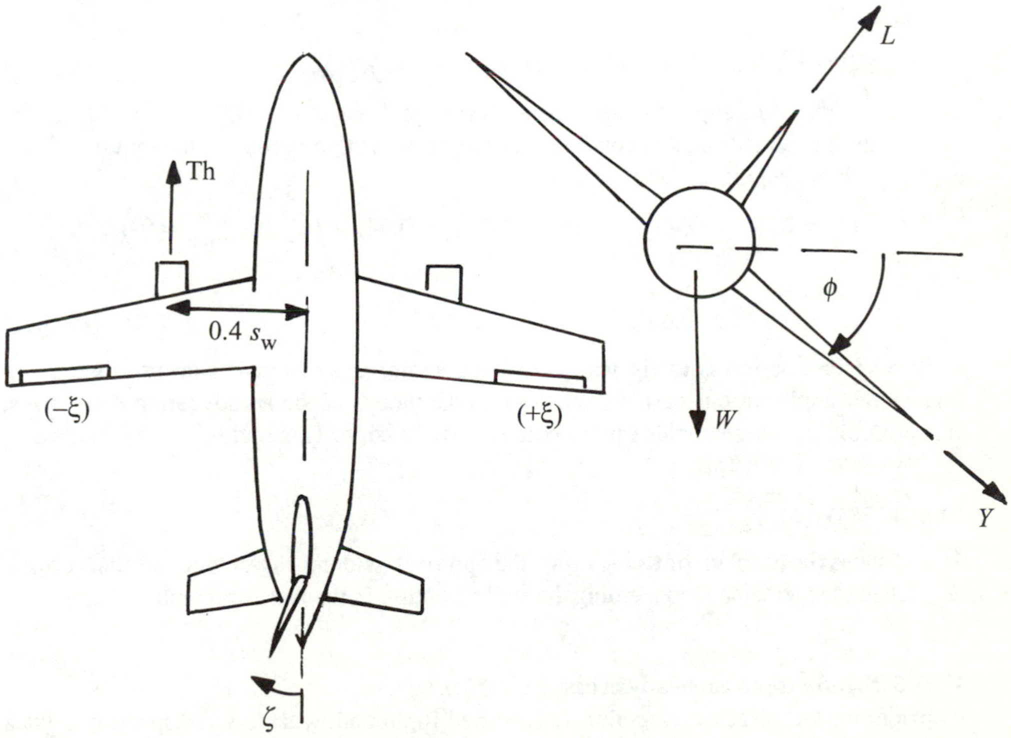

Fig. IV.28. Flight with engine out.

$$\begin{aligned}
\mathrm{Th}(0.4s_w) = D(0.4s_w) &= -\tfrac{1}{2}\rho_{at}U_{trim}^2 S_w\ 2s_w \quad (C_{n\beta}\beta + C_{n\xi}\xi + C_{n\zeta}\zeta) \\
0 &= \tfrac{1}{2}\rho_{at}U_{trim}^2 S_w\ 2s_w \quad (C_{l\beta}\beta + C_{l\xi}\xi + C_{l\zeta}\zeta) \\
W\sin\varphi &= -\tfrac{1}{2}\rho_{at}U_{trim}^2 S_w \quad (C_{Y\beta}\beta + C_{Y\xi}\xi + C_{Y\zeta}\zeta)
\end{aligned} \tag{IV.3.21}$$

In practice there can be a significant additional contribution to the asymmetric yawing moment from the defunct engine, arising from an increase in a turbo-fan spillage drag or from the windmilling of a propeller.

In principle there are two primary options: to fly either with zero sideslip with a bank angle, or to fly with zero bank angle with sideslip.

For the first option, to fly at zero sideslip, the control angles are

$$\begin{aligned}
\xi &= \left(C_{l\zeta}/(-C_{l\xi})\right)\zeta, \\
\left[(-C_{n\xi})\left(C_{l\zeta}/(-C_{l\xi})\right) + (-C_{n\zeta})\right]\zeta &= 0.2C_D,
\end{aligned} \tag{IV.3.22}$$

with bank angle

$$\sin\varphi = -(1/C_W)(C_{Y\xi}\xi + C_{Y\zeta}\zeta)$$

Typically

$$\zeta \simeq 1.3C_D, \quad \xi \simeq 0.2C_D, \quad \sin\varphi \simeq -0.4\,C_D/C_W.$$

For minimum bank angle the aeroplane should be flow at $(C_D/C_L)_{min}$, namely at the minimum drag condition; this condition is compatible with minimizing the required thrust from the single engine. Taking

$$C_D = 0.02 + 0.06C_L^2, \quad \text{with} \quad (C_D)_{min} = 0.04, \quad (C_D/C_L)_{min} = 0.07,$$

then

$$\zeta \simeq 3°, \quad \xi \simeq 0.45°, \quad \varphi \simeq -1.6°. \tag{IV.3.23}$$

The second option is to fly with zero bank angle, and non-zero sideslip; the aileron and rudder angles in this case are sensitive to the values of the aerodynamic derivatives; it is possible that these angles can become extremely large. This option is not preferred.

EXAMPLES IV.10

1. Discuss the problem of flying down the approach with an engine out and flaps down.
2. Check the statement concerning the second option in the last paragraph.

IV.3.5 Steady flight in steady crosswind

Consider an aeroplane moving along a specified flight path with forward speed U_{trim} in a steady crosswind of velocity v_g (= $\beta_g U_{trim}$), as shown in Fig. IV.29. The lateral equations of equilibrium are

$$\left(C_{n\beta}(\beta+\beta_g)+C_{n\xi}\xi+C_{n\zeta}\zeta\right)=0$$
$$\left(C_{l\beta}(\beta+\beta_g)+C_{l\xi}\xi+C_{l\zeta}\zeta\right)=0 \tag{IV.3.24}$$
$$\left(C_{Y\beta}(\beta+\beta_g)+C_{Y\xi}\xi+C_{Y\zeta}\zeta\right)=-C_W\sin\varphi.$$

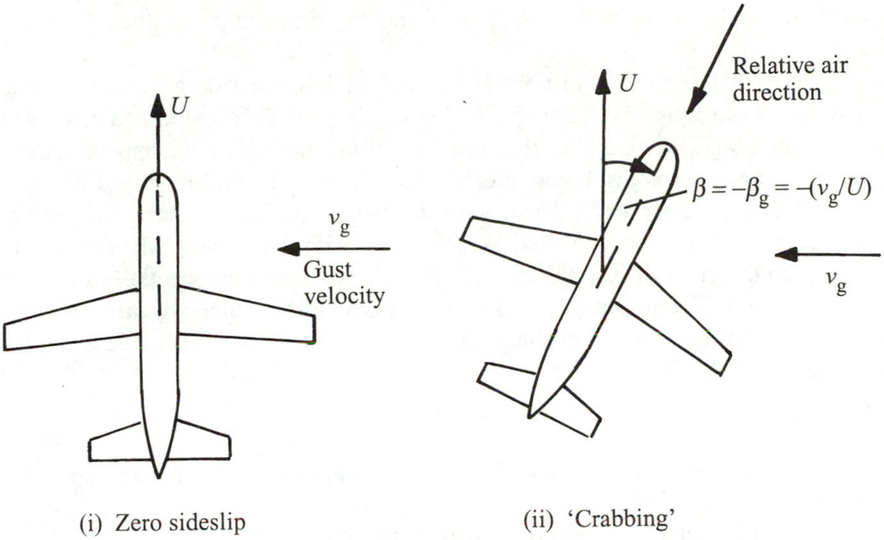

Fig. IV.29. Flight in crosswind.

Again there are two options for steady flight.

The first option is to point the aeroplane in the direction of the flight path (i.e. $\beta=0$) and to counteract the rolling moment, yawing moment and side force by the aileron, rudder and bank angles. From eqns. (IV.3.14), neglecting $C_{l\zeta}$ and $C_{n\zeta}$,

$$\zeta\simeq\left(C_{n\beta}/(-C_{n\zeta})\right)\beta_g\simeq+\beta_g$$
$$\xi\simeq\left((-C_{l\beta})/(-C_{l\xi})\right)\beta_g\simeq-(0.4+1.8C_W\tan\Lambda_w)\beta_g \tag{IV.3.25}$$
$$C_W\sin\varphi=\left[(-C_{Y\beta})+C_{Y\xi}\left(-\xi/\beta_g\right)-C_{Y\zeta}\left(\zeta/\beta_g\right)\right]\beta_g.$$

From eqns. (IV.3.25) the critical case for retaining lateral control occurs with flaps down with high C_W at maximum β_g. When

$$\Lambda_w=30°,\quad C_W=1.75,\quad \beta_g=10°,$$

then

$$\xi=22°,\quad \zeta=13°,\quad \varphi=2.5°.$$

This aileron angle is up against the stops.

It is a mandatory design criterion that the aileron angle given by

$$\xi \simeq -\big((-C_{l\beta})/(-C_{l\xi})\big)(\beta_g)_{max} \tag{IV.3.26}$$

shall be within the limits of the aileron stops in order to retain adequate roll control effectiveness in a crosswind throughout the flight envelope. For a swept wing configuration $C_{l\beta}$ can be reduced slightly by reducing the dihedral angle while $C_{l\xi}$ can be increased by an increase in the roll power and by supplementing the ailerons with spoilers.

The second flight option is to point the aeroplane into the side gust with β equal to $-\beta_g$, and then, from eqns. (IV.3.24), ξ, ζ and φ are all zero. This option in a cross wind is known as 'crabbing'. When a pilot flies this type of manoeuvre on the approach the pilot applies rudder and aileron just before touchdown to line up the undercarriage wheels with the centre line of the runway (except with the large Lockheed Galaxy C-5 aeroplane whose undercarriage can be swivelled to be lined up with the runway when the approach is crabbed). In the kick-off just before touchdown the manoeuvre essentially reverts back to the first option of zero sideslip and so it is essential that there is sufficient aileron power to maintain the required heading down the runway, hence the need for the design criterion of eqn. (IV.3.26).

EXAMPLES IV.11

1. How would a pilot fly an aeroplane on the approach with an engine out in a crosswind?
2. How would a pilot fly an aeroplane at cruise in a crosswind?
3. How would a pilot fly an aeroplane in steady wind which is inclined to direction to the flight path?

IV.4 LATERAL STATIC WEATHERCOCK STABILITY

Lateral static weathercock stability is analogous to the longitudinal static weathercock stability described in sect. III.7.

Consider an aeroplane, initially trimmed in steady level rectilinear flight, which is given a static angular disturbance,

$$\Delta\beta = -\Delta\psi > 0 \tag{IV.4.1}$$

as shown in Fig. IV.30, assuming that the aeroplane centre of mass continues on its initial trimmed flight path. The aeroplane will tend to return to its initial trimmed state (i.e. both $\Delta\beta$ and $\Delta\psi$ tend to zero) when, as indicated in the figure, the restoring perturbation yawing moment $\Delta\mathcal{N}$ satisfies the condition

$$\Delta\mathcal{N} > 0. \tag{IV.4.2}$$

If the static angular disturbance is negative, also shown in Fig. IV.30, namely

$$\Delta\beta = -\Delta\psi < 0 \tag{IV.4.3}$$

the aeroplane will tend to return to its initial trimmed state if

$$\Delta\mathcal{N} < 0. \tag{IV.4.4}$$

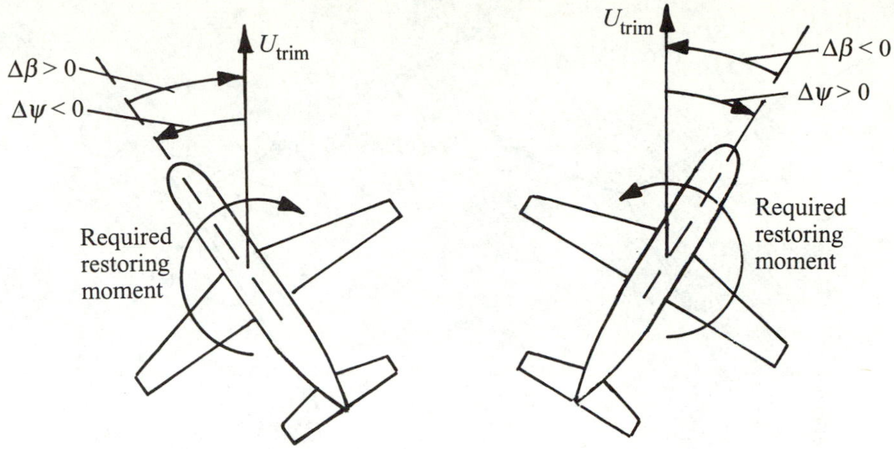

Fig. IV.30. Static lateral weathercock stability.

The condition of positive lateral weathercock stability which satisfies eqns. (IV.4.1)–(IV.4.4) is

$$\Delta\mathcal{N}/\Delta\beta > 0, \tag{IV.4.5}$$

that is,

$$C_{n\beta} > 0. \tag{IV.4.6}$$

It should be emphasized that lateral static weathercock stability refers to the particular combination of sideslip and yaw given by eqns. (IV.4.1), (IV.4.3), not to pure sideslip by itself with zero yaw, nor to pure yaw by itself with zero sideslip.

EXAMPLE IV.12

1. If $C_{n\beta} > 0$, what is the motion of an aeroplane when

$$\Delta\beta > 0, \quad \Delta\psi = 0; \qquad \Delta\beta < 0, \quad \Delta\psi = 0,$$
$$\Delta\beta = 0, \quad \Delta\psi > 0; \qquad \Delta\beta = 0, \quad \Delta\psi < 0?$$

IV.5 EQUATIONS OF MOTION FOR SMALL LATERAL PERTURBATIONS

In this section the equations of motion are derived for an aeroplane initially in steady equilibrium flight when disturbed laterally with time varying $\beta(t)$, $p(t)$ and $r(t)$ by control inputs $\xi(t)$ and $\zeta(t)$ and/or lateral winds and gusts.

In an initial equilibrium state of rectilinear trimmed flight, as shown in Fig. IV.31(i), the components of the absolute velocity of the centre of mass resolved in the direction of the fuselage body axes *oxyz* are, for small α_{trim}, $(U_{trim}, 0, U_{trim}\alpha_{trim})$, with zero rates of rotation about all three axes.

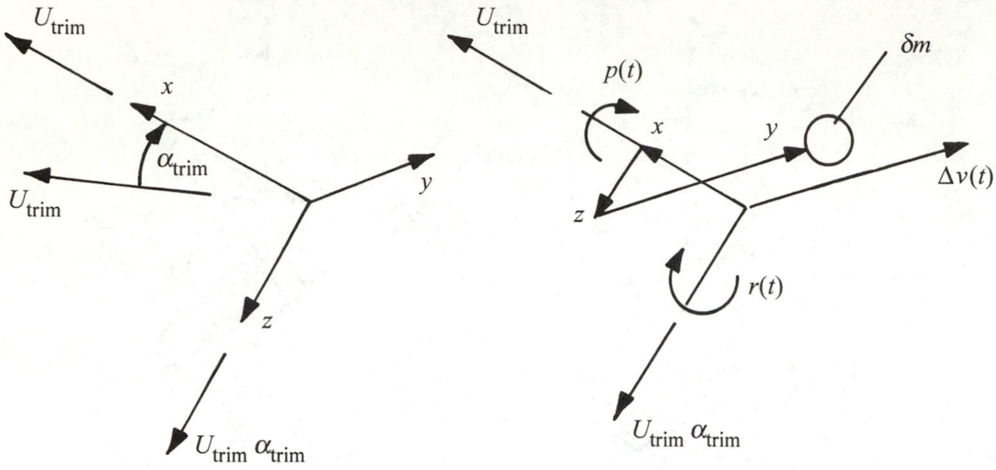

(i) Initial trim state (ii) Perturbed state

Fig. IV.31. Notation for small lateral perturbations.

When perturbed laterally the components of absolute velocity of the centre of mass are $(U_{\text{trim}}, \Delta v(t), U_{\text{trim}}\alpha_{\text{trim}})$, with rate of roll $p(t)$ about the ox fuselage body axis, zero rate of pitch about the oy axis, and rate of yaw, $r(t)$, about the oz fuselage body axis.

Consider a small element of mass δm located at $P(x, y, z)$.

By inspection of Fig. IV.31(ii) the absolute velocity components of this element of mass resolved in the directions of the body axis are

$$\begin{aligned} U_{Px}(t) &= U_{\text{trim}} - r(t)y \\ U_{Py}(t) &= \Delta v(t) + r(t)x - p(t)z \\ U_{Pz}(t) &= U_{\text{trim}}\alpha_{\text{trim}} + p(t)y. \end{aligned} \tag{IV.5.1}$$

By analogy with the analysis of the components of absolute acceleration of an element δm located at (x, y, z) in a planar longitudinal motion (see sect. III.4, eqns. (III.4.11) and (III.4.14)), the components of absolute acceleration relative to the $oxyz$ axis system are

$$\begin{aligned} A_{Px}(t) &= \dot{U}_{Px}(t) - r(t)U_{Py}(t) \\ A_{Py}(t) &= \dot{U}_{Py}(t) + r(t)U_{Px}(t) - p(t)U_{Pz}(t) \\ A_{Pz}(t) &= \dot{U}_{Pz}(t) + p(t)U_{Py}(t). \end{aligned} \tag{IV.5.2}$$

The overall equation of motion in the direction oy, deduced from Fig. IV.25, is

$$\Delta Y(t) + W\sin\Delta\varphi = \sum_{\text{aeroplane}} \delta m A_{Py} = m\big(\Delta\dot{v}(t) + r(t)U_{\text{trim}}\big) \tag{IV.5.3}$$

on substitution of eqns. (IV.5.1) and (IV.5.2), where $\Delta Y(t)$ is the perturbation aerodynamic side force; $W \sin \Delta\varphi$ ($\simeq W\Delta\varphi$, when $\Delta\varphi$ is small) is the component of the all-up weight in the oy direction; the summation is over all the elements of the aeroplane, remembering that $\sum\delta mx = \sum\delta my = \sum\delta mz = 0$ because the origin of the body axis system is located at the centre of mass; the quantities $r^2(t)$, $r(t)p(t)$ and $p(t)\alpha_{\text{trim}}$ are regarded as second order quantities and are neglected; and assuming that all internal forces between elements cancel out.

The overall equations of rotary motion are:

about the ox axis,

$$\begin{aligned}\mathscr{L}(t) &= \sum_{\text{aeroplane}} \left[\delta m\left[yA_{Pz}(t) - zA_{Py}(t)\right]\right] \\ &= I_{xx}\dot{p}(t) - I_{xz}\dot{r}(t),\end{aligned} \quad \text{(IV.5.4)}$$

about the oz axis,

$$\begin{aligned}\mathscr{N}(t) &= \sum_{\text{aeroplane}} \left[\delta m\left[xA_{Py}(t) - yA_{Px}(t)\right]\right] \\ &= -I_{xz}\dot{p}(t) + I_{zz}\dot{r}(t),\end{aligned} \quad \text{(IV.5.5)}$$

on substitution of eqns. (IV.5.1) and (IV.5.2), again neglecting second order terms, where $\mathscr{L}(t)$ and $\mathscr{N}(t)$ are the aerodynamic perturbation rolling moment and yawing moment respectively, I_{xx} and I_{zz} are the moments of inertia, and I_{xz} is the product of inertia, defined by

$$\begin{aligned}I_{xx} &= \sum_{\text{aeroplane}} \delta m(y^2 + z^2), \qquad I_{xz} = \sum_{\text{aeroplane}} \delta mxz, \\ I_{zz} &= \sum_{\text{aeroplane}} \delta m(x^2 + y^2).\end{aligned} \quad \text{(IV.5.6)}$$

By symmetry

$$I_{xy} = \sum_{\text{aeroplane}} \delta mxy = 0, \qquad I_{zy} = \sum_{\text{aeroplane}} \delta mzy = 0.$$

The equations of motion for small lateral perturbations $\Delta\beta(t)$, $\Delta\varphi(t)$ and $\Delta\psi(t)$ (eqns. (IV.5.3)–(IV.5.5)) are, in terms of the lateral derivatives,

$$\begin{aligned}&m\left(\Delta\dot{v}(t) + r(t)U_{\text{trim}}\right) \\ &\quad = \tfrac{1}{2}\rho_{\text{at}}U_{\text{trim}}^2 S_{\text{w}}\Big[C_{Y\beta}\,\Delta\beta(t) + C_{Y\dot{\beta}}\left(\Delta\dot{\beta}(t)s_{\text{w}}/U_{\text{trim}}\right) \\ &\qquad + C_{Yp}\left(p(t)s_{\text{w}}/U_{\text{trim}}\right) + C_{Y\dot{p}}\left(\dot{p}(t)(s_{\text{w}}/U_{\text{trim}})^2\right) \\ &\qquad + C_{Yr}\left(r(t)s_{\text{w}}/U_{\text{trim}}\right) + C_{Y\dot{r}}\left(\dot{r}(t)(s_{\text{w}}/U_{\text{trim}})^2\right)\Big] \\ &\qquad + W\Delta\varphi + [\text{side force due to control inputs and atmospheric gusts}];\end{aligned} \quad \text{(IV.5.7)}$$

$$I_{xx}\dot{p}(t) - I_{xz}\dot{r}(t)$$
$$= \tfrac{1}{2}\rho_{\text{at}}U_{\text{trim}}^2 S_{\text{w}}\ 2s_{\text{w}}\Big[C_{l\beta}\Delta\beta(t) + C_{l\dot{\beta}}\big(\Delta\dot{\beta}(t)s_{\text{w}}/U_{\text{trim}}\big)$$
$$+ C_{lp}\big(p(t)s_{\text{w}}/U_{\text{trim}}\big) + C_{l\dot{p}}\Big(\dot{p}(t)\big(s_{\text{w}}/U_{\text{trim}}\big)^2\Big)$$
$$+ C_{lr}\big(r(t)s_{\text{w}}/U_{\text{trim}}\big) + C_{l\dot{r}}\Big(\dot{r}(t)\big(s_{\text{w}}/U_{\text{trim}}\big)^2\Big)\Big]$$
$$+ \text{[rolling moment due to control inputs and atmospheric gusts];} \quad \text{(IV.5.8)}$$

$$-I_{xz}\dot{p}(t) + I_{zz}\dot{r}(t)$$
$$= \tfrac{1}{2}\rho_{\text{at}}U_{\text{trim}}^2 S_{\text{w}}\ 2s_{\text{w}}\Big[C_{n\beta}\Delta\beta(t) + C_{n\dot{\beta}}\big(\Delta\dot{\beta}(t)s_{\text{w}}/U_{\text{trim}}\big)$$
$$+ C_{np}\big(p(t)s_{\text{w}}/U_{\text{trim}}\big) + C_{n\dot{p}}\Big(\dot{p}(t)\big(s_{\text{w}}/U_{\text{trim}}\big)^2\Big)$$
$$+ C_{nr}\big(r(t)s_{\text{w}}/U_{\text{trim}}\big) + C_{n\dot{r}}\Big(\dot{r}(t)\big(s_{\text{w}}/U_{\text{trim}}\big)^2\Big)\Big]$$
$$+ \text{[rolling moment due to control inputs and atmospheric gusts];} \quad \text{(IV.5.9)}$$

where

$$\Delta\beta(t) = \Delta v(t)/U_{\text{trim}}$$

and, for small $\Delta\varphi(t)$ and $\Delta\psi(t)$,

$$p(t) \simeq \Delta\dot{\varphi}(t), \qquad r(t) \simeq \Delta\dot{\psi}(t).$$

Re-expressing and approximating these equations of motion,

$$\big(C_{\text{W}}/g\big)U_{\text{trim}}\big[\Delta\dot{\beta}(t) + r(t)\big]$$
$$\simeq \big[C_{Y\beta}\,\Delta\beta(t) + C_{Yp}\big(p(t)s_{\text{w}}/U_{\text{trim}}\big)\big] + C_{\text{W}}\Delta\varphi$$
$$+ \text{[non-dimensional side force due to control inputs and atmospheric gusts],} \quad \text{(IV.5.10)}$$

$$\big[i_{xx}\dot{p}(t) - i_{xz}\dot{r}(t)\big]\big(s_{\text{w}}C_{\text{W}}/2g\big)$$
$$\simeq \Big[C_{l\beta}\Delta\beta(t) + C_{l\dot{\beta}}\big(\Delta\dot{\beta}(t)\,s_{\text{w}}/U_{\text{trim}}\big)$$
$$+ C_{lp}\big(p(t)s_{\text{w}}/U_{\text{trim}}\big) + C_{lr}\big(r(t)s_{\text{w}}/U_{\text{trim}}\big)\Big]$$
$$+ \text{[non-dimensional rolling moment due to control inputs and atmospheric gusts],} \quad \text{(IV.5.11)}$$

$$[-i_{xz}\dot{p}(t)+i_{zz}\dot{r}(t)](s_W C_W/2g)$$
$$\simeq\Big[C_{n\beta}\Delta\beta(t)+C_{n\dot{\beta}}\big(\Delta\dot{\beta}(t)s_W/U_{\text{trim}}\big)$$
$$+\,C_{np}\big(p(t)s_W/U_{\text{trim}}\big)+C_{nr}\big(r(t)s_W/U_{\text{trim}}\big)\Big]$$
+ [non-dimensional yawing moment due to control inputs and atmospheric gusts] (IV.5.12)

where

(i) the aerodynamic terms involving $C_{Y\dot{\beta}}$, C_{Yr}, $C_{l\dot{p}}$ and $C_{n\dot{r}}$ are neglected in comparison with their inertial counterparts;
(ii) taking $C_{Y\dot{p}}$ and $C_{n\dot{p}}$ equal to zero from eqns. (IV.2.33);
(iii) assuming that the terms involving $C_{Y\dot{r}}$ and $C_{l\dot{r}}$ can be neglected; this assumption can be validated later in the coefficients of the characteristic equation;
(iv) i_{xx} = non-dimensional roll moment of inertia = $I_{xx}/(ms_W^2)$
i_{zz} = non-dimensional yaw moment of inertia = $I_{zz}/(ms_W^2)$ (IV.5.13)
i_{xz} = non-dimensional product of inertia = $I_{xz}/(ms_W^2)$.

Crudely

$$i_{xx}=\text{O}[0.10],\quad i_{zz}=\text{O}[0.25],\quad i_{xz}=\text{O}[0.01]. \tag{IV.5.14}$$

The implication of these orders of magnitude is that

radius of gyration in roll $\simeq 0.3s_W$, radius of gyration in yaw $\simeq 0.5s_W$.

The order-of-magnitude values of i_{xx} and i_{zz}, quoted in eqns. (IV.5.14), should be treated with caution; i_{xx}, in particular, depends on wing sweep, the location of the engines, a high or low tailplane, and on the amount of fuel in the wings, especially if fuel is held in wing tip tanks. More particularly,

single engine light aeroplane	$i_{xx}\simeq 0.035$,	$i_{zz}\simeq 0.075$	
large transport aeroplane	$i_{xx}\simeq 0.10$,	$i_{zz}\simeq 0.25$	(IV.5.15)
combat aeroplane	$i_{xx}\simeq 0.05$,	$i_{zz}\simeq 0.30$.	

The product of inertia relative to fuselage body axes tends to be positive due to underwing engines (which are located at positive x and positive z) and the fin (which is located at negative x and negative z).

Because the 'z' extent of an airframe is less than the 'x' or 'y' extents, $(\sum\delta m\,z^2)$ is much smaller than $(\sum\delta m\,x^2)$ or $(\sum\delta m\,y^2)$, so

$$I_{zz}\simeq I_{xx}+I_{yy}\quad\text{or}\quad i_{zz}\simeq i_{xx}+i_{yy}(2/\text{AR}_W)^2. \tag{IV.5.16}$$

The moments and product of inertia I_{xx}, I_{zz} and I_{xz} relative to the fuselage body axis system $oxyz$ are independent of the flight attitudes.

The equations of lateral perturbed motion from trimmed rectilinear flight expressed in terms of trim body axes are of exactly the same form as eqns. (IV.5.10)–(IV.5.12) with variables $p_1(t)$, $r_1(t)$ and $\Delta\varphi_1(t)$ replacing $p(t)$, $r(t)$ and $\Delta\varphi(t)$, and derivatives C_{l1p_1}, etc. replacing derivatives C_{lp}, etc. (see Appendix 9). However the moments of inertia $I_{x_1x_1}$, $I_{z_1z_1}$ and $I_{x_1z_1}$ relative to the trim body axis system ox_1yz_1 depend on α_{trim}, and so vary with the initial trimmed flight state; the transformation is

$$\begin{aligned} I_{x_1x_1} &= I_{xx}\cos^2\alpha_{\text{trim}} - I_{xz}\sin 2\alpha_{\text{trim}} + I_{zz}\sin^2\alpha_{\text{trim}} \\ I_{z_1z_1} &= I_{xx}\sin^2\alpha_{\text{trim}} + I_{xz}\sin 2\alpha_{\text{trim}} + I_{zz}\cos^2\alpha_{\text{trim}} \\ I_{z_1x_1} &= I_{xz}\cos 2\alpha_{\text{trim}} - \tfrac{1}{2}(I_{zz} - I_{xx})\sin 2\alpha_{\text{trim}}. \end{aligned} \qquad \text{(IV.5.17)}$$

The above analysis has been derived for small lateral perturbations relative to trimmed straight flight, where $(C_L)_{\text{trim}}$ is equal to C_W. The extension of this analysis to small lateral perturbations about a steady turn is described later in Part V.

EXAMPLES IV.13

1. Prove eqns. (IV.5.2).
2. Are the lateral perturbation equations affected by a steady angle of climb?
3. Does a high wing or low wing affect i_{xx}, i_{xz} and i_{zz}?
4. Prove the statement: 'The equations of lateral perturbed motion from trimmed rectilinear flight expressed in terms of trim body axes are of exactly the same form as eqns. (IV.5.10)–(IV.5.12) with variables $p_1(t)$, $r_1(t)$ and $\Delta\varphi_1(t)$ replacing $p(t)$, $r(t)$ and $\Delta\varphi(t)$, and derivatives C_{l1p_1}, etc. replacing derivatives C_{lp}, etc.'
5. Given $i_{xx} = 0.1$, $i_{xz} = 0.01$, $i_{zz} = 0.25$, $\alpha_{\text{trim}} = 10°$, determine $i_{x_1x_1}$, $i_{x_1z_1}$, $i_{z_1z_1}$.

IV.6 LATERAL STABILITY MODES

There are four lateral stability modes, which are now described in qualitative terms for an aeroplane initially in steady rectilinear flight.

IV.6.1 Roll rate mode

The roll mode involves primarily roll with little sideslip or yaw.

An approximation to the roll modal response is given by the transient response of the roll equation, eqn. (IV.5.11), when the input terms are put equal to zero, neglecting all sideslip and yaw terms, namely the non-zero solution of

$$\left[i_{xx}(U_{\text{trim}}C_W/2g)\,\mathrm{D} + (-C_{lp})\right]\left(p(t)s_w/U_{\text{trim}}\right) = 0 \qquad \text{(IV.6.1)}$$

where $\mathrm{D} = \mathrm{d}/\mathrm{d}t$.

The roll modal response is a pure subsidence of the roll rate (not the roll angle) with time to half amplitude

$$\begin{aligned} (t_{1/2})_{\text{roll}} &\simeq 0.7\left(i_{xx}/(-C_{lp})\right)\left(U_{\text{trim}}C_W/2g\right)\ \mathrm{s} \\ &= 0.7\left(i_{xx}/(-C_{lp})\right)\left((W/S_w)/(\rho_{\text{at}}U_{\text{trim}}g)\right)\ \mathrm{s}. \end{aligned} \qquad \text{(IV.6.2)}$$

Thus a rapid decay of the roll rate occurs with

low wing loading, low altitude, high forward speed,

small non-dimensional roll moment of inertia, i_{xx}, high $(-C_{lp})$.

Taking

$$W/S_w = 4\ \mathrm{kN/m^2}, \quad i_{xx}/(-C_{lp}) = 0.1/0.4$$

at sea level, when $U_{trim} = 50$ m/s ($\simeq 100$ knots), $(t_{1/2})_{roll} \simeq 1.14$ s

at sea level, when $U_{trim} = 170$ m/s ($M_\infty = 0.50$), $(t_{1/2})_{roll} \simeq 0.34$ s (IV.6.3)

at 11 km altitude, when $U_{trim} = 250$ m/s ($M_\infty = 0.85$), $(t_{1/2})_{roll} \simeq 0.76$ s

IV.6.2 Spiral mode

The spiral modal response is a slow motion.

An approximation to the spiral modal response is given by the transient response of the lateral equations of motion, eqns. (IV.5.10)–(IV.5.12),

(i) assuming that any turning motion is quasi-steady,
(ii) neglecting terms involving $\dot{p}(t)$ and $\dot{r}(t)$, since rates of change are assumed small.

In a quasi-steady turn the centripetal force due to the rate of yaw balances the side force due to the rotation of the lift vector, assuming the aerodynamic side force to be small (see sect. IV.4.3). This assumption is equivalent to neglecting the $\Delta\beta(t)$ and $p(t)$ terms in the side force equation, eqn. (IV.5.10), which reduces to, with zero input,

$$-\left(U_{trim}/g\right) r(t) + \Delta\varphi(t) = 0. \qquad \text{(IV.6.4)}$$

The roll and yaw equations, neglecting terms involving $\dot{p}(t)$ and $\dot{r}(t)$, with zero input, are

$$\left[C_{l\beta}\,\Delta\beta(t) + C_{lr}\left(r(t)s_w/U_{trim}\right) + C_{lp}\,\mathrm{D}\left(\Delta\varphi(t)s_w/U_{trim}\right)\right] = 0$$
$$\left[C_{n\beta}\,\Delta\beta(t) + C_{nr}\left(r(t)s_w/U_{trim}\right) + C_{np}\,\mathrm{D}\left(\Delta\varphi(t)s_w/U_{trim}\right)\right] = 0. \qquad \text{(IV.6.5)}$$

The stability characteristic equation of eqns. (IV.6.4) and (IV.6.5) is

$$\left(U_{trim}/g\right)\left[(-C_{l\beta})(-C_{np}) + (-C_{lp})(C_{n\beta})\right]\lambda + \left[(-C_{l\beta})(-C_{nr}) - C_{n\beta}C_{lr}\right] = 0. \qquad \text{(IV.6.6)}$$

Because the coefficient of λ is positive, the spiral modal response is stable as a pure subsidence when

$$(-C_{l\beta})(-C_{nr}) - C_{n\beta}C_{lr} > 0 \qquad \text{(IV.6.7a)}$$

and unstable as a pure divergence when

$$(-C_{l\beta})(-C_{nr}) - C_{n\beta}C_{lr} < 0. \qquad \text{(IV.6.7b)}$$

The dominant derivatives which determine the spiral mode stability are $(-C_{l\beta})$, which must not be too small, and $C_{n\beta}$, which must not be too large; $(-C_{l\beta})$ increases with dihedral angle and wing sweep while $C_{n\beta}$ increases with fin size.

The time to half amplitude for a stable spiral mode, from eqn. (IV.6.6) is

$$(t_{1/2})_{\text{spiral}} \simeq 0.7(U_{\text{trim}}/g)\left[\frac{(-C_{l\beta})(-C_{np})+(-C_{lp})(C_{n\beta})}{(-C_{l\beta})\,(-C_{nr})-C_{n\beta}C_{lr}}\right] \tag{IV.6.8}$$

$$= \mathrm{O}\left[2(U_{\text{trim}}/g)\ \mathrm{s}\right] = \mathrm{O}[30\ \mathrm{s}]. \tag{IV.6.9}$$

For a swept wing configuration $[(-C_{l\beta})\,(-C_{nr}) - C_{n\beta}\,C_{lr}]$ tends to decrease with decrease in C_{w}, while $[(-C_{l\beta})\,(-C_{np}) + (-C_{lp})\,(C_{n\beta})]$ is insensitive to $(C_{\mathrm{L}})_{\text{trim}}$, so $(t_{1/2})_{\text{spiral}}$ increases with increase in speed.

Note that $(t_{1/2})_{\text{spiral}}$ is independent of altitude, wing loading and moments of inertia.

Eqn. (IV.6.9) validates the initial assumption that rates of change during a spiral mode response are extremely slow.

For a stable spiral modal shape, from eqn. (IV.6.4),

$$\Delta\varphi(t) = \lambda(U_{\text{trim}}/g)\ \Delta\psi(t)$$

$$= -\left[\frac{(-C_{l\beta})(-C_{nr})-C_{n\beta}C_{lr}}{(-C_{l\beta})(-C_{np})+(-C_{lp})C_{n\beta}}\right]\Delta\psi(t) \tag{IV.6.10}$$

$$= \mathrm{O}[-0.4]\ \Delta\psi(t)$$

Because the motion develops so slowly, $r(t)s_{\mathrm{w}}/U_{\text{trim}}$ and $p(t)s_{\mathrm{w}}/U_{\text{trim}}$ are extremely small so the sideslip angle from eqns. (IV.6.5) is virtually zero, hence

$$\Delta\beta(t) \simeq 0. \tag{IV.6.11}$$

When the spiral mode is unstable, λ is positive, then from eqn. (IV.6.10) $\Delta\varphi(t)$ and $\Delta\psi(t)$ have the same sign, indicating a slow turn, gradually tightening, hence the phrase 'spiral'.

The following is a physical explanation of the spiral mode stability. If an aeroplane is disturbed into a positive rate of yaw, the negative C_{nr} is stabilizing in that it tends to reduce the rate of yaw whereas the positive C_{lr} is destabilizing in that it tends to roll the aeroplane with a positive bank angle, inducing the aeroplane into a positive sideslip. This positive sideslip introduces a negative $C_{l\beta}$ which is stabilizing in that the aeroplane is rolled in the negative sense, reducing the sideslip, and a positive $C_{n\beta}$ which is destabilizing in that it tends to increase the rate of yaw. This disturbance decays if the combination of stabilizing influences $[C_{nr}\,C_{l\beta}]$ is greater than the combination of destabilizing influences $[C_{lr}\,C_{n\beta}]$. Although $\Delta\beta$ is negligible compared with $\Delta\psi$ and $\Delta\varphi$, $\Delta\beta$ is comparable with $\Delta\dot{\psi}$ and $\Delta\dot{\varphi}$ for the slow rates of change associated with the spiral mode.

A spiral instability, like a phugoid instability, is not usually a problem for a pilot since a slow instability allows adequate time for the pilot to take remedial action, unless the pilot is distracted by more pressing tasks.

IV.6.3 Dutch roll, or lateral oscillation, mode

In the Dutch roll mode the centre of mass proceeds along the steady level flight path while the aeroplane oscillates in a dynamic lateral weathercock manner. According to folklore, the term Dutch roll originates from the observation that the aeroplane motion resembles that of a speed ice skater over the frozen canals in Holland.

In a lateral dynamic weathercock-type motion, as explained in sect. IV.4,

$$\Delta\beta(t) = -\,\Delta\psi(t). \qquad \text{(IV.6.12)}$$

As the aeroplane yaws the rate of yaw induces a rolling moment so the lateral weathercock motion is accompanied by a rolling motion.

The crudest approximation to the Dutch roll modal response is to neglect the effect of roll in the yaw equation, eqn. (IV.5.12). And then, eqn. (IV.5.12), neglecting i_{xz}, substituting $\Delta\beta(t)$ from eqn. (IV.6.12), with zero input, becomes

$$\left[\left(i_{zz}s_{\mathrm{w}}\,C_{\mathrm{W}}/2g\right)\mathrm{D}^2+\left((-C_{nr})\,s_{\mathrm{w}}/U_{\mathrm{trim}}\right)\mathrm{D}+C_{n\beta}\right]\Delta\psi(t)=0. \qquad \text{(IV.6.13)}$$

Because $(-C_{nr})$ and $C_{n\beta}$ are both positive, this second order system is a stable damped oscillation with

Dutch roll undamped frequency

$$=(\omega_0)_{\mathrm{Dr}}=\left[2gC_{n\beta}/(i_{zz}s_{\mathrm{w}}C_{\mathrm{W}})\right]^{1/2}\ \mathrm{rad/s} \qquad \text{(IV.6.14)}$$

Dutch roll damping ratio

$$=\zeta_{\mathrm{Dr}}=(-C_{nr})\left[(\mathrm{AR_w}/2)/(2C_{n\beta}i_{zz}\overline{m}\right]^{1/2}. \qquad \text{(IV.6.15)}$$

With typical values

$$i_{zz}=0.25,\quad s_{\mathrm{w}}=10\ \mathrm{m},\quad \mathrm{AR_w}=6,\quad \overline{m}=150,$$
$$C_{\mathrm{W}}=0.75,\quad C_{n\beta}=0.2,\quad (-C_{nr})=0.25,$$

$$(\omega_0)_{\mathrm{Dr}}=1.45\,\mathrm{rad/s}=0.23\ \mathrm{Hz}\quad(\text{period}=4.35\ \mathrm{s}),$$
$$\zeta_{\mathrm{Dr}}=0.11 \qquad \text{(IV.6.16)}$$

And then the time to half amplitude is

$$(t_{1/2})_{\mathrm{Dr}}\simeq 0.7/(\zeta\omega_0)_{\mathrm{Dr}}=4.4\ \mathrm{s}. \qquad \text{(IV.6.17)}$$

With these values the Dutch roll takes four periods to decay a lightly damped oscillation.

Note

(i) the Dutch roll undamped frequency depends on C_{W}, independent of altitude, whereas the Dutch roll damping ratio depends on altitude but is independent of C_{W};

(ii) an increase in aeroplane size (i.e. an increase in s_{w}) reduces the Dutch roll undamped frequency but does not affect the damping ratio.

The approximation for the Dutch roll stiffness in eqn. (IV.6.14) is reasonable but the approximation for the Dutch roll damping in eqn. (IV.6.15) is poor. A better approximation for the Dutch roll damping, derived in Appendix 10, extending the work of Thomas (ref. IV.3) replaces the derivative $(-C_{nr})$ in eqns. (IV.6.13) and (IV.6.15) by the more complicated form

$$0.5\Big[(-C_{nr})+(-C_{Y\beta})(i_{zz}/2)$$
$$+\Big[\big((-C_{lp})/(i_{xx}/2)\big)^2\big((-C_{nr})/C_{n\beta}\big)\big(i_{zz}\mathrm{AR_w}/4\overline{m}\big)\Big] \qquad \text{(IV.6.18)}$$
$$-\Big[\big(C_{\mathrm{L}}(i_{zz}/2)+(-C_{np})\big)\big((-C_{l\beta})/C_{n\beta}\big)\big(i_{zz}/i_{xx}\big)\Big]\Big]$$

This expression significantly reduces the Dutch roll damping ratio compared with eqn. (IV.6.15).

According to eqn. (IV.6.18), the Dutch roll damping

(i) increases with the derivatives $(-C_{nr})$, $(-C_{Y\beta})$ and $(-C_{lp})$,
(ii) decreases with altitude as $\overline{m}$ increases (this effect compounds the decrease with altitude in eqn. (IV.6.15)),
(iii) decreases significantly for higher values of C_{L}, that is at low speeds in straight flight, especially for swept aeroplanes where $(-C_{l\beta})$ is proportional to C_{L},
(iv) increases with decrease in i_{xx}, the non-dimensional roll inertia.

The ratio of derivatives $(-C_{l\beta})/C_{n\beta}$ is a key parameter in lateral stability; $(-C_{l\beta})/C_{n\beta}$ needs to be large enough to ensure positive spiral mode stability (see eqn. (IV.6.7)), but if $(-C_{l\beta})/C_{n\beta}$ is too large the Dutch roll damping can be reduced to an unacceptably low value, depending on the value of $(-C_{np})$.

IV.6.4 Neutral lateral stability mode

If an aeroplane with stable roll rate, spiral and Dutch roll modes is disturbed from a trimmed steady state flight condition, then the disturbance variables $\Delta\beta(t)$, $\Delta\varphi(t)$, $p(t)$ and $r(t)$ would return to zero but the perturbation angle of yaw, $\Delta\psi(t)$, would not return to zero but to a non-zero steady value; the heading of the aeroplane would not return to its initial heading.

This result, known as neutral lateral stability, is a consequence of the observation that an aeroplane has no preferred direction of flight. If an aeroplane is trimmed in steady level flight heading due north, and if the aeroplane is disturbed by a gust such that the heading is changed to north-east, then the aeroplane would continue flying north-east in the same trimmed state.

The author is reminded of one lecture during which, after explaining that an aeroplane had no preferred direction of flight, he was completely nonplussed and reduced to incoherence by the student who asked 'Is this true when a wind blows since the aerodynamic forces on the fin will then always align the aeroplane in the wind direction?' Perhaps the reader could answer this query.

EXAMPLES IV.14

1. What is the effect of Mach number on $(t_{1/2})_{\text{roll}}$?
2. What is the effect of Mach number on $(t_{1/2})_{\text{spiral}}$?
3. Deduce an approximation to the Dutch roll mode by considering the side force and yaw equations of motion only (eqns. (IV.5.10)–(IV.5.11)), together with the lateral weathercock assumption (eqn. (IV.6.12)). Derive the modal shape.
4. By taking typical values assess the orders of magnitude of the various terms in eqn. (IV.6.18); compare the value of eqn. (IV.6.18) with the value of $(-C_{nr})$ and deduce the effect on the Dutch roll damping ratio.
5. Are the lateral stability modes affected by an engine-out situation?
6. Are the lateral stability modes affected by propeller slipstream effects?
7. Are the lateral stability modes affected by underwing weapons?
8. Calculate the values of $(t_{1/2})_{\text{roll}}$, $(t_{1/2})_{\text{spiral}}$, $(\omega_0)_{\text{Dr}}$, ζ_{Dr} and $(t_{1/2})_{\text{Dr}}$ for the light aeroplane configuration (see Examples IV.3, IV.4 and IV.5).
9. Plot the variations of $(t_{1/2})_{\text{roll}}$, $(t_{1/2})_{\text{spiral}}$, $(\omega_0)_{\text{Dr}}$, ζ_{Dr} and $(t_{1/2})_{\text{Dr}}$ against Mach number for the transport aeroplane basic configuration:

   at sea level　　$0.15 < M_\infty < 0.5$

   at 11 km altitude　　$0.5 < M_\infty < 0.85$

   (see Examples IV.3, IV.4 and IV.5).
10. Plot the variations of $(t_{1/2})_{\text{roll}}$, $(t_{1/2})_{\text{spiral}}$, $(\omega_0)_{\text{Dr}}$, ζ_{Dr} and $(t_{1/2})_{\text{Dr}}$ against Mach number for the combat aeroplane basic configuration:

   at sea level　　$0.15 < M_\infty < 0.7$

   at 11 km altitude　　$0.5 < M_\infty < 1.8$

   (see Examples IV.3, IV.4 and IV.5).

IV.7 SMALL PERTURBATION LATERAL STABILITY

In this section the full lateral stability characteristics are derived in non-dimensional form for an aeroplane initially in steady rectilinear flight.

From sect. IV.5, eqns. (IV.5.10)–(IV.5.12), the equations of small perturbation lateral motion, relative to trimmed rectilinear steady flight, are

$$\left[(C_W/g)U_{\text{trim}}\,\mathrm{D} - C_{Y\beta}\right]\Delta\beta(t) + \left[(C_W/g)U_{\text{trim}}\right]\mathrm{D}\,\Delta\psi(t)$$
$$-\left[\left(C_{Yp}s_W/U_{\text{trim}}\right)\mathrm{D} + C_W\right]\Delta\varphi(t)$$
$$= \text{[non-dimensional side force due to control inputs and atmospheric gusts]} \qquad \text{(IV.7.1)}$$

$$-\left[\left(C_{l\dot{\beta}}s_{\mathrm{w}}/U_{\mathrm{trim}}\right)\mathrm{D}+C_{l\beta}\right]\Delta\beta(t)$$
$$-\left[\left(i_{xz}s_{\mathrm{w}}C_{\mathrm{W}}/2g\right)\mathrm{D}^2+\left(C_{lr}\,s_{\mathrm{w}}/U_{\mathrm{trim}}\right)\mathrm{D}\right]\Delta\psi(t)$$
$$+\left[\left(i_{xx}s_{\mathrm{w}}C_{\mathrm{W}}/2g\right)\mathrm{D}^2-\left(C_{lp}s_{\mathrm{w}}/U_{\mathrm{trim}}\right)\mathrm{D}\right]\Delta\varphi(t)$$

= [non-dimensional rolling moment due to control inputs and atmospheric gusts] (IV.7.2)

$$-\left[\left(C_{n\dot{\beta}}s_{\mathrm{w}}/U_{\mathrm{trim}}\right)\mathrm{D}+C_{n\beta}\right]\Delta\beta(t)$$
$$+\left[\left(i_{zz}s_{\mathrm{w}}C_{\mathrm{W}}/2g\right)\mathrm{D}^2-\left(C_{nr}\,s_{\mathrm{w}}/U_{\mathrm{trim}}\right)\mathrm{D}\right]\Delta\psi(t)$$
$$-\left[\left(i_{xz}s_{\mathrm{w}}C_{\mathrm{W}}/2g\right)\mathrm{D}^2+\left(C_{np}s_{\mathrm{w}}/U_{\mathrm{trim}}\right)\mathrm{D}\right]\Delta\varphi(t)$$

= [non-dimensional yawing moment due to control inputs and atmospheric gusts]. (IV.7.3)

The above equations of motion are now re-expressed in non-dimensional form. The unit of non-dimensional dynamic time, as previously defined, is

$$\hat{t}_{\mathrm{d}}=\overline{m}\,c_{\mathrm{w}}/U_{\mathrm{trim}}=\left(\overline{m}2/\mathrm{AR}_{\mathrm{w}}\right)s_{\mathrm{w}}/U_{\mathrm{trim}},$$
$$\overline{m}=m/\left(\tfrac{1}{2}\rho_{\mathrm{at}}c_{\mathrm{w}}S_{\mathrm{w}}\right). \tag{IV.7.4}$$

Non-dimensional dynamic time, $\bar{t}_{\mathrm{d}}$, is defined by

$$\bar{t}_{\mathrm{d}}=t/\hat{t}_{\mathrm{d}}. \tag{IV.7.5}$$

Defining $\mathrm{D}=\left(1/\hat{t}_{\mathrm{d}}\right)\overline{\mathrm{D}}$, where $\mathrm{D}=\mathrm{d}/\mathrm{d}t$ and $\overline{\mathrm{D}}=\mathrm{d}/\mathrm{d}\bar{t}_{\mathrm{d}}$, then

$$\mathrm{D}=\left(U_{\mathrm{trim}}\mathrm{AR}_{\mathrm{w}}/2\overline{m}s_{\mathrm{w}}\right)\overline{\mathrm{D}}=\left(\tfrac{1}{2}\rho_{\mathrm{at}}U_{\mathrm{trim}}S_{\mathrm{w}}/m\right)\overline{\mathrm{D}}=\left(g/(U_{\mathrm{trim}}C_{\mathrm{W}})\,\overline{\mathrm{D}}\right)$$
$$\mathrm{D}^2=\left(g\ \mathrm{AR}_{\mathrm{w}}/(2\overline{m}C_{\mathrm{W}}s_{\mathrm{w}})\right)\overline{\mathrm{D}}^2.$$

Eqns. (IV.7.1)–(IV.7.3) in non-dimensional form are:

$$\left[\overline{\mathrm{D}}-C_{Y\beta}\right]\Delta\beta(\bar{t}_{\mathrm{d}})+\overline{\mathrm{D}}\ \Delta\psi(\bar{t}_{\mathrm{d}})$$
$$-\left[\left(C_{Yp}\,\mathrm{AR}_{\mathrm{w}}/2\overline{m}\right)\overline{\mathrm{D}}+C_{\mathrm{W}}\right]\Delta\varphi(\bar{t}_{\mathrm{d}})$$

= [non-dimensional side force due to control inputs and atmospheric gusts] (IV.7.6)

$$-\left[C_{l\dot{\beta}}\,\overline{\mathrm{D}}+(2\overline{m}/\mathrm{AR_w})C_{l\beta}\right]\Delta\beta(\bar{t}_\mathrm{d})$$
$$-\left[(i_{xz}/2)\,\overline{\mathrm{D}}^2+C_{lr}\,\overline{\mathrm{D}}\right]\Delta\psi(\bar{t}_\mathrm{d})$$
$$+\left[(i_{xx}/2)\,\overline{\mathrm{D}}^2-C_{lp}\,\overline{\mathrm{D}}\right]\Delta\varphi(\bar{t}_\mathrm{d})$$
$$=(2\overline{m}/\mathrm{AR_w})\ [\text{non-dimensional rolling moment due to control inputs and atmospheric gusts}] \qquad \text{(IV.7.7)}$$

$$-\left[C_{n\dot{\beta}}\,\overline{\mathrm{D}}+(2\overline{m}\ \mathrm{AR_w})\,C_{n\beta}\right]\Delta\beta(\bar{t}_\mathrm{d})$$
$$+\left[(i_{zz}/2)\,\overline{\mathrm{D}}^2-C_{nr}\,\overline{\mathrm{D}}\right]\Delta\psi(\bar{t}_\mathrm{d})$$
$$-\left[(i_{xz}/2)\,\overline{\mathrm{D}}^2+C_{np}\,\overline{\mathrm{D}}\right]\Delta\varphi(\bar{t}_\mathrm{d})$$
$$=(2\overline{m}/\mathrm{AR_w})\ [\text{non-dimensional yawing moment due to control inputs and atmospheric gusts}] \qquad \text{(IV.7.8)}$$

The stability characteristic equation is

$$\begin{vmatrix} -\bar{\lambda}+C_{Y\beta} & -\bar{\lambda} & \left(C_{Yp}\ \mathrm{AR_w}/2\overline{m}\right)\bar{\lambda}+C_\mathrm{W} \\ C_{l\dot{\beta}}\bar{\lambda}+(2\overline{m}/\mathrm{AR_w})C_{l\beta} & (i_{xz}/2)\,\bar{\lambda}^2+C_{lr}\,\lambda & -(i_{xx}/2)\,\bar{\lambda}^2+C_{lp}\,\lambda \\ C_{n\dot{\beta}}\bar{\lambda}+(2\overline{m}/\mathrm{AR_w})C_{n\beta} & -(i_{zz}/2)\bar{\lambda}^2+C_{nr}\,\lambda & (i_{xz}/2)\,\bar{\lambda}^2+C_{np}\,\lambda \end{vmatrix}=0 \qquad \text{(IV.7.9)}$$

Expanding out this determinant

$$\left[A_4\bar{\lambda}^4+A_3\bar{\lambda}^3+A_2\bar{\lambda}^2+A_1\bar{\lambda}+A_0\right]\bar{\lambda}=0 \qquad \text{(IV.7.10)}$$

where

$$A_4=(i_{xx}/2)\,(i_{zz}/2)-(i_{xz}/2)^2$$
$$\simeq (i_{xx}/2)\,(i_{zz}/2)$$

$$A_3=(-C_{Y\beta}\,A_4)-(i_{zz}/2)C_{lp}-(i_{xx}/2)C_{nr}-(i_{xz}/2)(C_{lr}+C_{np})$$
$$+C_{l\dot{\beta}}\left[(i_{xz}/2)-(i_{zz}/2)\left(C_{Yp}\,\mathrm{AR_w}/2\overline{m}\right)\right]$$
$$+C_{n\dot{\beta}}\left[(i_{xx}/2)-(i_{xz}/2)\left(C_{Yp}\,\mathrm{AR_w}/2\overline{m}\right)\right]$$
$$\simeq(-C_{Y\beta})A_4+(i_{zz}/2)(-C_{lp})+(i_{xx}/2)\,(-C_{nr}),$$

$$
\begin{aligned}
A_2 = {} & C_{Y\beta}\left[(i_{zz}/2)C_{lp} + (i_{xx}/2)C_{nr} + (i_{xz}/2)(C_{lr} + C_{np})\right] \\
& + \left[C_{lp}C_{nr} - C_{lr}C_{np}\right] + \left[C_{l\dot{\beta}}C_{np} - C_{n\dot{\beta}}C_{lp}\right] \\
& + (2\bar{m}/\mathrm{AR_w})\left[(i_{xz}/2)C_{l\beta} + (i_{xx}/2)C_{n\beta}\right] \\
& - C_{\mathrm{W}}\left[(i_{zz}/2)C_{l\dot{\beta}} + (i_{xz}/2)C_{n\dot{\beta}}\right] \\
& - C_{Yp}\left[(i_{zz}/2)C_{l\beta} + (i_{xz}/2)C_{n\beta} - (C_{nr}C_{l\dot{\beta}} - C_{lr}C_{n\dot{\beta}})(\mathrm{AR_w}/2\bar{m})\right] \\
\simeq {} & (2\bar{m}/\mathrm{AR_w})\,(i_{xx}/2)C_{n\beta} + (-C_{lp})\,(-C_{nr})
\end{aligned}
$$

$$
\begin{aligned}
A_1 = {} & C_{Y\beta}[C_{lr}\,C_{np} - C_{nr}C_{lp}] + (2\bar{m}/\mathrm{AR_w})[C_{l\beta}C_{np} - C_{n\beta}C_{lp}] \\
& - (2\bar{m}/\mathrm{AR_w})C_{\mathrm{W}}\left[(i_{zz}/2)C_{l\beta} + (i_{xz}/2)C_{n\beta} - (C_{nr}C_{l\dot{\beta}} - C_{lr}C_{n\dot{\beta}})(\mathrm{AR_w}/2\bar{m})\right] \\
& + C_{Yp}[C_{l\beta}C_{nr} - C_{n\beta}C_{lr}] \\
\simeq {} & (2\bar{m}/\mathrm{AR_w})\left[\left(C_{\mathrm{W}}(i_{zz}/2)(-C_{l\beta})\right) + (-C_{l\beta})\,(-C_{np}) + C_{n\beta}(-C_{lp})\right]
\end{aligned}
$$

$$
A_0 = (2\bar{m}/\mathrm{AR_w})C_{\mathrm{W}}\left[(-C_{l\beta})(-C_{nr}) - C_{n\beta}C_{lr}\right]
$$

Note that A_j ($j = 1,\ldots, 4$) are all positive.

One characteristic root of the characteristic eqn. (IV.7.10) is

$$\bar{\lambda} = 0. \tag{IV.7.11}$$

A system with a zero characteristic root implies a stability mode of neutral equilibrium; in this case if the aeroplane is given a static displacement of the angle of yaw the aeroplane motion continues with that angle of yaw.

As an example, with the following data:

$$
\begin{array}{llll}
i_{xx} = 0.1, & i_{zz} = 0.25, & i_{xz} = 0.015, & (2\bar{m}/\mathrm{AR_w}) = 50, \\
C_{\mathrm{W}} = 0.6, & C_{Y\beta} = -0.6, & C_{Yp} = 0.3, & \\
C_{l\beta} = -0.13, & C_{l\dot{\beta}} = 0.02, & C_{lp} = -0.4, & C_{lr} = 0.11, \\
C_{n\beta} = 0.2, & C_{n\dot{\beta}} = -0.02, & C_{np} = -0.04, & C_{nr} = -0.30
\end{array}
\tag{IV.7.12}
$$

the characteristic equation, eqn. (IV.7.10) becomes, omitting the zero root,

$$\bar{\lambda}^4 + 10.8\bar{\lambda}^3 + 100\bar{\lambda}^2 + 765\bar{\lambda} + 81.6 = 0 \tag{IV.7.13}$$

which can be factorized into

$$(\bar{\lambda} + 9.012)(\bar{\lambda} + 0.108)(\bar{\lambda}^2 + 1.68\bar{\lambda} + 83.84) = 0. \tag{IV.7.14}$$

An algorithm for calculating these lateral roots is given in Appendix 5. Eqn. (IV.7.14) denotes a stable system.

The stability modes, their modal responses and modal shapes, can be identified.

(i) *Roll rate mode*

Substituting the characteristic root $\bar{\lambda} = -\,9.012$, which denotes the roll rate mode subsidence, into eqn. (IV.7.9) the associated modal shape is

$$(\Delta\varphi : \Delta\beta : \Delta\psi) = (1.00 : -0.07 : 0.03). \tag{IV.7.15}$$

In the roll rate mode approximation in sect. IV.6.1 sideslip ($\Delta\beta$) and yaw ($\Delta\psi$) are neglected, leading, from the roll equation in eqn. (IV.7.7), to the approximate (non-dimensional) root

$$\bar{\lambda} \simeq -(-C_{lp})/(i_{xx}/2) = -8.0 \tag{IV.7.16}$$

with the values in eqns. (IV.7.12). This approximation for the rate of roll subsidence underestimates the exact rate of roll subsidence by approximately 10%.

(ii) *Spiral mode*

Substituting the characteristic root $\bar{\lambda} = -\,0.108$, which denotes the spiral mode subsidence, into eqn. (IV.7.9) the associated modal shape is

$$(\Delta\varphi : \Delta\beta : \Delta\psi) = (-0.2 : 0.00 : 1.00). \tag{IV.7.17}$$

In the spiral mode approximation in sect. IV.6.2 the approximate (non-dimensional) root is

$$\bar{\lambda} \simeq -C_W \left[\frac{(-C_{l\beta})(-C_{nr}) - C_{n\beta}C_{lr}}{(-C_{l\beta})(-C_{np}) + (-C_{lp})(C_{n\beta})} \right] = -0.12$$

which overestimates the exact spiral mode rate of subsidence by approximately 10%.

(iii) *Dutch roll, or lateral oscillation, mode*

The characteristic equation of the damped oscillation mode, the Dutch roll mode, in eqn. (IV.7.14), namely

$$\bar{\lambda}^2 + 1.68\bar{\lambda} + 83.84 = 0 \tag{IV.7.18}$$

has roots

$$\bar{\lambda} = -0.84 \pm 9.1\mathrm{i} \tag{IV.7.19}$$

and associated modal shape

$$(\Delta\varphi : \Delta\beta : \Delta\psi) = (1.2\exp(\mathrm{i}\ 41^\circ) : 1.0 : 0.95\exp(-180^\circ)). \tag{IV.7.20}$$

Note that

(i) $\Delta\beta(t) \simeq -\,\Delta\psi(t)$, as assumed in the Dutch roll approximation in sect. IV.7.3,

(ii) the amplitude of the bank angle $\Delta\varphi(t)$ is slightly larger than the amplitudes of the yaw and bank angles, $\Delta\psi(t)$ and $\Delta\beta(t)$,

(iii) $\Delta\varphi(t)$ lags behind $\Delta\psi(t)$ by 139°.

The crude approximation for the Dutch roll described in sect. IV.6.3, given by eqn. (IV.6.13), expressed in non-dimensional form, is

$$\bar{\lambda}^2 + 2.4\bar{\lambda} + 80 = 0 \qquad \text{(IV.7.21)}$$

for the values in eqns. (IV.7.12). By comparison of eqns. (IV.7.18) and (IV.7.21) this approximation underestimates the undamped frequency of the Dutch roll oscillation by 5% and overestimates the damping by 50%; as the damping becomes lower at higher values of C_W this approximation for the damping becomes more inaccurate.

The second approximation for the Dutch roll introduced in sect. IV.6.3, eqn. (IV.6.18), is, in this case,

$$\bar{\lambda}^2 + 1.71\bar{\lambda} + 80 = 0. \qquad \text{(IV.7.22)}$$

By comparison of eqns. (IV.7.18) and (IV.7.22) this approximation predicts both damping and stiffness with reasonable accuracy. However, a word of warning; the excellent quantitative prediction of the Dutch roll damping by the approximation leading to eqn. (IV.7.22) is not universal; in other examples this approximation may underestimate the exact damping.

EXAMPLES IV.15

1. Check the approximations to the coefficients A_3, A_2, A_1 in eqn. (IV.7.10).
2. Repeat the above analysis and numerical example using trim body axes. Comment on the results.
3. Estimate the lateral stability modal responses and modal shapes for the basic light aeroplane configuration. Compare the exact characteristics with the approximate forms given in sect. IV.6.
4. Estimate the lateral stability modal responses and modal shapes for the basic combat aeroplane configuration at Mach 0.8 at 11 km altitude. Compare the exact characteristics with the approximate forms given in sect. IV.6.

IV.8 LATERAL RESPONSE TO CONTROL INPUTS

The full mathematical equations for the aeroplane lateral response to aileron and rudder are derived in Appendix 11. In this section these responses are described in qualitative terms.

IV.8.1 Lateral response to aileron input

Consider a step stick displacement to starboard, or a step clockwise wheel rotation, inducing a step aileron input in a negative sense, denoted by $(-\xi_s H(t))$. A positive rolling moment is generated, together with a much smaller positive yawing moment relative to the fuselage body axis (although a small negative yawing moment relative to trim body axes) and a small negative side force.

The aeroplane responds in three sequential phases: the roll rate mode response decays quickly, a Dutch roll mode response decays more slowly, and a spiral mode response which decays, if stable, or grows, if unstable, extremely slowly.

The initial roll rate mode response is given approximately by the roll mode approximation, eqn. (IV.6.1),

$$\left[i_{xx}U_{\text{trim}}\left(C_{\text{W}}/2g\right)\text{D}+(-C_{lp})\right]\left(p(t)s_{\text{w}}/U_{\text{trim}}\right)$$
$$\simeq C_{l\xi}\left(-\xi_{\text{s}}H(t)\right)=(-C_{l\xi})\,\xi_{\text{s}}H(t) \qquad \text{(IV.8.1)}$$

which gives the roll rate response

$$p(t)/\xi_{\text{s}} \simeq \left[U_{\text{trim}}/s_{\text{W}}\right]\left[(-C_{l\xi})/(-C_{lp})\right]\left[1-\exp(-\lambda t)\right] \qquad \text{(IV.8.2)}$$

where

$$\lambda=\left[2g/(U_{\text{trim}}C_{\text{W}})\right]\left[(-C_{lp})/i_{xx}\right]$$
$$=\left[g\,\rho_{\text{at}}U_{\text{trim}}/\left(W/S_{\text{w}}\right)\right]\left[(-C_{lp})/i_{xx}\right].$$

The steady state roll rate, $(p_{\text{roll}})_{\text{ss}}$, after the decay of the roll mode subsidence, is approximately

$$(p_{\text{roll}})_{\text{ss}}/\xi_{\text{s}} \simeq \left[U_{\text{trim}}/s_{\text{W}}\right]\left[(-C_{l\xi})/(-C_{lp})\right] \qquad \text{(IV.8.3)}$$

$(p_{\text{roll}})_{\text{ss}}$ is larger at higher speed and for configurations with lower span; the ratio $[(-C_{l\xi})/(-C_{lp})]$ is relatively insensitive to wing sweep and to subsonic Mach number.

Typically

$$\left[(-C_{l\xi})/(-C_{lp})\right]=\text{O}[0.5]$$

so when $U_{\text{trim}} = 100$ m/s, $s_{\text{w}} = 10$ m and $\xi_{\text{s}} = 5°$, then

$$(p_{\text{roll}})_{\text{ss}} \simeq 25°/\text{s}. \qquad \text{(IV.8.4)}$$

The time lag to the steady state roll rate is approximately $3(t_{1/2})_{\text{roll}}$, where $(t_{1/2})_{\text{roll}}$ is described in eqn. (IV.6.2).

The corresponding bank angle response, from eqn. (IV.8.2), is

$$\Delta\varphi(t)/\xi_{\text{s}}=\left[U_{\text{trim}}/s_{\text{W}}\right]\left[(-C_{l\xi})/(-C_{lp})\right]\left[t-\left(1-\left(\exp(-\lambda t)\right)/\lambda\right)\right]. \qquad \text{(IV.8.5)}$$

As the roll angle builds up the aeroplane begins to sideslip; this positive sideslip induces an opposing rolling moment proportional to $(-C_{l\beta})$ which tends to reduce the rate of roll and initiates a Dutch roll response, as sketched in Fig. IV.32.

The roll rate behaviour in Fig. IV.32 can be explained from the steady state roll rate response after the decay of the oscillatory Dutch roll mode, but before the ultimate decay of the spiral subsidence denoted by $(p_{\text{Dr}})_{\text{ss}}$. As derived in Appendix 11, eqn. (A11.14), re-expressed in dimensional form,

$$(p_{\text{Dr}})_{\text{ss}}/\xi_{\text{s}} \simeq \frac{U_{\text{trim}}}{s_{\text{W}}}\left[\frac{(-C_{l\xi})-C_{n\xi}\left((-C_{l\beta})/C_{n\beta}\right)}{(-C_{lp})+\left[(i_{zz}/2)\,C_{\text{W}}+(-C_{np})\right]\left[(-C_{l\beta})/C_{n\beta}\right]}\right].$$

(IV.8.6)

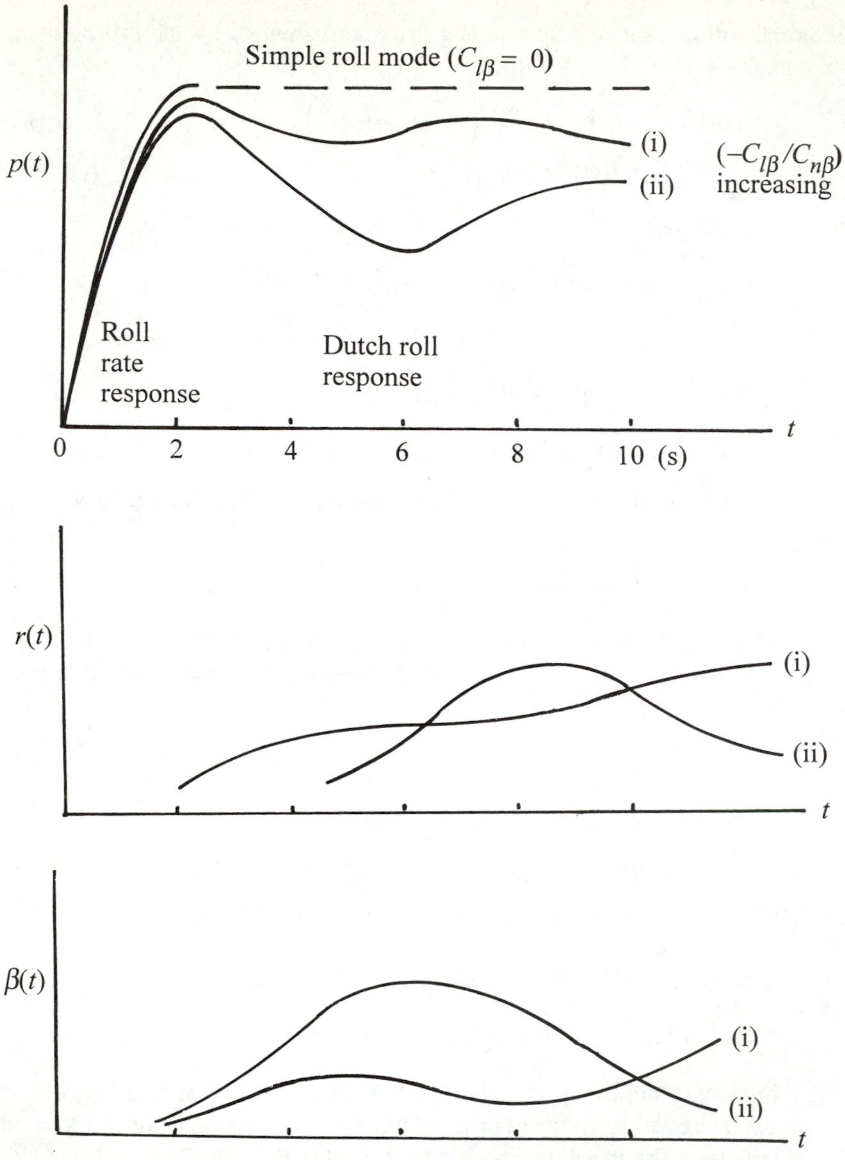

Fig. IV.32. Lateral responses to step aileron input.

According to eqns. (IV.8.3) and (IV.8.6),

(i) when $(-C_{l\beta})/C_{n\beta}$ is extremely small $(p_{\mathrm{Dr}})_{\mathrm{ss}}$ is virtually the same as $(p_{\mathrm{roll}})_{\mathrm{ss}}$;

(ii) as $(-C_{l\beta})/C_{n\beta}$ increases then $(p_{\mathrm{Dr}})_{\mathrm{ss}}$ decreases relative to $(p_{\mathrm{roll}})_{\mathrm{ss}}$;

(iii) a consequence of (ii) is that as $(-C_{l\beta})/C_{n\beta}$ increases there is more input into the Dutch roll mode;

(iv) also as $(-C_{l\beta})/C_{n\beta}$ increases, from eqn. (IV.7.18), the Dutch roll damping decreases, which contributes to the increase in amplitude in Fig. IV.32;

(v) as sketched in Fig. IV.32, the Dutch roll frequency decreases as $(-C_{l\beta})/C_{n\beta}$ increases; this trend is consistent with a decrease in $C_{n\beta}$ which determines the Dutch roll frequency, see sect. IV.6.3.

In the literature a common parameter is

$$(p_{\mathrm{Dr}})_{\mathrm{ss}}/(p_{\mathrm{roll}})_{\mathrm{ss}} = \omega_\varphi^2/(\omega_0^2)_{\mathrm{Dr}} \tag{IV.8.7}$$

Eqn. (IV.8.6), divided by eqn. (IV.8.3) however, gives $\omega_\varphi^2/(\omega_0^2)_{\mathrm{Dr}}$ in a more succinct form than that in the literature.

Typically when $\left((-C_{l\beta})/C_{n\beta}\right) = 1.0$ and $C_{\mathrm{w}} = 0.7$,

$$(p_{\mathrm{Dr}})_{\mathrm{ss}}/(p_{\mathrm{roll}})_{\mathrm{ss}} = \omega_\varphi^2/(\omega_0^2)_{\mathrm{Dr}} = \mathrm{O}[0.7]. \tag{IV.8.8}$$

The corresponding sideslip responses are sketched in Fig. IV.32, based on Babister (ref. P.16). Following the decay of the Dutch roll mode, from eqn. (A11.6), in dimensional form

$$\frac{(\Delta\dot{\beta}_{\mathrm{Dr}})_{\mathrm{ss}}}{(\mathrm{AR}_{\mathrm{w}}/2\overline{m})(U_{\mathrm{trim}}/s_{\mathrm{w}})} = \left[\frac{C_{\mathrm{W}}\left[(-C_{l\xi})(-C_{nr}) - C_{n\xi}C_{lr}\right]}{(-C_{l\beta})\left[C_{\mathrm{W}}(i_{zz}/2) + (-C_{np})\right] + C_{n\beta}(-C_{lp})}\right]\xi_{\mathrm{s}} \tag{IV.8.9}$$

which is positive. Note that $(\Delta\dot{\beta}_{\mathrm{Dr}})_{\mathrm{ss}}$ decreases as $(-C_{l\beta})/C_{n\beta}$ increases.

The corresponding rate of yaw responses are sketched in Fig. IV.32. As already mentioned (see sect. IV.3.6), there is an initial adverse yaw relative to stability body axes but not necessarily about fuselage body axes. Following the decay of the Dutch roll mode, comparing eqns. (A11.10) and (A11.14),

$$(\dot{r}_{\mathrm{Dr}})_{\mathrm{ss}} = (\mathrm{AR}_{\mathrm{w}}/2\overline{m})(U_{\mathrm{trim}}/s_{\mathrm{w}})C_{\mathrm{W}}(p_{\mathrm{Dr}})_{\mathrm{ss}}. \tag{IV.8.10}$$

For a stable aeroplane with a stable spiral mode the final steady state is, from eqns. (A11.7), (A11.11) and (A11.15)

$$p_{\mathrm{ss}} = 0$$

$$C_{\mathrm{W}}(\Delta\varphi_{\mathrm{ss}}) = \frac{r_{\mathrm{ss}}}{(\mathrm{AR}_{\mathrm{w}}/2\overline{m})(U_{\mathrm{trim}}/s_{\mathrm{w}})} = \left[\frac{(2\overline{m}/\mathrm{AR}_{\mathrm{w}})\left[(-C_{l\xi})C_{n\beta} + C_{n\xi}(-C_{l\beta})\right]}{\left[(-C_{l\beta})(-C_{nr}) - C_{n\beta}C_{lr}\right]}\right]\xi_{\mathrm{s}}$$

$$(\Delta\beta_{\mathrm{ss}}) = \left[\frac{(-C_{l\xi})(-C_{nr}) + C_{n\xi}C_{lr}}{(-C_{l\beta})(-C_{nr}) - C_{n\beta}C_{lr}}\right]\xi_{\mathrm{s}}. \tag{IV.8.11}$$

In this final steady state the bank angle, rate of yaw and sideslip angle are all positive.

Consider next the response to a pulse aileron input where the pilot applies an aileron angle $(-\xi_s)$ at a datum time ($t = 0$) and then returns the aileron angle to zero after a time delay t_1 (i.e. at time $t = t_1$).

The bank angle response for small $(-C_{l\beta})/C_{n\beta}$, from eqns. (IV.8.3), (IV.8.5), is

$$\Delta\varphi(t)/\xi_s \simeq (p_{\text{roll}})_{ss}\left[t_1 + \left(\exp(-\lambda t) - \exp\left(-\lambda(t - t_1)\right)/\lambda\right)\right]$$

which settles down to the steady state

$$(\Delta\varphi_{\text{roll}})_{ss}/\xi_s \simeq (p_{\text{roll}})_{ss}\left[(-C_{l\xi})/(-C_{lp})\right]t_1. \tag{IV.8.12}$$

With the typical values taken in eqn. (IV.8.4) a time t_1 of 2 s would result in a bank angle of 50°.

When $(-C_{l\beta})/C_{n\beta}$ is small there is little Dutch roll response and the bank angle remains close to the value in eqn. (IV.8.12). As $(-C_{l\beta})/C_{n\beta}$ increases the Dutch roll response increases, and as the Dutch roll mode decays the bank angle reduces to

$$(\Delta\varphi_{\text{Dr}})_{ss} = (p_{\text{Dr}})_{ss}t_1. \tag{IV.8.13}$$

The corresponding steady states of the yaw rate and sideslip angles after the decay of the Dutch roll are

$$\begin{aligned}(r_{\text{Dr}})_{ss} &= (\dot{r}_{\text{Dr}})_{ss}t_1\\ (\Delta\beta_{\text{Dr}})_{ss} &= (\Delta\dot{\beta}_{\text{Dr}})_{ss}t_1\end{aligned} \tag{IV.8.14}$$

where $(\Delta\dot{\beta}_{\text{Dr}})_{ss}$ and $(\dot{r}_{\text{Dr}})_{ss}$ are given by eqns. (IV.8.9) and (IV.8.10). Note that $(\Delta\beta_{\text{Dr}})_{ss}$ and $(r_{\text{Dr}})_{ss}$ are both positive.

Note that the final steady states of bank angle, rate of yaw and sideslip angle, following a 'pulse' aileron input, are all zero, assuming a stable spiral mode.

IV.8.2 Lateral response to rudder input

Typical lateral responses to a step change in the pedal displacement are sketched in Figs. IV.33 (based on ref. P.16) and can be explained in qualitative terms.

A right pedal down rotates the rudder in the negative sense (i.e. $\zeta(t) = -\zeta_s H(t)$), generating a fin side force in the negative y direction, a large positive yawing moment and a small negative rolling moment.

This input is virtually a pure input into a Dutch roll mode inducing positive yaw, negative sideslip (because the initial motion would be a lateral weathercock-type motion) and positive roll (because of the positive C_{lr} and negative $C_{l\beta}$).

After the decay of the Dutch roll, as deduced in Appendix 11, eqns. (A11.6), (A11.10) and (A11.14),

$$\frac{(\Delta\dot{\beta}_{\text{Dr}})_{ss}}{(\text{AR}_w/2\overline{m})(U_{\text{trim}}/s_w)} \simeq \left[\frac{C_W\left[(-C_{l\zeta})(-C_{nr}) + (-C_{n\zeta})C_{lr}\right]}{(-C_{l\beta})\left[C_W(i_{zz}/2) + (-C_{np})\right] + C_{n\beta}(-C_{lp})}\right]\zeta_s \tag{IV.8.15}$$

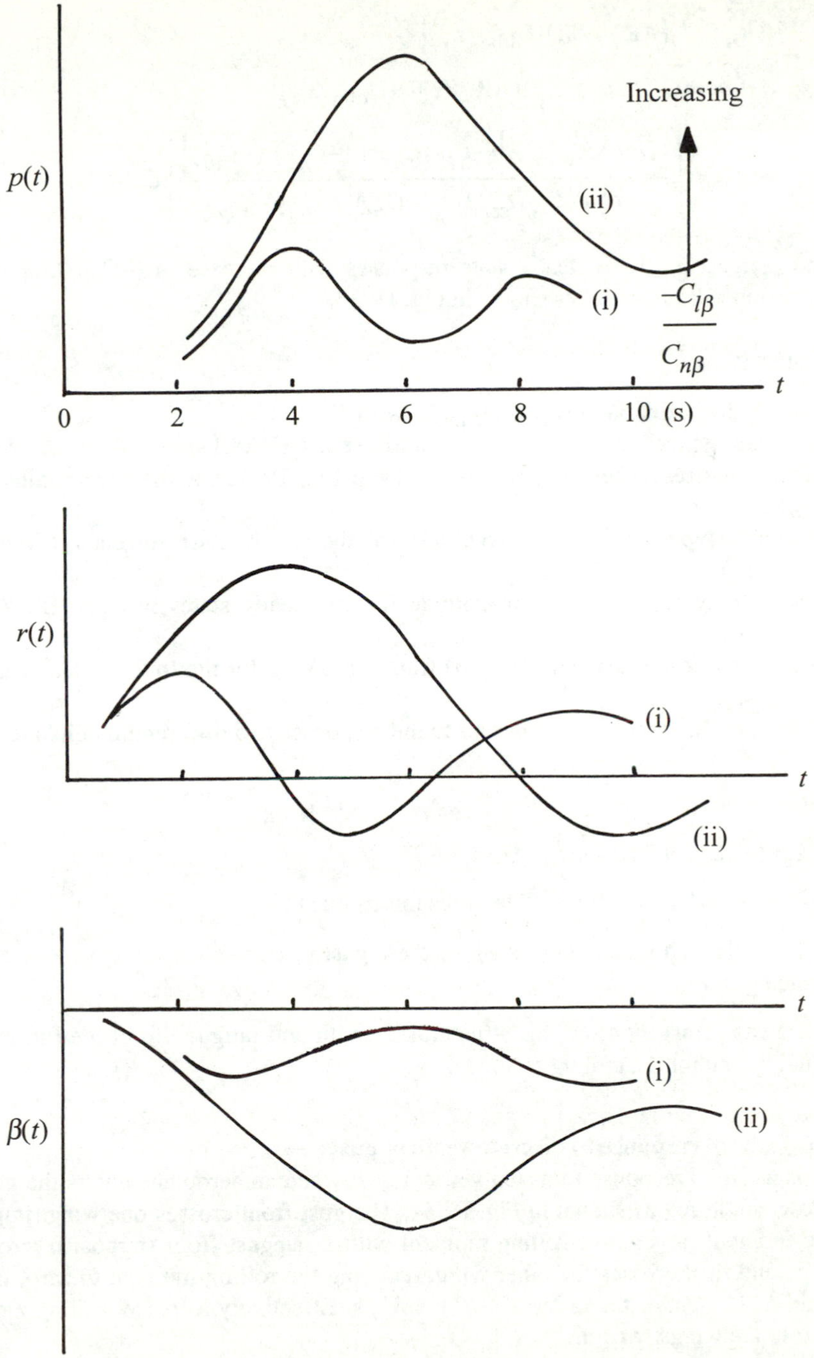

Fig. IV.33. Lateral responses to step rudder input.

$$(\dot{r}_{\mathrm{Dr}})_{\mathrm{ss}}\Big/\left[(\mathrm{AR_w}/2\overline{m})(U_{\mathrm{trim}}/s_{\mathrm{w}})\right]^2$$
$$= C_{\mathrm{W}}(\Delta\dot{\varphi}_{\mathrm{Dr}})_{\mathrm{ss}}\Big/\left[(\mathrm{AR_w}/2\overline{m})(U_{\mathrm{trim}}/s_{\mathrm{w}})\right]$$
$$= \left[\frac{(2\overline{m}/\mathrm{AR_w})\,C_{\mathrm{W}}\left[(-C_{l\zeta})\,C_{n\beta} + (-C_{n\zeta})\,(-C_{l\beta})\right]}{(-C_{l\beta})\left[C_{\mathrm{W}}(i_{zz}/2) + (-C_{np})\right] + C_{n\beta}(-C_{lp})}\right]\zeta_{\mathrm{s}}. \tag{IV.8.16}$$

The increase in these steady state responses with increase in $(-C_{l\beta})/C_{n\beta}$ implies a larger Dutch roll response, as shown in Fig. IV.33.

EXAMPLES IV.16

1. Sketch the variation of $(p_{\mathrm{Dr}})_{\mathrm{ss}}/(p_{\mathrm{roll}})_{\mathrm{ss}}$ with C_{W}.
2. Estimate typical values of the final states in eqns. (IV.8.11).
3. Sketch the responses $p(t)$, $r(t)$, $\Delta\beta(t)$ from Fig. IV.32 for the 'pulse' aileron input with $t_1 = 1$ s.
4. Estimate typical orders of magnitude for the steady states in eqns. (IV.8.13) and (IV.8.14).
5. Estimate typical orders of magnitude for the steady states in eqns. (IV.8.15) and (IV.8.16).
6. Sketch the responses $p(t)$, $r(t)$, $\beta(t)$ from Fig. IV.33 for the 'pulse' rudder input with $t_1 = 2$ s.
7. Compare the responses to ailerons to the responses to a differential tailplane.

IV.9 LATERAL RESPONSE TO GUSTS

Atmospheric turbulence causes lateral responses due to

(i) vertical and horizontal gusts where these gust velocities vary across the wing span,
(ii) side gusts.

Lateral gusts primarily affect the structural strength and fatigue life of the fin, passenger ride quality and pilot handling qualities.

IV.9.1 Lateral response to discrete vertical gusts

There is a lateral response to a step vertical gust when an aeroplane enters the gust front at a skew angle Λ_{g}, as shown in Fig. IV.34. The gust front crosses one wing, imposing a rolling moment (a negative rolling moment with an upgust from starboard), crosses the fuselage and then crosses the other wing, reducing the rolling moment to zero, in a time $(2s_{\mathrm{W}} \tan \Lambda_{\mathrm{g}}/U_{\mathrm{trim}})$, of the order of $(0.2 \tan \Lambda_{\mathrm{g}})$ s. Effectively a 'pulse' rolling moment is applied to the wings; writing

$$\text{applied rolling moment} = \mathscr{L}_{\mathrm{g}}\ \delta(t), \tag{IV.9.1}$$

where $\delta(t)$ is the delta function, then approximately

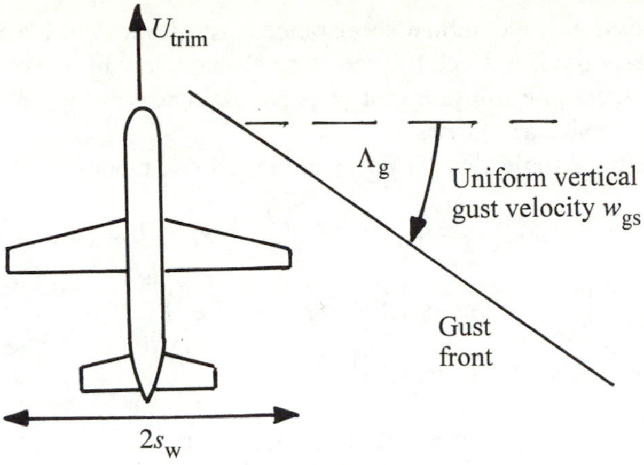

Fig. IV.34. Skew sharp-edged vertical gust.

$$\mathscr{L}_g \simeq -\tfrac{1}{2}[\text{maximum rolling moment}]\,[\text{time engulfed in gust}]$$

$$\simeq -\tfrac{1}{2}\left[\tfrac{1}{2}\rho_{at}U_{trim}^2(S_w/2)\,(a_\alpha)_w\left(w_{gs}/U_{trim}\right)(0.5s_w)\right] \times \left[(2s_w\tan\Lambda_g)/U_{trim}\right] \quad \text{(IV.9.2)}$$

where w_{gs} is the constant vertical gust velocity behind the gust front.

An approximate assessment of the initial response is given by the roll response. The roll equation, from eqn. (IV.7.2), is

$$\left[\left(i_{xx}U_{trim}C_W/2g\right)\mathrm{D}+(-C_{lp})\right]\left(p(t)s_w/U_{trim}\right) = \left(\mathscr{L}_g\,\delta(t)\right)/\left(\tfrac{1}{2}\rho_{at}U_{trim}^2S_w\,2s_w\right). \quad \text{(IV.9.3)}$$

The roll response for $t > 0$ is

$$\left(i_{xx}U_{trim}C_W/2g\right)\left(p(t)s_w/U_{trim}\right) = \left(\mathscr{L}_g/\left(\tfrac{1}{2}\rho_{at}U_{trim}^2S_w\,2s_w\right)\right)\exp(-\lambda t) \quad \text{(IV.9.4)}$$

where $\lambda = 2g\,(-C_{lp})/(i_{xx}U_{trim}C_W)$.

On substitution of eqn. (IV.9.2), eqn. (IV.9.4) becomes

$$\begin{aligned} p(t) &= -\left[\left((a_\alpha)_w\left(w_g/U_{trim}\right)\tan\Lambda_g\right)/8\right]\left[2g/\left(i_{xx}U_{trim}C_W\right)\right]\exp(-\lambda t) \\ &= -\left[g\tfrac{1}{2}\rho_{at}(a_\alpha)_w\tan\Lambda_g w_g/\left(4i_{xx}\left(W/S_w\right)\right)\right]\exp(-\lambda t). \end{aligned} \quad \text{(IV.9.5)}$$

The antisymmetric gust 'impulse' generates an 'instantaneous' change in $p(t)$ which then decays with time.

Again, as in the case of the normal acceleration gust response to a step vertical gust, the roll rate gust response is reduced by increasing altitude, low lift curve slope, and high wing loading. However, the roll rate gust response is increased by a small roll inertia, typical of light and combat aeroplanes.

The steady state bank angle after the decay of the roll rate mode is

$$
\begin{aligned}
(\varphi_{\text{roll}})_{\text{ss}} &= -\left[\left((a_\alpha)_{\text{w}}\left(w_{\text{g}}/U_{\text{trim}}\right)\tan\Lambda_{\text{g}}\right)/8\right]\left[2g/(i_{xx}U_{\text{trim}}C_{\text{W}})\right]/\lambda \\
&= -\left((a_\alpha)_{\text{w}}\left(w_{\text{g}}/U_{\text{trim}}\right)\tan\Lambda_{\text{g}}\right)/\left(8(-C_{lp})\right) \qquad \text{(IV.9.6)} \\
&= \mathrm{O}\left[\left(-w_{\text{g}}/U_{\text{trim}}\right)\tan\Lambda_{\text{g}}\right].
\end{aligned}
$$

The bank angle is directly proportional to the gust vertical velocity and $\tan\Lambda_{\text{g}}$, and inversely proportional to U_{trim}; eqn. (IV.9.6) is virtually independent of the type of aeroplane, Mach number and altitude.

It is of interest to note that when a pilot reduces forward speed to reduce the level of normal acceleration there is no change in the roll rate gust response but there is an increase in the bank angle gust response.

IV.9.2 Lateral response to continuous vertical gusts

The PSD analysis of sect. III.13 is now extended to two dimensions.

Denote the spatial variation of the 'frozen' vertical gust velocity field as the random variable $w_{\text{g}}(X, Y)$, where X and Y are spatial axes in a horizontal plane.

A two dimensional auto-correlation function $R_{\text{w}}(\chi, \nu)$ can be defined as

$$
\sigma_{\text{w}}^2 R_{\text{w}}(\chi,\nu) = \frac{1}{(X_N - X_0)(Y - Y_0)} \int_{Y_0}^{Y_N}\int_{X_0}^{X_N}\left(w_{\text{g}}(X,Y)\, w_{\text{g}}(X+\chi, Y+\nu)\, \mathrm{d}X\, \mathrm{d}Y\right) \qquad \text{(IV.9.7)}
$$

over the patch of turbulence ($X_N < X < X_0$, $Y_N < Y < Y_0$).

Assuming that $w_{\text{g}}(X, Y)$ is homogeneous in the patch of turbulence, then

$$
\left[\int_{X_0}^{X_N} w_{\text{g}}(X,Y)\, w_{\text{g}}(X+\chi,Y+\nu)\, \mathrm{d}X\right]_{Y=\text{ const}} \quad \text{is independent of } Y. \qquad \text{(IV.9.8)}
$$

Furthermore, assuming that eqn. (IV.9.7) is invariant with respect to the orientation of the OX, OY axes in the horizontal plane, then

$$
R_{\text{w}}(\chi,\nu) = R_{\text{w}}\left(\left[\chi^2+\nu^2\right]^{1/2}\right). \qquad \text{(IV.9.9)}
$$

where $R_{\text{w}}(\chi)$ is the one dimensional correlation defined in eqn. (III.13.36). Hence, combining eqns. (IV.9.7)–(IV.9.9)

$$
\sigma_{\text{w}}^2 R_{\text{w}}\left(\left[\chi^2+\nu^2\right]^{1/2}\right) = \left[\frac{1}{X_N - X_0}\int_{X_0}^{X_N} w_{\text{g}}(X,Y)\, w_{\text{g}}(X+\chi,Y+\nu)\, \mathrm{d}X\right]_{Y=\text{const}}. \qquad \text{(IV.9.10)}
$$

When the spatial wavelength is more than twice the wing span then it may be assumed that the vertical gust velocity varies linearly over the wing span; a representative spanwise gradient of gust velocity, represented as a gust-roll rate, is

$$p_g(X) = \left[w_g(X, +0.75s_w) - w_g(X, -0.75s_w)\right] / (1.5s_w) \tag{IV.9.11}$$

taking $1.5s_w$ as a representative wing span scale length.

An auto-correlation function R_p can be defined,

$$\sigma_{pg}^2 R_p(\chi) = \frac{1}{(X_N - X_0)} \int_{X_0}^{X_N} p_g(X)\, p_g(X+\chi)\, dX. \tag{IV.9.12}$$

On substitution of eqn. (IV.9.11), and by reference to eqn. (IV.9.10), eqn. (IV.9.12) becomes

$$\sigma_{pg}^2 R_p(\chi) = 2\sigma_w^2 \left[R_w(\chi) - R_w\left(\left[\chi^2 + (1.5s_w)^2\right]^{1/2}\right)\right] \Big/ (1.5s_w)^2. \tag{IV.9.13}$$

The power spectral density $\Phi_{pg}(\Omega)$ of the spanwise gust velocity gradient is given by

$$\begin{aligned} \Phi_{pg}(\Omega) &= \left(2\sigma_{pg}^2/\pi\right) \int_0^\infty R_p(\chi) \cos \Omega\chi \, d\chi, \\ \sigma_{pg}^2 &= \int_0^\infty \Phi_{pg}(\Omega)\, d\Omega. \end{aligned} \tag{IV.9.14}$$

An approximation derived by curve fitting (Roskam, ref. P.17) is

$$\Phi_{pg}(\Omega) = \frac{\sigma_w^2}{L} \frac{0.8\left(\pi L/8s_w\right)^{1/3}}{\left[1 + \left(8s_w\Omega/\pi\right)^2\right]}. \tag{IV.9.15}$$

Now the roll response $\Delta\varphi(t)$ to a time varying spanwise gust gradient $p_g(X = U_{trim}t)$, by reference to Appendix 10, in non-dimensional form, is

$$\begin{aligned} &(\bar{D} + \bar{\lambda}_{roll})(\bar{D} + \bar{\lambda}_{spiral})\left(\bar{D}^2 + (2\zeta\bar{\omega}_0)_{Dr}\, \bar{D} + (\bar{\omega}_0^2)_{Dr}\right) \Delta\varphi(\bar{t}_d) \\ &\quad \simeq -\frac{(-C_{lp})2\bar{m}}{(i_{xx}/2)\mathrm{AR_w}} \left[\bar{D}^2 + \left((-C_{Y\beta}) + \frac{(-C_{nr})}{(i_{zz}/2)}\right)\bar{D} + \frac{2\bar{m}}{\mathrm{AR_w}} \frac{C_{n\beta}}{(i_{zz}/2)}\right] \\ &\quad \times \left(p_g(\bar{m}\, c_w \bar{t}_d) s_w / U_{trim}\right) \end{aligned} \tag{IV.9.16}$$

taking

$$\kappa(\bar{t}_d) = p_g(U_{trim}t)\left(s_w/U_{trim}\right) = p_g(\bar{m} c_w \bar{t}_d)\left(s_w/U_{trim}\right)$$

$$C_{l\kappa} = C_{lp}, \quad C_{l\dot{\kappa}} = C_{n\dot{\kappa}} = C_{Y\dot{\kappa}} = 0$$

and neglecting the effects of $C_{n\kappa}$ $(= C_{np})$ and $C_{Y\kappa}$ $(= C_{Yp})$.

Now the bracket on the right hand side of eqn. (IV.9.16) is virtually the same as the Dutch roll term on the left hand side, hence

$$(\overline{D}+\overline{\lambda}_{\text{roll}})(\overline{D}+\overline{\lambda}_{\text{spiral}})\Delta\varphi(\overline{t}_{\text{d}})$$
$$\simeq -\left[(-C_{lp})(2\overline{m}/\text{AR}_{\text{w}})/(i_{xx}/2)\right]\left(p_{\text{g}}(\overline{m}c_{\text{w}}\overline{t}_{\text{d}})s_{\text{w}}/U_{\text{trim}}\right). \quad \text{(IV.9.17)}$$

Applying the PSD method, the power spectral density of the bank angle gust response is

$$\Phi_{\Delta\varphi}(\overline{\Omega})=\left(s_{\text{w}}/U_{\text{trim}}\right)^2\Phi_{\text{pg}}(\overline{\Omega})\left|G_{\Delta\varphi}(\text{i}\,\overline{\Omega})\right|^2. \quad \text{(IV.9.18)}$$

In the non-dimensional time domain,

$$\Phi_{\text{pg}}(\overline{\Omega})=\frac{\sigma_{\text{w}}^2}{L\overline{m}c_{\text{w}}}\,\frac{0.8\left(\pi L/8s_{\text{w}}\right)^{1/3}}{1+\left(4\text{AR}_{\text{w}}\overline{\Omega}/(\pi\overline{m})\right)^2}. \quad \text{(IV.9.19)}$$

[These transformations can be confusing; remember that

$$\sigma_{\text{pg}}^2=\int_0^\infty\Phi_{\text{pg}}(\Omega)\,\text{d}\Omega=\int_0^\infty\Phi_{\text{pg}}(\Omega_{\text{t}})\,\text{d}\Omega_{\text{t}}=\int_0^\infty\Phi_{\text{pg}}(\overline{\Omega})\,\text{d}\overline{\Omega} \quad \text{(IV.9.20)}$$

where

$$\Omega=2\pi/X,\quad \Omega_{\text{t}}=2\pi/t=\Omega U_{\text{trim}},\quad \overline{\Omega}=\Omega_{\text{t}}\hat{t}_{\text{d}}=\Omega_{\text{t}}\left(\overline{m}c_{\text{w}}/U_{\text{trim}}\right)=\Omega\overline{m}c_{\text{w}}.\Big]$$

At the knee of the power spectral density, where the spectrum decreases from its uniform, low frequency level, $\overline{\Omega}$ ($\simeq \pi\overline{m}/(4\text{AR}_{\text{w}})$) is of the order of 20.

And, from eqn. (IV.9.17)

$$G_{\Delta\varphi}(\text{i}\,\Omega)=-\frac{(-C_{lp})\left(2\overline{m}/\text{AR}_{\text{w}}\right)/\left(i_{xx}/2\right)}{\left(\text{i}\,\overline{\Omega}+\overline{\lambda}_{\text{roll}}\right)\left(\text{i}\,\overline{\Omega}+\overline{\lambda}_{\text{spiral}}\right)} \quad \text{(IV.9.21)}$$

where

$$\overline{\lambda}_{\text{roll}}\simeq(-C_{lp})/\left(i_{xx}/2\right)=\text{O}[8.0],\quad \overline{\lambda}_{\text{spiral}}=\text{O}[0.10].$$

Combining eqns. (IV.9.18), (IV.9.19) and (IV.9.21) the bank angle power spectral density is

(i) at low frequencies, $\overline{\Omega}\simeq 1$, proportional to $\left[\overline{m}c_{\text{w}}/\left(L^{2/3}s_{\text{w}}^{1/3}\right)\right]\left(\sigma_{\text{w}}/U_{\text{trim}}\right)^2$,

(ii) at higher frequencies, $\overline{\Omega}\simeq 16$, reduced relative to (i) by 80%.

For a more thorough and rigorous analysis, incorporating the smaller wavelengths comparable with the wing span, see Eggelston and Phillips (ref. IV.4).

IV.9.3 Lateral response to side gusts

The equations of the lateral responses to a time varying side gust of velocity $v_{\text{g}}(t)$ (= $\beta_{\text{g}}(t)U_{\text{trim}}$), can be deduced from Appendix 11, taking

$$\kappa(\bar{t}_d) = \beta_g(\bar{t}_d)$$

$$C_{Y\kappa} = C_{Y\beta}, \quad C_{l\kappa} = C_{l\beta}, \quad C_{n\kappa} = C_{n\beta},$$

and, for simplicity,

$$C_{Y\dot{\kappa}} = C_{l\dot{\kappa}} = C_{n\dot{\kappa}} = 0.$$

These equations are, in non-dimensional form, neglecting the spiral modal subsidence, retaining only the dominant terms,

roll:

$$\begin{aligned}(i_{xx}i_{zz}/4)\left[\bar{\mathrm{D}} + \bar{\lambda}_{\mathrm{roll}}\right]\left[\bar{\mathrm{D}}^2 + 2(\zeta\bar{\omega}_0)_{\mathrm{Dr}}\,\bar{\mathrm{D}} + (\bar{\omega}_0)^2_{\mathrm{Dr}}\right]\bar{\mathrm{D}}\,\Delta\varphi(\bar{t}_d) \\ = (2\pi/\mathrm{AR_w})\left[(i_{zz}/2)C_{l\beta}\bar{\mathrm{D}}^2\right. \\ \left. + \left(C_{l\beta}(-C_{nr}) + C_{n\beta}C_{lr}\right)\left(\bar{\mathrm{D}} + C_{Y\beta}\right)\right]\beta_g(\bar{t}_d)\end{aligned} \tag{IV.9.22}$$

yaw:

$$\left[\bar{\mathrm{D}}^2 + 2(\zeta\bar{\omega}_0)_{\mathrm{Dr}}\,\bar{\mathrm{D}} + (\bar{\omega}_0)^2_{\mathrm{Dr}}\right]\Delta\psi(\bar{t}_d) \simeq (\bar{\omega}_0)^2_{\mathrm{Dr}}\,\beta_g(\bar{t}_d) \tag{IV.9.23}$$

sideslip:

$$\begin{aligned}\left[\bar{\mathrm{D}}^2 + 2(\zeta\bar{\omega}_0)_{\mathrm{Dr}}\,\bar{\mathrm{D}} + (\bar{\omega}_0)^2_{\mathrm{Dr}}\right]\Delta\beta(\bar{t}_d) \\ \simeq \left[C_{Y\beta}\bar{\mathrm{D}} - (\bar{\omega}_0)^2_{\mathrm{Dr}}\right]\beta_g(\bar{t}_d).\end{aligned} \tag{IV.9.24}$$

The yaw and sideslip responses are virtually pure Dutch roll responses; the roll response includes a contribution from the roll mode.

On suddenly entering a sharp edge side gust, see Fig. IV.35, where

$$\beta_g(\bar{t}_d) = \beta_{gs}H(\bar{t}_d), \tag{IV.9.25}$$

the initial (non-dimensional) accelerations are, from eqns. (IV.9.22)–(IV.9.24),

$$\begin{aligned}\bar{\mathrm{D}}^2\,\Delta\varphi(+0) &= -\left[(2\bar{m}/\mathrm{AR_w})(-C_{l\beta})/(i_{xx}/2)\right]\beta_{gs}, \\ \bar{\mathrm{D}}^2\,\Delta\psi(+0) &= \left[(2\bar{m}/\mathrm{AR_w})C_{n\beta}/(i_{zz}/2)\right]\beta_{gs}, \\ \bar{\mathrm{D}}\,\Delta\beta(+0) &= -(-C_{Y\beta})\,\beta_{gs}.\end{aligned} \tag{IV.9.26}$$

The initial roll acceleration is negative, the initial yaw acceleration is positive, and the initial sideslip acceleration is negative, as intuitively expected. The initial roll and yaw accelerations are the same order of magnitude.

The subsequent response is primarily a Dutch roll modal response.

After the decay of the Dutch roll mode

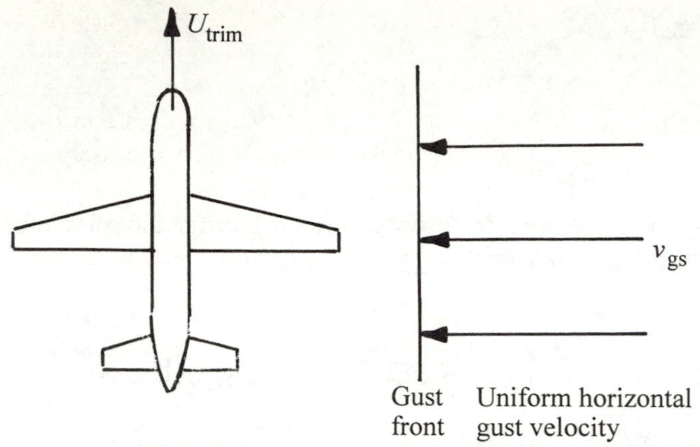

Fig. IV.35. Sharp-edged side gust.

$$\left((\bar{D}\Delta\varphi(\bar{t}_d)_{Dr}\right)_{ss} = \left[\frac{(2\pi/AR_w)\left[(-C_{l\beta})(-C_{nr}) - C_{n\beta}C_{lr}\right](-C_{Y\beta})}{(i_{xx}i_{zz}/4)\bar{\lambda}_{roll}(\bar{\omega}_0)^2_{Dr}}\right]\beta_{gs}$$

$$= O[0.1]\beta_{gs} \qquad \text{(IV.9.27)}$$

which converts, in real time, to

$$(\Delta\dot{\varphi}_{Dr})_{ss} = O[0.02]\beta_{gs}/s$$

and

$$(\Delta\psi_{Dr})_{ss} = -(\beta_{Dr})_{ss} \simeq \beta_{gs}. \qquad \text{(IV.9.28)}$$

For sinusoidal gusts

$$\beta_g(t_d) = \beta_{g0}\exp(i\bar{\Omega}\bar{t}_d) \qquad \text{(IV.9.29)}$$

the peak oscillatory responses will be when the gust frequency $\bar{\Omega}$ is equal to the Dutch roll undamped frequency $(\bar{\omega}_0)_{Dr}$. Then the peak amplitude ratios for the angles of sideslip and yaw are

$$\left|\frac{\Delta\beta}{\beta_{g0}}\right|_{max} \simeq \left|\frac{\Delta\psi}{\beta_{g0}}\right|_{max} \simeq \frac{1}{2\zeta_{Dr}} = O[4] \qquad \text{(IV.9.30)}$$

taking $C_{Y\beta} \ll (\bar{\omega}_0)_{Dr}$. And

$$\left|\frac{\Delta\varphi}{\beta_{g0}}\right|_{max} \simeq \frac{1}{2\zeta_{Dr}}\frac{(-C_{l\beta})}{C_{n\beta}}\frac{i_{zz}}{i_{xx}}\frac{1}{\left(1+\left(\bar{\lambda}_{roll}/(\bar{\omega}_0)_{Dr}\right)^2\right)^{1/2}} = O[7]. \qquad \text{(IV.9.31)}$$

Thus the peak yaw and sideslip responses to oscillatory side gusts depend only on the Dutch roll damping ratio. The peak roll response to oscillatory side gusts again depends on the Dutch roll damping, but in addition this peak roll response is increased by an increase in $(-C_{l\beta})/C_{n\beta}$, by an increase in i_{zz}/i_{xx} and by a decrease in $(-C_{lp})/C_{n\beta}$.

To obtain the statistical lateral response behaviour it is necessary to use the power spectral density of the side gust. The side gust power spectral density is the same as the vertical gust power spectral density because in both cases the aeroplane is flying into gusts which are normal to the flight path, hence the von Karman spectrum is, from eqn. (III.13.54),

$$\Phi_v(\Omega) = \frac{\sigma_v^2 L}{\pi} \frac{1+(8/3)(1.339L\Omega)^2}{\left[1+(1.339L\Omega)^2\right]^{11/6}}. \tag{IV.9.32}$$

As far as the author is aware, the SDG method has not been extended to the lateral case.

IV.9.4 Vortex wake interaction

So far the disturbances to an aeroplane arise within the natural environment. But another source of disturbance is the trailing vortex pattern left behind an aeroplane. The two counter-rotating wing tip vortices are remarkably stable for a long period of time in a calm atmosphere, as observed in the long vapour trails at altitude which can extend over a number of miles. The two vortices descend due to mutual interference effects, but as the downward motion enters an atmosphere of higher density an upward buoyancy force is created which opposes this downward motion and ultimately causes the vortices to break up. Near the ground the vortices move downward and apart, and drift in light winds.

Vortex wakes are a hazard in the vicinity of airports where aeroplanes of different sizes fly close to each other in sequential landing or in sequential take-off. If a smaller aeroplane encounters the swirling flow of one of the trailing vortices behind a larger aeroplane the smaller aeroplane can be thrown out of control, possibly flipped over—a potentially dangerous situation if it occurs close to the ground. To minimize the possibility of this type of incident there is a statutory separation time between take-offs and between landings of the order of $1\frac{1}{2}$ minutes.

For further information see refs. IV.5–IV.7.

EXAMPLES IV.17

1. Estimate the steady state bank angle from eqn. (IV.9.5) when an aeroplane meets a sharp-edged vertical gust at skew angle Λ_g at time $t = 0$ followed by a sharp-edged vertical gust at skew angle $-\Lambda_g$ at time $t = 0.2$ s.
2. Check the consistency of dimensions through eqns. (IV.9.11)–(IV.9.21).
3. Estimate $A_{\Delta\varphi w}$ and N_0 from eqn. (IV.9.18); see eqns. (III.13.64) and (III.13.68).
4. Plot out $\Phi_{\Delta\beta}(\Omega)$ using eqns. (IV.9.24) and (IV.9.32).
5. (i) By reference to eqns. (III.13.7)–(III.13.9) derive an expression for $C_{n\dot{\beta}g}$.
   (ii) Does the inclusion of $C_{n\dot{\beta}g}$ make any significant difference to eqns. (IV.9.30) and (IV.9.31)?

IV.10 LATERAL HANDLING QUALITIES

IV.10.1 Piloting

The main lateral piloting tasks are:

(i) to change the direction of the aeroplane heading; this manoeuvre is achieved by entering into, maintaining and exiting from a turn;
(ii) to maintain wings level in straight flight, or to maintain a steady bank angle in a turn, in turbulence.

As explained in sect. III.14, the human body is acutely aware of changes in accelerations of the head but the interpretation of these changes by the brain depends critically on simultaneous visual images. A pilot senses roll, pitch and yaw accelerations by virtue of the fact that the pilot's head is offset from the centre of mass and the axes of rotation. In addition the body feels 'heaviness' due to linear acceleration, including the normal acceleration in a sustained turn.

External visual cues are the horizon for bank angle, and ground reference for heading. Instrument cues are the Attitude Director for the bank angle and the Horizontal Situation Director for the heading.

The pilot is literally 'fixed' into the fuselage body axis system. However, a pilot tends to fly relative flight path axes, which, at small angles of incidence, are the same as trim body axes. It is the roll and yaw characteristics relative to flight path axes which influence pilot opinion.

To enter a coordinated turn to starboard from straight level flight the pilot moves the column stick to the right (or rotates a wheel right-hand-down), and pushes down, if necessary, the right pedal; the aeroplane rolls, and turns, to starboard. At approximately two-thirds of the required bank angle the stick and pedals are set at their appropriate positions for the required sustained turn, as quantified in sect. IV.3.3, eqns. (IV.3.13) and (IV.3.14). To retain the same speed and altitude in the turn as in the original straight flight the pilot also has to pull the stick back to increase angle of incidence in order to increase lift and to open the throttle in order to offset the increase in drag. Overall a complicated coordinated sequence of actions which needs practice for success.

A pilot can compensate to obtain a faster bank angle response.

In lateral manoeuvring, as in longitudinal manoeuvring, the pilot acts either in an open loop manner or in a closed loop manner. The above turn manoeuvre is an open loop action in that, by virtue of his training, the pilot knows what inputs are required to give a desired rate of turn. In a closed loop situation the pilot continually monitors the aeroplane response and moves the controls to maintain a particular flight condition, for example, minimizing bank angular excursions during an approach, or on a ground attack mission, or tracking in combat.

IV.10.2 Lateral stability under constraint

On the approach, or in a turn, a pilot attempts to maintain a zero, or constant, bank angle during any gust disturbances. This control of the bank angle modifies the stability characteristics.

The non-dimensional response equations are, from eqns. (IV.7.6)–(IV.7.8),

$$[\bar{\mathrm{D}} - C_{Y\beta}]\ \beta(\bar{t}_\mathrm{d}) + \bar{\mathrm{D}}\ \Delta\psi(\bar{t}_\mathrm{d}) - \left[\left(C_{Yp}\mathrm{AR}_\mathrm{w}/2\bar{m}\right)\bar{\mathrm{D}} + C_\mathrm{W}\right]\Delta\varphi(\bar{t}_\mathrm{d})$$
$$= C_{Y\xi}\ \xi(\bar{t}_\mathrm{d}) + \text{side gust input} \qquad \text{(IV.10.1)}$$

$$-(2\bar{m}/\mathrm{AR}_\mathrm{w})C_{l\beta}\ \beta(\bar{t}_\mathrm{d}) - \left[(i_{xz}/2)\bar{\mathrm{D}}^2 + C_{lr}\bar{\mathrm{D}}\right]\Delta\psi(\bar{t}_\mathrm{d})$$
$$+\left[(i_{xx}/2)\bar{\mathrm{D}}^2 - C_{lp}\bar{\mathrm{D}}\right]\Delta\varphi(\bar{t}_\mathrm{d})$$
$$= (2\bar{m}/\mathrm{AR}_\mathrm{w})C_{l\xi}\ \xi(\bar{t}_\mathrm{d}) + \text{roll gust input} \qquad \text{(IV.10.2)}$$

$$-(2\bar{m}/\mathrm{AR}_\mathrm{w})C_{n\beta}\ \beta(\bar{t}_\mathrm{d}) + \left[(i_{zz}/2)\bar{\mathrm{D}}^2 - C_{nr}\bar{\mathrm{D}}\right]\Delta\psi(\bar{t}_\mathrm{d})$$
$$-\left[(i_{xz}/2)\bar{\mathrm{D}}^2 + C_{np}\bar{\mathrm{D}}\right]\Delta\varphi(\bar{t}_\mathrm{d})$$
$$= (2\bar{m}/\mathrm{AR}_\mathrm{w})C_{n\xi}\ \xi(\bar{t}_\mathrm{d}) + \text{yaw gust input.} \qquad \text{(IV.10.3)}$$

When an aeroplane rolls due to gust disturbances, the pilot will move the aileron $\xi(t)$ to counter the roll disturbance. Suppose the pilot reacts to bank angle and applies an aileron angle

$$\xi(\bar{t}_\mathrm{d}) = \mathscr{K}_\varphi\ \Delta\varphi(\bar{t}_\mathrm{d}) \qquad \text{(IV.10.4)}$$

(remember a positive aileron angle gives a negative rolling moment as required to offset a positive bank angle). Then the roll equation becomes

$$-(\mathrm{AR}_\mathrm{w}/2\bar{m})C_{l\beta}\ \beta(\bar{t}_\mathrm{d}) - \left[(i_{xz}/2)\bar{\mathrm{D}}^2 + C_{lr}\bar{\mathrm{D}}\right]\Delta\psi(\bar{t}_\mathrm{d})$$
$$+\left[(i_{xx}/2)\bar{\mathrm{D}}^2 + (-C_{lp})\bar{\mathrm{D}} + \mathscr{K}_\varphi(2\bar{m}/\mathrm{AR}_\mathrm{w})(-C_{l\xi})\right]\Delta\varphi(\bar{t}_\mathrm{d})$$
$$= \text{roll gust input.} \qquad \text{(IV.10.5)}$$

The term $\left[\mathscr{K}_\varphi(2\bar{m}/\mathrm{AR}_\mathrm{w})(-C_{l\xi})\right]$ can be made much larger than any other term on the left hand side and the roll response $\Delta\varphi(\bar{t}_\mathrm{d})$ is reduced.

As a first approximation, if it assumed that $\Delta\varphi(\bar{t}_\mathrm{d})$ is ideally maintained at zero then the sideslip and yaw equations are coupled with zero roll. The corresponding characteristic equation becomes

$$(i_{zz}/2)\bar{\lambda}^2 + \left[(-C_{nr}) + (-C_{Y\beta})(i_{zz}/2)\right]\bar{\lambda}$$
$$+\left[(2\bar{m}/\mathrm{AR}_\mathrm{w})C_{n\beta} + (-C_{Y\beta})(-C_{nr})\right]$$
$$= 0. \qquad \text{(IV.10.6)}$$

The damping of this constrained Dutch roll response is significantly greater than the damping of the unconstrained Dutch roll.

Eliminating roll by the use of aileron is one piloting technique for damping out a Dutch roll response. This technique is even more effective on a combat aeroplane with a differential tailplane because of its large proverse yaw characteristics.

There is some confusion in the literature regarding the topic of 'stability under constraint'. In fact the classic papers by Neumark in the longitudinal case, and by Pinsker in the lateral case (ref. IV.8), do not strictly deal with stability under constraint but more precisely with the decoupling of equations, which does not, in itself, imply any constraints.

IV.10.3 Lateral handling qualities

When a pilot applies a rapid aileron input the pilot is influenced by the initial roll acceleration, the time lag to reach a steady roll rate and the steady state rate of roll after the decay of the roll rate mode. From eqn. (IV.8.1)

the initial roll acceleration to a step aileron input $(-\xi_s H(t))$ is

$$D^2\,\Delta\varphi(+0) \simeq \left(\left[2g(-C_{l\xi})\right]/\left[s_W i_{xx} C_W\right]\right)\xi_s \qquad \text{(IV.10.7)}$$

the time constant for the roll mode is

$$(t_c)_{\text{roll}} = 1/\lambda_{\text{roll}} \simeq \left[i_{xx} U_{\text{trim}} C_W/\left(2g(-C_{lp})\right)\right] \qquad \text{(IV.10.8)}$$

the steady state roll rate after about $2(t_c)_{\text{roll}}$ is

$$\begin{aligned}(p_{\text{roll}})_{\text{ss}} &\simeq \left[U_{\text{trim}}/s_W\right]\left[(-C_{l\xi})/(-C_{lp})\right]\xi_s \\ &= D^2\,\Delta\varphi(+0)(t_c)_{\text{roll}}.\end{aligned} \qquad \text{(IV.10.9)}$$

Hence

$$\ln\left(D^2\,\Delta\varphi(+0)\right) = \ln\left((p_{\text{roll}})_{\text{ss}}\right) - \ln\left((t_c)_{\text{roll}}\right) \qquad \text{(IV.10.10)}$$

Pilot opinion boundaries for the roll response of combat aeroplanes are shown in Fig. IV.36. It appears that pilots look for $(p_{\text{roll}})_{\text{ss}}$ from 60°/s to 300°/s with $(t_c)_{\text{roll}}$ less than 1.5 s. However, these overall opinion boundaries need to be broken down to relate the preferred rate of roll to different flight tasks. For combat aeroplanes, according to Burns (ref. IV.9):

(i) high rates of steady state roll imply sensitivity to aileron input, possibly leading to pilot induced oscillations;

(ii) in air-to-air combat (at high subsonic Mach number, at medium altitude) a bank angle of 90° in 1 s is desired; for a roll rate time constant of 1 s this manoeuvre requires $(p_{\text{roll}})_{\text{ss}}$ to be equal to 240°/s; for a roll rate time constant of 0.5 s $(p_{\text{roll}})_{\text{ss}}$ should be 160°/s; this roll performance must be available with asymmetric stores which impose an inertial rolling moment which must be reacted by an aileron (or differential taileron) angle, reducing the available aileron angle for manoeuvring;

(iii) a ground attack task (at high or medium subsonic Mach number, at low altitude) can be accomplished satisfactorily with $(p_{\text{roll}})_{\text{ss}}$ equal to 100°/s;

(iv) a long range missile interception task (supersonic speed, high altitude) can be accomplished satisfactorily with $(p_{\text{roll}})_{\text{ss}}$ equal to 40°/s;

(v) an approach can be accomplished satisfactorily with a bank angle response of 30° in 1 s which requires $(p_{roll})_{ss}$ equal to 80°/s with a roll rate time constant of 1 s; this roll rate performance is required in crosswind landings when a significant steady aileron angle is necessary to maintain wings level, leaving little remaining aileron for roll control.

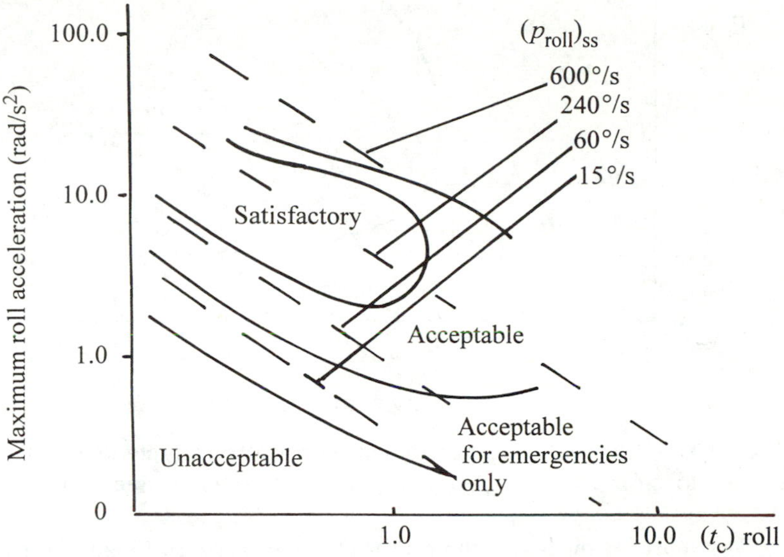

Fig. IV.36. Pilot opinion on roll performance.

As explained in sect. IV.8, the Dutch roll mode degrades the roll response to aileron input. The degree of Dutch roll mode response depends on the ratio $(p_{Dr})_{ss}/(p_{roll})_{ss}$, where $(p_{roll})_{ss}$ is the steady state roll rate after the decay of the roll rate mode, following a step aileron input, and $(p_{Dr})_{ss}$ is the subsequent steady state roll rate after the decay of the Dutch roll. The level of Dutch roll mode response increases as the ratio $(p_{Dr})_{ss}/(p_{roll})_{ss}$ decreases below unity. Pilot opinion of the significance of $(p_{Dr})_{ss}/(p_{roll})_{ss}$, which is equivalent to the ratio $\omega_\varphi^2/(\omega_0)_{Dr}^2$ used in the literature, and the Dutch roll damping ratio on the flying qualities, is shown in Fig. IV.37.

The spiral mode is not usually a problem in that the pilot has time to correct any spiral mode excursions; nevertheless pilot opinion is that a stable spiral mode is beneficial.

An additional, severe, manoeuvre concerns collision and debris avoidance; this manoeuvre involves both a high longitudinal *g* and a high rate of roll.

The derivative $(-C_{l\beta})$ plays an important role in lateral stability and response:

(i) for positive spiral mode stability, see eqn. (IV.6.7),

$$(-C_{l\beta})/C_{n\beta} > C_{lr}/(-C_{nr});$$

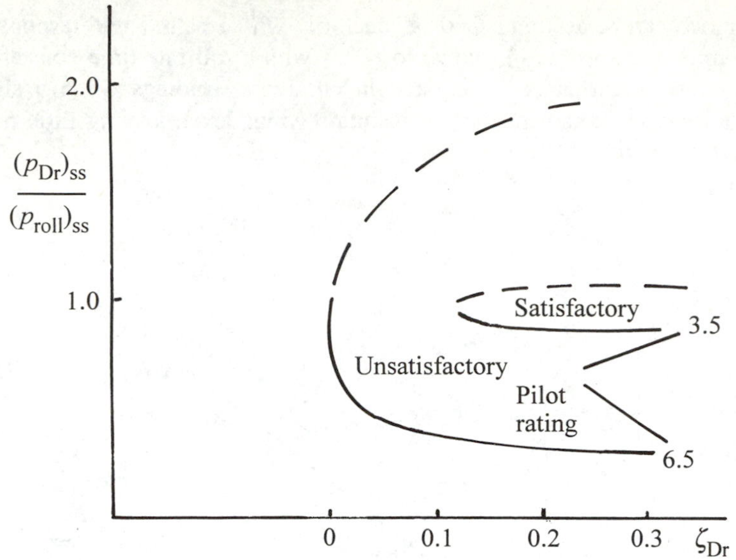

Fig. IV.37.

(ii) $(-C_{l\beta})/C_{n\beta}$ must be small to minimize oscillatory roll rate due to aileron input, that is, to ensure that $(p_{Dr})_{ss}/(p_{roll})_{ss}$ is close to unity, see eqns. (IV.8.3) and (IV.8.6);

(iii) $(-C_{l\beta})$ must be small to minimize bank angle response to side gusts, see eqns. (IV.9.26) and (IV.9.31);

(iv) $(-C_{l\beta})/(-C_{l\xi})$ must not be large in order to maintain roll power in a crosswind, see eqn. (IV.3.26).

Finally, an aeroplane must also be controllable on the ground after touchdown in a crosswind; factors which play a role are nose wheel steering sensitivity, state of the runway (dry, wet, flooded), braking procedures, thrust reversal or braking parachute, and aerodynamic control power from aileron and rudder.

IV.10.4 Lateral flying quality requirements

Some of the more important requirements are listed (for the definitions of aeroplane classes, flight phase categories, and flying quality levels 1, 2 and 3, see sect. III.14).

Roll time constant, $(t_c)_{roll}$

Class	Flight phase category	Maximum value of $(t_c)_{roll}$ (s)		
		Level 1	Level 2	Level 3
I, IV	A, C	1.0	1.4	Upper limit not specified
II, III	A, C	1.4	3.0	
All classes	B	1.4	3.0	

The roll response to side gusts, $(\Delta\phi/\beta_{gs})$, must be acceptable.

Roll performance

Class	Flight phase category	Roll performance Level 1	Level 2	Level 3
I	A	60° in 1.3 s	60° in 1.7 s	60° in 2.6 s
	B	60° in 1.7 s	60° in 2.5 s	60° in 3.4 s
	C	30° in 1.3 s	30° in 1.8 s	30° in 2.6 s
II	A	45° in 1.4 s	45° in 1.9 s	45° in 2.8 s
	B	45° in 1.9 s	45° in 2.8 s	45° in 3.8 s
	C	30° in 2.5 s	30° in 3.5 s	30° in 5.0 s
III	A	30° in 1.5 s	60° in 1.7 s	60° in 2.6 s
	B	30° in 2.0 s	30° in 3.0 s	30° in 4.0 s
	C	30° in 3.0 s	30° in 4.5 s	30° in 6.0 s
IV	A	90° in 1.3 s	90° in 1.7 s	90° in 2.6 s
	B	60° in 1.7 s	60° in 2.5 s	60° in 3.4 s
	C	30° in 1.0 s	30° in 1.3 s	30° in 2.6 s
	Air to air combat	90° in 1.0 s 360° in 2.5 s	90° in 1.3 s 360° in 3.7 s	90° in 1.7 s 360° in 4.4 s
	Ground attack	90° in 1.7 s	90° in 2.6 s	90° in 3.4 s

Dutch roll

Class	Flight phase category	Minimum values Level 1 ζ_{Dr}	$(\zeta\omega_0)_{Dr}$	$(\omega_0)_{Dr}$	Level 2 ζ_{Dr}	$(\zeta\omega_0)_{Dr}$	$(\omega_0)_{Dr}$	Level 3 ζ_{Dr}	$(\zeta\omega_0)_{Dr}$	$(\omega_0)_{Dr}$
IV	Combat ground attack	0.4	–	1.0	0.02	0.05	0.5	0.0	–	0.4
I, IV	A	0.19	0.35	1.0	0.02	0.05	0.5	0.0	–	0.4
II, III	A	0.19	0.35	0.5	0.02	0.05	0.5	0.0	–	0.4
All classes	B	0.08	0.15	0.5	0.02	0.05	0.5	0.0	–	0.4
I, IV	C	0.08	0.15	1.0	0.02	0.05	0.5	0.0	–	0.4
II, III	C	0.08	0.10	0.5	0.02	0.05	0.5	0.0	–	0.4

Flight phase category	Roll rate at first minimum as a percentage of roll rate at first peak; minimum percentage	
	Level 1	Level 2
A, C	60	25
B	25	0

Spiral mode

Flight phase category	Minimum time to double bank angle (s)		
	Level 1	Level 2	Level 3
A, C	12	8	5
B	20	8	5

The spiral mode response in turbulence must be acceptable.

EXAMPLES IV.18

1. What techniques are available to a pilot to damp out unwanted Dutch roll responses?
2. Relate the lateral flying quality requirements to the lateral handling criteria.

IV.11 LATERAL AUTOMATIC FLIGHT CONTROL SYSTEMS

IV.11.1 Lateral stability augmentation

The Dutch roll damping is usually unacceptably low to satisfy flying quality requirements. A limited authority yaw damper can be installed to improve this damping; a rate gyro senses the rate of yaw, a feedback signal is transmitted to the rudder actuator to rotate the rudder and a wash-out term is included in the feedback loop to reduce the effect of the yaw damper on a pilot input command for a yaw manoeuvre. The action of the yaw damper parallels that of the pitch damper described in sect. III.15.3, and so the description is not repeated here. One difference concerns the rudder hydraulic servo. Because rudder hinge moments tend to be larger than elevator or aileron hinge moments, the rudder hydraulic servo is more powerful, and more sluggish, than the other hydraulic units; it is therefore important that a full representation of the rudder actuator system be included in the design of the yaw damper.

In general aviation aeroplanes the yaw damper input to the manual control linkage moves the pilot pedals; this pedal motion can be disconcerting when manoeuvring on the approach so the pilot has the option of switching out the yaw damper. This problem does not occur with powered controls and the pilot cannot switch out the yaw damper.

A roll rate damper may also be installed to improve the roll damping for manoeuvring purposes and/or to reduce the roll response to side gusts. Again the design approach follows that of the pitch and yaw dampers. One problem is that by increasing the effective value of $(-C_{lp})$ the steady state roll rate after the decay of the roll rate mode, $(p_{\mathrm{roll}})_{\mathrm{ss}}$, is reduced and so the aileron control power might have to be increased to satisfy the flying quality requirements for roll.

In principle the spiral mode stability may be improved, or a spiral mode instability stabilized, by an aileron deflection given by a feedback signal depending on the rate of yaw (this statement follows directly from the yaw response to a control input in sect. IV.8). The feedback signal for the yaw damper can be used to drive the ailerons. In this case it would be necessary to examine the combined inputs of both the aileron and rudder on the effectiveness of the yaw damping and the spiral mode damping.

IV.11.2 Lateral command modes

Typical lateral auto-pilot modes are:

— bank angle hold or wing leveller
— heading hold
— track hold
— automatic turn coordination
— flat turn.

Typical lateral active controls are:

— roll rate command
— bank angle limiter.

Apart from listing these lateral systems it is not feasible to describe them in this book; further information is given by McLean (ref. P.21).

Part V

Flight dynamics at high angles of incidence

V.1 INTRODUCTION

High angles of incidence for light aeroplanes and transport aeroplanes refer to angles of incidence above the break angle of incidence; flight at these high angles of attack would be inadvertent.

For combat aeroplanes $C_{L\,max}$ occurs at high angles of attack, usually well above the break angle of incidence. Enhanced manoeuvrability is obtained by achieving as high a C_L as possible, thus flight at high angles of incidence is essential. Another benefit of being able to manoeuvre at high angles of incidence is the ability to point the aeroplane over a large angle relative to the flight path which improves the effectiveness of weapon aiming.

It is mandatory that aeroplanes should be flyable at all times; this requirement allows for the contingency that an aeroplane can go temporarily out of control as long as it can be demonstrated in flight tests that the aeroplane always returns to a controllable state, either naturally, without intervention by the pilot, or by the pilot applying standard recovery procedures.

The (temporary) loss of control as angle of incidence increases, defined in this book as the stall, occurs when an aeroplane

— either cannot sustain steady level flight as speed is decreased,
— or suddenly departs from controlled flight,
— or is unflyable because of an excessive level of buffeting.

It is mandatory that there should be a stall warning to the pilot that loss of control is imminent; the stall warning shall be either natural, with an increase in the level of buffeting, or artificial, by means for example of klaxon horns or stick shakers.

The stall associated with departure from controlled flight is usually abrupt, but the subsequent post-stall motions can range from gentle to violent. The immediate post-stall motions are known as post-stall gyrations. On transport aeroplanes and light general aviation aeroplanes the aim is to ensure that the post-stall gyrations are gentle and self-correcting, namely that the aeroplane returns naturally to a lower angle of incidence and controlled flight. On combat aeroplanes the post-stall gyrations can lead into a spin; it would be mandatory that a pilot should be able to recover from a spin. If the post-stall gyrations and subsequent motions are regarded as too dangerous the aeroplane is prevented from entering a stall, either by a stick-pusher, when the stick is suddenly forced forward out of the pilot's hands, inducing the aeroplane into a nose-down motion to reduce angle of incidence, or by an automatic stall-prevention system, which limits the range of the angle of incidence.

The aerodynamic phenomena which precipitate stall are flow separation, when the flow leaves the surface of a wing or fuselage, and flow breakdown, when a separated flow becomes unstable, developing large scale unsteadiness. As explained later, flow separation can occur without flow breakdown, but flow breakdown is always preceded by flow separation. Flow separations can be deliberately introduced into a flow field to delay, or control, flow breakdown (e.g. vortex generators).

Stall occurs sometimes at the onset of flow separation, sometimes at the onset of flow breakdown, and sometimes well after flow breakdown has become established—it all depends on the aeroplane configuration and the flight condition. For non-swept configurations stall is usually identified with maximum wing lift because stall, flow separation and flow breakdown, and maximum lift all occur together. But for swept wing configurations neither the stall, nor the onset of flow separation, nor the onset of flow breakdown are necessarily related to the maximum lift condition.

The word 'stall' does not have a universal meaning. In this book stall is defined as a flight dynamic phenomenon, recognized by the pilot. Flow separation and flow breakdown are aerodynamic phenomena. Stall, flow separation and flow breakdown, although interrelated, are distinct phenomena. The long established practice of aerodynamicists to use the word stall as synonymous with flow separation, or as synonymous with $C_{L\,max}$, should be discouraged.

The important aerodynamic phenomenon is flow breakdown; it is recommended that the word 'break' be used to denote the effect of flow breakdown with increasing angle of incidence, and also to denote the re-establishment of ordered flow with decreasing angle of incidence. As pointed out later, it may be necessary to distinguish between drag break, lift break and moment break.

V.2 SYMMETRIC AEROPLANE AERODYNAMICS AT HIGH ANGLES OF INCIDENCE

In this section a brief survey is presented on the steady and unsteady aerodynamic characteristics of steady and unsteady flows about aerofoils, wings and aeroplane configurations, assuming, at this stage, symmetric flow conditions. Understanding of this topic is far from complete, with continuing active research into most aspects, so the following presentation reflects the author's comprehension, which may well be flawed. As an introduction the flows about two dimensional aerofoils are described. It is well known that aerofoil characteristics bear little relationship to wing characteristics; nevertheless a study of aerofoil flows helps to establish a basic framework of language and appreciation of the mechanisms of flow separations and breakdown which can be extended subsequently to the more practical, and far more difficult, wing flows.

V.2.1 Introduction to steady, two dimensional flow separation

All fluids, including air, are viscous. The key hypothesis of a viscous fluid is that there is a no-slip condition between the fluid in contact with the surface of a body and that surface. When a wing is stationary in a moving stream of air the macroscopic elements of air in contact with the solid surface have zero velocity; alternatively when a solid body is moving with a velocity in still air the macroscopic elements of air in contact with the solid surface have the same velocity as the solid body (see Fig. V.1).

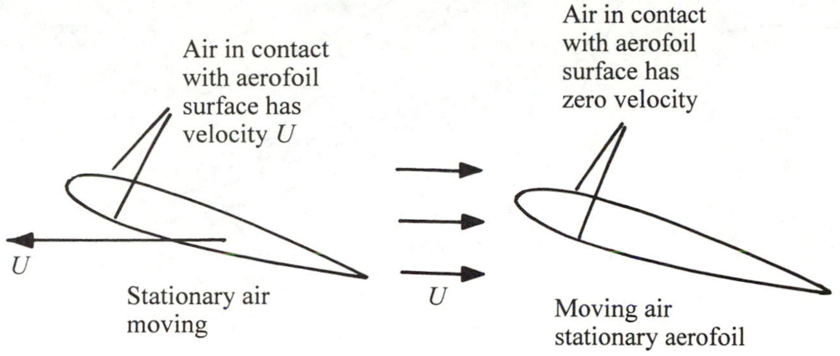

Fig. V.1. No-slip condition in viscous flow.

This hypothesis of no-slip is by no means self-evident, in fact its formal proposition by Stokes in 1845 (ref. V.1) evolved after many years of debate.

In attached flow the effect of viscosity is confined within a thin layer adjacent to the body surface, the boundary layer. In the case of a stationary wing in a moving stream, as shown in Fig. V.2, the tangential velocity changes from zero velocity at the surface to an outer velocity $q(s)$ at the outer edge of the boundary layer, where s is the coordinate along the surface.

The boundary layer starts with a small thickness at the front of the body and its thickness builds up along the length of a body. Initially the boundary layer is laminar (i.e. the streamlines follow well-defined paths), but as the boundary layer develops downstream and thickens, the boundary layer becomes unstable and breaks down into a turbulent random motion, comprising eddies and swirls, confined within the boundary layer, all moving downstream. The flow outside of the boundary layer remains laminar. The change from the laminar boundary layer to the turbulent boundary layer is known as transition. Because of the turbulent mixing the turbulent boundary layer is much thicker than the laminar boundary layer. The boundary layer thickness is approximately 3 cm in the neighbourhood of the trailing edge of a large transport aeroplane in high speed cruise.

Boundary layers induce a viscous shear stress on the body surface, tending to pull the body in the direction of the relative airstream (see Fig. V.2) which is the main contribution to the zero lift drag. A consequence of turbulent mixing is that the viscous shear stress on the wing surface due to a turbulent boundary layer is higher than the viscous shear stress on the wing surface due to a laminar boundary layer by a factor of the order of 8, hence the incentive to achieve a laminar flow wing in the cruise condition.

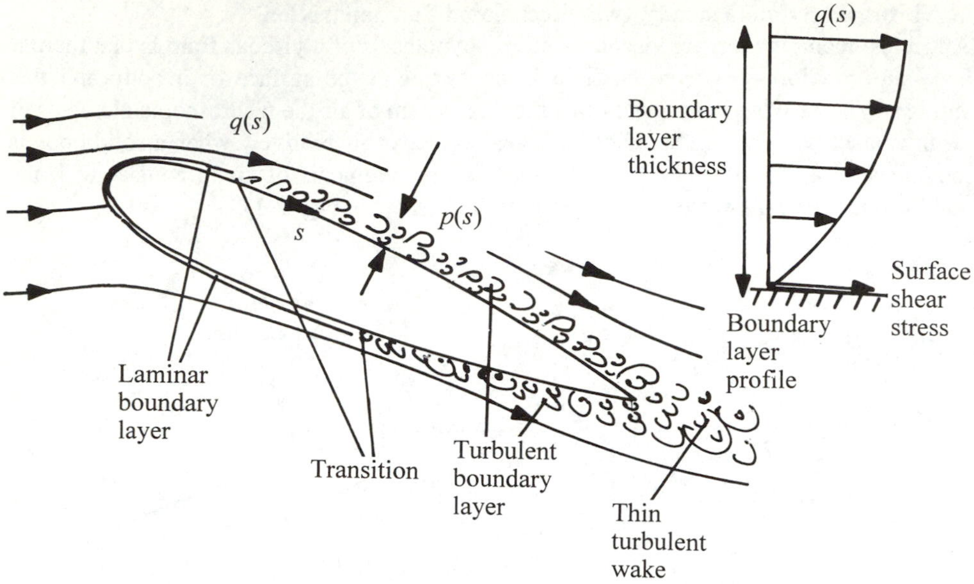

Fig. V.2. Boundary layer on two dimensional aerofoil in attached flow.

Because the boundary layer, whether laminar or turbulent, is relatively thin the static pressure is virtually constant through the boundary layer, normal to the boundary layer. The static pressure on the outside of the boundary layer, and hence the normal pressure on the wing surface, $p(s)$, depends on $q(s)$ and varies along the wing surface (see Fig. V.2).

The boundary layers on the upper and lower aerofoil surfaces merge at the trailing edge into a relatively thin wake.

Boundary layers are prone to separate in adverse pressure gradients on curved surfaces. Consider the flow shown in Fig. V.3:

(i) The flow velocity on the outside of the boundary layer decreases from q_A at station A to q_B at station B, so $q_A > q_B$.

(ii) This outer flow is slowing down so the static pressure must be increasing; the static pressure p_B must be greater than the static pressure p_A, $p_A < p_B$.

(iii) At station A, if the velocity inside the boundary layer is denoted by q_a, then $q_a < q_A$, so elements of air inside the boundary layer have less momentum than elements of air outside the boundary layer.

(iv) The static pressure difference $(p_B - p_A)$ which opposes the flow outside the boundary layer applies also to the flow inside the boundary layer, so the deceleration is the same inside and outside the boundary layer.

(v) Downstream of station A the flow inside the boundary layer, because of its lower initial momentum at station A, will come to rest before the flow outside the boundary layer, and then, further downstream, the flow inside the boundary layer reverses.

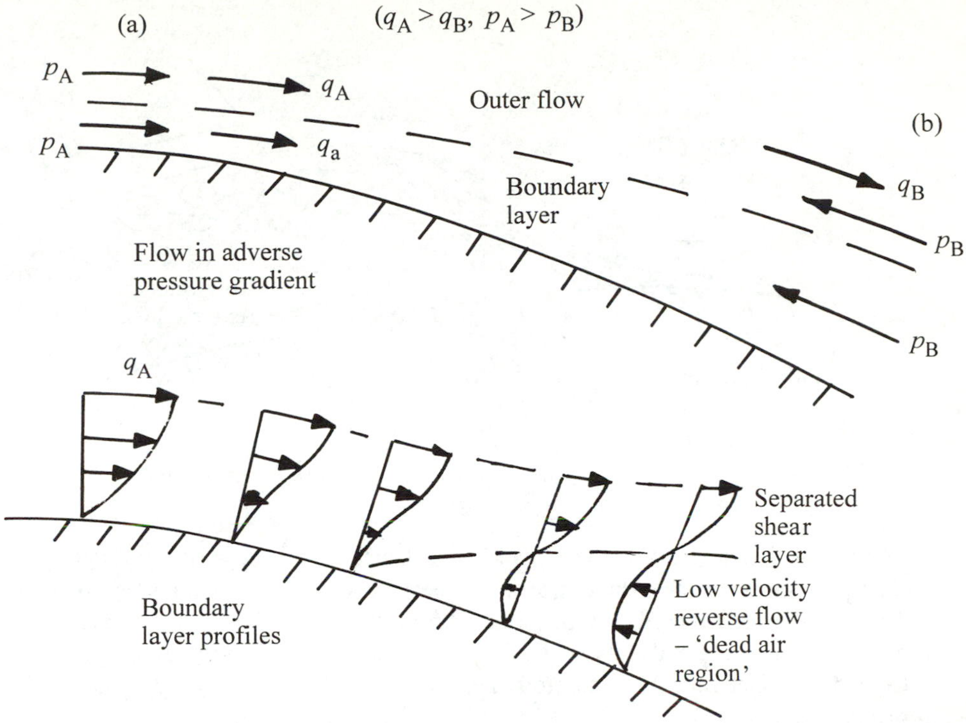

Fig. V.3. Flow separation from curved surface in two dimensions.

(vi) the separating boundary layer becomes a free shear flow above a slowly moving reverse flow region, or 'dead' air region.

This phenomenon, whereby the flow 'leaves' the surface, is known as flow separation.

Flow separation from a curved surface is always caused by an adverse pressure gradient; however, a weak adverse pressure gradient does not necessarily induce flow separation.

Flow separation from a curved surface can occur with either a laminar or turbulent boundary layer. By virtue of the turbulent mixing a turbulent boundary is better able to withstand an adverse pressure gradient than a laminar boundary layer, so, on a curve surface, a turbulent boundary layer tends to remain attached longer than a laminar boundary layer.

There is another type of flow separation. Flows separate from sharp corners with virtually no adverse pressure gradient ahead of the corner; in the example sketched in Fig. V.4 flow separates from the tip of a spoiler, a corner of 360°.

V.2.2 Static two dimensional aerofoils

To illustrate the complexities of steady flow separation the flow characteristics of static two dimensional aerofoils in a low speed stream of air are summarized.

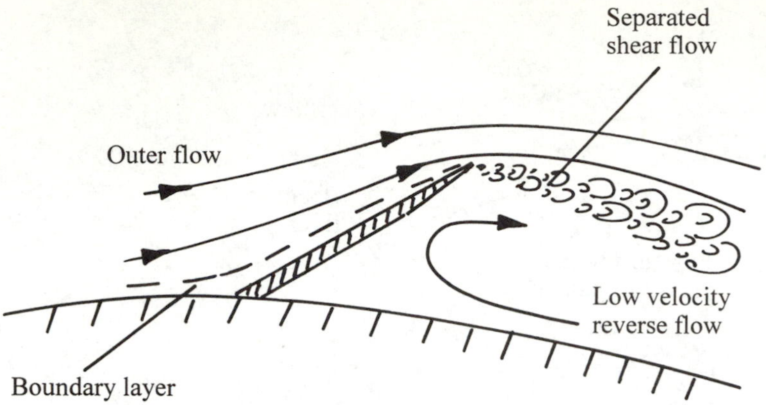

Fig. V.4. Flow separation from sharp corner.

Typical flow fields and pressure coefficient distributions $\left(c_p = (p - p_{at})/(\frac{1}{2}\rho_{at}U^2)\right)$ on the upper surface of two dimensional symmetric aerofoils over a range of static angle of incidence are shown in Figs. V.5, extracted from the exhaustive listing of conventional aerofoil characteristics in the classic book by Abbot and von Doenhoff (ref. V.2).

Consider a relatively thick aerofoil (i.e. thickness/chord ratio greater than 15°) as shown in Fig. V.5(i).

(i) In condition 1 at an angle of incidence, say 12°, the flow is attached; the adverse pressure gradient is insufficient to cause flow separation.

(ii) With increase in angle of incidence the adverse pressure gradient increases. At a critical angle of incidence there is onset of boundary layer separation on the upper surface in the vicinity of the trailing edge. As the angle of incidence is increased beyond this critical value the position of separation moves forward, to about the $\frac{2}{3}$ chord position in condition 2, at say 14°, and to about the $\frac{1}{3}$ chord position in condition 3, at say 16°. Once separation occurs the separated flow breaks down, creating a large region of random unsteady flow which extends beyond the trailing edge into a thick wake. Note that the boundary layer on the lower surface regards the trailing edge as a sharp corner and separates from there.

(iii) This type of separation is known as a trailing edge separation.

Consider next an aerofoil of medium thickness (e.g. 10% thickness/chord ratio) as shown in Fig. V.5(ii).

(i) At an angle of incidence of 8°, condition 1, a high suction peak around the nose is followed by a large adverse pressure gradient which is sufficient to cause the boundary layer to separate. But this separation occurs so close to the nose that the boundary layer is still laminar so it is a laminar boundary layer separation. Soon after the laminar shear layer leaves the aerofoil surface the laminar shear layer becomes unstable and transition to turbulence occurs. The mixing process associated with turbulence brings the turbulent shear layer back to the aerofoil surface, a

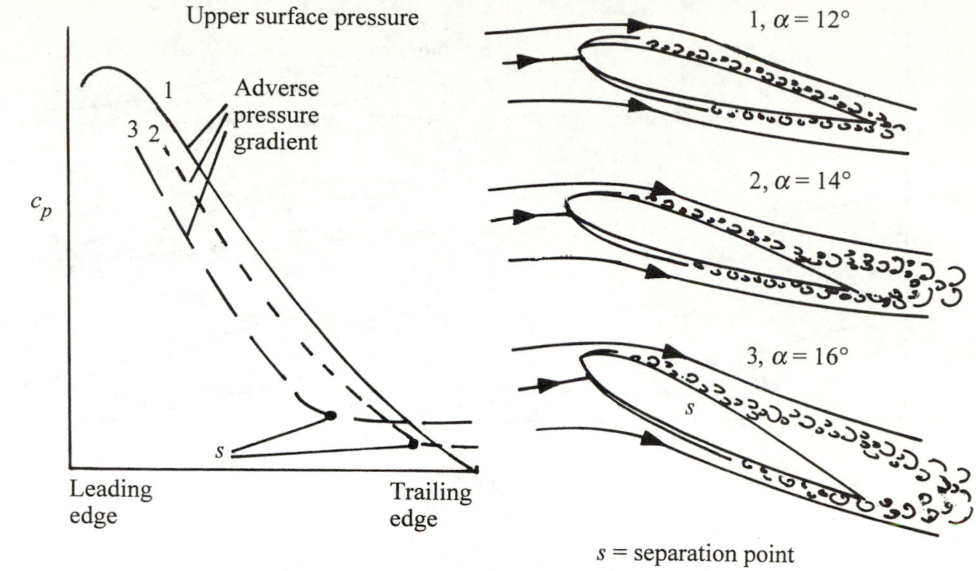
Upper surface pressure
1, $\alpha = 12°$
Adverse pressure gradient
1
3 2
c_p
2, $\alpha = 14°$
3, $\alpha = 16°$
s
s
Leading edge
Trailing edge
s = separation point

(i)

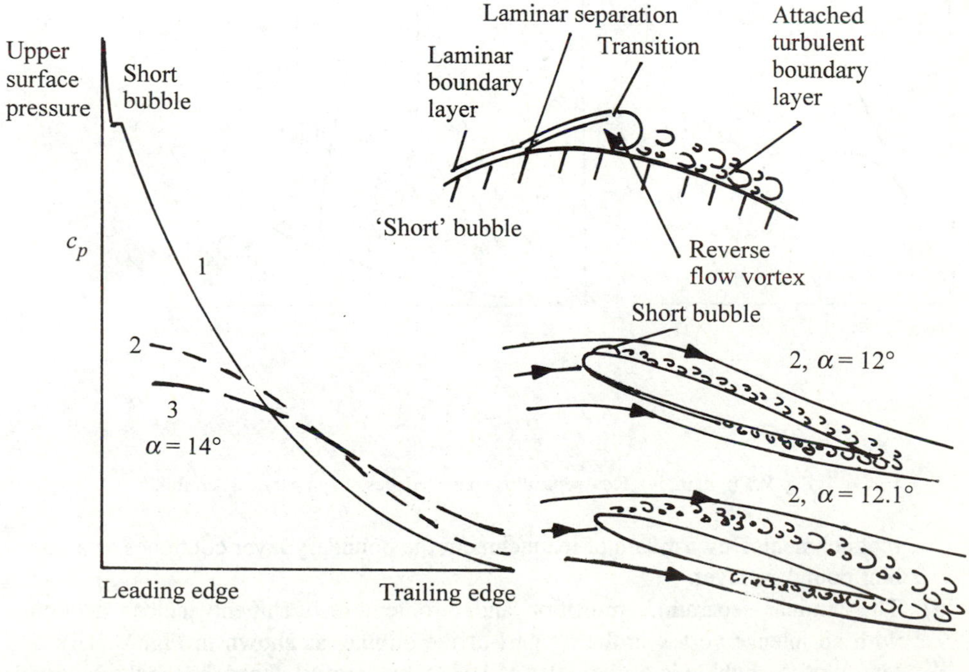
Laminar separation
Attached turbulent boundary layer
Transition
Laminar boundary layer
Upper surface pressure
Short bubble
'Short' bubble
Reverse flow vortex
c_p
1
Short bubble
2, $\alpha = 12°$
2
3
$\alpha = 14°$
2, $\alpha = 12.1°$
Leading edge
Trailing edge

(ii)

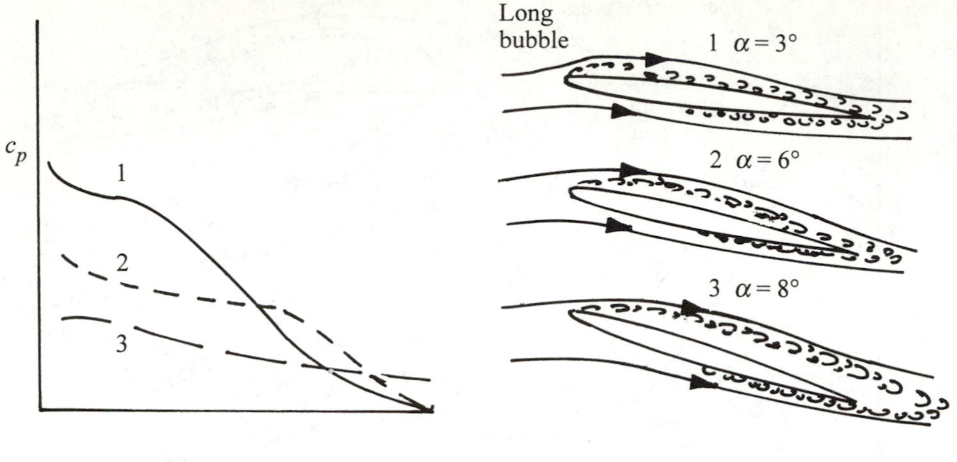

(iii)

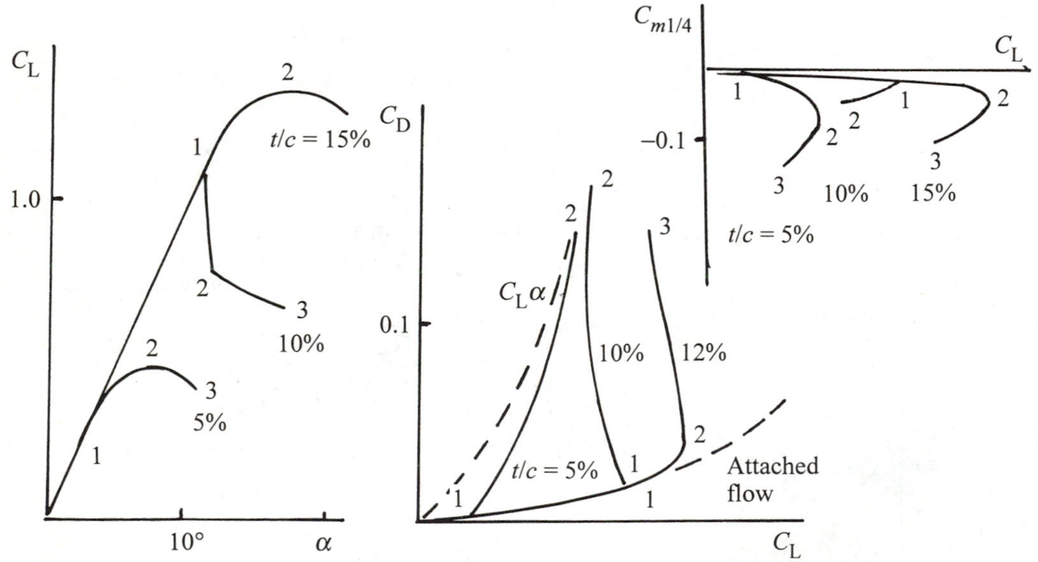

(iv)

Fig. V.5 (i, ii, iii, iv). Flow separation characteristics of symmetrical aerofoil.

reattachment. Downstream of reattachment the boundary layer continues as a turbulent boundary layer.

(ii) The laminar separation, transition and turbulent reattachment enclose a bubble, with an intense vortex in the aft part of the bubble, as shown in Fig. V.5(ii). The length of the bubble is of the order of 1% of the aerofoil chord, hence the bubble is known as a 'short bubble'.

(iii) This short bubble causes a small plateau in the pressure distribution under the laminar region before transition, see Fig. V.5(ii).

(iv) A flow with a short bubble within it is still regarded as attached flow; the short bubble identifies where transition occurs. The short bubble is an example where flow separation does not lead to flow breakdown or to detrimental effects on the aerodynamic loading.

(v) As the angle of incidence is increased the short bubble becomes shorter.

(vi) When the angle of incidence reaches a critical value, say 12°, the aft bubble reattachment process fails so the bubble 'bursts'; there is then complete separation from just behind the leading edge, with the flow possibly reattaching towards the trailing edge, as shown in condition 2.

(vii) When the short bubble bursts there is a loss in the leading edge suctions; at this angle of incidence the leading edge acts like a sharp edge, causing the flow to separate without the need of an adverse pressure gradient.

(viii) With further increase in angle of incidence the separation extends beyond the trailing edge, see condition 3.

(ix) This type of flow separation is known as a leading edge, short bubble, separation.

Consider a thin aerofoil (e.g. 5% thickness/chord ratio), as shown in Fig. V.5(iii).

(i) At angles of incidence up to approximately 3° the flow is attached with a short bubble, condition 1. This short bubble bursts at an angle of incidence of the order of 3°, but the separated shear layer reattaches about the 10% chord position, enclosing a so-called long bubble. Now the aerofoil leading edge behaves as a sharp edge so the flow separates from the leading edge as a laminar separation with a loss of the leading edge suctions. There is transition in the separated shear layer of the long bubble prior to reattachment.

(ii) With increasing angle of incidence, the long bubble lengthens, and the reattachment point moves aft, as shown in condition 2, until it reaches the aerofoil trailing edge, and then the separation region extends into the wake, as shown in condition 3.

(iii) This type of flow separation is known as a leading edge, long bubble, separation.

(iv) At those lower angles of incidence, when the long bubble reattaches before the trailing edge, the flow resembles the flow about a thicker aerofoil thus generating a reasonable level of lift; this is the reason that a flat plate generates a lift at low angles of incidence.

Note that when the boundary layer is attached at the trailing edge, irrespective of whether or not there is an upstream short or long bubble, c_p at the trailing edge is virtually zero (i.e. p is close to p_{at}). But c_p at the trailing edge changes from zero once flow separation extends beyond the trailing edge; this phenomenon is known as 'trailing edge pressure divergence'. Flow separation is often deduced from experimental surface pressure measurements by the trailing edge pressure divergence.

The lift, drag and pitching moment characteristics for these three aerofoils are shown in Fig. V.5(iv).

For the lift, below their respective break angles of incidence the lift curve slope is the same for the three aerofoils. In the region of the maximum lift the changes in lift are gradual for the trailing edge separation, and the leading edge, long bubble, separation, but there is a sudden loss of lift at the maximum lift when the short bubble bursts with the leading edge, short bubble, separation.

Separation always increases drag. Although aft of separation the viscous stresses on the surface are considerably reduced, flow separation modifies the normal pressure distribution around the whole surface, especially in the leading edge region, resulting in a significant increase in the normal pressure drag.

In attached flow the centre of pressure for all symmetric aerofoils lies close to the $\frac{1}{4}$ chord position so $C_{m\frac{1}{4}}$ is small. Once separation occurs the ratio $(-C_{m\frac{1}{4}}/C_L)$ gives the non-dimensional location of the centre of pressure aft of the $\frac{1}{4}$ chord position. Separation moves the centre of pressure aft, inducing a nose-down pitching moment.

For a given aerofoil the type of flow separation and the value of the maximum lift are dependent on the Reynolds number ($= \rho_{at} U c_w / \mu_{at}$, see eqn. (III.3.2)). With increasing Reynolds number boundary layers are more resistant to separation, long bubbles can be changed into short bubbles and trailing edge separations can be replaced by leading edge, short bubble, separations. As an illustration the effect of Reynolds number on a NACA 0012 aerofoil is shown in Fig. V.6, taken from Ericsson (ref. V.3); as Reynolds number increases the trailing edge stall changes into a leading edge, short bubble, separation and the maximum lift continues to increase with Reynolds number.

Camber on aerofoils of medium thickness/chord ratio tends to increase the loading in the central part of the aerofoil chord without affecting the high suctions in the neighbourhood of the nose. The 'central' loading due to camber tends to be independent of angle of

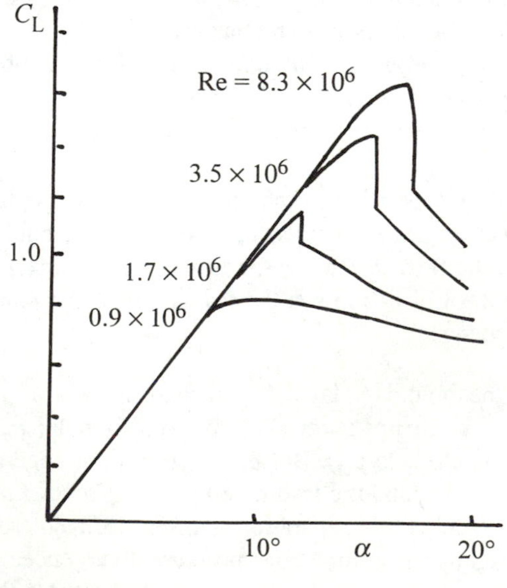

Fig. V.6. Effect of Reynolds number on flow separation for symmetric aerofoil.

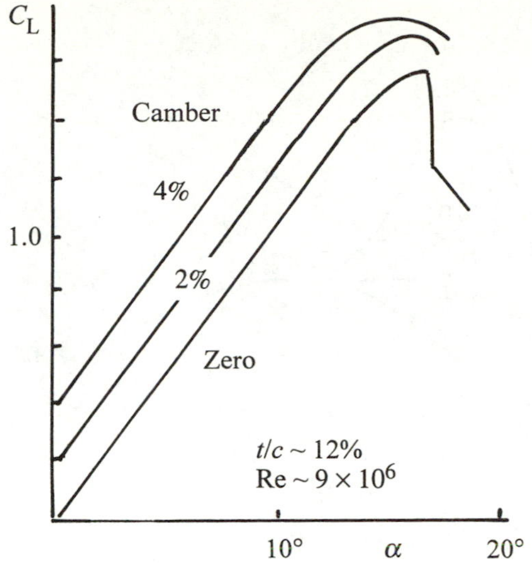

Fig. V.7. Effect of camber.

incidence, so, below the break angle of incidence, cambered aerofoils have a constant higher lift compared to symmetrical aerofoils, as shown in Fig. V.7. (This observation is equivalent to the observation that the lift curve slope is virtually independent of camber.) Fig. V.7, deduced from ref. V.2, shows the effect of camber on the separation characteristics for an aerofoil of 12% thickness/chord ratio. The break angle of incidence is virtually the same for the zero and 2% camber aerofoils; because the loading due to camber in this case is relatively small the suction pressures around the nose are independent of camber, so similar short bubble bursts occur at the same break angle of incidence. However, for the 4% cambered aerofoil the 'central' loading due to camber is sufficient to reduce the upper surface pressure gradients aft of the nose but to increase the pressure gradient towards the trailing edge, resulting in a trailing edge separation and reducing the break angle of incidence. Although camber increases $C_{L\,max}$ relative to zero camber, there is little difference between $C_{L\,max}$ for the 2% and 4% cambered aerofoils.

The details of flow separations depend on aerofoil geometry, not just on the thickness/chord ratio and camber but also on the nose radius, the form of the thickness distribution along the chord, and the trailing edge angle (see ref. V.2).

At higher angles of incidence, once flow separation extends from just behind the aerofoil leading edge into the wake, the resulting force on all aerofoils is the same normal force N, normal to the aerofoil chord, which acts near to the 40% chord point. And then

$$L = N\cos\alpha \qquad D = N\sin\alpha. \tag{V.2.1}$$

The variations of the normal force coefficient and associated lift coefficient with angle of incidence up to 90° are shown in Fig. V.8 (from Hancock, ref. V.4).

The flow breakdown following separation is not completely random; the separating shear layers from the separation point on the upper surface and from the lower surface at

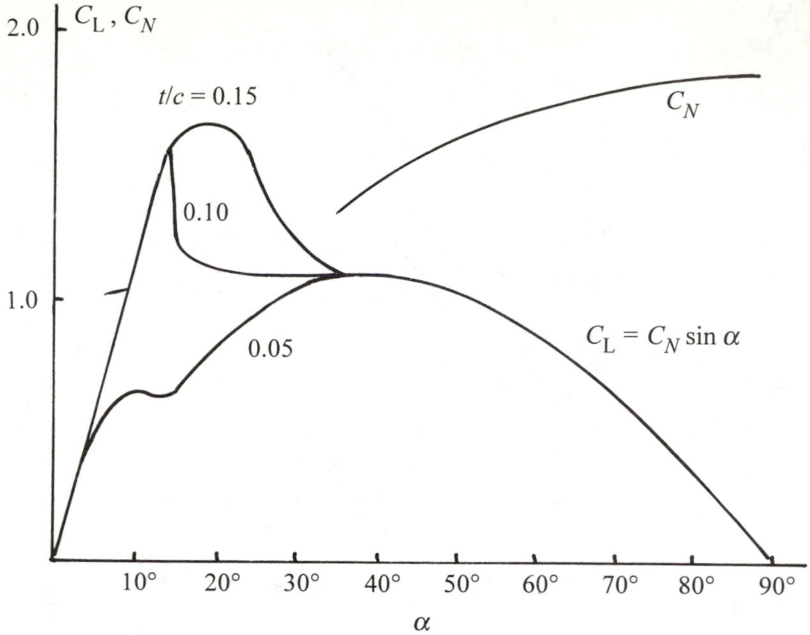

Fig. V.8. Variation of C_L for aerofoil at high angles of incidence.

the trailing edge tend to roll up, alternatively, to a sequence of vortex-type motions of opposite rotations, as shown in Fig. V.9. The strengths of the alternate shed vortices aft of the trailing edge, positive and negative, have equal magnitudes because the time average of the flow is constant. This unsteady pattern of vortex shedding appears to be independent of Reynolds number.

(i) The frequency of this vortex shedding, known as the Strouhal frequency, denoted as ω_{vs} rad/s, is given by (see ref. V.5)

$$\omega_{vs}\,(\text{wake thickness})/U \simeq 1.25. \qquad \text{(V.2.2)}$$

Taking the wake thickness as ($c_w \sin\alpha$) then

$$\omega_{vs}\,(c_w \sin\alpha)/U \simeq 1.25; \qquad \text{(V.2.3)}$$

(see Katz (ref. V.5)). For an aerofoil of chord $2m$ at 25° angle of incidence in a stream of 100 m/s this shedding frequency is of the order of 25 Hz. This frequency decreases with increase in angle of incidence to the order of 10 Hz at 90°.

(ii) The spatial wavelength between shed vortices from the upper surface is equal to $((2\pi/\omega_{vs})U)$ which is approximately equal to $(c_w \sin\alpha/0.2)$ which is of the order of $2c_w$ when α is 25°; this wavelength is consistent with the sketch in Fig. V.9.

(iii) The strength of the separating shear layers is insensitive to angle of incidence so the strength of the vortices is inversely proportional to frequency, that is, the strength of the vortices increases with incidence.

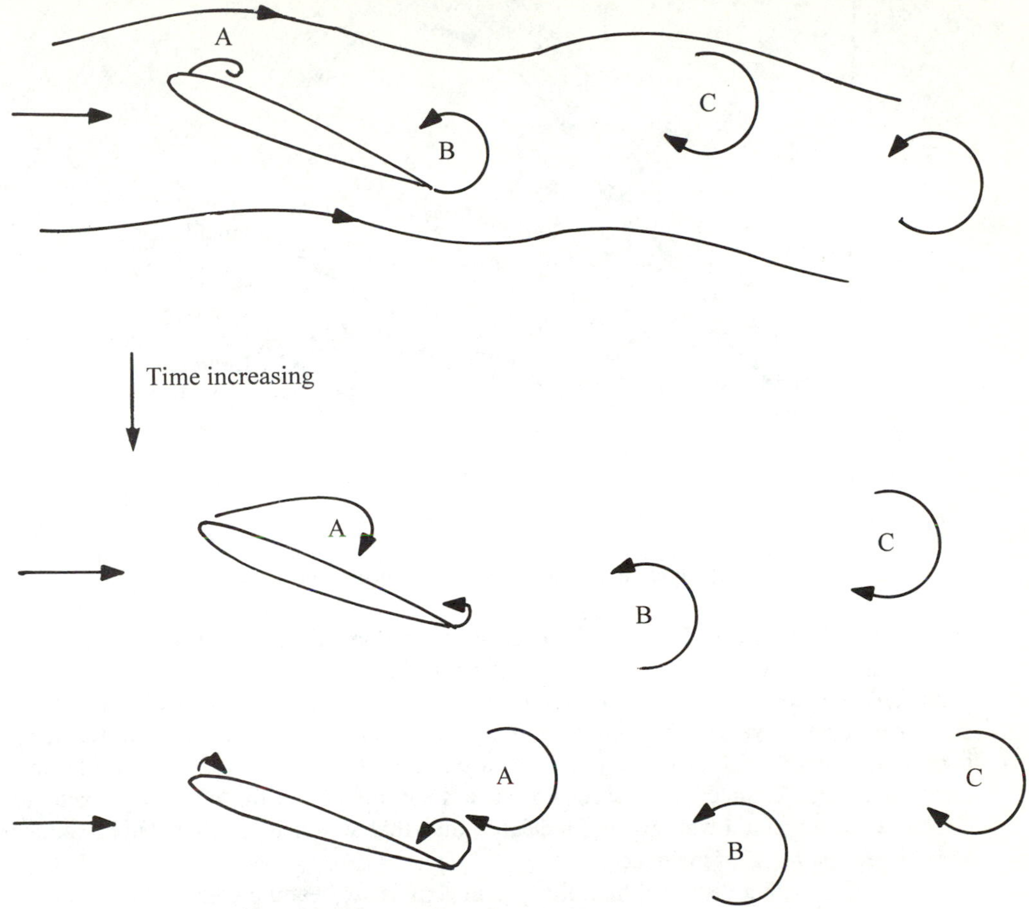

Fig. V.9. Strouhal vortex shedding.

(iv) A pulsating loading is applied to the aerofoil. The magnitude of this oscillatory component, which is proportional to the strength of the vortices, increases with angle of incidence; the amplitude of the oscillatory normal force coefficient is of the order of 0.1 at 90° angle of incidence. The frequency of the oscillatory loading at 90° angle of incidence is twice the Strouhal frequency because a peak response occurs with each shed vortex irrespective of its sign; however at 25° of incidence the dominant frequency of the oscillatory loading will be the Strouhal frequency.

The unsteady loading associated with flow breakdown is known as buffet; the response of the aerofoil to buffet is known as buffeting. This is a situation where unsteady aerodynamic loads are generated on a static aerofoil.

The lift variations with angle of incidence shown in Fig. V.5(iv) represent the (time averaged) lift variations as the angle of incidence is increased slowly. But when the angle

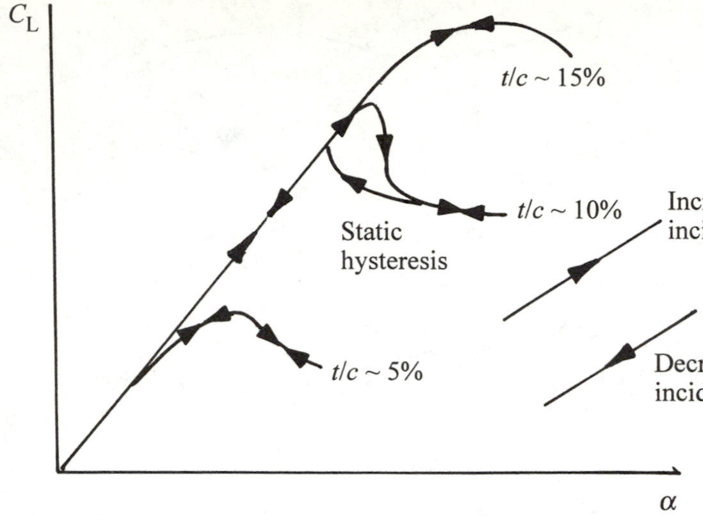

Fig. V.10. Effect of extremely slow variation of angle of incidence.

of incidence is decreased slowly from an initial value of 30°, say, the variation of decreasing lift does not necessarily retrace the variation of increasing lift, as sketched in Fig. V.10. For thick and thin aerofoils when decreasing the angle of incidence the lift usually retraces its values obtained when increasing the angle of incidence. But for those intermediate aerofoil thicknesses which feature a short bubble there is a (static) hysteresis; the return to attached flow, enclosing a short bubble, with decreasing angle of incidence occurs at a lower angle of incidence than that at which the short bubble bursts with increasing angle of incidence.

An aerofoil with a deployed high lift system comprising leading edge slat and trailing edge flap sustains the type of loading shown in Fig. V.11. There are regions of adverse pressure gradient on slat, aerofoil and flap. It is argued that the greatest maximum lift is obtained when the flows over the slat, aerofoil and flap all tend to separate simultaneously at the same angle of incidence. An aeroplane operates at an angle of incidence below that at which maximum lift occurs to give an adequate margin of safety for manoeuvring flight in turbulence. When landing, to obtain high drag, the flap is deployed at large angles and the flow separation must occur over the flap only. A useful reference is Smith (ref. V.6).

The variation of $C_{L\,max}$ with an increase in forward speed for an aerofoil with a trailing edge separation is sketched in Fig. V.12, taken from Wooton (ref. V.7). The initial increase in $C_{L\,max}$ at low free stream Mach numbers is a Reynolds number effect. The subsequent increase in Mach number tends to push the upper surface peak suction aft and hence increases the downstream pressure gradient, triggering an earlier separation.

$C_{L\,max}$ for an aerofoil with a short bubble separation is not significantly affected by low subsonic free stream Mach number. Although an increase in Mach number increases the upper surface pressures, the short bubble bursts at the same critical pressure gradient, which implies the same C_L.

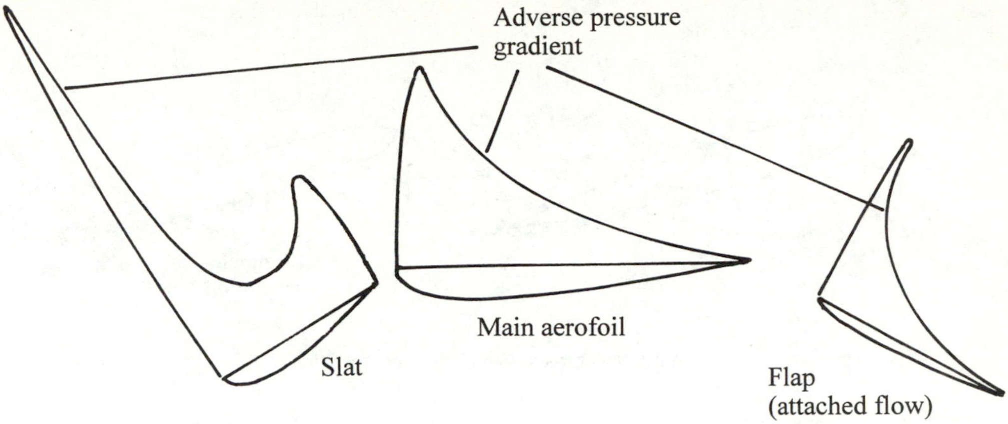

Fig. V.11. Pressure distribution on high lift system.

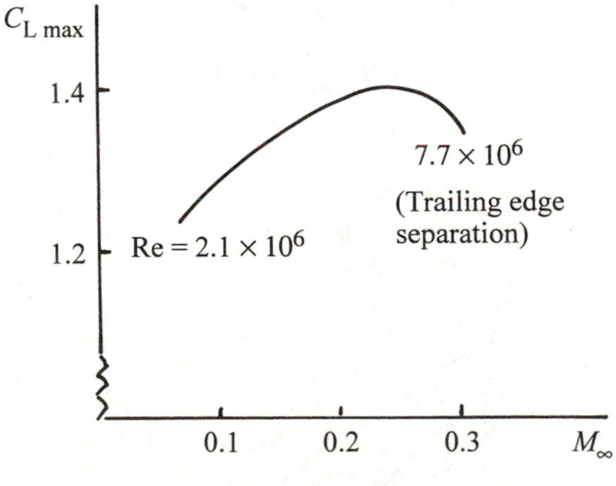

Fig. V.12. Effect of Mach number on $C_{L\,max}$.

Neither is $C_{L\,max}$ for an aerofoil with a long bubble separation seriously affected by low subsonic free stream Mach number. Mach number does not change the basic flow character.

At high subsonic free stream Mach numbers, as sketched in Fig. V.13, the flow over the upper surface expands continuously from subsonic ($M < 1.0$) to supersonic speeds ($M > 1.0$) up to the shock wave which compresses the flow back to subsonic speeds. Because there are no pressure gradients ahead of the shock no bubbles, either short or long, can be formed in the neighbourhood of the aerofoil nose. The abrupt adverse pressure increase across the shock wave acts on the boundary layer, and the boundary layer thickens and tends to separate. If the shock wave is weak any separation is followed by reattachment, forming a bubble. As the shock strength increases the bubble extends in

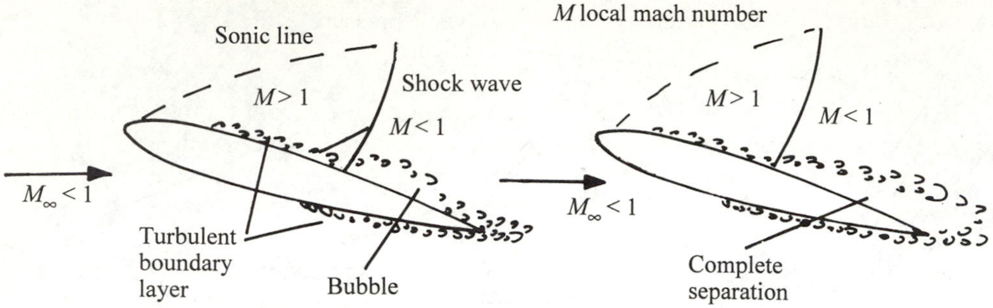

Fig. V.13. Shock wave–boundary layer separation.

length until it reaches the trailing edge and then there is complete separation with a thick wake and a trailing edge pressure divergence. Once separation is complete there is an interaction between the separation region and the outer flow which moves the shock wave forward, reducing its strength. Also with complete separation the intensity of the buffet associated with the Strouhal frequency is amplified by an unsteady interaction whereby the oscillations in the wake induce an unsteady oscillation in the position of the shock wave.

Fig. V.14 shows typical $C_{L\,max}$ and buffet boundaries for an aerofoil at high subsonic speeds.

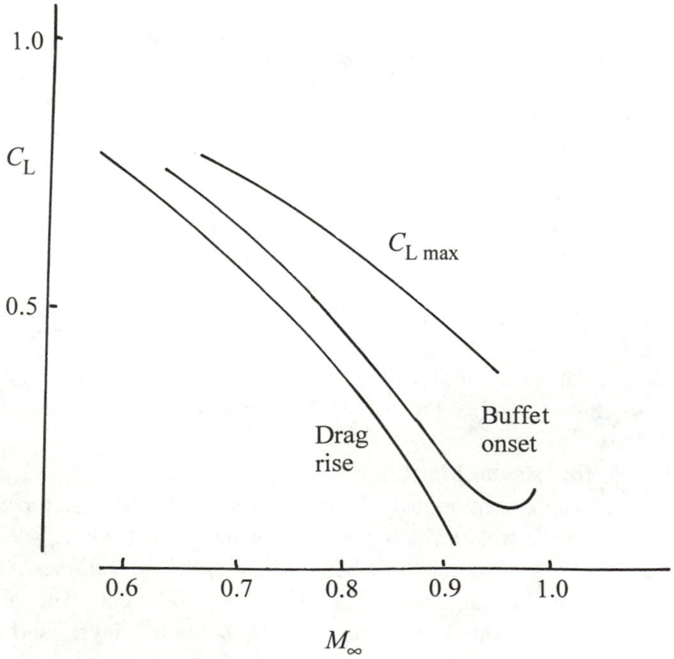

Fig. V.14. Transonic limits for aerofoil.

V.2.3 Dynamic two dimensional aerofoils

V.2.3.1 Unsteady attached flow

Consider, as shown in Fig. V.15(i), a symmetric aerofoil of chord c_w moving at a constant speed U of low Mach number at an angle of incidence, α, and pitch angle, $\theta\,(=\alpha)$; and then at time t equal to zero the aerofoil starts moving with an incremental time varying angle of incidence $\Delta\alpha\,(t)$ at a constant angle of pitch ($\theta=$ constant), a plunging motion.

In attached flow, when $\alpha(t)\ (=\alpha+\Delta\alpha(t))$ is below the static break angle of incidence (i.e. $\alpha(t)<\alpha_b$), the lift coefficient $C_L(\alpha(t),\ \theta|t)$ can be represented by the convolution integral

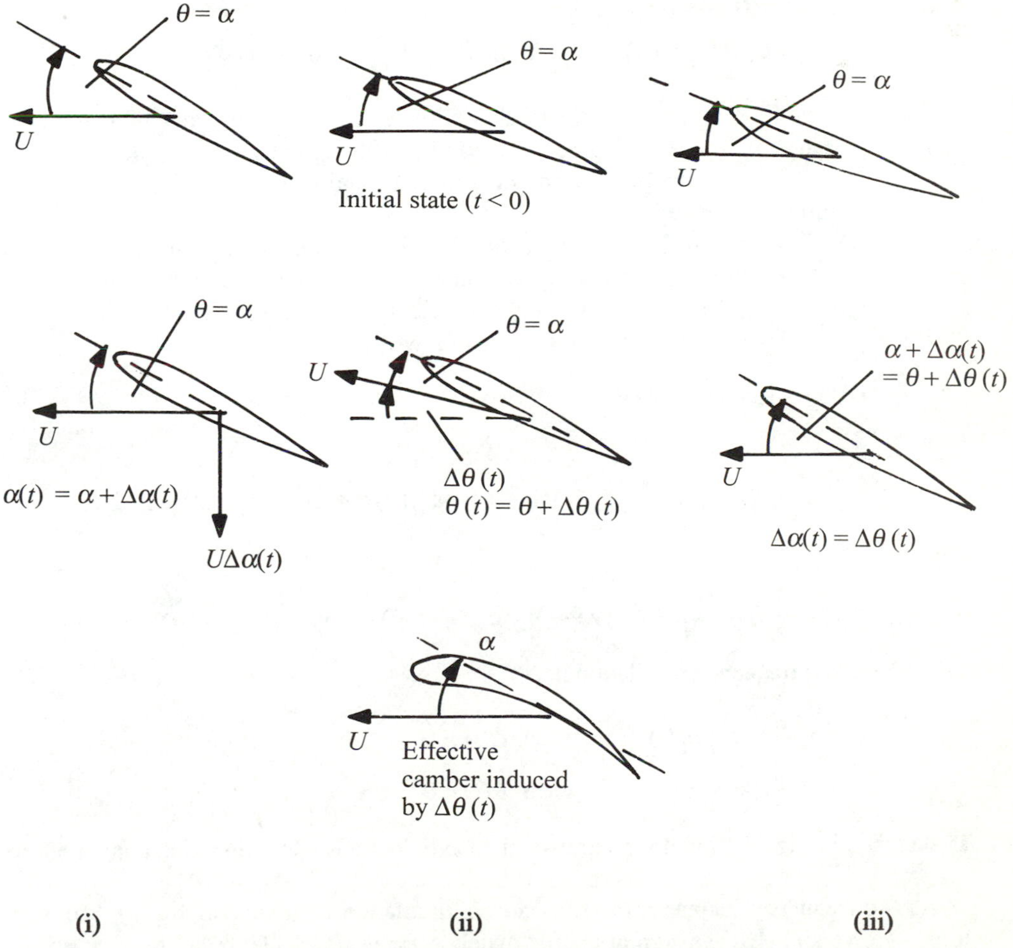

Fig. V.15. (i) Time variation in incidence (plunging motion). (ii) Time variation in 'pure' pitch. (iii) Time variation in 'weathercock' pitch.

$$C_L(\alpha + \Delta\alpha(t),\ \theta|t) = a_\alpha \alpha + \int_0^t C_L\big(H(t-\tau),\ 0|(t-\tau)\big),\ \Delta\alpha(\tau)\,\mathrm{d}\tau \qquad (\mathrm{V}.2.4)$$

where a_α is the static lift curve slope (for $\alpha < \alpha_b$), and $C_L(H(t), 0\,|\,t)$ is the incremental lift coefficient response to a unit step change in angle of incidence at a zero angle of pitch, as described in section III.3.3.

The above derivation of the incremental lift step response function $C_L(H(t)\,|\,t)$ neglects unsteady boundary layer effects. Hancock and Mabey (ref. V.8) argue that the unsteady boundary layer response to a step change in angle of incidence is faster than the circulation response, hence as a first approximation unsteady boundary layer effects can be neglected in eqn. (V.2.4).

For relatively slow motions, see sect. III.3.3, eqn. (V.2.4) can be expressed in the form

$$C_L(\alpha + \Delta\alpha(t),\ \theta|t)$$
$$= a_\alpha(\alpha + \Delta\alpha(t)) + a_{\dot\alpha}(t)\big(\Delta\dot\alpha(t)c_w/U\big), \qquad \text{for } \alpha(t) < \alpha_b. \qquad (\mathrm{V}.2.5)$$

In two dimensions it is not possible to approximate $a_{\dot\alpha}(t)$ by an order of magnitude constant because $a_{\dot\alpha}(t)$ is proportional to $(\ln t)$. Although the term $a_{\dot\alpha}(t)$ is large, $(\Delta\dot\alpha(t)c_w/U_{trim})$ is extremely small for slow motions and then $(a_{\dot\alpha}(t)(\Delta\dot\alpha(t)c_w/U))$ is small, as intuitively expected.

As explained in sect. III.3.3, the circulation lags behind the angle of incidence but the lift leads the circulation; the former lag is larger than the latter lead in slow motions so then there is a net lag between lift and angle of incidence, thus $a_{\dot\alpha}(t)$ is negative.

If the motion is a slow simple harmonic motion with

$$\alpha(t) = \alpha_m + \Delta\alpha_0 \sin\Omega t \qquad (\mathrm{V}.2.6)$$

then

$$C_L\big(\alpha(t)|t\big) = a_\alpha\alpha_m + \big[\tilde a_\alpha(v)\sin\Omega t + v\tilde a_{\dot\alpha}(v)\cos\Omega t\big]\,\Delta\alpha_0, \quad v = c_w\,\Omega/U$$

where

$$\tilde a_\alpha(v\to 0) = a_\alpha, \quad \tilde a_{\dot\alpha}(v\to 0) = a_{\dot\alpha}(t\to\infty) = -\infty, \quad \big(v\tilde a_{\dot\alpha}(v)\big)(v\to 0) \leqslant 0.$$

Thus, for a low frequency oscillation in $\alpha(t)$

$$\begin{aligned} C_L\big(\alpha(t)|t\big) &< a_\alpha\alpha(t) \qquad \text{when } \dot\alpha(t) > 0 \\ C_L\big(\alpha(t)|t\big) &> a_\alpha\alpha(t) \qquad \text{when } \dot\alpha(t) < 0 \end{aligned} \qquad (\mathrm{V}.2.7)$$

as sketched in Fig. V.16, with the arrows in an anticlockwise direction indicating a phase lag.

As the frequency increases the lift lead on circulation increases so $\tilde a_{\dot\alpha}(v)$ becomes less negative and changes sign at approximately $v\,(= 2k = \Omega c_w/U)$ equal to 0.65; above this frequency the arrows in Fig. V.16 go the other way around, indicating a lead, or phase advance.

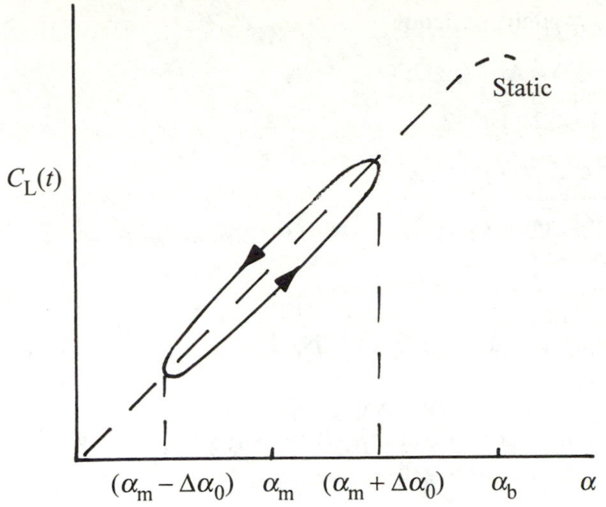

Fig. V.16. Oscillatory incidence in attached flow.

Next consider, as shown in Fig. V.15(ii), a symmetric aerofoil of chord c_w moving horizontally at a constant speed U of low Mach number at an angle of incidence, α, and pitch angle, $\theta\,(=\alpha)$, and then at time t equal to zero the aerofoil starts moving with an incremental time varying angle of pitch $\Delta\theta(t)$ at a constant angle of incidence (α = constant). This motion can be regarded as superimposing a time varying camber on an aerofoil at a constant angle of incidence. For a slow motion the lift coefficient can be expressed as

$$C_L\big(\alpha,\ \Delta\theta(t)\,|\,t\big) \simeq a_\alpha \alpha + a_q\big(q(t)c_w/U\big) + a_{\dot{q}}(t)\Big(\dot{q}(t)\big(c_w/U\big)^2\Big) \tag{V.2.8}$$

where $q(t) = \Delta\dot{\theta}(t)$, assuming that the flow remains attached. The derivative a_q is a constant and positive as implied by Fig. V.7. The derivative $a_{\dot{q}}(t)$ is again a function of time in two dimensions.

As a third motion consider, as shown in Fig. V.15(iii), a symmetric aerofoil of chord c_w moving horizontally at a constant speed U of low Mach number at an angle of incidence, α, and pitch angle, $\theta\,(=\alpha)$; and then at time t equal to zero the aerofoil starts moving with an incremental time varying weathercock pitch motion with $\Delta\alpha(t)$ equal to $\Delta\theta(t)$. Then, combining eqns. (V.2.5) and (V.2.8),

$$\begin{aligned} &C_L\big(\alpha+\Delta\alpha(t),\ \Delta\theta(t)=\Delta\alpha(t)\,|\,t\big) \\ &\quad = a_\alpha\big(\alpha+\Delta\alpha(t)\big) + \big(a_{\dot{\alpha}}(t)+a_q\big)\big(\Delta\dot{\alpha}(t)c_w/U\big) + a_{\dot{q}}(t)\Big(\Delta\ddot{\alpha}(t)\big(c_w/U\big)^2\Big). \end{aligned} \tag{V.2.9}$$

It is valid to replace $\Delta\alpha(t)$ by $\Delta\theta(t)$ in eqn. (V.2.9).

For a weathercock pitch oscillation

$$\Delta\alpha(t) = \Delta\theta(t) = \Delta\alpha_0 \sin \Omega t \tag{V.2.10}$$

about a mean α_{m}, from eqn. (V.2.9),

$$C_{\mathrm{L}}\left(\alpha + \Delta\alpha(t),\ \Delta\theta(t) = \Delta\alpha(t) \middle| t\right)$$
$$= a_\alpha \alpha_{\mathrm{m}}\left[\left(\tilde{a}_\alpha(\nu) - \nu^2 \tilde{a}_{\dot{q}}(\nu)\right)\sin\Omega t + \nu\left(\tilde{a}_{\dot{\alpha}}(\nu) + a_q(\nu)\right)\cos\Omega t\right]\Delta\alpha_0. \tag{V.2.11}$$

At low frequencies, with ν of the order of 0.05,

(i) in the in-phase term $(\nu^2 \tilde{a}_{\dot{q}}(\nu))$ is negligible compared with a_α,
(ii) in the out-of-phase term, because $\tilde{a}_{\dot{\alpha}}(\nu)$ is large and negative while a_q is positive, the term $(\tilde{a}_{\dot{\alpha}}(\nu) + a_q)$ is negative.

In an oscillatory weathercock pitch motion at a low frequency the variation of $C_{\mathrm{L}}(t)$ with $\Delta\alpha(t)$ resembles that of oscillatory angle of incidence as shown in Fig. V.16. As frequency increases $(\tilde{a}_{\dot{\alpha}}(\nu) + a_q)$ reduces in magnitude and becomes positive now at ν equal to 0.25, and then the arrows in Fig. V.16 are reversed.

The direction of the arrows in Fig. V.16 is a matter of some importance; a phase lag (i.e. anticlockwise arrows) implies positive damping while a phase advance (i.e. clockwise arrows) denotes negative damping. Nearly all of the work described in the literature refers to oscillatory weathercock motions with ν greater than 0.25, so the arrows are in the opposite sense to that shown in Fig. V.16, which means that the results are not directly applicable to aeroplane dynamics where ν is typically of the order of 0.05.

In flight dynamics the independent degrees of freedom are angle of incidence, $\alpha(t)$, and angle of pitch, $\theta(t)$, as defined and indicated in Figs. V.15(i) and (ii). A weathercock pitch motion is the particular motion when $\Delta\alpha(t)$ is equal to $\Delta\theta(t)$. In aeroelasticity and helicopter aerodynamics, the degrees of freedom are plunge, which is equivalent to change of angle of incidence, as shown in Fig. V.15(i), and 'pitch' which is, in flight dynamics terminology, a weathercock pitch motion. Thus 'pitch' in the literature can be ambiguous, and its context needs to be understood; this warning is mentioned because virtually all of the literature concerning the unsteady aerodynamics of two dimensional aerofoils is described in terms of plunge and (weathercock) pitch. In this book the term 'pitch', or 'pure pitch', refers to a change in θ with no change in α, and the term 'weathercock pitch' refers to a motion where the change in θ is equal to the change in α.

V.2.3.2 Unsteady separated flows

The next important question is: What happens when a dynamic motion proceeds into a regime of flow separation and flow breakdown?

Consider a motion involving $\Delta\alpha(t)$ only (i.e. $\Delta\theta(t)$ zero), where $\Delta\dot{\alpha}(t)$ is positive and constant, as $(\alpha + \Delta\alpha(t))$ approaches, and then exceeds, α_{b}, the static break angle of incidence.

First there is a delay in the onset of separation due to two effects.

(i) When $\Delta\dot{\alpha}(t)$ is positive, a normal pressure drag force acts on the aerofoil; conceptually the shed vorticity in the wake induces a downwash in the vicinity of the wing (as explained in sect. III.3.3) which rotates the lift vector, resulting in a drag component. This drag component acts when the lift reaches the static lift at which onset of separation occurs. Physically this normal pressure drag force manifests itself as a loss in leading edge suction pressures. A reduction in the leading edge suction pressures reduces the adverse pressure gradients around the aerofoil nose and delays the onset of separation.

(ii) As shown in Fig. V.17, the pressure gradient acting on the air in the boundary layer as it travels from A to B depends on $[p_B(t+\Delta t) - p_A(t)]$, where Δt is the time it takes for the boundary layer to travel from A to B. When $\Delta\dot{\alpha}(t)$ is positive, $p_B(t+\Delta t) < p_B(t)$, so the pressure gradient is relieved, further delaying the onset of separation.

The relative importance of these two factors to the delay in the onset of flow separation has yet to be explained.

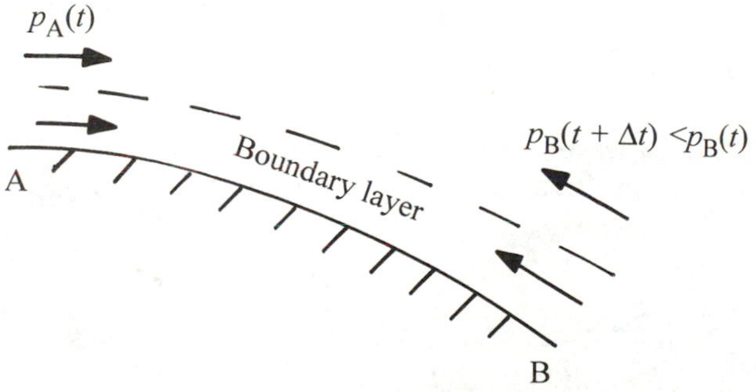

Fig. V.17. Unsteady adverse pressure gradient.

When onset of separation ultimately begins, the separating flow develops above the upper surface of the aerofoil, as shown in Fig. V.18. The shear layer from the separation rolls up and forms a vortex-type motion; usually the vortex forms over the front portion of the aerofoil but sometimes it can form further aft, depending on the aerofoil thickness, Reynolds number and the magnitude of $\dot{\alpha}(t)$. When the vortex reaches a certain size and intensity it moves downstream at about one third of the free stream velocity.

As the initial upper surface vortex moves downstream a vortex of opposite sign forms from the lower surface flow separation from the trailing edge. This mechanism is the start of the series of alternating vortices which constitute a fully developed wake, featuring the Strouhal frequency, indicated earlier in Fig. V.9.

One important result of a fully developed wake is that all of the wake vortices move downstream at approximately half the free stream velocity. Essentially the upper tier of clockwise separated vortices tend to slow down the lower tier of anticlockwise separated vortices, and *vice versa*, as sketched in Fig. V.19.

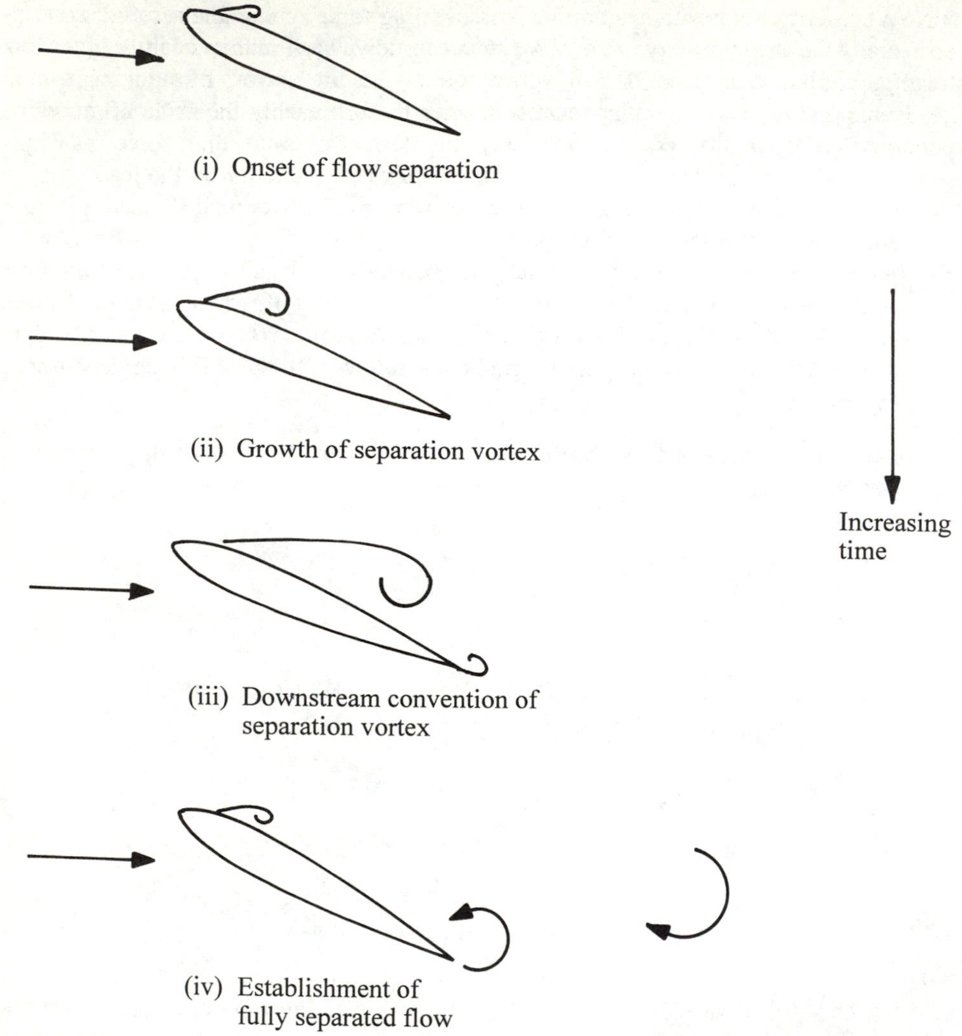

Fig. V.18. Development of unsteady flow separation.

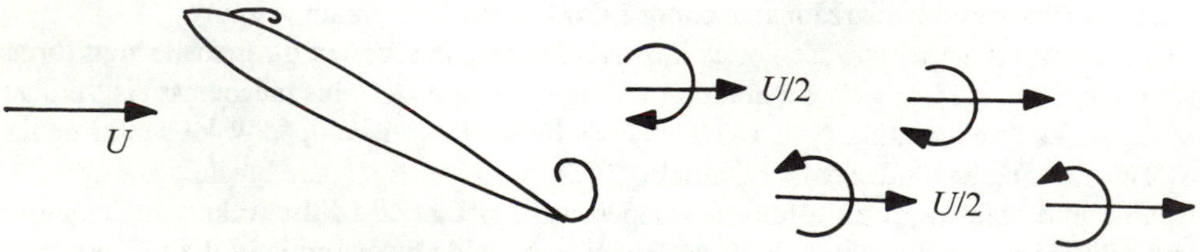

Fig. V.19. Downstream convection of shed vortices.

Now the lift continues to increase for $\alpha(t) > \alpha_b$ throughout the delay for the onset of separation and during the formation of the upper surface vortex and its convection downstream. Only when the upper surface vortex has moved downstream of the trailing edge (i.e. Fig. V.18(iii)) does the lift suddenly drop to approximately its static value corresponding to $\alpha(t)$; see Fig. V.20.

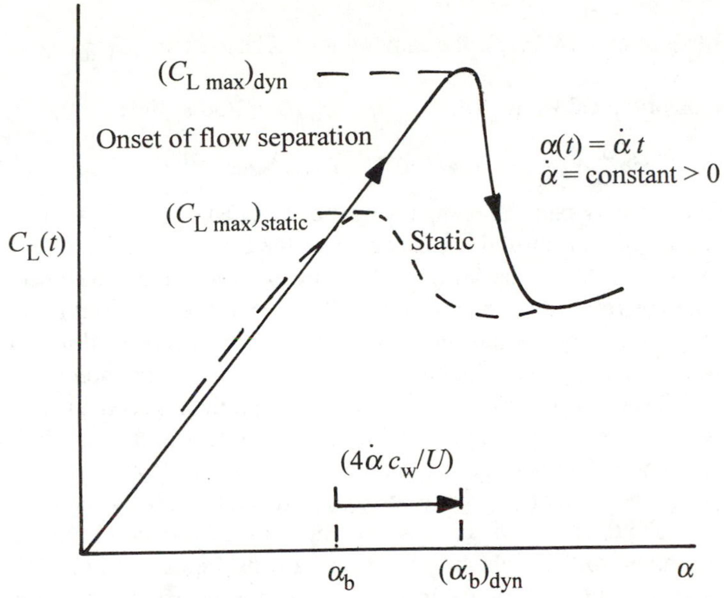

Fig. V.20. Dynamic overshoot with increasing incidence.

In broad terms:

(i) The increase in lift for $\alpha(t) > \alpha_b$ tends to follow an extrapolation of the attached flow $C_L \sim \alpha$ linear behaviour.
(ii) The time from when $\alpha(t)$ reaches α_b to the time when the dynamic break occurs and the lift drops is approximately $4\hat{t}$, where $\hat{t}$ is the unit of aerodynamic time (the time for the free stream to travel one chord $= c_w/U$), roughly a $2\hat{t}$ delay to the onset of separation and another $2\hat{t}$ delay for the formation and convection of the upper surface vortex.
(iii) The lift drops from $(C_{L\,max})_{dyn}$ to approximately the static lift associated with $\alpha(t)$ over a further time delay of $1\hat{t}$.

The overall delay time of $4\hat{t}$ to reach $(C_{L\,max})_{dyn}$ from the static break is a consistent value from experimental measurements and computations, see Kawashima & Yamasaki (ref. V.9), Francis & Keese (ref. V.10), Visbal (ref. V.11), Jumper *et al.* (ref. V.12), and Ericsson & Reding (ref. V.13).

Hence, as sketched in Fig. V.20, when $\dot{\alpha}(t) = \text{constant} > 0$, neglecting any $\ddot{\alpha}$ term,

$$C_L(t) \simeq a_\alpha \alpha(t) \qquad \text{for } \alpha(t) < \alpha_b + \dot{\alpha}(t)(4c_w/U)$$
$$\simeq C_L(\alpha(t))_{\text{static}} \qquad \text{for } \alpha(t) > \alpha_b + \dot{\alpha}(t)(5c_w/U). \tag{V.2.12}$$

Denoting $(\alpha_b)_{dyn} = \alpha_b + \dot{\alpha}(t)(4c_w/U)$, then for a symmetric aerofoil

$$(C_{L\,max})_{dyn} \simeq a_\alpha(\alpha_b)_{dyn}. \tag{V.2.13}$$

Note, according to eqn. (V.2.13), the important conclusion that $(C_{L\,max})_{dyn}$ increases with $\dot{\alpha}(t)$.

On substitution of typical values $\dot{\alpha}(t) = 15°/\text{s}$, $c_w/U = 1/30$ s, then

$$(\alpha_b)_{dyn} \simeq \alpha_b + 2°, \quad (C_{L\,max})_{dyn} \simeq (C_{L\,max})_{static} + 0.2. \tag{V.2.14}$$

Even at the relatively slow rates of change typical of aeroplane dynamics the increase in $C_{L\,max}$ of a two dimensional aerofoil is substantial, of the order of 20%.

Once $\alpha(t)$ exceeds $(\alpha_b)_{dyn}$ the wake can be regarded as fully developed, and the subsequent increasing $\alpha(t)$ does not fundamentally change the flow field. The mechanism for the unsteady lift, or normal force, is the same as in attached flow, namely the shedding of net vorticity into the wake as the circulation around the aerofoil increases, the convection of the net shed vorticity along the wake, and the induced downwash at the wing due to the wake net shed vorticity, leading to a lag effect in the circulation and in the lift. The rate of shedding net vorticity into the wake for slow motions is extremely low compared with the Strouhal frequency so there is no coupling between the alternative separation vortices and the net shed vorticity. But the net shed vorticity is convected with the Strouhal separation vortices which travel with half the free stream velocity. Hence, the lag effect in separated flow is twice the lag effect in attached flow. Thus, on the basis of the arguments in sect. III.3, for $\alpha(t) > (\alpha_b)_{dyn}$, as a crude approximation,

$$C_L(\alpha(t)|t) \simeq [C_L(\alpha(t))]_{\text{static}} + \left[(dC_L/d\alpha)_{\text{static}}\right|(\alpha = \alpha(t))$$
$$\times \left[2a_{\dot{\alpha}}\left(t - (t_b)_{dyn}\right)/a_\alpha\right]\left[\dot{\alpha}(t)c_w/U\right]\Big] \tag{V.2.15}$$

where $a_{\dot{\alpha}}(t)$ and a_α are the attached flow values. However, $(dC_L/d\alpha)_{static}$ is small at high angles of incidence, so the second term in eqn. (V.2.15) is probably negligible.

At higher angles of incidence with complete flow separations it is usual to switch to talking about the normal force, N, normal to the aerofoil chord, rather than the lift. And then

$$L(t) = N(t)\cos\alpha(t), \qquad D(t) = N(t)\sin\alpha(t). \tag{V.2.16}$$

This drag, a normal pressure drag, is virtually the total drag because the skin friction drag is relatively small.

As a further clarification: when referring to $L(t)$, $N(t)$ or $D(t)$ with a fully separated flow, it is implied that the high frequency loads associated with the Strouhal frequency have been filtered out.

Consider next the case when $\alpha(t)$ decreases, starting at a high angle of incidence with a fully developed wake. Although the delay mechanism of the onset of separation with

$\alpha(t)$ increasing has been researched and quantified in the literature, as described above, no corresponding attention appears to have been paid to the reattachment process. The following speculation is not inconsistent with experimental observation.

(i) The reasons listed for the delay in the onset of separation with $\alpha(t)$ increasing switch around and act to delay the onset of flow reattachment when $\alpha(t)$ is decreasing. And so a similar delay time of $2\hat{t}$ for the onset of reattachment may be assumed taken from when $\alpha(t)$ reaches α_b, the static break angle of incidence. If there is static hysteresis then it is necessary to refer to α_b+, the static break incidence at which flow separates when static α increases, and α_b-, the static break incidence at which flow reattaches when static α decreases.

(ii) Once the process of reattachment begins, the upper surface separation is swept downstream with the free stream velocity, so the flow becomes fully reattached in $1\hat{t}$ from the onset of reattachment.

The variation of lift incorporating the delay in the reattachment process is sketched in Fig. V.21.

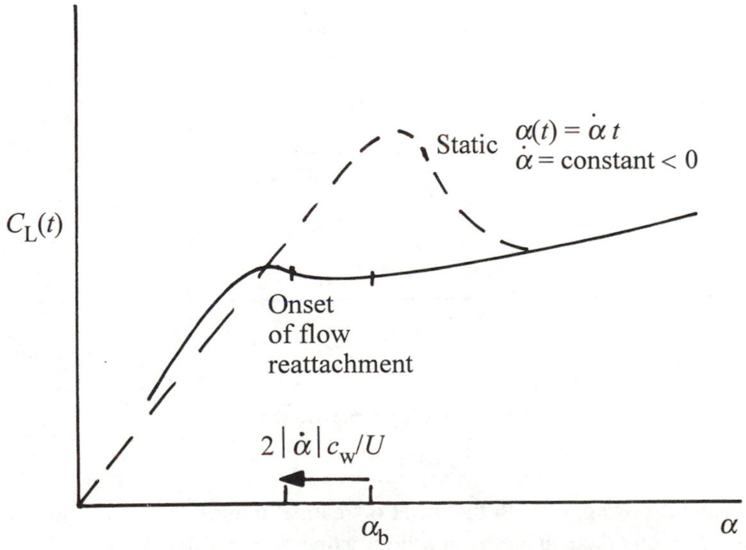

Fig. V.21. Dynamic overshoot with decreasing incidence.

The above descriptions have assumed that $\dot{\alpha}(t)$ is constant, either positive or negative; that is, $\ddot{\alpha}(t)$ zero.

Now consider a motion where the angle of incidence is increasing with $\alpha(t) > \alpha_b$, $\dot{\alpha}(t) > 0$ and $\ddot{\alpha}(t) < 0$, and denoting $\alpha(t_b) = \alpha_b$.

(i) If $\alpha(t)$ reaches α_{max} ($> \alpha_b$) in a time $t < t_b + 2\hat{t}$ the flow remains attached, the variation of $C_L(t)$ will be similar to that shown in Fig. V.16.

(ii) If $\alpha(t)$ reaches α_{max} ($> \alpha_b$), within the time $t + 2\hat{t} < t < t_b + 4\hat{t}$ then the onset of flow separation will begin. There are three possibilities:

(a) the onset of separation is followed sufficiently closely by the onset of reattachment that effectively the flow remains attached, see Fig. V.22(i);

(b) the onset of separation proceeds with the formation of the upper surface vortex, so initially the lift continues to rise (even though the angle of incidence is decreasing) before ultimately decreasing, as shown in Fig. V.22(ii);

(c) the separation, with the formation of the upper surface vortex, is virtually complete by α_{max}, and then fully developed separated flow occurs as the angle of incidence decreases, as shown in Fig. V.22(iii).

If $\dot{\alpha}(t_b + 4\hat{t}) > 0$, then the lift would behave as shown in Fig. V.20.

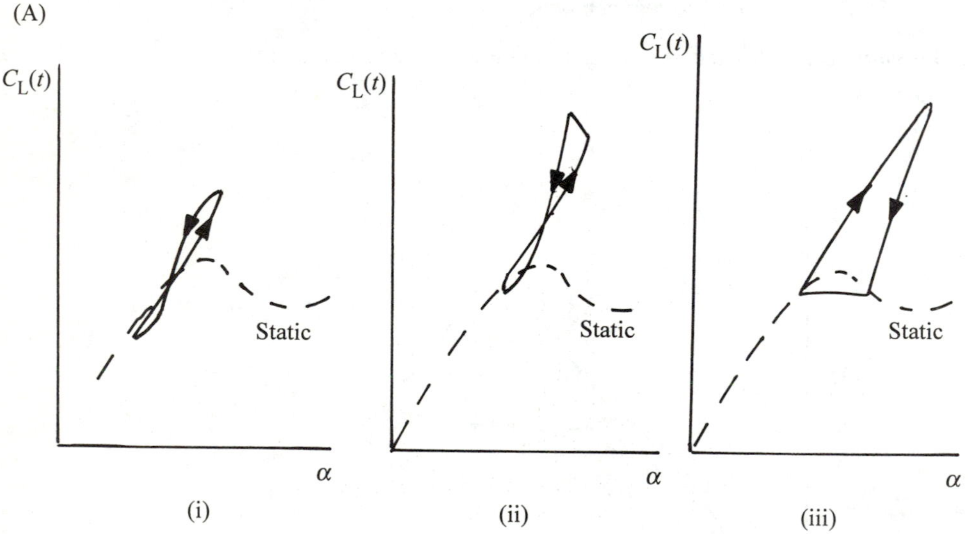

Fig. V.22. Types of dynamic overshoot.

Similar considerations apply with the onset of reattachment. Consider a motion where the angle of incidence is decreasing from a high value with a fully developed wake with $\ddot{\alpha}(t) > 0$ such that the flow is not reattached at α_{min}, when $\alpha(t)$ begins increasing. Usually the flow remains fully separated, although there is a possibility of partial reattachment followed immediately by flow separation.

To find out which type of flow would actually occur in practice it is necessary to turn to experiments on the particular aerofoil of interest, but remember that, unless the Reynolds number in the model experiment is comparable to the full scale Reynolds number, even the experimental results may be misleading. Contemporary computational aerodynamics based on the Navier–Stokes equations offers some insight (for example, ref. V.11) but at the time of writing such numerical solutions are limited in their Reynolds number range.

Consider next an oscillatory plunging motion where

$$\alpha(t) = \alpha_m + \Delta\alpha_0 \sin \Omega t \tag{V.2.17}$$

where α_m is the mean, below α_b, and $\Delta\alpha_0$ is a large amplitude of the order of 20°, at a low frequency. A measured periodic lift coefficient $C_L(t)$ would follow the type of variation shown in Fig. V.23.

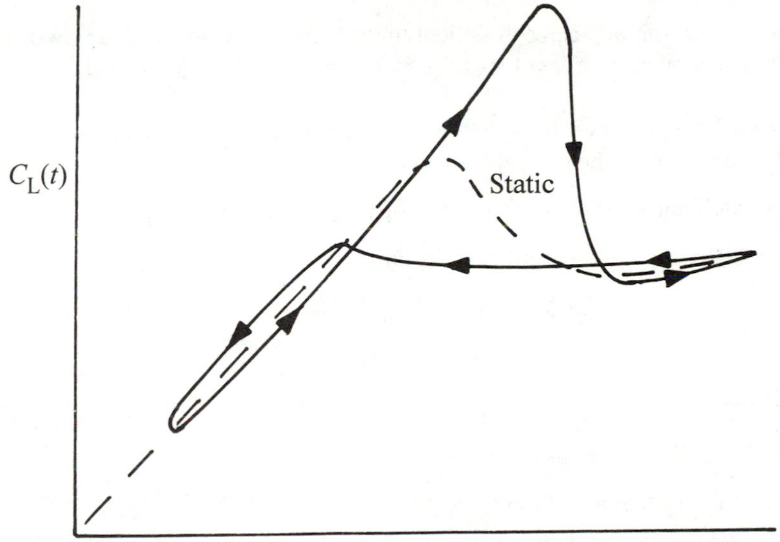

Fig. V.23. Typical lift variation for oscillatory incidence of large amplitude.

It is easier to measure the in-phase and out-of phase components of $C_L(t)$ than instantaneous $C_L(t)$, and then,

$$C_L(t) = C_{Lm} + \left[\tilde{a}_\alpha(\nu) \sin \Omega t + \nu \tilde{a}_{\dot{\alpha}}(\nu) \cos \Omega t\right] \Delta\alpha_0 \tag{V.2.18}$$

where

$$C_{Lm} = \int_0^1 C_L(t)\, d(\Omega t/2\pi), \qquad \tilde{a}_\alpha(\nu) = \int_0^1 C_L(t) \sin \Omega t\, d(\Omega t/2\pi)$$

$$\nu \tilde{a}_{\dot{\alpha}}(\nu) = \int_0^1 C_L(t) \cos \Omega t\, d(\Omega t/2\pi).$$

Eqn. (V.2.18) determines the components at the fundamental frequency; the lift response $C_L(t)$ shown in Fig. V.23 is far from simple harmonic so there are significant higher harmonic components.

Some important observations:

(i) If $\tilde{a}_\alpha$ and $\tilde{a}_{\dot{\alpha}}$ are the same order of magnitude, then at low frequencies, when $\nu\ (=\Omega c_w/U)$ is small, the $C_L(t)$ loop is shallow, similar to that shown in Fig. V.16. But the main loop in Fig. V.23 is wide which implies that $\tilde{a}_{\dot{\alpha}}$ is significantly greater than $\tilde{a}_\alpha$, 10 to 20 times greater.

(ii) From the direction of the arrows round the loops, and the dominance of the loop around separation and reattachment, $\tilde{a}_{\dot{\alpha}}$ is positive.

(iii) By inspection of Fig. V.23, C_{Lm} is greater than $(C_L(\alpha_m))_{static}$. The measured value of C_{Lm} is rarely quoted in the literature; unless C_{Lm} is measured and quoted together with $\tilde{a}_\alpha$ and $\tilde{a}_{\dot{\alpha}}$, application of the results is suspect.

The above description has been limited to the effects of changes in angle of incidence alone, but a general motion involves time variations in both angle of incidence and angle of pitch.

Now a positive pitch rate $q\ (=\dot{\theta}(t))$ induces an effective positive camber, as shown in Fig. V.15. According to the preamble to eqn. (III.3.29),

$$\text{a pitch rate } q \text{ induces a \% camber of } \left(qc_w/U_{trim}\right)/8. \tag{V.2.19}$$

Thus in a weathercock pitch oscillatory motion,

$$\begin{aligned} \Delta\alpha(t) = \Delta\theta(t) &= \Delta\alpha_0 \sin\Omega t \\ \text{maximum induced \% camber} &= \Delta\alpha_0\nu/8. \end{aligned} \tag{V.2.20}$$

With typical values of

$$\Delta\alpha_0 = 20^\circ\ (\simeq 0.3\ \text{rad}),\ \ \nu = 0.08,$$

$$\text{maximum camber} \simeq 0.3\%.$$

By reference to Fig. V.7, this small percentage camber hardly affects the static break angle of incidence, α_b, or the static $C_L(\alpha_b)$.

For slow motions, therefore, the effect of induced camber due to rate of pitch can be ignored on the dynamic onset of separation and on $(C_{L\,max})_{dyn}$. This conclusion does not apply at the higher frequencies associated with flutter; a frequency parameter of ν equal to 0.8 induces a 3% camber which, from Fig. V.7, lowers the break angle of incidence, increases the break lift coefficient, and changes the type of separation onset.

Once there is a fully developed wake it might be expected that the effect of the pitch rate would be negligible. It follows that the lift, or normal force, would be a function of incidence only.

Turning next to the pitching moment variation, for a static symmetric aerofoil the centre of pressure is approximately the 25% chord point (from the leading edge) in attached flow, moving aft to approximately the 35% chord point once fully developed separated flow is established, and moving further aft to approximately the 45% chord point at high angles of incidence.

With a motion involving a time varying increase in the angle of incidence with zero pitch the onset of separation is followed by the build-up of the upper surface vortex. As this vortex forms it induces a high suction underneath it on the aerofoil upper surface. Then, if this vortex forms initially in the leading edge region:

(i) the centre of pressure remains close to the 25% chord point as the upper surface vortex forms;

(ii) when the vortex is formed, it moves downstream along the chord upper surface and the associated suction moves with it so there is an aft shift of the centre of pressure with the most aft location, say around the 50% chord point, when the vortex reaches the trailing edge, remembering that this stage corresponds to $(C_{L\,max})_{dyn}$;

(iii) as the fully separated flow and wake develops, the centre of pressure moves forward to the 35% chord location;

(iv) as the angle of incidence continues to increase, the centre of pressure moves aft.

A typical time varying C_m about the 25% chord point, for an oscillatory angle of incidence, is sketched in Fig. V.24.

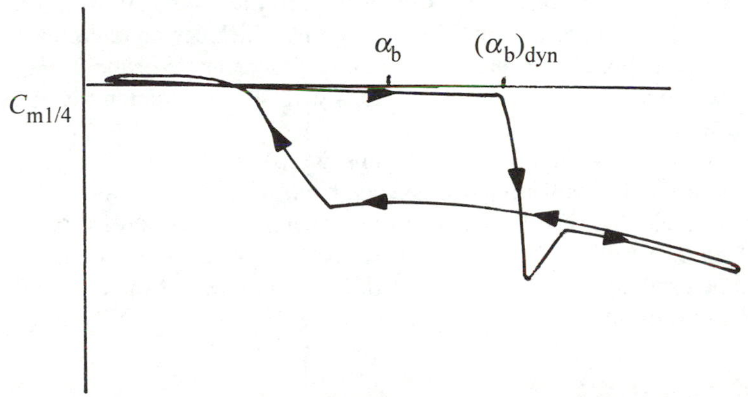

Fig. V.24. Typical pitching moment variation for oscillatory incidence of large amplitude.

The additional effect of rate of pitch may change the details of the pitching behaviour but not the fundamental trends.

As pointed out in the discussion of Fig. V.16, an anticlockwise loop indicates a lag, hence positive damping, while a clockwise loop indicates an advance, which implies negative damping. If the net effect of the C_m loops is a negative damping a single degree of weathercock oscillation in and out of separation, known as stall flutter, can occur.

It should be emphasized that the above outline of unsteady separation aerodynamics of two dimensional aerofoils is confined to the quasi-steady conditions associated with rigid aeroplane dynamics, in contrast to most of the literature which is concerned with higher frequency effects with applications to helicopter rotors and structural dynamic response. Furthermore, the outline here is necessarily elementary, omitting much of the detailed behaviour. For further reading see McCroskey (ref. V.14), and several papers in ref. V.15.

A final observation. The time taken for a dynamic overshoot is, from eqns. (V.2.12), of the order of $(5c_w/U_{trim})$, namely 0.2 s. From an aeroplane dynamics point of view the dynamic overshoot takes place in an extremely short time relative to aeroplane dynamic motions, hence it is not necessary to understand all of the fine detail of what happens during a dynamic overshoot; a broad quantitative framework is sufficient.

V.2.3.3 Unsteady two dimensional aerofoil characteristics at high subsonic speeds

In two dimensional attached flow the quasi-steady derivative $a_{\dot{\alpha}}(t)$ increases in magnitude substantially with increase in free stream Mach number, by a factor of 5 at Mach 0.8 compared with low Mach numbers, assuming shock free flow; it takes longer for information to pass upstream from the wake to the wing because the upstream speed of propagation of sound waves is $a_{at}(1 - M_\infty)$; see ref. V.8.

Once shock waves appear over the aerofoil surface there are additional delays, further increasing $a_{\dot{\alpha}}(t)$ by an additional factor of 2, according to ref. V.8, because the shock waves act as a barrier to the forward propagation of sound waves from the wake to the front of the aerofoil.

There is a large amount of data on oscillatory derivatives $\tilde{a}_\alpha(\nu)$ and $\tilde{a}_{\dot{\alpha}}(\nu)$, both computational and experimental (refs. V.16 and V.17), which can be interpolated down to small ν, for small amplitude oscillations about a low mean angle of incidence. This data includes shock wave–boundary layer interactions with flow separation aft of the foot of the shock wave.

Information on large amplitude oscillations is sparse. Experiments at low Mach numbers on aerofoils in oscillatory weathercock pitch with 10° amplitude about a mean angle of 15° indicate that shock waves can start appearing at free stream Mach numbers as low as Mach 0.35 (ref. V.18). As far as the author is aware there is no information on large amplitude oscillations of aerofoils at high Mach numbers of the order of Mach 0.8 to provide the type of information expressed in Fig. V.23.

V.2.4 Static finite wings

In this section some of the basic concepts relating to flow separation and flow breakdown on finite wings and their associated loadings are briefly summarized.

V.2.4.1 Static non-swept wings

Typical spanwise lift distributions

$$\left(L(y)/\tfrac{1}{2}\rho_{at}U^2\right)\left(= C_L(y)\, c(y)\right)$$

for a non-swept wing in attached flow at increasing angles of incidence below the break are shown in Fig. V.25(i).

To identify the spanwise location of the onset of flow separation the sectional lift coefficient distributions $C_L(y)$ should be plotted. For non-swept wings with small taper (i.e. with taper ratio $1 > \lambda > 0.75$) the $C_L(y)$ distribution will be similar to that shown in Fig. V.25(ii) with the maximum $C_L(y)$ in the central root region; with larger taper (i.e. $\lambda < 0.3$) and small chord lengths in the wing tip regions the maximum $C_L(y)$ occurs towards the wing tip regions, as shown in Fig. V.25(iii).

Flow separation occurs when, as angle of incidence is increased, the maximum $C_L(y)$ equals the sectional, two dimensional, (static) value of $C_{L\,max}$. This sectional value of $C_{L\,max}$ varies along the span depending on the thickness/chord ratio and camber. The

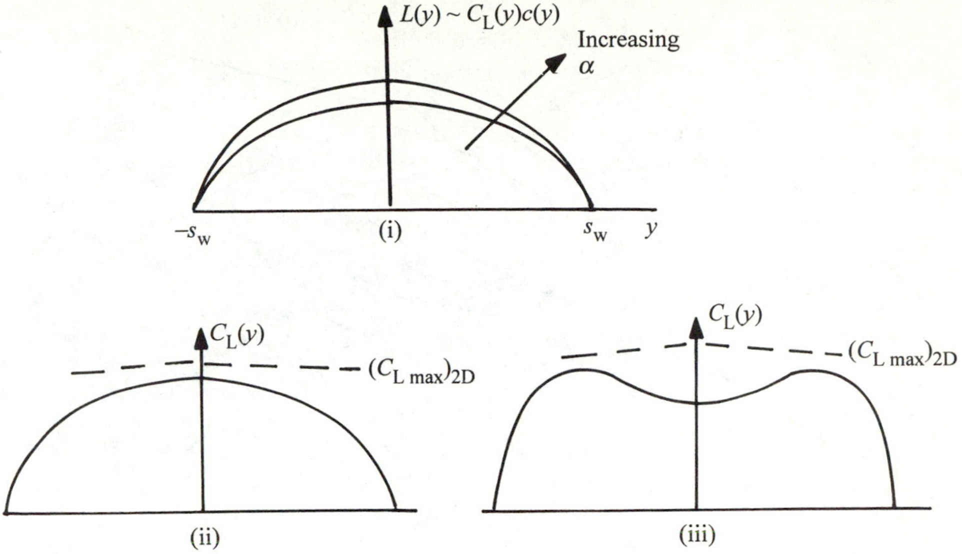

Fig. V.25. Onset of flow separation on non-swept wing.

onset of flow separation would probably occur inboard for the spanwise lift distribution given by Fig. V.25(ii) but outboard for the spanwise lift distribution given by Fig. V.25(iii).

The types of flow separation are similar to those described for two dimensional aerofoils—namely, trailing edge separation or short bubble burst. It is doubtful whether the sections would be so thin as to experience a long bubble type separation.

Flow separation on non-swept finite wings is not a process which develops gradually across the span with increase in angle of incidence; it occurs suddenly across a substantial part of the span. The onset of flow separation with a localized flow separation is a flow instability; the onset immediately spreads spanwise until a stable separated flow regime is established.

To understand this stable flow regime, refer to Fig. V.26. Suppose that the flow separates in the central region of the wing, resulting in the type of spanwise lift distribution shown. In the separated flow region there is an upper surface of (time average) shed vorticity from the leading edge, assuming a leading edge separation, with trailing vorticity at the side edge(s). And in the separated flow region there is a lower surface of equal and opposite (time average) shed vorticity from the trailing edge. At the edge of this lower surface of vorticity there is a trailing vorticity made up of two contributions, one from the shed vorticity from the separated flow region, the second from the change in spanwise loading on the wing from the attached to the separated flow regimes; both contributions act in the same direction. There is a net circulation of trailing vorticity, known as the part-span trailing vorticity.

The rotations of the part-span vorticity induce an upwash in the region of the centre span and a downwash in the region of the wing tips; the inboard upwash increases the inboard angle of incidence, reinforcing the flow separation, while the outboard

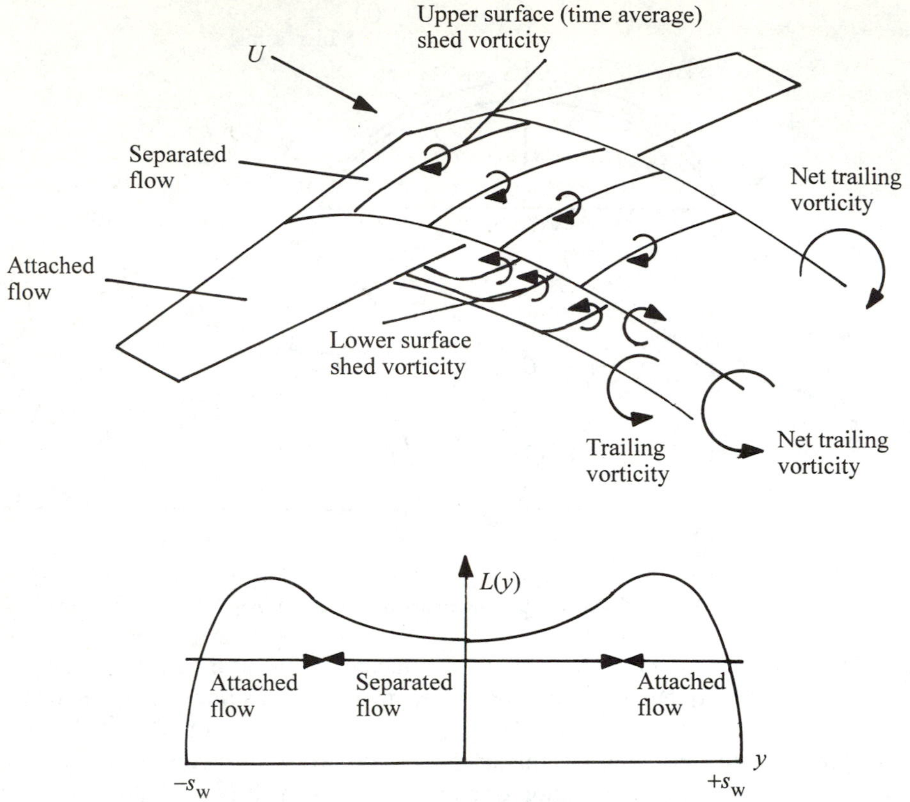

Fig. V.26. In-board flow separation on non-swept wing.

downwash decreases the outboard angle of incidence, maintaining attached flow. The strength of the part-span vorticity depends on the difference in the magnitude of the lift between the inboard separated region and the outboard attached flow region; this difference in the lift depends on the effective inboard angle of incidence and the effective outboard angle of incidence which, in turn, depend on the strength of the part-span vorticity. The matching of these interdependencies fixes the stable spanwise location of the part-span vortices at the onset of flow separation. These effects can be demonstrated mathematically by the application of non-linear lifting line theory (Shekar and Hancock, ref. V.19).

The same argument applies with an initial outboard onset of flow separation; the direction of the part-span trailing vorticity again stabilizes the inboard attached flow and the outboard separated flow.

Once the flow separation pattern is established at the break, the separated flow then expands gradually spanwise with further increase in angle of incidence.

At the break the centre of pressure of the lift in the separated region suddenly moves aft. For a non-swept wing the overall centre of pressure moves aft irrespective of whether the onset of separation is inboard or outboard, introducing a nose-down pitching moment.

With a non-swept wing the maximum lift and a nose-down pitch occur at the break. Such a combination of effects is beneficial from a flight dynamics point of view; if the aeroplane exceeds the break angle of incidence and suddenly loses some lift the aeroplane stalls, but the nose-down moment acts to rotate the aeroplane nose-down and to reduce the angle of incidence, thus restoring the aeroplane to an angle of incidence below the break. This behaviour denotes a natural stall recovery without the need for the pilot to intervene.

From the point of view of flight dynamics safety, the onset of flow separation should be inboard. With an outboard onset of flow separation there is the danger that in some flight conditions, or in some turbulence conditions, the outboard flow separation could occur on one wing only; the consequences would then be severe. A sudden loss of lift on one wing tip only imposes a sudden large rolling moment, causing a wing drop, and the aeroplane could spin out of control.

The required type of inboard flow separation characteristics can be obtained by appropriate sectional, plan form and washout design.

One point of interest: as far as the author is aware, there is no evidence that the Strouhal frequencies, which dominate the separated flow of two dimensional aerofoils, are present in the separated flow regions on three dimensional non-swept wings.

V.2.4.2 Static swept wings at low Mach numbers

For wings with sweep angles less than 20° the type of flow separation is similar to that described for the non-swept wing.

For planar wings (i.e. zero camber and wash-out) with sweep angle more than 20° and aspect ratio less than 8 the onset of flow separation occurs outboard in the wing tip regions due to two reasons. In attached flow:

(i) wing sweep decreases the chordwise pressure gradients in the wing root region and increases the streamwise pressure gradients in the wing tip regions (see Fig. III.8(ii));

(ii) there is an outward spanwise drift within the three dimensional boundary layers on the wing upper surface, creating thicker boundary layers on the upper surface in the wing tip regions; thicker boundary layers are more prone to flow separation.

The type of flow field for a swept case at the break differs from the type of flow separation described above for the non-swept wing. In the swept case the shed vorticity from the wing leading edge in the tip separated region veers into the stream direction above the wing surface, giving a flow field as sketched in Fig. V.27(i). The corresponding pattern of streamlines on the wing upper surface is sketched in Fig. V.27(ii). The vorticity at the edge of the separating vorticity above the wing upper surface induces a flow underneath it towards the wing tips; this flow is then swept forward due to the shed vorticity closer to the leading edge, and finally it moves inboard along the leading edge because the pressure is lower in the inboard unseparated region than in the outboard separated region.

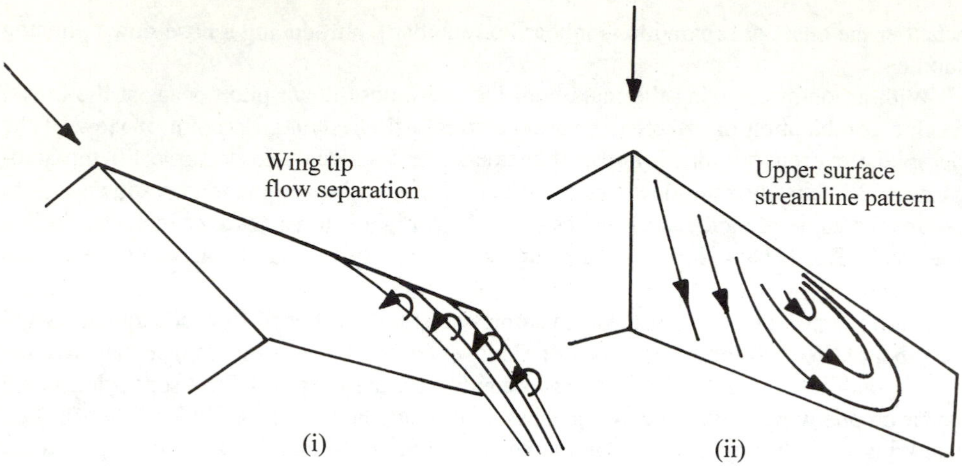

Fig. V.27. Swept wing flow separation (medium sweep).

Comparing Figs. V.26(ii) and V.27(i) it is observed that the edge vorticities from the upper surface flow separation from the wing leading edge for non-swept and swept wings are in opposite directions.

Surprisingly at the break, at the onset of flow separation and flow breakdown, there is little change in lift in the wing tip region of a swept wing, usually merely a redistribution of the chordwise loading distribution in that region, with little change in the lift inboard, hence the overall lift and its centre of pressure are almost unaffected.

From observation of experimental data the onset of flow separation on a swept wing, like the non-swept wing, is an unstable flow regime which suddenly expands inboard across a substantial part of the wing semi-span, about 30%, to establish a stable separated flow regime. The reason for the establishment of the stable separated region is probably broadly the same for the swept wing as for the non-swept wing, namely an increase in the effective incidence in the outboard separated region and decrease of effective incidence in the inboard attached flow region due to the part-span vorticity. However, it would appear that the part-span vorticity for the non-swept wing arises primarily from the trailing edge, according to Fig. V.26, whereas the part-span vorticity for a swept wing arises primarily from the leading edge, according to Fig. V.27.

With increase in angle of incidence above the break, the region of separation extends inboard gradually, the inboard lift in the unseparated region continues to rise whereas lift in the separated tip regions remains more or less constant independent of the angle of incidence. Thus

(i) the overall lift continues to increase, and maximum lift is no longer associated with the break;

(ii) the overall centre of pressure moves forward; this forward displacement of the centre of pressure gives an increasing incremental nose-up pitching moment with increase of angle of incidence.

At higher angles of incidence there is a more rapid progression of the separated flow inboard across the span and the lift attains a maximum value.

A set of results are shown in Fig. V.28, taken from Furlong and McHugh (ref. V.20). The planar wing of aspect ratio 8, sweep 45°, and taper ratio 0.5 has a break at angle of incidence of 12°. Note that below the break the pitching moment about the aerodynamic centre is small and constant, the lift is linear with respect to angle of incidence, and the drag increases with lift due to the vortex drag. With increasing angle of incidence above the break the pitching moment becomes increasingly positive, there is a large increase in drag, and the lift continues to rise almost linearly but with a reduced lift curve slope compared with the lift curve slope below the break. The maximum lift occurs at 24° angle of incidence.

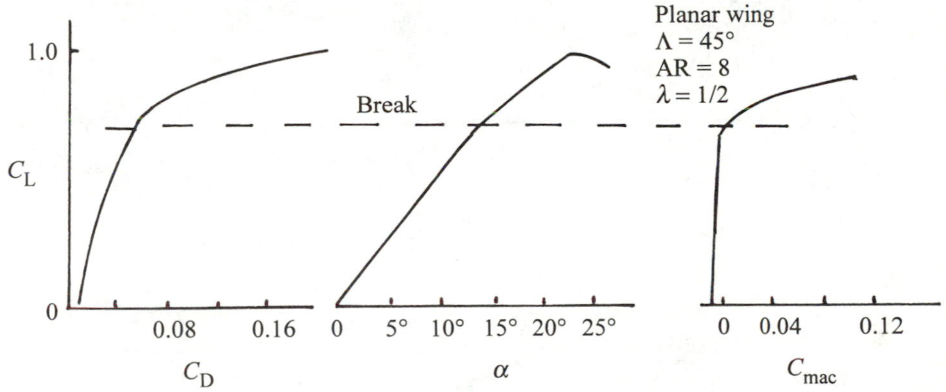

Fig. V.28. Swept wing at high angles of incidence.

The flight behaviour resulting from the nose-up pitching moment above the break is known as pitch-up. Following the break there is a small nose-up pitching moment which slowly rotates the aeroplane nose-up, but as the angle of incidence builds up the nose-up pitching moment increases so the aeroplane rotates nose-up more rapidly; a highly non-linear unstable flight condition.

The onset of pitch-up depends on aspect ratio and wing sweep; as aspect ratio increases the sweep angle for pitch-up decreases, as illustrated in Fig. V.29 (ref. V.21).

When the sweep angle exceeds 50° the form of the wing tip vorticity at the break changes. As sketched in Fig. V.30, the separating vorticity from the leading edge forms into a concentrated vortex, inducing a high suction underneath it which increases the lift in the wing tip region, resulting in a pitch-down at the break. With increase in angle of incidence above the break this concentrated vortex breaks down, as explained later; the flow pattern reverts to that shown in Fig. V.27, and then there is a sudden drop of wing tip lift, giving a sudden dramatic pitch-up.

The effects of sweep on the pitching moment characteristics for a thin wing of aspect ratio 4 and taper ratio 0.6 are shown in Fig. V.31. For sweep angles of 0° and 30° there is a pitch-down following the break (i.e. C_m decreases with increase in C_L). For the sweep angle of 45° there is a pitch-up following the break. For the sweep angle of 60° there is a small initial pitch-up followed by a severe pitch-down followed by a severe pitch-up. These trends are consistent with the above explanations.

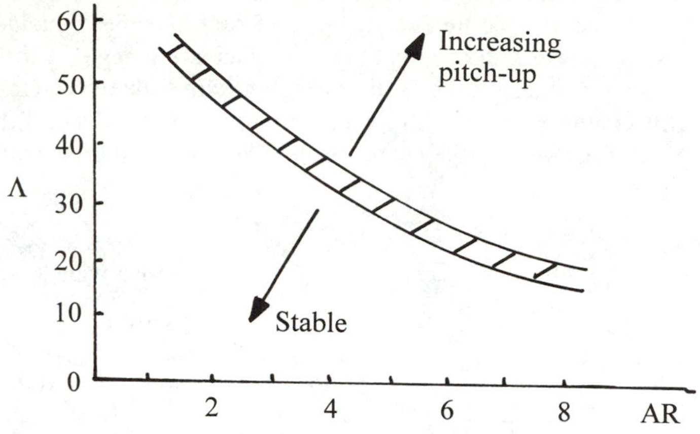

Fig. V.29. Pitch-up criterion.

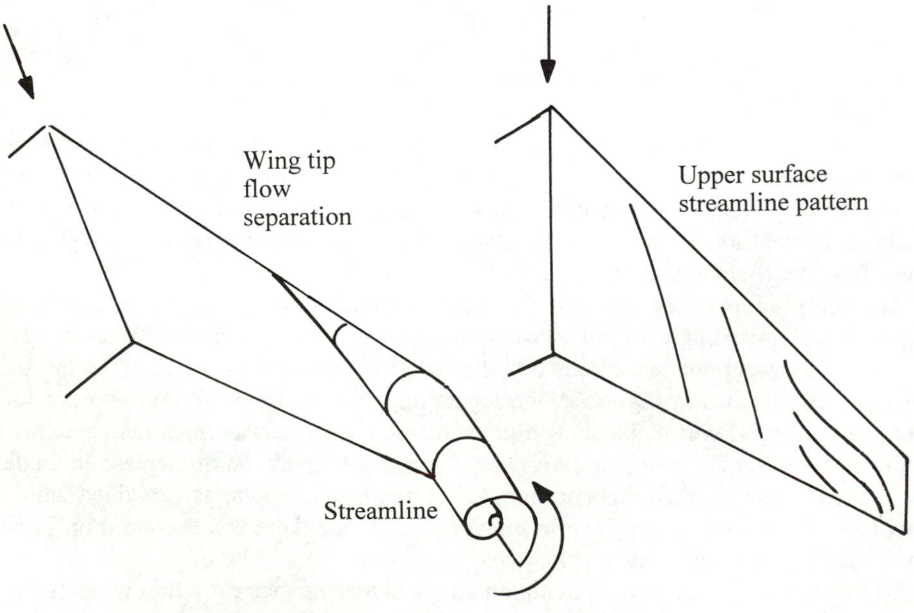

Fig. V.30. Swept wing flow separation (high sweep).

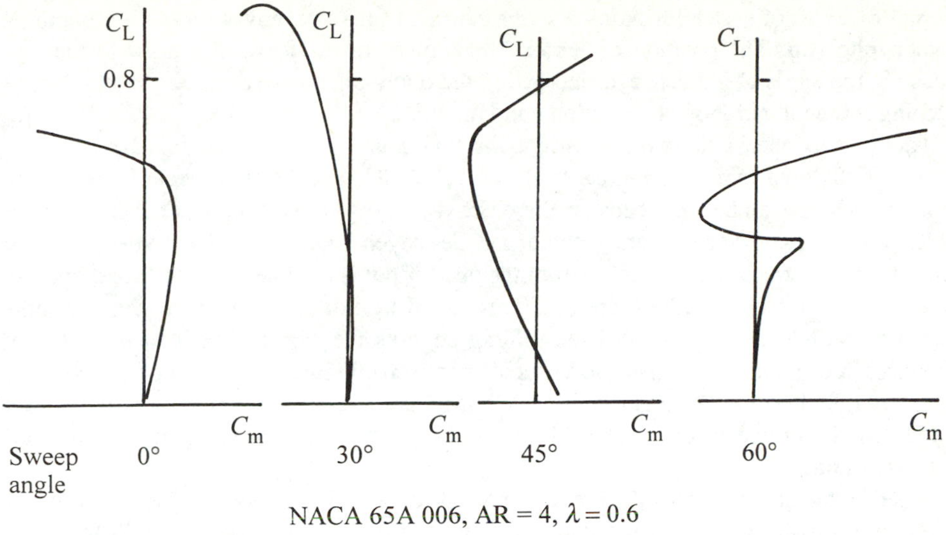

Fig. V.31. Variation in break characteristics with wing sweep angle.

V.2.4.3 Delta wings

For delta wings of thin section with high angles of leading edge sweep, above 60°, the flow tends to separate from the entire leading edge from low angles of incidence, forming a concentrated primary vortex, as sketched in Fig. V.32. This primary vortex induces peak suctions underneath it and a significant crossflow. As this crossflow moves towards the leading edge away from the peak suctions it slows down, creating an adverse pressure gradient which is sufficiently large to induce a secondary separation, forming a secondary, smaller, vortex in the opposite sense to that of the primary vortex.

With separation from the whole leading edge the main force on the wing is the force normal to the wing plan form; the lift and drag are then the components of the normal force at right angles and parallel to the relative airstream.

The streamline patterns on the wing upper surface are sketched in Fig. V.32. Inboard of the so-called reattachment line, the primary vortex has little effect so the streamlines lie in the stream direction. The primary vortices tend to dominate the flow underneath them. Outboard of the influence of the primary vortex the upper surface streamlines come up to the separation line induced by the secondary vortex and then proceed downstream. For further diagrams, and an extensive bibliography, see Rom (ref. V.22).

Both the primary and secondary vortices increase in strength and move inboard with increase in angle of incidence up to the order of 30°. Up to this angle of incidence the normal force increase with angle of incidence is mildly non-linear, as shown in conditions *a* and *b* in Fig. V.32. The location of the centre of pressure ($= C_m/C_N$, relative to the axis of C_m) lies approximately at 60% of the root chord from the wing apex, moving slightly forward with increase in lift between *a* and *b*.

At a critical angle of incidence the concentrated primary vortices burst slightly ahead of the wing trailing edge into a larger region of swirling turbulent flow. The high suctions on the wing upper surface aft of the vortex breakdown are then lost, there is a loss of aft normal force aft of vortex breakdown so the centre of pressure moves forward, inducing a sudden pitch-up. The position of vortex breakdown moves forward with a further increase in the angle of incidence, exacerbating the pitch-up. These trends are shown by the pitching moment variation at condition *c* in Fig. V.32.

There have been extensive investigations and many explanations for the cause of vortex breakdown (see Lambourne & Bryer, ref. V.23, and Escudier, ref. V.24); these explanations may all be valid because there is a wide range of conditions and situations in which concentrated vortices are created and destroyed. For the primary vortex over a delta wing the circulation builds up from the apex, flow is spiralled into the core, and the axial velocity along the core increases. This rolled-up vortex meets a growing adverse pressure gradient in the region of the trailing edge as the angle of incidence increases. This pressure gradient can disperse vorticity transversely away from its core to such an extent that it becomes unstable and the concentrated vortex breaks down (there is a fundamental theorem that a swirling flow is only stable as long as the vorticity does not decrease radially).

It is of interest to note that the break conditions on a highly swept wing are completely different to those on a delta wing with the same angle of sweep (see Fig. V.33 from ref. V.4). Perhaps the reader can explain why.

V.2.4.4 Finite wings at high speeds

At higher Mach numbers at transonic through to supersonic speeds upper surface shock wave patterns evolve as shown in Fig. V.34 (see Monnerie, ref. V.25). Flow separations tend to be induced aft of the outboard shocks in the tip region as incidence increases, with a localized loss in lift, a gentle pitch-up and an increase in drag.

Typical variations of C_L, C_m and $C_{D0}(= C_D - C_L^2/\pi\,\mathrm{AR})$ with α for a wing at high subsonic Mach number are shown in Fig. V.35. Note that the drag 'break' associated with the formation of shock waves occurs before the lift and moment breaks.

V.2.5 Stall delay devices

To delay pitch-up to higher angles of incidence many types of stall control devices, or fixes, have been used.

V.2.5.1 Fences

A fence extending over a full chord, situated about 50% semi-span, as shown in Fig. V.36, acts as a barrier creating effectively two wings of small aspect ratio, delaying the onset of pitch-up on each sub-wing, according to Fig. V.29. Fig. V.36, taken from ref. V.20, shows the beneficial effect of a full chord fence on the pitching moment; at a critical angle of incidence the separated flow 'jumps' the fence and the consequential pitch-up is especially severe.

A fence need not extend over the full chord; a fence extending over the front 25% of the chord is equally effective (Queijo *et al.*, ref. V.26). The reason is that such a fence generates, on its inboard side, high pressure gradients close to the wing leading edge, inducing a localized leading edge separation which forms into a concentrated streamwise

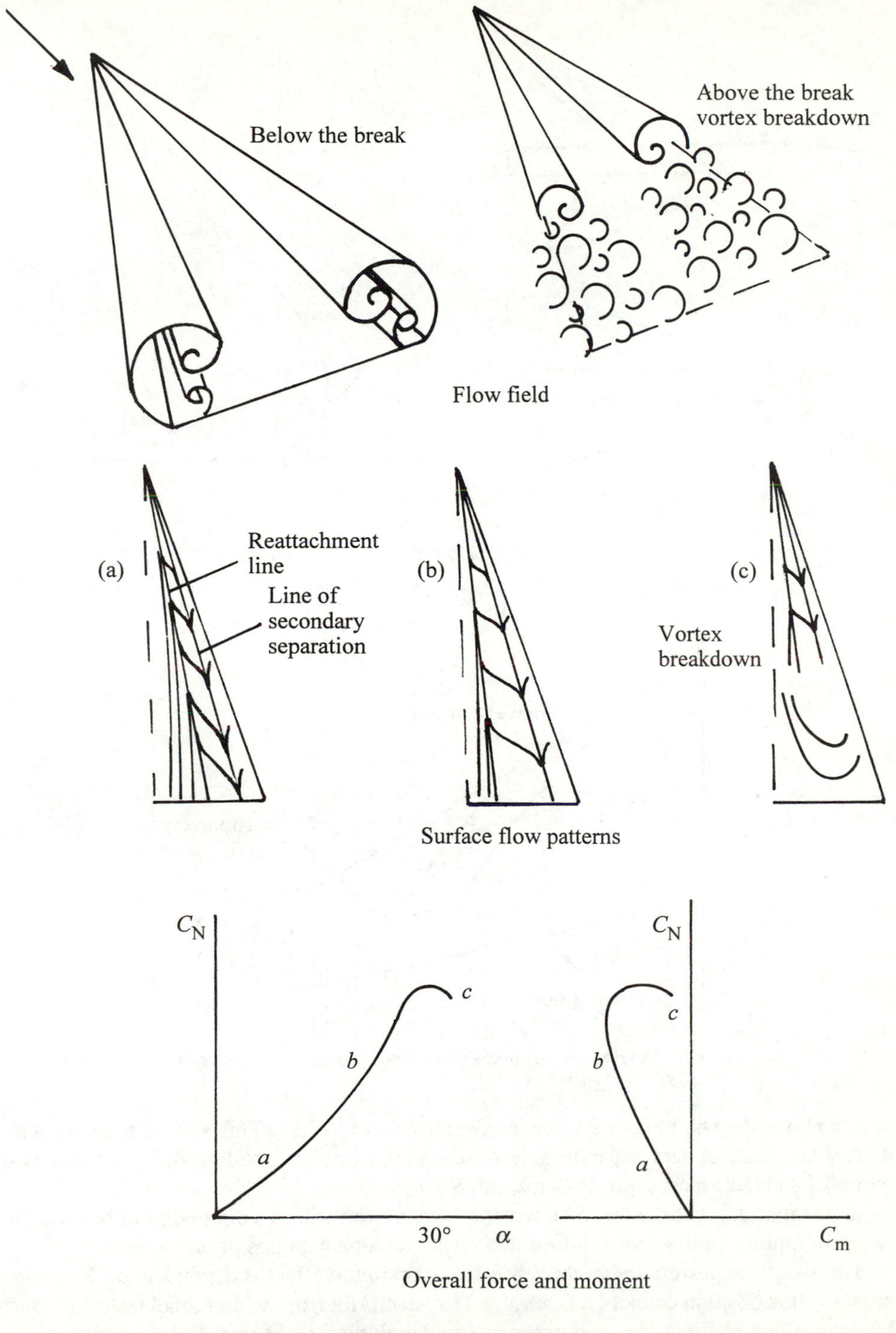

Fig. V.32. Characteristic of delta wing.

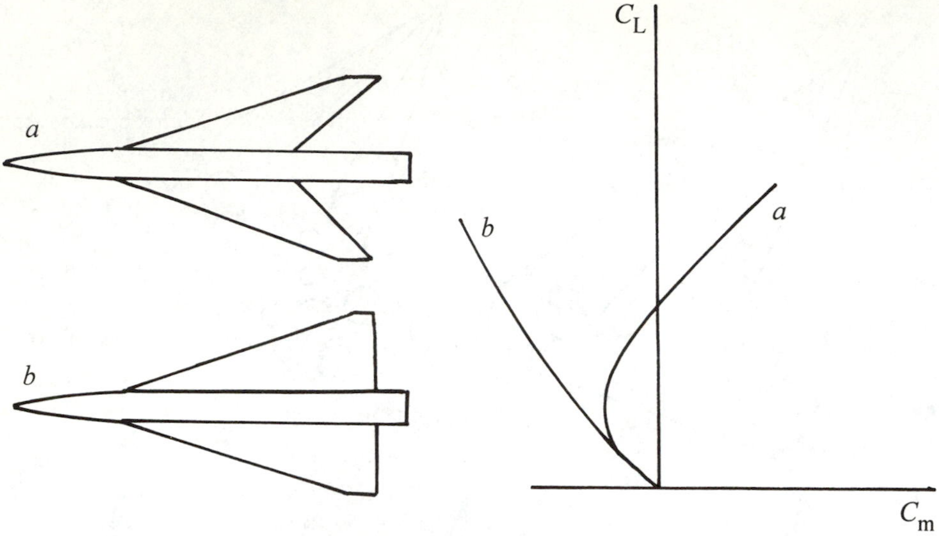

Fig. V.33. Effect of plan form on break characteristics.

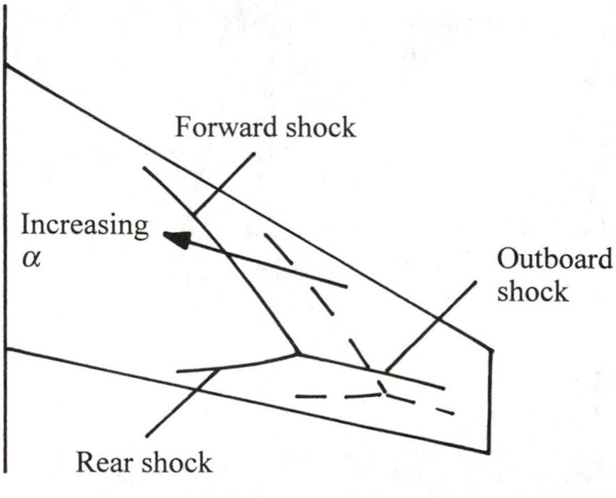

Fig. V.34. Development of upper surface shock pattern at transonic speeds.

vortex above the wing upper surface, as sketched in Fig. V.37. This vortex, together with its associated secondary separation, now acts as the barrier, dividing the wing into two wings of smaller aspect ratio (Pollatos, ref. V.27).

It is important that the fence be wrapped around the wing leading edge to beyond the stagnation point on the lower surface of the wing at higher angles of incidence.

The spanwise positioning of the fence for an optimum effect is dependent on Reynolds number; this position cannot be determined satisfactorily from wind tunnel tests and must be determined in flight tests, an expensive undertaking. Foster (ref. V.28) recalls that in

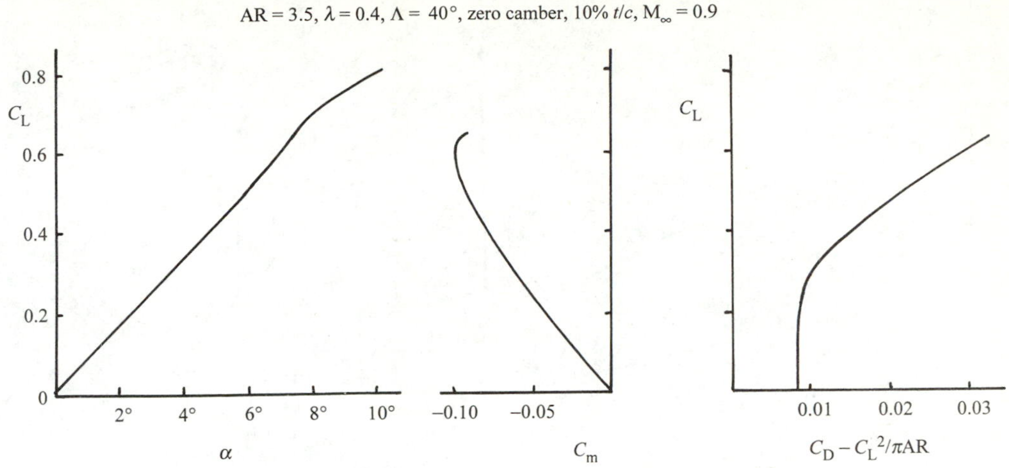

Fig. V.35. Wing break characteristics at high subsonic speeds.

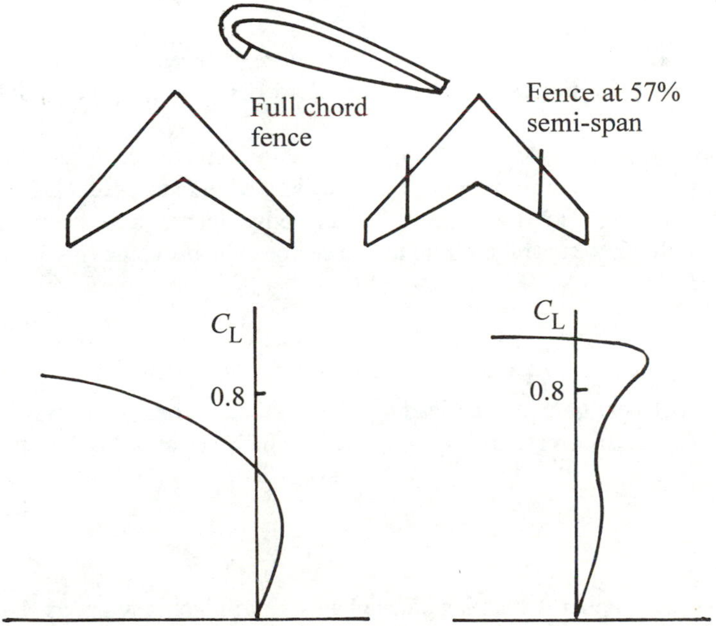

Fig. V.36. Effect of full chord fence.

the development stage of the Trident aeroplane, wind tunnel tests predicted the onset of flow breakdown outboard of the fence whereas in flight tests the onset of flow breakdown occurred inboard of the fence.

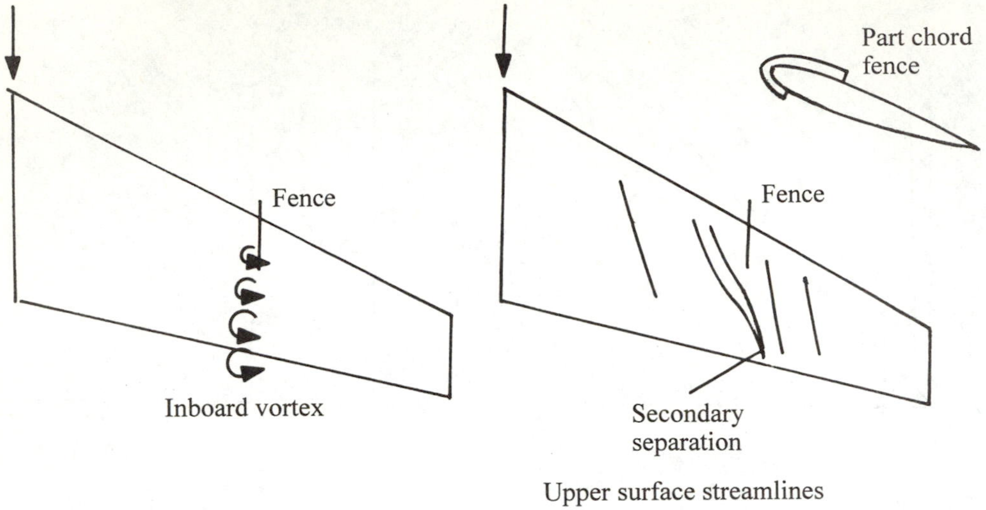

Fig. V.37. Flow behaviour induced by part-chord fence.

Aft fences have been tried to control shock wave induced separations (ref. V.29). Fences have also been suggested for application to delta wings (Rao & Johnson, ref. V.30).

Fences have their disadvantages. Drag penalties are created in take-off and cruise. Premature shock waves can form inboard of a leading edge fence, reducing the drag rise Mach number. At high subsonic speeds leading edge fences lose their effectiveness mainly because the flow separation from the fence does not affect the shock-wave boundary layer interactions.

V.2.5.2 Leading edge devices

Leading edge notches, or part-span leading edge outboard slats, or part-span outboard leading edge droop, all create part-span vortices, which act as a barrier similar to the fence vortex.

V.2.5.3 Strakes

A strake is a small slender delta wing situated ahead of the main wing, as shown in Fig. V.38. At higher angles of incidence the leading edge vortex from the strake passes over the main wing, inducing additional lift through high upper surface suctions, while a vortex from the kink appears to restrain any outboard separation. As sketched in Fig. V.38, pitch-up is delayed and higher lifts are obtained.

At the ultimate break condition of the strake–wing combination small changes in strake shape can lead to significant differences in behaviour, inducing either a destabilizing pitch-up or a stabilizing pitch-down (see Bradley, ref. III.12).

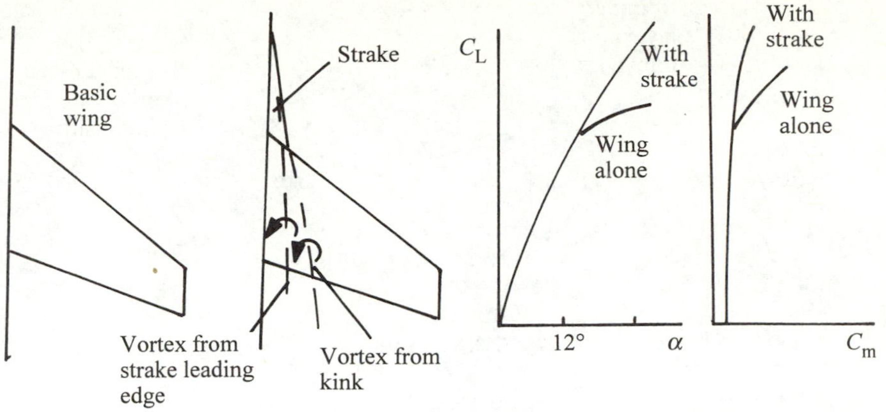

Fig. V.38. Effect of strake.

V.2.5.4 Engine nacelle

Underwing engines can strongly influence the pitch-up behaviour, as sketched in Fig. V.39 (ref. V.31). At angles of incidence approaching the break, flow separates from the upper surface of the nacelles, forming trailing vortices which pass over the wing upper surface. These vortices then act as barriers similar to the fence vortex.

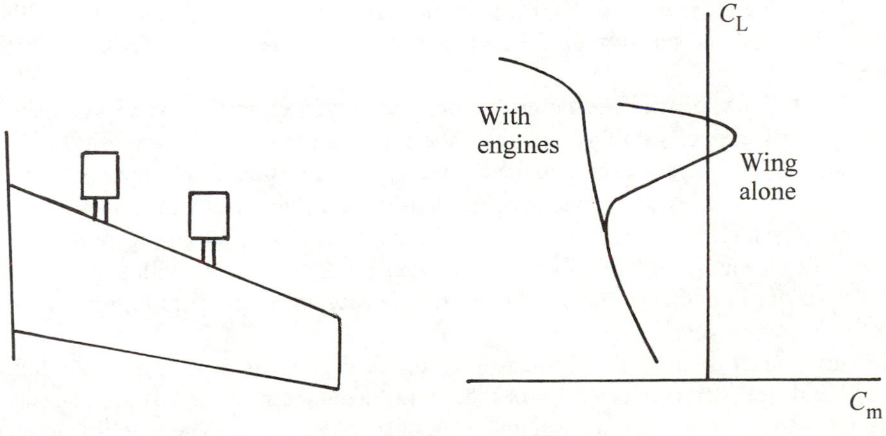

Fig. V.39. Effect of underwing engines.

V.2.5.5 Vortex generators

Vortex generators are usually small half delta wings of the size of the boundary layer thickness fixed on the wing upper surface, as sketched in Fig. V.40. The vortices from the leading edges of the delta wings mix outer air with boundary layer air to re-energize the boundary layer; the boundary layer is then more resistant to separation. Vortex generators

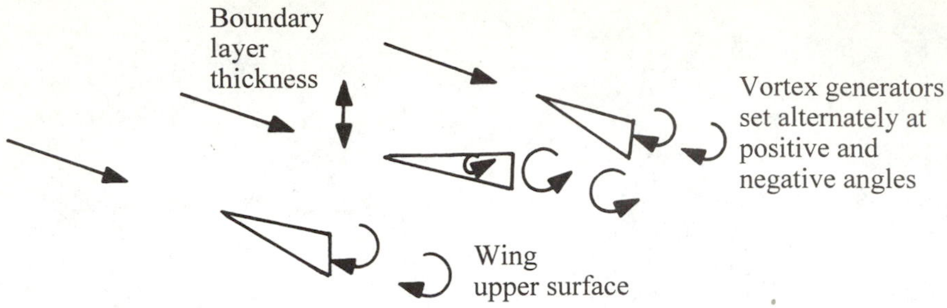

Fig. V.40. Vortex generators.

are useful for delaying separation over trailing edge flaps and for controlling shock induced separations at transonic speeds. For a full account of vortex generators, see Pearcey (ref. III.10).

V.2.6 Buffet and buffeting

Random turbulent motion which imposes unsteady loads on a wing which can be of sufficient intensity to shake the aeroplane, and the pilot. The aerodynamic excitation is known as 'buffet' and the aeroplane response, especially the flexible structural mode response, is known as 'buffeting'. An introduction to buffet and buffeting is presented in ref. V.25.

Local separations (e.g. leading edge short bubbles, vortex generators) and global separations which form into concentrated vortices (e.g. delta wings), may impose light buffeting. It is only when flow breakdown occurs that the level of buffet can become intense.

The buffet characteristics are described by: the power spectral densities of the unsteady pressures at points on the surface in the separated regions, the intensity and the length scales of the temperal and spatial correlations of the unsteady pressures.

A typical surface pressure power spectral density at a point aft of the shock induced separation on a full scale combat aeroplane at Mach 0.85 is sketched in Fig. V.41 (based on ref. V.25); the energy is primarily within the range of 20 to 200 Hz with a peak energy about 100 Hz. The integral of this power spectral density with respect to frequency gives the mean square pressure.

The variation of the root mean square pressure at a point on a wing at Mach 0.8 as angle of incidence increases is shown in Fig. V.41 (taken from ref. V.25); also shown is the extent of the flow breakdown as angle of incidence increases. The level of pressure excitation is high when the point lies just aft of the leading edge shock but the buffet level is low because the region of flow breakdown is restricted to a small bubble aft of that shock. Although the level of pressure excitation is lower at a higher angle of incidence the overall buffet level on the wing is increased as the flow breakdown region becomes more widespread.

To assess the overall level of buffet on a wing it is necessary to know how the pressures at different points on the wing upper surface are correlated. Unfortunately spatial correlations are extremely difficult to measure. There is little discussion of spatial

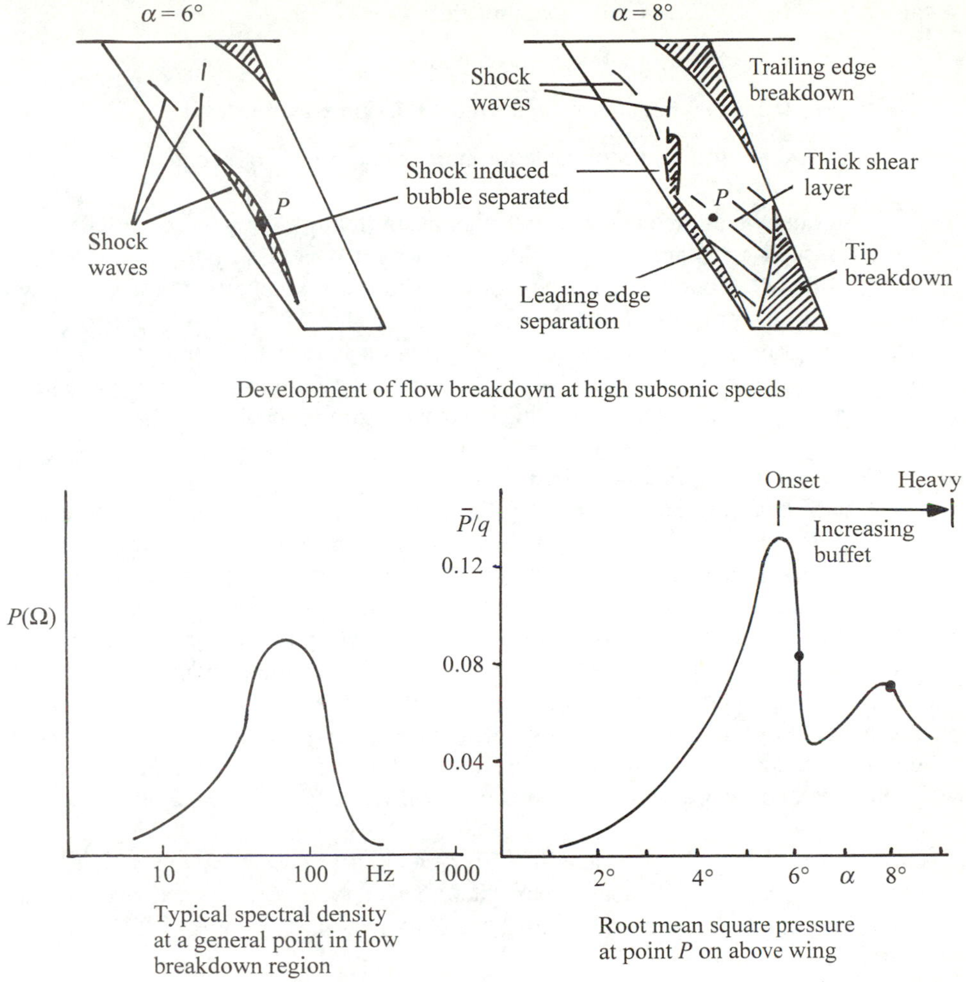

Fig. V.41. Buffet at high subsonic speeds.

correlations in the literature. It is thought that spatial correlations are related to frequency, and that at low buffet frequencies the random pressures can be correlated over the entire flow breakdown region.

Buffeting is a (random) shaking induced by the buffet described above. Most of the buffet excitation is in the frequency band above 10 Hz, which is in a higher frequency band than any of the rigid aeroplane dynamic response modes (e.g. short period, roll rate subsidence). The buffet excitation frequencies, however, extend over virtually all of the structural deformation modes, including wing bending and torsion modes. The intensity of buffeting depends on the aeroelastic dynamic response, thus a detailed explanation of the magnitude of buffeting is beyond the remit of this book.

Pilots' grading of buffeting is typically quoted in terms of peak '*g*' values:

onset	0.035	to $0.1g$ (often goes unnoticed)
light	0.1	to $0.2g$ (definitely perceptible)
moderate	0.2	to $0.6g$ (annoying, degrades mission effectiveness)
severe	0.6	to $1.0g$ (intolerable for more than one or two seconds).

These ratings depend on frequency and whether the buffeting is longitudinal or lateral.

For a transport aeroplane at high subsonic speeds it is necessary to know the Mach number for the buffet onset as a function of C_L. The Mach number for buffet onset will be greater than the drag rise Mach number at each value of C_L. It is a design aim to ensure an adequate margin between the cruise condition and any buffet onset.

For a combat aeroplane the design aim is to keep the buffeting within acceptable limits to as high a C_L as possible, thus enhancing the manoeuvring capability.

V.2.7 Finite wings in dynamic motion

In flight, stall is always approached at a finite rate, at a relatively low rate in a slow approach to the stall when gradually reducing speed, and at a relatively higher rate in accelerated stall manoeuvres. It is doubtful whether the static flow separation situation investigated in a wind tunnel has a practical application. An awareness that dynamic motions affect the stall of an aeroplane has been acknowledged for many years (see refs. V.33–V.39). But the topic of unsteady onset of flow separation and reattachment for finite wings, especially swept wings, has received little fundamental or systematic research attention, which contrasts starkly with the extensive work on the dynamic overshoot characteristics of two dimensional aerofoils, described in sect. V.2.3. More recent work on three dimensional wings, as explained below, has been confined mainly to delta wings.

Conner *et al.* (ref. V.39) measured the lift development on model wings undergoing a constant positive rate of weathercock pitch. The rate is low, typical of aeroplane dynamic response, and the main results are shown in Fig. V.42. A number of observations:

(i) For the non-swept wing model the static lift break is extremely gentle with little loss of lift beyond $(C_{L\,max})_{static}$.

(ii) In Fig. V.42(i), the increase in maximum lift for the non-swept model is consistent with a time lag of approximately $4c_w/U$, possibly slightly longer, to reach the dynamic break angle of incidence from the static break angle of incidence; this time delay is consistent with the time delay for the two dimensional aerofoils described in sect. V.2.3.

(iii) There appears to be a fundamental difference in the dynamic break characteristics between two dimensional aerofoils and three dimensional wings with low sweep angles. With two dimensional aerofoils there tends to be a sudden loss of lift after $(C_{L\,max})_{dyn}$, but for three dimensional wings the loss of lift after $(C_{L\,max})_{dyn}$ is much more gradual; in fact the dynamic lift seems to parallel the static lift.

(iv) In Fig. V.42(ii) the increase in $(C_{L\,max})_{dyn}$ relative to $(C_{L\,max})_{static}$ is virtually the same over the subsonic Mach number range.

(v) In Fig. V.42(iii) the increase in $(C_{L\,max})_{dyn}$ relative to $(C_{L\,max})_{static}$ is greater for the swept wing than for the unswept wing. This result suggests that the time lag from the static break to the dynamic break increases with wing sweep, especially when it is remembered that $(a_\alpha)_w$ is lower for a swept wing than for a non-swept wing.

(vi) In Fig. V.42(iv) the increase in $(C_{L\,max})_{dyn}$ relative to $(C_{L\,max})_{static}$ is greater for the lower aspect ratio unswept wing compared to the higher aspect ratio unswept wing. This result suggests that the time lag from the static break to the dynamic break increases as aspect ratio decreases, especially when it is remembered that $(a_\alpha)_w$ is lower for a low aspect ratio wing than for a high aspect ratio wing.

(vii) A parallel test flight programme confirmed the trends from the wind tunnel tests.

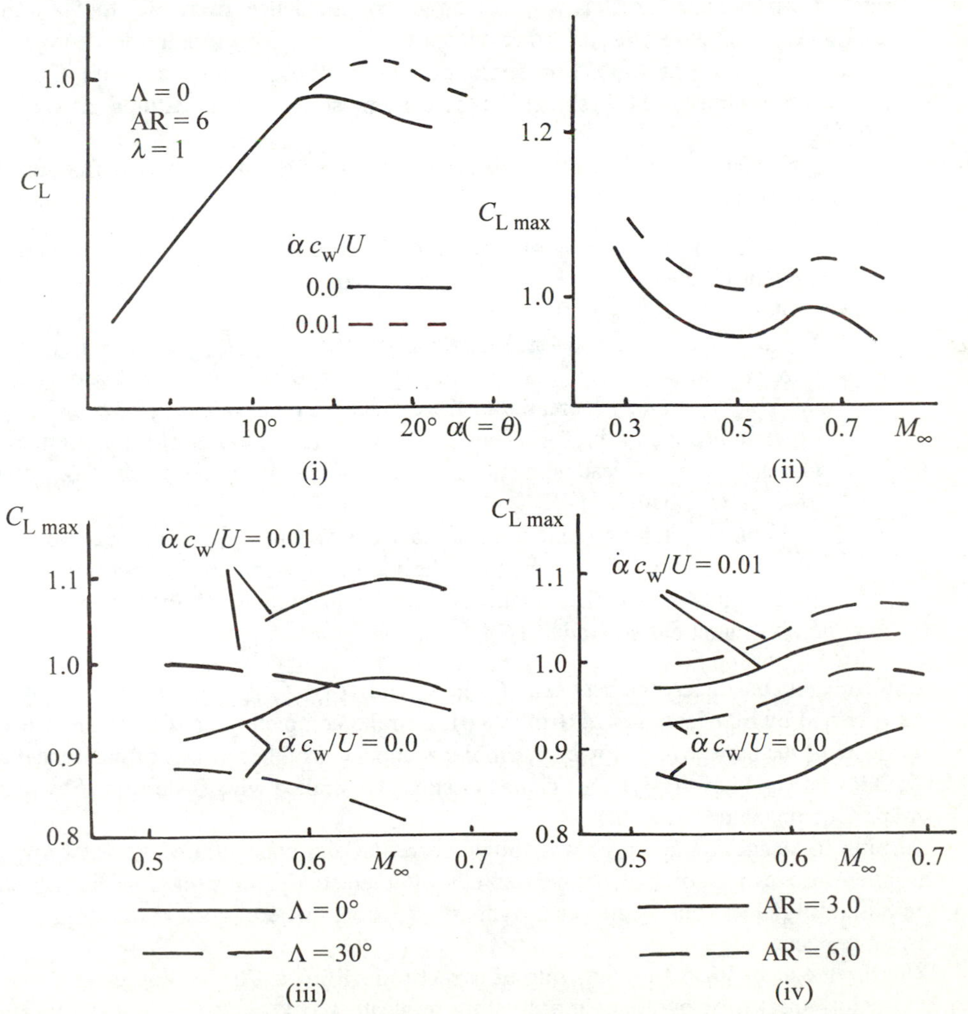

Fig. V.42. Effect of constant rate of pitch on finite wings.

Observations (v) and (vi) are confirmed later.

Further work on rectangular wings is reported by Robinson & Wissler (ref. V.40) and Costes (ref. V.41).

Measurements of the dynamic characteristics of a wing (45° sweep, aspect ratio 2.82, taper ratio 0.167) plus fuselage (i.e. no tail) are reported by Grafton & Libbey (ref. V.42) in oscillatory tests of weathercock pitch over a range of low frequencies ($\nu = 2k \simeq 0.1$) with amplitudes, $\Delta\theta$, from approximately 2.5° to 8.0° about a range of mean angles of incidence from –10° to +110°. A selection of results are presented in Fig. V.43.

(i) For the static tests results, the static break angle of incidence is approximately 15°. Above the break C_N continues to increase, albeit with a smaller $C_{N\alpha}$, accompanied by a weak pitch-up, as $C_{m\alpha}$ goes positive; the weak pitch-up is followed by a weak pitch-down at approximately 18°. At angles of incidence from 30° to 50°, C_N continues to increase with a further decrease in $C_{N\alpha}$, with virtually no change in the pitching moment $C_{m\alpha}$. For this configuration there is no maximum C_N, so $C_{L\,max}$ arises simply as $(C_N \sin\alpha)_{max}$; there are no aerodynamic features associated with $C_{L\,max}$.

(ii) For the oscillatory tests results, with amplitude approximately 5°, and frequency parameter (ν) equal to 0.13:

(a) the change in in-phase normal force oscillatory coefficient $\tilde{C}_{N\alpha}$ with mean angle of incidence is much more gradual than the static lift curve slope over the post-break region;

(b) the out-of-phase normal force oscillatory coefficient $(\tilde{C}_{N\dot{\alpha}} + \tilde{C}_{Nq})$ is of the order of –1.0 below the break, indicating the expected phase lag, but over the break $(\tilde{C}_{N\dot{\alpha}} + \tilde{C}_{Nq})$ increases to large peak positive values, of the order of +25.0, indicative of the lag effects associated with the onset of separation and with the onset of reattachment; this large variation arises from $\tilde{C}_{N\dot{\alpha}}$, the effect of $\tilde{C}_{Nq}$ being small;

(c) the in-phase pitching moment oscillatory coefficient $\tilde{C}_{m\alpha}$ is virtually identical to the static pitching moment derivative, as seen by inspection of the static results, while the break doubles the magnitude of the out-of phase pitching moment derivative $(\tilde{C}_{m\dot{\alpha}} + \tilde{C}_{mq})$.

Unfortunately the difference between $(\tilde{C}_N)_{mean}$ and $(C_N(\alpha_m))_{static}$ is not mentioned.

As reported by Staudacher *et al.* (ref. V.43), a strake completely eradicates the break phenomena of the basic wing. However, problems appear at higher angles of incidence; a detailed investigation of the dynamic characteristics of a straked wing is described by den Boer and Cunningham (ref. V.44).

Turning to slender delta wings with flow separation and concentrated vortex formations, there are two distinct dynamic regimes of interest: dynamic motions in which vortex bursting does not occur and dynamic motions where vortex bursting and reassembly occur.

Measurements of lift on a delta wing of aspect ratio 1.0 (i.e. 76° leading edge sweep angle) below the vortex burst angle oscillating in weathercock pitch at a low frequency and small amplitude about a range of mean angles of incidence by Schmidt (reported by

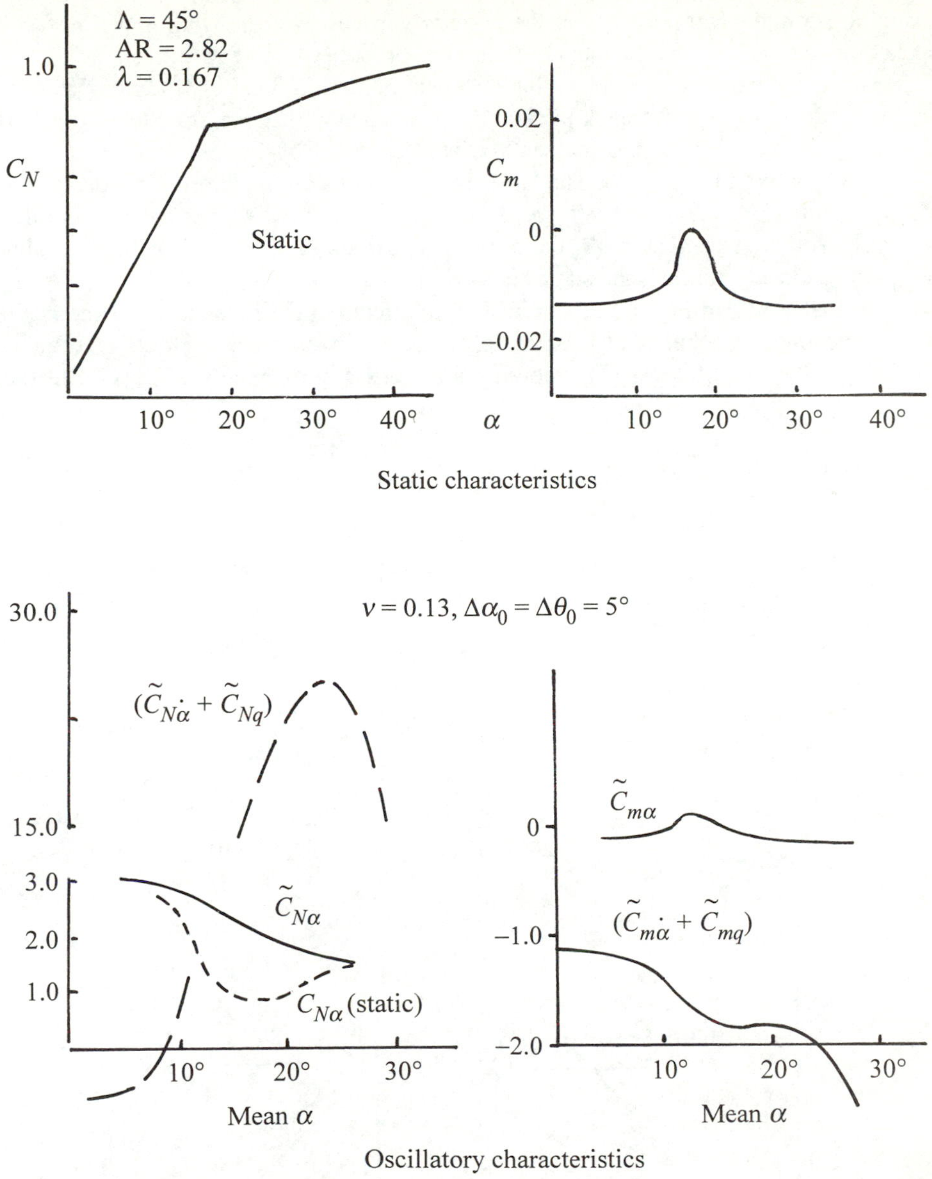

Fig. V.43. Low frequency oscillations of finite wing.

Schneider, ref. V.45) are sketched in Fig. V.44. The relative magnitudes of the damping derivatives to the stiffness derivatives are comparable to those for a wing in attached flow, as described in section III.3. However, the flow mechanisms are totally different. In attached flow the lags are associated with the formation of the wake and the effect of that wake on the wing loading, while for delta wings the lags are associated primarily with the changing strengths and positions of the primary vortices over the wing upper surface. It takes time to move around the mass of fluid in a vortex because of its inertia.

Measurements of lift on a delta wing of aspect ratio 1.46 (i.e. 70° leading edge sweep angle) oscillating in weathercock pitch at a low frequency of large amplitude (0 → 55°), involving vortex bursting and reassembly, are described by Soltani *et al.* (ref. V.46). Results are shown in Fig. V.45. The large dynamic loops are indicative of a delay in the onset of vortex breakdown as $\alpha(t)$ increases together with a delay in the reassembly of the vortex as $\alpha(t)$ decreases. Again it appears that the dynamic lift behaviour above $(C_{L\,max})_{dyn}$ closely parallels the static behaviour.

From the results in Fig. V.45, significant lag effects in the breakdown of the leading edge vortices occur at extremely low oscillatory pitch frequency ($\nu = \Omega c_w/U = \Omega c_r/2U = 0.015$), implying time lags approximately $20c_w/U$. But these

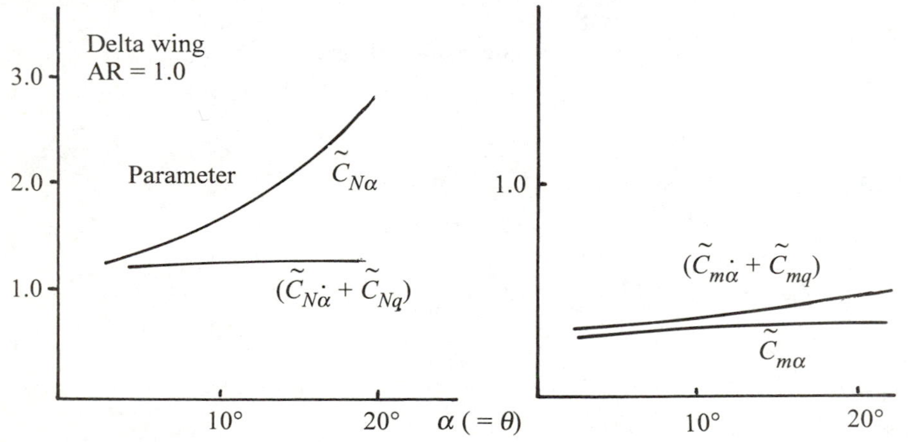

Fig. V.44. Delta wing characteristics below the break.

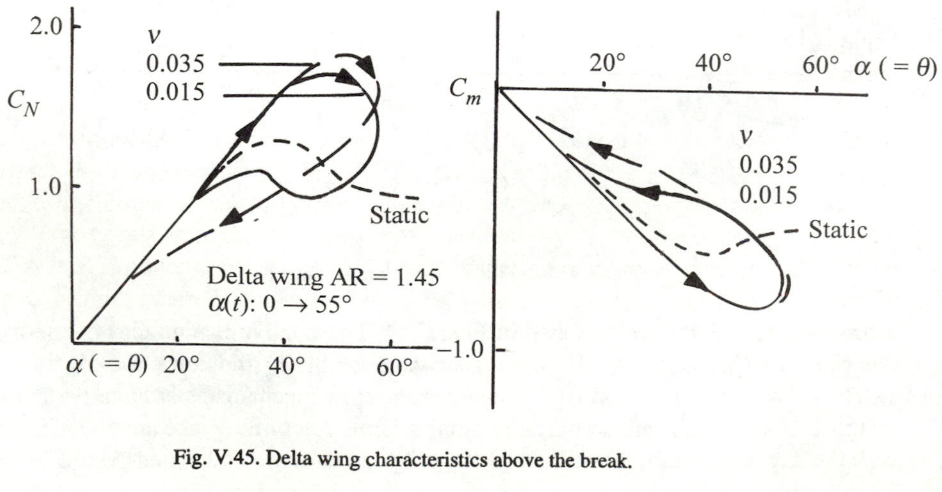

Fig. V.45. Delta wing characteristics above the break.

time lag effects are apparently highly non-linear; an increase in pitch frequency to ($\nu=$) 0.035 increases the time lag to approximately $28c_w/U$. However, these interpretations of Fig. V.45 should be treated with caution because the measured effects at $\nu=0.035$, in particular, may be determined more by the slowing down of $\alpha(t)$ as it approaches its maximum value of 55° rather than the lag in flow breakdown.

Physical explanations of the lag effects on unsteady vortex breakdown are virtually non-existent in the current literature. Vortex breakdown is an instability of the vortex core in a longitudinal adverse pressure gradient. Speculating, factors which might affect the delay in vortex breakdown:

(i) the core arises from the apex region and takes a time $2c_w yU$ to travel from the apex to the trailing edge;
(ii) the development of the core depends on the rate at which vorticity spirals into the core; because of its spiral path, vorticity from the front of the delta wing could take a time $4c_w yU$ to travel to the trailing edge;
(iii) the core involves a 'solid body' rotation at its centre which involves the action of viscous stresses which presumably take time to diffuse; a time lag in the diffusion process would make the core 'tighter' and hence more resistant to breakdown;
(iv) if there are time lag effects on the secondary separations the rate of shedding of leading edge vorticity could be affected.

Further work is needed to quantify these factors, and to identify others.

Of equal interest and importance is the reassembly of the leading edge vortex. It would appear from Fig. V.45 that the reassembly process is different for the two frequency parameters of these tests. Again the fundamental flow characteristics need to be investigated.

One word of advice to experimentalists: the appropriate experiments to conduct to investigate the fundamentals of unsteady effects are constant rate of pitch motions from 0 to 90°, both positive and negative rates, measuring transient normal force and pitching moment. In oscillatory experiments it is difficult to dissociate the effects from the time varying pitch rate of lag.

Measurements of lift on a delta wing of aspect ratio 4 (i.e. 45° leading edge sweep angle) oscillating in weathercock pitch over large amplitudes ($\Delta\alpha_0 = 8°$) about different mean angles of incidence at frequencies higher than $\nu = 0.1$, are described by Huyer *et al.* (ref. V.47). A delta wing of aspect ratio 4 has particular flow separation characteristics which resemble neither a slender delta wing with its well established primary vortex system nor a conventional swept back wing with its part-span flow separation characteristics. Furthermore, the frequencies are too high for application to aeroplane dynamics. Nevertheless this paper does introduce one interesting new facet, as shown in Fig. V.46; when the wing oscillates in the nominally fully developed flow about a high mean angle of incidence there appears to be a partial recovery of flow attachment; this effect may be a consequence of a higher value of $\nu (= 0.2)$. It is necessary to establish whether or not this phenomenon occurs at typical frequencies of aeroplane dynamics.

The time lag for the delay in the break with increasing angle of incidence for this delta wing of aspect ratio 4 appears to be approximately $8c_w/U$, which is not incompatible with the trends in Fig. V.42(iii) and (iv).

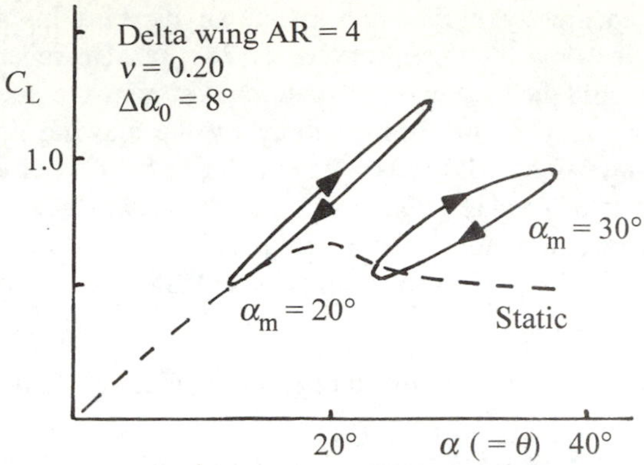

Fig. V.46. An unsteady effect above the break.

The one common feature of all types of wing is that the plot of the dynamic normal force versus angle of incidence in an oscillatory motion which includes the lag effects of onset of separation and reattachment is always a large clockwise loop, which implies a large positive $\tilde{C}_{N\dot{\alpha}}$.

However, plots of pitching moment versus angle of incidence in oscillatory motions across the break can be either clockwise or anticlockwise loops, or more complicated figures of eight. A net clockwise plot of $C_m(t) \sim \alpha(t)$ implies that $\tilde{C}_{m\dot{\alpha}} > 0$, which denotes negative damping, whereas an anticlockwise plot implies $\tilde{C}_{m\dot{\alpha}} < 0$, which denotes positive damping.

For wings with low sweep the onset of flow separation causes the centre of pressure to move aft, decreasing the pitching moment. But the plot of $C_m(t) \sim \alpha(t)$ which extends over the onset of flow separation can be similar to that shown for the two dimensional aerofoil in Fig. V.24, with a net clockwise behaviour, indicating negative pitch damping. This behaviour was noted by Wiley (ref. V.48) and Staudacher (ref. V.43).

It is somewhat paradoxical that for a wing with low sweep, although the centre of pressure moves aft at the onset of flow separation, inducing a nose-down pitching moment usually regarded as a stabilizing effect, the pitch damping can be negative and destabilizing. A mathematical explanation is that the nose-down stabilizing effect is contained in the relationship,

$$(\tilde{C}_m)_{\text{mean}} < (C_m(\alpha_{\text{m}}))_{\text{static}}$$

but the damping of the oscillation about $(\tilde{C}_m)_{\text{mean}}$ goes negative. Thus it is important to record $(\tilde{C}_m)_{\text{mean}}$.

For wings with high sweep, including delta wings, the onset of vortex breakdown causes the centre of pressure to move forward, increasing the pitching moment. Although there is a lag in vortex breakdown, typical plots of $C_m(t) \sim \alpha(t)$, which extend over the break, are anticlockwise—that is, stabilizing—as shown in Fig. V.45.

For wings of intermediate sweep there can be either little change in the positive pitch damping, or an increase in the positive pitch damping, across the break. The magnitude of the positive pitch damping can increase at higher angles of incidence (see Fig. V.43).

There appears to be little data on the effects of Mach number on the lift and moment characteristics in dynamic motions.

V.2.8 Wing–fuselage combinations

The usual interference effects between wing and fuselage, as explained in section III.3.4 are:

(i) an upwash around the side of the fuselage which increases the local angles of incidence along the wing span in the neighbourhood of the fuselage; this effect could modify the break angle;
(ii) a loss of lift across the fuselage compared with the wing alone; this loss of lift is compensated by the lift on the fuselage nose.

As the angle of incidence increases towards the break other phenomena occur, as sketched in Fig. V.47.

(i) With increasing angle of incidence symmetic flow separations occur in the region of the fuselage nose, these flow separations roll up into a pair of concentrated vortices, similar to the leading edge vortices on a delta wing, which pass over the upper surface of the fuselage. These vortices will induce localized high suctions which will contribute to a slight non-linear increase in lift.
(ii) In addition, further concentrated vortices may be created from flow separations at the cranks between the wing leading edge at its intersection with the fuselage.

These vortices may affect the break conditions on the wing; these vortices will affect the downwash field around the tailplane.

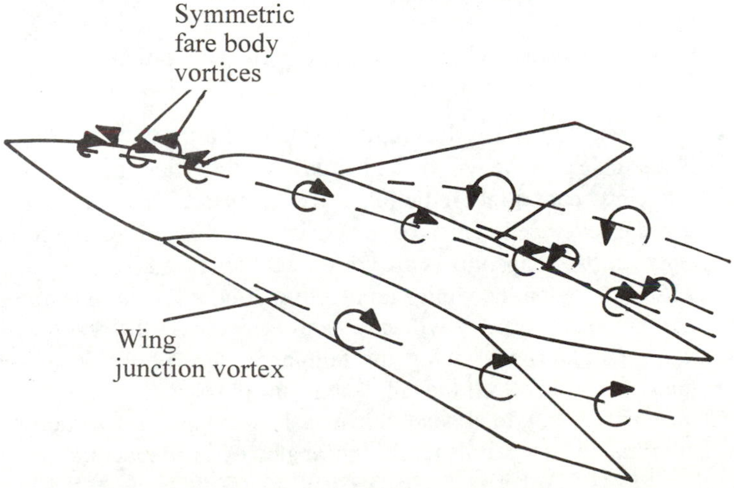

Fig. V.47. Wing–fuselage vortices.

Apart from some early work on the maximum lift characteristics of wing–fuselage combinations mentioned by Schlichting (ref. III.8), the author is unaware of any subsequent work on the effects of wing–fuselage interference on either the static or dynamic break, supported by measurements of dynamic derivatives.

V.2.9 Tailplane aerodynamics

For a conventional aeroplane with aft tailplane a design aim is to ensure that the flow over the tailplane remains attached when the flow initially separates on the wing; this aim is aided by the negative setting angle of the tailplane relative to the wing coupled with the downwash aft of the wing. For a combat aeroplane with all-moving tailplane the design aim is more concerned with ensuring adequate control power.

When the flow over the wing is attached the wake is relatively thin. The tailplane is located such that it does not enter the wing wake during operational flying. In general this objective is achieved with either a low tailplane (i.e. tailplane beneath the wing, e.g. Lightning), mid-tailplane (i.e. tailplane above the wing, for example on Airbus with its low wing on the underside of the fuselage and the tailplane on the mid aft fuselage) or high tailplane (i.e. tailplane half way up, or on top of, the fin, for example the VC 10 or Boeing 727).

Once there is flow breakdown over part of the wing there is a major change in the flow field in the wake. Fig. V.48 shows a flow field in the wake behind the semi-span of a $22\frac{1}{2}°$ swept, half-model, wing of aspect ratio 6 at 14° angle of incidence with an outboard separation, taken from some unpublished results by the author; note

(i) the vertical thickness of the wake in the wing tip region, of the order of c_w;
(ii) the distribution of total head deficit, which indicates the loss in dynamic pressure; the loss of total head at the centres of the tip vorticity and the part-span vorticity are clearly visible;
(iii) a large increase in downwash inboard due to the part-span vorticity.

At the break it would be hoped that the tailplane would be outside the wake, or at least on its periphery. Nevertheless, there will be an increase in downwash at the tailplane due to part-span vorticity, and hence a loss in tailplane effectiveness. If the tailplane becomes engulfed within a fully developed separated wake, its low dynamic pressure and high downwash, the tailplane lifting capabilities are considerably reduced.

With an inboard separation on the wing again there will be a loss in dynamic pressure in the wake but the part-span vorticity will now tend to decrease the downwash in the neighbourhood of the tailplane, increasing the tailplane angle of incidence—possibly increasing the tailplane effectiveness if the tailplane is just outside the wake.

Flow field characteristics (e.g. total head, downwash, sidewash and vorticity distributions) in the neighbourhood of a tailplane at high angles of incidence are described by Stone & Polhamus (ref. V.51), Kirby & Spence (ref. V.52), Shevell & Schaufele (ref. V. 53) and more recently by Komerath *et al.* (ref. V.54).

Dynamic effects on the tailplane arise from:

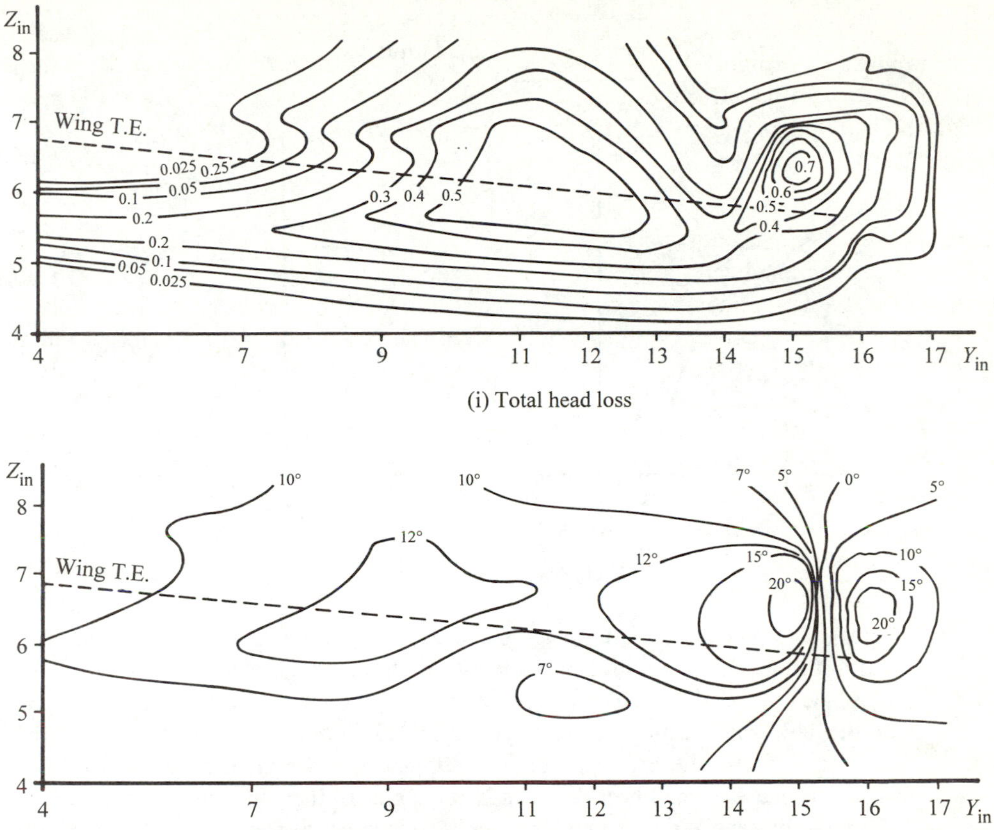

(ii) Downwash distribution

Fig. V.48. Flow field behind $22^1/_2°$ swept wing.

(i) the time lag for a separated wake, newly formed at the break, to convect from the wing to the downstream location of the tailplane; as explained in sect. V.2.3, in a fully separated wake shed vorticity is convected downstream at approximately half of the relative stream velocity, taking approximately $2l_t c_W/U$ to travel from the wing to the tailplane;

(ii) the time lag for the transient tailplane lift to build up in changing flow fields about the tailplane, especially if the tailplane angle of incidence exceeds its break value.

The author is unaware of any information on these topics.

V.2.10 Complete configurations at high angles of incidence

V.2.10.1 Transport aeroplanes

Trends of static variations of $C_m \sim \alpha$ are sketched in Fig. V.49 for transport aeroplanes of different configurations, based on Byrnes (ref. V.55).

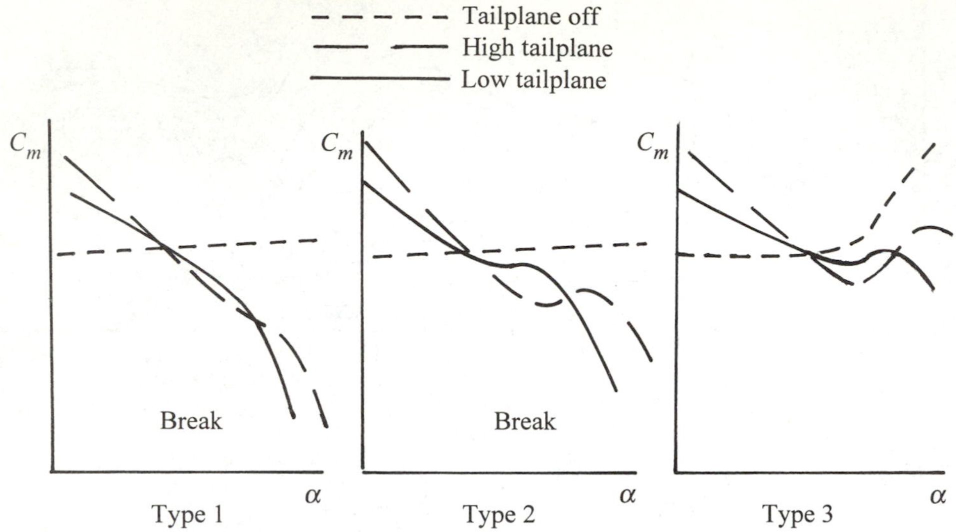

Fig. V.49. Effect of tailplane.

(i) Type 1 aeroplane represents an aeroplane configuration with a swept wing of aspect ratio of the order of 7 with either a low or high tailplane, relative to the wing, both tailplanes of equal area. There is no pitch-up at the break and $\partial\varepsilon/\partial\alpha$ downstream at the tailplane location remains less than 1.0 through the break. At angles of incidence below the break the higher tailplane has the greater effectiveness (i.e. $-C_{m\alpha}$) because of the lower downwash. At angles of incidence just above the break the effectiveness of the low tailplane tends to increase as it moves to the lower edge of the separated wake with a reduced downwash, whereas the high tailplane loses effectiveness as it moves into the wake with an increased downwash. At angles of incidence well above the break as the high tailplane emerges from the underside of the wake its effectiveness is restored; but now the lower tailplane has the greater effectiveness.

(ii) Type 2 aeroplane represents a similar configuration, where again there is no significant wing pitch-up at the break but now there is an increase in the downwash at the break, giving $\partial\varepsilon/\partial\alpha$ in the wake of the order of 1.0. The low tailplane loses effectiveness at the break but recovers its effectiveness as it moves below the wake with increase in angle of incidence. The high tailplane loses all of its effectiveness as it traverses the wake (its $C_m \sim a$ curve parallels the tail-off case) but recovers its effectiveness as it emerges from the underside of the wake.

(iii) Type 3 aeroplane represents a similar configuration but which has a severe wing pitch up at the break, and with $\partial\varepsilon/\partial\alpha$ greater than 1.0 in the wake. Neither the low nor higher tailplane can contain the large positive incremental pitching moment from the wing at the break until they emerge below the wake.

The Type 1 aeroplane would have a natural, nose-down, recovery at the break with the low tailplane, but could wallow about a constant angle with the high tailplane. However, there would be sufficient elevator control power to generate a nose-down pitching moment for the pilot to bring the aeroplane under control. The Type 2 aeroplane would need the intervention of the pilot to restore control beyond the break; it would be necessary to ensure that sufficient elevator control power was available above the break. For the Type 3 aeroplane it is feasible that sufficient elevator control power could not be provided, especially with the high tailplane; this aeroplane would not then be acceptable as airworthy.

A typical variation of $C_m \sim \alpha$ for a high T-tail configuration, that is a tailplane on top of the fin, over an extended angle of incidence range is sketched in Fig. V.50 for three cases, zero elevator angle, small negative elevator angle (stick slightly back), and maximum positive elevator angle down against its stops (stick forward to its extreme position). The main features are:

(i) an initial wing pitch-up occurs at the break, about 13° angle of incidence, increasing C_m;
(ii) the T-tail remains above the separated wake, generating a negative C_m, up to an angle of incidence about 26°, but gradually losing effectiveness as the downwash increases;
(iii) the T-tail loses virtually all of its effectiveness as it enters the extremely wide wing wake, encountering a loss in dynamic pressure and increase in downwash;
(iv) at an angle of incidence above 40° the T-tail comes out of the lower edge of the wake and the T-tail effectiveness is restored.

Configurations with T-tails can experience the phenomenon of 'deep stall'.

In Fig. V.50, with zero elevator the aeroplane is trimmed with zero pitching moment at trim state A at 10° angle of incidence. To reduce the trim speed the angle of incidence is increased by slowly decreasing the elevator angle (stick is slowly pulled back) and the trim state progresses from A to A_1, maintaining zero pitching moment. When the trim state reaches just beyond A_1 the positive nose-up pitching moment destabilizes the aeroplane and the aeroplane rotates nose-up, increasing the angle of incidence. The pitching moment becomes zero at state B_1 and between states B_1 and C_1 the pitching moment is negative. If the nose-up rotation induced by the positive pitching moment between A_1 and B_1 cannot be rectified by the nose-down pitching moment between B_1 and C_1 then the aeroplane will rotate nose-up beyond state C_1 into a regime of positive pitching moment, continuing the rotation, finally settling down at the stable state D_1. The pilot will want to recover by rotating the aeroplane nose-down, so the stick will be pushed forward as far as possible, but the aeroplane will only return to stable state D_2. The aeroplane is now locked into a stable state at high angle of incidence, of the order of 40°; there is no available elevator control power; the forward speed will be low because of the high drag; the low speed means that the lift is less than the weight so the aeroplane descends at a constant pitch attitude; a crash is inevitable.

To prevent the development of the deep stall the pilot should, immediately following the nose-up rotation at state A_1, push the stick forward, generating the negative pitching moment associated with state A_2. According to Thomas & Collingbourne (ref. V.56), for certain configurations prone to deep stall, a delay of half a second by the pilot in taking recovery action could be the difference between a safe recovery and disaster.

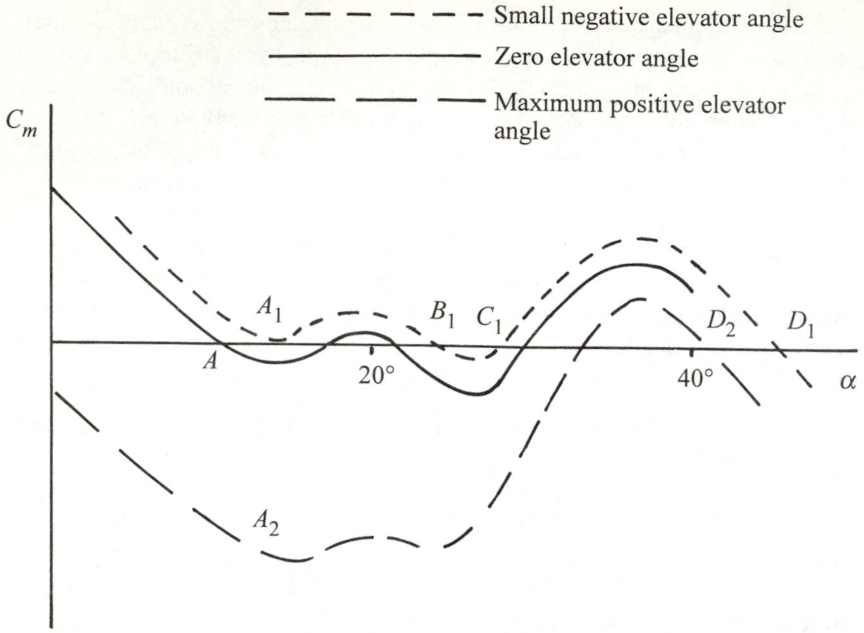

Fig. V.50. Deep stall phenomenon.

Design features such as an increase in the tailplane size and aft fuselage engines have been shown to restore some positive (nose-down) pitch control power. However, to preclude the possibility of danger the stick pusher has been introduced; at a critical angle of incidence before the break the stick is suddenly pushed forward out of the pilot's hands and the aeroplane is pitched nose-down to safety.

At low angles of incidence the overall short period damping, $[(-C_{mq})+(-C_{m\dot{\alpha}})]$ is dominated by the tailplane contribution to $(-C_{mq})$. At higher angles of incidence around and above the break, the overall pitch damping can be dominated by $(-C_{m\dot{\alpha}})$ from the wing. Overall pitch damping can either increase or decrease, possibly going negative, due to the wing contribution from $(-C_{m\dot{\alpha}})$.

The instability between states A_1 and B_1 in Fig. V.50 could be exacerbated by a loss in pitch damping.

V.2.10.2 Combat aeroplanes

A set of experimental results for a conventional model combat aeroplane is shown in Fig. V.51, taken from Grafton *et al.* (ref. V.57).

The configuration has a wing of low sweep, aspect ratio 3.68, with small strake. The aft tailplane is low, slightly below the plane of the wing.

For the wing–fuselage combination, without the tailplane, the static break occurs at an angle of incidence of 15°; there is a break in the lift but not in the pitching moment. The lift continues to rise with increases in angle of incidence above the break but at a slower rate; there is little change in the pitching moment. There is no pitch-up of the wing–fuselage; this result is consistent with the pitch-up criterion shown in Fig. V.29.

For the complete model, the tailplane at zero setting angle makes no contribution to the overall lift at low angles of incidence but then makes a substantial contribution to the lift at angles of incidence above the static break of the wing–fuselage combination. The variations of the total lift and pitching moment with angle of incidence are gradual. A possible explanation is that at low angles of incidence the downwash is large, of the order of the angle of incidence itself; at high angles of incidence the tailplane is well below the wing wake with the downwash decreasing with increase in angle of incidence; there may well be a sudden decrease in the downwash at the static break of the wing–fuselage.

The results when the tailplane is fixed at –25° show that pitch control power is retained up to 45° angle of incidence. According to Skow (ref. V.58), control power of an all-moving tailplane can be lost at angles of incidence approaching 60°.

The variations of oscillatory weathercock pitch derivatives with amplitude of 5° at a frequency parameter 0.112 as a function of the mean angle of incidence, with and without tailplane, are shown in Fig. V.51.

(i) All of the major unsteady effects arise from the wing.
(ii) The peak value of $\tilde{C}_{N\dot{\alpha}}$ ($\tilde{C}_{Nq}$ is relatively small), approximately +25, which conforms with the peak value of $\tilde{C}_{N\dot{\alpha}}$ in sect. V.2.4, occurs at 25° mean angle of incidence; this result is somewhat surprising because the break of the wing–fuselage combination occurs at 15° and the amplitude of oscillation is 5°.
(iii) The large positive value of $(\tilde{C}_{N\dot{\alpha}} + \tilde{C}_{Nq})$ at zero angle of incidence is unexpected, and inexplicable.
(iv) The pitch damping $(-[\tilde{C}_{m\dot{\alpha}} + \tilde{C}_{mq}])$ is reasonably constant up to, and through, the break, but then increases with further increase in angle of incidence.

Two alternative wing plan forms—a swept wing and delta wing, with the same fuselage and tailplane—were also investigated and reported in ref. V.57. The trends for all three configurations are similar apart from the elimination of the peak $\tilde{C}_{N\dot{\alpha}}$ for the delta wing, another surprising result because the delta wing–fuselage combination had the same break characteristics as the other two wing–fuselage combinations.

V.2.11 Small perturbation longitudinal stability at high angles of incidence

Consider an aeroplane in steady level flight at speed U_{trim} at a high angle of incidence α_{trim}. The longitudinal stability of this aeroplane can be assessed by assuming that perturbations about the steady state are small.

For the short period stability it is assumed that the forward speed does not change and that the perturbations involve small changes in angles of incidence and pitch. The appropriate equations of motion for the short period stability are the translational equation of motion in the vertical direction and the pitch equation of motion, namely

$$\begin{aligned} m\left[U_{\text{trim}}\,\Delta\dot{\alpha}(t) - U_{\text{trim}}\,\Delta\dot{\theta}(t)\right] &= -\Delta L(t) - D_{\text{trim}}\Delta\alpha(t) \\ I_{yy}\,\Delta\ddot{\theta}(t) &= \Delta\mathcal{M}(t). \end{aligned} \qquad \text{(V.2.21)}$$

Eqns. (V.2.21) can be rewritten in the form,

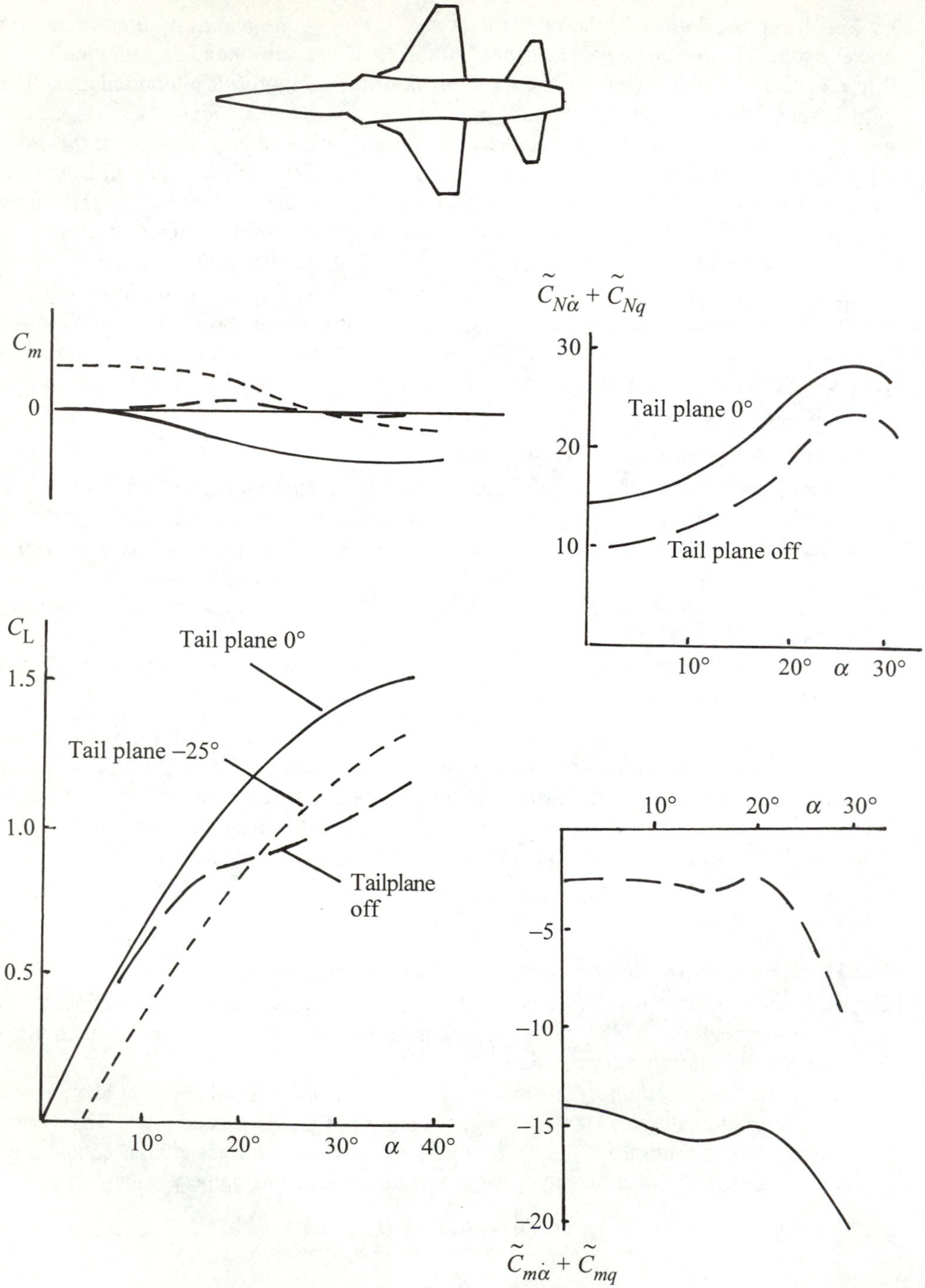

Fig. V.51. Characteristics of a combat aeroplane.

$$
\begin{aligned}
&(C_W U_{trim}/g)\big[\Delta\dot{\alpha}(t)-\Delta\dot{\theta}(t)\big] \\
&\quad = -\Big[\big[\tilde{C}_{L\alpha}(\nu,\alpha_{trim})+(C_D)_{trim}\big]\,\Delta\alpha(t)+\tilde{C}_{L\dot{\alpha}}(\nu,\alpha_{trim})\,\Delta\dot{\alpha}(t)\big(c_w/2U_{trim}\big) \\
&\qquad + C_{Lq}\big(q(t)c_w/2U_{trim}\big)\Big] \\
&\big(C_W i_{yy} c_w/g\big)\,\Delta\ddot{\theta}(t) \\
&\quad = -\Big[\tilde{C}_{m\alpha}(\nu,\alpha_{trim})\,\Delta\alpha(t)+\tilde{C}_{m\dot{\alpha}}(\nu,\alpha_{trim})\,\Delta\dot{\alpha}(t)\big(c_w/2U_{trim}\big) \\
&\qquad + C_{mq}\big(q(t)c_w/2U_{trim}\big)\Big]
\end{aligned}
\tag{V.2.22}
$$

taking the α derivatives to be the oscillatory derivatives over a range of low frequency parameters $\nu\,(=\omega c_w/U_{trim})$ of small amplitude, $\Delta\alpha_0$, say 3°, about the mean angle α_{trim}, evaluated, or measured, at the trim Mach number, and taking the q derivatives to be constant, equal to their value at low angles of incidence, and omitting the input terms.

Eqns. (V.2.22) become

$$
\begin{aligned}
&\big[1-\tilde{C}_{L\dot{\alpha}}(\nu,\alpha_{trim})/2\overline{m}\big]\,\Delta\dot{\alpha}(t) \\
&\qquad +\big(g/(C_W U_{trim})\big)\big[C_{L\alpha}(\nu,\alpha_{trim})+(C_D)_{trim}\big]\,\Delta\alpha(t)-\Delta\dot{\theta}(t)=0 \\
&\big(C_W i_{yy} c_w/g\big)\dot{q}(t)-C_{mq}\big(q(t)c_w/2U_{trim}\big) \\
&\qquad +\Big[\tilde{C}_{m\alpha}(\nu,\alpha_{trim})\,\Delta\alpha(t)+\tilde{C}_{m\dot{\alpha}}(\nu,\alpha_{trim})\,\Delta\dot{\alpha}(t)\big(c_w/2U_{trim}\big)\Big]=0
\end{aligned}
\tag{V.2.23}
$$

taking $C_{Lq}/2\overline{m} \ll 1$, but retaining $(C_D)_{trim}$ because of its higher value once there is flow breakdown.

The derivative $\tilde{C}_{L\dot{\alpha}}\,(\nu,\alpha_{trim})$ is positive and large, of the order of 30 when α_{trim} is slightly above the break. This damping term combines with the translational inertia term, reducing the effective mass of the aeroplane at sea level by approximately 10%.

From eqns. (V.2.23), and by reference to eqns. (III.9.4) and (III.9.7), the short period undamped frequency is given by

$$
(\omega_0)^2_{sp}=\frac{g\Big[\big(-\tilde{C}_{m\alpha}(\nu,\alpha_{trim})\big)+\big(\tilde{C}_{L\alpha}(\nu,\alpha_{trim})+(C_D)_{trim}\big)\big(-C_{mq}/2\overline{m}\big)\Big]}{c_w C_W i_{yy}\big[1-\tilde{C}_{L\dot{\alpha}}(\nu,\alpha_{trim})/2\overline{m}\big]}
\tag{V.2.24}
$$

$$
\nu=(\omega_0)_{sp}\,c_w/U_{trim}
\tag{V.2.25}
$$

and the short period damping is proportional to

$$
\frac{i_{yy}\Big[\big(\tilde{C}_{L\alpha}(\nu,\alpha_{trim})+(C_D)_{trim}\big)+\big(-\tilde{C}_{m\dot{\alpha}}(\nu,\alpha_{trim})\big)\Big]}{\Big[1-\big(\tilde{C}_{L\dot{\alpha}}(\nu,\alpha_{trim})/2\overline{m}\big)\Big]}+(-C_{mq})
\tag{V.2.26}
$$

The determination of the short period undamped frequency from eqns. (V.2.24) and (V.2.25) requires an iterative solution; guess a value of v, estimate the values of the derivatives in eqn. (V.2.24) at this value of v and obtain the value of $(\omega_0)_{sp}$, calculate a new value of v from eqn. (V.2.25), and repeat the process until the numbers are consistent.

For the short period damping, eqn. (V.2.26);

(i) the derivative $\tilde{C}_{L\alpha}(v, \alpha_{trim})$ should retain its attached flow value for several degrees above the static break, but $\tilde{C}_{L\alpha}(v, \alpha_{trim})$ will decrease at higher angles of α_{trim};
(ii) although it may be assumed that $(-C_{mq})$, due primarily to the tailplane, retains its attached flow value, this contribution from the tailplane is reduced by approximately 10% above the break;
(iii) the damping will probably be dominated by the variation of the wing contribution to $(-\tilde{C}_{m\dot{\alpha}}(v, \alpha_{trim}))$; this variation is configuration dependent, as an example see Fig. V.51.

An automatic control system to improve short period damping above the break is only feasible if there is sufficient control power at the higher angles of incidence.

V.2.12 Longitudinal dynamic motions at high angles of incidence: introducing the concept of aerodynamic modelling

The estimation of longitudinal dynamic motions is performed by direct numerical integration of the equations of motion.

The numerical solution follows a time marching process. The response at time $t_n + \Delta t$ (i.e. $\alpha(t_n + \Delta t)$, $q(t_n + \Delta t)$, $\theta(t_n + \Delta t)$, $U(t_n + \Delta t)$) is calculated from a known response at time t_n (i.e. $\alpha(t_n)$, $q(t_n)$, $\theta(t_n)$, $U(t_n)$) for a given input (i.e. where $\mathrm{Th}(t_n)$, $\eta(t_n)$, $\mathrm{Th}(t_n + \Delta t)$, $\eta(t_n + \Delta t)$ are all known). Once the response is calculated at time $t_n + \Delta t$ the process is repeated to obtain the response at $t_n + 2\Delta t$. And so on.

For the simple equation

$$mU_{trim}\dot{\alpha}(t) = -\tfrac{1}{2}\rho_{at}U_{trim}^2 S_W C_L\big(\alpha(t), \eta(t)\,|\,t\big) + W \qquad \text{(V.2.27)}$$

a crude algorithm is

$$(C_W U_{trim}/g)\alpha(t_n + \Delta t) = (C_W U_{trim}/g)\alpha(t_n) - \big[C_L\big(\alpha(t_n), \eta(t_n)\,|\,t_n\big) + C_W\big]\,\Delta t + C_W. \qquad \text{(V.2.28)}$$

More accurate algorithms, the Runge–Kutta or predictor–corrector algorithms (see ref. V.59) involve at least one iterative loop between t_n and $t_n + \Delta t$ to improve the estimation of $\alpha(t_n + \Delta t)$, incorporating values of $C_L(\alpha(t_n + \Delta t), \eta(t_n + \Delta t)|\,(t_n + \Delta t))$.

To solve eqns. (V.2.27) and (V.2.28) it is necessary to know $C_L(\alpha(t_n), \eta(t_n)|\,t_n)$. Remember that $C_L(\alpha(t_n), \eta(t_n)|\,t_n)$ denotes the value of C_L at time t_n; this value of C_L depends not only on $\alpha(t_n)$ and $\eta(t_n)$ but also on $\alpha(t)$ and $\eta(t)$ at earlier times, $t < t_n$, the past history. Below the break it is well established that the past history effects can be adequately represented by an expression of the form

$$C_L(t_n) = C_{L\alpha}\alpha(t_n) + C_{L\dot{\alpha}}\dot{\alpha}(t_n)\left(c_w/2U_{trim}\right). \qquad \text{(V.2.29)}$$

This formulation is possibly adequate for small perturbations about a steady state above the break, as described in sect. V.2.11, but not for large perturbations extending up to high angles of incidence.

The representation of the aerodynamic coefficients

$$C_D\left(\alpha(t), q(t), \eta(t) \,|\, t\right)$$
$$C_L\left(\alpha(t), q(t), \eta(t) \,|\, t\right)$$

and

$$C_M\left(\alpha(t), q(t), \eta(t) \,|\, t\right)$$

for application in estimating general longitudinal motions is known as aerodynamic modelling.

The concepts of aerodynamic modelling are now examined.

There are a number of basic premises underlying aerodynamic modelling.

(i) Aerodynamic modelling is a means to an end, namely to predict successfully all dynamic motions; aerodynamic modelling only has to be sufficiently accurate to meet this objective.
(ii) There should be a conceptual framework which embraces the understanding of the unsteady aerodynamic processes.
(iii) The empirical components should be measurable, or deducible, from standard experimental wind tunnel techniques, or, in the future, from computational aerodynamics.
(iv) The validity of the aerodynamic model is judged by the comparison of predictions of dynamic responses with flight measurements, over as wide a range of manoeuvres as possible; departures can be investigated on drop-model tests. Again, in the future, this validation may be done by computation.
(v) The approach should be universal, not developed and hence restricted to one type of configuration.

There is also an overriding consideration that the aerodynamic model, the associated experimental techniques and the representation of the equations of motion are all compatible.

Several observations arise from point (i).

Unsteady aerodynamic overshoots arise from the delays in flow separations and flow reattachments; these delays take a time of the order of $4c_w/U$ to $16c_w/U$, less than of the order of 0.6 s. Thus, from the point of view of aeroplane dynamics, which extends over 2–3 s, a detailed and precise time variation of the lift and moment during the onset and reattachment processes is unnecessary; all that is required of an aerodynamic model is that the magnitude and time scales are adequately incorporated.

There are two main aims for aerodynamic modelling: to build up understanding of general dynamic phenomena and to predict the actual dynamic behaviour of a particular configuration. The aerodynamic models may differ for these two objectives.

A qualitative understanding of the dynamics of deep stall, including recovery procedures, was comprehensively developed by Thomas & Collingbourne (ref. V.56) with an extremely simple model, namely

$$
\begin{aligned}
C_D\big(\alpha(t), q(t), \eta(t) \,|\, t\big) &= \big[C_D(\alpha(t))\big]_{\text{static}} \\
C_L\big(\alpha(t), q(t), \eta(t) \,|\, t\big) &= \big[C_L(\alpha(t), \eta(t))\big]_{\text{static}} \\
C_m\big(\alpha(t), q(t), \eta(t) \,|\, t\big) &= \big[C_m(\alpha(t), \eta(t))\big]_{\text{static}} \\
&\quad + C_{m\dot{\alpha}}\dot{\alpha}(t)c_w/2U_{\text{trim}} + C_{mq}\, q(t)c_w/2U_{\text{trim}}
\end{aligned}
\qquad (V.2.30)
$$

where the static terms were obtained from static wind tunnel tests and the $\dot{\alpha}$ and q moment derivatives were estimated on a quasi-steady basis, with empirical corrections, including an allowance for dynamic pressure losses in the wake.

However the quantitative prediction of stall, or departure, the post-stall gyrations, and the recovery of a particular configuration is much more demanding and challenging, especially for the real problem in six degrees of freedom. The current state-of-the-art is more a pragmatic approach aimed at meeting point (iv) above, achieving a fair measure of success, than an established and soundly based methodology. The following thoughts of the author, influenced by the classic ideas of Tobak & Schiff (ref. V.60) on the aerodynamic modelling of longitudinal motions, but extended later to coupled longitudinal–lateral motions, are proposed in order to stimulate the reader to ponder on how this important topic may be advanced.

First, the earlier observation, that there needs to be compatibility between feasible experimental techniques, equations of motion and aerodynamic modelling, is explored.

So far in this book the degrees of longitudinal freedom have been angle of incidence $\alpha(t)$, (pure) pitch $\theta(t)$ and forward speed $U(t)$, irrespective of the body axis system used. But from a dynamic point of view it might be thought that it would more natural to regard an aeroplane motion as an unsteady pitching motion of the aeroplane about the flight path superimposed on a curved flight path. These 'natural' degrees of freedom would be

weathercock pitch angle relative to the flight path $\Theta(t)$

flight path angle $\gamma(t)$ (V.2.31)

forward speed $U(t)$.

The relationships between the two sets of degrees of freedom are

$$
\begin{aligned}
\alpha(t) &= \Theta(t), \qquad & \theta(t) &= \Theta(t) + \gamma(t) \\
\Theta(t) &= \alpha(t), \qquad & \gamma(t) &= \theta(t) - \alpha(t).
\end{aligned}
\qquad (V.2.32)
$$

The appropriate equations of motion would be the translational equations relative to flight path axes, and the pitch equation about the fixed body axes, that is,

$$
\begin{aligned}
m\dot{U}(t) &= \mathrm{Th}(t)\cos\Theta(t) \\
&\quad -\left[\tfrac{1}{2}\rho_{\mathrm{at}}U(t)^2 S_{\mathrm{w}} C_{\mathrm{D}}\big(\Theta(t),\gamma(t),\eta(t)\,|\,t\big)\right] - W\sin\gamma(t) \\
mU(t)\dot{\gamma}(t) &= \mathrm{Th}(t)\sin\Theta(t) \\
&\quad +\left[\tfrac{1}{2}\rho_{\mathrm{at}}U(t)^2 S_{\mathrm{w}} C_{\mathrm{L}}\big(\Theta(t),\gamma(t),\eta(t)\,|\,t\big)\right] - W\cos\gamma(t) \\
I_{yy}\big(\ddot{\gamma}(t)+\ddot{\Theta}(t)\big) &= \left[\tfrac{1}{2}\rho_{\mathrm{at}}U(t)^2 S_{\mathrm{w}} c_{\mathrm{w}} C_m\big(\Theta(t),\gamma(t),\eta(t)\,|\,t\big)\right]
\end{aligned}
\qquad \text{(V.2.33)}
$$

assuming that the thrust acts along the fuselage axis and l_{Th} is 0.

These 'natural' degrees of freedom are not only more convenient for aerodynamic experiments, but they possibly reduce the levels of non-linear aerodynamic couplings between the degrees of freedom.

Wind tunnel experiments involving dynamic weathercock pitch motions are more straightforward than experiments involving dynamic incidence (i.e. plunging) motions. It is feasible to rotate a model through a dynamic weathercock pitch, including the extreme $0 \leftrightarrow 90°$, whereas plunging motions are limited to small changes in $\alpha(t)$ about a mean angle of incidence.

The aerodynamic effect of $\dot{\gamma}(t)$, which is a pure pitch rate when Θ is constant, can be measured either in a curved flow wind tunnel or on a whirling arm rig.

A curved flow wind tunnel, as sketched in Fig. V.52, exists in the Aerospace Department, Virginia Polytechnic Institute and State University, as described by Chambers *et al.* (ref. V.61). The curved flow is obtained by curving the wall of the tunnel and interjecting vorticity by means of wire grids (when an aeroplane travels along a curved flight path in still air with constant $\dot{\gamma}$, the airstream relative to the aeroplane has uniform vorticity). Because of the grids the turbulence level in the working section is higher than normal, but not prohibitively so. Furthermore, there is a small unwanted static pressure gradient normal to the curved stream. In spite of its shortcomings this unique facility is extremely useful.

A more direct experiment is to situate a model at the end of a whirling arm, as sketched in Fig. V.53. The model literally follows a curved flight path. One disadvantage is that the whirling arm generates a swirl so the model is not flying into still air. Another disadvantage is the low Reynolds number. Several whirling arm rigs were in use 50 years ago but are currently out of fashion; perhaps it would be timely to build a modern whirling rig with contemporary technology.

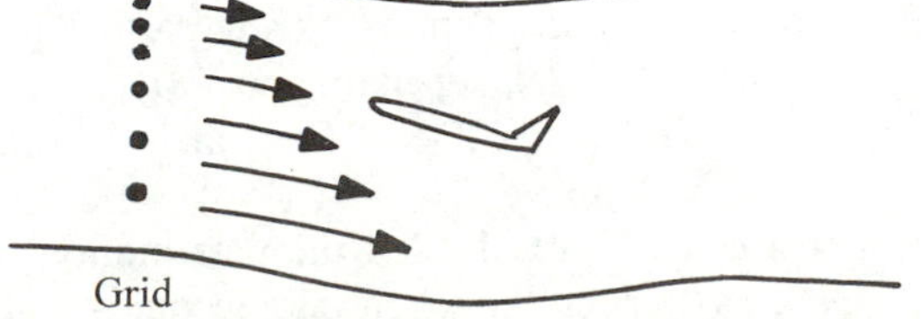

Fig. V.52. Curved flow tunnel.

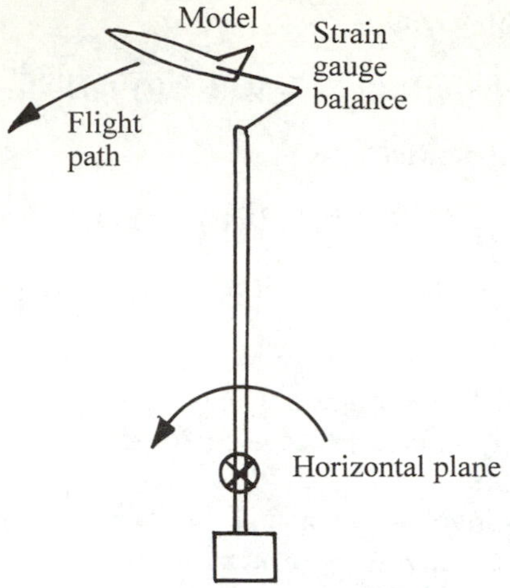

Fig. V.53. Whirling arm rig.

An aerodynamic model is now proposed.

Suppose that a dynamic weathercock pitch rig is available, capable of large amplitude oscillations on which instantaneous $C_N(t)$, $C_A(t)$, the axial force coefficient in the direction of the (–OX) axis, and $C_m(t)$, acting on a model, can be measured.

(i) Suppose the following oscillatory experiments were performed:

$\Theta(t)$	$0° \leftrightarrow 10°$,	$0° \leftrightarrow 20°$,	$0° \leftrightarrow 30°$,	$0° \leftrightarrow 40°$,	$0° \leftrightarrow 50°$,	$0° \leftrightarrow 60°$
		$10° \leftrightarrow 20°$,	$10° \leftrightarrow 30°$,	$10° \leftrightarrow 40°$,	$10° \leftrightarrow 50°$,	$10° \leftrightarrow 60°$
			$20° \leftrightarrow 30°$,	$20° \leftrightarrow 40°$,	$20° \leftrightarrow 50°$,	$20° \leftrightarrow 60°$
				$30° \leftrightarrow 40°$,	$30° \leftrightarrow 50°$,	$30° \leftrightarrow 60°$

all at the same low frequency (it may be necessary to repeat the larger amplitude tests at a secondary frequency). Static tests can also be carried out and can be regarded as the zero frequency case; static hysteresis would then be included.

(ii) Each of these experiments would give a $C_N(t) \sim \Theta(t)$ loop similar to those shown in Figs. V.45 and V.46; this information could be stored on a computer as a database with the ability to interpolate for intermediate loops.

(iii) From this amalgam of plots, by inspection, for any particular value of $\Theta(t)$ there would be a range of values of $C_N(t)$, depending on $\dot{\Theta}(t)$; in general, for a particular value of $\dot{\Theta}(t)$, at the particular value of $\Theta(t)$, there would be more than one value of $C_N(t)$.

(iv) The ambiguity of (iii) could be resolved if the past motion which preceded the combination of $(\Theta(t), \dot{\Theta}(t))$ could be taken into account—namely, if it could be decided which broad-park loop the motion was on.

(v) It is suggested that in a general motion $\Theta(t)$,

if, at time $t_{\min}$, $\dot{\Theta}(t_{\min}) = 0$, $\Theta(t_{\min}) = \Theta_{\min}$

followed by $\dot{\Theta}(t) > 0$ for $t > t_{\min}$ (V.2.34)

the value $C_N\left(\Theta_{\min}, \Theta(t), \dot{\Theta}(t)\right)$ is then unique.

For example, if $\Theta_{\min} = 10°$, then as $\Theta(t)$ increases according to the solution of the equations of motion C_N would gradually move up the loops (for example, from the $10° \leftrightarrow 20°$ loop, to the $10° \leftrightarrow 30°$ loop, to the $10° \leftrightarrow 40°$ loop), depending on $\dot{\Theta}(t)$, until $\Theta(t)$ reaches a local maximum.

(vi) Similarly,

if, at time $t_{\max}$, $\dot{\Theta}(t_{\max}) = 0$, $\Theta(t_{\max}) = \Theta_{\max}$

followed by $\dot{\Theta}(t) < 0$ for $t > t_{\max}$ (V.2.35)

the value $C_N\left(\Theta_{\max}, \Theta(t), \dot{\Theta}(t)\right)$ is then unique.

(vii) A sequence of $\Theta_{\min}$ and $\Theta_{\max}$ could appear in the numerical solution of the equations of motion; in particular, if the motion got locked into a limit cycle oscillation, the values of C_N would depend only on the most recent $\Theta_{\min}$ or $\Theta_{\max}$.

A similar procedure would give

$$C_m\left(\Theta_{\min}, \Theta(t), \dot{\Theta}(t) : \dot{\Theta}(t) > 0\right)$$

and

$$C_m\left(\Theta_{\max}, \Theta(t), \dot{\Theta}(t) : \dot{\Theta}(t) < 0\right).$$

And similarly for C_A.

Steady tests in a curved wind tunnel or on a whirling arm, with Θ and $\dot{\gamma}$ constant, would provide measurements of $C_N(\Theta, \dot{\gamma})$, $C_m(\Theta, \dot{\gamma})$ and $C_A(\Theta, \dot{\gamma})$. For relatively slow pitch rates it should be possible to express these measurements in the form

$$C_N(\Theta, \dot{\gamma}) = C_N(\Theta) + C_{N\dot{\gamma}}(\Theta)\left(c_w \dot{\gamma}/2U\right) \tag{V.2.36}$$

where $C_N(\theta)$ is given by the static tests on the weathercock pitch rig. Similar expressions can be obtained for C_m and C_A.

Static tests on the weathercock rig with constant Θ and η would provide measurements of $C_N(\Theta, \eta)$, $C_m(\Theta, \eta)$ and $C_A(\Theta, \eta)$. It should be possible to express these measurements in the form

$$C_N(\Theta, \eta) = C_N(\Theta) + C_{N\eta}(\Theta)\eta \tag{V.2.37}$$

with similar expressions for C_m and C_A.

Thus, for a general motion $\Theta(t)$ and $\gamma(t)$, with control input $\eta(t)$ the normal force coefficient may be expressed in the form

$$C_N\big(\Theta(t),\gamma(t),\eta(t)\,|\,t\big)$$
$$\simeq C_N\big(\Theta_{\min}\text{ or }\Theta_{\max},\Theta(t),\dot{\Theta}(t),\gamma(t)=0,\eta(t)=0\big)$$
$$+C_{N\dot{\gamma}}(\Theta(t))\big(c_{\mathrm{w}}\,\dot{\gamma}(t)/2U\big)+C_{N\eta}(\Theta(t))\,\eta(t). \tag{V.2.38}$$

Similar expressions would apply for C_m and C_A.

The assumptions underlying eqn. (V.2.38) are

(i) that $\dot{\gamma}(t)$ and $\eta(t)$ do not affect the dynamic break,
(ii) that $\dot{\Theta}(t)$ does not significantly affect $C_{N\dot{\gamma}}(\Theta(t))$ or $C_{N\eta}(\Theta(t))$,
(iii) that the aerodynamic effects of $\ddot{\gamma}(t)$ can be neglected.

On the basis of what has been said earlier, these assumptions appear to be reasonable; but fundamental research is needed to clarify the practicability of this proposal.

When automatic feedback systems are incorporated it might be necessary to include an unsteady term $C_{N\dot{\eta}}(\Theta(t))\;\dot{\eta}(t)$. Special rigs would then be required.

V.3 SMALL LATERAL PERTURBATION MOTIONS AT HIGH ANGLES OF INCIDENCE

In this section the lateral stability of an aeroplane trimmed at a high angle of incidence is described in general terms, assuming that the lateral perturbations in sideslip, bank and yaw angles are small. Under these conditions the concept of aerodynamic derivatives can be extended to higher angles of incidence as in sect. V.2.11. In this section high angles of incidence means up to approximately 35°.

V.3.1 Lateral aerodynamic derivatives at high angles of incidence

Lateral aerodynamics have not been investigated systematically at a fundamental level to the same extent as longitudinal aerodynamics as described in sect. V.2. A fund of qualitative understanding of lateral aerodynamics has evolved, complemented by an extensive database. One of the main difficulties at high angles of incidence is that lateral aerodynamics are highly configuration dependent, with significant differences in derivatives, even with change of sign, with small changes in configuration shape. At this stage the broad trends of the lateral aerodynamic characteristics are described; at a later stage some of the more important differences arising from configuration changes are reviewed.

All derivatives described below are relative to fuselage body axes.

Consider first the static sideslip derivatives. Measurements on models at a steady angle of incidence, α, show a reasonably linear variation of overall side force, rolling moment and yawing moment over a range of small steady sideslip angles, β, from which the derivatives can be determined from the gradients with respect to β.

A variation of the derivative $C_{n\beta}$ with α is shown in Fig. V.54(i) for the fuselage nose alone, the wing–fuselage without the fin, and the complete configuration. In this case the wing–fuselage break occurs at α about 15°.

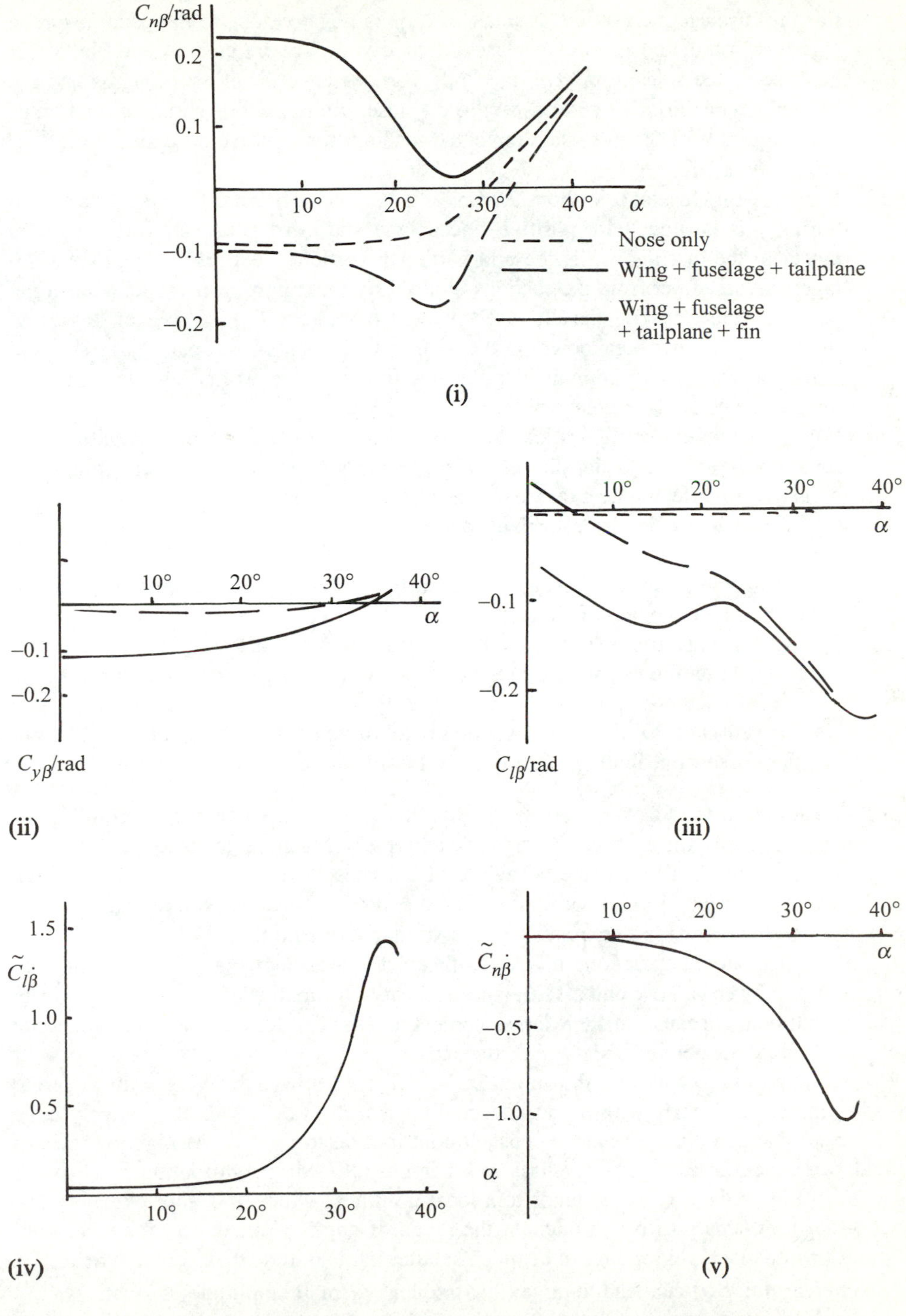

Fig. V.54. Typical variations of sideslip derivatives at high angles of incidence.

(i) For the fuselage nose alone: at small α, $C_{n\beta}$ is negative due to the usual negative side force on the nose; as α increases forebody vortices are created, see Fig. V.47; because of the sideslip the two forebody vortices have differing strengths and are located asymmetrically with respect to the nose, giving, in this case, a reduction of the magnitude of the nose side force and leading to a positive nose side force at α greater than 30°.

(ii) For the wing–fuselage, without the fin: as α increases beyond the break, part-span vorticity is created; with positive sideslip the starboard part-span vorticity veers closer to the fuselage while the port part-span vorticity veers away from the fuselage; the net effect from the suctions induced by these part-span vorticities is a net positive side force on the aft fuselage, which reduces $C_{n\beta}$; at higher angles of incidence the flow breakdown on the wing extends across the span, dispersing the part-span vorticity and diminishing the side forces on the aft fuselage, leaving only the side force on the fuselage nose.

(iii) For the complete configuration: at low angles of α the overriding negative side force on the fin due to sideslip results in a positive $C_{n\beta}$; as α increases through the break the fin effectiveness decreases for several reasons:

(a) an increase in the effective sweep angle of the fin decreases the fin 'lift curve' slope,

(b) an increase in the fuselage upper surface boundary layer immerses more of the fin in a region of reduced dynamic pressure,

(c) the asymmetric effects of the forebody vortices and the wing part-span vorticity act on the fin, similar to the effects on the aft fuselage as explained in (ii) above.

As α approaches 30° the fin loses virtually all of its effectiveness; the only remaining side force, contributing to the $C_{n\beta}$, is the side force on the fuselage nose.

The side force on the fuselage nose is therefore of crucial importance at high angles of incidence. But this force, even its sign, is extremely sensitive to nose geometry, as explained in more detail later; the behaviour of the nose force in Fig V.54(i) should not be regarded as a general trend but as a particular example. However, the dramatic loss of $C_{n\beta}$ through the break for a complete configuration is a general trend.

The corresponding variations of $C_{Y\beta}$ with α are shown in Fig. V.54(ii). The side forces on the fuselage nose and aft fuselage are relatively small (they generate significant yawing moments because of their large moment arms). The loss of fin effectiveness at angles of incidence above 30° is again indicated.

A variation of $C_{l\beta}$ with α is shown in Fig. V.54(iii). At low α the wing contribution to $(-C_{l\beta})$ increases linearly with α, as expected from sect. IV.2.3, and the relatively large fin for combat aeroplanes makes a constant contribution to $(-C_{l\beta})$. At higher angles of incidence the fin loses its effectiveness and then only the wing contribution remains. As shown in Fig. V.54(iii) $(-C_{l\beta})$ tends to a local minimum when α is approximately 25° but $(-C_{l\beta})$ remains positive throughout the range of angle of incidence; for other configurations this local minimum can be much smaller in magnitude than depicted here.

Time varying $\beta(t)$ can lead to large (low frequency, small amplitude) derivatives, $\tilde{C}_{l\dot{\beta}}$ and $\tilde{C}_{n\dot{\beta}}$, as sketched in Fig. V.54(iv) and (v), due to different delays in the onset of flow separation and reattachments on the port and starboard wings. Like $\tilde{C}_{m\dot{\alpha}}$, $\tilde{C}_{l\dot{\beta}}$ and $\tilde{C}_{n\dot{\beta}}$ can be either positive or negative, depending on the configuration; usually if $\tilde{C}_{n\dot{\beta}}$ is positive then $\tilde{C}_{l\dot{\beta}}$ is negative, and *vice versa*.

Next, for the roll rate derivatives. These are usually measured on an oscillatory roll rig which oscillates a model in roll about the fuselage body roll axis, the *ox* axis, through a small bank angle amplitude at a relatively low frequency, with the fuselage *ox* axis inclined at a static angle α to the airstream of velocity U. A small bank angle $\Delta\varphi$ induces a sideslip angle ($U \sin \alpha \Delta\varphi$). And so the rate derivatives which are measured are:

$$\tilde{C}_{lp} + \tilde{C}_{l\dot{\beta}} \sin\alpha, \quad \tilde{C}_{np} + \tilde{C}_{n\dot{\beta}} \sin\alpha, \quad \tilde{C}_{Yp} + \tilde{C}_{Y\dot{\beta}} \sin\alpha.$$

As demonstrated later, these combinations of derivatives appear in the equations of motion.

Typical variations of the roll rate derivatives are sketched in Fig. V.55. The large values above the break around 35° arise presumably from lag effects in the onset of flow separation and reattachment in both the p and β motions. Of particular significance is the loss in roll damping (i.e. $[-(\tilde{C}_{lp} + \tilde{C}_{l\dot{\beta}} \sin\alpha)]$) through the break, leading to a change in sign; a sign reversal does not always occur.

Finally, for the yaw rate derivatives which are measured on an oscillatory yaw rig which oscillates a model in yaw about the fuselage body yaw axis, the *oz* axis, through a small yaw angle amplitude at a relatively low frequency with the fuselage *ox* axis inclined at a static angle α to the airstream of velocity U. A small yaw angle $\Delta\psi$ induces a sideslip angle ($-U \cos \alpha \; \Delta\psi$). And so the rate derivatives which are measured are:

$$\tilde{C}_{lr} - \tilde{C}_{l\dot{\beta}} \cos\alpha, \quad \tilde{C}_{nr} - \tilde{C}_{n\dot{\beta}} \cos\alpha, \quad \tilde{C}_{Yp} - \tilde{C}_{Y\dot{\beta}} \cos\alpha.$$

Typical variations of the yaw rate derivatives are sketched in Figs. V.56. Again the fuselage nose forces due to rate of yaw play a prominent role in $(\tilde{C}_{lr} - \tilde{C}_{l\dot{\beta}} \cos\alpha)$ at high angles. In these sketches $(\tilde{C}_{lr} - \tilde{C}_{l\dot{\beta}} \cos\alpha)$ and $(\tilde{C}_{nr} - \tilde{C}_{n\dot{\beta}} \cos\alpha)$ change sign as α increases; this sign reversal does not always occur.

V.3.2 Small perturbation lateral stability

The following presentation follows that of Ross (ref. V.62).

Consider an aeroplane in trimmed steady level flight at forward speed U_{trim} and angle of incidence α_{trim}.

The equations of motion for small lateral perturbations are, extending eqns. (IV.5.10)–(IV.5.12),

$$\begin{aligned}(C_W/g)U_{\text{trim}}\left[\dot{\beta}(t) + \cos\alpha_{\text{trim}} r(t) - \sin\alpha_{\text{trim}} p(t)\right] \\ \simeq \left[C_{Y\beta}\beta(t) + C_{Yp}\left(p(t)s_W/U_{\text{trim}}\right)\right] + C_W \;\Delta\varphi(t)\cos\alpha_{\text{trim}} \\ + \text{[non-dimensional side force due to control inputs and atmospheric gusts]}\end{aligned} \qquad \text{(V.3.1)}$$

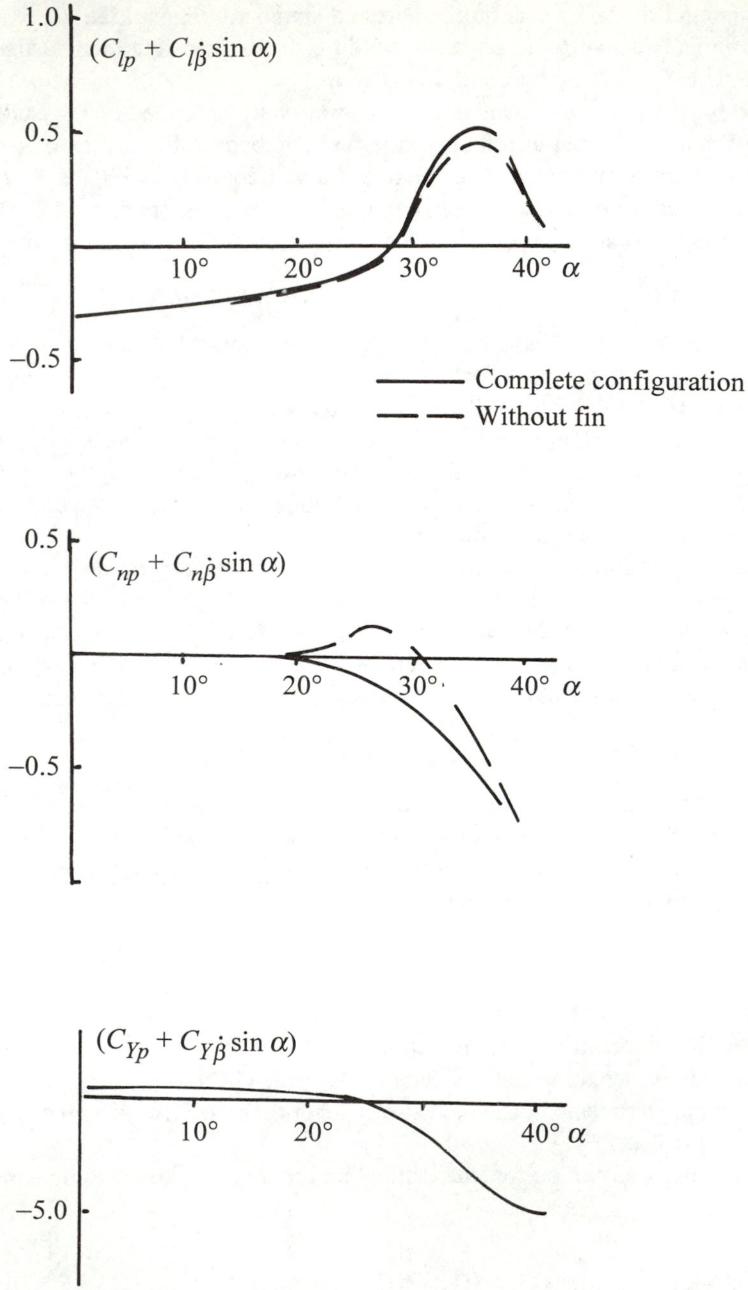

Fig. V.55. Typical variation of roll rate derivatives at high angles of incidence.

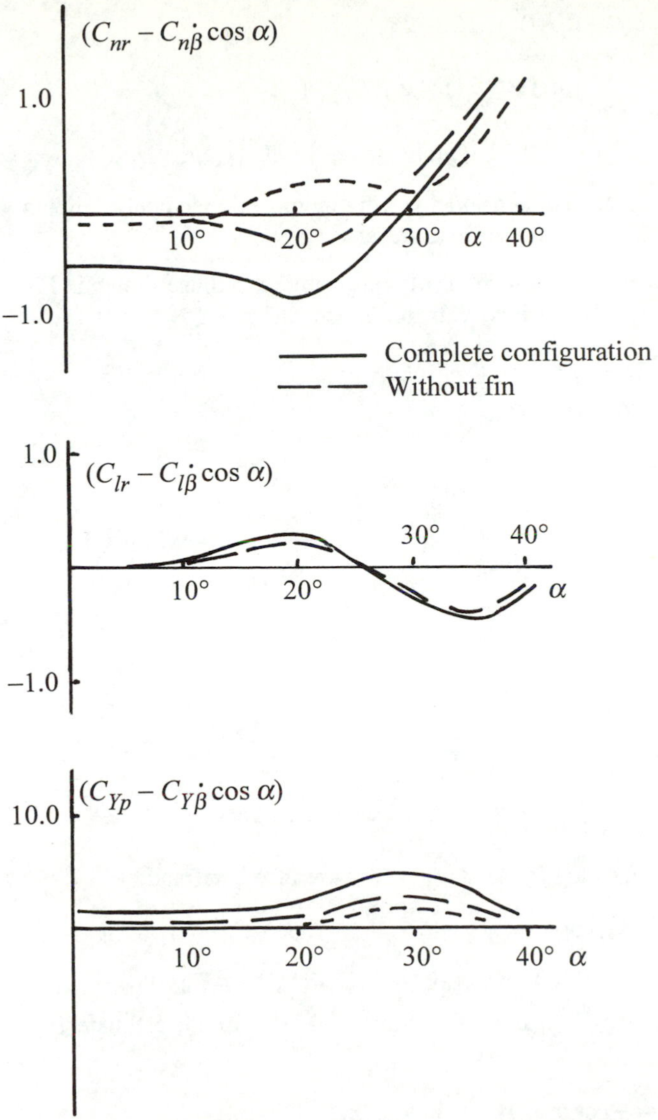

Fig. V.56. Typical variation of yaw rate derivatives at high angles of incidence.

$$
\begin{aligned}
&\left[i_{xx}\dot{p}(t) - i_{xz}\dot{r}(t)\right]\left(s_{\mathrm{w}}C_{\mathrm{W}}/2g\right) \\
&\quad \simeq \Big[C_{l\beta}\beta(t) + C_{l\dot{\beta}}\left(\dot{\beta}(t)s_{\mathrm{w}}/U_{\mathrm{trim}}\right) \\
&\qquad\qquad + C_{lp}\left(p(t)s_{\mathrm{w}}/U_{\mathrm{trim}}\right) + C_{lr}\left(r(t)s_{\mathrm{w}}/U_{\mathrm{trim}}\right)\Big] \qquad \text{(V.3.2)} \\
&\quad + [\text{non-dimensional rolling moment due to control inputs} \\
&\qquad \text{and atmospheric gusts}]
\end{aligned}
$$

$$\left[-i_{xz}\dot{p}(t)+i_{zz}\dot{r}(t)\right]\left(s_{\mathrm{w}}C_{\mathrm{W}}/2g\right)$$
$$\simeq\left[C_{n\beta}\beta(t)+C_{n\dot{\beta}}\left(\dot{\beta}(t)s_{\mathrm{w}}/U_{\mathrm{trim}}\right)\right.$$
$$\left.+\,C_{np}\left(p(t)s_{\mathrm{w}}/U_{\mathrm{trim}}\right)+C_{nr}\left(r(t)s_{\mathrm{w}}/U_{\mathrm{trim}}\right)\right] \qquad \text{(V.3.3)}$$
+[non-dimensional yawing moment due to control inputs and atmospheric gusts]

where all derivatives are functions of α_{trim}, similar to those shown in Figs. V.54–V.56.

At higher angles of incidence, by reference to Fig. V.57,

$$p(t)=\Delta\dot{\varphi}(t)-\Delta\dot{\psi}(t)\sin\alpha_{\mathrm{trim}},$$
$$r(t)=\Delta\dot{\psi}(t)\cos\alpha_{\mathrm{trim}} \qquad \text{(V.3.4)}$$

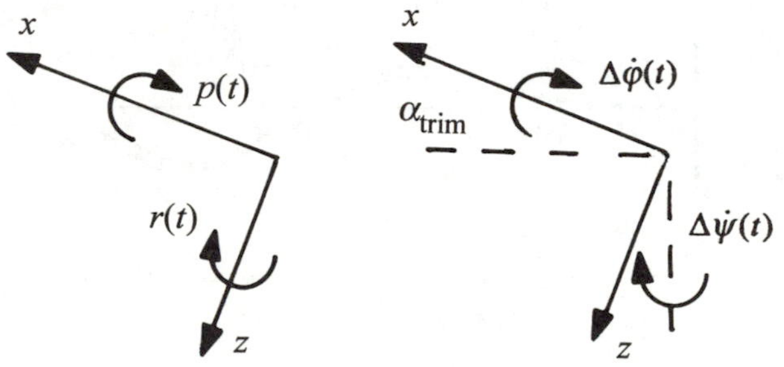

Fig. V.57. Resolution of rates of rotation.

Deviation angles $\Delta\varphi_{\mathrm{d}}(t)$ and $\Delta\psi_{\mathrm{d}}(t)$ are introduced, defined by

$$\Delta\varphi_{\mathrm{d}}(t)=\Delta\varphi(t)-\Delta\psi(t)\sin\alpha_{\mathrm{trim}},\quad \Delta\varphi(t)=\Delta\varphi_{\mathrm{d}}(t)+\Delta\psi_{\mathrm{d}}(t)\tan\alpha_{\mathrm{trim}}$$
$$\Delta\psi_{\mathrm{d}}(t)=\Delta\psi(t)\cos\alpha_{\mathrm{trim}},\quad \Delta\psi(t)=\Delta\psi_{\mathrm{d}}(t)\sec\alpha_{\mathrm{trim}} \qquad \text{(V.3.5)}$$

Because $(C_{\mathrm{W}}/g)U_{\mathrm{trim}}$ is of the order of 10.0 a crude estimate for $\dot{\beta}(t)$ from eqn. (V.3.1) is

$$\dot{\beta}(t)\simeq-\cos\alpha_{\mathrm{trim}}r(t)+\sin\alpha_{\mathrm{trim}}p(t). \qquad \text{(V.3.6)}$$

Combining eqns. (V.3.1)–(V.3.4) and (V.3.6), then

$$\left(C_{\mathrm{W}}/g\right)U_{\mathrm{trim}}\left[\dot{\beta}(t)+\cos\alpha_{\mathrm{trim}}r(t)-\sin\alpha_{\mathrm{trim}}p(t)\right]$$
$$\simeq\left[C_{Y\beta}\beta(t)+C_{Yp}\left(p(t)s_{\mathrm{w}}/U_{\mathrm{trim}}\right)\right]$$
$$+C_{\mathrm{W}}\left[\Delta\varphi_{\mathrm{d}}(t)\cos\alpha_{\mathrm{trim}}+\Delta\psi_{\mathrm{d}}(t)\sin\alpha_{\mathrm{trim}}\right] \qquad \text{(V.3.7)}$$
+[non-dimensional side force due to control inputs and atmospheric gusts]

$$\begin{aligned}&[i_{xx}\dot{p}(t) - i_{xz}\dot{r}(t)](s_{\mathrm{w}}C_{\mathrm{W}}/2g)\\&\quad\simeq \left[C_{l\beta}\beta(t) + (C_{lp})_{\mathrm{eff}}(p(t)s_{\mathrm{w}}/U_{\mathrm{trim}}) + (C_{lr})_{\mathrm{eff}}(r(t)s_{\mathrm{w}}/U_{\mathrm{trim}})\right]\\&\qquad+[\text{non-dimensional rolling moment due to control}\\&\qquad\quad\text{inputs and atmospheric gusts}]\end{aligned} \tag{V.3.8}$$

$$\begin{aligned}&[-i_{xz}\dot{p}(t) + i_{zz}\dot{r}(t)](s_{\mathrm{w}}C_{\mathrm{W}}/2g)\\&\quad\simeq \left[C_{n\beta}\beta(t) + (C_{np})_{\mathrm{eff}}(p(t)s_{\mathrm{w}}/U_{\mathrm{trim}}) + (C_{nr})_{\mathrm{eff}}(r(t)s_{\mathrm{w}}/U_{\mathrm{trim}})\right]\\&\qquad+[\text{non-dimensional yawing moment due to control}\\&\qquad\quad\text{inputs and atmospheric gusts}]\end{aligned} \tag{V.3.9}$$

$$p(t) = \Delta\dot{\varphi}_{\mathrm{d}}(t), \tag{V.3.10}$$

$$r(t) = \Delta\dot{\psi}_{\mathrm{d}}(t). \tag{V.3.11}$$

where

$$\begin{aligned}(C_{lp})_{\mathrm{eff}} &= C_{lp} + C_{l\dot{\beta}}\sin\alpha_{\mathrm{trim}}, &\quad (C_{lr})_{\mathrm{eff}} &= C_{lr} - C_{l\dot{\beta}}\cos\alpha_{\mathrm{trim}}\\(C_{np})_{\mathrm{eff}} &= C_{np} + C_{n\dot{\beta}}\sin\alpha_{\mathrm{trim}}, &\quad (C_{nr})_{\mathrm{eff}} &= C_{nr} - C_{n\dot{\beta}}\cos\alpha_{\mathrm{trim}}.\end{aligned} \tag{V.3.12}$$

These effective derivatives are the ones shown in Figs. V.55 and V.56; they are measured directly in conventional roll and yaw oscillatory rigs.

The stability characteristic equation of eqns. (V.3.7)–(V.3.11), which can be derived by following the same procedures as those described in section IV.8, is, in non-dimensional form

$$(A_4\bar{\lambda}^4 + A_3\bar{\lambda}^3 + A_2\bar{\lambda}^2 + A_1\bar{\lambda} + A_0)\bar{\lambda} = 0 \tag{V.3.13}$$

where, retaining only the main terms,

$$A_4 \simeq (i_{xx}/2)(i_{zz}/2)$$

$$A_3 \simeq (-C_{Y\beta})A_4 + (i_{zz}/2)(-C_{lp})_{\mathrm{eff}} + (i_{xx}/2)(-C_{nr})_{\mathrm{eff}}$$

$$\begin{aligned}A_2 \simeq{}& (2\overline{m}/\mathrm{AR}_{\mathrm{w}})\left[(i_{xx}/2)C_{n\beta}\cos\alpha_{\mathrm{trim}} + (i_{zz}/2)(-C_{l\beta})\sin\alpha_{\mathrm{trim}}\right]\\&+(-C_{lp})_{\mathrm{eff}}(-C_{nr})_{\mathrm{eff}}\end{aligned}$$

$$\begin{aligned}A_1 \simeq{}& (2\overline{m}/\mathrm{AR}_{\mathrm{w}})\Big[C_{n\beta}\big[(-C_{lp})_{\mathrm{eff}}\cos\alpha_{\mathrm{trim}} - (C_{lr})_{\mathrm{eff}}\sin\alpha_{\mathrm{trim}}\\&\qquad - C_{\mathrm{W}}(i_{xx}/2)\sin\alpha_{\mathrm{trim}}\big]\\&\quad+(-C_{l\beta})\big[(-C_{nr})_{\mathrm{eff}}\sin\alpha_{\mathrm{trim}} + (-C_{np})_{\mathrm{eff}}\cos\alpha_{\mathrm{trim}}\\&\qquad + C_{\mathrm{W}}(i_{zz}/2)\cos\alpha_{\mathrm{trim}}\big]\Big]\end{aligned}$$

$$A_0 \simeq (2\overline{m}/\mathrm{AR_w})C_W\Big[-\big[C_{n\beta}(-C_{lp})_{\mathrm{eff}}+(-C_{l\beta})(-C_{np})_{\mathrm{eff}}\big]\sin\alpha_{\mathrm{trim}} + \big[(-C_{l\beta})(-C_{nr})_{\mathrm{eff}} - C_{n\beta}(C_{lr})_{\mathrm{eff}}\big]\cos\alpha_{\mathrm{trim}}\Big].$$

From Appendix 10 for low angles of α_{trim} the characteristic equation, eqn. (V.3.13), can be expressed in terms of its factors

$$(\bar{\lambda}+\bar{\lambda}_{\mathrm{spiral}})(\bar{\lambda}+\bar{\lambda}_{\mathrm{roll}})\left(\bar{\lambda}^2+(2\zeta\overline{\omega}_0)_{\mathrm{Dr}}+(\overline{\omega}_0)^2_{\mathrm{Dr}}\right)=0 \qquad \text{(V.3.14)}$$

where

$$\begin{aligned}
\bar{\lambda}_{\mathrm{spiral}} &\simeq (A_0/A_1)\\
\bar{\lambda}_{\mathrm{roll}} &\simeq 0.5\big[(A_3/A_4)+(A_1/A_2)\big]\\
(2\zeta\overline{\omega}_0)_{\mathrm{Dr}} &\simeq 0.5\big[(A_3/A_4)-(A_1/A_2)\big]\\
(\overline{\omega}_0)^2_{\mathrm{Dr}} &\simeq (A_2/A_4)-0.5(A_3/A_4)\big[(A_3/A_4)-(A_1/A_2)\big].
\end{aligned} \qquad \text{(V.3.15)}$$

Although eqns. (V.3.14) and (V.3.15) become invalid as α_{trim} increases through the break, because the ball-park numbers change, it is thought that these equations indicate qualitative trends.

The coefficient A_3 plays a crucial role. From eqns. (V.3.15), as A_3 decreases, the Dutch roll damping can go negative. And the derivative which primarily affects A_3 is $(-C_{lp})_{\mathrm{eff}}$. A reduction of the effective roll rate damping can lead to an unstable Dutch roll. This conclusion needs care because a reduction of $(-C_{lp})_{\mathrm{eff}}$ reduces both A_3 and A_1, but the A_3 term appears to be the dominant one. Note that the roll rate modal damping remains positive as $(-C_{lp})_{\mathrm{eff}}$ tends to zero.

The other crucial coefficient is A_2. From eqns. (V.3.15), as A_2 decreases, the Dutch roll damping can go negative. And the 'derivative' which dominates A_2 is the so-called 'dynamic $C_{n\beta}$', where

$$(C_{n\beta})_{\mathrm{dyn}} = \left[C_{n\beta}\cos\alpha_{\mathrm{trim}} + (i_{zz}/i_{xx})(-C_{l\beta})\sin\alpha_{\mathrm{trim}}\right]. \qquad \text{(V.3.16)}$$

Also, as $(C_{n\beta})_{\mathrm{dyn}}$ decreases, the Dutch roll stiffness, and the Dutch roll undamped frequency, is reduced; it is not easy to deduce from eqns. (V.3.15) in qualitative terms exactly what happens to the Dutch roll stiffness as $(C_{n\beta})_{\mathrm{dyn}}$, and A_2, tend to zero.

As explained later, positive $(C_{n\beta})_{\mathrm{dyn}}$ is used as a design criterion.

For more accurate estimates of the stability characteristics it is necessary to plot out the variations of A_3, A_2, A_1 and A_0 with α_{trim} and evaluate the values of the roots (see Chambers & Anglin, ref. V.63).

V.3.3 Wing rock

Wing rock is a lightly damped rolling oscillation experienced by combat aeroplanes which affects controllability, impairs tracking and tactical effectiveness by preventing the full potential of the lifting capability to be exploited (see Ross & Nguyen, ref. V.63, and Ross, ref. V.64).

The author recommends that the reader treats the extensive literature on wing rock with critical scepticism; some of the mathematical models appear unconvincing and sometimes the relationship between cause and effect may not be the one described.

A key ingredient in wing rock is the loss of Dutch roll damping at high angles of incidence, as explained in the last section. And at high angles of incidence the Dutch roll mode can become primarily a roll motion with only a small yaw component. Now the Dutch roll damping may be negative for small amplitude oscillations but, as the amplitude builds up, the damping changes becoming positive; then small amplitude roll oscillations are unstable which build up to a stable roll oscillation of fixed large amplitude, a so-called limit cycle oscillation. This non-linear behaviour has been measured on the two most influential derivatives which affect the Dutch roll damping: $C_{n\beta}$ and $(-C_{lp})_{\text{eff}}$; in both cases, as shown in Fig. V.58, at higher angles of incidence these derivatives are negative for small amplitude, becoming positive at larger amplitudes.

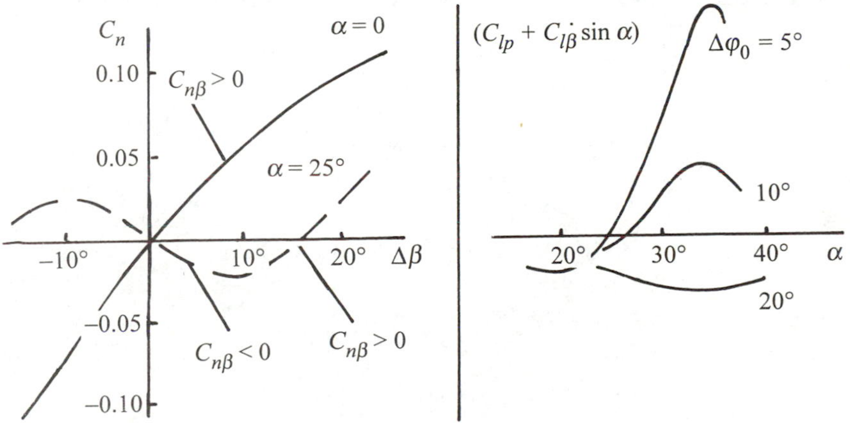

Fig. V.58. Variation of derivatives with amplitude.

Wing rock can occur in different forms.

(i) Wing rock can occur in flow regimes where lag effects are not prominent; this form of wing rock is repeatable.

(ii) Wing rock can occur in flow regimes where lag effects due to the onset of flow breakdown and reattachment, including vortex breakdown and reassembly, are prominent; this form of wing rock is sometimes random in occurrence with variations in amplitudes. Forebody vortices can play an influential role in this type of wing rock (see Ericsson, ref. V.66).

(iii) Persistent small amplitude irregular oscillations in roll can be generated at high subsonic speeds by the asymmetric fore and aft movements of shock waves on the upper surface of the wings.

Automatic flight control systems may be used to suppress the wing rock; such a system can only be effective if there is sufficient roll control power from the differential tailplane. But there should not be a problem at high angles of incidence for a low tailplane configuration.

V.4 COUPLED LONGITUDINAL–LATERAL MOTIONS

V.4.1 Equations of motion of a rigid aeroplane

To understand the complex motions of a rigid aeroplane involving coupled longitudinal and lateral degrees of freedom, it is first necessary to derive the full equations of motion. This derivation is a generalized extension of the derivations of the longitudinal and lateral motions outlined in Parts III and IV.

As shown in Fig. V.59, the position of the centre of mass relative to inertial *OXYZ* axes, taken for the present purposes as fixed earth axes, is denoted by the vector

$$\mathbf{R}_{\mathrm{cm}}(t) = \mathbf{I}X_{\mathrm{cm}}(t) + \mathbf{J}Y_{\mathrm{cm}}(t) + \mathbf{K}Z_{\mathrm{cm}}(t) \tag{V.4.1}$$

where **I**, **J**, **K** are the unit vectors in the directions of *OX*, *OY*, *OZ* respectively.

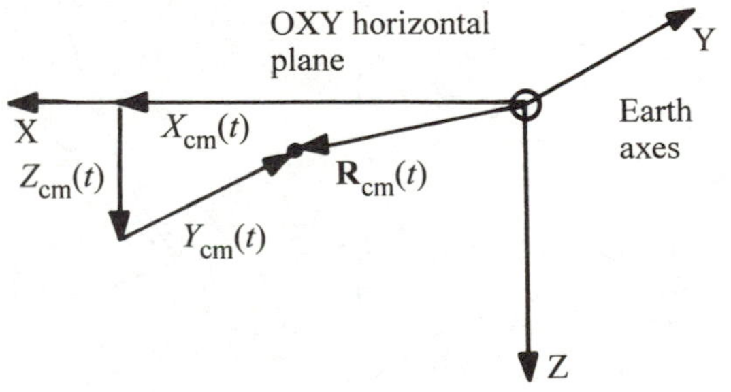

Fig. V.59. Definition of $\mathbf{R}_{\mathrm{cm}}(t)$.

The fuselage body axis system *oxyz* fixed in the rigid aeroplane has the origin at the centre of mass, the *ox* axis points forward along the fuselage, the *oz* axis points downward in the plane of symmetry, the *oy* axis points to starboard.

The angular rotation of the aeroplane is denoted by the vector

$$\mathbf{\Omega}(t) = \mathbf{i}p(t) + \mathbf{j}q(t) + \mathbf{k}r(t). \tag{V.4.2}$$

where **i**, **j**, **k** are the unit vectors in the directions *ox*, *oy*, *oz* respectively.

Because the unit vectors **i**, **j**, **k** are rotating in space, as shown in Fig. V.60, then

$$\mathrm{d}\mathbf{i}/\mathrm{d}t = \mathbf{j}r(t) - \mathbf{k}q(t), \quad \mathrm{d}\mathbf{j}/\mathrm{d}t = -\mathbf{i}r(t) + \mathbf{k}p(t), \quad \mathrm{d}\mathbf{k}/\mathrm{d}t = \mathbf{i}q(t) - \mathbf{j}p(t). \tag{V.4.3}$$

Consider a small element of mass δm located around point $P(x, y, z)$. The position of point P relative to the aeroplane centre of mass is the vector

$$P = \mathbf{i}x + \mathbf{j}y + \mathbf{k}z. \tag{V.4.4}$$

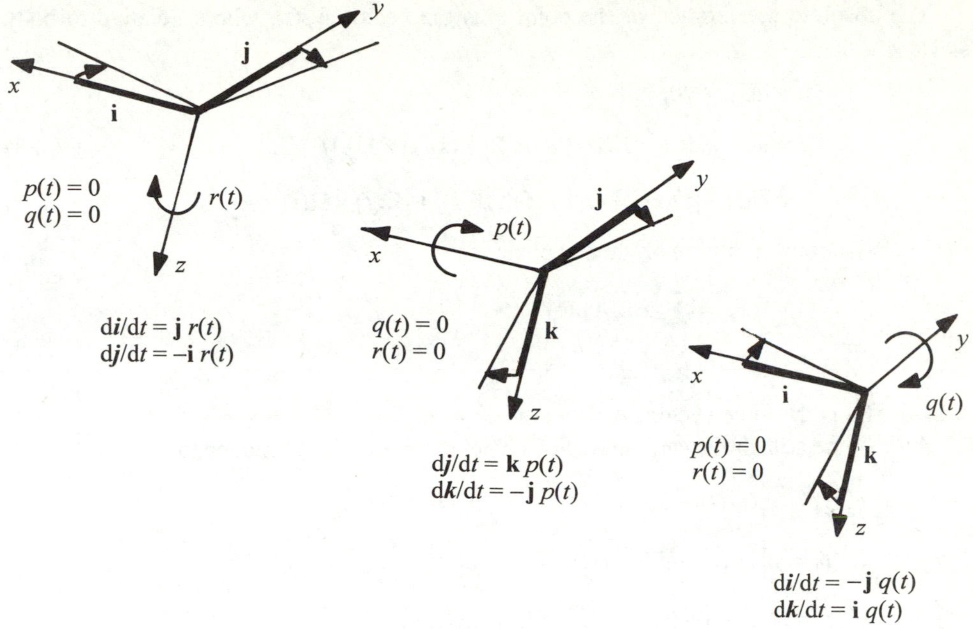

Fig. V.60. Rates of change of unit vectors.

The location of point P relative to earth axes is $(\mathbf{R}_{cm}(t) + P)$.

The absolute velocity of the point P is the vector $\mathbf{U}_P(t)$, where, relative to the body axes,

$$
\begin{aligned}
\mathbf{U}_P(t) &= \mathbf{i}U_{Px}(t) + \mathbf{j}U_{Py}(t) + \mathbf{k}U_{Pz}(t) \\
&= \mathrm{d}[\mathbf{R}_{cm}(t) + P]/\mathrm{d}t \\
&= \mathbf{U}(t) + \left[(\mathrm{d}\mathbf{i}/\mathrm{d}t)\,x + (\mathrm{d}\mathbf{j}/\mathrm{d}t)\,y + (\mathrm{d}\mathbf{k}/\mathrm{d}t)\,z\right] \\
&= \mathbf{U}(t) + (\mathbf{W}(t) \times P)
\end{aligned}
\qquad \text{(V.4.5)}
$$

where

$$
\begin{aligned}
\mathbf{U}(t) &= \text{absolute velocity of the aeroplane centre of mass} \\
&= \mathbf{I}\dot{X}_{cm}(t) + \mathbf{J}\dot{Y}_{cm}(t) + \mathbf{K}\dot{Z}_{cm}(t) \qquad \text{relative to } OXYZ \text{ axes} \\
&= \mathbf{i}U_x(t) + \mathbf{j}U_y(t) + \mathbf{k}U_z(t) \qquad \text{relative to } oxyz \text{ axes.}
\end{aligned}
\qquad \text{(V.4.6)}
$$

and

$$
\boldsymbol{\Omega}(t) \times P = \begin{vmatrix} \mathbf{i} & \mathbf{j} & \mathbf{k} \\ p(t) & q(t) & r(t) \\ x & y & z \end{vmatrix} \qquad \text{(V.4.7)}
$$

on substitution of eqn. (V.4.3).

The absolute acceleration of the point P is the vector $\mathbf{A}_P(t)$, where, relative to body axes,

$$\begin{aligned}\mathbf{A}_P(t) &= \mathrm{d}\mathbf{U}_P(t)/\mathrm{d}t \\ &= \mathrm{d}\mathbf{U}(t)/\mathrm{d}t + \big((\mathrm{d}\boldsymbol{\Omega}(t)/\mathrm{d}t)\times P\big) + \big(\boldsymbol{\Omega}(t)\times\mathbf{U}_P(t)\big) \\ &= \dot{\mathbf{U}}(t) + [\boldsymbol{\Omega}(t)\times\mathbf{U}(t)] + [\dot{\boldsymbol{\Omega}}(t)\times P] + [\boldsymbol{\Omega}(t)\times\boldsymbol{\Omega}(t)\times P].\end{aligned} \tag{V.4.8}$$

The equations of motion of the aeroplane are

$$\begin{aligned}\sum \delta\mathbf{F}_P &= \sum \delta m\,\mathbf{A}_P(t) \\ \sum (P\times\delta\mathbf{F}_P) &= \sum \delta m\big(P\times\mathbf{A}_P(t)\big)\end{aligned} \tag{V.4.9}$$

where $\delta\mathbf{F}_P$ is the force vector acting on the element δm.

After some straightforward but tedious algebra, eqns. (V.4.9) reduce to

$$\begin{aligned}F_x(t) &= m\big[\dot{U}_x(t) + U_z(t)\,q(t) - U_y(t)\,r(t)\big] \\ F_y(t) &= m\big[\dot{U}_y(t) + U_x(t)\,r(t) - U_z(t)\,p(t)\big] \\ F_z(t) &= m\big[\dot{U}_z(t) + U_y(t)\,p(t) - U_x(t)\,q(t)\big] \\ M_x(t) &= I_{xx}\dot{p}(t) - I_{xz}\big(\dot{r}(t) + p(t)\,q(t)\big) - (I_{yy} - I_{zz})q(t)r(t) \\ M_y(t) &= I_{yy}\dot{q}(t) - I_{xz}\big(r^2(t) - p^2(t)\big) - (I_{zz} - I_{xx})r(t)\,p(t) \\ M_z(t) &= I_{zz}\dot{r}(t) - I_{xz}\big(\dot{p}(t) - q(t)\,r(t)\big) - (I_{xx} - I_{yy})\,p(t)q(t)\end{aligned} \tag{V.4.10}$$

where

$$\begin{aligned}F_x(t) &= \text{total force component in direction } ox \text{ applied to the aeroplane} \\ &= -\mathbf{A}(t) + \big(F_x(t)\big)_{\mathrm{Th}} + \big(F_x(t)\big)_g\end{aligned}$$

$$\begin{aligned}F_y(t) &= \text{total force component in direction } oy \text{ applied to the aeroplane} \\ &= (Y(t)) + \big(F_y(t)\big)_g\end{aligned}$$

$$\begin{aligned}F_z(t) &= \text{total force component in direction } oz \text{ applied to the aeroplane} \\ &= (-N(t)) + \big(F_z(t)\big)_{\mathrm{Th}} + \big(F_z(t)\big)_g\end{aligned}$$

$$M_x(t) = \text{total moment component about } ox \text{ axis} = \mathscr{L}(t)$$

$$M_y(t) = \text{total moment component about } oy \text{ axis} = \mathscr{M}(t) + \big(M_y(t)\big)_{\mathrm{Th}}$$

$$M_z(t) = \text{total moment component about } oz \text{ axis} = \mathscr{N}(t) + \big(M_z(t)\big)_{\mathrm{Th}}$$

where A(t), $Y(t)$, $N(t)$, $\mathscr{L}(t)$, $\mathscr{M}(t)$, $\mathscr{N}(t)$ are the overall aerodynamic forces and moments; suffix 'Th' denotes the contribution from the thrust, the term $(M_z(t))_{Th}$ refers to an 'engine-out' case; suffix 'g' denotes the contribution from the gravitational body force; and m is the total aeroplane mass.

Moments of inertia are:

$$I_{xx} = \sum \delta m(y^2 + z^2), \quad I_{yy} = \sum \delta m(z^2 + x^2), \quad I_{zz} = \sum \delta m(x^2 + y^2).$$

Product of inertia:

$$I_{xz} = \sum \delta m\ xz.$$

The products of inertia

$$I_{zy}\left(= \sum \delta m\ zy\right) \quad \text{and} \quad I_{yx}\left(= \sum \delta m\ yx\right)$$

are assumed to be zero, assuming symmetry about the oxz plane.

The Euler angles $\psi(t)$, $\theta(t)$, $\varphi(t)$, defining the orientation of the body axes relative to the earth axes, are shown in Fig. V.61.

By reference to Fig. V.61,

$$\begin{aligned} (F_x(t))_g &= -mg \sin\theta(t) \\ (F_y(t))_g &= +mg \cos\theta(t) \sin\varphi(t) \\ (F_z(t))_g &= +mg \cos\theta(t) \cos\varphi(t). \end{aligned} \tag{V.4.11}$$

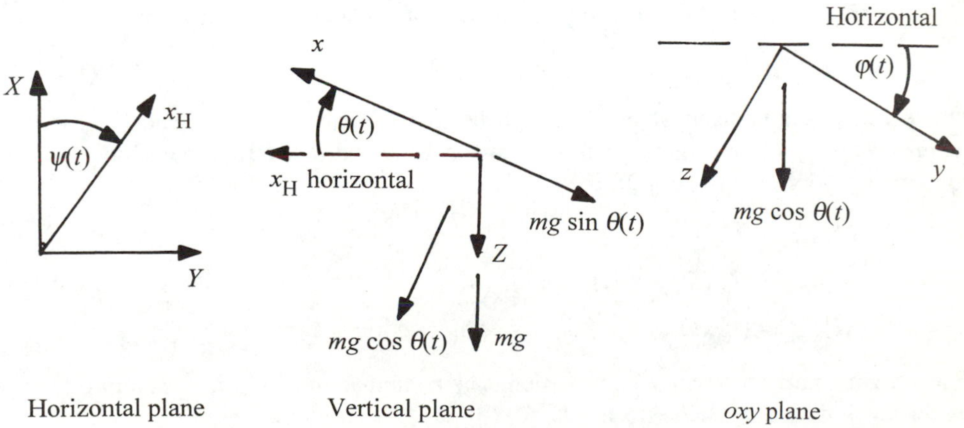

Fig. V.61. Definition of Euler angles.

Finally, the relationships between $p(t)$, $q(t)$ and $r(t)$ and $\dot{\psi}(t)$, $\dot{\theta}(t)$ and $\dot{\varphi}(t)$ are, by inspection of Fig. V.62,

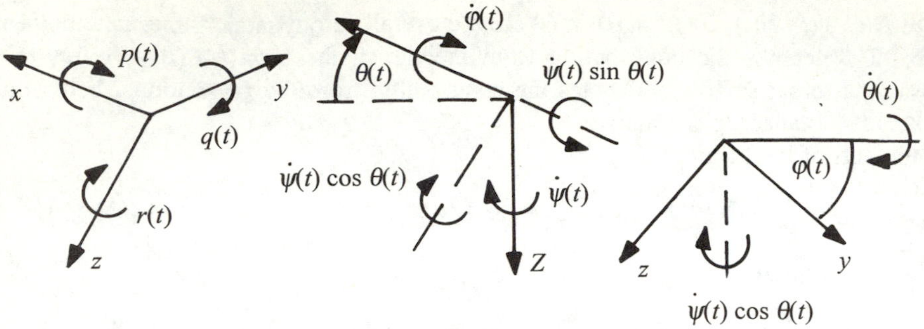

Fig. V.62. Transformation of angular velocities.

$$
\begin{aligned}
p(t) &= \dot{\varphi}(t) && -\dot{\psi}(t)\sin\theta(t) \\
q(t) &= && +\dot{\theta}(t)\cos\varphi(t)+\dot{\psi}(t)\cos\theta(t)\sin\varphi(t) \\
r(t) &= && -\dot{\theta}(t)\sin\varphi(t)\ +\dot{\psi}(t)\cos\theta(t)\cos\varphi(t).
\end{aligned}
\tag{V.4.12}
$$

$$
\begin{aligned}
\dot{\varphi}(t) &= p(t)+q(t)\sin\varphi(t)\tan\theta(t)+r(t)\cos\varphi(t)\tan\theta(t) \\
\dot{\theta}(t) &= \quad q(t)\cos\varphi(t) \qquad -r(t)\sin\varphi(t) \\
\dot{\psi}(t) &= \quad q(t)\sin\varphi(t)\sec\theta(t)+r(t)\cos\varphi(t)\sec\theta(t).
\end{aligned}
\tag{V.4.13}
$$

There are additional terms due to spinning rotors (e.g. propeller, compressors, turbines). If

angular momentum of a propeller or turbo-fan engine about the *ox* axis

$$= I_{\text{eng}}\Omega_{\text{eng}}, \tag{V.4.14}$$

where I_{eng} is the moment of inertia about the axis of engine rotation, and Ω_{eng} is the angular velocity of the engine, then the terms to be added to the right hand sides of the moment equations (eqns. (V.4.9)) are

$$
\begin{aligned}
(M_x)_{\text{eng}} &= 0, \\
(M_y)_{\text{eng}} &= (I_{\text{eng}}\Omega_{\text{eng}})\,r(t), \\
(M_z)_{\text{eng}} &= (I_{\text{eng}}\Omega_{\text{eng}})\,q(t).
\end{aligned}
\tag{V.4.15}
$$

Each engine makes a separate contribution. The combination of a pair of contra-rotating engines will have a zero net effect.

V.4.2 Kinematic coupling

When motions are specified there are relationships between the angular rates of rotation and the angles of incidence and sideslip; these relationships are known as kinematic coupling. This phraseology is somewhat misleading; the six degrees of freedom $U(t)$, $\alpha(t)$, $\beta(t)$, $p(t)$, $q(t)$ and $r(t)$ are independent degrees of freedom, they are only 'coupled' in the sense that there are relationships between them for specified motions, for example, in a longitudinal weathercock pitch motion $q(t) = \dot{\alpha}(t)$.

Two further examples.

Consider an aeroplane whose centre of mass is moving along a horizontal straight line with constant velocity U and the aeroplane is rolling with constant rate p (about the body ox axis), with q and r both zero. If, at datum time $t = 0$, angle of incidence > 0 and sideslip angle $= 0$, then

$$\begin{array}{lll} \text{at } t = \pi/2p & \text{angle of incidence} = 0, & \text{sideslip angle} > 0 \\ \text{at } t = \pi/p & \text{angle of incidence} < 0, & \text{sideslip angle} = 0 \\ \text{at } t = 3\pi/2p & \text{angle of incidence} = 0, & \text{sideslip angle} < 0 \\ \text{at } t = 2\pi/p & \text{angle of incidence} > 0, & \text{sideslip angle} = 0. \end{array} \tag{V.4.16}$$

Consider an aeroplane whose centre of mass is moving in a horizontal straight line with constant velocity U, rolling about the flight path with angular velocity $p_U(t)$ and with time varying longitudinal weathercock pitch ($\alpha(t) = \theta(t)$) and lateral weathercock yaw ($\beta(t) = -\psi(t)$). By reference to Fig. V.63,

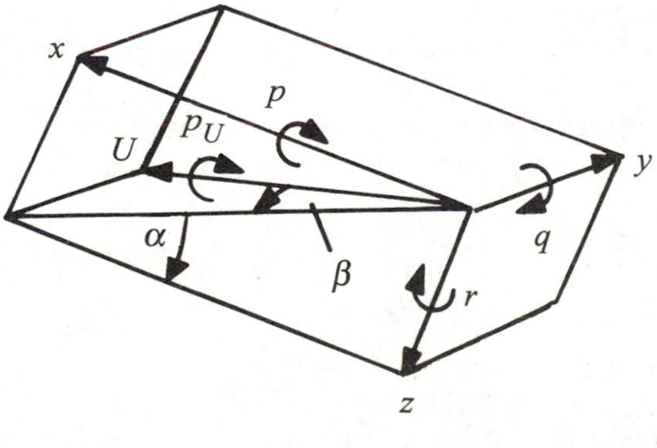

Fig. V.63. Kinematic coupling.

$$\begin{aligned} p(t) &= p_U(t)\cos\beta(t)\cos\alpha(t) + \dot{\beta}(t)\sin\alpha(t) \\ q(t) &= p_U(t)\sin\beta(t) + \dot{\alpha}(t) \\ r(t) &= p_U(t)\cos\beta(t)\sin\alpha(t) - \dot{\beta}(t)\cos\alpha(t). \end{aligned} \tag{V.4.17}$$

These equations can be inverted to give

$$\begin{aligned} \dot{\alpha}(t) &= q(t) - \big(p(t)\cos\alpha(t) + r(t)\sin\alpha(t)\big)\tan\beta(t) \\ \dot{\beta}(t) &= p(t)\sin\alpha(t) - r(t)\cos\alpha(t) \\ p_U(t) &= \big(p(t)\cos\alpha(t) + r(t)\sin\alpha(t)\big)\sec\beta(t). \end{aligned} \tag{V.4.18}$$

V.4.3 Aerodynamic cross-coupling

Aerodynamic cross-coupling refers to the dependency of the longitudinal derivatives on the lateral degrees of freedom and *vice versa*.

An illustration of aerodynamic cross-coupling is the variation of the set of the lateral derivatives with angle of incidence shown in Figs. V.54–V.56. The same data can be cross-plotted to give $C_{n\alpha}(\alpha, \beta)$ and $C_{l\alpha}(\alpha, \beta)$.

The most important example of aerodynamic cross-coupling concerns the behaviour of C_n at zero sideslip, as the angle of incidence increases. At angles of incidence below and through the break, C_n, at zero sideslip, is zero; see Fig. V.58. But at a critical high angle of incidence there is a second break where there is suddenly a finite C_n at zero sideslip, with a significant static hysteresis effect with respect to changes in β, as shown in Fig. V.64, taken from Skow & Titiriga (ref. V.67). This second break is due to the forebody vortices which change abruptly from a symmetric pattern of two forebody vortices symmetrically located about the fuselage nose, to an asymmetric pattern, where there are two vortices on one side of the nose and one vortex on the other side, as sketched in Fig. V.65. This asymmetric pattern of forebody vortices gives a side force on the fuselage nose, leading to a large yawing moment.

As shown in Fig. V.66, the sign of the nose side force can switch from one side to the other with increasing angle of incidence.

The asymmetric pattern of forebody vortices also affects the rolling moment by their downstream effect on the fin, see Fig. V.64.

The static hysteresis loop in Fig. V.64 will be enlarged in a dynamic sideslip oscillation at a typical low frequency, contributing to the large values of $\tilde{C}_{n\dot{\beta}}$ and $\tilde{C}_{l\dot{\beta}}$ at high angles of incidence shown in Fig. V.54(i).

Returning to the aerodynamic cross-coupling of conventional derivatives, the longitudinal derivatives can vary with sideslip angle, thus $C_{L\alpha}(\alpha, \beta)$, $C_{m\alpha}(\alpha, \beta)$,

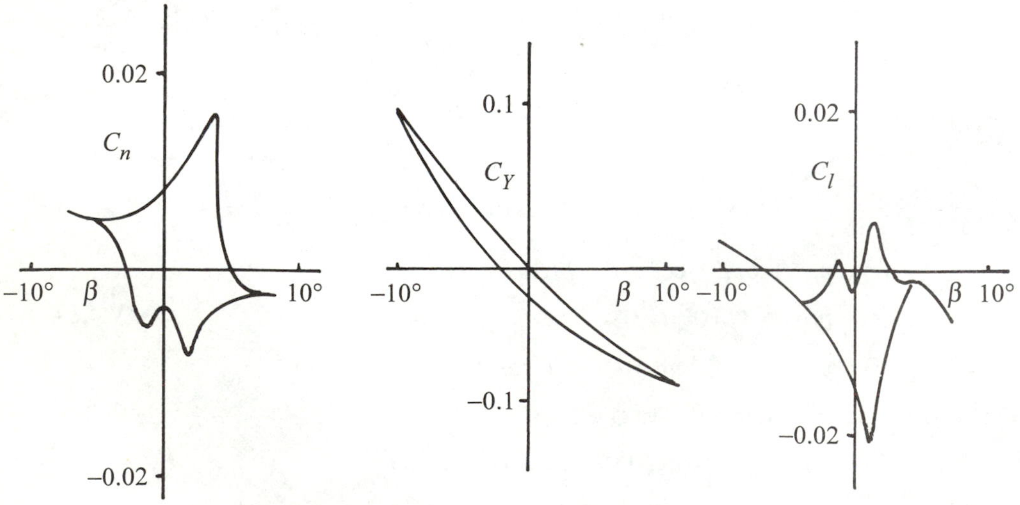

Fig. V.64. Static hysteresis from asymmetry of forebody vortices.

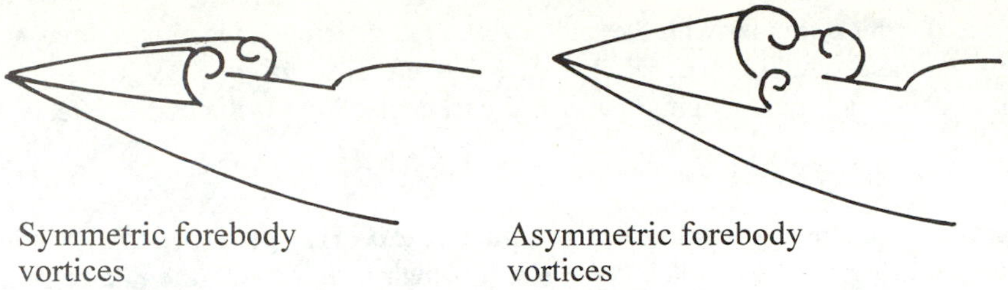

Fig. V.65. Forebody vortex patterns.

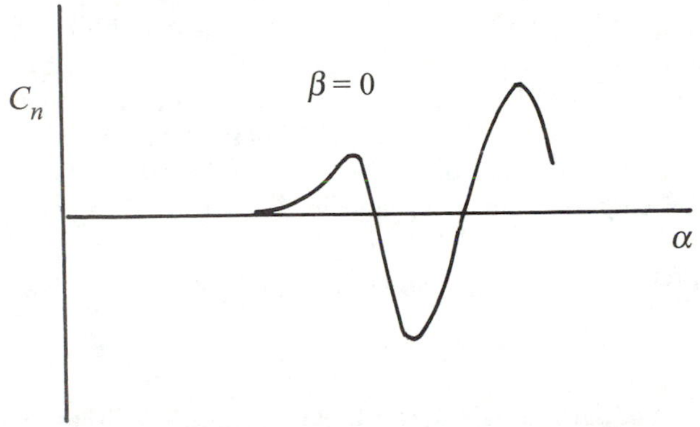

Fig. V.66. Variation of C_n with angle of incidence at zero sideslip.

$(\tilde{C}_{m\dot{\alpha}} + \tilde{C}_{mq})\ (\alpha, \beta)$, denote the dependency of these derivatives on α and β. Physically when an aeroplane sideslips there will be changes in the asymmetric loadings on the wings, which give a net change in the overall symmetric loads.

Of particular importance is the derivative $C_{m\beta}(\alpha)$; this derivative is obtained as an average of $\partial C_m/\partial\beta$ over a range of β, say 10°, at different α (sometimes this derivative is expressed as $C_{m|\beta|}$ because the variation is the same for β positive or negative). A positive $C_{m\beta}$ can amplify any pitch-up tendency.

Other cross derivatives which according to Orlik-Rückemann (ref. V.68) influence aeroplane dynamic motions at high angles of incidence are $(\tilde{C}_{lq} + \tilde{C}_{l\dot{\alpha}})$ and $(\tilde{C}_{nq} + \tilde{C}_{n\dot{\alpha}})$. Measurements of these two cross derivatives have been made by Orlik-Rückemann & Hanff (ref. V.69).

V.4.4 Inertial cross-coupling

In coupled longitudinal–lateral motions the inertial product terms in the moment equations of eqns. (V.4.10), so-called inertial cross-coupling, can lead to instability.

V.4.4.1 Stability of aeroplane in rapid rate of roll at low angles of incidence

Consider an aeroplane in a rate of roll p about the ox axis. Consider first a small static perturbation $\Delta\alpha$. This perturbation $\Delta\alpha$ induces a positive perturbation rate of yaw

Δr ($= p\,\Delta\alpha$), which couples with the rate of roll, p, to generate a reaction inertial nose-up pitching moment equal to $[(I_{zz} - I_{xx})\,p^2\,\Delta\alpha]$, by reference to eqns. (V.4.10). Thus the condition of overall static longitudinal stability is, neglecting Mach number effects,

$$C_{m\alpha}\left(Wc_{\mathrm{w}}/C_{\mathrm{W}}\right) + (I_{zz} - I_{xx})\,p^2 < 0. \tag{V.4.19}$$

Consider, secondly, a small static perturbation $\Delta\beta$. This perturbation $\Delta\beta$ induces a positive perturbation rate of pitch Δq ($= p\,\Delta\beta$), which couples with the rate of roll, p, to generate a reaction inertial yawing moment $[(I_{xx} - I_{yy})\,p^2\,\Delta\beta]$, by reference to eqns. (V.4.10). Thus the condition of overall static lateral stability is

$$C_{n\beta}\left(W\,2s_{\mathrm{w}}/C_{\mathrm{W}}\right) + (I_{xx} - I_{yy})\,p_{\mathrm{s}}^2 > 0. \tag{V.4.20}$$

Because $I_{zz} > I_{xx}$ and $I_{yy} > I_{xx}$ inertial cross-coupling destabilizes both of the static stabilities in eqns. (V.4.19) and (V.4.20).

A more complete analysis based on the stability of the incidence, sideslip, pitch and yaw perturbation equations (Phillips, ref. V.70; Pinsker, ref. V.71; ESDU, ref. V.72) shows that the stability depends only on the overall static stability of the coupled longitudinal–lateral degrees of freedom, namely,

$$\left[(-C_{m\alpha})\left(Wc_{\mathrm{w}}/C_{\mathrm{W}}\right) - (I_{zz} - I_{xx})\,p^2\right]\left[C_{n\beta}\left(W2s_{\mathrm{w}}/C_{\mathrm{W}}\right) - (I_{yy} - I_{xx})\,p^2\right] > 0 \tag{V.4.21}$$

which is the product of the two stabilities derived in eqns. (V.4.19) and (V.4.20).

Eqn. (V.4.21) can be re-expressed in the form, neglecting the phagoid mode,

$$\left[I_{yy}(\omega_0)_{\mathrm{sp}}^2 - (I_{zz} - I_{xx})\,p^2\right]\left[I_{zz}(\omega_0)_{\mathrm{Dr}}^2 - (I_{yy} - I_{xx})\,p^2\right] > 0 \tag{V.4.22}$$

where $(\omega_0)_{\mathrm{sp}}$ and $(\omega_0)_{\mathrm{Dr}}$ are the undamped short period and Dutch roll frequencies respectively for the uncoupled longitudinal and lateral motions.

Thus

(i) the system is stable (i.e. positive overall static stability) when

$$p^2 < \min\left[(\omega_0)_{\mathrm{sp}}^2 \frac{I_{yy}}{I_{zz} - I_{xx}},\quad (\omega_0)_{\mathrm{Dr}}^2 \frac{I_{zz}}{I_{yy} - I_{xx}}\right] \tag{V.4.23}$$

(ii) the system is unstable (i.e. negative overall static stability) when

$$\min\left[(\omega_0)_{\mathrm{sp}}^2 \frac{I_{yy}}{I_{zz} - I_{xx}},\quad (\omega_0)_{\mathrm{Dr}}^2 \frac{I_{zz}}{I_{yy} - I_{xx}}\right] < p^2 < \max\left[(\omega_0)_{\mathrm{sp}}^2 \frac{I_{yy}}{I_{zz} - I_{xx}},\quad (\omega_0)_{\mathrm{Dr}}^2 \frac{I_{zz}}{I_{yy} - I_{xx}}\right] \tag{V.4.24}$$

(iii) the system regains stability (i.e. positive overall static stability) when

$$p^2 > \max\left[(\omega_0)^2_{sp}\frac{I_{yy}}{I_{zz}-I_{xx}}, \quad (\omega_0)^2_{Dr}\frac{I_{zz}}{I_{yy}-I_{xx}}\right]. \tag{V.4.25}$$

Now

$$\begin{aligned}&\left[I_{yy}/(I_{zz}-I_{xx})\right]=\left[i_{yy}/(i_{zz}-i_{xx})\right](2/\mathrm{AR_w})^2 = O[1.0],\\ &\left[I_{zz}/(I_{yy}-I_{xx})\right]=\left[i_{zz}\Big/\left(\left(i_{yy}(2/\mathrm{AR_w})^2\right)-i_{xx}\right)\right]=O[2.0]\\ &(\omega_0)_{sp}=O[3\,\mathrm{rad/s}], \quad (\omega_0)_{Dr}=O[1.5\,\mathrm{rad/s}].\end{aligned} \tag{V.4.26}$$

With these numbers the aeroplane is unstable in the steady roll rate range

$$2\,\mathrm{rad/s} < p_s < 3\,\mathrm{rad/s}.$$

In the earlier description of static stability it was argued that overall static stability could be positive while the static stability of two modes could be negative and the system would then be unstable. It might therefore be conjectured that statement (iii) above (eqns. (V.4.22) and (V.4.25)) is suspect. However, the detailed investigation of stability in refs. V.70–V.72 shows that statement (iii) is correct.

V.4.4.2 Stability in rapid turn

In a rapid turn at a high bank angle the turn rate is essentially a pitch rate, q_{turn}. Small disturbances about this steady state separate out into distinct longitudinal and lateral perturbation motions.

In the lateral small disturbance moment equations, neglecting I_{xz},

$$\begin{aligned}&I_{xx}\dot{p}(t)-(I_{yy}-I_{zz})q_{turn}r(t)=\Delta\mathscr{L}\\ &I_{zz}\dot{r}(t)-(I_{xx}-I_{yy})q_{turn}p(t)=\Delta\mathcal{N}.\end{aligned} \tag{V.4.27}$$

Hence, by reference to eqns. (V.3.12), the effective rotary derivatives are now extended to the form

$$\begin{aligned}&(C_{lr})_{\text{eff}}=C_{lr}-C_{l\dot{\beta}}\cos\alpha_{\text{trim}}-(I_{zz}-I_{yy})\left(C_W/W\,2s_w\right)\left(q_{turn}U/s_w\right)\\ &(C_{np})_{\text{eff}}=C_{np}+C_{n\dot{\beta}}\sin\alpha_{\text{trim}}-(I_{yy}-I_{xx})\left(C_W/W\,2s_w\right)\left(q_{turn}U/s_w\right).\end{aligned} \tag{V.4.28}$$

The decrease in $(C_{np})_{\text{eff}}$ due to q_{turn} can be an important factor in the loss in Dutch roll damping, leading to a possible wing rock motion, see Ross (ref. V.62).

V.4.5 Departure

Departure occurs when an aeroplane goes rapidly, or suddenly, out of control, as a consequence of one, or more, of the following:

—pitch-up
—excessive, or divergent, wing rock oscillations

— wing drop
— nose slice
— loss of control power
— excessive buffeting.

Pitch-up and wing rock have already been described.

Wing drop describes an uncommanded roll divergence usually encountered at higher subsonic speeds. The roll rate is not usually too high, typically 10–20°/s, which is controllable by a pilot if a recovery action is taken sufficiently quickly.

It is possible that wing drop is a manifestation of a negative stiffness of the Dutch roll, possibly accompanied by a low damping. The motion could also be due to asymmetric shock wave developments and shock wave–boundary layer separations in the tip regions of the starboard and port wings, leading to asymmetric loadings and a rolling moment; the effects may be reinforced by the roll-out. Shock wave developments are known to be sensitive to Mach number and local angle of incidence variations so a small rate of yaw disturbance or a small rate of roll could be instrumental in initiating asymmetries.

Nose slice describes a fairly abrupt divergence in yaw, which is not usually controllable by the pilot. The main contributory factor is the sudden yawing moment created when the forebody vortices break into their asymmetric pattern, as sketched in Fig. V.65.

For the roll control effectiveness, the roll response to a differential tailplane input, which can be obtained from eqns. (V.3.6)–(V.3.11), takes the form, in non-dimensional terms,

$$(A_4\overline{\mathrm{D}}^4 + A_3\overline{\mathrm{D}}^3 + A_2\overline{\mathrm{D}}^2 + A_1\overline{\mathrm{D}} + A_0)\,\overline{\mathrm{D}}\,\Delta\varphi_\mathrm{d}(\bar{t}_\mathrm{d}) = (B_3\overline{\mathrm{D}}^3 + B_2\overline{\mathrm{D}}^2 + B_1\overline{\mathrm{D}} + B_0)\,\Delta\xi(\bar{t}_\mathrm{d}) \tag{V.4.29}$$

where the coefficients A_n are given in eqns. (V.3.13).

Positive roll response is obtained with $(\overline{\mathrm{D}}_{\Delta\varphi\mathrm{d}}(\bar{t}_\mathrm{d}) > 0)$ for an input $(\Delta\xi(t_\mathrm{d}) < 0)$; this condition is satisfied when

$$B_0 = -(2\bar{m}/\pi\,\mathrm{AR}_\mathrm{w})\,C_\mathrm{W}\sin\alpha_\mathrm{trim}(C_{n\beta}C_{l\xi} - C_{l\beta}C_{n\xi}) < 0,$$

assuming that the aeroplane is stable. Thus for roll control effectiveness

$$C_{n\beta} + (C_{n\xi}/C_{l\xi})(-C_{l\beta}) > 0. \tag{V.4.30}$$

Proverse yaw (i.e. $(C_{n\xi}/C_{l\xi}) > 0$) is beneficial; adverse yaw (i.e. $(C_{n\xi}/C_{l\xi}) < 0$) is detrimental. A proverse yaw at low angles of incidence can change into an adverse yaw at high angles of incidence.

V.4.5.1 Departure criteria

Two basic departure criteria, which have been proposed, are

$$(C_{n\beta})_\mathrm{dyn} = C_{n\beta} + (i_{zz}/i_{xx})(-C_{l\beta}) > 0 \tag{V.4.31}$$

$$\mathrm{LCDP} = C_{n\beta} + (C_{n\xi}/C_{l\xi})(-C_{l\beta}) > 0 \tag{V.4.32}$$

where LCDP is the lateral control departure parameter, as derived in eqns. (V.3.16) and (V.4.30).

There have been several investigations, for example Wiessman (ref. V.73), Greer (ref. V.74), Bihrle & Barnhart (ref. V.75), in which the departure of several aeroplanes have been compared with the criteria in eqns. (V.4.31) and (V.4.32). There is a consensus that these two criteria incorporate the correct trends, especially the trade-off of a positive $(-C_{l\beta})$ to compensate for a negative $C_{n\beta}$; some qualitative results are indicated in Fig. V.67. Although the success rate at predicting departure is fairly good the criteria are not regarded as completely satisfactory.

These two criteria are essentially based on separate longitudinal and lateral perturbations. Kalviste (ref. V.76) has extended the weathercock perturbation arguments to include coupling effects.

Consider an aeroplane in a steady linear motion with constant α and β and constant velocity U and zero angular rates; suppose the motion is disturbed with incremental changes $\Delta\alpha(t)$ and $\Delta\beta(t)$ but the centre of mass continues to travel along the initial flight path with velocity U. On differentiation of eqns. (V.4.18), neglecting all second order quantities,

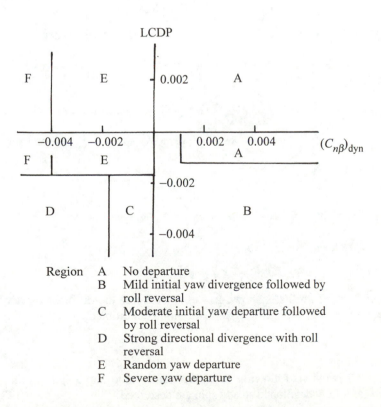

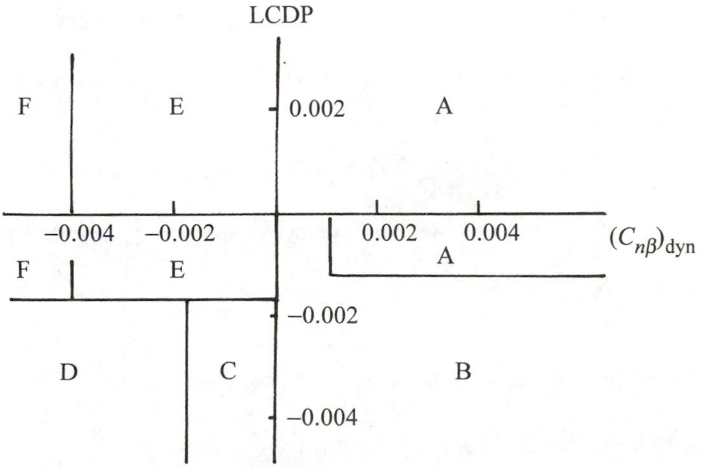

Region A No departure
B Mild initial yaw divergence followed by roll reversal
C Moderate initial yaw departure followed by roll reversal
D Strong directional divergence with roll reversal
E Random yaw departure
F Severe yaw departure

Fig. V.67. Effectiveness of departure criteria.

$$\Delta\ddot{\alpha}(t) = \dot{q}(t) - \big(\dot{p}(t)\cos\alpha + \dot{r}(t)\sin\alpha\big)\tan\beta$$
$$= \big(\Delta\mathcal{M}(t)/I_{yy}\big) - \big((\Delta\mathcal{L}(t)/I_{xx})\cos\alpha + (\Delta\mathcal{N}(t)/I_{zz})\sin\alpha\big)\tan\beta \quad \text{(V.4.33)}$$
$$= \big(Wc_{\text{w}}/(C_{\text{W}}I_{yy})\big)\big[(C_{m\alpha})_{\text{dyn}}\Delta\alpha(t) + (C_{m\beta})_{\text{dyn}}\Delta\beta(t)\big]$$

$$\Delta\ddot{\beta}(t) = \dot{p}(t)\sin\alpha - \dot{r}(t)\cos\alpha$$
$$= (\Delta\mathcal{L}(t)/I_{xx})\sin\alpha - (\Delta\mathcal{N}(t)/I_{zz})\cos\alpha \quad \text{(V.4.34)}$$
$$= \big(W2s_{\text{w}}/(C_{\text{W}}I_{zz})\big)\big[-(C_{n\alpha})_{\text{dyn}}\Delta\alpha(t) - (C_{n\beta})_{\text{dyn}}\Delta\beta(t)\big]$$

where

$$(C_{m\alpha})_{\text{dyn}} = C_{m\alpha} - \text{AR}_{\text{w}}\big[(I_{yy}/I_{xx})C_{l\alpha}\cos\alpha + (I_{yy}/I_{zz})C_{n\alpha}\sin\alpha\big]\tan\beta$$
$$(C_{m\beta})_{\text{dyn}} = C_{m\beta} - \text{AR}_{\text{w}}\big[(I_{yy}/I_{xx})C_{l\beta}\cos\alpha + (I_{yy}/I_{zz})C_{n\beta}\sin\alpha\big]$$
$$(C_{n\alpha})_{\text{dyn}} = C_{n\alpha}\cos\alpha - (I_{zz}/I_{xx})C_{l\alpha}\sin\alpha$$
$$(C_{n\beta})_{\text{dyn}} = C_{n\beta}\cos\alpha - (I_{zz}/I_{xx})C_{l\beta}\sin\alpha.$$

The stability of eqns. (V.4.33) and (V.4.34) is satisfied by the criteria

$$K > 0, \quad (C_{n\beta})_{\text{coup}} > 0, \quad (C_{m\alpha})_{\text{coup}} < 0 \quad \text{(V.4.35)}$$

where

$$X = (2s_{\text{w}}/I_{zz})(C_{n\beta})_{\text{dyn}} - (c_{\text{w}}/I_{yy})(C_{m\alpha})_{\text{dyn}}$$
$$Y = \big(c_{\text{w}}2s_{\text{w}}/(I_{yy}I_{zz})\big)\big((C_{n\alpha})_{\text{dyn}}(C_{m\beta})_{\text{dyn}} - (C_{n\beta})_{\text{dyn}}(C_{m\alpha})_{\text{dyn}}\big)$$
$$Z = X^2 - Y$$
$$K = \text{sign}[Z]$$
$$d = \text{sign}\big[(2s_{\text{w}}/I_{zz})(C_{n\beta})_{\text{dyn}} + (c_{\text{w}}/I_{yy})(C_{m\alpha})_{\text{dyn}}\big]$$
$$(C_{n\beta})_{\text{coup}} = (I_{zz}/2s_{\text{w}})\big(X + d\sqrt{Z}\big)$$
$$(C_{m\alpha})_{\text{coup}} = (I_{yy})/2c_{\text{w}}\big(-X + d\sqrt{Z}\big).$$

A typical set of results is shown in Fig. V.68. Note the different types of instability which can occur over a range of asymmetric flight conditions.

V.4.6 Spinning

The post-stall gyrations following departure can develop into a spin. In this section the condition for a fully developed steady spin are described.

Consider an aeroplane descending vertically downward at a steady speed U, at a steady angle of incidence α, with wings horizontal while the centre of mass rotates about

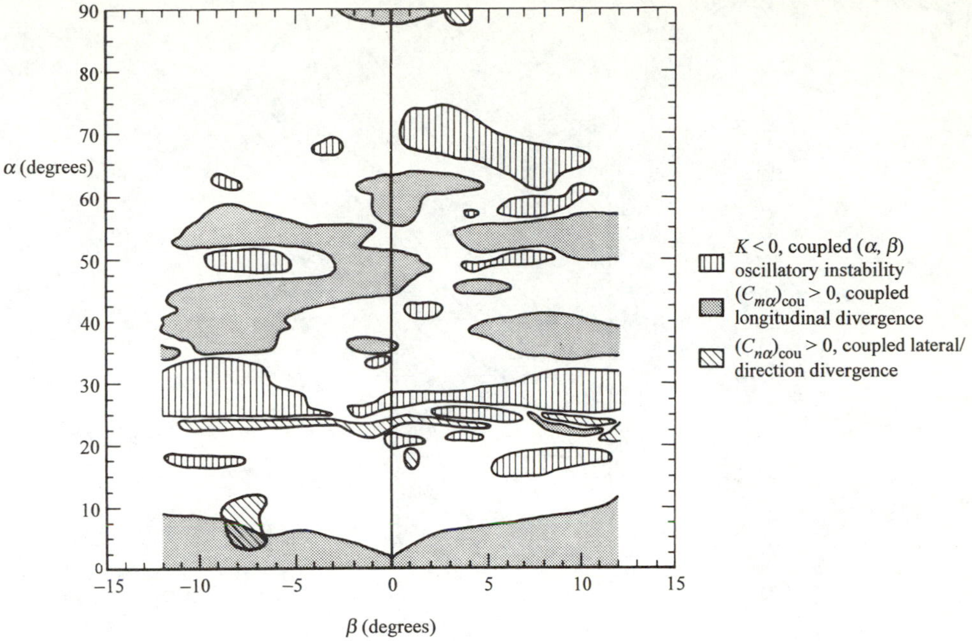

Fig. V. 68. Kalviste departure criteria for particular aeroplane configuration.

a vertical axis with steady angular velocity Ω rad/s with a radius of curvature R, the nose of the aeroplane pointing towards the vertical axis, as shown in Fig. V.69.

Thus

$$p = \Omega \cos \alpha, \qquad q = 0, \qquad r = \Omega \sin \alpha, \qquad U\beta = \Omega R. \tag{V.4.36}$$

The driving mechanism for a spin is auto-rotation.

Shown in Fig. V.70 is a typical variation of $C_L \sim \alpha$. When a wing rolls about the flight path with rate of roll Ω at a high angle of incidence, the increment of incidence across the wing span is

$$\Delta\alpha(y) = (\Omega \cos \alpha)\, y/(U \cos \alpha + \Omega \sin \alpha\, y). \tag{V.4.37}$$

At low angles of incidence the incremental angle of incidence on the starboard wing (i.e. $y > 0$) increases and its lift increases, while the incremental incidence on the port wing (i.e. $y < 0$) decreases and its lift decreases, giving a net wing negative rolling moment about the flight path. As sketched in Fig. V.70, at high angles of incidence, with a fast rate of roll, the net wing rolling moment can reverse and become positive.

This wing rolling moment about the flight path at a particular high angle of incidence, α, first increases with Ω, reaches a maximum and then decreases with further increase in Ω.

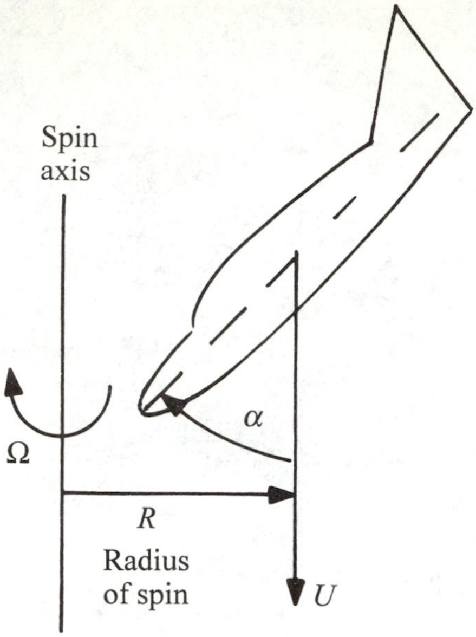

Fig. V.69. Steady spin.

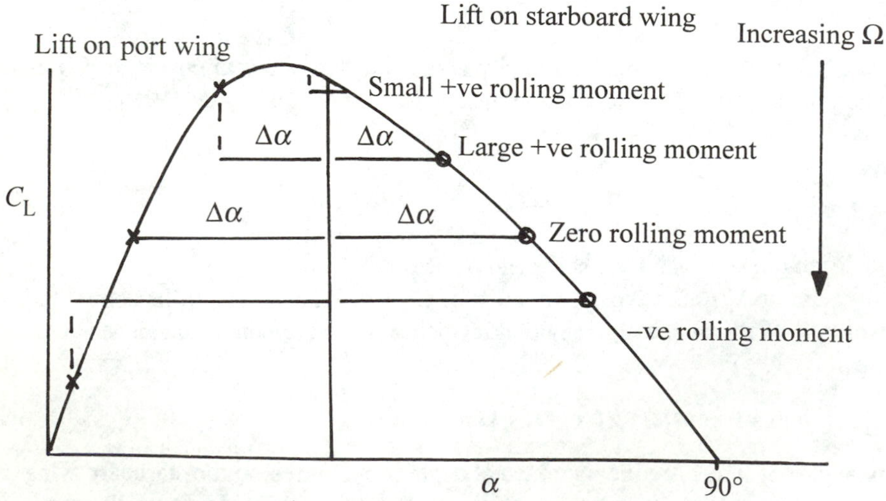

Fig. V.70. Aerodynamic rolling moment about flight path due to spin rate Ω.

As the aeroplane rolls about the flight path axis the cross-forces on the fuselage nose and aft fuselage fin induce a net fuselage–fin negative rolling moment about the flight path. This fuselage–fin rolling moment increases with Ω and with α.

Corresponding to each high angle of incidence there is a value of Ω at which the overall net rolling moment about the flight path axis is zero; the aeroplane then rolls about the flight path at the constant rate of roll Ω. This condition is known as auto-rotation.

The particular values of Ω and α are determined by satisfying the conditions of auto-rotation and equilibrium of the pitching moment, namely,

$$(I_{zz} - I_{xx})\Omega^2 \sin\alpha\cos\alpha = \tfrac{1}{2}\rho_{\mathrm{at}}U^2 S_{\mathrm{w}}c_{\mathrm{w}}\big(-C_m(\alpha)\big). \qquad \text{(V.4.38)}$$

See Fig. V.71.

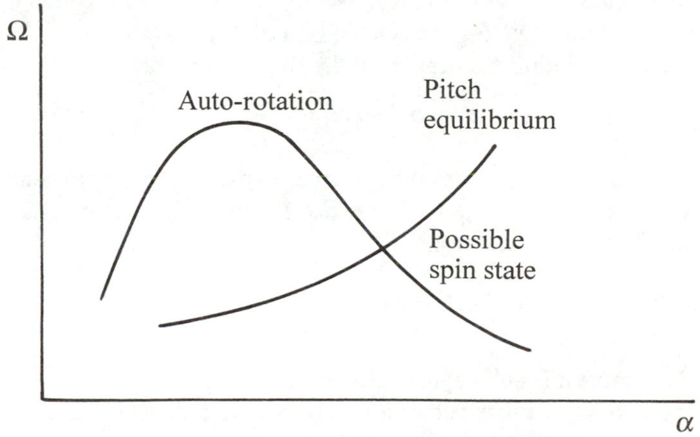

Fig. V.71. Determination of α and Ω in steady spin.

Once α is known, the speed of descent is determined by the condition of equilibrium in the vertical direction, namely

$$W + \mathrm{Th}\cos\alpha = \tfrac{1}{2}\rho_{\mathrm{at}}U^2 S_{\mathrm{w}}C_{\mathrm{D}}(\alpha). \qquad \text{(V.4.39)}$$

Once Ω, α and U are known, the radius of the spin R is determined by the condition of equilibrium in the horizontal direction. Assuming that the aerodynamic force on the aeroplane is primarily the normal force N, then

$$m\Omega^2 R \simeq N\cos\alpha \simeq (W/\sin\alpha)\cos\alpha$$

so

$$R \simeq g/(\Omega^2 \tan\alpha). \qquad \text{(V.4.40)}$$

So far four conditions of equilibrium have been satisfied: lift, drag, rolling moment about the flight path and pitching moment. For complete equilibrium two further conditions must be satisfied: zero side force and zero yawing moment of the flight path. Thus, there are two more variables:

(i) the wings are not horizontal as assumed initially; there is a steady bank angle, or tilt angle, φ;
(ii) there is an additional steady sideslip angle β_e which slews the nose of the aeroplane away from the axis of spin.

The tilt angle modifies the rates of rotation about body axes to

$$p = \Omega \cos\alpha \cos\varphi, \qquad q = \Omega \sin\varphi, \qquad r = \Omega \sin\alpha \cos\varphi.$$

The sign of the total sideslip angle $(\beta_e - \Omega R/U)$, given by the yawing moment equation, is influenced by the sign of $(I_{yy} - I_{xx})$; for slender configurations $I_{yy} > I_{xx}$ but for non-swept configurations with relatively heavy wings $I_{xx} > I_{yy}$. From the sideslip equation the sign of the tilt angle depends on the sign of $(\beta_e - g/\Omega U)$.

Now there is a inertia rolling moment about the flight path equal to

$$-\left[(I_{zz} - I_{yy})\Omega^2 \sin\alpha \sin\varphi \cos\varphi)\right]\cos\alpha \tag{V.4.41}$$

which, for a positive tilt angle, opposes the spin rate, a so-called anti-spin contribution.

The combined sideslip angle β $(= \beta_e - \Omega R/U)$ generates an aerodynamic rolling moment about the flight path equal to

$$\tfrac{1}{2}\rho_{at} U^2 S_w \; 2 s_w C_{l\beta}\left(\beta_e - g/\Omega U \tan\alpha\right)\cos\alpha. \tag{V.4.42}$$

If this moment is positive it is an in-spin contribution.

Without going into any further detail, a steady spin is a delicate balance of aerodynamic and gyroscopic moments, especially the latter.

In an oscillatory spin the aeroplane descends in a spiral motion but in addition there are oscillations in the angle of incidence, and other degrees of freedom.

Spins can range from fast and steep, with angles of incidence of the order of 40°, to slow and flat, with angles of incidence close to 90°. A configuration may have more than one spin mode, depending on the entry conditions.

Recovery from a spin is, in general, obtained by

(i) applying rudder to slow down the rate of spin;
(ii) applying forward stick to give a nose-down pitching moment to decrease the angle of incidence.

The combined effect of these two control actions tends to eliminate the possibility of a steady spin condition in Fig. V.71. Recovery from flat spins is more difficult to achieve than recovery from steep spins.

Spin experiments are carried out in spin tunnels in which the airstream is projected vertically upward and models are launched by hand from a balcony. The European tunnel is located at Lille in France and the USA tunnel is located at NASA (Langley).

Spin is potentially dangerous for combat aeroplanes when there is a significant loss in altitude before recovery is completed. If entry into the spin is at too low an altitude there could be insufficient altitude to recover.

Because spin is not a combat manoeuvre, contemporary combat aeroplanes have a spin prevention system which limits the maximum angle of incidence; the value of the maximum angle of incidence depends on the manoeuvre.

V.4.7 Longitudinal–lateral aerodynamic modelling

The ideas proposed in section V.2.12 for longitudinal aerodynamic modelling are now extended to the six degrees of freedom of coupled longitudinal–lateral motions. The aim of aerodynamic modelling is to predict manoeuvring flight, departure, post-stall gyrations and recovery procedures.

First it is necessary to define a set of 'natural' degrees of freedom to represent the aerodynamics; these 'natural' degrees of freedom should minimize kinetic coupling and be compatible with experimental techniques of model measurements. It is suggested that these 'natural' degrees of freedom comprise

(i) degrees of freedom describing the aeroplane motion relative to the flight path,
(ii) degrees of freedom describing the curvature of the flight path.

The three degrees of freedom describing the aeroplane motion relative to a straight flight path can (as sketched in Fig. V.72) be

(i) the weathercock pitch angle $\Theta(t)$, which is the angle of the *ox* (fuselage body) axis from the flight path (positive clockwise),
(ii) the bank angle $\Phi(t)$, which is the angular displacement of the *oy* axis, measured from the normal to the plane which defines $\Theta(t)$, by rotation about the *ox* axis,
(iii) the roll angle $\varphi_U(t)$, which is the roll angle of the *ox* axis (i.e. the plane which contains $\Theta(t)$) about the flight path, measured from the vertical plane.

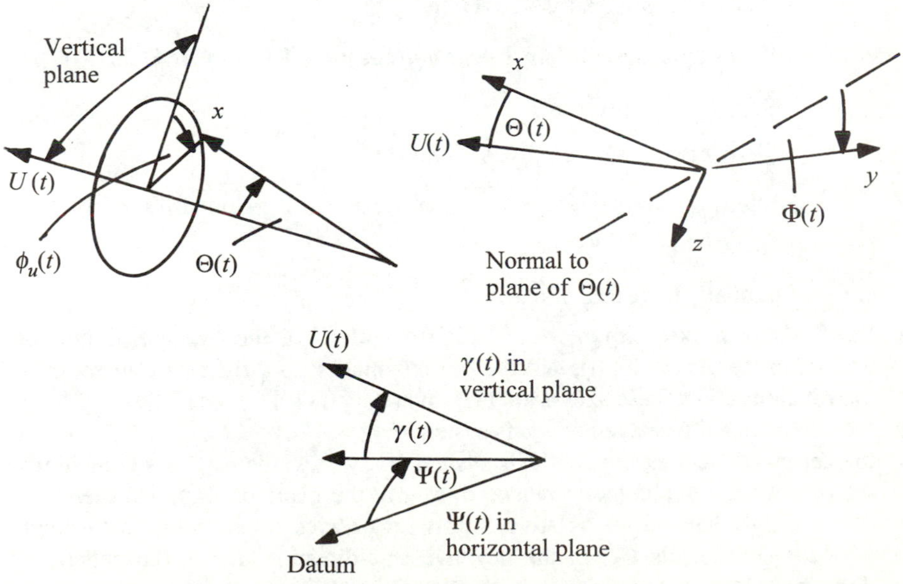

Fig. V.72. Definitions of degrees of freedom.

The three degrees of freedom describing the variation of the flight path are, as sketched in Fig. V.72:

(i) the forward speed $U(t)$,
(ii) $\gamma(t)$, the angle of climb, namely the inclination of the flight path from the horizontal in the vertical plane,
(iii) $\Psi(t)$, the angle of yaw of the projection of the flight path in the horizontal plane measured from a datum.

The relationships between (Θ, Φ) and (α, β) are

$$\begin{aligned} U_x &= U\cos\alpha\cos\beta = U\cos\Theta \\ U_y &= U\sin\beta \qquad\quad = U\sin\Theta\sin\Phi \\ U_z &= U\sin\alpha\cos\beta = U\sin\Theta\cos\Phi \end{aligned} \qquad \text{(V.4.43)}$$

so

$$\begin{aligned} \cos\Theta &= \cos\alpha\cos\beta & \tan\alpha &= \tan\Theta\cos\Phi \\ \tan\Phi &= \tan\beta/\sin\alpha & \sin\beta &= \sin\Theta\sin\Phi. \end{aligned} \qquad \text{(V.4.44)}$$

A nominal range $\quad 0 < \alpha < +90°, \quad -25° < \beta < +25°$

requires $\quad 0 < \Theta < +90°, \quad -90° < \Psi_U < +90°.$

The relationships between (p, q, r) and $(\dot{\Theta}, \dot{\Phi}, \dot{\varphi}_U, \dot{\gamma}, \dot{\Psi})$ are

$$\begin{aligned} p &= \dot{\Phi} + \dot{\varphi}_U\cos\Theta + \dot{\gamma}\sin\varphi_U\sin\Theta - \dot{\Psi}[-\cos\varphi_U\sin(\gamma+\Theta) + \sin\varphi_U\sin\gamma\cos\Theta\delta] \\ q &= \dot{\Theta}\cos\Phi + \dot{\varphi}_U\sin\Theta\sin\Phi \\ &\quad + \dot{\gamma}[\cos\varphi_U\cos\Phi - \sin\varphi_U\cos\Theta\sin\Phi] \\ &\quad + \dot{\Psi}[\cos\varphi_U\cos(\gamma+\Theta)\sin\Phi + \sin\varphi_U(\cos\gamma\cos\Phi - \sin\gamma\sin\Theta\sin\Phi)] \\ r &= -\dot{\Theta}\sin\Phi + \dot{\varphi}_U\sin\Theta\cos\Phi \\ &\quad + \dot{\gamma}[-\cos\varphi_U\sin\Phi - \sin\varphi_U\cos\Theta\cos\Phi] \\ &\quad + \dot{\Psi}[\cos\varphi_U\cos(\gamma+\Theta)\cos\Phi - \sin\varphi_U(\cos\gamma\sin\Phi + \sin\gamma\sin\Theta\cos\Phi)]. \end{aligned}$$

(V.4.45)

There are essentially three sets of axes:

(i) the flight path axes $ox_f y_f z_f$; ox_f is aligned with $U(t)$, the oy_f axis is horizontal, normal to the plane of $\gamma(t)$, and the oz_f axis makes up a right handed set of axes; the rotations about these axes are $(\dot{\Psi}(t)\sin\gamma(t),\ \dot{\gamma}(t),\ \dot{\Psi}(t)\cos\gamma(t))$;
(ii) the conventional fuselage body axis system $oxyz$,
(iii) the aerodynamic measurement axis system, $ox_m y_m z_m s$; the ox_m axis coincides with the ox axis, the oz_m is the 'downward' axis in the plane of $\Theta(t)$, and the oy_m axis forms a right handed set; relative to this set of axes experimental measurements give the coefficients C_N, in the negative oz_m direction, C_A in the negative ox_m direction, C_Y in the oy_m direction, and C_l, C_m and C_n about the ox_m, oy_m and oz_m axes respectively.

The translational equations of motion relative to flight path axes are

$$\begin{aligned}
m\dot{U}(t) &= \tfrac{1}{2}\rho_{\text{at}}U^2(t)S_{\text{w}}\left[-C_N(t)\sin\Theta(t) - C_A(t)\cos\Theta(t)\right] \\
&\quad + \text{Th}\cos\Theta(t) - mg\sin\gamma(t), \\
mU(t)\dot{\gamma}(t) &= \tfrac{1}{2}\rho_{\text{at}}U^2(t)S_{\text{w}}\left[C_N(t)\cos\Theta(t)\cos\varphi_U(t)\right. \\
&\quad \left.-C_A(t)\sin\Theta(t)\cos\varphi_U(t) - C_Y(t)\sin\varphi_U(t)\right] \\
&\quad + \text{Th}\sin\Theta(t)\cos\varphi_U(t) - mg\cos\gamma(t), \\
mU(t)\cos\gamma(t)\dot{\Psi}(t) &= \tfrac{1}{2}\rho_{\text{at}}U^2(t)S_{\text{w}}\left[C_N(t)\cos\Theta(t)\sin\varphi_U(t)\right. \\
&\quad \left.-C_A(t)\sin\Theta(t)\sin\varphi_U(t) + C_Y(t)\cos\varphi_U(t)\right].
\end{aligned} \tag{V.4.46}$$

The rotational equations are taken relative to the fuselage body axis system, namely from eqns. (V.4.10):

$$\begin{aligned}
&I_{xx}\dot{p}(t) - I_{xz}\big(\dot{r}(t) + p(t)q(t)\big) - (I_{yy} - I_{zz})q(t)r(t) \\
&\quad = \tfrac{1}{2}\rho_{\text{at}}U^2(t)S_{\text{w}}\ 2s_{\text{w}}C_l(t) \\
&I_{yy}\dot{q}(t) - I_{xz}\big(r^2(t) - p^2(t)\big) - (I_{zz} - I_{xx})r(t)p(t) \\
&\quad = \tfrac{1}{2}\rho_{\text{at}}U^2(t)S_{\text{w}}\ 2s_{\text{w}}[C_m(t)\cos\Phi(t) + C_n(t)\sin\Phi(t)] \\
&I_{zz}\dot{r}(t) - I_{xz}\big(\dot{p}(t) - q(t)r(t)\big) - (I_{xx} - I_{yy})p(t)q(t) \\
&\quad = \tfrac{1}{2}\rho_{\text{at}}U^2(t)S_{\text{w}}\ 2s_{\text{w}}[-C_m(t)\sin\Phi(t) + C_n(t)\cos\Phi(t)]
\end{aligned} \tag{V.4.47}$$

remembering that the moment derivatives are relative to the measurement axes.

The coefficients depend on all of the variables, and their past history; in the previous notation,

$$C_N(t) = C_N\big(\Theta(t), \Phi(t), \varphi_U(t), \dot{\gamma}(t), \dot{\Psi}(t), \xi(t), \eta(t), \zeta(t)\,\big|\,t\big).$$

Aerodynamic modelling is the formulation of the coefficients from measurements and computations.

An aerodynamic model of

$$C_N\big(\Theta(t), \Phi(t), \varphi_U(t), \dot{\gamma}(t), \dot{\Psi}(t)\,\big|\,t\big)$$

is proposed, omitting, for the time being, the dependency on the control angles. The same arguments apply to the other five coefficients, C_A, C_Y, C_l, C_m, C_n.

For an aeroplane in steady rectilinear flight C_N depends only on Θ and Φ, C_N is independent of φ_U, and $\dot{\varphi}_U$, $\dot{\gamma}$ and $\dot{\Psi}$ are zero. In this case the appropriate wind tunnel measurements are the conventional static balance measurements of $(C_N(\Theta,\Phi))_{\text{static}}$.

For an aeroplane in steady turning flight with Θ, Φ, φ_U, $\dot{\gamma}$ and $\dot{\Psi}$ constant, then it is reasonable to assume that C_N can be expressed as

$$C_N = \left(C_N(\Theta,\Phi)\right)_{\text{static}} + \left(C_{N\dot{\gamma}}(\Theta,\Phi,\varphi_U)\right)_{\text{static}}\dot{\gamma} + \left(C_{N\dot{\Psi}}(\Theta,\Phi,\varphi_U)\right)_{\text{static}}\dot{\Psi}. \tag{V.4.48}$$

If a model is set at $(\Theta, \Phi, \varphi_U)$ on a horizontal whirling arm which rotates at a constant rate $\dot{\sigma}$, $C_{N\dot{\sigma}}(\Theta,\Phi,\varphi_U)_{\text{static}}$ will be measured, then

$$\begin{aligned} C_{N\dot{\Psi}}(\Theta,\Phi,\varphi_U)_{\text{static}} &= C_{N\dot{\sigma}}(\Theta,\Phi,\varphi_U)_{\text{static}} \\ C_{N\dot{\gamma}}(\Theta,\Phi,\varphi_U)_{\text{static}} &= C_{N\dot{\sigma}}\left(\Theta,\Phi,(\varphi_U+90°)\right)_{\text{static}}. \end{aligned} \tag{V.4.49}$$

To measure dynamic effects, a number of rigs are proposed.

A large amplitude oscillatory weathercock pitch rig ($\Theta(t)$ from 0 to 90°), with the model at constant Φ; instantaneous $C_N(t)$ can be measured, over a range of amplitudes and mean angles of Θ at low frequencies, obtaining the range of dynamic loops similar to those described in the case of longitudinal modelling in section V.2.12. And then, as explained in section V.2.12, $C_N(t)$ can be expressed in the form

$$C_N(t) = C_N\left(\Theta_{\min} \text{ or } \Theta_{\max}, \Theta(t), \dot{\Theta}(t), \Phi\right). \tag{V.4.50}$$

A large amplitude oscillatory bank angle rig (i.e. roll about the *ox* axis, with $\Phi(t)$ from 0 to 90°) with the model set at constant Θ; instantaneous $C_N(t)$ can be measured over a range of amplitudes and mean angles at low frequencies obtaining a range of dynamic loops. And then

$$C_N(t) = C_N\left(\Theta, \Phi_{\min} \text{ or } \Phi_{\max}, \Phi(t), \dot{\Phi}(t)\right). \tag{V.4.51}$$

A constant rate of roll rig which rolls the model with constant Θ and Φ at a constant rate $\dot{\varphi}_U$ about the flight path; $(C_{N\dot{\varphi}U}(\Theta,\Phi))_{\text{static}}\dot{\varphi}_U$ can be measured. If there are strong non-linearities with respect to $\dot{\varphi}_U$ then an additional coefficient multiplying $\dot{\varphi}_U^2$ could be measured. This rotary motion is known as 'coning'.

The general time varying C_N may be expressed as

$$\begin{aligned} C_N(t) = {} & \left(C_N(\Theta(t),\Phi(t))\right)_{\text{dyn}} \\ & + \left(C_{N\dot{\varphi}U}(\Theta=\Theta(t),\Phi=\Phi(t))\right)_{\text{static}}\dot{\varphi}_U(t) \\ & + \left(C_{N\dot{\gamma}}(\Theta=\Theta(t),\Phi=\Phi(t),\varphi_U=\varphi_U(t))\right)_{\text{static}}\dot{\gamma}(t) \\ & + \left(C_{N\dot{\Psi}}(\Theta=\Theta(t),\Phi=\Phi(t),\varphi_U=\varphi_U(t))\right)_{\text{static}}\dot{\Psi}(t) \end{aligned} \tag{V.4.52}$$

where

$$\left(C_N(\Theta(t),\Phi(t))\right)_{\text{dyn}} = C_N\left(\Theta_{\min} \text{ or } \Theta_{\max}, \Theta(t), \dot{\Theta}(t), \Phi\right) + C_N\left(\Theta, \Phi_{\min} \text{ or } \Phi_{\max}, \Phi(t), \dot{\Phi}(t)\right) - \left(C_N(\Theta = \Theta(t), \Phi = \Phi(t))\right)_{\text{static}}.$$

In eqn. (V.4.52) the unsteady aerodynamic couplings between [$\Theta(t)$, $\Phi(t)$] and [$\varphi_U(t)$, $\Theta(t)$, $\Phi(t)$] have been ignored; these effects are not understood and need further research. As a pragmatic suggestion to cover these further couplings, if

$$F(t) = \left(C_N(\Theta(t), \Phi = \Phi(t))\right)_{\text{dyn}} \Big/ \left(C_N(\Theta = \Theta(t), \Phi = \Phi(t))\right)_{\text{static}}$$

then perhaps $C_N(t)$ can be expressed in the form

$$C_N(t) = \left(C_N(\Theta(t),\Phi(t))\right)_{\text{dyn}} + F(t)\left(C_{N\dot{\varphi}U}(\Theta = \Theta(t), \Phi = \Phi(t))\right)_{\text{static}} \dot{\varphi}_U(t) + F(t)\left(C_{N\dot{\gamma}}(\Theta = \Theta(t), \Phi = \Phi(t), \varphi_U = \varphi_U(t))\right)_{\text{static}} \dot{\gamma}(t) + F(t)\left(C_{N\dot{\Psi}}(\Theta = \Theta(t), \Phi = \Phi(t), \varphi_U = \varphi_U(t))\right)_{\text{static}} \dot{\Psi}(t). \tag{V.4.53}$$

In addition the control powers due to symmetric and asymmetric tailplane, spoilers and rudder need to be measured.

Somewhat stark references have been made to wind tunnel experimentation, a major activity embracing large wind tunnels, highly complex rigs, equipment and instrumentation, computer controlled experiments, computer processing of measured data, and sophisticated models, all extremely expensive. For further information see Orlik-Rückemann (ref. V.77), and refs. V.78 and V.79.

With all of the aerodynamic coefficients treated in the above manner a large database would be built up which needs to be systematically coded for rapid retrieval and used as inputs to the numerical solutions of the equations of motion (eqns. (V.4.46) and (V.4.47)). Sophisticated computers and software would be required.

Simplified approaches along the above lines have been extensively investigated, primarily in comparing predictions with flight behaviour of models dropped from helicopters or aeroplanes. There has been a measure of success in predicting post-stall gyrations from specified, high angle of incidence, starting conditions, and also in the validation of spin prevention systems (Ross & Edwards, ref. V.80), but predictions of motions through departure have yet to be satisfactorily resolved.

The study of dynamic motions requires both the small amplitude stability analyses of sections (V.2.11), (V.3.2), (V.4.4) and (V.4.5) and the large manoeuvre responses described in this section.

V.5 AGILITY

Agility is the measure of tactical manoeuvring which enhances effectiveness in either air-to-air or air-to-ground combat. Parameters which affect agility are

— maximum transient turn rate
— rates of longitudinal acceleration and deceleration
— rates of climb
— roll response to control input
— pitch response to control input
— ability to aim fuselage up to high angles of weathercock pitch independently of the flight path.

Requirements for these parameters are task dependent. For missile launch a target should lie within a cone of 20° half angle, but for gun firing the angle is down to 0.1°; thus for a missile launch a high turn rate is necessary to point the nose quickly into a ball-park direction with little need for precision in accurate aiming at the launch, whereas for gun firing the turn rate requirement is small but there is a need for a high degree of pitch and yaw control precision to maintain the nose in a desired direction.

The steady STR, the Sustained Turn Rate is described in sect. IV.3.3.

It is possible to obtain a higher transient turn rate than the maximum STR by flying at a higher C_L, keeping the load factor at, or below, its maximum, but then the drag is greater than the thrust so the forward speed U reduces with time. If a high C_L is maintained the normal acceleration and turn rate decrease during the turn.

For a high bank turn (i.e. $\sin\varphi \simeq 1.0$), from eqn. (IV.3.5),

$$\text{Turn rate} \simeq L/(mU) = g(L/W)\left[\tfrac{1}{2}\rho_{at}S_w C_L/L\right]^{1/2}$$

$$= g\left[\left(\tfrac{1}{2}\rho_{at}\right)(L/W)C_L/(W/S_w)\right]^{1/2} \qquad \text{(V.5.1)}$$

and

$$L/W = \text{load factor} = \tfrac{1}{2}\gamma\,\rho_{at}M_\infty^2\,C_L/(W/S_w). \qquad \text{(V.5.2)}$$

The ATR, the Attainable Turn Rate, at a given altitude and Mach number is given by

$$\begin{aligned} C_L &= C_{L\,max},\ \text{load factor} < \text{maximum load factor} \\ C_L &< C_{L\,max},\ \text{load factor} = \text{maximum load factor} \end{aligned} \qquad \text{(V.5.3)}$$

where maximum load factor = 9.

Hence, at a given altitude, maximum ATR is obtained with

$$C_L = C_{L\,max}\ \text{at}\ M_\infty = \left[9.0(W/S_w)/\left(\tfrac{1}{2}\gamma\,\rho_{at}C_{L\,max}\right)\right]^{1/2}. \qquad \text{(V.5.4)}$$

For overall maximum ATR, from eqn. (V.5.1) both the altitude and wing loading should be low, which implies, from eqn. (V.5.4), a subsonic Mach number. The reader should substitute typical numbers.

Typical variations of STR and ATR at 3 km (10 000 ft) altitude are shown in Fig. V.73. The variation of ATR with Mach number follows the trends predicted in the previous paragraph. The ATR is considerably faster than the STR from $0.5M_\infty$ up to $0.8M_\infty$ but at $0.9M_\infty$ the ATR and STR are virtually the same.

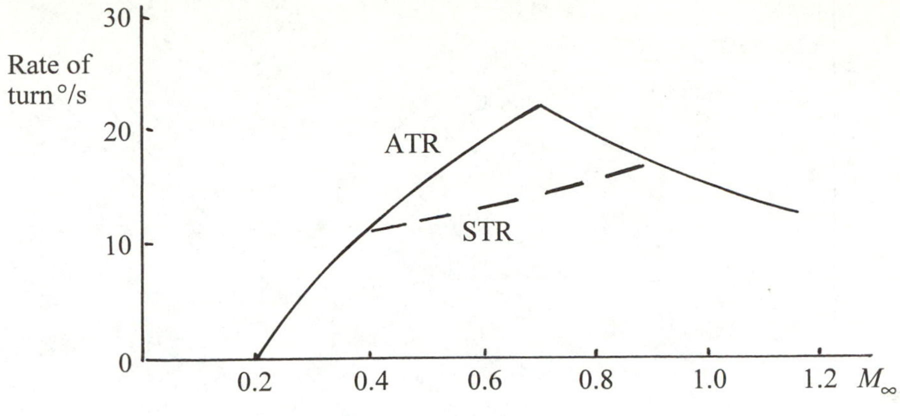

Fig. V.73. Comparison of rates of turn.

For longitudinal acceleration and climbing flight the basic equation is

$$\mathrm{Th} - D - W \sin \gamma(t) = m\, \mathrm{d}U(t)/\mathrm{d}t, \tag{V.5.5}$$

where $\gamma(t)$ is the flight path angle, positive for climb and $U(t)$ is the velocity along the flight path. Thus

$$\begin{aligned} [(\mathrm{Th} - D)/W]U(t) &= gU(t)\, \mathrm{d}U(t)/\mathrm{d}t + U(t) \sin \gamma(t) \\ &= \mathrm{d}\left[U^2(t)/2g + h(t)\right]/\mathrm{d}t \\ &= \mathrm{d}h_\mathrm{e}(t)/\mathrm{d}t \end{aligned} \tag{V.5.6}$$

where $h(t)$ is the altitude and $h_\mathrm{e}(t)$ $(= h(t) + U^2(t)/2g)$, the so-called energy height, is the (height) potential energy plus the kinetic energy per unit mass.

The specific excess power (SEP) is defined as

$$\mathrm{SEP} = [(\mathrm{Th} - D)/W]U(t) = \mathrm{d}h_\mathrm{e}(t)/\mathrm{d}t. \tag{V.5.7}$$

A positive SEP can be used to accelerate at constant altitude or to climb at constant speed, or to accelerate up a gradual climb.

A typical set of $\mathrm{Th}/p_\mathrm{at}$ and D/p_at against Mach number for different altitudes are shown in Fig. V.74, and a corresponding set of SEP contours, mapped on a Mach number/altitude grid with lines of constant energy height superimposed, are illustrated in Fig. V.75. At sea level the maximum thrust and drag curves are nearly parallel up to the drag rise Mach number so the SEP increases with Mach number due to the influence of the $U(t)$ term; above the drag rise Mach number the excess of thrust over drag diminishes rapidly and the SEP with it. The maximum SEP at an altitude decreases with altitude because both thrust and drag decrease with ambient pressure p_at. Above the tropopause the Th and D curves are nearly parallel from 1.0M to 1.6M so the SEP increases with Mach number over this Mach number range due to the influence of the '$U(t)$' term, moving the maximum SEP at a fixed altitude into the supersonic Mach number range.

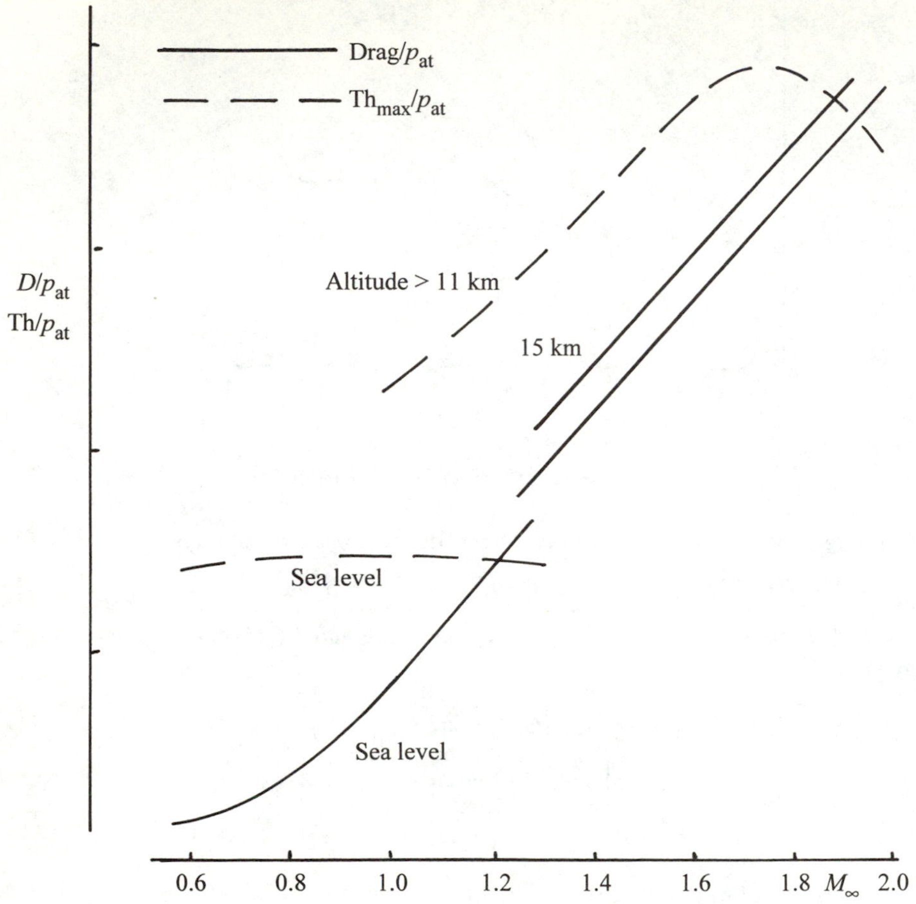

Fig. V.74. Typical thrust/drag characteristics.

Combat involves a combination of STR, ATR and SEP. Two basic combat scenarios are introduced.

(i) In the circular chase, shown in Fig. V.76, each aeroplane enters a sustained turn; as indicated, the aeroplane with the faster maximum STR is the victor.

(ii) In the 'scissors' engagement, shown in Fig. V.77 after a sustained turn skirmish, if neither aeroplane has a STR superiority, one aeroplane will break away; both aeroplanes will then enter an ATR in which energy is lost, followed by a straight dash in which the SEP increases the energy. If the SEP performance of the two aeroplanes is comparable the aeroplane with the faster ATR is the victor. If the aeroplane with the faster ATR has the lower SEP then there could be a stalemate.

Fine decisions are needed from the pilot on when to use a sustained turn or an attained turn or to accelerate. For example, from the data in Figs. V.73 and V.75 a 90° turn at $9g$ starting at $0.8M_\infty$ with an ATR of 19°/s would take 4.75 s, losing energy height at about

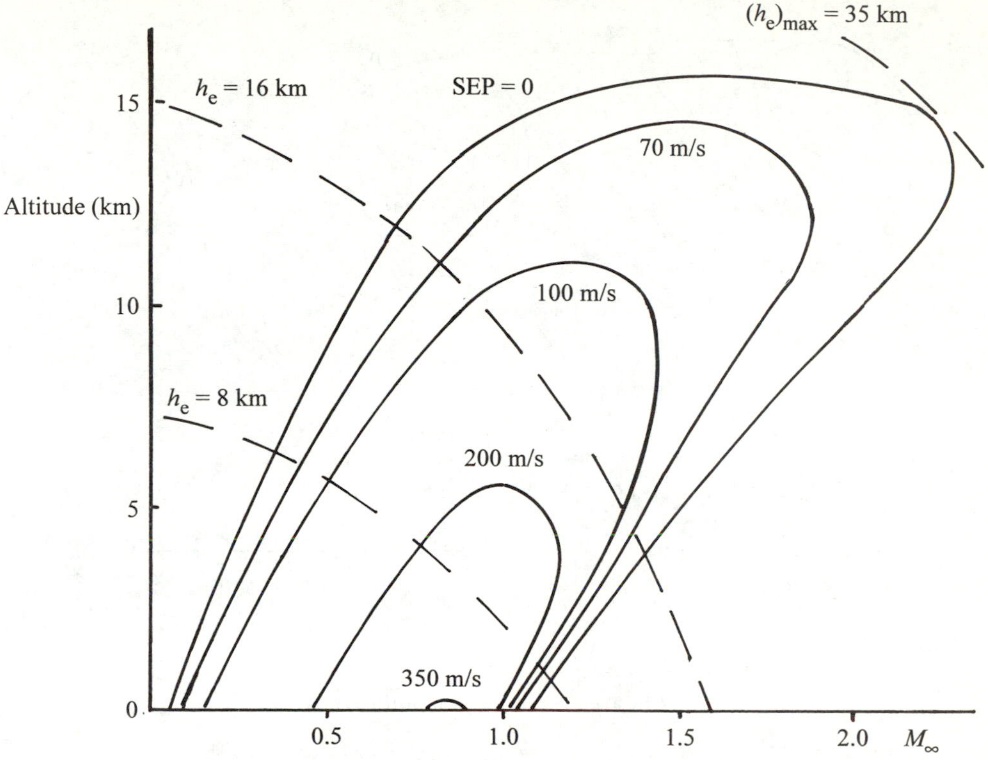

Fig. V.75. Typical contours of specific excess power in $1g$ flight.

350 m/s, so 1670 m of energy height would be lost. From the energy height curve the speed drops to about $0.6M_\infty$. With an SEP of 250 m/s it would take about 6.5 s in $1g$ flight to regain the lost energy, a long period of time in a vulnerable condition. Alternatively, the ATR could be maintained; energy would continue to be lost down to the (ATR = STR) corner where the turn rate is only 11°/s, another vulnerable situation. Manoeuvring with the ATR beyond the STR limit can be afforded for short periods only, preferably at the start of an engagement to gain a position of advantage and thereafter dominate the fight.

On-board computers can keep track of what is happening, analyse possible scenarios, and offer updated advice to the pilot (see Chin, ref. V.81).

Recent literature—for example, Dorn (ref. V.82), Skow (ref. V.83), Liefer *et al.* (ref. V.84)—is concerned with the identification of the 'metrics', or sets of groups of performance parameters, which quantify agility. A selection of proposed metrics are:

(i) dynamic speed turn—plot of SEP ~ turn rate;
(ii) pitch agility—time to pitch to maximum load factor plus time to pitch from maximum load factor to zero list;
(iii) T_{90}—time to roll to and capture a 90° bank angle change;
(iv) torsional agility—turn rate/T_{90};

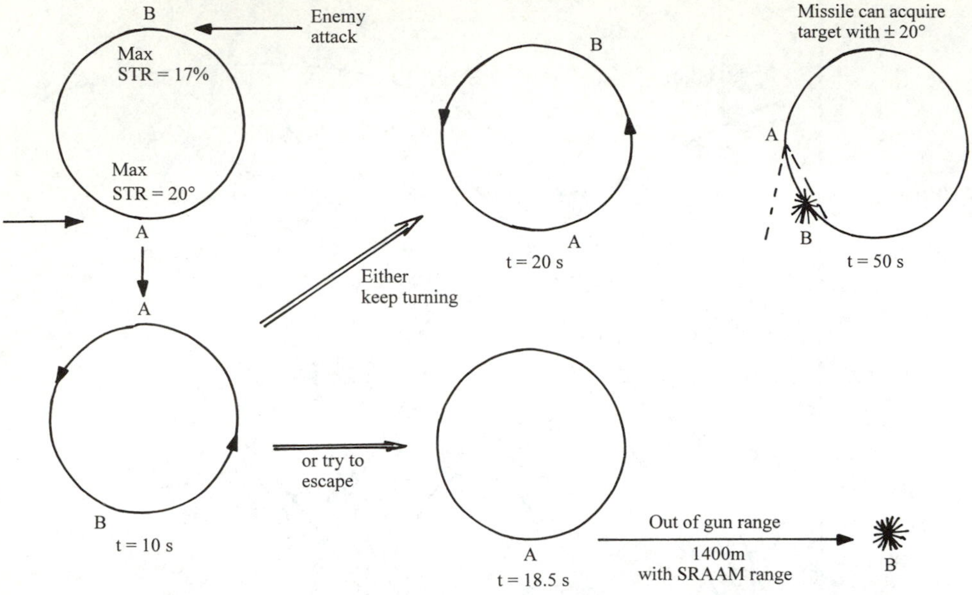

Fig. V.76. Tactics: importance of sustained turn rate.

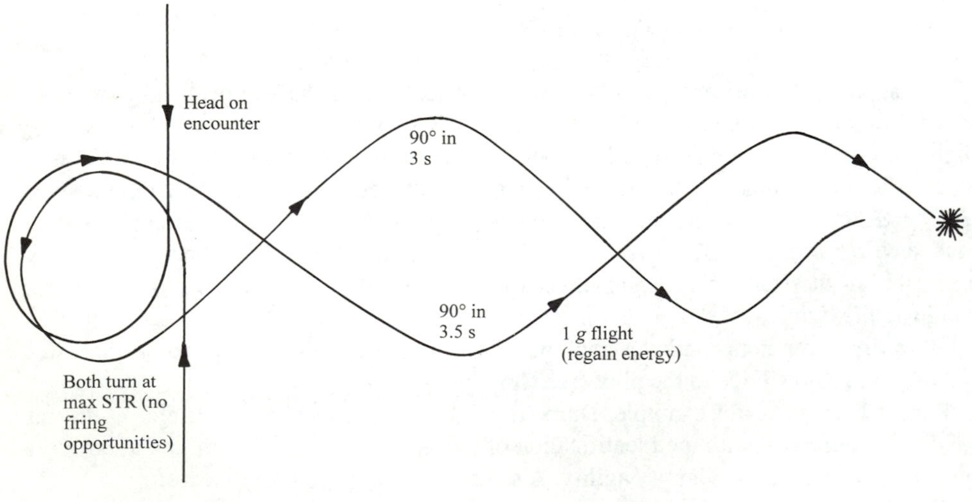

Fig. V.77. Tactics: importance of attained turn rate.

(v) axial agility—the difference between maximum and minimum SEP available at a given flight condition divided by the time of transition between the two levels;

(vi) combat cycle time—time to complete a maximum ATR and regain lost energy;

(vii) roll reversal agility parameter—product of the time required to reverse a turn and the cross-range displacement that occurs during the turn;

(viii) agility potential—$(\mathrm{Th}/W)/(W/S_w)$.

Supermanoeuvrability is a term to describe aeroplanes capable of rapid large angle of incidence excursions, up to 70°, relative to the flight path, the so-called cobra manoeuvre, and also capable of turning within small radii. An ultimate aspiration is an aeroplane which can pitch up to 90°, roll about the (vertical) roll axis through 180° and then pitch down; the aeroplane has then reversed direction in a zero radius turn without loss of altitude when the thrust/weight ratio is unity.

V.6 CONFIGURATION EFFECTS ON FLIGHT DYNAMIC CHARACTERISTICS

In this section a cursory summary is presented on the effects of configuration geometry on flight dynamic characteristics.

V.6.1 Conventional configurations

Conventional configurations are those with fuselage, wing and aft tailplane and fin.

One of the most important parts of the configuration is the shape of the cross-section of the fuselage nose and its effect on the break of the forebody vortices. As shown in Fig. V.78, reported by Woodcock & Weissman (ref. V.85), vertical ellipse cross-sections lead to an unstable break of the symmetric pattern of the forebody vortices to an asymmetric pattern, while horizontal ellipse cross-sections lead to a stable break. (It is not clear how a derivative $C_{n\beta}$ is obtained when there is a static hysteresis of C_n, as shown in Fig. V.64; hopefully $C_{n\beta}$ in Fig. V.78 is the in-phase oscillatory derivative $\tilde{C}_{n\beta}$.)

A comparison of the derivatives for a high wing and low wing in Fig. V.79 (taken from ref. V.85) shows the advantage of a low wing, due to a reduction in the interference effect of the wing on the fin.

A comparison of the effects of wing plan form on $(C_{n\beta})_{\mathrm{dyn}}$ and LCDP, due to aileron control, is shown in Fig. V.80 (taken from ref. V.57). Three plan forms were investigated:

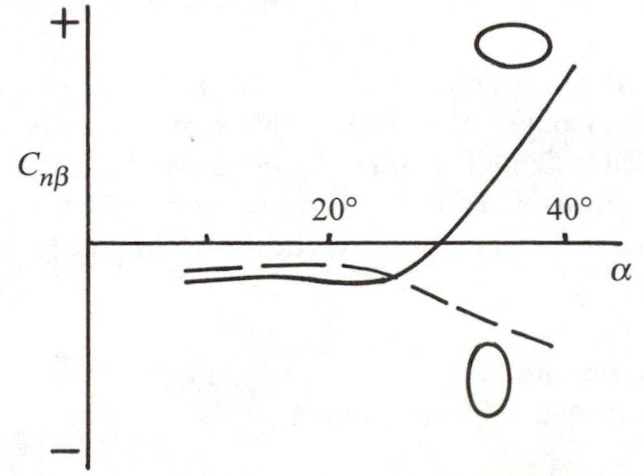

Fig. V.78. Effect of nose cross-section.

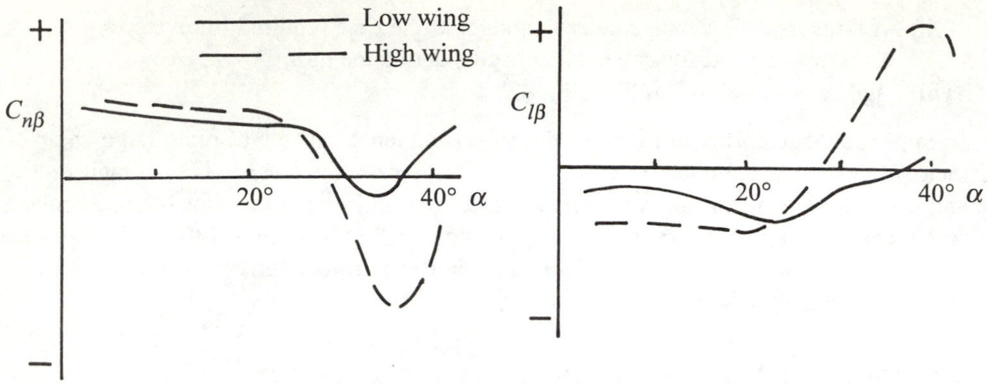

Fig. V.79. Effect of wing position.

the basic configuration has an aspect ratio of 3.68; the swept wing has a leading edge sweep of 45°, taper ratio 0.25 and an aspect ratio of 2.82; the delta wing has a leading edge sweep of 57.5° and an aspect ratio of 2.09. All three configurations have positive $(C_{n\beta})_{\text{dyn}}$ up to 40° angle of incidence; however, the LCDP goes to zero over a limited angle of incidence range for the swept wing configuration and goes negative at high angles of incidence for the delta wing configuration.

The effects of the above configurations on $(C_{lp} + C_{l\dot{\beta}} \sin \alpha)$ are shown in Fig. V.80(iii). The swept configuration shows excessive negative roll rate damping.

In an attempt to control the forebody vortices, strakes can be attached to the nose. As shown in Fig. V.81, a shorter strake is preferred. Forebody strakes can be combined with wing strakes to optimize the flight dynamic behaviour.

Forebody strakes, particularly longer ones, give a significant nose-up pitching moment which can contribute to a pitch-up. In addition, strakes may cause radar interference. An alternative way of controlling the forebody vortices is by blowing jets of air from the surface of the nose, see Malcolm *et al.* (ref. V.86).

Twin fins, splayed outward, are introduced primarily to reduce the interference between the fin(s) and the forebody vortices and any wing–fuselage, or wing strake, vortices.

Small ventral fins extending downward from the underside of the aft fuselage retain their effectiveness at high angles of incidence, unless in the wake of missiles or stores. But their spanwise extent is limited because of ground clearance at rotation at take-off.

Tailplane anhedral acts as additional fin area, also introducing a favourable aerodynamic advantage by channelling more air over the top of the rear fuselage in sideslip.

V.6.2 Modern configurations

There is a variety of contemporary configurations,

—tailless
—canard

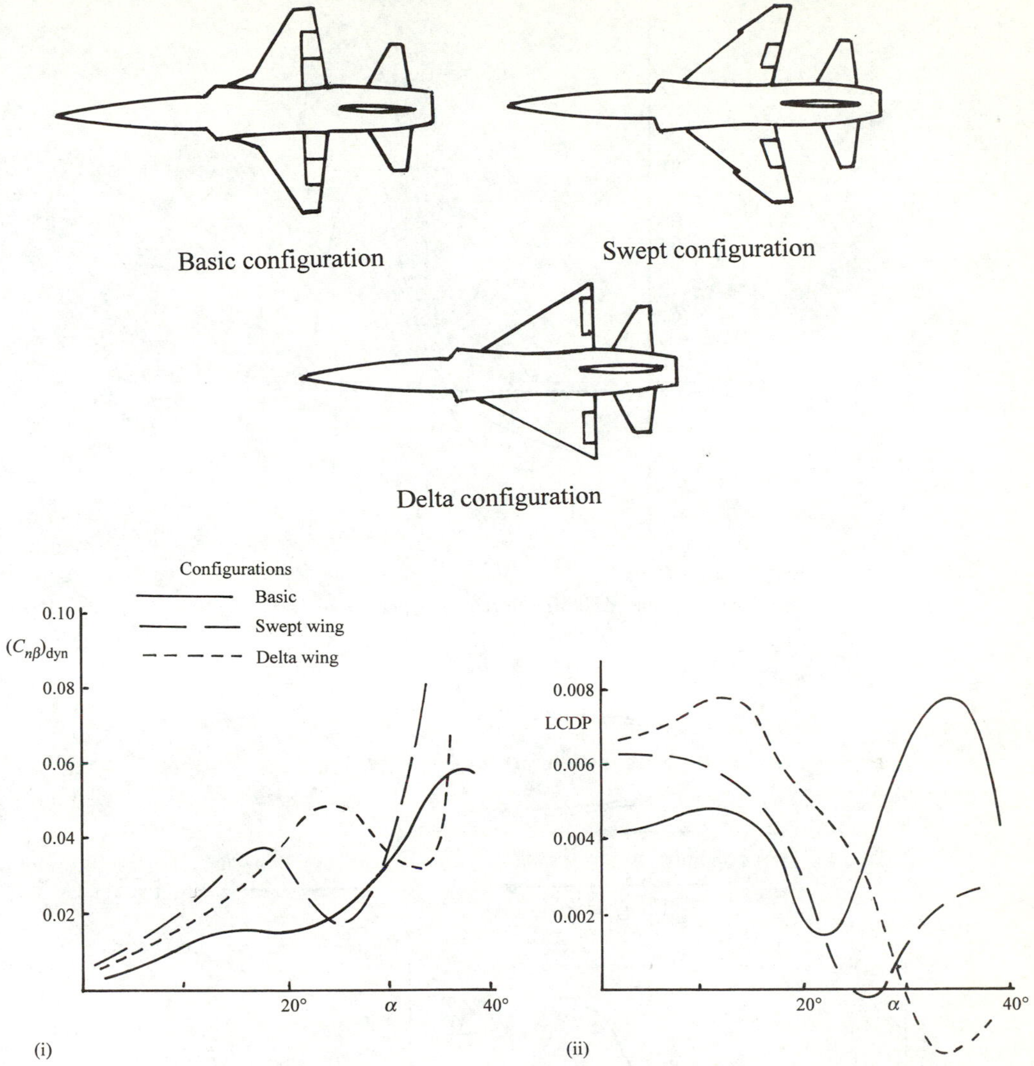

Fig. V.80 (i) and (ii). Effect of wing plan form.

— swept forward wing
— canard-wing-tailplane

all of which rely on artificial stability to optimize their performance potential.

The tailless configuration, usually a delta, or double-delta, which saves on the drag of the tailplane, is controlled via trailing edge controls, the elevons. Because the moment arm of the elevons from the centre of mass is relatively small the elevon power must be high. Furthermore, because the elevons occupy the wing trailing edge there is no room for trailing edge flaps to provide direct lift control.

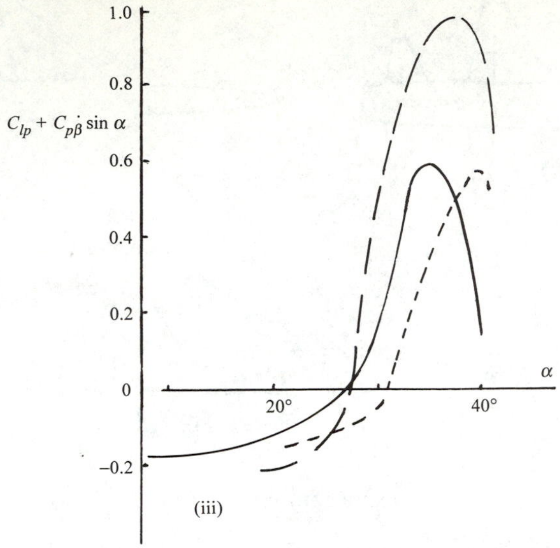

Fig. V.80(iii). Effect of wing plan form.

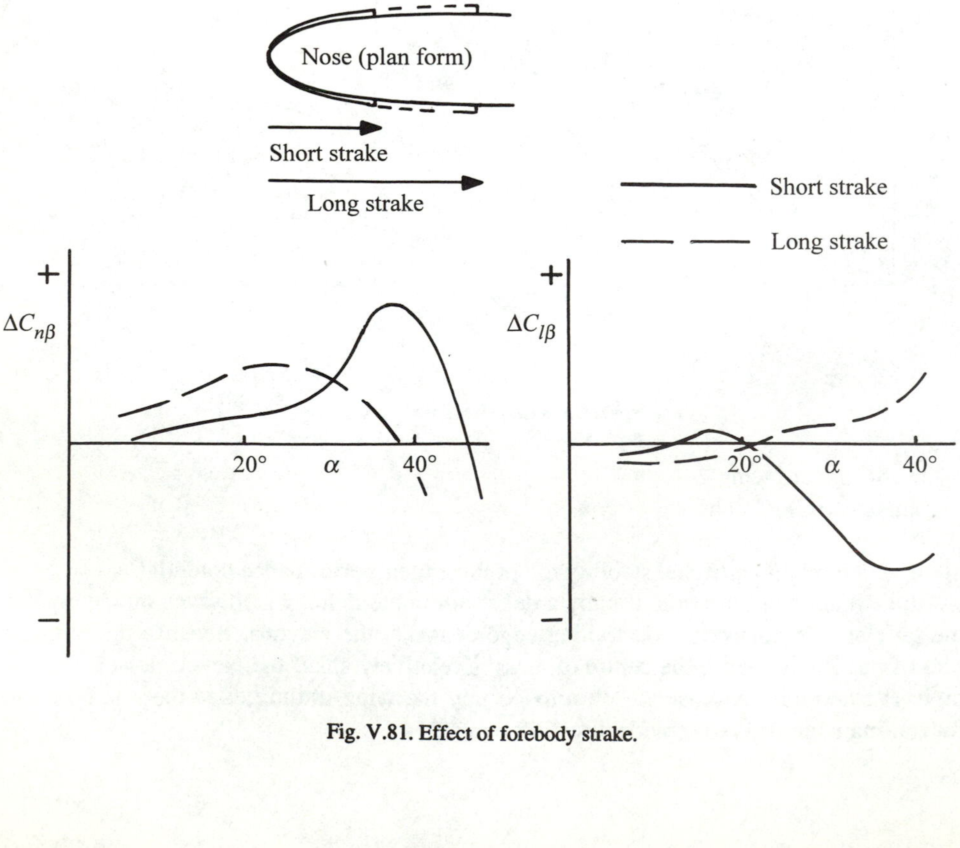

Fig. V.81. Effect of forebody strake.

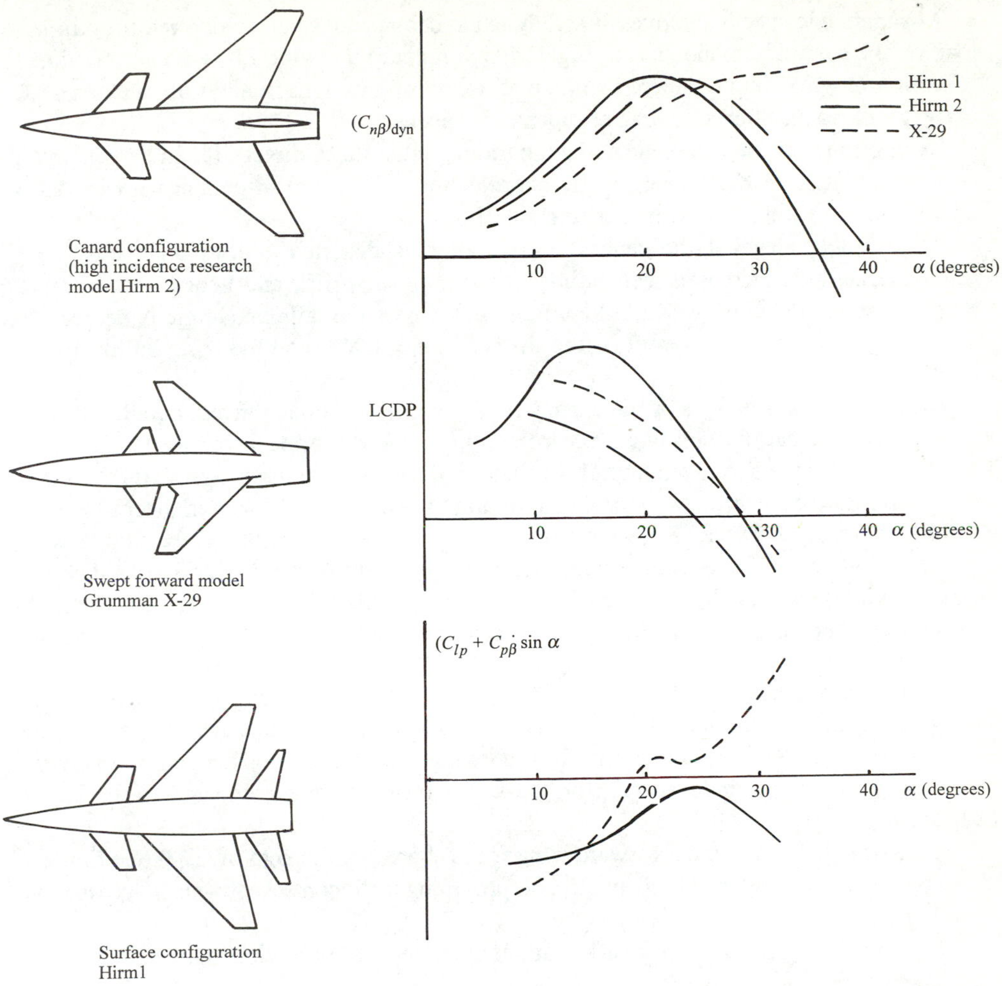

Fig. V.82. Lateral characteristics of modern configurations.

The canard configuration has a foreplane in front of the wing, replacing the aft tailplane (the term 'canard' originates from the Bleriot tail-first aeroplane of 1911 which resembled a duck in flight). Without artificial stability the centre of mass must lie forward of the overall aerodynamic centre, which implies a positive angle on the foreplane to trim, and a larger positive angle to manoeuvre; these large foreplane loads generate high drag. With artificial stability the centre of mass can be moved aft and the foreplane manoeuvre loads reduced.

At high angles of incidence there is a favourable interference between foreplane and main wing which enhances total lift.

At supersonic speeds the overall aerodynamic centre moves aft which requires an up-load on the canard in manoeuvring flight, which reduces the wing lift, with a consequent reduction in wave drag compared with an aft tail configuration. In addition, a cleaner aft body improves the afterbody drag at supersonic speeds.

By coordinating the foreplane and wing trailing edge flaps, direct lift can be generated at constant angle of incidence; and by coordinating differential foreplane with rudder a direct side force can be generated at zero sideslip.

Another advantage of the canard configuration is that in a pull-up manoeuvre the foreplane angle is increased, generating an initial positive lift, and hence a more rapid response compared with the aft tail configuration where the tailplane angle is decreased, generating an initial negative lift before the aeroplane rotates and the wing builds up the required positive lift.

Although the advantages of the canard configuration have been listed, detailed design studies suggest that the optimized canard configuration does not have any fundamental advantages over the optimized aft tail configuration (see, for example, Skow, ref. V.58).

Turning to the swept forward wing configuration, comparing a tapered swept forward wing with a tapered swept back wing with the same effective sweep (say, the same sweep of the mid-chord line) the leading edge sweep of the swept forward wing is less than the leading edge sweep of the swept back configuration. This effect increases the wing lift curve slope and reduces any pitch-up tendency, but might decrease the drag rise Mach number.

A forward swept wing is highly loaded towards the wing root, and so is prone to early wing root flow separation; this effect can be reduced with a canard layout where the downwash from the foreplane diminishes the wing loading. The difference in spanwise loading gives a lower induced drag on the swept forward wing compared to the swept back wing.

A major benefit of a swept forward wing is the change in the sign of ($C_{l\beta}$) due to wing sweep, which alleviates the difficulty of providing roll control power in crosswind landings.

Research into three surface configurations is aimed at optimizing manoeuvring performance.

A comparison of the lateral characteristics of three types of configurations is shown in Fig. V.82 (taken from Ross, ref. V.87). All configurations experience a loss in the LCDP at an angle of incidence close to 30°. Note the large loss in roll rate damping of the swept forward configuration.

Looking to the future, vectored thrust in flight is regarded as the next major development in the evolution of combat technology.

Appendix 1

Build up of circulation and lift following sudden change in incidence

In low speed two dimensional aerofoil theory the circulation around a planar aerofoil at a static angle of incidence, α_s, is given exactly by assuming that all of the aerofoil bound vorticity be concentrated into a vortex line of strength Γ_s located at the 1/4 chord point from the leading edge and then satisfying the downwash condition at the 3/4 point from the wing leading edge. To demonstrate this statement, by reference to Fig. A1.1, applying the two dimensional Biot–Savart law (see refs. III.7, III.8),

$$\Gamma_s/(2\pi c_w/2) = \text{downwash at the } 3/4 \text{ chord point} = U\alpha_s \tag{A1.1}$$

hence

$$C_L = \text{lift}/\left(\tfrac{1}{2}\rho U^2 c_w\right) = (\rho U \Gamma_s)/\left(\tfrac{1}{2}\rho U^2 c_w\right) = 2\pi\, \alpha_s. \tag{A1.2}$$

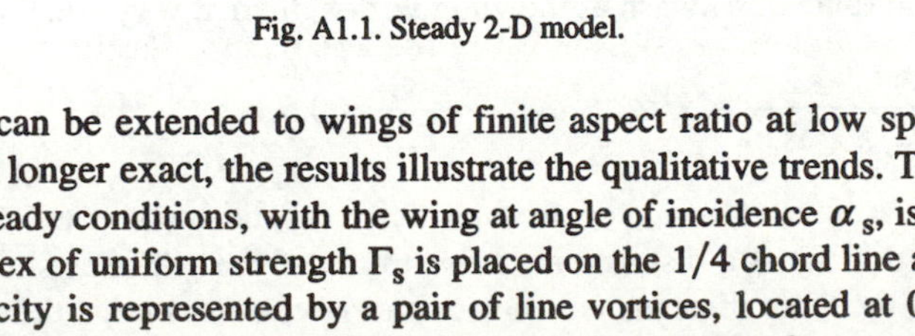

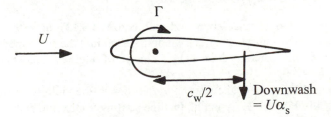

Fig. A1.1. Steady 2-D model.

This concept can be extended to wings of finite aspect ratio at low speeds; although the results are no longer exact, the results illustrate the qualitative trends. The model for a swept wing in steady conditions, with the wing at angle of incidence α_s, is shown in Fig. A1.2. A line vortex of uniform strength Γ_s is placed on the 1/4 chord line along the span, the trailing vorticity is represented by a pair of line vortices, located at 0.75 semi-span (this model is not mathematically consistent in that it does not conform to the principle of conservation of vorticity, but it is thought to be more representative for the calculation of induced velocities). The position where the downwash condition is to be satisfied is taken

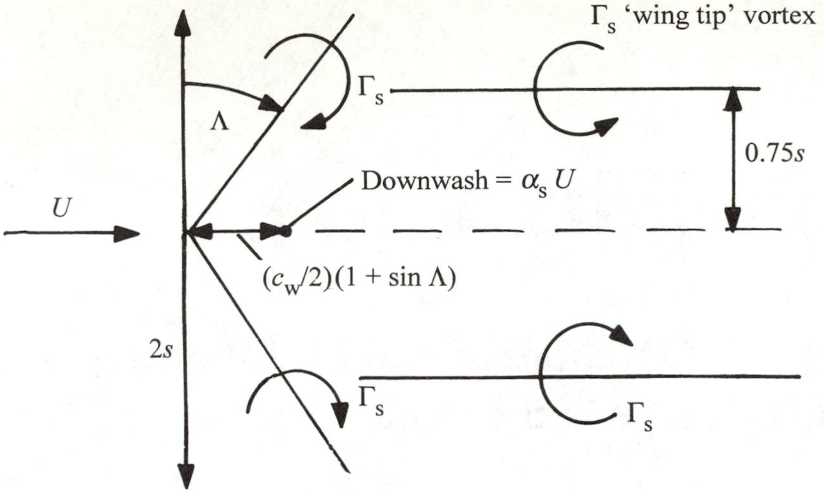

Fig. A1.2. Steady 3-D model.

to be $\{(1 + \sin \Lambda)c_w/2\}$ aft of the 1/4 chord point on the wing root chord; this position is chosen because it gives a more reasonable answer. On application of the three dimensional Biot–Savart law (see refs. III.7 and III.8), together with some crude rounding off,

$$\frac{\Gamma_s}{2\pi\ c_w/2}\left(\frac{1}{\cos\Lambda}+\frac{1}{0.75\text{AR}}\right) \simeq U\alpha_s \tag{A1.3}$$

which leads to the steady state lift coefficient

$$C_L = 2\pi\ \cos\Lambda\,\alpha_s/(1+1.3\cos\Lambda/\text{AR}). \tag{A1.4}$$

Eqn. (A1.4) is not too accurate compared with eqn. (III.3.13), nevertheless eqn. (A1.4) serves as a datum when unsteady effects are introduced into the same model.

Next consider the problem of the sudden change of angle of incidence (i.e. $\alpha = 0$ for $t < 0$, $\alpha = \alpha_s$ for $t > 0$).

For very small time, $t > 0$, the starting vortex lies in the vicinity of the wing trailing edge, as shown in Fig. A1.3. Assuming that the starting vortex and short trailing vortices induce about the same downwash as the wing vortex, then at very small times,

$$\frac{\Gamma(t)}{2\pi\ c_w/2}\,\frac{2}{\cos\Lambda} \simeq U\alpha_s \quad \text{thus} \quad \frac{\Gamma(t)}{\Gamma_s} \simeq 0.6. \tag{A1.5}$$

For very large time, $t \to \infty$, the shed vorticity can be lumped together into a single vortex of strength $\Gamma(t)$ at a distance Ut downstream of the wing, as shown in Fig. A1.4. Again applying the three dimensional Biot–Savart law, at very large times,

$$\frac{\Gamma(t)}{2\pi\ c_w/2}\left(\frac{1}{\cos\Lambda}+\frac{1}{0.75\text{AR}}+\frac{\text{AR}}{10\bar{t}^2}\right) \simeq U\alpha_s \quad \bar{t} = tU/C_w. \tag{A1.6}$$

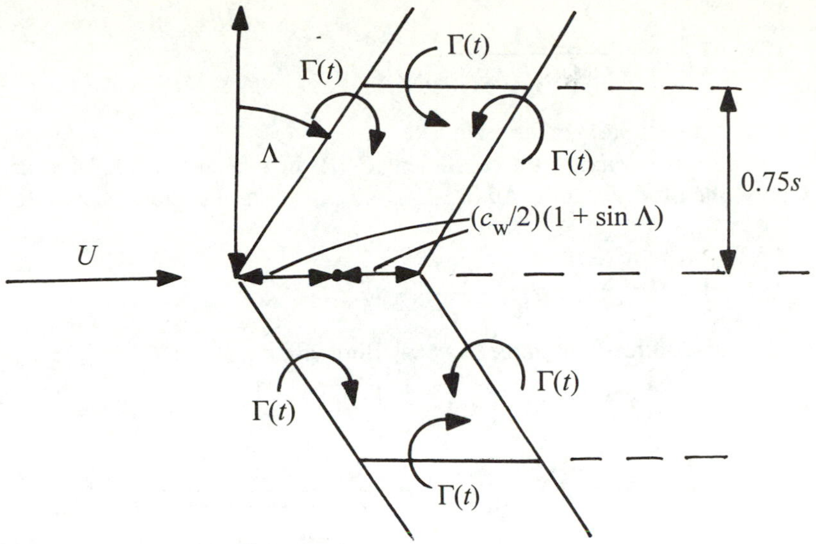

Fig. A1.3. Unsteady 3-D model at small time.

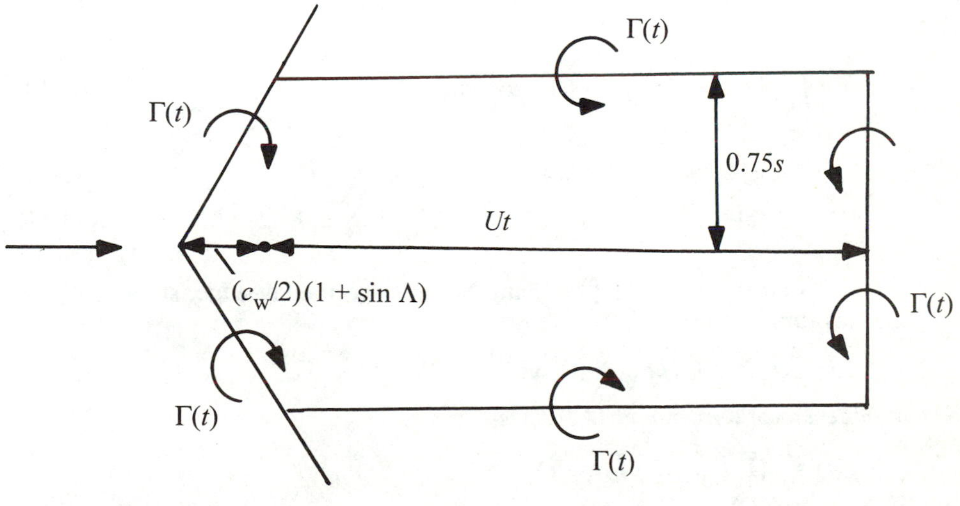

Fig. A1.4. Unsteady 3-D model at large time.

Hence, at very large times,

$$\Gamma(t) \simeq \Gamma_s\left(1-\left(\mathrm{AR}\ \cos\Lambda/10\bar{t}^2\right)\right). \tag{A1.7}$$

The number 10 is an order of magnitude.

An empirical formula for $\Gamma(t)$ for $t > 0$ embracing the correct behaviour at very small times, eqn. (A1.5), and very large times, eqn. (A1.7), is

$$\Gamma(t) = \Gamma_s\left(1 - \frac{1}{2.5 + \left(10\bar{t}^2/\text{AR}\cos\Lambda\right)}\right). \tag{A1.8}$$

Eqn. (A1.8) is eqn. (III.3.41) in the main text.

To obtain the time varying lift coefficient $C_L(t)$, in two dimensional linearized unsteady theory, the lift distribution Δp (= $p_{\text{lower}} - p_{\text{upper}}$) over the chord is, by reference to Fig. A1.5,

$$\Delta p(x,t) = \rho U \gamma(x,t) + \rho\int_0^x \frac{\partial(\gamma(\xi,t))}{\partial t}\,\mathrm{d}\xi. \tag{A1.9}$$

This equation arises directly from the unsteady Bernoulli equation.

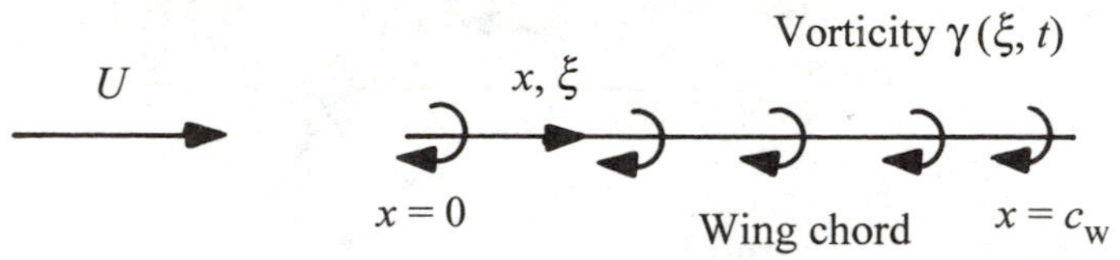

Fig. A1.5. Unsteady aerofoil vorticity.

Thus

$$\text{lift} = \int_0^{c_w} \Delta p(x,t)\,\mathrm{d}x = \rho U\Gamma(t) + \rho\int_0^{c_w}(c-\xi)\frac{\partial(\gamma(\xi,t))}{\partial t}\,\mathrm{d}\xi \tag{A1.10}$$

where

$$\Gamma(t) = \int_0^{c_w} \gamma(x,t)\,\mathrm{d}x. \tag{A1.11}$$

Now $\gamma(\xi,t)$ is large for small ξ reducing towards the trailing edge, so an order of magnitude for eqn. (A1.10) is

$$\text{lift} \simeq \rho U\Gamma(t) + 0.7\rho c_w\,\mathrm{d}\Gamma(t)/\mathrm{d}t. \tag{A1.12}$$

The non-dimensional form of eqn. (A1.12) is

$$C_L(t) \simeq 2\left(\bar{\Gamma}(\bar{t}) + 0.7\,\mathrm{d}\bar{\Gamma}(\bar{t})/\mathrm{d}\bar{t}\right)$$

$$\bar{\Gamma}(\bar{t}) = \Gamma(t)/c_w U, \quad \bar{t} = tU/c_w. \tag{A1.13}$$

Eqn. (A1.13) is eqn. (III.3.42) in the main text.

Appendix 2

Transformation from aeroelastic oscillatory aerodynamic derivatives to quasi-steady aerodynamic derivatives

The traditional degrees of freedom in aeroelasticity are weathercock pitch angle $\theta_e(t)$ and heave $h(t)$ as shown in Fig. A2.1; $h(t)$ refers to the vertical displacement of the wing apex from a datum.

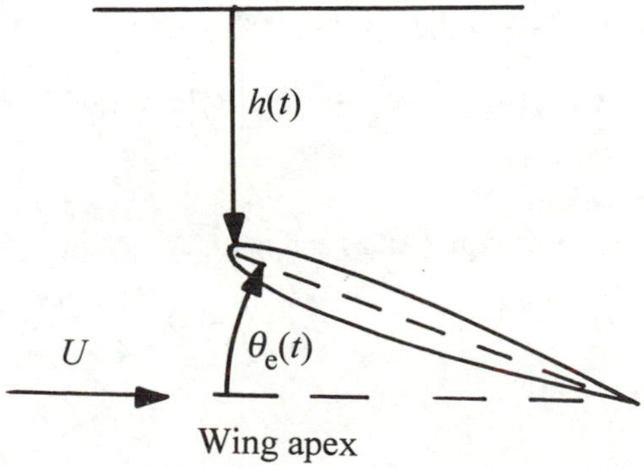

Fig. A2.1. Definition of aerofoil degrees of freedom.

The traditional degrees of freedom in aeroplane dynamics, keeping forward speed constant, are $\theta(t)$ and $\alpha(t)$.

The relationships between these degrees of freedom are

$$\begin{aligned} \theta(t) &= \theta_e(t) \\ \alpha(t) &= \theta_e(t) + \left(\dot{h}(t)/U\right). \end{aligned} \tag{A2.1}$$

Assuming simple harmonic motion

$$\begin{aligned} \theta_e(t) &= \theta_{e0}\exp(i\omega t), \qquad & h(t) &= h_0\exp(i\omega t) \\ \theta(t) &= \theta_0\exp(i\omega t), \qquad & \alpha(t) &= \alpha_0\exp(i\omega t). \end{aligned} \tag{A2.2}$$

so

$$\theta_0 = \theta_{e0}, \qquad \alpha_0 = \theta_{e0} + i\nu\left(h_0/c_w\right) \tag{A2.3}$$

where

$$\nu = \text{frequency parameter} = \omega c_w/U.$$

Outside the UK the reduced frequency parameter k is used instead of ν, where

$$k = \omega\left(c_w/2\right)/U = \nu/2.$$

The oscillatory lift derivatives used in aeroelasticity are expressed in the form

$$C_L(t) = -\Big[\left[\tilde{a}_{\theta e}(\nu) + i\nu\tilde{a}_{\dot{\theta}e}(\nu)\right]\theta_{e0} + \left[\tilde{a}_h(\nu) + i\nu\tilde{a}_{\dot{h}}(\nu)\right]\left(h_0/c_w\right)\Big]\exp(i\omega t). \tag{A2.4}$$

The negative sign is because in aeroelasticity the positive force is taken in the direction of $h(t)$ increasing.

The flight dynamics quasi-steady derivatives are defined as

$$\begin{aligned} C_L(t) &= a_\alpha\alpha(t) + a_{\dot{\alpha}}\dot{\alpha}(t)c_w/U + a_q q(t)c_w/U + a_{\dot{q}}\dot{q}(t)\left(c_w/U\right)^2 \\ &= \Big[\left[a_\alpha + i\nu a_{\dot{\alpha}}\right]\alpha_0 + \left[i\nu a_q - \nu^2 a_{\dot{q}}\right]\theta_0\Big]\exp(i\omega t) \end{aligned} \tag{A2.5}$$

in a low frequency oscillation.

Substituting eqn. (A2.3) into eqn. (A2.5) and comparing eqns. (A2.4) and (A2.5), then

$$\begin{aligned} a_\alpha &= -\tilde{a}_{\dot{h}}(\nu) & \nu &\to 0 \\ a_{\dot{\alpha}} &= \left(\tilde{a}_h(\nu)/\nu^2\right) & \nu &\to 0 \\ a_q &= -\left[\tilde{a}_{\dot{\theta}e}(\nu) + \left(\tilde{a}_h(\nu)/\nu^2\right)\right] & \nu &\to 0 \\ \nu^2 a_{\dot{q}} &= \tilde{a}_{\theta e}(\nu) + \tilde{a}_{\dot{h}}(\nu) & \nu &\to 0. \end{aligned} \tag{A2.6}$$

Similar relationships apply for the pitching moment derivatives but with the opposite signs, since positive pitching moment is nose-up in both systems. These derivatives refer to a pitching moment about a pitch axis through the wing apex.

There are additional hazards.

The normal force coefficient in aeroelasticity is sometimes obtained by non-dimensionalizing with respect to $(\rho U^2 S_w)$, rather than the usual $(\frac{1}{2}\rho U^2 S_w)$, so there may be a factor of 2 between C_L and the aeroelastic normal force coefficient.

As an example for the reader, obtain expressions for the oscillatory derivatives when the pitch axis is located $0.25c_W$ aft of the apex. (Note: $h(t)$ is affected by location of the pitch axis.)

Appendix 3

Effect of aspect ratio on downwash lag

Assume that the time varying circulation around a non-swept wing is concentrated into a line vortex from wing tip to wing tip, and assume that a mean value of the strength is taken, namely $\Gamma(t)$, along the span, as shown in Fig. A3.1. Assume that

$$\Gamma(t) = \Gamma_0 t, \quad \text{where} \quad \Gamma_0 = \text{constant.} \tag{A3.1}$$

In accordance with Helmholtz theorem, bound vorticity of strength

$$(\mathrm{d}\Gamma(t)/\mathrm{d}t)\,\delta t \; \left(= \Gamma_0 \delta t = \Gamma_0\, \delta\xi/U\right),$$

shed continuously from the wing trailing edge, moves downstream of the wing with relative velocity U, forming an associated trailing vortex field.

The downwash, $w_{\mathrm{bd}}(t)$, induced at location distance lc_{w} downstream of the wing due to the wing vortex and the shed bound vorticity field, see Fig. A3.1, is, from the Biot–Savart law,

$$\begin{aligned} w_{\mathrm{bd}}(t) &= \frac{\Gamma(t)}{4\pi\, lc_{\mathrm{w}}} \frac{2s}{\left((lc_{\mathrm{w}})^2 + s^2\right)^{1/2}} + \frac{\Gamma_0}{U} \int_{\xi=2lc_{\mathrm{w}}}^{\infty} \frac{1}{4\pi(\xi - lc_{\mathrm{w}})} \frac{2s\, \mathrm{d}\xi}{\left((\xi - lc_{\mathrm{w}})^2 + s^2\right)^{1/2}} \\ &= \frac{\Gamma(t)}{4\pi\, lc_{\mathrm{w}}} \frac{\mathrm{AR}}{\left(l^2 + (\mathrm{AR}/2)^2\right)^{1/2}} + \frac{\Gamma_0}{2\pi U} \ln\left[\frac{\left(1 + (2l/\mathrm{AR})^2\right)^{1/2} + (2l/\mathrm{AR}) + 1}{\left(1 + (2l/\mathrm{AR})^2\right)^{1/2} + (2l/\mathrm{AR}) - 1}\right]. \end{aligned} \tag{A3.2}$$

The trailing vortices are assumed to be concentrated vortices located at spanwise station $0.7s$, as shown in Fig. A3.1; for consistency with the bound vorticity, the strength of the trailing vortices is $(\Gamma(t) - \Gamma_0\xi/U)$. The downwash $w_{\mathrm{tg}}(t)$ due to the trailing vorticity is

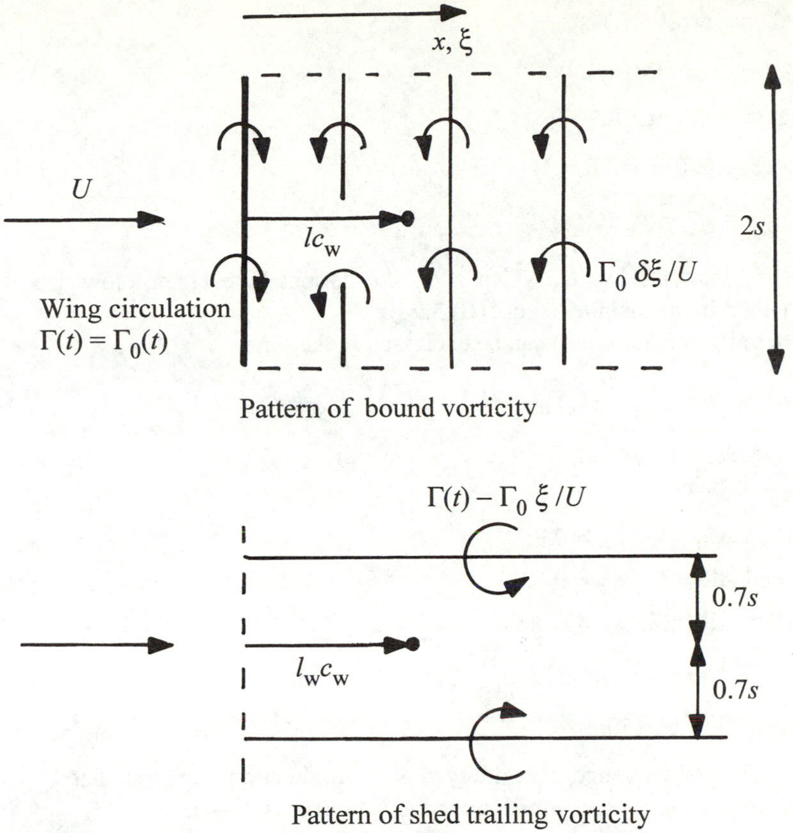

Fig. A3.1. Unsteady wake vorticity.

$$
\begin{aligned}
w_{tg}(t) &= \frac{\Gamma(t)}{4\pi}\frac{2}{(0.7s)}\left[1+\frac{lc_w}{\left((lc_w)^2+(0.7s)^2\right)^{1/2}}\right] \\
&\quad -\frac{\Gamma_0}{U}\int_{\xi=0}^{\infty}\left[\frac{2(0.7s)}{4\pi\left((\xi-lc_w)^2+(0.7s)^2\right)^{3/2}}\right]\xi\,d\xi \\
&= \frac{\Gamma(t)}{4\pi\,lc_w}\frac{2l}{(0.35\text{AR})}\left[1+\frac{l}{\left(l^2+(0.35\text{AR})^2\right)^{1/2}}\right] \\
&\quad -\frac{\Gamma_0}{4\pi U}\frac{2l}{(0.35\text{AR})}\left[1+\left(1+(0.35\text{AR}/l)^2\right)^{1/2}\right].
\end{aligned}
\tag{A3.3}
$$

The total downwash $w(t)$ is

$$w(t) = w_{\rm bd}(t) + w_{\rm tg}(t).$$

Note that in the limit $\mathrm{AR} \to 0$,

$$\begin{aligned} w(t) &\to \left(1/(0.35\pi \mathrm{AR} c_{\rm w})\right)\left(\Gamma(t) - \Gamma_0 l c_{\rm w}/U\right) \\ &\propto \Gamma\left(t - l c_{\rm w}/U\right) \end{aligned} \tag{A3.4}$$

for small time intervals $lc_{\rm w}/U$, which gives the correct time lag for low aspect ratio wings, as quoted in the main text, eqn. (III.3.98).

For a general aspect ratio $w(t)$ can be expressed in the form

$$w(t) = \mathrm{const}\left(\Gamma(t) - k_\varepsilon \Gamma_0 l c_{\rm w}/U\right) = \mathrm{const}\left(\Gamma\left(t - k_\varepsilon l c_{\rm w}/U\right)\right) \tag{A3.5}$$

where k_ε depends on l and AR.

Taking $l = 3$, then

$$\begin{aligned} &\text{when AR} = 3, \quad k_\varepsilon = 0.9; \\ &\text{when AR} = 7, \quad k_\varepsilon = 0.62; \\ &\text{when AR} = 10, \quad k_\varepsilon = 0.39. \end{aligned} \tag{A3.6}$$

Hence a crude approximation for k_ε, when $\mathrm{AR} < 10$, is

$$k_\varepsilon \simeq 1 - \mathrm{AR}^2/150. \tag{A3.7}$$

Although outside of its range of validity this approximation suggests that $k_\varepsilon \to 0$ as $\mathrm{AR} \to 12$, from the more exact equations above $k_\varepsilon \to 0$ as $\mathrm{AR} \to 15$.

In slender wing theory the parameter which defines 'slenderness' is $\mathrm{AR}^2(1 - M_\infty^2)$, hence it is thought that the Mach number effect at subsonic speeds can be incorporated by the modification

$$k_\varepsilon \simeq 1 - \mathrm{AR}^2(1 - M_\infty^2)/150. \tag{A3.8}$$

The combination of eqns. (A3.5) and (A3.8) is eqn. (III.3.100) in the main text.

Appendix 4

Derivation of E_{trim}

The trim equations, eqns. (III.5.6), are

$$
\begin{aligned}
&(C_{\text{L}})_{\text{trim}} + (C_{\text{D}})_{\text{trim}}\alpha_{\text{trim}} \\
&\qquad = C_{\text{L0}}(M_\infty) + \left(C_{\text{L}\alpha}(M_\infty) + (C_{\text{D}})_{\text{trim}}\right)\alpha_{\text{trim}} + C_{\text{L}\eta}(M_\infty)\eta_{\text{trim}} = C_{\text{W}} \\
&(C_m)_{\text{trim}} + l_{\text{Th}}(C_{\text{D}})_{\text{trim}} \\
&\qquad = C_{m0}(M_\infty) + l_{\text{Th}}(C_{\text{D}})_{\text{trim}} + C_{m\alpha}(M_\infty)\alpha_{\text{trim}} + C_{\text{L}\eta}(M_\infty)\eta_{\text{trim}} = 0 \\
&(C_{\text{Th}})_{\text{trim}} = (C_{\text{D}})_{\text{trim}} \simeq \left(C_{\text{D0}} + C_{\text{W}}^2/\pi\,\text{AR}\right)
\end{aligned}
\tag{A4.1}
$$

where

$$
M_\infty = U_{\text{trim}}/a_{\text{at}}, \quad C_{\text{W}} = (W/S_{\text{w}})/\left(\tfrac{1}{2}\rho_{\text{at}}U_{\text{trim}}^2\right).
$$

Consider the nearby trim state

$$
\left(U_{\text{trim}} + \Delta U_{\text{trim}}\right), \quad \left(\alpha_{\text{trim}} + \Delta\alpha_{\text{trim}}\right), \quad \left(\eta_{\text{trim}} + \Delta\eta_{\text{trim}}\right).
$$

Then the perturbation lift and moment trim equations are

$$
\begin{aligned}
&\left[\frac{\partial C_{\text{L0}}(M_\infty)}{\partial M_\infty} + \left(\frac{\partial(C_{\text{L}\alpha}(M_\infty))}{\partial M_\infty} + \frac{\partial(C_{\text{D}})_{\text{trim}}}{\partial M_\infty}\right)\alpha_{\text{trim}}\right. \\
&\qquad\qquad\qquad \left. + \frac{\partial C_{\text{L}\eta}(M_\infty)}{\partial M_\infty}\eta_{\text{trim}}\right]\left[M_\infty\ \Delta U_{\text{trim}}/U_{\text{trim}}\right] \\
&\qquad + \left(C_{\text{L}\alpha}(M_\infty) + C_{\text{D}}(M_\infty)\right)\Delta\alpha_{\text{trim}} + C_{\text{L}\eta}(M_\infty)\ \Delta\eta_{\text{trim}} \\
&\quad = -2C_{\text{W}}\left[1 - \text{d}((C_{\text{D}})_{\text{trim}}/\text{d}C_{\text{W}})\alpha_{\text{trim}}\right]\left(\Delta U_{\text{trim}}/U_{\text{trim}}\right) \\
&\quad \simeq -2C_{\text{W}}\left(\Delta U_{\text{trim}}/U_{\text{trim}}\right)
\end{aligned}
\tag{A4.2a}
$$

$$\left[\frac{\partial C_{m0}(M_\infty)}{\partial M_\infty} + l_{\text{Th}}\frac{\partial (C_{\text{D}})_{\text{trim}}}{\partial M_\infty} + \frac{\partial C_{m\alpha}(M_\infty)}{\partial M_\infty}\alpha_{\text{trim}} + \frac{\partial C_{m\eta}(M_\infty)}{\partial M_\infty}\eta_{\text{trim}}\right]\left[M_\infty\ \Delta U_{\text{trim}}/U_{\text{trim}}\right]$$
$$+ l_{\text{Th}}\left(\text{d}(C_{\text{D}})_{\text{trim}}/\text{d}C_{\text{W}}\right)\left[-2(C_{\text{W}})\left(\Delta U_{\text{trim}}/U_{\text{trim}}\right)\right]$$
$$+ C_{m\alpha}(M_\infty)\Delta\alpha_{\text{trim}} + C_{m\eta}(M_\infty)\Delta\eta_{\text{trim}} = 0 \qquad \text{(A4.2b)}$$

Eqns. (A4.2a and b) are rearranged.

$$\left(C_{\text{L}\alpha}(M_\infty) + (C_{\text{D}})_{\text{trim}}\right)\Delta\alpha_{\text{trim}} + C_{\text{L}\eta}(M_\infty)\Delta\eta_{\text{trim}}$$
$$= -(C_{\text{L}U} + C_{\text{D}U}\alpha_{\text{trim}})\left(\Delta U_{\text{trim}}/U_{\text{trim}}\right)$$
$$C_{m\alpha}(M_\infty)\Delta\alpha_{\text{trim}} + C_{m\eta}(M_\infty)\Delta\eta_{\text{trim}}$$
$$= -\left(C_{mU} + l_{\text{Th}}\left[C_{\text{D}U} - 2\left(C_{\text{W}}\left(\text{d}(C_{\text{D}})_{\text{trim}}/\text{d}C_{\text{W}}\right)\right)\right]\right)\left(\Delta U_{\text{trim}}/U_{\text{trim}}\right) \qquad \text{(A4.3)}$$

where

$$C_{\text{L}U} = 2(C_{\text{L}})_{\text{trim}} + \left(M_\infty\ \partial C_{\text{L}}/\partial M_\infty\right)_{\text{trim}}$$
$$\left[\frac{\partial C_{\text{L}}}{\partial M_\infty}\right]_{\text{trim}} = \left[\frac{\partial C_{\text{L}0}(M_\infty)}{\partial M_\infty} + \frac{\partial C_{\text{L}\alpha}(M_\infty)}{\partial M_\infty}\alpha_{\text{trim}} + \frac{\partial C_{\text{L}\eta}(M_\infty)}{\partial M_\infty}\eta_{\text{trim}}\right]$$
$$C_{mU} = 2(C_m)_{\text{trim}} + \left(M_\infty \partial C_m/\partial M_\infty\right)_{\text{trim}}$$
$$\left[\frac{\partial C_m}{\partial M_\infty}\right]_{\text{trim}} = \left[\frac{\partial C_{m0}(M_\infty)}{\partial M_\infty} + \frac{\partial C_{m\alpha}(M_\infty)}{\partial M_\infty}\alpha_{\text{trim}} + \frac{\partial C_{m\eta}(M_\infty)}{\partial M_\infty}\eta_{\text{trim}}\right]$$
$$C_{\text{D}U} = 2(C_{\text{D}})_{\text{trim}} + \left(M_\infty \partial C_{\text{D}}/\partial M_\infty\right)_{\text{trim}}$$

are the perturbation speed derivatives introduced in sect. III.3.11.

On elimination of $\Delta\alpha_{\text{trim}}$ from eqns. (A4.3)

$$\left[(-C_{m\eta})\left(1 + (C_{\text{D}}/C_{\text{L}\alpha}) - K_\alpha C_{\text{L}\eta}\right)\right]\Delta\eta_{\text{trim}}$$
$$= \Big[K_\alpha(C_{\text{L}U} + C_{\text{D}U}\alpha_{\text{trim}})$$
$$+ \left(1 + (C_{\text{D}}/C_{\text{L}\alpha})\right)\left(C_{mU} + l_{\text{Th}}\left[C_{\text{D}U} - 2\left(C_{\text{W}}\left(\text{d}(C_{\text{D}})_{\text{trim}}/\text{d}C_{\text{W}}\right)\right)\right]\right)\left[\Delta U_{\text{trim}}/U_{\text{trim}}\right]\Big]$$
$$= \Big[K_\alpha(C_{\text{L}U} + C_{\text{D}U}\alpha_{\text{trim}})$$
$$+ \left(1 + (C_{\text{D}}/C_{\text{L}\alpha})\right)\left(C_{mU} + l_{\text{Th}}\left[C_{\text{D}U} - 2\left(C_{\text{W}}\left(\text{d}(C_{\text{D}})_{\text{trim}}/\text{d}C_{\text{W}}\right)\right)\right]\right)\Big]\left[-\Delta C_{\text{W}}/(2C_{\text{W}})\right].$$

$$\text{(A4.4)}$$

Thus the full formula for $E_{trim}(=-\Delta\eta_{trim}/\Delta C_W)$ is

$$2C_W\Big[(-C_{m\eta})\big(1+((C_D)_{trim}/C_{L\alpha})-K_\alpha C_{L\eta}\big)\Big]E_{trim}$$
$$=\Big[K_\alpha(C_{LU}+C_{DU}\alpha_{trim})+\big(1+((C_D)_{trim}/C_{L\alpha})\big)C_{mU}$$
$$+l_{Th}\big(1+((C_D)_{trim}/C_{L\alpha})\big)\Big[C_{DU}-2\big(C_W(d(C_D)_{trim}/dC_W)\big)\Big]\Big]. \quad (A4.5)$$

Neglecting small terms

$$(C_D)_{trim}/C_{L\alpha} \ll 1, \quad C_{DU}\alpha_{trim} \ll C_{LU} \quad \text{and} \quad \big(K_\alpha C_{L\eta}/(-C_{m\eta})\big) \ll 1$$

then

$$2C_W(-C_{m\eta})E_{trim} \simeq K_\alpha C_{LU}+C_{mU}+l_{Th}\Big[C_{DU}-2\big(C_W(d(C_D)_{trim}/dC_W)\big)\Big]$$
$$\simeq K_\alpha\Big[2C_W+M_\infty(\partial C_L/\partial M_\infty)_{trim}\Big]+M_\infty(\partial C_m/\partial M_\infty)_{trim}$$
$$-l_{Th}\Big[2C_W(d(C_D)_{trim}/dC_W)-M_\infty(\partial C_D/\partial M_\infty)_{trim}\Big]. \quad (A4.6)$$

Next, approximate expressions are developed for

$$\left[\frac{\partial C_L}{\partial M_\infty}\right]_{trim}=\left[\frac{\partial C_{L0}(M_\infty)}{\partial M_\infty}+\frac{\partial C_{L\alpha}(M_\infty)}{\partial M_\infty}\alpha_{trim}+\frac{\partial C_{L\eta}(M_\infty)}{\partial M_\infty}\eta_{trim}\right]$$

and

$$\left[\frac{\partial C_m}{\partial M_\infty}\right]_{trim}=\left[\frac{\partial C_{m0}(M_\infty)}{\partial M_\infty}+\frac{\partial C_{m\alpha}(M_\infty)}{\partial M_\infty}\alpha_{trim}+\frac{\partial C_{m\eta}(M_\infty)}{\partial M_\infty}\eta_{trim}\right].$$

It is reasonable to assume that the lift coefficients $(a_\alpha)_w$, $(a_\alpha)_t$, a_η, and the downwash gradient $\partial\varepsilon/\partial\alpha$ all vary with Mach number in the same manner.

Assuming that the downwash effects on C_L are small then,

$$(\partial C_L/\partial M_\infty)_{trim} \simeq (C_L)_{trim}\big(\partial(a_\alpha)_w/\partial M_\infty\big)/(a_\alpha)_w \quad (A4.7)$$

Including the effects of the downwash in the $C_{m\alpha}$ term, then

$$(\partial C_m/\partial M_\infty)_{trim} \simeq \big[(C_m)_{trim}+\alpha_{trim}\, l_t(a_\alpha)_t(S_t/S_w)(\partial\varepsilon/\partial\alpha)\big]$$
$$\times\big((\partial(a_\alpha)_w/\partial M_\infty)/(a_\alpha)_w\big). \quad (A4.8)$$

where $\alpha_{trim}=(C_W/C_{L\alpha})-i_w-\alpha_{0w}$.

At subsonic speeds, from eqn. (III.3.13)

$$(a_\alpha)_w=2\pi\frac{AR_w}{(AR^2+4)^{1/2}+2}\,\frac{(AR_w\cos\Lambda_w)+1}{AR(1-M_\infty^2\cos^2\Lambda_w)^{1/2}+1}$$

hence

$$\left(\partial(a_\alpha)_w/\partial M_\infty\right)/(a_\alpha)_w \simeq \frac{M_\infty \cos^2\Lambda}{(1-M_\infty^2\cos^2\Lambda)^{1/2}\left[(1-M_\infty^2\cos^2\Lambda)^{1/2}+(1/\text{AR})\right]^2}. \tag{A4.9}$$

At supersonic speeds, from eqn. (III.3.14)

$$(a_\alpha)_w \simeq \frac{\pi\,\text{AR}/2}{\left[1+(M_\infty^2-1)^{1/2}/\pi\right][1+0.2\lambda]}$$

hence

$$\left(\partial(a_\alpha)_w/\partial M_\infty\right)/(a_\alpha)_w \simeq \frac{-M_\infty}{\pi(M_\infty^2-1)^{1/2}\left[1+(M_\infty^2-1)^{1/2}/\pi\right]^2} \tag{A4.10}$$

Finally

$$\left(\text{d}C_D/\text{d}C_L\right)_{\text{trim}} = 2(C_L)_{\text{trim}}/\pi\text{AR} \tag{A.4.11}$$

$$\left(\partial C_D/\partial M_\infty\right)_{\text{trim}} = \left(\partial C_{D0}/\partial M_\infty\right) + \left(2(C_L)_{\text{trim}}/\pi\,\text{AR}\right)\left(\partial C_L/\partial M_\infty\right)_{\text{trim}}. \tag{A4.12}$$

Appendix 5

Quartic solutions

A5.1 SOLUTION OF LONGITUDINAL QUARTIC

The following algorithm is taken from Babister (ref. P.16).

When the longitudinal quartic characteristic equation

$$i_{yy}\lambda^4 + A_3\lambda^3 + A_2\lambda^2 + A_1\lambda + A_0 = 0$$

satisfies the Routh criteria, eqns. (II.91), the quartic equation can usually be factorized into the form

$$(i_{yy}\lambda^2 + B_j\lambda + C_j)(\lambda^2 + D_j\lambda + E_j) = 0$$

by the iterative process $(j \geqslant 2)$:

$$B_1 = A_3, \quad C_1 = A_2, \quad D_1 = [A_1A_2 - A_3A_0]/A_2^2, \quad E_1 = A_0/A_2;$$
$$B_j = A_3 - i_{yy}D_{j-1},$$
$$C_j = A_2 - B_{j-1}D_{j-1} - i_{yy}E_{j-1},$$
$$D_j = [C_jA_1 - B_jA_0]/C_j^2,$$
$$E_j = A_0/C_j.$$

A5.2 SOLUTION OF THE LATERAL QUARTIC

When the lateral quartic characteristic equation

$$\lambda^4 + A_3\lambda^3 + A_2\lambda^2 + A_1\lambda + A_0 = 0$$

satisfies the Routh criteria, eqns. (II.91), the quartic equation can usually be factorized into the form

$$(\lambda + B_j)(\lambda + C_j)(\lambda^2 + D_j\lambda + E_j) = 0$$

by the iterative process $(j \geqslant 2)$:

$$B_1 = A_3, \quad C_1 = A_0/A_1,$$
$$B'_j = A_3 - A_2\big/B_{j-1} + A_1\big/B_{j-1}^2 + A_0\big/B_{j-1}^3$$
$$B_j = \tfrac{1}{2}(B_{j-1} + B'_j)$$
$$C_j = (A_0/A_1) - (A_2/A_1)C_{j-1} + (A_3/A_1)C_{j-1}^2 - C_{j-1}^3.$$

When B_j and C_j have converged

$$D_j = A_3 - B_j - C_j$$
$$E_j = A_0/(B_jC_j).$$

Appendix 6

Derivation of control response equations

From sect. III.9 the equations of the short period response are

$$\left[\mathrm{D}+\left(g/(U_{\text{trim}}C_{\mathrm{W}})\right)C_{\mathrm{L}\alpha}\right]\Delta\alpha(t)-q(t)$$
$$=-\left(g/(U_{\text{trim}}C_{\mathrm{W}})\right)\left[C_{\mathrm{L}\dot{\eta}}\left(c_{\mathrm{w}}/2U_{\text{trim}}\right)\mathrm{D}+C_{\mathrm{L}\eta}\right]\Delta\eta(t), \tag{A6.1}$$

$$\left[(-C_{m\dot{\alpha}})(c_{\mathrm{w}}/2U_{\text{trim}})\mathrm{D}+(-C_{m\alpha})\right]\Delta\alpha(t)$$
$$+\left[\left(c_{\mathrm{w}}C_{\mathrm{W}}i_{yy}/g\right)\mathrm{D}+(-C_{mq})\left(c_{\mathrm{w}}/2U_{\text{trim}}\right)\right]q(t)$$
$$=\left[\left(C_{m\dot{\eta}}\left(c_{\mathrm{w}}/2U_{\text{trim}}\right)\right)\mathrm{D}+C_{m\eta}\right]\Delta\eta(t) \tag{A6.2}$$

where D is the differential operator $\mathrm{d}/\mathrm{d}t$, and l_{Th} is taken to be zero.

On elimination of $\Delta\alpha(t)$ between eqns. (A6.1) and (A6.2), the pitch rate response is given by, neglecting all terms involving $(1/U_{\text{trim}})^2$ and $(-C_{m\alpha})C_{\mathrm{L}\eta}$ compared with $C_{\mathrm{L}\alpha}(-C_{m\eta})$,

$$\left[\mathrm{D}^2+2\zeta_{\text{sp}}(\omega_0)_{\text{sp}}\,\mathrm{D}+(\omega_0)_{\text{sp}}^2\right]q(t)$$
$$\simeq\left(g/(i_{yy}c_{\mathrm{w}}C_{\mathrm{W}})\right)\left[\left(c_{\mathrm{w}}/2U_{\text{trim}}\right)C_{m\dot{\eta}}\mathrm{D}^2+C_{m\eta}\,\mathrm{D}\right.$$
$$\left.+\left(g/(U_{\text{trim}}C_{\mathrm{W}})\right)C_{\mathrm{L}\alpha}C_{m\eta}\right]\Delta\eta(t) \tag{A6.3}$$

$$\simeq\left((\omega_0)_{\text{sp}}^2/E_{\mathrm{m}}\right)\left[-\left(\left((C_{m\dot{\eta}}/2)/(-C_{m\eta})\right)\left(c_{\mathrm{w}}/(U_{\text{trim}}C_{\mathrm{L}\alpha})\right)\right)\mathrm{D}^2\right.$$
$$\left.+\left(1/C_{\mathrm{L}\alpha}\right)\,\mathrm{D}+g/(U_{\text{trim}}C_{\mathrm{W}})\right](-\Delta\eta(t)) \tag{A6.4}$$

where

$$(\omega_0)^2_{sp} = \left[g/(c_w C_W i_{yy})\right] C_{L\alpha} H_m$$
$$= \left[g/(c_w C_W i_{yy})\right] C_{L\alpha}(-C_{m\eta}) E_m$$
$$2\zeta_{sp}(\omega_0)_{sp} = (g/U_{trim} C_W)\left[C_{L\alpha} + \left[\left((-C_{m\dot{\alpha}}/2) + (-C_{mq}/2)\right)/i_{yy}\right]\right]$$

On eliminating $q(t)$ between eqns. (A6.1) and (A6.2), the angle of incidence response is given by

$$\left[D^2 + 2\zeta_{sp}(\omega_0)_{sp} D + (\omega_0)^2_{sp}\right]\Delta\alpha(t)$$
$$\simeq \left(g/(i_{yy} c_w C_W)\right)\left[\left[\left((c_w/2)/U_{trim}\right) C_{m\dot{\eta}} - \left(g/(U_{trim} C_W)\right) \times \left(i_{yy} c_w C_W/g\right) C_{L\eta}\right] D + C_{m\eta}\right](\Delta\eta(t)) \qquad \text{(A6.5)}$$

again neglecting all terms involving $(1/U_{trim})^2$.

The normal acceleration response $g\,\Delta n(t)(= U_{trim}(q(t) - D\,\Delta\alpha(t))$, from eqns. (A6.4) and (A6.5), is given by

$$\left[D^2 + 2\zeta_{sp}(\omega_0)_{sp} D + (\omega_0)^2_{sp}\right]\Delta n(t)$$
$$\simeq \left[-\left(C_{L\eta}/C_W\right) D^2 + (\omega_0)^2_{sp}/(E_m C_W)\right](-\Delta\eta(t)). \qquad \text{(A6.6)}$$

The left hand sides of eqns. (A6.4) –(A6.6) are the same because all of these responses have the same short period stability characteristics.

Appendix 7

Derivation of gust response equations

The short period response equations for the gust input $\Delta\alpha_g(t)$ are, from eqns. (III.8.14), with the gust input terms from eqns. (III.13.7),

$$\left[D+\left(g/(U_{trim}C_W)\right)C_{L\alpha}\right]\Delta\alpha(t)-q(t)$$
$$=-\left(g/(U_{trim}C_W)\right)\left[(C_{L\dot{\alpha}}+C_{L\dot{\alpha}g})\left((c_w/2)/U_{trim}\right)D+C_{L\alpha}\right]\Delta\alpha_g(t)$$

$$\left[(-C_{m\dot{\alpha}})\left((c_w/2)/U_{trim}\right)D+(-C_{m\alpha})\right]\Delta\alpha(t) \tag{A7.1}$$
$$+\left[\left((c_w C_W i_{yy})/g\right)D+(-C_{mq})\left((c_w/2)/U_{trim}\right)\right]q(t)$$
$$=\left[(C_{m\dot{\alpha}}+C_{m\dot{\alpha}g})\left((c_w/2)/U_{trim}\right)D+C_{m\alpha}\right]\Delta\alpha_g(t).$$

The set of responses, $q(t)$, $\Delta\theta(t)$, $\Delta\alpha(t)$, $\Delta n(t)$ $\left(=(U_{trim}/g)(q(t)-D\Delta\alpha(t))\right)$, and $\Delta\gamma(t)$ $\left(=(g/U_{trim})\int\Delta n(t)\,dt\right)$, neglecting small terms, are listed.

(i)
$$\left[D^2+2\zeta_{sp}(\omega_0)_{sp}D+(\omega_0^2)_{sp}\right]q(t)$$
$$\simeq\left(g/(c_w C_W i_{yy})\right)\left[(C_{m\dot{\alpha}}+C_{m\dot{\alpha}g})(c_w/2U_{trim})\right]D^2$$
$$+\left(C_{m\alpha}+\left(g/(U_{trim}C_W)\right)(c_w/2U_{trim})C_{m\dot{\alpha}g}C_{L\alpha}\right)D\Big]\Delta\alpha_g(t) \tag{A7.2}$$
$$=\left[2\zeta_{\theta g}(\omega_0)_{sp}D^2-\frac{K_\alpha-C_{m\dot{\alpha}g}/\overline{m}}{K_\alpha+(-C_{mq})/\overline{m}}(\omega_0^2)_{sp}\,D\right]\Delta\alpha_g(t),$$

where

$$2\zeta_{sp}(\omega_0)_{sp} = \big(g/(U_{trim}C_W)\big)\Big[C_{L\alpha} + \Big(\big((-C_{m\dot{\alpha}}) + (-C_{mq})\big)\big/2i_{yy}\Big)\Big],$$

$$(\omega_0^2)_{sp} = gC_{L\alpha}\Big(K_\alpha + \big(-C_{mq}/\overline{m}\big)\Big)\Big/(c_w C_W i_{yy}),$$

$$\frac{\zeta_{\theta g}}{\zeta} = \frac{-(-C_{m\dot{\alpha}}) + C_{m\dot{\alpha}g}}{2i_{yy}C_{L\alpha} + (-C_{m\dot{\alpha}}) + (-C_{mq})} = O[0.2],$$

$$C_{m\dot{\alpha}g} \simeq (-C_{mq}).$$

(ii)
$$\Big[D^2 + 2\zeta_{sp}(\omega_0)_{sp}D + \omega_0^2\Big]\Delta\theta(t)$$

$$\simeq \left[2\zeta_{\theta g}(\omega_0)_{sp}D - \frac{K_\alpha - C_{m\dot{\alpha}g}/\overline{m}}{K_\alpha + (-C_{mq})/\overline{m}}(\omega_0^2)_{sp}\right]\Delta\alpha_g(t), \tag{A7.3}$$

(iii)
$$\Big[D^2 + 2\zeta_{sp}(\omega_0)_{sp}D + (\omega_0^2)_{sp}\Big]\Delta\alpha(t)$$

$$\simeq \big(g/(c_w C_W i_{yy})\big)\Big[\big(-(2i_{yy}C_{L\alpha}) + C_{m\alpha} + C_{m\dot{\alpha}g}\big)\big(c_w/2U_{trim}\big)D$$

$$+C_{m\alpha} - \big(g/(U_{trim}C_W)\big)\big(c_w/2U_{trim}\big)(-C_{mq})C_{L\alpha}\Big]\Delta\alpha_g(t) \tag{A7.4}$$

(iv)
$$\Big[D^2 + 2\zeta_{sp}(\omega_0)_{sp}D + (\omega_0^2)_{sp}\Big]\Delta n(t)$$

$$= \big(U_{trim}/(c_w C_W i_{yy})\big)\Big[\big(c_w/2U_{trim}\big)\, 2i_{yy}C_{L\alpha}D^2$$

$$+\big(g/(U_{trim}C_W)\big)\big(c_w/2U_{trim}\big)C_{L\alpha}\big((-C_{mq}) + C_{m\dot{\alpha}g}\big)D\Big]\Delta\alpha_g(t)$$

$$= \big(C_{L\alpha}/C_W\big)\Big[D^2 + 2\zeta_{ng}\omega_0 D\Big]\Delta\alpha_g(t) \tag{A7.5}$$

where

$$\frac{\zeta_{ng}}{\zeta_{sp}} = \frac{(-C_{mq}) + C_{m\dot{\alpha}g}}{2C_{L\alpha}i_{yy} + (-C_{m\dot{\alpha}}) + (-C_{mq})} = O[1.0]$$

(v)
$$\Big[D^2 + 2\zeta_{sp}(\omega_0)_{sp}D + (\omega_0^2)_{sp}\Big]\Delta\gamma(t)$$

$$= \big(g/U_{trim}\big)\big(C_{L\alpha}/C_W\big)\Big[D + 2\zeta_{ng}\omega_0\Big]\Delta\alpha_g(t). \tag{A7.6}$$

Appendix 8

Side load on fin due to differential tailplane

The lift on the starboard tailplane deflected through angle ξ is from eqn. (IV.2.96)

$$\begin{aligned} L_t &= \tfrac{1}{2}\rho_{at}U_{trim}^2(S_t/2)(a_\alpha)_t\ 0.65\xi \\ &= \rho_{at}U_{trim}\Gamma_t s_t \end{aligned} \qquad \text{(A8.1)}$$

where Γ_t is the mean spanwise circulation around the starboard tailplane. Thus

$$\Gamma_t/U_{trim} = \tfrac{1}{2}c_t(a_\alpha)_t\ 0.65\xi. \qquad \text{(A8.2)}$$

The sidewash velocity at the fin semi-span, by reference to Fig. A8.1, is, by application of the Biot–Savart law,

$$v \simeq \left[2\Gamma_t/\left(4\pi(s_f/2)\right)\right]0.5.$$

The term in the square brackets is the sidewash induced by the semi-infinite central trailing vortex; the factor 0.5 accounts for the opposite sidewash induced by the tip vortices and interference effects of the aft fuselage.

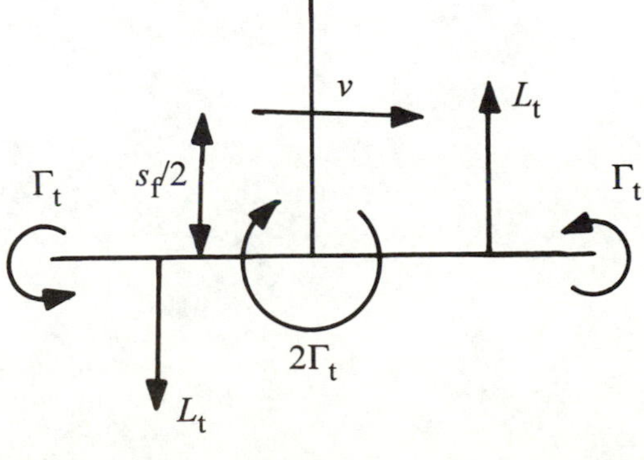

Fig. A8.1. Sidewash on fin due to differential tailplane.

The fin side force is therefore

$$
\begin{aligned}
(Y_\xi)_\mathrm{f} &= \tfrac{1}{2}\rho_\mathrm{at}U_\mathrm{trim}^2 S_\mathrm{f}(a_\beta)_\mathrm{f}\left(v/U_\mathrm{trim}\right) \\
&\simeq \tfrac{1}{2}\rho_\mathrm{at}U_\mathrm{trim}^2 S_\mathrm{w}\left[\left(S_\mathrm{f}/S_\mathrm{w}\right)(a_\beta)_\mathrm{f}\left(0.5/(\pi\, s_\mathrm{f})\right)\right]\left[\tfrac{1}{2}c_\mathrm{t}(a_\alpha)_\mathrm{t}\,0.65\xi\right] \qquad \text{(A8.3)} \\
&\simeq \tfrac{1}{2}\rho_\mathrm{at}U_\mathrm{trim}^2 S_\mathrm{w}\left[0.05(a_\beta)_\mathrm{f}(a_\alpha)_\mathrm{t}\left(S_\mathrm{f}/S_\mathrm{w}\right)\left(c_\mathrm{t}/s_\mathrm{f}\right)\right]\xi.
\end{aligned}
$$

Appendix 9

Axis transformation for lateral derivatives

Relative to the fuselage body axis system *oxyz* (see Fig. A9.1), the angular rates of rotation about the *ox* and *oz* axes are *p* and *r*. The rolling and yawing moments about the *ox* and *oz* axes, and the side force, are

$$\begin{aligned}
\mathcal{L} &= \tfrac{1}{2}\rho_{\mathrm{at}}U^2 S_{\mathrm{w}}\ 2s_{\mathrm{w}}\ \left[C_{l\beta}\beta + C_{lp}\left(ps_{\mathrm{w}}/U\right) + C_{lr}\left(rs_{\mathrm{w}}/U\right)\right] \\
\mathcal{N} &= \tfrac{1}{2}\rho_{\mathrm{at}}U^2 S_{\mathrm{w}}\ 2s_{\mathrm{w}}\ \left[C_{n\beta}\beta + C_{np}\left(ps_{\mathrm{w}}/U\right) + C_{nr}\left(rs_{\mathrm{w}}/U\right)\right] \\
Y &= \tfrac{1}{2}\rho_{\mathrm{at}}U^2 S_{\mathrm{w}}\ \left[C_{Y\beta}\beta + C_{Yp}\left(ps_{\mathrm{w}}/U\right) + C_{Yr}\left(rs_{\mathrm{w}}/U\right)\right]
\end{aligned} \tag{A9.1}$$

omitting the time variation for convenience.

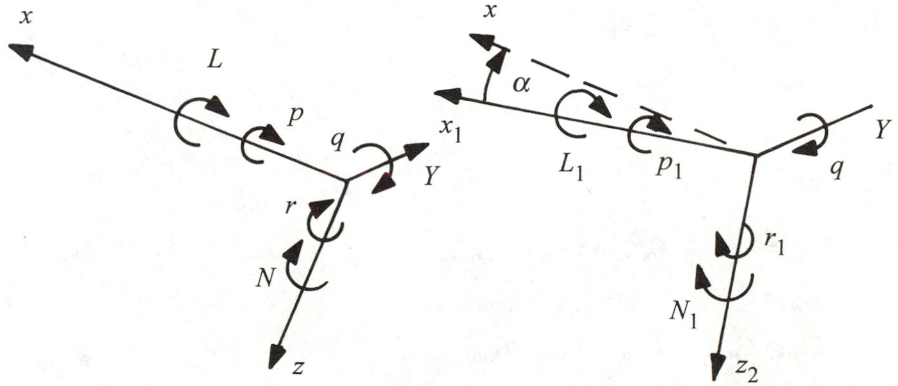

Fig. A9.1. Definition of axes.

Relative to the trim body axis system ox_1yz_1, see Fig. A9.1, the angular rates of rotation about the ox_1 and oz_1 axes are p_1 and r_1. The rolling and yawing moments about the ox_1 and oz_1 axes, and the side force, are

$$
\begin{aligned}
\mathscr{L}_1 &= \tfrac{1}{2}\rho_{\text{at}}U^2S_{\text{w}}\ 2s_{\text{w}}\left[C_{l_1\beta}\beta + C_{l_1p_1}(p_1s_{\text{w}}/U) + C_{l_1r_1}(r_1s_{\text{w}}/U)\right]\\
\mathscr{N}_1 &= \tfrac{1}{2}\rho_{\text{at}}U^2S_{\text{w}}\ 2s_{\text{w}}\left[C_{n_1\beta}\beta + C_{n_1p_1}(p_1s_{\text{w}}/U) + C_{n_1r_1}(r_1s_{\text{w}}/U)\right]\\
Y &= \tfrac{1}{2}\rho_{\text{at}}U^2S_{\text{w}}\ \left[C_{Y\beta}\beta + C_{Yp_1}(p_1s_{\text{w}}/U) + C_{Yr_1}(r_1s_{\text{w}}/U)\right].
\end{aligned}
\tag{A9.2}
$$

For small α_{trim},

$$
\begin{aligned}
\mathscr{L}_1 &\simeq \mathscr{L} + \mathscr{N}\alpha_{\text{trim}}, & \mathscr{N}_1 &\simeq \mathscr{N} - \mathscr{L}\alpha_{\text{trim}}\\
p_1 &\simeq p + r\alpha_{\text{trim}}, & r_1 &\simeq r - p\alpha_{\text{trim}}.
\end{aligned}
\tag{A9.3}
$$

Combining eqns. (A9.1)–(A9.3):

$$
\begin{aligned}
C_{l_1p_1} &= C_{lp} + (C_{np} + C_{lr})\alpha_{\text{trim}}\\
C_{l_1r_1} &= C_{lr} + (C_{nr} - C_{lp})\alpha_{\text{trim}}\\
C_{n_1p_1} &= C_{np} - (C_{lp} - C_{nr})\alpha_{\text{trim}}\\
C_{n_1r_1} &= C_{nr} - (C_{lr} + C_{np})\alpha_{\text{trim}}\\
C_{Yp_1} &= C_{Yp} + C_{Yr}\alpha_{\text{trim}}\\
C_{Yr_1} &= C_{Yr} - C_{Yp}\alpha_{\text{trim}}\\
C_{l_1\beta} &= C_{l\beta} + C_{n\beta}\alpha_{\text{trim}}\\
C_{n_1\beta} &= C_{n\beta} - C_{l\beta}\alpha_{\text{trim}}
\end{aligned}
\tag{A9.4}
$$

or the inverse,

$$
\begin{aligned}
C_{lp} &= C_{l_1p_1} - (C_{n_1p_1} + C_{l_1r_1})\alpha_{\text{trim}}\\
C_{lr} &= C_{l_1r_1} - (C_{n_1r_1} - C_{l_1p_1})\alpha_{\text{trim}}\\
C_{np} &= C_{n_1p_1} + (C_{l_1p_1} - C_{n_1r_1})\alpha_{\text{trim}}\\
C_{nr} &= C_{n_1r_1} + (C_{l_1r_1} + C_{n_1p_1})\alpha_{\text{trim}}\\
C_{Yp} &= C_{Yp_1} - C_{Yr_1}\alpha_{\text{trim}}\\
C_{Yr} &= C_{Yr_1} + C_{Yp_1}\alpha_{\text{trim}}\\
C_{l\beta} &= C_{l_1\beta} - C_{n_1\beta}\alpha_{\text{trim}}\\
C_{n\beta} &= C_{n_1\beta} + C_{l_1\beta}\alpha_{\text{trim}}.
\end{aligned}
\tag{A9.5}
$$

As an example, take α_{trim} equal to 0.2 ($\simeq$ 11.5°), and $(C_L)_{\text{trim}}$ equal to 1.0, with

$$\begin{aligned}
C_{lp} &= -0.40 \quad \text{then} \quad & C_{l_1p_1} &= -0.41 \\
C_{lr} &= 0.20 & C_{l_1r_1} &= 0.22 \\
C_{np} &= -0.15 & C_{n_1p_1} &= -0.13 \\
C_{nr} &= -0.30 & C_{n_1r_1} &= -0.31 \\
C_{Yp} &= 0.60 & C_{Yp_1} &= 0.68 \\
C_{Yr} &= 0.40 & C_{Yr_1} &= 0.28 \\
C_{l\beta} &= -0.27 & C_{l_1\beta} &= -0.23 \\
C_{n\beta} &= 0.20 & C_{n_1\beta} &= 0.25.
\end{aligned} \tag{A9.6}$$

Note:

(i) the values of the direct rate derivatives, C_{lp} and C_{nr}, in the two axis systems are virtually the same;
(ii) there is approximately a 10% difference in the values of the cross rate derivatives, C_{lr} and C_{np}, in the two axis systems;
(iii) there is approximately a 20% difference in the values of the side force derivatives, C_{Yr} and C_{Yp}, in the two axis systems.

Finally, for the control derivatives

$$\begin{aligned}
C_{l_1\xi} &= C_{l\xi} + C_{n\xi}\alpha_{\text{trim}}, & C_{l\xi} &= C_{l_1\xi} - C_{n_1\xi}\alpha_{\text{trim}} \\
C_{n_1\xi} &= C_{n\xi} - C_{l\xi}\alpha_{\text{trim}}, & C_{n\xi} &= C_{n_1\xi} + C_{l_1\xi}\alpha_{\text{trim}} \\
C_{l_1\zeta} &= C_{l\zeta} + C_{n\zeta}\alpha_{\text{trim}}, & C_{l\zeta} &= C_{l_1\zeta} - C_{n_1\zeta}\alpha_{\text{trim}} \\
C_{n_1\zeta} &= C_{n\zeta} - C_{l\zeta}\alpha_{\text{trim}}, & C_{n\zeta} &= C_{n_1\zeta} + C_{l_1\zeta}\alpha_{\text{trim}}.
\end{aligned} \tag{A9.7}$$

The values of the side force derivatives due to control deflections are not affected by the axis system.

Taking

$$\alpha_{\text{trim}} = 0.2, \qquad C_L = 1.0,$$

with

$$C_{l\xi} = -0.2, \qquad C_{n\xi} = -0.02, \qquad C_{l\zeta} = 0.03, \qquad C_{n\zeta} = -0.15$$

then

$$C_{l_1\xi} = -0.2, \qquad C_{n_1\xi} = +0.02, \qquad C_{l_1\zeta} = 0.0, \qquad C_{n_1\zeta} = -0.15. \tag{A9.8}$$

The values of the direct control derivatives, $C_{l\xi}$ and $C_{n\zeta}$, are not affected by the change in axis system. But the cross derivatives, $C_{n\xi}$ and $C_{l\zeta}$, although small, are significantly affected. In particular the adverse yaw due to aileron with respect to stability body axes (i.e. $C_{n_1\xi} > 0$), becomes a proverse yaw due to aileron with respect to fuselage body axes (i.e. $C_{n\xi} < 0$).

Appendix 10

Derivation of approximation for Dutch roll stability roots

This derivation is an extension of the ideas of Thomas in ref. IV.3.

The lateral small perturbation characteristic equation, omitting the zero root, is a quartic of the form

$$\lambda^4 + \bar{A}_3\lambda^3 + \bar{A}_2\lambda^2 + \bar{A}_1\lambda + \bar{A}_0 = 0 \tag{A10.1}$$

where

$$\bar{A}_3 = A_3/A_4, \quad \bar{A}_2 = A_2/A_4, \quad \bar{A}_1 = A_1/A_4, \quad \bar{A}_0 = A_0/A_4$$

and where A_0, A_1, A_2, A_3 and A_4 are defined in sect. IV.7, eqn. (IV.7.11).

Eqn. (A10.1) can be re-expressed in the form

$$(\lambda^2 + g\lambda + h)(\lambda^2 + G\lambda + H) = 0. \tag{A10.2}$$

The bracket $(\lambda^2 + g\lambda + h)$ denotes the product of the stability roots of the roll rate and spiral modes, while $(\lambda^2 + G\lambda + H)$ gives the roots of the Dutch roll.

Equating coefficients from eqns. (A10.1) and (A10.2)

$$\begin{aligned} \bar{A}_3 &= g + G \\ \bar{A}_2 &= h + gG + H \\ \bar{A}_1 &= gH + Gh \\ \bar{A}_0 &= hH. \end{aligned} \tag{A10.3}$$

Now

$$\begin{aligned} \bar{A}_1 - \bar{A}_2 G + gG^2 &= H(g - G) \\ -\bar{A}_1 + \bar{A}_2 g - g^2 G &= h(g - G). \end{aligned} \tag{A10.4}$$

Multiplying eqns. (A10.4):

$$\bar{A}_0(g-G)^2=(\bar{A}_1-\bar{A}_2G+gG^2)(-\bar{A}_1+\bar{A}_2g-g^2G) \tag{A10.5}$$

substituting for hH $(=\bar{A}_0)$.

Expanding out eqn. (A10.5) and substituting eqns (A10.3)

$$\begin{aligned}&(gG)^3-2\bar{A}_2(gG)^2+(-4\bar{A}_0+\bar{A}_2^2+\bar{A}_1\bar{A}_3)(gG)\\&\quad-(\bar{A}_1\bar{A}_2\bar{A}_3-\bar{A}_1^2-\bar{A}_0\bar{A}_3^2)=0.\end{aligned} \tag{A10.6}$$

Taking the orders of magnitudes, from sect. IV.7, eqn. (IV.7.13),

$$\bar{A}_3=\mathrm{O}[10],\quad \bar{A}_2=\mathrm{O}[100],\quad \bar{A}_1=\mathrm{O}[1000],\quad \bar{A}_0=\mathrm{O}[50] \tag{A10.7}$$

the approximate value of gG is

$$\begin{aligned}gG&\simeq\left(\bar{A}_1\bar{A}_2\bar{A}_3-\bar{A}_1^2\right)/\left(\bar{A}_2^2+\bar{A}_1\bar{A}_3\right)\\&=\left(\bar{A}_1/\bar{A}_2\right)\left(\bar{A}_3-\left(\bar{A}_1/\bar{A}_2\right)\right)/\left(1+\left(\bar{A}_1\bar{A}_3/\bar{A}_2^2\right)\right).\end{aligned} \tag{A10.8}$$

Because G is small compared with g, as deduced from eqn. (IV.7.14), then from eqns. (A10.3),

$$\begin{aligned}G&\simeq gG/\bar{A}_3\\&\simeq\left[\left(\bar{A}_1/(\bar{A}_2\bar{A}_3)\right)/\left(1+\left(\bar{A}_1\bar{A}_3/\bar{A}_2^2\right)\right)\right]\left[\bar{A}_3-\left(\bar{A}_1/\bar{A}_2\right)\right]\\&\simeq 0.5\left[\bar{A}_3-\left(\bar{A}_1/\bar{A}_2\right)\right].\end{aligned} \tag{A10.9}$$

In the example in sect. IV.7, eqn. (IV.7.14),

$$\begin{aligned}&\text{exact } G=1.68;\\ \text{from eqn. (A10.9)}\quad &\text{approximate } G=1.58,\end{aligned} \tag{A10.10}$$

a reasonable agreement.

For the stiffness of the Dutch roll, because

$$H\gg h$$

again deduced from eqn. (IV.7.14), then, from eqn. (A10.9)

$$\begin{aligned}H&\simeq\bar{A}_2-gG\\&\simeq\bar{A}_2-0.5\bar{A}_3\left[\bar{A}_3-\left(\bar{A}_1/\bar{A}_2\right)\right].\end{aligned} \tag{A10.11}$$

In the example in sect. IV.7, eqn. (IV.7.14),

$$\begin{aligned}&\text{exact } H=83.84,\\ \text{from eqn. (A10.11)}\quad &\text{approximate } H=82.99,\end{aligned} \tag{A10.12}$$

a close agreement.

Further approximations can be introduced for G and H by using the approximate forms of $\overline{A}_3$, $\overline{A}_2$ and $\overline{A}_1$, in terms of the lateral derivatives given in eqn. (IV.7.10),

$$\begin{aligned} G \simeq\ & 0.5\Big[(-C_{Y\beta}) + \big((-C_{nr})/(i_{zz}/2)\big) + \big((-C_{lp})/(i_{xx}/2)\big) \\ & - \frac{(2\overline{m}/\mathrm{AR_W})\big[(-C_{l\beta})\big(C_W(i_{zz}/2) + (-C_{np})\big) + C_{n\beta}(-C_{lp})\big]}{\big[(2\overline{m}/\mathrm{AR_W})(i_{xx}/2)C_{n\beta} + (-C_{lp})(-C_{nr})\big]} \\ \simeq\ & 0.5\Big[(-C_{Y\beta}) + \big((-C_{nr})/(i_{zz}/2)\big) \\ & + \big((-C_{lp})/(i_{xx}/2)\big)^2\big((-C_{nr})/C_{n\beta}\big)\big(\mathrm{AR_W}/2\overline{m}\big) \\ & - \big(C_W(i_{zz}/2) + (-C_{np})\big)\big(-C_{l\beta}/C_{n\beta}\big)/(i_{xx}/2)\Big], \end{aligned} \tag{A10.13}$$

assuming

$$(2\overline{m}/\mathrm{AR_W})(i_{xx}/2)C_{n\beta} \gg (-C_{lp})(-C_{nr})$$

and expanding by the binomial theorem

$$H \simeq (2\overline{m}/\mathrm{AR_W})C_{n\beta}/(i_{zz}/2). \tag{A10.14}$$

This simple approximation for H arises because collections of smaller terms which are not negligible in themselves are of opposite signs and tend to cancel.

Again the example in sect. IV.7,

$$\begin{aligned} &\text{exact } G = 1.68, \quad \text{approximate (eqn. (A10.13)) } G = 1.71, \\ &\text{exact } H = 83.84, \quad \text{approximate (eqn. (A10.14)) } H = 80, \end{aligned} \tag{A10.15}$$

again a reasonable agreement.

The above approximations lead to an approximation for the roll rate damping. Because the spiral root is small

$$\begin{aligned} \text{roll rate damping} &\simeq g \\ &= \overline{A}_3 - G \\ &= 0.5\big[\overline{A}_3 + (\overline{A}_1/\overline{A}_2)\big] \end{aligned} \tag{A10.16}$$

from eqns. (A10.3) and (A10.9).

In the example in sect. IV.7

$$\begin{aligned} &\text{exact roll rate damping} = 9.01 \\ &\text{approximate roll rate damping, from eqn. (A10.16)} = 9.22. \end{aligned} \tag{A10.17}$$

The above approximations can be applied qualitatively; agreement between approximate values and exact values is not always as close as those quoted above.

Appendix 11

Lateral response equations

The lateral responses to control surface and side gust inputs are given by the non-dimensional eqns. (IV.7.6)–(IV.7.8), namely

$$\left[\overline{\mathrm{D}} - C_{Y\beta}\right] \Delta\beta(\bar{t}_{\mathrm{d}}) + \overline{\mathrm{D}}\ \Delta\psi(\bar{t}_{\mathrm{d}}) - \left[\left(C_{Yp}\mathrm{AR}_{\mathrm{w}}/2\overline{m}\right)\overline{\mathrm{D}} + C_{\mathrm{W}}\right] \Delta\varphi(\bar{t}_{\mathrm{d}})$$
$$= \left[\left(C_{Y\dot{\kappa}}\mathrm{AR}_{\mathrm{w}}/2\overline{m}\right)\overline{\mathrm{D}} + C_{Y\kappa}\right]\kappa(\bar{t}_{\mathrm{d}}) \tag{A11.1}$$

$$-\left[(C_{l\dot{\beta}})\overline{\mathrm{D}} + \left(2\overline{m}/\mathrm{AR}_{\mathrm{w}}\right)C_{l\beta}\right] \Delta\beta(\bar{t}_{\mathrm{d}})$$
$$-\left[\left(i_{xz}/2\right)\overline{\mathrm{D}}^2 + C_{lr}\overline{\mathrm{D}}\right] \Delta\psi(\bar{t}_{\mathrm{d}})$$
$$+\left[\left(i_{xx}/2\right)\overline{\mathrm{D}}^2 - C_{lp}\overline{\mathrm{D}}\right] \Delta\varphi(\bar{t}_{\mathrm{d}})$$
$$= \left(2\overline{m}/\mathrm{AR}_{\mathrm{w}}\right)\left[\left[\left(C_{l\dot{\kappa}}\ \mathrm{AR}_{\mathrm{w}}/2\overline{m}\right)\overline{\mathrm{D}} + C_{l\kappa}\right]\kappa(\bar{t}_{\mathrm{d}})\right] \tag{A11.2}$$

$$-\left[(C_{n\dot{\beta}})\overline{\mathrm{D}} + \left(2\overline{m}/\mathrm{AR}_{\mathrm{w}}\right)C_{n\beta}\right] \Delta\beta(\bar{t}_{\mathrm{d}})$$
$$+\left[\left(i_{zz}/2\right)\overline{\mathrm{D}}^2 - C_{nr}\overline{\mathrm{D}}\right] \Delta\psi(\bar{t}_{\mathrm{d}})$$
$$-\left[\left(i_{xz}/2\right)\overline{\mathrm{D}}^2 + C_{np}\overline{\mathrm{D}}\right] \Delta\varphi(\bar{t}_{\mathrm{d}})$$
$$= \left(2\overline{m}/\mathrm{AR}_{\mathrm{w}}\right)\left[\left[\left(C_{n\dot{\kappa}}\ \mathrm{AR}_{\mathrm{w}}/2\overline{m}\right)\overline{\mathrm{D}} + C_{n\kappa}\right]\kappa(\bar{t}_{\mathrm{d}})\right] \tag{A11.3}$$

where

$\kappa(\bar{t}_{\mathrm{d}}) = \beta_{\mathrm{g}}(\bar{t}_{\mathrm{d}})$, a time varying side gust

or $= \xi(\bar{t}_{\mathrm{d}})$, a time varying aileron input

or $= \zeta(\bar{t}_{\mathrm{d}})$, a time varying rudder input.

A11.1 SIDESLIP RESPONSE

$$\left(A_4\overline{\mathrm{D}}^4 + A_3\overline{\mathrm{D}}^3 + A_2\overline{\mathrm{D}}^2 + A_1\overline{\mathrm{D}} + A_0\right)\Delta\beta(\bar{t}_\mathrm{d})$$
$$= \left(B_{\beta 4}\overline{\mathrm{D}}^4 + B_{\beta 3}\overline{\mathrm{D}}^3 + B_{\beta 2}\overline{\mathrm{D}}^2 + B_{\beta 1}\overline{\mathrm{D}} + B_{\beta 0}\right)\kappa(\bar{t}_\mathrm{d}) \tag{A11.4}$$

where

$$B_{\beta 4} = C_{Y\dot{\kappa}}\left(\mathrm{AR_w}/2\overline{m}\right)B_{\beta 31}$$
$$B_{\beta 3} = C_{Y\kappa}B_{\beta 31} + C_{Y\dot{\kappa}}\left(\mathrm{AR_w}/2\overline{m}\right)B_{\beta 21} + C_{l\dot{\kappa}}B_{\beta 22} + C_{n\dot{\kappa}}B_{\beta 23}$$
$$B_{\beta 2} = C_{Y\kappa}B_{\beta 21} + \left(2\overline{m}/\mathrm{AR_w}\right)C_{l\kappa}B_{\beta 22} + \left(2\overline{m}/\mathrm{AR_w}\right)C_{n\kappa}B_{\beta 23}$$
$$+ C_{Y\dot{\kappa}}\left(\mathrm{AR_w}/2m\right)B_{\beta 11} + C_{l\dot{\kappa}}B_{\beta 12} + C_{n\dot{\kappa}}B_{\beta 13}$$
$$B_{\beta 1} = C_{Y\kappa}B_{\beta 11} + \left(2\overline{m}/\mathrm{AR_w}\right)C_{l\kappa}B_{\beta 12} + \left(2\overline{m}/\mathrm{AR_w}\right)C_{n\kappa}B_{\beta 13}$$
$$+ C_{l\dot{\kappa}}B_{\beta 02} + C_{n\dot{\kappa}}B_{\beta 03}$$
$$B_{\beta 0} = \left(2\overline{m}/\mathrm{AR_w}\right)C_{l\kappa}B_{\beta 02} + \left(2\overline{m}/\mathrm{AR_w}\right)C_{n\kappa}B_{\beta 03}$$
$$B_{\beta 31} = \left(i_{xx}/2\right)\left(i_{zz}/2\right) - \left(i_{xz}/2\right)^2$$
$$B_{\beta 21} = -\left(i_{xz}/2\right)\left(C_{np} + C_{lr}\right) - \left(i_{xx}/2\right)C_{nr} - \left(i_{zz}/2\right)C_{lp}$$
$$B_{\beta 22} = -\left(i_{xz}/2\right) + \left(i_{zz}/2\right)\left(C_{Yp}\,\mathrm{AR_w}/2\overline{m}\right)$$
$$B_{\beta 23} = -\left(i_{xx}/2\right) + \left(i_{xz}/2\right)\left(C_{Yp}\,\mathrm{AR_w}/2\overline{m}\right)$$
$$B_{\beta 11} = -C_{lr}C_{np} + C_{lp}C_{nr}$$
$$B_{\beta 12} = -C_{np} + \left(i_{zz}/2\right)C_\mathrm{W} - C_{nr}\left(C_{Yp}\,\mathrm{AR_w}/2m\right)$$
$$B_{\beta 13} = C_{lp} + \left(i_{xz}/2\right)C_\mathrm{W} + C_{lr}\left(C_{Yp}\,\mathrm{AR_w}/2m\right)$$
$$B_{\beta 02} = -C_{nr}C_\mathrm{W}$$
$$B_{\beta 03} = C_{lr}C_\mathrm{W}.$$

With a step input $\kappa(t) = \kappa_\mathrm{s}H(t)$

(i) initial response (for qualitative behaviour neglect all time lags)

$$\Delta\beta(0+) \simeq 0, \qquad \overline{\mathrm{D}}\,\Delta\beta \simeq \left(B_{\beta 31}/A_4\right)\kappa_\mathrm{s} \simeq C_{Y\kappa}\kappa_\mathrm{s} \tag{A11.5}$$

(ii) 'steady state' after decay of Dutch roll (i.e. neglecting A_0),

$$\overline{\mathrm{D}}\,\Delta\beta \simeq \left(B_{\beta 0}/A_1\right)\kappa_\mathrm{s} \simeq \left[\frac{C_\mathrm{W}\left[C_{l\kappa}(-C_{nr}) + C_{n\kappa}C_{lr}\right]}{(-C_{l\beta})\left[C_\mathrm{W}\left(i_{zz}/2\right) + (-C_{np})\right] + \left(C_{n\beta} - C_{lp}\right)}\right]\kappa_\mathrm{s} \tag{A11.6}$$

(iii) steady state after decay of spiral mode,

$$\Delta\beta = \left(B_{\beta 0}/A_0\right)\kappa_s \simeq \left[\frac{C_{l\kappa}(-C_{nr}) + C_{n\kappa}C_{lr}}{(-C_{l\beta})\,(-C_{nr}) - C_{n\beta}C_{lr}}\right]\kappa_s \qquad \text{(A11.7)}$$

A11.2 YAW RESPONSE

$$\left(A_4\overline{D}^4 + A_3\overline{D}^3 + A_2\overline{D}^2 + A_1\overline{D} + A_0\right)\bar{r}(\bar{t}_d)$$
$$= \left(B_{\psi 4}\overline{D}^4 + B_{\psi 3}\overline{D}^3 + B_{\psi 2}\overline{D}^2 + B_{\psi 1}\overline{D} + B_{\psi 0}\right)\kappa(t_d) \qquad \text{(A11.8)}$$

where $\bar{r}(\bar{t}_d) = \overline{D}\,\Delta\psi(\bar{t}_d)$

$$B_{\psi 4} = C_{Y\dot{\kappa}}\left(\mathrm{AR_w}/2\overline{m}\right)B_{\psi 31} + C_{l\dot{\kappa}}B_{\psi 32} + C_{n\dot{\kappa}}B_{\psi 33}$$

$$B_{\psi 3} = C_{Y\kappa}B_{\psi 31} + \left(2\overline{m}/\mathrm{AR_w}\right)C_{l\kappa}B_{\psi 32} + \left(2\overline{m}/\mathrm{AR_w}\right)C_{n\kappa}B_{\psi 33}$$
$$+ C_{Y\dot{\kappa}}\left(\mathrm{AR_w}/2m\right)B_{\psi 21} + C_{l\dot{\kappa}}B_{\psi 22} + C_{n\dot{\kappa}}B_{\psi 23}$$

$$B_{\psi 2} = C_{Y\kappa}B_{\psi 21} + \left(2\overline{m}/\mathrm{AR_w}\right)C_{l\kappa}B_{\psi 22} + \left(2\overline{m}/\mathrm{AR_w}\right)C_{n\kappa}B_{\psi 23}$$
$$+ C_{Y\dot{\kappa}}\left(\mathrm{AR_w}/2m\right)B_{\psi 11} + C_{l\dot{\kappa}}B_{\psi 12} + C_{n\dot{\kappa}}B_{\psi 13}$$

$$B_{\psi 1} = C_{Y\kappa}B_{\psi 11} + \left(2\overline{m}/\mathrm{AR_w}\right)C_{l\kappa}B_{\psi 12} + \left(2\overline{m}/\mathrm{AR_w}\right)C_{n\kappa}B_{\psi 13}$$
$$+ C_{l\dot{\kappa}}B_{\psi 02} + C_{n\dot{\kappa}}B_{\psi 03}$$

$$B_{\psi 0} = +\left(2\overline{m}/\mathrm{AR_w}\right)\left[C_{l\kappa}B_{\psi 02} + C_{n\kappa}B_{\psi 03}\right]$$

$$B_{\psi 31} = C_{l\dot{\beta}}\left(i_{xz}/2\right) + C_{n\dot{\beta}}\left(i_{xx}/2\right)$$

$$B_{\psi 32} = i_{xz}/2$$

$$B_{\psi 33} = i_{xx}/2$$

$$B_{\psi 21} = C_{l\dot{\beta}}C_{np} - C_{n\dot{\beta}}C_{lp} + \left(\mathrm{AR_w}/2\overline{m}\right)\left[C_{n\beta}\left(i_{xx}/2\right) + C_{l\beta}\left(i_{xz}\right)\right]$$

$$B_{\psi 22} = -C_{Y\beta}\left(i_{xz}/2\right) + C_{np} + C_{n\dot{\beta}}\left(C_{Yp}\ \mathrm{AR_w}/2\overline{m}\right)$$

$$B_{\psi 23} = -C_{Y\beta}\left(i_{xx}/2\right) - C_{lp} - C_{l\dot{\beta}}\left(C_{Yp}\ \mathrm{AP_w}/2\overline{m}\right)$$

$$B_{\psi 11} = \left(2\overline{m}/\mathrm{AR_w}\right)\left[C_{l\beta}C_{np} - C_{n\beta}C_{lp}\right]$$

$$B_{\psi 12} = -C_{Y\beta}C_{np} + C_{n\beta}C_{Yp} + C_W C_{n\dot{\beta}}$$

$$B_{\psi 13} = C_{Y\beta}C_{lp} - C_{l\beta}C_{Yp} - C_W C_{l\dot{\beta}}$$

$$B_{\psi 02} = \left(2\overline{m}/\mathrm{AR_w}\right)C_W C_{n\beta}$$

$$B_{\psi 03} = -\left(2\overline{m}/\mathrm{AR_w}\right)C_W C_{l\beta}.$$

With a step input $\kappa(t) = \kappa_s H(t)$,

(i) initial response (for qualitative behaviour ignoring all time lags)

$$\bar{r}(0+) \simeq 0, \quad \bar{\mathrm{D}}\bar{r}(0+) = \left(B_{\psi 3}/A_4\right)\kappa_s \simeq \left(2\bar{m}/\mathrm{AR_w}\right)\left(C_{n\kappa}/\left(i_{zz}/2\right)\right)\kappa_s \quad \text{(A11.9)}$$

(ii) 'steady state' after decay of Dutch roll (i.e. neglecting A_0),

$$\bar{\mathrm{D}}\bar{r} \simeq \left(B_{\beta 0}/A_1\right)\kappa_s \simeq \left[\frac{\left(2\bar{m}/\mathrm{AR_w}\right)C_{\mathrm{W}}\left[C_{l\kappa}C_{n\beta} + C_{n\kappa}(-C_{l\beta})\right]}{(-C_{l\beta})\left[C_{\mathrm{W}}\left(i_{zz}/2\right) + (-C_{np})\right] + C_{n\beta}(-C_{lp})}\right]\kappa_s \quad \text{(A11.10)}$$

(iii) steady state after decay of spiral mode,

$$\bar{r} = \left(B_{\beta 0}/A_0\right)\kappa_s \simeq \left[\frac{\left(2\bar{m}/\mathrm{AR_w}\right)\left[C_{l\kappa}C_{n\beta} + C_{n\kappa}(-C_{l\beta})\right]}{(-C_{l\beta})(-C_{nr}) - C_{n\beta}C_{lr}}\right]\kappa_s. \quad \text{(A11.11)}$$

A11.3 ROLL RESPONSE

$$\left(A_4\bar{\mathrm{D}}^4 + A_3\bar{\mathrm{D}}^3 + A_2\bar{\mathrm{D}}^2 + A_1\bar{\mathrm{D}} + A_0\right)\Delta\varphi(\bar{t}_d)$$
$$= \left(B_{\varphi 3}\bar{\mathrm{D}}^3 + B_{\varphi 2}\bar{\mathrm{D}}^2 + B_{\varphi 1}\bar{\mathrm{D}} + B_{\varphi 0}\right)\kappa(\bar{t}_d) \quad \text{(A11.12)}$$

where

$$B_{\varphi 3} = C_{Y\dot{\kappa}}\left(\mathrm{AR_w}/2\bar{m}\right)B_{\varphi 21} + C_{l\dot{\kappa}}B_{\varphi 22} + C_{n\dot{\kappa}}B_{\varphi 23}$$

$$B_{\varphi 2} = C_{Y\kappa}B_{\varphi 21} + \left(2\bar{m}/\mathrm{AR_w}\right)C_{l\kappa}B_{\varphi 22} + \left(2\bar{m}/\mathrm{AR_w}\right)C_{n\kappa}B_{\varphi 23}$$
$$+ \left(C_{Y\dot{\kappa}}\ \mathrm{AR_w}/2\bar{m}\right)B_{\varphi 11} + C_{l\dot{\kappa}}B_{\varphi 12} + C_{n\dot{\kappa}}B_{\varphi 13}$$

$$B_{\varphi 1} = C_{Y\kappa}B_{\varphi 11} + \left(2\bar{m}/\mathrm{AR_w}\right)C_{l\kappa}B_{\varphi 12} + \left(2\bar{m}/\mathrm{AR_w}\right)C_{n\kappa}B_{\varphi 13}$$
$$+ \left(C_{Y\dot{\kappa}}\ \mathrm{AR_w}/2m\right)B_{\varphi 01} + C_{l\dot{\kappa}}B_{\varphi 02} + C_{n\dot{\kappa}}B_{\varphi 03}$$

$$B_{\varphi 0} = C_{Y\kappa}B_{\varphi 01} + \left(2\bar{m}/\mathrm{AR_w}\right)C_{l\kappa}B_{\varphi 02} + \left(2\bar{m}/\mathrm{AR_w}\right)C_{n\kappa}B_{\varphi 03}$$

$$B_{\varphi 21} = \left(i_{zz}/2\right)C_{l\dot{\beta}} + \left(i_{xz}/2\right)C_{n\dot{\beta}}$$

$$B_{\varphi 22} = \left(i_{zz}/2\right)$$

$$B_{\varphi 23} = \left(i_{xz}/2\right)$$

$$B_{\varphi 11} = \left(2\bar{m}/\mathrm{AR_w}\right)\left[\left(i_{zz}/2\right)C_{l\beta} + \left(i_{xz}/2\right)C_{n\beta}\right] - C_{l\dot{\beta}}C_{nr} + C_{lr}C_{n\dot{\beta}}$$

$$B_{\varphi 12} = -\left(i_{zz}/2\right)C_{Y\beta} - C_{nr} + C_{n\dot{\beta}}$$

$$B_{\varphi 13} = -\left(i_{xz}/2\right)C_{Y\beta} + C_{lr} - C_{l\dot{\beta}}$$

$$B_{\varphi 01} = -(2\overline{m}/\mathrm{AR_w})\left[C_{l\beta}C_{nr} - C_{n\beta}C_{lr}\right]$$

$$B_{\varphi 02} = (2\overline{m}/\mathrm{AR_w})C_{n\beta} + C_{Y\beta}C_{nr}$$

$$B_{\varphi 03} = -(2\overline{m}/\mathrm{AR_w})C_{l\beta} - C_{Y\beta}C_{lr}.$$

With a step input $\kappa(t) = \kappa_s H(t)$

(i) 'steady state' after decay of roll rate subsidence

$$\overline{\mathrm{D}}\Delta\varphi \simeq (2m/\mathrm{AR_w})\left(C_{l\kappa}/(-C_{lp})\right)\kappa_s \tag{A11.13}$$

(ii) 'steady state' after decay of Dutch roll (i.e. neglecting A_0),

$$\overline{\mathrm{D}}\Delta\varphi \simeq \left(B_{\varphi 0}/A_1\right)\kappa_s \simeq \left[\frac{(2\overline{m}/\mathrm{AR_w})\left[C_{l\kappa}C_{n\beta} + C_{n\kappa}(-C_{l\beta})\right]}{(-C_{l\beta})\left[C_\mathrm{W}(i_{zz}/2) + (-C_{np})\right] + C_{n\beta}(-C_{lp})}\right]\kappa_s \tag{A11.14}$$

(iii) steady state after decay of spiral mode,

$$\Delta\varphi = \left(B_{\beta 0}/A_0\right)\kappa_s \simeq \left[\frac{(2\overline{m}/\mathrm{AR_w})\left[C_{l\kappa}C_{n\beta} + C_{n\kappa}(-C_{l\beta})\right]}{C_\mathrm{W}\left[(-C_{l\beta})(-C_{nr}) - C_{n\beta}C_{lr}\right]}\right]\kappa_s. \tag{A11.15}$$

References

PREFACE

P.1 G. H. Bryan, *Stability in Aviation*, Macmillan, London, 1911.

P.2 B. Melvile Jones, *Dynamics of the Airplane*, Vol. 5, *Aerodynamic Theory* (ed. W. F. Durand), Julius Springer, 1935 (Dover Publications, 1963; Peter Smith, 1976).

P.3 C. D. Perkins & R. E. Hale, *Airplane Performance, Stability and Control*, Wiley, London, 1949.

P.4 W. J. Duncan, *Principles of the Stability and Control of Aircraft*, Cambridge University Press, 1952.

P.5 B. Etkin, *Dynamics of Flight, Stability and Control*, Wiley, 1958.

P.6 H. N. Abramson, *Introduction to the Dynamics of Aeroplanes*, Ronald Press, 1958.

P.7 W. R. Kolk, *Modern Flight Mechanics*, Prentice-Hall, 1961.

P.8 A. W. Babister, *Aircraft Stability and Control*, Pergamon Press, 1961.

P.9 C. L. Gillis & T. A. Toll, *Stability and Control of High Speed Aircraft*, Vol. VIII, *High Speed Aerodynamics and Jet Propulsion*, Oxford University Press, 1961.

P.10 J. Arnall, *Stability and Control. Supersonic Engineering* (ed. D. Henshall), Heinemann Press, 1962.

P.11 E. Seckel, *Stability and Control of Airplanes and Helicopters*, Academic Press, 1964.

P.12 F. Irving, *An Introduction to the Longitudinal Static Stability of Low Speed Aircraft*, Pergamon Press, 1966.

P.13 B. Dickinson, *Aircraft Stability and Control for Pilots and Engineers*, Pitman, 1968.

P.14 T. Hacker, *Flight Stability and Control*, Elsevier, 1970.

P.15 B. Etkin, *Dynamics of Atmospheric Flight*, Wiley, 1972.

P.16 A. W. Babister, *Aircraft Dynamic Stability and Response*, Pergamon Press, 1980.

P.17 J. Roskam, *Airplane Flight Dynamics and Automatic Flight Controls*, Roskam Aviation Press, 1982.

P.18 R. C. Nelson, *Flight Stability and Automatic Control*, McGraw-Hill, 1989.

P.19 J. H. Blackelock, *Automatic Control of Aircraft and Missiles*, Wiley, New York, 1965.

P.20 D. McRuer, I. Ashkenas & D. Graham, *Aircraft Dynamics and Automatic Control*, Princeton University Press, New Jersey, 1973.

P.21 D. McLean, *Automatic Flight Control Systems*, Prentice-Hall International, 1990.

P.22 B. L. Stevens & F. L. Lewis, *Aircraft Control and Simulation*, Wiley, 1992.

P.23 H. R. Hopkins, A scheme of notation and nomenclature for aircraft dynamics and associated aerodynamics. ARC R&M 3562, 1970.

PART II

II.1 L. S. Pontryagin, *Ordinary Differential Equations*, Addison Wesley, 1962.

II.2 *N(ational) A(lgorithm) G(group); Fortran Library Manual.*

II.3 W. H. Press, S. A. Teukolsky, B. P. Flannery & W. T. Vetterling, *Numerical Recipes; the Art of Scientific Computing*, Cambridge University Press, 1986.

II.4 J. H. Wilkinson & C. Reinsch, *Handbook for Automatic Computation*, Vol. 2, *Linear Algebra*, Springer-Verlag, 1971.

PART III

III.1 W. L. Green, *Aircraft Hydraulic Systems*, Wiley, 1985.

III.2 W. A. Neese, *Aircraft Hydraulic Systems*, 3rd edn., Krieger, 1991.

III.3 D. K. Bird, The all-electric aircraft. ICAS-80-5-1, 1980.

III.4 *Advanced Actuator Systems*, NASA SP, 1980.

III.5 M. J. Cronin, All electric vs conventional aircraft; the production/operational aspects. *J. Aircraft* **20** (6), 1983.

III.6 ESDU Data Sheets, *Aerodynamics*, Vol. 1(b).

III.7 B. W. McCormick, *Aerodynamics, Aeronautics, and Flight Mechanics*, Wiley, 1979.

III.8 H. Schlichting & E. Truckenbrodt, *Aerodynamics of the Airplane*, McGraw-Hill, 1979.

III.9 J. Moran, *An Introduction to Theoretical and Computational Aerodynamics*, Wiley, 1984.

III.10 G. V. Lachmann (ed.), *Boundary Layer and Flow Control; Its Principles and Applications*, Pergamon Press, 1961.

III.11 D. Kuchemann, *The Aerodynamic Design of Aircraft*, Pergamon Press, 1978.

III.12 D. Nixon, *Transonic Aerodynamics*, Vol. 81, *Progress in Astronautics and Aeronautics*, AIAA, 1982.

III.13 ESDU Data Sheets, *Aerodynamics*, Vols. 2(c), 2(d).

III.14 E. W. E. Rogers & I. M. Hall, An introduction to the flow about plane swept back wings at transonic speeds, *J. Roy. Aero. Soc.* (Aug.), 1960.

III.15 R. Vepa, Vortex doublet method. In-house program, Queen Mary and Westfield College.

III.16 ESDU Data Sheets, *Aerodynamics*, Vol. 9(a).

III.17 M. Tobak, On the use of the indicial function concept in the analysis of unsteady motions of wings and wing-tail combinations. NACA Report 1188, 1954.
III.18 ESDU Data Sheets, *Aerodynamics*, Vol. 10.
III.19 R. L. Bisplinghoff, H. Ashley & R. L. Halfman, *Aeroelasticity*, Addison Wesley, 1955.
III.20 G. J. Hancock, Some introductory concepts based on the unsteady flows about circular cylinders. Lecture Series: Unsteady Aerodynamics. AGARD Report 679. 1980.
III.21 H. C. Garner & R. D. Milne, Asymptotic expansion for transient forces from quasi-steady subsonic wing theory. *Aero. Quarterly* **XVII** (Nov.), 1966.
III.22 ESDU Data sheets, *Aerodynamics*, Vol. 9(a).
III.23 ESDU Data sheets, *Aerodynamics*, Vol. 5(b).
III.24 M. J. Sheu & G. J. Hancock, A simplified model for the external loading on an engine nacelle, enclosing an engine: Part 1, At a steady incidence; Part II, In oscillatory motion. *J. Roy. Aero. Soc.* (Dec.), 1984.
III.25 M. R. Spearman, Some effects of external stores of the static stability of fighter aeroplanes. NASA TN D6775, 1972.
III.26 J. M. Whoric, Effects of various external stores on the static longitudinal stability, longitudinal control, and drag characteristics of model F4 c airplane. AEDC TR 73 186, 1973.
III.27 *Drag and other aerodynamic effects of external stores*, AGARD AR 107, 1977.
III.28 J. L. Meriam & L. J. Kraige, *Engineering Mechanics*, Vol. 12, *Dynamics*, Wiley, 1900.
III.29 *Handbook of Aviation Meteorology*, HMSO, 1991.
III.30 B. W. Atkinson, *Dynamic Meteorology, an Introduction*, Methuen, 1991.
III.31 J. K. Zbrozek, Atmospheric gusts. *J. Roy. Aero. Soc.* **69** (Jan.), 1965.
III.32 P. Donely, Atmospheric turbulence and the air transport system. *R. Ae. S/CASI/ AIAA International Conference on Turbulence*, 1971.
III.33 ESDU Data Sheets, *Dynamics*, Vol. D32.
III.34 A. Popoulis, *Probability, Random Variables and Stochastic Processes*, McGraw-Hill, 1965.
III.35 J. C. Houbolt, Atmospheric turbulence. *AIAA J.* **11** (April), 1973.
III.36 J. G. Jones, UK Research on Aeronautical Effects of Surface Winds and Gusts. AGARD Report 626, 1974.
III.37 H. N. Murrow, W. E. McCain & R. H. Rhyne, Power spectral measurements of clear air turbulence to long wavelengths for altitudes up to 14 000 m. NASA TP 1979, 1982.
III.38 H. Press & J. C. Houbolt, Some applications of generalized harmonic analysis to gust loads on aeroplanes. *J. Aero. Sci.*, **22** (1), 1955.
III.39 J. C. Houbolt, R. Steiner & K. G. Pratt, Dynamic response of airplanes to atmospheric turbulence, including flight data on input and response. NASA TR R199, 1964.
III.40 S. O. Rice, Mathematical analysis of random noise. *Selected Papers on Noise and Stochastic Processes* (ed. Nelson Wax), Dover Publications, 1954.

III.41 I. W. Kaynes, Aircraft centre of gravity response to two-dimensional spectra of turbulence. ARC R&M 3665, 1970.

III.42 R. Noback, A non-stationary model for atmospheric turbulence patches for the prediction of aircraft design loads. NLR TR 76131U, 1976.

III.43 J. G. Jones, Statistical–Discrete–Gust method for predicting aircraft loads and dynamic response. *J. Aircraft* **26** (April), 1989.

III.44 B. Perry III, A. S. Pototzky & J. A. Woods, NASA investigation of a claimed 'overlap' between two gust response analysis methods. *J. Aircraft* **27** (July), 1990.

III.45 W. Frost, Flight in low level wind shear. NASA CR 3678, March 1983.

III.46 A. A. Woodfield, Wind shear topics at RAE Flight Systems Dept., TN FS132, 1985.

III.47 K. U. Hahn, Takeoff and landing in a downburst. *J. Aircraft* **24** (Aug.), 1987.

III.48 R. C. Wingrove & R. E. Bach, Jr., Severe winds in the Dallas/Fort Worth Microburst measured from two aircraft. *J. Aircraft* **26** (March), 1989; Analysis of windshear from airline flight data. *J. Aircraft* **26** (Feb.), 1989.

III.49 R. L. Bowles, Reducing wind shear through airborne systems technology. ICAS CP, 1990.

III.50 O. H. Gerlach, G. A. H. van de Moesdijk & J. C. van der Vaart, Progress in the mathematical modelling of flight in turbulence. AGARD CP 140, 1973.

III.51 P. M. Reeves, A non-Gaussian turbulence simulation. USAF AFFDL TR 67, 1969.

III.52 B. N. Tomlinson, Developments in the simulation of atmospheric turbulence. AGARD CP 198, 1975.

III.53 J. A. Dutton, Present challenges in prediction of the effects of atmospheric turbulence on aeronautical systems. *Progr. Aeronaut. Sci.* **2**, 1971.

III.54 B. Etkin, Turbulent wind and its effect on flight. *J. Aircraft* **18** (May), 1981.

III.55 D. W. Camp & W. Frost (eds.), Proceedings of the workshop on atmospheric turbulence relative to aviation, missile, and space programs. NASA CP 2468, 1987.

III.56 J. Houbolt (ed.), Manual on the flight of flexible aircraft in turbulence. AGARD AG 317, 1991.

III.57 C. R. Chalk, T. P. Neal & T. M. Harris, Background information and user guide for Mil-F-8785 B(ASG). Military specifications. Flying qualities of piloted aeroplanes. Air Force Flight Dynamics Laboratory, TR 69 72, 1969; and D. J. Moorhouse & R. J. Woodcock, Background information and user guide for Mil-F-8785 C(ASG). Military specifications. Flying qualities of piloted aeroplanes. Air Force Flight Dynamics Laboratory, TR 81 3109, 1981.

III.58 E. L. Wiener & D. C. Nagel (eds.), *Human Factors in Aviation.*

III.59 S. Neumark, Longitudinal stability below the minimum drag speed and theory of stability under constraint. ARC R&M 2983, 1957.

III.60 P. Painleve, Etude sur le régime normal d'un aéroplane, in *La Technique Aéronautique*, Vol. 1, pp. 3–11, Paris, 1910.

III.61 R. von Mises, *Fluglehre*, Springer-Verlag, Berlin, 1915.

III.62 R. Fuchs & L. Hopf, *Aerodynamik*, Springer-Verlag, Berlin, 1922.

III.63 Handling qualities criteria. AGARD CP 106, 1972.

III.64 I. L. Ashkenas, Twenty five years of handling qualities research. *J. Aircraft* **21** (May), 1984.

III.65 R. P. Harper, Jr. & G. E. Cooper, Handling qualities and pilot evaluation. *J. Guidance, Control and Dynamics* **9** (Sept./Oct.), 1986.

III.66 J. C. Gibson, Handling qualities for unstable combat aircraft. ICAS Congress, 1986.

III.67 Advances in flying qualities. AGARD LS 157, 1988.

III.68 H. J. Kranenborg, A survey of gyroscopes and accelerometers with particular application to modern developments. NLRL (Amsterdam) Report, V1959, 1967.

III.69 J. Andresen, *Fundamentals of Aircraft Flight and Engine Instruments*, Hayden Book Co., New York, 1969.

III.70 R. F. Demiel, *Mechanics of the Gyroscope*, Dover Publications, 1950.

III.71 B. R. A. Burns, Control configured combat aircraft. AGARDgraph 234, 1978.

III.72 Active control systems—review, evaluation and projections. AGARD CP 384, 1900.

III.73 Impact of active control technology to airplane design. AGARD CP 157, 1974.

III.74 D. McRuer, D. Johnson & T. Myers, A perspective of superaugmented flight control advantages and problems. AGARD CP 384, 1984.

III.75 J. G. Jones & D. E. Fry, Aircraft ride bumpiness and the design of ride-smoothing systems. AGARD CP240, 1977.

PART IV

IV.1 ESDU Data sheets, Vols. 9(b), 9(c).

IV.2 D. E. Hoak, USAF stability and control DAT(a) COM(pendium). Flight Control Division, Flight Dynamics Laboratory, Wright Patterson Air Force Base, 1970.

IV.3 H. H. B. M. Thomas, A brief introduction to aircraft dynamics. Lecture series, 'Aircraft stability and control'. Von Karman Institute of Fluid Dynamics, 1975.

IV.4 J. M. Eggleston & W. H. Philips, The lateral-directional response of airplanes to random atmospheric turbulence. NASA TR-R-74, 1960.

IV.5 J. A. Zalovcik & R. E. Dunham, Jr., Vortex wake research flight in turbulence. AGARD CP 140, 1973.

IV.6 H. A. Verstynen, Jr. & R. E. Dunham, Jr., A flight investigation of the trailing vortices generated by a jumbo jet transport. NASA TN D7172, 1973.

IV.7 W. H. Andrews, G. R. Robinson & R. R. Larson, Exploratory flight investigation of aircraft response to the wing vortex wake generated by jet transport aircraft. NASA TN D6655, March 1972.

IV.8 W. J. G. Pinsker, Directional stability in flight with bank angle constraint. ARC R&M 3556, 1968.

IV.9 B. R. A. Burns, Design considerations for the satisfactory stability and control of military combat aeroplanes. AGARD CP 119, 1972.

PART V

V.1 Sir G. G. Stokes, On the theories of the internal friction of fluids in motion. *Cambridge Trans. (viii)* **287**, 1845.

V.2 I. H. Abbot & A. E. von Doenhoff, *Theory of Wing Sections* (*including a Summary of Airfoil Data*), Dover Publications, 1960.

V.3 L. E. Ericsson, A critical look at dynamic simulation of viscous flow. AGARD CP 386, 1985.

V.4 G. J. Hancock, Problems of aircraft behaviour at high angles of attack. AGARDgraph 136, 1969.

V.5 J. Katz, A discrete vortex model for the non-steady separated flow over an airfoil. *J. Fluid Mechanics* **102**, 315 (1981).

V.6 A. M. O. Smith, Aerodynamics of high-lift systems. AGARD CP 102, 1972.

V.7 L. R. Wooton, Effect of compressibility on the maximum lift coefficient of aerofoils at subsonic speeds. *J. Roy. Aero. Soc.* **71** (July), 1967.

V.8 G. J. Hancock & D. Mabey, Unsteady aerodynamics of controls. AGARD CP 465, 1989.

V.9 S. Kawashima & M. Yamasaki, Aerodynamic response for the aerofoil experiencing a sudden change in angle of attack. *Trans. Japan Soc. Aeronaut. Space Sci.* (Aug.), 1978.

V.10 S. Francis & E. Keese, Airfoil dynamic stall performance with large amplitude motions. *AIAA J.* **23** (Nov.), 1985.

V.11 M. R. Visbal, Dynamic stall of constant rate pitching aerofoil. *J. Aircraft* **27** (May), 1990.

V.12 E. J. Jumper, S. J. Shreck & R. L. Dimmick, Lift curve characteristics for an airfoil pitching at constant rate. *J. Aircraft* **24** (Oct.), 1987.

V.13 L. E. Ericsson & J. P. Reding, Dynamic overshoot of the static stall angle. *J. Aircraft* **22** (July), 1985.

V.14 W. J. McCroskey, The phenomenon of dynamic stall. NASA Tech Memo. 81264, 1981.

V.15 Unsteady aerodynamics—fundamentals and applications to aircraft aerodynamics. AGARD CP 386, 1985.

V.16 Unsteady aerodynamics. AGARD LS 1988-07, 1988.

V.17 N. C. Lambourne, Compendium of unsteady aerodynamic measurements. AGARD Report 702, 1982.

V.18 L. E. Ericsson, Shock-induced dynamic stall. *J. Aircraft* **21** (May), 1984.

V.19 P. Shekar & G. J. Hancock, Extension of lifting line theory to separated flows of finite wings. QMC EP 1025, 1977.

V.20 G. C. Furlong & J. C. McHugh, A summary and analysis of the low speed longitudinal characteristics of swept wings at high Reynolds numbers. NACA Report 1339, 1957.

V.21 Manoeuvre limitations of combat aeroplanes 1979. AGARD Advisory Report 155A, 1979.

V.22 J. Rom, *High Angle of Attack Aerodynamics*, Springer-Verlag, 1992.

V.23 N. C. Lambourne & D. W. Bryer, The bursting of leading edge vortices, some observations and discussion of the phenomenon. ARC, R&M 3282, 1965.

V.24 M. Escudier, Vortex breakdown: observation and explanations. *Progr. Aeronaut. Sci.* **25**, 1988.

V.25 The effects of buffeting and other transonic phenomena on manoeuvring combat aircraft. AGARD AR 82, 1975.

V.26 M. J. Queijo, B. M. Jaquet & W. D. Wolhart, Wind tunnel investigation at low speed of the effects of chordwise wing fences and horizontal tail position on the static longitudinal stability characteristics of an airplane model with a 35° sweptback wing. NACA Report 1203, 1954.

V.27 D. Pollatos, Fence effects on a low speed wing. Ph.D. thesis, University of London, 1977.

V.28 D. N. Foster, The low speed stalling of wings with high lift devices. AGARD CP 102, 1972.

V.29 R. S. Bray, The effects of fences on the high speed longitudinal stability of a swept wing airplane. NACA RM A53 F23, NACA TIB 3854, 1953.

V.30 D. M. Rao & T. D. Johnson, Jr., Alleviation of the subsonic pitch up of delta wings. *J. Aircraft* **20** (June), 1983.

V.31 G. S. Schairer, Pod mounting of jet engines. *4th Anglo-American Conference*, 1953.

V.32 C. E. Lemley & R. E. Mullans, Buffeting pressures on a swept wing in transonic flight—comparison of model and full scale. AIAA Paper 73-311, 1973.

V.33 M. Kramer, Increase in the maximum lift of an airplane due to a sudden increase in the effective angle of attack resulting from a gust. *Z. Flugtechn. Motorluft.* **27** (7), 1932. Translated as NACA TM 678, 1932.

V.34 W. S. Farren, The reaction on a wing whose angle of incidence is changing rapidly. ARC R&M 1648, 1935.

V.35 A. Silverstein, Comparative flight and full scale wind tunnel measurements of the maximum lift of an aeroplane. NACA Report 618, 1938.

V.36 P. W. Harper & R. E. Flanigan, Investigation of the variation of maximum lift for a pitching airplane model and comparison with flight results. NACA TN 1734, 1948.

V.37 P. W. Harper & R. E. Flanigan, Effect of rate of change of angle of attack on the maximum lift of a small model. NACA TN 1061, 1950.

V.38 B. L. Gradeburg, Effect of rate of change of angle of attack on the maximum lift coefficient of a pursuit airplane. NACA TN 2525, 1951.

V.39 F. Conner, C. Willey & W. Twomeny, A flight and wind tunnel investigation of the effect of angle attack rate on maximum lift coefficient. NASA CR 321, 1965.

V.40 M. C. Robinson & J. B. Wissler, Pitch rate and Reynolds Number effects on a pitching rectangular wing. AIAA Paper 88-2577, June 1988.

V.41 J. J. Costes, Unsteady three-dimensional stall on rectangular wing. ONERA TP 119, 1986.

V.42 S. B. Grafton & C. E. Libbey, Dynamic stability derivatives of a twin jet fighter model for angles of attack from –10° to 110°. NASA TN D6091, 1971.

V.43 W. Staudacher, B. Laschka, B. Schulze, P. Poisson-Quinton & M. Canu, Some factors affecting the dynamic stability derivatives of a fighter type model. AGARD CP 235, 1978.

V.44 R. G. den Boer & A. M. Cunningham, Jr., Low speed unsteady aerodynamics of a pitching straked wing at high incidence: Part I, Test program; Part II, Harmonic analysis. *J. Aircraft* **27** (Jan.), 1990.

V.45 S. C. Schneider, Analytical determination of dynamic stability parameters. AGARD Lecture Series 114, 1981.

V.46 M. R. Soltani, M. B. Bragg & J. M. Brandon, Measurements on an oscillating 70° delta wing in subsonic flow. *J. Aircraft* **27** (March), 1990.

V.47 S. A. Huyer, M. C. Robinson & M. W. Luttges, Unsteady loading produced by a sinusoidally oscillating delta wing. *J. Aircraft* **29** (May–June), 1992.

V.48 H. G. Wiley, Significance of non-linear damping trends determined for current aircraft configurations. AGARD CP 17, 1966.

V.49 Unsteady aerodynamics. AGARD LS 1988-07.

V.50 D. Nixon, *Unsteady transonic flows*, Progress in Astronautics and Aeronautics, AIAA, 1992.

V.51 R. W. Stone, Jr. & E. C. Polhamus, Some effects of shed vortices on the flow fields around stabilising tail surfaces. AGARD Report 108, 1957.

V.52 D. Kirby & A. Spence, Low speed tunnel model tests on the flow structure behind a delta wing aircraft and a 40° swept aircraft at high incidence. ARC R&M 3078, 1958.

V.53 R. S. Shevell & R. D. Schaufele, Aerodynamic design features of the DC-9. *J. Aircraft* **3** (Nov.–Dec.), 1966.

V.54 N. M. Komerath, S. G. Liou, R. J. Schwartz & J. M. Kim, Flow over a twin tailed aircraft at angle of attack. *J. Aircraft* **29** (May–June), 1992.

V.55 A. L. Byrnes, Effect of horizontal stabilizer vertical location on the design of large transport aircraft. *J. Aircraft* **3** (March–April), 1966.

V.56 H. H. B. M. Thomas & Collingbourne, Longitudinal motions of aircraft involving high angles of attack. ARC R&M 3753 (1973).

V.57 S. B. Grafton, J. R. Chambers & P. L. Coe, Jr., Wind tunnel free-flight investigation of a model of a spin-resistant fighter configuration. NASA TN D7716, 1974.

V.58 A. M. Skow, Control of advanced fighter aircraft. AGARD Report 711, 1983.

V.59 L. D. Lambert, *Computational Methods in Ordinary Differential Equations*, Wiley, 1974.

V.60 M. Tobak & L. Schiff, Aerodynamic mathematical modelling, basic concepts. Some applications of aerodynamic formulations to problems in aircraft dynamics. AGARD LS 114, 1981.

V.61 J. R. Chambers, S. B. Grafton & F. H. Lutze, Curved flow, rolling flow and oscillatory pure-yawing test methods for determination of dynamic stability derivatives. AGARD LS 114, 1981.

V.62 A. J. Ross, Lateral stability at high angles of attack, particularly wing rock. AGARD CP 260, 1979.

V.63 J. R. Chambers & E. L. Anglin, Analysis of lateral-directional stability characteristics of a twin jet fighter airplane at high angles of attack. NASA D5361, 1969.

V.64 A. J. Ross & L. T. Nguyen, Some observations regarding wing rock oscillations at high angles of attack. AIAA Paper 88-4371 CP, Aug. 1988.

V.65 A. J. Ross, Review and extension of analysis of wing rock oscillations. RAE TR 89051, 1989.

V.66 L. E. Ericsson, Further analysis of wing rock generated by forebody vortices. *J. Aircraft* **26** (Dec.), 1989.

V.67 A. M. Skow & A. Titiriga, Jr., A survey of analytical and experimental techniques to predict aircraft dynamic characteristics at high angles of attack. AGARD CP 235, 1978.

V.68 K. J. Orlik-Rückemann, Sensitivity of aircraft motion to cross-coupling and acceleration derivatives. AGARD LS 114, 1981.

V.69 K. J. Orlik-Rückemann & E. S. Hanff, Experiments on cross-coupling and translational acceleration derivatives. AGARD CP 235, 1978.

V.70 H. Phillips, Effect of steady rolling on longitudinal and directional stability. NACA TN 1627, 1948.

V.71 W. J. G. Pinsker, Charts of peak amplitudes in incidence and sideslip in rolling manoeuvres due to inertia cross-coupling. ARC R&M 3293, 1962.

V.72 ESDU Data Sheet, *Dynamics*, Vol. 1.

V.73 R. Wiessman, Preliminary criteria for predicting departure characteristics/spin susceptibility of fighter type aircraft. *J. Aircraft* **10** (April), 1973.

V.74 H. D. Greer, Summary of directional divergence characteristics of several high-performance aircraft configurations. NASA TN D6993, 1972.

V.75 W. Bihrle & B. Barnhart, Departure susceptibility and uncoordinated roll-reversal boundaries for fighter configurations. *J. Aircraft* **19** (Nov.), 1982.

V.76 J. Kalviste, Aircraft stability characteristics at high angles of attack. AGARD CP 235, 1978.

V.77 K. J. Orlik-Rückemann, Review of techniques for determination of dynamic stability parameters in wind tunnels. AGARD LS 114, 1981.

V.78 Unsteady aerodynamics—fundamentals and applications to aircraft dynamics. AGARD CP 386, 1985.

V.79 Manoeuvring aerodynamics. AGARD CP 497, 1991.

V.80 A. J. Ross & G. F. Edwards, Correlations of predicted and free-flight responses near departure conditions of a high incidence research model. AGARD CP 386, 1985.

V.81 H. H. Chin, Knowledge based system of supermanoeuvre selection for pilot aiding. *J. Aircraft* **26** (Dec.),1989.

V.82 M. Dorn, Aircraft agility; the science and opportunities. AIAA Paper 89-2015, 1989.

V.83 A. M. Skow, Agility as a contributor to design balance. *J. Aircraft* **29** (Jan.–Feb.), 1992.

V.84 R. K. Liefer, J. Valasek, D. P. Eggold & D. R. Downing, Fighter agility metrics, research and test. *J. Aircraft* **29** (May–June), 1992.

V.85 R. J. Woodcock & R. Weissman, The stall/spin problem. AGARD CP 199, 1975.
V.86 G. N. Malcolm, T. T. Ng, L. C. Lewis & D. G. Murri, Development of non-conventional control methods for high angle of attack flight using vortex manipulation. AGARD CP 465, 1990.
V.87 A. J. Ross, High incidence—the challenge to control systems. RAE Tech Memo, Aero 2175, 1990.

Notation

a, a_j	arbitrary constants
(a_α), $(a_{\dot\alpha})$	component quasi-steady lift derivatives due to incidence
(a_q), $(a_{\dot q})$	component quasi-steady lift derivatives due to pitch rate (suffixes: w, wing; wf, wing fuselage; t, tailplane; nac, nacelles)
$(a_\beta)_\mathrm{f}$, $(a_{\dot\beta})_\mathrm{f}$	quasi-steady derivatives of fin 'lift'
(a_η), $(a_{\dot\eta})$	quasi-steady lift derivatives due to elevator
(a_ξ), $(a_{\dot\xi})$	quasi-steady lift derivatives due to aileron, or differential tailplane
(a_ζ), $(a_{\dot\zeta})$	quasi-steady 'lift' derivatives due to rudder
$\tilde a_\alpha(\nu)$, $\tilde a_{\dot\alpha}(\nu)$	in-phase and out-of-phase oscillatory wing derivatives due to oscillating angle of incidence
a_at	speed of sound in atmosphere at altitude h
$(a_\mathrm{at})_\mathrm{sl}$	speed of sound at sea level
$A(t)$	time varying 'axial' force in $-ox$ direction
A_j	coefficients of differential operator; coefficients in characteristic equation
$A_X(t)$, $A_Y(t)$, $A_Z(t)$	components of absolute acceleration of c.m. resolved in OX, OY, OZ directions
$A_x(t)$, $A_y(t)$, $A_z(t)$	components of absolute acceleration of c.m. resolved in ox, oy, oz directions
$A_{PX}(t)$, $A_{PY}(t)$, $A_{PZ}(t)$	compoents of absolute acceleration of point P resolved in OX, OY, OZ directions
$A_{Px}(t)$, $A_{Py}(t)$, $A_{Pz}(t)$	components of absolute acceleration of point P resolved in ox, oy, oz directions
$A_\mathrm{N}(t)$, $A_\mathrm{T}(t)$	components of absolute acceleration resolved normal and tangential to the flight path in planar motion
$[\mathbf{A}]$, $\mathbf{A}$, $[\mathbf{A}_0]$, $[\mathbf{A}_1]$	matrices $(n \times n)$
AR	aspect ratio $= 2s/c = (2s)^2/S$ (suffixes: w, wing; t, tailplane)
$\mathrm{AR_f}$	aspect ratio of fin $(= s_\mathrm{f}/c_\mathrm{f})$
$A_{n\mathrm{w}}$	factor relating σ_w to $\sigma_{\Delta n}$
ATR	attained turn rate

b, b_j	arbitrary constants
$\mathcal{b}_\alpha, \mathcal{b}_\eta, \mathcal{b}_\delta$	static elevator hinge moment derivatives due to angles of incidence, elevator and tab
[**B**], [$\mathbf{B}_0$], **B**	matrices ($n \times m$)
B_j	coefficients in differential operator of input
c, c_j	arbitrary constants
c_w, c_t, c_f	mean chords of wing, tailplane, fin
c_e	mean chord of elevator
c_r	wing root chord
$c(y)$	spanwise variation of chord
c.m.	centre of mass
$c_p(x, y)$	wing surface pressure coefficient $= \left(p(x,y) - p_{at}\right) / \left(\frac{1}{2}\rho_{at}U^2\right)$
CAA	Civil Aviation Authority
CAP	Control Anticipation Parameter
$(C_L)_w$	wing lift coefficient $= \text{wing lift} / \left(\frac{1}{2}\rho_{at}U^2 S_w\right)$ $= (a_\alpha)_w\left(\alpha(t) + i_w - \alpha_{0w}\right) + (a_{\dot{\alpha}})_w\left(\dot{\alpha}(t)c_w/U(t)\right) + (a_q)_w\left(q(t)c_w/U(t)\right) + (a_{\dot{q}})_w\left(\dot{q}(t)(c_w/U(t))^2\right)$
$(C_L)_{wf}$	wing–fuselage lift coefficient $= \text{wing–fuselage lift} / \left(\frac{1}{2}\rho_{at}U^2 S_w\right)$ $= (C_{L0})_{wf} + (a_\alpha)_{wf}\left(\alpha(t) + i_w - \alpha_{0w}\right) + (a_{\dot{\alpha}})_{wf}\left(\dot{\alpha}(t)c_w/U(t)\right) + (a_q)_w\left(q(t)c_w/U(t)\right) + (a_{\dot{q}})_w\left(\dot{q}(t)(c_w/U(t))^2\right)$
$(C_L)_t$	tailplane lift coefficient $= \text{tailplane lift} / \left(\frac{1}{2}\rho_{at}U^2 S_t\right)$ $= (a_\alpha)_t\left(\alpha(t) + i_t + q(t)l_t c_w/U(t)\right) - \varepsilon(t) + (a_{\dot{\alpha}})_t\left(\left[\dot{\alpha}(t) + \dot{q}(t)l_t\, c_w/U(t) - \dot{\varepsilon}(t)\right]c_w/U(t)\right) + a_\eta \eta(t) + a_{\dot{\eta}}\left(\dot{\eta}(t)c_w/U(t)\right)$
$C_L(y)$	using spanwise lift distribution $= L(y) / \left(\frac{1}{2}\rho_{at}U^2 c_w\right)$
C_A, C_N, C_Y	overall force coefficients $= A / \left(\frac{1}{2}\rho_{at}U^2(t)S_w\right),\ N / \left(\frac{1}{2}\rho_{at}U^2(t)S_w\right),\ Y / \left(\frac{1}{2}\rho_{at}U^2(t)s_w\right)$

$C_L(M_\infty(t), \alpha(t), \theta(t)|t)$ time varying overall lift coefficient

$= \text{total aerodynamic lift force}/\left(\frac{1}{2}\rho_{at}U^2(t)S_w\right);$

(at low angles of incidence)

$$= C_{L0} + C_{L\alpha}\alpha(t) + C_{L\dot{\alpha}}(\dot{\alpha}(t)c_w/2U(t)) + C_{Lq}\left(q(t)(c_w/2U(t)) + C_{L\dot{q}}\dot{q}(t)(c_w/2U(t))^2\right) + C_{L\eta}\eta(t) + C_{L\dot{\eta}}\left(\dot{\eta}(t)c_w/(2U(t))^2\right)$$

$$= \text{total aeroplane lift}/\left(\tfrac{1}{2}\rho_{at}U_{trim}^2 S_w\right)$$

$$= (C_L)_{trim} + C_{LU}(\Delta U(t)/U_{trim}) + C_{L\alpha}\Delta\alpha(t) + C_{L\dot{\alpha}}(\Delta\dot{\alpha}(t)c_w/2U(t)) + C_{Lq}(q(t)c_w/2U(t)) + C_{L\dot{q}}\dot{q}(t)(c_w/2U(t))^2 + C_{L\eta}\Delta\eta(t) + C_{L\dot{\eta}}\left(\Delta\dot{\eta}(t)c_w/(2U(t))^2\right)$$

C_D overall drag coefficient $= D/\left(\frac{1}{2}\rho_{at}U^2S_w\right) = C_{D0} + C_{DL}$

C_{D0} drag coefficient at zero lift

C_{DL} lift-dependent drag coefficient $\left(\simeq C_L^2/(\pi\, AR_w) \text{ at subsonic speeds}\right)$

C_{Th} thrust coefficient $= Th/\left(\frac{1}{2}\rho_{at}U_{trim}^2S_w\right)$

$(C_m)_w$ wing aerodynamic pitching moment coefficient

= wing aerodynamic pitching moment about wing aerodynamic centre$/\left(\frac{1}{2}\rho_{at}U^2(t)S_wc_w\right)$

$$= (m_0)_w + (m_{\dot{\alpha}})_w(\alpha(t)c_w/U(t)) + (m_q)_w(q(t)c_w/U(t)) + (m_{\dot{q}})_w\left(q(t)(c_w/U(t))^2\right)$$

$(C_m)_{wf}$ wing–fuselage aerodynamic pitching moment coefficient

= (wing–fuselage aerodynamic pitching moment about wing–fuselage aerodynamic centre)$/\left(\frac{1}{2}\rho_{at}U^2S_wc_w\right)$

$$= (m_0)_{wf} + (m_{\dot{\alpha}})_{wf}(\alpha(t)c_w/U(t)) + (m_q)_{wf}(q(t)c_w/U(t)) + (m_{\dot{q}})_{wf}\left(q(t)(c_w/U(t))^2\right)$$

$C_l(t)$ time varying overall rolling moment about fuselage body *ox* axis

$$= \mathcal{L}(t)\Big/\left(\tfrac{1}{2}\rho_{\mathrm{at}}U^2(t)S_{\mathrm{w}}2s_{\mathrm{w}}\right)$$

at low angles of incidence

$$\begin{aligned}
&= C_{l\beta}\beta(t) + C_{l\dot\beta}\dot\beta(t)s_{\mathrm{w}}/U(t)\\
&\quad + C_{lp}\left(p(t)s_{\mathrm{w}}/U(t)\right) + C_{l\dot p}\left(\dot p(t)s_{\mathrm{w}}^2/U^2(t)\right)\\
&\quad + C_{lr}\left(r(t)s_{\mathrm{w}}/U(t)\right) + C_{l\dot r}\left(\dot r(t)s_{\mathrm{w}}^2/U^2(t)\right)\\
&\quad + C_{l\xi}\xi(t) + C_{l\dot\xi}\dot\xi(t)s_{\mathrm{w}}/U(t)\\
&\quad + C_{l\zeta}\zeta(t) + C_{l\dot\zeta}\dot\zeta(t)s_{\mathrm{w}}/U(t)
\end{aligned}$$

$C_m\left(M_\infty(t),\ \alpha(t),\ \theta(t)\,|\,t\right)$ time varying overall pitching moment coefficient about the *oy* axis

$$= \mathcal{M}\Big/\left(\tfrac{1}{2}\rho_{\mathrm{at}}U^2(t)S_{\mathrm{w}}c_{\mathrm{w}}\right)$$

(at low angles of incidence)

$$\begin{aligned}
&= C_{m0} + C_{m\alpha}\alpha(t) + C_{m\dot\alpha}\left(\dot\alpha(t)c_{\mathrm{w}}/2U(t)\right)\\
&\quad + C_{mq}\left(q(t)c_{\mathrm{w}}/2U(t)\right) + C_{m\dot q}\left(\dot q(t)c_{\mathrm{w}}/2U(t)\right)^2\\
&\quad + C_{m\eta}\eta(t) + C_{m\dot\eta}\left(\dot\eta(t)c_{\mathrm{w}}/(2U(t))^2\right)
\end{aligned}$$

$$\begin{aligned}
&= \mathcal{M}\Big/\left(\tfrac{1}{2}\rho_{\mathrm{at}}U_{\mathrm{trim}}^2S_{\mathrm{w}}c_{\mathrm{w}}\right)\\
&= (C_m)_{\mathrm{trim}} + C_{mU}\left(\Delta U(t)/U_{\mathrm{trim}}\right)\\
&\quad + C_{m\alpha}\,\Delta\alpha(t) + C_{m\dot\alpha}\left(\Delta\dot\alpha(t)c_{\mathrm{w}}/2U(t)\right)\\
&\quad + C_{mq}\left(q(t)(c_{\mathrm{w}}/2U(t)) + C_{m\dot q}\left(\dot q(t)c_{\mathrm{w}}/2U(t)\right)^2\right)\\
&\quad + C_{m\eta}\,\Delta\eta(t) + C_{m\dot\eta}\left(\Delta\dot\eta(t)c_{\mathrm{w}}/(2U(t))^2\right)
\end{aligned}$$

$C_n(t)$ time varying overall yawing moment about fuselage body oz axis

$$= \mathcal{N}(t)\Big/\left(\tfrac{1}{2}\rho_{\rm at}U^2(t)S_{\rm w}2s_{\rm w}\right)$$

at low angles of incidence

$$= C_{n\beta}\beta(t) + C_{n\dot\beta}\dot\beta(t)s_{\rm w}/U(t)$$
$$+ C_{np}\big(p(t)s_{\rm w}/U(t)\big) + C_{n\dot p}\left(\dot p(t)s_{\rm w}^2/U^2(t)\right)$$
$$+ C_{nr}\big(r(t)s_{\rm w}/U(t)\big) + C_{n\dot r}\left(\dot r(t)s_{\rm w}^2/U^2(t)\right)$$
$$+ C_{n\xi}\xi(t) + C_{n\dot\xi}\dot\xi(t)s_{\rm w}/U(t)$$
$$+ C_{n\zeta}\zeta(t) + C_{n\dot\zeta}\dot\zeta(t)s_{\rm w}/U(t)$$

$\tilde C_{N\alpha}(\nu, M_\infty)$, $\tilde C_{N\dot\alpha}(\nu, M_\infty)$

$\tilde C_{M\alpha}(\nu, M_\infty)$, $\tilde C_{M\dot\alpha}(\infty, M_\infty)$

in-phase and out-of-phase oscillatory small amplitude derivatives

$C_{{\rm L}\dot\alpha g}$, $C_{{\rm mL}\dot\alpha g}$ gust input derivatives

$C_{\rm W}$ weight coefficient = all-up weight$\Big/\left(\tfrac{1}{2}\rho_{\rm at}U_{\rm trim}^2 S_{\rm w}\right)$

D operator $\mathrm{d}/\mathrm{d}t$

D^j operator $\mathrm{d}^j/\mathrm{d}t^j$

$\overline{\mathrm{D}}$ operator $\mathrm{d}/\mathrm{d}\bar t_{\rm d}$

D drag force (in direction of resultant relative airstream)

$E_{\rm trim}$ elevator trim margin $= -\mathrm{d}\eta_{\rm trim}/\mathrm{d}C_{\rm W}$

$E_{\rm m}$ elevator manoeuvre margin $= -\Delta\eta/(\Delta n C_{\rm W})$

$f_{\rm H}(t)$ lift response function to step change in angle of incidence

$$\left(= ((C_{\rm L})_{\rm w})_{\rm ss} - \big(C_{\rm L}(\alpha(t) = H(t)|t)\big)_{\rm w}\right)$$

FAA Federal Aviation Authority

$F_X(t)$, $F_Y(t)$, $F_Z(t)$ components of resultant force resolved about earth axes

$F_x(t)$, $F_y(t)$, $F_z(t)$ components of resultant force resolved about fuselage body axes

$G_{\Delta n}(\mathrm{i}\Omega)$ steady state harmonic response of gust, normal acceleration

h altitude

$H(t)$ step function (= 0 for $t < 0$, = 1 for $t > 0$)

$H_{\rm g}$ spatial length of ramp in a ramp-step gust

$H_{\rm max}$ value of $H_{\rm g}$ for tuned gust

$H_{\rm m}$ conventional manoeuvre margin = $E_{\rm m}(-C_{m\eta})$

$h_{\rm ac}c_{\rm w}$ distance of overall aerodynamic centre aft of wing–fuselage aerodynamic centre

$h_{\rm wac}c_{\rm r}$ distance of wing aerodynamic centre aft of wing apex

$h_{trim}c_w$	distance of trim point aft of wing–fuselage aerodynamic centre
$h_m c_w$	distance of overall aerodynamic centre aft of wing–fuselage aerodynamic centre
i	$\sqrt{-1}$
i_w, i_t	wing setting angle, tailplane setting angle, relative to fuselage centre line
i_d	wing dihedral angle
I_{xx}, I_{yy}, I_{zz}	direct moments of inertia about fuselage body axis system $\left(=\sum \delta m(y^2+z^2),\ \sum \delta m(z^2+x^2),\ \sum \delta m(x^2+y^2) \text{ respectively}\right)$
I_{xz}	product of inertia $\left(=\sum \delta m\ xz\right)$
i_{xx}, i_{yy}, i_{zz}	non-dimensional direct moments of inertia $\left(=I_{xx}/ms_w^2,\ I_{yy}/mc_w^2,\ I_{zz}/ms_w^2 \text{ respectively}\right)$
i_{xz}	non-dimensional product of inertia $=I_{xz}/ms_w^2$
$I_{x_1x_1}$, $I_{y_1y_1}$, $I_{z_1z_1}$	moments of inertia about trim body axis system
[I]	unit diagonal matrix
JAR	Joint Airworthiness Requirements
k	reduced frequency parameter $(=\Omega c_w/2U)$
k_H	integral of $f_H(t)$ over $0<t<\infty$
k_ε	downwash factor
K_α	incidence stiffness $(=(-C_{m\alpha})/C_{L\alpha})$
K_g	gust alleviation factor
$\overline{K}_{\alpha g}$	gust stiffness term
$\mathcal{K}$	feedback gains (subscripts α, θ, q)
$l_{wf}c_w$	distance of centre of mass aft of wing–fuselage aerodynamic centre
$l_t c_w$	distance of tailplane aerodynamic centre aft of centre of mass
lc_w	distance from wing–fuselage aerodynamic centre to tailplane aerodynamic centre $(=(l_{wf}+l_t)c_w)$
$l_{eng}c_w$	length of engine/nacelle
$l_{fus}c_w$	distance of centre of mass aft of centre of area of fuselage plan form
$l_{nac}c_w$	distance of centre of mass aft of leading edge of engine nacelle
$l_{prop}c_w$	distance of centre of mass aft of propeller disc
$l_{Th}c_w$	moment arm of thrust–drag pitching moment
$l_f c_w$	fin moment arm, distance of fin aerodynamic centre aft of c.m.
$l_n c_w$	fuselage nose moment arm, distance of c.m. aft of nose load centre of pressure
L	total lift force (in direction normal to resultant relative air stream)
L	spatial scale length of turbulence
$\mathcal{L}$	rolling moment about fuselage body ox axis
$\mathcal{L}_1$	rolling moment about trim body ox_1 axis
L_w	wing lift
L_{wf}	wing–fuselage lift

L_{nac}	nacelle lift
L_{t}	tailplane lift
L_{g}	lift due to vertical gust
$L(y)$	wing spanwise lift distribution $\left(L_{\mathrm{w}} = \int_{\text{wing span}} L(y)\,\mathrm{d}y\right)$
$\Delta L_{p_1}(y)$	wing spanwise lift distribution due to $\Delta\alpha_{p_1}(y)$
ΔL_{g}	incremental lift due to vertical gust
m	total aeroplane mass
$\overline{m}$	relative density $\left(= m/\left(\frac{1}{2}\rho_{\mathrm{at}} c_{\mathrm{w}} S_{\mathrm{w}}\right)\right)$
m_n	nth moment of random variable, eqn. (III.13.46)
m_{Th}	mass flow rate through propeller of turbo-fan engine
(m_0) $(m_{\dot{\alpha}})$	component quasi-steady moment derivatives due to incidence
(m_q) $(m_{\dot{q}})$	component quasi-steady moment derivatives due to pitch rate (suffixes: w, wing; wf, wing–fuselage)
M	total pitching moment about *oy* axis
$\mathcal{M}$	aerodynamic pitching moment about *oy* axis
M_{∞}	aeroplane Mach number $\left(= U(t)/a_{\mathrm{at}}\right)$
M_{D}	drag divergence Mach number
$\Delta\mathcal{M}_{\mathrm{g}}$	incremental pitching moment due to vertical gust
Δn	incremental normal acceleration
$n(t)$	rate of yaw about fuselage *oz* axis
$n_1(t)$	rate of yaw about trim oz_1 axis
N	force normal to *ox* axis, in the plane of Θ
N_{prop}	normal force on propeller disc
N_{nac}	normal force on engine nacelle
$N(\Delta n)$	average number of peaks of normal acceleration per unit time greater than $(g\,\Delta n)$
N_0	number of increasing crossings of level zero
$\mathcal{N}$	yawing moment about the fuselage *oz* axis
$\mathcal{N}_1$	yawing moment about trim body axis
ox, *oy*, *oz*	fuselage body axes, origin at centre of mass, *ox* and *oz* in plane of symmetry, *ox* forward along fuselage axis, *oy* to starboard, *oz* downwards
ox_1, oy_1, oz_1	trim body axes
ox_{f}, oy_{f}, oz_{f}	flight path axes
OX, *OY*, *OZ*	fixed earth axes, *OX* and *OY* horizontal, *OZ* vertically downwards
$p(t)$	rate of roll about fuselage body *ox* axis
$p_1(t)$	rate of roll about trim body ox_1 axis
p_{at}	atmospheric pressure at altitude h
$(p_{\mathrm{at}})_{\mathrm{sl}}$	atmospheric pressure at sea level
$p(x, y)$	static pressure distribution
$p(w_{\mathrm{g}})$	probability density of $w_{\mathrm{g}}(t)$
$(p_{\mathrm{roll}})_{\mathrm{ss}}$	steady state roll rate after decay of roll-rate modal response

$(p_{Dr})_{ss}$	steady state roll rate after decay of Dutch roll modal response
$q(t)$	pitch rate about fuselage body oy axis
$q_1(t)$	pitch rate about trim body oy_1 axis $(= q(t))$
q_{ss}	steady pitch rate response to step elevator after the decay of the short period mode
q_{com}	command rate of pitch
$r_{fus}(x)$	fuselage radius along fuselage
r_{max}	$(r_{fus}(x))_{max}$
r_{prop}	radius of propeller disc
r_{nac}	radius of nacelle
$r(t)$	yaw rate about fuselage body oz axis
$r_1(t)$	yaw rate about trim body oz_1 axis
Re	Reynolds number $(= \rho_{at} U c_w / \mu_{at} = U c_w / \nu_{at})$
$R(\chi)$	auto-correlation function
s_w, s_t	semi-span of wing, tailplane
s_f	fin span
S_w	wing area
S_t, S_e	tailplane area (which includes elevator area)
S_f	fin area (which includes rudder)
SEP	specific excess power $(= (\text{Th} - D)U/W)$
STR	sustained turn rate
t	time
$\hat{t}$	unit of aerodynamic time $(= c_w/U)$
$\bar{t}$	non-dimensional aerodynamic time $(= t/\hat{t})$
$\hat{t}_d$	unit of dynamic time $(= \overline{m}\hat{t})$
$\bar{t}_d$	non-dimensional dynamic time $(= t/\hat{t}_d)$
$t_{1/2}$	time to half amplitude
t_2	time to double amplitude
$t_{0.95}$	time to 95% of steady state value
$t_{0.99}$	time to 99% of steady state value
t_c	time constant of first order system
t_R	rate of ramp input (ramp input $= t/t_R$)
t_n	time at time $t = n\,\Delta t$
T	temporal gust scale length $(= L/U_{trim})$
T_{at}	atmospheric temperature at altitude h
$(T_{at})_{sl}$	atmospheric temperature at sea level
T_γ	time lag of steady state flight path angle response relative to datum response $q_{ss}t$
$T_{\theta 2}$	time lag of flight path steady state response relative to steady state pitch attitude response
Th	total thrust on aeroplane
u_p	excess velocity in propeller slipstream
u_j	downstream exhaust velocity of jet behind a turbo-fan engine, relative to the engine
u_{gs}	amplitude of horizontal step gust

u_k	defines family of similar discrete gusts
$U(t)$	absolute velocity of aeroplane centre of mass
$U_X(t)$, $U_Y(t)$, $U_Z(t)$	components of $U(t)$ in directions of earth axes *OXYZ*
$U_x(t)$, $U_y(t)$, $U_z(t)$	components of $U(t)$ in directions of fuselage body axes *oxyz*
$U_g(t)$	absolute velocity of atmosphere in vicinity of aeroplane
U_{TAS}	aeroplane speed relative to atmosphere
U_{EAS}	equivalent airspeed $\left(=(\rho_{at}/(\rho_{at})_{sl})^{1/2} U_{TAS}\right)$
$w_g(X)$	spatial two dimensional vertical gust
$\overline{w}_g$	mean of $w_g(X)$
w_{gs}	amplitude of ramp-step gust
x	coordinate in *ox* direction
$x(t)$	system input
$\mathbf{x}(t)$	column vector $(n \times 1)$ of n input functions
$X_0 < X < X_N$	spatial length of patch of turbulence
$X_{cm}(t)$, $Y_{cm}(t)$, $Z_{cm}(t)$	coordinates of centre of mass relative to earth axes
y	coordinate in *oy* direction
$y(t)$	system response
$y_a(t)$, $y_H(t)$	impulse response, step response
$y_R(t)$, $y_{RH}(t)$	ramp response, ramp-step response
$y_O(t)$	oscillatory response
$y_{tr}(t)$	transient response
$(y(t))_{ss}$	steady state response $(= y(t)$ as $t \to \infty)$
$(y_O(t))_{ss}$	steady state frequency response
$\mathbf{y}(t)$	column vector $(n \times 1)$ of n response functions
$\mathbf{y}_j$	column vector $(n \times 1)$, or eigenvector, of the modal shape corresponding to characteristic root, or eigenvalue, λ_j
Y_p	side force due to rate of roll p about *Ox* axis
Y_{p_1}	side force due to rate of roll p_1 about ox_1 axis
z	coordinate in *oz* direction
$\alpha(t)$	angle of incidence of *ox* axis $\left(= \tan^{-1}(U_z(t)/U_x(t))\text{ in still air}\right)$
$\Delta\alpha(t)$	incremental angle of incidence
$\Delta\alpha_{p_1}(y)$	incremental spanwise distribution of angle of incidence due to rate of roll p_1
α_b	break incidence (suffixes static, dynamic)
α_{0w}	wing angle of zero lift
$\Delta\alpha_g(t)$	gust angle
$\alpha_R(t)$	angle of incidence in turbulent air
$\beta(t)$	sideslip angle $\left(= \sin^{-1} U_y(t)/U(t)\right)$
γ	ratio of specific heats (= 1.4)
$\gamma(t)$	flight path angle; angle from horizontal in vertical plane to direction of $U(t)$; positive for climb, negative for descent

$\gamma(H_g)$	peak acceleration from discrete gust of ramp length H_g from family $u_k = 1.0$ m/s
γ_{max}	$\left(\gamma(H_g)\right)_{max}$
$\Gamma(y)$	circulation distribution along wing span
Γ	mean value of circulation
$\overline{\Gamma}$	non-dimensional mean circulation $\left(= \Gamma/(c_w U)\right)$
$\delta(t)$	impulse function $\left(\delta(t) = 0 \text{ for } t > 0,\ \ t < 0;\ \int_{t=0+}^{t=0-} \delta(t)\,\mathrm{d}t = 1.0\right)$
Δt, $\Delta\alpha$, ΔS_w	incremental changes
$\varepsilon(t)$	downwash angle
ζ	damping ratio ($=\mu/\omega_0$) (suffixes: sp, short period; ph, phugoid; Dr, Dutch roll)
ζ_{ng}, $\zeta_{\theta g}$	damping ratios in gust input, eqn. (III.13.18)
$\zeta(t)$	rudder angle
$\eta(t)$	elevator, or all-moving tailplane, angle
$\Delta\eta_p(t)$	elevator input from human pilot
$\Delta\eta_{stab}(t)$	elevator input for stability feedback
$\Delta\eta_{auto}(t)$	elevator input for auto-pilot feedback
$\Delta\eta_{comm}(t)$	elevator angle for manoeuvre demand system
$\theta(t)$	pitch angle (pure)
$\Theta(t)$	weathercock pitch angle, angle between *ox* axis and direction of U
λ_w, λ_t	taper ratio (= tip chord/root chord) (suffixes: w, wing; t, tailplane)
λ	characteristic variable
$\overline{\lambda}$	non-dimensional characteristic variable
λ_j, $\overline{\lambda}_j$	characteristic root, or eigenvalue
Λ	sweep of 1/4 chord line (suffixes: w, wing; t, tailplane; f, fin)
Λ_{le}	leading edge sweep
$\Lambda_{1/2}$	sweep of $\frac{1}{2}$ chord line
μ	real part of λ (damping)
μ_{at}	coefficient of viscosity
ν	frequency parameter ($= \Omega c_w/U$)
ν_{at}	kinematic viscosity
$\xi(t)$	aileron or differential tailplane angle
ρ_{at}	atmospheric density at altitude h
$(\rho_{at})_{sl}$	atmospheric density at sea level
σ_w, σ_v	gust intensities
τ	time
φ	phase angle
$\varphi(t)$	bank angle about *ox* axis
$\varphi_U(t)$	bank angle of plane of $\Theta(t)$ about flight path from vertical datum
$\psi(t)$	yaw angle of *oxyz* axes
$\Psi(t)$	yaw angle of flight path axes
ω	imaginary part of λ (frequency)

ω_0	undamped natural frequency (suffixes: sp, short period; ph, phugoid; Dr, Dutch roll)
Ω	input frequency

Index